Consumer Behavior

Building Marketing Strategy   10/e

Consumer Behavior

Building Marketing Strategy 10/e

Del I. Hawkins
University of Oregon

David L. Mothersbaugh
University of Alabama

Roger J. Best
University of Oregon

McGraw-Hill Irwin

Boston   Burr Ridge, IL   Dubuque, IA   Madison, WI   New York   San Francisco   St. Louis
Bangkok   Bogotá   Caracas   Kuala Lumpur   Lisbon   London   Madrid   Mexico City
Milan   Montreal   New Delhi   Santiago   Seoul   Singapore   Sydney   Taipei   Toronto

McGraw-Hill
Irwin

CONSUMER BEHAVIOR: BUILDING MARKETING STRATEGY

Published by McGraw-Hill/Irwin, a business unit of The McGraw-Hill Companies, Inc., 1221 Avenue of the Americas, New York, NY, 10020. Copyright © 2007 by The McGraw-Hill Companies, Inc. All rights reserved. No part of this publication may be reproduced or distributed in any form or by any means, or stored in a database or retrieval system, without the prior written consent of The McGraw-Hill Companies, Inc., including, but not limited to, in any network or other electronic storage or transmission, or broadcast for distance learning.

Some ancillaries, including electronic and print components, may not be available to customers outside the United States.

This book is printed on acid-free paper.

1 2 3 4 5 6 7 8 9 0 DOW/DOW 0 9 8 7 6

ISBN-13: 978-0-07-310137-8
ISBN-10: 0-07-310137-0

Editorial director: *John E. Biernat*
Publisher: *Andy Winston*
Sponsoring editor: *Barrett Koger*
Managing developmental editor: *Nancy Barbour*
Executive marketing manager: *Trent Whatcott*
Producer, Media technology: *Janna Martin*
Project manager: *Marlena Pechan*
Production supervisor: *Gina Hangos*
Senior designer: *Adam Rooke*
Photo research coordinator: *Lori Kramer*
Photo researcher: *Mike Hruby*
Media project manager: *Joyce J. Chappetto*
Typeface: *10/12 Times Roman*
Compositor: *Interactive Composition Corporation*
Printer: *R. R. Donnelley*

Library of Congress Cataloging-in-Publication Data

Consumer behavior : building marketing strategy / Delbert I. Hawkins . . . [et al.].—10th ed.
    p. cm. — (McGraw-Hill/Irwin series in marketing)
   Includes index.
   ISBN-13: 978-0-07-310137-8 (alk. paper)
   ISBN-10: 0-07-310137-0 (alk. paper)
   1. Consumer behavior—United States. 2. Market surveys—United States. 3. Consumer behavior—United States—Case studies. I. Hawkins, Del I. II. Series.
HF5415.33.U6.C653 2007
658.8'3420973—dc22

2005054357

www.mhhe.com

Preface

Marketing attempts to influence the way consumers behave. These attempts have implications for the organizations making them, the consumers they are trying to influence, and the society in which these attempts occur. We are all consumers and we are all members of society, so consumer behavior, and attempts to influence it, are critical to all of us. This text is designed to provide an understanding of consumer behavior. This understanding can make us better consumers, better marketers, and better citizens.

MARKETING CAREERS AND CONSUMER BEHAVIOR

A primary purpose of this text is to provide the student with a usable, managerial understanding of consumer behavior. Most students in consumer behavior courses aspire to careers in marketing management, sales, or advertising. They hope to acquire knowledge and skills that will be useful to them in these careers. Unfortunately, some may be seeking the type of knowledge gained in introductory accounting classes; that is, a set of relatively invariant rules that can be applied across a variety of situations to achieve a fixed solution that is known to be correct. For these students, the uncertainty and lack of closure involved in dealing with living, breathing, changing, stubborn consumers can be very frustrating. However, if they can accept dealing with endless uncertainty, utilizing an understanding of consumer behavior in developing marketing strategy will become tremendously exciting.

It is our view that the utilization of knowledge of consumer behavior in the development of marketing strategy is an art. This is not to suggest that scientific principles and procedures are not applicable; rather, it means that the successful application of these principles to particular situations requires human judgment that we are not able to reduce to a fixed set of rules.

Let us consider the analogy with art in some detail. Suppose you want to become an expert artist. You would study known principles of the visual effects of blending various colors, of perspective, and so forth.

Then you would practice applying these principles until you developed the ability to produce acceptable paintings. If you had certain natural talents, the right teacher, and the right topic, you might even produce a masterpiece. The same approach should be taken by one wishing to become a marketing manager, a salesperson, or an advertising director. The various factors or principles that influence consumer behavior should be thoroughly studied. Then, one should practice applying these principles until acceptable marketing strategies result. However, while knowledge and practice can in general produce acceptable strategies, great marketing strategies, like masterpieces, require special talents, effort, timing, and some degree of luck (what if Mona Lisa had not wanted her portrait painted?).

The art analogy is useful for another reason. All of us, professors and students alike, tend to ask, "How can I use the concept of, say, social class to develop a successful marketing strategy?" This makes as much sense as an artist asking, "How can I use blue to create a great picture?" Obviously, blue alone will seldom be sufficient for a great work of art. Instead, to be successful, the artist must understand when and how to use blue in conjunction with other elements in the picture. Likewise, the marketing manager must understand when and how to use a knowledge of social class in conjunction with a knowledge of other factors in designing a successful marketing strategy.

This book is based on the belief that knowledge of the factors that influence consumer behavior can, with practice, be used to develop sound marketing strategy. With this in mind, we have attempted to do three things. First, we present a reasonably comprehensive description of the various behavioral concepts and theories that have been found useful for understanding consumer behavior. This is generally done at the beginning of each chapter or at the beginning of major subsections in each chapter. We believe that a person must have a thorough understanding of a concept in order to successfully apply that concept across different situations.

Second, we present examples of how these concepts have been utilized in the development of marketing strategy. We have tried to make clear that these examples are not "how you use this concept." Rather, they are presented as "how one organization facing a particular marketing situation used this concept."

Third, at the end of each chapter and each major section, we present a number of questions, activities, or cases that require the student to apply the concepts.

CONSUMING AND CONSUMER BEHAVIOR

The authors of this book are consumers, as is everyone reading this text. Most of us spend more time buying and consuming than we do working or sleeping. We consume products such as cars and fuel, services such as haircuts and home repairs, and entertainment such as television and concerts. Given the time and energy we devote to consuming, we should strive to be good at it. A knowledge of consumer behavior can be used to enhance our ability to consume wisely.

Marketers spend billions of dollars attempting to influence what, when, and how you and I consume. Marketers not only spend billions attempting to influence our behavior but also spend hundreds of millions of dollars studying our behavior. With a knowledge of consumer behavior and an understanding of how marketers use this knowledge, we can study marketers. A television commercial can be an annoying interruption of a favorite program. However, it can also be a fascinating opportunity to speculate on the commercial's objective, target audience, and the underlying behavior assumptions. Indeed, given the ubiquitous nature of commercials, an understanding of how they are attempting to influence us or others is essential to understand our environment.

Throughout the text, we present examples that illustrate the objectives of specific marketing activities. By studying these examples and the principles on which they are based, one can develop the ability to discern the underlying logic of the marketing activities encountered daily.

SOCIAL RESPONSIBILITY AND CONSUMER BEHAVIOR

What are the costs and benefits of direct-to-consumer (DTC) advertising of pharmaceutical products? How much more needs to be done to protect the online privacy of children? These issues are currently being debated by industry leaders and consumer advocacy groups. As educated citizens, we have a responsibility to take part in these sorts of debates and work toward positive solutions. However, developing sound positions on these issues requires an understanding of such factors as information processing as it relates to advertising—an important part of our understanding of consumer behavior.

The debates described above are just a few of the many that require an understanding of consumer behavior. We present a number of these topics throughout the text. The objective is to develop the ability to apply consumer behavior knowledge to social and regulatory issues as well as to business and personal issues.

FEATURES OF THE TENTH EDITION

Marketing and consumer behavior, like the rest of the world, are changing at a rapid pace. Both the way consumers behave and the practices of studying that behavior continue to evolve. In order to keep up with this dynamic environment, the tenth edition includes a number of important features.

Internet and Technology

The Internet and technology are rapidly changing many aspects of consumer behavior. We have integrated the latest research and practices concerning the Internet and technology throughout the text and the cases. Examples include:

- Multi-channel shopping
- e-fluentials and Internet mavens
- Behavioral targeting and viral marketing
- Technographics segments

Continued Global Emphasis

Previous editions have included a wealth of global material, and this edition is no exception. Most chapters contain multiple global examples woven into the text. In addition, Chapter 2 and several of the cases are devoted to global issues. New global examples include:

- Bollywood (India) goes global
- Roper Starch global lifestyle segments
- Starbucks in Asia
- Renault taps emerging global markets

Updated DDB Life Style Study™ Data

The DDB Life Style Study™ Data is completely new for this edition. It comes from DDB's 2004 survey (the most recent data we can get you access to!) and is packed with exciting new variables of interest relating to culture, self-concept, decision making, marketing regulation, technology, and Internet shopping. We think this update offers an improved learning experience for students.

Addition of a New Author to the Team

Our book is now in its tenth edition. We continue to strive to provide the most current, relevant, and balanced presentation of consumer behavior in the context of building marketing strategy. As part of that ongoing tradition, we are pleased to announce the addition of a new author to our team—David L. Mothersbaugh from The University of Alabama. David brings the same passion, enthusiasm, and devotion to the book's core mission that we have been nurturing for nearly three decades.

CHAPTER FEATURES

Each chapter contains a variety of features designed to enhance students' understanding of the material as well as to make the material more fun.

Opening Vignettes

Each chapter begins with a practical example that introduces the material in the chapter. These involve situations in which businesses, government units, or nonprofit organizations have used or misused consumer behavior principles.

Consumer Insights

These boxed discussions provide an in-depth look at a particularly interesting consumer study or marketing practice. Each has several questions with it that are designed to encourage critical thinking by the students.

Integrated Coverage Ethical/Social Issues

Marketers face numerous ethical issues as they apply their understanding of consumer behavior in the marketplace. We describe and discuss many of these issues. These discussions are highlighted in the text via an "ethics" icon in the margin. In addition, Chapter 20 is devoted to social and regulation issues relating to marketing practice. Several of the cases are also focused on ethical or regulatory issues, including all of the cases following Part Six.

Internet Exercises

The Internet is a major source of data on consumer behavior and a medium in which marketers use their knowledge of consumer behavior to influence consumers. A section at the end of each chapter has Internet assignments to enhance students' understanding of how marketers are approaching consumers using this medium.

DDB Life Style Study™ Data Analyses (*New Data for the Tenth Edition!*)

Each relevant chapter poses a series of questions that require students to analyze data from the annual DDB Life Style Study™ survey. These data are available in spreadsheet format on the disk that accompanies this text. These exercises increase students' data analysis skills as well as their understanding of consumer behavior. The DDB data have been completely updated for this edition to include results of their 2004 survey. A major advantage of this new data is that it includes information on behaviors related to Internet use and shopping.

Four-Color Illustrations

Print ads, Web pages, storyboards, and photos of point-of-purchase displays and packages appear throughout the text. Each is directly linked to the text material both by text references to each illustration and by the descriptive comments that accompany each illustration.

These illustrations, which we've continued to update with the tenth edition, provide vivid examples and applications of the concepts and theories presented in the text.

Review Questions

The review questions at the end of each chapter allow students or the instructor to test the acquisition of the facts contained in the chapter. The questions require memorization, which we believe is an important, though insufficient, part of learning.

Discussion Questions

These questions can be used to help develop or test the students' understanding of the material in the chapter. Answering these questions requires the student to utilize the material in the chapter to reach a recommendation or solution. However, they can generally be answered without external activities such as customer interviews; therefore, they can be assigned as in-class activities.

Application Activities

The final learning aid at the end of each chapter is a set of application exercises. These require the students to utilize the material in the chapter in conjunction with external activities such as visiting stores to observe point-of-purchase displays, interviewing customers or managers, or evaluating television ads. They range in complexity from short evening assignments to term projects.

OTHER LEARNING AIDS IN THE TEXT

Three useful sets of learning material are presented outside the chapter format—cases, an overview of consumer research methods, and a format for a consumer behavior audit.

Cases

There are cases at the end of each major section of the text except the first. Many of the cases can be read in class and used to generate discussion of a particular topic. Students like this approach, and many instructors find it a useful way to motivate class discussion.

Other cases are more complex and data intense. They require several hours of effort to analyze. Still others can serve as the basis for a term project. We have used several cases in this manner with success (the assignment is to develop a marketing plan clearly identifying the consumer behavior constructs that underlie the plan).

Each case can be approached from a variety of angles. A number of discussion questions are provided with each case. However, many other questions can be used. In fact, while the cases are placed at the end of the major sections, most lend themselves to discussion at other points in the text as well.

Consumer Research Methods Overview

Appendix A provides a brief overview of the more commonly used research methods in consumer behavior. While not a substitute for a course or text in marketing research, it is a useful review for students who have completed a research course. It can also serve to provide students who have not had such a course with relevant terminology and a very basic understanding of the process and major techniques involved in consumer research.

Consumer Behavior Audit

Appendix B provides a format for doing a consumer behavior audit for a proposed marketing strategy. This audit is basically a list of key consumer behavior questions that should be answered for every proposed marketing strategy. Many students have found it particularly useful if a term project relating consumer behavior to a firm's actual or proposed strategy is required.

SUPPLEMENTAL LEARNING MATERIALS

We have developed a variety of learning materials to enhance the student's learning experience and to facilitate the instructor's teaching activities. Please contact your local Irwin/McGraw-Hill sales representative for assistance in obtaining ancillaries. Or visit the McGraw-Hill Higher Education Web site at www. mhhe.com.

Instructor's Presentation CD ROM

The *Instructor's CD ROM to Accompany Consumer Behavior* includes all of the instructor's resources available for *Consumer Behavior* in electronic form and an easy interface that makes it even easier to access the specific items the instructor wants to use:

- **Instructor's Manual**
  The Instructor's Manual contains suggestions for teaching the course, learning objectives for each chapter, additional material for presentation, lecture tips and aids, answers to the end-of-chapter questions, suggested case teaching approaches, and discussion guides for each case.

- **Test Bank and Computerized Test Bank (All New for the 10th Edition!)**

  The test bank for the tenth edition is completely new and improved. Laurie Babin (University of Southern Mississippi) has created over 2000 questions ranging from multiple-choice, to true-false, to short-answer. These questions are coded according to degree of difficulty and are designed with the flexibility to suit your students' needs and your teaching style. These questions cover all the chapters, including material in the opening vignettes and in the Consumer Insights. Questions are marked with a page number so that instructors can make quick reference back to the book.

- **Digital Four-Color Ad Set**

  A set of digital four-color images of ads, picture boards, point-of-purchase displays, and so forth is included. These items are keyed to specific chapters in the text. The Instructor's Manual relates theses items to the relevant concepts in the text.

- **PowerPoint Program (All New for the 10th Edition!)**

  The tenth edition comes with a completely new and more comprehensive set of PowerPoint slides for each chapter. They include the key material from each chapter as well as additional illustrations and examples to enhance the overall classroom experience. These PowerPoints can be used "off the shelf," in combination with the instructor's own materials, and/or can be combined with the digital four-color ad set to create powerful presentations which include both text and non-text materials.

Video Cases

A set of video cases is available to adopters. These videos describe firm strategies or activities that relate to material in the text. A guide for teaching from the videos is contained in the Instructor's Manual.

Text Web site

The book-specific Online Learning Center, located at **www.mhhe.com/hawkins10e,** offers comprehensive classroom support by providing resources for both instructors and students. For instructors, it gives access to downloadable teaching supplements (Instructor's Manual and PowerPoint slides), resource links, and PageOut. For students, it offers resource links and quizzes for self-testing.

ACKNOWLEDGMENTS

We enjoy studying, teaching, consulting, and writing about consumer behavior. Most of the faculty we know feel the same. As with every edition of this book, our goal for the tenth edition has been to make a book that students enjoy reading and that excites them about a fascinating topic.

Numerous individuals and organizations helped us in the task of writing this edition. We are grateful for their assistance. At the risk of not thanking all who deserve credit, we would like to thank Martin Horn at DDB, Tom Spencer at Claritas, Shannon McDonald at eMarketer, Rick Bruner at DoubleClick, and Carrie Hollenberg at SRI Consulting Business Intelligence. Alexa Martinez Given and Tracy Bradshaw (The University of Alabama) deserve special thanks for their countless hours of research and analysis.

We would also like to thank the many members of the McGraw-Hill Higher Education team, including Barrett Koger, Nancy Barbour, Marlena Pechan, Gina Hangos, Joyce Chappetto, Adam Rooke, and Janna Martin. Particular thanks are also due to the many people who helped us in the development of this text. We believe that the tenth edition is improved because of your efforts: Jurgita Baltrusaityte, University of Illinois; Robert Bergman, Lewis University; Sheri Bridges, Wake Forest University; Hongsik John Cheon, Frostburg State University; Sharon Delay, Hondros College; David Hagenbuch, Messiah College; Lee Hibbitt, Freed-Hardeman University; Martie R. Kazura, Berea College; Nora Martin, Claflin University; George Miaoulis, Jr., Lynchburg College; Carlos Moore, Baylor University; Patricia Pulliam, Benedictine College; Patrick Quinlan, Adrian College; Esmeralda de los Santos, University of Incarnate Word; Lois Smith, University of Wisconsin-Whitewater; Mita Sujan, Tulane University; William Williamson, Govenors State University; Alan R. Wiman, Rider University; Joseph Wisenblit, Seton Hall University; David Wright, Abilene Christian University.

Finally, to our colleagues at Oregon and Alabama— Thanks for your ongoing support, encouragement and friendship.

Del I. Hawkins
David L. Mothersbaugh
Roger J. Best

Walkthrough

KNOWING CONSUMER BEHAVIOR

Marketing attempts to influence the way consumers behave. These attempts have implications for the organizations making the attempt, the consumers they are trying to influence, and the society in which these attempts occur. We are all consumers: the authors of this book are consumers, as is everyone reading this text, and we are all members of society, so consumer behavior, and attempts to influence it, are critical to all of us. This text is designed to provide an understanding of consumer behavior. This understanding can make us better consumers, better marketers, and better citizens.

Throughout the text, we present examples that illustrate the objectives of specific marketing activities. By studying these examples and the principles on which they are based, one can develop the ability to discern the underlying logic of the marketing activities encountered daily. Given the time and energy we devote to consuming, we should strive to be good at it, and a knowledge of consumer behavior can be used to enhance our ability to consume wisely.

Opening Vignette

The chapter openers feature vignettes that focus on practical examples that introduce the consumer behavior concepts covered in the chapter.

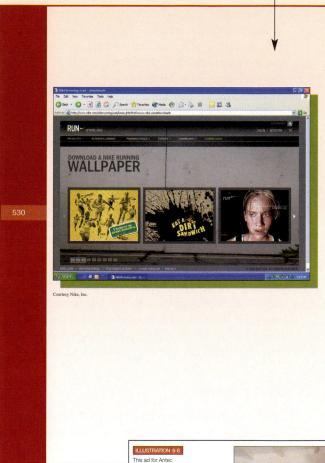

Courtesy Nike, Inc.

Four-Color Illustrations

Print ads, Web pages, storyboards, and photos of point-of-purchase displays and packages appear throughout the text.

ILLUSTRATION 6-8
This ad for Antec computers recognizes that teens often play an important role in influencing family decisions relating to technology.

Courtesy Lewis P.R., Inc.

Part-Ending Cases

There are cases at the end of each major section of the text that can be approached from a variety of angles. They can be utilized for class discussion, more intense efforts of analysis, or as the basis for a term project.

part two

Cases

CASE 2-1   Starbucks Keeps It Brewing in Asia

Asia, particularly China, is well known for its love of tea. So it may be a bit surprising how enthusiastic Starbucks is about the Chinese market. Consider the following quote from a Starbucks executive:

I am so excited about China right now I can hardly stand it. I was in Shanghai a few weeks ago. The stores there are full of customers. I thought China would always be a great

In a population so large, it might surprise you to know that as of 2005, Starbucks has only around 150 outlets in China, a small drop in the bucket compared to around 4,600 in the United States. Various factors will influence the Chinese coffee market and must be considered in Starbucks' marketing strategy.

Demographics and Geography

15

Ethical/Social Issues

The discussions regarding the numerous ethical issues facing marketers are highlighted in the margin throughout the text.

What Are the Ethical Implications of Marketing This Product in This Country?
All marketing programs should be evaluated on ethical as well as financial dimensions. As discussed at the beginning of the chapter, international marketing activities raise many ethical issues. The ethical dimension is particularly important and complex in marketing to Third World and developing countries. Consider Kellogg's attempt to introduce cold cereal as a breakfast food in a developing country. An ethical analysis would consider various factors including:

If we succeed, will the average nutrition level be increased or decreased?

If we succeed, will the funds spent on cereal be diverted from other uses with more beneficial long-term impacts for the individuals or society?

If we succeed, what impact will this have on the local producers of currently consumed breakfast products?

Such an ethical analysis not only is the right thing to do; it may head off conflicts with local governments or economic interests. Understanding and acting on ethical considerations in international marketing is a difficult task. However, it is also a necessary one.

Information Search

The ability of consumers to search for information has increased radically since the advent of the Internet. The Internet allows easy access to manufacturers' Web sites, to other consumers, and to third parties such as consumer groups and government agencies. It also greatly expands the ability of marketers to provide information to consumers. Marketers can provide information to consumers who are directly seeking information about the firm's products, typically through the company's or brand's home page or Web site. Marketers can also provide consumers information that they are not explicitly seeking by placing ads on other sites on the Web.

Internet strategies continue to evolve. However, most companies go well beyond simply providing company and product information in an electronic format. Consider the following.¹

Nike's ... its sh ... well b ...

tion about shoes. For example, runners can create their own online training log, learn about upcoming events, learn about runner communities, download running-related Nike wallpaper, and become a member and receive access to members-only services and the NikeRunning.com Newsletter.

- Kodak's site has various sections which provide product information to both amateur consumers and professional users. For cinematographers (and aspiring film students), Kodak offers film-comparison software, interviews with cinematographers, and information about their student film program. For their consumer market, they offer Kodak EasyShare Gallery, where digital pictures can be stored, printed, and shared online for free. For ...

DDB Life Style Study™ Data Analyses

Each relevant chapter poses a series of questions geared toward helping students increase their data analysis skills as well as their understanding of consumer behavior.

DDB LIFE STYLE STUDY™ DATA ANALYSES

1. Based on the DDB data in Table 5A, which heavier-user categories have the greatest differences across the ethnic subcultures? Why is this the case?
2. For which products does ownership differ the most across ethnic groups (Table 5A)? Why is this the case?
3. For which types of television shows (Table 5A) do preferences differ the most across the ethnic subcultures? Why is this the case?

ethnic subcultures. What might explain these differences?
a. Enjoy shopping for items influenced by other cultures.
b. Religion is a big part of my life.
c. Try to maintain a youthful appearance.
d. When making family decisions, consideration of kids comes first.
e. There is not enough ethnic diversity in commercials today.

APPLICATION ACTIVITIES

38. Watch two hours of prime-time major network (ABC, CBS, FOX, or NBC) television. What subculture groups are portrayed in the programs? Describe how they are portrayed. Do these portrayals match the descriptions in this text? How would you explain the differences? Repeat these tasks for the ads shown during the programs.
39. Pick a product of interest and examine the Simmons Market Research Bureau or MediaMark studies on the product in your library (these are often in the journalism library on CD-ROM).

e. Asian-Indian Americans
f. Native Americans

42. Interview three members of the following subcultures and ascertain the extent to which they identify with the core American culture, their ethnic subculture within America, or their nationality subculture. Also determine the extent to which they feel others of their ethnic/race group feel as they do and the reasons for any differences.
a. African Americans
b. Asian Americans

Consumer Insight   2-1

Bollywood Goes Global

In 2003, India produced 1,100 movies, and cinema admissions were 3.4 billion. Called Bollywood, a nod to America's Hollywood, India is the leading movie producer and consumer in the world (the United States was second with 593 movies and 1.6 billion admissions).¹¹⁵ No wonder then that Indian culture is hot stuff especially among global teens. Consider the following:

With riffs off India's cultural cachet showing up everywhere—from Madonna's use of mendhi, the traditional Indian henna art, to bhangra rhythms from northern India mixed into a Britney Spears single, advertisers are far from alone in embracing the colors and sounds of the subcontinent. The trend is even more entrenched overseas, where major campaigns with Bollywood themes are popping up from the Mediterranean to the South China Sea.

Marketers have not been shy about tapping this global hip status to market to teens in the United States, Asia, and Europe. A few examples include:

- In the United States, Absolut vodka has a 12-minute online "Bollywood ad" called Absolut

man standing on the side of the road. Alighting, they start gyrating to pulsating Indian music, while the man looks on in astonishment."
- In Spain, Italy, and Portugal, Coca-Cola runs an ad in which a Hindu waiter gets everyone at a stuffy European party to dance and liven up by singing a Bollywood-style song after drinking a Coke.¹¹⁶

Not everything coming out of Bollywood is good, however. A World Health Organization (WHO) study finds that over three-quarters of films coming out of Bollywood over the past 10 years contain smoking of some sort. In a country that accounts for 1 in 3 smoking-related deaths, WHO appears to have valid concerns.¹¹⁷

Critical Thinking Questions

1. What cultural values are companies like Absolut, Nokia, and Coke tapping into in their advertising appeals?
2. How are these values different from or similar to traditional values in the countries where they are operating?

Consumer Insight

These boxed discussions provide an in-depth look at a particularly interesting consumer study or marketing practice.

End-of-Chapter Materials

At the end of each chapter are a series of learning tools including Internet Exercises, Review Questions, Discussion Questions, and Application Activities.

DDB Life Style Study™ Data Analyses

DDB Worldwide is one of the leading advertising agencies in the world. One of the many services it provides for its clients, as well as to support its own creative and strategy efforts, is a major annual lifestyle survey. This survey is conducted using a panel maintained by Synovate. In a panel such as this, consumers are recruited such that the panel has demographic characteristics similar to the U.S. population. Members of the panel agree to complete questions on a periodic basis.

THE DATA

The 2004 DDB Life Style Study™ involved more than 3,300 completed questionnaires. These lengthy questionnaires included hundreds of attitude, activity, interest, opinion, and behavior items relating to consumers, their consumption, and their lifestyles. The questionnaires also contained numerous questions collecting demographic and media preference data.

DDB has allowed us to provide a portion of these data in spreadsheet format in the disk that accompanies this text. The data are presented in the form of cross-tabulations at an aggregate level with the cell values being percents. For example,

	Household Size			
	1	2	3–5	6+
Number in Sample	523	1294	1351	133
Own a DVD player	49.0%	68.2%	84.3%	88.5%
Purchased clothes online	11.0	12.4	15.3	13.1
Visited a fast-food restaurant	46.6	54.1	69.1	74.7

The example indicates that 49.0 percent of the 523 respondents from one-person households own a DVD player, compared with 68.2 percent of the 1,294 from two-person households, 84.3 percent of those from households with three, four, or five members, and 88.5 percent of those from households with six or more members.

It is possible to combine columns within variables. That is, we can determine the percent of one- and two-person households combined that purchased clothes online. Because the number of respondents on which the percentages are based differs across columns, we can't simply average the cell percentage figures. Instead, we need to convert the cell percentages to numbers by multiplying each cell percentage times the number in the sample for that column. Add the numbers for the cells to be combined together and divide the result by the sum of the number in the sample for the combined cells' columns. The result is the percentage of the combined column categories that engaged in the behavior of interest.

The data available on the disk are described below.

COLUMN VARIABLES FOR THE DATA TABLES

Tables

1A & 1B Household size, marital status, number of children at home, age of youngest child at home, age of oldest child at home.

2A & 2B For married female respondents, their spouse's level of employment. For married male respondents, their spouse's level of employment.

3A & 3B Household income, education level of respondent, perceived tech savvy.

4A & 4B Occupation of respondent.

5A & 5B Ethnic subculture, age, cognitive age (feel a lot younger than my age).

6A & 6B Gender, geographic region.

7A & 7B   Ideal self-concept traits (adventurous, affectionate, ambitious, assertive, careful, competitive, easy-going, independent, masculine, sensitive, tolerant, traditional, youthful).

ROW VARIABLES FOR TABLES 1A THROUGH 7A

Heavier User Behaviors and Product Ownership

General Behaviors

Read books/articles about health

Visited gourmet coffee bar or café

Visited fast-food restaurant

Went on weight reducing diet

Went dancing at a club

Played bingo

Worked in the garden

Jogged

Went camping

Rented a DVD

Traveled to another country

Attended church/place of worship

Consumption Behaviors

Dessert

Diet sodas

Sports drinks

Cordials, liqueurs or other after-dinner drinks

Chocolate bars

Premium ice cream

Shopping Activities

Purchased from mail order catalog

Shopped at a convenience store

Purchased items for home at discount retailer

Bought a store's own brand

Used a price coupon

Product Ownership

DVD

PVR

MP3 Player

Personal computer

Cellular phone

Individual retirement account

Car

Home

ATV or off-road motorcycle

Dog

Cat

Types of TV Shows Watched Regularly

Children's shows

Comedy

Drama

Home improvement

News/political

Religious programming

Sports

Weather

ROW VARIABLES FOR TABLES 1B THROUGH 7B

Attitude/Activity/Interest/ Behavior Relating to . . .

Culture

Enjoy shopping for items influenced by other cultures

Interested in the cultures of other countries

Values

I work hard most of the time

Religion is a big part of my life

Men concerned with latest styles and fashions aren't masculine

Make a special effort to buy from environmentally friendly businesses

Work at trying to maintain a youthful appearance

A commercial that features people of my race speaks more directly to me

There is not enough ethnic diversity in commercials today

I make a strong effort to recycle

Gender and Family

Individuality is an important value to pass down to kids

A woman's place is in the home

When making family decisions, consideration of the kids comes first

Brands, Innovators, and Opinion Leadership

Friends and neighbors come to me for advice about brands and products

I am usually among the first to try a new product

I try to stick to well-known brand names

Motivation, Personality, and Extended Self

View shopping as a form of entertainment

Want to look a little different from others

Have more self-confidence than friends

Brands I buy are a reflection of who I am

The car I drive is a reflection of who I am

Clothes I wear reflect who I am as a person

Information Search and Decision Making

Consult consumer reports before making a major purchase

Nutritional information on label influences what I buy

Information in advertising helps me to make better decisions

The Internet is the best place to get information about products and services

Consider myself tech savvy

In making big decisions, I go with my heart rather than my head

Making purchases with a credit card over the Internet is too risky

Worry about others getting private information about me

Shopping and Loyalty

Am an impulse buyer

Stick with favorite brand even if something else is on sale

Pay more for better service

Our family is in too much debt

Marketing Regulation

Avoid buying products advertised on shows with sex or violence

TV commercials place too much emphasis on sex

Most big companies are just out for themselves

Advertising directed at children should be taken off TV

Internet Use and Purchase

Used the Internet in the past 12 months

Purchased auto insurance online

Purchased clothes online

Purchased concert/play/sports tickets online

Brief Contents

Contents

Part Three
Internal Influences   278

CHAPTER EIGHT
Perception   281

CHAPTER NINE
Learning, Memory, and Product Positioning   321

CHAPTER TEN
Motivation, Personality, and Emotion   363

Part Five
Organizations as Consumers   682

CHAPTER NINETEEN
Organizational Buyer Behavior   685

Part Six
Consumer Behavior and Marketing Regulation   714

CHAPTER TWENTY
Marketing Regulation and Consumer Behavior   717

Consumer Behavior

Building Marketing Strategy   10/e

part one

Introduction

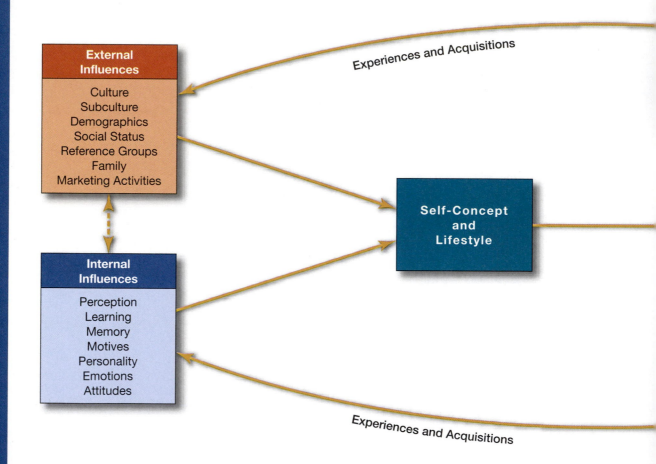

External Influences

Culture
Subculture
Demographics
Social Status
Reference Groups
Family
Marketing Activities

Internal Influences

Perception
Learning
Memory
Motives
Personality
Emotions
Attitudes

Self-Concept and Lifestyle

Experiences and Acquisitions

Experiences and Acquisitions

■ What is consumer behavior? Why should we study it? Do marketing managers, regulators, and consumer advocates actually use knowledge about consumer behavior to develop strategies and policy? How? Will a sound knowledge of consumer behavior help you in your career? Will it enable you to be a better citizen? How does consumer behavior impact the quality of all of our lives and the environment? How can we organize our knowledge of consumer behavior to understand and use it more effectively?

Chapter 1 addresses these and a number of other interesting questions, describes the importance and usefulness of the material to be covered in this text, and provides an overview of the text. Chapter 1 also explains the logic of the model of consumer behavior shown below, which is presented again in Figure 1-3 and discussed toward the end of the chapter.

3

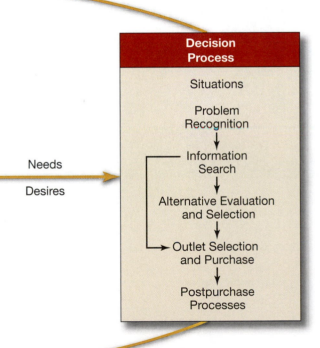

Courtesy The Coca-Cola Company.

Consumer Behavior and Marketing Strategy

■ Marketers face exciting and daunting challenges as the forces that drive and shape consumer behavior evolve at a rapid pace. Domestic firms confront the challenges of international competition but also the opportunities of vast emerging consumer markets such as China and India. In the United States, companies are responding to increased diversity in numerous areas including expansion of the Hispanic market. Retailers face the challenges and opportunities of technology such as online shopping. Marketers and regulators struggle with tough ethical and social aspects of marketing including marketing to children. And this only scratches the surface of the subject of this book—consumer behavior! Let's take a more in-depth look at a few of these areas.

Global marketing—China's massive population, rising income, and emerging youth market make it very attractive to marketers around the world. Consider the following:

Urban Chinese teens download hip-hop tunes to trendy Nokia cell phones, guzzle icy Cokes after shooting hoops in Nike shoes and munch fries at McDonald's after school.

If this sounds like an American marketer's dream, you are partly right. However, there are challenges to marketing to this segment. Chinese history, values, and culture are factors that cannot be ignored. They create a unique teen market that U.S. marketers must understand and adapt to. As one marketing expert puts it:

Successful advertising for youth brands carefully navigates the respect young consumers feel for their family, peer groups and country with their cautious desire to express individuality.

Still, key "passion points" exist—music, fashion, sports, and technology. These passion points are similar for teens around the globe, but U.S. companies must adapt to the Chinese culture by identifying specific trends among urban Chinese teens. For example:

Coke . . . has combined its partnerships with a popular girl band in China called S.H.E.; athletes like Liu Xiang; and the current video game hit in China, "World of Warcraft" to hit two or three passion points at the same time.[1]

Social marketing—The American Legacy Foundation (www.americanlegacy.org) is the national, independent public health foundation established by the 1998 tobacco settlement. Legacy is dedicated to reducing tobacco use in the United States with major initiatives reaching youth, women, and minority populations through grant awards, research initiatives, marketing campaigns, training programs, and collaboration with national and local partners. It faces the monumental task of convincing people to change addiction-driven behaviors and preventing young people from consuming a product that often seems glamorous and mature to them. It spends approximately $115 million per year on marketing programs, most of which are aimed at teens.

The foundation's Truth campaign has used humor, shock tactics, and appeals to peer pressure to influence teenagers. It airs television and print ads, and sponsors a tour, a Web site, and activities by teenagers to call attention to facts about smoking. For example, in Miami teens put small signs next to dog poop on city streets that stated: "Ammonia is found in dog poop. Tobacco companies add it to cigarettes."

Online marketing—Cohort management involves bundling multiple brands into a single online marketing effort aimed at a common consumer group. It represents a collective approach to marketing in contrast to the traditional individualistic brand management approach. Procter & Gamble is using cohort marketing on its Web site HomeMadeSimple.com. The site offers an online guide to home and lifestyle issues while promoting five P&G brands—Cascade, Dawn, Mr. Clean, Swiffer, and Febreze. Other P&G brands are also promoted on the site. The key issue facing online marketers in the "post–dot-com bubble" era is not just the challenge of driving traffic to their Web sites (which HomeMadeSimple does very well) but driving sales. As Andy Walter, director of the project, states: "The thing I've preached to my team is HomeMadeSimple can be more successful than MarthaStewart (in terms of number of visitors). But we will end it next month if that's all we attain. We have to sell those brands."

HomeMadeSimple has regular sections on getting organized, interior decoration, cooking, outside activities, celebrating the small things in life, and kids activities. But for its Web site to continue to attract visitors and enhance the sales and image of its products, P&G must understand much more about its customers than their cleaning requirements![2]

The field of **consumer behavior** is *the study of individuals, groups, or organizations and the processes they use to select, secure, use, and dispose of products, services, experiences, or ideas to satisfy needs and the impacts that these processes have on the consumer and society.* This view of consumer behavior is broader than the traditional one, which focused more narrowly on the buyer and the immediate antecedents and consequences of the purchasing process. Our broader view will lead us to examine more indirect influences on consumption decisions as well as far-reaching consequences that involve more than just the purchaser and seller.

The opening examples above summarize some attempts to apply an understanding of consumer behavior in order to develop an effective marketing strategy or influence socially desirable behavior. Throughout this text, we will explore the factors and trends shaping consumer behavior and how marketers and regulators can utilize this information. The examples cited above in the chapter opener reveal four key aspects regarding consumer behavior. First and most basic, successful marketing decisions by commercial firms, non-profit organizations, and regulatory agencies require extensive information about consumer behavior. It should be obvious from the examples that *organizations are applying theories and information about consumer behavior on a daily basis.* Knowledge of consumer behavior is critical for influencing not only product purchase decisions but people's decisions about which college to attend, which charities to support, how much recycling to do, whether to seek help for an addiction or behavioral problem, and a world of other choices.

Second the examples indicate the need to collect information about the *specific* consumers involved in the marketing decision at hand. At its current state of development, consumer behavior theory provides the manager with the proper questions to ask. Given the importance of the specific situation or product category, it will often be necessary to *conduct research* to find the relevant answers to these questions. One executive explains the importance of consumer behavior research this way:

> Understanding and properly interpreting consumer wants is a whole lot easier said than done. Every week our marketing researchers talk to more than 4,000 consumers to find out
>
> - What they think of our products and those of our competitors.
> - What they think of possible improvements in our products.
> - How they use our products.
> - What attitudes they have about our products and our advertising.
> - What they feel about their roles in the family and society.
> - What their hopes and dreams are for themselves and their families.
>
> Today, as never before, we cannot take our business for granted. That's why understanding—and therefore learning to anticipate—consumer behavior is our key to planning and managing in this ever-changing environment.[3]

Marketers approach consumer research in a variety of ways (as discussed in Appendix A at the end of the text). An emerging approach involves online research. One estimate is that 60 percent of all product and service concept testing is done online. The most prominent reason is its efficiency in terms of time and money. Kellogg hired BuzzBack Market Research to conduct online research on kids and moms about their new Pop-Tarts Yogurt Blasts. They focused on picking a brand name and selecting key product benefits to feature in their promotions. They found that by having colorful and interesting packaging (kids) and emphasizing key health benefits (moms) they could satisfy both groups.[4]

Third, the examples in the chapter's opener reveal that *consumer behavior is a complex, multidimensional process.* Coke, the American Legacy Foundation, and P&G have invested substantial time, money, and effort researching consumer behavior and much more trying to influence it; yet none of them are completely successful. Careful research is no guarantee—it simply increases the odds of success. Think of the complexity involved in Kellogg's new Yogurt Blasts, where both kids and parents must be satisfied and the benefits they want differ dramatically. Or ask people if they want to drive cars that are better for the environment, and although many say yes, these same consumers are trading off environmental concerns against their desire for performance. Early attempts to market environmentally friendly automobiles failed because they failed to consider these competing trade-offs.

Finally, the examples cited above suggest that *marketing practices designed to influence consumer behavior involve ethical issues that affect the firm, the individual, and society.*

Courtesy Bombardier, Inc.

Courtesy Crownline Boats, Inc.

The issues are not always obvious and many times involve trade-offs at different levels. Coke, while providing benefits to individual consumers and profits for the company, raises resource use, disposition, and other issues that affect all of society. Coke may provide individual consumers with an enjoyable experience; however, the dietary consequences of consuming sugar-laden beverages also exist at both the individual and societal level as highlighted, for example, by increases in juvenile diabetes. More obvious concerns arise around marketing products such as cigarettes and alcohol, as well as marketing practices that target children. We will explore such ethical issues throughout the text.

Sufficient knowledge of consumer behavior currently exists to provide a usable guide to marketing practice for commercial firms, nonprofit organizations, and regulators, but the state of the art is not sufficient for us to write a cookbook with surefire recipes for success. We will illustrate how some organizations were able to combine certain ingredients for success under specific conditions. However, as conditions change, the quantities and even the ingredients required for success may change. It is up to you as a student and future marketing manager to develop the ability to apply this knowledge to specific situations. To assist you, we provide a variety of questions and exercises at the end of each chapter and a series of short cases at the end of each main part of the text that can be used to develop your application skills. Appendix B at the end of the text provides a list of key questions for a consumer behavior audit for developing marketing strategy.

Remember that *all marketing decisions and regulations are based on assumptions and knowledge about consumer behavior.* It is impossible to think of a marketing decision for which this is not the case. For example, Legacy's decisions to use certain types of advertising appeals in targeting teen smoking must be based on various assumptions about how teens perceive their social environment, how teens view advertising, and so forth. Likewise, a decision to match a competitor's price reduction must be based on some assumption about how consumers evaluate prices and how they would respond to a price differential between the two brands. Examine Illustration 1-1. Both these ads appeared in the same issue of *Boating World* magazine and are targeted at the same consumers. *What assumptions about consumer behavior underlie each ad? Which approach is best? Why?*

APPLICATIONS OF CONSUMER BEHAVIOR

Marketing Strategy

All marketing strategies and tactics are based on explicit or implicit beliefs about consumer behavior. Decisions based on explicit assumptions and sound theory and research are more likely to be successful than are decisions based solely on hunches or intuition. Thus, knowledge of consumer behavior can be an important competitive advantage. It can greatly reduce the odds of bad decisions and market failures such as the following:

> S.C. Johnson recently pulled the plug on its Ziploc TableTops, a line of semi-disposable plates. TableTops was one of the company's most expensive launches with $65 million spent on marketing. A number of factors appear to have contributed to the failure including relatively high prices (which made consumers less likely to throw them away) and the fact that the products really weren't all that disposable. As one retailer explained, "There are no repeat purchases. The things last forever."[5]
>
> Nestea launched a yellowish carbonated beverage named Tea Whiz. As you might suspect, it failed as did Miller Clear Beer and Gerber adult foods.

A primary goal in this book is to help you obtain a usable managerial understanding of consumer behavior. The key here is *usable understanding*—we want to increase your understanding of consumer behavior in order to help you become a more effective marketing manager. Before we take a look at marketing strategy and consumer behavior, let's examine regulatory policy, social marketing, and the importance of being an informed individual.

Regulatory Policy

Various regulatory bodies exist to develop, interpret, and/or implement policies designed to protect and aid consumers. For example, the Food and Drug Administration (FDA) administers the Nutrition Labeling and Education Act (NLEA). Among other things, NLEA requires that packaged foods prominently display nutrition information in the form of the "Nutrition Facts" panel.

A major goal of NLEA was to improve consumer dietary decisions by providing them with more nutritional information. Has it succeeded? A recent study suggests that it depends. For example, the Nutrition Facts panel appears to be the most beneficial to highly motivated consumers who are low in nutritional knowledge. Regulations have both costs and benefits. For example, the benefits of NLEA can be viewed in light of the estimated $2 billion in compliance costs. The comparisons get increasingly difficult as one tries to place a dollar value on individual and societal benefits.[6]

Clearly, effective regulation of many marketing practices requires an extensive knowledge of consumer behavior. We will discuss this issue throughout the text and provide a detailed treatment in Chapter 20.

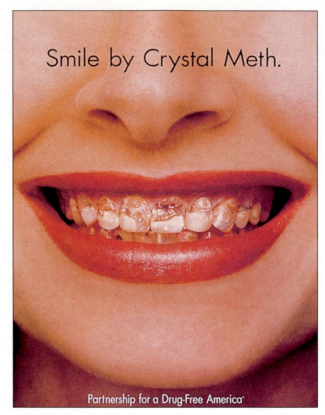

Courtesy Partnership for a Drug-Free America.

Social Marketing

Some states now invest cigarette tax revenues in high-quality, prime-time antismoking television commercials. Researchers at the University of Vermont spent $2 million on a four-year television campaign that showed popular kids disdaining cigarettes or smokers being unable to get dates. Smoking rates among teenagers were 35 percent lower in communities where the campaign was shown than in similar communities without the campaign. The effect was still strong two years after the campaign quit airing.[7]

How did these researchers decide to stress negative social consequences of smoking rather than negative health consequences? The decision was based on their knowledge and assumptions about the consumer behavior of teenagers.

Social marketing is *the application of marketing strategies and tactics to alter or create behaviors that have a positive effect on the targeted individuals or society as a whole.*[8] Social marketing has been used in attempts to reduce smoking, as noted above; to increase the percentage of children receiving their vaccinations in a timely manner; to encourage environmentally sound behaviors such as recycling; to reduce behaviors potentially leading to AIDS; to enhance support of charities; to reduce drug use; and to support many other important causes.

Just as for commercial marketing strategy, successful social marketing strategy requires a sound understanding of consumer behavior. For example, the Partnership for a Drug-Free America uses a fear-based campaign in its efforts to discourage the use of crystal meth. Illustration 1-2 shows one of its milder ads. In Chapter 11, we will analyze the conditions under which such campaigns are likely to succeed.

Informed Individuals

Most economically developed societies are legitimately referred to as consumption societies. Most individuals in these societies spend more time engaged in consumption than in any other activity, including work or sleep (both of which also involve consumption). Therefore, knowledge of consumer behavior can enhance our understanding of our environment and ourselves. Such an understanding is essential for sound citizenship, effective purchasing behavior, and reasoned business ethics.

Literally thousands of firms are spending millions of dollars to influence you, your family, and your friends. These attempts to influence you occur in ads, on packages, as product features, in sales pitches, and in store environments. They also occur in the content of many television shows, in the products that are used in movies, and in the materials presented to children in schools.[9] Given the magnitude of these direct and indirect influence attempts, it is important that consumers accurately understand the strategies and tactics being used. It is equally important that all of us, as citizens, understand the consumer behavior basis of these strategies so that we can set appropriate limits on them when required.

MARKETING STRATEGY AND CONSUMER BEHAVIOR

The applications of consumer behavior described above focus on the development of, regulation of, or effects of marketing strategy. We will now examine marketing strategy in more depth.

To survive in a competitive environment, an organization must provide its target customers more value than is provided to them by its competitors. **Customer value** is *the difference between all the benefits derived from a total product and all the costs of acquiring those benefits.* For example, owning a car can provide a number of benefits, depending on the person and the type of car, including flexible transportation, image, status, pleasure, comfort, and even companionship. However, securing these benefits requires paying not only for the car, but for gasoline, insurance, registration, maintenance, and parking fees, among others, as well as risking injury from an accident, adding to environmental pollution, and dealing with traffic jams and other frustrations. It is the difference between the total benefits and the total costs that constitutes customer value.

It is critical that a firm consider value *from the customer's perspective.* Ziploc's TableTop failure referred to earlier demonstrates this. The product was overpriced relative to products of other competitors in the category and much higher priced than truly disposable tableware. The high price made consumers hesitant to buy in the first place, or if they did buy, made them uncomfortable with throwing them away. TableTop was too expensive and durable to be maximally useful to consumers and profitable for Ziploc.

Providing superior customer value requires the organization to do a better job of anticipating and reacting to customer needs than the competition does. This is the essence of a good marketing strategy. As Figure 1-1 indicates, an understanding of consumer behavior is the basis for marketing strategy formulation. Consumers' reactions to the marketing strategy determine the organization's success or failure. However, these reactions also determine the success of the consumers in meeting their needs, and they have significant impacts on the larger society in which they occur.

Marketing strategy, as described in Figure 1-1, is conceptually very simple. It begins with an analysis of the market the organization is considering. This requires a detailed analysis of the organization's capabilities, the strengths and weaknesses of competitors, the

| FIGURE 1-1 | Marketing Strategy and Consumer Behavior |

economic and technological forces affecting the market, and the current and potential customers in the market. On the basis of the consumer analysis undertaken in this step, the organization identifies groups of individuals, households, or firms with similar needs. These market segments are described in terms of demographics, media preferences, geographic location, and so forth. Management then selects one or more of these segments as target markets based on the firm's capabilities relative to those of its competition (given current and forecast economic and technological conditions).

Next, marketing strategy is formulated. Marketing strategy seeks to provide the customer with more value than the competition while still producing a profit for the firm. Marketing strategy is formulated in terms of the marketing mix; that is, it involves determining the product features, price, communications, distribution, and services that will provide customers with superior value. This entire set of characteristics is often referred to as the **total product.** The total product is presented to the target market, which is consistently

Photo by David McNew/Getty Images.

engaged in processing information and making decisions designed to maintain or enhance its lifestyle (individuals and households) or performance (businesses and other organizations).

Look at Illustration 1-3. What is the Starbucks' total product? Clearly, it is much more than coffee. Places like Starbucks and the Hard Rock Cafe are selling experiences as much as or perhaps more than food and beverages—and they are doing so around the world. An "experience" occurs when a company intentionally creates a memorable event for customers. While products and services are to a large extent external to the customer, an experience is largely internal to each customer. The experience exists in the mind of an individual who has been engaged on an emotional, physical, intellectual, or even spiritual level. Today, many firms are wrapping experiences around their traditional products and services in order to sell them better. Niketown, the Sharper Image, Cabella's, and REI all draw customers to their outlets in part because of the experiences that are available at those outlets.[10] Consumer Insight 1-1 shows how traditional retailers are drawing on this notion to develop lifestyle centers.

For the firm, the reaction of the target market to the total product produces an image of the product/brand/organization, sales (or lack thereof), and some level of customer satisfaction among those who did purchase. Sophisticated marketers seek to produce satisfied customers rather than mere sales—because satisfied customers are more profitable in the long run. For the individual, the process results in some level of need satisfaction, financial expenditure, attitude development/change, and/or behavioral changes. For society, the cumulative effect of the marketing process affects economic growth, pollution, social problems (e.g., illnesses caused by smoking and alcohol), and social benefits (e.g., improved

Beyond Transactions: Retailers Build Lifestyle Centers

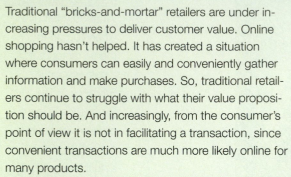

Traditional "bricks-and-mortar" retailers are under increasing pressures to deliver customer value. Online shopping hasn't helped. It has created a situation where consumers can easily and conveniently gather information and make purchases. So, traditional retailers continue to struggle with what their value proposition should be. And increasingly, from the consumer's point of view it is not in facilitating a transaction, since convenient transactions are much more likely online for many products.

To add additional value and remain competitive, retail developers have been moving to what are called lifestyle centers.[11] **Lifestyle centers** are "small, convenient, open-air retailing complexes laid out to evoke the small-town shopping districts of previous generations." In contrast to traditional enclosed malls with anchor stores, these lifestyle centers are anchored by more experiential offerings such as restaurants and movie theaters, and also allow a relaxing stroll along the way. Lifestyle centers are on the increase while traditional malls are declining. The following excerpt about a typical lifestyle shopper (Kristen Kratus, a 29-year-old working professional and mother) helps to explain why:

> [Kristen] avoids the hassles of mall parking by making half her purchases online. Most of the rest is

done at Broadway Plaza, a lifestyle center about 10 miles away in Walnut Creek with easy access to parking. "It's more convenient," says Kratus, who has a 10-month-old son, Charlie. "I can buy things, take them back to the car, and then shop again." She says the center has a better selection of restaurants and attractive pedestrian walkways, making shopping more enjoyable: "I can walk around with Charlie, drink a coffee outside, window shop, and see what's out there. It's like being at a park."

Clearly, shopping goes beyond transactions, and traditional retailers have responded in various ingenious ways including lifestyle centers that add an experiential component hard to match online.

Critical Thinking Questions

1. How do lifestyle centers add value hard to match by online retailers?

2. Can you see any negative aspects of lifestyle centers compared to traditional malls?

3. Do you think *virtual* lifestyle centers might be possible online? What would they look like?

nutrition, increased education). Since individual and societal impacts may or may not be in the best interests of the individual or society, the development and application of consumer behavior knowledge has many ethical implications.

Note again that an *analysis of consumers* is a key part of the foundation of marketing strategy, and *consumer reaction* to the total product determines the success or failure of the strategy. Before providing an overview of consumer behavior, we will examine marketing strategy formulation in more detail.

MARKET ANALYSIS COMPONENTS

Market analysis requires a thorough understanding of the organization's own capabilities, the capabilities of current and future competitors, the consumption process of potential customers, and the economic, physical, and technological environment in which these elements will interact.

The Consumers

It is not possible to anticipate and react to customers' needs and desires without a complete understanding of consumer behavior. Discovering customers' needs is a complex process, but it can often be accomplished by marketing research. For example, Target wanted to tap into the $210 billion college market. In particular Target was looking at the furnishings and accessories market and was interested in the specific needs and motivations of students making the transition from home to college dorm life. Jump Associates conducted the research for Target and they took a unique approach:

> [Jump Associates] sponsored a series of "game nights" at high school grads' homes, inviting incoming college freshmen as well as students with a year of dorm living under their belts. To get teens talking about dorm life, Jump devised a board game that involved issues associated with going to college. The game naturally led to informal conversations—and questions—about college life. Jump researchers were on the sidelines to observe, while a video camera recorded the proceedings.

Based on this research (which is a variation of focus groups—see Appendix A), Target launched the Todd Oldham Dorm Room line which includes such products as Kitchen in a Box and Bath in a Box—"all-in-one" assortments of the types of products needed by college freshmen. The line has been a success, fueling double-digit revenue increases.[12]

Knowing the consumer requires understanding the behavioral principles that guide consumption behaviors. These principles are covered in depth in the balance of this text.

The Company

A firm must fully understand its own ability to meet customer needs. This involves evaluating all aspects of the firm, including its financial condition, general managerial skills, production capabilities, research and development capabilities, technological sophistication, reputation, and marketing skills. Marketing skills would include new-product development capabilities, channel strength, advertising abilities, service capabilities, marketing research abilities, market and consumer knowledge, and so forth.

Failure to adequately understand one's own strengths can cause serious problems. IBM's first attempt to enter the home computer market with the PC Jr. was a failure in part for this reason. Although IBM had an excellent reputation with large business customers and a very strong direct sales force for serving them, these strengths were not relevant to the household consumer market.

The Competitors

It is not possible to consistently do a better job of meeting customer needs than the competition without a thorough understanding of the competition's capabilities and strategies. This requires the same level of knowledge of a firm's key competitors that is required of one's own firm. In addition, for any significant marketing action, the following questions must be answered:

1. If we are successful, which firms will be hurt (lose sales or sales opportunities)?
2. Of those firms that are injured, which have the capability (financial resources, marketing strengths) to respond?
3. How are they likely to respond (reduce prices, increase advertising, introduce a new product)?
4. Is our strategy (planned action) robust enough to withstand the likely actions of our competitors, or do we need additional contingency plans?

The Conditions

The state of the economy, the physical environment, government regulations, and technological developments affect consumer needs and expectations as well as company and competitor capabilities. The deterioration of the physical environment has produced not only consumer demand for environmentally sound products but also government regulations affecting product design and manufacturing.

International agreements such as NAFTA (North America Free Trade Agreement) have greatly reduced international trade barriers and raised the level of both competition and consumer expectations for many products. And technology is changing the way people live, work, deal with disease, and so on. Blogging, podcasting, instant messaging, MP3s, and Apple's astounding success with the iPod are just some of the ways technology is changing the way consumers communicate and access media.

Clearly, a firm cannot develop a sound marketing strategy without anticipating the conditions under which that strategy will be implemented.

MARKET SEGMENTATION

Perhaps the most important marketing decision a firm makes is the selection of one or more market segments on which to focus. A **market segment** is *a portion of a larger market whose needs differ somewhat from the larger market.* Since a market segment has unique needs, a firm that develops a total product focused solely on the needs of that segment will be able to meet the segment's desires better than a firm whose product or service attempts to meet the needs of multiple segments.

To be viable, a segment must be large enough to be served profitably. To some extent, each individual or household has unique needs for most products (a preferred color combination, for example). The smaller the segment, the closer the total product can be to that segment's desires. Historically, the smaller the segment, the more it costs to serve the segment. Thus, a tailor-made suit costs more than a mass-produced suit. However, flexible manufacturing and customized media (including online) are making it increasingly cost effective to develop products and communications for small segments or even individual consumers, as the following example shows:

> Fingerhut, a catalog retailer with $2 billion in sales, has a database that stores over 500 pieces of information on each of more than 50 million potential customers. The data include not only past purchases and credit information but demographics such as age, marital status, and number of children and personal data such as hobbies and birthdays. This database enables Fingerhut to send consumers individualized catalogs at times when they are most likely to buy.[13]

Behavioral targeting, in which consumers' online activity is tracked and specific banner ads are delivered based on that activity, is another example of how technology is making individualized communication increasingly cost-effective.

Market segmentation involves four steps:

1. Identifying product-related need sets.
2. Grouping customers with similar need sets.
3. Describing each group.
4. Selecting an attractive segment(s) to serve.

Product-Related Need Sets

Organizations approach market segmentation with a set of current and potential capabilities. These capabilities may be a reputation, an existing product, a technology, or some other skill

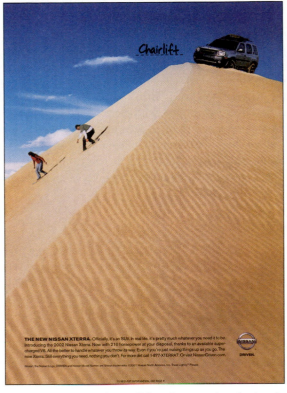

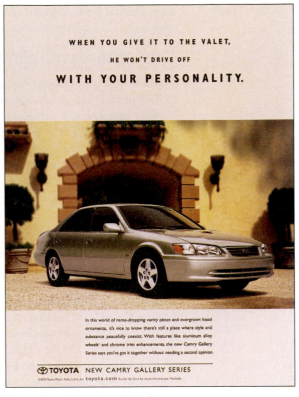

Courtesy Nissan (2001). Nissan and Nissan logo are registered trademarks of Nissan.

Courtesy Toyota Motor Sales, U.S.A., Inc.

set. The first task of the firm is to identify need sets that the organization is capable, or could become capable, of meeting. The term **need set** is used to reflect the fact that most products in developed economies satisfy more than one need. Thus, an automobile can meet more needs than just basic transportation. Some customers purchase cars to meet transportation and status needs. Others purchase them to meet transportation and fun needs. Still others purchase automobiles to meet status, fun, and transportation needs. Illustration 1-4 shows two ads for automobiles. What needs does the Toyota ad appeal to? The Nissan ad? These ads differ because the firms are pursuing different market segments with distinct need sets.

Customer needs are not restricted to product features. They also include types and sources of information about the product, outlets where the product is available, the price of the product, services associated with the product, the image of the product or firm, and even where and how the product is produced. For example, in the 1990s Nike lost sales as a result of publicity about child labor and abusive working conditions at some of the factories in developing countries where many of its products are made. In response, it changed practices and engaged in a variety of public relations activities. As a result it seems to have turned its image around in the area of Corporate Social Responsibility (CSR).[14]

Identifying the various need sets that the firm's current or potential product might satisfy typically involves consumer research, particularly focus groups and depth interviews, as well as logic and intuition. These need sets are often associated with other variables such as age, stage in the household life cycle, gender, social class, ethnic group, or lifestyle, and many firms start the segmentation process focusing first on one or more of the groups defined by one of these variables. Thus, a firm might start by identifying various ethnic groups and then attempt to discover similarities and differences in consumption-related needs across these groups. While better-defined segments will generally be discovered by

ILLUSTRATION 1-4

The Nissan Xterra and the Toyota Camry are both automobiles. Both provide flexible, individual transportation. Yet, as these ads show, they are designed to meet different sets of needs in addition to basic transportation.

focusing first on needs, then on consumer characteristics associated with those needs, both approaches are used in practice and both provide a useful basis for segmentation.

Customers with Similar Need Sets

The next step is to group consumers with similar need sets. For example, the need for moderately priced, fun, sporty automobiles appears to exist in many young single individuals, young couples with no children, and middle-aged couples whose children have left home. These consumers can be grouped into one segment as far as product features and perhaps even product image are concerned despite sharply different demographics.

This step generally involves consumer research, including focus group interviews, surveys, and product concept tests (see Appendix A). It could also involve an analysis of current consumption patterns.

Description of Each Group

Once consumers with similar need sets are identified, they should be described in terms of their demographics, lifestyles, and media usage. In order to design an effective marketing program, it is necessary to have a complete understanding of the potential customers. It is only with such a complete understanding that we can be sure we have correctly identified the need set. In addition, we cannot communicate effectively with our customers if we do not understand the context in which our product is purchased and consumed, how it is thought about by our customers, and the language they use to describe it. Thus, while many young single individuals, young couples with no children, and middle-aged couples whose children have left home may want the same features in an automobile, the media required to reach each group and the appropriate language and themes to use with each group would likely differ.

Attractive Segment(s) to Serve

Once we are sure we have a thorough understanding of each segment, we must select our **target market**—*that segment(s) of the larger market on which we will focus our marketing effort.* This decision is based on our ability to provide the selected segment(s) with superior customer value at a profit. Thus, the size and growth of the segment, the intensity of the current and anticipated competition, the cost of providing the superior value, and so forth are important considerations. Table 1-1 provides a simple worksheet for use in evaluating and comparing the attractiveness of various market segments.

TABLE 1-1

Market Segment
Attractiveness
Worksheet

Criterion	Score*
Segment size	_____
Segment growth rate	_____
Competitor strength	_____
Customer satisfaction with existing products	_____
Fit with company image	_____
Fit with company objectives	_____
Fit with company resources	_____
Distribution available	_____
Investment required	_____
Stability/predictability	_____
Cost to serve	_____
Sustainable advantage available	_____
Communications channels available	_____
Risk	_____
Other (_____)	_____

*Score on a 1 to 10 scale, with 10 being most favorable.

It is important to remember that each market segment requires its own marketing strategy. Each element of the marketing mix should be examined to determine if changes are required from one segment to another. Sometimes each segment will require a completely different marketing mix, including the product. At other times, only the advertising message or retail outlets may need to differ.

MARKETING STRATEGY

It is not possible to select target markets without simultaneously formulating a general marketing strategy for each segment. A decisive criterion in selecting target markets is the ability to provide superior value to those market segments. Since customer value is delivered by the marketing strategy, the firm must develop its general marketing strategy as it evaluates potential target markets.

Marketing strategy is basically the answer to the question: *How will we provide superior customer value to our target market?* The answer to this question requires the formulation of a consistent marketing mix. The **marketing mix** is *the product, price, communications, distribution, and services provided to the target market.* It is the combination of these elements that meets customer needs and provides customer value. For example, in Illustration 1-1, Crownline boats promise superior value compared to competitors in terms of quality and service. Their J.D. Power and Associates award backs up these claims.

The Product

A **product** is *anything a consumer acquires or might acquire to meet a perceived need.* Consumers are generally buying need satisfaction, not physical product attributes.[15] As the former head of Revlon said, "in the factory we make cosmetics, in the store we sell hope." Thus, consumers don't purchase quarter-inch drill bits but the ability to create quarter-inch holes. Federal Express lost much of its overnight letter delivery business not to UPS or Airborne but to fax machines and the Internet because these technologies could meet the same consumer needs faster, cheaper, or more conveniently.

We use the term *product* to refer to physical products and primary or core services. Thus, an automobile is a product, as is a transmission overhaul or a ride in a taxi. Packaged goods alone (food, beverages, pet products, household products) account for over 30,000 new product introductions each year.[16] Obviously, many of these will not succeed. To be successful, products must meet the needs of the target market better than the competition does.

Consider the Chinese computer market. A few years ago, a state-owned company—Legend—appeared headed for oblivion as China opened its market to Western firms. Today, it is a major player. How? According to its general manager, "We have much more insight into the needs of Chinese customers." U.S. companies are learning that while attractive, the Chinese market is also a challenge. A joint venture between Legend and AOL to provide broadband access and service never became viable. As a consequence, Legend broke with AOL and formed an alliance to bundle their computers with China Telecom's China Vnet broadband service.[17]

Communications

Marketing communications include *advertising, the sales force, public relations, packaging, and any other signal that the firm provides about itself and its products.* An effective communications strategy requires answers to the following questions:

1. *With whom, exactly, do we want to communicate?* While most messages are aimed at the target-market members, others are focused on channel members or those who

Courtesy The Coca-Cola Company.

influence the target-market members. For example, pediatric nurses are often asked for advice concerning diapers and other nonmedical infant care items. A firm marketing such items would be wise to communicate directly with these individuals.

Often it is necessary to determine who within the target market should receive the marketing message. For a children's breakfast cereal, should the communications be aimed at the children or the parents or both? The answer depends on the target market and varies by country.

2. *What effect do we want our communications to have on the target audience?* Often a manager will state that the purpose of advertising and other marketing communications is to increase sales. While this may be the ultimate objective, the behavioral objective for most marketing communications is often much more immediate. That is, it may seek to have the audience learn something about the product, seek more information about the product, like the product, recommend the product to others, feel good about having bought the product, or a host of other communications effects.

3. *What message will achieve the desired effect on our audience?* What words, pictures, and symbols should we use to capture attention and produce the desired effect? Marketing messages can range from purely factual statements to pure symbolism. The best approach depends on the situation at hand. Developing an effective message requires a thorough understanding of the meanings the target audience attaches to words and symbols, as well as knowledge of the perception process. Consider Illustration 1-5. Many older consumers may not relate to the approach of this ad. However, it communicates clearly to its intended youth market.

4. *What means and media should we use to reach the target audience?* Should we use personal sales to provide information? Can we rely on the package to provide needed information? Should we advertise in mass media, use direct mail, or rely on consumers to find us on the Internet? If we advertise in mass media, which media (television, radio, magazines, newspapers, Internet) and which specific vehicles (television programs, specific magazines, Web sites, banner ads, and so forth) should we use? Answering these questions requires an understanding both of the media that the target audiences use and of the effect that advertising in those media would have on the product's image.

   Starburst recently launched a sweepstakes promotion targeting teens. The sweepstakes was promoted on 60 million packages and offered two ways to enter—via their cell phone (using the code word "juicy") or online. Notice how the media fits the target audience.[18]

5. *When should we communicate with the target audience?* Should we concentrate our communications near the time that purchases tend to be made or evenly throughout the week, month, or year? Do consumers seek information shortly before purchasing our product? If so, where? Answering these questions requires knowledge of the decision process used by the target market for this product.

Price

Price is *the amount of money one must pay to obtain the right to use the product.* One can buy ownership of a product or, for many products, limited usage rights (i.e., one can rent or lease the product such as a video). Economists often assume that lower prices for the same product will result in more sales than higher prices. However, price sometimes serves as a signal of quality. A product priced "too low" might be perceived as having low quality. Owning expensive items also provides information about the owner. If nothing else, it indicates that the owner can afford the expensive item. This is a desirable feature to some consumers. Starbucks charges relatively high prices for its coffee. Yet it understands that the Starbucks brand allows consumers to "trade up" to a desired image and lifestyle without breaking the bank.[19] Therefore, setting a price requires a thorough understanding of the symbolic role that price plays for the product and target market in question.

It is important to note that the price of a product is not the same as the cost of the product to the customer. **Consumer cost** is *everything the consumer must surrender in order to receive the benefits of owning/using the product.* As described earlier, the cost of owning/using an automobile includes insurance, gasoline, maintenance, finance charges, license fees, parking fees, time and discomfort while shopping for the car, and perhaps even discomfort about increasing pollution, in addition to the purchase price. One of the ways firms seek to provide customer value is to reduce the nonprice costs of owning or operating a product. If successful, the total cost to the customer decreases while the revenue to the marketer stays the same or even increases.

Distribution

Distribution, *having the product available where target customers can buy it,* is essential to success. Only in rare cases will customers go to much trouble to secure a particular brand. Obviously, good channel decisions require a sound knowledge of where target customers shop for the product in question, as the following example shows:

Huffy bikes created a *Cross Sport* bike which was a hybrid between a traditional lightweight 10-speed and a mountain bike. Research suggested strong consumer acceptance. However, Huffy distributed the bike through mass merchandisers like K-Mart when the target buyer was more likely to go to a specialty bike shop—a mistake that cost them millions.[20]

Today's distribution decisions also require an understanding of cross-channel options. Savvy retailers are figuring out ways to let each distribution channel (e.g., online versus offline) do what it does best. For example, Coldwater Creek keeps retail inventories low by having in-store Internet kiosks where consumers can shop and get free shipping. Barnes and Noble bookstores use a similar approach. Obviously, retailers who adopt this approach have to choose an appropriate merchandising strategy where fast-moving, high-profit, seasonal items are in-store to attract customers while other merchandise is available online.[21]

Service

Earlier, we defined *product* to include primary or core services such as haircuts, car repairs, and medical treatments. Here, **service** refers to *auxiliary or peripheral activities that are performed to enhance the primary product or primary service.* Thus, we would consider car repair to be a product (primary service), while free pickup and delivery of the car would be an auxiliary service. Although many texts do not treat service as a separate component of the marketing mix, we do because of the critical role it plays in determining market share and relative price in competitive markets. A firm that does not explicitly manage its auxiliary services is at a competitive disadvantage.

Auxiliary services cost money to provide. Therefore, it is essential that the firm furnish only those services that provide value to the target customers. Providing services that customers do not value can result in high costs and high prices without a corresponding increase in customer value.

CONSUMER DECISIONS

As Figure 1-1 illustrated, the consumer decision process intervenes between the marketing strategy (as implemented in the marketing mix) and the outcomes. That is, the outcomes of the firm's marketing strategy are determined by its interaction with the consumer decision process. The firm can succeed only if consumers see a need that its product can solve, become aware of the product and its capabilities, decide that it is the best available solution, proceed to buy it, and become satisfied with the results of the purchase. A significant part of this entire text is devoted to developing an understanding of the consumer decision process (Chapters 14–18).

OUTCOMES

Firm Outcomes

Product Position   The most basic outcome for a firm of a marketing strategy is its **product position**—*an image of the product or brand in the consumer's mind relative to competing products and brands.* This image consists of a set of beliefs, pictorial representations, and feelings about the product or brand. It does not require purchase or use for it to develop. It is determined by communications about the brand from the firm and other sources, as well as by direct experience with it. Most marketing firms specify the product position they want their brands to have and measure these positions on an ongoing basis. This is because a brand whose position matches the desired position of a target market is likely to be purchased when a need for that product arises.

Courtesy Domecq Importers, Inc.

Sauza Conmemorativo tequila attempts to build a product position as a smooth, light-hearted tequila by running a series of humorous ads all with the tag line: "Life is harsh. Your tequila shouldn't be" (see Illustration 1-6). This positioning has helped the brand's sales grow at more than twice the industry average.[22]

Sales   Sales are a critical outcome, as they produce the revenue necessary for the firm to continue in business. Therefore, virtually all firms evaluate the success of their marketing programs in terms of sales. As we have seen, sales are likely to occur only if the initial consumer analysis was correct and if the marketing mix matches the consumer decision process.

Customer Satisfaction   Marketers have discovered that it is generally more profitable to maintain existing customers than to replace them with new customers. Retaining current customers requires that they be satisfied with their purchase and use of the product. Thus, **customer satisfaction** is a major concern of marketers.

As Figure 1-2 indicates, convincing consumers that your brand offers superior value is necessary in order to make the initial sale. Obviously, one must have a thorough understanding of the potential consumers' needs and of their information acquisition processes to succeed at this task. However, *creating satisfied customers,* and thus future sales, requires that customers continue to believe that your brand meets their needs and offers superior value *after they have used it.* You must deliver as much or more value than your customers initially expected, and it must be enough to satisfy their needs. This requires an even greater understanding of consumer behavior.

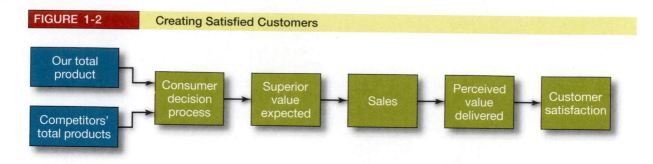

FIGURE 1-2   **Creating Satisfied Customers**

Individual Outcomes

Need Satisfaction   The most obvious outcome of the consumption process for an individual, whether or not a purchase is made, is some level of satisfaction of the need that initiated the consumption process. This can range from none (or even negative if a purchase increases the need rather than reduces it) to complete. Two key processes are involved—the actual need fulfillment and the perceived need fulfillment. These two processes are closely related and are often identical. However, at times they differ. For example, people might take a food supplement because they believe it is enhancing their health while in reality it could have no direct health effects or even negative effects. One objective of government regulation and a frequent goal of consumer groups is to ensure that consumers can adequately judge the extent to which products are meeting their needs.

Injurious Consumption   While we tend to focus on the benefits of consumption, we must remain aware that consumer behavior has a dark side. **Injurious consumption** occurs *when individuals or groups make consumption decisions that have negative consequences for their long-run well-being.*

For most consumers, fulfilling one need affects their ability to fulfill other needs, because of either financial or time constraints. For example, some estimates indicate that most Americans are not saving at a level that will allow them to maintain a lifestyle near their current one when they retire.[23] The cumulative impact of many small decisions to spend financial resources to meet needs now will limit their ability to meet what may be critically important needs after retirement. For other consumers, readily available credit, unrelenting advertising, and widespread, aggressive merchandising result in a level of expenditure that cannot be sustained by their income.[24] The result is often financial distress, delayed or bypassed medical or dental care, family stress, inadequate resources for proper child care, bankruptcy, or even homelessness.

Cigarette consumption is encouraged by hundreds of millions of dollars in marketing expenditures, as is the consumption of alcoholic beverages, snacks with high sugar or fat content, and other potentially harmful products. These expenditures cause some people to consume these products or to consume more of them. Some of these people, and their families, in turn are then harmed by this consumption.[25] Companies are not the only entities that promote potentially harmful products. Most states in the United States now promote state-sponsored gambling, which has caused devastating financial consequences for some individuals.

While these are issues we should be concerned with and we will address throughout this text, we should also note that alcohol consumption seems to have arisen simultaneously with civilization and evidence of gambling is nearly as old. Consumers smoked and chewed tobacco long before mass media or advertising as we know it existed, and illegal drug consumption continues to grow worldwide despite the absence of large-scale marketing, or at least advertising. Thus, though marketing activities based on knowledge of consumer behavior undoubtedly exacerbate some forms of injurious consumption, they are not the sole cause and, as we will see shortly, may also be part of the cure.

Society Outcomes

Economic Outcomes   The cumulative impact of consumers' purchase decisions, including the decision to forgo consumption, is a major determinant of the state of a given country's economy. Their decisions on whether to buy or save affect economic growth, the availability and cost of capital, employment levels, and so forth. The types of products and brands purchased influence the balance of payments, industry growth rates, and wage levels. Decisions made in one society, particularly large wealthy societies like the United States, Western Europe, and Japan, have a major impact on the economic health of many other countries. A recession in the United States or a strong shift toward purchasing only American-made products would have profound negative consequences on the economies of many other countries, both developed and developing.

Physical Environment Outcomes   Consumers make decisions that have a major impact on the physical environments of both their own and other societies. The cumulative effect of American consumers' decisions to rely on relatively large private cars rather than mass transit results in significant air pollution in American cities as well as the consumption of nonrenewable resources from other countries. The decisions of people in most developed and in many developing economies to consume meat as a primary source of protein result in the clearing of rain forests for grazing land, the pollution of many watersheds due to large-scale feedlots, and an inefficient use of grain, water, and energy to produce protein. It also appears to produce health problems for many consumers. The destruction of the rain forests and other critical habitat areas receives substantial negative publicity. However, these resources are being used because of consumer demand, and consumer demand consists of the decisions you and I and our families and our friends make!

As we will see in Chapter 3, many consumers now recognize the indirect effects of consumption on the environment and are altering their behavior to minimize environmental harm.

Social Welfare   Consumer decisions affect the general social welfare of a society. Decisions concerning how much to spend for private goods (personal purchases) rather than public goods (support for public education, parks, health care, and so forth) are generally made indirectly by consumers' elected representatives. These decisions have a major impact on the overall quality of life in a society.

Injurious consumption, as described above, affects society as well as the individuals involved. The social costs of smoking-induced illnesses, alcoholism, and drug abuse are staggering. To the extent that marketing activities increase or decrease injurious consumption, they have a major impact on the social welfare of a society. Consider the following:

According to the U.S. Public Health Service, of the 10 leading causes of death in the United States, at least 7 could be reduced substantially if people at risk would change just 5 behaviors: compliance (e.g., use of antihypertensive medication), diet, smoking, lack of exercise, and alcohol and drug abuse. Each of these behaviors is inextricably linked with marketing efforts and the reactions of consumers to marketing campaigns. The link between consumer choices and social problems is clear.[26]

However, the same authors conclude: "Although these problems appear daunting, they are all problems that are solvable through altruistic [social] marketing." Thus, marketing and consumer behavior can both aggravate and reduce serious social problems.

THE NATURE OF CONSUMER BEHAVIOR

Figure 1-3 is the model that we use to capture the general structure and process of consumer behavior and to organize this text. It is a **conceptual model.** It does not contain sufficient detail to predict particular behaviors; however, it does reflect our beliefs about the general nature of consumer behavior. Individuals develop self-concepts and subsequent lifestyles based on a variety of internal (mainly psychological and physical) and external

FIGURE 1-3 Overall Model of Consumer Behavior

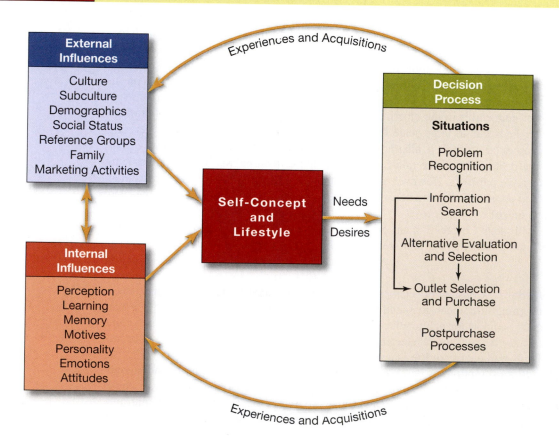

(mainly sociological and demographic) influences. These self-concepts and lifestyles produce needs and desires, many of which require consumption decisions to satisfy. As individuals encounter relevant situations, the consumer decision process is activated. This process and the experiences and acquisitions it produces in turn influence the consumers' self-concept and lifestyle by affecting their internal and external characteristics.

The model in Figure 1-3, while simple, is both conceptually sound and intuitively appealing. Each of us has a view of ourselves (self-concept), and we try to live in a particular manner given our resources (lifestyle). Our view of ourselves and the way we try to live are determined by internal factors (such as our personality, values, emotions, and memory) and external factors (such as our culture, age, friends, family, and subculture). Our view of ourselves and the way we try to live results in desires and needs that we bring to the multitude of situations we encounter daily. Many of these situations will cause us to consider a purchase. Our decision, and even the process of making it, will cause learning and may affect many other internal and external factors that will change or reinforce our current self-concept and lifestyle.

Of course life is rarely so structured as Figure 1-3 and our discussion of it so far may seem to suggest. Consumer behavior is hardly ever so simple, structured, conscious, mechanical, or linear. A quick analysis of your own behavior and that of your friends will reveal that on the contrary consumer behavior is frequently complex, disorganized, nonconscious, organic, and circular. Remember—Figure 1-3 is only a model, a starting point for our analysis. It is meant to aid you in thinking about consumer behavior. As you look at the model and read the following chapters based on this model, continually relate the descriptions in the text to the rich world of consumer behavior that is all around you.

The factors shown in Figure 1-3 are given detailed treatment in the subsequent chapters of this book. Here we provide a brief overview so that you can initially see how they work and fit together. Our discussion here and in the following chapters moves through the model from left to right.

External Influences (Part Two)

Dividing the factors that influence consumers into categories is somewhat arbitrary. For example, we treat learning as an internal influence despite the fact that much human learning involves interaction with, or imitation of, other individuals. Thus, learning could also be considered a group process. In Figure 1-3, the two-directional arrow connecting internal and external influences indicates that each set interacts with the other.

We organize our discussion of external influences from large-scale macrogroups to smaller, more microgroup influences. *Culture* is perhaps the most pervasive influence on consumer behavior. We begin our consideration of culture in Chapter 2 by examining differences in consumption patterns across cultures. In Chapters 3 through 6, we focus on American culture in detail. In Chapter 3, we examine cultural values. As we will see, while Americans share many values and consumption behaviors, there is also rich diversity and ongoing change in this society that create both marketing opportunities and unique social energy. Illustration 1-7 shows how marketers are embracing this diversity in their advertisements.

Chapter 4 continues our examination of American society by analyzing its demographics (the number, education, age, income, occupation, and location of individuals in a society) and social stratification. Chapter 5 considers ethnic, religious, and regional subcultures. Chapter 6 analyzes families and households, including discussions of how they evolve over time, the role of families in teaching children how to consume, and household decision making. Finally, in Chapter 7, we look at the processes by which groups influence

America is increasingly diverse. Ads such as this one reflect and embrace such diversity.

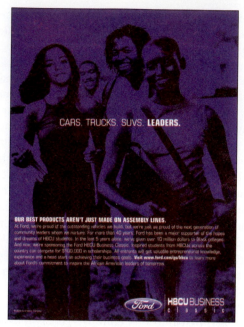

CARS. TRUCKS. SUVS. **LEADERS.**

OUR BEST PRODUCTS AREN'T JUST MADE ON ASSEMBLY LINES.
At Ford, we're proud of the outstanding vehicles we build, but we're just as proud of the next generation of community leaders whom we nurture. For more than 40 years, Ford has been a major supporter of the hopes and dreams of HBCU students. In the last 5 years alone, we've given over 10 million dollars to Black colleges. And now, we're sponsoring the Ford HBCU Business Classic. Inspired students from HBCUs across the country can compete for $100,000 in scholarships. All entrants will get valuable entrepreneurial knowledge, experience and a head start on achieving their business goals. Visit **www.ford.com/go/hbcu** to learn more about Ford's commitment to inspire the African American leaders of tomorrow.

Ford   HBCU BUSINESS
         c l a s s i c

Courtesy Ford Motor Company.

consumer behavior and group communication, including the role of groups in the acceptance of new products and technologies. Taken together, Chapters 2 through 7 provide a means of comparing and contrasting the various external factors that influence consumer behavior in America—and around the world: Cross-cultural variations are highlighted when possible throughout the text.

Internal Influences (Part Three)

Internal influences begin with perception, the process by which individuals receive and assign meaning to stimuli (Chapter 8). This is followed by learning—changes in the content or structure of long-term memory (Chapter 9). Chapter 10 covers three closely related topics: motivation—the reason for a behavior; personality—an individual's characteristic response tendencies across similar situations; and emotion—strong, relatively uncontrolled feelings that affect our behavior. We conclude our coverage of internal influences by examining attitudes in Chapter 11. An attitude is an enduring organization of motivational, emotional, perceptual, and cognitive processes with respect to some aspect of our environment. In essence an attitude is the way one thinks, feels, and acts toward some aspect of his or her environment such as a retail store, television program, or product. As such, our attitudes are heavily influenced by the external and internal factors that we will have discussed in the preceding chapters.

Self-Concept and Lifestyle

Chapter 12 concludes Part Three with a detailed discussion of the key concepts of self-concept and lifestyle around which our model revolves. As a result of the interaction of the internal and external variables described earlier, individuals develop a self-concept that is reflected in a lifestyle. **Self-concept** is *the totality of an individual's thoughts and feelings about him- or herself.* **Lifestyle** is, quite simply, *how one lives,* including the products one buys, how one uses them, what one thinks about them, and how one feels about them. Lifestyle is the manifestation of the individual's self-concept, the total image the person has of him- or herself as a result of the culture he or she lives in and the individual situations and experiences that comprise his or her daily existence. It is the sum of the person's past decisions and future plans.

Both individuals and families exhibit distinct lifestyles. We often hear of "career-oriented individuals," "outdoor families," or "devoted parents." One's lifestyle is determined by both conscious and unconscious decisions. Often we make choices with full awareness of their impact on our lifestyle, but generally we are unaware of the extent to which our decisions are influenced by our current or desired lifestyle. Our model shows that consumers' self-concepts and lifestyles produce needs and desires that interact with the situations in which consumers find themselves to trigger the consumer decision process.

We do not mean to imply that consumers think in terms of lifestyle. None of us consciously thinks, "I'll have an Evian bottled water in order to enhance my lifestyle." Rather, we make decisions consistent with our lifestyles without deliberately considering lifestyle. Most consumer decisions involve very little effort or thought on the part of the consumer. They are what we call *low-involvement decisions.* Feelings and emotions are as important in many consumer decisions as logical analysis or physical product attributes. Nonetheless, most consumer purchases involve at least a modest amount of decision making, and most are influenced by the purchaser's current and desired lifestyle.

Consumer Decision Process (Part Four)

Consumer decisions result from perceived problems ("I'm thirsty") and opportunities ("That looks like it would be fun to try"). We will use the term *problem* to refer both to problems and to opportunities. Consumer problems arise in specific situations and the nature of the situation influences the resulting consumer behavior. Therefore, we provide a detailed discussion of situational influences on the consumer decision process in Chapter 13.

As Figure 1-3 indicates, a consumer's needs/desires may trigger one or more levels of the consumer decision process. It is important to note that for most purchases, consumers devote very little effort to this process, and emotions and feelings often have as much or more influence on the outcome as do facts and product features. Despite the limited effort that consumers often devote to this process, the results have important effects on the individual consumer, the firm, and the larger society. Therefore, we provide detailed coverage of each stage of the process: problem recognition (Chapter 14), information search (Chapter 15), alternative evaluation and selection (Chapter 16), outlet selection and purchase (Chapter 17), and use, disposition, and purchase evaluation (Chapter 18). The increasing role of technology, particularly the Internet, in consumer decision making is highlighted throughout these chapters.

Organizations (Part Five) and Regulation (Part Six)

In Chapter 19, we show how our model of individual and household consumer behavior can be modified to help understand the consumer behavior of organizations.

Chapter 20 focuses our attention on the regulation of marketing activities, especially those targeting children. We pay particular attention to the role that knowledge of consumer behavior plays or could play in regulation.

"I (Andre Hank) worked eight-hour shifts at one restaurant, then drove to the other one for another eight-hour shift. One day I came home and my girlfriend and our six-year-olds were gone. When she left, I fell apart. I stopped going to work, stopped sleeping. I wasn't doing anything, just going crazy . . . they took me to the hospital where I got a shot to help me sleep. I woke up in a psyche ward. After three or four months, they released me.

"When I came out of the hospital I didn't have anything. I wanted to get my old job back, but they wouldn't give me a second chance. I tried to get another job but it's hard when you don't have a phone, or an answering machine, or a pager. And I was sleeping in abandoned buildings, then on the El for a long time.

"One day more than three years ago I was hungry and didn't have any money and I saw a guy selling newspapers. I asked him what he was selling and he told me about *StreetWise* (a nonprofit, independent newspaper sold by the homeless, formerly homeless, and economically disadvantaged men and women of Chicago). So I [began to sell *StreetWise*]. . . . I don't make a lot of money but I'm good at saving it. Right now I'm saving for a coat for next winter.

"I'm no longer homeless. I've got a nice little room in a hotel . . . I can buy food . . . I even saved for [and bought] Nikes."

Andre is not unique among low-income consumers in wanting and buying items such as Nike shoes. As one expert says: "These people (low-income consumers) want the same products and services other consumers want." He suggests that marketing efforts reflect those desires. Another expert states: "There's this stereotype that they don't have enough money for toothpaste, and that's just not true. There has to be some significance to them being called lower-income, but they do buy things."

The working poor are forced to spend a disproportionate percent of their income on housing, utilities, and medical care (due to a lack of insurance). They generally rely on public transportation. They spend a smaller portion of their relatively small incomes on meals away from home and on all forms of entertainment such as admissions, pets, and toys. They spend very little on their own financial security. However, as Andre illustrated, they spend the same percent of their income (though a smaller dollar amount) on apparel and accessories.[27]

Critical Thinking Questions

1. What does the consumption of a product like Nikes mean to Andre?

2. What does this story say about our society and the impact and role of marketing?

THE MEANING OF CONSUMPTION

As we proceed through this text, we will describe the results of studies of consumer behavior, discuss theories about consumer behavior, and present examples of marketing programs designed to influence consumer behavior. In reading this material, however, do not lose sight of the fact that consumer behavior is not just a topic of study or a basis for developing marketing or regulatory strategy. Consumption frequently has deep meaning for the consumer.[28]

Consider Consumer Insight 1-2. Andre, just escaping homelessness, is clearly proud that he was able to save and buy a pair of Nikes. He could undoubtedly have purchased a different brand that would have met his physical needs as well for much less money. While he does not say why he bought the more expensive Nikes, a reasonable interpretation is that they serve as a visible symbol that Andre is back as a successful member of society. In fact, Nike is sometimes criticized for creating, through its marketing activities, symbols of success or status that are unduly expensive. *What do you think? Does Nike manipulate people like Andre into spending more than necessary for a product because of its symbolism? If*

ads were banned or restricted to showing only product features, would products and brands still acquire symbolic meaning?

Perhaps some insight into these questions can be found in the following description of the attitudes of several goatherders in a narrow mountain valley in northeastern Mexico in 1964. Modern advertising was not part of their environment.

> I asked Juan what were his major economic concerns. He answered very quickly, "food and clothes," he said. "How about housing?" I asked. "That is never a problem," he said, "for I can always make a house." For Juan and the others, a house is not a prestige symbol but simply a place to sleep, a place to keep dry in, a place for family privacy, and a place in which to store things. It is not a place to live, as the word is so meaningfully used in the United States.
>
> It seems difficult to overestimate the importance of clothing. A clean set of clothes is for a pass into town or a fiesta. Clothes are the mark of a man's self-respect, and the ability of a man to clothe his family is in many ways the measure of a man. I once asked Mariano . . . why he wanted the new pair of trousers he had just purchased, when the pair he was wearing in the field seemed perfectly acceptable. He told me that while they were acceptable for the field, they could not be worn into town, for they were much too shabby. "They would call me a hick," he said, "if they saw me go into town this way."[29]

Thus, as you read the chapters that follow, keep in mind that we are dealing with real people with real lives, not mere abstractions.

SUMMARY

This should be a fascinating course for you. The fact that you are enrolled in this class suggests that you are considering marketing or advertising as a possible career. If that is the case, you should be immensely curious about why people behave as they do. Such curiosity is essential for success in a marketing-related career. That is what marketing is all about—understanding and anticipating consumer needs and developing solutions for those needs.

Even if you do not pursue a career in marketing, analyzing the purpose behind advertisements, package designs, prices, and other marketing activities is an enjoyable activity. In addition, it will make you a better consumer and a more informed citizen.

Finally, much of the material is simply interesting. For example, it is fun to read about China's attempt to market Pansy brand men's underwear in America, or that Kellogg struggled in Sweden where Bran Buds translated to "burned farmer." So have fun, study hard, and expand your managerial skills as well as your understanding of the environment in which you live.

KEY TERMS

Conceptual model   26
Consumer behavior   6
Consumer cost   21
Customer satisfaction   23
Customer value   11
Distribution   21
Injurious consumption   24
Lifestyle   29

Lifestyle centers   14
Marketing communications   19
Marketing mix   19
Marketing strategy   19
Market segment   16
Need set   17
Price   21
Product   19

Product position   22
Self-concept   29
Service   22
Social marketing   10
Target market   18
Total product   12

INTERNET EXERCISES

1. Market segmentation is one of the most important parts of developing a marketing strategy. Many commercial firms provide information and services to help define and/or describe market segments. One is Yankelovich. Visit their Web site (www.yankelovich.com). Prepare a report on how their MindBase tool segments consumers. Also take the Mindbase survey to see which segment you fall into. How accurate is their profile of you? How valuable do you think this service would be to a marketer?

2. Visit the WorldOpinion Web site (www.worldopinion.com). What information can you find that is relevant to understanding consumer behavior?

3. Marketers are increasingly looking at the opportunities offered by older consumers. How will the number of adults 65 and over change between 2005 and 2010? What about 2005 and 2020? (Hint: visit www.census.gov and look under statistical abstract.)

4. Examine magazine ads for a product category that interests you. Visit two Web sites identified in the ads. Which is most effective? Why? What beliefs about consumer behavior are reflected in the ads?

5. What ethical and legal issues involving the interaction of consumers and marketing are currently the concern of the following?
   a. Federal Trade Commission (www.ftc.gov)
   b. Better Business Bureau (www.bbb.org)

6. Visit the FDA's Center for Food Safety and Applied Nutrition (www.cfsan.fda.gov). What food-related issues are currently of concern? While there visit the food labeling and nutrition section and take the quiz on food labeling (go to www.cfsan.fda.gov/label.html and click on "Quiz Yourself"). How important do you feel the NLEA's Nutritional Facts Panel is in helping consumers make better food choices? Can this information still be misleading?

7. Evaluate several of PETA's Web sites (www.peta-online.org, www.circuses.com, www.nofishing.net, www.taxmeat.com, and www.furisdead.com).

8. Evaluate Apple's Web site (www.apple.com). What assumptions about consumer behavior are reflected in this Web site?

DDB LIFE STYLE STUDY™ DATA ANALYSES

1. Examine the DDB data in Tables 1A through 7A for differences among heavier consumers of the following. Why do you think these differences exist? How would you use these insights to develop marketing strategy?
   a. Gourmet coffee bar
   b. DVD rental
   c. Sports drinks
   d. Mail order catalog

2. Some people are more prone to be influenced by nutritional labels than others. Use the DDB data (Tables 1B through 7B) to examine possible characteristics of these consumers. How might this information be used by the FDA in developing marketing campaigns related to nutrition?

REVIEW QUESTIONS

1. How is the field of consumer behavior defined?
2. What conclusions can be drawn from the examples at the beginning of this chapter?
3. What are the four major uses or applications of an understanding of consumer behavior?
4. What is *social marketing?*
5. What is *customer value,* and why is it important to marketers?
6. What is required to provide superior customer value?
7. What is a *total product?*

8. What is involved in the *consumer* analysis phase of market analysis in Figure 1-1?

9. What is involved in the *company* analysis phase of market analysis in Figure 1-1?

10. What is involved in the *competitor* analysis phase of market analysis in Figure 1-1?

11. What is involved in the *conditions* analysis phase of market analysis in Figure 1-1?

12. Describe the process of *market segmentation.*

13. What is *marketing strategy?*

14. What is a *marketing mix?*

15. What is a *product?*

16. What does an effective communications strategy require?

17. What is a *price?* How does the price of a product differ from the *cost of the product to the consumer?*

18. How is *service* defined in the text?

19. What is involved in creating satisfied customers?

20. What are the major outcomes for the firm of the marketing process and consumers' responses to it?

21. What are the major outcomes for the individual of the marketing process and consumers' responses to it?

22. What are the major outcomes for society of the marketing process and consumers' responses to it?

23. What is *product position?*

24. What is meant by *injurious consumption?*

25. What is meant by *consumer lifestyle?*

26. Describe the consumer decision process.

DISCUSSION QUESTIONS

27. Why would someone shop on the Internet? Buy an iPod? Eat at TGI Friday's frequently?
    a. Why would someone else not make those purchases?
    b. How would you choose one outlet, brand, or model over the others? Would others make the same choice in the same way?

28. Respond to the questions in Consumer Insight 1-1.

29. Of what use, if any, are models such as the one in Figure 1-3 to managers?

30. What changes would you suggest in the model in Figure 1-3? Why?

31. Describe your lifestyle. How does it differ from your parents' lifestyle?

32. Do you anticipate any changes in your lifestyle in the next five years? What will cause these changes? What new products or brands will you consume because of these changes?

33. Describe a recent purchase you made. To what extent did you follow the consumer decision-making process described in this chapter? How would you explain any differences?

34. Describe several *total products* that are more than their direct physical features.

35. Describe the needs that the following items might satisfy and the total cost to the consumer of obtaining the benefits of the total product.
    a. Digital video recorder (e.g., TiVo)
    b. Botox treatments
    c. Motorcycle
    d. Camera phone

36. How would you define the product that the Hard Rock Cafe provides? What needs does it meet?

37. To what extent, if any, are marketers responsible for injurious consumption involving their products?

38. How could social marketing help alleviate some of society's problems?

39. Respond to the questions in Consumer Insight 1-2.

40. Is the criticism of Nike for creating a shoe that is symbolic of success to some groups (see Consumer Insight 1-2) valid? Why or why not?

41. Robert's American gourmet snack foods produces herbal-based snacks such as Spirulina Spirals and St. Johns Wort Tortilla Chips. According to the company president, "We're selling like crazy. We don't do research. We react as sort of a karma thing."[30] How would you explain the firm's success? What are the advantages and risks of this approach?

APPLICATION ACTIVITIES

42. Interview the manager or marketing manager of a retail firm. Determine how this individual develops the marketing strategy. Compare this person's process with the approach described in the text.

43. Interview the managers of a local charity. Determine what their assumptions about the consumer behavior of their supporters are. To what extent do they use marketing strategy to increase support for the organization or compliance with its objectives?

44. Interview five students. Have them describe the last three restaurant meals they consumed and the situations in which they were consumed. What can you conclude about the impact of the situation on consumer behavior? What can you conclude about the impact of the individual on consumer behavior?

45. Visit one or more stores that sell the following items. Report on the sales techniques used (point-of-purchase displays, store design, salesperson comments, and so forth). What beliefs concerning consumer behavior appear to underlie these techniques? It is often worthwhile for a male and

a female student to visit the same store and talk to the same salesperson at different times. The variation in salesperson behavior is sometimes quite revealing.
   a. Books and magazines
   b. Cellular phones
   c. Home office supplies
   d. Expensive art
   e. Camping equipment
   f. Personal computers

46. Interview individuals who sell the following items. Try to discover their personal "models" of consumer behavior for their products.
   a. Pleasure boats
   b. Pets
   c. Expensive jewelry
   d. Plants and garden supplies
   e. Flowers
   f. Life insurance

47. Interview three individuals who recently made a major purchase and three others who made a minor purchase. In what ways were their decision processes similar? How were they different?

REFERENCES

1. N. Madden, "Report From China," *AdAge.com*, May 31, 2005 (at www.adage.com).

2. J. Neff, "P&G vs. Martha," *Advertising Age*, April 8, 2002, p. 24.

3. "Marketing-Oriented Lever Uses Research," *Marketing News*, February 10, 1978, p. 9; see also B. O'Connor, "How Deep-Dive Consumer Research Defined an Emerging Market and Helped to Create a Brand," *Design Management Review*, Summer 2004, p. 64.

4. B. Light, "Kellogg's Goes Online for Consumer Research," *Packaging Digest*, July 2004, p. 40.

5. J. Neff, "S. C. Johnson Likely to Bag ZipLoc Table Tops," *Advertising Age*, November 25, 2002, p. 3; and J. Neff, "S. C. Johnson Faces a Clean-up Job," *Advertising Age*, November 29, 2004, p. 8.

6. See W. I. Ghani and N. M. Childs, "Wealth Effects of the Passage of the Nutrition Labeling and Education Act of 1990 for Large U.S. Multinational Food Corporations," *Journal of Public Policy and Marketing*, Fall 1999, pp. 147–58; and S. K. Balasubramanian and C. Cole, "Consumers' Search and Use of Nutrition Information," *Journal of Marketing*, July 2002, pp. 112–27.

7. "Slick TV Ads Divert Child Smoking," *Marketing News*, August 29, 1994, p. 30. See also C. Pechmann and S. Ratneshwar, "The

Effects of Antismoking and Cigarette Advertising on Young Adolescents' Perceptions of Peers Who Smoke," *Journal of Consumer Research*, September 1994, pp. 236–51.

8. See A. R. Andreasen, "Social Marketing," *Journal of Public Policy & Marketing*, Spring 1994, pp. 108–14; and P. Kotler, N. Roberto, and N. Lee, *Social Marketing* (Thousand Oaks, CA: Sage, 2002).

9. See, e.g., C. A. Russell, "Investigating the Effectiveness of Product Placements in Television Shows," *Journal of Consumer Research*, December 2002, pp. 306–18.

10. B. J. Pine, Jr., and J. H. Gilmore, "Welcome to the Experience Economy," *Harvard Business Review*, July–August 1998, pp. 97–105.

11. This insight is based on J. Weber and A. T. Palmer, "How the Net Is Remaking the Mall," *BusinessWeek Online*, May 9, 2005. See also A. Serwer, "Hot Starbucks to Go," *Fortune*, January 26, 2004, pp. 61–74; and P. Bhatnagar, "Supermarkets Strike Back," *CNNMoney* (online), May 2, 2005.

12. A. S. Wellner, "The New Science of Focus Groups," *American Demographics*, March 2003, pp. 29–33.

13. S. Chandler, "Data Is Power," *BusinessWeek*, June 3, 1996, p. 69.

14. See W. McCall, "Nike Battles Backlash from Overseas Sweatshops," *Marketing News,* November 9, 1998, p. 14; and A. Hill, "Nike's Reputation in Spotlight Again," *PR Week,* April 1, 2005, p. 13.

15. T. F. McMahon, "What Buyers Buy and Sellers Sell," *Journal of Professional Services Marketing,* no. 2 (1996), pp. 3–16.

16. "'Build a Better Mousetrap' 2004 New Product Innovations of the Year," *Productscan Online* (press release), December 27, 2004 (at www.productscan.com).

17. D. Roberts, "How Legend Lives Up to Its Name," *BusinessWeek,* February 15, 1999, pp. 75–76; and "China Industry," *EIU ViewsWire* (online), January 22, 2004 (at www.viewswire.com).

18. P. Odell, "Starburst Puts Texting Promo on 60 Million Wrappers," *Promo* (online), June 6, 2005 (at www.promomagazine.com).

19. Serwer, "Hot Starbucks to Go."

20. C. Power, "Flops," *BusinessWeek,* August 16, 1993, pp. 79–80.

21. See, e.g., Weber and Palmer, "How the Net Is Remaking the Mall."

22. T. Pruzan, "Sauza Tequila Ads," *Advertising Age,* July 8, 1996, p. 29.

23. B. Morris, "The Future of Retirement," *Fortune,* August 19, 1996, pp. 86–94.

24. See D. N. Hassey and M. C. Smith, "Compulsive Buying," *Psychology & Marketing,* December 1996, pp. 741–52; and N. A. Mendoza and J. W. Pracejus, "Buy Now, Pay Later," *Advances in Consumer Research XXIV,* ed. M. Bruck and D. J. MacInnis (Provo, UT: Association for Consumer Research, 1997), pp. 499–503.

25. See P. Mergenhagen, "People Behaving Badly," *American Demographics,* August 1997, pp. 37–43.

26. R. E. Petty and J. T. Cacioppo, "Addressing Disturbing and Disturbed Consumer Behavior," *Journal of Marketing Research,* February 1996, pp. 1–8.

27. C. Miller, "The Have-Nots," *Marketing News,* August 1, 1994, pp. 1–2; P. Mergenhagen, "What Can Minimum Wage Buy?" *American Demographics,* January 1996, pp. 32–36; and A. Hank, "Hank Finds Two Families," *StreetWise,* May 16–31, 1996, p. 7.

28. See M. L. Richins, "Special Possessions and the Expression of Material Values," *Journal of Consumer Research,* December 1994, pp. 522–33.

29. J. F. Epstein, "A Shirt for Juan Navarro," in *Foundations for a Theory of Consumer Behavior,* ed. W. T. Tucker (New York: Holt, Rinehart & Winston, 1967), p. 75.

30. M. W. Fellman, "New Age Dawns for Product Niche," *Marketing News,* April 27, 1998, p. 1.

part two

External Influences

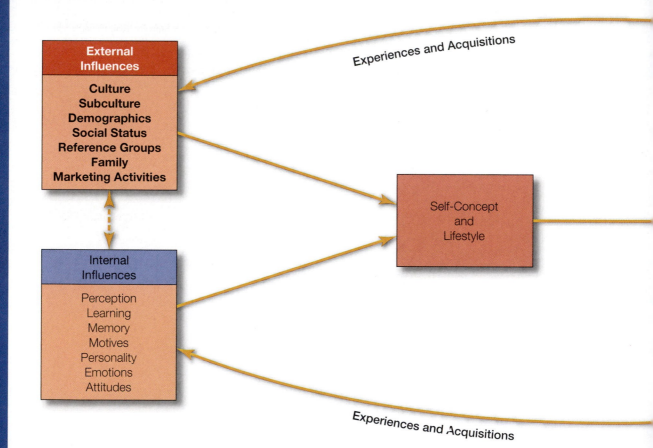

External Influences

Culture
Subculture
Demographics
Social Status
Reference Groups
Family
Marketing Activities

Internal Influences

Perception
Learning
Memory
Motives
Personality
Emotions
Attitudes

Self-Concept
and
Lifestyle

Experiences and Acquisitions

Experiences and Acquisitions

■ The external influence area of our model shown at the left is the focal point of this part of the text. Any division of the factors that influence consumer behavior into separate and distinct categories is somewhat arbitrary. For example, we will consider learning in Part Three of the text, which focuses on internal influences. However, a substantial amount of learning involves interaction with, or imitation of, other individuals. Thus, learning clearly in-volves external influences such as family and peers. Our focus in this part is on the functioning of the various external groups, not the processes by which individuals react to these groups.

In this part, we begin with large-scale, macrogroup influences and move to smaller, more microgroup influences. As we progress, the nature of the influence exerted changes from general guidelines to explicit expectations for specific behaviors. In Chapter 2, we examine how cultures cause differing behaviors across countries and other cultural units. Chapters 3 through 6 focus primarily on the American society, examining its values, demographics, social stratification, subcultures, and family structure. Chapter 7 examines the mechanisms by which groups influence consumer behaviors. In combination, these chapters allow for a comparison and contrast of how external influences operate in America and around the world.

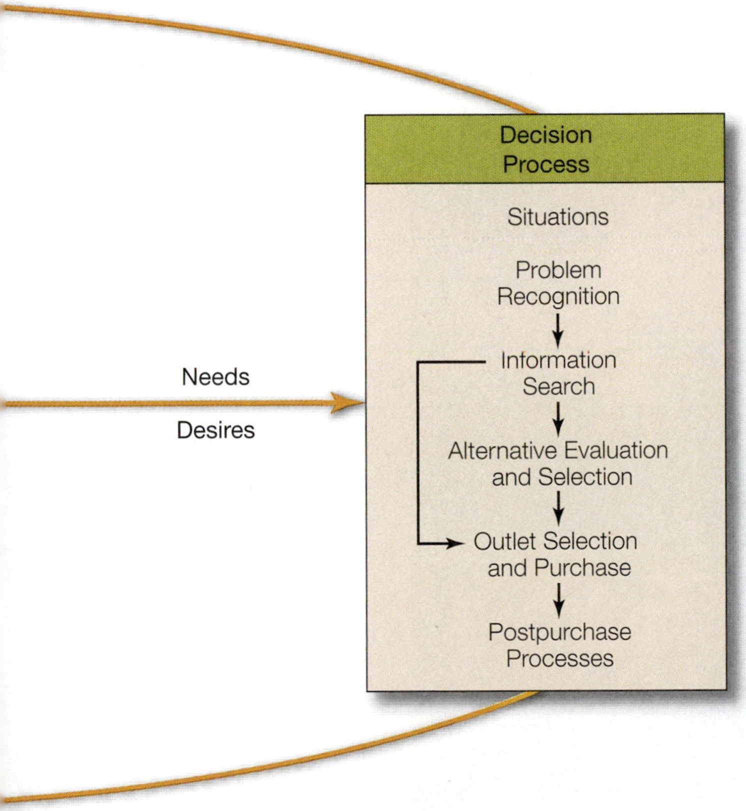

Decision Process

Situations

Problem Recognition
↓
Information Search
↓
Alternative Evaluation and Selection
↓
Outlet Selection and Purchase
↓
Postpurchase Processes

Needs

Desires

2

Cross-Cultural Variations in Consumer Behavior

■ FedEx, while one of the top express shipping companies in the region, is not nearly as well known in Latin America and the Caribbean as it is in other parts of the world. Therefore, it decided to launch an advertising campaign to build brand awareness among small and medium-sized shippers. The ad agency was challenged to create a commercial that would work across this broad region with its differing cultures and languages. In addition, it would need to be presented in English and Portuguese in addition to Spanish without looking "dubbed." (It would cost too much to shoot three or four versions of the ad.) The ad would have to capture attention and convey the message and meaning desired.

The 30-second commercial shows a young equipment manager for a soccer team, the dominant sport in the region, worried about the delivery of five boxes of uniforms he had shipped to Madrid for a major match. An older man assures him that all will be fine as long as he had shipped them via FedEx, which he had not. The next scene is a soccer field where the opponents are about to attempt a penalty kick. As the camera reveals the defenders, the audience sees that they are defending the goal without their uniforms or any other clothing. The tagline for the ad is: "Let FedEx take the load off your shoulders."

Two versions of the last scene were shot, the nude version and a version with the men in their underwear. The underwear version was run in Mexico due to local restrictions on nudity in prime time. According to Karine Skobinsky, manager of pan-divisional advertising for FedEx Latin America and Caribbean Division: "We wanted to choose a theme that our target could relate to. And soccer is the national pastime in most Latin American markets. The script was designed to portray a realistic situation depicted from a customer's standpoint. Of course, we added a twist at the end to keep things entertaining and memorable. The tone of the advertising is in line with our brand identity, which uses humor to convey the message." Depending on the market, FedEx brand awareness increased 7 to 17 percent. "Not only did people specifically remember the ad, they could replay the message, the story, and who the sponsor was," said Skobinsky.[1]

Marketing across cultural boundaries is a difficult and challenging task. As Figure 2-1 indicates, cultures may differ in demographics, languages, nonverbal communications, and values. The success of FedEx in Latin America and elsewhere depends on how well the company understands and adapts to these differences.

In this chapter, we focus on cultural variations in *values* and *nonverbal communications*. In addition, we briefly describe how *demographic variations* across countries and cultures influence consumption patterns.

Before we begin our discussion, we need to point out an increasingly significant ethical issue. Not only is marketing strategy heavily influenced by cultural factors such as values, demographics, and languages, but in turn it also influences aspects of cultures. For example, television advertising in countries such as China and India is extensive and reflects many Western values such as individualism and an emphasis on youth. Over time, such advertising will influence not only how many Chinese and Indians choose to live (lifestyle) but also what they value and how they think and feel.[2]

Thus, the massive export and multinational advertising of consumer goods, particularly heavily symbolic goods such as cigarettes, soft drinks, clothing, and athletic gear, as well as experiential goods such as music, movies, and television programming, impact the

FIGURE 2-1   **Cultural Factors Affect Consumer Behavior and Marketing Strategy**

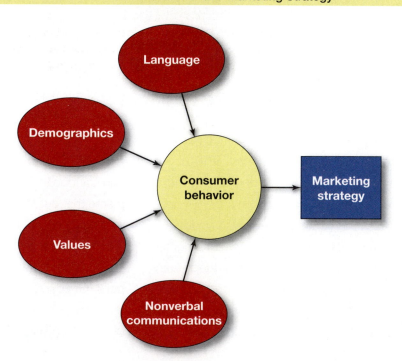

culture and desired lifestyles of the importing countries.[3] Often these products are adapted to the local culture and assume meanings and uses that greatly enrich the culture and the lives of its members. For example, many American holiday traditions are spreading throughout the world. Halloween originated in Ireland, Britain, and northwest France. Over time, its celebration became limited to the United States, Canada, and Ireland. Now, however, it is becoming global:

- The Abominable Giant Man Eating Zombie Tea Party is the theme for a costume bash at a Singapore nightclub.
- Japan recently held a Hello Halloween Pumpkin Parade in Tokyo.
- In Paris, shops decorate their windows with goblins, spider webs, and skeletons; pumpkins are on sale at open-air markets; bakeries produce decorated Halloween cakes; McDonald's gives out masks with kids' meals; and some children go trick-or-treating.[4]

When such holidays do not replace local traditions and are adapted to the local culture, they can enrich the lives of the populations that adopt them. However, such imports can also be disruptive or controversial. For example, American-style celebrations of Valentine's Day are spreading throughout the world; but in countries such as India, they are being met with protests. Hindu and Indian beliefs generally restrict public displays of affection and many find Valentine cards that show young couples embracing to be offensive.[5]

In fact, many countries, both developed and developing, are concerned about the *Westernization,* and particularly the *Americanization,* of their cultures. This has led to attempts to ban or limit the importation of various American products. Europe has attempted to limit the importation of American movies, and Canada has restricted the Nashville-based Country Music Television channel. Both the French and Chinese governments have tried to restrict the use of English in brand names or advertising. American goods and services are often controversial and laced with political meaning in Islamic cultures.[6]

Despite concerns such as those described above, most categories of American products are generally prized throughout the world, as are those of Japan and Europe.[7] The American tobacco industry has taken advantage of this. American tobacco companies are aggressively marketing their products internationally, where government restrictions and public attitudes are more favorable. For example, the required label on the side of a cigarette package in Japan is relatively weak: "As smoking might injure your health, be careful not to smoke too much."[8] Perhaps not surprisingly, Japan ranks among the highest countries in per-capita smoking.[9]

As Illustration 2-1 shows, tobacco firms have been particularly aggressive in the developing countries of Asia, Latin America, Africa, and Eastern Europe. Their advertising and promotions, frequently using Western models and alluring settings, along with the marketing activities of local tobacco firms, have been quite successful.[10] Despite sharp drops in consumption in the United States, Canada, and much of Western Europe, cigarette consumption in much of the world including Africa, Asia, South America, and the Middle East is increasing.[11] Smoking-related deaths are now a leading killer in Asia, where alarming increases in female smoking are a major concern.[12] As one World Health Organization (WHO) official notes:

> Here in Japan we see Western cigarette brands marketed as a kind of liberation tool. We see cigarette companies calling on young Japanese women to assert themselves, shed their inhibitions and smoke.[13]

Clearly, there are both subtle (exported ads and products influencing other cultures' values) and direct (exporting harmful products) ethical issues involved in international marketing.

© Munshi Ahmed.

THE CONCEPT OF CULTURE

Culture is the complex whole that includes knowledge, belief, art, law, morals, customs, and any other capabilities and habits acquired by humans as members of society.

Several aspects of culture require elaboration. First, culture is a comprehensive concept. It includes almost everything that influences an individual's thought processes and behaviors. While culture does not determine the nature or frequency of biological drives such as hunger or sex, it does influence if, when, and how these drives will be gratified. It influences not only our preferences but how we make decisions[14] and even how we perceive the world around us. Second, culture is acquired. It does not include inherited responses and predispositions. However, since much of human behavior is learned rather than innate, culture does affect a wide array of behaviors.

Third, the complexity of modern societies is such that culture seldom provides detailed prescriptions for appropriate behavior. Instead, in most industrial societies, culture supplies boundaries within which most individuals think and act. Finally, the nature of cultural influences is such that we are seldom aware of them. One behaves, thinks, and feels in a manner consistent with other members of the same culture because it seems "natural" or "right" to do so.

Imagine a pizza that you and some friends are sharing. If you are an American, odds are you envisioned pepperoni on your pizza. However, in Japan, squid is the most popular topping; in England, it's tuna and corn; in Guatemala, black bean sauce; in Chile, mussels and clams; in the Bahamas, barbecued chicken; in Australia, eggs; and in India, pickled ginger.[15]

Some of these toppings probably seem strange or disgusting to you but are perfectly natural to members of other cultures. This is the nature of culture. We don't think about the fact that our preference for pizza topping, as well as most of our other preferences, is strongly influenced by our culture.

Values, Norms, Sanctions, and Consumption Patterns   FIGURE 2-2

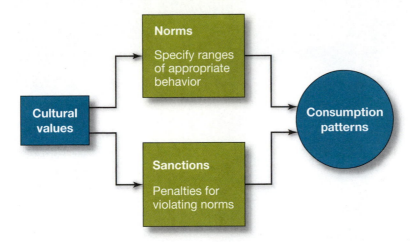

Culture operates primarily by setting rather loose boundaries for individual behavior and by influencing the functioning of such institutions as the family and mass media. Thus, culture provides the framework within which individual and household lifestyles evolve.

The boundaries that culture sets on behavior are called **norms,** which are simply rules that specify or prohibit certain behaviors in specific situations. Norms are derived from **cultural values,** or widely held beliefs that affirm what is desirable. Violation of cultural norms results in **sanctions,** or penalties ranging from mild social disapproval to banishment from the group. Thus, as Figure 2-2 indicates, cultural values give rise to norms and associated sanctions, which in turn influence consumption patterns.

The preceding discussion may leave the impression that people are aware of cultural values and norms and that violating any given norm carries a precise and known sanction. This is seldom the case. We tend to "obey" cultural norms without thinking because to do otherwise would seem unnatural. For example, we are seldom aware of how close we stand to other individuals while conducting business. Yet this distance is well defined and adhered to, even though it varies from culture to culture.

Cultures are not static. They typically evolve and change slowly over time. Marketing managers must understand both the existing cultural values and the emerging cultural values of the societies they serve. A failure to understand cultural differences can produce negative consequences such as:

- A U.S. electronics firm landed a major contract with a Japanese buyer. The U.S. firm's president flew to Tokyo for the contract-signing ceremony. Then the head of the Japanese firm began reading the contract intently. The scrutiny continued for an extraordinary length of time. At last, the U.S. executive offered an additional price discount. The Japanese executive, though surprised, did not object. The U.S. executive's mistake was assuming that the Japanese executive was attempting to reopen negotiations. Instead, he was demonstrating his personal concern and authority in the situation by closely and slowly examining the document.
- An article entitled "All about Sake" in the Air Canada magazine focused on how to select Japanese sake and how to become a Japanese sake connoisseur. The accompanying photograph showed Chinese ceramic and bamboo steamers with Chinese writing—not a sound way to impress either their Japanese or Chinese customers.

Malaysian shoppers buy American products at Makro, a Dutch-owned retail chain. The combination of low price, wide selection, and world brands is changing traditional shopping patterns around the world.

© Munshi Ahmed.

- Lipton created a line of instant meals named *Side Dishes*. The meals sold well in the United States but not in Latin America, a large market that Lipton had hoped would fuel growth for the line. Latin American housewives, with more traditional views of their family role, felt that "instant" meals implied they were lazy or poor caretakers for their families.[16]

Starbucks' CEO offers this cautionary note for American businesses going global: "The biggest lesson is not to assume that the market or the consumers are just like Americans, even if they speak English or otherwise behave as if they were. They're not. This happened in the U.K., [and] it has even happened in Canada. The Canadians are not Americans. They are different."[17] However, as Illustration 2-2 indicates, with appropriate strategies and an eye toward the needs and wants of local consumers, sophisticated retailers and manufacturers can and do succeed throughout the world.

VARIATIONS IN CULTURAL VALUES

Cultural values are widely held beliefs that affirm what is desirable. These values affect behavior through norms, which specify an acceptable range of responses to specific situations. A useful approach to understanding cultural variations in behavior is to understand the values embraced by different cultures.

There are numerous values that vary across cultures and affect consumption. We will present a classification scheme consisting of three broad forms of cultural values—*other-oriented, environment-oriented,* and *self-oriented*. The cultural values that have the most impact on consumer behavior can be classified in one of these three general categories.

Other-oriented values reflect a society's view of the appropriate relationships *between individuals and groups* within that society. These relationships have a major influence on marketing practice. For example, if the society values collective activity, consumers will look toward others for guidance in purchase decisions and will not respond favorably to promotional appeals to "be an individual."

Environment-oriented values prescribe a society's relationship *to its economic and technical as well as its physical environment.* As a manager, you would develop a very different marketing program for a society that stressed a problem-solving, risk-taking, performance-oriented approach to its environment than you would for a fatalistic, security- and status-oriented society.

Self-oriented values reflect the objectives and approaches to life *that the individual members of society find desirable.* Again, these values have strong implications for marketing management. For instance, the acceptance and use of credit is very much determined by a society's position on the value of postponed versus immediate gratification.

Table 2-1 provides a list of 18 values that are important in most cultures. Most of the values are shown as dichotomies (e.g., materialistic versus nonmaterialistic). However, this is not meant to represent an either/or situation but a continuum. For example, two societies can each value tradition, but one may value it more than the other. For several of the values, a natural dichotomy does not seem to exist. For a society to place a low value on cleanliness does not imply that it places a high value on dirtiness. These 18 values are described in the following paragraphs.

TABLE 2-1

Cultural Values of
Relevance to
Consumer Behavior

Other-Oriented Values

- *Individual/Collective.* Are individual activity and initiative valued more highly than collective activity and conformity?
- *Youth/Age.* Is family life organized to meet the needs of the children or the adults? Are younger or older people viewed as leaders and role models?
- *Extended/Limited family.* To what extent does one have a lifelong obligation to numerous family members?
- *Masculine/Feminine.* To what extent does social power automatically go to males?
- *Competitive/Cooperative.* Does one obtain success by excelling over others or by cooperating with them?
- *Diversity/Uniformity.* Does the culture embrace variation in religious belief, ethnic background, political views, and other important behaviors and attitudes?

Environment-Oriented Values

- *Cleanliness.* To what extent is cleanliness pursued beyond the minimum needed for health?
- *Performance/Status.* Is the culture's reward system based on performance or on inherited factors such as family or class?
- *Tradition/Change.* Are existing patterns of behavior considered to be inherently superior to new patterns of behavior?
- *Risk taking/Security.* Are those who risk their established positions to overcome obstacles or achieve high goals admired more than those who do not?
- *Problem solving/Fatalistic.* Are people encouraged to overcome all problems, or do they take a "what will be, will be" attitude?
- *Nature.* Is nature regarded as something to be admired or overcome?

Self-Oriented Values

- *Active/Passive.* Is a physically active approach to life valued more highly than a less active orientation?
- *Sensual gratification/Abstinence.* To what extent is it acceptable to enjoy sensual pleasures such as food, drink, and sex?
- *Material/Nonmaterial.* How much importance is attached to the acquisition of material wealth?
- *Hard work/Leisure.* Is a person who works harder than economically necessary admired more than one who does not?
- *Postponed gratification/Immediate gratification.* Are people encouraged to "save for a rainy day" or to "live for today"?
- *Religious/Secular.* To what extent are behaviors and attitudes based on the rules specified by a religious doctrine?

Other-Oriented Values

Individual/Collective   Does the culture emphasize and reward individual initiative, or are cooperation with and conformity to a group more highly valued? Are individual differences appreciated or condemned? Are rewards and status given to individuals or to groups? Answers to these questions reveal the individual or collective orientation of a culture. Individualism is a defining characteristic of American culture. Australia, the United Kingdom, Canada, New Zealand, and Sweden are also relatively individualistic. Taiwan, Korea, Hong Kong, Mexico, Japan, India, and Russia are more collective in their orientation.[18]

This value is a key factor differentiating cultures, and it heavily influences the self-concept of individuals. Not surprisingly, consumers from cultures that differ on this value differ in their reactions to foreign products,[19] advertising,[20] and preferred sources of information.[21] Examples include:

- Eating alone is more prevalent in individualistic cultures such as the United States and Hungary than in collectivist cultures such as Russia and Romania.[22] *What are the implications of such a difference for food marketers?*
- In services such as health care and hair stylist, consumers in Thailand place greater importance on relationship aspects such as social benefits and special treatment than U.S. consumers. These relationship benefits also tend to drive loyalty more for consumers in Thailand.[23]
- Consumers from more collectivist countries tend to be more imitative and less innovative in their purchases than those from individualistic cultures.[24] Thus, ad themes such as "be yourself," and "stand out," are often effective in the United States but generally are not in Japan, Korea, or China.

Interestingly, you might expect luxury items to be less important in collectivist cultures. However, they are quite important, but for different reasons. In individualistic cultures, luxury items are purchased as a means of self-expression or to stand out.[25] This is often not the case in more collectivist Asian societies. As one expert describes:

> Brands take on roles as symbols that extend well beyond the intrinsic features of the category. One is not buying a watch, or even a status brand, one is buying club membership, or an "I am just like you" (symbol).[26]

As useful as such generalizations are, it is important to realize that cultural values can and do evolve. This is particularly true among young, urban consumers in the developed and developing countries of Asia, where individualism is on the rise.[27] For example, 26 percent of Chinese teens consider individuality an important trait, more than double the rate of older Chinese.[28] Although this number is substantially lower than that of Western cultures, it represents an important shift. Consider the following description of a young Japanese woman:

> Mizuho Arai knows what she likes. A 20-year-old uniformed office worker by day, at night she wears loafers, a sweater, Levi's 501s, and a black parka. Shopping with an L. L. Bean bag over her shoulder, she prefers bargain outlets to traditional department stores and designer boutiques. "I don't like to be told what's trendy. I can make up my own mind."[29]

Arai is typical of the younger generation of Asian consumers, where traditional appeals may not work as they once did. For example, in the late 1980s, Shiseido Co. launched its very successful Perky Jean makeup line with the theme: "Everyone is buying it." "That would never work now," says a company executive.

Photo by Marie Hornbein.

The different values held by younger and older Asian consumers illustrate that few cultures are completely homogeneous. Marketers must be aware of differences both *between* cultures and *within* cultures.[30]

Youth/Age   To what extent do the primary family activities focus on the needs of the children instead of those of the adults? What role, if any, do children play in family decisions? What role do they play in decisions that primarily affect the child? Are prestige, rank, and important social roles assigned to younger or older members of society? Are the behavior, dress, and mannerisms of the younger or older members of a society imitated by the rest of the society?

While American society is clearly youth oriented, many Asian cultures have traditionally valued the wisdom that comes with age. Thus, mature spokespersons would tend to be more successful in these cultures than would younger ones. However, some Asian cultures are becoming increasingly youth oriented with increases in youth-oriented ads designed to target them.[31] Consider the following description of Taiwan:

> Taiwan is very, very youth-oriented, and it is a very hip culture. . . . You have a consumer-based economy that is quite potent, and pitching to the youth is a good way of ensuring that your products are going to be bought.[32]

Illustration 2-3 demonstrates 7-Up's use of a youth theme in China. These unique outdoor "light pole" signs are common in China's major cities.

This youth trend can also be seen in Arab countries. One study of Arab consumers from Saudi Arabia, Bahrain, Kuwait, and the United Arab Emirates shows the rapid emergence of several youth segments. The largest (35 percent) consists of younger, more liberal, individualistic married couples living in nuclear (versus communal) families in which women are more likely to work outside the home and thus demand a greater voice in family decisions.[33]

Children's influence on purchases and the tactics they use vary according to the youth versus age value and this has implications for marketers.[34] For example, one study compared the tactics used by children in the Fiji Islands to those of children in the United States. The Fiji Islands (and other Pacific Island nations) can be characterized as less individualistic and higher in respect for authority and seniority. As a consequence, Fiji children were more likely to "request" than "demand" and Fiji parents responded more favorably (i.e., bought the item) to "requests." In contrast, American children were more likely to demand than request and American parents responded more positively to demands.[35]

China's policy of limiting families to one child has produced a strong focus on the child, a shift toward youth, and increasing Westernization of children's commercials. In fact, many Chinese children receive so much attention that they are known in Asia as "little emperors."[36] Consider the following description of the Zhou family and their 10-year-old daughter Bella, who live in Shanghai:

> Under traditional Confucian teachings, respecting and obeying one's elders were paramount. In today's urban China, it is increasingly children who guide their parents through a fast-changing world. When the Zhous bought a new television set last year, Bella chose the brand. When they go out to eat, Bella insists on Pizza Hut.[37]

Obviously, while changes to traditional cultures such as those in Asia and the Gulf are occurring, it is important to remember that traditional segments and values still remain and that marketers must adapt not only across but within cultures.

Extended/Limited Family   The family unit is the basis for virtually all societies. Nonetheless, the definition of the family and the rights and obligations of family members vary widely across cultures. As we will see in Chapter 6, our families have a lifelong impact on all of us, both genetically and through our early socialization, no matter what culture we come from. However, cultures differ widely in the obligations one owes to other family members at various stages of life as well as who is considered to be a member of the family.

In the United States, the family is defined fairly narrowly and is less important than in many other cultures. In general, strong obligations are felt only to immediate family members, and these diminish as family members establish new families. In many other countries and regions including South America, Fiji, Israel, and Asia, the role of the family is much stronger. Families, and obligations, often extend to cousins, nieces, nephews, and beyond. One has responsibilities to one's parents, grandparents, and even ancestors that must be fulfilled. The following description indicates the complexity and extent of the extended Chinese family.

> The family is critically important in all aspects of Chinese life and there is a distrust of non-family members. In response to this, the Chinese have developed family-like links to a greater extent than almost any other culture. Thus the family in the Chinese context is different from the western conceptualization. It stretches to the furthest horizons, from close family, to slightly distant, to more distant, embracing people who are not really family but are connected to someone in one's family and to all their families. As such, the family is really a system of contacts, rather than purely an emotional unit as in the west.[38]

Clearly, marketers need to understand the role of families in the cultures they serve and adapt accordingly. For example:

- In Mexico, compared to the United States, adolescents are much more likely to seek parental advice or to respond positively to ads with parental figures in the purchase of items ranging from candy to movies to fashion clothing.[39]

- Young adults living on their own in Thailand, compared to the United States, are more likely to continue to be influenced by their parents and family in terms of consumption values and purchases.[40]
- Due to the fact that Indian consumers tend to shop in groups and with their families, Biyani (a large discounter similar to Wal-Mart) has U- and C-shaped aisles to provide private corners where families can discuss their purchase decisions.[41]

Masculine/Feminine   Are rank, prestige, and important social roles assigned primarily to men? Can a female's life pattern be predicted at birth with a high degree of accuracy? Does the husband, wife, or both, make important family decisions? Basically, we live in a masculine-oriented world, yet the degree of masculine orientation varies widely, even across the relatively homogeneous countries of Western Europe.

This value dimension influences both obvious and subtle aspects of marketing (see Chapter 3). Obviously, the roles and manner in which one would portray women in advertisements in Muslim countries would differ from those in the United States.[42] However, suppose you were going to promote furniture in Taiwan or Japan. Would you focus on the husband, the wife, or both? Would it vary by country? Research indicates that a moderate focus on the wife would be best in both countries.[43] How would you portray a teenage Japanese girl in an ad to this audience? A more "girlish" (childlike, approval seeking) portrayal than is common in U.S. ads (a more sultry, explicitly sexual portrayal) would be appropriate.[44]

Consider the following data on participating in sports and exercise.

	Never Participate			Frequently Participate		
	Male	Female	Difference	Male	Female	Difference
United States	34%	44%	10%	46%	39%	−7%
United Kingdom	40	41	1	45	43	−2
South Korea	53	73	20	37	23	−14
Mexico	42	72	30	44	18	−26
Japan	66	72	6	16	16	0
Brazil	46	66	20	47	27	−20
China	45	51	6	38	32	−6
France	45	57	12	44	29	−15
Germany	30	34	4	55	48	−7
Italy	59	72	13	32	25	−7

World Monitor, 2nd Quarter, 2001, published by Ipsos. Reprinted by permission.

While males are somewhat more likely to exercise across all the countries, the differences between male and female participation are quite large in traditionally masculine countries.[45] *What does this imply for marketing activities in those countries?*

The roles of women are changing and expanding throughout much of the world.[46] This is creating new opportunities as well as challenges for marketers.[47] For example, the increasing percentage of Japanese women who continue to work after marriage has led to increased demand for time-saving products as well as other products targeted at the working woman:

- Many Japanese women feel guilty preparing frozen vegetables in a microwave rather than preparing fresh vegetables. In promoting its Green Giant frozen vegetables in Japan, Pillsbury emphasized convenience and nutrition and attempted to position them as part of "modern up-to-date cooking." Sales increased 50 percent. The company has

ILLUSTRATION 2-4

The changing role of women creates new needs and products even in relatively traditional cultures such as Japan. This lipstick is targeted at Japan's new working women.

© Shiseido Cosmetics (America) Ltd.

followed up with Dough Boy frozen bite-sized meat pies for busy mothers to pack in their children's school lunches.

- Long-lasting, no-smear lipstick didn't exist in Japan over a decade ago, but now is a huge market (see Illustration 2-4). Targeted at working women, Shiseido's brand, Reciente Perfect Rouge, features a popular model racing through her busy day wearing the no-smear lipstick.[48]

Again, it is important to remember that traditional segments and values certainly do still remain and that marketers must adapt not only across but within cultures. For example, a recent study of women in mainland China found both traditionalist and modern segments.[49] The challenge is to sort them out for marketing purposes.

Competitive/Cooperative   Is the path to success found by outdoing other individuals or groups, or is success achieved by forming alliances with other individuals or groups? Does everyone admire a winner? Cultures with more masculine and individualistic orientations such as the United Kingdom, the United States, and Australia tend to value competitiveness and demonstrate it openly. Collectivist cultures, even if high in masculinity (e.g., Japan), tend to find *openly* competitive gestures offensive as they cause others to "lose face."[50]

Variation on this value can be seen in the way different cultures react to comparative advertisements. For example the United States encourages them, while their use in other cultures can lead to consumer (and even legal) backlash. As one would expect, the more collectivist Japanese have historically found comparative ads to be distasteful, as do the Chinese, although Pepsi found Japanese youth somewhat more receptive if comparisons are done in a frank and funny way.[51] As a rule, comparative ads should be used with care and only after considerable testing.

Diversity/Uniformity   Do members of the culture embrace variety in terms of religions, ethnic backgrounds, political beliefs, and other important behaviors and attitudes? A culture that values diversity not only will accept a wide array of personal behaviors and attitudes but is also likely to welcome variety in terms of food, dress, and other products and services. In contrast, a society valuing uniformity is unlikely to accept a wide array of tastes and product preferences, though such a society may be subject to fads, fashions, and other changes over time.

Japan and other collectivist cultures tend to place a strong value on uniformity and conformity,[52] whereas more individualistic cultures such as Canada and Holland tend to value diversity. While many important aspects of these cultures are affected by the differences in this value, one obvious to any tourist is the relative absence of "ethnic" (Mexican, Italian, Indian, and so forth) restaurants in Japan compared to Canada and Holland. Obviously, however, economic and social changes associated with the youth movement in many collectivist societies mean relatively more acceptance of diversity than has been traditionally found, even if absolute levels trend lower than in their individualistic counterparts.

Environment-Oriented Values

Cleanliness   Is cleanliness next to godliness, or is it a rather minor matter? Are homes, offices, and public spaces expected to be clean beyond reasonable health requirements? In the United States, a high value is placed on cleanliness, where germ-fighting liquid soaps alone are a $16 billion market.[53] In fact, people from many cultures consider Americans to be paranoid on the subject of personal hygiene.

While there are differences in the value placed on cleanliness among the economically developed cultures, the largest differences are between these cultures and many of the underdeveloped nations. In many poorer countries, cleanliness is not valued at a level sufficient to produce a healthy environment. This is true even in large parts of rapidly developing countries such as China and India, where a lack of basic hygiene still causes significant health problems.[54] While often criticized for having a negative impact on local cultures, McDonald's has been credited with introducing more hygienic food preparation and toilets in several East Asian markets, including China.[55]

Performance/Status   Are opportunities, rewards, and prestige based on an individual's performance or on the status associated with the person's family, position, or class? Do all people have an equal opportunity economically, socially, and politically at the start of life, or are certain groups given special privileges? Are products and brands valued for their ability to accomplish a task or for the reputation or status of the brand?

Performance/status is closely related to the concept of **power distance,** which refers to *the degree to which people accept inequality in power, authority, status, and wealth as natural or inherent in society*. India, China, Brazil, Mexico, France, Hong Kong, and Japan are relatively high in their acceptance of power. Austria, Denmark, New Zealand, Sweden, and the United States are relatively low. In which of these countries would an expert source have the greatest impact in an advertisement? Research indicates that expert sources have a greater impact in a high power distance country than in a low one.[56] In addition, consumers in high power distance countries are more likely to seek the opinions of others in making decisions.[57]

A status-oriented society is more likely to prefer "quality" or established brand names and high-priced items to functionally equivalent items with unknown brand names or lower prices (e.g., private label or store brands). This is the case in Japan, China, Hong Kong, Singapore, the Philippines, Malaysia, Indonesia, Thailand, India, and most Arab countries, where consumers are attracted by prestigious, known brands.[58] As a result, compared to the United States, advertising in Japan, China, and India tend to involve more appeals to status or wealth.[59]

Tradition/Change   Is tradition valued simply for the sake of tradition? Is change or "progress" an acceptable reason for altering established patterns? Compared to Americans, Korean and Chinese consumers have traditionally been much less comfortable dealing with new situations or ways of thinking.[60] Britain, too, has a culture laden with tradition. This value is reflected in their advertising where, compared to ads in America, those in Britain and China are more likely to emphasize tradition and history.[61]

It is important to note once again that change can and does live alongside traditional values. For example, both the Korean and Chinese cultures are now enthusiastically embracing change. In China, "modernness" (often symbolized by a Western name) is an important product attribute, particularly among younger, urban Chinese. A recent study found that advertisers in China segment their advertising depending on audience. For the mainstream audiences targeted by television, traditional appeals are used more. In magazines targeted at younger Chinese (e.g., *Elle, Cosmopolitan,* and *Sanlian*), modern appeals focusing on technology, fashion, and leisure are used more.[62]

A focus on technology as an indicator of change illustrates some dramatic differences. Obviously these differences are a function of economic development as well as culture. The following represent Internet users and cell phones as a percentage of total population.[63]

	Internet	Cell Phone
Brazil	8%	25%
Mexico	10	27
China	7	21
Japan	45	68
South Korea	60	69
United Kingdom	42	82
United States	54	54

The United States lags much of the developed world in cell phones. In addition, given China's large population, the absolute market potential is staggering (China has 269 million cell phones compared to just 34 million in South Korea). China's continued development will fuel massive growth in this market. And Vodafone has found out just how demanding tech-hungry Asian consumers can be. Their market share in Japan has plummeted recently because of their failure to innovate and stay cutting edge.[64]

Risk Taking/Security   Do the "heroes" of the culture meet and overcome obstacles? Is the person who risks established position or wealth on a new venture admired or considered foolhardy? This value relates to tolerance for ambiguity and uncertainty avoidance. It has a strong influence on entrepreneurship and economic development as well as new-product acceptance. A society that does not admire risk taking is unlikely to develop enough entrepreneurs to achieve economic change and growth. New-product introductions, new channels of distribution, and advertising themes are affected by this value.[65]

Problem Solving/Fatalistic   Do people react to obstacles and disasters as challenges to be overcome, or do they take a "what will be, will be" attitude? Is there an optimistic, "we can do it" orientation? In the Caribbean, difficult or unmanageable problems are often dismissed with the expression "no problem." This actually means: "There is a problem, but we don't know what to do about it—so don't worry!" Western Europe and the United States tend to fall toward the problem-solving end of the continuum, whereas Mexico and most Middle-East countries fall toward the fatalistic end. Fatalists tend to feel they don't have control over the outcome of events. This has been shown to reduce consumer expectations of quality and decrease the likelihood that consumers make formal complaints when faced with an unsatisfactory purchase.[66]

Nature   Is nature assigned a positive value, or is it viewed as something to be overcome, conquered, or tamed? Americans historically considered nature as something to be overcome or improved. Most northern European countries place a high value on the environment. Packaging and other environmental regulations are stronger in these countries than in America. In fact, a British company recently developed a zero-emissions motorcycle that runs on hydrogen. They worry, however, because it also makes no sound! *Would you want a motorcycle that didn't growl when you revved it up?*[67]

In turn, Americans and Canadians appear to place a higher value on the environment than the southern European countries and most developing countries, though this may reflect variations in the financial ability to act on this value rather than in the value itself. These differences in attitudes are reflected in consumers' purchase decisions, consumption practices, and recycling efforts.[68]

As with all the values we are discussing, there are wide ranges within as well as between countries, which create market opportunities. For example, overall China does not have a strong environmental orientation. However, there are segments of the country that do have such an orientation and the means to buy products and services that reflect this focus.[69]

Self-Oriented Values

Active/Passive   Are people expected to take a physically active approach to work and play? Are physical skills and feats valued more highly than nonphysical performances? Is emphasis placed on doing? Americans are much more prone to engage in physical activities and to take an action-oriented approach to problems. "Don't just stand there, do something" is a common response to problems in America. Participation in active exercise varies widely across countries, especially for women (see our discussion earlier in this chapter). While this obviously limits the market for exercise equipment in these countries, it also affects advertising themes and formats. For example, an exercise/sport theme for bottled water would not be appropriate in a country such as Japan, where two-thirds of the men and three-fourths of the women exercise less than twice a year.

Sensual Gratification/Abstinence   Is it acceptable to pamper oneself, to satisfy one's desires for food, drink, or sex beyond the minimum requirement? Is one who forgoes such gratification considered virtuous or strange? Muslim cultures are extremely conservative on this value as are many Asian cultures including Hong Kong and India. A full 37 percent of Saudis indicated modesty is important, compared to 9 percent in the United States.[70] Perhaps not surprisingly, compared to U.S. and Australian ads, ads in Hong Kong and India contain fewer sex appeals.[71] And, China has put legal restrictions on the use of sex appeals in ads.[72] Consider the following:

> In U.S. cigarette advertisements, it is not uncommon to find sensual models, males and females holding hands, and couples in intimate situations. In the eastern culture of India, such open display of intimacy between opposite sexes is not socially acceptable.[73]

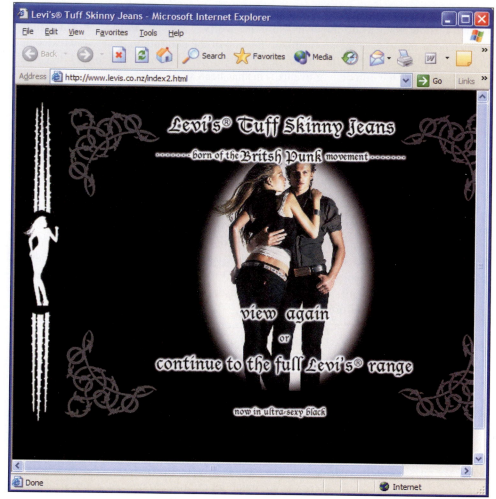

Courtesy Levi Strauss Pty Ltd.

In Arab countries advertisements, packaging, and products must carefully conform to Muslim standards. Polaroid's instant cameras gained rapid acceptance because they allowed Arab men to photograph their wives and daughters without fear that a stranger in a film laboratory would see the women unveiled.

In contrast, Brazilian and European advertisements contain nudity and blatant (by U.S. standards) appeals to sensual gratification. Consider the following billboard ad for Gossard women's underwear appearing throughout the United Kingdom:

> The picture shows the upper half of a nude woman lying on a bed with her arms above her head, her back arched. Her bra and panties are on the floor along with a man's shoe and shirt. The text says "Bring him to his knees." The tagline is "*Gossard.* Find your *G* spot." Another version has the copy line—"If he's late you can always start without him."[74]

Illustration 2-5 shows a page from Levi's New Zealand Web site that makes use of sensuality and the British punk rock counterculture. While quite appropriate for New Zealand, it would not be successful in a culture that did not accept sensual gratification.

Material/Nonmaterial   Is the accumulation of material wealth a positive good in its own right? Does material wealth bring more status than family ties, knowledge, or other activities? Consider the following conclusion from a study of Chinese television ownership:

> The television one owns is very much a representation of one's own self-worth. For most, the television had become almost as much a part of getting married as saying their vows. One engaged man (age 24), who was saving for his TV so he could get married, noted that he wanted a 25" or 29" Japanese model. He was willing to save for up to two years (a commonly quoted time frame) before revising his sights downward. Price was not nearly as important as projecting "a good image" to others. He was concerned about getting off to a good start. Several respondents noted that the purchase of the appropriate television set was more important than having furniture when considering marriage.[75]

There are two types of materialism. **Instrumental materialism** is *the acquisition of things to enable one to do something.* Skis can be acquired to allow one to ski. **Terminal materialism** is *the acquisition of items for the sake of owning the item itself.* Art is generally acquired for the pleasure of owning it rather than as a means to another goal. Cultures differ markedly in their relative emphasis on these two types of materialism.[76]

Hard Work/Leisure   Is work valued for itself, independent of external rewards, or is work merely a means to an end? Will individuals continue to work hard even when their minimum economic needs are satisfied, or will they opt for more leisure time? For example, in parts of Latin America, work has traditionally been viewed as a necessary evil. However, generational gaps exist. For example, in Mexico, 100 percent of the older generation agreed with the statement "Today's emphasis on work is a bad thing" compared to only 28 percent of the younger generation. The trend was just the opposite in the U.K., Netherlands, France, Canada, and Australia, where agreement by the older generation was around 55 percent while agreement by the younger generation was around 80 percent. In the United States and Hong Kong younger and older generations were roughly the same (about 50 percent agreeing) on this value.[77]

These attitudes do not necessarily reflect *actual* work patterns. For example, hours worked per week are highest in Hong Kong (48.6 hours) and Mexico (41.6) and lowest in France (34.1) and Canada (34.8).[78] Nonetheless, this value has important consequences for lifestyle and demand for leisure activities.

Postponed Gratification/Immediate Gratification   Is one encouraged to "save for a rainy day," or should one "live for today"? Is it better to secure immediate benefits and pleasures, or is it better to suffer in the short run for benefits in the future, or in the hereafter or for future generations? The United States, the U.K., and Australia tend to have short-term orientations, while India, Hungary, Brazil, Hong Kong, and China have long-term orientations. This value has implications for business strategies, efforts to encourage savings, and the use of credit. For example, valued business goals in short-term cultures tend to include "this year's profits" while those in long-term cultures included "profits 10 years from now."[79] In addition, use of credit is lower in long-term oriented cultures where cash and debit card usage is more common.[80]

Religious/Secular   To what extent are daily activities determined by religious doctrine? The United States is relatively secular. Many Islamic cultures as well as some Catholic cultures are much more religiously oriented.[81] In contrast, religion plays a very small role in Chinese culture. However, even in a country such as China where few are actively involved with a formal religion, many of the culture's values were formed in part by historical religious influences. The same is true for the secular nations of the West. Understanding the extent and type of religious influences operating in a culture is essential for effectively designing all elements of the marketing mix.[82]

Clearly, the preceding discussion has not covered all of the values operating in the various cultures. However, it should suffice to provide a feel for the importance of cultural values and how cultures differ along value dimensions.

CULTURAL VARIATIONS IN NONVERBAL COMMUNICATIONS

Differences in **verbal communication systems** (languages) are immediately obvious to anyone entering a foreign culture. An American traveling in Britain or Australia will be able to communicate, but differences in pronunciation, timing, and meaning will still occur. For example, Dogpile, a U.S.-based meta search engine (www.dogpile.com), changed its name in Europe to WebFetch after realizing that in the U.K. "pile" means hemorrhoids or the result of a dog relieving itself![83]

Attempts to translate marketing communications from one language to another can result in ineffective communications, as Ford Motor Company is painfully aware. For example, Fiera (a low-cost truck designed for developing countries) faced sales problems since *fiera* means "terrible, cruel, or ugly" in Spanish.[84] Table 2-2 indicates that Ford is not the only company to encounter translation problems.

The problems of literal translations and slang expressions are compounded by symbolic meanings associated with words, the absence of some words from various languages, and the difficulty of pronouncing certain words:[85]

- Mars addressed the problem of making the M&M's name pronounceable in France, where neither ampersands nor the apostrophe "s" plural form exists, by advertising extensively that M&M's should be pronounced "aimainaimze." Whirlpool is facing a similar problem in Spain, as its name is virtually unpronounceable in Spanish.
- To market its Ziploc food storage bags in Brazil, Dow Chemical had to use extensive advertising to actually create the word *zipar,* meaning to zip, since there was no such term in Portuguese.

Coca-Cola Company avoided the problems that many companies have encountered by realizing that *enjoy,* which is part of its famous logo Enjoy Coca-Cola, has sensual

TABLE 2-2

Translation Problems in International Marketing

- Colgate's Cue toothpaste had problems in France, as *cue* is a crude term for "butt" in French.
- Sunbeam attempted to enter the German market with a mist-producing curling iron named the Mist-Stick. Unfortunately, *mist* translates as "dung" or "manure" in German.
- Parker Pen mistook *embarazar* (to impregnate) to mean to embarrass and ran an ad in Mexico stating "It won't leak in your pocket and make you pregnant."
- Pet milk encountered difficulties in French-speaking countries where *pet* means, among other things, "to break wind."
- Esso found that its name pronounced phonetically meant "stalled car" in Japanese.
- Kellogg's Bran Buds translates to "burned farmer" in Swedish.
- United Airlines' in-flight magazine cover for its Pacific Rim routes showed Australian actor Paul Hogan in the outback. The caption stated, "Paul Hogan Camps It Up." "Camps it up" is Australian slang for "flaunts his homosexuality."
- China attempted to export Pansy brand men's underwear to America.
- General Motors' "Body by Fisher" was translated as "corpse by Fisher" in Flemish.
- American Airlines introduced its new leather first-class seats in Mexico with the theme "Fly in Leather" which, when translated literally, read "Fly Naked."

Factors Influencing Nonverbal Communications   **FIGURE 2-3**

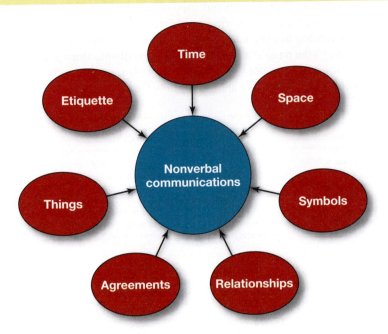

connotations in Russian and several other languages. Coca-Cola solved this problem by changing the logo to Drink Coca-Cola where appropriate. It also altered the successful "The real thing" theme to "I feel Coke" in Japan and several other countries with great success and "Life tastes good" in many countries where *tastes* would not convey the same meaning it does in English.

Additional communication factors that can cause problems include humor, style, and pace for which preferences vary across cultures, even those speaking the same basic language.[86] Nonetheless, verbal language translations generally do not present major problems as long as we are careful. What many of us fail to recognize, however, is that each culture also has nonverbal communication systems or languages that, like verbal languages, are specific to each culture. **Nonverbal communication systems** are the *arbitrary meanings a culture assigns actions, events, and things other than words.*

The following discussion examines the seven variables shown in Figure 2-3, all of which influence nonverbal communications: time, space, symbols, relationships, agreements, things, and etiquette.

Time

The meaning of time varies between cultures in two major ways. First is what we call time perspective: this is a culture's overall orientation toward time.[87] The second is the interpretations assigned to specific uses of time.

Time Perspective   Most Americans, Canadians, Western Europeans, and Australians tend to view time as inescapable, linear, and fixed in nature. It is a road reaching into the future with distinct, separate sections (hours, days, weeks, and so on). Time is seen almost as a physical object: we can schedule it, waste it, lose it, and so forth. Believing that a person does one thing at a time, we have a strong orientation toward the present and the short-term future. This is known as a **monochronic time perspective.**

Most Latin Americans, Asians, and Indians tend to view time as being less discrete and less subject to scheduling. They view simultaneous involvement in many activities as natural. People and relationships take priority over schedules, and activities occur at their own pace rather than according to a predetermined timetable. Such cultures have an orientation toward the present and the past. This is known as a **polychronic time perspective.**

Some important differences between individuals with a monochronic perspective and those with a polychronic perspective are listed below.[88]

Monochronic Culture	Polychronic Culture
Do one thing at a time	Do many things at once
Concentrate on the job	Highly distractible and subject to interruptions
Take deadlines and schedules seriously	Consider deadlines and schedules secondary
Committed to the job or task	Committed to people and relationships
Adhere religiously to plans	Change plans often and easily
Emphasize promptness	Base promptness on the relationship
Accustomed to short-term relationships	Prefer long-term relationships

How would marketing activities vary between monochronic and polychronic cultures? Personal selling and negotiation styles and strategies would need to differ, as would many advertising themes. Contests and sales with deadlines would generally be more effective in monochronic than in polychronic cultures. Convenience foods frequently fail when positioned in terms of timesaving and convenience in polychronic cultures where "saving time" is not part of the cultural thought processes. The following quote illustrates the impact of time perspective on the positioning strategy of fast-food outlets in polychronic cultures:

> In Argentina, McDonald's has an image of an expensive, modern restaurant where the majority of the customers are teenagers and young adults who patronize McDonald's to express their modern and liberated value systems. This is equally true in Turkey. In fact, a major reason for the popularity of fast-food restaurants in many developing countries is neither convenience nor reasonable prices. Time savings does not have the same priority in these countries as it does in the United States. What makes these restaurants popular in developing countries such as Argentina, Turkey, and many others is their "Americanness." Patronization of these restaurants enables consumers to express their "aspirational" links with developed nations.[89]

Interestingly, even within a culture, time perspectives can vary by age and by situation. For example, in Japan, work is approached in terms of monochronic time whereas leisure is approached, as their culture might suggest, in terms of polychronic time.[90] Also, while Americans have tended to be monochronic, younger consumers appear to demonstrate elements of polychronic time. This so-called MTV generation seems to have no attention span and may simultaneously be found doing homework, watching TV, and surfing the net! Not surprisingly, U.S. advertisers find it hard to capture and hold the attention of this audience.

Meanings in the Use of Time   Specific uses of time have varying meanings in different cultures. In much of the world, the time required for a decision is proportional to the importance of the decision. Americans, by being well prepared with ready answers, may adversely downplay the importance of the business being discussed. Likewise, both Japanese and Middle-Eastern executives are put off by Americans' insistence on coming to the point directly and quickly in business transactions.

Promptness is considered very important in America and Japan. Furthermore, promptness is defined as being on time for appointments, whether you are the person making the call or the person receiving the caller. According to one expert:

> Time is money and a symbol of status and responsibility. To be kept waiting is offensive in monochronic cultures, it is perceived as a message. It is not in polychronic cultures.[91]

What is meant by "being kept waiting" also varies substantially by culture. Thirty minutes might seem like an eternity in the United States, but seem like very little time in other countries such as those in the Middle-East. As you can see, understanding such differences *prior* to doing business in a given country is critical.

Space

The use people make of space and the meanings they assign to their use of space constitute a second form of nonverbal communication.[92] In America, "bigger is better." Thus, office space in corporations generally is allocated according to rank or prestige rather than need. The president will have the largest office, followed by the executive vice president, and so on.

A second major use of space is **personal space.** It is the nearest that others can come to you in various situations without your feeling uncomfortable. In the United States, normal business conversations occur at distances of 3 to 5 feet and highly personal business from 18 inches to 3 feet. In parts of northern Europe, the distances are slightly longer; in most of Latin America, they are substantially shorter.

An American businessperson in Latin America will tend to back away from a Latin American counterpart in order to maintain his or her preferred personal distance. In turn, the host will tend to advance toward the American in order to maintain his or her personal space. The resulting "chase" would be comical if it were not for the results. Both parties generally are unaware of their actions or the reasons for them. Furthermore, each assigns a meaning to the other's actions according to what the action means in his or her own culture. Thus, the North American considers the Latin American to be pushy and aggressive. The Latin American, in turn, considers the North American to be cold, aloof, and snobbish.

Symbols

An American seeing a baby wearing a pink outfit would most likely assume the child to be female. If the outfit were blue, the assumed gender would be male. These assumptions would be accurate most of the time in the United States but not in many other parts of the world, such as Holland. Colors, animals, shapes, numbers, and music have varying meanings across cultures. Failure to recognize the meaning assigned to a symbol can cause serious problems:

- Most Chinese business travelers were shocked during the inauguration of United's concierge services for first-class passengers on its Pacific Rim routes. To mark the occasion, each concierge was proudly wearing a white carnation—an Asian symbol of death.
- AT&T had to change its "thumbs-up" ads in Russia and Poland, where showing the palm of the hand in this manner has an offensive meaning. The change was simple. The thumbs-up sign was given showing the back of the hand.

Kellogg's tiger is an effective symbol in many cultures. Here the tiger and a contest work as well in Japan as they do in America.

KELLOGG'S FROSTED FLAKES® is a registered trademark of Kellogg Company. All rights reserved. Used with permission.

TABLE 2-3

The Meaning of Numbers, Colors, and Other Symbols

• White	Symbol for mourning or death in the Far East; happiness, purity in the United States.
• Purple	Associated with death in many Latin American countries.
• Blue	Connotation of femininity in Holland; masculinity in Sweden, United States.
• Red	Unlucky or negative in Chad, Nigeria, Germany; positive in Denmark, Rumania, Argentina. Brides wear red in China, but it is a masculine color in the United Kingdom and France.
• Yellow flowers	Sign of death in Mexico; infidelity in France.
• White lilies	Suggestion of death in England.
• 7	Unlucky number in Ghana, Kenya, Singapore; lucky in Morocco, India, Czechoslovakia, Nicaragua, United States.
• Triangle	Negative in Hong Kong, Korea, Taiwan; positive in Colombia.
• Owl	Wisdom in United States; bad luck in India.
• Deer	Speed, grace in United States; homosexuality in Brazil.

- Mont Blanc has a white marking on the end of its pens meant to represent the snow-capped Alpine mountain peaks. However, Arab consumers reacted negatively because it looked like the "Star of David," which is Israel's national symbol. Mont Blanc worked to clear up the misunderstanding.[93]

Table 2-3 presents additional illustrations of varying meanings assigned to symbols across cultures.[94] Despite frequent cultural differences in symbols, many symbols work well across a wide range of cultures. Kellogg's Tony the Tiger works in the United States, Japan (see Illustration 2-6), and many other cultures.

Relationships

The rights and obligations imposed by relationships and friendship are another nonverbal cultural variable. Americans, more so than most other cultures, form relationships and make friends quickly and easily and drop them easily also. In large part, this may be because America has always had a great deal of both social and geographic mobility. People who move every few years must be able to form friendships in a short time period and depart from them with a minimum of pain. In many other parts of the world, relationships and friendships are formed slowly and carefully because they imply deep and lasting obligations. As the following quote indicates, friendship and business are deeply intertwined in most of the world:

> To most Asians and Latin Americans, good personal relationships and feelings are all that really matter in a long-term agreement. After all, the written word is less important than personal ties. Once personal trust has been established, cooperation increases. The social contacts developed between the parties are often far more significant than the technical specifications and the price. In many countries the heart of the matter, the major point of the negotiations, is getting to know the people involved. Americans negotiate a contract; the Japanese negotiate a relationship. In many cultures, the written word is used simply to satisfy legalities. In their eyes, emotion and personal relations are more important than cold facts.[95]

In addition, long-run success in many cultures involves more than just "getting to know" someone in the Western sense of the expression. For example, Chinese relationships are complex and described under the concept of **guanxi:**

> *Guanxi* is literally translated as personal connections/relationships on which an individual can draw to secure resources or advantages when doing business as well as in the course of social life. Its main characteristics are (1) the notion of a continuing reciprocal relationship over an indefinite period of time, (2) favors are banked, (3) it extends beyond the relationship between two parties to include other parties within the social network (it can be transferred), (4) the relationship network is built among individuals not organizations, (5) status matters—relationships with a senior will extend to his subordinates but not vice versa, and (6) the social relationship is prior to and a prerequisite to the business relationship.[96]

Agreements

Americans rely on an extensive and, generally, highly efficient legal system for ensuring that business obligations are honored and for resolving disagreements. Many other cultures have not developed such a system and rely instead on relationships, friendship, and kinship, local moral principles, or informal customs to guide business conduct. For example, the Chinese "tend to pay more attention to relationships than contracts."[97] Under the American system, we would examine a proposed contract closely. Under the Chinese system, we would examine the character of a potential trading partner closely. In the words of an American CEO based in China,

> Relationships are everything in China, more so than in the United States, which is more focused on business. The Chinese want to know and understand you before they buy from you.[98]

Americans generally assume that, in almost all instances, prices are uniform for all buyers, related to the service rendered, and reasonably close to the going rate. We order many products such as taxi rides without inquiring in advance about the cost. In many Latin American, Asian, and Middle East countries, the procedure is different. Virtually all prices are negotiated prior to the sale, including industrial products.[99] If a product such as a taxi ride is consumed without first establishing the price, the customer must pay what the seller demands. Likewise, assuming that a price list exists or has real meaning for industrial products can lead to incorrect conclusions concerning the actual price.

Things

The cultural meaning of things leads to purchase patterns that one would not otherwise predict. One observer noted a strong demand for expensive, status brands whose absolute cost was not too high among those Russians beginning to gain economically under capitalism. He concluded,

> They may stick to their locally produced toothpaste, but they want the Levi's, the Mont Blanc pens, the Moet Chandon champagne to establish their self-esteem and their class position.[100]

The differing meanings that cultures attach to things, including products, make gift-giving a particularly difficult task.[101] For example, giving a Chinese business customer or distributor a nice desk clock—a common gift in many countries—would be inappropriate. Why? In China, the word for *clock* is similar to the word for *funeral,* making clocks inappropriate gifts. When does receipt of a gift "require" a gift in return? In China this depends on the closeness of the relationship between the parties—the closer the relationship, the less a return gift is required.[102]

The business and social situations that call for a gift, and the items that are appropriate gifts, vary widely. For example, a gift of cutlery is generally inappropriate in Russia, Japan, Taiwan, and Germany. In Japan, small gifts are required in many business situations, yet in China they are less appropriate. In China, gifts should be presented privately, but in Arab countries they should be given in front of others.

Etiquette

Etiquette represents generally accepted ways of behaving in social situations. Assume that an American is preparing a commercial that shows people eating an evening meal, with one person about to take a bite of food from a fork. The person will have the fork in the right hand, and the left hand will be out of sight under the table. To an American audience this will seem natural. However, in many European cultures, a well-mannered individual would have the fork in the left hand and the right hand on the table.

Behaviors considered rude or obnoxious in one culture may be quite acceptable in another. The common and acceptable American habit, for males, of crossing one's legs while sitting, such that the sole of a shoe shows, is extremely insulting in many Eastern cultures. In these cultures, the sole of the foot or shoe should never be exposed to view. While most Americans are not hesitant to voice dissatisfaction with a service encounter, many Asians are. This also appears to be true of the British who have traditionally been characterized by their reserved nature. Such factors can lead U.S. managers to misjudge customer response to their services abroad.[103]

Normal voice tone, pitch, and speed of speech differ among cultures and languages, as does the use of gestures. Westerners often mistake the seemingly loud, volatile speech of some Asian cultures as signifying anger or emotional distress (which it would if it were being used by a Westerner) when it is normal speech for the occasion.

As American trade with Japan increases, we continue to learn more of the subtle aspects of Japanese business etiquette. For example, a Japanese executive will seldom say *no* directly during negotiations, as this would be considered impolite. Instead, he might say, "That will be very difficult," which would mean *no*. A Japanese responding *yes* to a request often means, "Yes, I understand the request," not "Yes, I agree to the request." Many Japanese find the American tendency to look straight into another's eyes when talking to be aggressive and rude.

Another aspect of Japanese business etiquette is *meishi,* epitomized by "A man without a *meishi* has no identity in Japan." The exchange of meishi is the most basic of social rituals in a nation where social ritual matters very much. The act of exchanging meishi is weighted with meaning. Once the social minuet is completed, the two know where they stand in relation to each other and their respective statures within the hierarchy of corporate or government bureaucracy. What is "meishi"? It is the exchange of business cards when two people meet! A fairly common, simple activity in America, it is an essential, complex social exchange in Japan.

Other cultures also find it necessary to learn about the subtleties of doing business with Westerners. Business leaders in China are developing training programs to help sensitize Chinese businesspeople to other cultures. According to Jack Ma who runs one such program:

> Chinese businessmen are shrewd, but they need to learn to be more polished. At a World Economic Forum held in Bejing, Mr. Ma was depressed at how many conducted themselves, noting— Many smoked constantly and held loud cellphone conversations, even during meetings.[104]

The importance of proper, culture-specific etiquette is obvious. Although people recognize that etiquette varies from culture to culture, there is still a strong emotional feeling that "our way is natural and right."

Conclusions on Nonverbal Communications

Can you imagine yourself becoming upset or surprised because people in a different culture spoke to you in their native language, say Spanish or German, instead of English? Of course not. We all recognize that verbal languages vary around the world. Yet we generally feel that our nonverbal languages are natural or innate. Therefore, we misinterpret what is being "said" to us because we think we are hearing English when in reality it is Japanese, Italian, or Russian. It is this error that marketers can and must avoid.

GLOBAL CULTURES

An important issue facing marketers is the extent to which one or more global consumer cultures or segments are emerging. Evidence suggests that there is indeed movement in this direction.[105] Such a culture would have a shared set of consumption-related symbols with common meaning and desirability among members. One such proposed global culture is that portion of local cultures that view themselves as cosmopolitan, knowledgeable, and modern. Such individuals share many values and consumption-related behaviors with similar individuals across a range of national cultures.

Such cultures are being created by the globalization of mass media, work, education, and travel. Some product categories (cell phones, Internet) and brands (Sony, Nike) have become symbolically related to this culture. This does not imply that these brands use the same advertising globally but rather that the underlying theme and symbolism may be the same. Thus, a combined shampoo/conditioner could be positioned as a time-saver for the time-pressured modern career woman. The advertisement might portray the shampoo being used in the context of a gym in the United States or Germany, where many females exercise, but in a home context in Japan, where few women visit gyms. Philips Electronic is one firm that has developed a global positioning strategy based on such a global culture.[106]

Perhaps the closest thing to a global culture today are urban teenagers, which we examine next.

A Global Teenage Culture?

Consider _____, a 19-year old hip-hop music producer scouting for a new pair of Air Force 1 sneakers at the Nike shop. . . . _____, who prefers to be addressed by his street name, "Jerzy King"—moved to _____ three years ago. . . . A music school dropout who has never set foot outside of _____, he totes a mini-disc player loaded with Eminem, Puff Daddy, and Fabolous. On this particular day he's looking phat in a blue-and-white fleece jacket bearing the logo of the Toronto Maple Leafs.[107]

Can you fill in the blanks in the above story with any degree of confidence? The young man is Wang Qi and he lives in Beijing. However, many of his behaviors and possessions echo that of millions of other teenagers in Europe, North and South America, and Asia. One study videotaped the bedrooms of teens from 25 countries. The conclusion:

From the gear and posters on display, it's hard to tell whether the rooms are in Los Angeles, Mexico City, or Tokyo. Basketballs sit alongside soccer balls. Closets overflow with staples from an international, unisex uniform: baggy Levi's or Diesel jeans, NBA jackets, and rugged shoes from Timberland or Doc Martens.[108]

"Teenagers—who make up a huge and growing part of the population around the world—represent the first truly international market in history," according to Larry McIntosh, Pepsi-Cola's vice president for international advertising.[109] Consider the following data on teenage clothing ownership around the world (the data for Asia exclude China).[110]

	U.S.	Europe	Asia	Latin America
Jeans	93%	94%	93%	86%
T-shirt	93	94	96	59
Running shoes	80	89	69	65
Blazer	42	43	27	30
Denim jacket	39	57	23	41

The World's Teenagers (New York: D'Arcy Masius Benton & Bowles, 1994).

Teenagers around the world not only tend to dress alike, but are very similar in the things they find enjoyable.[111]

What is causing this movement toward uniformity? The largest single influence is worldwide mass media. Teenagers around the world watch many of the same shows, see the same movies and videos, and listen to the same music. They not only idolize the same musicians, but copy these musicians' dress styles, mannerisms, and attitudes, which provide them with many shared characteristics. This interconnectedness is rapidly increasing with the growth of the Internet. Sports and sports figures are another unifying force. Products used or endorsed by global sports figures often find quick acceptance among teenagers around the world.

Marketers are using the similarities among teenagers across cultures to launch global brands or to reposition current brands to appeal to this large market. For example, Pepsi

そぎ落とすと、こうなる。

Courtesy BBH/Tokyo.

Max was introduced around the world with a single set of commercials aimed at teenagers. The ads showed a quartet of teens vying to perform the most outrageous feats, such as sky-diving from Big Ben, rollerblading off the Sphinx, or surfing down the dunes of the Sahara. Levi's, reacting to the growing online trend among global teens, launched an online campaign in Asia targeted at "young, tech-savvy trendsetters." The Web site plays heavily on Western music and style to promote its Levi's re-cut 501 Re-Born jeans. The theme emphasizes that the jeans have been re-cut for today, with one page showing a teen being "reborn" or transformed by the new Levi's jeans.[112] Illustration 2-7 provides another example of a Levi's ad using a global teen appeal.

It is important to note that teenagers also have a great many culturally unique behaviors, attitudes, and values. As one expert states, "European teens resent being thought of as Americans with an accent."[113] Also, the similarities described above are most noticeable among middle-class teens living in urban areas. Poorer, rural teens often conform more closely to their society's traditional culture. For example, Coke distinguishes between major urban centers and smaller cities and towns in China. Consider the following:

> In the smaller cities and towns Coke uses a famous Chinese actor traveling the countryside in a hot bus and stresses taste and price. In China's largest markets its TV spot "features a hip Taiwanese VJ . . . who shows off his dance moves as he pretends his Coke can magnetically draw him to an attractive lady across the street." According to a Coke executive, "The (urban TV) ad is aimed at young adults who want to do things their own way, as opposed to following a famous actor as in the bus spot."[114]

Chapter 1's opening ad shows Coke's urban TV spot. It is fascinating to watch how teens across cultures continue to search for the new and interesting, and how different cultures influence each other. A recent example is India and its growing influence on teens worldwide as discussed in Consumer Insight 2-1.

GLOBAL DEMOGRAPHICS

Economies such as India and China have seen rapid growth, which has led to increased personal disposable income and strong and growing middle classes that are the envy of marketers worldwide.[118] Such expansion not only creates opportunities, it can also create challenges.

For example, the initial explosion in the use of motorbikes as replacements for bicycles in China triggered demand for gasoline in cities with no gasoline stations and few available sites. Illustration 2-8 shows how one firm dealt with this challenge by developing and deploying "mobile" service stations in the form of trucks with attached gasoline pumps. More recently, an increase in automobile use (expected to increase 10 percent per year between 2005 and 2010) is creating environmental concerns related to emissions as well.[119]

Disposable income is one aspect of demographics. **Demographics** *describe a population in terms of its size, structure, and distribution. Size* refers to the number of individuals in the society. *Structure* describes the society in terms of age, income, education, and occupation. *Distribution* refers to the physical location of individuals in terms of geographic region and rural, suburban, and urban location.

Demographics are both a result and a cause of cultural values. Densely populated societies are likely to have more of a collective orientation than an individualistic one because

© Delbert Hawkins.

a collective orientation helps such societies function smoothly. Cultures that value hard work and the acquisition of material wealth are likely to advance economically, which alters their demographics both directly (income) and indirectly (families in economically advanced countries tend to be smaller).

A critical aspect of demographics for marketers is income, particularly the distribution of income. One country with a relatively low average income can have a sizable middle-income segment, while another country with the same average income may have most of the wealth in the hands of a few individuals. As shown below, by one measure (per capita gross domestic product expressed as purchasing power parity), Brazil's average per capita income is slightly higher than Romania's.[120] However, the distribution of that income differs sharply. Almost half of the income generated in Brazil goes to just 10 percent of the population. In contrast, the top 10 percent of households in Romania command only 25 percent of that country's income. *How will these and the other differences shown below affect consumption?*

	GDP per Capita	Percentage of Total Income to Top 10%		GDP per Capita	Percentage of Total Income to Top 10%
Brazil	$ 7,600	48%	Japan	$28,200	22%
Canada	29,800	24	Kenya	1,000	37
Chile	9,900	41	South Korea	17,800	23
China	5,000	30	Mexico	9,000	36
Egypt	4,000	30	Romania	7,000	25
France	27,600	25	United Kingdom	27,700	28
India	2,900	34	United States	37,800	31

Marketers increasingly use **purchasing power parity (PPP)** rather than average or median income to evaluate markets. PPP is based on the cost of a standard market basket of products bought in each country. An average household in one country may have a lower income in U.S. dollars. However, these households may be able to buy *more* than other countries with higher income in U.S. dollars because of a lower local cost structure, government-provided health care, and so forth. The World Bank describes all countries in terms of PPP in its annual World Bank Atlas. Notice how Brazil's purchasing power is substantially higher than its per capita income would suggest. In fact, according to The World Bank, in PPP terms Brazil is a middle-income country. Consider the following figures:[121]

	Per Capita Income	Per Capita PPP
Brazil	$ 2,710	$ 7,480
China	1,100	4,990
Egypt	1,390	3,940
India	530	2,880
Japan	34,510	28,620
Mexico	6,230	8,950
Romania	2,310	7,140
United Kingdom	28,350	27,650
United States	37,610	37,500

WORLD BANK ATLAS, 03 by WORLD BANK. Copyright 2003 by WORLD BANK. Reproduced with permission of WORLD BANK in the format Textbook via Copyright Clearance Center.

The estimated age distributions of the United States, the Philippines, Japan, and Canada are shown below.[122] Note that almost half the population of the Philippines is less than 20 years of age compared to less than a third for the United States, one-fourth for Canada, and about one-fifth for Japan. In the Middle-East, a massive baby boom is under way, with two-thirds of the population under 25, fueling the youth movement in this region that we discussed earlier.[123] What product opportunities do this and the other age differences among these countries suggest?

Age	United States	Philippines	Japan	Canada
<10	13.6%	26.6%	9.2%	11.3%
10–19	14.3	22.6	10.3	13.3
20–29	13.7	17.5	13.3	13.8
30–39	14.5	13.4	14.2	14.5
40–49	15.4	8.9	12.4	16.6
50–59	12.0	5.5	15.0	13.0
>60	16.5	5.4	25.5	17.7

CROSS-CULTURAL MARKETING STRATEGY

There is continuing controversy over the extent to which cross-cultural marketing strategies, particularly advertising, should be standardized.[124] Standardized strategies can result in substantial cost savings. This was an important consideration in the FedEx ad strategy described at the opening of this chapter. Likewise, Maybelline's Manhattan line of cosmetics designed for the Asian market used one ad campaign in China, Taiwan, Hong Kong, Thailand, and Singapore. The ads featured an attractive Asian model in a low-cut, short

ILLUSTRATION 2-9

McDonald's offers both family and singles sections in Muslim countries to accommodate the cultural norms governing interactions between men and women. The singles section is for single men only.

Christopher Morris/VII Agency.

dress against the Manhattan skyline at night. This combination of appeals to youth, beauty, and sophistication could be used in many other countries, though this ad would be inappropriate, and probably banned, in most Islamic countries.

McDonald's used to strive for uniformity around the globe. Now it adapts its products as appropriate, adding fried eggs to burgers in Japan, offering Samurai pork burgers with a sweet barbecue sauce in Thailand, and stressing chicken and rice dishes in Indonesia. Consider its approach in India:

> Eighty percent of Indians are Hindu who don't eat beef so there will be no Big Macs in India. Instead, the menu will feature the Maharaja Mac—"two all mutton patties, special sauce, lettuce, cheese, pickles, onions on a sesame-seed bun."[125]

McDonald's also adapts its store layout. As shown in Illustration 2-9, separate sections for families and singles are provided in Muslim countries.

In general, most companies will blend standardization and customization. A recent surge in people's pride in their local cultures (up 11 percent in Brazil and France and up 20 percent in Japan) means that at least some customization is necessary.[126] A critical success factor is achieving the right balance and determining where standardization is possible and where customization is critical.

Considerations in Approaching a Foreign Market

There are seven key considerations for each geographic market that a firm is contemplating. An analysis of these seven variables provides the background necessary for deciding whether or not to enter the market and to what extent, if any, an individualized marketing strategy is required. A small sample of experts, preferably native to the market under consideration, often will be able to furnish sufficient information on each variable.

Is the Geographic Area Homogeneous or Heterogeneous with Respect to Culture?
Marketing efforts are generally directed at defined geographic areas, primarily political and economic entities. Legal requirements and existing distribution channels often encourage this approach. However, it is also supported by the implicit assumption that geographical or political boundaries coincide with cultural boundaries. As we have seen, country boundaries represent general tendencies, but differences *within* a given country are also critical to consider. For example, research suggests that strategies in Latin America need to consider not only cross-country (e.g., Brazil vs. Chile) but also within-country (e.g., region, urban/rural) differences.[127]

Likewise, China has strong regional cultures (one authority has identified eight), urban/rural cultures, as well as sharp differences associated with income, age, and education.[128] Thus, marketing campaigns must be developed for cultural and demographic groups, not just countries.

What Needs Can This Product or a Version of It Fill in This Culture?
Most firms examine a new market with an existing product or product technology in mind. The question they must answer is what needs their existing or modified product can fill in the culture involved. For example, bicycles and motorcycles serve primarily recreational needs in the United States, but they provide basic transportation in many other countries.

General Foods successfully positioned Tang as a substitute for orange juice at breakfast in the United States. However, in analyzing the French market, it found that the French drink little orange juice and almost none at breakfast. Therefore, a totally different positioning strategy was used; Tang was promoted as a new type of refreshing drink for any time of the day.

Can Enough of the People Needing the Product Afford the Product?
An initial demographic analysis is required to determine the number of individuals or households that might need the product who can actually afford it. For example, while China has over 1.3 billion consumers, the effective market for most Western goods is estimated to be less than 20 percent of this total.[129] Future economic expansion in countries like China and India is expected to enhance their market potential in coming years. In addition, the possibilities of establishing credit, obtaining a government subsidy, or making a less expensive version should be considered. This latter approach is being used by P&G in China, where a tiered pricing system was designed to help reach consumers with relatively low incomes.[130]

What Values or Patterns of Values Are Relevant to the Purchase and Use of This Product?
The first section of this chapter focused on values and their role in consumer behavior. The value system should be investigated for influences on purchasing the product, owning the product, using the product, and disposing of the product. Much of the marketing strategy will be based on this analysis.

What Are the Distribution, Political, and Legal Structures for the Product?
The legal structure of a country can have an impact on each aspect of a firm's marketing mix. The chapter opening example described how FedEx had to produce two endings for its Latin America/Caribbean ad because of legal restrictions in Mexico. China recently banned sex appeals, and ads for so-called "offensive" products such as feminine-hygiene products and hemorrhoid ointments have been banned during the three daily meal times (when families, including children, watch). The U.K. is threatening to ban junk-food ads, and Brazil has put laws in place that limit the amount of alcohol advertising.[131] Such legal restrictions limit the ability of companies to use standardized approaches to their marketing efforts.

What effect would China's ban on sex appeals have on Maybelline's advertising for its Manhattan line in Asia?

Regulations also affect distribution channels. Until recently, Japan prohibited yen-based transactions on the Internet, which slowed the development of this distribution channel.[132] China recently announced a ban on direct sales to consumers, which has major consequences for Amway, Avon, Mary Kay, and other direct marketers in China.[133]

In What Ways Can We Communicate about the Product?

This question requires an investigation into (1) available media and who attends to each type, (2) the needs the product fills, (3) values associated with the product and its use, and (4) the verbal and nonverbal communications systems in the culture(s). All aspects of the firm's promotional mix—including packaging, nonfunctional product design features, personal selling techniques, and advertising—should be based on these four factors. For example, Whirlpool uses bright colors for the refrigerators it markets in Thailand and other Asian countries. Whirlpool does so because many consumers in these countries keep their refrigerators in their living rooms (the kitchens are too small) and want them to serve as attractive pieces of furniture, not just as appliances.

The Internet seems like a natural media through which to communicate to consumers. However, as we saw earlier, Internet access varies widely across a country as does the percentage of consumers who will actually buy online.[134] Moreover, research suggests that tailoring Web sites to specific countries is critical to online marketing success because of cultural variations in Web site dimensions driving purchase and loyalty.[135]

What Are the Ethical Implications of Marketing This Product in This Country?

All marketing programs should be evaluated on ethical as well as financial dimensions. As discussed at the beginning of the chapter, international marketing activities raise many ethical issues. The ethical dimension is particularly important and complex in marketing to Third World and developing countries. Consider Kellogg's attempt to introduce cold cereal as a breakfast food in a developing country. An ethical analysis would consider various factors including:

If we succeed, will the average nutrition level be increased or decreased?

If we succeed, will the funds spent on cereal be diverted from other uses with more beneficial long-term impacts for the individuals or society?

If we succeed, what impact will this have on the local producers of currently consumed breakfast products?

Such an ethical analysis not only is the right thing to do; it may head off conflicts with local governments or economic interests. Understanding and acting on ethical considerations in international marketing is a difficult task. However, it is also a necessary one.

SUMMARY

Culture is defined as the complex whole that includes knowledge, beliefs, art, law, morals, customs, and any other capabilities acquired by humans as members of society. It includes almost everything that influences an individual's thought processes and behaviors.

Culture operates primarily by setting boundaries for individual behavior and by influencing the functioning of such institutions as the family and mass media. The boundaries, or *norms,* are derived from *cultural values.* Values are widely held beliefs that affirm what is desirable.

Cultural values are classified into three categories: other, environment, and self. *Other-oriented values* reflect a society's view of the appropriate relationships between individuals and groups within that society. Relevant values of this nature include *individual/collective, youth/age, extended/limited family, masculine/femi-nine, competitive/cooperative,* and *diversity/uniformity. Environment-oriented values* prescribe a society's relationships with its economic, technical, and physical environments. Examples of environment values are *cleanliness, performance/status, tradition/change, risk taking/security, problem solving/fatalistic,* and *nature. Self-oriented values* reflect the objectives and approaches to life that individual members of society find desirable. These include *active/passive, sensual gratification/abstinence, material/nonmaterial, hard work/leisure, postponed gratification/ immediate gratification,* and *religious/secular.*

Differences in *verbal communication systems* are immediately obvious across cultures and must be taken into account by marketers wishing to do business in those cultures. Probably more important, however, and certainly more difficult to recognize are *nonverbal communication systems.* Major examples of nonverbal communication variables that affect marketers are *time,* *space, symbols, relationships, agreements, things,* and *etiquette.*

There is evidence that urban teenagers around the world share at least some aspects of a common culture. This is driven by worldwide mass media and common music and sports stars. *Demographics* describe a population in terms of its size, structure, and distribution. Demographics differ widely across cultures and influence cultural values (and are influenced by them) as well as consumption patterns.

Seven questions are relevant for developing a cross-cultural marketing strategy: (1) Is the geographic area homogeneous or heterogeneous with respect to culture? (2) What needs can this product fill in this culture? (3) Can enough people afford the product? (4) What values are relevant to the purchase and use of the product? (5) What are the distribution, political, and legal structures for the product? (6) How can we communicate about the product? (7) What are the ethical implications of marketing this product in this country?

KEY TERMS

Cultural values 43	Nonverbal communication	Purchasing power parity (PPP) 68
Culture 42	systems 57	Sanctions 43
Demographics 66	Norms 43	Self-oriented values 45
Environment-oriented values 45	Other-oriented values 44	Terminal materialism 55
Guanxi 61	Personal space 59	Verbal communication
Instrumental materialism 55	Polychronic time perspective 58	systems 56
Monochronic time perspective 57	Power distance 51	

INTERNET EXERCISES

1. Visit the Michigan State University international business resources Web site (www.globaledge. msu.edu/index.asp). Which of the resources listed is most useful for the following (hint: the global resources section is a good place to start)?
   a. Worldwide consumer data
   b. Data on consumer markets in China
   c. Data on consumer markets in Brazil
   d. Data on industrial markets in Canada

2. Using the Michigan State University site in Exercise 1 above, select and describe one of the sources listed. Evaluate its usefulness for understanding international markets and other cultures.

3. Using the Internet, prepare a brief report on the following as a market for automobiles. Provide addresses for all Web sites used.
   a. India
   b. Germany
   c. Qatar
   d. China

4. Prepare a report that describes how useful, if at all, the information available at the World Bank Web site (www.worldbank.org) is in terms of helping you understand the following as a market for cell phones:
   a. United Kingdom
   b. South Korea
   c. Australia
   d. Argentina

5. Visit the CIA site (www.odci.gov). Evaluate the usefulness of this site for international marketers.

6. Visit the Kwintessential Web site (www.kwintessential.co.uk). Click on the "Online Test: How Culturally Aware are You?" Pick several topics/countries and take a quiz. Prepare a report on what you learned.

7. Visit Lands' End's various international sites (you can start at www.landsend.com). Beyond adapting to language differences, how much adapting have they done for each country? Based on your understanding of the cultural differences would you have expected more or less adaptation?

DDB LIFE STYLE STUDY™ DATA ANALYSES

1. What characterizes U.S. consumers who are interested in other cultures and interested in shopping for items influenced by other cultures? (Use the DDB data in Tables 1B through 7B.) How might travel agents use this in developing marketing strategies involving international travel?

REVIEW QUESTIONS

1. What are some of the ethical issues involved in cross-cultural marketing?

2. What is meant by the term *culture?*

3. What does the statement "Culture sets boundaries on behaviors" mean?

4. What is a *norm?* From what are norms derived?

5. What is a *cultural value?*

6. What is a *sanction?*

7. Cultural values can be classified as affecting one of three types of relationships—other, environment, or self. Describe each of these, and differentiate each one from the others.

8. How does the first of the following paired orientations differ from the second?
   a. Individual/Collective
   b. Performance/Status
   c. Tradition/Change
   d. Limited/Extended family
   e. Active/Passive
   f. Material/Nonmaterial
   g. Hard work/Leisure
   h. Risk taking/Security
   i. Masculine/Feminine
   j. Competitive/Cooperative
   k. Youth/Age
   l. Problem solving/Fatalistic
   m. Diversity/Uniformity
   n. Postponed gratification/Immediate gratification
   o. Sensual gratification/Abstinence
   p. Religious/Secular

9. What is meant by *nonverbal communications?* Why is this a difficult area to adjust to?

10. What is meant by each of the following as a form of nonverbal communication?
    a. Time
    b. Space
    c. Symbols
    d. Relationships
    e. Agreements
    f. Things
    g. Etiquette

11. What is *guanxi?*

12. What is the difference between *instrumental* and *terminal* materialism?

13. What are the differences between a *monochronic* time perspective and a *polychronic* time perspective?

14. What forces seem to be creating a global teenage culture?

15. What are *demographics?* Why are they important to international marketers?

16. What is *purchasing power parity?*

17. What are the seven key considerations in deciding whether or not to enter a given international market?

18. What does determining if a geographic area or political unit is homogeneous or heterogeneous with respect to culture mean? Why is this important?

DISCUSSION QUESTIONS

19. Why should we study foreign cultures if we do not plan to engage in international or export marketing?

20. Is a country's culture more likely to be reflected in its art museums or its television commercials? Why?

21. Are the cultures of the world becoming more similar or more distinct?

22. Why do values differ across cultures?

23. The text lists 18 cultural values (in three categories) of relevance to marketing practice. Describe and place into one of the three categories two additional cultural values that have some relevance to marketing practice.

24. Select two cultural values from each of the three categories. Describe the boundaries (norms) relevant to that value in your society and the sanctions for violating those norms.

25. What are the most relevant cultural values affecting the consumption of each of the following? Describe how and why these values are particularly important.
    a. Internet
    b. MP3 player
    c. Jewelry
    d. Fast food
    e. Hybrid car
    f. Vodka

26. What variations between the United States and other societies, *other than cultural variations,* may affect the relative level of usage of the following?
    a. Internet
    b. MP3 player
    c. Jewelry
    d. Fast food
    e. Hybrid car
    f. Vodka

27. Is the European Union likely to become a relatively homogeneous culture by 2025?

28. What values underlie the differences between Fiji Island and U.S. children in terms of the strategies they use to influence their parents' decisions? What marketing implications emerge?

29. What are the marketing implications of the differences in the *masculine/feminine orientation* across countries?

30. Respond to the questions in Consumer Insight 2-1.

31. Why do nonverbal communication systems vary across cultures?

32. Which, if any, nonverbal communication factors might be relevant in the marketing of the following?
    a. Luxury automobiles
    b. Women's shoes
    c. Laptop computers
    d. Laundry detergent
    e. Lip balm
    f. Charity giving

33. What are the implications of *guanxi* for a Western firm entering the Chinese market?

34. To what extent do you think teenagers are truly becoming a single, global culture?

35. Will today's teenagers still be a "global culture" when they are 40? Why or why not?

36. How do demographics affect a culture's values? How do a culture's values affect its demographics?

37. What causes the differences between purchasing power parity and income as shown in the text on page 68?

38. The text provides a seven-step procedure for analyzing a foreign market. Using this procedure, analyze your country as a market for
    a. Cell phones from China
    b. Automobiles from Mexico
    c. Sunglasses from Italy
    d. Wine from Australia

39. What are the major ethical issues in introducing prepared foods such as fast foods to developing countries?

40. Should U.S. tobacco firms be allowed to market cigarettes in developing countries? Why or why not?

41. How can developing countries keep their cultures from being overly Westernized or Americanized?

APPLICATION ACTIVITIES

42. Interview two students from two different cultures. Determine the extent to which the following are used in those cultures and the variations in the values of those cultures that relate to the use of these products:
    a. Mountain bikes
    b. Energy drinks (like Red Bull)
    c. Beer
    d. DVDs
    e. Music
    f. Internet

43. Interview two students from two different foreign cultures. Report any differences in nonverbal communications they are aware of between their culture and your culture.

44. Interview two students from two different foreign cultures. Report their perceptions of the major differences in cultural values between their culture and your culture.

45. Interview a student from India. Report on the advice that the student would give an American firm marketing consumer products in India.

46. Interview two students from EU (European Union) countries. Report on the extent to which they feel the EU will be a homogeneous culture by 2025.

47. Imagine you are a consultant working with your state or province's tourism agency. You have been asked to advise the agency on the best promotional themes to use to attract foreign tourists. What would you recommend if Germany and Australia were the two target markets?

48. Analyze a foreign culture of your choice, and recommend a marketing program for a brand of one of the following made in your country:
    a. MP3 player
    b. Fast-food outlets
    c. Wine
    d. Discount retailer
    e. Sport watches
    f. Cosmetics

REFERENCES

1. P. L. Andruss, "FedEx Kicks Up Brand," *Marketing News,* July 30, 2001, pp. 4–5.

2. See T. Srivastava and D. D. Schoenbachler, "An Examination of the Information and Thematic Content of Consumer Print Advertising in India," *Journal of International Consumer Marketing,* no. 2 (1999), pp. 63–85; and A. T. Shao, M. A. Raymond, and C. Taylor, "Shifting Advertising Appeals in Taiwan," *Journal of Advertising Research,* November 1999, pp. 61–68.

3. C. Miller, "Not Quite Global," *Marketing News,* July 3, 1995, p. 9.

4. S. Gutkin, "Spooky Fun Creeping around Globe," *Register-Guard,* October 29, 2000, p. 16A.

5. "Hindus Torch Valentines," *Register-Guard,* February 14, 2002, p. 6A.

6. J. Solomon, "Amid Anti-American Protests," *The Wall Street Journal,* October 26, 2001, p. 1; and O. Sandikci and G. Ger, "Fundamental Fashions," *Advances in Consumer Research,* vol. 28, ed. M. C. Gilly and J. Meyers-Levy (Provo, UT: Association for Consumer Research, 2001), pp. 146–50.

7. See W. Bailey, "Country of Origin Attitudes in Mexico," *Journal of International Consumer Marketing,* no. 3 (1997), pp. 25–41; and J. Marcoux, P. Filiatrault, and E. Cheron, "The Attitudes

Underlying Preferences of Polish Consumers toward Products Made in Western Countries," *Journal of International Consumer Marketing,* no. 4 (1997), pp. 5–29.

8. S. Mulley, "Young Women's Smoking Crisis Declared in Asia," *Medical Post,* January 11, 2000, p. 68.

9. J. Mackay and M. Eriksen, *The Tobacco Atlas* (Brighton, U.K.: The World Health Organization, 2002), p. 31.

10. M. E. Goldberg and H. Baumgartner, "Cross-Country Attraction as a Motivation for Product Consumption," *Journal of Business Research* 55 (2002), pp. 901–6.

11. Mackay and Eriksen, *The Tobacco Atlas,* p. 89.

12. S. Efron, "Smokers Light Up All over the World," *Register-Guard,* September 9, 1996, p. 1; and Mulley, "Young Women's Smoking Crisis Declared in Asia."

13. Mulley, "Young Women's Smoking Crisis Declared in Asia."

14. See, e.g., J. L. Aaker and J. Sengupta, "Additivity versus Attenuation," *Journal of Consumer Psychology,* no. 2 (2000), pp. 67–82; and D. A. Briley, M. W. Morris, and I. Simonson, "Reasons as Carriers of Culture," *Journal of Consumer Research,* September 2000, pp. 157–77.

15. "And Then There's Global Pizza," *Register-Guard,* August 25, 1996, p. C1.

16. For this and other global missteps see M. D. White, *A Short Course in International Marketing Blunders* (California: World Trade Press, 2002).

17. "It's a Grande-Latte World," *The Wall Street Journal,* December 15, 2003, p. B1.

18. G. Hofstede, *Culture's Consequences,* 2nd ed. (Thousand Oaks, CA: Sage, 2001).

19. Z. Gurhan-Canli and D. Maheswaran, "Cultural Variations in Country of Origin Effects," *Journal of Marketing Research,* August 2000, pp. 309–17.

20. C. Pornpitakpan and J. N. P. Francis, "The Effect of Cultural Differences, Source Expertise, and Argument Strength on Persuasion," *Journal of International Consumer Marketing,* no. 1 (2001), pp. 77–101.

21. R. B. Money, M. C. Gilly, and J. L. Graham, "Explorations of National Culture and Word-of-Mouth Referral Behavior," *Journal of Marketing,* October 1998, pp. 76–87.

22. Based on data presented in *The Little Global Fact Book* (Ipsos World Monitor, 2004) at www.ipsos-insight.com; and Hofstede, *Culture's Consequences.*

23. P. G. Patterson and T. Smith, "Relationship Benefits in Service Industries," *Journal of Services Marketing* 15, no. 6 (2001), pp. 425–43.

24. J. E. M. Steenkamp, F. Ter Hofstede, and M. Wedel, "A Cross-National Investigation into the Individual and National Cultural Antecedents of Consumer Innovativeness," *Journal of Marketing,* April 1999, pp. 55–69; and I. S. Yaveroglu and N. Donthu, "Cultural Differences on the Diffusion of New Products," *Journal of International Consumer Marketing* 14, no. 4 (2002), pp. 49–63.

25. N. Y. Wong and A. C. Ahuvia, "Personal Taste and Family Face," *Psychology & Marketing,* August 1998, pp. 423–41.

26. C. Robinson, "Asian Culture," *Journal of the Market Research Society,* January 1996, pp. 55–62.

27. See, e.g., J. Zhang and S. Shavitt, "Cultural Values in Advertisements to the Chinese X-Generation," *Journal of Advertising* 32, no. 1 (2003), pp. 23–33.

28. "Global Teen Culture," *Brand Strategy,* January 2003, pp. 37–38.

29. K. L. Miller, "You Just Can't Talk to These Kids," *BusinessWeek,* April 19, 1993, pp. 104–6.

30. See, e.g., K. C. C. Yang, "The Effects of Allocentrism and Idiocentrism on Consumers' Product Attribute Evaluation," *Journal of International Consumer Marketing* 16, no. 4 (2004), pp. 63–84.

31. B. Barak et al., "Perceptions of Age-Identity," *Psychology & Marketing,* October 2001, pp. 1003–29; C. A. Lin, "Cultural Values Reflected in Chinese and American Television Advertising," *Journal of Advertising,* Winter 2001, pp. 83–94; and D. H. Z. Khairullah and Z. Y. Khairullah, "Dominant Cultural Values," *Journal of Global Marketing* 16, no. 1/2 (2002), pp. 47–70.

32. P. L. Andruss, "Groups Make Fruits Apple of Taiwan's Eye," *Marketing News,* December 4, 2000, p. 5.

33. H. Fattah, "The New Arab Consumer," *American Demographics,* September 2002, p. 58.

34. J. Sherry, B. Greenberg, and H. Tokinoya, "Orientations to TV Advertising among Adolescents and Children in the U.S. and Japan," *International Journal of Advertising,* no. 2 (1999), pp. 233–50; and A. Shoham and V. Dalakas, "Family Consumer Decision Making in Israel," *Journal of Consumer Marketing* 20, no. 3 (2003), pp. 238–51.

35. J. Wimalasiri, "A Comparison of Children's Purchase Influence and Parental Response in Fiji and the United States," *Journal of International Consumer Marketing,* no. 4 (2000), pp. 55–73.

36. M. F. Ji and J. U. McNeal, "How Chinese Children's Commercials Differ from Those of the United States," *Journal of Advertising,* Fall 2001, pp. 79–92; K. Chan and J. U. McNeal, "Parent-Child Communications about Consumption and Advertising in China," *Journal of Consumer Marketing* 20, no. 4 (2003), pp. 317–34; and "Little Emperors," *Fortune,* October 4, 2004, pp. 138–50.

37. L. Chang, "The New Stresses of Chinese Society Shape a Girl's Life," *The Wall Street Journal,* December 4, 2003, pp. A1 and A13.

38. P. Kotler, S. W. Ang, and C. T. Tan, *Marketing Management: An Asian Perspective* (Singapore: Prentice Hall Pergamon, 1996), p. 524.

39. B. D. Keillor, R. S. Parker, and A. Schaffer, "Influences on Adolescent Brand Preferences in the United States and Mexico," *Journal of Advertising Research,* May–June 1996, pp. 47–56.

40. M. Viswanathan, T. L. Childers, and E. S. Moore, "The Measurement of Intergenerational Communication and Influence on Consumption," *Journal of the Academy of Marketing Science,* Summer 2000, pp. 406–24.

41. M. Kripalani, "Here Come the Wal-Mart Wannabes," *BusinessWeek,* April 4, 2005, p. 56.

42. See F. S. Al-Olayan and K. Karande, "A Content Analysis of Magazine Advertisements from the United States and the Arab World," *Journal of Advertising,* Fall 2000, pp. 69–82.

43. C.-N. Chen, M. Lai, and D. D. C. Tarn, "Feminism Orientation, Product Attributes, and Husband-Wife Decision Dominance," *Journal of Global Marketing,* no. 3 (1999), pp. 23–39. See also A. K. Lalwani, S. C. Mehta, and T. C. Tiong, "Family Roles in the Selection for Schools in Multiracial Singapore," *Journal of Professional Services Marketing,* no. 2 (1999), pp. 73–92; and C. Webster, "Is Spousal Decision Making a Culturally Situated Phenomenon?" *Psychology & Marketing,* December 2000, pp. 1035–58.

44. M. L. Maynard and C. R. Taylor, "Girlish Images across Cultures," *Journal of Advertising,* Spring 1999, pp. 39–47.

45. From Ipsos's global consumer and civic trends reporting service, *World Monitor,* 2nd quarter, 2001. Profiled data were collected on Ipsos's Global Express omnibus survey in 34 countries in November–December of 2000. Never less than twice a year; frequently at least once a week.

46. S. M. Sidin et al., "The Effects of Sex Role Orientation on Family Purchase Decision Making in Malaysia," *Journal of Consumer Marketing* 21, no. 6 (2004), pp. 381–90; and "Rate of Chinese Businesswomen Higher than World Average," *China Daily,* March 20, 2005, at www.chinadaily.com.

47. L. M. Milner and J. M. Collins, "Sex-Role Portrayals and the Gender of Nations," *Journal of Advertising,* Spring 2000, pp. 67–78; and G. Fowler, "China Cracks Down on Commercials," *The Wall Street Journal,* February 19, 2004, p. B7.

48. J. Russell, "Working Women Give Japan Culture Shock," *Advertising Age,* January 16, 1995, p. I24.

49. L. Y. Sin and O. H. Yau, "Female Role Orientation and Consumption Values," *Journal of International Consumer Marketing* 13, no. 2 (2001), pp. 49–75.

50. For a related discussion see M. de Mooij, *Global Marketing and Advertising* (Thousand Oaks, CA: Sage, 1998), pp. 252–53.

51. See Miller, "You Just Can't Talk to These Kids," p. 106; P. Sellers, "Pepsi Opens a Second Front," *Fortune,* August 8, 1994, pp. 70–76; and N. Donthu, "A Cross-Country Investigation of Recall of and Attitude toward Comparative Advertising," *Journal of Advertising,* Summer 1998, pp. 111–22.

52. See M. de Mooij, *Consumer Behavior and Culture* (Thousand Oaks, CA: Sage, 2004), pp. 162–64.

53. L. Shannahan, "Bugging Out over Germs," *Brandweek,* November 22, 2004, p. 17.

54. See, e.g., V. Kurian, " 'Hand Wash' Campaign in Kerala Raises a Stink," *Businessline,* November 6, 2002, p. 1.

55. J. L. Watson, *Golden Arches East* (Stanford, CA: Stanford University Press, 1997).

56. Pornpitakpan and Francis, "The Effect of Cultural Differences, Source Expertise, and Argument Strength on Persuasion"; see also B. R. Barnes et al., "Investigating the Impact of International Cosmetics Advertising in China," *International Journal of Advertising* 23 (2004), pp. 361–87.

57. C. Pornpitakpan, "Factors Associated with Opinion Seeking," *Journal of Global Marketing* 17, no. 2/3 (2004), pp. 91–113.

58. For the related role of individualism/collectivism see M. de Mooij and G. Hofstede, "Convergence and Divergence in Consumer Behavior," *Journal of Retailing* 78 (2002), pp. 61–69; see also S. H. C. Tai and R. Y. K. Chan, "Cross-Cultural Studies on the Information Content of Service Advertising," *Journal of Services Marketing* 15, no. 7 (2001), pp. 547–64.

59. H. Cheng and J. C. Schweitzer, "Cultural Values Reflected in Chinese and U.S. Television Commercials," *Journal of Advertising Research,* May/June 1996, pp. 27–45; Lin, "Cultural Values Reflected in Chinese and American Television Advertising"; and Khairullah and Khairullah, "Dominant Cultural Values."

60. D. Kim, Y. Pan, and H. S. Park, "High- versus Low-Context Culture," *Psychology & Marketing,* September 1998, pp. 507–21.

61. Z. Caillat and B. Mueller, "The Influence of Culture on American and British Advertising," *Journal of Advertising Research,* May–June 1996, pp. 79–88; and Lin, "Cultural Values Reflected in Chinese and American Television Advertising."

62. Zhang and Shavitt, "Cultural Values in Advertisements to the Chinese X-Generation."

63. Table based on *World Fact Book* (Washington, DC: Central Intelligence Agency, 2004).

64. G. Parker, "Going Global Can Hit Snags," *The Wall Street Journal,* June 16, 2004, p. B1.

65. See Steenkamp, Ter Hofstede, and Wedel, "A Cross-National Investigation"; Pornpitakpan and Francis, "The Effect of Cultural Differences, Source Expertise, and Argument Strength on Persuasion"; and J. M. Jung and J. J. Kellaris, "Cross-National Differences in Proneness to Scarcity Effects," *Psychology & Marketing,* September 2004, pp. 739–53.

66. See, e.g., P. Raven and D. H. B. Welsh, "An Exploratory Study of Influences on Retail Service Quality," *Journal of Services Marketing* 18, no. 3 (2004), pp. 198–214.

67. "Quiet Motorcycle Seeks Added Vroom," *CNN.com,* March 17, 2005, at www.cnn.com.

68. T. S. Chan, "Concerns for Environmental Issues," *Journal of International Consumer Marketing,* no. 1 (1996), pp. 43–55.

69. See R. Y. K. Chan, "Environmental Attitudes and Behavior of Consumers in China," *Journal of International Consumer Marketing,* no. 4 (1999), pp. 25–74; and R. Y. K. Chan, "Determinants of Chinese Consumers' Green Purchase Behavior," *Psychology & Marketing,* April 2001, pp. 389–413.

70. "Saudis and Americans," *NOP World* (New York: United Business Media), January 6, 2003, at www.nopworld.com.

71. S. L. M. So, "A Comparative Content Analysis of Women's Magazine Advertisements from Hong Kong and Australia on Advertising Expressions," *Journal of Current Issues and Research in Advertising,* Spring 2004, pp. 47–58; and Khairullah and Khairullah, "Dominant Cultural Values."

72. K. Chen and L. Chang, "China Takes Aim at Racy, Violent TV Shows," *The Wall Street Journal,* May 24, 2004, p. B1.

73. Khairullah and Khairullah, "Dominant Cultural Values," p. 64.

74. "G, What Unusual Undie Ads," *Advertising Age,* October 23, 2000, p. 28.

75. K. B. Doran, "Symbolic Consumption in China," *Advances in Consumer Research,* vol. 24, ed. M. Bruck and D. J. MacInnis (Provo, UT: Association for Consumer Research, 1997), pp. 128–31.

76. C. Webster and R. C. Beatty, "Nationality, Materialism, and Possession Importance," *Advances in Consumer Research,* vol. 24, ed. Brucks and MacInnis, pp. 204–10.

77. P. Paul, "Global Generation Gap," *American Demographics,* March 2002, pp. 18–19.

78. "Work Hard? Play Hard? It's Not the Countries You Might Think," *NOP World* (New York: United Business Media), November 8, 2004, at www.nopworld.com.

79. G. Hofstede et al., "What Goals Do Business Leaders Pursue?" *Journal of International Business Studies* 33, no. 4 (2002), pp. 785–803.

80. de Mooij and Hofstede, "Convergence and Divergence in Consumer Behavior."

81. See S. S. Al-Makaty, "Attitudes toward Advertising in Islam," *Journal of Advertising Research,* May–June 1996, pp. 16–25; and "Saudis and Americans."

82. See L. C. Huff and D. L. Alden, "An Investigation of Consumer Response to Sales Promotions in Developing Markets," *Journal of Advertising Research,* May–June 1998, pp. 47–56.

83. "Dogpile," *Kwintessential* at www.kwintessential.co.uk/translation/articles/cross-cultural-issues.htm, accessed March 20, 2005.

84. D. A. Ricks, *Big Business Blunders* (Burr Ridge, IL: Richard D. Irwin, 1983), p. 39.

85. See S. Zhang and B. H. Schmitt, "Creating Local Brands in Multilingual International Markets," *Journal of Marketing Research,* August 2001, pp. 313–25.

86. See M. F. Toncar, "The Use of Humor in Television Advertising," *International Journal of Advertising* 20 (2001), pp. 521–39.

87. See N. Spears, X. Lin, and J. C. Mowen, "Time Orientation in the United States, China, and Mexico," *Journal of International Consumer Marketing* 1 (2001), pp. 57–75.

88. C. J. Kaufman, P. M. Lane, and J. D. Lindquist, "Exploring More than 24 Hours a Day," *Journal of Consumer Research,* December 1991, pp. 392–401; and L. A. Manrai and A. K. Manrai, "Effect of Cultural-Context, Gender, and Acculturation on Perceptions of Work versus Social/Leisure Time Usage," *Journal of Business Research,* February 1995, pp. 115–28.

89. Manrai and Manrai, "Effect of Cultural-Context, Gender, and Acculturation on Perceptions of Work versus Social/Leisure Time Usage." See also M. Lee and F. M. Ulgado, "Consumer Evaluations of Fast-Food Services," *Journal of Services Marketing* 1 (1997), pp. 39–52; and G. H. Brodowsky and B. B. Anderson, "A Cross-Cultural Study of Consumer Attitudes toward Time," *Journal of Global Marketing,* no. 3 (2000), pp. 93–109.

90. de Mooij, *Global Marketing and Advertising.*

91. Ibid., p. 71.

92. See M. Chapman and A. Jamal, "Acculturation," *Advances in Consumer Research,* vol. 24, ed. Bruck and MacInnis, pp. 138–44.

93. This example is from White, *A Short Course in International Marketing Blunders,* p. 39.

94. See also de Mooij, *Global Marketing and Advertising;* and T. J. Madden, K. Hewett, and M. S. Roth, "Managing Images in Different Cultures," *Journal of International Marketing* 8, no. 4 (2000), pp. 90–107.

95. P. A. Herbig and H. E. Kramer, "Do's and Don'ts of Cross-Cultural Negotiations," *Industrial Marketing Management,* no. 4 (1992), p. 293; see also P. Fan and Z. Zigang, "Cross-Cultural Challenges When Doing Business in China," *Singapore Management Review* 26, no. 1 (2004), pp. 81–90.

96. M. Ewing, A. Caruana, and H. Wong, "Some Consequences of *Guanxi,*" *Journal of International Consumer Marketing,* no. 4 (2000), p. 77.

97. Fan and Zigang, "Cross-Cultural Challenges When Doing Business in China," p. 85.

98. G. Brewer, "An American in Shanghai," *Sales and Marketing Management,* November 1997, p. 42.

99. See H. McDonald, P. Darbyshire, and C. Jevons, "Shop Often, Buy Little," *Journal of Global Marketing,* no. 4 (2000), pp. 53–72; and A. G. Abdul-Muhmin, "The Effect of Perceived Seller Reservation Prices on Buyers' Bargaining Behavior in a Flexible-Price Market," *Journal of International Consumer Marketing,* no. 3 (2001), pp. 29–45.

100. Miller, "Not Quite Global."

101. S. Y. Park, "A Comparison of Korean and American Gift-Giving Behaviors," *Psychology & Marketing,* September 1998, pp. 577–93.

102. A. Joy, "Gift Giving in Hong Kong and the Continuum of Social Ties," *Journal of Consumer Research,* September 2001, pp. 239–54. See also J. Wang, F. Piron, and M. V. Xuan, "Faring One Thousand Miles to Give Goose Feathers," *Advances in Consumer Research,* vol. 28, ed. M. C. Gilly and J. Meyers-Levy (Provo, UT: Association for Consumer Research, 2001), pp. 58–63.

103. A. S. Mattila, "The Role of Culture and Purchase Motivation in Service Encounter Evaluations," *Journal of Services Marketing,* no. 4–5 (1999), pp. 376–89; M. K. Hui and K. Au, "Justice Perceptions of Complaint Handling," *Journal of Business Research* 52 (2001), pp. 161–73; and C. A. Voss et al., "A Tale of Two Countries' Conservatism, Service Quality, and Feedback on Customer Satisfaction," *Journal of Service Research,* February 2004, pp. 212–30.

104. M. Fong, "Chinese Charm School," *The Wall Street Journal,* January 13, 2004, pp. B1 and B6.

105. B. D. Keillor, M. D'Amico, and V. Horton, "Global Consumer Tendencies," *Psychology & Marketing,* January 2000, pp. 1–19; and F. Ter Hofstede, M. Wedel, and J. E. M. Steenkamp, "Identifying Spacial Segments in International Markets," *Marketing Science,* Spring 2002, pp. 160–77.

106. C. Edy, "The Olympics of Marketing," *American Demographics,* June 1999, pp. 47–48.

107. "Little Emperors," p. 143.

108. S. Tully, "Teens," *Fortune,* May 1994, pp. 90–97.

109. B. G. Yovovich, "Youth Market Going Truly Global," *Advertising Age,* March 27, 1995, p. 10.

110. *The World's Teenagers* (New York: D'Arcy Masius Benton & Bowles, 1994).

111. Ibid.

112. N. Madden, "Levi's Enjoys 'Rebirth' on the Web in Asia," *Advertising Age,* April 19, 2004, p. N-10.

113. L. Bertagnoli, "Continental Spendthrifts," *Marketing News,* October 22, 2001, p. 15.

114. N. Madden, "Coke Targets Second Cities," *Advertising Age,* August 16, 2004, p. 22.

115. S. Elder, "The Reel World," *National Geographic,* March 2005.

116. Examples and excerpt from C. Prystay, "It Is a Walk of Fame for Bollywood," *The Wall Street Journal Online,* December 24, 2004, at www.wsj.com.

117. "Bollywood Told to Stub It Out," *BBC News* (online), February 18, 2003, at http://news.bbc.co.uk, accessed March 21, 2005.

118. See, e.g., L. Tong, "Consumerism Sweeps the Mainland," *Marketing Management,* Winter 1998, pp. 32–35; and J. Slater, "In India, a Market Unleashed," *The Wall Street Journal,* March 12, 2004, p. A13.

119. J. L. Lee, "China Senses Need for Cleaner Fuel," *The Wall Street Journal,* December 11, 2003, p. A16.

120. *The World Fact Book* (Washington DC: Central Intelligence Agency, 2004).

121. *World Bank Atlas* (World Bank, 2003) at www.worldbank.org/data/quickreferences; per capita income in U.S. dollars, per capita PPP in international dollars.

122. *Statistical Abstract of the United States* (2004–5) at www.census.gov/prod/www/statistical-abstract-04.html; *2000 Philippine Statistical Yearbook* (Makati City: National Statistical Information Center, 2000), p. 1.18; *Statistics Canada* (2004) at http://www.statcan.ca/english/Pgdb/demo10a.htm; *Japan Statistical Yearbook* (2003) at www.stat.go.jp/english/data/nenkan/1431-02.htm.

123. H. Fattah, "The Middle East Baby Boom," *American Demographics,* September 2002, pp. 55–60.

124. S. Onkvisit and J. J. Shaw, "Standardized International Advertising," *Journal of Advertising Research,* November 1999, pp. 19–34; K. Sirisagul, "Global Advertising Practices," *Journal of Global Marketing,* no. 3 (2000), pp. 77–87; J. Neff, "Rethinking Globalism," *Advertising Age,* October 9, 2000, p. 1; de Mooij and Hofstede, "Convergence and Divergence in Consumer Behavior"; and A. Kanso and R. A. Nelson, "Advertising Localization Overshadows Standardization," *Journal of Advertising Research,* January/February 2002, pp. 79–89.

125. D. Bryson, "Hindus Eat Mutton in Their Macs," *Register-Guard,* October 12, 1996, p. 1.

126. "Local Pride," *American Demographics,* September 2003, p. 16.

127. C. Rubel, "Survey," *Marketing News,* July 15, 1996, p. 5; and D. Barros, "Create Unique Strategy for Each Brazilian Culture," *Marketing News,* September 1, 2004, pp. 17–18.

128. G. Cui, "Segmenting China's Consumer Market," *Journal of International Consumer Marketing,* no. 1 (1999), pp. 55–76.

129. P. L. Andruss, "Slow Boat to China," *Marketing News,* September 10, 2001, p. 11.

130. N. Madden and J. Neff, "P&G Adapts Attitude toward Local Markets," *Advertising Age,* February 23, 2004, p. 28.

131. Chen and Chang, "China Takes Aim at Racy, Violent TV Shows"; G. A. Fowler, "China Cracks Down on Commercials," *The Wall Street Journal,* February 19, 2004, p. B7; "Molson Airs Ad under New Rules," *Advertising Age,* February 23, 2004, p. 12; and A. Jardine, "U.K. Threatens Ban on 'Junk-Food' Ads," *Advertising Age,* November 22, 2004, p. 12.

132. M. Haffenberg, "Report from Tokyo," *Marketing News,* May 25, 1998, p. 2.

133. N. Madden, "China's Direct Sales Ban," *Advertising Age,* May 18, 1998, p. 56.

134. R. Gardyn, "Full Speed Ahead," *American Demographics,* October 2001, p. 12.

135. P. D. Lynch, R. J. Kent, and S. S. Srinivasan, "The Global Internet Shopper," *Journal of Advertising Research,* May/June 2001, pp. 15–23.

Photo by Jamie Squire/Getty Images.

3

The Changing American Society: Values

■ Gender roles and perceptions continue to evolve in the United States. At home, at work, and at play, women continue to redefine and reinvent themselves and their roles. This is the case at every level in the world of sports. Some major examples in professional sports include:[1]

- The Women's United Soccer Association (WUSA)—WUSA began in 2001 and has been relaunched to capture the increasing popularity of the sport, which began with a United States win in the 1999 women's World Cup. Momentum has continued with a Gold Medal win by the U.S. Women's Soccer Team in the 2004 Olympics in Athens. Millions of girls in the United States play soccer in leagues, as they and their parents learn about the game and become fans. Major corporate sponsors of WUSA include Coca-Cola, Adidas, and Under Armour.

- Women's National Basketball Association (WNBA)—WNBA began in 1996 and represents a major force in professional sports. Its popularity is such that the 2005 draft was televised on ESPN2. The WNBA audience attests to its broad-based appeal, with 70 percent of stadium attendance and 50 percent of the TV audience being male. As a consequence of this broad appeal, major endorsement contracts flow to WNBA stars such as Sue Bird of the Seattle Storm, who has contracts with Nike, American Express, and Minute Maid.

- Ladies Professional Golf Association (LPGA)—The LPGA has gained considerable attention recently in part due to superstars such as Annika Sorenstam. Annika not only dominates the LPGA but also has seen success in crossing over to the PGA tour. Such appearances are a marketing dream since they boost excitement and ratings.

Women are also active in amateur sports. Almost two-thirds engage in some general fitness activity, compared to only a third of males. Almost a third participate in a sport of some type. Half of women surveyed watch sports on television weekly, compared to 75 percent of males. Moreover, women do not confine their sports viewing to "women" sports. The top three "first mentions" to the question "What are the main sports you watch on TV?" were football (40 percent), baseball (19 percent), and basketball (12 percent).[2]

Spending on women's sports sponsorship grew from $285 million in 1992 to $1.1 billion in 2000.[3] Clearly, sports are no longer an exclusively male domain.

In Chapter 2, we discussed how variations in values influence consumption patterns *across* cultures. In this chapter, we will describe how changes in values over time influence consumption patterns *within* cultures, specifically the U.S. culture. The changing role of women in American society reflects changes in the "masculine/feminine" value described in Chapter 2. Obviously, cultural values are not constant. Rather, they evolve over time. In the first section of this chapter, we will examine the evolution of American values in general. Next, we examine four marketing trends that have evolved in response to changing values: green marketing, cause-related marketing, marketing to gay consumers, and gender-based marketing.

CHANGES IN AMERICAN CULTURAL VALUES

Observable shifts in behavior, including consumption behavior, often reflect underlying shifts in **cultural values,** *widely held beliefs that affirm what is desirable.* Therefore, it is necessary to understand the underlying *value shifts* in order to understand current and future consumer behavior.[4] Thus, a shift away from a masculine-dominated to a more nearly balanced masculine/feminine value has produced a wide array of changes in the consumption behaviors of both men and women. Consumer Insight 3-1 describes an evolving trend in the United States: vegetarianism. Knowing which cultural values underlie it and how they are evolving enhances understanding of such a trend and its likely future course.

Although we discuss American values as though every American has the same values, in fact there is substantial variance in values across individuals and groups. In addition, changes in values tend to occur slowly and unevenly across individuals and groups. While traumatic events such as the September 11, 2001, attack on the World Trade Center and Pentagon and the resultant military actions can produce value shifts, a slow evolution is more common. Caution should be used in assuming that short-term behavioral or attitudinal changes in response to such events represent long-lasting value shifts.

Figure 3-1 presents our estimate of how American values are changing. These are the same values used to describe different cultures in Chapter 2 (see page 45 for definitions). It must be emphasized that Figure 3-1 is based on the authors' *subjective* interpretation of the American society. You should feel free, indeed compelled, to challenge these judgments.

Self-Oriented Values

Traditionally, Americans have been active, materialistic, hardworking, religious people inclined toward abstinence and postponed gratification. Beginning after the end of World War II and accelerating rapidly during the 1970s and early 1980s, Americans placed increased emphasis on leisure, immediate gratification, and sensual gratification. An

Vegetarianism: A Fad or the Future?

Vegetarianism—ranging from avoiding only red meat to avoiding all animal products—is clearly on the rise in the United States. The vegetarian market includes adults, adolescents, and teens. One study estimates that 4 to 10 percent of the U.S. population is vegetarian. Another study estimates that the vegetarian market will grow by 60 percent over the next several years and reach $2.5 billion in revenues by 2008. In addition, many more people have adopted a "vegetarian orientation"— a preference for vegetarian meals while still consuming some meat.

Most vegetarians in the United States have made a conscious decision to adopt the practice, as opposed to having been raised a vegetarian. Several studies have explored the motives for this decision. One found four primary motives: (1) moral—focused on animal welfare and suffering, (2) gustatory—relating to a negative reaction to the taste or texture of meat, (3) health—the belief that meat consumption is bad for one's health, and (4) ecological—concern that the practice of raising animals for food is not good for the environment. Another study found the first three motives listed above but identified reference group influence as a fourth motive.

Being a vegetarian now is easier than in the past, but it still requires considerable commitment. It is difficult and time consuming to be sure that purchased food products, particularly restaurant meals, are indeed vegetarian. Food options for vegetarians are still limited in terms of recipes, restaurant meal choices, and pre-

pared foods. Most vegetarians face social pressures to conform to the "normal" eating practices of the majority. Sometimes these pressures can be quite strong:

> My dad was very prickly about it (my being vegetarian) because he thought this was like a value judgment against him. He thought that by disagreeing with his dietary choice I was kind of saying that his food wasn't good enough for me.

Vegetarianism is produced by a complex set of motives, which differ between males and females. For example, male vegetarians are more independent or nonconforming than are female vegetarians. This is probably due to a cultural belief that red meat is a "man's" food while vegetables and other light foods are for women. Thus, a male vegetarian is going more against social norms than is a female. There are also noticeable differences in motives between vegetarians and those with a strong vegetarian orientation. For example, vegetarians are motivated in part by a concern for the environment. This does not appear to influence those with a strong vegetarian orientation.[5]

Critical Thinking Questions

1. To what extent are vegetarianism and a vegetarian orientation influenced by values?

2. What factors do you think are contributing to the growth in the vegetarian market?

3. Will vegetarianism ever become "the norm" in the United States? Why or why not?

examination of American advertising, product features, and personal debt levels indicates that these changes have significantly affected consumer behaviors and marketing practice. It appears that several of these trends have reversed direction and are moving back toward their traditional positions, however.

Religious/Secular   America is basically a secular society. A religious group does not control the educational system, government, or political process and most people's daily behaviors are not guided by strict religious guidelines. Nonetheless, 79 percent of all Americans believe in God, 36 percent claim to attend a religious service at least once a month,[6] and more than 50 percent state that religion is very important in their lives. There was an upsurge in religious interest in the wake of the World Trade Center tragedy, but behaviors seem to have reverted to their prior patterns.[7]

While Americans often profess to be more religious than their behaviors would suggest, religious-based beliefs do influence decisions.[8] Many Americans for whom religion is

FIGURE 3-1   Traditional, Current, and Emerging American Values

Self-Oriented

Left	Markers (left → right)	Right
Active	ECT*	Passive
Material	T · C · E	Nonmaterial
Hard work	T · C · E	Leisure
Postponed gratification	T · · · EC	Immediate gratification
Sensual gratification	· C · E · · T	Abstinence
Religious	· · T · · EC	Secular

Environment-Oriented

Left	Markers (left → right)	Right
Maximum cleanliness	TC · E	Minimum cleanliness
Performance	T · E · C	Status
Tradition	· · · · EC · T	Change
Risk taking	T · E · C	Security
Problem solving	T · CE	Fatalistic
Admire nature	· · E · C · · T	Overcome nature

Other-Oriented

Left	Markers (left → right)	Right
Individual	T · CE	Collective
Limited family	· · TEC	Extended family
Diversity	· · EC · · · T	Uniformity
Competition	T · C · E	Cooperation
Youth	T · · C · E	Age
Masculine	T · · C · E	Feminine

*T = Traditional, E = Emerging, and C = Current.

especially important are conservative in their beliefs. They are quite active politically and as consumers. Their political activism involves attempts to regulate various marketing activities, including products (particularly "sin" products such as liquor, gambling, and pornography) and advertising. Their consumption patterns include both positive consumption (purchasing religious objects and books) and negative consumption (avoiding or boycotting products and companies).

When it comes to key policy issues such as abortion, gay rights, the death penalty, and welfare, devoutly religious consumers appear increasingly to want less compromise by their elected officials. Among those attending religious services once a week in 2004, only 63 percent agreed that "Even elected officials who are deeply religious sometimes have to make compromises and set their convictions aside to get results while in government," compared to 82 percent in 2000 (a 19 percent shift). By comparison, there was only a 10 percent shift in the general population and a 3 percent shift among those who never attend religious services.[9]

While conservative religious groups generate substantial publicity and have considerable political power, the culture remains relatively secular. Indeed, one expert estimates the devoutly religious at only 25 percent of the U.S. population, with the remainder made up of those mildly interested in religion (50 percent), and the secular (25 percent).[10] Increasing secularism is cited as one reason for the increase in interfaith marriages.[11] We treat religion and its impact on our society in considerable depth in Chapter 5 when we discuss subcultures.

Sensual Gratification/Abstinence   Closely tied to America's traditional religious orientation was a belief in the virtue of abstinence. As American society became more secular, sensual gratification became more acceptable. By the 1960s, sensual gratification was an important objective for many consumers. Now, sensual gratification is somewhat less acceptable than in the recent past. While it is still perfectly acceptable to consume products for the sensual pleasures they provide, the range of products and occasions for which this is acceptable has narrowed. In the advertising and fashion industries, there are signs that blatant appeals to sexuality *may* be losing their luster. According to one New York advertising executive,

> Everyone's gotten a little tired of in-your-face sexuality. Now there is an appreciation of things that are more prim and proper, with just a hint of depths lurking underneath.[12]

While sensual and suggestive advertising is often used in an effective manner, some ads can go too far. For example, "Monday Night Football" and "Desperate Housewives" teamed up to do a joint promotion during prime time in which a scantily clad Nicollette Sheridan tries to seduce Terrell Owens of the Philadelphia Eagles. There was considerable backlash from the viewing public, who felt the ad was too racy for family viewing. In response to growing concerns over sex and violence on TV, the FCC has begun stepping up its efforts to curb indecency.[13]

In the food industry, tension between gratification and abstinence can be seen in consumers' seemingly contradictory behaviors toward food and diet. Even in the face of ongoing diet concerns and popular dietary programs, consumption of desserts and snacks remains strong. A recent study shows that roughly 90 percent of Americans eat dessert at least once a week with the average being three times a week.[14] And while the overall cookie category has taken recent hits, sales of premium cookies such as Pepperidge Farm's Distinctive Cookies have gone up. According to one executive,

> What we're finding even in the midst of low-carb mania is that people still have a need for indulgence. Minis (one of their premium cookies) offer a small indulgence anytime, anywhere.[15]

Illustration 3-1 shows an ad that appeals to sensual gratification.

Postponed/Immediate Gratification   In line with the value they generally place on sensual gratification, Americans seem unwilling to delay pleasures. While concern about personal debt is high[16] and more consumers are shopping for value and waiting for sales, personal debt, personal bankruptcies, and credit sales continue to climb. In fact, while Americans will postpone gratification to an extent during economic downturns, their willingness to consume even in these conditions has been a major force in maintaining a relatively strong economy. Virtually all major purchases in America are made on credit, and many of these involve credit card debt that is extremely expensive.

Hard Work/Leisure   Americans continue their strong tradition of hard work, leading much of the industrialized world in hours worked. Average weekly hours worked is around 39, with 28 percent of workers clocking more than 40 hours per week. The percentage of married women who work outside the home for wages has increased by 50 percent since 1970, from 41 to 61 percent of all married women.[17] A recent survey found that Americans work long hours for many reasons. One is clearly their material orientation. Americans work in order to have such things as a large home, two cars, and a nice vacation. Others work long hours because they lack the skills or job opportunities to provide even a moderate lifestyle without doing so. However, Americans also work long and hard because work is

Courtesy of Campbell Soup Company.

meaningful and valuable to them. They gain self-esteem and the respect of their peers in part by the work that they do.

Partly in response to the increase in work hours, the value placed on work relative to leisure has dropped over the past two decades. For example, a recent study found that 81 percent of employed consumers felt the need to simplify their lives and create more time for home and family.[18] This opens up opportunities for marketers to enhance value by creating products and services that deliver convenience. Still, we can't seem to get away from work even when we are away from work. Forty-three percent of people in a recent survey check in with the office while on vacation![19] Thus, we have a situation where hard work and leisure are both valued (often by the same people) and commingled in people's lives.

Material/Nonmaterial   Americans have maintained a strong material orientation. An outcome of America's focus on materialism is a consumption-driven society. As we have seen, Americans are working longer hours, in part, to afford material possessions. That is, Americans are trading time and energy for things and services such as cars and travel. Consider that the size of the average American family has dropped sharply over the past 30 years while the size of the average American home has dramatically increased. There is some evidence that this strong value on material possessions is moderating, however, at least among some consumers. Role overload, burnout, and emotional exhaustion are causing some to rethink their priorities and consciously simplify their lives. Consider the following comment,

> I had all the stuff that was supposed to make me successful—my car and my clothes, the house in the right neighborhood and belonging to the right health club. All the external framework was excellent and inside I kind of had this pit eating away at me.[20]

Consumers' efforts to reduce their reliance on consumption and material possessions have been termed **voluntary simplicity.** Voluntary simplicity can span a continuum from

ILLUSTRATION 3-2

This ad is consistent with American values for leisure, activeness, sensual gratification, and risk taking.

Courtesy Aspen Skiing Company.

minor life adjustments and reduced spending to drastic lifestyle adjustments including downsized jobs, incomes, houses, and spending. A major influence in the decision to simplify appears to be reduced stress and increased life satisfaction, although other motivations including environmentalism can be involved. While the voluntary simplicity movement appears to represent a relatively small proportion of the U.S. population, its growth certainly holds economic and marketing consequences, including the market for second-hand products and green products.[21]

Active/Passive   Americans continue to value an active approach to life. While less than half of all American adults exercise regularly, most Americans take an active approach to both leisure and problem-solving activities. Television viewing as a primary form of entertainment has dropped sharply from its peak in the mid-1980s (Young men (18–24 years) seem to be moving away from TV faster than any other group[22]). Alternative activities including surfing the net, sports, cooking, and gardening are popular. And, the amount of time children spend in scheduled activities continues to increase.[23] The following quote illustrates that Americans differ on this value, but most would agree more with the second speaker than the first.

My idea of a vacation is a nice oceanfront resort, a beach chair, and a piña colada.

Mine too. For a day or two. Then I'd go bug spit. I'd feel like I was in prison. I'd *do* something.[24]

Illustration 3-2 describes a resort designed for active leisure.

Environment-Oriented Values

Environment-oriented values prescribe a society's relationship with its economic, technical, and physical environments. Americans have traditionally admired cleanliness, change, performance, risk taking, problem solving, and the conquest of nature. While this cluster of values remains basically intact, there are some significant shifts occurring.

Americans continue
to place a high
value on cleanli-
ness, as this ad
demonstrates.

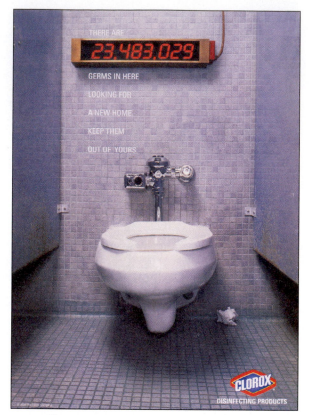

CLOROX® is a registered trademark of The Clorox Company. Used with
permission. © 2005 The Clorox Company. Reprinted with permission.

Cleanliness

Americans have long valued cleanliness. This strong focus seems to be declining somewhat, particularly in terms of our homes. Likely due to increased time demands caused by work, messier homes are more acceptable.[25] However, such shifts don't
appear to suggest major changes. The popularity of TV shows like "Clean Sweep" suggest
that while Americans may accept messier homes they are not happy about them. This obviously presents marketing opportunities.[26] For example, the recent development of robotic
vacuum cleaners such as Sharper Image's Roomba tap the desire for cleanliness while
offering much needed convenience and time savings.

Personal hygiene, another aspect related to cleanliness, remains very important to most
Americans. A recent study shows that antibacterial hand sanitizers such as Purell are a new
addition to the arsenal of products carried around by mothers.[27] Illustration 3-3 demonstrates the emphasis Americans place on cleanliness.

Tradition/Change

Americans have always been very receptive to change. *New* has
traditionally been taken to mean *improved*. While still very appreciative of change,
Americans are now less receptive to change for its own sake. New-product recalls, the expense and the failure of various government programs, and the energy required to keep
pace with rapid technological changes are some of the reasons for this shift. Another reason is the aging of the American population. As we will see in the next chapter, the average
age of the population is increasing, and people generally become somewhat less accepting
of change as they age. Still, much of America continues to embrace change, as evidenced
by a growing segment of workers that one expert calls the *creative class*. The creative class

includes those who work in such professions as architecture, science, engineering, and health care and business who generate new ideas and technologies for a living or engage in complex problem solving. This group now constitutes about 33 percent of the workforce compared to just 10 percent in 1900.[28]

Risk Taking/Security   Americans' risk-taking orientation seems to have changed somewhat over time. There was an increased emphasis on security during the period from 1930 through the mid-1980s. This attitude was a response to the tremendous upheavals and uncertainties caused by the Depression, World War II, and the Cold War. However, risk taking remains highly valued and is gaining appreciation as Americans look to entrepreneurs for economic growth and to smaller firms and self-employment to obtain desired lifestyles. Increasing interest and investment in space tourism, culminating recently in the first successful private spacecraft named SpaceShipOne, is just one more example of America's spirit of change, innovation, and risk taking.[29]

Problem Solving/Fatalistic   Americans take great pride in being problem solvers, and as we saw earlier, as a percentage of the workforce, problem solvers and creative types are on the increase. By and large, Americans believe that virtually anything can be fixed given sufficient time and effort. For example, over two-thirds of Americans believe that they can continue to grow the economy *and* improve environmental quality.[30] Marketers introduce thousands of new products each year with the theme that they will solve a problem better than existing products will. We will examine the results of this value later in this chapter in the sections on green marketing and cause marketing.

Admire/Overcome Nature   Traditionally, nature was viewed as an obstacle. Americans attempted to bend nature to fit their desires without realizing the negative consequences this could have for both nature and humanity. However, this attitude has shifted dramatically over the past 30 years.

Although the percentage of Americans who consider themselves to be environmentalists has dropped from 76 to 50 percent over the last decade, the statistics show that environmental concerns are still strong:

- More than 80 percent of the public are concerned about the condition of the environment.
- Ninety percent have engaged in activities to protect the environment.
- Over 70 percent have purchased a product/brand because it was better for the environment.
- Forty percent have contributed to an environmental agency.[31]

One firm classifies consumers into the following segments in terms of their environmental activism:[32]

- *True Naturals* (11 percent): express deeply felt environmental concerns and tailor their actions and purchases to these beliefs.
- *New Green Mainstream* (17 percent): concerned about the environment but alter their actions and purchases only when it is convenient.
- *Affluent Healers* (11 percent): most concerned about environmental issues that relate to their personal health; are less inclined to consider the environment when shopping.
- *Young Recyclers* (14 percent): most concerned about environmental issues that relate to solid waste; are less inclined to consider the environment when shopping.
- *Overwhelmed* (22 percent): feel too caught up in life's demands to worry about the environment; are unlikely to favor a product for environmental reasons.
- *Unconcerned* (25 percent): do not pay attention to environmental issues, or do not feel that the environment is seriously threatened.

Firms that convince environmentally concerned consumers that their products are environmentally sound can reap huge rewards. Tom's of Maine markets environmentally sound personal care products. Its products command a 20 to 50 percent price premium and its sales have been growing rapidly. According to an executive, the firm gains additional advantages as well:

> Our environmental and social responsibility policies are a barrier to competitive advances. Even a competitor with much greater resources cannot just replicate our formula and expect to take our market share. Our corporate practices add a richness and depth to our product appeal that creates an unusually strong brand loyalty.[33]

We describe the marketing response to this value in the section of this chapter on green marketing.

Performance/Status   Americans are shifting back to a focus on performance rather than status. Although consumers are still willing to purchase "status" brands, these brands must provide style and functionality in addition to the prestige of the name. This has led to substantial increases in sales at stores that combine price, service, and quality, such as Wal-Mart and Target stores, and for quality retailer private-label brands such as those offered by Albertson's and Wal-Mart. In contrast, outlets with inappropriate cost structures or images, such as The Gap, Kmart, and Montgomery Ward, have struggled or failed.[34]

Other-Oriented Values

Other-oriented values reflect a society's view of the appropriate relationships between individuals and groups within that society. Historically, American society has been oriented toward individualism, competitiveness, masculinity, youth, limited families, and uniformity. However, several aspects of this orientation are undergoing change.

Individual/Collective   A strong emphasis on individualism is one of the defining characteristics of American society. Watch any American hit movie. The leading character will virtually always behave as an individual, often despite pressures to compromise to the group. Americans believe in "doing your own thing." Even the "uniforms" that each generation of teenagers invents for itself allow ample room for individual expression. This value affects incentive systems for salespeople, advertising themes, product design, and customer complaining behavior.[35] For example, consumers higher in individualism are more likely to complain, switch, or engage in negative word-of-mouth when faced with poor service performance.[36] Individualism is also evident in the customization craze for cars, trucks, and motorcycles, currently a market worth over $2 billion a year. Discovery Channel has tapped into this trend with shows like "Monster Garage" and "American Chopper," which attract the highly elusive younger male audience.[37]

Diversity/Uniformity   While American culture has always valued individualism, it has also valued a degree of uniformity, particularly with respect to groups. America was founded in part by people seeking religious freedom or fleeing from various forms of persecution. The Constitution and many laws seek to protect diverse religions, political beliefs, and so forth. Nonetheless, Americans historically insisted that immigrants quickly adopt the language, dress, values, and many other aspects of the majority. Those who did not were often subject to various forms of discrimination. This was particularly true for racial and some religious minorities.

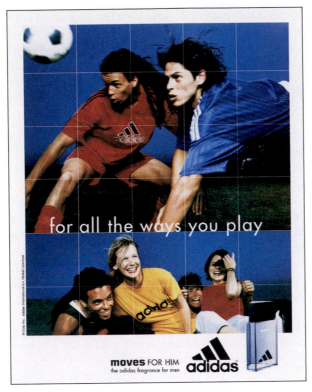

Americans increasingly value diversity. As a result, diversity is portrayed as the norm in many ads.

Courtesy Coty, Inc.

Since World War II, Americans have increasingly valued diversity. For example, a recent study concludes,

[There] is an equally strong respect for religious diversity that translates into a strong tolerance of other people's beliefs. Americans seem to expect that they will encounter people of different faiths in their daily lives, and have absorbed the idea of respect into their social conduct. This recognition of the importance of both religious faith and religious diversity is underscored repeatedly in the study.[38]

While far from free from racial, religious, ethnic, or class prejudice, American culture is evolving toward valuing diversity more than uniformity. A recent study finds that 56 percent of Americans feel that over the past year they have become more likely to respect cultures with different values.[39] The Adidas ad shown in Illustration 3-4 reflects the positive view of diversity held by most Americans. We examine one aspect of America's increasing acceptance of diversity–marketing to gay and lesbian consumers—in the marketing strategy section of this chapter.

Limited/Extended Family   America was settled by immigrants, people who left their extended families behind. As the nation grew, the western movement produced a similar phenomenon. Even today, frequent geographic moves as well as differential rates of social mobility mean that few children grow up in close interaction with aunts, uncles, cousins, nieces, or nephews.[40] It is also common for children to leave their hometowns and parents once they begin their own careers. The physical separation of traditional family members often reduces the sense of family among those members. This, in turn, reduces the impact that the family has on the individual.

This is not to say that Americans do not love their family members or that how an American is raised does not influence the person for life. Rather, it means that a 35-year-old American is unlikely to have a cousin who would feel obligated to respond positively to a loan request (this is not the case in many other cultures). Likewise, this 35-year-old would be unlikely to have one or more cousins, aunts, or nephews live with him or her for an extended time period. The role of families in the American culture is covered in depth in Chapter 6.

Youth/Age   Traditionally, older people were considered wiser than young people and were, therefore, looked to as models and leaders in almost all cultures. This has never been as true in American culture, probably because transforming a wilderness into a new type of producing nation required characteristics such as physical strength, stamina, youthful vigor, and imagination. The value on youth continued as America became an industrial nation. Since World War II, it has increased to such an extent that products such as cars, clothing, cosmetics, and hairstyles seem designed for and sold only to the young! For example, youth appeals in American advertising still appear to outstrip appeals to age and tradition.[41]

But a slow reversal of this value on youth seems to be occurring. Because of their increasing numbers and disposable income, older citizens have developed political and economic clout and are beginning to use it. As one expert says,

> It used to be that 25-year-old women drove the fashion industry; now it's 45-year-old women. Because when you are 45, you already know what you look good in. If a designer says, "Crepe is in," this group may confidently answer that "crepe is crap."[42]

Cosmetics, medicines, and hair care products are being marketed specifically to older consumers, and ads for these products increasingly utilize older models such as Julianne Moore who are closer in age to the target audience. However, most of these products still have either a direct or indirect appeal of creating a younger appearance.

Age portrayal in advertising is a difficult issue. Since people often feel younger than their actual age, ads utilizing younger models might generate a more positive reaction. In addition, for youth-oriented or conspicuously consumed products, using older models in ads may alienate younger consumers.[43] These two factors help to explain the overrepresentation of younger models in ads over the last three decades.[44] There is the worry, however, that at some point older consumers may feel ignored by ads that portray overly young users. Clearly marketers have a lot to learn in this area.[45]

Competition/Cooperation   America has long been a competitive society, and this value remains firmly entrenched. It is reflected in our social, political, and economic systems. We reward particularly successful competitors in business, entertainment, and sports with staggering levels of financial compensation. While there is increased focus on cooperation and teamwork in schools and businesses, this is generally done so that the team or group can outperform some other team or group. It is no wonder that America was one of the first countries to allow comparative advertising.

Masculine/Feminine   American society, like most others, has reflected a masculine orientation for a long time. But as indicated by this chapter's opening story, this orientation is changing as are gender roles. While American society is becoming less masculine oriented, however, it still clearly leans in this direction. For example, 42 percent of parents indicate that they would prefer a boy if they could have only one child, compared to 27 percent who would opt for a girl.[46] Likewise, boys receive larger allowances than do girls.[47] Still, there is a shift taking place in this value and the marketing implications resulting from it are discussed in detail later in the next section of this chapter.

MARKETING STRATEGY AND VALUES

We have examined a number of marketing implications of American values and changes in these values. It is critical that all aspects of the firm's marketing mix be consistent with the value system of its target market. We will now examine four marketing responses to evolving American values: green marketing, cause-related marketing, marketing to gay and lesbian consumers, and gender-based marketing.

Green Marketing

Marketers have responded to Americans' increasing concern for the environment with an approach called **green marketing.**[48] Green marketing generally involves (1) developing products whose production, use, or disposal is less harmful to the environment than the traditional versions of the product; (2) developing products that have a positive impact on the environment; or (3) tying the purchase of a product to an environmental organization or event. For example,[49]

- Wal-Mart has launched several "eco-stores." The stores carry Wal-Mart's usual merchandise but highlight environmentally superior products as well as environmental innovations in store design. For example, the stores are designed to be energy efficient and use recycled materials.
- General Mills, through its Nature Valley Granola brand, is a corporate sponsor of the National Park Foundation, giving $150,000 a year for trail restoration. In addition, Nature Valley Granola packaging features promotions for other environmental causes through its partnership with The Nature Conservancy.
- Estée Lauder launched, under the Origins label, a complete line of cosmetics that are made of natural ingredients, are not tested on animals, and are packaged in recyclable containers.
- Office Depot offers Envirocopy Recycled Copy Paper which contains 35 percent post-consumer recycled fibers with green-colored packaging to emphasize the environment.
- Prang Crayons are made from soybeans rather than petroleum-based wax.

As concern for the environment grew throughout the 1980s and 1990s, many firms began to improve their products and processes relative to the environment and to advertise those improvements. Unfortunately, different marketers used the same claims, such as *environmentally friendly* or *environmentally safe,* to refer to vastly differing performance levels. The Federal Trade Commission (FTC) issued a set of voluntary guidelines for green claims to guide companies and protect consumers. The general guidelines include dozens of examples of acceptable and unacceptable practices to guide marketers, including:

- Labels promoting products as "environmentally safe" or "environmentally friendly" must specify what portion of the product is being referred to; otherwise, they would be deceptive.
- An ad calling a trash bag "recyclable" without qualification would be deemed misleading because bags aren't ordinarily separated from other trash at landfills or incinerators.
- A shampoo advertised as "biodegradable" without qualification wouldn't be deceptive if the marketer has competent and reliable scientific support showing it will decompose in a short time.[50]

Green marketing is complex. Confusing terminology is a contributing factor. For example, "sustainable" products are a hot trend in food marketing. However, inconsistent use of the term makes it hard for consumers to make informed judgments. An emerging

Hybrid automobiles are increasingly popular. This ad for the Honda Civic Hybrid goes beyond environmental benefits to emphasize a key consumer benefit.

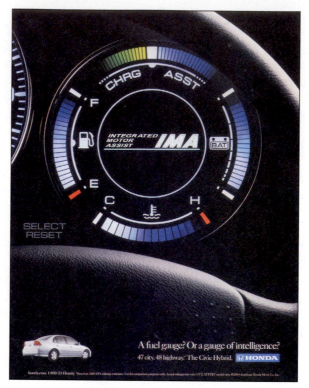

Courtesy American Honda Motor Co., Inc.

consensus is that **sustainability** involves methods that are (*a*) profitable for the farmer, (*b*) environmentally sound, and (*c*) socially responsible. The sustainability movement has become important in industries such as coffee.[51] In addition, environmental concerns are only one factor in consumer decisions.[52] Even among those who are environmentally concerned, factors such as lack of convenience, higher prices, skepticism about green claims, quality concerns, lack of availability, and a sense that individuals can't make a difference can inhibit green behaviors and purchases.[53] Overcoming these obstacles is critical to the success of green marketing. For example, Philips struggled in the compact fluorescent light (CFL) market until it effectively communicated the consumer benefits in terms of a $26 savings in energy costs (which is also environmentally friendly) over the lifetime of the bulb. This was critical given its high price. The Environmental Protection Agency's (EPA) "Energy Star" label also added credibility.[54] As discussed in Consumer Insight 3-2, the automotive industry is working hard to put these lessons to work on hybrid automobiles (also see Illustration 3-5).

Cause-Related Marketing

The term *cause marketing* is sometimes used interchangeably with *social marketing* to refer to the application of marketing principles and tactics to advance a cause such as a charity (United Way), an ideology (environmental protection), or an activity (breast cancer exams). Social marketing differs from traditional marketing in the intangible and abstract nature of the "product" and in the absence of a profit motive. At one extreme, such as a

The Emerging Hybrid

American consumers are torn between their love for automobiles and their concern for the environment.[55] On the one hand, 60 percent favor energy conservation and 62 percent think that the environment should be a legislative priority. On the other hand, large trucks and sport-utility vehicles (SUVs) remain extremely popular even in the face of rising prices at the gas pump.

Americans, it seems, want it all. And auto manufacturers are working hard to deliver. Early attempts involving electric automobiles and other super–high mileage or low pollution cars failed to penetrate the U.S. market. Problems included poor driving performance and high sticker prices. The emerging breed of hybrids is another thing altogether.

Performance, styling, and luxury are becoming the name of the game. Consider the Lexus RX 400h, which gets 29 MPG and does 0 to 60 in 7.3 seconds, which compares favorably to the all-wheel drive conventional Lexus RX 330 AWD, which gets 21 MPG and does 0 to 60 in 7.7 seconds. Comparisons for the Honda Civic hybrid and the conventional model are equally attractive in that driving performance is comparable while fuel economy is higher.

Toyota's Prius was the first model to make a major move in the hybrid market. Celebrities such as Charlize Theron, Sting, and Leonardo DiCaprio were early adopters who helped generate momentum. Other efforts included product placements in shows like the "Gilmore Girls" and "The West Wing." However the real key to success has been creating a car that doesn't require consumers to compromise on driving performance. The Prius appears to have been a right step in that direction, so much so that consumer demand has outstripped supply and waiting lists are common.

Currently, hybrids represent .5 percent of the 17 million annual U.S. car buyers. Most major brands plan to enter the hybrid market and Toyota's goal is a hybrid version of most of its models. According to industry experts, in order to maintain sustained growth, continued improvements in battery quality and related engine performance, comfort, and price will be necessary.

What's on the horizon for hybrids? Can you say hybrid GMC Yukon?

Critical Thinking Questions

1. Why is there so much demand for conventional SUVs, which are not environmentally friendly, when American values strongly support environmental protection?

2. What lessons does the Philips struggle in the compact fluorescent light (CFL) market referred to in the text provide for automobile manufacturers?

3. How important will continued high gasoline prices be to the growth of the hybrid market?

---

health-related campaign, there are potential direct benefits to the individual. However, in general, the benefits to the individual are indirect (a better society in which to live). Often, the benefit is purely or primarily emotional. Individuals are requested to change beliefs or behaviors or provide funds because it is "the right thing to do" and they will "feel good" or "be a better person" because of it.

Examine the two ads in Illustration 3-6. *What are the benefits being promised to those who respond? Why might an individual "buy" one of these "products"?* As noted in Chapter 1, social marketing is marketing done to enhance the welfare of individuals or society without direct benefit to a firm. In contrast, cause marketing or **cause-related marketing (CRM)** is *marketing that ties a company and its products to an issue or cause with the goal of improving sales or corporate image while providing benefits to the cause.*[56] Companies associate with causes to create long-term relationships with their customers, building corporate and brand equity that should eventually lead to increased sales. The Christian Children's Fund in Illustration 3-6 is an example of social marketing, as it promotes a benefit to the world community without advancing the profits or image of a commercial

Courtesy Christian Children's Fund.

Courtesy Yoplait USA, Inc.

firm. The Yoplait ad in Illustration 3-6 is an example of cause-related marketing. It attempts to benefit a cause *and* to enhance the image and sales of a commercial firm.

The foundation of CRM is marketing to consumers' values, and it can be very effective. Consumer acceptance and response to CRM has increased dramatically over the past decade. Consider the following statistics (to learn more visit the Cause Marketing Forum at www.causemarketingforum.com):

- Eighty percent say that corporate support of a cause increases their trust in the company.
- Seventy-four percent claim that a company's commitment to a social issue is important when deciding which products and services to recommend to other people.
- Eighty-six percent are likely to switch brands based on CRM when price and quality are equal (up from 66 percent in 1993).[57]

Cause-related marketing is often effective because it is consistent with strongly held American values.[58] For example, a common theme in most CRM programs taps America's problem-solving orientation by presenting a problem, such as breast cancer, AIDS, or pollution, and an action that individuals can take to help solve the problem. Given consumer receptivity to CRM, it is not surprising that corporate spending on it is on the rise. One area of spending, cause-related sponsorship, has grown from $120 million in 1990 to $1.08 billion in 2005![59] Consumer skepticism and apathy remain a challenge, however, as illustrated by the following descriptions and quotes of four consumer groups based on their responses to CRM.[60]

Skeptic (doubt sincerity or effectiveness of CRM): I think those are fake, most of them. Because what they give is so little it doesn't amount to anything.

Balancer (believe in CRM but generally don't act accordingly): I hate to say this, but, as far as grocery stores, I go to the one that is closest to me. It makes me feel better . . . about Food Lion that they were willing to do this (participate in CRM) . . . but, sometimes I don't put out that extra effort, but I guess I really should.

Attribution-oriented (concerned about motives behind CRM): I always approach them with a skeptical eye, but I try and use good judgment and common sense based on who they are, what they're doing and try to see the end result.

Socially concerned (driven by desire to help): I mean, as long as they're doing it, the motives can be questionable as far as I'm concerned. . . . Even if there's questionable motives, it's that much more important to support companies who do those things. Just to reinforce that good behavior.

An emerging consensus is that a "fit" between the company and the cause can improve results.[61] For example ConAgra (a food marketing company) launched *Feeding Children Better* to combat child hunger while Crest and the Boys and Girls Club of America partnered to form *Healthy Smiles 2010* to teach kids about oral hygiene. In both cases there is a business-cause fit.[62]

Marketing to Gay and Lesbian Consumers

As Americans in general are shifting to valuing diversity, they are increasingly embracing ethnic, religious, and racial diversity. Another group gaining increased public acceptance is the gay and lesbian community (we follow business press convention and refer to gay and lesbian consumers as the gay market). In 2004, 54 percent of respondents to a large survey felt that homosexuality should be considered an acceptable lifestyle, compared to only 34 percent in 1982.[63] Interestingly, the value that Americans place on individual rights and protection appears to transcend personal opinions about lifestyle. For example, over 70 percent support hate-crime protection laws and same-sex couple rights such as hospital visitation. These numbers are even stronger among younger consumers.[64] The emergence and popularity of TV shows with openly gay or lesbian characters such as "Will and Grace" and "The L Word" is additional evidence of increased public acceptance.

Before we begin, it is important to emphasize that gay consumers, like heterosexuals, vary in terms of ethnicity, geographic region, occupation, and age. These and other factors influence their behavior and, in most instances, play a much larger role in their consumption process than does their sexual orientation.

Estimating the size of the gay market has proven difficult, in part because market researchers have been hesitant to ask explicit questions about sexual orientation, and in part because of underreporting by respondents based on concerns of prejudice and discrimination. Current estimates vary, but common benchmarks put the size of the gay market at 5 to 7 percent of the adult U.S. population or between 11 to 16 million people over the age of 18. Gauging income and occupational status of the gay market has also been a challenge. Some research suggests that the gay market is wealthier and in higher-status occupations than the general population, while other research suggests that they are relatively similar. A recent analysis, which assumes that the gay population mirrors the general population in terms of income, estimates the purchasing power of the gay market at $610 billion.[65]

Not surprisingly many companies have concluded that the gay market is a highly attractive segment to pursue and are investing resources to research and target them. For example, American Express spent $250,000 on a study of this market and then committed additional marketing efforts. Likewise, Subaru conducted a major study and decided the market warranted a special effort.[66] This focused effort produced impressive results: Subscribers to the gay magazines in which Subaru advertised were 2.6 times more likely to buy a Subaru than nonsubscribers.[67]

Any firm that desires to capture the loyalty of the gay community must have internal policies that do not discriminate against gay employees. A recent survey found that 82 percent of gay consumers are more likely to buy from companies they know are gay friendly.[68] The Human Rights Campaign Foundation (www.hrc.org) helps provide such information through its corporate equality index (CEI), which measures how equitably a company treats its GLBT (Gay, Lesbian, Bisexual, and Transgender) employees, customers, and investors.

Additional product and communication issues in serving this market include:

- Does the product need to be modified to meet the needs of this market?
- Should the firm advertise in gay-oriented media using its standard ads?
- Should it advertise in gay media using ads with gay themes?
- To what extent should the firm be involved in gay community activities?
- Should its major media ads include ads with gay themes?

Product Issues   In many cases the lifestyles of gay consumers do not differ sufficiently from other consumers to require product modifications. For example, IBM, United Airlines, Coors, and Procter & Gamble have programs that target the gay market using their standard products. However, product modification opportunities are sometimes possible and beneficial. For example, MTV includes advertising and programming aimed at the gay market as a way to broaden its appeal. In addition, with the increased focus on same-sex marriage, companies such as Pottery Barn and Tiffany's are modifying their bridal registries to be gender neutral, and Web sites such as Gayweddings (www.gayweddings.com) are emerging to serve this market.

Another area in which product modifications are often necessary is financial services. As the director of segment marketing for American Express explains,

> Often, gay couples are very concerned about issues like Social Security benefits and estate planning, since same-sex marriages often are not recognized under the law.[69]

The following ad content reflects one of American Express's product offerings targeting the gay market.

> When you're ready to plan a future together, who can you trust to understand the financial challenges that gay men and lesbians face?
>
> At American Express Financial Advisors we offer Domestic Partner Planning services that can help you address issues like protecting assets from unnecessary taxation and getting around restrictions placed on unmarried couples. We offer you the expertise and insight you need to make smart decisions.

Communication Issues   There are a large number of gay-oriented print media in the United States and Canada. Rivendell Marketing Co. is a national advertising representative for over 200 such publications with a combined circulation of over 3.5 million. The National Gay Newspaper Guild has 12 publications with a readership of over 750,000. There are a number of gay-oriented magazines, with *Out* and *The Advocate* being two of the largest with circulations of around 100,000 each. Given the size and spending power of the gay market, it is not surprising that spending in gay-oriented print media has doubled since 1997 to its current level of over $200 million. Over 150 Fortune 500 companies now advertise in gay media, up from 19 in 1994.[70]

Ads targeting the gay community can range from standard ads run in gay-oriented media to ads with clear gay themes. This ad takes the approach of showing a gay couple in a daily activity without a unique gay theme.

Courtesy Brown & Company.

Compared to the general population, gay consumers tend to be more tech savvy, are more likely to be online, are more likely to have broadband access, and spend more hours online. Marketers are taking this into account in developing their Web sites.[71] For example, IBM has a GLBT Business Community page on their Web site, Orbitz has a gay and lesbian page on their travel site, and American Express often features financial issues specific to the gay market in their online advice columns. In addition, numerous gay Web sites have emerged. PlanetOut.com and Gay.com (now merged) are highly successful examples. With over 3 million active members and over 4 million unique visits each month they have amazing access to the gay market. EarthLink, Visa, MG-Rover, Ford, American Express, and ING are among the firms that advertise on them.[72]

Since most products don't require alteration for the gay market, firms may decide to approach the market by placing one of their standard ads in gay-oriented media. Anheuser-Busch, Miller Brewing, Baileys Original Irish Cream, and American Express are among the firms that first approached this market with standard ads. However, these and other firms are increasingly creating ads specifically for this market, with 2004 being the first time a majority of the ads (59 percent) in gay print media were specifically created for gay consumers.[73] The ads may portray a gay couple instead of a heterosexual couple in a standard ad, as shown in Illustration 3-7. Or the entire ad may contain a gay theme. For example, Hartford Financial Services developed Diverse Household Auto Insurance that offers discounts to both heterosexual and gay couples (not all companies do so). In a humorous ad, two blue cars are shown side-by-side with the caption, "The Hartford offers auto insurance discounts to gay couples." Beneath these cars are two side-by-side pink cars with the caption, "We also offer discounts to lesbian couples." At the bottom of the ad, a blue and a pink car are side-by-side with the caption, "Heck, we even offer discounts to heterosexual couples. (Not that there's anything wrong with that.)"

It has been estimated that slightly more than a fourth of the gay community does not use gay-oriented media. Those who do use gay-oriented media also spend considerable time using standard media. As one gay man stated, "We are not only reading *Out* and *The Advocate* all the time. If you go into any gay man's apartment you're very likely to see *Vanity Fair* and *People* as well."[74] This is also true online, where 8 of the 10 top visited Web sites by gay consumers are general sites such as Yahoo!, Google, Amazon, CNN, and eBay, which are not specifically devoted to gay issues.[75]

However, firms generally remain reluctant to use ads with gay themes in standard mass media. The Hartford ad described earlier appeared on billboards and some local newspapers. This was unusual enough to generate an article in *Advertising Age* entitled "Insurer Places Gay-Themed Ads in Mainstream Media." Concern about backlash from the portion of the market that does not accept the gay community as well as a desire to have ads that directly appeal to the largest number of viewers are the primary reasons for the general lack of gay-themed ads on mainstream media.[76]

Finally, in addition to advertising in gay media, support of gay community events such as Gay Pride week is another important avenue firms use in approaching this market.

Gender-Based Marketing

As we saw in the chapter's opening vignette, gender roles in the United States are shifting. It's hard to imagine that just one or two generations ago, the prevailing stereotype of an automobile purchase involved a male making the purchase alone. Today, women influence 80 percent of all vehicles sold, make over half of all new vehicle purchases (up from 20 percent in 1984), and purchase 40 percent of all SUVs.[77]

Changes in gender roles for women have been dramatic, with increased participation in the workforce, increased wealth and purchase power, and increased participation in active lifestyles, to name just a few. Marketers of products and services ranging from automobiles, to sportswear, to financial services clearly understand the importance of women as a market segment. Consider the following examples:

- Women represent 40 percent of the market for casual lifestyle athletic shoes. Skechers, K-Swiss, and Reebok maintain strong positions in this market by offering products specifically tailored to the needs of active women.[78]
- Merrill Lynch recently launched its Women's Business Development Unit to target wealthy women investors who are entrepreneurs and executives.[79]
- *Good Housekeeping* now offers a "Women's Automobile Satisfaction Award" to brands that score 5 percent or more above the average satisfaction rating among female owners.

The terms *sex* and **gender** are used interchangeably to refer to *whether a person is biologically a male or female.* **Gender identity** refers to the traits of *femininity* (expressive traits such as tenderness and compassion) and *masculinity* (instrumental traits such as aggressiveness and dominance). These traits represent the ends of a continuum, and individuals have varying levels of each trait, with biological males tending to be toward the masculine end of the continuum and biological females toward the feminine end.[80]

Gender roles are *the behaviors considered appropriate for males and females in a given society.* As the previous discussion of automobile purchasing indicates, gender roles in America have undergone massive changes over the past 30 years. The general nature of this shift has been for behaviors previously considered appropriate primarily for men to be acceptable for women too.[81]

Gender roles are ascribed roles. An **ascribed role** is based on *an attribute over which the individual has little or no control.* This can be contrasted with **achievement roles,** which are based on *performance criteria over which the individual has some degree of control.* Individuals can, within limits, select their occupational role (achievement role), but they cannot generally determine their gender (ascribed role).

Researchers find it useful to categorize women into **traditional** or **modern gender orientations** on the basis of their preference for one or the other of two contrasting lifestyles:

• *Traditional.* A marriage with the husband assuming the responsibility for providing for the family and the wife running the house and taking care of the children.
• *Modern.* A marriage where husband and wife share responsibilities. Both work, and they share homemaking and child care responsibilities.

Americans have certainly moved toward a *preference* for a modern lifestyle, from only 35 percent in 1977 to 58 percent in 2002.[82] In addition, only 25 percent agree that women should return to their traditional roles and 87 percent agree that fathers are just as capable as mothers of caring for their children.[83] However, while males and females both express strong preferences for the modern lifestyle as a general concept, most recognize that it comes with a cost, and attitudes and behaviors toward specific aspects of that lifestyle remain very conservative in some cases. For example, almost 70 percent of both women and men believe it would be best if mothers would "stay at home and just take care of the house and children."[84] And 80 percent of mothers with children age 5 or under would prefer to stay home with their children if it were totally up to them.[85]

There is still disparity between men and women in terms of participation in household duties although men's participation is on the rise. For example, recent research suggests that married men spend 50 percent more time on housework than they did 25 years ago. However, one study estimates that working men spend only half as much time per day on housework as their working wives (45 minutes versus 90 minutes), while another estimates it at around 66 percent (2 hours versus 3).[86] In the grocery shopping arena, change has been much slower with men currently the principal shoppers for groceries and kids' clothing in only 21 percent of households, up from 13 percent in 1985.[87]

While gender roles are evolving and there is a more equitable distribution of household duties particularly when both spouses work, men often resent and resist housework. Consider the following excerpt about one couple's battle over housework:

"It's a blowout fight every month," Hope (32 and a book editor) confesses. "It's the only thing we fight about." Hope says getting Cohen (34 and a medical resident) to do his agreed-upon tasks requires constant reminders. "He'll tell me he'll wash the dishes before we go to bed, and maybe he will," she says. "But by around 9:30, with dirty dishes still in the sink, I'm broiling." It's not like Cohen makes her feel "like a mom" on purpose. As she points out, "He had no household responsibilities growing up."[88]

Conflict exists not only across gender groups but also within individuals who are torn between the two orientations. Many mothers who work outside the home experience considerable guilt, role conflict, and emotional burnout related to the heavy demands of their numerous roles.[89]

In fact, many Americans are realizing that they can't have it all, and where there is a choice, some are opting for change. Sometimes the change is toward the nontraditional, as in the increasing numbers of "stay-at-home" dads, which by one estimate has increased by

Courtesy Logitech, Inc.

© The Procter & Gamble Company. Used by permission.

Women fulfill a multitude of roles today and have a wide range of attitudes about their roles in society. These two ads take radically different approaches to their portrayal of women and women's attitudes.

70 percent since 1990.[90] Sometimes the change is toward the traditional as in the recent increase in "stay-at-home" moms, which reverses a three-decade trend of increasing numbers of young mothers in the workforce.[91]

As we have seen, women have a variety of role options and a range of attitudes concerning their gender roles. The ads in Illustration 3-8 reflect two sharply contrasting views of the female role. Next, we examine some of the marketing implications of the changing roles of women in American society.

Market Segmentation   Neither the women's nor the men's market is as homogeneous as it once was. At least four significant female market segments exist.[92]

1. *Traditional housewife.* Generally married. Prefers to stay at home. Very home and family centered. Desires to please husband and children. Seeks satisfaction and meaning from household and family maintenance as well as volunteer activities. Experiences strong pressure to work outside the home and is well aware of forgone income opportunity. Feels supported by family and is generally content with role.
2. *Trapped housewife.* Generally married. Would prefer to work, but stays at home due to young children, lack of outside opportunities, or family pressure. Seeks satisfaction and meaning outside the home. Does not enjoy most household chores. Has mixed feelings about current status and is concerned about lost opportunities.
3. *Trapped working woman.* Married or single. Would prefer to stay at home, but works due to economic necessity or social/family pressure. Does not derive satisfaction or

meaning from employment. Enjoys most household activities, but is frustrated by lack of time. Feels conflict about her role, particularly if younger children are home. Resents missed opportunities for family, volunteer, and social activities. Is proud of financial contribution to family.

4. *Career working woman.* Married or single. Prefers to work. Derives satisfaction and meaning from employment rather than, or in addition to, home and family. Experiences some conflict over her role if younger children are at home, but is generally content. Views home maintenance as a necessary evil. Feels pressed for time.

While the above descriptions are oversimplified, they indicate the diverse nature of the adult female population. Notice that women may move in and out of these categories over their lifetimes. For example, an otherwise career working woman may feel more like a trapped working woman if she finds it necessary to work while her children are young. And while the career working woman category has grown significantly over the past three decades, the other segments are still sizable, unique, and important.

The male market is likewise diverse in both its attitudes and behaviors toward gender roles, work, and household chores.

Product Strategy Many products are losing their traditional gender typing. Guns, cars, motorcycles, computer games and equipment, golf equipment, financial services, and many other once-masculine products are now specifically designed with women in mind. The expanding wealth, independence, and purchase power of women, and the time pressure on them, make them an important target market. Consider the following:

*   Women-headed households are expected to represent 28 percent of all households in 2010. The Barbara K tool line targeted at women was launched in 2003 and had sales of $5 million in 2004. According to CEO Barbara Kavovit, "Women have made so many strides but can't fix things in their homes." The tools are designed to be stylish and functional, have special features targeting women such as cushioned handles, but don't come in "girly" colors.[93]

*   Assaults against women are a major social problem. Smith & Wesson launched Lady-Smith, a line of guns designed specifically for women. They found that "if a woman is going to pull out a gun for personal protection, she doesn't want a cute gun." So rather than "feminize" men's guns with colored handles, Smith & Wesson targeted a key success criterion by redesigning its guns to fit women's hands.

*   More women work more hours outside the home today than at any time in our history.[94] This has created great time pressures on most households. As one working mother says, "The poor kids have to make do with you know, canned ravioli, or fish sticks or whatever I can round up."[95] A wealth of time-saving products and services has emerged to meet this need. For example, General Mills' Betty Crocker brand has responded with products and a Web site that make meal planning and preparation easier. Illustration 3-9 demonstrates how companies are designing products to meet the need of reducing meal preparation time.

As women's roles have expanded, the consumption of potentially harmful products has become socially acceptable for women. This of course raises the ethical issue of targeting groups that have not historically been heavy users of products such as alcohol or tobacco.

Marketing Communications There is considerable research suggesting that males and females process and respond differently to various communications elements including

As time pressure has mounted for women, firms have responded with new products and positioning strategies.

Courtesy Barilla America, Inc.

sexual appeals, music, verbal style, and so forth.[96] As just one example, females respond more favorably to a "help-others" type of appeal for a charity, whereas males respond best to a "self-help" appeal.[97] This is caused by differing worldviews that affect a range of communications responses as well as consumption behaviors.

Men and women also consume different media. For example, while men and women are similar in their readership of news magazines, their top magazine category preferences vary dramatically:[98]

Women	Men
General women's	Automotive
Parenting/child rearing	General men's
Health	Fishing/hunting
Home/home Service	Sports
Epicurean	Motorcycles

Reprinted with permission from the February 2002 issue of American Demographics. Copyright Crain Communications Inc. 2004.

Since women are quite diverse as a group, marketers must also consider such factors as ethnicity, age, life stage, and employment status differences when designing marketing communications. For example, State Farm Insurance targets working mothers who have children or who are expecting a child as prospects for their life insurance products. Its ads

Fisher-Price designs the first diaper pail you can open without passing out.

Most diaper pails have a nice little fragrance tablet in the lid. But it's not *that* fragrance you usually notice first.

That's why the Fisher-Price® Diaper Pail has a unique odor barrier: an inner lid that helps keep odor from sneaking out, even when you open the top.

Our exclusive design makes diaper disposal a very tidy one-way task.

And so, when you're in the nursery, surprise! All you smell is fresh air.

A second, inner lid helps keep the room fresh.

Courtesy Fisher-Price.

in magazines such as *Working Mother, Working Woman,* and *American Baby* have featured a picture of a woman life insurance agent with her own child. The copy from one ad reads,

> A mother's love knows no bounds. And there's no better way to show how much you love them than with State Farm life insurance. Nobody knows better than Gail Coleman—a State Farm agent and mom. When she sits down with you to talk about life insurance, she knows you need a plan designed for working moms. One that will grow as your needs grow. And she's always there to answer your questions. So when it comes to life there are two things you can always count on. A mother's love and your State Farm agent. Like a good neighbor, State Farm is there.

Advertisements portraying women must be careful about offending any of the various segments.[99] For example, an ad that implied that housework was unimportant or that women who work outside the home are somehow superior to those who do not could insult traditional housewives. Ads that show women primarily as decoration or as clearly inferior to males tend to produce negative responses across all female segments.[100] Despite such negative reactions, many ads still use these tactics. However, some companies are hitting this issue straight on. Dove launched its "Real Beauty" campaign which features realistic depictions of women. This has been in response to idealized and unrealistic portrayals of women in advertising that have been shown to reduce self-esteem.

Finally, in terms of gender role portrayal, there are still relatively few ads showing men using products traditionally designed for women or performing tasks traditionally performed by women. Illustration 3-10 shows an exception. Given the increased acceptance of various activities across gender, such ads are likely to become increasingly common.

Retail Strategy   As we have seen, men are increasingly shopping for household and other products traditionally purchased by females,[101] and females are shopping for "masculine" products such as lawn mowers and power tools. In response to these changes, retailers such as Kmart have begun showing very masculine men shopping for household products at their stores, while stores such as Bloomingdales and Target carry power tools targeted at women such as the Barbara K line discussed earlier.

In addition, men and women react differently to various aspects of retail and service environments. For example, when there is a service failure, men appear to focus mostly on problem resolution, whereas women also focus on the process by which the problem is resolved. Being able to have a voice in the resolution process is much more important for women than men. Such differences need to be built into employee training programs.[102]

SUMMARY

American values have evolved and will continue to evolve. In terms of those values that influence an individual's relationship with *others,* Americans remain individualistic. We have substantially less of a masculine orientation now than in the past. We also place a greater value on older persons and diversity.

Values that affect our relationship to our *environment* have become somewhat more performance-oriented and slightly less oriented toward change. There is a strong and growing value placed on protecting the natural environment, and we increasingly value risk taking.

Self-oriented values have also undergone change. We place somewhat less emphasis on hard work as an end in itself and on sensual gratification, although we tend to desire immediate gratification considerably more than has been traditionally true. While religion is important and is perhaps becoming more so, America remains a relatively secular culture.

Americans assign a high value to the environment. Marketers have responded to this concern with *green marketing:* (1) developing products whose production, use, or disposition is less harmful to the environment than the traditional versions of the product; (2) developing products that have a positive impact on the environ-

ment; or (3) tying the purchase of a product to an environmental organization or event.

Cause-related marketing is marketing that ties a company and its products to an issue or cause with the goal of improving sales and corporate image while providing benefits to the cause. Companies associate with causes to create long-term relationships with their customers, building corporate and brand equity that should eventually lead to increased sales.

The *gay market* is estimated at 11 to 16 million people over the age of 18 with a purchase power of $610 billion. Many companies view the gay market as highly attractive and have committed considerable resources to targeting this market with specific products and promotional efforts. Supportive internal policies toward gay employees as well as support for important gay causes are among the critical factors in approaching this market.

Gender roles have undergone radical changes in the past 30 years. A fundamental shift has been for the female role to become more like the traditional male role. Male roles are also evolving, with men taking on what have traditionally been considered female tasks. Virtually all aspects of our society, including marketing activities, have been affected by these shifts.

KEY TERMS

Achievement role 101
Ascribed role 101
Cause-related marketing
  (CRM) 95
Cultural values 82

Gender 100
Gender identity 100
Gender role 100
Green marketing 93
Modern gender orientation 101

Sustainability 94
Traditional gender
  orientation 101
Voluntary simplicity 86

INTERNET EXERCISES

1. Visit a site such as the Internet Newspaper (www.trib.com/NEWS). What value does it have in helping track American values? What other sites are useful for this?

2. Search for a newsgroup that is relevant for understanding the following. Report on the insights that it can provide.
   a. American values in general
   b. Cause-related marketing
   c. Green marketing
   d. Gender roles

3. Visit www.publicagenda.org. Pick an issue that is relevant to one or more of the values discussed in this chapter and report on the data available relevant to that value.

4. Use the Internet to discover what, if any, cause-related marketing activities the following firms are involved with:
   a. Toyota
   b. Starbucks

   c. Estée Lauder Cosmetics
   d. A firm for which you would like to work

5. Evaluate an online green shopping mall or community (such as www.ecomall.com or www.envirolink.org). What value do these malls and communities provide consumers? Advertisers? What types of firms advertise here? How would you characterize their ads?

6. Use the Internet to explore key issues facing GLBT (gay, lesbian, bisexual, transgender) consumers (one useful site is the Human Rights Campaign at www.hrc.org).

7. Use the Internet to determine the role of women in purchasing the following:
   a. Houses
   b. Motorcycles
   c. Greeting cards

DDB LIFE STYLE STUDY™ DATA ANALYSES

1. What characterizes individuals with a traditional view of the female role? How do these individuals differ from those with a more modern view? (Use the DDB data in Tables 1B through 7B.)

2. Based on the data in the DDB Tables 1B through 7B, what characterizes individuals who believe that individuality is an important value to pass on to kids?

3. What characterizes consumers who are particularly responsive to green marketing? What are the marketing strategy implications of this? (See DDB data in Tables 1B through 7B.)

4. Examine the DDB data in Tables 1B through 7B. What characterizes individuals who are active recyclers? What are the marketing strategy implications of this?

REVIEW QUESTIONS

1. What is a *cultural value?* Do all members of a culture share cultural values?

2. Describe the current American culture in terms of each of the 18 values discussed in this chapter.

3. How is *voluntary simplicity* related to the materialism value? What are the marketing implications of voluntary simplicity? Do these implications vary by product class?

4. What is *green marketing?*

5. What values underlie green marketing?

6. What problems did the questionable use of environmental claims by some firms cause for consumers? For other firms? How did the Federal Trade Commission respond?

7. Describe the basic conflict between the environmental movement and many businesses.

8. What is *cause-related marketing?* Why is it often successful?

9. What are the major decisions a firm faces with respect to the gay market?

10. What is meant by *gender?*

11. What is *gender identity?*

12. What is a *gender role?*

13. How does an *ascribed role* differ from an *achievement role?*

14. What is happening to male and female gender roles in America?

15. What are the differences between a traditional and a modern gender role orientation?

16. Describe a segmentation system for the female market based on employment status and gender role orientation.

17. What are some of the major marketing implications of the changing role of women?

DISCUSSION QUESTIONS

18. Describe additional values you feel could, or should, be added to Figure 3-1. Describe the marketing implications of each.

19. Pick the three values you feel the authors of this book were most *in*accurate about in the chapter in describing the *current* American values. Justify your answers.

20. Pick the three values you feel the authors were most *in*accurate about in describing the *emerging* American values. Justify your answers.

21. Respond to the questions in Consumer Insight 3-1.

22. Which values are most relevant to the purchase or use of the following? Are they currently favorable or unfavorable for ownership/use? Are they shifting at all? If so, is the shift in a favorable or unfavorable direction?
    a. Electric toothbrush
    b. Christian Children's Fund contribution
    c. Financial investments (stocks, mutual funds, etc.)
    d. Sports car

    e. Tanning salon
    f. Visa card

23. Do you believe Americans' concern for the environment is a stronger value than their materialism?

24. What are the primary ethical issues involved in green marketing?

25. Respond to the questions in Consumer Insight 3-2.

26. Cause-related marketing is done to enhance a firm's sales or image. Some critics consider such marketing to be unethical. What is your position?

27. In which of the four categories of responders to cause-related marketing (see pages 96 and 97) are you? Why?

28. Suppose AT&T showed a gay couple using its long-distance service or P&G showed a gay couple using one of its laundry products in ads on network television. Is a backlash by those who do not accept the gay community a likely response? How are such consumers likely to respond? Why?

29. Do you think housewives may be defensive or sensitive about not having employment outside of the home? If so, what implications will this have for marketing practice?

30. Develop an advertisement for the following for each of the four female market segments described in the chapter (see pages 102 and 103).

a. Power tools
b. Online banking
c. Dentist
d. Breakfast cereal
e. Vacations
f. Cosmetics

APPLICATION ACTIVITIES

31. Find and copy or describe an advertisement for an item that reflects Americans' position on the following values.
    a. Active/Passive
    b. Material/Nonmaterial
    c. Hard work/Leisure
    d. Postponed/Immediate gratification
    e. Sensual gratification/Abstinence
    f. Religious/Secular
    g. Cleanliness
    h. Performance/Status
    i. Tradition/Change
    j. Risk taking/Security
    k. Problem solving/Fatalistic
    l. Admire/Overcome nature
    m. Individual/Collective
    n. Limited/Extended family
    o. Diversity/Uniformity
    p. Competition/Cooperation
    q. Youth/Age
    r. Masculine/Feminine

32. Interview a vegetarian and a person with a strong vegetarian orientation. What values influence their decision to adopt this eating pattern?

33. Interview a salesperson who has been selling the following for at least 10 years. See if this individual has noticed a change in the purchasing roles of women over time.
    a. Cellular phones
    b. Automobiles
    c. Computers
    d. Homes
    e. Financial services

34. Interview a career-oriented working wife and a traditional housewife of a similar age. Report on differences in attitudes toward shopping, products, and so forth.

35. Form a team of five. Have each team member interview five married adult males. Based on these interviews, develop a typology that classifies them by their attitude toward and participation in household or child-rearing activities.

36. Pick two different environmental activism segments (e.g., True Naturals versus Overwhelmed). Find one advertisement you think is particularly appropriate or effective for each. Copy or describe each ad and justify its selection.

37. Interview a salesperson for each of the following. Ascertain the interest shown in the item by males and females. Determine if males and females are concerned with different characteristics of the item and if they have different purchase motivations.
    a. Art
    b. Computers
    c. Golf clubs
    d. Pets
    e. Televisions
    f. Flowers

38. Interview 10 male and 10 female students. Ask each to describe the typical owner or consumer of the following. If they do not specify, ask for the gender of the typical owner. Then probe to find out why they think the typical owner is of the gender they indicated. Also determine the perceived marital and occupational status of the typical owner and the reasons for these beliefs.
    a. Dog
    b. Digital camera
    c. Large life insurance policy
    d. Power tools
    e. Habitat for Humanity contributor
    f. Motorcycle

REFERENCES

1. Sources include J. Batsell, "Seattle Basketball Guard to Appear on Local Nike Billboard," *Knight Ridder Tribune Business News,* September 30, 2003, p. 1; and information about the various associations garnered from their Web sites at www.wusa.com, www.wnba.com, and www.lpga.com.

2. From Ipsos's global consumer and civic trends reporting service, *World Monitor,* 2nd quarter, 2001. Profiled data were collected on Ipsos's *Global Express* omnibus survey in 34 countries in November–December 2000.

3. S. G. Edry, "No Longer Just Fun and Games," *American Demographics,* May 2001, p. 38.

4. See, e.g., M. W. Allen and S. H. Ng, "The Direct and Indirect Influences of Human Values on Product Ownership," *Journal of Economic Psychology,* February 1999, pp. 5–39.

5. This Consumer Insight is based on M. Grimm, "Veggie Delight," *American Demographics,* August 2000, p. 66; S. Janda and P. J. Trocchia, "Vegetarianism," *Psychology & Marketing,* December 2001, pp. 1205–40; S. Blake, "Vegetarian Food in the U.S.," *Just-Food,* July 2004, pp. 9–10; and K. Weisberg, "Vegetarian Delight," *Foodservice Director,* October 15, 2004, pp. 46–50.

6. H. Taylor, "While Most Americans Believe in God, Only 36% Attend a Religious Service Once a Month or More Often," *The Harris Poll®,* Number 59, October 15, 2003, at www.harrisinteractive.com.

7. B. A. Robinson, "How Many People Go Regularly to Weekly Religious Services?" Ontario Consultants on Religious Tolerance, November 26, 2001, at www.religioustolerance.org.

8. See P. S. La Barbera and Z. Gurhan, "The Role of Materialism, Religiosity, and Demographics in Subjective Well-Being," *Psychology & Marketing,* January 1997, pp. 71–97.

9. "New Survey Shows Religious Americans Less Likely to Support Compromise," press release by Public Agenda, January 23, 2005, at www.publicagenda.org.

10. Robinson, "How Many People Go Regularly to Weekly Religious Services?"

11. R. Gardyn, "Breaking the Rules of Engagement," *American Demographics,* July/August 2002, p. 35.

12. R. La Ferla, "Sex Doesn't Sell," *The Tuscaloosa News,* February 16, 2004, p. B1.

13. J. Flint, "Angry NFL Slams ABC's 'Desperate Housewives' Promo," *The Wall Street Journal Online,* November 17, 2004, at www.wsj.com.

14. "What (and Who) Is Really Cooking at Your House?" *Parade Magazine,* November 16, 2003, pp. 4–5.

15. S. Thompson, "Minor Indulgence Keeps Cookies from Tanking," *Advertising Age,* June 28, 2004, p. S-18.

16. See, e.g., "Paper or Plastic," *American Demographics,* May 2003, p. 14.

17. These statistics drawn from *Statistical Abstract of the United States* (Washington, DC: U.S. Census Bureau, 2004), Section 12, Labor Force, Employment, and Earnings, tables 582, 584, and 578, respectively.

18. A. Miller, "The Millennial Mind-Set," *American Demographics,* January 1999, pp. 62–63.

19. R. Gardyn, "Nowhere to Hide," *American Demographics,* July/August 2002, pp. 12–13.

20. S. Zavestoski, "The Social-Psychological Bases of Anticonsumption Attitudes," *Psychology & Marketing,* February 2002, p. 155.

21. A. Etzioni, "Voluntary Simplicity," *Journal of Economic Psychology* 19 (1998), pp. 619–43; Zavestoski, "The Social-Psychological Bases of Anticonsumption Attitudes"; and M. Craig-Lees and C. Hill, "Understanding Voluntary Simplifiers," *Psychology & Marketing,* February 2002, pp. 197–210.

22. See P. Paul, "Targeting Boomers," *American Demographics,* March 2003, pp. 24–26; and J. Consoli, "Where Have All the Young Men Gone?" *Mediaweek,* October 20, 2003, pp. 4–5.

23. M. Slatalla, "Overscheduled?" *Time,* July 24, 2000, p. 79.

24. T. Cahill, "Exotic Places Made Me Do It," *Outside,* March 2002, p. 60.

25. See J. P. Robinson and M. Milke, "Dances with Dust Bunnies," *American Demographics,* January 1997, pp. 37–40; and Miller, "The Millennial Mind-Set."

26. P. Tyre, "Clean Freaks," *Newsweek,* June 7, 2004, p. 42.

27. "Cash and Carry," *American Demographics,* May 2000, p. 45.

28. "Creativity at Work," *American Demographics,* December 2002/January 2003, pp. 22–23.

29. J. Lovell, "Burt Rutan," *Time,* April 18, 2005, p. 103.

30. "Earth in the Balance," *American Demographics,* January 2001, p. 24.

31. *Public Agenda Online,* February 28, 2002, at www.publicagenda.org.

32. D. J. Lipke, "Good for Whom?" *American Demographics,* January 2001, p. 37.

33. J. Ottman, "Environmental Branding Blocks Competitors," *Marketing News,* August 17, 1998, p. 8.

34. A. C. Cuneo, "What's in Store," *Advertising Age,* February 25, 2002, p. 1.

35. M. J. Dutta-Bergman and W. D. Wells, "The Values and Lifestyles of Idiocentrics and Allocentrics in an Individualistic Culture," *Journal of Consumer Psychology* 12, no. 3 (2002), pp. 231–42.

36. B. S. C. Liu, O. Furrer, and D. Sudharshan, "The Relationship between Culture and Behavioral Intentions toward Services," *Journal of Service Research,* November 2001, pp. 118–29.

37. J. Halliday, "Tuners Fit In with Customizer Fare," *Advertising Age,* May 31, 2004, p. S-8.

38. *For Goodness Sakes,* Public Agenda, 2001, at www.publicagenda.org.

39. "Americans See Themselves as More Respectful than They Were a Year Ago toward Cultures with Different Values," *Ipsos News Center,* press release, November 7, 2002, at www.ipsosna.com/news/pressrelease.

40. R. Suro, "Movement at Warp Speed," *American Demographics,* August 2000, pp. 61–64.

41. See, e.g., C. A. Lin, "Cultural Values Reflected in Chinese and American Television Advertising," *Journal of Advertising,* Winter 2001, pp. 83–94.

42. Miller, "The Millennial Mind-Set," p. 65.

43. E. Day and M. R. Stafford, "Age-related Cues in Retail Services Advertising," *Journal of Retailing,* Summer 1997, pp. 211–33.

44. C. R. Wiles, J. A. Wiles, and A. Tjernlund, "The Ideology of Advertising," *Journal of Advertising Research,* May–June 1996, pp. 57–66.

45. For a discussion, see M. Carrigan and I. Szmigin, "The Usage and Portrayal of Older Consumers in Contemporary Consumer Advertising," *Journal of Marketing Practice* 4, no. 8 (1998), pp. 231–48.

46. J. Fetto and D. J. Lipke, "Gender Bias," *American Demographics,* March 2001, p. 80.

47. J. Rosenberg, "Brand Loyalty Begins Early," *Advertising Age,* February 12, 2001, p. S2.

48. J. Ottman, "Innovative Marketers Give New Products the Green Light," *Marketing News,* March 1998, p. 10.

49. This and additional information on the environmental practices of these companies is available through their corporate Web sites.

50. S. W. Colford, "FTC Green Guidelines May Spark Ad Efforts," *Advertising Age,* August 3, 1992, p. 11. See also D. L. Scammon and R. N. Mayer, "Agency Review of Environmental Marketing Claims," *Journal of Advertising,* Summer 1995, pp. 33–54.

51. "Environmental Groups Unveil Eco-Friendly Coffee Guidelines," *Gourmet News,* July 2001, p. 5; and K. McLaughlin, "Is Your Grocery List Politically Correct?" *The Wall Street Journal,* February 17, 2004, p. D1.

52. See J. A. Lee and S. J. S. Holden, "Understanding the Determinants of Environmentally Conscious Behavior," *Psychology & Marketing,* August 1999, pp. 373–92; and A. Biswas et al., "The Recycling Cycle," *Journal of Public Policy & Marketing,* Spring 2000, pp. 93–105.

53. J. Cohen and J. Darian, "Disposable Products and the Environment," *Research in Consumer Behavior* 9 (2000), pp. 227–57; H.-K. Bang et al., "Consumer Concern, Knowledge, Belief, and Attitude toward Renewable Energy," *Psychology & Marketing,* June 2000, pp. 449–68; R. Gardyn, "Being Green," *American Demographics,* September 2002, pp. 10–11; and R. Gardyn, "Eco-Friend or Foe?" *American Demographics,* October 2003, pp. 12–13.

54. J. A. Ottman, "Green Marketing, Eco-innovation and Your Consumer," available at www.greenmarketing.com/articles/Green-Graveyard.html.

55. This insight based on M. Grimm, "Earth Crunch," *American Demographics,* June 2002, pp. 46–47; L. Guyer, "Hybrids Soar via Word-of-Mouth," *Advertising Age,* February 21, 2005, p. 36; K. Greenberg, "Green Is Good," *Brandweek,* January 3, 2005, pp. 16–20; "The Environment," *Public Agenda,* accessed April 18, 2005, at www. publicagenda.org/issues; and L.

Armstrong, "Are You Ready for a Hybrid?" and D. Welch and C. Dawson, "Itching to Ditch the Slow Lane," both in *BusinessWeek,* April 25, 2005, pp. 118–26 and p. 126, respectively.

56. See, e.g., P. S. Bronn and A. B. Vrioni, "Corporate Social Responsibility and Cause-Related Marketing," *International Journal of Advertising,* no. 2 (2001), pp. 207–21.

57. "Multi-Year Study Finds 21% Increase in Americans Who Say Corporate Support for Social Issues is Important in Building Trust," Cone Incorporated Press Release, December 8, 2004, at www.coneinc.com.

58. See also M. Strahilevitz, "The Effects of Product Type and Donation Magnitude on Willingness to Pay More for a Charity-Linked Brand," *Journal of Consumer Psychology,* no. 3 (1999), pp. 215–41; M. J. Barone, A. D. Miyazaki, and K. A. Taylor, "The Influence of Cause-Related Marketing on Consumer Choice," *Journal of the Academy of Marketing Science,* Spring 2000, pp. 248–62; and S. Sen and C. B. Bhattacharya, "Does Doing Good Always Lead to Doing Better?" *Journal Marketing Research,* May 2001, pp. 225–43.

59. "The Growth of Cause Marketing," available from Cause Marketing Forum, accessed April 22, 2005, at www.causemarketingforum.com.

60. D. J. Webb and L. A. Mohr, "A Typology of Consumer Responses to Cause-Related Marketing," *Journal of Public Policy and Marketing,* Fall 1998, pp. 226–38.

61. R. P. Hamlin and T. Wilson, "The Impact of Cause Branding on Consumer Reactions to Products," *Journal of Marketing Management,* September 2004, pp. 663–81; and J. W. Pracejus and G. D. Olsen, "The Role of Brand/Cause Fit in the Effectiveness of Cause-Related Marketing Campaigns," *Journal of Business Research* 57 (2004), pp. 635–40.

62. Additional information about these programs can be found on each company's Web site. See also the Cause Marketing Forum at www.causemarketingforum.com.

63. "Gay Rights: Acceptance of Homosexuality Has Grown Significantly" *Public Agenda Online,* accessed April 18, 2005, at www.publicagenda.org.

64. "Gay Rights: Seven in 10 Americans Say They Would Favor Hate Crime Laws to Protect Gays and Lesbians," *Public Agenda Online,* accessed April 18, 2005, at www.publicagenda. org; and "Everything but the Ring," *American Demographics,* December 2002/January 2003, p. 20.

65. Size and income estimates based on D. M. Smith and G. J. Gates, *Gay and Lesbian Families in the United States* (Washington, DC: Human Rights Campaign, August 22, 2001); and "Gay Buying Power Projected at $610 Billion in 2005," *Witeck-Combs Communications,* press release, January 31, 2005, at www.witeckcombs.com.

66. M. Wilke, "Ads Targeting Gays Rely on Real Results," *Advertising Age,* June 22, 1998, p. 3.

67. J. Halliday, "GayRide," *Advertising Age,* February 25, 2002, p. 18.

68. D. L. Vence, "Pride Power," *Marketing News,* September 1, 2004, pp. 1 and 13.

69. L. Koss-Feder, "Out and About," *Marketing News,* May 25, 1998, pp. 1 and 20.

70. *2004 Gay Press Report* (Mountainside, NJ: 11th Annual Report by Prime Access Inc. and Rivendell Media Company Inc., 2004), available at www.gaymarket.com/agency_reports.html; see also S. Yin, "Coming Out in Print," *American Demographics,* February 2003, pp. 18–21.

71. R. Greenspan, "Advertisers May Find Gay Dollars Online," July 30, 2003, at www.clickz.com.

72. Information from corporate Web site at www.planetoutinc.com.

73. *2004 Gay Press Report;* see also S. M. Kates, "Making the Ad Perfectly Queer," *Journal of Advertising,* Spring 1999, pp. 25–35.

74. R. Gardyn, "A Market Kept in the Closet," *American Demographics,* November 2001, pp. 37–42; see also, J. J. Burnett, "Gays," *Journal of Advertising Research,* January 2000, pp. 75–83.

75. R. Greenspan, "Gays Access News, Influenced by Ads," May 17, 2004, at www.clickz.com.

76. S. Bhat, T. W. Leigh, and D. L. Wardlow, "The Effect of Consumer Prejudices on Ad Processing," *Journal of Advertising,* Winter 1998, pp. 9–28; S. A. Grier and A. M. Brumbaugh, "Noticing Cultural Differences," *Journal of Advertising,* Spring 1999, pp. 79–91; J. L. Aaker, A. M. Brumbaugh, and S. A. Grier, "Nontarget Market and Viewer Distinctiveness," *Journal of Consumer Psychology,* no. 3 (2000), pp. 127–40; and G. Oakenfull and T. Greenlee, "The Three Rules of Crossing Over from Gay Media to Mainstream Media Advertising," *Journal of Business Research* 57 (2004), pp. 1276–85.

77. For these and other statistics go to the *About 4-Wheel Drive/Offroading* Web site at http://4wheeldrive.about.com.

78. M. Powell, "Eye on Footwear," *Sporting Goods Business,* December 2002, p. 38.

79. J. B. Bernstal, "The Power of the Purse," *ABA Bank Marketing,* November 2004, pp. 18–23.

80. E. Fischer and S. J. Arnold, "Sex, Gender Identity, Gender Role Attitudes, and Consumer Behavior," *Psychology & Marketing,* March 1994, pp. 163–82; see also K. M. Palan, C. S. Areni, and P. Kiecker, "Gender Role Incongruity and Memorable Gift Exchange Experiences," in *Advances in Consumer Research,* ed. M. Gilly and J. Meyers-Levy (Provo, UT: Association for Consumer Research, 2001), pp. 51–57.

81. See P. Ireland, *What Women Want* (New York: E. P. Dutton, 1996); D. J. Swiss, *Women Breaking Through* (Princeton: Peterson's/Pacesetter Books, 1996); and P. McCorduck and N. Ramsey, *The Futures of Women* (Reading, MA: Addison-Wesley, 1996).

82. J. S. Grigsby, "Women Change Places," *American Demographics,* November 1992, p. 48; and N. Speulda and M. McIntosh, *Global Gender Gaps,* Pew Research Center for the People & the Press, Commentary, released May 13, 2004, at http://people-press.org/commentary/display.php3?AnalysisID=90.

83. "Child Care: Most People Say Fathers Can Be Just as Caring as Mothers and that Women Should Not Return to Their Traditional Roles," *Public Agenda Online,* accessed April 24, 2005, at www.publicagenda.org.

84. "The Family," *Public Agenda Online,* accessed February 28, 2002, at www.publicagenda.org.

85. "Child Care: Most Women Say that Mothers Who Work Outside the Home Are under More Stress than Mothers Who Stay Home and Most Mothers Say They Would Prefer to Stay at Home," *Public Agenda Online,* accessed April 24, 2005, at www.publicagenda.org.

86. P. Paul, "Whose Job Is This Anyway?" *Time,* October 4, 2004, p. 83.

87. J. Fetto, "Are Men the New Women?" *Forecast,* October 2002, pp. 7–8.

88. P. Paul, "Whose Job Is This Anyway?"

89. See, e.g., M. Posig and J. Kickul, "Work-Role Expectations and Work Family Conflict," *Women in Management Review* 19, no. 7/8 (2004), pp. 373–86; J. Warner, "Mommy Madness," *Newsweek,* February 21, 2005, p. 42; and "The Female Midlife Crisis," *The Wall Street Journal,* April 7, 2005, p. D1.

90. A. Taylor, "Many Fathers Begin to Stay at Home with Children," *Knight Ridder Tribune Business News,* June 20, 2004, p. 1.

91. A. Rock, "From Two Incomes to One," *Money,* January 2005, p. 34.

92. These segments are similar to the four categories popularized by Bartos. See C. M. Schaninger, M. C. Nelson, and W. D. Danko, "An Empirical Evaluation of the Bartos Model," *Journal of Advertising Research,* May 1993, pp. 49–63; and R. Bartos, "Bartos Responds to 'The Bartos Model,'" *Journal of Advertising Research,* January 1994, pp. 54–56.

93. A. Tsao, "Retooling Home Improvement," *BusinessWeek Online,* February 15, 2005, at www.businessweek.com.

94. See J. Larson, "The New Homemakers," *American Demographics,* September 1997, pp. 45–50.

95. C. J. Thompson, "Caring Consumers," *Journal of Consumer Research,* March 1996, pp. 388 and 395–96.

96. See, e.g., L. D. Wolin, "Gender Issues in Advertising," *Journal of Advertising Research,* March 2003, pp. 111–29.

97. F. F. Brunel and M. R. Nelson, "Explaining Gender Responses to 'Help-Self' and 'Help-Others' Charity Ad Appeals," *Journal of Advertising,* Fall 2000, pp. 15–28.

98. From Simmons Market Research Bureau, found in A. S. Wellner, "The Female Persuasion," *American Demographics,* February 2002, p. 25.

99. See L. J. Jaffe, "The Unique Predictive Ability of Sex-Role Identity in Explaining Women's Response to Advertising," *Psychology & Marketing,* September 1994, pp. 467–82; J. B. Ford and M. S. LaTour, "Contemporary Female Perspectives of Female Role Portrayals in Advertising," *Journal of Current Issues and Research in Advertising,* Spring 1996, pp. 81–95; and R. Widgery, M. G. Angur, and R. Nataraajan, "The Impact of Employment Status on Married Women's Perceptions of Advertising Message Appeals," *Journal of Advertising Research,* January 1997, pp. 54–62.

100. M. S. LaTour, T. L. Henthorne, and A. J. Williams, "Is Industrial Advertising Still Sexist?" *Industrial Marketing Management,*

1998, pp. 247–55; and M. Y. Jones, A. J. S. Stanaland, and B. D. Gelb, "Beefcake and Cheesecake," *Journal of Advertising,* Summer 1998, pp. 33–51.

101. For a description and theory of male shopping behavior, see C. Otnes and M. A. McGrath, "Perceptions and Realities of Male Shopping Behavior," *Journal of Retailing,* Spring 2001, pp. 111–37.

102. J. R. McColl-Kennedy, C. S. Daus, and B. A. Sparks, "The Role of Gender in Reactions to Service Failure and Recovery," *Journal of Service Research,* August 2003, pp. 66–82; see also, A. S. Mattila, A. A. Grandey, and G. M. Fisk, "The Interplay of Gender and Affective Tone in Service Encounter Satisfaction," *Journal of Service Research,* November 2003, pp. 136–43.

© Shooting Star.

4

The Changing American Society: Demographics and Social Stratification

■ How did a movie tentatively entitled *Cheer Fever* and forecast to be a financial disaster become the remarkably successful ($17.4 million in the first week) teenage movie *Bring It On?* Initial tests showed that 62 percent of its target (teens) said they would "definitely not" see a movie about cheerleading. Universal wanted to repeat the success of *American Pie* with the movie, but it lacked its raunchy sexual jokes and edgy content. As Universal's head of marketing stated: "With that title, we are saying, 'We are the cheerleading movie, and we know that 62 percent of you reject us, so now go find something else to do that weekend.'"

Universal decided to play up the overall high school experience in the movie and changed its name to *Made You Look*. The movie's one-sheet marketing poster showed the cheerleaders in a traditional cheerleading position but wearing their street clothes. "We chose to shoot them as human beings." This positioning was also a failure.

In reviewing the movie for marketing options, an executive noticed a somewhat buried subplot about a rivalry between the white cheerleading squad from the suburbs and a black squad from the inner city. A decision was made to rename the film *Bring It On* and to position it as a contest between these two squads even though it would mean substantial reshooting. This focus on the competition and the infusion of the black squad and its hip-hop culture produced huge enthusiasm among white, black, and Hispanic girls.

Next an intense marketing campaign began. The studio promoted Kirsten Dunst, the star, on the cover of *Maxim*. Over $10 million was spent on media advertising during such teen TV favorites as "Buffy the Vampire Slayer" and MTV as well as an aggressive radio campaign. Extensive grassroots marketing was done at Britney Spears and Christina Aguilera concerts.

Internet efforts were focused on Alloy.com. Alloy created a microsite for the movie, ran a sweepstakes, and sent e-zines telling teens where and when the movie's stars would appear. Ethnic sites such as 360hiphop.com, BlackVoices.com, and Hookt.com were also used. Universal also partnered with malls around the country to arrange cheerleading contests and fashion shows.

Seven days before the opening, male teens still showed no great interest in seeing the film. The studio quickly prepared a racy spot aimed at young men and aired it on a preseason "Monday Night Football" game and on ESPN2. This succeeded in generating considerable interest among teenage males.[1]

Turning the apparent disaster *Cheer Fever* into the successful *Bring It On* required substantial knowledge not only of teens' movie preferences but of how and where to communicate with them. The approach used with this age group would not succeed with older groups, since different generations have different values and ways of living. This is one aspect of demographics.

In this chapter, we will discuss the closely related concepts of demographics and social status. As we will see, several demographic variables—income, education, and occupation—serve as dimensions of social status, and they combine with others to determine social class. We will first take a broad look at the demographics of the American society, with particular attention to age and its related concept, generations. Then we will consider social status and the role that demographics play in social status.

DEMOGRAPHICS

Demographics *describe a population in terms of its size, distribution, and structure* (see also Chapter 2). Demographics influence consumption behaviors both directly and by affecting other attributes of individuals, such as their personal values and decision styles.[2] Consider the demographics of the devoted high-end coffee shop crowd:

> Today's most devoted coffee shop patrons are 18- to 34-year-olds and those with annual incomes over $75,000. Forty-two percent of the 18- to 34-year-olds and 46 percent of those who earn more than $75,000 say that when they drink coffee away from home, they head straight for Starbucks-like shops, compared with just 32 percent of all away-from-home coffee drinkers. The younger folks are attracted to the coffee-bar atmosphere, music selections and what tends to be a younger customer base, while the wealthy simply want the best.[3]

Not surprisingly, marketers frequently segment markets on the basis of demographics and use that information to select appropriate media and develop effective promotional themes.

Population Size and Distribution

The population of the United States is approximately 298 million today and is expected to surpass 320 million by 2015. The population has grown steadily since 1960 despite a declining birthrate because of longer life expectancies, the large baby boom generation moving through their child-bearing years, and significant immigration. This growth has not been even throughout the United States, nor is it expected to be so in the future. For example, from 2005 to 2015, states like Arizona, Nevada, Texas, and Florida are predicted to grow by at least 15 percent. Growth in these states is being fueled in part by the retirement and migration of older consumers. In contrast, states like New York, Ohio, Iowa, and North Dakota are expected to grow by less than 2 percent.[4] As we discuss in the next chapter, regions of the country serve as important subcultures whose members have unique tastes and preferences. Several examples of these differences are shown in Figure 4-1.

Occupation

Occupation is probably the most widely applied single cue we use to initially evaluate and define individuals we meet. This should be obvious when you stop to think of the most common bit of information we seek from a new acquaintance: "What do you do?" Almost invariably we want to know someone's occupation to make inferences about his or her probable lifestyle. Occupation is strongly associated with education (which to some extent determines occupation) and income (which to some extent is determined by occupation).

One's occupation provides status and income. In addition, the type of work one does and the types of individuals one works with over time also directly influence one's values, lifestyle, and all aspects of the consumption process. Differences in consumption between occupational classes have been found for products such as beer, detergents, dog food, shampoo, and paper towels. Media preferences, hobbies, and shopping patterns are also influenced by occupational class (see Table 4-1).

Education

Approximately 85 percent of Americans have a high school degree, and 27 percent have completed college. Education is increasingly critical for a "family wage" job. Traditional high-paying manufacturing jobs that required relatively little education are rapidly disappearing. High-paying jobs in the manufacturing and service sectors today require technical

TABLE 4-1

Occupational Influences on Consumption

	Administrative/Managerial	Technical/Clerical/Sales	Precision/Craft
Products			
Domestic beer	104	79	183
Cigarettes	82	102	125
Diet colas	118	102	85
Laptop/notebook	223	128	72
Activities			
Sailing	192	90	97
Archery	101	90	221
Listen to music	112	110	93
Movies (frequent)	104	121	89
Shopping			
Wal-Mart	96	101	106
Ann Taylor	197	129	32
Olive Garden	133	128	80
Bonanza	82	81	164
Media			
Sports Afield	99	54	196
Outside	215	68	77
Jazz radio	191	85	65
Religious radio	91	110	80

Note: 100 = Average level of use, purchase, or consumption.

Source: *Mediamark Reporter 2002—University* (New York: Mediamark Research Inc., March 2002).

FIGURE 4-1   A Tale of Three Cities

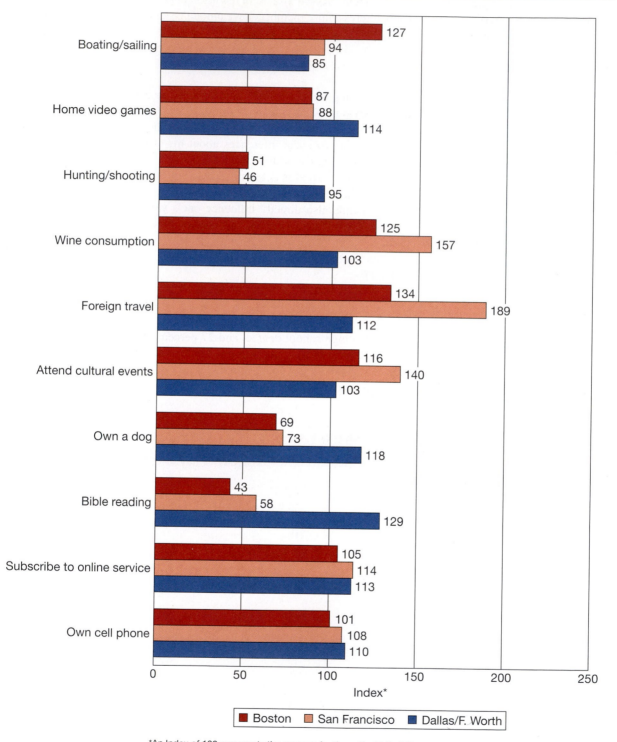

*An Index of 100 represents the average for the entire United States

Source: Reprinted from the 2004 edition of "The Lifestyle Analyst," published by SRDS, with data supplied by Polk.

skills, abstract reasoning, and the ability to read and learn new skills rapidly. Individuals without these skills are generally forced into minimum wage and often part-time jobs, which will rarely keep a family above the poverty level.[5] As the following data show, education clearly drives income in today's economy.

Since individuals tend to have spouses with similar education levels, these differences are magnified when spousal income is considered.

Mean Income: Workers 18 and Older[6]

Education Level	Males	Females
No high school degree	$22,091	$13,459
High school degree	32,673	21,141
Associate's degree	42,392	27,341
Bachelor's degree	63,503	37,909
Master's degree	73,629	47,368
Professional degree	138,827	61,583

Education influences what one can purchase by partially determining one's income and occupation. It also influences how one thinks, makes decisions, and relates to others.[7] Those with a limited education are generally at a disadvantage not only in earning money but in spending it wisely.[8] Not surprisingly, education has a strong influence on one's tastes and preferences, as shown in Table 4-2. However, education seldom provides a complete explanation for consumption patterns. For example, a lawyer earning $30,000 per year as a public defender will have a different lifestyle from a lawyer earning $250,000 per year in private practice, despite similar educational backgrounds.

	Graduated College	Attended College	Graduated High School	Did Not Graduate High School
Products				
Champagne	148	107	82	63
Laptop/notebook	206	116	56	24
Soy sauce	124	110	91	73
Shortening (frequent)	49	81	115	164
Activities				
Mountain biking	165	135	65	30
Lottery (frequent)	84	100	115	93
Wrestling (attended)	67	108	107	117
Recycle products	137	110	89	60
Shopping				
Ames	84	82	125	102
Eddie Bauer	180	109	69	44
Ponderosa	70	104	126	83
TGI Friday's	143	114	83	55
Media				
National Enquirer	44	105	126	118
Men's Journal	154	136	74	23
Nick at Nite	77	115	110	88
CNN	133	106	90	66

TABLE 4-2

Education Level Influences on Consumption

Note: 100 = Average level of use, purchase, or consumption.

Source: *Mediamark Reporter 2002—University* (New York: Mediamark Research Inc., March 2002).

Income

A household's income level combined with its accumulated wealth determines its purchasing power. While many purchases are made on credit, one's ability to buy on credit is ultimately determined by one's current and past income (wealth).

Most of American history has been characterized by consistently increasing real per capita income. For most middle- and lower-income Americans, this increasing trend stopped in the 1980s and household incomes were stagnant or declining until they increased again in 1995.[9] The economic boom from 1995 through 2000 enhanced the purchasing power of most Americans. The economic downturn at the beginning of this century reduced the wealth of many Americans, reduced the earnings of others, and, along with the September 11, 2001, attack on the World Trade Center, created economic uncertainty for most. The resultant downturn in consumer spending hurt manufacturers and retailers alike.

The economy has shown positive signs, however, with retail sales increasing by almost 8 percent between 2001 and 2003, and new home sales at historical highs.[10] In addition, even consumers with modest incomes want to "trade up" to luxury brands and are willing to make trade-offs to do so. For example, a consumer might shop at Wal-Mart for staple items in order to be able to afford a more expensive Gucci watch. Companies, in a movement termed **class to mass,** have responded by expanding opportunities for less affluent consumers to afford luxury. According to one expert, consumers are looking for affordable or "new luxury" goods:

> New luxury goods range in price from a $6 Tuscan chicken sandwich at Panera to a $26,000 Mercedes CLK. What they have in common is that they enable less affluent consumers to trade up to higher levels of quality, taste, and aspiration. These are luxuries that continue to sell even when the economy is shaky, because they often meet very powerful emotional needs.[11]

Income *enables* purchases but *does not generally cause or explain them.* For example, a college professor or lawyer may have the same income as a truck driver or plumber. Nonetheless, it is likely that their consumption processes for a variety of products will differ. Occupation and education directly influence preferences for products, media, and activities; income provides the means to acquire them.[12] Thus, income is generally more effective as a segmentation variable when used in conjunction with other demographic variables.

An example of using income with other demographic variables is provided by Vons, a West Coast grocery chain. Vons analyzed the demographics and purchase patterns of consumers in the shopping area of each of its outlets. It found that the income and age distribution, along with ethnicity, of each area had a major influence on the types and amounts of items purchased at each store. As a result, it moved from a single store format to five distinct store types based on the shopping area demographics, particularly income and ethnicity.[13]

How wealthy one feels may be as important as actual income for some purchases.[14] **Subjective discretionary income (SDI)** is *an estimate by the consumer of how much money he or she has available to spend on nonessentials.* Several studies show that SDI adds considerable predictive power to actual total family income (TFI) measures.[15]

Age

Proper age positioning is critical for many products. Age carries with it culturally defined behavioral and attitudinal norms.[16] It affects our self-concept and lifestyles.[17] Not surprisingly, age influences the consumption of products ranging from beer to toilet paper to vacations. Our age shapes the media we use, where we shop, how we use products, and how we think and feel about marketing activities.[18] Table 4-3 illustrates some consumption behaviors that vary with age. Illustration 4-1 shows an ad with the type of humor appreciated by many young adults.

Tougher than you.

www.bolle.com

bollé

Performance Eyewear

Courtesy Bushnell Performance Optics.

ILLUSTRATION 4-1

Age affects how individuals think, feel, and behave. The humor in this ad would be appreciated more by younger consumers than by older consumers.

TABLE 4-3

Age Influences on Consumption

	18–24	25–34	35–44	45–54	55–64	65+
Products						
Tequila	168	130	114	83	66	33
Scotch	71	84	95	126	122	106
Laptop/notebook	107	95	133	142	82	23
Laserdisc players	127	124	115	95	98	35
Activities						
Barbecuing	67	106	134	130	103	37
Aerobics	140	125	115	104	64	38
Cruise ship	61	78	88	128	139	117
Volunteer work	80	83	116	122	100	90
Shopping						
J.C. Penney	84	88	104	113	109	102
Banana Republic	190	157	102	75	41	26
Hooters	176	159	102	92	44	12
Marie Callender's	64	80	91	129	153	96
Media						
Reader's Digest	65	72	93	116	124	137
Maxim	337	200	52	31	6	1
Comedy Central	194	140	108	83	46	23
CNN	55	80	99	119	126	121

Note: 100 = Average level of use, purchase, or consumption.

Source: *Mediamark Reporter 2002—University* (New York: Mediamark Research Inc., March 2002).

The estimated age distributions (millions in each age category) of the U.S. population for 2005 and 2015 are[19]

Age Category	2005	2015	Percentage Change
<10	38.3	41.5	+8.3%
10–19	41.6	41.1	−1.2
20–29	38.5	42.5	+10.4
30–39	38.6	39.9	+3.3
40–49	44.9	39.4	−12.2
50–59	36.5	43.3	+18.7
60–69	22.9	33.9	+47.9
>69	26.3	30.5	+16.2

Even a quick look at these age distributions indicates that momentous changes are occurring. Some of the profound marketing implications of these changes are

- Demand for children's products such as toys, diapers, and clothes will grow moderately, as the population less than 10 years of age will grow 8 percent over this period.
- Products consumed by twentysomethings will increase moderately in demand. Since this is the prime age of household formation and childbirth, this group will have an important impact on the overall market. Demand for higher education, homes, family cars, insurance, and so forth should be strong.
- Products consumed by those aged 40 to 49 will decline as this population group grows smaller. This will have significant implications for such industries as financial services for which this is a key age group.
- The largest impact will be caused by the huge increase (11 million) in the number of individuals between 60 and 69. These will represent primarily one- or two-person households, with many retired or near retirement. Vacations, restaurants, second homes, and financial services aimed at this market should flourish.
- The large growth in the number of individuals over 69 will also create many opportunities for marketers ranging from beauty aids and travel and leisure to retirement homes and health care.

Age groups as defined by the census and as presented above can be useful as a means of understanding and segmenting a market. For example, P&G recently launched the Oil of Olay ProVital line targeting women over 50 years old, the fastest-growing segment of the population. The spokeswoman for the product was 51-year-old actress Anne Roberts. However, the product line will not be positioned as just an antiwrinkle solution:

Age is just a number. Many women 50 and over have told us that as they age, they feel more confident, wiser, and freer than ever before. These women are redefining beauty. Our research shows that when it comes to skin, dryness and vitality are their key concerns, not just a few wrinkles.[20]

While age groups as defined by the census are often a useful way to understand and segment a market, analyzing age cohort groups or generations will often provide more meaningful segments and marketing strategies. This approach is covered in depth in the next section. In addition, as Consumer Insight 4-1 describes, age as determined by the calendar may not be the best concept of age.

Cognitive Age: As Young as You Feel?

One's age is a chronological fact but, more important, a social construct.[21] That is, the time that has passed since one's birth is directly observable and uniform. However, the meaning of age, how it is perceived, the behaviors and attitudes expected at differing ages, how one feels about aging, and so forth are constructed by cultures and within cultures by individuals.

> I'm not my mother's 52. I'm not in the second half of my life. I'm in the first chapter of a whole new book.

This quote reflects the increasingly recognized fact that, in the United States at least, as consumers' chronological age increases, their subjective or cognitive age lags behind. In fact, for older consumers, cognitive age is often 10 to 15 years less than chronological age. And, at least for some behaviors, it appears that you are indeed as young as you feel.

Cognitive age is defined as *one's perceived age, a part of one's self-concept.* It is most commonly measured by the following scale.

1. I *feel* like I'm in my _____.
2. I *look* like I'm in my _____.
3. My *interests* are those of a person in his/her _____.
4. I *do* the things a person does in his/her _____.

Respondents are asked to indicate a decade for each question (20s, 30s, 40s, etc.). The midpoint of the decade given in response to each question is used to compute an average age based on the four responses. This is one's cognitive age. Though both the adequacy of this operationalization and the validity of the concept itself have been challenged, it is gaining widespread use in marketing.

While cognitive age varies with chronological age, it is also influenced by such factors as one's health, education, income, and social support—the more of each, the lower the cognitive age. In turn, it affects a wide range of attitudes and consumption behaviors.

Cognitive age, while an artificial concept, is one with which people readily identify. Consumers have no trouble indicating how old they feel rather than how old they "are."

Critical Thinking Questions

1. Cognitive age is measured on four dimensions. What additional dimensions, if any, do you think should be added?
2. Do you think cognitive age is a valid concept? Why?
3. If the meaning of age is a cultural concept, how would the concept and measurement of cognitive age change across cultures?
4. How can marketers use cognitive age?

UNDERSTANDING AMERICAN GENERATIONS

A **generation** or **age cohort** is *a group of persons who have experienced a common social, political, historical, and economic environment.* Age cohorts, because their shared histories produce unique shared values and behaviors, often function as unique market segments.[22]

Cohort analysis is *the process of describing and explaining the attitudes, values, and behaviors of an age group as well as predicting its future attitudes, values, and behaviors.*[23] A critical fact uncovered by cohort analysis is that each generation behaves differently from other generations as it passes through various age categories. For example, in 2010 the baby boom generation will be entering retirement. However, it would be a mistake to assume that retiring baby boomers will behave like the pre-Depression generation does today. The forces that shaped the lives of these generations were different, and their behaviors will differ throughout their life cycles. As just one example, the computer and Internet skills that baby boomers have acquired will make them much heavier Internet

Targeting the Mature Market

One approach to segmenting older consumers is geron-tographics, based on the theory that people change their outlook on life when they experience major life events such as becoming a grandparent, retiring, losing a spouse, or developing chronic health conditions. Individuals who have confronted similar events are likely to have a similar outlook on life and, given similar economic resources, similar lifestyles. Gerontographics has identified four segments of the mature market. Interestingly, age is not the major distinguishing factor across segments (for example, frail recluses can be in any age range from 55 and above), which attests to the power of life events, health, and financial status.[24]

Healthy Indulgers   This segment (7 million and rapidly growing as boomers age) is physically and mentally healthy, has the most in common with the baby boomers than any other segment, and will increasingly be composed of baby boomers as they age. Both spouses are generally still alive. They have prepared for retirement both financially and psychologically. They are basically content and set to enjoy life. They often sell their fairly large homes and move into apartments, townhouses, or condos. They like activities, convenience, personal service, and high-tech home appliances. They are a strong part of the market for cruises and group travel.

Ailing Outgoers   These people (18 million) have experienced health problems which limit their physical abilities and frequently their financial capability. Ailing outgoers are a key market for retirement communities and assisted-living housing. People in this group acknowledge their limits, maintain positive self-esteem, and seek to get the most out of life. Independence and socializing are important as is remaining stylish in their dress. However, limited funds are an issue as are physical limitations. Thus, value pricing and discounts are viewed positively as are ease and convenience such as Velcro fasteners on clothes.

Healthy Hermits   People in this group (20 million) retain their physical health, but life events, often the death of a spouse, have reduced their self-concept. They have reacted by becoming withdrawn. Many then resent the isolation and the feeling that they are expected to act like old people. This group does not want to stand out. They prefer clothing styles that are popular with other seniors. They will pay a premium for well-known brands. They tend to stay in the homes in which they raised their families, and they are an important part of the do-it-yourself market.

Frail Recluses   Those in this segment (18 million) have accepted their old-age status and have adjusted

users in their retirement years than is currently true of their parents, who in many cases were bypassed by the most recent technology revolution.

In the following sections, we will examine the six generations that compose the primary American market.[25] It is important to emphasize that generation is only one factor influencing behavior and the differences within generations are often larger than the differences across generations. In addition, generations do not have sharp boundaries. Those near the age breaks between generations often do not clearly belong to either generation.

The Pre-Depression Generation

The pre-Depression generation is composed of those individuals born before 1930. Some 18 million Americans are in this generation. These individuals grew up in traumatic times. Most were children during the Depression and entered young adulthood during World War II. They have witnessed radical social, economic, and technological change. As a group, they are conservative and concerned with financial and personal security.

As with all generations, the pre-Depression generation is composed of many distinct segments, and marketing to it requires a strategy that incorporates such factors as gender, their lifestyles to reflect reduced physical capabilities and social roles. They focus on becoming spiritually stronger. Frail recluses may have been in any one of the other categories at an earlier age. They tend to stay at home, and many require home and lawn care services. They are a major market for health care products, home exercise and health testing equipment, and emergency response systems. Locational convenience is often a critical factor for this group.

One recent study found striking differences across these market segments in terms of how they choose physicians and surgeons. The following table examines the importance of several key criteria (numbers represent percentage in each group who indicate that the criterion is important):[26]

Not surprisingly, what drives patronage for one group is not necessarily a key factor for others, a finding that is true across a variety of products and services including restaurants and financial services.

Critical Thinking Questions

1. The percentage of the American population that is mature is going to increase dramatically over the next 20 years. How is this going to change the nature of American society?

2. What explains the key differences in the importance of criteria used to select physicians and surgeons across the segments?

3. What ethical and social responsibilities do marketers have when marketing to older consumers?

	Healthy Hermits	Healthy Indulgers	Ailing Outgoers	Frail Recluses
Reasonable fees	25%	24%	43%	29%
Convenient location	54	57	53	62
Related services at same location	39	36	35	34
Staff explanation of services	34	45	39	35

ethnicity, and social class.[27] In fact, this generation is part of a broader category of consumers called the **mature market.** The mature market (often categorized as 55 years of age and over) now spans three generations (pre-Depression, Depression, and baby boom) and is a large and growing market with numerous subsegments. **Gerontographics** is *one segmentation approach to the mature market that incorporates aging processes and life events related to the physical health and mental outlook of older consumers* (see Consumer Insight 4-2).

The pre-Depression generation faces numerous consumption-related decisions. One is the disposition of valued belongings that they no longer use or that are not appropriate in nursing or retirement homes. These can be emotional decisions for both the elderly person and their family members.

> The pin means a great deal to me. I would love for my granddaughter to have it. It will be strange not seeing it in my jewelry box anymore.[28]

Communications strategies need to consider media selection, message content, and message structure. For example, some aspects of information processing, memory, and cognitive performance decline with age. The rapid, brief presentation of information that younger consumers respond to is generally not appropriate for older consumers.[29]

Products related to the unique needs of this segment range from health services to single-serving sizes of prepared foods. As this generation continues to age, assisted-living services are growing rapidly. As more members of this generation experience reduced mobility, shopping will become an increasing problem. Although Internet shopping would seem a good solution, relatively few members of this generation use the Internet.

Depression Generation

This is the cohort born between 1930 and 1945. These people were small children during the Depression or World War II. They matured during the prosperous years of the 1950s and early 60s. They discovered both Sinatra and Presley. They "invented" rock and roll and grew up with music and television as important parts of their lives.

There are about 32 million individuals in this group. Most have or will soon retire. Many have accumulated substantial wealth in the form of home equity and savings. Those who still work often dominate the top positions in both business and government. Members of this generation are also grandparents with sufficient incomes to indulge their grandchildren, making them a major market for upscale children's furniture, toys, strollers, car seats, and clothing.

Many in this generation are still in excellent health and are quite active. Active lifestyles translate into demand for recreational vehicles, second homes, new cars, travel services, and recreational adult education. For example, this generation spends at least 11 percent more on travel than the average household, making them an important target segment for the travel industry.[30] So-called "active adult communities" such as Sun City in Phoenix, Arizona, are also a major growth arena and will continue to be so as the baby boomers enter their retirement years. These age-restricted communities offer an amazing array of activities and attract relatively wealthy households, many of whom can pay cash for their homes.[31]

Marketers targeting this segment are increasingly utilizing themes that stress an active lifestyle and breaking with stereotypical portrayals of older consumers. Illustration 4-2 contains an ad from *Modern Maturity* magazine that uses a mature spokesperson. The copy stresses health benefits, but for an active lifestyle rather than just for staying well. The stated message, as well as the message implied by using Big John in the ad, positions this product for the "Healthy Indulger" segment described in Consumer Insight 4-2.

Nonetheless, this generation is dealing with the physical effects of aging. In terms of clothing, comfort as well as style is important. Levi's Action Slacks have been a major success with this generation. These slacks, which have an elastic waistband, are cut for the less lean, more mature body. Easy Spirit shoes also targets this segment with comfort in mind. Health care is a major concern and a major expenditure. Of those over the age of 65 (includes Depression and pre-Depression), 40 percent are expected to spend time in a nursing home and 75 percent are expected to need some form of in-home care.[32]

Asset management is important to this group and firms such as Merrill Lynch have developed products and services to meet these needs.[33] Lawyers, accountants, and financial planners have also been attracted to the "wealth transfer" that is expected to occur as the baby boomers inherit the wealth accumulated by their parents. Numbers vary dramatically due to stock market fluctuations and rising health care costs. However, even the most conservative estimate puts the value at $1 trillion over the next decade.[34]

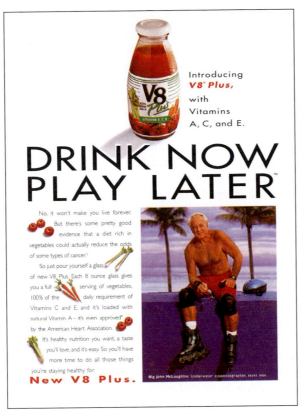

Courtesy of Campbell Soup Company.

In addition, this group of consumers is downsizing homes and possessions just like the pre-Depression generation. And increasing numbers are becoming more tech savvy, even to the point of using eBay to help them downsize! As one sixtysomething eBay user jokes:

> The end of the bidding cycle is quite exciting, especially for older people whose lives like mine are not that exciting anymore.

SeniorNet is a nonprofit group that helps older consumers learn about computers by offering classes in nursing homes and recreation centers. eBay has donated over $5 million to SeniorNet to help them expand their classes and computer centers.[35]

Baby Boom Generation

The baby boom generation refers to those individuals born during the dramatic increase of births between the end of World War II and 1964. There are almost 80 million baby boomers, which is substantially more than the two preceding generations combined. Most of this group grew up during the prosperous 1950s and 1960s. They were heavily influenced by the Kennedy assassination, the Vietnam War, recreational drugs, the sexual revolution, the energy crisis, the rapid growth of divorce, and the Cold War, as well as rock and roll and the Beatles. Although there are significant differences between the boomers born early in this generation and those born later, boomers are considered to be more self-centered, individualistic, economically optimistic, skeptical, suspicious of authority, and focused on the present than other generations.[36]

Baby boomers are characterized by high education levels, high incomes, and dual-career households. They are also often characterized by time poverty (particularly young boomers) as they try to manage two careers and family responsibilities. In 2010 their age range will be 46 to 64, a range characterized by children leaving home, marrying, and producing grandchildren. The "empty nest" is rapidly becoming the norm for this generation, a circumstance that is providing them with both increased discretionary income and time. In fact, aging baby boomers are expected to boost the percentage of households in the 55–74-year-old category with incomes over $100,000 by some 61 percent through 2007.[37] As a result, sales of adventure vacations, expensive restaurant meals, second homes, recreational vehicles, maintenance free homes, personal chefs, personal trainers, and even motorcycles should continue to grow rapidly.[38]

TV is still a major route through which to target this generation. However, baby boomers are more tech savvy than previous generations, a trend that will increasingly make the mature market an important target for online marketers, particularly given their high level of discretionary income.[39] The Internet offers the convenience and customization that this generation will increasingly demand. In addition, the Internet allows access to health information of importance to this aging segment. Currently, only 21 percent of consumers 65 and older (mostly pre-Depression and Depression) have accessed health information online, compared to 53 percent of those between 50 and 64 years of age. Much of this difference is likely driven by the higher Internet usage of baby boomers.[40]

Retirement is no longer something in the distant future, and many have already made that step. However, surveys indicate that boomers plan to continue and expand the concept of "active retirement" begun by the Depression generation. For example, households in this age segment spend 21 percent more on travel than the average household.[41] However, baby boomers don't just want to travel, they want to learn new skills, work actively both for pay and in charities, and otherwise continue to grow. Two-thirds of a recent survey of 50- to 75-year-olds selected as a definition of retirement: To begin a new, active, and involved chapter in life, starting new activities and setting new goals.[42] Or as one boomer who recently took early retirement stated: "I'm not retiring; I'm re-engineering my life."

In fact, it is expected that the baby boom generation will continue to work longer than previous generations. The reasons vary from necessity among those with lower incomes or poor pension plans, to changes in Social Security which are increasing the age at which full benefits can be drawn, to an increased desire to stay active in interesting and rewarding careers.[43]

Boomers are also facing the aging and often failing health of their parents. Becoming the caregiver rather than the care-receiver is a major challenge for this group. One result of this is the rapid growth of assisted-living centers. This type of living arrangement is a major innovation, and it arose because many baby boomers did not want their parents living with them and the healthy and active pre-Depression and Depression generations did not want to be dependent on or impose on their children.[44]

As boomers age, their physical needs are changing. Weight gain has become an increasing concern, and demand for plastic surgery, baldness treatments, health clubs, cosmetics for both men and women, hair coloring, health foods, and related products is exploding.

When lotions failed to smooth the crow's feet around Cheryl Hoover's eyes and restore the firmness to her skin, the 41-year-old turned to Botox, collagen, and laser treatments. "I try to be proactive in heading off things. You want, as you get older, to appear youthful or at least look your age and not older. Our generation is looking for the fountain of youth, where it would have been more acceptable to age in previous generations."[45]

© The Procter & Gamble Company. Used by permission.

Illustration 4-3 shows an ad focused on the needs of this group. Other examples of firms focusing on the maturing needs of this generation include

- Kellogg Co. dropped its Special K ads featuring young, slim, attractive women putting on tight fitting jeans or short skirts. Research revealed that boomers were alienated by these ads: "They told us they couldn't relate to advertising techniques that used unrealistic body images."[46]
- Sony is spending $25 million to target what they call the "zoomers," a name that reflects the active lifestyle of this generation. One of their ads is a spot which features a "grey-haired astronaut filming earth with his own camcorder." The tagline: "When your kids ask where the money went, show them the tape." Sony credits the recent surge in camcorder sales to their renewed focus on this increasingly important segment.[47]

Generation X

Generation X, often referred to as the baby bust generation, was born between 1965 and 1976. It is a smaller generation than its predecessor (about 45 million). This generation reached adulthood during difficult economic times. It is the first generation to be raised mainly in dual-career households, and 40 percent spent at least some time in a single-parent household before the age of 16. The divorce of their parents is often a cause of stress and other problems for the children involved.[48] However, these changes have also caused many members of Generation X to have a very broad view of a family, which may include parents, siblings, stepparents, half-siblings, close friends, live-in lovers, and others.

This is the first American generation to seriously confront the issue of "reduced expectations." These reduced expectations are based on reality for many "busters" as wages and job opportunities for young workers were limited until the economic boom that started in the mid-90s.[49] This relative lack of opportunity was in part responsible for this generation's tendency to leave home later and also to return home to live with their parents as younger adults. Not only has the path to success been less certain for this generation, but many Generation Xers do not believe in sacrificing time, energy, and relations to the extent the boomers did for the sake of career or economic advancement.

This generation faces a world racked by regional conflicts and terrorism, an environment that continues to deteriorate, and an AIDS epidemic that threatens their lives. Members of this group tend to blame the "me generation" and the materialism associated with the baby boom generation for the difficult future they see for themselves.

However, Generation X is highly educated with more college attendance and graduates than previous generations. And Xer women are more highly educated than men, giving them increased leverage in the workforce. Given their early economic challenges, it is perhaps not surprising that this generation appears to be more entrepreneurial in its approach to jobs and less prone to devote their lives to large public corporations. For example, a recent survey found that Xers are 25 percent more likely than previous generations to be self-employed professionals.[50] The empowerment of Xer women extends beyond their careers. One study shows that across all generations, Xer women are the highest viewers of home improvement media and the most likely to engage in home-improvement projects including adding a room onto the house.[51]

This generation is moving into the middle and latter stages of the vaunted 18–49 demographic that advertisers and marketers covet. Considerable attention has recently focused on the inability of traditional network TV to attract this demographic, particularly men in the 18–34 range. One explanation is the explosion of media options including cable and the Internet which are increasingly luring these consumers away. Both Xers and their younger counterparts in Generation Y are more avid users of the Internet and related technologies than previous generations. Advertisers are responding by increasingly utilizing alternative media to reach these consumers.[52]

In 2010, this generation will be 34 to 45 years old. While they tended to delay marriage, 63 percent of Xer households are now families with children under 18.[53] This is one of the reasons the housing market remained strong throughout the recent economic decline. It is also the reason that this generation increasingly feels the time crunch typical of child-rearing years. This generation will be a major force in the market for cars, appliances, and children's products. The ad for AstraZeneca in Illustration 4-4 targets Xer parents and capitalizes on the fact that this audience is a heavy user of the Internet.

While an important market, Generation X is not always easy to reach. It is both cynical and sophisticated about products, ads, and shopping. It is materialistic and impatient. In many aspects, its tastes are "not baby boom." Thus, it created the grunge look and snowboarding. Magazines such as *Spin, Details,* and *Maxim* were created for this generation as was the X Games. It responds to irreverence in advertising but not always as well to traditional approaches. Generation Xers want products and messages designed uniquely for their tastes and lifestyles. Marketers are increasingly targeting this group:

- Volvo is redesigning its marketing mix for the S40 sedan to go after the Generation X market and some older Generation Yers. They are doing tie-ins with Microsoft's Xbox and Virgin Group as well as creating commercials with a hip-hop feel using the band Dilated Peoples. Signs and banners of the S40 will be posted at Virgin's Megastores.[54]
- State Farm began targeting Generation Xers with media buys on MTV, ESPN, and Comedy Central. They also placed banner ads on Web sites such as Rollingstone.com.[55]

As these examples suggest, companies are beginning to understand that Generation Xers are moving into a new life stage accompanied by increased buying power and families to

Everydaykidz is a trademark of the AstraZeneca group of companies.
© 2004 AstraZeneca LP. All rights reserved.

care for. However, these companies are also adapting their media strategies beyond traditional approaches to speak to this segment on its own terms.

Generation Y

Traditional mass-marketing approaches that were so successful with older generations often don't work well with younger consumers including those in Generation Y. Companies must continually push the creative envelope with respect to media and promotional themes to capture this audience. Event sponsorships and electronic media are just a few of the ways marketers are finding to connect with this generation. Music and fashion are often key touchpoints. Illustration 4-5 shows how Pepsi is leveraging music on its Web site. Pepsi also hit it big with this generation with the "P-Diddy Driving Pepsi" commercial spot in which the rapper catches a ride to an awards ceremony in a Diet Pepsi truck and unwittingly starts a pop-icon frenzy that is mimicked by other stars. The ad helped Pepsi win the 2005 Super Bowl ad wars with 63 percent awareness among 14–24-year-olds.[56]

Today's 30-year-olds are the leading edge of this generation of 71 million members, a number that rivals that of the baby boom. These children of the original baby boomers were born between 1977 and 1994 and are sometimes referred to as the "echo boom." Overall, it is the first generation to grow up with virtually full-employment opportunities for women, with dual-income households the standard, with a wide array of family types seen as normal, with significant respect for ethnic and cultural diversity, with computers in the home and schools, and with the Internet. It has also grown up with divorce as the norm,[57] AIDS,

ILLUSTRATION 4-5

Attracting Generation Y often requires unique and creative marketing approaches. Pepsi's Web site is a great example of this.

Courtesy Pepsi-Cola North America.

visible homelessness (including many teenagers), drug abuse, gang violence, and economic uncertainty. The Columbine shootings, the Oklahoma City bombing, the Clinton/Lewinsky scandal, the collapse of the Soviet Union, and Kosovo were key events for this generation.[58] Global terrorism and its consequences will have an as yet unknown impact, particularly on the younger members of this generation.[59]

Generation Y is characterized by a strong sense of independence and autonomy. They are assertive, self-reliant, emotionally and intellectually expressive, innovative, and curious. They understand that advertisements exist to sell products and are unlikely to respond to "marketing hype." They prefer ads that use humor or irony and have an element of truth about them. They like the ability to customize products to their unique needs. Brand names are important to them.[60]

While considered a single generation, Generation Y is much less a single market than the other generations. Its age range in 2010 will be from 16 to 33. This market is easily composed of at least two age subsegments, namely, (*a*) the so-called "twentysomethings," a term often used to refer to young adults, and (*b*) teens. This generation, as a whole, is expected to be the highest-educated generation to date with incomes that should follow.

The older members of this generation which include late teens and twentysomethings are in college or have entered the workforce. These consumers are Internet savvy and use e-mail, cell phones, and text messaging to communicate. Over 80 percent of the 18–29 group is online, which is higher than any preceding generation[61] and the 18–24 group leads all other age groups in every cell phone data service from text messaging to Web browsing.[62] This group is accustomed to media and TV programs designed for them such as "American Idol," "Big Brother 4," "CSI," MTV, and *Maxim*. Notice the overlap in media usage and lifestyles between older Yers and younger Xers.

The older members of this generation are also becoming a major market for automobiles. It is expected Generation Y as a whole will represent 40 percent of the auto market in 10 years, a number that has automakers like Toyota and Ford clamoring to attract this group early and earn its loyalty. Toyota's Scion has been successful in attracting a younger crowd by offering lower pricing and edgy styling. Scion's marketing is also eclectic and edgy with an "Urban Youth" touch including hosting dance parties with emerging DJs and artists.[63]

Another growth market for Generation Yers is apparel, for which 18- to 34-year-olds spend the most of all age categories.[64] Abercrombie & Fitch has achieved great success by focusing on the middle- and upper-income portion of this group. Its stores blast contemporary music at corporate-specified decibel levels designed to discourage conversation. And finally, as this group gets married and has children, they should fuel growth in housing and child-related products as well.

The teenage segment of this generation also receives a lot of attention. Many reside in dual-income or single-parent households and have grown up assisting in household management, including shopping. Coupled with the ubiquitous presence of advertising throughout their lives, this has made them savvy shoppers. They are also tech savvy and cell phones are an important communication tool.

The teenage market is attractive to marketers for two reasons. First, preferences and tastes formed during the teenage years can influence purchases throughout life. As the Ford Focus brand manager states, "Although very few of [teenagers] are car buyers now, it is vital to create a relationship with them so they'll think of Ford when it is time to buy a car."[65] Second, teenagers currently spend over $150 billion annually for personal consumption,[66] spend billions more while doing the household shopping, and influence the purchase of many additional items such as cars and vacations.

Marketers targeting teens need to use appropriate language, music, and images. Retailers are realizing that they need to constantly adjust and update their offerings to drive traffic among this active shopper segment that is also easily bored. Consider the following statement by a retail consultant:

> This is the challenge for any store catering to mall rats—the kids come back so often that you're forced to constantly change the displays. Otherwise they get bored and stop coming at all. It's one reason stores need to know how often the regulars return—to see whether the windows and front tables should be changed every week or every seventeen days.[67]

Honesty, humor, uniqueness, and information appear to be important to teens.[68] The ad shown in Illustration 4-6 appeals to teens through its humor and openness. Toyota ran a series of humorous ads in teen magazines entitled "Driver's Ed," which featured a geeky Toyota employee dispensing driving tips such as

> Attention Nose Pickers: Just because you are alone in your car—NEWS FLASH—you are not invisible.

Ads targeting this generation must be placed in appropriate magazines and on appropriate Internet sites, television and radio programs, and even videogames—a strategy called *advergaming*.[69] The portrayal of multiple racial and ethnic groups in ads aimed at this generation is common. This is a multiethnic generation, and single-race ads would seem unnatural to them. In addition, urban African American teenagers and Hispanic teenagers are frequently the style leaders of this generation.[70] As important as effective advertising are public relations (e.g., creating buzz) and event sponsorship.

Successful approaches to targeting this market include

- Cover Girl is a remarkable success among teens. It maintains a steady flow of teen-oriented products and it is the largest advertiser in teen magazines. Its coverGirl.com Web site gets over 250,000 unique hits a month. Teens can enter information about their skin color and other preferences and receive free samples. It advertises heavily on teen portal Alloy.com and offers e-mail newsletters to teens.[71]

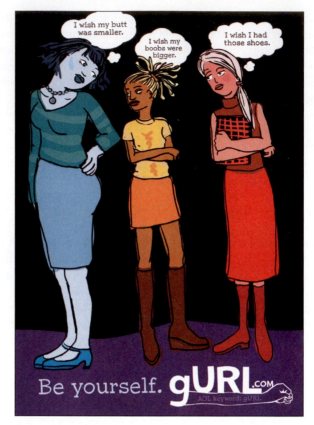

Courtesy Prime Media.

• Heinz's Bagel Bites were originally marketed only to mothers (to buy for their teens and others). Heinz revamped its strategy to focus directly on teens. It signed on as a sponsor of ESPN's Winter X Games and sales jumped 25 percent.[72]

Millennials

This newest generation was born after 1994. The oldest members of this group, who are just now entering their early teen years, will turn 16 in 2010. This generation could be in the range of 62 million people in 2010, depending on where the boundary is ultimately set. It is generally too early to characterize this group. However, Millennials will likely continue trends in increased education, diversity, and technology usage. For example, 4 percent of 6–8-year-olds and 9 percent of 9–12-year-olds already have their own personal Web sites and many more plan to have one in the future![73] Consider also that Mattel is launching a personal media player called the Juice Box targeted at older kids.[74]

The oldest of this group, now in the so-called "tween" years (8–14) have many of the same characteristics as the teens discussed earlier. And marketers are increasingly targeting consumers at younger ages, going after early loyalty and hefty allowances. Consider the following excerpt:

Cosmetic and personal care companies are targeting kids and tweens this fall with products that include tasty lip balm branded Dairy Queen and Snapple, Bratz cosmetics and toothpaste featuring characters from Blues Clues, Looney Tunes and Dragon Tales.[75]

We discuss marketing to children in more detail in Chapter 6 in our discussion of families.

SOCIAL STRATIFICATION

We are all familiar with the concept of social class, but most of us would have difficulty explaining our class system to a foreigner. The following quote illustrates the vague nature of social class:

> Like it or not, all of us are largely defined, at least in the eyes of others, according to a complex set of criteria—how much we earn, what we do for a living, who our parents are, where and how long we attended school, how we speak, what we wear, where we live, and how we react to the issues of the day. It all adds up to our socioeconomic status, our ranking in U.S. society.[76]

The words *social class* and *social standing* are used interchangeably to mean **societal rank**—*one's position relative to others on one or more dimensions valued by society.* How do we obtain a social standing? Your social standing is a result of characteristics you possess that others in society desire and hold in high esteem. Your education, occupation, ownership of property, income level, and heritage (racial/ethnic background, parents' status) influence your social standing, as shown in Figure 4-2. Social standing ranges from the lower class, those with few or none of the socioeconomic factors desired by society, to the upper class, who possess many of the socioeconomic characteristics considered by society as desirable. Individuals with different social standings tend to have different needs and consumption patterns. Thus, a **social class system** can be defined as *a hierarchical division of a society into relatively distinct and homogeneous groups with respect to attitudes, values, and lifestyles.*

"Pure" social classes do not exist in the United States or most other industrialized societies. However, it is apparent that these same societies do have hierarchical groups of individuals and that individuals in those groups do exhibit unique behavior patterns that are different from behaviors in other groups.

What exists is *not a set of social classes* but a *series of status continua.*[77] These status continua reflect various dimensions or factors that the overall society values. In an achievement-oriented society such as the United States, *achievement-related factors* constitute the primary status dimensions. Thus, education, occupation, income, and, to a lesser extent, quality of residence and place of residence are important status dimensions in the United States. Race and gender are *ascribed* dimensions of social status that are not related to achievement but still influence status in the United States. Likewise, the status of a person's parents is an ascribed status dimension that also exists in the United States. However, heritage is a more important factor in a more traditional society such as England.[78]

The various status dimensions are clearly related to each other. In a functional sense, the status of one's parents influences one's education, which in turn influences occupation that

| Social Standing Is Derived and Influences Behavior | FIGURE 4-2 |

Socioeconomic factors	Social standing	Unique behaviors
Occupation	Upper class	Preferences
Education	Middle class	Purchases
Ownership	Working class	Consumption
Income	Lower class	Communication
Heritage		

generates income, which sets limits on one's lifestyle, including one's residence. Does this mean that an individual with high status based on one dimension will have high status based on the other dimensions? This is a question of **status crystallization.** The more consistent an individual is on all status dimensions, the greater the degree of status crystallization for the individual. Status crystallization is moderate in the United States. For example, many blue-collar workers (such as plumbers and electricians) earn higher incomes than many professionals (such as public school teachers).

SOCIAL STRUCTURE IN THE UNITED STATES

The moderate level of status crystallization in the United States supports the contention that a social class system is not a perfect categorization of social position. However, this does not mean that the population cannot be subdivided into status groups whose members share similar lifestyles, at least with respect to particular product categories or activities. Furthermore, there are many people with high levels of status crystallization who exhibit many of the behaviors associated with a class system. It is useful for the marketing manager to know the characteristics of these relatively pure class types, even though the descriptions represent a simplified abstraction from reality.

A number of different sets of social classes have been proposed to describe the United States. We will use the one developed by Coleman and Rainwater.[79] In their system, shown in Table 4-4, the *upper class* (14 percent) is divided into three groups primarily on

---

TABLE 4-4

The Coleman-Rainwater Social Class Hierarchy

Upper Americans
- Upper-Upper (0.3%). The "capital S society" world of inherited wealth, aristocratic names.
- Lower-Upper (1.2%). The newer social elite, drawn from current professional, corporate leadership.
- Upper-Middle Class (12.5%). The rest of college graduate managers and professionals; lifestyle centers on careers, private clubs, causes, and the arts.

Middle Americans
- Middle Class (32%). Average pay white-collar workers and their blue-collar friends; live on "the better side of town," try to "do the proper things."
- Working Class (38%). Average pay blue-collar workers; lead "working-class lifestyle" whatever the income, school background, and job.

Lower Americans
- Upper-Lower (9%). "A lower group of people but not the lowest"; working, not on welfare; living standard is just above poverty.
- Lower-Lower (7%). On welfare, visibly poverty-stricken, usually out of work (or have "the dirtiest jobs").

Typical Profile				
Social Class	**Percent**	**Income**	**Education**	**Occupation**
Upper Americans				
Upper-upper	0.3%	$600,000	Master's degree	Board chairman
Lower-upper	1.2	450,000	Master's degree	Corporate president
Upper-middle	12.5	150,000	Medical degree	Physician
Middle Americans				
Middle class	32.0	28,000	College degree	High school teacher
Working class	38.0	15,000	High school	Assembly worker
Lower Americans				
Upper-lower	9.0	9,000	Some high school	Janitor
Lower-lower	7.0	5,000	Grade school	Unemployed

Source: R. P. Coleman, "The Continuing Significance of Social Class in Marketing," *Journal of Consumer Research,* December 1983, p. 267. Copyright 1983 by the University of Chicago. Used by permission.

differences in occupation and social affiliations. The *middle class* (70 percent) is divided into a middle class (32 percent) of average-income white- and blue-collar workers living in better neighborhoods and a working class (38 percent) of average-income blue-collar workers who lead a "working-class lifestyle." The *lower class* (16 percent) is divided into two groups, one living just above the poverty level and the other visibly poverty-stricken. Note that the average income associated with each class will have increased, in some cases dramatically, since Table 4-4 was developed. For example, the top 1 percent income group in the United States averages in excess of $1 million, while middle Americans likely fall in the $30,000 to $70,000 range.[80]

The percentage of the American population assigned to each class in the Coleman-Rainwater system closely parallels the way Americans classify themselves. In one study, Americans were asked to classify themselves into one of five classes.[81] The results were

Poor	8%
Working	37
Middle	43
Upper-middle	8
Upper	1

The Coleman-Rainwater groups are described in more detail in the following sections.

Upper Americans

The Upper-Upper Class   Members of the upper-upper social class are aristocratic families who make up the social elite. Members with this level of social status generally are the nucleus of the best country clubs and sponsors of major charitable events. They provide leadership and funds for community and civic activities and often serve as trustees for hospitals, colleges, and civic organizations.

The Kennedy family is a national example of the upper-upper class. Most communities in America have one or more families with significant "old money." These individuals live in excellent homes, drive luxury automobiles, own original art, and travel extensively. They generally stay out of the public spotlight unless it is to enter politics or support a charity or community event.

The Lower-Upper Class   The lower-upper class is often referred to as "new rich—the current generation's new successful elite." These families are relatively new in terms of upper-class social status and have not yet been accepted by the upper crust of the community. In some cases, their incomes are greater than those of families in the upper-upper social strata. Bill Gates, founder of Microsoft, and Ted Turner, founder of CNN, are national examples of the lower-upper class. Most communities have one or more families who have acquired great wealth during one generation, many from the high-tech and dot-com boom of the 1990s.

Many members of this group continue to live lifestyles similar to those of the upper-middle class. Other members of the lower-upper class strive to emulate the established upper-upper class. Entrepreneurs, sports stars, and entertainers who suddenly acquire substantial wealth often engage in this type of behavior. However, they are frequently unable to join the same exclusive clubs or command the social respect accorded the true "blue bloods." Many respond by aggressively engaging in **conspicuous consumption;** that is, they purchase and use automobiles, homes, yachts, clothes, and so forth primarily to demonstrate their great wealth.[82] Thus, it is not unusual to read about a star professional

This private jet ser-
vice would appeal
strongly to the
upper classes.

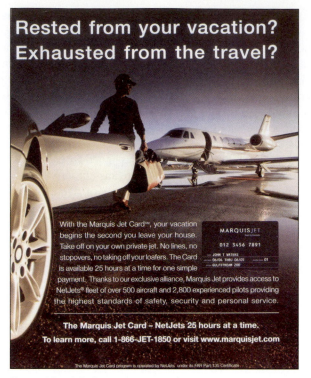

Courtesy Marquis Jet Partners, Inc.

athlete who owns 5 or 10 luxury cars, multiple homes, and so forth. These individuals are referred as the **nouveaux riches.** Doing the "in thing" on a grand scale is important to this group. High-status brands and activities are actively sought out by the nouveaux riches.

Although small, these groups serve as important market segments for some products and as a symbol of "the good life" to the upper-middle class. Illustration 4-7 shows a service that would appeal to the upper classes.

The Upper-Middle Class   The upper-middle class consists of families who possess neither family status derived from heritage nor unusual wealth. Occupation and education are key aspects of this social stratum, as it consists of successful professionals, independent businesspeople, and corporate managers. As shown in Table 4-4, members of this social class are typically college graduates, many with professional or graduate degrees.

Upper-middle-class individuals tend to be confident and forward looking. They worry about the ability of their children to have the same lifestyle they enjoy. They realize that their success depends on their careers, which in turn depend on education. As a result, having their children get a sound education from the right schools is very important to them.

This group is highly involved in the arts and charities of their local communities. They belong to private clubs where they tend to be quite active. They are a prime market for financial services that focus on retirement planning, estate planning, and college funding issues. They consume fine homes, expensive automobiles, quality furniture, good wines, and nice resorts. Illustration 4-8 contains an advertisement aimed at this group.

This segment of the U.S. population is highly visible, and many Americans would like to belong to it. Because it is aspired to by many, it is an important positioning variable for some products. Figure 4-3 describes the upward-pull strategy often associated with the *class to mass* approach discussed earlier in the chapter. The ad for Kahlua shown in

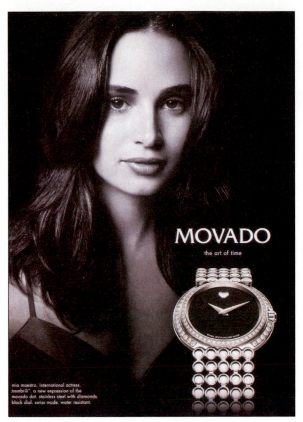

Courtesy Movado Group.

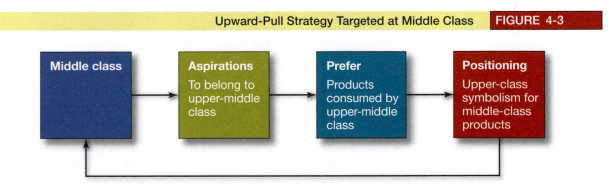

Upward-Pull Strategy Targeted at Middle Class   FIGURE 4-3

Middle class	Aspirations To belong to upper-middle class	Prefer Products consumed by upper-middle class	Positioning Upper-class symbolism for middle-class products

Illustration 4-9 is an example of the upward-pull strategy. Kahlua, a relatively inexpensive liqueur, is shown being consumed in very elegant surroundings. Thus, a product readily affordable by the middle and working class is positioned as one that will allow its users to experience some elements of the upper-middle-class lifestyle.

Middle Americans

The Middle Class   The middle class is composed of white-collar workers (office workers, schoolteachers, lower-level managers) and high-paid blue-collar workers (plumbers,

By positioning a moderately priced product as one that will allow its users to experience some elements of the upper-middle-class lifestyle, Kahlua is using an upward-pull strategy.

Courtesy Hiram Walker, Inc.

factory supervisors). Thus, the middle class represents the majority of the white-collar group and the top of the blue-collar group. The middle-class core typically has some college education though not a degree, a white-collar or a factory supervisor position, and an average income. Many members of this class feel very insecure because of reductions in both government and private workforces during the recent recession.

The middle class is concerned about respectability. They care what the neighbors think. They generally live in modest suburban homes. They are deeply concerned about the quality of public schools, crime, drugs, the weakening of "traditional family values," and their family's financial security. Retirement is an increasing concern as firms reduce pension plans and health care costs escalate.

Members of the middle class are likely to get involved in do-it-yourself projects. They represent the primary target market for the goods and services of home improvement centers, garden shops, automotive parts houses, as well as mouthwashes and deodorants. With limited incomes, they must balance their desire for current consumption with aspirations for future security. Illustration 4-10 shows how Lowe's meets the needs of this segment.

The Working Class   The working class consists of skilled and semiskilled factory, service, and sales workers. Though some households in this social stratum seek advancement, members are more likely to seek security for and protection of what they already have. This segment suffered seriously during the first half of the 1990s as their average real earnings declined. Automation and the movement of manufacturing activities to developing countries also led to economic insecurity. Few of these individuals benefited from the stock market boom of the late 1990s, but many were negatively affected by the most recent economic downturn.

Working-class families live in modest homes or apartments that are often located in marginal urban neighborhoods, decaying suburbs, or rural areas. They are greatly concerned about crime, gangs, drugs, and neighborhood deterioration. They generally cannot afford to move to a different area should their current neighborhood or school become unsafe or otherwise undesirable. With modest education and skill levels, the more marginal

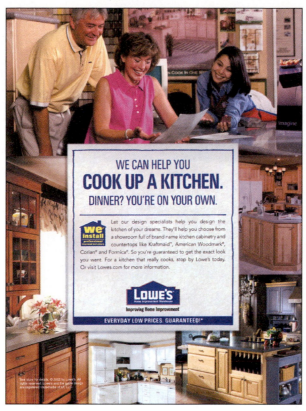

Courtesy Lowe's Companies.

ILLUSTRATION 4-10
This ad will appeal
to the middle class's
focus on their
homes as well as
their desire for
value.

members of this class are in danger of falling into one of the lower classes. The ad shown in Illustration 4-11 would appeal to those members of this class seeking advancement as well as those concerned about downward mobility and workforce reductions.

Many **working-class aristocrats** dislike the upper-middle class and prefer products and stores positioned at their social-class level.[83] These individuals are proud of their ability to do "real work" and see themselves as the often-unappreciated backbone of America. They are heavy consumers of pickups and campers, hunting equipment, power boats, and beer. Miller Brewing Company gave up attempts to attract a broad audience for its Miller High Life beer. Instead, it is targeting working-class aristocrats with ads that feature bowling alleys, diners, and country music. The ad shown in Illustration 4-12 would appeal to this group.

Lower Americans

The Upper-Lower Class   The upper-lower class consists of individuals who are poorly educated, have very low incomes, and work as unskilled laborers.[84] Most have minimum-wage jobs. A full-time, 50-week-a-year minimum-wage job is not enough to keep a one-earner family of three above the poverty level. In fact, it keeps the family almost 30 percent below the poverty line—this is a major change from the late 1960s, when the minimum wage would support a family of three. Compounding the problem is that many of these jobs are part-time and few provide benefits such as health insurance or a retirement plan.

This ad would appeal to members of the working class seeking advancement as well as to those concerned about downward social mobility caused by the changing economy. It would also appeal to some members of the upper-lower classes as well as marginal members of the middle class.

Courtesy Olsten Corporation.

This product and ad would appeal to the working class, particularly the working-class aristocrats.

Courtesy Bartle Bogle Hegarty/New York.

Consider John Gibson, a 50-year-old part-time janitor in Nashville who makes somewhat more than minimum wage:

"I'd like to work more," John says. However, he is not qualified for many jobs. "I have to make sacrifices but I get by. When I get my check, the first thing I do is pay my rent." John lives alone in a small efficiency apartment. One of the things John sacrifices in order to get by is eating at fast-food restaurants. Although he likes the food and the convenience, a co-worker convinced him that it was much cheaper to prepare food at home. He minimizes his expenses on clothing by shopping at thrift stores such as the one operated by the Salvation Army.

As a part-time employee, he has no company health insurance, but he is now eligible for some coverage from the state of Tennessee. A few years before he had this coverage he was hospitalized. Afterward, his wages were garnished to cover his bills, and he was forced to rely on social service agencies. Today he spends a great deal of his spare time volunteering at these same agencies. He would enjoy golf but is seldom able to play. He has no pension plan or personal insurance and wonders what his retirement years will be like.[85]

This group is 66 percent white, 18 percent black, and 12 percent Hispanic, close to the national average. Two-thirds have two adults present in the household, and 80 percent have children at home (40 percent have three or more children). Lack of education is the defining characteristic—almost 70 percent have a high school degree or less, compared to 40 percent of the nonpoor.[86]

Members of the upper-lower class live in marginal housing that is often located in depressed and decayed neighborhoods. Crime, drugs, and gangs are often close at hand and represent very real threats. They are concerned about the safety of their families and their children's future. The lack of education, role models, and opportunities often produces despair that can result in harmful consumption such as cigarettes and alcohol. It may also produce inefficient purchasing and a short-term time focus.[87]

The marketing system has not served this group effectively. They have a particularly difficult time securing financial services, and many do not have bank accounts. This means that they generally must pay a fee for cashing pay and other checks, which is estimated to cost them $180 per year. However, research indicates substantial marketing opportunities in this group. They tend to be value-oriented rather than just cost-focused. They tend to be very brand loyal. Firms such as Wal-Mart, Dollar General, and Radio Shack have done a good and profitable job serving these consumers.[88]

The Lower-Lower Class Members of the lower-lower social stratum have very low incomes and minimal education. This segment of society is often unemployed for long periods of time and is the major recipient of government support and services provided by nonprofit organizations. Andre Hank, as described in Chapter 1 in Consumer Insight 1-2, is an example of an individual who was in the upper-lower class and then wound up in the lower-lower class when he lost his job.

Marketing to the lower classes is frequently controversial. The rent-to-own business flourishes by renting durable goods such as televisions and refrigerators to lower-class households who frequently cannot afford to acquire them for cash and lack the credit rating to charge the purchases at regular outlets. While this service appears to meet a real need, the industry is frequently criticized for charging exorbitant interest rates on the purchases.[89]

The marketing of "sin" products to this group is even more controversial. Malt liquors and fortified wines sell heavily in lower-class neighborhoods. However, firms that actively promote such products to this market risk significant negative publicity. When R. J.

Reynolds tried to market its Uptown cigarettes to lower-class urban blacks, public protests became so strong that the product was withdrawn. Although some might applaud this outcome, the unstated assumption of the protest is that these individuals lack the ability to make sound consumption decisions and thus require protections that other social classes do not require—an assumption that is certainly controversial.

Other firms are criticized for not marketing to the lower classes. Major retail chains, particularly food chains, and financial firms seldom provide services in lower-class neighborhoods. Critics argue that such businesses have a social responsibility to locate in these areas. The businesses thus criticized respond that this is a problem for all of society and the solution should not be forced on a few firms. However, a few sophisticated chain retailers such as Dollar General Corporation have begun to meet the unique needs of this segment. As one specialist in this area said,

> People with lower household incomes are still consumers. They still have to buy food. They still wear clothing. They still have to take care of their kids.[90]

The challenge for business is to develop marketing strategies that will meet the needs of these consumers efficiently and at a reasonable profit to the firm.

THE MEASUREMENT OF SOCIAL CLASS

There are two basic approaches to measuring social status: a single-item index and a multi-item index.

Single-item indexes estimate social status on the basis of a single dimension. Since an individual's overall status is influenced by several dimensions, single-item indexes are generally less accurate at predicting an individual's social standing or position in a community than are well-developed multi-item indexes. The three most common single-item indexes are (1) education, (2) occupation, and (3) income. Each of these provides an individual with social status. However, marketers generally think of them as direct influencers of consumption behavior, not as determinants of status that then influence behavior.

The use of social class as an explanatory consumer behavior variable has been heavily influenced by two studies, each of which developed a **multi-item index** to measure social class.[91] The basic approach in each of these studies was to determine, through a detailed analysis of a relatively small community, the classes into which the community members appeared to fit. Then more objective and measurable indicators or factors related to status were selected and weighted in a manner that would reproduce the original class assignments.

Multi-Item Indexes

Hollingshead Index of Social Position   The Hollingshead **Index of Social Position (ISP)** is a two-item index that is well developed and widely used. The item scales, weights, formulas, and social-class scores are shown in Table 4-5.

Warner's Index of Status Characteristics   Another multi-item scale of social status is Warner's **Index of Status Characteristics (ISC).** Warner's system of measurement is based on four socioeconomic factors: occupation, source of income, house type, and

TABLE 4-5

Hollingshead Index of
Social Position (ISP)

Occupation Scale (Weight of 7)	
Description	**Score**
Higher executives of large concerns, proprietors, and major professionals	1
Business managers, proprietors of medium-sized businesses, and lesser professionals	2
Administrative personnel, owners of small businesses, and minor professionals	3
Clerical and sales workers, technicians, and owners of little businesses	4
Skilled manual employees	5
Machine operators and semiskilled employees	6
Unskilled employees	7

Education Scale (Weight of 4)	
Description	**Score**
Professional (MA, MS, ME, MD, PhD, LLD, and the like)	1
Four-year college graduate (BA, BS, BM)	2
One to three years college (also business schools)	3
High school graduate	4
Ten to 11 years of school (part high school)	5
Seven to nine years of school	6
Less than seven years of school	7

ISP score = (Occupation score × 7) + (Education score × 4)

Classification System	
Social Strata	**Range of Scores**
Upper	11–17
Upper-middle	18–31
Middle	32–47
Lower-middle	48–63
Lower	64–77

Source: Adapted from A. B. Hollingshead and F. C. Redlich, *Social Class and Mental Illness* (New York: John Wiley & Sons, 1958).

dwelling area. Each of these dimensions of status is defined over a range of seven categories and each carries a different weight. This system classifies individuals into one of six social status groups:

Category	Percentage of Population
Upper-upper	1.4%
Lower-upper	1.6
Upper-middle	10.2
Lower-middle	28.8
Upper-lower	33.0
Lower-lower	25.5

Census Bureau's Index of Socioeconomic Status   The U.S. Bureau of the Census
uses a three-factor social status index based on occupation, income, and education. This

scale, referred to as the **Socioeconomic Status Scale (SES),** produces four social status categories:

Category	Percentage of Population
Upper	15.1%
Upper-middle	34.5
Middle	34.1
Lower-middle	16.3

It is important to note that multi-item indexes were designed to measure or reflect *an individual's or family's overall social position within a community.* Because of this, it is possible for a high score on one variable to offset a low score on another. Thus, the following three individuals would all be classified as middle class on the ISP scale: (1) someone with an eighth-grade education who is a successful owner of a medium-sized firm; (2) a four-year college graduate working as a salesperson; and (3) a graduate of a junior college working in an administrative position in the civil service. All of these individuals may well have similar standing in the community. However, it seems likely that their consumption processes for at least some products will differ, pointing out the fact that overall status may mask potentially useful associations between individual status dimensions and the consumption process for particular products.

Another important aspect of these measures is that *they were developed before the rapid expansion of the role of women.* Traditionally, women acquired the status of their husbands. They had few opportunities outside the home and had limited access to education or careers. This has changed radically. Now women bring educational, financial, and occupational prestige to the household just as males do. No scale has been developed that fully accounts for the new reality of dual sources of status for a household.

Demographics or Social Status?

Social status is largely derived from demographics; that is, one's income, education, and occupation go a long way toward determining one's social class or status. Should marketers use an overall measure of social status (a multi-item index) or a demographic variable such as income? Multi-item measures of social status are clearly superior for indicating a person's or family's overall standing in a community. If this is the issue of concern, perhaps in a study of opinion leadership, a multi-item index such as the Warner's or Hollingshead's instrument would be most appropriate. However, marketers are rarely interested in social standing per se. Instead, they are more likely to focus on demographic characteristics as direct influencers on consumer behavior. Thus, research on taste and intellectually oriented activities such as magazine readership or television viewing should consider education as the most relevant dimension. Occupation might be most relevant for studies focusing on leisure-time pursuits. And as we saw earlier, marketers frequently combine demographic measures, not to produce a measure of status but to provide a more complete understanding of the target market.

SOCIAL STRATIFICATION AND MARKETING STRATEGY

While social stratification does not explain all consumption behaviors, it is certainly relevant for some product categories. For clear evidence of this, visit a furniture store in a working-class neighborhood and then an upper-class store such as Ethan Allen Galleries.

The consumption of imported wine, liqueurs, and original art varies with social class. Beer is consumed across all social classes, but Michelob is more popular at the upper end and Pabst is more popular at the lower end. A product/brand may have different meanings to members of different social strata. Blue jeans may serve as economical, functional clothing items to working-class members and as stylish, self-expressive items to upper-class individuals. Likewise, different purchase motivations for the same product may exist between social strata. Individuals in higher social classes use credit cards for convenience (they pay off the entire balance each month); individuals in lower social classes use them for installment purchases (they do not pay off the entire bill at the end of each month).

Figure 4-4 illustrates how Anheuser-Busch covers more than 80 percent of the U.S. population by carefully positioning three different brands. Table 4-6 indicates that consumers perceive these brands very clearly in terms of social class.

Anheuser-Busch Positioning to Social Class Segments   FIGURE 4-4

Upper-class lifestyle

Aspiring

Upper-middle-class target market (12.5%)

Contented

Aspiring

Upper-middle-class lifestyle

Michelob

Upper-middle-class product position:

super premium price; prestige themes; status/professional backgrounds

Middle-class target market (36%)

Contented

Aspiring

Middle-class lifestyle

Budweiser

Middle-class product position:

premium price; achievement, sharing themes; middle-class backgrounds

Working-class target market (38%)

Contented

Working-class lifestyle

Busch

Working-class product position:

popular price; sports themes; working-class backgrounds

TABLE 4-6

Perceived Social Class Appeal of Various Beer Brands

Brand	Social Class*				
	Upper/Upper Middle	Middle	Lower Middle	Upper Lower/Lower	All Classes
Coors	22%	54%	16%	2%	3%
Budweiser	4	46	37	7	4
Miller	14	50	22	6	6
Michelob	67	23	4	1	2
Old Style†	3	33	36	22	1
Bud Light	22	53	14	3	5
Heineken	88	9	1	—	1

*Percentage classifying the brand as most appropriate for a particular social class.

†Local beer on tap.

Source: K. Grønhaug and P. S. Trapp, "Perceived Social Class Appeals of Branded Goods," *Journal of Consumer Marketing,* Winter 1989, p. 27.

SUMMARY

American society is described in part by its *demographics,* which include a population's size, distribution, and structure. The structure of a population refers to its age, income, education, and occupation makeup. Demographics are not static. At present, the rate of population growth is moderate, average age is increasing, southern and western regions are growing, and the workforce contains more women and white-collar workers than ever before. Marketers frequently segment markets based on a combination of two or more demographic descriptors.

In addition to actual measures of age and income, subjective measures can provide additional understanding of consumption. *Cognitive age* is how old a person feels. Many older consumers feel 10 to 15 years younger than their chronological age. *Subjective discretionary income,* which measures how much money consumers feel they have available for nonessentials, has been found to be a better predictor of some purchases than actual income.

An *age cohort* or *generation* is a group of persons who have experienced a common social, political, historical, and economic environment. *Cohort analysis* is the process of describing and explaining the attitudes, values, and behaviors of an age group as well as predicting its future attitudes, values, and behaviors. There are six major generations functioning in America

today—pre-Depression, Depression, baby boom, Generation X, Generation Y, and Millennials.

A *social class system* is defined as the hierarchical division of a society into relatively permanent and homogeneous groups with respect to attitudes, values, and lifestyles. A tightly defined social class system does not exist in the United States. What does seem to exist is a series of status continua that reflect various dimensions or factors that the overall society values. Education, occupation, income, and, to a lesser extent, type of residence are important status dimensions in this country. *Status crystallization* refers to the consistency of individuals and families on all relevant status dimensions (e.g., high income and high educational level).

While pure social classes do not exist in the United States, it is useful for marketing managers to know and understand the general characteristics of major social classes. Using Coleman and Rainwater's system, we described American society in terms of seven major categories—*upper-upper, lower-upper, upper-middle, middle, working class, upper-lower,* and *lower-lower.*

There are two basic approaches to the measurement of social classes: (1) use a combination of several dimensions, a *multi-item index;* or (2) use a single dimension, a *single-item index.* Multi-item indexes are designed to measure an individual's overall rank or social position within the community.

KEY TERMS

Age cohort 123
Class to mass 120
Cognitive age 123

Cohort analysis 123
Conspicuous consumption 137
Demographics 116

Generation 123
Gerontographics 125
Index of Social Position (ISP) 144

INTERNET EXERCISES

1. Use the Internet to describe the following characteristics of the U.S. population in 2020 (www.census.gov is a good place to start). How will this differ from the way it is today? What are the marketing strategy implications of these shifts?
   a. Total size and size by major census region
   b. Age distribution
   c. Education level
   d. Occupation structure
   e. Income level

2. Evaluate the services and data provided at www.easidemographics.com.

3. Visit www.freedemographics.com. Register for their free demographic information. Pick two cities of interest and use the site to develop a demographic comparison using the most recent data available.

4. Compare and evaluate two teen Web sites such as about.com/teens, delias.com, alloy.com, teenpeople.com, gurl.com, bolt.com, and seventeen.com.

5. Visit the Tripod Web site (www.tripod.lycos.com). Evaluate this site in terms of its potential appeal to Generation X.

6. Visit AARP'S Web site (www.aarp.org). On the basis of what you read there, do you think AARP is doing a good job of appealing to baby boomers?

DDB LIFE STYLE STUDY™ DATA ANALYSES

1. Which demographic variables are most closely associated with heavier consumption of the following? What would explain this association? Which contributes most to causing the consumption? (See Tables 1A through 6A.)
   a. Dessert
   b. DVD rental
   c. Fast-food restaurant
   d. Read books/articles about health

2. Which demographic variables are most closely associated with ownership of the following? What would explain this association? Which contributes most to causing the ownership? (See Tables 1A through 6A.)
   a. MP3 player
   b. Personal computer
   c. Individual retirement account
   d. Dog

3. Examine the DDB data in Tables 1A through 6A. Which demographic variables are most closely associated with watching the following types of shows on a regular basis? What would explain this association? Which contributes most to causing this enjoyment?
   a. News
   b. Children's shows
   c. Home improvement
   d. Sports

4. Which demographic variables are most closely associated with the following? What would explain this association? Which contributes most to causing each? (See Tables 1B through 6B.)
   a. Working hard
   b. View shopping as a form of entertainment
   c. View self as tech savvy
   d. Purchase clothes online

5. Using the DDB data in Table 5A, create age groups that approximate the generations described in the text. For which products and activities are there the greatest differences in heavier consumption across the generations? Why is this the case?

6. Using the DDB data in Table 5A, examine how actual age and cognitive age relate (positive, negative, no relationship) to the following behaviors. Compare and contrast the effects of actual age and cognitive age. Explain any similarities and differences you find.

   a. Read books/magazines about health
   b. Visit gourmet coffee bar
   c. Own cell phone
   d. Own personal computer
   e. Watch sports regularly

REVIEW QUESTIONS

1. What are demographics?
2. Why is population growth an important concept for marketers?
3. What trend(s) characterizes the occupational structure of the United States?
4. What trend(s) characterizes the level of education in the United States?
5. What trend(s) characterizes the level of income in the United States?
6. What is meant by subjective discretionary income? How does it affect purchases?
7. What trend(s) characterizes the age distribution of the American population?
8. What is cognitive age? How is it measured?
9. What is an *age cohort?* A *cohort analysis?*
10. Describe each of the major generations in America.
11. What is a social class system?
12. What is meant by the statement, "What exists is not a set of social classes but a series of status continua"?

13. What underlying cultural value determines most of the status dimensions in the United States?
14. What is meant by *status crystallization?* Is the degree of status crystallization relatively high or low in the United States? Explain.
15. Briefly describe the primary characteristics of each of the classes described in the text (assume a high level of status crystallization).
16. What is meant by the phrase *class to mass* and how does it relate to *upward-pull?*
17. What ethical issues arise in marketing to the lower social classes?
18. What are the two basic approaches used by marketers to measure social class?

19. What are the advantages of multi-item indexes? The disadvantages?
20. Describe the Hollingshead Index of Social Position.

DISCUSSION QUESTIONS

21. Which demographic shifts, if any, do you feel will have a noticeable impact on the market for the following in the next 10 years? Justify your answer.
    a. Upscale restaurants
    b. Lasik eye surgery
    c. Prescription drugs
    d. Internet shopping
    e. Green products
    f. Magazines
    g. Charity contributions
22. Given the projected changes in America's demographics, name five products that will face increasing demand and five that will face declining demand.

23. Why do the regional differences shown in Figure 4-1 exist? What are the implications of such differences for marketers of products such as soft drinks?
24. Will the increasing median age of our population affect the general tone of our society? In what ways?
25. Respond to the questions in Consumer Insight 4-1.
26. Which demographic variable, if any, is most related to the following?
    a. Watching extreme sports on TV
    b. Skiing
    c. Listening to public radio
    d. Hybrid automobile ownership

e. Spa treatments

f. Going to a NASCAR event

27. Describe how each of the following firms' product managers should approach the (*i*) pre-Depression generation, (*ii*) Depression generation, (*iii*) baby boom generation, (*iv*) Generation X, (*v*) Generation Y, and (*vi*) Millennials.

  a. Pepsi
  b. TGI Fridays
  c. The Golf Channel
  d. About.com
  e. The Humane Society
  f. iPod
  g. eBay.com
  h. Colgate toothpaste

28. Respond to the questions in Consumer Insight 4-2.

29. How will your lifestyle differ from your parents' when you are your parents' age?

30. How could a knowledge of social stratification be used in the development of a marketing strategy for the following?

  a. Boots
  b. Expensive jewelry
  c. Home security system
  d. Breakfast cereal
  e. International travel
  f. Habitat for Humanity

31. Do you think the United States is becoming more or less stratified over time?

32. Do your parents have a high or low level of status crystallization? Explain.

33. Based on the Hollingshead two-item index, what social class would your father be in? Your mother? What class will you be in at their age?

34. Name two products for which each of the three following demographic variables would be most influential in determining consumption. If you could combine two of the three, which would be the second demographic you would add to each? Justify your answer.

  a. Income
  b. Education
  c. Occupation

35. Name three products for which subjective discretionary income might be a better predictor of consumption than actual income. Justify your answer.

36. How do you feel about each of the ethical issues or controversies the text describes with respect to marketing to the lower classes? What other ethical issues do you see in this area?

37. Is it ethical for marketers to use the mass media to promote products that most members of the lower classes and working class cannot afford?

38. Would your answer to Question 37 change if the products were limited to children's toys?

39. Name five products for which the upward-pull strategy shown in Figure 4-3 would be appropriate. Name five for which it would be inappropriate. Justify your answers.

40. What causes the results shown in Table 4-6?

APPLICATION ACTIVITIES

41. On the basis of the demographics of devoted coffee shop patrons (p. 116), select two magazines in which the industry should advertise (use Standard Rate and Data (SRDS), Mediamark, or Simmons Research Bureau data). Justify your answer.

42. Interview a salesperson at the following locations and obtain a description of the average purchaser in demographic terms. Are the demographic shifts predicted in the text going to increase or decrease the size of this average-purchaser segment?

  a. Volvo dealership
  b. Electronics store
  c. Life insurance agent (vacation travel)
  d. The Gap
  e. Harley-Davidson dealership
  f. Pet store

43. Using Standard Rate and Data, Mediamark, or Simmons Research Bureau studies, pick three magazines that are oriented toward the different groups listed below. Analyze the differences in the products advertised and in the types of ads.

a. Income groups
b. Age groups
c. Occupation groups
d. Education levels

44. Interview three people over 50. Measure their cognitive age and the variables that presumably influence it. Do the variables appear to "cause" cognitive age? Try to ascertain if cognitive age or their chronological age is most influential on their consumption behavior.

45. Interview two members of the following generations. Determine the extent to which they feel the text description of their generation is accurate and how they think their generation differs from the larger society. Also determine what they think about how they are portrayed in the mass media and how well they are served by business today.
   a. Pre-Depression
   b. Depression
   c. Baby boom
   d. Generation X
   e. Generation Y
   f. Millenial

46. Interview a salesperson from an expensive, moderate, and inexpensive outlet for the following. Ascertain their perceptions of the social classes or status of their customers. Determine if their sales approach differs with differing classes.
   a. Men's clothing
   b. Women's clothing
   c. Furniture
   d. Wine

47. Examine a variety of magazines/newspapers and clip or copy an advertisement that positions a product as appropriate for each of the seven social classes described in the text (one ad per class). Explain how each ad appeals to that class.

48. Interview an unskilled worker, schoolteacher, retail clerk, and successful businessperson all in their 30s or 40s. Measure their social status using one of the multi-item measurement devices. Evaluate their status crystallization.

49. Visit a bowling alley and a golf course parking lot. Analyze the differences in the types of cars, dress, and behaviors of those patronizing these two sports.

50. Volunteer to work two days or evenings at a homeless shelter, soup kitchen, or other program aimed at very low income families. Write a brief report on your experiences and reactions.

REFERENCES

1. W. Friedman, "Tinkering Turns Movie into Must-See for Teens," *Advertising Age,* October 9, 2000, p. 26.

2. See, e.g., M. R. Stafford, "Demographic Discriminators of Service Quality in the Banking Industry," *Journal of Services Marketing,* no. 4 (1996), pp. 6–22; and I. M. Rosa-Diaz, "Price Knowledge," *Journal of Product and Brand Management* 13, no. 6 (2004), pp. 406–28.

3. K. Dawidowska, "Caffeine Overload," *American Demographics,* April 2002, p. 16.

4. U.S. Census Bureau, Population Division, Interim State Population Projections, April 21, 2005.

5. P. Mergenhagen, "What Can Minimum Wage Buy?" *American Demographics,* January 1996, pp. 32–36; and W. O'Hare and J. Schwartz, "One Step Forward, Two Steps Back," *American Demographics,* September 1997, pp. 53–56.

6. "Mean Earnings by Highest Degree Earned," *Education* (Washington, DC: U.S. Bureau of the Census, 2004), Table 215; data for 2002.

7. See, e.g., M. Mittila, H. Karjaluoto, and T. Pento, "Internet Banking Adoption among Mature Consumers," *Journal of Services Marketing* 17, no. 5 (2003), pp. 514–28; and V. Mittal, W. A. Kamakura, and R. Govind, "Geographic Patterns in Customer Service and Satisfaction," *Journal of Marketing,* July 2004, pp. 48–62.

8. See A. D. Mathios, "Socioeconomic Factors, Nutrition, and Food Choice," *Journal of Public Policy & Marketing,* Spring 1996, pp. 45–54.

9. S. Fulwood III, "Americans Draw Fatter Paychecks," *Register-Guard,* September 27, 1996, p. 1; and E. Kacapyr, "Are You Middle Class?" *American Demographics,* October 1996, pp. 31–35.

10. P. Francese, "A New Era of Cold Hard Cash," *American Demographics,* June 2004, pp. 40–41.

11. R. Gardyn, "Oh, The Good Life," *American Demographics,* November 2002, pp. 30–35.

12. For an example, see F. J. Mulhern, J. D. Williams, and R. P. Leone, "Variability of Brand Price Elasticities across Retail Stores," *Journal of Retailing,* no. 3 (1998), pp. 427–45.

13. M. Johnson, "The Application of Geodemographics to Retailing," *Journal of the Market Research Society,* January 1997, p. 212.

14. Consumer confidence indexes also consider the subjective nature of spending and represent "leading indicators" of consumer spending. For a discussion, see M. J. Weiss, "Inside Consumer Confidence Surveys," *American Demographics,* February 2003, pp. 22–29.

15. T. C. O'Guinn and W. D. Wells, "Subjective Discretionary Income," *Marketing Research,* March 1989, pp. 32–41; see also P. L. Wachtel and S. J. Blatt, "Perceptions of Economic Needs and of Anticipated Future Income," *Journal of Economic Psychology,* September 1990, pp. 403–15; and J. R. Rossiter, "'Spending Power' and the Subjective Discretionary Income (SDI) Scale," *Advances in Consumer Research,* vol. 22, eds. F. R. Kardes and M. Sujan (Provo, UT: Association for Consumer Research, 1995), pp. 236–40.

16. P. L. Alreck, "Consumer Age Role Norms," *Psychology & Marketing,* October 2000, pp. 891–909.

17. P. Henry, "Modes of Thought That Vary Systematically with Both Social Class and Age," *Psychology & Marketing,* May 2000, pp. 421–40.

18. For example, see R. Gardyn, "Shopping Attitudes by Life Stage," *American Demographics,* November 2002, p. 33.

19. "Population by Age Group," *Statistical Abstract of the United States 2001* (Washington, DC: U.S. Bureau of the Census, 2001), p. 16.

20. P. Sloan and J. Neff, "With Aging Boomers in Mind, P&G, Den-Mat Plan Launches," *Advertising Age,* April 13, 1998, p. 3.

21. This section is based on K. P. Gwinner and N. Stephens, "Testing the Implied Mediational Role of Cognitive Age"; D. Guiot, "Antecedents of Subjective Age Biases among Senior Women"; E. Sherman, L. G. Schiffman, and A. Mathur, "The Influence of Gender on the New-Age Elderly's Consumption Orientation"; I. Szmigin and M. Carrigan, "Time, Consumption, and the Older Consumer"; and M. Catterall and P. Maclaran, "Body Talk," all in *Psychology & Marketing,* October 2001, pp. 1031–48, 1049–71, 1073–90, 1091–1116, and 1117–33, respectively.

22. See A. S. Wellner, "Generational Divide," *American Demographics,* October 2000, pp. 53–58.

23. A. Rindfleisch, "Cohort Generational Influences on Consumer Socialization," in *Advances in Consumer Research,* vol. 21, eds. C. T. Allen and D. R. John (Provo, UT: Association for Consumer Research, 1994), pp. 470–76; and R. T. Rust and K. W. Y. Yeung, "Tracking the Age Wave," *Advances in Consumer Research,* vol. 22, ed. Kardes and Sujan, pp. 680–85.

24. G. P. Moschis, "Life Stages of the Mature Market," *American Demographics,* September 1996, pp. 44–51; G. P. Moschis, "Marketing to Older Adults"; G. P. Moschis, C. F. Curasi, and D. Bellenger, "Restaurant-Selection Preferences of Mature Consumers," *Cornell Hotel and Restaurant Administration Quarterly,* August 2003, pp. 51–60; and G. P. Moschis, C. F. Curasi, and D. Bellenger, "Patronage Motives of Mature Consumers in the Selection of Food and Grocery Stores," *Journal of Consumer Marketing* 21, no. 2 (2004), pp. 123–33. For an alternative segmentation scheme, see C. M. Morgan and D. J. Levy, "The Boomer Attitude," *American Demographics,* October 2002, pp. 42–45.

25. For a detailed treatment, see J. W. Smith and A. Clurman, *Rocking the Ages* (New York: Harper Business, 1997).

26. Table adapted from G. P. Moschis, D. N. Bellenger, and C. F. Curasi, "What Influences the Mature Consumer?" *Marketing Health Services,* Winter 2003, p. 19.

27. See N. Long, "Broken Down by Age and Sex," *Journal of the Market Research Society,* April 1998, pp. 73–91; and G. P. Moschis, "Life Stages of the Mature Market," *American Demographics,* September 1996, pp. 44–51.

28. L. L. Price, E. J. Arnould, and C. F. Curasi, "Older Consumers' Disposition of Special Possessions," *Journal of Consumer Research,* September 2000, p. 192.

29. See C. Yoon, "Age Differences in Consumers' Processing Strategies," *Journal of Consumer Research,* December 1997, pp. 329–40; S. Law, S. A. Hawkins, and F. I. M. Craik, "Repetition-Induced Belief in the Elderly," *Journal of Consumer Research,* September 1998, pp. 91–107; G. P. Moschis, "Consumer Behavior in Later Life," *Research in Consumer Behavior* 9 (2000), pp. 103–28; and G. Moschis, "Marketing to Older Adults," *Journal of Consumer Marketing* 20, no. 6 (2003), pp. 516–25.

30. P. Francese, "The Exotic Travel Boom," *American Demographics,* June 2002, pp. 48–49.

31. J. Schleimer, "Active Adults Uncovered," *Builder,* February 2001, pp. 336–40.

32. M. J. Weiss, "Great Expectations," *American Demographics,* May 2003, pp. 26–35.

33. K. Parker, "Reaping What They've Sown," *American Demographics,* December 1999, pp. 34–38; and R. G. Javalgi, E. G. Thomas, and S. R. Rao, "Meeting the Needs of the Elderly in the Financial Services Market," *Journal of Professional Services Marketing* 2, no. 2 (2000), pp. 87–105.

34. M. J. Weiss, "Great Expectations."

35. J. Saranow, "Online Deaccessioning," *The Wall Street Journal,* June 28, 2004, pp. B1–B2.

36. C. Gibson, "The Four Baby Booms," *American Demographics,* November 1993, pp. 36–41; and P. Braus, "The Baby Boom at Mid-Decade," *American Demographics,* April 1995, pp. 40–45.

37. P. Francese, "Older and Wealthier," *American Demographics,* November 2002, pp. 40–41.

38. J. Raymond, "The Joy of Empty Nesting," *American Demographics,* May 2000, pp. 49–54; P. Francese, "Big Spenders," *American Demographics,* September 2001, pp. 30–31; P. Francese, "The Coming Boom in Second-Home Ownership," *American Demographics,* October 2001, pp. 26–27; S. Yin, "More at Home on the Road," *American Demographics,* June 2003, pp. 26–27; and S. Yin, "Full Speed Ahead," *American Demographics,* September 2003, pp. 20–21.

39. P. Paul, "Targeting Boomers," *American Demographics,* March 2003, pp. 24–26.

40. "Online Health Information Poised to Become Important for Seniors," press release, Kaiser Family Foundation, January 12, 2005, at www.kff.org.

41. P. Francese, "The Exotic Travel Boom."

42. See R. Gardyn, "Retirement Redefined," *American Demographics,* November 2000, pp. 52–57.

43. P. Francese, "Working Women," *American Demographics,* March 2003, pp. 40–41.

44. J. Raymond, "Senior Living," *American Demographics,* November 2000, pp. 58–63.

45. L. Singhania, "Boomers Spend Big on Skin," *Register-Guard,* February 27, 2002, p. E1; see also J. Taylor, "A Second Coming of Age," *American Demographics,* June 2004, pp. 36–38.

46. D. Goodman, "Special K Drops Thin Models for Health Theme," *Marketing News,* March 2, 1998, p. 8.

47. K. Greene, "Marketing Surprise," *The Wall Street Journal,* April 6, 2004, pp. A1 and 12.

48. N. Zill and J. Robinson, "The Generation X Difference," *American Demographics*, April 1995, pp. 24–33.

49. Ibid.

50. C. Reynolds, "Gen X," *American Demographics,* May 2004, pp. 8–9.

51. "Farther ALONG the X Axis," *American Demographics,* May 2004, pp. 20–24.

52. J. Engebretson, "Odd Gen Out," *American Demographics,* May 2004, pp. 14–17; B. Barnes, "TV Ratings Show Stable Viewership by Young Males," *The Wall Street Journal,* May 27, 2004, p. B6; and C. Atkinson, "NBC's Grip on Prime Time Slips as Young Viewers Flee," *Advertising Age,* November 8, 2004, pp. 4 and 65.

53. P. Francese, "In the Shadow of the Boom," *American Demographics,* May 2004, pp. 40–41.

54. J. Halliday, "Volvo Goes After Younger Buyers," *Advertising Age,* January 19, 2004, p. 12.

55. M. Grimm, "Insurance Gets Hip," *American Demographics,* January 2002, pp. 48–49.

56. "P. Diddy Helps Pepsi Win the Super Bowl Ad Wars among Young Adults," press release, *STRATEGiY,* February 14, 2005, at www.strategiy.com.

57. For a discussion of the consequences of this, see A. Rindfleisch, J. E. Burroughs, and F. Denton, "Family Structure, Materialism, and Compulsive Consumption," *Journal of Consumer Research,* March 1997, pp. 312–25.

58. P. Paul, "Getting Inside Gen Y," *American Demographics,* September 2001, pp. 43–49.

59. E. O. Lawler, "Optimistic, Empowered Kids Back to Being Kids," *Advertising Age,* February 4, 2002, p. S2.

60. J. Napoli and M. T. Ewing, "The Net Generation," *Journal of International Consumer Marketing* 13, no. 1 (2001), pp. 21–34.

61. M. Madden, *America's Online Pursuits,* Pew Internet and American Life Project, December 22, 2003, at www.pewinternet.org.

62. N. R. Brier, "Coming of Age," *American Demographics,* November 2004, pp. 16–19.

63. N. Shirouzu, "Scion Plays Hip-Hop Impresario to Impress Younger Drivers," *The Wall Street Journal Online,* October 5, 2004, at www.wsj.com.

64. P. Paul, "Echo Boomerang," *American Demographics,* June 2001, pp. 45–49; and A. Merrick, "Gap's Greatest Generation?" *The Wall Street Journal Online,* September 15, 2004, at www.wsj.com.

65. N. Shepherdson, "New Kids on the Lot," *American Demographics,* January 2000, p. 47.

66. M. Harvey, "Let's Hear it for the Boys," *American Demographics,* August 2000, p. 30; and "TRU Projects Teens Will Spend $169 Billion in 2004," TRU press release, December 1, 2004.

67. P. Underhill, *Call of the Mall* (New York: Simon and Schuster, 2004), p. 160; see also D. L. Haytko and J. Baker, "It's All at the Mall," *Journal of Retailing* 80 (2004), pp. 67–83.

68. D. Chaplin, "The Truth Hurts," *American Demographics,* April 1999, pp. 68–69; for discussion of other issues related to Generation Y and advertising see Y. Bao and A. T. Shao, "Nonconformity Advertising to Teens," *Journal of Advertising Research,* May/June 2002, pp. 56–65; and A. J. Bush, C. A. Martin, and V. D. Bush, "Sports Celebrity Influence on the Behavioral Intentions of Generation Y," *Journal of Advertising Research,* March 2004, pp. 108–18.

69. C. La Ferle, S. M. Edwards, and W. Lee, "Teens' Use of Traditional Media and the Internet," *Journal of Advertising Research,* May 2000, pp. 55–65; and H. Fattah and P. Paul, "Gaming Gets Serious," *American Demographics,* May 2002, pp. 38–43.

70. M. Spiegler, "Marketing Street Culture," *American Demographics,* November 1996, pp. 29–34; and J. D. Zbar, "Hispanic Teens Set Urban Beat," *Advertising Age,* June 25, 2001, p. S6.

71. J. Neff, "P7G Crawls the Malls," *Advertising Age,* February 4, 2002, p. S3.

72. K. Cleland, "Action Sports Form Fabric of Generation," *Advertising Age,* April 16, 2001, p. S22.

73. "Internet Usage," *IT Facts,* accessed April 30, 2005, at www.itfacts.biz.

74. B. S. Bulik, "Mattel Rolls Out Juice Box MP3 Player Just for Tweens," *Advertising Age,* September 27, 2004, p. 9.

75. S. Thompson, "Cosmetic Change," *Advertising Age,* June 28, 2004, p. 4.

76. K. Labich, "Class in America," *Fortune,* February 7, 1994, p. 114.

77. J. E. Fisher, "Social Class and Consumer Behavior," in *Advances in Consumer Research,* vol. 14, ed. M. Wallendorf and P. Anderson (Provo, UT: Association for Consumer Research, 1987), pp. 492–96.

78. See R. P. Health, "The New Working Class," *American Demographics,* January 1998, pp. 51–55.

79. R. Coleman, "The Continuing Significance of Social Class in Marketing," *Journal of Consumer Research,* December 1983, p. 265.

80. R. Greenstein and I. Shapiro, *The New Definitive CBO Data on Income and Tax Trends,* Report by the Center on Budget and Policy Priorities, September 23, 2003, at www.cbpp.org; and T. G. Williams, "Social Class Influences on Purchase Evaluation Criteria," *Journal of Consumer Marketing* 19, no. 3 (2002), pp. 249–76.

81. See Heath, "The New Working Class."

82. See A. M. Kerwin, "Brands Pursue Old, New Money," *Advertising Age,* June 11, 2001, p. S1.

83. See J. P. Dickson and D. L. MacLachlan, "Social Distance and Shopping Behavior," *Journal of the Academy of Marketing Science,* Spring 1990, pp. 153–62.

84. See also D. Watson, "In Search of the Poor," *Journal of Economic Psychology* 21 (2000), pp. 495–515.

85. Mergenhagen, "What Can Minimum Wage Buy?"

86. H. Fattah, "The Rising Tide," *American Demographics,* April 2001, pp. 48–53.

87. For a theoretical examination, see P. Henry, "Hope, Hopelessness, and Coping," *Psychology & Marketing,* May 2004, pp. 375–403.

88. Fattah, "The Rising Tide."

89. R. H. Hill, D. L. Ramp, and L. Silver, "The Rent-to-Own Industry and Pricing Disclosure Tactics," *Journal of Public Policy & Marketing,* Spring 1998, pp. 1–10.

90. C. Miller, "The Have-Nots," *Marketing News,* August 1, 1994, p. 2.

91. See A. B. Hollingshead, *Elmstown's Youth* (New York: John Wiley & Sons, 1949); and W. L. Warner, M. Meeker, and K. Eels, *Social Class in America: A Manual of Procedure for the Measurement of Social Status* (Chicago: Science Research Associates, 1949).

Courtesy Girl Scouts of The United States of America.

5

The Changing American Society: Subcultures

■ Slightly less than 7 percent of the Girl Scouts are Hispanic, compared to 17 percent of the girls in the appropriate age range (5 to 17). It would seem that the Girl Scouts would be very appealing to new immigrants, offering direction and building on the strong sense of community that is central to Hispanic culture.

However, attracting Hispanic youth to the Girl Scouts will require significant understanding and training. For example, although the green Girl Scout uniform may remind many non-Hispanic moms of good times and cookie sales, it may trigger memories of immigration officers in many Hispanic moms. In addition, some Hispanic parents may feel that the Girl Scouts don't teach the kids proper respect for adults by having them address troop leaders by their first names.

To address these issues and recruit more Hispanic girls, the organization recently launched a program entitled "For Every Girl, Everywhere." A spokesperson stated, "We couldn't just go in and make some ads. We had to start from within." This meant, in part, identifying the unique needs of Hispanics and the common elements between their culture and the Girl Scouts. This resulted in a major training effort for volunteers in areas with Hispanic populations.

The training focused on such basic issues as how to address a Hispanic woman (señora) and the importance of building a relationship. Hard-sell approaches and large meetings with parent groups were ruled out. Instead, soft-sell chats over coffee were encouraged.

The programming (the product) was also altered. Brothers were encouraged to attend some events. Camping, an uncommon activity for Hispanic girls, began including the entire family. Elements of Hispanic traditions are also being incorporated into Scouting. Las Posadas, a Hispanic Christmas tradition that pays homage to Mary and Joseph's search for an inn, is being conducted by Girl Scout troops in some areas.

The Girl Scouts have also recognized that there is not a single best approach to this group because Hispanics are not a single culture. As the national director states, "It's a grassroots enterprise, and the grass is different in every location."[1]

In the previous chapter, we described how changes in American demographics are creating challenges and opportunities for marketers. Another extremely important aspect of the American society is its numerous subcultures such as the Hispanic subculture described above. Although American society has always contained numerous subcultures, until recently many marketers treated it as a homogeneous culture based primarily on Western European values. This view of America was never very accurate, and it is even less so today as non-European immigration, differential birthrates, and increased ethnic identification accentuate the heterogeneous nature of our society.

An array of racial, ethnic, nationality, religious, and regional groups or subcultures characterize American society today. These subcultures are growing at different rates and are themselves undergoing change. In this chapter, we describe the more important subcultures in America. We also highlight the marketing strategy implications of a heterogeneous rather than a homogeneous society.

THE NATURE OF SUBCULTURES

A **subculture** is *a segment of a larger culture whose members share distinguishing values and patterns of behavior.* The unique values and patterns of behavior shared by subculture group members are based on the social history of the group as well as on its current situation. Subculture members are also part of the larger culture in which they exist, and they generally share most behaviors and beliefs with the core culture. As Figure 5-1 indicates, the degree to which an individual behaves in a manner unique to a subculture depends on the extent to which the individual identifies with that subculture.

America has traditionally been viewed as a melting pot or a soup bowl. Immigrants from various countries came to America and quickly (at least by the second generation) surrendered their old languages, values, behaviors, and even religions. In their place, they acquired American characteristics that were largely a slight adaptation of Western European, particularly British, features. The base American culture was vast enough that new immigrants did not change the flavor of the mixture to any noticeable extent. Although this is a reasonable approximation of the experience of most Western European immigrants, it

| FIGURE 5-1 | Identification with a Subculture Produces Unique Market Behaviors |

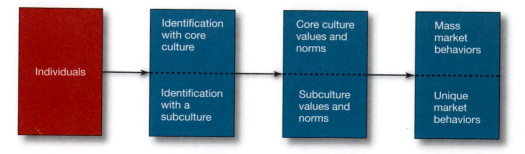

isn't very accurate for African, Hispanic, Asian, or Arabic immigrants. Nor does it accurately describe the experience of Native Americans.

Today, America is perhaps better described as a salad rather than a melting pot or a soup bowl.[2] When a small amount of a new ingredient is added to a soup, it generally loses its identity completely and blends into the overall flavor of the soup. In a salad, each ingredient retains its own unique identity while adding to the color and flavor of the overall salad.[3] However, even in the salad bowl analogy, we should add a large serving of salad dressing, which represents the core American culture and blends the diverse groups into a cohesive society. As one expert stated,

> The future of diversity is not multiculturalism—separate and distinct ethnic enclaves—but a mixing, blurring, and blending of racial and ethnic traits.[4]

Ethnic groups are the most commonly described subcultures, but religions and geographic regions are also the bases for strong subcultures in the United States. Generations, as described in the previous chapter, also function like subcultures. Thus, *we are all members of several subcultures*. Each subculture may influence different aspects of our lifestyle. Our attitudes toward new products or imported products may be strongly influenced by our regional subculture, our taste in music by our generation subculture, our food preferences by our ethnic subculture, and our alcohol consumption by our religious subculture. The communications manager at Miller Brewing describes his firm's view of the influence of ethnicity and age on consumption:

> We used to have an ethnic marketing department up until several years ago. . . . [But now we believe] the things that young Hispanic or young African American or young white people have in common are much stronger and more important than any ethnic difference.[5]

This manager believes that age is more important than ethnicity in influencing the behaviors of the members of his target market for his product. The Jeep ad shown in Illustration 5-1 takes more of a middle-ground approach. This ad, targeting young Hispanics, speaks to their cultural heritage and youth simultaneously using Spanish copy.

Identifying which subculture, if any, is an important determinant of behavior for a specific product is a key task for marketing managers. In the sections that follow, we describe the major ethnic, religious, and regional subcultures in America. While we will describe the general nature of these subcultures, it must be emphasized that *there are very large variations within each subculture*. Our focus in this chapter is on America, but all countries have a variety of subcultures that marketers must consider.

ETHNIC SUBCULTURES

Until the 2000 Census, the Bureau of the Census used the terms black, white, Asian/Pacific Islander, and American Indian/Alaskan Native/Aleut and Other to describe America's major racial groups. Hispanic was used as an ethnic term to describe individuals from Spanish-speaking cultures regardless of race. Under this system, people of Arab background were considered white and people from China, India, and Samoa were grouped together. There were obvious problems with such a system, and more than 10 million Americans refused to place themselves into one of the racial categories used in the 1990 Census. In addition, many younger Hispanics do not consider themselves to be white or black, but Hispanics or Latinos. Other individuals have parents from two different races and are

ILLUSTRATION 5-1

The degree to
which an ad needs
to be customized
for an ethnic audi-
ence varies by
product and strat-
egy. This ad for
Jeep blends His-
panic and youth
themes.

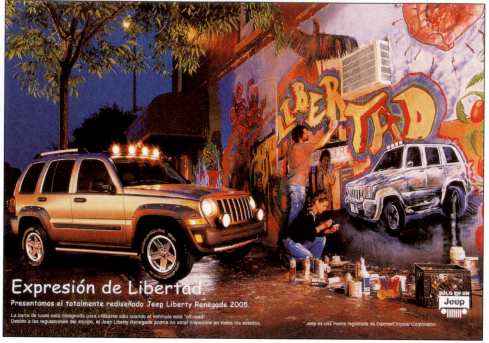

Courtesy DaimlerChrysler.

proud of their mixed heritage.[6] Romona Douglas, of white, black, and American Indian descent, described her feelings thusly:

> The assumption is that black people are a certain way, and white people are a particular way, and
> Asians are a certain way. Well, what about multi-racial families? I don't appreciate a McDonald's
> commercial with a street-wise black person. That is not me, that is not my upbringing. A lot of
> marketing campaigns are based on stereotypes of mono-racial communities.[7]

In the 2000 Census, the Hispanic question appeared before the race question. Respondents were asked if they were *Spanish/Hispanic/Latino*. To answer yes, respondents had
to select a nationality group as well (*Mexican/Mexican American/Chicano, Puerto Rican,
Cuban, Other*). In the race question that followed, respondents could make multiple selections from 15 categories (*White; Black/African American/Negro; American Indian/Alaskan
Native; Asian Indian; Chinese; Filipino; Japanese; Korean; Vietnamese; Native Hawaiian;
Guamanian/Chamorro; Samoan; Other Pacific Islander; Other Race*). With this system,
Douglas could accurately identify herself. However, Americans of Arab or Middle-Eastern
descent had to choose Other Race. The new system has produced 57 race categories that
render comparison of the 2000 data with prior data difficult if not impossible.[8] Despite such
shortcomings, the new data provide a much richer understanding of the American society.

We define **ethnic subcultures** broadly as *those whose members' unique shared behaviors are based on a common racial, language, or national background.* Figure 5-2 provides
the current and projected sizes of the major ethnic groups in America. As this figure makes
clear, non-European ethnic groups constitute a significant and growing part of our population, from 32 percent in 2005 to 38 percent by 2020. The percentages shown in the figure
understate the importance of these ethnic groups to specific geographic regions.[9] Thus,
Hispanics are the largest population group in parts of Arizona, California, Florida, New

Major Ethnic Subcultures in the United States: 2005–2020   FIGURE 5-2

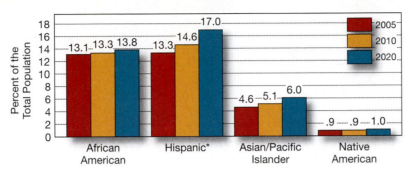

*May be of any race.

Source: "Table 10 Resident Population," *Statistical Abstract of the United States* (Washington, DC: U.S. Bureau of the Census, 2001), p. 13.

Mexico, and Texas; Asian Americans are the largest group in Honolulu; and African Americans are a majority in parts of the South and urban areas in the Northeast and Midwest. In contrast, states such as Maine, Vermont, and West Virginia are more than 95 percent white.

The relatively faster growth rate of non-European groups is due to a higher birthrate among some of these groups and to greater immigration. Immigration has accounted for over a third of the U.S. population growth over the past several decades. Between 700,000 and 1.1 million legal immigrants arrive each year. In 2003, the sources of these immigrants were as follows (these percentages have been relatively stable over the past several decades).[10]

Asia	34.7%
Mexico	16.4
Europe	14.3
Caribbean	9.7
Central/South America	15.5
Africa	6.9

The influx of ethnic immigrants not only increases the size of ethnic subcultures, but also reinforces the unique behaviors and attitudes derived from the group's home culture. In the following sections, we describe the major ethnic subcultures. It is critical to remember that *all subcultures are very diverse, and general descriptions do not apply to all of the members.*[11]

Although one's ethnic heritage is a permanent characteristic, its influence is situational. That is, the degree to which a person's consumption is influenced by his or her ethnicity depends on such factors as who he or she is with, where he or she is, and other physical and social cues.[12] Thus, one's ethnicity might play no role in a decision to grab a quick bite for lunch during a business meeting and a large role in deciding what to prepare for family dinner.

In addition, ethnicity is only one factor that influences an individual's behavior. As we saw in the previous chapter, demographic factors also play a role. For example, a 45-year-old black doctor earning $90,000 per year and a 45-year-old white doctor with the same income would probably have more consumption behaviors in common than they would with members of their own race who were low-income service workers. As shown below, the various ethnic groups have distinct demographic profiles.[13] Thus, one must use caution in

TABLE 5-1

Ethnic Subcultures
and Consumption

	White	Black	Hispanic
Products			
Ground coffee	110	47	64
Colas (frequent)	98	120	111
Aftershave lotion/cologne	94	150	102
Wok	101	64	115
Activities			
Barbequing	111	35	83
Picnic	110	17	114
Soccer	105	48	230
Movies (frequent)	93	141	125
Shopping			
TJ Maxx	90	167	92
ShopKo	114	14	61
Red Robin	100	68	119
Red Lobster	95	145	86
Media			
Cosmopolitan	103	95	156
GQ	78	238	108
Jazz radio	93	163	86
MTV	95	138	129

Note: 100 = Average level of use, purchase, or consumption.

Source: *Mediamark Reporter 2002—University* (New York: Mediamark Research Inc., March 2002).

assuming that observed consumption differences between ethnic groups are caused by their ethnicity. These differences often disappear when demographic variables such as income are held constant.

	Whites	Blacks	Hispanics	Asian/Pacific Islander
Median age (2010)	38	31	27	36
High school or more (25 or older)	85%	80%	57%	88%
Bachelor's or more (25 or older)	28%	17%	11%	50%
Children under 18	46%	56%	63%	N/A
Growth rate (2000–2020)	13%	10%	25%	11%
Median household income	$45,086	$29,026	$33,103	$52,626

Examine Table 5-1. *Which of these differences are mainly caused by ethnicity or race and which are caused by other factors?*

Astute marketers are aggressively pursuing opportunities created by increased ethnic diversity. Bank of America spent $40 million marketing to the Hispanic, Asian, and African American markets in 2002. AT&T runs broadcast and print ads in 20 different languages in the United States. EABC, a cable and satellite network, broadcasts programming in Arabic, Asian, Indian, Chinese, Filipino, Greek, Italian, Korean, Polish, and Russian. Chrysler advertises its New Yorker model by emphasizing safety features to the general market, styling to African Americans, and aspiration and achievement to Hispanics. However, marketing to ethnic groups requires a thorough understanding of the attitudes and values of each group.[14] For example, a New York Life Insurance ad designed to appeal to Koreans was a disaster because it used a Chinese model.[15]

AFRICAN AMERICANS

Debra Sandler, director of Flavor Brands (Slice, Mountain Dew, Mug Root Beer, and others) for PepsiCo, recently discussed the differences in marketing to the overall market and marketing to African Americans.

The strategy does not differ, the tactics differ. For example, if we say we want to be the beverage of choice to all teens, one of the things we have to do if we want to get to where teens are, to where they live and breathe, is to be wherever they are. We want to be available; we also want to be seen as part of their lifestyle. The difference is we may go about that differently for an 18-year-old Anglo male who lives in the suburbs than for an 18-year-old African American male who happens to live in an urban environment.

For example, we did a promotion where we gave away prizes—jet skis and convertibles. One thing we heard loud and clear from the urban teens was that they didn't participate in the promotion because they didn't think the prizes were relevant. So sometimes the tactics must change. . . . While we, African American consumers, are our own segment, we are also very much a part of the mainstream. In fact, in many cases we are driving the mainstream. . . . Again, in reaching teens, if I can produce television creative that appeals to an urban 18-year-old male, chances are that creative will appeal to all teens. It doesn't always work the other way around.[16]

African Americans, or blacks (surveys do not indicate a clear preference for either term among African Americans),[17] constitute 13 percent of the American population. Concentrated in the South and the major metropolitan areas outside the South, African Americans represent $723 billion in buying power, which is expected to grow by over 30 percent over the next five years.[18] Thus, it is not surprising that marketers are very interested in this group.

On average, African Americans are younger than the white population and tend to have less education and lower household income levels. However, stereotyping African Americans as being of low income would not be accurate.[19] Nearly one-third of black households have incomes above the median level for whites:

African American Household Income	Percentage
>$75,000	13%
$50,000–$74,999	14
$25,000–$49,999	29
$15,000–$24,999	16
<$15,000	27

Education, income, and purchasing power have risen dramatically among African Americans over the past several decades and marketers are responding. Jaguar North America recently targeted the wealthier portion of this group with a direct-mail campaign to a list of 675,000 African Americans between the ages of 35 and 54 with annual incomes over $75,000 who do not own Jaguars. Spike Lee's agency created the mailing, which included a lifestyle-oriented brochure and an eight-minute video. The video showed a black female surgeon and her sculptor husband preparing for a jaunt to Martha's Vineyard from

New York's Harlem in their Jaguar. The theme to the campaign was, "It's not luck that got you where you are."

Many of the consumption differences noted between African Americans and other groups relate as much to age, education, and economic circumstances as to race.[20] However, other differences are caused by differing values and lifestyles associated with the group's unique African American identity.

Consumer Groups

It would be a mistake to treat African Americans as a single segment. Numerous distinct segments exist as a function of demographics, life stage, and lifestyle. For example, Market Segment Research found four segments relating to aspirations, occupation, income, and life stage. The segments were *Contented* (mature and content with life, followers not leaders, not status conscious); *Upwardly Mobile* (active, status-conscious professionals, financially secure, optimistic about future); *Living for the Moment* (young, socially active, carefree, and image conscious); and *Living Day to Day* (low education and income, price conscious, pessimistic about future).[21]

Marketers are also finding important differences in terms of brand and style consciousness. While African Americans are more brand and style conscious than Whites, research by Yankelovich finds wide differences *among* African Americans represented by two distinct segments labeled "market leaders" and "market followers":[22]

- *Market leaders* want to be on the cutting edge and to set trends. This group tends to have higher incomes that allow them to buy the "latest and greatest." This group has a relatively strong need to be seen as "hip and cool," and sees brands as communicating their unique style and identity. This group tends not to be price sensitive and tends to be brand loyal.
- *Market followers* tend to follow trends rather than lead the way. Compared to market leaders, this group has less of a need to be seen as "hip and cool," and they are considerably less likely to see brands as an indicator of their style and identity. This group often has financial constraints that make them more conservative, more price sensitive, and less brand loyal.

Generational differences also exist and have important marketing implications.[23] African American Baby Boomers and aging Generation Xers are driving growth in income and purchase power through education and professional achievement. Many of these consumers are migrating to the suburbs surrounding major metropolitan areas.[24] Such changes are creating challenges and opportunities for marketers. Consider the following quote by Pepper Miller, president of Hunter-Miller Group, an African American consulting firm:

Black Generation Xers spawned one of the greatest marketing and lifestyle phenomena: the Hip Hop Culture. However, not all African American Generation Xers are Hip Hoppers. Yet marketing communications targeting the African American Generation X segment continue to reflect typical and often stereotypical images of Hip Hop's rap culture.[25]

Moreover, the aging Xers are increasingly focused on professional accomplishments and leveraging their higher educations toward higher incomes. The challenge for marketers is how to reflect these ongoing generational changes while still embracing core cultural values.[26]

Obviously these are just some of the ways that the African American market can be segmented, reflecting the diversity that exists both within and across ethnic subcultures. Marketing strategies that target African Americans as a single market are likely to fail.

Media Usage

African Americans make greater use of mass media than do whites, have different preferences, and report more influence by mass media ads than do whites.[27] In the spring of 2000,
there was little overlap between the 10 most popular evening shows among black and white
audiences (excluding sports specials):[28]

Blacks' Top 10	Whites' Top 10
1. Jamie Foxx Show (WB)	1. Friends (NBC)
2. Moesha (UPN)	2. Frasier (NBC)
3. Malcolm & Eddie (UPN)	3. 60 Minutes (CBS)
4. Showtime at the Apollo (SYN)	4. E.R. (NBC)
5. Law and Order (NBC)	5. Law and Order (NBC)
6. Fresh Prince of Bel Air (SYN)	6. Wheel of Fortune (SYN)
7. Walker, Texas Ranger (CBS)	7. Touched by an Angel (CBS)
8. 60 Minutes (CBS)	8. World News Tonight (ABC)
9. Martin (SYN)	9. Drew Carey Show (ABC)
10. The Simpsons (FOX)	10. Walker, Texas Ranger (CBS)

Source: Mediamark Research, Inc.

As this information suggests, African Americans prefer shows with African American
themes or performers, although there is evidence that TV preferences are much more similar among teenagers across ethnicity.[29] Consider comments from an advertiser in the automobile industry who has worked with Black Entertainment Television (BET):

> We've been working with BET for 15 years. There are precious few TV outlets that specifically
> target the African American audience. BET is far and away the flagship operation for that. What
> we like about BET is that it has continued to evolve and diversify its programming. The African
> American market isn't really one big monolithic market, even though that's what people think.
> There's a lot of diversity in the market. BET's current programming speaks to the old, the young,
> and everyone in between.[30]

Likewise, radio stations that play music popular with African Americans and magazines
like *Essence* and *Ebony* focused on African American concerns receive most of the attention from this segment. Areas with large black populations will also often have a black-
owned and -focused newspaper with substantial black readership.

African Americans have historically lagged behind in terms of computer ownership and
Internet usage. This gap is rapidly decreasing and in some cases, African Americans outstrip the general population. For example, computer ownership by African Americans
(60 percent) in 2003 was roughly that of the general population (64 percent). And Internet
penetration among African Americans is estimated at 69 percent in 2007 (compared to
81 percent white), up from 45 percent in 2001.[31] Not surprisingly, Black-focused sites such
as NetNoir (www.netnoir.net) and BlackVoices (www.blackvoices.com) are attracting
advertisers such as IBM, Hewlett-Packard, Wells Fargo, Walt Disney, and McDonalds.

Some interesting aspects regarding African American Internet usage include:[32]

- Research by AOL finds that African Americans who are online are more likely to use
  broadband connections (43 percent) than the general online population (36 percent).
- Research by Digital Marketing Service finds that most African Americans read online
  ads and are more likely to find them informative (46 percent) than the general online
  population (26 percent).

- African Americans prefer a Black perspective on news and information. BlackPlanet.com is currently the largest online community for African Americans. It features news, entertainment, and career information from a Black perspective and has over 14 million members.
- African Americans are more likely to search for job and career information online than Whites, and more likely to purchase clothing and apparel, listen to music, and watch videos online than the general online population.

Clearly there are ongoing opportunities for marketing to African Americans in a host of media outlets, some of which are specifically tailored to the needs of this market.

Marketing to African Americans

Marketing to African Americans should be based on the same principles as marketing to any other group. That is, the market should be carefully analyzed, relevant needs should be identified among one or more segments of the market, and the entire marketing mix should be designed to meet the needs of the target segments. At times, the relevant segment of the African American market will require a unique product. At other times, it will require a unique package, advertising medium, or message. Or no change may be required from the marketing mix used to reach a broader market. However, it is critical that the decision on how to appeal to this market be based on a sound understanding of the needs of the selected segments.

Products   African Americans have different skin tones and hair from white Americans. Cosmetics and similar products developed for white consumers are often inappropriate for black consumers. Recognition of this fact by major firms has created aggressive competition for the $6.2 billion that African Americans spend each year on personal care products and services including cosmetics, hair care, and skin care.[33] L'Oréal created their Soft-Sheen-Carson Division to specifically serve women in this market. Iman's line of cosmetics which are sold through Walgreens and Target is similarly targeted to this market (www.i-iman.com). Illustration 5-2 shows a print advertisement for a product designed specifically for the unique needs of the African American market and another for a product designed to meet the needs of all ethnic groups but that is being promoted to African Americans.

Numerous companies have found it worthwhile to alter their products to meet unique social needs of African Americans. Hallmark has a Mahogany line of greeting cards that features black characters and sayings. Mattel, Tyco Toys and others now offer a variety of African American dolls. Bank of America offers Kente checks with Kente cloth borders and the option of several symbols of relevance to the black community in the center of the check. And, AG Mobile (www.agmobile.com) has launched Def Jam Mobile to offer products targeted at young African Americans and the hip-hop market such as rap-inspired downloadable ring tones (an important means of self-expression) and games such as Cleo, a hip-hop card game. As one senior executive for AG Mobile notes, "You need to have multiple brands to support what America really looks like."[34]

Communications   A common mistake when communicating with any ethnic group is to assume that its members are the same as the larger culture except for superficial differences. Failure to recognize this often results in commercials targeted at African Americans that simply place the firm's standard ad in black media or that replace white actors with black actors, without changing the script, language, or setting. For example, Greyhound Bus targeted blacks by placing its standard commercials on black radio stations. Unfortunately,

Courtesy of Alberto-Culver Company.

Used with permission of the Procter & Gamble Company.

the soundtrack for the commercials was country and western, which is not popular with most black audiences.

Not all messages targeted at African Americans need to differ significantly from those targeted at other groups, though the use of black actors and spokespersons is important.[35] This is particularly the case for ethnically relevant products such as cosmetics and for those with strong ethnic identities.[36] The appeal of the Motions ad in Illustration 5-2 is to the desire for attractiveness that is the same for whites and blacks, though the product is designed to meet the unique grooming needs of black women. In other instances, advertisers can simply change the race of the models in the ads and perhaps the consumption setting to help indicate that the product is appropriate for the needs of African Americans. This works when the product, the appeal, and the appropriate language are the same for the black target market and the other groups being targeted. The Tide ad in Illustration 5-2 is a good example of this approach. This ad also recognizes the life-stage transition of many Generation Xers as they age and have families. Such ads can be effectively run in both black and general media.

In contrast, the ad for Stove Top Stuffing shown in Illustration 5-3 is used specifically to target African Americans. Research revealed that many African Americans refer to foods of this type as dressing rather than stuffing. Thus, in ads targeting this segment the word *dressing* is used. Note also the use of the term *Mama* and the outdoor basketball court setting.

Another means of communicating with the African American and other ethnic communities is **event marketing,** which involves *creating or sponsoring an event that has a particular appeal to a market segment.* Honey Nut Cheerios sponsors the Soul Fest music event that travels to 30 urban markets each year.

ILLUSTRATION 5-2

African American consumers have both unique and shared needs relative to other ethnic groups.

This product is widely used by African Americans and white Americans. However, this ad was designed to reflect the fact that African Americans generally refer to this product category as *dressing* while whites term it *stuffing*.

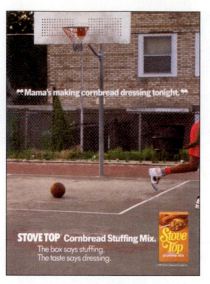

Used with permission of Kraft Foods, Inc.

Retailing Retailers often adjust the merchandising mix to meet the needs of African American shoppers. JCPenney Co. had great success with its Authentic African boutiques in stores located near significant African American populations. These small shops, located inside JCPenney stores, featured clothing, handbags, hats, and other accessories imported from Africa. Albertson's, a national grocery retailer, adapts its merchandising mix in African American neighborhoods. One store in Oak Cliff Texas has a full grocery aisle devoted to African American hair care products. And, their food selections also cater to African American tastes with products such as offal (organ meat) and brands such as Glory.[37]

Surveys reveal that a major difference between white and black shoppers' store selection criteria is respect. More than 60 percent of African American shoppers say that one of their most important reasons for choosing a store is that it treats its customers with respect.[38] This focus on respect is caused by the sad fact that many black shoppers still encounter obviously disrespectful acts such as being closely watched while shopping as well as more subtle discrimination such as slower service.[39] Another study showed that middle-class African Americans felt unwelcome at a variety of leisure activities.[40] The need for cultural sensitivity training for retail and service employees is clear.[41]

African Americans also use shopping as a form of recreation more than whites.[42] This suggests that stores with black customers should pay particular attention to providing a pleasant and fun shopping environment. Blacks also respond to sales differently than whites and have differing desires with respect to credit card, cash, and check payments.[43] Thus, all aspects of the shopping experience need to be carefully aligned to the needs of the target shoppers.

HISPANICS

The Bureau of the Census defines **Hispanic** as *a person of Cuban, Mexican, Puerto Rican, South or Central American, or other Spanish culture or origin regardless of race.* It is measured by a person's response to the question: Are you Spanish/Hispanic/Latino? The Hispanic market is now the largest and fastest growing ethnic subculture in the United States. By 2020 Hispanics are expected to represent 17 percent of the U.S. population. Marketers are definitely taking notice.

Like the other ethnic groups in America, Hispanics are diverse. Many marketers feel that the Hispanic subculture is not a single ethnic subculture but instead is three main and several minor nationality subcultures: Mexican Americans (66 percent), Puerto Ricans (9 percent), Cubans (4 percent), and other Latinos, mainly from Central America (14 percent). Each group speaks a slightly different version of Spanish and has somewhat distinct values and lifestyles. Further, each group tends to live in distinct regions of the country: Mexican Americans in the Southwest and California, Puerto Ricans in New York and New Jersey, Cubans in Florida, and other Latinos in California, New York, and Florida. Income levels also vary across the groups, with Cuban Americans having incomes well above the others.

Others argue that while one must be sensitive to nationality-based differences, the common language, common religion (Roman Catholic for most Hispanics), and the emergence of national Spanish-language media and entertainment figures create sufficient cultural homogeneity for most products and advertising campaigns. However, at a minimum, the decision to treat Hispanics as a single ethnic subculture needs to take into consideration factors relating to acculturation, language, and generational influences, which we discuss next.

Acculturation, Language, and Generational Influences

Given that over 40 percent of growth in the Hispanic population is attributable to immigration, the level of acculturation plays a major role in the attitudes and behaviors of Hispanic consumers.[44] **Acculturation** is *the degree to which an immigrant has adapted to his or her new culture*.[45] Acculturation is highly related to language use and both are strongly influenced by generational factors. A recent study by the Pew Hispanic Center identifies three generations of Hispanic adults:

First generation adults (63 percent) are those born outside the United States. This generation has the lowest income and education, is most likely to identify themselves as Hispanic (including country of origin), is most likely to have Spanish as their primary language (72 percent), and is most likely to possess traditional values including a masculine view of the family decision hierarchy.

Second generation adults (19 percent) are those born in the United States to immigrant parents. Compared to the first generation, this generation has higher income and education, is more likely to identify themselves as Americans (though 62 percent still identify as Hispanic), is equally split between bilingual and English as primary language, and is somewhat less likely to ascribe to traditional values.

Third generation (and beyond) adults (17 percent) are those born in the United States to U.S.-born parents. This group has the highest education and income, is most likely to identify as Americans (57 percent, versus 41 percent who identify themselves as Hispanic), is most likely to have English as the primary language (only 22 percent are bilingual; none are Spanish only), and is also somewhat less likely to ascribe to traditional values.[46]

As this discussion indicates, income, education, language, and identification with Hispanic culture change across generations. However, it is also important to note that most Hispanic adults identify more or less strongly with a Hispanic culture.[47] This strong cultural identity is also true of Hispanic teens, many of whom were born in the United States and would thus be classified as second and third generation teens.[48] As discussed in Consumer Insight 5-1, Hispanic teens are blending language and culture, setting cultural trends in the general U.S. population, and living truly bicultural and bilingual experiences.

The Hispanic culture is heavily influenced by the Roman Catholic religion. It is family oriented, with the extended family playing an important role across generations (unlike the general U.S. population where extended family has lost its importance). It is also a masculine culture, and sports are very important to Hispanics, particularly boxing, baseball, and soccer. This masculine orientation manifests itself in many ways, including husband-dominant household decision making.[49] Examine Illustration 5-4. Note the family focus and the strong presence of the male.

The Hispanic culture generally has a fairly traditional view of the appropriate role of women. For example, the wife is expected to prepare the food for the family. This produces challenges and opportunities for marketers. Church's Chicken encountered resistance to its

Hispanic Teens Rule

Hispanic teens constitute about 15 percent of all teenagers but are far more important to marketers than that percentage suggests.[50] First, they spend more than other teenagers. Hispanic teens spend an average of $375 per month. Hispanic teenage girls spend 60 percent more on makeup and twice as much on hair products as other teenagers. More important, these teens are joining black teenagers as fashion and style leaders for the overall teenage market.

Hispanic teens often differ from their parents, who in many cases felt strong pressures to blend in and "be American" (i.e., act and speak like white Americans). These teens don't. As three experts describe,

> I'm always amazed by the "Hispanicness" of Hispanic teens. They're speaking Spanish at home, both with friends, English for college and the Internet, but they're very much into the Hispanic culture. Even when they're born here. It's downright breathtaking.

> It's not about being bilingual. It's about being bicultural. They are engrossed in the American culture, but they take an incredible amount of pride in being Latino.

> It's very cool to be Hispanic at this age. It almost makes them more attractive, exotic. Hispanic teens are brushing up on their Spanish and celebrating their culture.

These bilingual teens read the same English language magazines and watch the same television programs as their non-Hispanic counterparts. In fact, they are much more likely to read such teen magazines as *Seventeen* and *YM*. One of the magazines targeting the female Hispanic teenager, *Latina,* is mostly English,

though most of the ads are in Spanish. However, they also utilize Spanish language magazines, television, and radio. They grew up listening not only to hip-hop and other popular music but to Hispanic-based rhythms as well—mariachi, banda, and norteño in California; tejano in Texas; salsa in Florida; and meringue in New York. Now they are helping popularize these sounds and variations of them throughout the larger teen population.

One of the core values that differentiates Hispanic teens is *familismo,* or a strong family orientation. This influences many aspects of their behavior. Family activities and events play a larger role in their lives than for non-Hispanics. Family means an extended family, not just the nuclear family. Children, including teenagers, are encouraged to be dependent longer. The Office of National Drug Control Policy attempts to capitalize on this value in an antidrug campaign targeting this group. It uses the theme, "If you do drugs, you are letting down your family."

Inspired by stars such as Jennifer Lopez and Ricky Martin, teenagers throughout America are adopting styles long popular with Hispanic youth. "Spanglish" is "in" in many areas. Hispanic youth are also in the vanguard of the movement away from colas toward sweeter, flavored drinks.

Critical Thinking Questions

1. To what extent are Hispanic teenagers leading the teenage market? Justify your response.

2. Many Hispanic teenagers are truly bicultural. What challenges does this present marketers?

3. Why are Hispanic teenage girls heavier readers of magazines such as *Cosmopolitan* and heavier users of cosmetics than white teenagers?

restaurant and takeout foods among Hispanic consumers. Church's vice president of marketing stated, "In the Latino community, there are a number of cultural barriers to not cooking." A result of these barriers is a social stigma against women who do not prepare meals for their families. To counter this, Church's launched an advertising campaign to make eating out more acceptable. The campaign positioned the chain as a place that provides a value-price dinner that frees up consumers to engage in more pressing activities.[51]

Language is clearly important to the Hispanic market and often strongly intertwined with cultural identity. Despite generational differences which are clearly emerging, a recent

ILLUSTRATION 5-4

The family is very important to the Hispanic subculture, and the male plays a major role. This Pepsi ad has a strong family theme with a strong male presence.

study finds that 69 percent of Hispanic households speak mostly Spanish at home and 83 percent speak at least some. Perhaps even more important is that Spanish-language ads are often more effective.[52] Consider the following:

> When asked about advertising effectiveness, 38% of Hispanics surveyed found English language ads less effective than Spanish ads in terms of recall and 70% less effective than Spanish ads in terms of persuasion. Many younger and acculturated Latinos mix languages in the form of "Spanglish," in which they speak English peppered with Spanish words. But, when it comes to selling, 56% of Latino adults respond best to advertising when it is presented in Spanish.[53]

Given these numbers, it should not be surprising that Univision, a Spanish-language network, is the fifth largest network in the United States[54] and that there are over 30 cable stations targeted at the Hispanic market. In addition, recent research shows that the top 53 TV shows watched by Hispanics in the 18 to 49 demographic were in Spanish.[55]

Marketing to Hispanics

Although average Hispanic household income is relatively low, the purchase power of the Hispanic market is estimated at $686 billion and is expected to grow by 45 percent over the next five years.[56] In addition, Hispanic consumers tend to be highly brand loyal, particularly to marketers who they feel are working to adapt their products and services to meet their distinctive needs. Price is important, but so too is the availability of high quality national brands. Hispanics tend to be less receptive than the general market to store brands.[57] Marketers are responding with adaptations to various aspects of their marketing mix.

Communications   As we saw earlier, Hispanics often speak Spanish and often prefer Spanish-language media. Therefore, although it is possible to reach part of this market using mass media, serious attempts to target Hispanics will often involve Spanish-language media as well. Univision, Telefutura, and Telemundo are the top three Spanish-language TV networks in the United States. Spanish language radio is widespread, with both local and network stations. And there are numerous Spanish-language magazines, including Spanish versions of *Cosmopolitan, National Geographic, Maxim, Men's Health, People,* and *Reader's Digest. Latina* targets younger, affluent Hispanic women and *Latina Style* targets more mature but contemporary Hispanic women. There are also many Spanish-language newspapers.

With respect to communication and media, it is important to note that a youth trend is emerging which will likely shape the future of Hispanic media strategy. Specifically, the 14- to 24-year-old demographic (which will grow rapidly over the next decade)[58] spends more time viewing English-language TV, radio, and print media than Spanish. This group tends to be U.S. born and more English-dominant in terms of language. In addition, the 18 to 34 demographic views Spanish- and English-language media about equally. In response, Univision and Telemundo are offering both bilingual and Spanish-language programming and are developing shows more in touch with the Hispanic youth market such as the reality show "Protagonistas de Novela." SiTV is a relatively new cable network that creates and delivers English-language programming with a Latino theme targeted toward a younger demographic.[59]

Hispanics have historically lagged behind the general population in terms of Internet usage. However, that is quickly changing, with Internet penetration among Hispanics estimated at 68 percent in 2007 (compared to 81 percent white), up from 45 percent in 2005.[60] In response, new sites focused on Hispanics such as Univision.com are rapidly coming online (see Illustration 5-5). Gateway, Colgate-Palmolive, Coca-Cola, MasterCard, and GM are some of the firms that advertise on these sites. Online sports are available through such sites as ESPNdeportes.com and Spanish-language versions of Yahoo! and AOL have been developed. Online Spanish-language communities such as CiudadFutura.com are also emerging. Hispanic Internet users tend to be relatively young, frequent both English- and Spanish-language sites, and in many cases prefer English-language media.[61] As with traditional media providers, online Hispanic providers will be challenged to deliver content that is relevant to acculturated Hispanics, regardless of language.

Successfully communicating to Hispanic consumers involves more than directly translating ad copy from English to Spanish. For example, Mattel recently launched BarbieLatina.com, a Spanish version of its extremely successful Barbie.com. Although it is very similar to the English version, it is not merely a translation. While both Hispanic and non-Hispanic girls aged three to eight have a passion for fantasy and nurturing behavior, the Hispanic girls had less interest in games and more interest in activity-based play. The content of the two sites reflects these differences.[62]

However, language translation is a challenge. For example, Tang introduced itself in its Spanish ads as *jugo de chino,* which worked well with Puerto Ricans, who knew it meant orange juice, but the phrase had no meaning to most other Hispanics. Other examples of

ILLUSTRATION 5-5

Use of the Internet by Hispanics is exploding. Sites such as this one by Univision are being developed to appeal to the unique needs of this market.

translation difficulties include the following:

- Frank Perdue's chicken slogan, "It Takes a Tough Man to Make a Tender Chicken," was translated as "It Takes a Sexually Excited Man to Make a Chick Affectionate."
- Budweiser's slogan ended up being "The Queen of Beers," and Miller's was "Filling; Less Delicious."
- Coors' recent campaign uses the word "guey," which in modern slang terms can mean the equivalent of "dude." However, the word can also be used as slang for idiot or stupid. According to one expert, whether or not consumers get the humor is generational.[63]

Successful marketing to Hispanics moves beyond accurate translations into unique appeals and symbols. It requires marketers to be "in-culture," that is, to understand the value system and the overall cultural context of the various Hispanic groups. In fact, value congruence has been found to overcome persuasion shortfalls for second-language ads (e.g., English-language ads to bilingual Hispanics).[64]

- Sears recognized the importance of the extended family in a successful ad for baby furniture. In the English ad, a husband and wife are shown selecting the furniture. In the Spanish ad, a teenage daughter and the grandparents join the expectant couple.
- Hispanic teens are particularly difficult to target with effective communications. Frito-Lay's successful campaign for Doritos was themed *Sabor a todo volumen* (roughly, "The loudest taste on earth"). TV ads featured loud Hispanic music and Hispanic teens with an emphasis on Doritos' bold and spicy taste. Research revealed that the music was key to the success of the campaign. According to a spokesperson, "Music is one of the

major attributes of Hispanic teens that bind them together. The styles differ from salsa to Latin pop, but all are based on Latin roots."[65]

- Best Buy created a TV spot designed to bridge the gap between younger tech-savvy Hispanic teens and their older less acculturated fathers who often are uncomfortable with technology but, given the patriarchal hierarchy, must "sign off" on the purchase. The slogan reads "If you're far away, get closer with Best Buy." Best Buy says they designed the spot to get kids and their fathers talking.[66]

Products   Historically, other than specialty food products, few marketers developed unique products or services for the Hispanic market. However, given the size and growth of this market, that is changing. For example:

- In Colorado, Wal-Mart created Denver Bronco T-shirts specifically targeting Hispanic consumers. One version had the phrase "de todo corazón," meaning with all my heart in Spanish. Wal-Mart's goal was to combine American sports tradition with symbols of Hispanic culture. The T-shirts became the most popular Denver Bronco's merchandise of the season.[67]
- Ford Motor Company is tapping into the increasingly lucrative Hispanic auto market by offering the F-150 Lobo truck. *Lobo* means "wolf" in Spanish and the Lobo truck, offered only in bright red, features a monochrome exterior and Lobo badging. Ford is leveraging the fact that the Lobo is made in Mexico and that many Hispanics are from Mexico. It has also signed Pablo Montero (a popular Mexican singer) as a celebrity spokesperson.[68]
- In addition, marketers are capturing the loyalty developed with their products in Central and South America by distributing them in areas of the United States with large Hispanic populations. For example, Colgate-Palmolive distributes its Mexican household cleaner Fabuloso in Los Angeles and Miami.

Some attempts at adapting products to the Hispanic market have failed because of a failure to truly understand the needs of this market. For example, many Hispanics find the current trend in houses of having the kitchen open onto the family room to be repugnant (Hispanics tend to be uncomfortable having strangers in their kitchens) and find the homes built for Hispanic buyers to be too stereotypical.[69]

Retailing   The primary retailing responses to this market have been increasing the number of bilingual salespeople; the use of Spanish language signs, directions, and point-of-purchase displays; and merchandise assortments that reflect the needs of the local Hispanic community. The following examples describe more focused responses:

- Tiangus, a grocery chain aimed at the Mexican American market in southern California, was launched with a fiesta atmosphere. Stands served a wide variety of Mexican foods, the walls were splashed with bright colors, and shoppers were serenaded with mariachi bands. The shelves were stocked with empanadas, handmade tortillas, and other items typically found only in specialty stores.

  The stores are not just standard stores with a Latin flair and a few specialty items. The chain is based on extensive research. For example, it was found that the Hispanic shopper "is fussier about freshness, so she shops more frequently and uses less refrigeration. She may have less disposable income but she'll spend a higher share of it on food." On the basis of these findings, Tiangus stores emphasize fresh food. Half the selling space is devoted to fresh food with reduced space for packaged items and freezer foods.[70]
- Warehouse Entertainment launched a chain of Tu Música (Your Music) stores catering to Hispanic consumers. The stores carry music ranging from Hispanic rock to pop

ILLUSTRATION 5-6

Ads on this site would appeal to many Chinese consumers but would not reach most other Asian Americans.

crossover to Mexican favorites. The logic of starting the stores was simple according to the firm's president: "The market in which we operated was changing and we needed to change with it." Tu Música targets first- to third-generation Hispanics who speak Spanish and seek Latino music. It advertises on Spanish-language TV, radio, and newspapers. It uses Spanish-speaking sales personnel. About one-third of its titles (more than 10,000) are in Spanish, compared to 2 percent in a typical outlet.[71]

- Bank of America converted its 5,000 ATM machines into a bilingual format. In regions of the country with large Hispanic populations, its branches have a Spanish language service line, first-time homebuyer education programs in Spanish, and a Spanish language loan-by-phone program. Its brochures are available in a bilingual format. These and other activities are tied together in an image campaign called *Cerca de ti,* or "Close to you."

ASIAN AMERICANS

Asian Americans represent an important subculture. While relatively small in size this group will continue to grow. Of particular importance to marketers is that Asian Americans are the highest educated and highest income group with substantial purchasing power. Asian American purchase power is estimated at $363 billion and is expected to grow by 45 percent over the next five years.[72] However, Asian Americans are also the most diverse group, with numerous nationalities, languages, and religions. The U.S. Census includes Asian-Indians in their summary figures for this group. However, we will discuss them separately in the next section.

Asian Americans are not a single subculture. Consider the Web site in Illustration 5-6. Ads on this site are probably quite effective with many of the Chinese members of this subculture. However, as Figure 5-3 shows, Chinese represent only a little over a fourth of all Asian Americans and they share neither a common language nor culture with most of the other groups.

As with Hispanics, language is a major factor. One estimate is that 80 percent of Asian Americans can be reached with "in-language" promotions. Two-thirds of Asian Americans are immigrants and the percentage of each nationality group that primarily uses its native

FIGURE 5-3
National Background of Asian Americans

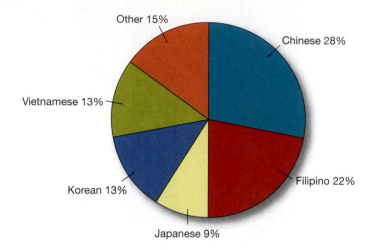

language is high, except for Filipinos.[73] In addition, the percentage who prefer "in-language" communication is also high, even for Filipinos.[74]

Country	Primarily Use Native Language	Prefer Communication in Native Language
Vietnam	85%	93%
Hong Kong	82	N/A
China	64	83
Korea	64	81
Taiwan	64	N/A
Japan	46	42
Philippines	27	66

More than languages differ among the groups. In fact, the concept and term *Asian American* was developed and used by marketers and others who study these groups rather than the members themselves. Members of the various nationalities involved generally refer to themselves by their nationality without the term *American,* that is, Vietnamese, not Vietnamese American. An exception are Japanese Americans.[75]

While each nationality group is a distinct culture with its own language and traditions, there are some commonalities across most of these groups. All have experienced the need to adjust to the American culture while being physically distinct from the larger population. Most come from home cultures influenced by Confucianism. Confucianism emphasizes subordination of the son to the father, the younger to the elder, and the wife to the husband. It values conservatism and prescribes strict manners. Their base cultures have also typically placed a very strong value on traditional, extended families. Education, collective effort, and advancement are also highly valued.[76]

Consumer Segments and Trends

Market Segment Research found three groups of Asian Americans on the basis of their demographics and attitudes that cut across nationality groups. Such commonalities can be useful starting points when designing marketing campaigns even if language and cultural symbols must be adapted. *Traditionalists* are older, often retired, have strong identification with original culture, native language tends to be primary language, and are not concerned about status. *Established* are older conservative professionals, are well educated with strong incomes, have relatively weak identification with native culture, have less need or desire for native-language programming, and will pay premium prices for high quality. *Living for the Moment* are younger, have moderate identification with native culture, tend to be bilingual, are spontaneous, materialistic, and impulsive shoppers who are concerned with status and quality.[77]

Several emerging trends are worth watching, some of which will make the Asian American population somewhat easier to target over time. First is geographic concentration, which has historically been high and appears to be increasing. In 1990, for example, 54 percent of Asian Americans resided in just five cities (Los Angeles, San Francisco, New York, Honolulu, and Chicago). In 2000 that number had increased to 59 percent. The concentration is even higher if you look at the state level, with roughly 75 percent of all Asian Americans living in just six states (California, New York, New Jersey, Hawaii, Texas, and Illinois).[78]

Immigration is one of the factors fueling the growth of the Asian American population. One trend is toward an increase in skilled workers from Mandarin-speaking regions of mainland China. This trend appears to be causing a "gradual shift to Mandarin from Cantonese in Chinese communications."[79]

A final trend is one which is common to all subcultures, and that is the youth trend. Roughly 33 percent of Asian Americans are under the age of 18, which is higher than that of whites.[80] In addition, this second generation (sometimes referred to as Generation 2.0), which was born in the United States, is, like the African American and Hispanic youth, still tied to their roots, but blending languages and cultures, influencing general U.S. culture, and fueling trends in fashion and music. As in the Hispanic market, English-language media options with Asian American content targeted at this second generation are increasing. Pepsi is airing ads in English on one such venue called *Stir* TV.[81] Also consider the Honda initiative:

> Honda Motor Co. chose to piggyback on Boba, a beverage developed in Taiwan that is all the rage in Asian youth circles. The beverage, also known as bubble tea, consists of "pearls" of black, gummy, tapioca balls that float in the mixture of sweetened iced tea. It has quickly caught on as the soft drink of Asian youth. Honda's idea was to develop drink sleeves that surround hot beverages in the U.S. to promote its youth-oriented cars, like the Civic and Acura RSX. Ponce (manager of emerging markets) got the idea from one of her young Asian co-workers who frequents Boba stores and noticed the number of young Asians who pulled up in Hondas.[82]

Marketing to Asian Americans

As we've seen, there are several Asian American markets, based primarily on nationality and language. Each of these in turn can be further segmented on degree of acculturation,[83] social class, generation, lifestyle, and other variables. And while this creates challenges for marketers, the purchase power of this group and its various segments is increasingly attractive to marketers and causing them to address these niche markets with creative product, merchandising, and media approaches.

Geographic concentration is increasing which helps marketing efficiency. Where there is a concentration of any of the nationality groups, there are native-language television and radio stations as well as newspapers.[84] Thus, targeted nationalities can be efficiently reached with native-language ads. For example, in San Francisco, KTSF presents a live one-hour newscast in Cantonese every weeknight. It covers both mainstream news and news of particular interest to the Chinese community. Many KTSF advertisers, such as

Courtesy Bank of America.

McDonald's, dub their existing ads in Cantonese. Others, such as Colgate-Palmolive, run the ads they are using for the same products in Asia.

Direct broadcast satellite (DBS) is also an important TV option. DBS provides a means of reaching virtually all of the native-language speakers of any nationality nationwide. For example, EchoStar's Dish network offers a "Chinese Package" called the "Great Wall TV Package" which started with three channels several years ago and is now at over 25 channels. DirecTV offers the gamut of language options to the Asian American audience including three services for South Asian languages, VietnameseDirect, and three Chinese-language services in both Cantonese and Mandarin which are broadcast from China, Hong Kong, and Taiwan.[85]

Asian Americans are highly tech savvy and heavy users of the Internet. Over 85 percent of households have computers and Internet penetration of Asian Americans is estimated at 82 percent (compared to 81 percent white) in 2007.[86] Internet-based marketing to the Asian community is growing rapidly. Firms can reach Chinese consumers in their native language on Sinanet.com (see Illustration 5-6). Similar sites are gaining popularity among other Asian nationality groups, and firms such as Charles Schwab are using them as communications channels.

Marketing to the various Asian nationality groups should follow the same basic guidelines discussed earlier for Hispanics. Thus, effective communication is more than simply translating ad copy. It also requires adopting and infusing ads with cultural symbols and meanings relevant to each nationality segment. Examine Illustration 5-7. It is bilingual and can communicate to Vietnamese with differing language preferences. More important, it is a special promotion based on the Lunar New Year that is meaningful to this group. It shows that Bank of America is doing more than just translating an ad used for the broader market but is focusing special attention on the Vietnamese market.

Other examples of successful marketing to Asian Americans include,

- A Los Angeles chain selected four outlets with large numbers of Chinese and Vietnamese customers. At the time of the Moon Festival (an important holiday in many Asian cultures), the store ran ads and distributed coupons for free moon cakes and lanterns. Sales increased by 30 percent in these stores during the promotion. Likewise, Sears advertises the Moon Festival in Mandarin, Cantonese, Vietnamese, or Korean, depending on the population near each outlet. It provides nationality-relevant gifts and entertainment such as traditional dances.
- Western Union sponsors numerous Asian cultural events such as the Asian-American Expo for the Chinese New Year in Los Angeles. They also partnered with World Journal to publish the *Chinese Immigrant Handbook* to offer practical guidance to new immigrants. These represent grassroot, community-based efforts to target the very specific needs of various nationality groups. These efforts supplement their more traditional mass-media approaches using TV, radio, and magazines.[87]

NATIVE AMERICANS

The number of Native Americans (American Indians and Alaska Natives in U.S. Census terms) depends on the measurement used. The Census reports three numbers for Native Americans: (1) one tribe only, (2) one tribe only or in combination with another tribe, and (3) number 2 plus in combination with any other race. The first definition produces an estimate of 2.8 million Native Americans; the total jumps to 4.1 million when the third definition is used. Nearly half live in the West, and 30 percent reside in the South. While many Native Americans live on or near reservations, others are dispersed throughout the country.

There are approximately 550 Native American tribes, each with its own language and traditions. Many of the tribes have reservations and quasi-independent political status. In general, Native Americans have limited incomes,[88] but this varies widely by tribe. The overall buying power of this group is estimated at $47.7 billion and is expected to grow by 38 percent in the next five years.[89] The larger tribes are as follows:

Tribes	One Tribe Only	Multiracial
Cherokee	281,000	730,000
Navajo	269,000	298,000
Sioux	109,000	153,000
Chippewa	106,000	150,000
Choctaw	87,000	159,000
Pueblo	60,000	74,000
Apache	57,000	97,000
Eskimo	46,000	55,000

In recent years, Native Americans have taken increasing pride in their heritage and are less tolerant of inaccurate stereotypes of either their history or their current status. Thus, marketers using Native American names or portrayals must ensure accurate and appropriate use. Native American cuisine is making its way into the American mainstream with efforts from Native American chefs like Arnold Olson. Olson blends European and Native American styles to create interesting dishes such as bison carpaccio and caribou bruschetta. As American interest in and acceptance of diversity continues to grow, unique Native American offerings such as this will become increasingly relevant and popular.[90]

The larger tribes all have their own newspapers and radio stations. In addition, there are two national Native American–oriented newspapers and several national radio shows and magazines.[91] Although each tribe is small relative to the total population, the geographic concentration of each tribe provides easy access for marketers. Sponsorship of tribal events and support for tribal colleges, training centers, and community centers can produce good results for firms that do so over time. For example, Nike has teamed up with the Indian Health Service to set up educational programs to teach and promote health and fitness on reservations.[92]

ASIAN-INDIAN AMERICANS

There are approximately 1.7 million Americans of Indian heritage (from India). This segment of the population is growing rapidly due to immigration. Asian-Indian Americans are concentrated in New York and California, with significant numbers in New Jersey, Illinois, and Texas as well. As a group, they are well educated, affluent, and fluent in English; yet most retain cultural ties to their Indian background.

Those unfamiliar with India often assume that it is a homogeneous country. However, in some ways it is more like Europe than America. It has 25 states, 7 union territories, 15 official languages, and dozens of other languages and dialects. Thus, while those who immigrate to America have much in common, they also have many differences based on their background in India.

While diverse in many ways, most share a number of important cultural traits:

- They place great value on education, particularly their children's education.
- They are concerned with financial security and save at a rate much higher than the average American.
- They do not have a "throw-away" mentality. They shop for value and look for quality and durability.
- Husbands tend to have a dominant role in family decisions.

Asian-Indian Americans attend to the general mass media. They can also be targeted via specialty magazines such as *Masal* and *India Abroad,* online sites such as IndiaAbroad.com, as well as cable TV, radio stations, and newspapers in regions with significant populations. For example, Western Union advertises to this segment on Eye on Asia, a cable channel focused on this group. National reach is now possible through EchoStar's Dish Network's South Asia Package with various channels from India. Long-term involvement in the Indian community is an effective way to gain support from this segment:

> Metropolitan Life was a major sponsor of a Navaratri, a religious festival that attracted 100,000 participants from around New York and New Jersey. As one participant said, "One of the chief executives of the company attended the festival, and the company took out a series of ads in the souvenir program. Now we feel we should reward the company for taking an interest in us."[93]

The Internet is also an effective way to market to these consumers. However, such an effort requires a sound knowledge of the community:

> It's December but Namaste.com's holiday rush has been over for two months. Christmas is not the big season for its customers. "To suggest gifting to Indians around Christmas time doesn't make sense. It's the wrong marketing message. Diwali [a festival of lights that happens in late October] is the Indian 'Christmas.' "[94]

ARAB AMERICANS

The 2000 Census identified 1.25 million self-identified Arab Americans in the United States. However the Arab American Institute (the Census Bureau's official designee for analyzing data related to Arab Americans) estimates underreporting by a factor of three and based on additional research has estimated the Arab American population at about 3.5 million. Perhaps no group in America has a more inaccurate stereotype. For example: What is the most common religion of Arab Americans? Sixty-six percent identify themselves as Christians (up from about 50 percent in the early 1990s), and 24 percent are Muslim (down from about 50 percent in the early 1990s).

Arab Americans come from a variety of countries, including Morocco, Algeria, Egypt, Lebanon, Jordan, Saudi Arabia, and Kuwait. They share a common Arabic heritage and the Arabic language. Since World War II, many Arab immigrants have been business proprietors, landowners, or influential families fleeing political turmoil in their home countries. Many of these individuals attended Western or Westernized schools and were fluent in English before arriving.

More than 80 percent of Arab Americans are U.S. citizens, and a recent study finds that 75 percent were born in the United States. They are somewhat younger than the general population, better educated, and have a higher than average income. They are also much more likely to be entrepreneurs. A third of all Arab Americans live in California, New York, and Michigan.

Most Arab Americans are tired of negative stereotyping and misrepresentations about their culture. Even the film *Aladdin* contained insults and mistakes. Aladdin sings about the "barbaric" country from which he came. A guard threatened to cut off a young girl's hand for stealing food for a hungry child. Such an action would be contrary to Islamic law. The storefront signs in the mythical Arabic land had symbols that made no sense in Arabic or any other language. The aftermath of the September 11, 2001, attack on the World Trade Center has aroused some prejudice against these citizens—as well as some enhanced knowledge of their backgrounds and beliefs.

The first rule in reaching this market is to treat its members with respect and accuracy. There are specialized newspapers, magazines, and radio and television stations focused on this market. EchoStar's Dish Network offers an Arabic-language package. Attention to the unique traditions of this community can pay large dividends.[95]

RELIGIOUS SUBCULTURES

As discussed in Chapter 3, America is basically a **secular society.** That is, the educational system, government, and political process are not controlled by a religious group, and most people's daily behaviors are not guided by strict religious guidelines. Nonetheless, 79 percent of all Americans believe in God, 36 percent claim to attend a religious service at least once a month,[96] and more than 50 percent state that religion is very important in their lives.[97]

The fact that the American culture is largely secular is not viewed as optimal by all of society. Many conservative Christians would prefer a society and legal system more in line with their faith. The intense debates over abortion, prayer in schools, the teaching of evolution versus creationism, homosexual rights, and a host of other issues are evidence of this division in American society.

Religion is important to, and directly influences the behaviors of, many Americans. This includes consuming religiously themed products[98] and avoiding the consumption of other products such as alcohol. The different religions in America prescribe differing values and behaviors. Thus, a number of **religious subcultures** exist in America.

© C28.com

Christian Subcultures

Much of the American value system and the resultant political and social institutions are derived from the Christian, and largely Protestant, beliefs of the early settlers. Although American culture is basically secular, many of its traditions and values are derived from the Judeo–Christian heritage of the majority of Americans. Most of the major American holidays, including Christmas, Easter, and Thanksgiving, have a religious base. However, except for Easter, the pure religious base of these holidays is no longer the central theme that it once was.

Although the United States is predominantly Christian, the percentage of American adults claiming Christianity as their religion was 76.5 percent in 2001, down from 86.2 percent in 1990.[99] However, Yankelovich has been tracking a psychographic segment they call the "young religious" composed of Gen X and Y. Following up on the huge success of the movie *The Passion of the Christ,* clothing firms have begun marketing trendy fashions with an edge to this younger audience including T-shirts with the slogan "Jesus is my homeboy." Some retailers have embraced this trend while others, concerned about offending customers, have declined.[100] The C28 Web site shown in Illustration 5-8 appears to be targeting this group.

Christianity takes many forms in this country, each with some unique beliefs and behaviors as discussed next.

Roman Catholic Subculture   Roughly 25 percent of American adults are Roman Catholic. The Catholic church is highly structured and hierarchical. The pope is the central religious authority, and individual interpretation of scripture and events is minimal. A basic tenet of the Catholic church is that a primary purpose of a marital union is procreation.

Therefore, the use of birth control devices is prohibited, though many Catholics deviate from this. A result of this is a larger average family size for Catholics than for Protestants or Jews. The larger family size makes economic gains and upward social mobility more difficult. It also has a major influence on the types of products consumed by Catholics relative to many other religions.

The Catholic church is ethnically diverse, with 35 percent of its adult membership coming from ethnic subcultures. Recall from our earlier discussion that the predominant religion among Hispanics is Catholicism. Hispanics have fueled much of the Catholic growth since 1960. Twenty-nine percent of adult Catholics are Hispanic, 3 percent are African American, and 3 percent are Asian.[101] Catholics tend to be concentrated in the Northeast and in areas with large Hispanic populations. *Encuentro* is one manifestation of this cultural diversity. It is a gathering of U.S. Hispanic Catholics held every few years. *Encuentro 2000: Many Faces in God's House* was a special event that embraced people of all ethnic and racial backgrounds. The conference included Latin music, an ethnic village, workshops reflecting the Asian experience, and speakers from various ethnic backgrounds.[102]

Like Protestants, Catholics vary in their commitment and conservatism. The more conservative members share many values and behaviors with Protestant religious conservatives. Catholics have few consumption restrictions or requirements associated with their religion. Marketers targeting this group can reach the more committed members through specialized magazines and radio programs.

Protestant Subcultures   Approximately 52 percent of American adults identify themselves as Protestant. While there are many types of Protestant faiths with significant differences between them, most emphasize direct individual experience with God as a core tenet. In general, Protestant faiths emphasize individual responsibility and control. This focus has been credited with creating a strong work ethic, desire for scientific knowledge, a willingness to sacrifice for the future, and relatively small families. These characteristics in turn have created upward social mobility and produced the majority of the ruling elite in America.

Protestant values and attitudes have tended to shape the core American culture. This is particularly true for white Protestants of Western European heritage—WASPs (white Anglo-Saxon Protestants). This group has historically dominated America in terms of numbers, wealth, and power, with power historically belonging to the male members of this group.

Although Protestants constitute the basic core culture of America, the diversity across and within denominations creates numerous subcultures within the larger group. Many of these religious groups have unique beliefs of direct relevance to marketers. These generally involve the consumption of products containing stimulants such as caffeine (prohibited by the Mormon Church) or alcohol (prohibited by the Southern Baptist church, among others). However, the basic distinction among Protestants, as among Catholics, is the degree of conservatism in their religious beliefs. The majority of Protestants are middle of the road in terms of conservatism. This is consistent with America's dominant cultural values. However, a sizable minority are very conservative and, along with conservative Catholics, represent a significant subculture.

The Born-Again Christian Subculture   Born-again Christians have been referred to as the Christian Right, Religious Right, Conservative Christians, Evangelical Christians, and Fundamentalist Christians. **Born-again Christians** are *characterized by a strong belief in the literal truth of the Bible, a very strong commitment to their religious beliefs, having had a "born-again" experience, and encouraging others to believe in Jesus Christ.*

Born-again Christians tend to have somewhat lower education and income levels than the general population. They tend to have a more traditional gender role orientation.

Born-again Christians are best known for their political stands on issues such as abortion, homosexual rights, and prayer in the schools.

Their beliefs also influence their consumption patterns. They generally oppose the use of alcohol and drugs. They do not consume movies or television programs that are overly focused on sex or other activities that they consider to be immoral. In fact, various groups of born-again Christians have organized boycotts against advertisers that sponsor shows they find inappropriate.

In contrast, they are very receptive to programs, books, and movies that depict traditional (i.e., Protestant) family (husband, wife, children) values. Firms with a reputation for supporting similar values are well received by this segment. In contrast, Disney products have faced boycotts because of Disney's personnel policies which extend some benefits to same-sex couples.

Non-Christian Subcultures

Jewish Subculture
Judaism represents 1.3 percent of American adults and is unique in that historically it has been an inseparable combination of ethnic and religious identity. Historically, Jews in America tended to marry other Jews, although that has changed somewhat over time.[103] In fact, a recent study of Match.com members found that 81 percent of Jewish single men and 72 percent of Jewish single women said they would date outside their race, ethnicity, or religion (these percentages were similar to those found for most other religions).[104]

Jews are heavily concentrated in the Northeast but are increasingly dispersing throughout the United States, particularly into the Sunbelt.[105] American Jews tend to have higher-than-average incomes and education levels. In most ways, Jewish consumption patterns are similar to those of other Americans with similar education and income levels.

Like other religious groups, the committed, conservative Jews represent a subculture distinct from mainstream Jews. Orthodox Jews have strict dietary rules that prohibit some foods such as pork and specify strict preparation requirements for other foods (see Illustration 5-9). They also strictly observe Jewish holidays, and many do not participate in even the secular aspects of the major Christian holiday, Christmas. Reformed Jews and Jews less committed to the strict interpretations of Judaism are less influenced by these practices.[106]

Muslim Subculture
It is important to recall from our earlier discussion that Arab Americans are often not Muslims, and by the same token Muslims in America are not necessarily Arabs. Muslims in America (representing roughly .5 percent of the American adult population)[107] are culturally diverse, including Arab Americans, African Americans, Asian Americans, and Hispanics. Like the Protestants, there are a variety of Muslim sects with varying belief patterns, though all are based on the Koran. Like Protestants, Catholics, and Jews, the most obvious division among Muslims is the degree of conservatism and the importance attached to the literal teachings of the religion. As with the other religious groups in America, most Muslims' lives are centered on work, family, school, and the pursuit of success and happiness.

In general, Muslims tend to be conservative with respect to drug and alcohol use and sexual permissiveness. In fact, many oppose dating. They also place considerable emphasis on the family, with the eldest male as the head of the family, and on respect for elders. The more devout Muslims avoid not only pork products but also any foods that have not been prepared in accordance with the strict rules of Islam. The following quote from a

© H.J. Heinz Company, L.P. Used with permission.

devout Pakistani Muslim on why he does not eat in Western restaurants illustrates the stress this can cause:

> Well, how can I be sure that the cook who has cooked pork or bacon in a pan did not cook my vegetables in the same pan? How can I be sure that even if he used different pans he washed his hands in between cooking bacon and a vegetable? I do not think there is any way I can get a pure food out there.[108]

These beliefs conflict with the practices in the larger society and the images portrayed on television and in the movies and are also a source of conflict between older Muslims who immigrated to America and their children who were raised here.[109] Muslims in America have their own magazines, schools, social clubs, marriage services, and bookstores. There are more than 1,100 Muslim mosques and sanctuaries in America. In general, this subculture has not attracted the attention of marketers except as it overlaps with the Arab American subculture.

Buddhist Subculture   There are nearly as many Buddhists in America as there are Muslims. They are primarily Asian American or white, although Asian Americans are more likely to be Christian (roughly 43 percent) than Buddhist (roughly 6 percent). Buddhists tend to be slightly above average in income and education, and they are concentrated in the West.

There are a variety of Buddhist sects in America. All emphasize the basic idea that all beings are caught in *samsara,* a cycle of suffering and rebirth that is basically caused by desire and actions that produce unfavorable *karma.* Samsara can be escaped and a state of *nirvana* reached by following the noble *Eightfold Path.* This combines ethical and disciplinary practices, training in concentration and meditation, and the development of enlightened wisdom.

Thus far, marketers have largely ignored this market. Its small size and diverse ethnic composition make it difficult to target. However, as specialized media evolve to serve Buddhists, opportunities will exist for astute marketers.

REGIONAL SUBCULTURES

Distinct **regional subcultures** arise as a result of climatic conditions, the natural environment and resources, the characteristics of the various immigrant groups that have settled in each region, and significant social and political events. These distinct subcultures present numerous opportunities and challenges for marketers. Examples include,

- TGI Friday's has a customizable menu which includes a set of 70 standard items plus 30 regional items, including chicken-fried steak, which is a hit in the Southeast but not in some other regions, and a baked brie cheese appetizer that is offered only in Michigan.
- Many national magazines run regional editions. *TV Guide,* for example, had 25 different regional covers for their NFL preview issue. And, *Sports Illustrated* often offers special issues devoted to sports in a specific city such as the *Sports Illustrated Boston Collection.*[110]
- Wahoo's, a restaurant in Southern California and Colorado (and also now online at www.wahoos.com), offers fish tacos, a menu item that may sound a bit odd to some, but which is popular among Hispanic consumers.

Although the most effective regional marketing strategies are often based on small geographic areas, we can observe significant consumption differences across much larger regions. Table 5-2 illustrates some of the consumption differences across the four U.S.

TABLE 5-2

Regional Consumption Differences

	Northeast	North Central	South	West
Media				
Elle	99	65	86	164
Outdoor Life	69	126	115	71
Ebony	88	81	155	42
Gourmet	121	87	86	118
Classic rock radio	103	129	85	91
Country radio	55	110	131	80
Hobbies/Activities				
Hunting (with rifle)	80	118	118	69
Tennis	116	91	78	130
In-line skating	124	117	67	115
Auto race (attend)	82	115	103	94
Product Use				
Imported wine	144	88	96	80
Domestic wine	118	91	86	116
Candy (frequent)	83	105	107	99
Laptop/notebook	92	88	92	134
Restaurants/Shopping				
Dominos	81	85	119	103
Wal-Mart	74	106	119	86
Eddie Bauer	94	155	67	101
Banana Republic	145	55	77	144

Note: 100 = Average consumption or usage.

Source: *Mediamark Reporter 2002—University* (New York: Mediamark Research Inc., March 2002).

census regions. Given such clear differences in consumption patterns, marketers realize that, for at least some product categories, the United States is no more a single market than the European Union. Since specialized (regional) marketing programs generally cost more than standardized (national) programs, marketers must balance potential sales increases against increased costs. This decision process is exactly the same as described in the section on multinational marketing decisions in Chapter 2.

SUMMARY

The United States is becoming increasingly diverse. Much of this diversity is fueled by immigration and an increase in ethnic pride and by identification with non-European heritages among numerous Americans. Most members of a culture share most of the core values, beliefs, and behaviors of that culture. However, most individuals also belong to several subcultures. A *subculture* is a segment of a larger culture whose members share distinguishing patterns of behavior. An array of ethnic, nationality, religious, and regional subcultures characterizes American society. The existence of these subcultures provides marketers with the opportunity to develop unique marketing programs to match the unique needs of each.

Ethnic subcultures are defined broadly as those whose members' unique shared behaviors are based on a common racial, language, or nationality background. Non-European ethnic groups constitute a significant and growing part of the U.S. population, from 24 percent in 1990 to 38 percent by 2020.

African Americans represent a substantial non-European ethnic group at roughly 13 percent of the U.S. population. While African Americans are younger and tend to have lower incomes than the general population, their rapidly growing education, income, purchasing power, and cultural influence continues to attract marketers to this large and diverse subculture.

Hispanics represent the largest and fastest growing ethnic subculture in the United States. It is currently slightly larger than the African American segment but the gap is expected to grow substantially by 2020. While Hispanics have a variety of national backgrounds (Mexico, 66 percent; Puerto Rico, 9 percent; Cuba, 4 percent), the Spanish language, a common religion (Roman Catholic), and national Spanish-language media and entertainment figures have created a somewhat homogeneous Hispanic subculture.

Asian Americans are the most diverse of the major ethnic subcultures. They are characterized by a variety of nationalities, languages, and religions. From a marketing perspective, it is not appropriate to consider Asian Americans as a single group. Instead, Asian Americans are best approached as a number of nationality subcultures.

Native Americans, Asian-Indian Americans, and *Arab Americans* are smaller but important subcultures. Each is diverse yet shares enough common values and behaviors to be approached as a single segment for at least some products. Geographic concentration and specialized media allow targeted marketing campaigns.

Although the United States is a relatively secular society, roughly 80 percent of American adults claim a religious affiliation and a majority state that religion is important in their lives. A majority of American adults identify themselves as Christian although the percentage has declined over time. And a variety of *religious subcultures* exist within both the Christian faiths and the Jewish, Muslim, and Buddhist faiths. Within each faith, the largest contrast is the degree of conservatism of the members.

Regional subcultures arise as a result of climatic conditions, the natural environment and resources, the characteristics of the various immigrant groups that have settled in each region, and significant social and political events. Regional subcultures affect all aspects of consumption behavior, and sophisticated marketers recognize that the United States is composed of numerous regional markets.

KEY TERMS

Acculturation   169
Born-again Christians   183
Ethnic subcultures   160
Event marketing   167
Hispanic   168
Regional subcultures   186
Religious subcultures   181
Secular society   181
Subculture   158

INTERNET EXERCISES

1. Visit the U.S. Census Web site (www.census.gov). What data are available there on the following? Which of this is most useful to marketers? Why?
   a. Native Americans
   b. African Americans
   c. Hispanics
   d. Asian Americans

2. Use the Internet to determine the cities in the United States that have the largest population of the following. Why is this useful to marketers?
   a. Native Americans
   b. African Americans
   c. Hispanics
   d. Asian-Indian Americans
   e. Arab Americans

3. Visit www.adherents.com. Evaluate its usefulness as an information source on the following.
   a. Roman Catholic subculture
   b. Protestant subcultures
   c. Jewish subculture
   d. Muslim subculture
   e. Buddhist subculture

4. Visit Native Nations Network (www.nativenationsnet.net). Based on this site, what seem to be some of the major issues facing Native Americans today?

5. Visit Hispanic Works (a Hispanic advertising agency) at www.hispanicworks.com. Click on "Our Work" to view examples of major campaigns they have created. Prepare a brief report on one of these campaigns and how the agency has customized its ads to the unique needs of this segment.

6. Visit Kang & Lee Advertising (an Asian American advertising agency) at www.kanglee.com. Use the resources they provide to learn more about the Asian American market.

DDB LIFE STYLE STUDY™ DATA ANALYSES

1. Based on the DDB data in Table 5A, which heavier-user categories have the greatest differences across the ethnic subcultures? Why is this the case?

2. For which products does ownership differ the most across ethnic groups (Table 5A)? Why is this the case?

3. For which types of television shows (Table 5A) do preferences differ the most across the ethnic subcultures? Why is this the case?

4. Use the DDB data in Table 5B to examine differences in the following characteristics across ethnic subcultures. What might explain these differences?
   a. Enjoy shopping for items influenced by other cultures.
   b. Religion is a big part of my life.
   c. Try to maintain a youthful appearance.
   d. When making family decisions, consideration of kids comes first.
   e. There is not enough ethnic diversity in commercials today.
   f. Want to look a little different from others.

REVIEW QUESTIONS

1. What is a *subculture?*

2. What determines the degree to which a subculture will influence an individual's behavior?

3. Is the American culture more like a soup or a salad?

4. What is an *ethnic subculture?*

5. How large are the major ethnic subcultures in America? Which are growing most rapidly?

6. What countries/regions are the major sources of America's immigrants?

7. Are the various ethnic subcultures homogeneous or heterogeneous?

8. Describe the income distribution of African Americans. What are the marketing implications of this distribution?

9. Describe the two African American consumer groups found by the Yankelovich group.

10. What are the basic principles that should be followed in marketing to an African American market segment?

11. To what extent is the Spanish language used by American Hispanics?

12. Can Hispanics be treated as a single market?

13. Describe the three Hispanic generational groups identified by the Pew Hispanic Center.

14. How homogeneous are Asian Americans?

15. To what extent do Asian Americans use their native language?

16. Describe three emerging trends which may make the Asian American population somewhat easier to target.

17. Why is the United States considered to be a *secular society?*

18. Describe the *Roman Catholic subculture.*

19. Describe the *born-again Christian subculture.*

20. Describe the *Jewish subculture.*

21. Describe the *Muslim subculture.*

22. Describe the *Buddhist subculture.*

23. What is a regional subculture? Give some examples.

DISCUSSION QUESTIONS

24. Examine Table 5-1. Which of these differences are mainly caused by ethnicity or race and which are caused by other factors?

25. Do you agree that America is becoming more like a salad than a soup in terms of the integration of ethnic groups? Is this good or bad?

26. Do you agree with Miller Brewing that "the things that young Hispanic or young African American or young white people have in common are much stronger and more important than any ethnic difference"? For what types of products is this view most correct? Least correct?

27. Most new immigrants to America are non-European and have limited English-language skills. What opportunities does this present to marketers? Does this raise any ethical issues for marketers?

28. Does a firm's social responsibility play a role in marketing to consumers from various ethnic subcultures whose incomes fall below the poverty line? If so, what?

29. Respond to the questions in Consumer Insight 5-1.

30. Although many of the following have very limited incomes, others are quite prosperous. Does marketing to prosperous members of these groups require a marketing mix different from the one used to reach other prosperous consumers?
    a. African Americans
    b. Hispanics
    c. Asian Americans

31. Describe how each of the following firms' product managers should approach (*i*) the African American, (*ii*) the Hispanic, (*iii*) the Asian American, (*iv*) the Asian-Indian American, (*v*) the Arab American, or (*vi*) the Native American markets.
    a. Red Bull
    b. Wendy's
    c. NBA
    d. *Maxim* magazine
    e. The United Way
    f. Dell laptops
    g. eBay.com
    h. Coach handbags

32. What, if any, unique ethical responsibilities exist when marketing to ethnic subcultures?

33. Do you agree that the United States is a secular society? Why or why not?

34. Describe how each of the following firms' product managers should approach the (*i*) Catholic, (*ii*) Protestant, (*iii*) born-again Christian, (*iv*) Jewish, (*v*) Muslim, and (*vi*) Buddhist subcultures.
    a. Red Bull
    b. Wendy's
    c. NBA
    d. *Maxim* magazine
    e. The United Way
    f. Dell laptops
    g. eBay.com
    h. Coach handbags

35. Will regional subcultures become more or less distinct over the next 20 years? Why?

36. Select one product, service, or activity from each category in Table 5-2 and explain the differences in consumption for the item across the regions shown.

37. Why does the consumption of laptop/notebook computers differ across regions? Are regions a better explanation for laptop/notebook use than the demographic factors identified in Chapter 4 (see Tables 4-1, 4-2, and 4-3)?

APPLICATION ACTIVITIES

38. Watch two hours of prime-time major network (ABC, CBS, FOX, or NBC) television. What subculture groups are portrayed in the programs? Describe how they are portrayed. Do these portrayals match the descriptions in this text? How would you explain the differences? Repeat these tasks for the ads shown during the programs.

39. Pick a product of interest and examine the Simmons Market Research Bureau or MediaMark studies on the product in your library (these are often in the journalism library on CD-ROM). Determine the extent to which its consumption varies by ethnic group and region. Does consumption also vary by age, income, or other variables? Are the differences in ethnic and regional consumption due primarily to ethnicity and region or to the fact that the ethnic group or region is older, richer, or otherwise different from the larger culture?

40. Examine several magazines or newspapers aimed at a non-European ethnic or nationality group. What types of products are advertised? Why?

41. Interview three members of the following subcultures and ascertain their opinions of how their ethnic or nationality group is portrayed on network television shows and in national ads.
    a. African Americans
    b. Asian Americans
    c. Hispanics
    d. Arab Americans

    e. Asian-Indian Americans
    f. Native Americans

42. Interview three members of the following subcultures and ascertain the extent to which they identify with the core American culture, their ethnic subculture within America, or their nationality subculture. Also determine the extent to which they feel others of their ethnic/race group feel as they do and the reasons for any differences.
    a. African Americans
    b. Asian Americans
    c. Hispanics
    d. Arab Americans
    e. Asian-Indian Americans
    f. Native Americans

43. Interview three members of the following religious subcultures and determine the extent to which their consumption patterns are influenced by their religion.
    a. Catholics
    b. Protestants
    c. Born-again Christians
    d. Jews
    e. Muslims
    f. Buddhists

44. Interview two students from other regions of the United States and determine the behavior and attitudinal differences they have noticed between their home and your present location. Try to determine the causes of these differences.

REFERENCES

1. C. P. Taylor, "Girl Scouts Extend Multicultural Reach," *Advertising Age,* January 28, 2002, p. 18.

2. See R. Suro, "Recasting the Melting Pot," *American Demographics,* March 1999, pp. 30–32.

3. For conflicting data, see S. Reese, "When Whites Aren't a Mass Market," *American Demographics,* March 1997, pp. 51–54.

4. L. Wentz, "Reverse English," *Advertising Age,* November 19, 2001, p. S1.

5. M. G. Briones, "Coors Turns Up the Heat," *Marketing News,* June 22, 1998, p. 15.

6. See R. Suro, "Mixed Doubles," *American Demographics,* November 1999, pp. 57–62.

7. C. Fisher, "It's All in the Details," *American Demographics,* April 1998, p. 45.

8. A. S. Wellner and J. Fette, "Technical Difficulties," *American Demographics,* May 2001, pp. 24–25.

9. W. H. Frey, "Micro Melting Pots," *American Demographics,* June 2001, pp. 20–23.

10. *2003 Yearbook of Immigration Statistics* (Washington, DC: U.S. Department of Homeland Security, September 2004), p. 8.

11. See L. R. Oswald, "Culture Swapping," *Journal of Consumer Research,* March 1999, pp. 303–18.

12. M. R. Forehand and R. Deshpande, "What We See Makes Us Who We Are," *Journal of Marketing Research,* August 2001, pp. 336–48.

13. *Statistical Abstract of the United States 2004–2005* (Washington, DC: U.S. Census Bureau, 2004–2005); except growth rate from *Hispanics: A People in Motion* (Washington, DC: Pew Research Center, 2005).

14. J. Holland and J. W. Gentry, "Ethnic Consumer Reaction to Targeted Marketing," *Journal of Advertising,* Spring 1999, pp. 65–76.

15. T. McCarroll, "It's a Mass Market No More," *Time,* Fall 1993, p. 80.

16. M. L. Rossman, *Multicultural Marketing* (New York: American Management Association, 1994), pp. 153–57.

17. E. Morris, "The Difference in Black and White," *American Demographics,* January 1993, p. 46.

18. J. M. Humphreys, "The Multicultural Economy 2004," *Georgia Business and Economic Conditions* 64, no. 3 (2004).

19. Table below based on "Money Income of Households," *Statistical Abstract of the United States 2004–2005* (Washington, DC: U.S. Bureau of the Census, 2004–2005), p. 443.

20. For example, see B. E. Bryant and J. Cha, "Crossing the Threshold," *Marketing Research,* Winter 1996, pp. 21–28.

21. *The 1993 Minority Market Report* (Coral Gables, FL: Market Segment Research, Inc., 1993).

22. D. M. Ayers, "What Does Brand Have to Do With It?" *Market Snapshot* (Chicago, IL: The Hunter-Miller Group, Inc., July 2004), at www.huntermillergroup.com.

23. See A. S. Wellner, "The Forgotten Baby Boom," *American Demographics,* February 2001, pp. 47–51.

24. D. M. Ayers, "Moving On Up," *Market Snapshot,* January 2004, at www.huntermillergroup.com.

25. P. Miller, *African Americans Are a Heterogeneous, Not a Homogeneous Market* (Cablevision Advertising Bureau, 2005), available at www.onetvworld.org.

26. "Black Baby Boomers," *Market Snapshot,* May 2002, at www.huntermillergroup.com.

27. Y. K. Kim and J. Kang, "The Effects of Ethnicity and Product on Purchase Decision Making," *Journal of Advertising Research,* March 2001, pp. 39–48.

28. *Mediamark Reporter 2002—University* (New York: Mediamark Research Inc., March 2002).

29. J. Hodges, "Black, White Teens Show Similarity in TV Tastes," *Advertising Age,* May 13, 1996, p. 24.

30. J. Adler, "Marketers, Agencies Praise BET's Savvy," *Advertising Age,* April 11, 2005, p. B16.

31. *Wow! 2004 U.S. Multicultural Markets* (Washington, DC: Diversity Best Practices/Business Women's Network, 2004).

32. Based on information found in R. Greenspan, "African-Americans Create Online Identity," *ClickZ.com,* September 26, 2003, at www.clickz.com; and D. M. Ayers, "African Americans on the Internet," *Market Snapshot,* March 2005, at www.huntermillergroup.com.

33. "African-American Buying Power 2002 vs. 2001," *Marketing News,* July 15, 2004, p. 11.

34. L. Wentz, "AG Tailors Mobile Entertainment," *Advertising Age,* September 27, 2004, p. 38.

35. E. M. Simpson et al., "Race, Homophily, and Purchase Intentions and the Black Consumer," *Psychology & Marketing,* October 2000, pp. 877–99. See also L. A. Perkins, K. M. Thomas, and G. A. Taylor, "Advertising and Recruitment," *Psychology & Marketing,* March 2000, pp. 235–55.

36. C. L. Green, "Ethnic Evaluations of Advertising," *Journal of Advertising,* Spring 1999, pp. 49–63; O. Appiah, "Ethnic Identification on Adolescents' Evaluations of Advertisements," *Journal of Advertising Research,* September 2001, pp. 7–21; and T. E. Whittler and J. S. Spira, "Model's Race," *Journal of Consumer Psychology* 12, no. 4 (2002), pp. 291–301.

37. D. Howell, "Albertson's Caters to Different Ethnic Markets," *DSN Retailing Today,* October 1, 2001, p. 18.

38. C. Fisher, "Black, Hip and Primed to Shop," *American Demographics,* September 1996, p. 56. See also K. P. Marshall and J. R. Smith, "Race-Ethnic Variations in the Importance of Service Quality Issues," *Journal of Professional Services Marketing* 18, no. 2 (1999), pp. 119–31.

39. T. L. Ainscough and C. M. Motley, "Will You Help Me Please?" *Marketing Letters,* May 2000, pp. 129–36.

40. S. F. Philipp, "Are We Welcome," *Journal of Leisure Research* 31, no. 4 (1999), pp. 385–403.

41. See V. D. Bush et al., "Managing Culturally Diverse Buyer–Seller Relationships," *Journal of the Academy of Marketing Science,* Fall 2001, pp. 391–404.

42. M. F. Floyd and K. J. Shinew, "Convergence in Leisure Style and Whites and African Americans," *Journal of Leisure Research* 31, no. 4 (1999), pp. 359–84.

43. N. Delener, "Consumer Payment System Attribute Perceptions and Preferences," *Journal of Professional Services Marketing,* no. 1 (1995), pp. 53–71; and F. J. Mulhern, J. D. Williams, and R. P. Leone, "Variability of Brand Price Elasticities across Retail Stores," *Journal of Retailing,* no. 3 (1998), pp. 427–45.

44. W. R. Ortiz, "Answering the Language Question," CableTelevision Advertising Bureau, press release, accessed May 9, 2005, at www.onetvworld.org.

45. An excellent description of this process for Mexican immigrants appears in L. Penaloza, "*Atravesando Fronteras*/Border Crossings," *Journal of Consumer Research,* June 1994, pp. 32–54.

46. *Generational Differences* (Washington, DC: Pew Hispanic Center/Kaiser Family Foundation), March 2004 (Source: © 2004, Pew Hispanic Center, www.pewhispanic.org).

47. G. Berman, *Portrait of the New America* (Coral Gables, FL: The Market Segment Group, 2002), p. 21.

48. See *Hispanics: A People in Motion.*

49. C. Webster, "The Effects of Hispanic Identification on Marital Roles in the Purchase Decision Process," *Journal of Consumer Research,* September 1994, pp. 319–31.

50. Based on R. X. Weissman, "Los Ninos Go Shopping," *American Demographics,* May 1999, pp. 37–39; H. Stapinski, "Generacion Latino," *American Demographics,* July 1999, pp. 63–68; R. Gardyn, "Habla English," *American Demographics,* April 2001, pp. 54–57; J. D. Zbar, "Hispanic Teens Set Urban Beat," *Advertising Age,* June 2001, p. S6; and H. Chura, "Sweet Spot," *Advertising Age,* November 12, 2001, p. 1.

51. L. Kramer, "Church's Chicken Chain Courts Latino Audience," *Advertising Age,* October 19, 1998, p. 12.

52. *The U.S. Hispanic Market* (New York: Package Facts, October 2003).

53. L. Sonderup, "Hispanic Marketing," *Advertising & Marketing Review,* April 2004, at www.ad-mkt-review.com.

54. Ibid.

55. Ortiz, "Answering the Language Question."

56. Humphreys, "The Multicultural Economy 2004."

57. *The U.S. Hispanic Market.*

58. L. Wentz, "Rapid Change Sweeps Hispanic Advertising Industry," *AdAge.com,* May 3, 2005, at www.adage.com.

59. *The U.S. Hispanic Market.*

60. *Wow! 2004 U.S. Multicultural Markets.*

61. "YupiMSN and ESPNdeportes.com Team Up to Deliver the Best in Online Sports to Spanish-Speaking Fans throughout the Americas," Microsoft press release, June 4, 2002; and "A Year in Review," ComScore Networks press release, November 12, 2003.

62. C. P. Taylor, "BarbieLatina Says 'Hola' to Net," *Advertising Age,* October 1, 2001, p. 54.

63. For these and other examples see "Marketing to Hispanics," *Advertising Age,* February 8, 1987, p. S23; M. Westerman, "Death of the Frito Bandito," March 1989, pp. 28–32; and L. Wentz, "Debate Swirls over Slang in Coors Spot," *Advertising Age,* May 17, 2004, p. 6.

64. See D. Luna, L. A. Peracchio, and M. D. de Juan, "The Impact of Language and Congruity on Persuasion in Multicultural E-Marketing," *Journal of Consumer Psychology* 13, no. 1/2 (2003), pp. 41–50; see also Gardyn, "Habla English."

65. L. Giegoldt, "Brand Loyalty Opportunities Abound," *Advertising Age,* August 24, 1998, p. S10. See also S. Shim and K. C. Gehrt, "Hispanic and Native American Adolescents," *Journal of Retailing,* no. 3 (1996), pp. 307–24.

66. L. Wentz, "Best Buy Targets Hispanic Patriarchs," *Advertising Age,* August 2, 2004, p. 20.

67. J. Garcia and R. Gerdes, "To Win Latino Market, Know Pitfalls, Learn Rewards," *Marketing News,* March 1, 2004, pp. 14 and 19.

68. J. Halliday, "Ford Unveils First Truck for U.S. Hispanic Market," *AdAge.com,* April 26, 2005, at www.adage.com; and "Ford Celebrates Cinco de Mayo with 'Lobo' F-150," *Edmunds.com* press release, April 26, 2005.

69. A. S. Wellner, "Gen X Homes In," *American Demographics,* August 1999, p. 61.

70. M. Johnson, "The Application of Geodemographics to Retailing," *Journal of the Market Research Society,* January 1997, p. 213.

71. J. D. Zbar, "Latinization Catches Retailers' Ears," *Advertising Age,* November 16, 1998, p. S22.

72. Humphreys, "The Multicultural Economy 2004."

73. See B. Edmundson, "Asian Americans in 2001," *American Demographics,* February 1997, pp. 16–17.

74. "Asia Rising," *American Demographics,* July/August 2002, pp. 38–43.

75. M. C. Tharp, *Marketing and Consumer Identity in Multicultural America* (Thousand Oaks, CA: Sage, 2001), p. 259.

76. Ibid., pp. 253–57.

77. *The 1993 Minority Market Report.*

78. D. L. Vence, "Growth in Asian-Am. Spending Fuels Targeted Marketing," *Marketing News,* June 1, 2004, pp. 11–13.

79. "Asia Rising."

80. "Asian American Diversity," *Advertising Age,* July/August 2002, p. 41.

81. Vence, "Growth in Asian-Am. Spending Fuels Targeted Marketing."

82. "Reaching Generation 2.0," *Advertising Age,* July/August 2002, p. 42.

83. S. F. Ownby and P. E. Horridge, "Acculturation Level and Shopping Orientations of Asian American Consumers," *Psychology & Marketing,* January 1997, pp. 1–18; D. D'Rozario and S. P. Douglas, "Effects of Assimilation on Prepurchase External Information-Search Tendencies," *Journal of Consumer Psychology* 8, no. 2 (1999), pp. 187–209; and Y.-K. Kim and J. Kang, "Effects of Asian-Americans' Ethnicity and Acculturation on Personal Influences," *Journal of Current Issues and Research in Advertising,* Spring 2001, pp. 43–53.

84. See P. Paul, "Mediachannels," *American Demographics,* November 2001, pp. 26–31.

85. Information accessed from corporate Web sites.

86. *Wow! 2004 U.S. Multicultural Markets.*

87. Vence, "Growth in Asian-Am. Spending Fuels Targeted Marketing."

88. "Diversity in America," *American Demographics,* November 2002, p. S17.

89. J. M. Humphreys, "Minority Buying Power," *Marketing News,* July 2, 2001, p. 17.

90. "Native American Food Goes Haute Cuisine," *CNN.com,* September 30, 2004, at www.cnn.com.

91. See A. S. Wellner, "Discovering Native America," *American Demographics,* August 2001, p. 21.

92. A. M. Peterson, "Nike Boosts Indians' Health, Its Reputation," *Marketing News,* June 1, 2004, p. 10.

93. This section was based on M. Mogelonsky, "Asian Indian Americans," *American Demographics,* August 1995, pp. 32–39; see also M. M. Cardona, "Segment Marketing Grows as Tool for Financial Services Leaders," *Advertising Age,* November 20, 2000, p. S1.

94. A. S. Wellner, "Every Day's a Holiday," *American Demographics,* December 2000, p. 63.

95. This section was based on S. El-Badry, "The Arab-American Market," *American Demographics,* January 1994, pp. 22–30; L. P. Morton, "Segmenting to Target Arab Americans," *Public Relations Quarterly,* Winter 2001, pp. 47–48; "Survey Reveals

Arab American Experiences and Reactions Following 9/11," Arab American Institute press release, August 19, 2002; and "Arab American Demographics," Arab American Institute, accessed May 14, 2005, at www.aaiusa.org/demographics.htm.

96. H. Taylor, "While Most Americans Believe in God, Only 36% Attend a Religious Service Once a Month or More Often," *The Harris Poll*®, October 15, 2003, at www.harrisinteractive.com.

97. B. A. Robinson, "How Many People Go Regularly to Weekly Religious Services?" Ontario Consultants on Religious Tolerance, November 26, 2001, at www.religioustolerance.org.

98. See R. Cimino and D. Lattin, "Choosing My Religion," *American Demographics,* April 1999, pp. 6–65.

99. This and other statistical information on religion in the United States can be found at Adherents.com (www.adherents.com) which collects and disseminates statistics from various sources including two of the most comprehensive surveys of religion in the U.S., namely the National Survey of Religious Identification (NSRI: 1990) and the American Religious Identity Survey (ARIS: 2001) conducted by B. A. Kosmin, S. P. Lachman and associates.

100. B. Ebenkamp, "The Young and Righteous," *Brandweek,* April 5, 2004, p. 18; and S. Kang, "Pop Culture Gets Religion," *The Wall Street Journal,* May 5, 2004, pp. B1 and B2.

101. Information on ethnic diversity from ARIS research briefs at www.gc.cuny.edu.

102. Information on *Encuentro 2000* from press releases by the United States Conference of Catholic Bishops (Washington, DC), including "Growing Asian Impact on Church to Be Felt at *Encuentro 2000,*" May 22, 2000; "Latin Music, Movie on Cuba, Hispanic Cultural Expressions Part of *Encuento 2000* Celebration of Multi-ethnic Church," May 30, 2000; and "Bishops' Agenda Includes Pastoral Framework for Hispanic Ministry," October 11, 2002, at www.usccb.org.

103. B. A. Kosmin and P. Lachman, *One Nation under God* (New York: Harmony Books, 1993), p. 245.

104. "Breaking the Rules of Engagement," *American Demographics,* July/August 2002, p. 35.

105. R. Thau, "The New Jewish Exodus," *American Demographics,* June 1994, p. 11.

106. Kosmin and Lachman, *One Nation under God,* p. 12.

107. Estimates here have been hotly debated. For an excellent discussion, see "The Largest Religious Groups in the United States of America," at www.adherents.com.

108. M. Chapman and A. Jamal, "The Floodgates Open," *Enhancing Knowledge Development in Marketing* (Chicago: American Marketing Association, 1996), p. 198.

109. See S. El-Badry, "Understanding Islam in America,"*American Demographics,* January 1994, p. 10.

110. B. Horovitz, "Down-home Marketing," *USA Today,* October 3, 1997, p. 1B.

© M. Hruby

6

The American Society: Families and Households

■ Americans spend approximately $150 billion a year on babies and children. For infants, the marketing task is relatively clear: Parents and grandparents are the key decision makers and buyers. One study reached the following conclusions:

- Gifts are a significant part of the market.
- New mothers look to other mothers in deciding what to buy.
- Mothers want a special look for their baby that is different from other kids.
- Collections and coordination are not critical.
- Comfort is important, durability less so.
- Practical features such as ease of dressing are very important.
- Price/value is important, as the baby quickly outgrows the clothing.

However, even by age two, children begin to influence the purchase of items bought for them. By six, many are insisting on "cool" clothes, foods, and other items. By their early teens, they may play the dominant role in purchasing electronics and computers for the household.

Marketers are increasingly pursuing this market. But it's not easy. Both children and parents must be satisfied. Eddie Bauer tested a line of children's clothes in its catalogs and stores. The clothes were basically downsized versions of its adult lines. Several years after this experiment failed, Eddie Bauer reentered the market with "cooler" styles for kids and an eddiebauer.com Internet site. The site was marketed in the *Disney* magazine, *Family PC, Family Fun,* and *Working Mother* as well as in Eddie Bauer stores and catalogs. However, a visit to that site today connects you to Eddie Bauer's main home page. It is difficult to become cool with kids.

In contrast, the Nautica Kids line is doing well as are many others that target this group. Limited Too targets 7- to 14-year-old girls. It sells through both an Internet site and a rapidly expanding set of retail stores. Rave Girl, targeting tweens, is also growing rapidly.

Abercrombie & Fitch is quickly expanding its line of stores focused on 7- to 16-year-olds. Wal-Mart launched a line of fashionable clothing for 6- to 14-year-old girls under the Mary-Kate and Ashley Olsen brands.

Jell-O has shifted focus from marketing primarily to mothers to reaching kids directly. It launched X-treme Jell-O in flavors such as Green Apple, Watermelon, Blue Raspberry, and Tangerine to appeal to this market. A spokesperson said, "X-treme Jell-O gelatin is a logical next step for us—particularly when kids are so interested in dialed up tastes, flavors, and colors."[1]

How do eight-year-olds acquire X-treme Jell-O? They might buy it at a store with their own money, they might request a parent to buy it for them, or a parent might buy it without a request. Most of the time, such a purchase will involve more than just the child. Even if the child has the money for the purchase, the parent might prohibit it. Such purchases are made in the context of a family or household.

The household is the basic consumption unit for most consumer goods. Major items such as housing, automobiles, and appliances are consumed more by household units than by individuals. Furthermore, the consumption patterns of individual household members seldom are independent from those of other household members. For example, deciding to grant a child's request for a bicycle may mean spending discretionary funds that could have been used to purchase a weekend away for the parents, new clothing for a sister or brother, or otherwise used by another member of the household. Therefore, it is essential that marketers understand the household as a consumption unit, as shown in Figure 6-1.

Households are important not only for their direct role in the consumption process but also for the critical role they perform in socializing children. The family household is the primary mechanism whereby cultural and subcultural values and behavior patterns are passed on to the next generation. Purchasing and consumption patterns are among those attitudes and skills strongly influenced by the family household unit.

This chapter examines (1) the nature and importance of families and households in contemporary American society, (2) the household life cycle, (3) the nature of the family decision process, and (4) consumer socialization.

THE NATURE OF AMERICAN HOUSEHOLDS

Types of Households

There are a variety of types of households. The Census Bureau defines a **household** as *all the people who occupy a housing unit* (a house, apartment, group of rooms, or single room designed to be occupied as separate living quarters). It defines a **family household** as one having *at least two members related by birth, marriage, or adoption, one of whom is the householder* (householder owns or rents the residence). A **nonfamily household** is a *householder living alone or exclusively with others to whom he or she is not related.* Table 6-1 indicates the current distribution of household types in the United States.

These definitions are important because the Census Bureau, which provides most of the available data on households, uses them. Unfortunately, these terms do not capture the richness of the American family structure. The **blended family**—*a family consisting of a couple, one or both of whom were previously married, their children, and the children from the previous marriage of one or both parents*—is one missing form.[2] While more than 40 percent of first marriages end in divorce, most of these divorced individuals remarry.[3] Thus, a

The Household Influences Most Consumption Decisions	FIGURE 6-1

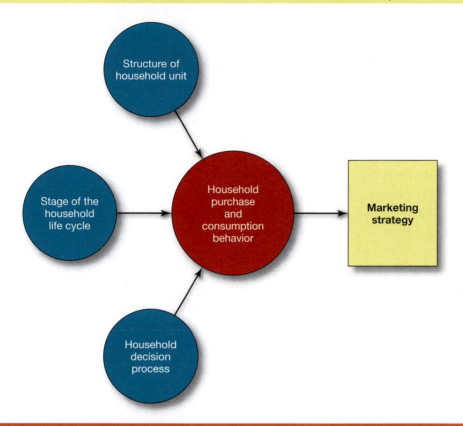

Type of Household	Number (000)	Percentage
All households	**111,278**	**100.0%**
Family households	**75,596**	**67.9**
Married couples	57,320	51.5
Children under 18 at home	*25,914*	*23.3*
No children under 18 at home	*31,406*	*28.2*
Single fathers (children under 18 at home)	1,915	1.7
Single mothers (children under 18 at home)	8,139	7.3
Other families	8,222	7.4
Nonfamily households	**35,682**	**32.1**
Male householder	16,020	14.4
Living alone	*12,511*	*11.2*
Female householder	19,662	17.7
Living alone	*16,919*	*15.2*

TABLE 6-1

Family and Nonfamily Households, 2003

Source: *America's Families and Living Arrangements* (Washington, DC: U.S. Census Bureau, November 2004), p. 3.

significant percentage of American children grow up with stepparents and stepsiblings. Many of these children spend significant time in two such families, one formed by their mother and the other by their father.

The term **traditional family** refers to *a married couple and their own or adopted children living at home*. Much publicity has been given to its demise and this type of family has clearly declined over time. This is particularly true if one considers a traditional family to be one headed by a never-divorced couple. However, over half (52 percent) of all households are headed by married couples (down from 71 percent in 1970) and roughly

Unmarried Families[4]

There are over 4 million unmarried, opposite-sex households in the United States. This number is forecast to grow rapidly. For some, cohabitation is a temporary arrangement before marriage; for others, it represents a long-term relationship:

> Our relationship has lasted longer than those of any of our friends near our own age—married or not. We are actually looked up to as a model couple. I don't want to mess with what works.

Unmarried couples increasingly resemble the general population. Forty-five percent are 35 or older, and less than 20 percent are under 25. A third have one or more children under the age of 15 living with them. And, in many ways, the needs of unmarried couples are the same as those of married couples with similar demographics. However, there are exceptions, such as finding knowledgeable assistance with legal and financial issues concerning joint home ownership, estate planning, and so forth.

> When Dorain and Marshall—both twentysomething and cohabiting for eight years—applied for joint tenants insurance, they were told by a local agent that their only choice was to apply for individual policies at almost twice the cost. They eventually found an agency catering to the gay and lesbian community that signed them up for joint tenants and auto insurance with no problem. In fact, many heterosexual couples turn to gay professionals who are better equipped to navigate the complex legal and financial issues that unmarried couples often face.

One reason marketers rarely target unmarried couples is that they are not easy to identify or reach. There are no media dedicated to this audience, and they are not demographically unique. Another reason is that cohabitation is not fully accepted:

> Companies that might benefit from targeting this group—banks, lawyers, and so forth—don't want to be viewed as doing anything that undermines marriage because they could be viewed as promoting an uncommitted lifestyle.

Most unmarried couples realize and deal with the difficulties and prejudices associated with their status. However, they would also like some recognition that they matter. Hallmark Cards is one firm that has responded. It recently launched a "Ties That Bind" line of greeting cards aimed at nontraditional families, including unmarried partnerships:

> Our cards reflect the times. Relationships today are so nebulous that they are hard to pin down, but in creating products, we have to be aware that they are there. Companies need to respect and be sensitive to how people are truly living their lives now, and not how they might wish or hope for them to live.

Critical Thinking Questions

1. Do you agree that unmarried couples will become increasingly more common?
2. What needs do unmarried couples have that demographically similar married couples do not have?
3. Should firms such as banks develop and advertise products to meet the unique needs of this group?

70 percent of households with children under 18 are headed by a married couple.[5] The decline in traditional families is due in part to an increase in single parent households as a result of divorce. A larger cause is a significant increase in single individuals. This increase has been largely a result of the overall delay in the median age of marriage—from 23.2 and 20.8 years for males and females in 1970 to 27.1 and 25.3 in 2003—and by an increase in sole survivors as the percentage of the population over 65 has grown significantly.

Other common household structures are also not adequately captured by Census reports or other major data sources such as Mediamark, Simmons, or Nielsen. Unmarried couples, both same sex and opposite sex, have consumption patterns similar to married couples but, in the absence of children, would not be classified as a family household by the Census. Consumer Insight 6-1 describes one subset of unmarried families, namely opposite-sex households, and some of the marketing issues and opportunities these consumers create.

Kraft recognizes the diversity and importance of families. Its ads portray various family types in scenarios revolving around food. A recent spot features a father and his daughter enjoying a quiet conversation.

Recognizing and adapting to the differing needs of various family members can be a critical success factor (see Illustration 6-1).

THE HOUSEHOLD LIFE CYCLE

The traditional view of the American household life cycle was quite simple. People married by their early 20s; they had several children; these children grew up and started their own families; the original couple retired; and the male would eventually

Courtesy Campbell Soup Company.

die, followed after a few years by the female. This was known as the *family life cycle,* and it was a useful tool for segmenting markets and developing marketing strategy. The basic assumption underlying the family life cycle approach is that most families pass through an orderly progression of stages, each with its own characteristics, financial situation, and purchasing patterns.

However, as described earlier, American households follow much more complex and varied cycles today. Therefore, researchers have developed several models of the **household life cycle (HLC).**[6] All are based on the age and marital status of the adult members of the household and the presence and age of children. A useful version is shown in Figure 6-2.

The HLC assumes that households move into a variety of relatively distinct and well-defined categories over time. There are a variety of routes into most of the categories shown in Figure 6-2, and movement from one category into another frequently occurs. For example, it is common for singles to marry and then divorce within a few years without having children (move from single to young married back to young single). Or one can become a single parent through divorce or through birth or adoption without a cohabiting partner.

Each category in the household life cycle poses a set of problems that household decision makers must solve. The solution to these problems is bound intimately to the selection and maintenance of a lifestyle and, thus, to consumption. For example, all young couples with no children face a need for relaxation or recreation. Solutions to this common problem differ, with some opting for an outdoors-oriented lifestyle and others choosing a sophisticated urban lifestyle. As these families move into another stage in the HLC such as the "full nest I" stage, the problems they face change. The amount of time and resources available for recreation usually diminishes. New problems related to raising a child become more urgent.

Each stage presents unique needs and wants as well as financial conditions and experiences. Thus, the HLC provides marketers with relatively homogeneous household segments that share similar needs with respect to household-related problems and purchases.

FIGURE 6-2   Stages of the Household Life Cycle

Stage	Marital Status		Children at Home		
	Single	Married	None	<6 years	>6 years
Younger (<35)					
Single I	✗		✗		
Young married		✗	✗		
Full nest I		✗		✗	
Single parent I	✗			✗	
Middle-aged (35–64)					
Single II	✗		✗		
Delayed full nest I		✗		✗	
Full nest II		✗			✗
Single parent II	✗				✗
Empty nest I		✗	✗		
Older (>64)					
Empty nest II		✗	✗		
Single III	✗		✗		

While Figure 6-2 categorizes households into married and unmarried, it is "coupleness" rather than the legal status of the relationship that drives most of the behavior of the household. Committed couples, same sex or opposite sex, tend to exhibit most of the category-specific behaviors described below whether or not they are married.

Single I   This group consists of young (18–34), unmarried individuals. In 2003, there were roughly 66.5 million people in this age group, with 69 percent of men and 60 percent of women being single. Single I is basically the unmarried members of the younger Generation Xers and older Generation Yers, as described in Chapter 4. The aging of the larger Generation Y cohort along with continued delay of marriage is fueling growth in this market.[7] During this time, individuals generally leave home and establish their own distinct identities. It is a time of growth and change, both exciting and positive and frightening and painful. As one thirtysomething said,

> I wouldn't go through my 20s again for all the money in the world. You are out of undergraduate school and it's like, "What's expected of me?" You still haven't come to know yourself, and it's like that there is this gigantic world out there and you must somehow get all the experiences you can under your belt before you can get to know yourself. So you try on a lot of labels and I guess that somehow you think that assemblage is you, when it isn't.[8]

This group can be subdivided into those who live with one or both parents and those who live alone or with other individuals. The roughly 43 million single individuals in this age range live as follows:

	Males	Females	Total
Live alone	13%	12%	12%
Live with parent(s)	45	38	42
Live with others	42	50	46

Ad courtesy of Club Med a Publicís US.

ILLUSTRATION 6-2

Young singles are active and often have significant discretionary income. They are an excellent market for a wide array of recreational and leisure items. This ad would appeal to their desire for action and romance.

Those who live with parents tend to be younger; 78 percent are under 25. A significant number are in school or have recently graduated from high school or college and are beginning their working careers. Though people in this group have low incomes, they also have few fixed expenses. They lead active, social lives. They go to bars, movies, and concerts, and purchase sports equipment, clothes, and personal care items.

Although some of those who live with others are involved with a partner, many share quarters with one or more housemates. These individuals have more fixed living expenses than do those who live with their parents, but they generally have ample disposable income as they share rent and other fixed housing costs.

These singles are a good market for the same types of products as those who live at home as well as for convenience-oriented household products. They are also a prime market for nice apartments, sports cars, Club Med vacations, and similar activities. They are beginning to develop financial portfolios such as life insurance, savings, and stocks or mutual funds. The ad shown in Illustration 6-2 would appeal to both groups.

Singles who live alone are older; 71 percent are over 25. In general they have higher incomes than the others but also have much higher expenses as they have no one with whom to share the fixed cost of a house or apartment. They are a good market for most of the same products and services as the other singles.

Young Couples: No Children   The decision to marry, or to live together, brings about a new stage in the household life cycle. Marriage is much more likely for the 25- to 34-year-olds (52 percent) than it is for the under 25 crowd (12 percent). The lifestyles of two young singles are greatly altered as they develop a shared lifestyle. Joint decisions and shared roles in household responsibilities are in many instances new experiences.[9] Savings,

This ad positions Falling Rock as an ideal resort for couples to escape the pressure of a hectic work schedule for relaxation and romance.

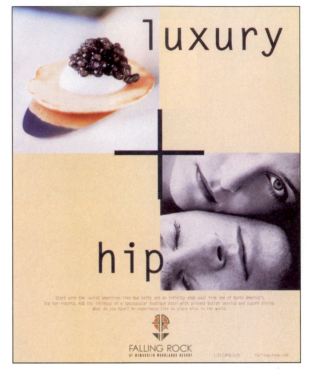

Courtesy Falling Rock at Nemacolin Woodlands Resort.

household furnishings, major appliances, and more comprehensive insurance coverage are among the new areas of problem recognition and decision making to which a young married couple must give serious consideration.

Like the young single stage, the time spent by a young couple in this stage of the HLC has grown as couples either delay their start in having children or choose to remain childless.

Most households in this group have dual incomes and thus are relatively affluent. Compared to full nest I families, this group spends heavily on theater tickets, expensive clothes, luxury vacations, restaurant meals, and alcoholic beverages. They can afford nice cars, stylish apartments, and high-quality home appliances.

Illustration 6-3 contains an ad that would appeal to this group as well as to some members of the single I and full nest I segments. Note that romance plays a major role in the ad. It also plays on the desire to escape worries and everyday responsibilities.

Full Nest I: Young Married with Children   Roughly 7 percent of households are young married couples with children. The addition of the first child to a family creates many changes in lifestyle and consumption. Naturally, new purchases in the areas of baby clothes, furniture, food, and health care products occur in this stage. Lifestyles are also greatly altered. The wife often withdraws fully or partly from the labor force (in less than 60 percent of married couples with a child under three does the wife work outside the home)[10] for several months to several years, with a resulting decline in household income. The couple may have to move to another place of residence since their current apartment may not be appropriate for children. Likewise, choices of vacations, restaurants, and automobiles must be changed to accommodate young children.

Some of the changes in income and annual expenditures that occur as a household moves from childless to the young child stage include the following (based on no child

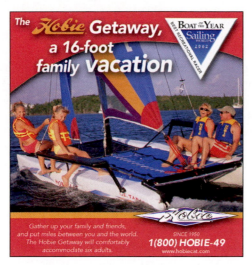

Courtesy The Hobie Cat Company.

versus one child for 25- to 35-year-old couples):[11]

Expenditure	Percentage Change
Income	−9.3%
Food at home	11.8
Meals out	−34.7
Alcoholic beverages	−43.4
Adult apparel	−28.4
Health care	7.9
Pets, toys	23.0
Education	−48.1
Personal care products	−8.5

As shown above, discretionary and adult expenditures are reduced by the need to spend on child-related products such as food, health care, and toys as well as to offset the decline in income.

Obtaining competent child care becomes an issue at this stage and remains a major concern of parents at all HLC stages. Households with a stay-at-home spouse confront this issue mainly for evenings out or weekends away. Single-parent and dual-earner households generally require daily child care, which is expensive and often requires parents to make trade-offs from their ideal situation.

ClubMom is an online loyalty program aimed at the $1.7 trillion in spending power of moms (across all HLC stages). Among other things, it provides advice, resources, and discounts to moms. Chrysler is the exclusive automobile partner of ClubMom. Chrysler promotes ClubMom in its ads and, in turn, ClubMom gives "points" that provide discounts on other products to members who purchase Dodge brands like the Durango.[12] McDonald's attempts to attract this segment by providing recreational equipment at its outlets that cater heavily to families with young children. Illustration 6-4 contains an ad aimed at this market segment. It shows how the choice of recreational activities may change with the addition of young children.

Single Parent I: Young Single Parents   Birth or adoption by singles is increasingly common. Roughly one-third of children are born to unmarried mothers, a number that has been relatively stable since 1995.[13] However, as many as 40 percent of these children may actually be born to cohabiting unmarried parents.[14] Divorce, while on the decline since 1980, also continues to be a significant part of American society with 40 percent of first marriages ending in divorce.[15] Although most divorced individuals remarry and most women who bear children out of wedlock eventually get married, 9 percent of American households are single-parent families, and 81 percent of these are headed by women.

The younger members of this group, particularly those who have never been married, tend to have a limited education and a very low income. These individuals are often members of one of the lower social classes, as described in Chapter 4. The older members of this segment and the divorced members receiving support from their ex-spouses are somewhat better off financially, but most are still under significant stress as they raise their young children without the support of a partner who is physically present.

This type of family situation creates many unique needs in the areas of child care, easy-to-prepare foods, and recreation. The need to work and raise younger children creates enormous time pressures and places tremendous demands on the energy of these parents. Most are renters and so are not a major market for home appliances and improvements. Their purchases focus on getting by and time- and energy-saving products and services that are not overly expensive.

Few firms have developed marketing campaigns that explicitly focus on this group. An exception is John Hancock Financial Services, which targeted divorced mothers with this ad:

In a dimly lit suburban kitchen, a divorced couple is quarreling bitterly. The thirtysomething woman tells her ex-husband that he's not doing enough for their son. He retaliates that he's never missed a payment. She responds that he just doesn't get it. And then, almost as if he's trying to prove her point, the man says that his girlfriend wants him to move to California. "You tell Joey that, you tell him," she replies.[16]

Middle-Aged Single   The middle-aged single category is made up of people who have never married and those who are divorced and have no child-rearing responsibilities. These individuals are in the 35 to 64 age category.

Middle-aged singles often live alone. In fact, living alone is increasingly viewed as a lifestyle choice that many are willing and able to make given higher incomes. Middle-aged singles who live alone represented roughly 13.5 million households in 2003, which is about 46 percent of all single-person households. Middle-aged singles have higher incomes than young singles. However, all live-alone singles suffer from a lack of scale economies. That is, a couple or family needs only one dishwasher, clothes dryer, and so forth for everyone in the household; but the single-person household needs the same basic household infrastructure even though only one person uses it. Likewise, many foods and other items come in sizes inappropriate for singles, or the small sizes are disproportionately expensive. Thus, opportunities appear to exist to fill unmet needs among this important and growing market.[17]

The needs of middle-aged singles in many ways reflect those of young singles. But middle-aged singles are likely to have more money to spend on their lifestyles and they are willing to indulge themselves. Thus, they may live in nice condominiums, frequent expensive restaurants, own a luxury automobile, and travel often. They are a major market for gifts, and the males buy significant amounts of jewelry as gifts.

Empty Nest I: Middle-Aged Married with No Children   The lifestyle changes in the 1980s and 1990s influenced many young couples to not have children.[18] In other cases, these households represent second marriages in which children from a first marriage are not living with the parent. This group also includes married couples whose children have

Ad created by Tinsley Advertising for Super Clubs Resorts.

left home. These three forces have produced a huge market consisting of middle-aged couples without children at home. Roughly 52 percent of married couples in this age group (35 to 64) don't have children under the age of 18. The size of this segment will grow rapidly over the next 10 years as the baby boomers continue to move into the latter stages of middle age.

Both adults typically will have jobs, so they are very busy. However, the absence of responsibilities for children creates more free time than they have enjoyed since their youth. They also have money to spend on dining out, expensive vacations, second homes, luxury cars, and time-saving services such as house-cleaning, laundry, and shopping. They are a prime market for financial services. Less obviously, they are also heavy purchasers of upscale children's products, as gifts for nieces, nephews, grandchildren, and friends' children. One estimate puts baby boomer spending on grandchildren at $35 billion a year. They are purchasing products ranging from clothing and books to electronics products and represent a growing market for upscale brands.[19]

The ad and product in Illustration 6-5 would appeal to this group, as well as the full nest II and empty nest II segments.

Delayed Full Nest I: Older Married with Young Children   Many members of the baby boom generation delayed having their first child until they were in their mid-30s. This produced the new phenomenon of a large number of middle-aged, established families entering into parenthood for the first time. Recall that married couples with children under 18 make up 23.3 percent of all households. And young married couples make up only 7 percent of all households. However, middle-aged (35 to 64) married couples with children (both delayed full nest I and full nest II) make up roughly 16 percent of all households and represent 69 percent of all married couples with children under 18.

A major difference between delayed full nest I and younger new parents is income. Older new parents' incomes are significantly larger than those of younger new parents. They have had this income flow longer and so have acquired more capital and possessions. They spend heavily on child care, mortgage payments, home maintenance, lawn care, and household furnishings. In addition, they want only the best for their children and are willing and able to spend on them. For example, the specialty diaper and toiletries market is expected to grow by 21 percent between 2001 and 2006. Brands like Estée Lauder are getting into the game. And, traditional mass marketers such as Kimberly-Clark are pushing high-end products like "pull-up" diapers with glow-in-the-dark animated characters such as Buzz Lightyear.[20] In addition to child-focused spending, delayed full nest I can also spend more on nonchild expenditures such as food, alcohol, and entertainment and can make more savings and retirement contributions than can younger new parents.

Full Nest II: Middle-Aged Married with Children at Home

A major difference between this group and delayed full nest I is age of the children. The children of full nest II are generally over six years old and are becoming more independent. The presence of older children creates unique consumption needs, however. Families with children six and older are the primary consumers of lessons of all types (piano, dance, gymnastics, and so on), dental care, soft drinks, presweetened cereals, and a wide variety of snack foods.

Greater demands for space create a need for larger homes and cars. Transporting children to multiple events places time demands on the parents and increases transportation-related expenditures. These factors, coupled with heavy demand for clothing and an increased need to save for college, create a considerable financial burden on households in this stage of the HLC. This is offset somewhat by the tendency of the wife to return to work as the children enter school. This return to work usually entails greater time pressures. ConAgra has found great success tapping parents' desire to simplify mealtime with their easy-to-prepare Banquet Crock-Pot Classics, which have all needed ingredients and can cook all day and be ready to eat in the evening with minimal hassle.[21]

As we saw in Chapter 4, the teenage members of this segment, as well as teens in the single parent II segment, are important consumers in their own right as well as important influencers on household consumption decisions.

Single Parent II: Middle-Aged Single with Children at Home

Single individuals in the 35 to 64 age group who have children are often faced with serious financial pressures. The same demands that are placed on the middle-aged married couple with children are present in the life of a middle-aged single with children. However, the single parent often lacks some or all of the financial, emotional, and time support that the presence of a spouse generally provides. Many individuals in this position are thus inclined to use time-saving alternatives such as ready-to-eat food, and they are likely to eat at fast-food restaurants. The children of this segment are given extensive household responsibilities.

It is important to note that becoming a single parent (through adoption or conception) is increasingly viewed as a lifestyle choice for older, more financially secure women who may or may not plan to marry in the future. Single Mothers by Choice (http://mattes.home. pipeline.com) is an organization that recognizes this and offers support and assistance. According to the organization, single women by choice are well-educated, career-oriented women in their 30s and 40s. As a consequence, they often have higher income and financial security than many single parents.[22]

Empty Nest II: Older Married Couples

There are about 10 million households in this segment, and it is expected to grow rapidly over the next 10 years as baby boomers age. For

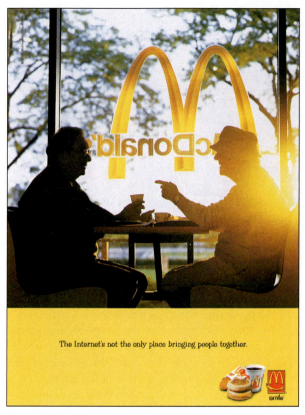

Courtesy McDonald's Corporation.

the most part, couples in the over-64 age group are either fully or partially retired. However, as we discussed in Chapter 4, improvements in health care and longevity, desire to stay active, and changes in Social Security may push retirement age upward over the decades to come. The younger members of this group are healthy, active, and often financially well-off. They have ample time. They are a big market for RVs, cruises, and second homes. They also spend considerable time and money on grandchildren. Increasingly, they take their grandchildren and occasionally their children on vacations. As described in Chapter 4, as they advance in age, health care and assisted living become more important. Illustration 6-6 shows an ad for a product designed to meet one of this segment's needs.

Older Single   There are more than 15 million older singles in the United States, and this group is growing rapidly. Roughly three-fourths of all older singles are female and roughly two-thirds of all older singles live alone. The conditions of being older, single, and generally retired create many unique needs for housing, socialization, travel, and recreation. Many financial firms have set up special programs to work with these individuals. They often have experienced a spouse's death and now are taking on many of the financial responsibilities once handled by the other person. A recent study labeled consumers who were single due to the death of a spouse as "single by circumstance" rather than single by choice. Many older singles would fall into the single by circumstance category. Results of the research suggest that older singles who are single by circumstance will be less innovative, more risk averse, more price sensitive, and will engage in coping behaviors such as spending more time watching television than their single by choice counterparts.[23] *What are the social and ethical issues involved in marketing to older consumers who are single by circumstance?*

MARKETING STRATEGY BASED ON THE HOUSEHOLD LIFE CYCLE

The preceding sections have illustrated the power of the HLC as a segmentation variable. The purchase and consumption of many products are driven by the HLC. The reason for this is that each stage in the HLC poses unique problems or opportunities to the household members; and the resolution of these problems often requires the consumption of products or services. Our earlier discussion and illustrations indicated how marketers are responding to the unique needs of each stage in the HLC.

While a stage in the HLC causes many of the problems or opportunities individuals confront as they mature, it does not provide solutions. For example, while all full nest I families face similar needs and restrictions with respect to recreation, such factors as their income, occupation, and education heavily influence how they will meet those needs. Thus, it makes sense to combine stage in the HLC with one of these variables to aid in market segmentation and strategy formulation.

For example, think of how the need for vacations differs as one moves across the stages of the household life cycle. Young singles often desire vacations focused on activities, adventure, and the chance for romance. Young married couples without children would have similar needs but without the desire to meet potential romantic partners. Full nest I and single parent I families need vacations that allow both parents and young children to enjoy themselves. The manner in which these needs will be met will vary sharply across occupational, income, and educational categories. For example, a young professional couple may vacation in Paris or at a resort in the tropics. A white-collar couple may visit a domestic ski resort or visit Hawaii on a package deal. A young blue-collar couple may visit family or go camping.

Table 6-2 presents the **HLC/occupational category matrix.** The vertical axis is the particular stage in the HLC, which determines the problems the household will likely

| TABLE 6-2 | HLC/Occupational Category Matrix |

HLC Stage	Occupational Category				
	Executive/ Elite Professional	Administrative/ Professional	Technical/ Sales/Clerical	Crafts	Unskilled/ Manual
Single I					
Young Married					
Full nest I					
Single parent I					
Single II					
Delayed full nest I					
Full nest II					
Single parent II					
Empty nest I					
Empty nest II					
Single III					

encounter; the horizontal axis is a set of occupational categories, which provide a range of acceptable solutions. While this version has been found to be useful across a range of products, using income, education, or social class instead of occupation should be considered for some product categories.

This matrix can be used to segment the market for many products and to develop appropriate marketing strategies for the targeted segments. An effective use of the matrix is to isolate an activity or problem of interest to the firm, such as preparing the evening meal, snacks, weekend recreation, vacations, and so forth. Research, often in the form of focus group interviews, is used to determine the following information for each relevant cell in the matrix:

1. What products or services are now being used to meet the need or perform the activity?
2. What, if any, symbolic or social meaning is associated with meeting the need or using the current products?
3. Exactly how are the current products or services being used?
4. How satisfied are the segment members with the current solutions, and what improvements are desired?

Attractive segments are those that are large enough to meet the firm's objectives and that have needs that current products are not fully satisfying. This approach has been used successfully for movies, regional bakeries, and financial services.[24] *What type of automobile would be best suited for each cell and what type of ad should promote it?*

FAMILY DECISION MAKING

Family decision making is *the process by which decisions that directly or indirectly involve two or more family members are made.* Decision making by a group such as a family differs in many ways from decisions made by an individual. Consider the purchase of a breakfast cereal that children, and perhaps the adults, will consume. Who recognizes the need for the product? How is a type and brand selected? Does everyone consider the same attributes? A parent typically makes the actual *purchase;* does that mean that the parent also makes the *choice?* Or is the choice made by the children, the other parent, or some combination? Which parents are involved, and how does this change across products and over time? How does it differ by stage in the household life cycle?

Family purchases are often compared to organizational buying decisions. Although this can produce useful insights, it fails to capture the essence of family decision making. Organizations have relatively objective criteria, such as profit maximization, that guide purchases. Families generally lack such explicit, overarching goals. Most industrial purchases are made by strangers or have little impact on those not involved in the purchase. Most family purchases directly affect the other members of the family.

Most important, *many family purchases are inherently emotional and affect the relationships between the family members.*[25] The decision to buy a child a requested toy or new school clothes is more than simply an acquisition. It is a symbol of love and commitment to the child. The decision to take the family to a restaurant for a meal or to purchase a new television has emotional meaning to the other family members. Disagreements about how to spend money are a major cause of marital discord. The processes families use to make purchase decisions and the outcomes of those processes have important effects on the well-being of the individual family members and the family itself. Thus, while family decision making has some things in common with organizational decision making, it is not the same.

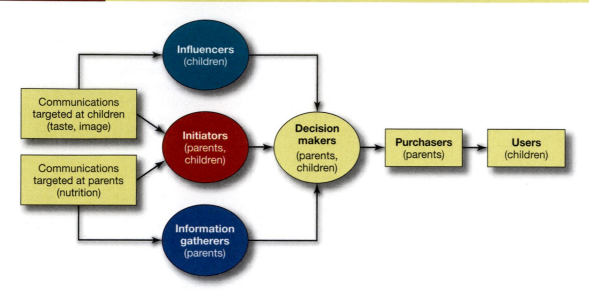

FIGURE 6-3   **The Household Decision-Making Process for Children's Products**

The Nature of Family Purchase Roles

Figure 6-3 illustrates the six roles that frequently occur in family decision making, using a cereal purchase as an example.[26] It is important to note that individuals will play various roles for different decisions.

- *Initiator(s).* The family member who first recognizes a need or starts the purchase process.
- *Information gatherer(s).* The individual who has expertise and interest in a particular purchase. Different individuals may seek information at different times or on different aspects of the purchase.
- *Influencer(s).* The person who influences the alternatives evaluated, the criteria considered, and the final choice.
- *Decision maker(s).* The individual who makes the final decision. Of course, joint decisions also are likely to occur.
- *Purchaser(s).* The family member who actually purchases the product. This is typically an adult or teenager.
- *User(s).* The user of the product. For many products there are multiple users.

Marketers must determine who in the family plays which role before they can affect the family decision process. After thorough study, Crayola shifted its advertising budget from children's television to women's magazines. Its research revealed that mothers rather than children were more likely to recognize the problem, evaluate alternatives, and make the purchase. Illustration 6-7 shows a product designed for use by children that is selected by both the children and the parents and purchased by parents.

Family decision making has been categorized as *husband-dominant, wife-dominant, joint,* or *individualized.* Husband-dominant decisions have traditionally occurred with the purchase of such products as automobiles, liquor, and life insurance. Wife-dominant decisions were more common in the purchase of household maintenance items, food, and kitchen appliances. Joint decisions were most likely when buying a house, living room furniture, and vacations. These patterns are much less pronounced today. As women's occupational roles have expanded, so has the range of family decisions in which they participate or dominate.[27]

A moment's reflection will reveal that the above four categories omit critical participants in many family decisions. Until recently, most studies have ignored the influence of children.[28] Yet children, particularly teenagers, often exert a substantial influence on family purchase decisions.[29] Thus, we need to recognize that *child-dominant* and various combinations of *husband, wife,* and *child joint decisions* are also common.

Studies of family decisions have focused on direct influence and ignored indirect influence. For example, a wife might report that she purchased an automobile without discussing it with any member of her family. Yet she might purchase a van to meet her perceptions of the desires of the family rather than the sports car that she personally would prefer. Most research studies would classify the above decision as strictly wife-dominated. Clearly, however, other family members influenced the decision.

Different family members often become involved at different stages of the decision process. Figure 6-4 shows the influence of wives and husbands at each stage of the decision process for a variety of services. As can be seen, roles vary across services and across stages in the decision process.

Family decisions also allow different members to make specific subdecisions of the overall decision. When an individual makes a decision, he or she evaluates all the relevant attributes of each alternative and combines these evaluations into a single decision. In a family decision, different members often focus on specific attributes. For example, a child

ILLUSTRATION 6-7

Children often determine the products and brands they use. At other times, they influence these choices but the parents play the dominant role. In such cases, the marketer must meet the needs of both the child and the parents.

Courtesy The Dannon Company, Inc.

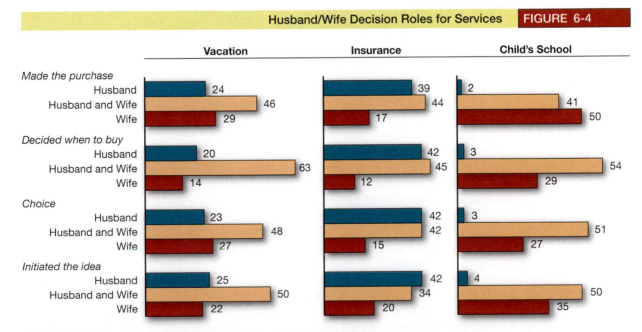

Husband/Wife Decision Roles for Services   FIGURE 6-4

	Vacation	Insurance	Child's School
Made the purchase			
Husband	24	39	2
Husband and Wife	46	44	41
Wife	29	17	50
Decided when to buy			
Husband	20	42	3
Husband and Wife	63	45	54
Wife	14	12	29
Choice			
Husband	23	42	3
Husband and Wife	48	42	51
Wife	27	15	27
Initiated the idea			
Husband	25	42	4
Husband and Wife	50	34	50
Wife	22	20	35

Note: Totals do not add to 100 because other individuals were involved in some decisions.

Source: M. R. Stafford, G. K. Ganesh, and B. C. Garland, "Marital Influence in the Decision-Making Process for Services." *Journal of Services Marketing* 10, no. 1 (1996), p. 15.

Courtesy Lewis P.R., Inc.

may evaluate the color and style of a bicycle while one or both parents evaluate price, warranty, and safety features.

Determinants of Family Purchase Roles

How family members interact in a purchase decision is largely dependent on the *culture and subculture* in which the family exists, the *role specialization* of different family members, the degree of *involvement* each has in the product area of concern, and the *personal characteristics* of the family members.[30]

Today, America has less of a masculine orientation than many other cultures. As one would expect, wives are more involved in a wider range of decisions in the United States than they are in cultures with a more masculine focus.[31] However, subcultures and other groups in the United States vary on this value. As we saw in Chapter 5, the Hispanic subculture has more of a masculine orientation than the broader culture. Research indicates that Hispanics who identify strongly with the Hispanic culture tend to make more husband-dominant decisions than do others.

Over time, each spouse develops more specialized roles as a part of the family lifestyle and family responsibilities. Husbands traditionally specialized in mechanical and technical areas, while wives specialized in home care and child rearing. Although particular roles are no longer automatically assigned to one gender in the marriage, they still tend to evolve over time. It is simply much more efficient for one person to specialize in some decisions than it is to have to reach a joint decision for every purchase.

Involvement or expertise in a product area is another major factor that affects how a family purchase decision will be made. Naturally, the more involved a spouse or other family member is with a product area, the more influence this person will have. For example,

Teen Internet Mavens as Family Influencers

The influence and purchase power of teens are well documented. So too is their heavy online and technology usage. So, it shouldn't be surprising that one area where teens have influence in family decisions is in technology-related categories like computers and the Internet.

However, research is now finding that technology is giving teens more power in family purchase decisions *not* directly related to technology such as family vacations.[32] The idea is that the Internet provides a wealth of information access that can be used in making family decisions of all kinds. Tech savvy teens who can provide their families with access to this world should have greater influence on the decision-making process. These teens are called Internet mavens and have the following characteristics:

- Greater enjoyment and interest in the Internet in general.
- Greater knowledge about the Web-based marketplace (e.g., new sites, where to get deals).
- More expertise in searching out and finding information and resources on the Web.
- Greater enjoyment and desire to help others by providing information found on the Web.

Not all teens are Internet mavens. Teen Internet mavens are more likely to be heavy users of the Internet than nonmavens and are more likely to use the Internet for fun. Interestingly, teens who perceive themselves as Internet mavens are usually seen as mavens by their parents, who in turn seek them out as a gateway to the Internet marketplace.

Research looking specifically at family vacation decisions finds that teen Internet mavens had greater influence than nonmavens at both the earlier (initiation and search) and later stages (evaluation and choice) of the decision process. Teen influence was lower at the later stages even for the Internet mavens, suggesting that the maven's primary role is in information search and access. However, the Internet mavens also maintained a stronger influence at the later stages than did nonmavens, perhaps a carry-over from their involvement in earlier stages.

Clearly family decision making presents unique challenges to marketers including how to simultaneously and effectively communicate with diverse members of a household unit.

Critical Thinking Questions

1. Were you or any of your siblings the Internet maven in your household?

2. What role does parent online expertise play in terms of the power of teen Internet mavens in the family decision process?

3. What unique challenges does the existence of teen Internet mavens present to marketers?

---

when children are the primary users of a product (e.g., toys, snacks, breakfast cereal), they tend to have more influence. Teenagers who are involved with computers often strongly influence the decision for a family computer or the choice of an Internet access service.[33] Antec recognizes the strong role that teens can play in technology decisions and has designed their ads to appeal to this group (Illustration 6-8).

As Consumer Insight 6-2 shows, teenagers are also garnering increased power over nontechnology purchases through their tech savvy status within the family.

Several personal characteristics have an effect on the influence individuals will have on purchase decisions.[34] Education is one such personal characteristic. The higher a wife's education, the more she will participate in major decisions.[35] Personality is an important determinant of family decision roles. Traits such as aggressiveness, locus of control (belief in controlling one's own situation), detachment, and compliance influence family decision power.[36] For children, age matters, with older children and teens playing an increasingly stronger role. For example, one study found that 40 percent of kids age 12 to 14 told their parents to buy a certain kind of furniture, compared to only 25 percent of kids age 6 to 8. Marketers are responding. Ikea makes references to "living with parents" in its catalogs and Pottery Barn has children and teen lines and a teen catalog *PBteen* with products to fit the teen lifestyle.[37]

Finally, stage of the decision process influences decision roles. Purchase decisions evolve from the early stages of problem recognition and information search through choice and purchase. Children and teens tend to have more influence on earlier stages of the family decision process than on later stages.[38]

Conflict Resolution

Given the number of decisions families make daily, disagreements are inevitable. How they are resolved is important to marketers as well as to the health of the family unit. One study revealed six basic approaches that individuals use to resolve purchase conflicts after they have arisen (most couples generally seek to avoid open conflicts):[39]

- *Bargaining.* Trying to reach a compromise.
- *Impression management.* Misrepresenting the facts in order to win.
- *Use of authority.* Claiming superior expertise or role appropriateness (the husband/wife should make such decisions).
- *Reasoning.* Using logical argument to win.
- *Playing on emotion.* Using the silent treatment or withdrawing from the discussion.
- *Additional information.* Getting additional data or a third-party opinion.

Another study found that spouses adapt their strategies across decisions and that when they use coercive means (e.g., silent treatment) to get their way they are satisfied with the decision *outcome* but dissatisfied with the decision *process*.[40] Although neither study included children, a study focused on how children and parents attempt to influence each other found a similar though more complex set of influence strategies.[41]

Conclusions on Family Decision Making

Much remains to be learned about family decision making. But we can offer five general conclusions:

1. Different family members are often involved at different stages of the decision process.
2. Different family members often evaluate different attributes of a product or brand.
3. The direct involvement of family members in each stage of the decision process represents only a small part of the picture. Taking into account the desires of other family members is also important, though seldom studied.
4. Who participates at each stage of the decision process and the method by which conflicts are resolved are primarily a function of the product category and secondarily a function of the characteristics of the individual family members and the characteristics of the family. The product category is important because it is closely related to who uses the product.
5. Overt conflicts in decision making are less common than agreement.

MARKETING STRATEGY AND FAMILY DECISION MAKING

Formulating an effective marketing strategy for most consumer products requires a thorough understanding of the family decision-making process in the selected target markets with respect to that product. Table 6-3 provides a framework for such an analysis.

TABLE 6-3

Marketing Strategy
Based on the Family
Decision-Making
Process

Segment: _____

Stage in the Decision Process	Family Members Involved	Family Members' Motivation and Interests	Marketing Strategy and Tactics
Problem recognition			
Information search			
Alternative evaluation			
Purchase			
Use/consumption			
Disposition			
Evaluation			

The family decision-making process often varies across market segments such as stages in the family life cycle or subculture. Therefore, a marketer must analyze family decision making *within* each of the firm's defined target markets. Within each target market, the marketer needs to

- Discover which family members are involved at each stage of the decision process.
- Determine what their motivations and interests are.
- Develop a marketing strategy that will meet the needs of each participant.

For example, younger children are often involved in the problem recognition stage related to breakfast. They may note a new cartoon character–based cereal or discover that their friends are eating a new cereal. They are interested in identifying with the cartoon character or being like their friends. When they request the new cereal, the parents, generally the mother, may become interested. However, she is more likely to focus on nutrition and price. Thus, a marketer needs to communicate fun, taste, and excitement to children—and nutrition, value, and taste to parents. The children can be reached on Saturday cartoons, appropriate Internet sites, and similar media, while the mother may be more effectively communicated with through magazine ads and package information.

CONSUMER SOCIALIZATION

The family provides the basic framework in which consumer socialization occurs. **Consumer socialization** is *the process by which young people acquire skills, knowledge, and attitudes relevant to their functioning as consumers in the marketplace.*[42] We are concerned with understanding both the content of consumer socialization and the process of consumer socialization. The content of consumer socialization refers to what children learn with respect to consumption; the process refers to how they learn it. Before we address these two issues, we need to consider the ability of children of various ages to learn consumption-related skills.

The Ability of Children to Learn

Younger children have limited abilities to process certain types of information. **Piaget's stages of cognitive development** are a widely accepted set of stages of cognitive development:

> *Stage 1: The period of sensorimotor intelligence (0 to 2 years).* During this period, behavior is primarily motor. The child does not yet "think" conceptually, though cognitive development is seen.

> *Stage 2: The period of preoperational thoughts (3 to 7 years).* This period is characterized by the development of language and rapid conceptual development.

> *Stage 3: The period of concrete operations (8 to 11 years).* During these years, the child develops the ability to apply logical thought to concrete problems.

> *Stage 4: The period of formal operations (12 to 15 years).* During this period, the child's cognitive structures reach their greatest level of development, and the child becomes able to apply logic to all classes of problems.

Other researchers have proposed other stages, with learning rather than aging as the underlying cause of observed differences. However, the general pattern of less ability to deal with abstract, generalized, unfamiliar, or large amounts of information by younger children is common to all approaches.[43]

The changing capabilities of children to process information as they age present challenges to parents who are attempting to teach their children appropriate consumption behaviors.[44] As we will discuss shortly, this also poses ethical and practical issues for marketers.[45] Children's limited learning capacity is the basis for substantial regulation of advertising to children. We describe existing and proposed regulations of marketing to children in depth in Chapter 20.

The Content of Consumer Socialization

The content of consumer learning can be broken down into three categories: consumer skills, consumption-related preferences, and consumption-related attitudes.[46] **Consumer skills** are *those capabilities necessary for purchases to occur such as understanding money, budgeting, product evaluation, and so forth.* A child has to learn how to shop, how to compare similar brands, how to budget available income, and so forth. The following example shows an attempt by a parent to teach her adolescent appropriate, from the parent's perspective, shopping rules:

> Son, look at this. This is just going to wash nicer, it will come through the laundry nicer, and you do a lot of the laundry yourself, and I just would rather that it's something that would wash easy, that doesn't have to be ironed, that isn't 100 percent cotton. (Mother with son, age 13)[47]

Consumption-related preferences are *the knowledge, attitudes, and values that cause people to attach differential evaluations to products, brands, and retail outlets.* For example, some parents through their comments and purchases may "teach" their children that Calvin Klein is a prestigious brand name and that prestigious brands are desirable. This information about Calvin Klein's prestige is not necessary to carry out the actual purchase (consumer skills), but it is extremely important in deciding to purchase and what to purchase (consumption-related preferences).[48]

Consumption-related attitudes are *cognitive and affective orientations toward marketplace stimuli such as advertisements, salespeople, warranties, and so forth.*[49] For example, children may learn from their parents or other family members that "you get what you pay for." This would lead them to assume a strong price–quality relationship. Or they may be taught that salespeople are not trustworthy. These attitudes will influence how they react to the various activities undertaken by marketers. What type of attitude is being formed in the following interaction?

> I'm always trying to get her to learn the relative value of things and particularly the impact of advertising and its effect on driving purchases and desires. So we try to talk about that. I point out manipulative or deceptive advertising, and give her a sense of being a critical consumer. (Father with daughter, age 13)[50]

The Process of Consumer Socialization

Consumer socialization occurs through a number of avenues including advertising and friends. However, family is a primary source of consumer socialization. For example, a recent study of eating patterns found that children cite parents as the most important influence regarding the kinds of foods they eat. This was even true of teenagers, where parental influence was highest and friends and advertising played a much lesser role.[51] Parents teach their children consumer skills, consumption-related preferences, and consumption-related attitudes. They do so both deliberately and casually through instrumental training, modeling, and mediation.

Instrumental training *occurs when a parent or sibling specifically and directly attempts to bring about certain responses through reasoning or reinforcement.* In other words, a parent may try directly to teach a child which snack foods should be consumed by explicitly discussing nutrition. Or a parent may establish rules that limit the consumption of some snack foods and encourage the consumption of others. The following example shows an approach used with older children:

> One thing that we always talk about when we're looking at something is the price of it. "For what you're buying, is the price worth the quality of what you're buying?" (Mother with son, age 13)[52]

Parents often worry that marketing messages will simply drown out any instrumental training they try to provide. In Illustration 6-9 Wendy's positions itself as a partner in the socialization process by offering nutritional options for kids that parents can live with.

Modeling *occurs when a child learns appropriate, or inappropriate, consumption behaviors by observing others.* Modeling generally, though not always, occurs without direct instruction from the role model and frequently without conscious thought or effort on the part of the child. Modeling is an extremely important way for children to learn relevant skills, knowledge, and attitudes. Children learn both positive and negative consumption patterns through modeling. For example, children whose parents smoke are more likely to start smoking than are children whose parents do not smoke.

Mediation *occurs when a parent alters a child's initial interpretation of, or response to, a marketing or other stimulus.* This can easily be seen in the following example.

CHILD: Can I have one of those? See, it can walk!

PARENT: No. That's just an advertisement. It won't really walk. They just make it look like it will so kids will buy them.

The advertisement illustrated a product attribute and triggered a desire, but the parent altered the belief in the attribute and in the believability of advertising in general. This is not

Wendy's clearly recognizes the concerns of parents in the socialization process. Their updated menu provides healthy choices and ample opportunities for parents to engage in instrumental training in a fast-food environment.

© 2004 Oldemark, LLC. Reprinted with permission. The Wendy's name, design and logo are registered trademarks of Oldemark, LLC and are licensed to Wendy's International, Inc.

to suggest that family members mediate all commercials. However, children often learn about the purchase and use of products during interactions with other family members. Thus, a firm wishing to influence children must do so in a manner consistent with the values of the rest of the family.

The Supermarket as a Classroom

Professor James McNeal developed a five-stage model of how children learn to shop by visiting supermarkets and other retail outlets with a parent.[53]

Stage I: Observing　Parents begin taking children to the store with them at a median age of two months. During this stage, children make sensory contact with the marketplace and begin forming mental images of marketplace objects and symbols. In the early months, only sights and sounds are being processed. However, by 12 to 15 months, most children can begin to recall some of these items. This stage ends when children understand that a visit to the market may produce rewards beyond the stimulation caused by the environment.

Stage II: Making Requests　At this stage (median age is two years), children begin requesting items in the store from their parents. They use pointing and gesturing as well as statements to indicate that they want an item. Throughout most of this stage, children make requests only when the item is physically present, as they do not yet carry mental images of the products in their minds. In the latter months of stage II, they begin to make requests for items at home, particularly when they are seen on television.

Stage III: Making Selections   Actually getting an item off the shelf without assistance is the first act of an independent consumer (median age is three and a half years). At its simplest level, a child's desire is triggered by an item in his or her immediate presence and this item is selected. Soon, however, children begin to remember the store location of desirable items, and they are allowed to go to those areas independently or to lead the parent there.

Stage IV: Making Assisted Purchases   Most children learn by observing (modeling) that money needs to be given in order to get things from a store. They learn to value money given to them by their parents and others as a means to acquire things. Soon they are allowed to select and pay for items with their own money. They are now primary consumers (median age is five and a half years).

Stage V: Making Independent Purchases   Making a purchase without a parent to oversee it requires a fairly sophisticated understanding of value as well as the ability to visit a store, or a section of a store, safely without a parent. Most children remain in stage IV a long time before their parents allow them to move into stage V (median age is eight years).

McNeal's research indicates that children learn to shop, at least in part, by going shopping. Retailers are developing programs based on these learning patterns. Examples include child-sized shopping carts and kids' clubs.

MARKETING TO CHILDREN

Children are a very large market. Spending by children aged 5 to 14 is estimated to be $35 billion, and they influence about $200 billion of their parents' purchases.[54] Brand loyalties developed at this age may produce returns for many years. Thus, it is no surprise that marketers are aggressively pursuing these young consumers.

However, marketing to children is fraught with ethical concerns. The major source of these concerns is the limited ability of younger children to process information and to make informed purchase decisions. There are also concerns that marketing activities, particularly advertising, produce undesirable values in children, result in inappropriate diets, and cause unhealthy levels of family conflict. We will examine questionable marketing practices focused on children and the regulations designed to control them in detail in Chapter 20.

Although marketers need to be very sensitive to the limited information-processing skills of younger consumers, ethical and effective marketing campaigns can be designed to meet the needs of children and their parents. All aspects of the marketing mix must consider the capabilities of the child. Consider the following ad and the responses to the ad from children of different ages:

The ad reads "Inhale a lethal dose of carbon monoxide and it's called suicide. Inhale a smaller amount and it's called smoking. Believe it or not, cigarette smoke contains the same poisonous gas as automobile exhaust. So if you wouldn't consider sucking on a tailpipe, why would you want to smoke?" A picture of a smoking exhaust pipe was below the copy.

Seven- and eight-year-old responses:
"Never stand behind a bus because you could get poisonous in your face."
"People sometimes get sick from exhaust."

Nine- and ten-year-old responses:
"The person who is driving is smoking."
"No matter what kind of smoking it is, it can always make you sick."

Eleven-year-old responses:
"You could hurt yourself with that stuff. The same stuff in car exhaust is in cigarettes."
"The tailpipe of a car is like the same as smoking and smoking could kill you . . . both of them could kill you."

Only the older children could fully engage in the analogical reasoning required to completely understand the ad. In contrast, a simpler ad that showed a dirty, grimy sock next to an ashtray full of cigarette butts with the word *gross* under the sock and *really gross* under the ashtray was understood by children of all ages (7 through 11).[55]

Reaching children used to mean advertising on Saturday morning cartoons. Now there are many more options, even for the very young. *National Geographic Kids, Martha Steward Kids,* and *Discovery Girls* are just a few of the many magazines with strong readership among children. In fact at www.themagazinesite.com, you can find over 1,000 magazines targeted at kids. CD-ROMs with interactive capabilities and titles such as "The Magic School Bus" are becoming big sellers. They provide the opportunity to offer entertainment, education, and commercial messages to children and their parents. Children as young as three are active Internet users. Sites such as Foxkids.com, Cartoonnetwork.com, Nick.com, Pokemon.com, and Barbie.com are visited by millions of children aged 2 to 11. And, Yahooligans! (www.yahooligans.yahoo.com) is an online Web guide designed specifically for kids including games, news, and music videos. Radio is popular with older children who are very much into pop music and stars such as Britney Spears.

Direct mail can be an effective means to reach even very young children. Many firms target children or families with young children by forming "kids' clubs." Unfortunately, these clubs sometimes engage in sales techniques that are controversial if not clearly unethical. If done properly, however, they can be fun and educational for the children while delivering responsible commercial messages.

SUMMARY

The household is the basic purchasing and consuming unit and is, therefore, of great importance to marketing managers of most products. Family households are also the primary mechanism whereby cultural and social-class values and behavior patterns are passed on to the next generation.

The *family household* consists of two or more related persons living together in a dwelling unit. *Nonfamily households* are dwelling units occupied by one or more unrelated individuals.

The *household life cycle* is the classification of the household into stages through which it passes over time based on the age and marital status of the adults and the presence and age of children. The household life cycle is a valuable marketing tool because members within each stage or category face similar consumption problems. Thus, they represent potential market segments.

The *household life cycle/occupational category matrix* is a useful way to use the HLC to develop marketing strategy. One axis is the stages in the HLC, which determine the problems the household will likely encounter; the other is a set of occupational categories, which provide a range of acceptable solutions. Each cell represents a market segment.

Family decision making involves consideration of questions such as who buys, who decides, and who uses. Family decision making is complex and involves emotion and interpersonal relations as well as product evaluation and acquisition.

Marketing managers must analyze the household decision process separately for each product category within each target market. Household member participation in the decision process varies by *involvement with the specific product, role specialization, personal characteristics,* and one's *culture and subculture.* Participation also varies by stage in the decision process. Most decisions are reached by consensus. If not, a variety of conflict resolution strategies may be employed.

Consumer socialization deals with the processes by which young people (from birth until 18 years of age) learn how to become consumers. Children's learning abilities are limited at birth, then slowly evolve with experience over time. Consumer socialization deals with the learning of consumer skills, consumption-related preferences, and consumption-related attitudes. Families influence consumer socialization through direct *instrumental training, modeling,* and *mediation.* Young consumers appear to go through five stages of learning how to shop. This learning takes place primarily in retail outlets in interaction with the parents.

Marketing to children is fraught with ethical issues. The main source of ethical concern is the limited ability of children to process information and make sound purchase decisions or requests. There are also concerns about the role of advertising in forming children's values, influencing their diets, and causing family conflict. However, ethical and effective marketing programs can be developed for children.

KEY TERMS

Blended family 196
Consumer skills 216
Consumer socialization 215
Consumption-related attitudes 216
Consumption-related
  preferences 216
Family decision making 209

Family household 196
HLC/occupational category
  matrix 208
Household 196
Household life cycle (HLC) 199
Instrumental training 217
Mediation 217

Modeling 217
Nonfamily household 196
Piaget's stages of cognitive
  development 216
Traditional family 197

INTERNET EXERCISES

1. Prepare a report on the information available on the Internet concerning the percentage of the U.S. population that is in each stage of the household life cycle. Provide the addresses for all sites used.

2. Search Canadian government Web sites and compare the U.S. Census household definitions with those of the Canadian government. Which country seems to be best adapting to the evolution of household structures?

3. Visit the Federal Trade Commission (www.ftc.gov) and Better Business Bureau (www.bbb.org) sites. What ethical and legal issues involving marketing to children appear?

4. Visit one of the sites listed below. Evaluate the effectiveness of the site in terms of marketing to children and the degree to which it represents an ethically sound approach to marketing to children.

a. www.kelloggs.com
b. www.fritolay.com
c. www.warnerbros.com
d. www.crayola.com
e. www.nabisco.com
f. www.barbie.com

5. Visit one of the sites listed below. Evaluate the effectiveness of the site in terms of marketing to children and the degree to which it represents an ethically sound approach to marketing to children. What ages is it best suited for?

a. www.kids.gov
b. www.pbskids.org
c. www.disney.com
d. www.nick.com
e. www.cartoonnetwork.com
f. www.mtv.com

6. Find and describe two sites targeting children under six. What is your evaluation of these sites?

DDB LIFE STYLE STUDY™ DATA ANALYSES

1. Using the data in Table 1A examine which of the following vary the most by *household size.* Why is this the case?
   a. Heavier user (general, consumption, and shopping)

   b. Product ownership
   c. Types of TV shows watched
2. Repeat Question 1 for *marital status.*
3. Repeat Question 1 for *number of children at home.*

4. Using the data in Table 1B examine the relationship between *number of children at home* with each of the following statements. For each, explain the possible underlying cause(s).
   a. Religion is a big part of my life.
   b. When making family decisions, consideration of the kids comes first.
   c. Willing to pay more for better service.
   d. Our family is in too much debt.

REVIEW QUESTIONS

1. The household is described as "the basic consumption unit for consumer goods." Why?
2. What is a *traditional family?* Can a single-parent family be a nuclear family?
3. How does a *nonfamily household* differ from a *family household?*
4. Describe the *blended family.*
5. How has the distribution of household types in the United States been changing? What are the implications of these shifts?
6. What is meant by the *household life cycle?*
7. What is meant by the following statement? "Each stage in the household life cycle poses a series of problems that household decision makers must solve."
8. Describe the general characteristics of each of the stages in the household life cycle.
9. Describe the *HLC/occupational category matrix.* What is the logic for this matrix?
10. What is meant by *family decision making?* How can different members of the household be involved with different stages of the decision process?
11. How does family decision making differ from most organizational decision making?
12. The text states that the marketing manager must analyze the family decision-making process separately within each target market and for each product. Why?
13. What factors influence involvement of a household member in a purchase decision?
14. How do family members attempt to resolve conflict over purchase decisions?
15. What is *consumer socialization?* How is knowledge of it useful to marketing managers?
16. What are Piaget's stages of cognitive development?
17. What do we mean when we say that children learn consumer skills, consumption-related attitudes, and consumption-related preferences?
18. What processes do parents use to teach children to be consumers?
19. Describe each of the five stages children go through as they learn to shop at stores.
20. What ethical issues arise in marketing to children?

DISCUSSION QUESTIONS

21. Respond to the questions in Consumer Insight 6-1.
22. Canada has legislation giving cohabiting couples who have been living together for one year or more the same federal rights and responsibilities as married couples. Should the United States have similar legislation?
23. Rate the stages of the household life cycle in terms of their probable purchase of the following. Justify your answers.
    a. Designer jeans
    b. Trip to Cancun
    c. Jump drive
    d. Breakfast bars
    e. Contribution to SPCA
    f. Satellite radio
24. Pick two stages in the household life cycle. Describe how your marketing strategy for the following would differ depending on which group was your primary target market.
    a. Minivan
    b. Razors
    c. Broadway show
    d. Casino
25. Do you think the trend toward nonfamily households will continue? Justify your response.

26. What are the primary marketing implications of Table 6-1?

27. How would the marketing strategies for the following differ by stage of the HLC? (Assume each stage is the target market.)
    a. Surf board
    b. Contact lenses
    c. Power tools
    d. Hair gel
    e. Detergent
    f. Colleges

28. What are the marketing implications of Figure 6-4?

29. What type of the following would be best suited for each cell in Table 6-2?
    a. Hotel
    b. Television program
    c. Restaurant for the entire household
    d. Lawn mower

30. Name two products for which the horizontal axis in Table 6-2 should be the following. Justify your response.
    a. Occupational category
    b. Income
    c. Education
    d. Social class

31. How can a marketer use knowledge of how family members seek to resolve conflicts?

32. Describe a recent family purchase in which you were involved. Use this as a basis for completing Table 6-3 for a marketer attempting to influence that decision.

33. Describe four types of activities or situations in which direct *instrumental training* is likely to occur.

34. Describe four types of activities or situations in which *modeling* is likely to occur.

35. Describe four types of activities or situations in which *mediation* is likely to occur.

36. Respond to the questions in Consumer Insight 6-2.

37. Are Piaget's stages of cognitive development consistent with the five stages of learning to shop that McNeal identified?

APPLICATION ACTIVITIES

38. Interview a middle school student and determine and describe the household decision process involved in the purchase of his or her
    a. Backpack
    b. Snack foods
    c. Bedroom furniture
    d. Laptop computer
    e. Scooter

39. Interview two sporting goods salespersons from different price-level outlets. Try to ascertain which stages in the household life cycle constitute their primary markets and why this is so.

40. Interview one individual from each stage in the household life cycle. Determine and report the extent to which these individuals conform to the descriptions provided in the text.

41. Interview a family with a child under 13 at home. Interview both the parents and the child, but interview the child separately. Try to determine the influence of each family member on the following products *for the child's use*. In addition, ascertain what method(s) of conflict resolution are used.
    a. Toothbrush
    b. Clothes
    c. Cereal
    d. Major toys, such as Nintendo Game Boy
    e. Television viewing
    f. Fast-food restaurant

42. Interview a couple who have been married for the following periods. Ascertain and report the degree and nature of role specialization that has developed with respect to their purchase decisions. Also determine how conflicts are resolved.
    a. Less than 1 year
    b. 1–5 years
    c. 6–10 years
    d. More than 10 years

43. Pick a product and market segment of interest and interview three households. Collect sufficient data to complete Table 6-3.

44. Pick a product of interest and with several fellow students complete enough interviews to fill the relevant cells in Table 6-2 using the four questions in the text (see p. 209). Develop an appropriate marketing strategy based on this information.

45. Interview several parents of preschool children. Determine the extent to which they agree with Piaget's four stages and McNeal's five stages.

46. Watch several hours of Saturday morning cartoons. What ethical concerns, if any, do they cause?

REFERENCES

1. S. Chandler, "Kids' Wear Is Not Child's Play," *BusinessWeek*, June 19, 1995, p. 118; M. M. Cardona and A. Z. Cuneo, "Retailers Reaching Out to Capture Kids' Clout," *Advertising Age*, October 9, 2000, p. 16; and S. Thompson, "Jell-O Taken to 'X-tremes,'" *Advertising Age*, November 19, 2001, p. 4.

2. See P. Kiecker and N. R. McClure, "Redefining the Extended Family in Recognition of Blended Family Structures," *Enhancing Knowledge Development in Marketing* (Chicago: American Marketing Association, 1996), pp. 242–43.

3. See F. F. Furstenberg, Jr., "The Future of Families," *American Demographics*, June 1996, pp. 34–40; R. Gardyn, "Unmarried Bliss," *American Demographics*, December 2000, pp. 56–61; S. Raymond, "The Ex-Files," *American Demographics*, February 2001, pp. 60–64; and P. Paul, "Millennial Myths," *American Demographics*, December 2001, p. 20.

4. This Consumer Insight is based on Gardyn, "Unmarried Bliss."

5. Statistics in this section drawn primarily from *America's Families and Living Arrangements: 2003* (Washington, DC: U.S. Census Bureau, November 2004).

6. See C. M. Schaninger and W. D. Danko, "A Conceptual and Empirical Comparison of Alternative Household Life Cycle Models," *Journal of Consumer Research*, March 1993, pp. 580–94; R. E. Wilkes, "Household Life-Cycle Stages, Transitions, and Product Expenditures," *Journal of Consumer Research*, June 1995, pp. 27–42; and C. M. Schaninger and D. H. Lee, "A New Full-Nest Classification Approach," *Psychology & Marketing*, January 2002, pp. 25–58.

7. See, e.g., N. Donthu and D. I. Gilliland, "The Single Consumer," *Journal of Advertising Research*, November–December 2002, pp. 77–84.

8. G. J. Thompson, "Interpreting Consumers," *Journal of Marketing Research*, November 1997, p. 448.

9. See J. Raymond, "For Richer or Poorer," *American Demographics*, July 2000, pp. 59–64.

10. "Labor Force Participation Rates for Wives, Husband Present by Age of Own Youngest Child: 1975 to 2003," *Statistical Abstract of the United States 2004–2005* (Washington, DC: U.S. Bureau of the Census), p. 377; see also R. Rosenwein, "The Baby Sabbatical," *American Demographics*, February 2002, pp. 36–38.

11. Estimated from *Consumer Expenditure Survey* (Washington, DC: U.S. Bureau of Labor Statistics, 2000).

12. S. Thompson, "ClubMom Prepares National Rollout," *Advertising Age*, May 3, 2004, p. 24.

13. "Births to Teens, Unmarried Mothers, and Prenatal Care: 1990–2002," *Statistical Abstract of the United States 2004–2005*, p. 64.

14. Gardyn, "Unmarried Bliss," p. 61.

15. For a discussion, including differences across groups, see www.divorcereform.org; and D. Hurley, "Divorce Rate," *The New York Times*, April 19, 2005, p. F7.

16. Raymond, "The Ex-Files," p. 60.

17. See, e.g., J. Morrow, "A Place for One," *American Demographics*, November 2003, pp. 25–29; and P. Francese, "Well Enough Alone," *American Demographics*, November 2003, pp. 32–33.

18. P. Paul, "Childless by Choice," *American Demographics*, November 2001, pp. 45–50.

19. P. Paul, "Make Room for Granddaddy," *American Demographics*, April 2002, pp. 40–45.

20. J. Fetto, "The Baby Business," *American Demographics*, May 2003, p. 40; and J. Neff, "P&G Challenges Rival K-C in Trainers Battle," *Advertising Age*, May 17, 2004, p. 10.

21. "New Survey Finds Parents and Children Alike Crave More Time to Talk and Relax Together," ConAgra press release, January 17, 2005.

22. Information from organization's Web site at http://mattes.home.pipeline.com.

23. Donthu and Gilliland, "The Single Consumer."

24. For a different approach, see L. G. Pol and S. Pak, "Consumer Unit Types and Expenditures on Food Away from Home," *Journal of Consumer Affairs*, Winter 1995, pp. 403–28.

25. See J. Park, P. Tansuhaj, and E. R. Spangenberg, "An Emotion-Based Perspective of Family Purchase Decisions," *Advances in Consumer Research*, vol. 22, eds. F. R. Kardes and M. Sujan (Provo, UT: Association for Consumer Research, 1995), pp. 723–28.

26. C. Lackman and J. M. Lanasa, "Family Decision-Making Theory," *Psychology & Marketing*, March–April 1993, pp. 81–113.

27. For an expanded view of this in an international context, see J. Ruth and S. R. Commuri, "Shifting Roles in Family Decision Making," *Advances in Consumer Research*, vol. 25, eds. J. W. Alba and J. W. Hutchinson (Provo, UT: Association for Consumer Research, 1998), pp. 400–6. See also W. Na, Y. Son, and R. Marshall, "An Empirical Study of the Purchase Role Structure in Korean Families," *Psychology & Marketing*, September 1998, pp. 563–76.

28. An exception is S. E. Beatty and S. Talpade, "Adolescent Influence in Family Decision Making," *Journal of Consumer Research*, September 1994, pp. 332–41.

29. See B. Dellaert, M. Prodigalidad, and J. Louviere, "Family Members' Projections of Each Other's Preference and Influence," *Marketing Letters*, no. 2 (1998), pp. 135–45; K. M. Palan, "Relationships between Family Communication and Consumer Activities of Adolescents," *Journal of the Academy of Marketing Science*, Fall 1998, pp. 338–49; L. A. Williams and A. C. Burns, "Exploring the Dimensionality of Children's Direct Influence Attempts," *Advances in Consumer Research*, vol. 27, eds. S. J. Hoch and R. J. Meyer (Provo, UT: Association for Consumer Research, 2000), pp. 64–71; and J. B. Schor, *Born to Buy* (New York: Scribner, 2004).

30. See R. Madrigal and C. M. Miller, "Construct Validity of Spouses' Relative Influence Measures," *Journal of the Academy of Marketing Science*, Spring 1996, pp. 157–70; C.-N. Chen, M. Lai, and D. D. C. Tarn, "Feminism Orientation, Product Attributes and Husband-Wife Decision Dominance," *Journal of Global Marketing* 12, no. 3 (1999), pp. 23–39; and C. Webster and M. C. Reiss, "Do Established Antecedents of Purchase Decision-Making Power Apply to Contemporary Couples?" *Psychology & Marketing*, September 2001, pp. 951–72.

31. J. B. Ford, L. E. Pelton, and J. R. Lumpkin, "Perception of Marital Roles in Purchase Decision Processes," *Journal of the Academy of Marketing Science,* Spring 1995, pp. 120–31.

32. This insight is based on M. A. Belch, K. A. Krentler, and L. A. Willis-Flurry, "Teen Internet Mavens," *Journal of Business Research* 58 (2005), pp. 569–75.

33. See C. K. C. Lee and S. E. Beatty, "Family Structure and Influence in Family Decision Making," *Journal of Consumer Marketing* 19, no. 1 (2002), pp. 24–41; and G. Slattery and J. Butler, "Teens Are Primary Influencer on Holiday Technology Purchases," *Business Wire,* November 23, 2004, p. 1.

34. See C. Webster and S. Rice, "Equity Theory and the Power Structure in a Marital Relationship," *Advances in Consumer Research,* vol. 23, eds. K. P. Corfman and J. G. Lynch (Provo, UT: Association for Consumer Research, 1996), pp. 491–97; M. C. Reiss and C. Webster, "Relative Influence in Purchase Decision Making," *Advances in Consumer Research,* vol. 24, eds. M. Bruck and D. J. MacInnis (Provo, UT: Association for Consumer Research, 1997), pp. 42–47; and C. Webster, "The Meaning and Measurement of Marital Power," *Advances in Consumer Research,* vol. 25, eds. Alba and Hutchinson, pp. 395–99.

35. D. Crispell, "Dual-Earner Diversity," *American Demographics,* July 1995, pp. 32–37.

36. C. Webster, "Is Spousal Decision Making a Culturally Situated Phenomenon?" *Psychology & Marketing,* December 2000, pp. 1035–58.

37. T. Meyers, "Kids Gaining Voice in How Home Looks," *Advertising Age,* March 29, 2004, p. S-4.

38. See, e.g., Belch, Krentler, and Willis-Flurry, "Teen Internet Mavens."

39. C. Kim and H. Lee, "A Taxonomy of Couples Based on Influence Strategies," *Journal of Business Research,* June 1996, pp. 157–68.

40. C. Su, E. F. Fern, and K. Ye, "A Temporal Dynamic Model of Spousal Family Purchase-Decision Behavior, *Journal of Marketing Research,* August 2003, pp. 268–81.

41. K. M. Palan and R. E. Wilkes, "Adolescent–Parent Interaction in Family Decision Making," *Journal of Consumer Research,* September 1997, pp. 159–69; see also A. Aribarg, N. Arora, and H. O. Bodur, "Understanding the Role of Preference Revision and Concession in Group Decisions," *Journal of Marketing Research,* August 2002, pp. 336–49.

42. For a thorough review, see D. R. John, "Consumer Socialization of Children," *Journal of Consumer Research,* December 1999, pp. 183–209. See also, G. M. Rose, V. Dalakas, and F. Kropp, "Consumer Socialization and Parental Style across Cultures," *Journal of Consumer Psychology* 13, no. 4 (2003), pp. 366–76; and J. Cotte and S. L. Wood, "Families and Innovative Consumer Behavior," *Journal of Consumer Research,* June 2004, pp. 78–86.

43. See J. Gregan-Paxton and D. R. John, "The Emergence of Adaptive Decision Making in Children," *Journal of Consumer Research,* June 1997, pp. 43–56; T. Davis, "What Children Understand about Consumption Constellations," *Advances in Consumer Research,* vol. 27, eds. Hoch and Meyer, pp. 72–78; and E. S. Moore and R. J. Lutz, "Children, Advertising, and Product Experiences," *Journal of Consumer Research,* June 2000, pp. 31–47.

44. Parental responses differ across cultures; see G. M. Rose, "Consumer Socialization, Parental Style, and Developmental Timetables in the United States and Japan," *Journal of Marketing,* July 1999, pp. 105–19.

45. For example, see M. C. Macklin, "Preschoolers' Learning of Brand Names from Visual Cues," *Journal of Consumer Research,* December 1996, pp. 251–61; and D. R. Pawlowski, D. M. Badzinski, and N. Mitchell, "Effects of Metaphors on Children's Comprehension and Perception of Print Advertisements," *Journal of Advertising,* Summer 1998, pp. 83–98.

46. M. Viswanathan, T. L. Childers, and E. S. Moore, "The Measurement of Intergenerational Communication and Influence on Consumption," *Journal of the Academy of Marketing Science,* Summer 2000, pp. 406–24.

47. Palan and Wilkes, "Adolescent–Parent Interaction in Family Decision Making."

48. M. F. Ji, "Children's Relationships with Brands," *Psychology & Marketing,* April 2002, pp. 369–87; and E. S. Moore, W. L. Wilkie, and R. J. Lutz, "Passing the Torch," *Journal of Marketing,* April 2002, pp. 17–37.

49. See G. M. Rose, V. D. Bush, and L. R. Kahle, "The Influence of Family Communication Patterns on Parental Reactions toward Advertising," *Journal of Advertising,* Winter 1998, pp. 71–85; T. F. Mangleburg and T. Bristol, "Socialization and Adolescents' Skepticism toward Advertising," *Journal of Advertising,* Fall 1998, pp. 11–20; and L. Carlson, R. N. Laczniak, and J. E. Keith, "Socializing Children about Television," *Journal of the Academy of Marketing Science,* Summer 2001, pp. 276–88.

50. Palan and Wilkes, "Adolescent–Parent Interaction in Family Decision Making."

51. P. Dando, "Healthier Fast-Food a Reality," *Advertising Age,* March 29, 2004, p. S-7.

52. Palan and Wilkes, "Adolescent–Parent Interaction in Family Decision Making."

53. J. U. McNeal, *Kids as Consumers* (New York: Lexington Books, 1992); and J. U. McNeal and C. Yeh, "Born to Shop," *American Demographics,* June 1993, pp. 34–39. See also J. B. Schor, *Born to Buy* (New York: Scribner, 2004).

54. J. Rosenberg, "Brand Loyalty Begins Early," *Advertising Age,* February 12, 2001, p. S2.

55. L. A. Peracchio and D. Luna, "The Development of an Advertising Campaign to Discourage Smoking Initiation among Children and Youth," *Journal of Advertising,* Fall 1998, pp. 49–56.

Courtesy of Jeep Jamboree USA.

226

7

Group Influences on Consumer Behavior

■ For most products and brands, a consumer or family makes a purchase decision, acquires the item, and consumes it. The basic purchase motivation relates to the ability of the product or service itself to meet a need of the consumer.

Other purchases are fundamentally different. The consumer buys more than the product or brand. Membership in a group is also being purchased. A prime example of this is the purchase of a Harley-Davidson motorcycle. Most purchasers of a Harley-Davidson acquire not only the bike and some aspect of the image that comes with it; they also join a group or subculture. While there are a number of distinct Harley-Davidson groups, most share a core ethos or value system.

An important part of the biker identity involves product consumption. Obviously, one must own a Harley; however, just owning a Harley isn't enough. People, both other bikers and the general public, have expectations about the dress and behaviors of Harley bikers. As one study found: "The newcomer becomes acutely aware of another aspect of Harley ownership, performance before an audience. Much of what guides the newcomer's purchases of protective clothing, footwear, helmets, and accessories can be explained as tasks of impression management driven by perceptions of audience expectation."[1]

Likewise, some Jeep owners elect to become members of a "Jeep community." These owners attend "brandfests" such as Jeep Jamborees, Jeep 101, and Camp Jeep. At these events, they meet and form relationships with other, geographically dispersed owners, deepen their involvement with their Jeeps and with the manufacturer (DaimlerChrysler), and become acculturated into the rituals and traditions of the community. The following quote illustrates how Susan, a first-time Jeep owner, began to become a member of this community.

I've been very happy. I get a lot of communications from Jeep, which I've been so impressed with. Usually you buy a car and you're a forgotten soul. It's kinda like they want you to be part of the family. As soon as I got the invitation for Jeep 101, I registered. I was very excited. But I was also nervous. I didn't think I would end up driving. I was very relieved to see someone in the car with you, 'cause it gave you the confidence to do what you're supposed to. Otherwise, I had

visions of abandoning the truck on the hill and saying, "I can't do it!" I thought I might wimp out, but I didn't (smiles).[2]

Of course, other Jeep owners elect not to join this community and may even remain unaware that it exists.

Purchasing a Harley and "becoming a biker" or joining the Jeep "family" is clearly a group-based process. Even in an individualistic society like America, group memberships and identity are very important to all of us. And while we don't like to think of ourselves as conformists, most of us conform to group expectations most of the time.

When you decided what to wear to the last party you attended, you probably based your decision in part on the anticipated responses of the other individuals at the party. Likewise, your behavior at an anniversary celebration for your grandparents probably would differ from your behavior at a graduation party for a close friend. These behaviors are responses to group influences and expectations.

TYPES OF GROUPS

The terms *group* and *reference group* need to be distinguished. A **group** is defined as *two or more individuals who share a set of norms, values, or beliefs and have certain implicitly or explicitly defined relationships to one another such that their behaviors are interdependent.* A **reference group** is *a group whose presumed perspectives or values are being used by an individual as the basis for his or her current behavior.* Thus, a reference group is simply a group that an individual uses as a guide for behavior in a specific situation.

Most of us belong to a number of different groups and perhaps would like to belong to several others. When we are actively involved with a particular group, it generally functions as a reference group. As the situation changes, we may base our behavior on an entirely different group, which then becomes our reference group. We may belong to many groups simultaneously, but we generally use only one group as our primary point of reference in any given situation. This is illustrated in Figure 7-1.

Groups may be classified according to a number of variables. Four criteria are particularly useful: (1) membership, (2) strength of social tie, (3) type of contact, (4) attraction.

The *membership* criterion is dichotomous: Either one is a member of a particular group or one is not a member of that group. Of course, some members are more secure in their membership than others are; that is, some members feel they really belong to a group, while others lack this confidence.

Strength of social tie refers to the closeness and intimacy of the group linkages. **Primary groups,** such as family and friends, involve strong ties and frequent interaction. Primary groups often wield considerable influence. **Secondary groups** such as professional and neighborhood associations involve weaker ties and less frequent interaction.

Type of contact refers to whether the interaction is direct or indirect. Direct contact involves face-to-face interaction while indirect contact does not. The Internet, in particular, has increased the importance of indirect reference groups in the form of *virtual communities,* which are discussed in more detail later in the chapter.

Reference Groups Change as the Situation Changes   FIGURE 7-1

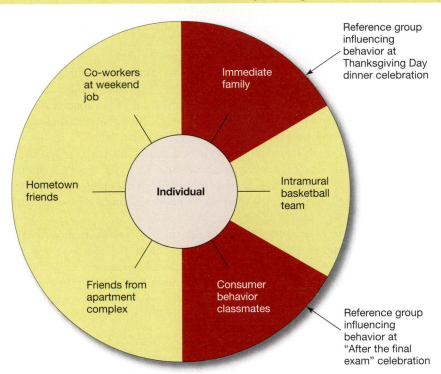

Attraction refers to the desirability that membership in a given group has for the individual. This can range from negative to positive. Groups with negative desirability—**dissociative reference groups**—can influence behavior just as do those with positive desirability. For example, teenagers tend to avoid clothing styles associated with older consumers. Nonmembership groups with a positive attraction—**aspiration reference groups**—also exert a strong influence. Individuals frequently purchase products thought to be used by a desired group in order to achieve actual or symbolic membership in the group.

Recent research has identified various groups of teens, including influencers and conformers. *Influencers* are seen by themselves and others as cool and at the center of the action. Influencers are an aspirational group for many teens, particularly the *conformers,* who have a high need for acceptance and adapt their behaviors and purchases to fit in with the influencers.[3]

Teens are not the only ones susceptible to group influence. Golf equipment companies make heavy use of symbolic aspiration group influence in targeting adults. They get their equipment in the hands of the professionals and allow them, as a group, to exert their influence on the amateur players and weekend duffers with no illusions of turning pro. The influence revolves around identifying with core values and traits of the pros as well as their expertise.[4] Titleist has a clever ad in which various professional golfers talk about all their differences (right handed versus left, fade versus draw, boxers versus briefs) but one key similarity—their use of the Titleist golf ball.

Consumption Subcultures

A consumption-based group, often termed a **consumption subculture,** is *a distinctive subgroup of society that self-selects on the basis of a shared commitment to a particular* *product class, brand, or consumption activity.* These groups have (1) an identifiable, hier-archical social structure; (2) a set of shared beliefs or values; and (3) unique jargon, rituals, and modes of symbolic expression.[5] Thus, they are reference groups for their members as well as those who aspire to join or avoid them.

A number of such subcultures ranging from "punk" culture to skydiving have been examined. Activity-based subcultures are common. Snowboarding, golfing, home brewing (beer), and gardening all have consumption subcultures built around them. Each has a set of self-selecting members. They have hierarchies at the local and national levels. And they also have shared beliefs and unique jargon and rituals. Most hobbies and participation sports have consumption-based group subcultures built around them.

Consumption need not be shared physically to be a shared ritual that creates and sustains a group.[6] Serious fans of professional football or "Star Trek" form consumption subcul-tures. For example, following a team gives a fan something in common with other fans of the same team, and enthusiasm for the sport itself provides a common ground for all mem-bers of the group.[7]

Note that not all, or even most, product owners or participants in an activity become members of the consumption subculture associated with it. For example, one can enjoy the "Star Trek" TV shows without becoming a member of the associated subculture. Self-selecting into a consumption subculture involves more than merely participating in the activity or owning the product. Commitment is required, as are the acquisition of the group's beliefs and values, participation in its indirect activities, and use of its jargon and rituals.

> It is a feeling of family. When I visit other dojos for a judo competition, I feel like I came back home. No other sports that I know do this and have the community judo has.[8]

As with other types of groups, members of consumption subcultures vary in their com-mitment to and interpretation of the group's values and norms. Members of the Star Trek consumption subculture tend to vary along a continuum from fandom to Trekkers to Trekkies (varying in part by when and how much Star Trek symbols, such as clothing, are worn). Members are quite cognizant of these gradients:

> You have to learn to be yourself, to feel secure at expressing what you're really all about. When I tell people that the uniform symbolizes my devotion to the series, to Gene's vision, and I tell them the philosophy behind the show . . . they want to know more.
>
> To me, a "Trekkie" is someone who is pretty much lost in the fantasy world of "Star Trek," some-one who has taken an escapist approach to the show and almost literally "escaped" into it. I like to think I am a fan with a more appropriate detachment to the show.[9]

Marketing and Consumption Subcultures

Consumption subcultures based on ac-tivities obviously are markets for the requirements of the activity itself, such as golf clubs for golfers. However, these groups develop rituals and modes of symbolic communication that often involve other products or services. Golf is renowned for the "uniform" that many of its adherents wear. Clothes, hats, and other items designed for golfers are based as much on providing symbolic meaning as they are for functional benefits.

While these subcultures adopt consumption patterns in large part to affirm their unique identity, the larger market often appropriates all or parts of their symbols, at least for a time.

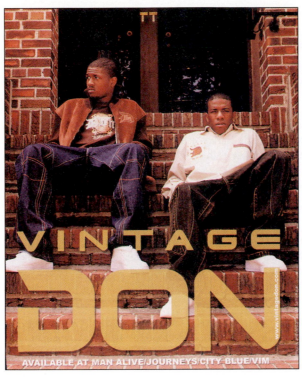

Courtesy Vintage Don.

Thus, clothing initially worn by a consumption subculture such as snowboarders or surfers for functional or symbolic reasons may emerge as a style for a much larger group (see Illustration 7-1). Marketers such as Nike observe such groups closely for clues to new trends.

Participating in a shared consumption experience is a means of developing and maintaining social relationships among individuals. When two or more individuals share a consumption event such as attending a performance, the consumption experience is not just the direct effect of seeing the performance. It includes the social interactions with the other individuals, the fact of sharing, and the meanings attached to these interactions. Thus, organizations marketing the arts, as well as sports marketers and others, should focus on providing and promoting the social, group aspects of the experience as well as the artistic and entertaining features.

Brand Communities

Consumption subcultures focus on the interactions of individuals around an activity, product category, or occasionally a brand. A **brand community** is *a nongeographically bound community, based on a structured set of social relationships among owners of a brand and the psychological relationship they have with the brand itself, the product in use, and the firm.*[10] A **community** is *characterized by consciousness of kind, shared rituals and traditions, and a sense of moral responsibility.*[11]

Both Jeep and Harley-Davidson have created brand communities as described at the beginning of this chapter, as have Saab, Ford Bronco, and Macintosh. The following examples illustrate the nature of brand communities:[12]

Consciousness of Kind

Who else drives Broncos? Guys like myself and guys who like engines.

A lot of people actually purchased the cars [Saabs] who I feel shouldn't have purchased them.

There's a certain type of owner who is proper for the car.

To get down to task, there are several new classes of riders fouling the wind with the misapprehension that merely owning a Harley will transform them into a biker. This is the same type of dangerous ignorance that suggests that giving a dog an artichoke turns him into a gourmet.

Rituals and Traditions

If you drove a Saab, whenever you passed someone else driving a Saab, you beeped or flashed your headlights.

You can find out more about the history of Apple, but arguably its greatest contribution to the world was introduced on January 24, 1984, under the leadership of founder and chairman Steve Jobs. Apple introduced Macintosh, the machine that would change the world [from an individual's Macintosh Web site].

Moral Responsibility

Yeah, we see another Saab on the side of the road; we pull over to help, no matter what it is.

In Colorado, a longtime Jeep owner spent time at an intimidating stream crossing, loudly guiding drivers along the correct route through the rough water. He encouraged inexperienced drivers and reassured them about the capabilities of their vehicles.

Marketing and Brand Communities

Brand communities can add value to the ownership of the product and build intense loyalty. A "mere" Jeep owner derives the functional and symbolic benefits associated with owning a Jeep. A member of the Jeep community derives these benefits plus increases in self-esteem from gaining skill in the off-road operation of a Jeep, the ability and confidence to use the Jeep in a wider range of situations, new friendships and social interactions, a feeling of belongingness, a positive association with DaimlerChrysler, and a deeper relationship with his or her Jeep.

If a consumer anticipates these benefits in advance and values them, he or she is much more likely to buy the brand. Once a consumer becomes a member of a brand community, remaining in the community generally requires continuing to own and use the brand. This can create a very intense brand loyalty. Thus, a "mere" Jeep owner who needed to replace his Jeep might compare a new Jeep with other competing brands by comparing attributes across the brands. However, a Jeep community member would also consider the social and psychological costs of leaving the Jeep community.

A number of firms work diligently to foster brand communities. An initial question a manager must ask is, Does a brand community make sense for this product and brand? Brand communities seem most relevant for high-involvement, activity-based products.

A second condition for a strong brand community appears to be a degree of uniqueness to the brand itself. Harley-Davidson has its historical association with "outlaw bikers." Jeep conjures up images from endless World War II movies. Saab has its unique design and foreign origin. It would certainly be more difficult to build a strong brand community around a mundane brand.

Given that a brand community is feasible, what is required to foster one? Saturn faced that question when it was launched as a new brand with a unique approach to the market.

Saturn works to create a community through the image it portrays of its customers in its advertising; the barbecues, workshops, and other events local dealers sponsor for owners; and the annual "vacation get-together at the factory" program. Saturn also sponsors CarClubs through its dealers, as described on its Web site:

> Buy a Saturn and chances are you'll suddenly start noticing all the other Saturns already out on the road. Even if you think of yourself as being pretty restrained behind the wheel, you might find that every Saturn driver you see sparks a nearly uncontrollable impulse to wave hello. That feeling of being connected to other Saturn owners was the inspiration behind the CarClub.
>
> You're probably wondering, "What exactly do CarClub chapters do?" Hard to say exactly, since no two are alike. But in the past year, club chapters have held community fund-raisers for animal shelters, cancer research, and Habitat for Humanity; gone on short road trips to local vineyards and longer ones to Spring Hill; organized barbecues and road rallies; and learned more about their cars at special Saturn Customer Clinics.

Fostering a community requires the firm to establish a relationship with the owner. Saturn attempts this through portraying itself as a customer-focused firm, by direct mail sent to owners, and by dealer-organized events. It helps owners understand and value their cars through its Customer Clinics. It encourages the formation of social relationships among owners through its sponsorship of CarClubs, the annual vacation get-together, and dealership-sponsored activities.

One important tool for community building that Saturn does not utilize is the "brandfest." A brandfest is *a gathering of owners and others for the purposes of interacting with one another in the context of learning about and using the brand*. Jeep makes extensive use of its brandfests with its Jeep Jamborees and Camp Jeep.

Virtual Communities

A **virtual community** is *a community that interacts over time around a topic of interest on the Internet*.[13] These interactions can take place in various forms and forums including the Usenet (Internet-based message boards), blogs (interconnected online personal journals), professional sites, and sites for nonprofit groups. Examples would include Saturn owners, scuba divers, *Star Wars* fans, and Planned Parenthood.

While it is easy to imagine that true communities are evolving on the Internet, the evidence is less clear. Such groups lack the wide range of functions and interactions that characterize "real" communities. Many participants in virtual communities lack any ongoing commitment to the group. And the lack of face-to-face or even voice-to-voice interaction can remove much of the symbolic and emotional meaning conveyed in real communities.

Despite these distinctions, research indicates that virtual communities do exist for many participants and that there is often a sense of community online, which moves beyond mere interactions to include an affective or emotional attachment to the online group. Studies have found ongoing communications among subsets of these interest groups. In addition, the patterns of communication indicate a group structure, with the more experienced members serving as experts and leaders and the newer members seeking advice and information. These groups develop unique vocabularies, netiquette, and means for dealing with behaviors deemed inappropriate.

Extent of connection can vary dramatically across members. Many members observe the group discussions without participating. Others participate but only at a limited level. For example, one of the authors of this text visits a scuba diving interest group once a year or so. He inquires about dive sites and other recreational opportunities in the area of his

Courtesy Meredith Corporation.

planned vacation. Along these lines, a recent study distinguishes three types of virtual group members:[14]

- *Leaders* are a relatively small group who are highly influential and take on the most responsibility for community maintenance. They are active members in that they both post and respond to messages.
- *Participants* are a larger group who are active members but not deemed (by themselves or others) as leaders.
- *Lurkers* are the largest group and only passively peruse the group discussions without being active participants.

Illustration 7-2 shows how *Parents* magazine (online) promotes the formation of a virtual community for parents who are members.

Marketing and Virtual Communities

Marketing in virtual communities is both possible and potentially beneficial. However, the approach taken has to be tailored to the type of virtual community. More commercial sites, including portals such as iVillage.com (women's issues), which have community message boards, operate under more traditional standards where advertising is expected and tolerated. The main reason mentioned by such portals for using these community areas on their site is to "drive repeat traffic" to their Web site.[15]

However, many online groups, particularly those started and maintained by individuals, are sensitive to "commercial" interference and companies have to be careful not to overstep. Google Groups, which offers members easy access to online groups and Usenet without special software, is careful to conform to these norms. As their Web site indicates, "As always, Google Groups never displays pop-ups or banner ads. You see only relevant text ads of interest."

In addition, these groups often expect that the company will be part of the community and not just market to it. A recent study examined an online newsgroup devoted to those interested in multisport events such as triathlons (MSN—or multisport network—with 17,000 daily readers). Some members of this community were sporting goods vendors who had to play a delicate balancing act:

> These sporting goods members . . . are expected to be "community members" first and vendors second. Other MSN members appreciate their views on equipment, but vendors lose their credibility if they appear to participate in MSN primarily to promote their own products. By adhering to this "good member" policy, one vendor reported that on days he posted a message to MSN, he could expect an additional 4000 hits on his Web site.[16]

Being part of the community has been an important part of the success for Biogen, maker of the multiple sclerosis (MS) drug Avonex. Biogen created a branded site as well as a nonbranded virtual community to provide information and support for MS patients and their caregivers.[17]

REFERENCE GROUP INFLUENCES ON THE CONSUMPTION PROCESS

We all conform in a variety of ways to numerous groups. Look around your classroom. The odds are that, except for gender differences, most of you will be dressed in a similar manner. In fact, a student who comes to class dressed in a suit will generally be asked about the job interview that others will assume is the cause of the more formal clothing. Note that we, as individuals, do not generally consider these behaviors to constitute conformity. Normally, we conform without even being aware of doing so, although we also frequently face conscious decisions as to whether or not to go along with the group. Reference groups have been found to influence a wide range of consumption behaviors. Before examining the marketing implications of these findings, we need to examine the nature of reference group influence more closely.

The Nature of Reference Group Influence

Reference group influence can take three forms: *informational, normative,* and *identification*. It is important to distinguish among these types since the marketing strategy required depends on the type of influence involved.

Informational influence *occurs when an individual uses the behaviors and opinions of reference group members as potentially useful bits of information.* This influence is based on either the similarity of the group's members to the individual or the expertise of the influencing group member.[18] Thus, a person may notice that runners on the track team use a specific brand of nutrition bar. He or she may then decide to try that brand because these healthy and active runners use it. Use by the track team members thus provides indirect information about the brand.

Sometimes the informational influence is more direct, as in Illustration 7-3. Notice that the text of the ad indicates that one of the friends engaged in a fairly extensive search process and sought information from an expert before using Cetaphil. Then she told her friends about the recommendation and how well the product worked for her. There are two important aspects here. First, dermatologists represent a positive nonmember expert referent group for this product. Second, the friends represent a positive member referent group in which the members trust each others opinions and suggestions.

ILLUSTRATION 7-3

Group members often use other members as a source of information for their purchase decisions. This is known as informational influence. This ad shows how this works.

Courtesy Galderma Laboratories, LP; Agency: J. Walter Thompson.

Normative influence, sometimes referred to as *utilitarian* influence, *occurs when an individual fulfills group expectations to gain a direct reward or to avoid a sanction.*[19] You may purchase a particular brand of wine to win approval from a colleague. Or you may refrain from wearing the latest fashion for fear of teasing by friends or to fit in with or be accepted by them. As you might expect, normative influence is strongest when individuals have strong ties to the group and the product involved is socially conspicuous.[20] This type of influence appears particularly important to younger consumers:

Some of my friends would be unbelievably mad at me if I ever did start to smoke.

I wanted to fit in with older people and everyone else was smoking.[21]

Girls can like the Spice Girls and not get called lesbian or anything but if boys like boy bands they get called gay.[22]

Ads that promise social acceptance or approval if a product is used are relying on normative influence. Likewise, ads that suggest group disapproval if a product is not used, such as a mouthwash or deodorant, are based on normative influence.

Identification influence, also called *value-expressive* influence, *occurs when individuals have internalized the group's values and norms.* These then guide the individuals' behaviors without any thought of reference group sanctions or rewards. The individual has accepted the group's values as his or her own. The individual behaves in a manner consistent with the group's values because his or her values and the group's values are the same.

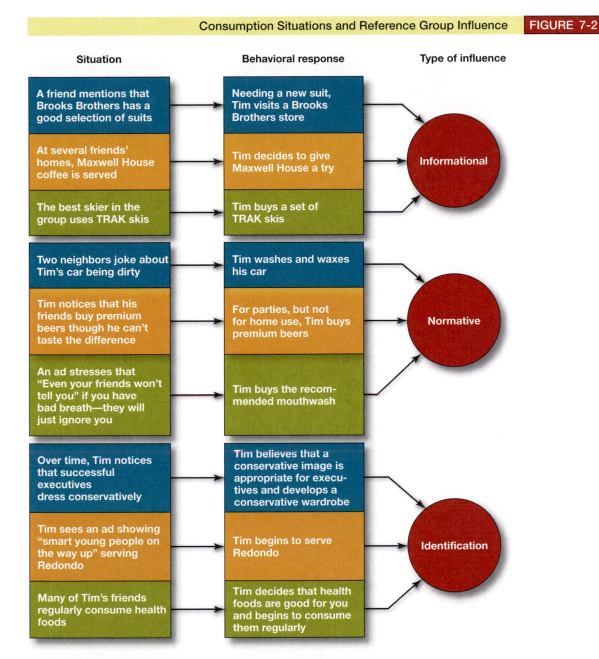

FIGURE 7-2 Consumption Situations and Reference Group Influence

Figure 7-2 illustrates a series of consumption situations and the type of reference group influence that is operating in each case.

Degree of Reference Group Influence

Reference groups may have no influence in a given situation, or they may influence usage of the product category, the type of product used, or the brand used. Brand influence is most likely to be a category influence rather than a specific brand; that is, a group is likely to approve, or disapprove, a range of brands such as imported beers or luxury automobiles.

TABLE 7-1

Two Consumption
Situation
Characteristics and
Product/Brand
Choice

	Degree Needed	
	Necessity	**Nonnecessity**
Consumption	Weak reference group influence on product	Strong reference group influence on product

Visible
Strong reference group influence on brand
	Public Necessities
	Influence: Weak product and strong brand
	Examples:
	    Shoes
	    Automobile
		Public Luxuries
		Influence: Strong product and brand
		Examples:
		    Snow board
		    Health club

Private
Weak reference group influence on brand
	Private Necessities
	Influence: Weak product and brand
	Examples:
	    Clothes washer
	    Insurance
		Private Luxuries
		Influence: Strong product and weak brand
		Examples:
		    Hot tub
		    Home theater system

Table 7-1 shows how two consumption situation characteristics—necessity/nonnecessity and visible/private consumption—combine to affect the degree of reference group influence likely to operate in a specific situation. In the following paragraphs, we will discuss these two characteristics and three additional determinants of reference group influences.

1. Group influence is strongest *when the use of product or brand is visible to the group*. For a product such as running shoes, the product category (shoes), product type (running), and brand (Reebok) are all visible. The consumption of other products, such as vitamins, is generally private. Reference group influence typically affects only those aspects of the product (category, type, or brand) that are visible to the group.[23]

2. Reference group influence is higher *the less of a necessity an item is*. Thus, reference groups have strong influence on the ownership of products such as snowboards and designer clothes, but much less influence on necessities such as refrigerators.

3. In general, *the more commitment an individual feels to a group, the more the individual will conform to the group norms*. People are much more likely to consider group expectations when dressing for a dinner with a group they would like to join (stay with) than for dinner with a group that is unimportant to them.

4. *The more relevant a particular activity is to the group's functioning, the stronger the pressure to conform to the group norms concerning that activity*. Thus, style of dress may be important to a social group that frequently eats dinner together at nice restaurants and unimportant to a group that meets for basketball on Thursday nights.

5. The final factor that affects the degree of reference group influence is *the individual's confidence in the purchase situation*. One study found the purchase of color televisions, automobiles, home air conditioners, insurance, refrigerators, medical services, magazines or books, clothing, and furniture to be particularly susceptible to reference group influence. Several of these products such as insurance and medical services are neither visible nor important to group functioning. Yet they are important to the individual and are products about which most individuals have limited information. Thus, group influence is strong because of the individual's lack of confidence in purchasing these products. In addition to confidence in the purchase situation, there is evidence that individuals differ in their tendency to be influenced by reference groups.[24]

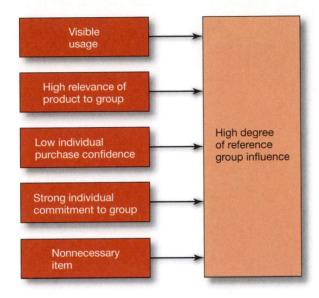

Figure 7-3 summarizes the major determinants of the degree to which a reference group is likely to influence product and brand usage. Marketing managers can use this structure to determine the likely degree of group influence on the consumption of their brand.

MARKETING STRATEGIES BASED ON REFERENCE GROUP INFLUENCES

The first task a manager faces in using reference group influence is to determine the degree and nature of the influence that exists, *or can be created,* for the product in question. Figure 7-3 provides the starting point for this analysis.

Personal Sales Strategies

The power of groups was initially demonstrated in a classic series of studies. Eight subjects are shown four straight lines on a board—three unequal lines are grouped close together, and another appears some distance from them. The subjects are asked to determine which one of the three unequal lines is closest to the length of the fourth line shown some distance away. The subjects are to announce their judgments publicly. Seven of the subjects are working for the experimenter, and they announce incorrect matches. The order of announcement is arranged so that the naive subject responds last. The naive subject almost always agrees with the incorrect judgment of the others. This is known as the **Asch phenomenon.**

This study has been repeated in a variety of formats and has generally achieved the same results. For example, student evaluations of the nutritional value of a new diet food were strongly affected by the stated opinions of other students even when they did not know the other students.[25] Imagine how much stronger the pressures to conform are among friends or when the task is less well defined, such as preferring one brand or style to another.

French champagne is viewed by many as being appropriate only for very special occasions. This ad indicates that it is appropriate for fun, casual group activities.

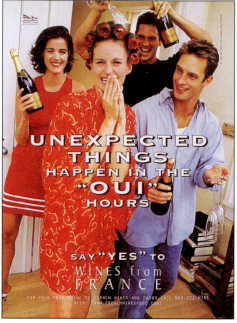

Courtesy of Food & Wines from France, Inc.

Consider this direct application of the Asch phenomenon in personal selling. A group of potential customers are brought together for a sales presentation. As each design is presented, the salesperson scans the expressions of the people in the group, looking for the one who shows approval (e.g., head nodding) of the design. The salesperson then asks that person for an opinion, since the opinion is certain to be favorable. The person is asked to elaborate. Meanwhile, the salesperson scans the faces of the other people, looking for more support, and then asks for an opinion of the person now showing most approval. The salesperson continues until the person who initially showed the most disapproval is reached. In this way, by using the first person as a model, and by social group pressure on the last person, the salesperson gets all or most of the people in the group to make a positive public statement about the design. *Do you see any ethical issues in using group influences in this way?*

Advertising Strategies

Marketers often position products as appropriate for group activities. French wines gained an image of being somewhat expensive and snobbish. Many consumers viewed them as appropriate only for very special occasions. A trade group, Food and Wines from France, launched a campaign to broaden their appeal. Illustration 7-4 shows an ad that positions French champagne as appropriate for casual group parties.

Marketers use all three types of reference group influence when developing advertisements. Informational influence in advertising was shown earlier in Illustration 7-3. Ads using informational influence typically show members of a group using a product. The message, generally unstated, is that "these types of people find this brand to be the best; if you are like them, you will too."

Normative group influence is not portrayed in ads as much as it once was. It involves the explicit or implicit suggestion that using, or not using, the brand will result in members of a group you belong to or wish to join rewarding, or punishing, you. One reason for the reduced use of this technique is the ethical questions raised by implying that a person's friends would base their reactions to the individual due to his or her purchases. Ads showing a person's friends saying negative things about them behind their back because their coffee was not great (yes, there was such an ad campaign) were criticized for playing on people's insecurities and fears.

Identification influence is based on the fact that the individual has internalized the group's values and attitudes. The advertising task is to demonstrate that the product is consistent with the group's and therefore the individual's beliefs. This often involves showing the brand being used by a particular type of group such as socially active young singles or parents of young children.

Teenagers and preteenagers are strongly influenced by peer pressure, or normative and identification group influences.[26] Unfortunately, these influences sometimes lead to injurious consumption involving cigarettes, alcohol, drugs, sexual activities, and so forth. Organizations working to combat these behaviors are up against a powerful foe. It is difficult to "just say no to drugs" if your friends are doing them and you face teasing and being ostracized if you don't join them.

One way to succeed in such a situation is to alter the group norms; that is, engaging in the injurious behavior needs to become a violation of the group norms. The text below is from a 30-second Partnership for a Drug-Free America commercial targeted at preteens. The visual showed a teenage boy smoking a joint and looking at two nearby girls. It clearly defines smoking pot as inappropriate group behavior subject to group sanctions (girls won't like you). Similar antismoking ads targeting teenagers have been very effective (one said, "Your friends won't come near you").[27]

TOMMY: Whoa, look at . . .

GIRLS: Tommy. He's so stoned.

TOMMY: This is totally . . .

GIRLS: Look what's happened to him.

TOMMY: You know I look like . . .

GIRLS: . . . such a mess. What a loser.

TOMMY: Yeah, this weed is definitely . . .

GIRLS: Gross. Ever since he started smoking pot, he's gross.

TOMMY: Like everybody's doing it.

GIRLS: And it's so uncool.

TOMMY: They're really into me. They think I'm so . . .

GIRLS: Out of it.

GIRLS: He's really out of it.

COMMUNICATIONS WITHIN GROUPS AND OPINION LEADERSHIP

We learn about new products, services, and brands, as well as retail and information outlets from our friends and other reference groups in two basic ways. First is by observing or participating with them as they use products and services. Second is by seeking or receiving advice and information from them in the form of **word-of-mouth (WOM) communications.** WOM involves *individuals sharing information with other individuals in a verbal form including face-to-face, phone, and the Internet.* It is estimated that two-thirds of all consumer product decisions are influenced by WOM.[28] Consider the following:

Delores Sotto, a longtime resident of a large apartment building on Manhattan's West End Avenue, is explaining the problem with dry cleaning in her neighborhood. "If you ask me," she says, "none of the dry cleaners in this area is any good. They all should have gone out of business long ago." Over the course of the next 10 minutes, Delores relays horror stories about ruined Armani ("Collezion, for God's sake!"), shrunken custom-made shirts now suitable for only a pre-teen nephew, and stains mysteriously appearing on garments days after they have been cleaned.

It turns out that Delores's information comes not from direct experience but from the collective wisdom of her apartment building. In the laundry room, hallways, and elevators of her building, Delores's neighbors pass on the negative experiences they have with neighborhood vendors.[29]

As this example suggests, negative experiences are powerful motivators of WOM, a factor that must be considered by marketers since negative WOM can strongly influence recipients' attitudes and behaviors.[30] Negative experiences are highly emotional, memorable and motivate consumers to talk. While the number varies by situation and product, it is not at all uncommon to find that dissatisfied consumers tell twice as many people about their experience than do satisfied consumers.[31] While merely satisfying consumers (delivering what they expected) may not always motivate WOM, going beyond satisfaction to deliver more than was expected appears to also have the potential to generate substantial WOM. Thus, companies may consider strategies for "delighting" consumers or otherwise creating positive emotional experiences that consumers are motivated to pass along in the form of positive WOM (see Chapter 18).[32] Obviously, it is imperative for companies to provide both consistent product and service quality and quick, positive responses to consumer complaints.

Consumers generally trust the opinions of people (family, friends, acquaintances) more than marketing communications because, unlike marketing communications, these personal sources have no reason not to express their true opinions and feelings. As a consequence, WOM via personal sources such as family and friends can have a critical influence on consumer decisions and business success. Recent research shows just how much faith consumers put in personal WOM versus advertising across a number of products and services. The information below shows the percentage of adults who put people (WOM from friends, family, or other people) at the top of their list of best sources for information compared to advertising:

	People	Advertising
Restaurants	83%	35%
Places	71	33
Prescription drugs	71	21
Hotels	63	27
Health tips	61	19
Movies	61	67
Best brands	60	33
Retirement planning	58	9
Automobiles	58	36
Clothes	50	59
Computer equipment	40	18
Web sites to visit	37	12

Source: Adapted with the permission of The Free Press, a Division of Simon & Schuster Adult Publishing Group, from The Influentials by Ed Keller and Jon Berry. Copyright © 2003 by Roper ASW, LLC. All rights reserved. Percentages across can sum to greater than 100 percent due to the multi-source nature of people and advertising.

As this information suggests, the importance of WOM is generally high, and its importance relative to advertising varies somewhat across product types. In addition, traditional mass-media advertising still plays a role, particularly at the earlier stages of the decision process including building brand awareness. Moreover, it is important to note that not all personal sources are equal in value. Some folks are known in their circles as the "go to

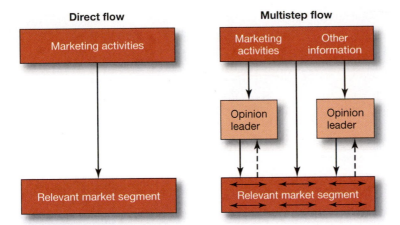

person" for specific types of information. These individuals actively filter, interpret, or provide product and brand-relevant information to their family, friends, and colleagues. An individual who does this is known as an **opinion leader.** The process of one person receiving information from the mass media or other sources and passing it on to others is known as the **two-step flow of communication.** The two-step flow explains some aspects of communication within groups, but it is too simplistic to account for most communication flows. What usually happens is a multistep flow of communication. Figure 7-4 contrasts the direct flow of information from a firm to customers with the more realistic multistep flow of mass communications.

The **multistep flow of communication** involves opinion leaders for a particular product area who actively seek relevant information from the mass media as well as other sources. These opinion leaders process this information and transmit their interpretations of it to some members of their groups. These group members also receive information from the mass media as well as from group members who are not opinion leaders. Figure 7-4 also indicates that these non–opinion leaders often initiate requests for information and supply feedback to the opinion leaders. Likewise, opinion leaders receive information from their followers as well as from other opinion leaders.

Situations in Which WOM and Opinion Leadership Occur

The exchange of advice and information between group members can occur *directly* in the form of WOM when (1) one individual seeks information from another or (2) when one individual volunteers information. It can also occur *indirectly* through observation as a by-product of normal group interaction.[33]

Imagine that you are about to make a purchase in a product category with which you are not very familiar. Further imagine that the purchase is important to you—perhaps a new sound system, skis, or a bicycle. How would you go about deciding what type and brand to buy? Chances are you would, among other things, ask someone you know who you believe to be knowledgeable about the product category. This person would be an opinion leader for you. Notice that we have described a *high-involvement* purchase situation in which the purchaser had limited product knowledge about an important decision. Figure 7-5 illustrates how these factors lead to varying levels of opinion leadership.[34]

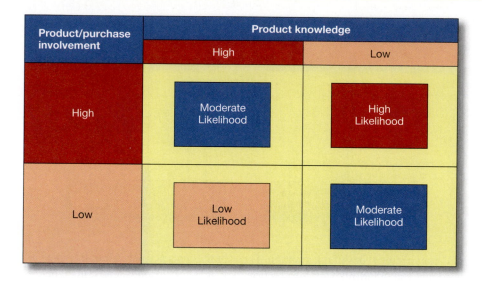

FIGURE 7-5   Likelihood of Seeking an Opinion Leader

In addition to *explicitly* seeking or volunteering information, group members provide information to each other through observable behaviors. Consider Hard Candy nail polish:

> Dinah Mohajer, a student at the University of Southern California, made some funky-colored nail polish to match a pair of sandals. Other students saw her and wanted similar polishes. Soon she and her boyfriend were making nail polish in her bathtub. Next she obtained distribution for the polish, now named Hard Candy, in trendy local salons. News photos showing Quentin Tarantino and Drew Barrymore wearing it generated more interest. The actress Alicia Silverstone wore and praised the product on David Letterman. In three years sales grew to $30 million.[35]

Hard Candy succeeded mainly through observation. Stylish individuals were seen wearing it on campus (Dinah and her friends). Then other individual style leaders used it (by being distributed through trendy salons it was seen and purchased by style-conscious individuals). Finally, celebrities were seen in mass media wearing Hard Candy.

Obviously, observation and direct WOM often operate together. For example, you might be in the market for a digital camera and notice that a friend uses an Olympus. This might jump-start a conversation about digital cameras, the Olympus brand, and where to find the best deals. And while Hard Candy's success depended heavily on observation, WOM was also involved as friends told other friends.

Characteristics of Opinion Leaders

What characterizes opinion leaders? The most salient characteristic is greater long-term involvement with the product category than the non–opinion leaders in the group. This is referred to as **enduring involvement,** and it leads to enhanced knowledge about and experience with the product category or activity.[36] This knowledge and experience makes opinion leadership possible.[37] Thus, an individual tends to be an opinion leader only for specific product or activity clusters.

Opinion leadership functions primarily through interpersonal communications and observation. These activities occur most frequently among individuals with similar demographic characteristics. Thus, it is not surprising that opinion leaders are found within all demographic segments of the population and seldom differ significantly on demographic variables from the people they influence. Opinion leaders tend to be more gregarious than others are which may explain their tendency to provide information to others. They also have higher levels of exposure to relevant media than do non–opinion leaders. And, opinion leaders around the world appear to possess similar traits.[38]

Opinion leaders can be identified using self-designating questionnaires with questions such as "I often persuade other people to buy the————that I like," which allow researchers to adapt the area of opinion leadership to fit their needs. While such measures allow you to identify opinion leaders through direct research, what if you want to know who the opinion leaders are for a product on a national scale? Opinion leaders are hard to identify a priori because they tend to be demographically similar to those they influence.

The fact that opinion leaders are heavily involved with the mass media, particularly media that focus on their area of leadership, provides a partial solution to the identification problem. For example, Nike could assume that many subscribers to *Runner's World* serve as opinion leaders for jogging and running shoes.[39] Likewise, the fact that opinion leaders tend to be gregarious and tend to belong to clubs and associations suggests that Nike could also consider members, and particularly leaders, of local running clubs to be opinion leaders.

Some product categories have professional opinion leaders. For products related to livestock, county extension agents are generally very influential. Barbers and hair stylists serve as opinion leaders for hair care products. Pharmacists are important opinion leaders for a wide range of health care products.

Market Mavens, Influentials, and e-Fluentials

Opinion leaders tend to be specialists. That is, their knowledge and involvement tend to be product or activity specific. Therefore, while a person might be an opinion leader for motorcycles, they are likely to be opinion seekers for other products such as cell phones or stereo equipment. However, some individuals have information about many different kinds of products, places to shop, and other aspects of markets. They both initiate discussions with others about products and shopping and respond to requests for market information. These generalized market influencers are **market mavens.** In essence, then, market mavens are a special type of opinion leader.

Market mavens provide significant amounts of information to others across a wide array of products, including durables and nondurables, services, and store types. They provide information on product quality, sales, usual prices, product availability, store personnel characteristics, and other features of relevance to consumers. Market mavens are extensive users of media.[40] They are also more extroverted and conscientious, which drives their tendency to share information with others.[41] Demographically, market mavens tend to be similar to those they influence.

Roper Starch (a market research company) has been tracking a group of generalized market influencers for over 30 years that are very similar in nature to market mavens. These consumers, which they call the *Influentials,* represent about 10 percent of the population and have broad social networks that allow them to influence the attitudes and behaviors of the other 90 percent of the population. Influentials are heavy users of print media such as newspapers, magazines, and the Internet and are more likely than the general population to engage in WOM recommendations about products, services, brands, and even what new Web sites to visit.[42]

Internet mavens also exist. As we saw in Chapter 6, teen Internet mavens are able to in-fluence family decisions that their parents make by operating as important gatekeepers to information on the Web.[43] Roper Starch and Burston-Marsteller have identified a related group of consumers they call *e-fluentials*. E-fluentials represent about 10 percent of the adult online community, but their influence is extensive as they communicate news, infor-mation, and experiences to a vast array of people both online and offline. These e-fluentials actively use the Internet to gather and disseminate information through online bulletin boards, newsgroups, listservs, and corporate Web sites. Their number one factor in open-ing unsolicited e-mails is brand familiarity. Clearly a trusted brand and solid online pres-ence are critical to targeting e-fluentials.[44]

Marketing Strategy, WOM, and Opinion Leadership

Marketers are increasingly relying on WOM and influential consumers as part of their mar-keting strategies. Driving factors include fragmented markets that are more difficult to reach through traditional mass media, greater consumer skepticism toward advertising, and a realization that opinion leaders can provide invaluable insights in the research and devel-opment process. For example, *Teen People* has a group of 4,000 young "trend spotters" on call. The magazine encourages them to submit story ideas and respond to published arti-cles. It invites them to monthly meetings at regional offices to discuss what's cool and what is not.

This is not to say that marketers have given up on traditional advertising and mass-media approaches. Instead they realize that in many cases they could make their traditional media spending go a lot further if they could tap into these influential consumers who will spread the word either indirectly through observation or directly through WOM. We ex-amine some marketing strategies designed to generate WOM and encourage opinion lead-ership next.

Advertising   Advertising can stimulate and simulate WOM and opinion leadership. *Stimulation* can involve themes designed to encourage current owners to talk about the brand (tell a friend about) or prospective owners to ask current owners (ask someone who owns one) for their impressions. Ads can attempt to stimulate WOM by generating interest and excitement. For example, Dodge launched its Pontiac G6 campaign during the 2004 Olympics, using short "teaser" ads with an edgy rock theme and the G6 logo but no car! Dove generated interest using a combination of advertising and so-called "pass-it-on" tools to stimulate WOM. They ran an ad offering two free bars of Dove to anyone who would recommend three friends who also got a free bar of soap that was gift-wrapped with the name of the initiating friend on the outside. So instead of a sample from a giant company it felt like a gift from a friend.[45]

Simulating opinion leadership involves having an acknowledged opinion leader—such as Shaquille O'Neal or Sheryl Swoopes for basketball equipment—endorse a brand. Illustration 7-5 is an example of this approach for performance sports eyewear. Or it can involve having an apparent opinion leader recommend the product in a "slice of life" commercial. These commercials involve an "overheard" conversation between two indi-viduals in which one person provides brand advice to the other. Finally, advertising can present the results of surveys showing that a high percentage of either knowledgeable in-dividuals ("9 out of 10 dentists surveyed recommend . . .") or typical users recommend the brand.[46]

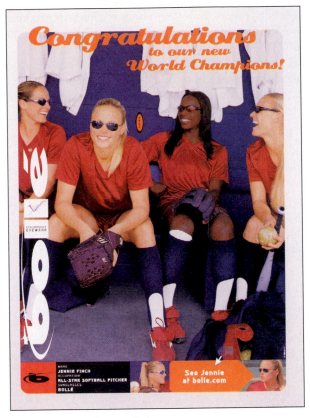

Courtesy Bushnell Performance Optics.

Product Sampling   *Sampling,* sometimes called "seeding," involves getting a sample of a product into the hands of a group of potential consumers. Sampling can be a particularly potent WOM tool when it involves individuals likely to be opinion leaders.

In an attempt to increase the preference for Dockers among the key 24- to 35-year-old urban market, Levi Strauss has created the position of "urban networker" in key cities. The urban networker identifies emerging trendsetters in their cities and ties them to Dockers. This could involve noticing a new band that is beginning to catch on and providing Dockers to the members. The objective is to be associated with emerging urban "happenings" and young influentials as they evolve.[47]

BzzAgent (www.BzzAgent.com) recruits everyday people to actively spread WOM about products they like. BzzAgent is adamant that their "agents" acknowledge their association with BzzAgent and provide honest opinions. Most of the WOM occurs offline in normal conversations. Agents receive a free product sample to use and are coached on various WOM approaches. Agents report back to BzzAgent about each WOM episode and redeemable points are rewarded. Importantly, the motive of most is not the points since many don't redeem them. BzzAgent's client list is long and growing and includes Kraft Foods, Goodyear, and Wharton School Publishing. Companies hire BzzAgent to create and field a WOM campaign. Costs vary, but a 12-week campaign involving 1,000 agents can cost $100,000.[48]

Retailing/Personal Selling   Numerous opportunities exist for retailers and sales personnel to use opinion leadership. Clothing stores can create "fashion advisory boards" composed of likely style leaders from their target market. An example would be cheer-leaders and class officers for a store like Abercrombie & Fitch, which caters to older teens and college students.

Retailers and sales personnel can encourage their current customers to pass along information to potential new customers. For example, an automobile salesperson, or the dealership, might provide a free car wash or oil change to current customers who send friends in to look at a new car.[49]

Creating Buzz   **Buzz** can be defined as *the exponential expansion of WOM.* It happens when "word spreads like wildfire" with no or limited mass media advertising supporting it. "Buzz" drove demand for Hard Candy nail polish, as described earlier. It also made massive successes of Pokémon, Beanie Babies, the original *Blair Witch Project,* and the Harry Potter books.[50] Marketers create buzz by providing opinion leaders advance information and product samples, having celebrities use the product, placing the product in movies, sponsoring "in" events tied to the product, restricting supply, courting publicity, and otherwise generating excitement and mystique about the brand. Consider the following:

> When Julia Roberts won the Academy Award for best actress, she waved to the audience with a snowflake-designed Van Cleef & Arpels diamond bracelet on her right wrist. That image was not only broadcast worldwide via television but also appeared in numerous magazine photos of the event. It generated widespread interest and was mentioned by brand in many newspaper and magazine articles.[51]

Van Cleef & Arpels' PR agent was critical in getting Julia Roberts to wear their jewelry suggesting the importance of good PR and event marketing.

Buzz is generally not supported by large advertising budgets, but it is often created by marketing activities. In fact, creating buzz is a key aspect of *guerrilla marketing*—marketing with a limited budget using nonconventional communications strategies. Guerrilla marketing is about making an "intense connection with individuals and speed[ing] up the natural word-of-mouth process."[52] Examples of guerrilla techniques include:

- Sony Ericsson hired attractive actors to pose as tourists in various metro areas. They would then hand their cell phone/digital camera to locals and ask them to take a picture in an attempt to get the camera in their hands and get them talking about it.
- Blue Cross Blue Shield (BC/BS) hired people to be painted blue and then asked to roam around Pittsburgh. Nobody knew what the "Blue Crew" campaign was about and it generated enormous buzz. When BC/BS revealed its linkage to the campaign, Web site traffic increased.[53]

Buzz is not just guerrilla marketing and guerrilla tactics must be used with care. Consumer advocates are increasingly concerned about certain guerrilla tactics. *What ethical concerns surround "hired representatives" who do not identify their affiliation with the company? How is BzzAgent's approach different from Sony Ericsson's?*

Creating buzz is often part of a larger strategy that includes significant mass media advertising. Clairol attempted to create WOM for its True Intense Color line via an online sampling program. It also launched a sweepstakes, "Be the Attraction," with a grand prize of an all-expenses-paid trip for four to the premiere of *Legally Blond* to fuel the buzz. However, these efforts were soon supplemented with a major mass media advertising campaign.[54]

Consumer Insight 7-1

Online Strategies to Leverage Buzz and WOM

The Internet continues to change the nature of interpersonal communications. People can seek and receive advice from strangers about brands and activities in various ways including chat rooms and Usenet groups. In fact, these weak-tie communications, whether by Internet or other means, may have more total impact on behavior than strong-tie (between close acquaintances) communications.[55] New avenues are rapidly evolving and the rewards can be huge for companies who can harness the speed and ease of interconnectivity that the Internet allows. Here are a few examples.

- **Viral marketing** is an online "pass-it-along" strategy. It "uses electronic communications to trigger brand messages throughout a widespread network of buyers." Viral marketing comes in many forms, but often involves e-mail. Honda U.K. developed a successful viral marketing campaign that started with "cutting-edge" creative in the form of a two-minute advertisement called "The Cog." The ad aired in the U.K. during the Brazilian Formula 1 Grand Prix to hit likely opinion leaders and was available on Honda's Web site. That's when the viral kicked in as people "wowed" by the ad e-mailed it to friends and acquaintances around the world. Honda had record sales in the U.K., and buzz spread to America where Web traffic and sales jumped. Honda, Volvo, and Gillette are among a growing list of companies using viral techniques.[56]

- **Online guides** are online opinion leaders. About.com utilizes online guides to provide original consumer information and advice. They are highly knowledgeable and passionate experts (e.g., the Table Tennis guide is a two-time Olympian). About.com has over 450 guides, over 50,000 topics, and more than 1 million pieces of original content. The Web site is also a portal for additional topic-relevant resources and includes discussion boards. One of the authors of this text frequents the guitar area where Dan Cross is the guide. Dan sends a regular newsletter with useful links and playing tips. About.com attracts one in five Internet users and has 21 million unique hits per month. Its popularity with opinion leaders makes it an important site for marketers such as Microsoft, Earthlink, and Nationwide Insurance.[57]

- **Blogs** are personalized journals where people and organizations can keep a running dialogue. Software exists (e.g., www.blogger.com) to make these journals easy to create and update from any device with e-mail including cell phones. People can read, comment on, and connect to your blog creating a powerful network which also includes other topical and news blogs. When Gizmodo (electronics blog) endorsed DiscHub's new storage device its Web traffic soared from 20 to 10,000! Marketers can place banner ads in blogs and Yahoo 360° will package ads with blog feeds. Vespa Scooters is creating two blogs which will be developed and maintained by four passionate Vespa "evangelists." Vespa has had scooter clubs for years and feels that blogs can tap the loyalty of its online customer base.[58]

Clearly marketers are learning how to leverage the WOM potential of the Internet. It will be interesting to see what the future brings!

Critical Thinking Questions

1. What other Internet alternatives exist for interpersonal communication?

2. Do you trust online sources to provide accurate information? What can marketers do to increase consumer trust in online sources?

3. What do you think are typical characteristics of those who are heavy bloggers?

Buzz and WOM are not confined to traditional offline strategies. As discussed in Consumer Insight 7-1, marketers are leveraging increasing numbers of online strategies as well.

Illustration 7-6 shows how Hershey's used viral marketing to encourage positive buzz about its Take 5 candy bar.

Positive buzz can be a critical component of the success of a firm. Here, Hershey's leverages the Internet and viral marketing to generate buzz for its new Take 5 candy bar.

Courtesy of Hershey Corporation.

DIFFUSION OF INNOVATIONS

An **innovation** is *an idea, practice, or product perceived to be new by the relevant individual or group.* Whether or not a given product *is* an innovation is determined by the perceptions of the potential market, not by an objective measure of technological change. The manner by which a new product is accepted or spreads through a market is basically a group phenomenon. In this section, we will examine this process in some detail.[59]

Categories of Innovations

Try to recall new products that you have encountered in the past two or three years. As you reflect on these, it may occur to you that there are degrees of innovation. For example, the MP3 players are more of an innovation than a new fat-free snack. The changes required in one's behavior, including attitudes and beliefs, or lifestyle if a person adopts the new product or service determine the degree of innovation, not the technical or functional changes in the product.

We can place any new product somewhere on a continuum ranging from no change to radical change, depending on the target market's perception of the item. This continuum is often divided into three categories or types of innovations.

Continuous Innovation
Adoption of this type of innovation requires relatively minor changes in behavior or changes in behaviors that are unimportant to the consumer. Examples include Crest Dual Action Whitening toothpaste, Wheaties Energy Crunch cereal, Pria (an afternoon snack bar), and DVD players. Note that several of these products are complex technological breakthroughs. However, their use requires little change in the owner's behavior or attitude. Illustration 7-7 is another example of a continuous innovation.

Reprinted with permission and courtesy of Bayer Corporation.

Dynamically Continuous Innovation   Adoption of this type of innovation requires a moderate change in an important behavior or a major change in a behavior of low or moderate importance to the individual. Examples include digital cameras, personal navigators, and Jergens' Naturally Smooth (a moisturizer designed to also make the hair on a woman's legs finer and less noticeable, reducing the need for shaving). Illustration 7-8 shows a product that is a dynamically continuous innovation for most consumer groups.

Discontinuous Innovation   Adoption of this type of innovation requires major changes in behavior of significant importance to the individual or group. Examples would include Norplant contraceptive, becoming a vegetarian, and the Segway Human Transporter (see Illustration 7-9).

Most of the new products or alterations introduced each year tend toward the no-change end of the continuum. Much of the theoretical and empirical research, however, has been based on discontinuous innovations. For example, individual consumers presumably go through a series of distinct steps or stages known as the **adoption process** when purchasing an innovation. These stages are shown in Figure 7-6.

Figure 7-6 also shows the steps in extended decision making described in Chapter 1. As can be seen, the *adoption process* is basically a term used to describe extended decision making when a new product is involved. As we will discuss in detail in Chapter 14, extended decision making occurs when the consumer is *highly involved* in the purchase. High purchase involvement is likely for discontinuous innovations such as the decision to purchase a hybrid car, and most studies of innovations of this nature have found that consumers use extended decision making.

ILLUSTRATION 7-8

Using this product would require a major change in an area of moderate importance for most individuals. For these individuals, it would be a dynamically continuous innovation.

Courtesy of Light Years Ahead: Den-Mat Corporation.

ILLUSTRATION 7-9

Buying and using the Segway for transportation would involve a major change in an important activity. Most consumers will react to this as a discontinuous innovation.

Photo by Business Wire via Getty Images.

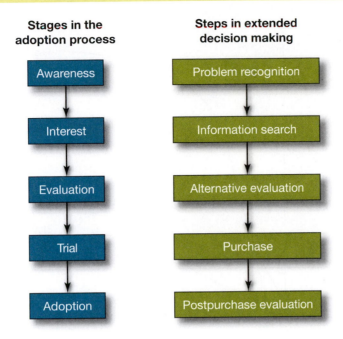

Adoption Process and Extended Decision Making   FIGURE 7-6

Stages in the adoption process

Awareness

Interest

Evaluation

Trial

Adoption

Steps in extended decision making

Problem recognition

Information search

Alternative evaluation

Purchase

Postpurchase evaluation

However, it would be a mistake to assume that all innovations are evaluated using extended decision making (the adoption process). In fact, most continuous innovations probably trigger limited decision making. As consumers, we generally don't put a great deal of effort into deciding to purchase innovations such as Dr. Pepper's new Cherry Vanilla cola or the new Hefty HandySaks.

Diffusion Process

The **diffusion process** is *the manner in which innovations spread throughout a market.* The term *spread* refers to purchase behavior in which the product is purchased with some degree of regularity.[60] The market can range from virtually the entire society (for a new soft drink, perhaps) to the students at a particular high school (for an automated fast-food and snack outlet).

For most innovations, the diffusion process appears to follow a similar pattern over time: a period of relatively slow growth, followed by a period of rapid growth, followed by a final period of slower growth. This pattern is shown in Figure 7-7. However, there are exceptions to this pattern. In particular, it appears that for continuous innovations such as new ready-to-eat cereals, the initial slow-growth stage may be skipped.

An overview of innovation studies reveals that the time involved from introduction until a given market segment is saturated (i.e., sales growth has slowed or stopped) varies from a few days or weeks to years. This leads to two interesting questions: (1) What determines how rapidly a particular innovation will spread through a given market segment? and (2) In what ways do those who purchase innovations relatively early differ from those who purchase them later?

| FIGURE 7-7 | Diffusion Rate of an Innovation over Time |

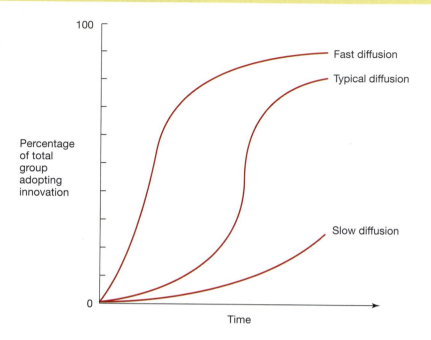

Factors Affecting the Spread of Innovations   The rate at which an innovation is diffused is a function of the following 10 factors.

1. *Type of group.* Some groups are more accepting of change than others. In general, young, affluent, and highly educated groups accept change, including new products, readily. Thus, the target market for the innovation is an important determinant of the rate of diffusion.[61]

2. *Type of decision.* The type of decision refers to an individual versus a group decision. The fewer the individuals involved in the purchase decision, the more rapidly an innovation will spread.

3. *Marketing effort.* The rate of diffusion is heavily influenced by the extent of marketing effort involved. Thus, the rate of diffusion is not completely beyond the control of the firm.[62]

4. *Fulfillment of felt need.* The more manifest or obvious the need that the innovation satisfies, the faster the diffusion. Rogaine, a cure for some types of hair loss, gained rapid trial among those uncomfortable with thin hair or baldness.

5. *Compatibility.* The more the purchase and use of the innovation are consistent with the individual's and group's values or beliefs, the more rapid the diffusion.[63]

6. *Relative advantage.* The better the innovation is perceived to meet the relevant need compared to existing methods, the more rapid the diffusion. Both the performance and the cost of the product are included in relative advantage. The digital audio tape (DAT) had neither advantage compared to CDs and DVDs and never took off.

7. *Complexity.* The more difficult the innovation is to understand and use, the slower the diffusion. The key to this dimension is ease of use, *not* complexity of product. Specialized blogging software is making an otherwise complex task easy and fun.[64]

8. *Observability.* The more easily consumers can observe the positive effects of adopting an innovation, the more rapid its diffusion will be. Cell phones are relatively visible. Laser eye surgery, while less visible, may be a frequent topic of conversation. On

Diffusion Rates for Consumer Electronics   FIGURE 7-8

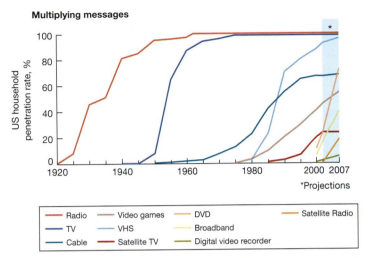

Source: "Crowned at Last," *Economist,* April 2, 2005, p. 14. © 2005 The Economist Ltd. All rights reserved.

the other hand, new headache remedies are less obvious and generally less likely to be discussed.

9. *Trialability.* The easier it is to have a low-cost or low-risk trial of the innovation, the more rapid is its diffusion. The diffusion of products like laser eye surgery has been hampered by the difficulty of trying out the product in a realistic manner. This is much less of a problem with low-cost items such as headache remedies, or such items as camera phones which can be borrowed or tried at a retail outlet.

10. *Perceived risk.* The more risk associated with trying an innovation, the slower the diffusion. Risk can be financial, physical, or social. Perceived risk is a function of three dimensions: (1) *the probability that the innovation will not perform as desired;* (2) *the consequences of its not performing as desired;* and (3) *the ability (and cost) to reverse any negative consequences.*[65] Thus, many consumers may feel a need for the benefits offered by laser eye surgery and view the probability of its working successfully as being quite high. However, they perceive the consequences of failure as being extreme and irreversible and therefore do not adopt this innovation.

Figure 7-8 shows the diffusion curves for various consumer electronic products. How would you explain the differences in diffusion rates across these products in U.S. households?

Characteristics of Individuals Who Adopt an Innovation at Varying Points in Time

The curves shown in Figures 7-7 and 7-8 are cumulative curves that illustrate the increase in the percentage of adopters over time. If we change those curves from a cumulative format to one that shows the percentage of a market that adopts the innovation at any given point in time, we will have the familiar bell-shaped curves shown in Figure 7-9.

Figure 7-9 reemphasizes the fact that a few individuals adopt an innovation very quickly, another limited group is reluctant to adopt the innovation, and the majority of the group adopts at some time in between the two extremes. Researchers have found it useful to divide the adopters of any given innovation into five groups based on the relative time

FIGURE 7-9   Adoptions of an Innovation over Time

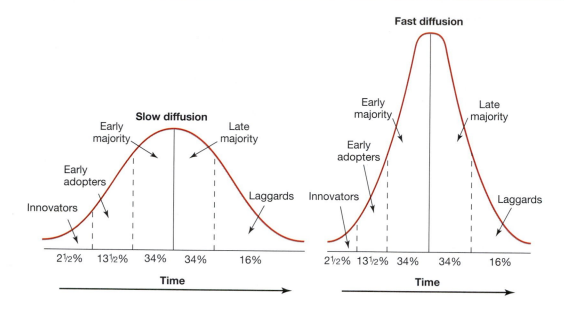

at which they adopt. These groups, called **adopter categories,** are shown in Figure 7-9 and defined below:

Innovators: The first 2.5 percent to adopt an innovation.

Early adopters: The next 13.5 percent to adopt.

Early majority: The next 34 percent to adopt.

Late majority: The next 34 percent to adopt.

Laggards: The final 16 percent to adopt.

How do these five groups differ? The first answer is: It depends on the product category being considered. Table 7-2 illustrates the rather dramatic differences between early purchasers of home computers and VCRs. Thus, although we propose some broad generalizations, they may not hold true for a particular product category.

Innovators are venturesome risk takers. They are capable of absorbing the financial and social costs of adopting an unsuccessful product. They are cosmopolitan in outlook and use other innovators rather than local peers as a reference group. They tend to be younger, better educated, and more socially mobile than their peers. Innovators make extensive use of commercial media, sales personnel, and professional sources in learning of new products.

Early adopters tend to be opinion leaders in local reference groups. They are successful, well educated, and somewhat younger than their peers. They are willing to take a calculated risk on an innovation but are concerned with failure. Early adopters also use commercial, professional, and interpersonal information sources, and they provide information to others.

Early majority consumers tend to be cautious about innovations. They adopt sooner than most of their social group but also after the innovation has proven successful with others. They are socially active but seldom leaders. They tend to be somewhat older, less well

TABLE 7-2

Early Purchasers of
Home Computers
and VCRs

	Home Computer	VCR
Age*		
18–24	103	163
25–34	113	91
35+	94	84
Education*		
College graduate	179	152
Attended college	125	86
High school	77	92
Marital status*		
Married	209	92
Single	107	136
Products owned†		
Tennis clothing	0	+
Squash racquet	0	−
Water skis	−	+
Target gun	−	+
Bowling ball	−	+
Ski boots	−	0
Luxury car	−	0
Men's diamond ring	−	+
Classical folk records/tapes	0	−
Contemporary jazz records/tapes	−	0
Book club	0	−
Solar heating	+	−
Food dehydrator	+	−
Electric ice cream maker	−	+

*Results are index numbers where 100 equals average consumption.

†+ = Heavy consumption; 0 = Moderate consumption; and − = Light consumption

Source: A. J. Kover, "Somebody Buys New Products Early—But Who?" Unpublished paper prepared for Cunningham & Walsh, Inc.

educated, and less socially mobile than the early adopters. The early majority relies heavily on interpersonal sources of information.

Late majority members are skeptical about innovations. They often adopt more in response to social pressures or a decreased availability of the previous product than because of a positive evaluation of the innovation. They tend to be older and have less social status and mobility than those who adopt earlier.

Laggards are locally oriented and engage in limited social interaction. They tend to be relatively dogmatic and oriented toward the past. Laggards adopt innovations only with reluctance.

Marketing Strategies and the Diffusion Process

Market Segmentation   Since earlier purchasers of an innovation differ from later purchasers, firms should consider a "moving target market" approach. That is, after selecting a general target market, the firm should initially focus on those individuals within the target market most likely to be innovators and early adopters.[66] Messages to this group can often emphasize the newness and innovative characteristics of the product as well as its functional features. Since this group is frequently very involved with, and knowledgeable about, the product category, marketing communications may be able to focus on the new

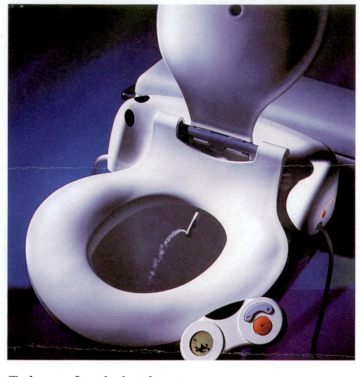

Take a fresh look at the most important seat in the house.

You're looking at Zoë, the first real advance in toilet design since its invention. At the touch of a button, the new washlet bathes your body with a soft, cleansing, aerated stream of water. Zoë also draws in odors, breaks down their molecules, and leaves you with an odor-free environment. There's an optional warming feature for the comfortable, ergonomically designed seat. Zoë doesn't take up any extra space and can be installed quickly and easily. Usually you just remove your existing toilet seat and replace it with Zoë. Zoë is made by Toto, the world's largest manufacturer of bathroom products. You can find Zoë at the following kitchen and bath showrooms listed below, or contact TOTO KIKI USA, INC. for the dealer nearest you at (800) 938-1541. **TOTO**

Community Home Supply, Chicago, IL
(312) 281-7010
Max Gerber, Chicago, IL
(312) 342-7600

Vanity City, Evanston, IL
(708) 869-2111
Infinity Kitchen & Bath, Hindsdale, IL
(708) 789-6659

Advantage Plumbing Supply, Niles, IL
(708) 965-4444

Courtesy of Toto U.S.A.

technical features of the product and rely on the audience to understand the benefits these features will provide.[67]

As the innovation gains acceptance, the focus of attention should shift to the early and late majority. This will frequently require different media. In addition, message themes should generally move away from a focus on radical newness. Instead, they should emphasize the acceptance the product has gained and its proven performance record.

Diffusion Enhancement Strategies   Table 7-3 provides a framework for developing strategies to enhance the market acceptance of an innovation. The critical aspect of this process is to analyze the innovation *from the target market's perspective*. This analysis will indicate potential obstacles—*diffusion inhibitors*—to rapid market acceptance. The manager's task is then to overcome these inhibitors with *diffusion enhancement strategies*. Table 7-3 lists a number of potential enhancement strategies, but many others are possible.

Consider the innovation shown in Illustration 7-10. Which factors will inhibit its diffusion, and what strategies can be used to overcome them?

Diffusion Determinant	Diffusion Inhibitor	Diffusion Enhancement Strategies
1. Nature of group	Conservative	Search for other markets
		Target innovators within group
2. Type of decision	Group	Choose media to reach all deciders
		Provide conflict reduction themes
3. Marketing effort	Limited	Target innovators within group
		Use regional rollout
		Leverage buzz
4. Felt need	Weak	Extensive advertising showing importance of benefits
5. Compatibility	Conflict	Stress attributes consistent with normative values
6. Relative advantage	Low	Lower price
		Redesign product
7. Complexity	High	Distribute through high-service outlets
		Use skilled sales force
		Use product demonstrations
		Extensive marketing efforts
8. Observability	Low	Use extensive advertising
		Target visible events when appropriate
9. Trialability	Difficult	Use free samples to early adopter types
		Special prices to rental agencies
		Use high-service outlets
10. Perceived risk	High	Success documentation
		Endorsement by credible sources
		Guarantees

TABLE 7-3

Innovation Analysis and Diffusion Enhancement Strategies

SUMMARY

A *group* in its broadest sense includes two or more individuals who share a set of norms, values, or beliefs and have certain implicit or explicit relationships such that their behaviors are interdependent. Some groups require membership; others (e.g., aspiration groups) do not. *Primary groups* are those with strong social ties and frequent interaction, while *secondary groups* involve weaker ties and less frequent interaction. *Attraction* refers to the degree of positive or negative desirability the group has to the individual.

The degree of *conformity* to a group is a function of (1) the visibility of the usage situation, (2) the level of commitment the individual feels to the group, (3) the relevance of the behavior to the functioning of the group, (4) the individual's confidence in his or her own judgment in the area, and (5) the necessity/nonnecessity nature of the product.

A *consumption subculture* is a group that self-selects on the basis of a shared commitment to a particular product or consumption activity. These subcultures also have (1) an identifiable, hierarchical social structure; (2) a set of shared beliefs or values; and (3) unique jargon, rituals, and modes of symbolic expression.

A *brand community* is a nongeographically bound community, based on a structured set of social relationships among owners of a brand and the psychological relationship they have with the brand itself, the product in use, and the firm. Brand communities can add value to the ownership of the product and build intense loyalty. A *virtual community* is a community that interacts over time around a topic of interest on the Internet. Virtual communities exist and are important for many participants, although the level of connection and participation can vary dramatically.

Group influence varies across situations. *Informational influence* occurs when individuals simply acquire information shared by group members. *Normative influence* happens when an individual conforms to group expectations to gain approval or avoid disapproval. *Identification influence* exists when an individual identifies with the group norms as a part of his or her self-concept and identity.

Communication within groups is a major source of information about certain products. It is a particularly important source when an individual has a high level of *purchase involvement* and a low level of *product knowledge*. In such cases, the consumer is likely to seek information from a more knowledgeable group member. This person is known as an *opinion leader*. Opinion leaders are product-category or activity-group specific. They tend to have greater product knowledge, more exposure to relevant media, and more gregarious personalities than their followers. They tend to have demographics similar to their followers.

The terms *market maven* and *Influentials* describe individuals who are general market influencers. They have information about many different kinds of products, places to shop, and other aspects of markets. *Internet mavens* and *e-fluentials* describe their online counterparts. Information is communicated within groups either directly through *word-of-mouth (WOM)* communication or indirectly through observation. Negative experiences are a strong driver of negative WOM for all consumers.

Marketers attempt to identify opinion leaders primarily through their media habits and social activities. Identified opinion leaders then can be used in marketing research, product sampling, retailing/personal selling, advertising, and creating buzz. Various offline and online strategies exist for stimulating WOM, opinion leadership, and buzz. Online strategies include viral marketing, guides, and blogs.

Groups greatly affect the diffusion of innovations. *Innovations* vary in degree of behavioral change required and the rate at which they are diffused. The first purchasers of an innovative product or service are termed *innovators;* those who follow over time are known as *early adopters, early majority, late majority,* and *laggards.* Each of these groups differs in personality, age, education, and reference group membership. These characteristics help marketers identify and appeal to different classes of adopters at different stages of an innovation's diffusion.

The time it takes for an innovation to spread from innovators to laggards is affected by several factors: (1) nature of the group involved, (2) type of innovation decision required, (3) extent of marketing effort, (4) strength of felt need, (5) compatibility of the innovation with existing values, (6) relative advantage, (7) complexity of the innovation, (8) ease in observing usage of the innovation, (9) ease in trying the innovation, and (10) perceived risk in trying the innovation.

KEY TERMS

Adopter categories 256
Adoption process 251
Asch phenomenon 239
Aspiration reference groups 229
Blogs 249
Brand community 231
Buzz 248
Community 231
Consumption subculture 229
Diffusion process 253
Dissociative reference
 groups 229
Early adopters 256

Early majority 256
Enduring involvement 244
Group 228
Identification influence 236
Informational influence 235
Innovation 250
Innovators 256
Laggards 257
Late majority 257
Market mavens 245
Multistep flow of
 communication 243
Normative influence 236

Opinion leader 243
Online guide 249
Primary group 228
Reference group 228
Secondary group 228
Two-step flow of
 communication 243
Viral marketing 249
Virtual community 233
Word-of-mouth (WOM)
 communications 241

INTERNET EXERCISES

1. Monitor a chat group or bulletin board on a topic that interests you for a week. Are the participants in this activity a group? A reference group? A virtual community?

2. Find a consumption-based group or subculture that uses the Internet as one means of communication. What can you learn about this group by monitoring the Internet?

3. Find and describe an example of a marketer using the Internet to encourage the formation of or communications of a brand community.

4. Visit the Web sites for the following and describe the firms' efforts to foster brand communities.
   a. Pontiac G6
   b. Harley-Davidson

c. Jeep
d. Volvo
e. Hewlett-Packard
f. Hobie lifejackets
g. NASCAR

5. Find and describe evidence of market maven and/or opinion leadership on the Internet.
6. Pick a recent innovation of interest. Prepare a report on the information available about this innovation on the Internet.

DDB LIFE STYLE STUDY™ DATA ANALYSES

1. Use the DDB data (Tables 1B through 7B) to determine the characteristics of new-product innovators. Why is this the case? What are the marketing implications?
2. Use the DDB data (Tables 1B through 7B) to determine the characteristics of opinion leaders. Why is this the case? What are the marketing implications?

3. What are the characteristics of those who like to "play it safe" by *sticking with well-known brand names* (Tables 1B through 7B)? How do these consumers compare with the innovators you found in Question 1?

REVIEW QUESTIONS

1. How does a *group* differ from a *reference group?*
2. What criteria are used by marketers to classify groups?
3. What is a *dissociative reference group?* In what way can dissociative reference groups influence consumer behavior?
4. What is an *aspiration reference group?* How can an aspiration reference group influence behavior?
5. What is a *consumption-based group* or a *consumption subculture?* What are the characteristics of such a group?
6. How can marketers develop strategy based on consumption subcultures?
7. What is a *brand community?* What are the characteristics of such a group?
8. For what products are brand communities most appropriate? How can a marketer foster a brand community?
9. What types of group influence exist? Why must a marketing manager be aware of these separate types of group influence?
10. What five factors determine the strength of reference group influence in a situation?
11. What is the *Asch phenomenon* and how do marketers utilize it?

12. How can a marketer use knowledge of reference group influences to develop advertising strategies?
13. What is an *opinion leader?* How does an opinion leader relate to the *multistep flow of communication?*
14. What characterizes an opinion leader?
15. What determines the likelihood that a consumer will seek information from an opinion leader?
16. How does a *market maven* differ from an *opinion leader?*
17. Explain the role of *enduring involvement* in driving opinion leadership.
18. How can marketing managers identify opinion leaders?
19. How can marketers utilize opinion leaders?
20. What is *buzz?* How can marketers create it?
21. What is a *blog?*
22. What is an *innovation?* Who determines whether a given product is an innovation?
23. What are the various categories of innovations? How do they differ?
24. What is the *diffusion process?* What pattern does the diffusion process appear to follow over time?

25. Describe the factors that affect the diffusion rate for an innovation. How can these factors be utilized in developing marketing strategy?

26. What are *adopter* categories? Describe each of the adopter categories.

27. How can a marketer use knowledge of adopter categories to develop marketing strategy?

DISCUSSION QUESTIONS

28. Respond to the questions in Consumer Insight 7-1.

29. Using college students as the market segment, describe the most relevant reference group(s) and indicate the probable degree of influence on decisions for each of the following:
    a. Brand of toothpaste
    b. Purchase of a Segway
    c. Usenet participation
    d. Becoming a vegetarian
    e. Choice of music DVD

Answer Questions 30–33 using (a) shoes, (b) HDTV, (c) car, (d) an Internet connection, (e) pet, and (f) volunteering with a nonprofit organization.

30. How important are reference groups to the purchase of the above-mentioned products or activities? Would their influence also affect the brand or model? Would their influence be informational, normative, or identification? Justify your answers.

31. What reference groups would be relevant to the decision to purchase the product or activity (based on students on your campus)?

32. What are the norms of the social groups of which you are a member concerning the product or activity?

33. Could an Asch-type situation be used to sell the product or activity?

34. Describe two groups that serve as aspiration reference groups for you. In what ways, if any, have they influenced your consumption patterns?

35. Describe two groups to which you belong. For each, give two examples of instances when the group has exerted (*a*) informational, (*b*) normative, and (*c*) identification influence on you.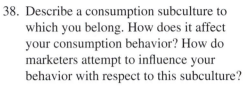

36. Develop two approaches using reference group theory to reduce drug, alcohol, or cigarette consumption among teenagers.

37. What ethical concerns arise in using reference group theory to sell products?

38. Describe a consumption subculture to which you belong. How does it affect your consumption behavior? How do marketers attempt to influence your behavior with respect to this subculture?

39. Do you belong to a brand community? If so, describe the benefits you derive from this group and how it affects your consumption.

40. Do you belong to a virtual community? If so, describe the benefits you derive from this group and how it affects your consumption.

41. Answer the following questions for: (*i*) MP3 players, (*ii*) space flight, (*iii*) wireless Internet connection.
    a. Is the product an innovation Justify your answer.
    b. Using the student body on your campus as a market segment, evaluate the perceived attributes of the product.
    c. Who on your campus would serve as opinion leaders for the product?
    d. Will the early adopters of the product use the adoption process (extended decision making), or is a simpler decision process likely?

42. Describe two situations in which you have served as or sought information from an opinion leader. Are these situations consistent with the discussion in the text?

43. Are you aware of market mavens on your campus? Describe their characteristics, behaviors, and motivation.

44. Have you used a blog recently? Why? How did it work? What marketing implications does this suggest?

45. Identify a recent (*a*) continuous innovation, (*b*) dynamically continuous innovation, and (*c*) discontinuous innovation. Justify your selections.

46. Analyze the Roomba (robotic vacuum cleaner) in terms of the determinants in Table 7-3 and suggest appropriate marketing strategies.

47. Conduct a diffusion analysis and recommend appropriate strategies for the innovation shown in Illustration 7-10.

48. Assume that you are a consultant to firms with new products. You have members of the appropriate market segments rate innovations on the 10 characteristics described in Table 7-3. Based on these ratings, you develop marketing strategies. Assume that a rating of 9 is extremely favorable (e.g., strong relative advantage or a lack of complexity), and 1 is extremely unfavorable. Suggest appropriate strategies for each of the following consumer electronic products (see table).

	Product								
Attribute	A	B	C	D	E	F	G	H	I
Fulfillment of felt need	9	7	3	8	8	5	7	8	9
Compatibility	8	8	8	8	9	2	8	9	8
Relative advantage	9	2	8	9	7	8	9	8	8
Complexity	9	9	9	9	9	3	8	8	7
Observability	8	8	9	1	9	4	8	8	8
Trialability	8	9	8	9	9	2	9	2	9
Nature of group	3	8	7	8	9	9	7	7	3
Type of decision	3	7	8	8	6	7	7	3	7
Marketing effort	6	7	8	7	8	6	3	8	7
Perceived risk	3	8	7	7	3	7	8	8	5

APPLICATION ACTIVITIES

49. Find two advertisements that use reference groups in an attempt to gain patronage. Describe the advertisement, the type of reference group being used, and the type of influence being used.

50. Develop an advertisement for (*i*) breath strips, (*ii*) energy drink, (*iii*) upscale club, (*iv*) Habitat for Humanity, (*v*) scooters, or (*vi*) watches using the following.
    a. An informational reference group influence
    b. A normative reference group influence
    c. An identification reference group influence

51. Interview two individuals who are strongly involved in a consumption subculture. Determine how it affects their consumption patterns and what actions marketers take toward them.

52. Interview an individual who is involved in a brand community. Describe the role the firm plays in maintaining the community, the benefits the person gets from the community, and how it affects his or her consumption behavior.

53. Identify and interview several opinion leaders on your campus for the following. To what extent do they match the profile of an opinion leader as described in the text?
    a. Local restaurants
    b. Sports equipment
    c. Music
    d. Computer equipment

54. Interview two salespersons for the following products. Determine the role that opinion leaders play in the purchase of their product and how they adjust their sales process in light of these influences.
    a. Cell phones
    b. In-line skates
    c. Computers
    d. Art
    e. Gifts
    f. Sunglasses

REFERENCES

1. J. W. Schouten and J. H. McAlexander, "Subcultures of Consumption," *Journal of Consumer Research,* June 1995, pp. 43–61.

2. J. H. McAlexander, J. W. Schouten, and H. F. Koenig, "Building Brand Community," *Journal of Marketing,* January 2002, pp. 38–54.

3. "'Getting Wiser to Teens' Offers a Snapshot of Teen Social Hierarchy," Teenage Research Unlimited (TRU) press release, June 21, 2004.

4. For the role that consumer self-enhancement needs play in the process, see J. E. Escalas and J. R. Bettman, "You Are What They Eat," *Journal of Consumer Psychology* 13, no. 3 (2003), pp. 339–48.

5. Schouten and McAlexander, "Subcultures of Consumption," p. 43.

6. B. Gainer, "Ritual and Relationships," *Journal of Business Research,* March 1995, pp. 253–60. See also E. J. Arnould and

P. L. Price, "River Magic," *Journal of Consumer Research,* June 1993, pp. 24–45.

7. See R. J. Fisher, "Group-Derived Consumption," *Advances in Consumer Research,* vol. 25, eds. J. W. Alba and J. W. Hutchinson (Provo, UT: Association for Consumer Research, 1998), pp. 283–88; and R. J. Fisher and K. Wakefield, "Factors Leading to Group Identification," *Psychology & Marketing,* January 1998, pp. 23–40.

8. J. H. McAlexander, K. Fushimi, and J. W. Schouten, "A Cross-Cultural Examination of a Subculture of Consumption," *Research in Consumer Behavior* 9 (2000), p. 66.

9. R. V. Kozinets, "Utopian Enterprise," *Journal of Consumer Research,* June 2001, p. 72.

10. Based on McAlexander, Schouten, and Koenig, "Building Brand Community."

11. A. M. Muniz Jr. and T. C. O'Guinn, "Brand Community," *Journal of Consumer Research,* March 2001, p. 413. See also R. P. Bagozzi, "On the Concept of Intentional Social Action in Consumer Behavior," *Journal of Consumer Research,* December 2000, pp. 388–96; and A. M. Muniz Jr. and H. J. Schau, "Religiosity in the Abandoned Apple Newton Brand Community," *Journal of Consumer Research,* March 2005, pp. 737–47.

12. Bronco and Saab examples come from Muniz Jr. and O'Guinn, "Brand Community." Harley example comes from Schouten and McAlexander, "Subcultures of Consumption." Jeep example comes from McAlexander, Schouten, and Koenig, "Building Brand Community."

13. Q. Jones, "Virtual Communities, Virtual Settlements, and Cyber-Archaeology," *Journal of Computer-Mediated Communication* 3, no. 3 (1997), at www.ascusc.org/jcmc/vol3/issue3/jones.html; C. Okleshen and S. Grossbart, "Usenet Groups, Virtual Community and Consumer Behaviors" and S. Dann and S. Dann, "Cybercommuning," both in *Advances in Consumer Research,* vol. 25, eds. Alba and Hutchinson, pp. 276–82 and 379–85, respectively; C. L. Beau, "Cracking the Niche," *American Demographics,* June 2000, pp. 38–40; and P. Maclaran and M. Catterall, "Researching the Social Web," *Marketing Intelligence and Planning* 20, no. 6 (2002), pp. 319–26.

14. A. L. Blanchard and M. L. Markus, "The Experienced 'Sense' of a Virtual Community," *Database for Advances in Information Systems,* Winter 2004, pp. 65–79.

15. Beau, "Cracking the Niche."

16. Blanchard and Markus, "The Experienced 'Sense' of a Virtual Community."

17. S. Shalo, "Virtual Community Generates Real ROI," *Pharmaceutical Executive,* March 2002, p. 118.

18. See T. F. Mangleburg and T. Bristol, "Socialization and Adolescents' Skepticism toward Advertising," *Journal of Advertising,* Fall 1998, pp. 11–20. See also, T. F. Mangleburg, P. M. Doney, and T. Bristol, "Shopping with Friends and Teens' Susceptibility to Peer Influence," *Journal of Retailing* 80 (2004), pp. 101–16.

19. See R. J. Fisher and D. Ackerman, "The Effects of Recognition and Group Need on Volunteerism," *Journal of Consumer Research,* December 1998, pp. 262–77.

20. See K. R. Lord, M.-S. Lee, and P. Choong, "Differences in Normative and Informational Social Influence," *Advances in Consumer Research,* vol. 28, eds. M. C. Gilly and J. Meyers-Levy (Provo, UT: Association for Consumer Research, 2001), pp. 280–85.

21. L. A. Peracchio and D. Luna, "The Development of an Advertising Campaign to Discourage Smoking Initiation among Children and Youth," *Journal of Advertising,* Fall 1998, pp. 49–56.

22. M. K. Hogg and E. N. Banister, "The Structure and Transfer of Cultural Meaning," *Advances in Consumer Research,* vol. 27, eds. S. J. Itoch and R. J. Meyer (Provo, UT: Association for Consumer Research, 2000), pp. 19–23.

23. See E. Day and M. R. Stafford, "Age-Related Cues in Retail Services Advertising." *Journal of Retailing,* no. 2 (1997), pp. 211–33.

24. Y.-K. Kim and J. Kang, "Effects of Asian-Americans' Ethnicity and Acculturation on Personal Influences," *Journal of Current Issues and Research in Advertising,* Spring 2001, pp. 44–52; D. D'Rozario, "The Structure and Properties of the Consumer Susceptibility to Interpersonal Influence Scale," *Journal of International Consumer Marketing* 13, no. 2 (2001), pp. 77–101; and R. Batra, P. M. Homer, and L. R. Kahle, "Values, Susceptibility to Normative Influence, and Attribute Importance Weights," *Journal of Consumer Psychology* 11, no. 2 (2002), pp. 115–28.

25. D. N. Lascu, W. O. Bearden, and R. L. Rose, "Norm Extreme and Interpersonal Influences on Consumer Conformity," *Journal of Business Research,* March 1995, pp. 201–13. See also P. F. Bone, "Word-of-Mouth Effects on Short-Term and Long-Term Product Judgments," *Journal of Business Research,* March 1995, pp. 213–23.

26. See S. Auty and R. Elliot, "Being Like or Being Liked," *Advances in Consumer Research,* vol. 28, eds. Gilly and Meyers-Levy, pp. 235–41.

27. C. Pechmann, "The Effects of Antismoking and Cigarette Advertising on Young Adolescents' Perceptions of Peers Who Smoke," *Journal of Consumer Research,* September 1994, pp. 236–51. See also D. D. Schoenbachler and T. E. Whittler, "Adolescent Processing of Social and Physical Threat Communications," *Journal of Advertising,* Winter 1996, pp. 37–54. For a discussion of how *perceived* peer influence can backfire see R. L. Rose, W. O. Bearden, and K. C. Manning, "Attributions and Conformity in Illicit Consumption," *Journal of Public Policy and Marketing,* Spring 2001, pp. 84–92.

28. M. Gladwell, "Alternative Marketing Vehicles," *Consumer Insight Magazine* (an ACNielsen Publication), Spring 2003, pp. 6–11, at www2.acnielsen.com.

29. C. Walker, "Word of Mouth," *American Demographics,* July 1995, p. 38.

30. See e.g., R. N. Laczniak, T. E. DeCarlo, and S. N. Ramaswami, "Consumers' Responses to Negative Word-of-Mouth Communication," *Journal of Consumer Psychology* 11, no. 1 (2001), pp. 57–73.

31. E. Rosen, *The Anatomy of Buzz* (New York: Doubleday, 2000); see also D. S. Sundaram, K. Mitra, and C. Webster, "Word-of-Mouth Communications," *Advances in Consumer Research,* vol. 25, eds. Alba and Hutchinson, pp. 527–31; and A. A. Bailey, "The Interplay of Social Influence and Nature of Fulfillment," *Psychology & Marketing,* April 2004, pp. 263–78.

32. M. Johnson, G. M. Zinkhan, and G. S. Ayala, "The Impact of Outcome, Competency, and Affect on Service Referral," *Journal of Services Marketing,* no. 5 (1998), pp. 397–415.

33. See W. G. Mangold, F. Miller, and G. R. Brockway, "Word-of-Mouth Communication in the Service Marketplace," *Journal of Services Marketing* 13, no. 1 (1999), pp. 73–89.

34. For a thorough discussion, see D. F. Duhan, S. D. Johnson, J. B. Wilcox, and G. D. Harrell, "Influences on Consumer Use of Word-of-Mouth Recommendation Sources," *Journal of the Academy of Marketing Science,* Fall 1997, pp. 283–95; and C. Pornpitakpan, "Factors Associated with Opinion Seeking," *Journal of Global Marketing* 17, no. 2/3 (2004), pp. 91–113.

35. R. Dye, "The Buzz on Buzz," *Harvard Business Review,* November 2000, p. 145.

36. G. M. Rose, L. R. Kahle, and A. Shoham, "The Influence of Employment-Status and Personal Values on Time-Related Food Consumption Behavior and Opinion Leadership," in *Advances in Consumer Research,* vol. 22, eds. F. R. Kardes and M. Sujan (Provo, UT: Association for Consumer Research, 1995), pp. 367–72; and U. M. Dholakia, "Involvement-Response Models of Joint Effects," *Advances in Consumer Research,* vol. 25, eds. Alba and Hutchinson, pp. 499–506.

37. See M. C. Gilly, J. L. Graham, M. F. Wolfinbarger, and L. J. Yale, "A Dyadic Study of Interpersonal Information Search," *Journal of the Academy of Marketing Science,* Spring 1998, pp. 83–100.

38. R. Marshall and I. Gitosudarmo, "Variation in the Characteristics of Opinion Leaders across Borders," *Journal of International Consumer Marketing* 8, no. 1 (1995), pp. 5–22.

39. See I. M. Chaney, "Opinion Leaders as a Segment for Marketing Communications," *Marketing Intelligence and Planning* 19, no. 5 (2001), pp. 302–8.

40. L. F. Feick and L. L. Price, "The Market Maven," *Journal of Marketing,* January 1987, pp. 83–97. See also R. A. Higie, L. F. Feick, and L. L. Price, "Types and Amount of Word-of-Mouth Communications about Retailers," *Journal of Retailing,* Fall 1987, pp. 260–78; K. C. Schneider and W. C. Rodgers, "Generalized Marketplace Influencers' Attitudes toward Direct Mail as a Source of Information," *Journal of Direct Marketing,* Autumn 1993, pp. 20–28; and J. E. Urbany, P. R. Dickson, and R. Kalapurakal, "Price Search in the Retail Grocery Market," *Journal of Marketing,* April 1996, pp. 91–104.

41. T. A. Mooradian, "The Five Factor Model and Market Mavenism," *Advances in Consumer Research,* vol. 23, eds. K. P. Corfman and J. G. Lynch (Provo, UT: Association for Consumer Research, 1996), pp. 260–63. For additional motivations driving mavens, see G. Walsh, K. P. Gwinner, and S. R. Swanson, "What Makes Mavens Tick?" *Journal of Consumer Marketing* 21, no. 2 (2004), pp. 109–22.

42. E. Keller and J. Berry, *The Influentials* (New York: Free Press, 2003). See also D. Godes and D. Mayzlin, "Firm-Created Word-of-Mouth Communication," *Harvard Business School Marketing Research Papers,* no. 04-03 (July 2004).

43. M. A. Belch, K. A. Krentler, and L. A. Willis-Flurry, "Teen Internet Mavens," *Journal of Business Research* 58 (2005), pp. 569–75.

44. I. Cakim, "E-Fluentials Expand Viral Marketing," *iMedia Connection* October 28, 2002 at www.imediaconnection.com; see

also information on Burson-Marsteller's Web site at www.efluentials.com.

45. Rosen, *The Anatomy of Buzz.*

46. See C. S. Areni, M. E. Ferrell, and J. B. Wilcox, "The Persuasive Impact of Reported Group Opinions on Individuals Low vs. High in Need for Cognition," *Psychology & Marketing,* October 2000, pp. 855–75.

47. A. Z. Cuneo, "Dockers Strives for Urban Credibility," *Advertising Age,* May 25, 1998, p. 6.

48. See R. Walker, "The Hidden (In Plain Sight) Persuaders," *New York Times Magazine,* December 5, 2004; and materials on BzzAgent's Web site at www.BzzAgent.com.

49. See E. Biyalogorsky, E. Gerstner, and B. Libai, "Customer Referral Management," *Marketing Science,* Winter 2001, pp. 82–95.

50. Dye, "The Buzz on Buzz," p. 140.

51. B. S. Bulik, "Well-Heeled Heed the Need for PR," *Advertising Age,* June 11, 2001, p. S2.

52. T. F. Lindeman, "More Firms Use Unique 'Guerrilla Marketing' Techniques to Garner Attention," *Knight Ridder Tribune Business News,* January 18, 2004, p. 1.

53. Ibid.

54. K. Fitzgerald, "Bristol-Meyers Builds Buzz," *Advertising Age,* April 23, 2001, p. 18.

55. A. Goldenberg, B. Libai, and E. Muller, "Talk of the Net," *Marketing Letters,* August 2001, pp. 211–23.

56. A. Dobele, D. Toleman, M. Beverland, "Controlled Infection!" *Business Horizons* 48 (2005), pp. 143–49.

57. Information from their corporate Web site at www.about.com.

58. S. Baker and H. Green, "Blogs Will Change Your Business," *BusinessWeek,* May 2, 2005, pp. 56–67; M. V. Copeland and A. Tilan, "Leverage the Hype Machine," *Business 2.0,* June 2005, pp. 92–94; and information on Yahoo and Vespa accessed June 2005, at www.yahoo.com and www.vespablogs.com, respectively.

59. See also V. Mahajan, E. Muller, and F. M. Bass, "New Product Diffusion Models in Marketing," *Journal of Marketing,* January 1990, pp. 1–26; E. M. Rogers, *Diffusion of Innovations,* 4th ed. (New York: Free Press, 1995). For an alternative to the traditional adoption diffusion model, see C.-F. Shih and A. Venkatesh, "Beyond Adoption," *Journal of Marketing,* January 2004, pp. 59–72.

60. See M. I. Nabith, S. G. Bloem, and T. B. C. Poiesz, "Conceptual Issues in the Study of Innovation Adoption Behavior," *Advances in Consumer Research,* vol. 24, eds. M. Bruck and D. J. MacInnis (Provo, UT: Association for Consumer Research, 1997), pp. 190–96.

61. See, e.g., S. L. Wood and J. Swait, "Psychological Indicators of Innovation Adoption," *Journal of Consumer Psychology* 12, no. 1 (2002), pp. 1–13.

62. See, e.g., E.-J. Lee, J. Lee, and D. W. Schumann, "The Influence of Communication Source and Mode on Consumer Adoption of Technological Innovations," *Journal of Consumer Affairs,* Summer 2002, pp. 1–27.

63. See N. Y.-M. Siu and M. M.-S. Cheng, "A Study of the Expected Adoption of Online Shopping," *Journal of International Consumer Marketing* 13, no. 3 (2001), pp. 87–106.

64. For a discussion of how type of innovation and consumer expertise interact see C. P. Moreau, D. R. Lehmann, and A. B. Markman, "Entrenched Knowledge Structures and Consumer Response to New Products," *Journal of Marketing Research,* February 2001, pp. 14–29.

65. For a more complete analysis, see U. M. Dholakia, "An Investigation of the Relationship between Perceived Risk and Product Involvement," *Advances in Consumer Research,* vol. 24, eds. Bruck and MacInnis, pp. 159–67.

66. For a discussion of when this is not appropriate, see V. Mahajan and E. Muller, "When Is It Worthwhile Targeting the Majority instead of the Innovators in a New Product Launch," *Journal of Marketing Research,* November 1998, pp. 488–95.

67. See, e.g., Chaney, "Opinion Leaders as a Segment for Marketing Communications."

Cases

CASE 2-1 Starbucks Keeps It Brewing in Asia

Asia, particularly China, is well known for its love of tea. So it may be a bit surprising how enthusiastic Starbucks is about the Chinese market. Consider the following quote from a Starbucks executive:

> I am so excited about China right now I can hardly stand it. I was in Shanghai a few weeks ago. The stores there are full of customers. I thought China would always be a great market for us eventually. But it is clearly a tea-drinking society—unlike Japan, which we think of as a tea-drinking society but they also drink a lot of coffee. In China, that really isn't true. I thought it would be a much longer education process. But they're picking that up so fast.

And there certainly is reason for excitement. China is a major consumer market. With an overall population of around 1.3 billion, rising incomes, and increasingly global attitudes particularly in the major cities, numerous companies around the world are clamoring to tap this goldmine.

However, the reality of China's coffee market is still far behind the hype. Consider the fact that despite a 90 percent growth in coffee sales in China over the past five years, per capita consumption is still under 1 kg per person compared to 4 kg in the United States. Tea is still the number one beverage in China (by volume), is a part of China's national heritage, and is strongly embedded in their culture. Here is how one expert on food marketing put it:

> Despite the potential of a 1.3 billion population base, coffee marketers are wary of the difficulty in transforming a tea-drinking nation into a coffee-drinking nation. Tea is the Chinese national drink and deemed to have medicinal qualities that coffee does not have, which means that it will continue to be an integral part of Chinese daily life in the next two or three decades. Added to this the fact that coffee is still prohibitively expensive and not familiar to the majority of the population, the indications are that despite potential being massive, the growth of coffee will continue to be slow.

In a population so large, it might surprise you to know that as of 2005, Starbucks has only around 150 outlets in China, a small drop in the bucket compared to around 4,600 in the United States. Various factors will influence the Chinese coffee market and must be considered in Starbucks' marketing strategy.

Demographics and Geography

Pure population statistics don't tell the whole story. The potential 1.3 billion population base is largely rural and lower income. The economy is growing and the middle class is increasing in size. The middle- and upper-class Chinese tend to be located in the major cities such as Guangzhou, Beijing, and Shanghai, where incomes have risen substantially. One estimate puts the number of Chinese with "middle-class" incomes at 50 million and income is expected to double by 2012. The coastal market between Shanghai and Shenzhen represents roughly 200 million people and is therefore highly attractive.

Competition

Beyond tea, which is clearly a major "beverage" competitor, challengers in terms of the "fresh-ground" market include Pacific Coffee (Hong Kong), Blenz Coffee (Canada), Figaro (Phillipines), and McCafe (a McDonald's coffee house). However, instant coffee is the major player. According to one report, this is because coffee is just taking off and the Chinese don't yet appreciate the taste of coffee or the taste difference among types of coffee. Currently, inexpensive mixes (coffee, milk, and sugar) are popular as a time-saving device among time-pressed professionals. In fact, Nescafé (a Nestlé brand) holds nearly half the market share and has become the Chinese generic term for coffee.

Culture, Habits, and Perceptions

Obviously, a population of 1.3 billion is impossible to generalize. However, some interesting information is available as a guide. General insights come from a recent survey of consumers in the four Chinese cities of Beijing, Shanghai, Chengdu, and Shenyang by Kurt Salmon Associates. The survey found that the top five factors in choosing a brand were high quality, good for health, cares about customer, fits self-image, and fair price. Given the highly collectivist nature of Chinese culture, the self-image component is significant.

Another general insight regarding foods and beverages is the notion of balance as embodied by the concepts of yin versus yang. Frito-Lay learned their lesson when they found that certain flavors and colors are associated with yin and some with yang. In terms of seasonal marketing, the difference is critical since yin is associated with cool and yang is associated with hot. Frito-Lay developed a cool lemon chip with pastel packaging to highlight yin for summer months since their traditional fried potato chip was associated with yang.

More specific insights in terms of the coffee and food market especially for younger, wealthier, professional Chinese include:

- Enjoy eating out
- Associate coffee with Western lifestyles
- See coffee as a fashionable drink
- Associate Starbucks with wealth and status
- Prefer food products from local (versus foreign) merchants
- Enjoy sweet tasting foods and beverages, particularly desserts

As if the Chinese market were not enough, Starbucks is finalizing a deal to enter India. Clearly they are betting on the Asian market to fuel growth as the U.S. market matures. Whether they can fully capitalize on this bet remains to be seen.

Discussion Questions

1. What are the barriers facing Starbucks as they try to "teach" people to change their consumption habits from tea and instant coffee?

2. To what extent can/should Starbucks customize their offerings to local tastes and preferences? What are the risks of extreme customization?

3. What values are involved in the Starbucks "experience"?

4. Examine the 10 factors that influence the spread of innovations from Chapter 7, pages 254–255 (thinking now that Starbucks is still quite novel and an innovative concept as is coffee to many in China), and create a grid for the Chinese market relative to coffee and Starbucks.

5. Based on your analysis in Question 4, what can Starbucks do to successfully encourage greater coffee consumption? Develop an advertising campaign that not only would encourage greater coffee consumption in general, but also more demand for Starbucks. Specify key themes, copy points, and visuals.

6. Develop a marketing strategy for taking Starbucks into smaller Chinese cities and communities. What barriers would be faced? Could they be successful?

7. Discuss the demographic, cultural, and media factors that make India more attractive for Starbucks than it was 10 years ago. Compare and contrast India and China in terms of the key elements Starbucks must address.

Source: "It's a Grande-Latte World," *The Wall Street Journal,* December 15, 2003, p. B1 and B4; G. A. Fowler and R. Setoodeh, "Outsiders Get Smarter about China's Tastes," *The Wall Street Journal,* August 5, 2004, p. B1; L. Chang, "China's Consumers Put Product Quality over Price," *The Wall Street Journal,* August 6, 2004, p. A7; "China Wakes Up to Instant Coffee," *AP-Foodtechnology.com,* September 27, 2004; D. Farkas, "China Patterns," *Chain Leader,* March 2005, pp. 20 and 22; M. S. Ouchi, "Starbucks Ventures that China Will Like Java, Too," *Knight Ridder Business News,* June 10, 2005, p. 1; "Starbucks Lifts Stake in South China Venture," *The Wall Street Journal,* June 10, 2005, p. 1; J. Harrison et al., "Exporting a North American Concept to Asia," *Cornell Hotel and Restaurant Administration Quarterly,* May 2005, pp. 275–83.

CASE 2-2   Norelco's Advantage Razor Introduction

While electric razors represent a $400 million plus market, less than a third of U.S. males use electric shavers, and only one in seven females use them. Norelco dominates the men's segment, followed by Remington, Braun, and Panasonic.

In the early 1990s, electric razor marketers sharply increased their marketing efforts, but this had little impact on electric razors' share of shavers. In fact, the percentage of both men and women using electric razors declined slightly between 1991 and 1993. By

1996, Norelco had well over 50 percent of the electric market. In late 1996, Pat Dinley, Norelco's president, described the firm's new approach:

> Over the years, we've fought the market share battle with other electric shavers. Long term, the big opportunity is in converting people who use blades to electric.

Norelco used a two-pronged approach to gain share in the overall shaving market, focusing on younger shavers and directly targeting blade users. According to Dinley,

> Traditionally, our target market has been 35-plus. We believe we've got a real opportunity to bring some new people into the category, so we're going after 18- to 54-year-olds.

Targeting younger consumers has involved using different media and themes. Some of the media used include ESPN sports, "Monday Night Football," and "Friends," as well as select men's magazines. The creative theme focused heavily on the irritation that can be associated with blade shaving. One television ad featured sneering blade razors that turn into dragons and snakes. The comfort of a Norelco shave was emphasized with the tagline "Anything closer would be too close for comfort."

In 1998, Philips Electronics, Norelco's parent company, made two major moves. First, it focused Norelco strictly on men's products. Women's electric razors and other products targeting women were redesigned and introduced under the Philips Personal Care name.

Norelco then launched a new flagship razor, the Advantage. The Advantage has a Nivea for Men shaving lotion cartridge built inside the razor chamber. This unique system dispenses the lotion while shaving, offering a wet shave experience without the hassle associated with water and lather. The razor comes with five lotion cartridges, can be used wet or dry, and can be rinsed clean with tap water.

The product was launched with an estimated $35 million campaign. The ads take a humorous approach that challenges consumers to put the razor "to the test." One ad makes this offer: "If you don't make it part of your routine after 21 days, we'll give you your money back, guaranteed." According to VP–marketing Rich Sorota, "The advertising is part of our holistic approach to get consumers to put it to the test. [The

objective] is to get really dissatisfied blade users to trade up to electrics. [Marketing research has found] over 10 million dissatisfied blade users out there."

A spokesperson for the ad agency says the ads also try to eliminate the perception that electric razors are "some old razor your grandmother gave you in high school" and instead position them as the "high-tech way to shave." Advantage commercials will run on network, cable, and syndicated TV and in such magazines as *Rolling Stone, Details, Spin,* and *Sports Illustrated.*

Table A provides demographic data on the users of electric razors, disposable razors, and replaceable-blade razors and on the users of Remington, Norelco, and Braun electric shavers.

Discussion Questions

1. Prepare a two-page summary, accompanied by no more than four graphs, that conveys the key information in Table A to a manager.
2. Describe the typical user of an electric razor, a disposable razor, and a blade razor, in one paragraph each.
3. Conduct an innovation analysis of the Advantage using Table 7-3 as the basis. What insights does the innovation analysis provide into its probable sales growth?
4. Which of the demographic factors are most relevant for developing marketing strategy for the Advantage? Why?
5. Using demographics, describe the best target market for the Advantage.
6. What additional demographic data would you like to have in order to develop marketing strategy for the Advantage? Justify your answer.
7. Why would "10 million dissatisfied blade users" continue to use blades?
8. Evaluate Norelco's objective to, and strategy for, switching dissatisfied blade users to electric razors.
9. Using the available data, develop a marketing strategy for the Advantage.

Source: R. A. Davis, "Electric Razors Plan Aggressive Fourth-Quarter," *Advertising Age,* October 12, 1992, p. 20; L. Petrecca, "Norelco Courts Younger Crowd," *Advertising Age,* September 1996, p. 64; L. Petrecca, "Norelco Puts New Shaver to the Test," *Advertising Age,* August 31, 1998, p. 10; "Electric Razors Retain Strong Category Position," *MMR,* January 1999, p. 30; and R. Lee, "Gillette's New Wet Shaver to Challenge Norelco, Schick," *Knight Ridder Tribune Business News,* January 22, 2004.

TABLE A

Demographics and
Razor Use

Variable	Type			Brand		
	Electric	Disposable	Blades	Norelco	Remington	Braun
Percent adults using	**29.8%**	**54.4%**	**44.9%**	**16.0%**	**5.3%**	**4.6**
Age						
18–24 years	92	97	120	66	95	107
25–34	93	103	111	81	89	125
35–44	88	108	101	86	86	89
45–54	90	105	96	93	91	89
55–64	109	93	94	121	111	89
>64	143	86	75	173	146	100
Education						
College graduate	105	95	107	109	90	141
Some college	102	96	107	100	109	98
High school graduate	94	104	97	96	102	85
No degree	101	105	87	95	97	75
Occupation						
Professional	99	96	113	95	88	141
Managerial/administrative	95	100	107	100	78	133
Technical/Clerical/Sales	92	102	113	94	71	107
Precision/Craft	95	106	105	94	92	93
Race/Ethnic group						
White	103	100	102	108	101	103
Black	77	102	85	41	103	67
Spanish speaking	86	106	101	78	56	114
Region						
Northeast	89	99	103	86	102	90
North Central	115	98	101	108	130	125
South	95	104	101	97	92	77
West	103	97	95	109	81	118
Household Income						
<$10,000	97	111	76	105	62	49
$10,000–19,999	98	102	85	90	108	47
$20,000–29,999	104	103	84	99	98	99
$30,000–39,999	99	101	98	108	122	75
$40,000–49,999	110	100	99	108	143	74
$50,000–59,999	93	97	108	99	91	109
$60,000–74,999	105	99	107	93	105	152
$75,000+	96	97	113	100	77	127
Household Structure						
Single	92	99	110	70	97	111
Married	103	100	98	111	103	99

Note: 100 = Average use or consumption unless a percent is indicated. Base = All males.

Source: Spring 2000 Mediamark Research Inc.

CASE 2-3   Crest Rejuvenating Effects

Procter & Gamble spent $50 million to launch a cosmetic-style toothpaste called Crest Rejuvenating Effects. Targeting women aged 30 to 44, it was the first attempt to position a toothpaste for a relatively narrow adult market. The effort was headed by three women executives who referred to themselves as "chicks in charge."

This sub-brand provides multibenefit whitening, a glimmering "pearlescent" box, and sparkly, teal-toned toothpaste with vanilla and cinnamon notes. It also leaves a slight tingling sensation that Crest hopes will serve as a "sensory signal" of gum health and fresh breath. However, it does not provide any functional benefits not available in other toothpastes.

It was priced similarly to other multifunctional toothpastes.

One of the "chicks in charge" stated,

> This is one of the few categories [in personal care] where there are no products specifically marketed to women. I think times are changing and women want products specifically for themselves.

The introductory campaign featured actress/singer Vanessa Williams. The general market campaign differed from the one targeting African American consumers. The general market ads positioned Rejuvenating Effects as a natural extension of the many other things women do for beauty care. Thus, it is part of a beauty routine, not just a dental hygiene activity. However, P&G's research indicated that, compared to white women, black women don't age as noticeably, don't have as involved beauty-care routines, and are more likely to see aging as desirable and conferring respect. Ads specifically targeting this audience showed scenes from various times in Ms. Williams' life, noting that she hasn't aged much and praising a toothpaste "that cares for her mouth and allows it to look as good as her face."

Discussion Questions

1. Has Rejuvenating Effects succeeded? Why or why not?
2. Is Rejuvenating Effects an innovation? If so, what type?
3. What values are relevant to the success or failure of Rejuvenating Effects?
4. Why would women want "their own" toothpaste?
5. How would you market Rejuvenating Effects to Hispanic consumers?
6. Why do you think the age range of 30 to 44 was selected as the primary target market?
7. What social classes are most likely to purchase this product? Why?
8. How would you market this product and how likely would it be to succeed in the following countries?
   a. Germany
   b. Japan
   c. France
   d. Brazil

Source: J. Neff, "Crest Spinoff Targets Women," *Advertising Age,* June 3, 2002, p. 1; and "Crest Dresses Up for Women Users," *Advertising Age,* June 10, 2002, p. 28.

CASE 2-4   Renault's Logan Taps Emerging Global Markets

In 1999, Renault bought Romanian auto maker Dacia. The idea was to retool the plant and manufacture an ultra-low-priced automobile that would be attractive to consumers in developing countries where 80 percent have never owned a car. Renault's chairman at the time, Louis Schweitzer indicates that he had

> . . . always been slightly nervous about the constant escalating costs of ordinary family cars. Adding more and more features just pushed up costs with no real benefit for buyer or carmaker.

The move was a bold one. Consider that in 1999, with gasoline prices still in check, consumer demand was still high for larger and more powerful automobiles. And cars often are an important status symbol for at least some consumers. Many luxury brands continue to tap this "aspirational" market with lower-priced versions of their luxury brands. These aspirational buyers pay a lower but still hefty price for the status of owning a luxury name plate.

Renault's Logan is anything but luxury. However, it is a well-designed, reliable, and easy-to-repair car. It is a roomy sedan that can seat five people, but has simple design features such as a flat windshield, minimal electronics, a single-piece dashboard, and so on to reduce manufacturing costs. Simple, low-cost manufacturing which can be executed in factories located in countries like Russia, Morocco, Colombia, and Iran has been the goal, since production close to their key markets also reduces costs.

The Logan has been an unqualified success, beating even Renault's most optimistic projections. Perhaps not so surprising is Logan's success in developing countries like Romania. The automobile is currently priced at about 5,000 euros (or $6,000). This puts the Logan at the ultra-low end of the price spectrum, but also, into the price range of large masses of consumers in developing countries. Consider these two illustrative statistics:

- In Poland, entry-level autos account for 30 percent of the market.

- In Russia, 90 percent of the auto market falls in the 8,000 to 10,000 euro range.

Renault's goal for the Logan is 1 million units worldwide by 2010, an amazing number, particularly when you consider the time frame involved (also that the best selling auto in the United States in 2004 sold only 400,000 units). Obviously, large developing countries with increasing incomes, such as India and China, are part of the plan.

However, what has really surprised Renault is that buyers in Western Europe are also flocking to the Logan. In response, Renault has added some additional features, but still kept the price well below comparable competitors. These Western European buyers are far from aspirational in their view of cars. Consider the following comment by one happy owner in France (where there is now a three-month wait to get a Logan): "For me a car is only a means of transportation. The Logan is a genius idea."

Not surprisingly, given Renault's success, competitors are on their way, including Volkswagen (going after China) and Tata (an Indian auto manufacturer).

Discussion Questions

1. Beyond income, can you see other barriers to selling cars to consumers in developing countries where 80 percent have *never* owned a car? Be as specific as you can about the consumer behavior–related barriers including culture, values, new-product adoption, etc.

2. Based on your answer to Question 1, develop an action plan for Renault that would help them to overcome these barriers.

3. Do you think the Logan would be successful in the United States? If Renault thought it could be successful, would it make sense for them to put resources here given their goal of 1 million units per year worldwide?

4. Develop an advertising campaign to market the Logan in the following countries. Be specific with respect to core theme, copy points, and visuals. Detail the role you think different media (e.g., TV, print, radio, mobile phone, Internet) might play in these different countries.
   a. Russia
   b. India
   c. China

5. Do you think a branding strategy that includes Renault's name (e.g., Logan by Renault) is wise? What are the potential risks and benefits?

6. What sorts of word-of-mouth strategies might be effective in marketing the Logan?

7. As incomes in the developing countries increase, do you expect these consumers to continue to have strong demand for ultra-low-priced cars such as the Logan?

Source: A. Lewis, "Renault's Romanian Route," *Automotive Industries,* February 2005, pp. 6–7; "Renault's Logan 'World Car' Begins Production in Moscow," www.edmunds.com, April 4, 2005; "Got 5,000 Euros?" *BusinessWeek,* July 4, 2005, p. 49; "Renault's Low-cost Logan Beats Sales Forecasts," www.Forbes.com, July 10, 2005; and "Renault's $6,000 Sedan," www.biz-architect.com, July 18, 2005.

CASE 2-5   Office Depot Leads in Green

In 2004, Office Depot issued its first annual *Environmental Stewardship Report*. It was audited by an independent third party, namely the sustainability experts at PricewaterhouseCoopers LLP. Their report was the "office supply industry's first independently verified report of environmental performance." The report details key policy initiatives and achievements and also details the key guiding principles underlying their *Environmental Paper Procurement Policy*. The three core areas and 10 key guiding principles as detailed in the report are as follows.

Recycling and Pollution Reduction

- Give preference to paper products made with postconsumer recycled fiber and unbleached paper and paper made with advanced processes or technologies that reduce or eliminate the use of chlorine compounds.
- Increase the scope of products and services containing recycled materials.
- Increase the total volume of paper recovered from recycling.

- Increase the amount of recycled materials in the paper products distributed by the Company.
- Encourage suppliers to continue to reduce pollution, including the phasing out of elemental chlorine bleaching agents in the paper-making process.

Responsible Forest Management and Conservation

- Promote and advance responsible forest management and the conservation of forests and the biodiversity they contain.
- Identify products sourced from forest operations that are congruent with Office Depot's principles of sustainable forest management and increasingly source paper products from these preferred sources . . . ; and progressively phase out paper products derived from nonpreferred sources as they are identified and alternate sources of supply are secured.

Issue Awareness and Market Development

- Increase the general level of knowledge, understanding, and popular consciousness of environmental issues, including the implications of purchasing decisions and the benefits of Office Depot's policies as well as the advantage of purchasing environmentally preferred products.
- Grow the markets for environmentally preferred products by stimulating demand and supply, while demonstrating that environmental performance and a collaborative, ethical, science-based approach can create economic benefits from improved environmental outcomes.

- Address the needs for improved information, methods, tools, and standards to advance environmental stewardship and increase the role and value of conservation science in business and resource management decision making.

Discussion Questions

1. Review materials on Office Depot's Web site (www.officedepot.com) pertaining to their environmental stewardship efforts, including their ongoing reports. Prepare a report that details accomplishments that Office Depot has made relating to its 10 guiding principles. How would you judge Office Depot's environmental stewardship?

2. Based on your review in Question 1, do you think that consumers are generally aware of the positive things that Office Depot does? If not, should it more heavily promote these positive activities? If it decided to do so, how should it go about it?

3. What effect does PricewaterhouseCoopers' auditing have on your overall evaluation of Office Depot's efforts in the area of the environment?

4. Office Depot argues that being "green" makes both environmental and business sense. What consumer values does environmental stewardship tap into and how do you think these can translate to the "bottom line" of businesses?

5. Develop promotional materials that would help Office Depot achieve its goal of "increasing demand for environmentally preferred products" to a consumer target market.

Source: *2004 Environmental Stewardship Report* (Delray Beach, FL: Office Depot, 2004).

CASE 2-6   Dixon Ticonderoga's Prang Soybean Crayon

In a contest held by Purdue University to develop new uses for soybeans, one entrant used them to make crayons. As a result, Dixon Ticonderoga entered into an agreement to develop and market the new crayon. After years of research, the product was launched as the "first new crayon in 100 years."

Named Prang Fun Pro Soybean Crayons, they promise a number of advantages over traditional crayons:

- They are made from soybeans, a renewable resource. Most crayons are made from paraffin, a petroleum product.

- They don't flake like petroleum-based crayons.
- They don't create a waxy build-up.
- Prang crayons allow users to blend or layer colors, which is not possible with traditional crayons.

While Prang crayons have a number of desirable features, they also face a serious obstacle. Crayola is virtually synonymous with crayons. It dominates the market in terms of sales, distribution, and advertising. Crayola features many products in addition to traditional crayons, including Crayola Construction Paper crayons that provide consistent, true color across all types of paper, including black construction paper, brown paper bags, and colored poster board; Crayola Washable highlighters and Crayola Erasable highlighters; Crayola Poster markers; Crayola School glue; Crayola Student scissors; Crayola Metallic colored pencils; Crayola Computer & Craft Paper; Crayola Color WipeOffs Whiteboard Combo sets; and Crayola Color WipeOffs washable dry erase markers.

Crayola Kids' Katchalls designed for organizing kids' crayons, markers, and supplies are durable plastic boxes with a snap-close top and handle that makes them easy for kids to grip and carry. Crayola backpacks come in a variety of colors and sizes, and some styles include a matching lunch bag. Crayola shoes are available in infant size 1 through children's size 12.

Discussion Questions

1. What type of innovation is the new Prang crayon? Evaluate it as an innovation using Table 7-3 as a structure.

2. How can the firm use opinion leaders to help the Prang crayon succeed?

3. How can the firm use reference group influence to help the Prang crayon succeed?

4. What values will help this product succeed?

5. Would you target children or adults? How would your approach differ between the two groups?

6. What demographic groups would you target?

7. How would you compete against Crayola?

8. How would you market the Prang crayon in these countries?
   a. Japan
   b. European Union
   c. Mexico
   d. Egypt

Source: www.prang.com; D. Gardner, "Soy-Based Crayons Color the Countryside," *Agri Marketing,* February 1998, pp. 18–19; and "Soybean Crayons Add Color," *PR Newswire,* August 31, 1999.

CASE 2-7   The Mosquito Magnet

Female mosquitoes bite humans and other creatures to acquire blood for the protein they need to lay eggs. They are attracted to humans by the carbon dioxide and other compounds in their breath as well as body heat, moisture, and organic compounds on the skin. Mosquitoes typically do not fly more than a few hundred yards from where they are hatched (unless windblown) during their short (several weeks) lives. Thus, if most females are continuously killed in an area, the population should collapse in six to eight weeks.

American Biophysics recently introduced the Mosquito Magnet on the basis of these facts. It looks a bit like a small gas barbecue grill, complete with propane tank. It mimics a large mammal by emitting a plume of carbon dioxide, heat and moisture, and octenol (a chemical in human breath). This plume attracts female mosquitoes, no-see-ums, biting midges, black flies, and sand flies. It attracts only blood-sucking insects. As the insects approach the Magnet, they are vacuumed into a net where they dehydrate and die. A variety of tests indicate that this system does indeed work and is the most effective available (see www.mosquitomagnet.com).

The system needs to operate 24 hours a day as it works by creating a mosquito-free (or low-density) area. It takes about two weeks for there to be a noticeable decrease in the mosquito population. The company claims that the population will typically collapse

in four to six weeks, leaving only occasional, windblown mosquitoes in the area.

The 20-gallon propane tank will need to be refilled approximately every three weeks (approximately $10). The octenol cartridge (which is not essential but improves the attraction power of the system) also needs to be replaced every three weeks (about $6 each). The net needs to be emptied when half full (frequency depends on the mosquito density in the area).

Mosquito Magnet initially launched with three models as described below (prices do not include the propane tank, which costs less than $50).

- *Liberty:* covers three-quarters of an acre; needs a 110-volt plug to operate the vacuum fan; $495.
- *Freedom:* covers three-quarters of an acre; generates its own electricity; $795.
- *Pro:* covers one acre; generates its own electricity; $1,295.

Discussion Questions

1. Is the Mosquito Magnet an innovation? If so, what type?

2. Conduct an innovation analysis on the Mosquito Magnet, and develop appropriate marketing strategies based on this analysis.

3. How can the firm use the test results in marketing the Mosquito Magnet?

4. How can the firm encourage word-of-mouth communications about the Mosquito Magnet?

5. Who do you think the opinion leaders will be for this product, and how can the firm use them?

6. What, if any, values are relevant to marketing this product?

7. List the top five countries outside the United States in order of their attractiveness as an export market for this product. Justify your selection.

8. Which family members will be involved in the purchase decision? What roles will they play?

Source: www.mosquitomagnet.com; J. E. Guyette, "Easing Summer's Sting," *LP/Gas,* August 2001, p. 1; F. Antowiewicz, "Mosquitoes Help Save Firm from Bankruptcy," *Plastics News,* June 24, 2002, p. 1; and S. O'Neill, "Skeeter Snuffers," *Kiplinger's Personal Finance,* June 2002, p. 3.

CASE 2–8   Tapping the Ethnic Housing Market

Fannie Mae was established in 1968 and provides financial products and services that help low, moderate, and middle income households buy homes. Their goal is to increase home ownership, particularly among underserved populations. They recently commissioned a survey to look at the perceptions and knowledge of the home-buying process across ethnic subcultures. Three major areas were assessed, namely (*a*) reasons to buy a home, (*b*) knowledge about the home-buying process, and (*c*) confidence in the home-buying process. Results were as follows.

Home-Buying Reasons

Key reasons for buying or wanting to buy a home are shown in Table A. (Note that English Hispanics are those for whom English is the dominant language, and

Spanish Hispanics are those for whom Spanish is dominant.)

Home-Buying Knowledge

Knowledge about the home-buying process was assessed by the percentage of respondents who identified each of the following statements (S) as false (which they are) as shown in Table B.

S1: Information on buying a home is only available in English.

S2: You need to hire an attorney to fill out your paperwork when you buy a house.

S3: If you want a mortgage, you have to accept a 30-year commitment.

	Safe Investment with Potential	Renting is Bad	Feeling of Ownership	Can Pick Neighborhood	Always My Dream
General population	61%	77%	74%	67%	65%
African American	54	67	82	66	67
English Hispanic	67	77	82	71	77
Spanish Hispanic	60	75	79	65	63

TABLE A

Key Reasons to Purchase a Home by Ethnicity

Key Reasons to Purchase a Home by Ethnicity from Understanding America's Homeownership Gaps: 2003 Fannie Mae National Housing Survey (Washington, DC: Fannie Mae, 2003). Used by permission.

	S1	S2	S3	S4	S5	S6
General population	89%	70%	74%	59%	48%	73%
African American	92	53	60	36	34	57
English Hispanic	93	70	65	42	47	64
Spanish Hispanic	60	39	27	25	23	22

TABLE B

Home-Buying Knowledge by Ethnicity

Note: Read each column as percentage who know the statement is false. For example, 89 percent of the general population know that Statement 1 is false.

Home-buying Knowledge by Ethnicity from Understanding America's Homeownership Gaps: 2003 Fannie Mae National Housing Survey (Washington, DC: Fannie Mae, 2003). Used by permission.

Perceptions of
Home-Buying
Confidence by
Ethnicity

	Understand Process Well*	Process too Complex	Avoiding Discrimination**
General population	33%	13%	4.0
African American	23	25	3.4
English Hispanic	29	18	3.9
Spanish Hispanic	18	23	3.6

*Think they have above average knowledge of the home-buying process.

**Measured on a 1–5 scale, where 1 is lowest confidence and 5 is highest confidence that they will avoid discrimination in the home-buying process.

Perceptions of Home Buying Confidence by Ethnicity from Understanding America's Homeownership Gaps: 2003 Fannie Mae National Housing Survey (Washington, DC: Fannie Mae, 2003). Used by permission.

S4: Housing lenders are required by law to give you the best possible rates on loans.

S5: The person buying the home pays the real estate professional.

S6: You need to have a perfect credit rating to qualify for a mortgage.

Home-Buying Confidence

Confidence in home-buying skill and in avoiding discrimination were examined as shown in Table C.

Discussion Questions

1. What are the opportunities and challenges facing housing lenders and real-estate agents across ethnic subcultures?

2. Based on the information in Tables A, B, and C develop an overall marketing strategy for targeting each of the following groups:
   a. African Americans

   b. English Hispanics
   c. Spanish Hispanics

3. Based on the information in Tables A, B, and C develop advertising campaigns including (a) overall positioning strategy and core theme, (b) key advertising copy points, (c) visual elements, and (d) key media outlets for:
   d. African Americans
   e. English Hispanics
   f. Spanish Hispanics

4. Based on the information in Tables A, B, and C develop training materials for lenders and real-estate agents to enhance their interactions with consumers from various ethnic backgrounds. Analyze lenders and real-estate agents separately and develop materials relating to both verbal (written and oral) and nonverbal communications.

Source: Tables from *Understanding America's Homeownership Gaps: 2003 Fannie Mae National Housing Survey* (Washington, DC: Fannie Mae, 2003). General information about Fannie Mae found at www.fanniemae.com.

CASE 2-9   Fighting Obesity in Kids

In the mid-60s, less than 5 percent of children aged 6 to 11 or 12 to 19 were significantly overweight. By the end of the century, the percentage for both groups was approaching 15 percent. A diet rich in high-fat, high-calorie foods coupled with limited physical activity is acknowledged as the cause.

In July 2002, the Centers for Disease Control (CDC) launched a $125 million campaign, including $50 million for media purchases and $43 million for various marketing and public relations activities; funding for subsequent years was to be substantial but less. The funding legislation from Congress directed the CDC to target childhood obesity but left it wide

latitude as to how. It did require that the CDC "communicate messages that help foster good health over a lifetime, including diet, physical activity, and avoidance of illicit drugs, tobacco and alcohol."

The CDC opted to narrow the approach to increased physical activity, particularly among 9- to 13-year-olds. Mike Greenwell, communications director for the CDC, stated, "What we want is behavior change. That would be success for us."

The barriers to physical activity for kids are substantial. First, nonphysical entertainment options have exploded in recent years. Not only has cable television greatly expanded the number of television channels targeting kids, but magazines focusing on them have also expanded. Videos and video games are now a major recreational choice for children. Of course, the time spent online has grown dramatically as well.

Coupled with the vast growth in nonphysical exercise options, there has been a radical decline in required physical education in school. CDC estimates that the number of kids getting physical education in schools has dropped from 50 percent to 21 percent in the past decade.

An initial 15-second spot launched in July showed computer animation of action words turning into an image of a boy running. The theme was "Verb: It's what you do." This and similar teaser spots ran on kid-targeted network and cable TV shows. In September, the full campaign began. The ads all promoted the fun of a physically active lifestyle rather than warning about the dangers of not exercising or of excess weight.

The CDC campaign was the exclusive sponsor of a weekly live-action Nickelodeon show called "WACK" (Wild & Crazy Kids), a related nine-city tour, Nick.com's WACK Web site, and a "Nick News" special program.

There is controversy about the positive-lifestyle approach of the campaign. Antidrug ads targeting the same age were not successful. In explaining why, the Partnership for a Drug-Free America argued that the positive-lifestyle approach does not motivate nearly as well as ads warning about drug dangers.

Discussion Questions

1. The campaign focused primarily on children, with limited attention to parents. Teachers and other potential influencers were not directly targeted. What do you think is the appropriate balance among these groups? Why?

2. Is the positive approach better than the negative approach in this situation? Why?

3. Describe a series of three positive-lifestyle ads you would use to encourage physical activity among 9- to 13-year-olds.

4. Describe a series of three warning ads you would use to encourage physical activity among 9- to 13-year-olds.

5. Describe a series of three positive-lifestyle ads targeting parents that you would use to encourage physical activity among their 9- to 13-year-old children.

6. Describe a series of three warning ads targeting parents that you would use to encourage physical activity among their 9- to 13-year-old children.

Source: I. Teinowitz and W. Friedman, "U.S. Launches $125 Mil Push to Combat Obesity," *Advertising Age,* July 17, 2002, p. 4; and www.cdc.gov.

Internal Influences

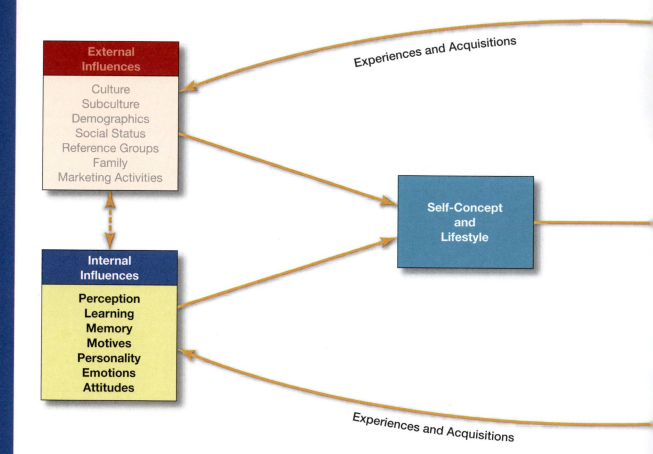

External Influences

Culture
Subculture
Demographics
Social Status
Reference Groups
Family
Marketing Activities

Internal Influences

**Perception
Learning
Memory
Motives
Personality
Emotions
Attitudes**

**Self-Concept
and
Lifestyle**

Experiences and Acquisitions

Experiences and Acquisitions

The highlighted areas of our model, internal influences and self-concept and lifestyle, are the focal points of this part of the text. Our attention shifts from forces that are basically outside the individual to processes that occur primarily within the individual.

Part Three begins with a discussion of perception, the process by which individuals access and assign meaning to environmental stimuli. In Chapter 9, we consider learning and memory. Chapter 10 covers motivation, personality, and emotions. Chapter 11 focuses on the critical concept of attitudes and the various ways attitudes are formed and changed.

As a result of the interaction of the external influences described in the previous part of the text and the internal processes examined in this part, individuals form self-concepts and desired lifestyles, as discussed in Chapter 12. These are the hub of our model of consumer behavior. Self-concept refers to the way individuals think and feel about themselves as well as how they would like to think and feel about themselves. Their actual and desired lifestyles are the way they translate their self-concepts into daily behaviors, including consumption behaviors.

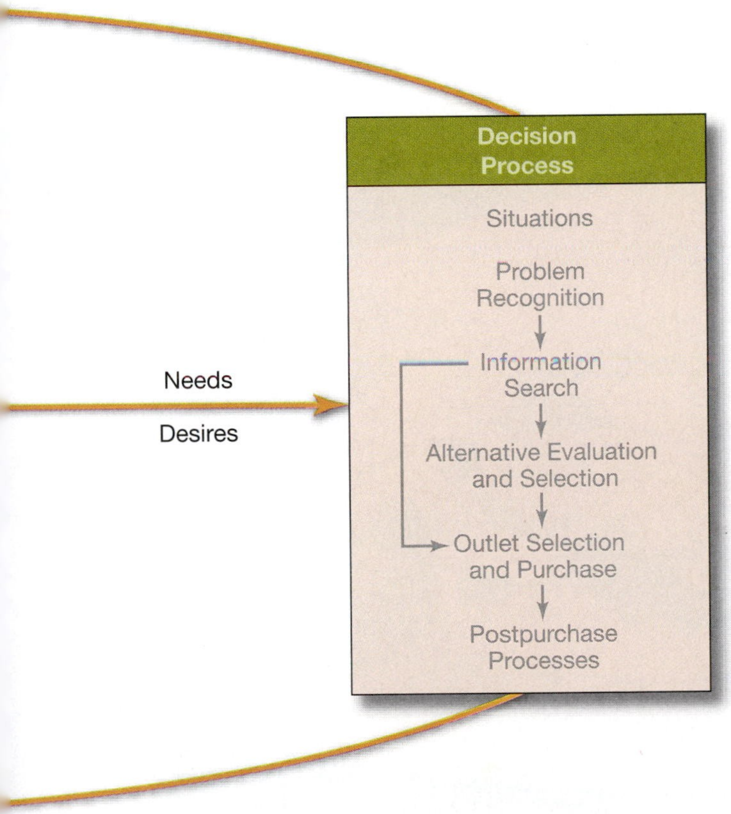

Decision Process

Situations

Problem Recognition

Information Search

Alternative Evaluation and Selection

Outlet Selection and Purchase

Postpurchase Processes

Needs

Desires

Courtesy Gardenburger, Inc.

8

Perception

■ Consumers on vegetarian and vegan diets are searching for foods that balance taste and dietary requirements. In response, Gardenburger introduced its first "meatless" patty in 1985 and has gone on to create other meatless alternatives including Meatless Meatloaf and Buffalo Chik'n Wings. Their products substitute grain-based proteins and vegetables for meat. Many of their meatless patties include mushrooms as a key ingredient.

In early 2002, Gardenburger became concerned when a competitor introduced foods containing mycoprotein and wanted to claim they were "mushroom in origin." As Gardenburger's CEO Scott Wallace explained it, "After extensive consumer research and discussion with scientific experts, we feel that this labeling is misleading, and could potentially damage those who legitimately use mushrooms in their products."

To understand Gardenburger's concern, you might ask yourself the following question: "What does it mean to me if a product claims it is 'mushroom in origin'?" Gardenburger launched an extensive survey to answer this very question. Sixty percent of the consumers they surveyed believed that a product labeled as "mushroom in origin" would contain actual mushrooms! Is that what you thought it meant as well? If so, look more carefully at the phrase. It never explicitly states that the product contains mushrooms.

Gardenburger's concerns were justified. Labeling mycoprotein as "mushroom in origin" rather than with the more accurate "edible protein derived from fungus" increases the odds that consumers will infer the presence of mushrooms when they aren't there. It also enhances consumer perceptions and willingess to try the product over that garnered by the more accurate label. As a consequence, Gardenburger has petitioned the Food and Drug Administration to regulate the labeling of mycoprotein.[1]

Perception is a process that begins with consumer exposure and attention to marketing stimuli and ends with consumer interpretation. As we will see, exposure and attention are highly selective—meaning that consumers process only a small fraction of the available information. And as the opening example suggests, interpretation can be a highly subjective process. Thus reality and consumer perceptions of that reality are often quite different. Marketers wishing to communicate their brand message effectively to consumers must understand the nature of perception and the many factors influencing it.

THE NATURE OF PERCEPTION

Information processing is a series of activities by which stimuli are perceived, transformed into information, and stored. Figure 8-1 illustrates a useful information-processing model having four major steps or stages: exposure, attention, interpretation, and memory. The first three of these constitute **perception.**

Exposure occurs when a stimulus such as a banner ad comes within range of a person's sensory receptor nerves—vision, in this example. *Attention* occurs when the stimulus

FIGURE 8-1   Information Processing for Consumer Decision Making

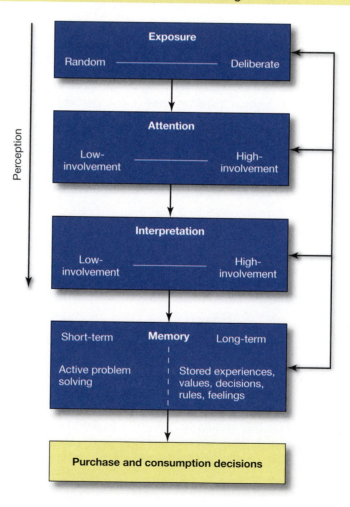

(banner ad) is "seen" (the receptor nerves pass the sensations on to the brain for processing). *Interpretation* is the assignment of meaning to the received sensations. *Memory* is the short-term use of the meaning for immediate decision making or the longer-term retention of the meaning.

Figure 8-1 and the above discussion suggest a linear flow from exposure to memory. However, *these processes occur virtually simultaneously and are clearly interactive.* For example, a person's memory influences the information he or she is exposed to and attends to and the interpretations the person assigns to that information. At the same time, memory itself is being shaped by the information it is receiving.

Both perception and memory are extremely selective. Of the massive amount of information available, individuals can be exposed and attend to only a limited amount. The meaning assigned to a stimulus is as much or more a function of the individual as it is the stimulus itself. Further, much of the interpreted information will not be available to active memory when the individual makes a purchase decision.

This selectivity, sometimes referred to as **perceptual defenses,** means that *individuals are not passive recipients of marketing messages.* Rather, consumers largely determine the messages they will encounter and notice as well as the meaning they will assign them. Clearly, the marketing manager faces a challenging task when communicating with consumers.

EXPOSURE

Exposure *occurs when a stimulus is placed within a person's relevant environment and comes within range of their sensory receptor nerves.* Exposure provides consumers with the *opportunity* to pay attention to available information but in no way guarantees it. For example, have you ever been watching television and realized that you were not paying attention to the commercials being aired? In this case, exposure occurred, but the commercials will probably have little influence due to your lack of attention.

An individual can be exposed to only a minuscule fraction of the available stimuli. There are now hundreds of television channels, thousands of radio stations, and innumerable magazines and Web sites. In-store environments are also cluttered with tens of thousands of individual items and in-store advertising. Even in today's multi-tasking society there are limits.

So, what determines exposure? Is it a random process or purposeful? Most of the stimuli to which individuals are exposed are "self-selected." That is, people deliberately seek out exposure to certain stimuli and avoid others. Generally, people seek *information that they think will help them achieve their goals.* Immediate goals could involve seeking stimuli such as a television program for amusement or a Web site to make a purchase. Long-range goals might involve examining corporate Web sites to determine how environmentally friendly they are in hopes of making your community a safer place to live. An individual's goals and the types of information needed to achieve those goals are a function of that person's existing and desired lifestyle and such short-term motives as hunger or curiosity.

Of course, people are also exposed to a large number of stimuli on a more or less random basis during their daily activities. While driving, they may hear commercials, see billboards and display ads, and so on that they did not purposefully seek out.

Selective Exposure

The highly selective nature of consumer exposure is a major concern for marketers since failure to gain exposure results in lost communication and sales opportunities. For example, consumers are highly selective in the way they shop once they enter a store. One study found that only 21 percent of U.S. shoppers visited each aisle in the store. The remainder avoided exposure to products in aisles they didn't shop. Consumers in France, Belgium and Holland are also highly selective shoppers, while consumers in Brazil and the U.K. are more likely to shop all the aisles.[2]

Media exposure is also of great concern to marketers. Media are where marketers put their commercial messages and include television, radio, magazines, direct mail, billboards, and the Internet. The impact of the active, self-selecting nature of media exposure can be seen in the zipping, zapping, and muting of television commercials. **Zipping** occurs when one fast-forwards through a commercial on a prerecorded program. **Zapping** involves switching channels when a commercial appears. **Muting** is turning the sound off during commercial breaks. Zipping, zapping, and muting are simply mechanical ways for consumers to selectively avoid exposure to advertising messages, often referred to as **ad avoidance.**

The nearly universal presence of remote controls makes zipping, zapping, and muting very simple. Indeed, existing and emerging technologies give consumers more and more control over exposure to television commercials. One such technology is the *digital video recorder (DVR)* offered by companies such as TiVo. DVRs allow for digital recording of programs and "time-shifted" viewing in much the same way as VCRs only easier. And while DVRs are currently in only a small fraction of U.S. households, adoption is expected to increase dramatically over the next several years.[3]

A major concern for marketers is that the DVR will increase ad avoidance. One study by TiVo found that when viewers watch prerecorded programs they zipped through the commercials 77 percent of the time.[4] Some feel that this signals the end of TV advertising as we know it. However, another study has found a possible upside in that a majority of viewers who zip through DVR commercials still "notice" the ads. As a consequence, companies are now trying to devise ways of compressing ads so consumers are exposed to a shortened version which plays in real time during fast forwarding.[5] Other strategies include more repetitions to enhance recall of zipped ads.[6] Clearly, marketers need to think beyond traditional models as technology continues to transform how consumers watch TV.

Avoidance of commercials is a global phenomenon which extends beyond TV to include radio, the Internet, magazines, and newspapers. Ad avoidance depends on numerous psychological and demographic factors. A recent study by Initiative examined ad avoidance globally and across various media. They found that ad avoidance is increased by lifestyle (busy and hectic lifestyle), social class (higher social class), and demographics (men and younger consumers).[7]

In addition, ad avoidance appears to increase as advertising clutter increases and as consumer attitudes toward advertising become more negative. Consumers tend to dislike (and actively avoid) advertising when it is perceived to be boring, uninformative, and intrusive.[8] In China, for example, where the novelty of advertising and product variety is wearing off, ad avoidance is on the rise and feelings about advertising are becoming more negative.[9] In online settings, marketers have devised "pop-up" ads that are difficult or impossible for viewers to eliminate. At the extreme, movie theaters have begun airing ads *prior* to the movie since the theater provides a captive audience and enhances ad recall beyond that of TV.[10] Such techniques should be used with care, however, since consumers may react very negatively to such forced exposure.[11] In fact, one study found that between 20 and 37 percent of online users are so turned off by pop-up ads that they download "anti-pop-up" software to avoid them completely![12]

In response to consumers' tendency to avoid ads, marketers increasingly seek to gain exposure by placing their messages in unique media such as on the side of trucks and taxis

Courtesy mobileoutdoor.com advertising.

(see Illustration 8-1), in airplanes, in television programs and movies, at events, in video games, and inside taxis. For example, CabTV places interactive touch-screen TVs in cabs. These TVs hold 75 minutes of video, much of which is a tour guide to the city. If the screen isn't touched, it runs a 12-minute loop of 30-second commercials. As an executive explained,

> Most travelers know where they are going to stay, but they don't know where they're going to eat, shop, gamble, etc. So it's very compelling. It's a 10-inch screen less than two feet from your face.[13]

Firms expend tremendous effort placing their products within entertainment media such as in movies. Such **product placement** provides exposure that consumers don't try to avoid, it shows how and when to use the product, and it enhances the product's image (see Consumer Insight 8-1).

Voluntary Exposure

Although consumers often avoid commercials and other marketing stimuli, sometimes they actively seek them out for various reasons including purchase goals, entertainment, and information. As we saw earlier, consumers actively seek out aisles containing items they want to buy.[14] And, many viewers look forward to the commercials developed for the Super Bowl. Perhaps more impressive is the positive response consumers have to

Brands as Movie Stars[15]

Product placement involves incorporating brands into movies, television programs, and other entertainment venues in exchange for payment or promotional or other consideration. Product placement agents read scripts and meet with set designers to find scenes where their clients' brand names and products can be placed or written into the dialogue. The goal is to add realism to the scene, give subtle exposure to the brand, and influence consumers in an unobtrusive manner. In general, product placement in movies is unrestricted, but in television, sponsor identification rules may apply (the Federal Communications Commission is the regulatory authority).

While product placements have probably been used since the advent of movies, they really caught marketers' attention when sales of Reese's Pieces candy jumped 6 percent in the three months following the release of *E.T.,* in which they were featured. However, merely obtaining presence in a movie or program does not guarantee success. Placements appear to work best when the principal actor is present and the placement is well integrated into the scene. Ideally, it seems that one would want to have the principal character use the product in a noticeable but positive, natural way. For example, as hybrid cars began taking hold in the United States, Toyota's Prius was featured prominently in an episode of the political drama "The West Wing." The Prius was integral to a principle character in the episode and positively woven into the core plot dealing with fuel economy standards for the auto industry.

Many consumers appear to understand and even appreciate the use of branded products in movies and TV shows. The use of brands can make scenes more realistic, provoke feelings of nostalgia, and help establish the lifestyle of the characters. However, consumer receptiveness to product placements can be reduced by overemphasizing the brand or by using ethically charged products such as cigarettes.

Interestingly, a study by WPP Group suggests that younger consumers are the most likely age group to consider buying products they see in movies. This may be of concern to regulators as product placement moves into "youth" venues such as video games.

Global considerations are also important since receptivity to product placements differs by region (Asia-Pacific region is higher in receptivity than others) and since the portrayal must be appropriate across the countries in which the brand is sold.

Critical Thinking Questions

1. What ethical questions, if any, do you see in using product placement as a marketing tool? Are your feelings the same across all product categories?

2. Are there unique issues and perhaps rules that should govern product placements in movies targeting children?

3. How could a marketer determine how much to pay for a brand placement in a particular movie or television program episode?

---

infomercials—program-length commercials with an 800 number and/or Web address through which to order or request additional information. These positively affect brand attitudes and purchase intentions.[16] And they are more likely to be viewed by early adopters and opinion leaders.[17] This latter effect implicates a critical indirect influence of infomercials through word-of-mouth communications. It also highlights the role that information and relevance play in driving voluntary exposure to marketing messages.

Exposure to online messages and advertising can also be voluntary or involuntary. As we saw earlier, exposure to banner ads and pop-ups is generally *involuntary,* as consumers encounter them while seeking other information or entertainment. However, a consumer who clicks on the banner or pop-up (*clickthrough*) is now *voluntarily* being exposed to the target site and its marketing message.

Consumers also voluntarily expose themselves to marketing messages by deliberately visiting firms' home pages and other marketer sites. For example, if you are buying a new car you might visit manufacturer sites such as www.toyota.com and independent sites such as www.edmunds.com. In fact, recent car buyers using the Web visited up to seven sites and spent almost five hours online![18] You might also register online to receive coupons or regular updates/newsletters about a company's products and services. When you register at www.eversave.com the site provides you with coupons and newsletters from various consumer goods marketers like Procter & Gamble. The voluntary and self-selected nature of such online offerings, where consumers "opt in" to receive e-mail-based promotions, is often referred to as **permission-based marketing**.[19] Consumers control the messages they are exposed to and consequently are more receptive and responsive to those messages.

ATTENTION

Attention *occurs when the stimulus activates one or more sensory receptor nerves, and the resulting sensations go to the brain for processing.* Attention requires consumers to allocate limited mental resources toward the processing of incoming stimuli such as packages seen on store shelves or banner ads on the Web. As we discussed earlier, the marketing environment is highly cluttered and consumers are constantly bombarded by thousands of times more stimuli than they can process. Therefore, consumer attention is selective.

This selectivity has major implications for marketers. As the following example illustrates, after obtaining exposure, anyone wishing to communicate effectively with consumers must understand how to gain their attention.

> The Federal Crop Insurance Corporation (FCIC) spent $13.5 million over a four-year period on an advertising campaign to increase awareness and knowledge among farmers of the federal crop insurance program. The campaign included radio ads, direct mail brochures, and news releases. However, "farmers ended up knowing no more about this program after the ad campaign than they did before." A spokesperson described the problem: "It was very good and very effective advertising. The trouble is that we had a hard time getting people to read it."[20]

"Very good and very effective advertising" that no one reads is neither good nor effective. People must attend to the messages. As one advertising agency director stated,

> Every year it gets more and more important to stand out and be noticed, to be loud but simple, and to say something relevant and compelling because there is less and less opportunity to talk to consumers and you can't waste any chances.[21]

The ad in Illustration 8-2 is very likely to attract attention. What factors determine and influence attention? Perhaps you are in the market for a DVD player. Once in the DVD aisle you focus your attention on the various brands to make a purchase. However, a loud announcement briefly pulls your attention away from the display. Later, you lose concentration and begin focusing on nearby products you hadn't noticed before. These products were available all the time but were not processed until a deliberate effort was made to do so. As this example demonstrates, attention always occurs within the context of a situation. The *same individual* may devote different levels of attention to the *same stimulus* in *different situations*. Attention is determined by these three factors: the *stimulus,* the *individual,* and the *situation*.

Courtesy Overture Services.

Stimulus Factors

Stimulus factors are physical characteristics of the stimulus itself. Stimulus characteristics such as ad size and color are under the marketer's control and can attract attention independent of individual or situational characteristics. The attention garnered by stimulus factors tends to be relatively automatic. So, even if you *think* you are not interested in a car (individual characteristic), a large and colorful car ad (stimulus characteristics) may be hard to ignore.

Size Larger stimuli are more likely to be noticed than smaller ones. This is certainly the case on store shelves where shelf space is at a premium and more shelf space can translate into greater attention and sales.[22] As a consequence, consumer-products companies often pay what are called *slotting allowances* to retailers in order to secure shelf space. The Federal Trade Commission estimates that companies spend 9 billion dollars annually on such slotting fees.[23]

Size also affects attention to advertising. Figure 8-2 indicates the relative attention-attracting ability of various sizes of magazine ads, with larger ads garnering more attention than smaller ads. Larger banner ads also attract more attention, which might help to explain why banner and online ads continue to increase in size.[24] And, larger Yellow Page ads garner more attention and higher call rates. In one study, consumers seeking a business from the Yellow Pages attended to more than 90 percent of the quarter-page ads but only a quarter of the small listings.[25]

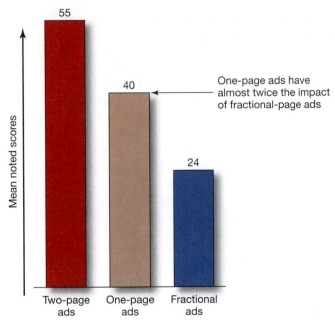

The Impact of Size on Advertising Readership*   FIGURE 8-2

One-page ads have almost twice the impact of fractional-page ads

*Based on an analysis of 85,000 ads.

Source: *Cahners Advertising Research Report 110.1B* (Boston: Cahners Publishing, undated).

Intensity   The *intensity* (e.g., loudness, brightness, length) of a stimulus can increase attention. For instance, the longer a scene in an advertisement is held on-screen, the more likely it is to be noticed and recalled.[26] In online contexts, one aspect of intensity is *intrusivensess,* or the degree to which one is forced to see or interact with a banner ad or pop-up in order to see the desired content. A study in which the banner ad was the only thing on the screen for a brief period before the consumer was connected to the sought-after site produced over three times the level of noticing the ad compared with a standard banner format, and almost 25 times the clickthrough rate.[27] As we saw earlier, however, caution is advised in using intrusiveness due to negative attitudes and avoidance.

Repetition is related to intensity. It is the number of times an individual is exposed to a given stimulus, such as an ad or brand logo, over time. Attention generally decreases across repeated exposures, particularly when those exposures occur in a short period of time (intensity is high). For example, attention to multiple inserts of the same print ad within the same magazine issue has been found to drop by 50 percent from the first to the third exposure.[28]

However, the decrease in overall attention caused by repetition needs to be interpreted in light of two factors. First, consumers may shift the *focus* of their attention from one part of the ad to another across repetitions. Have you ever noticed something new about an ad after you've seen it a couple of times? This is a result of a shift in your attention as you become more familiar with the ad. One study suggests that consumers shift their attention away from the brand component of the ad (name, logo, etc.) and toward the text component.[29] This *attention reallocation* is important since many of a brand's features can be communicated through the ad's text, but convincing consumers to read is difficult. The second factor is that repetition often increases recall.[30] As we discuss in Chapter 9, subsequent exposures, while generating less attention, appear to reinforce the learning that occurred on the first exposure.

Attractive Visuals   Individuals tend to be attracted to pleasant stimuli and repelled by unpleasant stimuli. This explains the ability of *attractive visuals* such as mountain scenes and attractive models to draw consumer attention to an advertisement. In fact, an ad's visual or pictorial component can have a strong influence on attention independent of other characteristics. In one study of over 1,300 print ads, the ad's picture garnered more attention than any other ad element (e.g., brand and text elements) regardless of its size. This *picture superiority* effect on attention demonstrates the importance of an ad's visual component and suggests why the heavy use of pictures in contemporary print advertising may be justified. However, since attention is limited, drawing attention to one element of an ad can detract from others. For example, increasing picture size in a print ad reduces the amount of attention consumers pay to the brand.[31]

Any factor that draws attention to itself and away from the brand and its selling points has to be used with caution. An ad's visual component represents one such factor. Attractive models represent another. One company found that putting a provocatively dressed model in their print ad drew attention away from their product and toward the model. As a consequence, consumer recall of their brand name 72 hours after exposure to the ad was reduced by 27 percent![32]

Color and Movement   Both *color* and *movement* serve to attract attention, with brightly colored and moving items being more noticeable. Certain colors and color characteristics create feelings of excitement and arousal, which are related to attention. Brighter colors are more arousing than dull. And, *warm* colors such as reds and yellows are more arousing than *cool* colors such as blues and grays.[33]

In-store, a brightly colored package or display is more apt to receive attention. Retailers interested in encouraging impulse purchases may utilize red in their displays given its ability to attract attention and generate feelings of excitement.[34] Also, point-of-purchase displays with moving parts and signage are more likely to draw attention and increase sales. Thus, companies like Eddie Bauer are choosing dynamic digital signage over static displays.[35]

Color and movement are also important in advertising. Thus, banner ads with dynamic animation attract more attention than similar ads without dynamic animation.[36] In a study of Yellow Page advertising, color ads were attended to sooner, more frequently, and longer than noncolor ads.[37] Figure 8-3 shows the relative attention-attracting ability of black-and-white and of four-color magazine ads of different sizes.

Illustration 8-3 shows two ads that are identical except for the use of color. The ad with the color was noticed by significantly more readers than was the black-and-white ad.

Position   *Position* refers to the placement of an object in physical space or time. In retail stores, items that are easy to find or that stand out are more likely to attract attention. End-caps and kiosks are used for this reason. In addition, since items near the center of a consumer's visual field are more likely to be noticed than those on the periphery, consumer goods manufacturers compete fiercely for eye-level space in grocery stores.[38]

Position effects in advertising often depend on the medium and how consumers normally interact with that medium. In print contexts, ads on the right-hand page receive more attention than those on the left based on how we peruse magazines and newspapers. Attention within an ad is also affected by the positioning of elements[39] and how we read. U.S. readers tend to scan print ads from top left to bottom right, much the same way we read. As a consequence, so-called *high-impact* zones in print ads and other print documents

Color and Size Impact on Attention* | **FIGURE 8-3**

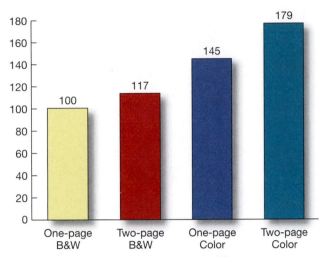

*Readership of a 1-page black and white ad was set at 100.
Source: "How Important Is Color to an Ad?" *Starch Tested Copy,* February 1989, p. 1, Roper Starch Worldwide, Inc.

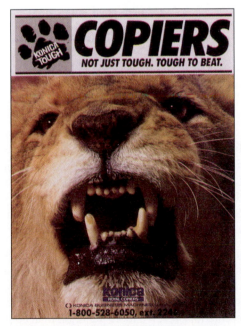 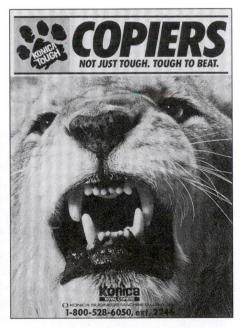

Courtesy of Konica Business Machines, U.S.A.

ILLUSTRATION 8-3

Color can attract attention to an ad. In this case, the color ad had a noted score of 62 percent, compared with 44 percent for the identical black-and-white ad.

tend to be more toward the top and left of the ad. In online contexts, vertical banners attract more attention then horizontal banners, perhaps because they stand out from the typically horizontal orientation of most print communications.[40] In television, the probability of a commercial being viewed and remembered drops sharply as it moves from being the first to air during a break to the last to air since consumers often engage in other activities during commercial breaks.[41]

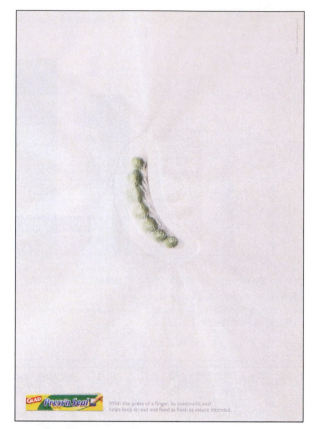

"GLAD® and PRESS'N'SEAL® are registered trademarks of The Glad
Products Company. Used with permission." "© 2005 The Glad Products
Company. Reprinted with permission."

Isolation   *Isolation* is separating a stimulus object from other objects. In-store, the use of stand-alone kiosks is based on this principle. In advertising, the use of "white space" (placing a brief message in the center of an otherwise blank or white advertisement) is based on this principle, as is surrounding a key part of a radio commercial with a brief moment of silence.[42] Illustration 8-4 shows an effective print ad that uses isolation and contrast (discussed shortly). This ad for Glad Press'n Seal contains only the peapod-shaped outline of peas in the Glad wrapping surrounded by a white background.

Format   Catalog merchants wishing to display multiple items per page often create an environment in which the competition for attention across items reduces attention to all of the items. However, with proper arrangement and formatting, this competition for attention can be reduced and sales improved.[43] *Format* refers to the manner in which the message is presented. In general, simple, straightforward presentations receive more attention than complex presentations. Elements in the message that increase the effort required to process the message tend to decrease attention. Advertisements that lack a clear visual point of reference or have inappropriate movement (too fast, slow, or "jumpy") increase the processing effort and decrease attention. Likewise, audio messages that are difficult to understand due to foreign accents, inadequate volume, or a speech rate which is too fast[44] also reduce attention.

Contrast and Expectations   Consumers pay more attention to stimuli that *contrast* with their background than to stimuli that blend with it. Nissan's use of color ads for its Infinity G35 in newspapers demonstrates an effective use of contrast.[45]

Contrast is related to the idea of expectations. Expectations drive our perceptions of contrast. Packaging, in-store displays, and ads that differ from our expectations tend to get noticed. For example, ads that differ from the type of ad consumers *expect* for a product category often motivate more attention than ads that are more typical for the product category.[46]

One concern of marketers is that once a promotion becomes familiar to consumers it will lose its ability to attract attention. **Adaptation level theory** suggests that if a stimulus doesn't change, over time we adapt or habituate to it and begin to notice it less. Thus, an ad that we initially notice when it's new may lose its ability to capture our attention as we become familiar with it. This familiarity effect is not uncommon. However, one study finds that by being original (that is, unexpected, surprising, unique), an advertisement can continue to attract attention even after consumers are familiar with it.[47] Illustration 8-5 shows a print ad that is unique and original compared to typical ads in the soda category.

Diet Sunkist is a registered trademark of Sunkist Growers, Inc. Used under license by Dr. Pepper/Seven Up, Inc. © 2005 Dr. Pepper/Seven Up, Inc.

Interestingness   What one is interested in is generally an individual characteristic. Snowboarders would be likely to attend to ads or shop in stores related to that activity, whereas nonboarders would not. However, there are characteristics of the message, store, and in-store display themselves that cause them to be of interest to a large percentage of the population. For example, in-store displays that utilize "tie-ins" to sporting events and movies appear to generate considerably more interest, attention, and sales than a simple brand sign.[48]

In advertising, factors that increase curiosity such as a plot, the possibility of a surprise ending, and uncertainty as to the point of the message until the end, can increase interest and the attention paid to the ad. Folgers' series of ads concerning the evolving relationship between a man and woman (virtually a soap opera) attracted a great deal of attention even among people not at all interested in coffee. In fact, while many DVR users skip commercials, one study found that more than 90 percent watched *certain* ads because they found them interesting.[49] Another study found that consumers were more likely to continue watching TV ads that were highly entertaining.[50]

Information Quantity   A final stimulus factor, *information quantity,* represents the number of cues in the stimulus field. Cues can relate to the features of the brand itself, typical users of the brand, typical usage situations, and so on. This information can be provided on packaging, in displays, on Web sites, and in ads.

Information helps consumers make decisions. But is more information better? In advertising, the answer is that it depends on a number of factors including the media used. In print advertising, information appears to attract attention, while in TV advertising information appears to reduce attention. One explanation is that increases in information quantity in TV ads quickly lead to **information overload** since (unlike print ads) consumers have no control over the pace of exposure.[51] Information overload occurs when consumers are confronted with so much information that they cannot or will not attend to all of it. The result can be suboptimal decisions.

Individual Factors

Individual factors are characteristics which distinguish one individual from another. Generally speaking, consumer motivation and ability are the major individual factors affecting attention.

Motivation   *Motivation* is a drive state created by consumer *interests* and *needs*. Interests are a reflection of overall lifestyle as well as a result of goals (e.g., becoming an accomplished guitar player) and needs (e.g., hunger). *Product involvement* indicates motivation or interest in a specific product category. Product involvement can be temporary or enduring. You might be temporarily involved with dishwashers if yours stops working, but involved with guitars and music your entire life. Either way, product involvement motivates attention. For example, one study found that product involvement increases the amount of attention paid to print ads.[52] Another study found that consumers were more likely to click on banners for products they were involved with. *External* stimulus characteristics like animation had less influence on these consumers since they were already *internally* motivated.[53]

One way marketers have responded to consumer interests and involvement is by developing smart banners for the Internet. **Smart banners** are *banner ads that are activated based on terms used in search engines.*[54] Such *behavioral targeting* strategies are available for general Web sites as well and they appear to be quite effective. For example, during one ad campaign, surfers on www.wsj.com who visited travel-related columns were targeted as potential travelers and "were 'followed' around the site and served American Airlines ads, no matter what section of wsj.com they were reading."[55] Attention was higher for these targeted ads, as was brand and message recall.

Ability   *Ability* refers to the capacity of individuals to attend to and process information. Ability is related to knowledge and familiarity with the product, brand, or promotion. An audiophile, for example, is more capable of attending to highly detailed product information about stereo equipment than a novice. As a consequence, experts can attend to more information, more quickly and more effectively than novices and tend to be less plagued by information overload. One study found that consumers with higher education and greater health-related experience were more likely to pay attention to the highly detailed technical information in "direct-to-consumer" pharmaceutical ads.[56]

Brand familiarity is an ability factor related to attention. Those with high brand familiarity may require less attention to the brand's ads due to their high existing knowledge. For example, one exposure appears to be all that is needed to capture attention and generate click through with banner ads when brand familiarity is high. In contrast, the clickthrough rate is very low on the first exposure when brand familiarity is low, but increases dramatically on the fifth exposure.[57] Consumers with low brand familiarity appear to require more banner attention to yield the knowledge and trust needed to drive further attention via clickthrough to the site.

Situational Factors

Situational factors include stimuli in the environment other than the focal stimulus (i.e., the ad or package) and temporary characteristics of the individual that are induced by the environment, such as time pressures or a crowded store. Clutter and program involvement are two major situational factors affecting attention.

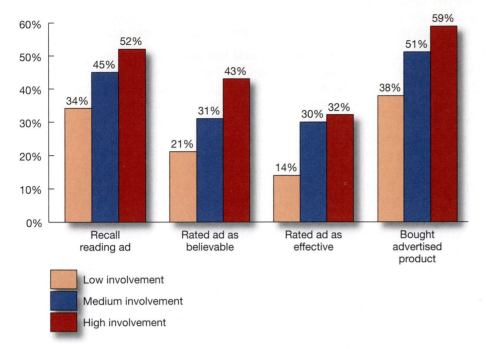

Source: *Cahners Advertising Research Report 120.1 and 120.12* (Boston: Cahners Publishing, undated).

Clutter   *Clutter* represents the density of stimuli in the environment. In-store research suggests that cluttering the environment with too many point-of-purchase displays decreases the attention consumers pay to a given display. This explains why companies such as Wal-Mart have made a concerted effort to reduce the number of displays in their stores.[58] In advertising, consumers pay less attention to a commercial in a large cluster of commercials than they do to one in a smaller set.[59] You may have noticed cable channels moving more to a single-sponsor format and actually promoting the fact that their programs will have fewer commercials!

Program Involvement   *Program involvement* refers to how interested viewers are in the program or editorial content surrounding the ads (as opposed to involvement with the ad or brand). In general, the audience is attending to the medium because of the program or editorial content, not the advertisement. In fact, as we saw earlier, many individuals actively avoid commercials by zapping them. Does the nature of the program or editorial content in which an ad appears influence the attention that the ad will receive? The answer to this question is clearly yes.[60] Figure 8-4 demonstrates the positive impact that involvement with a magazine has on attention to print ads.

Nonfocused Attention

Thus far we have been discussing a fairly high involvement attention process in which the consumer focuses attention on some aspect of the environment due to stimulus, individual, or situational factors. However, stimuli may be attended to without deliberate or conscious focusing of attention. A classic example is the *cocktail party effect* whereby an individual engaged in a conversation with a friend isn't consciously aware of other conversations at a crowded party until someone in another group says something relevant such as mentioning her name. This example suggests we are processing a host of stimuli at a subconscious level and mechanisms in our brain evaluate this information to decide what warrants deliberate and conscious attention. In fact, the idea behind *hemispheric lateralization* is that different parts of our brain are better suited for focused versus nonfocused attention.

Hemispheric Lateralization   **Hemispheric lateralization** is a term applied to activities that take place on each side of the brain. The left side of the brain is primarily responsible for verbal information, symbolic representation, sequential analysis, and the ability to be conscious and report what is happening. It controls those activities we typically call *rational thought*. The right side of the brain deals with pictorial, geometric, timeless, and nonverbal information without the individual being able to verbally report it. It works with images and impressions.

The left brain needs fairly frequent rest. However, the right brain can easily scan large amounts of information over an extended time period. This led Krugman to suggest that "it is the right brain's picture-taking ability that permits the rapid screening of the environment—to select what it is the left brain should focus on."[61] One study of banner ads found evidence of preconscious screening. Web surfers seem able to spot a banner ad without actually looking directly at it. As a consequence, direct attention to banner ads occurred only 49 percent of the time. It seems that experience with the Web allows consumers to build up knowledge about banner characteristics (typical size and location) that is used to avoid direct attention.[62]

However, just because consumers don't pay direct attention to an advertisement doesn't mean it can't influence them. For example, brands contained in ads to which subjects are exposed but pay little or no attention (incidental exposure) nonetheless have an enhanced probability of being considered for purchase.[63]

Subliminal Stimuli   A message presented so fast or so softly or so masked by other messages that one is not aware of seeing or hearing it is called a **subliminal stimulus.** A subliminal ad is different from a "normal" ad in that it "hides" key persuasive information within the ad by making it so weak that it is difficult or impossible for an individual to physically detect. Normal ads present key persuasive information to consumers so that it is easily perceived.

Subliminal advertising has been the focus of intense study and public concern. It's one thing for consumers to decide not to pay attention to an ad. It's quite another for advertisers to try to bypass consumers' perceptual defenses by using subliminal stimuli.

Two books triggered public interest in masked subliminal advertising.[64] The author "documents" numerous advertisements that, once you are told where to look and what to look for, appear to contain the word *sex* in ice cubes, phalli in mixed drinks, and nude bodies in the shadows. Such masked symbols, deliberate or accidental, do not appear to affect standard measures of advertising effectiveness or influence consumption behavior.[65] Research on messages presented too rapidly to elicit awareness indicates that such messages have little or no effect.[66] In addition, there is no evidence marketers are using subliminal messages.[67]

INTERPRETATION

Interpretation is *the assignment of meaning to sensations.* Interpretation is related to how we comprehend and make sense of incoming information. It is a function of the *gestalt,* or pattern, formed by the characteristics of the stimulus, the individual, and the situation.

Several aspects of interpretation are important to consider. First, it is generally a relative process rather than absolute, often referred to as **perceptual relativity.** It is often difficult for people to make interpretations in the absence of some reference point. Consider the following actual scenario:

> An episode of QVC Network's *Extreme Shopping* program offers Muhammad Ali's boxing robe (priced at over $12,000), followed by Jane Mansfield's former mansion (almost $3.5 million), and a Volkswagen Beetle painted by Peter Max ($100,000). Then, signed and personalized Peter Max prints were offered for about $200.

In line with the notion of relativity, consumers interpreted the print price as lower when it followed the higher priced items.[68]

A second aspect of interpretation is that it tends to be subjective and open to a host of psychological biases. The subjective nature of interpretation can be seen in the distinction between *semantic meaning,* the conventional meaning assigned to a word such as found in the dictionary, and *psychological meaning,* the specific meaning assigned a word by a given individual or group of individuals based on their experiences, expectations, and the context in which the term is used.

Marketers must be concerned with psychological meaning as it is the subjective experience, not objective reality, that drives consumer behavior. A firm may introduce a high-quality new brand at a lower price than competitors because the firm is more efficient. However, if consumers interpret the lower price to mean lower quality (and they often do), the new brand will not be successful regardless of the objective reality.[69]

A final aspect of interpretation is that it can be a cognitive "thinking" process or an affective "emotional" process. **Cognitive interpretation** is *a process whereby stimuli are placed into existing categories of meaning.*[70] As we saw earlier, consumers categorize ads as expected or unexpected, a process which can vary by culture and individual.[71] In countries like France where ads are more sexually explicit, nudity may be seen as more appropriate than in the United States. However, individual assessments will also vary as a function of age, religiosity, gender, and so on.

Products can also be categorized. When DVD players were first introduced, most consumers probably grouped them in the general category of video players. With further experience, consumers likely formed "finer-grained" subcategories for various types and altered their categorization for VCRs in the process. The more radically "new" a product is (a discontinuous innovation), the more difficult it is to categorize and interpret.[72] Unless consumers are provided explicit help by marketers, this may slow their understanding and acceptance of the product.[73]

Affective interpretation is *the emotional or feeling response triggered by a stimulus such as an ad*. Emotional responses can range from positive (upbeat, exciting, warm) to neutral (disinterested) to negative (anger, fear, frustration). Like cognitive interpretation, there are "normal" (within-culture) emotional responses to many stimuli (e.g., most Americans experience a feeling of warmth when seeing pictures of young children with kittens). Likewise, there are also individual variations to this response (a person allergic to cats might have a negative emotional response to such a picture). Consumers confronting new products or brands often assign them to emotional as well as cognitive categories.[74] The ad shown in Illustration 8-6 is likely to trigger an emotional interpretation as well as a cognitive one.

Individual Characteristics

Marketing stimuli have meaning *only* as individuals interpret them.[75] Individuals are not passive interpreters of marketing and other messages but actively assign meaning based on their needs, desires, experiences, and expectations.

Consumers have emotional responses to or interpretations of ads as well as cognitive ones. This ad is likely to produce an emotional or feeling response in many members of its target audience.

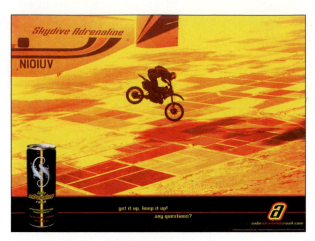

Courtesy Pepsi; Agency: Jager di Paola Kemp Design.

Traits Inherent physiological and psychological traits, which drive our needs and desires, influence how a stimulus is interpreted. From a *physiological* standpoint, consumers differ in their sensitivity to stimuli. Some children are more sensitive to the bitter taste of certain chemicals found in green leafy vegetables such as spinach.[76] Tab (a diet cola containing saccharine) maintains a small but fiercely loyal customer base, most likely among those who (unlike most of us) don't physiologically perceive saccharine as bitter.

From a *psychological* standpoint, consumers have natural cognitive, emotional, and behavioral predispositions. As just one example, some people experience emotions more strongly than others, a trait known as *affect intensity*. A number of studies have found that consumers who are higher in affect intensity experience stronger emotional reactions to any given advertisement.[77] We discuss other personality differences in Chapter 10.

Learning and Knowledge The meanings attached to such "natural" things as time, space, relationships, and colors are learned and vary widely across cultures, as we saw in Chapter 2. Consumers also learn about marketer-created stimuli like brands and promotions through their experiences with them. This experience and knowledge affects interpretations. One general finding is that consumers tend to interpret information in ways that favor their preferred brands. In one study, those higher in loyalty to a firm tended to discredit negative publicity about the firm and thus were less affected by it.[78] Similarly, another study found that consumers infer more positive motives to a company's price increase if it has a strong reputation.[79]

The ad in Illustration 8-7 uses color to reinforce an interpretation that Godiva truffles are "rich" and "luscious." This works because we have learned to assign this type of meaning to the color gold.

Expectations Individuals' interpretations of stimuli tend to be consistent with their *expectations,* an effect referred to as the *expectation bias*. Most consumers expect dark brown pudding to taste like chocolate, not vanilla, because dark pudding is generally chocolate flavored and vanilla pudding is generally cream colored. In a taste test, 100 percent of a sample of college students accepted dark brown *vanilla* pudding as chocolate.[80] Thus, their expectations, cued by color, led to an interpretation that was inconsistent with objective reality.

Consumers' expectations are the result of learning and can be formed very quickly, as the old saying "first impressions matter" suggests. Once established, these expectations can

Courtesy Godiva Chocolatiers, Inc.

ILLUSTRATION 8-7

Colors are often used to convey product characteristics and meanings. The use of gold in this ad conveys a meaning of richness.

wield enormous influence[81] and can be hard to change. Many consumers expect, for example, that well-known brands are higher quality. As a consequence consumers frequently evaluate the performance of a well-known brand as higher than that of an *identical* product with an unknown brand name. Many consumers have also come to expect that brands with some sort of in-store signage are on sale. As a consequence, one study found that brands with promotional signs on them in retail stores are interpreted as having reduced prices even though the signs don't indicate a price reduction and the prices aren't actually reduced.[82]

Situational Characteristics

A variety of situational characteristics impact interpretation, including temporary characteristics of the individual such as time pressure and mood[83] and the physical characteristics of the situation such as the number and characteristics of other individuals present, the nature of the material surrounding the message in question, and so on.

Basically, the situation provides a context within which the focal stimulus is interpreted. The **contextual cues** present in the situation play a role in consumer interpretation *independent* of the actual stimulus. There are innumerable contextual cues in any given marketing context—here we examine just a few examples. *Color* can be a contextual cue. A recent study of online advertising examined various aspects of background color present during Web page loads. Certain color characteristics were found to elicit feelings of relaxation (blue more relaxing than red) and these feelings increased perceptions of faster Web page loading even when actual speed was identical.[84]

The *nature of the programming* surrounding a brand's advertisements can also be a contextual cue. Both Coca-Cola and General Foods have refused to advertise some products during news broadcasts because they believe that "bad" news might affect the interpretation of their products. According to a Coca-Cola spokesperson,

> It's a Coca-Cola corporate policy not to advertise on TV news because there's going to be some bad news in there, and Coke is an upbeat, fun product.[85]

The previous example expresses a concern about the impact that the content of the material surrounding an ad will have on the interpretation of the ad. As Coca-Cola suspects, it appears that ads are evaluated in a more positive light when surrounded with positive programming.[86]

Stimulus Characteristics

The stimulus is the basic entity to which an individual responds and includes the product, package, advertisement, in-store display, and so on. Consumers react to and interpret basic traits of the stimulus (size, shape, color), the way the stimulus is organized, and changes in the stimulus. As we have seen, all of these processes are likely to be heavily influenced by the individual and situation.

Traits Specific traits of the stimulus such as size, shape, and color affect interpretation. The meaning of many stimulus traits is learned. Canada Dry's sugar-free ginger ale sales increased dramatically when the can was changed to green and white from red. Red is interpreted as a "cola" color and thus conflicted with the taste of ginger ale.[87] Other aspects of stimulus interpretation are more innate. For example, people tend to interpret tall or elongated packages as containing more than that of a shorter package of equal volume. This in turn appears to affect both consumption and subsequent satisfaction with the brand.[88]

Beyond specific traits, stimuli can also be generally categorized as easier or harder to process. *Ease of processing* has important implications for consumer categorization and interpretation. Consumers appear to prefer stimuli that they perceive as easy to process. In addition, a number of studies have found that making a statement easier to process increases the chances that consumers will perceive the statement to be true regardless of its actual truth. Various strategies, including repetition, can be used to increase perceived ease of processing.[89]

Another general trait is the extent to which the stimulus is unexpected, a trait sometimes referred to as *incongruity*. Incongruity increases attention, as we saw earlier. However, it also increases liking, in part because of the pleasure consumers derive from "solving the puzzle" presented by the incongruity. As a consequence, products and ads that deviate somewhat from established norms (without going too far) are often better liked. Incongruity often requires that consumers go beyond what is directly stated or presented in order to make sense of the stimulus. These inferences, which we discuss later in the chapter, are an important part of interpretation. Consumer Insight 8-2 provides a closer look at how *rhetorical figures* can be used to enhance incongruity and influence both attention and interpretation.

Organization **Stimulus organization** refers to *the physical arrangement of the stimulus objects*. Organization affects consumer interpretation and categorization. For example, you likely perceive the letters that make up the words you are reading as words rather than as

Examine the ad in Illustration 8-8. Is this ad unique in any way? How does it impact your thoughts and feelings? As media outlets become more cluttered, companies struggle to find advertising tactics that grab consumer attention and draw them into the ad. One tactic that seems to have potential is the use of rhetorical figures. **Rhetorical figures** *involve the use of an unexpected twist or artful deviation in how a message is communicated either visually in the ad's picture or verbally in the ad's text or headline.*[90] Common rhetorical figures include rhymes such as Bounty's "quicker, picker, upper," or uni-ball's "write the good write," and metaphors such as Kiwi's "Unpolished shoes are the open fly of footwear" or Srixon's (golf ball) "Fire in the hole."

The unexpected nature of rhetorical figures attracts and holds attention as consumers decipher the ad's meaning. In one study of over 800 print ads, rhetorical figures in the ad's headline increased readership (a measure of total attention) between 15 and 42 percent over literal headlines. Clearly rhetorical figures have the power to attract and hold attention!

Rhetorical figures also influence how consumers interpret an ad. Unpolished shoes aren't *literally* an unzipped garment (open fly). However, the meanings associated with "open fly" (embarrassing, distasteful, bad for your image) are what Kiwi hopes consumers will relate to unpolished shoes. Such meaning would be harder to communicate and probably less convincing if directly stated in the ad. In addition, the artful twist or deviation of rhetorical figures tends to generate more positive attitudes toward the ad.

Marketers need to be careful when using rhetorical figures across ethnic subcultures since their interpretation often requires an understanding of embedded cultural meanings which don't always transfer across cultures. Thus, the "open fly" in Kiwi's ad might work well with native English speakers but not so well with first generation Asian Americans.

Marketers also need to be careful not to overuse rhetorical figures within an ad. Overuse can trigger perceptual defenses by heightening consumer skepticism toward the advertiser's motives.

Critical Thinking Questions

1. How do rhetorical figures work?
2. What other types of rhetorical figures can you think of?
3. Besides ethnicity, what other factors might influence the effectiveness of rhetorical figures?
4. What ethical concerns, if any, can you see with the use of rhetorical figures?

individual letters. This effect is enhanced by the fact that each word has letters that are close together and is separated by larger spaces, a principle called proximity. We discuss this and other principles next.

Proximity refers to the fact that *stimuli positioned close together are perceived as belonging to the same category.* Sometimes proximity comes from the stimulus itself. For example, the ad in Illustration 8-9 involves a billboard and a mannequin. Consumers don't see these as unrelated stimuli, but rather see the proximity of the vacuum hose and the woman and interpret the billboard as meaning that the AEG Vampyr Rosso is a powerful vacuum cleaner.

Sometimes proximity results from the relationship of the stimulus to its context as in ambush marketing. **Ambush marketing** involves *any communication or activity that implies, or from which one could reasonably infer, that an organization is associated with an event, when in fact it is not.* A common form of ambush marketing is to advertise heavily during the event. Proximity would lead many to believe that the company was a sponsor of the event even if it was not.[91]

Closure involves *presenting an incomplete stimulus with the goal of getting consumers to complete it and thus become more engaged and involved.* Advertisers will often use

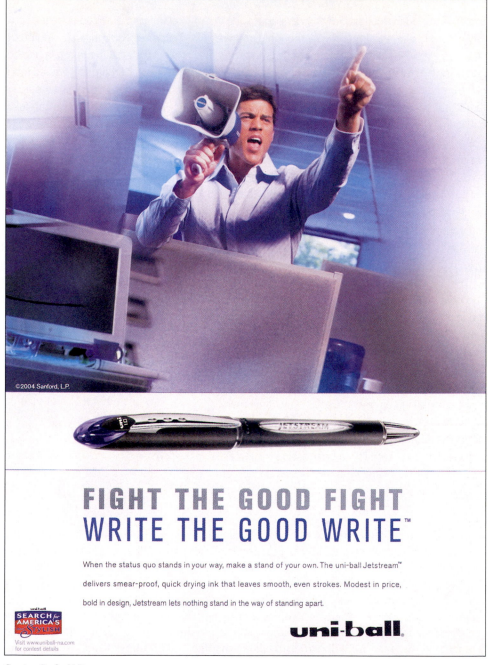

Courtesy Sanford LP.

incomplete stimuli in this manner since closure is often an automatic response engaged in by consumers in order to interpret message meaning. Not surprisingly, increasing consumer ad involvement also increases recall, as we will discuss more in Chapter 9.[92] Illustration 8-10 demonstrates the closure concept. Interpretation is enhanced by perceiving the three parallel lines as the letter E. The red color of the lines draws attention to the incompleteness and also reinforces the core meaning of the ad.

Courtesy HVR/FCB Advertising/The Netherlands.

Courtesy General Motors Archives.

Figure-ground involves *presenting the stimulus in such a way that it is perceived as the focal object to be attended to and all other stimuli are perceived as the background.* This strategy is often used in advertising, where the goal is to make the brand stand out as the prominent focal object to which consumers will attend. Absolut, a Swedish vodka, uses figure-ground very effectively. Each ad uses the natural elements in the ad to "form" the figure of a bottle, as with Absolut Mandarin where the bottle is formed by pieces of orange peel.

Changes   In order to interpret stimulus change, consumers must be able to categorize and interpret the new stimulus relative to the old. Interpreting change requires both the ability to detect change and then assign meaning to that change. Sometimes consumers won't be able to detect a change. Sometimes they can detect a change but interpret it as unimportant.

The physiological ability of an individual to distinguish between similar stimuli is called **sensory discrimination.** This involves such variables as the sound of stereo systems, the taste of food products, or the clarity of display screens. The minimum amount that one brand can differ from another (or from its previous version) with the difference still being noticed is referred to as the **just noticeable difference (j.n.d.).** The higher the initial level of an attribute, the greater that attribute must be changed before the change will be noticed. Thus, a small addition of salt to a pretzel would not likely be noticed unless that pretzel contained only a small amount of salt to begin with.

As a general rule, *individuals typically do not notice relatively small differences between brands or changes in brand attributes.* Makers of candy bars have utilized this principle for years. Since the price of cocoa fluctuates widely, they simply make small adjustments in the size of the candy bar rather than altering price. Since marketers want some product changes, such as reductions in the size, to go unnoticed, they may attempt to make changes that fall below the j.n.d. This strategy, sometimes referred to as *weighting out,* appears to be on the increase. However, if and when consumers do notice, the potential backlash may be quite severe.[93] *What is your evaluation of the ethics of this practice?*

After *noticing* a change or difference, consumers must *interpret* it. Some changes are meaningful and some are not. The relationship between change and consumers' valuation of that change tends to follow the pattern discussed for j.n.d. The higher the initial level of an attribute, the greater the attribute must change before it is seen as meaningful. Change is often interpreted with respect to some *referent state.* The referent state might be a brand's prior model or a competitor model. *Reference price* is also a referent state. Consumers can bring *internal* reference prices with them based on prior experience. Also, marketers can provide a reference in the form of *manufacturer suggested retail price (MSRP).* Consumers then are more likely to interpret the sale price with respect to the MSRP which, if favorable, should increase perceived value of the offer and likelihood of purchase.[94]

Consumer Inferences

When it comes to marketing, "what you see is not what you get." That's because interpretation often requires consumers to make inferences. An **inference** *goes beyond what is directly stated or presented.* Consumers use available data *and* their own ideas to draw conclusions about information that is not provided.

Quality Signals   Inferences are as numerous and divergent as consumers themselves. However, some inferences related to product quality are relatively consistent across consumers. Here consumers use their own experiences and knowledge to draw inferences about product quality based on a nonquality cue.

Price-perceived quality is an inference based on the popular adage "you get what you pay for." Consumers often infer that higher-priced brands possess higher quality than do lower-priced brands.[95] Consumers sometimes take price discounts as a signal of lower quality, which is a major concern for companies such as General Motors who rely heavily on such tactics.[96]

Advertising intensity is also a quality signal. Consumers tend to infer that more heavily advertised brands are higher quality.[97] One reason is that effort is believed to predict success, and ad spending is seen as an indicator of effort. Any factor related to advertising expense such as medium, use of color, and repetition, can increase quality perceptions and choice.[98]

Warranties are another quality signal, with longer warranties generally signaling higher quality. Consumers infer that a firm wouldn't offer a longer warranty if it weren't confident in the quality of its products, since honoring the warranty would be expensive.[99]

Price, advertising, and warranties are just a few quality cues. Others include *country of origin (COO)* in which consumers interpret products more positively when they are manufactured in a country they perceive positively,[100] as well as *brand* effects, where well-known brands are perceived as higher quality than are unknown brands.

In general, quality signals operate more strongly when consumers lack the expertise to make informed judgments on their own, when consumer motivation or interest in the decision is low, and when other quality-related information is lacking.

Interpreting Images   Consumer inferences from visual images are becoming increasingly important as advertisers increase their use of visual imagery.[101] Note how visuals dominate many print ads. For example, Clinique ran an ad that pictured a tall, clear glass of mineral water and ice cubes. A large slice of lime was positioned on the lip of the glass. In the glass with the ice cubes and mineral water were a tube of Clinique lipstick and a container of cheek base. Nothing else appeared in the ad. *What does this mean?*

Obviously, in order to interpret the Clinique ad, consumers must infer meaning. Until recently, pictures in ads were thought to convey reality. If so, the Clinique ad is nonsensical. Is Clinique guilty of ineffective advertising? No. All of us intuitively recognize that pictures do more than represent reality; they supply meaning. Thus, one interpretation of the Clinique ad is "Clinique's new summer line of makeup is as refreshing as a tall glass of soda with a twist."

The verbal translation of the meaning conveyed by images is generally incomplete and inadequate. A picture is worth a thousand words not just because it may convey reality more efficiently than words but because it may convey meanings that words cannot adequately express.

Marketers must understand the meanings their audiences assign to various images and words, and use them in combination to construct messages that will convey the desired meaning. They must be sensitive to cultural differences since interpretation is highly contingent on shared cultural experience. For example, consumers in some cultures (termed high-context cultures) tend to "read between the lines." These consumers are very sensitive to cues in the communications setting such as tone of voice. On the other hand, consumers in low-context cultures tend to ignore such cues and focus more on the message's literal or explicit meaning. A recent study finds that consumers in high-context cultures such as the Philippines are more likely to infer implicit meanings from ad visuals than are those in low-context cultures such as the United States.[102] Illustration 8-11 is an example of an ad based heavily on imagery. *What does this ad mean to you? Would it mean the same to older consumers? Consumers from other cultures?*

Missing Information and Ethical Concerns   When data about an attribute are missing, consumers may assign it a value based on a presumed relationship between that attribute and one for which data are available; they may assign it the average of their assessments of the available attributes; they may assume it to be weaker than the attributes for which data are supplied; or any of a large number of other strategies may be used.[103]

Consider the following hypothetical ad copy:

- The Subaru Outback gets better gas mileage than the Pontiac Aztek.
- It has more cargo space than the Saturn VUE.
- It has more power than the Toyota RAV4.

Pictures and imagery do more than merely represent reality. They convey feelings and meanings that often cannot be expressed in words.

Courtesy Pfizer, Inc.

Some consumers would infer from this that the Subaru gets better gas mileage than the VUE and the RAV4; has more cargo space than the Aztek and the RAV4; and has more power than the Aztek and the VUE.[104] These claims are not stated in the ad, making it clear that certain types of information portrayal may lead to incorrect inferences and suboptimal consumer decisions. Thus, a factually correct ad could still mislead some consumers. *Are such ads ethical?*

As we saw in the opening example, consumers can be misled in a number of different ways. One way is that companies can make *direct claims* that are false. Claiming that something is mushroom in origin when it is really a fungus or mold appears to fall into this category. This is the easiest form of deception to detect and prosecute under the law. However, other types of deception are more subtle. These fall under the broad category of *claim-belief discrepancies,* whereby a communication leads consumers to believe something about the product that is not true even though it doesn't present a direct false claim. For example, the Federal Trade Commission (FTC) felt that Kraft Foods' early ads for Kraft Cheese Singles might be misleading based on claim-belief discrepancy. That's because their ads focused on the importance of calcium and the fact that each slice was made from 5 ounces of milk. The FTC's concern was that reasonable consumers would infer that Kraft Cheese Singles contained the same amount of calcium as five ounces of milk even though this was not directly stated in their ads. This inference is wrong since processing milk into cheese reduces calcium content. Since parents might use Kraft Cheese Singles as a calcium source for their kids, this was of particular concern. Although more difficult from a legal standpoint, the FTC can and does hold companies responsible for claim-belief discrepancies as we see with Kraft.[105] Our understanding and regulation of deception continues to evolve as we gain a better understanding of consumer information processing. This is discussed in more detail in Chapter 20.

PERCEPTION AND MARKETING STRATEGY

Perception holds critical implications for marketing strategy in a number of areas. We turn to these next.

Retail Strategy

Retailers often use exposure very effectively. Store interiors are designed with frequently purchased items (canned goods, fresh fruits/vegetables, meats) separated so that the average consumer will travel through more of the store. This increases total exposure. High-margin items are often placed in high-traffic areas to capitalize on increased exposure.

Shelf position and amount of shelf space influence which items and brands are allocated attention. Point-of-purchase displays also attract attention and boost sales.[106] Stores are designed with highly visible shelves and overhead signs to make locating items (an information-processing task) as easy as possible. And **cross-promotions,** whereby signage in one area of the store promotes complementary products in another (milk signage in the cookie aisle), can also be effective.

In recent years, many retailers have felt a need to reduce the number of SKUs (stock keeping units—individual items such as brands, sizes, and versions) within product categories in order to reduce operating costs. Category managers at companies such as Kraft Foods have felt a similar pressure.[107] However, they have been reluctant to do so for fear that consumers will perceive this as a reduction in choice and shop elsewhere. What should they do? One study shows that eliminating low-preference items while holding total product category shelf space constant does not have a negative impact on consumer perceptions.[108] Another study finds that reducing the number of SKUs in a category can actually *increase* category sales! The key seems to be eliminating brands or attributes that are perceived as relatively unimportant or redundant in the category.[109]

Brand Name and Logo Development

Shakespeare notwithstanding, marketers do not believe that "a rose by any other name would smell as sweet." *Would you rather have a soft drink sweetened with NutraSweet or with aspartame?* Mountain Dew's marketing director ascribes part of the success of Code Red to its name: "Had it been called 'Mountain Dew Cherry' it would've done very differently."[110] Brand names can influence anything from food taste to color preference. One study found that people preferred avocado to light green even though the actual color was exactly the same![111] Effects such as this can be related back to expectation biases. That is, the name sets up an expectation which, in turn, biases people's perceptions of the actual experience. Given the tendency toward global brands, it is easy to imagine how complex creating an appropriate name can be.[112]

Linguistic Considerations   Sometimes brand names start out having no inherent meaning, but gain associations over time as consumers gain experience with them. Ford and Toyota are examples. However, marketers increasingly tap into linguistic characteristics of words to create brand names with inherent meaning right from the start. One aspect is inherent *semantic meaning* or *morpheme*. NutraSweet took advantage of morphemes to imply nutritious and sweet. And Dodge has brought back its "Hemi" engine, a name associated with high performance.[113] A second aspect is sound or *phonemes*. Sounds of letters and words can symbolize product attributes. For example, heavier sounding vowels

(Frosh) might be better used to suggest richer creamier ice cream than lighter sounding vowels (Frish).[114]

Lexicon and other naming companies such as NameLab use these concepts to create names that convey appropriate meanings. Lexicon selected the Blackberry name for Research in Motion's handheld device because Berry suggests small, the "b" sound is associated strongly with relaxation, and the two b sounds at the beginning of black and berry are light and crisp suggesting speed. Thus, a name that suggests a handheld that is small, easy to use, and fast—every consumer's dream![115]

Branding Strategies   Marketers engage in numerous strategies to leverage strong existing brand names. One is **brand extension** where an existing brand extends to a new category with the same name such as Levi Strauss putting its Levi name on a line of upscale men's suits. Another is **co-branding,** an alliance in which two brands are put together on a single product. An example is "Intel Inside" Compaq computers. Brand extensions and co-branding can be positive or negative, as we'll discuss in Chapter 9. A key issue is *perceived fit* between the core brand and the extension or the two co-brands. Really poor fit (too much incongruity) is bad, as people find it hard to categorize and make sense of the new brand. For example, the Levi men's suit was a flop because the core Levi image of relaxed and casual did not fit a formal, upscale suit.[116]

Logo Design and Typographics   How a product or service name is presented—its *logo*—is also important.[117] Figure 8-5 shows the additional positive or negative impact the graphic part of a logo can have on the image associated with a name. Image was an overall measure based on such attributes as "trustworthy" and "high quality." One rating was obtained from consumers who saw only the company name; the second was in response to the full logo including the name.[118] *What advice would you offer these firms?*

Perhaps in trying to answer this last question, you realized that you don't have any criteria for making suggestions. Such criteria are hard to come by and we are just now

FIGURE 8-5   Logos Influence the Image Consumers Have of Firms

Name Only	Rated Very High	Name and Logo	Rated Very High	Percent Change
UPS	68%	UPS	58%	−15%
FedEx	67	FedEx	50	−25
Federal Express	62	FEDERAL EXPRESS	68	+10
United States Postal Service	53	UNITED STATES POSTAL SERVICE	54	+2

Note: The percentage shown on the Name and Logo columns is average top-box ratings ("agree strongly") within a 5-point rating scale on the image contribution attributes, based only on respondents who are aware of the company or brand.

beginning to understand why some logos work better than others. One study provides guidance, finding that logo symbols (such as Prudential's Rock) which are natural, moderately elaborate, and symmetrically balanced lead to higher levels of logo liking. *Natural* logos depict commonly experienced objects; *elaborate* logos entail complexity; *symmetrical* logos are visually balanced.

Beyond the logo symbol is also the shape and form of the letters in their name which relates to typeface and type font. Intuitively, for example, you might think that a fancy *scripted* font signals elegance and is better suited for a fountain pen than for a mountain bike. Turns out you would be right! Different fonts do evoke different meanings and an appropriate fit between the font and product can increase choice of the brand, independent of the name.[119] *Given these various criteria, can you now make suggestions to the firms?*[120]

Media Strategy

The explosion of media alternatives makes it difficult and expensive to gain exposure to key target audiences.[121] However, the fact that the exposure process is often selective rather than random is the underlying basis for effective media strategies. Specifically, determine to which media the consumers in the target market are most frequently exposed and place ad messages in those media. As one executive stated,

> We must look increasingly for matching media that will enable us best to reach carefully targeted, emerging markets. The rifle approach rather than the old shotgun.[122]

Consumer involvement can drive media exposure and strategy. For high-involvement products, ads should be placed in media outlets with content relevant to the product. Specialized media such as *Runner's World* or *Vogue* tend to attract readers who are interested in and receptive to ads for related products. In contrast, ads for low-involvement products should be placed in reputable media independent of content, as long as it is frequented by the target market.[123] In a situation such as this, the marketer must find media that the target market is interested in and place the advertising message in those media. Target markets as defined by age, ethnic group, social class, or stage in the family life cycle have differing media preferences which can then be used to select media outlets. Table 8-1 illustrates selective exposure to several magazines based on demographic characteristics.

Many marketers want consumers to visit their Web sites. These sites are often online magazines offering entertainment and education to attract consumers. For example, P&G's girls' health advice feature "Ask Iris" at BeingGirl.com gets 30,000 e-mail queries a week.[124] Technology continues to radically alter media choices beyond the Internet. Consider the impact of GPS technology on outdoor mobile ads in the following example.

> While a cab travels from one end of a city to the other, an electronic billboard on top changes according to location and time of day. Thanks to a satellite feed and Global Positioning System, the bright, attention-getting ads on the taxi roof keep changing. As the cab passes by a college, an ad for a bookstore appears. While the cab moves through the business district at noon, an ad for a local deli fills the screen. As the cab travels through a Hispanic neighborhood, a Spanish-language ad for a snack food is shown.[125]

Advertisements

Advertisements must perform two critical tasks—capture attention and convey meaning. Unfortunately, the techniques appropriate for accomplishing one task are often counterproductive for the other.

TABLE 8-1

Selective Exposure to Magazines Based on Demographic Characteristics*

Demographic Characteristics	Better Homes & Gardens	Cosmopolitan	Maxim	National Geographic	Family Circle
Gender					
Male	45	34	172	114	19
Female	151	161	34	87	175
Age					
18–24	56	217	337	98	38
25–34	91	151	200	80	77
35–44	112	99	52	106	105
45–54	119	77	31	124	124
55–64	117	32	6	101	123
65+	96	21	1	90	127
Education					
College graduate	108	100	111	154	80
High school graduate	101	92	61	74	111
Household income					
$75,000+	119	119	147	128	94
$40,000–$49,999	96	105	82	103	109
$20,000–$29,999	89	78	66	82	111

*100 represents an average level of usage.

Source: *Mediamark Reporter 2002—University* (New York: Mediamark Research Inc., March 2002).

What if you had to design a campaign to increase users for your firm's toilet bowl freshener but research shows your target market has little inherent interest in the product. What do you do? Two strategies seem reasonable. One is to *utilize stimulus characteristics* such as bright colors or surrealism to attract attention. The second is to *tie the message to a topic in which the target market is interested.*

However, using factors unrelated to the product category to attract attention must be used with caution. First, it may detract attention away from the core brand message since stimuli compete for limited attention. That's why companies often try to use humor, sex appeal, and celebrities in ways that are relevant to the product or message. Second, it may negatively affect *interpretation.* For example, humor in an insurance ad may result in the brand being interpreted as unreliable.

The ad shown in Illustration 8-12 appeared in *Outside* magazine. It uses color, contrast, and size (two full pages) to attract attention. However, the connection between these attention-attracting devices and the brand's features or image is not clear. *Does this ad inspire you to want to ski Mt. Bachelor?* (Management states that the ad was designed to attract snowboarders who it believes relate to the ad.)

Package Design and Labeling

Packages must also attract attention and convey information. Packaging has functional and perceptual components. Consider the candy coating of M&M's. It is functional because it keeps the chocolate from melting in your hands. But it is also perceptual. The bright colors are interesting and unique even though they don't taste different. One study varied the color variety (7 versus 10 colors) in a bowl of M&M's and found that as variety went up consumers ate more![126] M&M's has refocused on color by introducing bolder colors and emphasizing color in its ads. As one executive states, "We've always had color as a unique

Courtesy Mt. Bachelor.

point of difference, but we wanted to reinforce that message in a fresh, contemporary way."[127]

Bright colors, taller packages, and unusual shapes can be used to attract attention, convey meaning, and influence consumption.[128] Research also shows that unusual or uniquely shaped packages are perceived to be larger volume than an equal size package that is more typical or expected. That is, the very fact that a container attracts consumer attention causes them to infer that it must have been because it was larger in volume.[129]

Packages also contain product information and warnings. Ethical and legal considerations require marketers to place warning labels on a wide array of products such as cigarettes, alcoholic beverages, and many over-the-counter drugs. On the one hand there is the desire to effectively alert users to potential risks. On the other hand, there is a desire to avoid detracting unduly from product image. The key from an ethical and legal standpoint is to not err on the side of image at the expense of the consumer. Well-designed warnings appear to be at least somewhat effective. Factors reducing their effectiveness include overly technical or complex language and a failure to indicate the positive consequences of compliance.[130]

ILLUSTRATION 8-12

What is this ad for? It will attract attention. The critical questions are: Will it draw the reader into the message itself? and Will it convey the type of image the area wants readers of *Outside* magazine to have of Mt. Bachelor?

SUMMARY

Perception consists of those activities by which an individual acquires and assigns meaning to stimuli. Perception begins with *exposure*. This occurs when a stimulus comes within range of one of an individual's primary sensory receptors. People are exposed to only a small fraction of the available stimuli, and this is usually the result of self-selection as evidenced by high levels of *ad avoidance.* Marketers try to overcome avoidance by using tactics such as *product placement.*

Attention occurs when the stimulus activates one or more of the sensory receptors and the resulting sensations go into the brain for processing. People *selectively attend* to stimuli as a function of stimulus, individual, and situational factors. *Stimulus factors* are physical characteristics of the stimulus itself, such as contrast, size, intensity, attractiveness, color, movement, position, isolation, format, and information quantity. *Individual factors* are characteristics of the individual, such as motivation and ability. *Situational factors* include stimuli in the environment other than the focal stimulus and temporary characteristics of the individual that are induced by the environment. Clutter and program involvement are situational factors of particular interest to marketers.

Nonfocused attention occurs when a person takes in information without deliberate effort. *Hemispheric lateralization* is a term applied to activities that take place on each side of the brain. The left side of the brain is concerned primarily with those activities typically called rational thought and the ability to be conscious and report what is happening. The right side of the brain deals with pictorial, geometric, timeless, and nonverbal information without the individual being able to verbally report it.

A message presented so fast or so softly or so masked by other messages that one is not aware of seeing or hearing it is called a *subliminal message.* Subliminal messages have generated a great deal of interest but are not generally thought to affect brand choice or other aspects of consumer behavior in a meaningful way.

Interpretation is the assignment of meaning to stimuli that have been attended to. Interpretation tends to be relative rather than absolute (perceptual relativity) and subjective rather than objective. Two general forms of interpretation are cognitive and affective. *Cognitive interpretation* appears to involve a process whereby new stimuli are placed into existing categories of meaning. *Affective interpretation* is the emotional or feeling response triggered by the stimulus.

Interpretation is largely a function of individual traits, learning, and expectations that are triggered by the stimulus and moderated by the situation. Stimulus characteristics are critical. *Stimulus organization* is the physical arrangement of the stimulus objects and relates to the perceptual principles of *proximity, closure,* and *figure-ground.* Marketers can use these principles to design effective communication strategies. *Stimulus change* and consumer reactions to it are also of concern and have consequences in relation to such strategies as "weighting out" whereby marketers attempt to reduce the quantity offered in increments that consumers won't detect.

Interpretation often involves consumer inferences. *Inferences* go beyond what is directly stated or presented and help to explain consumer use of *quality signals* (e.g., higher price means higher quality), their *interpretation of images,* and how they deal with *missing information.* Inferences also help to explain how consumers can be misled by marketing messages even when those messages are *literally* true.

Marketers use their knowledge of perception to enhance strategies in a number of areas including media, retailing, branding, advertising, and package design.

KEY TERMS

Ad avoidance 284
Adaptation level theory 293
Affective interpretation 297
Ambush marketing 301
Attention 287
Brand extension 308
Brand familiarity 294
Closure 301
Co-branding 308
Cognitive interpretation 297
Contextual cues 299
Cross-promotions 307

Exposure 283
Figure-ground 303
Hemispheric lateralization 296
Inference 304
Infomercials 286
Information overload 293
Information processing 282
Interpretation 296
Just noticeable difference
  (j.n.d.) 304
Muting 284
Perception 282

Perceptual defenses 283
Perceptual relativity 296
Permission-based marketing 287
Product placement 285
Proximity 301
Rhetorical figures 301
Sensory discrimination 304
Smart banners 294
Stimulus organization 300
Subliminal stimulus 296
Zapping 284
Zipping 284

INTERNET EXERCISES

1. Examine several magazines. Copy two ads that do a good job of encouraging the reader to visit a Web site. Justify your selection using the principles of perception described in this chapter.

2. Visit one of the following Web sites. Evaluate the site on the principles of perception covered in this chapter.
   a. www.fandango.com
   b. www.skyy.com
   c. www.people.com
   d. www.excite.com
   e. www.cyberpet.com

3. Visit several company Web sites until you find one that you feel makes effective use of the principles of perception that we have covered and one that violates these principles. Provide the URL of each and justify your selections.

DDB LIFE STYLE STUDY™ DATA ANALYSES

1. Examine the DDB data in Tables 1B through 7B. What characterizes a person who *avoids buying products advertised on shows with sex or violence?* Why is this the case? What does it suggest about the importance of *programming context?*

REVIEW QUESTIONS

1. What is *information processing?* How does it differ from *perception?*

2. What is meant by *exposure?* What determines which stimuli an individual will be exposed to? How do marketers utilize this knowledge?

3. What are *zipping, zapping,* and *muting?* Why are they a concern to marketers?

4. What are *infomercials?* How effective are they?

5. What is *ad avoidance?* How are marketers dealing with this phenomenon?

6. What is meant by *attention?* What determines which stimuli an individual will attend to? How do marketers utilize this?

7. What stimulus factors can be used to attract attention? What problems can arise when stimulus factors are used to attract attention?

8. What is *adaptation level theory?*

9. What is *information overload?* How should marketers deal with information overload?

10. What impact does *program involvement* have on the attention paid to commercials embedded in the program?

11. What is a *contextual cue?* Why is it of interest to marketers?

12. What is meant by *nonfocused attention?*

13. What is meant by *hemispheric lateralization?*

14. What is meant by *subliminal perception?* Is it a real phenomenon? Is it effective?

15. What is meant by *interpretation?*

16. What determines how an individual will interpret a given stimulus?

17. What is the difference between *cognitive* and *affective* interpretation?

18. What is the difference between *semantic* and *psychological* meaning?

19. What is *sensory discrimination?* What is a *just noticeable difference* (j.n.d.)?

20. What is a *consumer inference?* Why is this of interest to marketers?

21. How does a knowledge of information processing assist the manager in the following?
    a. Formulating retail strategy
    b. Developing brand names and logos
    c. Formulating media strategy
    d. Designing advertisements
    e. Package design and labels

22. What is *co-branding?* Is it effective?

23. What is a *cross-promotion* retail strategy? Provide two examples.

24. How can *rhetorical figures* enhance attention?

25. What is a *smart banner?* How does this relate to selective attention?

26. What is *figure-ground?*

27. What ethical concerns arise in applying knowledge of the perceptual process?

28. What is *ambush marketing?*

DISCUSSION QUESTIONS

29. Given that smoking scenes in movies increase the positive image and intention to smoke among youth, what regulations, if any, should apply to this?

30. How could a marketing manager for the following use the material in this chapter to guide the development of a national advertising campaign (choose one)? To assist local retailers or organizations in developing their promotional activities? Would the usefulness of this material be limited to advertising decisions?
    a. Salvation Army
    b. Tennis equipment
    c. Qdoba Mexican Grill
    d. Windex
    e. Belkin WiFi equipment

31. Respond to the questions in Consumer Insight 8-1.

32. Anheuser-Busch test-marketed a new soft drink for adults called Chelsea. The product was advertised as a "not-so-soft drink" that Anheuser-Busch hoped would become socially acceptable for adults. The advertisements featured no one under 25 years of age, and the product contained 0.5 percent alcohol (not enough to classify the product as an alcoholic beverage). The reaction in the test market was not what the firm expected or hoped for. The Virginia Nurses Association decided to boycott Chelsea, claiming that it "is packaged like a beer and looks, pours, and foams like beer, and the children are pretending the soft drink is beer." The Nurses Association claimed the product was an attempt to encourage children to become beer drinkers later on. The secretary of health, education and welfare urged the firm to "rethink their marketing strategy." Others made similar protests. Although Anheuser-Busch reformulated the product and altered the marketing mix substantially, the product could not regain momentum and was withdrawn. Assuming Anheuser-Busch was in fact attempting to position Chelsea as an adult soft drink, which appears to have been its objective, why do you think it failed?

33. Pick three brand names that utilize a *morphemic* approach and three that utilize a *phonetic* approach. Are the morphemes and phonetics consistent with the overall positioning of these brands?

34. Develop a brand name for (*a*) the iPod, (*b*) an R&B music store, (*c*) an Internet grocery shopping service, (*d*) a national magazine for adults over 50, or (*e*) a pet walking service. Justify your name.

35. Develop a logo for (*a*) the iPod, (*b*) an R&B music store, (*c*) an Internet grocery shopping service, (*d*) a national magazine for adults over 50, or (*e*) a pet walking service. Justify your design.

36. Evaluate the in-text ads in Illustrations 8-1 through 8-12. Analyze the attention-attracting characteristics and the meaning they convey. Are they good ads? What risks are associated with each?

37. Develop three co-branded products: one that would be beneficial to both individual brands, one that would benefit one brand but not the other, and one that would benefit neither brand. Explain your logic.

38. Respond to the questions in Consumer Insight 8-2.

39. Find an ad that you feel might mislead consumers through a *claim-belief discrepancy.* What inference processes are you assuming?

APPLICATION ACTIVITIES

40. Find and copy or describe examples of advertisements that specifically use stimulus factors to attract attention. Look for examples of each of the various factors discussed earlier in the chapter and try to find their use in a variety of promotions. For each example, evaluate the effectiveness of the stimulus factors used.

41. Repeat Question 40, but this time look for advertisements using individual factors.

42. Complete Question 34 and test your names on a sample of students. Justify your testing procedure and report your results.

43. Complete Question 35 and test your logos on a sample of students. Justify your testing procedure and report your results.

44. Find two brand names that you feel are particularly appropriate and two that you feel are not very appropriate. Explain your reasoning for each name.

45. Find and describe a logo that you feel is particularly appropriate and one that you feel is not very appropriate. Explain your reasoning.

46. Interview three students about their behavior during television and radio commercial breaks. What do you conclude?

47. Interview three students about how they respond to banner ads and the extent to which they attend to various commercial messages on the Internet.

48. Go to a health food or alternative medicines store or section of a store. Find three products that make health claims. Evaluate the likely effectiveness of any disclaimers that they contain.

49. Find and copy or describe an ad or other marketing message that you think makes unethical use of the perceptual process. Justify your selection.

50. Develop an ad but omit information about some key product attributes. Show the ad to five students. After they have looked at the ad, give them a questionnaire that asks about the attributes featured in the ad and about the missing attributes. If they provide answers concerning the missing attributes, ask them how they arrived at these answers. What do you conclude?

REFERENCES

1. Based on K. Weisberg, "Vegetarian Delight," *Foodservice Director*, October 15, 2004; "Gardenburger Takes a Stand against Deceptive Labeling," corporate press release, April 10, 2002; and additional information from Gardenburger's corporate Web site at www.gardenburger.com, including a "Roper ASW Study," March 15, 2002.

2. R. Liljenwall, "Global Trends in Point-of-Purchase Advertising," in *The Power of Point-of-Purchase Advertising,* ed. R. Liljenwall (Washington, DC: Point-of-Purchase Advertising International 2004), chap. 10.

3. R. Grover, T. Lowry, G. Khermouch, C. Edwards, and D. Foust, "Can Mad Ave. Make Zap-Proof Ads?" *BusinessWeek,* February 2, 2004, p. 36.

4. E. Ephron, "Live TV Is Ready for Its Closeup," *Advertising Age,* March 22, 2004, p. 19.

5. J. Mandese, "Study: DVRs 'Recapture' 96% of TV Ad Zapping," *MediaPost's Media Daily News* (online), May 25, 2004 at www.mediapost.com.

6. B. A. S. Martin, V. T. L. Nguyen, J.-Y. Wi, "Remote Control Marketing," *Marketing Intelligence & Planning* 20, no. 1 (2002), pp. 44–48.

7. "Ad Avoidance Highest among Key Target Groups, Says Study," *Businessline,* October 21, 2004, p. 1.

8. S. M. Edwards, H. Li, and J.-H. Lee, "Forced Exposure and Psychological Reactance," *Journal of Advertising,* Fall 2002, pp. 83–95; H. Li, S. M. Edwards, and J.-H. Lee, "Measuring the Intrusiveness of Advertisements," *Journal of Advertising,* Summer 2002, pp. 37–47; S. Shavitt, P. Vargas, and P. Lowrey, "Exploring the Pole of Memory for Self-Selected Ad Experiences," *Psychology & Marketing,* December 2004, pp. 1011–32.

9. A. C. B. Tse and R. P. W. Lee, "Zapping Behavior during Commercial Breaks," *Journal of Advertising Research,* May 2001, pp. 25–28; M. Savage, "China Turning On, but Tuning Out," *Media,* May 7, 2004, p. 19.

10. P. Paul, "Coming Soon: More Ads Tailored to Your Tastes," *American Demographics,* August 2001, pp. 28–31.

11. Edwards, Li, and Lee, "Forced Exposure and Psychological Reactance."

12. "Pop-Ups—End of an Era?" *NOP World United Business Media* (online), at www.unitedbusinessmedia.com, September 29, 2003.

13. K. Strauss, "Pedestrian Cab Reborn as Ad Star," *Advertising Age,* July 9, 2001, p. S6.

14. Liljenwall, "Global Trends in Point-of-Purchase Advertising."

15. This Consumer Insight is based on C. Pechmann and D.-F. Shih, "Smoking Scenes in Movies and Antismoking Advertisements before Movies," *Journal of Marketing,* July 1999, pp. 1–13; S. J. Gould, P. B. Gupta, and S. Grabner-Krauter, "Product Placements in Movies," *Journal of Advertising,* Winter 2000, pp. 42–56; R. Ferraro and R. J. Avery, "Brand Appearances on Prime-Time Television," A. d'Astous and F. Chartiere, "A Study of Factors Affecting Consumer Evaluations and Memory of Product Placements in Movies," and P. B. Gupta, S. K. Balasubramanian, and M. L. Klassen, "Viewers' Evaluations of Product Placements in Movies," all in *Journal of Current Issues and Research in Advertising,* Fall 2000, pp. 1–25, 31–40, and 41–52, respectively; S. Law and K. A. Braum, "I'll Have What She's Having," *Psychology & Marketing,* December 2000, pp. 1059–75; C. R. Morton and M. Friedman, "I Saw It in the Movies," *Journal of Current Issues and Research in Advertising,* Fall 2002, pp. 33–40; C. A. Russell, "Investigating the Effectiveness of Product Placements in Television Shows," *Journal of Consumer Research,* December 2002, pp. 306–18; S. A. McKechnie and J. Zhou, "Product Placement in Movies," *International Journal of Advertising* 22, no. 3 (2003), pp. 349–74;

and E. Hall, "Young Consumers Receptive to Movie Product Placement," *Advertising Age,* February 29, 2004, p. 8.

16. M. Singh, S. K. Balasubramanian, and G. Chakraborty, "A Comparative Analysis of Three Communication Formats," *Journal of Advertising,* Winter 2000, pp. 59–75.

17. M. T. Elliot and P. S. Speck, "Antecedents and Consequences of Infomercials," *Journal of Direct Marketing,* Spring 1995, pp. 39–51.

18. R. Park, "Consumers Kick the Tires on the Web before They Drive New Cars off the Lot," *iMedia Connection.com,* September 23, 2004, at imediaconnection.com.

19. "DoubleClick's 2004 Consumer Email Study," October 2004, at www.doubleckick.com.

20. "Farm Ads Win Golden Fleece," *Stars and Stripes,* July 10, 1984, p. 6.

21. S. Thompson, "Media Recipe," *Advertising Age,* October 23, 2000, p. 42.

22. K. Bouffard, "Analyst Says Grocers' Cut in Shelf Space for Orange Juice Hurts Citrus Sales," *Knight Ridder Tribune Business News,* July 22, 2004, p. 1.

23. M. Rappaport, "Food Product Makers Secure Supermarket Shelf Space by Paying Slotting Fees," *Knight Ridder Tribune Business News,* January 14, 2004, p. 1.

24. X. Drèze and F. Xavier Hussherr, "Internet Advertising," *Journal of Interactive Marketing,* Autumn 2003, pp. 8–23; and "A Not-So-Banner Year," *Marketing News,* April 29, 2002, p. 3.

25. G. L. Lohse, "Consumer Eye Movement Patterns on Yellow Pages Advertising," *Journal of Advertising,* Spring 1997, pp. 61–73; and A. M. Abernethy and D. N. Laband, "The Customer Pulling Power of Different-sized Yellow Pages Advertisements," *Journal of Advertising Research,* May/June 2002, pp. 66–72.

26. J. R. Rossiter and R. B. Silberstein, "Brain-Imaging Detection of Visual Scene Encoding in Long-Term Memory for TV Commercials," *Journal of Advertising Research,* March 2001, pp. 13–21. See also S. L. Crites, Jr., and S. N. AikmanEckenrode, "Making Inferences Concerning Physiological Responses," *Journal of Advertising Research,* March 2001, p. 25; and J. R. Rossiter et al., "So What?" *Journal of Advertising Research,* May 2001, pp. 59–61.

27. C.-H. Cho, J.-G. Lee, and M. Tharp, "Different Forced-Exposure Levels to Banner Ads," *Journal of Advertising Research,* July 2001, pp. 45–54.

28. R. Pieters, E. Rosbergen, and M. Wedel, "Visual Attention to Repeated Print Advertising," *Journal of Marketing Research,* November 1999, pp. 424–38.

29. R. Pieters and Michel Wedel, "Attention Capture and Transfer in Advertising," *Journal of Marketing,* April 2004, pp. 36–50.

30. S. N. Singh et al., "Does Your Ad Have Too Many Pictures," *Journal of Advertising Research,* January 2000, pp. 11–27.

31. Pieters and Wedel, "Attention Capture and Transfer in Advertising."

32. *What the Eye Does Not See, the Mind Does Not Remember,* Telecom Research, Inc., undated.

33. G. J. Gorn, A. Chattopadhyay, T. Yi, and D. W. Dahl, "Effects of Color as an Executional Cue in Advertising," *Management Science,* October 1997, pp. 1387–99.

34. L. Haugen and C. Weems, "P-O-P Advertising Design and Creativity," in *The Power of Point-of-Purchase Advertising,* chap. 6.

35. L. Rostoks, "Sales from POP Advertising are Measureable," *Canadian Grocer,* July/August 2001, p. 19; and J. McCarthy, "Point of Purchase Last Chance to Dance," *Marketing Magazine,* March 2004, p. 33.

36. C.-H. Cho, "How Advertising Works on the WWW," *Journal of Current Issues and Research in Advertising,* Spring 1999, pp. 33–49.

37. Lohse, "Consumer Eye Movement Patterns." See also K. V. Fernandez and D. L. Rosen, "The Effectiveness of Information and Color in Yellow Pages Advertising," *Journal of Advertising,* Summer 2000, pp. 62–73.

38. D. Alexander, "Food Industry Giants Spend Big Money for Prime Supermarket Shelf Space," *Knight Ridder Tribune Business News,* December 14, 2003, p. 1.

39. C. Garcia, V. Ponsoda, and H. Estebaranz, "Scanning Ads," *Advances in Consumer Research,* vol. 27, eds. S. J. Hoch and R. J. Meyer (Provo, UT: Association for Consumer Research, 2000), pp. 104–9.

40. Drèze and Hussherr, "Internet Advertising."

41. D. D. McAdams, "Is Anybody Paying Attention?" *Broadcasting & Cable,* August 7, 2000, p. 38.

42. See G. D. Olsen, "Creating the Contrast," *Journal of Advertising,* Winter 1995, pp. 29–44.

43. C. Janiszewski, "The Influence of Display Characteristics on Visual Exploratory Search Behavior," *Journal of Consumer Research,* December 1998, pp. 290–301.

44. A. Chattopadhyay, D. W. Dahl, R. J. B. Ritchie, and K. N. Shahin, "Hearing Voices," *Journal of Consumer Psychology* 13, no. 3 (2003), pp. 198–204.

45. J. Roumelis, "How to Get Noticed . . . Fast," *Marketing Magazine,* May 6, 2002, p. 26.

46. R. C. Goodstein, "Category-Based Applications and Extensions in Advertising," *Journal of Consumer Research,* June 1993, pp. 87–99; see also Y. H. Lee, "Manipulating Ad Message," *Journal of Advertising,* Summer 2000, pp. 29–43.

47. R. Pieters, L. Warlop, and M. Wedel, "Breaking through the Clutter," *Management Science,* June 2002, pp. 765–81.

48. "Signposts," *Advertising Age,* May 21, 2001, p. 3.

49. T. Elkin, "PVR Not Yet a Big Threat," *Advertising Age,* May 6, 2002, p. 55. See also L. F. Allwitt, "Effects of Interestingness on Evaluations of TV Commercials," *Journal of Current Issues and Research in Advertising,* Spring 2000, pp. 41–53; and W. Friedman, "72.3% of PVR Viewers Skip Commercials," *AdAge.com,* July 2, 2002, at www.adage.com.

50. J. W. Elpers, M. Wedel, and R. Pieters, "Why Do Consumers Stop Viewing Television Commercials?" *Journal of Marketing Research,* November 2003, pp. 437–53.

51. Pieters, Warlop, and Wedel, "Breaking through the Clutter"; and Elpers, Wedel, and Pieters, "Why Do Consumers Stop Viewing Television Commercials?"

52. Pieters and Wedel, "Attention Capture and Transfer in Advertising."

53. C.-H. Cho, "The Effectiveness of Banner Advertisements," *Journalism and Mass Communication Quarterly,* Autumn 2003, pp. 623–45.

54. See W. Dou, R. Linn, and S. Yang, "How Smart Are 'Smart Banners'?" *Journal of Advertising Research,* July 2001, pp. 31–43.

55. K. Oser, "Targeting Web Behavior Pays, American Airlines Study Says," *Advertising Age,* May 17, 2004, p. 8; see also L. Sherman and J. Deighton, "Banner Advertising," *Journal of Interactive Marketing,* Spring 2001, pp. 60–64.

56. A. M. Menon, A. D. Deshpande, M. Perri III, and G. M. Zinkhan, "Consumers' Attention to the Brief Summary in Print Direct-to-Consumer Advertisements," *Journal of Public Policy and Marketing,* Fall 2003, pp. 181–91.

57. M. Dahlen, "Bannar Advertisements through a New Lens," *Journal of Advertising Research,* July 2001, pp. 23–30.

58. J. Spaeth, "Post-Promotion Evaluation," chap. 6, and Liljenwall, "Global Trends in Point-of-Purchase Advertising," chap. 10, both in *The Power of Point-of-Purchase Advertising.*

59. R. G. M. Pieters and T. H. A. Bijmolt, "Consumer Memory for Television Advertising," *Journal of Consumer Research,* March 1997, pp. 362–72.

60. See D. L. Hoffman and R. Batra, "Viewer Response to Programs," *Journal of Advertising Research,* August–September 1991, pp. 46–56; K. G. Celuch and M. Slama, "Program Content and Advertising Effectiveness," *Psychology & Marketing,* July–August 1993, pp. 285–99; and K. R. Lord and R. E. Burnkrant, "Attention versus Distraction," *Journal of Advertising,* March 1993, pp. 47–60.

61. H. E. Krugman, "Sustained Viewing of Television," *Journal of Advertising Research,* June 1980, p. 65; and H. E. Krugman, "Low Recall and High Recognition of Advertising," *Journal of Advertising Research,* February–March 1986, pp. 79–86.

62. Drèze and Hussherr, "Internet Advertising."

63. S. Shapiro, D. J. MacInnis, S. E. Heckler, "The Effects of Incidental Ad Exposure on the Formation of Consideration Sets," *Journal of Consumer Research,* June 1997, pp. 94–104; and S. Shapiro, "When an Ad's Influence Is beyond Our Conscious Control," *Journal of Consumer Research,* June 1999, pp. 16–36.

64. W. B. Key, *Subliminal Seduction* (Englewood Cliffs, NJ: Prentice Hall, 1973); and W. B. Key, *Media Sexploitation* (Englewood Cliffs, NJ: Prentice Hall, 1976).

65. D. L. Rosen and S. N. Singh, "An Investigation of Subliminal Embed Effect on Multiple Measures of Advertising Effectiveness," *Psychology & Marketing,* March–April 1992, pp. 157–73; and K. T. Theus "Subliminal Advertising and the Psychology of Processing Unconscious Stimuli," *Psychology & Marketing,* May 1994, pp. 271–90. In contrast, see A. B. Aylesworth, R. C. Goodstein, and A. Kalra, "Effect of Archetypical Embeds on Feelings," *Journal of Advertising,* Fall 1999, pp. 73–81.

66. C. L. Witte, M. Parthasarathy, and J. W. Gentry, "Subliminal Perception versus Subliminal Persuasion," in *Enhancing Knowledge Development in Marketing,* eds. B. B. Stern and

G. M. Zinkhan (Chicago: American Marketing Association, 1995), pp. 133–38; and C. Trappey, "A Meta-Analysis of Consumer Choice and Subliminal Advertising," *Psychology & Marketing,* August 1996, pp. 517–30.

67. M. Rogers and C. A. Seiler, "The Answer Is No," *Journal of Advertising Research,* March 1994, pp. 36–45.

68. T. F. Stafford, "Alert or Oblivious?" *Psychology & Marketing,* September 2000, pp. 745–60.

69. See D. Grewal, K. B. Monroe, and R. Krishnan, "The Effects of Price-Comparison Advertising," *Journal of Marketing,* April 1998, pp. 46–59; and D. Grewal, R. Krishnan, J. Baker, and N. Borin, "The Effects of Store Name, Brand Name, and Price Discounts," *Journal of Retailing,* no. 3 (1998), pp. 331–52.

70. S. S. Liu, "When the Irrelevant Becomes Relevant," *Journal of Current Issues and Research in Advertising,* Fall 1999, pp. 31–47; and M. Viswanathan and T. L. Childers, "Understanding How Product Attributes Influence Product Categorization," *Journal of Marketing Research,* February 1999, pp. 75–94.

71. Goodstein, "Category-Based Applications and Extensions in Advertising."

72. G. P. Moreau, D. R. Lehmann, and A. B. Markman, "Entrenched Knowledge Structures and Consumer Responses to New Products," *Journal of Marketing Research,* February 2001, pp. 14–29.

73. G. Page Moreau, A. B. Markham, and D. R. Lehmann, "'What Is It?' Categorization Flexibility and Consumers' Responses to Really New Products," *Journal of Consumer Research,* March 2001, pp. 489–98.

74. J. Z. Sojka and J. L. Giese, "Thinking and/or Feeling," *Advances in Consumer Research,* vol. 24, eds. M. Bruck and D. J. MacInnis (Provo, UT: Association for Consumer Research, 1997), pp. 438–42; and J. A. Ruth, "Promoting a Brand's Emotional Benefits," *Journal of Consumer Psychology* 11, no. 2 (2001), pp. 99–113.

75. See S. Ratneshwar, "Goal-Derived Categories," *Journal of Consumer Psychology* 10, no. 3 (2001), pp. 147–57.

76. B. Turnbull and E. Matisoo-Smith, "Taste Sensitivity to 6-*n*-propylthiouracil Predicts Acceptance of Bitter-Tasting Spinach in 3–6-y-Old Children," *American Journal of Clinical Nutrition* 76 (2002), pp. 1101–5.

77. For a discussion, see J. E. Escalas, M. C. Moore, and J. E. Britton, "Fishing for Feelings?" *Journal of Consumer Psychology* 14, nos. 1 & 2 (2004), pp. 105–14.

78. R. Ahluwalia, R. E. Burnkrant, and H. R. Unnava, "Consumer Response to Negative Publicity," *Journal of Marketing Research,* May 2000, pp. 203–14; see also J. E. Russo, M. G. Meloy, and V. H. Medvec, "Predecisional Distortion of Product Information," *Journal of Marketing Research,* November 1998, pp. 438–52.

79. M. C. Campbell, "Perceptions of Price Unfairness," *Journal of Marketing Research,* May 1999, pp. 187–99; see also L. Xia, K. B. Monroe, and J. L. Cox, "The Price is Unfair!" *Journal of Marketing,* October 2004, pp. 1–15.

80. G. Tom et al., "Cueing the Consumer," *Journal of Consumer Marketing,* Spring 1987, pp. 23–27. See also D. S. Kempf and R. N. Laczniak, "Advertising's Influence on Subsequent

Product Trial Processing," *Journal of Advertising,* Fall 2001, pp. 27–40.

81. See K. R. Evans et al., "How First Impressions of a Customer Impact Effectiveness in an Initial Sales Encounter," *Journal of the Academy of Marketing Science,* Fall 2000, pp. 512–26.

82. J. J. Inman, L. McAlister, and W. D. Hoyer, "Promotion Signal," *Journal of Consumer Research,* June 1990, pp. 74–81.

83. See M. G. Meloy, "Mood-Driven Distortion of Product Information," *Journal of Consumer Research,* December 2000, pp. 345–58.

84. G. J. Gorn, A. Chattopadhyay, J. Sengupta, and S. Tripathi, "Waiting for the Web," *Journal of Marketing Research,* May 2004, pp. 215–25.

85. "GF, Coke Tell Why They Shun TV News," *Advertising Age,* January 28, 1980, p. 39.

86. K. R. France and C. W. Park, "The Impact of Program Affective Valence and Level of Cognitive Appraisal on Advertisement Processing and Effectiveness," *Journal of Current Issues and Research in Advertising,* Fall 1997, pp. 1–21; A. B. Aylesworth and S. B. MacKenzie, "Context Is Key," *Journal of Advertising,* Summer 1998, pp. 17–31; Q. Chen and W. D. Wells, "Attitude toward the Site," *Journal of Advertising Research,* September 1999, pp. 27–37; and B. M. Tennis and A. B. Bakker, "Stay Tuned—We Will Be Right Back after These Messages," *Journal of Advertising,* Fall 2001, pp. 15–25. See also S. Shapiro, D. J. MacInnis, and C.W. Park, "Understanding Program-Induced Mood Effects," *Journal of Advertising,* Winter 2002, pp. 15–26.

87. R. Alsop, "Color Grows More Important in Catching Consumers' Eyes," *The Wall Street Journal,* November 29, 1989, p. B1.

88. P. Raghubir and A. Krishna, "Vital Dimensions in Volume Perception," *Journal of Marketing Research,* August 1999, pp. 313–26.

89. C. Janiszewski and T. Meyvis, "Effects of Brand Logo Complexity, Repetition, and Spacing on Processing Fluency and Judgment," *Journal of Consumer Research,* June 2001, pp. 18–32; A. Y. Lee and A. A. Labroo, "The Effect of Conceptual and Perceptual Fluency on Brand Evaluation," *Journal of Marketing Research,* May 2004, pp. 151–65; and N. Schwarz, "Metacognitive Experiences in Consumer Judgment and Decision Making," *Journal of Consumer Psychology* 14, no. 4 (2004), pp. 332–48.

90. This insight is based on M. F. Toncar and J. M. Munch, "Consumer Response to Tropes in Print Advertising," *Journal of Advertising,* Spring 2001, pp. 55–65; D. L. Mothersbaugh, B. A. Huhmann, and G. R. Franke, "Combinatory and Separative Effects of Rhetorical Figures on Consumers' Effort and Focus in Ad Processing," *Journal of Consumer Research,* March 2002, pp. 589–602; E. F. McQuarrie and D. Glenn Mick, "Visual and Verbal Rhetorical Figures under Directed Processing versus Incidental Exposure to Advertising," *Journal of Consumer Research,* March 2003, pp. 579–87; and R. Ahluwalia and R. E. Burnkrant, "Answering Questions about Questions," *Journal of Consumer Research,* June 2004, pp. 26–42.

91. T. Meenaghan, ed., special issue, "Ambush Marketing," *Psychology & Marketing,* July 1998.

92. J. Sengupta and G. J. Gorn, "Absence Makes the Mind Grow Sharper," *Journal of Marketing Research,* May 2002, pp. 186–201.

93. T. Howard, "Pay the Same, Get Less as Package Volume Falls," *USA Today,* March 17, 2003, p. 3b.

94. D. Grewal, K. B. Monroe, and R. Krishnan, "The Effects of Price-Comparison Advertising on Buyers' Perceptions of Acquisition Value, Transaction Value, and Behavioral Intentions," *Journal of Marketing* 62 (1998), pp. 46–59; D. R. Bell, and R. E. Bucklin, "The Role of Internal Reference Points in the Category Purchase Decision," *Journal of Consumer Research,* September 1999, pp. 128–43; S. Han, S. Gupta, and D. R. Lehmann, "Consumer Price Sensitivity and Price Thresholds," *Journal of Retailing* 77 (2001), pp. 435–56; A. Krishna, R. Briesch, D. R. Lehmann, and H. Yuan, "A Meta-Analysis of the Impact of Price Presentation on Perceived Savings," *Journal of Retailing* 78 (2002), pp. 101–18; and L. D. Compeau, J. Lindsey-Mullikin, D. Grewal, and R. D. Petty, "Consumers' Interpretations of the Semantic Phrases Found in Reference Price Advertisements," *Journal of Consumer Affairs,* Summer 2004, pp. 178–87.

95. P. Raghubir, "Free Gift with Purchase," *Journal of Consumer Psychology* 14, nos. 1 & 2 (2004), pp. 181–86.

96. S. Chatterjee, T. B. Heath, and S. Basuroy, "Failing to Suspect Collusion in Price-Matching Guarantees," *Journal of Consumer Psychology* 13, no. 3 (2003), pp. 255–67; and J. Halliday, "GM Incentive Plans Could Damage Brand," *Advertising Age,* September 27, 2004, p. 1.

97. A. Kirmani, "Advertising Repetition as a Signal of Quality," *Journal of Advertising,* Fall 1997, pp. 77–86.

98. G. L. Lohse and D. L. Rosen, "Signaling Quality and Credibility in Yellow Pages Advertising," *Journal of Advertising,* Summer 2001, pp. 73–85.

99. A. Kirmani and A. R. Rao, "No Pain, No Gain," *Journal of Marketing,* April 2000, pp. 66–79; and D. Soberman, "Simultaneous Signaling and Screening with Warranties," *Journal of Marketing Research,* May 2003, pp. 176–92.

100. Z. Gurhan-Canli and D. Maheswaran, "Cultural Variations in Country of Origin Effects," *Journal of Marketing Research,* August 2000, pp. 309–17; and Z. Gurhan-Canli and D. Maheswaran, "Determinants of Country-of-Origin Effects," *Journal of Consumer Research,* June 2000, pp. 96–108.

101. B. J. Phillips and E. F. McQuarrie, "The Development, Change, and Transformation of Rhetorical Style in Magazine Advertisements 1954–1999," *Journal of Advertising* 31, no. 4 (2003), pp. 1–13.

102. B. J. Phillips, "The Impact of Verbal Anchoring on Consumer Response to Image Ads," *Journal of Advertising,* Spring 2000, pp. 15–24; E. F. McQuarrie and D. G. Mick, "Visual Rhetoric in Advertising," *Journal of Consumer Research,* June 1999, pp. 37–54; and M. Callow and L. Schiffman, "Implicit Meaning in Visual Print Advertisements," *International Journal of Advertising,* 21, 2002, pp. 259–77.

103. See R. Kivetz and I. Simonson, "The Effects of Incomplete Information on Consumer Choice," *Journal of Marketing Research,* November 2000, pp. 427–48.

104. G. V. Johar, "Consumer Involvement and Deception from Implied Advertising Claims," *Journal of Marketing Research,* August 1995, pp. 267–79; C. Pechmann, "Do Consumers Overgeneralize One-Sided Comparative Price Claims?" *Journal of Marketing Research,* May 1996, pp. 150–62; M. J. Barone and P. J. Miniard, "How and When Factual Ad Claims Mislead Consumers," *Journal of Marketing Research,* February 1999, pp. 58–74; M. J. Barone et al., "Enhancing the Detection of Misleading Comparative Advertising," *Journal of Advertising Research,* September 1999, pp. 43–50; and M. J. Barone, K. M. Palan, and P. W. Miniard, "Brand Usage and Gender as Moderators of the Potential Deception Associated with Partial Comparative Advertising," *Journal of Advertising,* Spring 2004, pp. 19–28.

105. For an excellent discussion, see I. L. Preston, *The Tangled Web They Weave* (Madison, WI: The University of Madison Press, 1994).

106. L. Petrak, "Capturing Consumer Attention," *National Provisioner,* October 2003, pp. 52–53.

107. S. Thompson, "Kraft Vows to Kick Addiction to Extensions," *Advertising Age,* August 23, 2004, p. 1.

108. S. M. Broniarcyzk, W. D. Hoyer, and L. McAlister, "Consumers' Perceptions of the Assortment Offered in a Grocery Category," *Journal of Marketing Research,* May 1998, pp. 166–76.

109. I. Simonson, "The Effect of Product Assortment on Buyer Preferences," *Journal of Retailing* 75, no. 3 (1999), pp. 347–70; and P. Boatwright and J. C. Nunes, "Reducing Assortment," *Journal of Marketing,* July 2001, pp. 50–63. See also E. van Herpen and R. Pieters, "The Variety of an Assortment," and S. J. Hoch, E. T. Bradlow, and B. Wansink, "Rejoinder to 'The Variety of an Assortment,'" both in *Marketing Science,* Summer 2002, pp. 331–41 and pp. 342–46, respectively; and A. Chernev, "When More Is Less and Less Is More," *Journal of Consumer Research,* September 2003, pp. 170–83.

110. H. Chura, "Pepsi-Cola's Code Red Is White Hot," *Advertising Age,* August 27, 2001, p. 24.

111. "What's in a Name?" *Global Cosmetics Industry,* August 2002, p. 42.

112. S. Zhang and B. H. Schmitt, "Creating Local Brands in Multilingual International Markets," *Journal of Marketing Research,* August 2001, pp. 313–25.

113. S. Freeman, "Revived 'Hemi' Engine Helps Chrysler Juice Up Its Sales," *The Wall Street Journal,* April 30, 2004, p. B1.

114. R. R. Klink, "Creating Brand Names with Meaning," *Marketing Letters* 11, no. 1 (2000), pp. 5–20; and E. Yorkston and G. Menon, "A Sound Idea," *Journal of Consumer Research,* June 2004, pp. 43–51.

115. S. Begley, "New ABCs of Branding," *The Wall Street Journal,* August 26, 2002, p. B1.

116. B. L. Simonin and J. A. Ruth, "Is a Brand Known by the Company It Keeps?" *Journal of Marketing Research,* February 1998, pp. 30–42; I. P. Levin and A. M. Levin, "Modeling the Role of Brand Alliances in the Assimilation of Product Evaluations," *Journal of Consumer Psychology* 9, no. 1 (2000), pp. 43–52; and K. K. Desai and K. I. Keller, "The Effects of Ingredient Branding Strategies on Host Brand Extendibility," *Journal of Marketing,* January 2002, pp. 73–93.

117. See J. Tantillo, J. D. Lorenzo-Aiss, and R. E. Mathisen, "Quantifying Perceived Differences in Type Styles," *Psychology & Marketing,* August 1995, pp. 447–57; and C. Janiszewski and T. Meyvis, "Effects of Brand Logo Complexity, Repetition, and Spacing on Processing Fluency and Judgment," *Journal of Marketing Research,* June 2001, pp. 18–32.

118. A. H. Schechter, "Measuring the Value of Corporate and Brand Logos," *Design Management Journal,* Winter 1993, pp. 33–39.

119. T. L. Childers and J. Jass, "All Dressed Up with Something to Say," *Journal of Consumer Psychology* 12, no. 2 (2002), pp. 93–106; and J. R. Doyle and P. A. Bottomley, "Font Appropriateness and Brand Choice," *Journal of Business Research* 57 (2004), pp. 873–80.

120. P. W. Henderson and J. A. Cote, "Guidelines for Selecting or Modifying Logos," *Journal of Marketing,* April 1998, pp. 14–30; and J. T. Landry, "Making Logos Matter," *Harvard Business Review,* March–April 1998, pp. 16–17.

121. M. Peers, "Buddy, Can You Spare Some Time?" *The Wall Street Journal,* January 26, 2004, p. B1; and B. Frank, "'Missing' Men Prove Prescient," *Advertising Age,* August 23, 2004, p. 16.

122. "Ford Boss Outlines Shift to 'Rifle' Media," *Advertising Age,* October 26, 1981, p. 89. See also P. J. Danaher, "Wearout Effects in Target Marketing," *Marketing Letters,* no. 3 (1996), pp. 275–87.

123. P. N. Shamdasani, A. J. S. Stanaland, and J. Tan, "Location, Location, Location," *Journal of Advertising Research,* July 2001, pp. 7–20.

124. J. Neff, "P&G Reins in Its Domains," *Advertising Age,* October 29, 2001, p. 32.

125. J. Guterman, "Outdoor Interactive," *American Demographics,* August 2001, p. 32.

126. B. E. Kahn and B. Wansink, "The Influence of Assortment Structure on Perceived Variety and Consumption Quantities," *Journal of Consumer Research,* March 2004, pp. 519–33.

127. S. Thompson, "M&M's Wraps Up Promo with Color," *Advertising Age,* March 8, 2004, p. 4.

128. B. Wansink and K. Van Ittersum, "Bottoms Up!" *Journal of Consumer Research,* December 2003, pp. 455–63.

129. V. Folkes and S. Matta, "The Effect of Package Shape on Consumers' Judgments of Product Volume," *Journal of Consumer Research,* September 2004, pp. 390–401.

130. L. Nohre et al., "The Association between Adolescents' Receiver Characteristics and Exposure to the Alcohol Warning Label," *Psychology & Marketing,* May 1999, pp. 245–59; E. Lepkowska-White and A. L. Parsons, *Journal of Consumer Affairs,* Winter 2001, pp. 278–94; and V. A. Taylor and A. B. Bower, "Improving Product Instruction Compliance," *Psychology & Marketing,* March 2004, pp. 229–45.

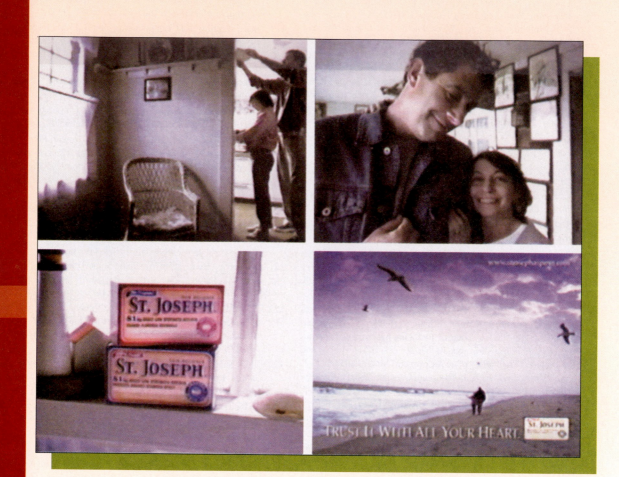

9

Learning, Memory, and Product Positioning

■ Imagine a company buying a brand whose sales had declined 90 percent over the past 15 years in large part because its use was linked with a deadly disease. Further imagine that for all of its 110-year history it has been marketed exclusively as a children's product, and you are going to market it to baby boomers and older adults. A foolish idea? Johnson & Johnson doesn't think so.

Johnson & Johnson recently acquired St. Joseph Aspirin, which, since its beginning in the late 1800s, had been sold strictly as a children's aspirin. It is sold only in orange-flavored, 81-milligram doses, compared with 325 milligrams in standard aspirin. It was quite successful until the 1980s, when using aspirin to treat viral infections in children was linked to Reye's syndrome (a disease that affects all organs of the body, but most lethally the liver and the brain).

Johnson & Johnson hopes to reposition St. Joseph as the best source for a low-dosage aspirin regime to reduce the risk of heart attacks and strokes in adults. The firm hopes to capture the positive memories many adults have of St. Joseph while teaching them that it is the optimal source for low-dosage aspirins. Thus, the firm faces the dual challenge of reviving old memories and positive feelings while teaching consumers that the product is uniquely appropriate for this use by adults.

The marketing team asked itself, How would baby boomers remember St. Joseph? They went on eBay and bought old St. Joseph packages and posters, they redesigned the package using elements from its old packages, when the brand was at its strongest. Of course, any reference to children was removed and adult usage was emphasized. Evidence indicated that most adults had heard the message that aspirin is good for one's heart. The challenge was to teach consumers that St. Joseph was the best aspirin to use.

The first commercial in a $10 million campaign featured a caring, middle-aged couple, with the man much taller than the woman. The background music was the old tune "Mr. Sandman." The wife states, "We both take St. Joseph because its low dose is safe for every size adult." The commercial ends with the tagline: "Trust it with all your heart."[1]

Johnson & Johnson is spending more than $10 million in an advertising campaign designed to teach consumers that St. Joseph is the best aspirin for adults to use in a low-dosage aspirin regime. Since most adults think of St. Joseph as a children's aspirin, this will require what is called *product repositioning*. Its success will depend on how well the marketing team understands and uses learning principles.

As the St. Joseph example illustrates, brands seek to reinforce existing positive associations (e.g., comfort), reduce existing negative associations (e.g., may cause Reye's Syndrome), and create new positive associations (e.g., safe for adults to use). These associations are at the heart of learning. They are also the key to successful brand image development, positioning, and repositioning.

In this chapter, we discuss the nature of learning and memory, conditioning and cognitive theories of learning, and factors affecting retrieval. Implications for marketing managers are discussed throughout, culminating with an examination of product positioning and brand equity in the final sections.

NATURE OF LEARNING AND MEMORY

Learning is essential to the consumption process. In fact, consumer behavior is largely *learned* behavior. People acquire most of their attitudes, values, tastes, behaviors, preferences, symbolic meanings, and feelings through learning. Culture, family, friends, mass media, and advertising provide learning experiences that affect the type of lifestyle people seek and the products they consume. Consider, for example, how often your movie choices are influenced by what you read online and discussions you have with friends.

Learning is *any change in the content or organization of long-term memory or behavior*[2] and is the result of information processing. In the previous chapter, we described information processing as *a series of activities by which stimuli are perceived, transformed into information, and stored*. The four activities in the series are exposure, attention, interpretation, and memory.

FIGURE 9-1	Information Processing, Learning, and Memory

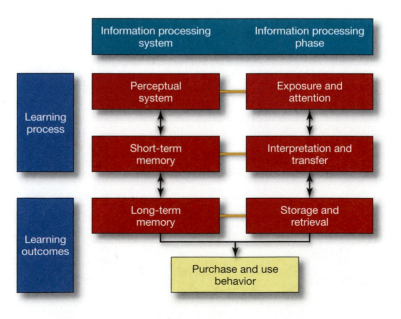

As Figure 9-1 indicates, different information processing systems handle different aspects of learning. The perceptual system deals with information intake through exposure and attention and, as we discussed in Chapter 8, may be conscious or unconscious. Short-term memory (STM) deals with holding information temporarily while it is interpreted and transferred into long-term memory. Long-term memory (LTM) deals with storing and retrieving information to be used in decisions.

These processes are highly interrelated. For example, a consumer may notice their favorite brand of soda on the store shelf because of a purchase goal stored in long-term memory. The soda's current price is brought into short-term memory through the perceptual system for processing. But, a reference price may also be retrieved from long-term memory as a comparison point to help make the decision. Finally, price perceptions associated with their favorite brand may be updated and stored in long-term memory as a consequence of the comparison process.

MEMORY'S ROLE IN LEARNING

Memory is the total accumulation of prior learning experiences. As Figure 9-1 suggests, memory is critical to learning. It consists of two interrelated components: short-term and long-term memory.[3] These are *not* distinct physiological entities. Instead, **short-term memory** (STM) or *working memory* is that portion of total memory that is currently activated or in use. **Long-term memory** (LTM) is that portion of total memory devoted to permanent information storage.

Short-Term Memory

Short-term memory has a limited capacity to store information and sensations. In fact, it is not used for storage in the usual sense of that term. It is more like a computer file that is currently in use. Active files hold information while it is being processed. After processing is complete, the reconfigured information is printed or returned to more permanent storage such as the hard drive. A similar process occurs with short-term memory. Individuals use short-term memory to hold information while they analyze and interpret it. They may then transfer it to another system (write or type it), place it in long-term memory, or both. Thus, short-term memory is closely analogous to what we normally call thinking. *It is an active, dynamic process, not a static structure.*

STM Is Short Lived   The short-lived nature of STM means that consumers must constantly refresh information through **maintenance rehearsal** or it will be lost. Maintenance rehearsal is the continual repetition of a piece of information in order to hold it in current memory for use in problem solving or transferal to long-term memory. Repeating the same formula or definition several times before taking an exam is an example. Marketers frequently simulate this by repeating the brand name or a key benefit in a prominent manner several times in an ad.

STM Has Limited Capacity   The limited capacity of STM means that consumers can only hold so much information in current memory. The capacity of STM is thought to be in the range of 5 to 9 bits of information. A bit can be an individual item or a related set of items. Organizing individual items into groups of related items that can be processed as a single unit is called *chunking*. Chunking can greatly aid in the transfer (and recall) of information from memory. A recent study of toll-free *vanity numbers* shows the power of chunking. Memory for completely numeric numbers was 8 percent, memory for combinations of numbers and words (800-555-HOME) was 44 percent, and memory for all words (800-NEW-HOME) was 58 percent! The number of bits goes down as the words become meaningful chunks replacing meaningless numbers.[4]

Successful new products and brands must enter into memory in a favorable manner, and they must be recalled when required. In this case, the brand name, the visual in the ad, and the ad text will enhance elaborative activities appropriate for the product.

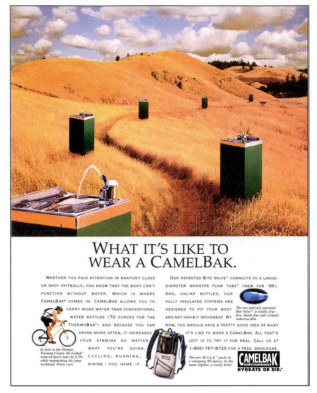

© Fasttrack Systems, Inc. 1996. Created by Mizuno & Associates/ Westlake Village, CA.

Marketers can help consumers to chunk product information by organizing detailed attribute information in messages around the more general benefits that they create. Interestingly, consumers who are product experts are better able to chunk due to highly organized memory structures. As a consequence, experts are better able to learn information and avoid information overload.[5]

Elaborative Activities Occur in STM   STM is often termed working memory because that's where information is analyzed, categorized, and interpreted—that is, STM is where **elaborative activities** take place. Elaborative activities are *the use of previously stored experiences, values, attitudes, beliefs, and feelings to interpret and evaluate information in working memory as well as to add relevant previously stored information*. Elaborative activities serve to redefine or add new elements to memory.

Suppose your firm has developed a new product targeted initially at bike riders. The product is a water bottle that one wears strapped to the back with a tube from which the rider can drink without using hands. How will this product be categorized or assigned meaning by the market? The answer depends in large part on *how* it is presented. How it is presented will influence the nature of the elaborative activities that will occur, which in turn will determine how the product is remembered.

Illustration 9-1 shows how CamelBak® introduced such a product. First, it used an image-rich name that conveys much of the product's function. Camels are known for their ability to store water, and this system is worn on one's back. The visual in the ad clearly, if symbolically, shows the product's primary benefit. The text expands on this theme. Thus, this ad should help trigger elaborative activities that will allow consumers to define this as a new and useful product for providing fluids on bike trips. The high-imagery name should help retention and recall of the key benefits of the product.

Elaborative activities can involve both concepts and imagery. **Concepts** are abstractions of reality that capture the meaning of an item in terms of other concepts. They are similar to a dictionary definition of a word. Thus, a consumer might bring to mind concepts such as water bottle and backpack when first processing the new concept CamelBak.

Imagery involves concrete sensory representations of ideas, feelings, and objects. It permits a direct recovery of aspects of past experiences. Thus, imagery processing involves the recall and mental manipulation of sensory images, including sight, smell, taste, and tactile (touch) sensations.

Pictures can increase imagery, particularly when they are relatively concrete representations of reality rather than an abstraction. In the CamelBak ad, for example, the visual of water pouring from the fountain is contrasted with the dry arid surroundings of the bike trail. These concrete images may induce some consumers to recall the experience of thirst they felt on their last ride and the feeling of cool water quenching that thirst. Pictures are not the only factor to increase imagery, however. Words and phrases in an ad can also encourage consumers to conjure up their own images (e.g., "picture it . . . ," "feel it . . . ," "imagine . . .").[6]

Whether consumers are processing concepts or images, a key issue in learning and memory is the *extent of elaboration*. A major determinant of elaboration is consumer motivation or involvement. Elaboration is enhanced when consumers are more involved or interested in the brand, product, or message at hand (as we saw earlier, it also is facilitated by consumer expertise). Elaboration increases the chances that information will be transferred to LTM and be retrieved at a later time by increasing the processing attention directed at that information and by establishing meaningful linkages between the new information and existing information. These linkages or associations are an important part of LTM as discussed next.

Long-Term Memory

Long-term memory is viewed as *an unlimited, permanent storage.* It can store numerous types of information such as concepts, decision rules, processes, affective (emotional) states, and so forth. Marketers are particularly interested in **semantic memory,** which is *the basic knowledge and feelings an individual has about a concept.* It represents the person's understanding of an object or event at its simplest level. At this level, a brand such as Acura might be categorized as "a luxury car."

Another type of memory of interest to marketers is **episodic memory.** This is *the memory of a sequence of events in which a person participated.* These personal memories of events such as a first date, graduation, or learning to drive can be quite strong. They often elicit imagery and feelings. Marketers frequently attempt to evoke episodic memories either because their brand was involved in them or to associate the positive feelings they generate with the brand.

Marketers worry not only about *what* information is stored in LTM but also *how* this information is organized. Two important memory structures are schemas and scripts.

Schemas   Both concepts and episodes acquire depth of meaning by becoming associated with other concepts and episodes. A pattern of such associations around a particular concept is termed a **schema** or *schematic memory,* sometimes called a *knowledge structure.* Schematic memory is a complex web of associations. Figure 9-2 provides a simplified example of a schema by showing how one might associate various concepts with Mountain

FIGURE 9-2   A Partial Schematic Memory for Mountain Dew

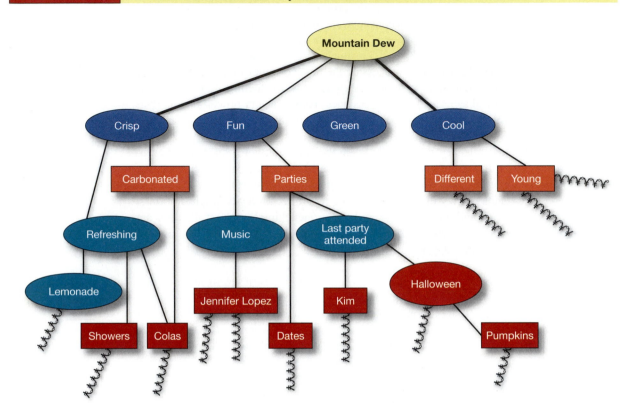

Dew to form a network of meaning for that brand. Notice that our hypothetical schema contains *product characteristics, usage situations, episodes,* and *affective reactions*. The source of some of the schema is personal experience, but other aspects may be completely or partially based on marketing activities.[7] The schematic memory of a brand is the same as the brand image, which we discuss later in the chapter. It is what the consumer thinks of and feels when the brand name is mentioned.

In the partial schema shown in Figure 9-2, concepts, events, and feelings are stored in *nodes* within memory. Thus, the concept "cool" is stored in a node, as are "music," "fun," and "Halloween." Each of these is associated either directly or indirectly with Mountain Dew. *Associative links* connect various concepts to form the complete meaning assigned to an item.

Associative links vary in terms of how strongly and how directly they are associated with a node. In our example, crisp, fun, green, and cool are directly associated with Mountain Dew. However, one or two of these may be strongly associated with the brand, as crisp and cool are shown to be by the bold lines in our example. Other nodes may have weaker links, such as fun and green. Without reinforcement, the weaker links may disappear or fade over time (e.g., the Halloween party linkage). Over the longer run, so will the stronger ones (e.g., the cool linkage). Marketers spend enormous effort attempting to develop strong, easily activated links between their brands and desirable product benefits.[8] The various ways in which these linkages are established and strengthened (reinforced) are discussed in the next section on learning.

The memory activation shown in Figure 9-2 originated with the name of a particular brand. If the activation had begun with the concept "cool," would Mountain Dew arise as a node directly linked to cool? It would depend on the total context in which the memory was being activated. In general, multiple memory nodes are activated simultaneously.

Thus, a question like "What is a cool soft drink?" might quickly activate a memory schema that links Mountain Dew directly to cool. However, a more abstract question like "What is cool?" might not due to its relatively weak and indirect connection to beverages and sodas.[9] Marketers expend substantial effort to influence the schema consumers have for their brands. We will discuss this process in detail later in the chapter.

Marketers also strive to influence the schema consumers have for consumption situations. For example, consumers likely have very different beverage schemas for situations like jogging where thirst is a key component than for a party where socializing and relaxing are key components. The beverage schema for jogging might include products such as water and soda and brands such as Dasani and Pepsi. The beverage schema for a party might include products such as wine and beer and brands such as Yellow Tail and Budweiser. Brands in the schematic memory that come to mind (are recalled) for a specific problem or situation such as thirst are known as the *evoked set*.

The usage situation schema a brand attaches itself to can have major ramifications. For example, if Canada Dry Ginger Ale associated itself strongly with a "party" situation as a mixer for cocktails, then it is much less likely to be retrieved as part of the evoked set when consumers are thinking of other usage situations, such as those involving thirst.[10] We will discuss how the evoked set influences consumer decision making in Chapter 15.

Scripts   *Memory of how an action sequence should occur,* such as purchasing and drinking a soft drink in order to relieve thirst, is a special type of schema known as a **script.** Scripts are necessary for consumers to shop effectively. One of the difficulties new forms of retailing have is teaching consumers the appropriate script for acquiring items in a new manner. This is the problem facing firms wanting to sell products via the Internet. Before these firms can succeed, their target markets must learn appropriate scripts for Internet shopping.

Marketers and public policy officials want consumers to develop scripts for appropriate product acquisition, use, and disposal behavior. For example, using a product or service requires one to learn a process. This process often includes the disposition of the package or some part of the product.[11] Unfortunately, many consumers have learned consumption scripts that do not include appropriate disposition activities such as recycling. Thus, both government agencies and environmental groups spend substantial effort attempting to teach consumers consumption scripts that include recycling.

Retrieval from LTM   The likelihood and ease with which information can be recalled from LTM is termed **accessibility.** Every time an informational node or a link between nodes is activated (accessed) in memory it is strengthened. Thus, accessibility can be enhanced by rehearsal, repetition, and elaboration. For example, Coca-Cola might be one of the brands that always comes to mind (is retrieved) when you think of sodas because you have seen so many ads for that brand. This accessibility effect for brands is called *top-of-mind awareness*. In addition, accessibility is related to the strength and number of incoming linkages. In essence, when a concept is linked to other concepts in memory its accessibility increases due to multiple retrieval pathways. Thus, elaboration enhances retrieval by creating a rich associative network. Finally, accessibility is related to the strength and directness of links to nodes, with stronger and more direct linkages being more accessible. Thus, cool and crisp are highly accessible associations related to Mountain Dew, while parties and refreshing are less accessible. Clearly, marketers want strong and direct linkages between their brand and critical product features.

Retrieving information from LTM is not a completely objective or mechanical task. If asked to recall the sponsor of the last summer Olympics, some consumers will not remember instantly and certainly. These individuals may *construct* a memory based on limited recall and a series of judgments or inferences. For example, many might "recall" Nike because it is a dominant firm in sports equipment and apparel. Thus, it would "make sense"

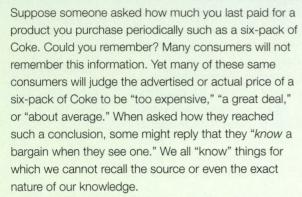

Suppose someone asked how much you last paid for a product you purchase periodically such as a six-pack of Coke. Could you remember? Many consumers will not remember this information. Yet many of these same consumers will judge the advertised or actual price of a six-pack of Coke to be "too expensive," "a great deal," or "about average." When asked how they reached such a conclusion, some might reply that they "*know* a bargain when they see one." We all "know" things for which we cannot recall the source or even the exact nature of our knowledge.

Traditionally, we have thought of remembering, and thus memory, as the ability to recall specific items or events. If you read this chapter and then try to answer the review questions at the end without referring back to the chapter, you are engaging in traditional memory recall. This is referred to as **explicit memory,** which is characterized by *the conscious recollection of an exposure event*. In contrast to remembering, "knowing" utilizes implicit memory. **Implicit memory** involves *the nonconscious retrieval of previously encountered stimuli*. It is a sense of familiarity, a feeling, or a set of beliefs about an item without conscious awareness of when and how they were acquired.[12]

The distinction between explicit memory (remembering) and implicit memory ("knowing") is important for marketing research, pricing, and advertising strategy.

For example, it suggests that measuring the effectiveness of ads using advertising recall (explicit memory) may not work for ads aimed at establishing a brand image. Much of a brand image will take the form of an implicit memory. A consumer will "know" Mountain Dew is cool, that Levi's are old-fashioned, and that Volkswagen is fun without being able to explain how he or she acquired this knowledge. Thus, recall of the ad or any of its features is not as relevant as its long-term impact on what consumers "know" about the brand.

It is also important for marketers to understand and monitor what their target consumers "know" relative to their firm and brand. This is because consumers' knowledge about a product, brand, or process frequently does not correspond with reality. For example, a consumer may "know" that Bayer aspirin provides superior inflammation reduction compared with less expensive store brands. If that is not the actual case, Bayer benefits, but other brands and the consumer lose.

Critical Thinking Questions

1. What is the relationship between explicit and implicit memory?

2. Why do marketers rely so much on measuring of advertising recall?

for Nike to be the sponsor, which could lead some consumers to believe that Nike was indeed a sponsor of the event even if they were not.[13] Therefore, memory is sometimes shaped and changed as it is accessed. Likewise, memory of an actual event may be altered as new or additional information about that event is received.[14] In fact, one study found that an ad which prompted imagery responses about a childhood trip to Disney increased consumers' confidence that they had actually experienced an event at Disney (shaking hands with a non-Disney character such as Bugs Bunny) that could not have happened.[15] *What are the ethical concerns relating to this sort of memory construction and distortion?*

Finally, retrieval may involve *explicit* memories (memories of specific events or objects) or *implicit* memories (generalized memories about events or objects). Consumer Insight 9-1 highlights this distinction.

LEARNING UNDER HIGH AND LOW INVOLVEMENT

We have described learning as any change in the content or organization of long-term memory or behavior. In addition, we have described long-term memory in terms of schemas or associational networks. So how do people *learn* these associations? For

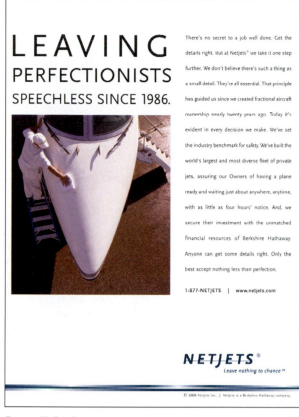

Courtesy NetJets, Inc.

Courtesy Unilever United States, Inc.

example, how do consumers *learn* that Mountain Dew is cool or that Wal-Mart has low prices?

A moment's reflection will reveal that people learn things in different ways.[16] For example, buying a car or stereo generally involves intense, focused attention and processing. The outcome of these efforts is rewarded by better choices. However, most learning is of a much different nature. Most people know who is playing in the World Series each year even if they don't care for baseball because they hear about it frequently. And people can identify clothes that are stylish even though they never really think much about clothing styles.

As just described, learning may occur in either a high-involvement or a low-involvement situation. Recall from Chapter 8 that information processing (and therefore learning) may be conscious and deliberate in high-involvement situations. Or it may be nonfocused and even nonconscious in low-involvement situations. A **high-involvement learning** situation is one in which *the consumer is motivated to process or learn the material*. For example, an individual reading *Laptop Buyer's Guide* prior to purchasing a computer is probably highly motivated to learn relevant material dealing with the various computer brands. A **low-involvement learning** situation is one in which *the consumer has little or no motivation to process or learn the material*. A consumer whose television program is interrupted by a commercial for a product he or she doesn't currently use or feel a desire for generally has little motivation to learn the material presented in the commercial. Much, if not most, consumer learning occurs in relatively low-involvement contexts.[17]

As we will see in the following sections, the way a communication should be structured differs depending on the level of involvement the audience is expected to have.[18] Illustration 9-2 shows one ad that assumes high-involvement learning and another based on

FIGURE 9-3   Learning Theories in High- and Low-Involvement Situations

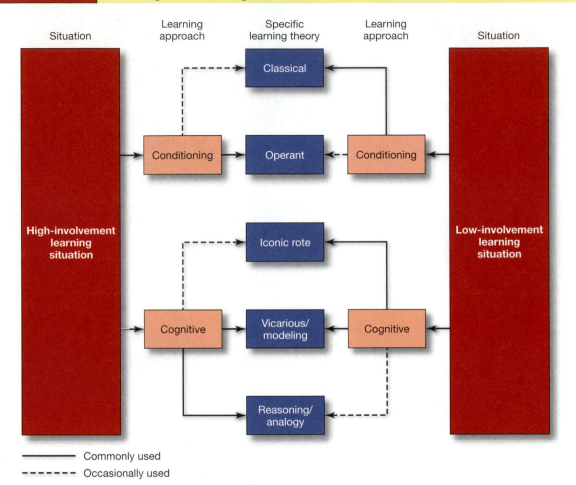

low-involvement learning. *Why does one ad assume a highly involved audience and the other a low-involvement audience? What differences do you notice between these two ads? Do those differences make sense?*

Figure 9-3 shows the two general situations and the five specific learning theories that we are going to consider. *Level of involvement is the primary determinant of how material is learned.* The solid lines in the figure indicate that operant conditioning and analytical reasoning are common learning processes in high-involvement situations. Classical conditioning and iconic rote learning tend to occur in low-involvement situations. And, vicarious learning/modeling is common in both low- and high-involvement situations. We will discuss each of these theories in the following pages.

Conditioning

Conditioning is probably most appropriately described as a set of procedures that marketers can use to increase the chances that an association between two stimuli is formed or learned. The word *conditioning* has a negative connotation to many people and brings forth images of robot-like humans. However, the general procedure simply involves presenting two stimuli

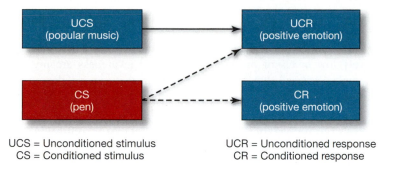

Consumer Learning through Classical Conditioning   FIGURE 9-4

UCS = Unconditioned stimulus   UCR = Unconditioned response
CS = Conditioned stimulus   CR = Conditioned response

in close proximity so that eventually the two are perceived (consciously or unconsciously) to be related or associated. That is, consumers learn that the stimuli go (or do not go) together.

There are two basic forms of conditioned learning—classical and operant. *Classical conditioning* attempts to create an association between a stimulus (e.g., brand name) and some response (e.g., behavior or feeling). *Operant conditioning* attempts to create an association between a response (e.g., buying a brand) and some outcome (e.g., satisfaction) that serves to reinforce the response.

Classical Conditioning   Imagine that you are marketing a new brand of pen and want consumers to feel positively about that pen. How might classical conditioning help you to associate positive feelings with your unfamiliar brand? The classical conditioning procedure would have you pair the unknown brand repeatedly together with some other stimulus that you know already *automatically* elicits positive feelings or emotions, such as popular music in an ad. The goal would be that, eventually, after repeatedly pairing the brand name and the music, the brand name alone will elicit the same positive feelings produced by the music.

The process of using an established relationship between one stimulus (music) and response (pleasant feelings) to bring about the learning of the same response (pleasant feelings) to a different stimulus (the brand) is called **classical conditioning.** Figure 9-4 illustrates this type of learning. Hearing popular music (unconditioned stimulus) automatically elicits a positive emotion (unconditioned response) in many individuals. If this music is consistently paired with a particular brand of pen or other product (conditioned stimulus), the brand itself may come to elicit the same positive emotion (conditioned response).[19] In addition, some features, such as the masculine/feminine qualities of the unconditioned stimulus, may also become associated with the conditioned stimulus. That is, using a scene showing males or females in an activity that elicits positive emotions may not only cause a positive emotional response to a brand consistently paired with it, but also cause the brand to have a masculine or a feminine image.[20] For example, Marlboro cigarettes are presented on billboards and, in countries where it is legal, in media ads showing the brand name or package and a beautiful outdoor scene. Part of the objective of such ads is to associate the positive emotional response to the outdoor scene with the brand. This in turn will increase the likelihood that the individual will like the brand. This is an important *learning* outcome since, as we will see in later chapters, attitudes influence information search, trial, and brand choice.

Other marketing applications of classical conditioning include:

- Consistently advertising a product on exciting sports programs may result in the product itself generating an excitement response.

- An unknown political candidate may elicit patriotic feelings by consistently playing patriotic background music in his or her commercials and appearances.
- Christmas music played in stores may elicit emotional responses associated with giving and sharing, which in turn may increase the propensity to purchase.

Learning via classical conditioning is most common in low-involvement situations, where relatively low levels of processing effort and awareness are involved.[21] In the Marlboro example described above, it is likely that many consumers devote little or no focused attention to the advertisement, since cigarette ads are low-involvement messages even for most smokers. However, after a sufficient number of low-involvement "scannings" or "glances at" the advertisement, the association may be formed or learned.

Operant Conditioning **Operant conditioning** (or instrumental learning) involves rewarding desirable behaviors such as brand purchases with a positive outcome that serves to reinforce the behavior.[22] The more often a response is reinforced, the more likely it will be repeated in the future as consumers *learn* that the response is associated with a positive outcome.

Imagine that you are marketing a snack called Pacific Snax's Rice Popcorn. You believe your product has a light, crisp taste that consumers will like. But how can you influence them to learn to consume your brand? One option based on the operant conditioning procedure would be to distribute a large number of free samples through the mail, at shopping malls, or in stores. Many consumers would try the free sample (desired response). To the extent that the taste of Rice Popcorn is indeed pleasant (a positive outcome that serves as a reinforcement), the probability of continued consumption is increased. This is shown graphically in Figure 9-5.

Unlike the relatively automatic associations created by classical conditioning, operant conditioning requires that consumers first engage in a deliberate behavior and come to understand its power in predicting positive outcomes that serve as reinforcement. As suggested in Figure 9-3, such learning is common under conditions of higher involvement.

Operant conditioning often involves influencing consumers to purchase a specific brand or product (desired response). Thus, a great deal of marketing strategy is aimed at securing an initial trial. Free samples (at home or in the store), special price discounts on new products, and contests all represent rewards offered to consumers to try a particular product or brand. If they try the brand under these conditions and like it (reinforcement), they are likely to take the next step and purchase it in the future. This process of encouraging partial responses leading to the final desired response (consume a free sample, buy at a discount, buy at full price) is known as **shaping** and is illustrated in Figure 9-6.

In one study, 84 percent of those given a free sample of a chocolate while in a candy store made a purchase, whereas only 59 percent of those not provided a sample made a purchase. Thus, shaping can be very effective. Illustration 9-3 shows an ad designed to induce trial, the first step in shaping.

FIGURE 9-5	Consumer Learning by Operant Conditioning

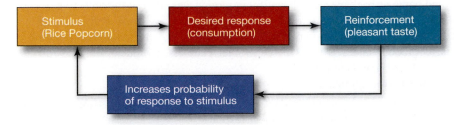

The Process of Shaping in Purchase Behavior   FIGURE 9-6

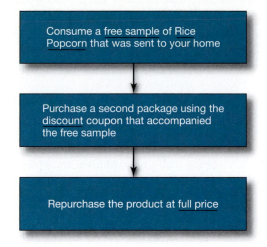

Consume a free sample of Rice Popcorn that was sent to your home

↓

Purchase a second package using the discount coupon that accompanied the free sample

↓

Repurchase the product at full price

Courtesy Sara Lee Food & Beverage.

While reinforcement increases the likelihood of behavior such as a purchase being repeated, a negative consequence (punishment) has exactly the opposite effect. Thus, the purchase of a brand that does not function properly greatly reduces the chances of future purchases of that brand. This underscores the critical importance of consistent product quality.

Operant conditioning is used widely by marketers. The most common application is to offer consistent-quality products so that the use of the product to meet a consumer need is reinforcing. Other applications include:

- Direct-mail or personal contact after a sale that congratulates the purchaser for making a wise purchase.
- Giving extra reinforcement for shopping at a store, such as trading stamps, rebates, or prizes.
- Giving extra reinforcement for purchasing a particular brand, such as rebates, toys in cereal boxes, or discount coupons.
- Giving free product samples or introductory coupons to encourage product trial (shaping).
- Making store interiors, shopping malls, or downtown areas pleasant places to shop (re-inforcing) by providing entertainment, controlled temperature, exciting displays, and so forth.

The power of operant conditioning was demonstrated by an experiment conducted by an insurance company. More than 2,000 consumers who purchased life insurance over a one-month period were randomly divided into three groups. Two of the groups received rein-forcement after each monthly payment in the form of a nice "thank-you" letter or telephone call. The third group received no such reinforcement. Six months later, 10 percent of the members of the two groups that received reinforcement had terminated their policies, while 23 percent of those who had not received reinforcement had done so! Reinforcement (being thanked) led to continued behavior (sending in the monthly premium).[23]

Cognitive Learning

Cognitive learning encompasses all the mental activities of humans as they work to solve problems or cope with situations. It involves learning ideas, concepts, attitudes, and facts that contribute to our ability to reason, solve problems, and learn relationships without direct experience or reinforcement. Cognitive learning can range from very simple infor-mation acquisition (as in iconic rote learning) to complex, creative problem solving (as in analytical reasoning). Three types of cognitive learning are important to marketers.

Iconic Rote Learning
Learning *a concept or the association between two or more concepts in the absence of conditioning* is known as **iconic rote learning.** For example, one may see an ad that states "Ketoprofin is a headache remedy" and associate the new concept "ketoprofin" with the existing concept "headache remedy." Notice the distinction from conditioning in that there is neither an unconditioned stimulus (classical) nor a direct reward or reinforcement (operant) involved.

Also, it is important to point out that unlike more complex forms of cognitive learning, iconic rote learning generally involves considerably less cognitive effort and elaboration.[24] A substantial amount of low-involvement learning involves iconic rote learning. Numerous repetitions of a simple message that occur as the consumer scans the environment may result in the essence of the message being learned. Through iconic rote learning, consumers may form beliefs about the characteristics or attributes of products without being aware of the source of the information. When the need arises, a purchase may be made based on those beliefs.[25]

Vicarious Learning/Modeling
It is not necessary for consumers to directly experience a reward or punishment to learn. Instead, they can observe the outcomes of others' behav-iors and adjust their own accordingly.[26] Similarly, they can use imagery to anticipate the outcome of various courses of action. This is known as **vicarious learning** or **modeling.**

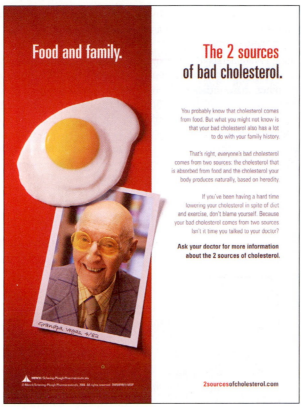

ILLUSTRATION 9-4

Ads not only convey information and elicit feelings; they can challenge existing assumptions and cause readers to think and reexamine their beliefs.

This type of learning is common in both low- and high-involvement situations. In a high-involvement situation, such as purchasing a new suit shortly after taking a job, a consumer may deliberately observe the styles worn by others at work or by role models from other environments, including advertisements. Many ads encourage consumers to imagine the feelings and experience of using a product.[27] Such images not only enhance learning about the product, but may even influence how the product is evaluated after an actual trial.

A substantial amount of modeling also occurs in low-involvement situations. Throughout the course of their lives, people observe others using products and behaving in a great variety of situations. Most of the time they pay little attention to these behaviors. However, over time they learn that certain behaviors, and products, are appropriate in some situations and others are not.

Analytical Reasoning   The most complex form of cognitive learning is **analytical reasoning.** In reasoning, individuals engage in creative thinking to restructure and recombine existing information as well as new information to form new associations and concepts. Information from a credible source that contradicts or challenges one's existing beliefs will often trigger reasoning.[28] The ad for Merck in Illustration 9-4 challenges consumer beliefs regarding the sources of bad cholesterol.

One form of analytical reasoning is the use of analogy. **Analogical reasoning** allows consumers to use an existing knowledge base to understand a new situation or object. That is, it allows consumers to use knowledge about something they are familiar with to help them understand something they are not familiar with. For example, suppose you were hearing about software programs called off-line Web readers for the first time. These off-line Web readers are designed to download Web pages to PCs. You might learn about this software by analogical reasoning such as,

> relating it to something you understand better such as VCRs. You notice that the Web readers and VCRs are designed to retrieve media content. Given this similarity of purpose, you may logically expect them to share other characteristics. Since VCRs record TV programs onto a videocassette that allows them to be replayed on other VCR players at any desired time, you may conclude that the Web readers will record Web pages onto a disk that can then be accessed from other computers as desired. You may also believe that VCR players are difficult to program and assume that the new Web readers will also be difficult to use properly. At the end of this process, you may have a fairly complete set of beliefs about the new Web reader without having seen or used the product or read or viewed any information about its characteristics.[29]

Learning to Generalize and Differentiate

Regardless of which approach to learning is applicable in a given situation, consumers' ability to differentiate and generalize from one stimulus to another (for example one brand to another) is critical to marketers.

Stimulus discrimination or differentiation refers to the *process of learning to respond differently to similar but distinct stimuli*. This is critical for marketers who want consumers to perceive their brands as possessing unique and important features compared to other brands. For example, the management of Bayer aspirin feels that consumers should not see its aspirin as being the same as other brands. In order to obtain a premium price or a large market share, Bayer must teach consumers that its aspirin is distinct from other brands. Stimulus discrimination is an important consideration in brand image and product positioning and we devote a major section to these issues later in the chapter.

Stimulus generalization, often referred to as the *rub-off effect, occurs when a response to one stimulus is elicited by a similar but distinct stimulus.*[30] Thus, a consumer who learns that Nabisco's Oreo Cookies taste good and therefore assumes that the company's new Oreo Chocolate Cones will also taste good has engaged in stimulus generalization. Stimulus generalization is common and provides a major source of brand equity and brand extensions based on leveraging brand equity. This area is so important that we devote the last major section of this chapter to it.

Summary of Learning Theories

Theories of learning help us understand how consumers learn across a variety of situations. We have examined five specific learning theories: classical conditioning, operant conditioning, iconic rote learning, vicarious learning/modeling, and analytical reasoning. Each of these learning theories can operate in a high- or a low-involvement situation, although some are more common in one type of situation than another. Table 9-1 summarizes these theories and provides examples from both high- and low-involvement contexts.

LEARNING, MEMORY, AND RETRIEVAL

Gillette's growth slowed considerably in the early 2000s,[31] as did Saturn's in the early 1990s,[32] and L&M cigarettes' in the 1980s.[33] In each case, at least some of the decline in growth was attributed to sharply reduced advertising. As one executive stated,

> Some time after the company moved away from advertising and marketing, it became clear that people would quickly forget about our products if we didn't support them in the marketplace.[34]

Summary of Learning Theories with Examples of Involvement Level   **TABLE 9-1**

Theory	Description	High-Involvement Example	Low-Involvement Example
Classical Conditioning	A response elicited by one object is elicited by a second object if both objects frequently occur together.	The favorable emotional response elicited by the word *America* comes to be elicited by a car brand after repeated exposure to its *Made in America* campaign. This response is in addition to any cognitive learning that may have occurred.	The favorable emotional response elicited by a song in an ad for a new breath mint comes to be elicited by that brand after repeated pairing with the song even though the consumer pays little attention to the ad.
Operant Conditioning	A response that is reinforced is more likely to be repeated when the same (or similar) situation arises in the future.	A suit is purchased after extensive thought and the consumer finds that it is comfortable and doesn't wrinkle. A sport coat made by the same firm is later purchased because of the positive experience with their suits.	A familiar brand of peas is purchased without much thought due to the low importance of the decision. The peas taste "fresh" so the consumer continues to purchase this brand.
Iconic Rote Learning	A concept or the association between two concepts is learned without conditioning.	A consumer with little expertise about CD players tries hard to learn brand information by examining it carefully several times. Learning is limited, however, because his or her lack of expertise inhibits elaboration.	A consumer learns a company's most recent jingle because it is catchy and can't stop replaying it in his or her head.
Vicarious Learning or Modeling	Behaviors are learned by watching the outcomes of others' behaviors or by imagining the outcome of a potential behavior.	A consumer carefully watches the reactions that other co-workers have to her friend's new briefcase before deciding to buy one.	A child learns that people dress up for special occasions without really ever thinking about it.
Analytical Reasoning	Individuals use thinking to restructure and recombine existing and new information to form new associations and concepts.	A consumer buying a car carefully processes information about a new gas/electric hybrid car by using the analogy of homes powered by solar energy.	When a store is out of black pepper, a consumer buys white pepper instead based on the quick reasoning that "pepper is pepper."

These examples emphasize that marketers want consumers to learn *and* remember positive features, feelings, and behaviors associated with their brands. However, consumers forget. In conditioned learning, forgetting is often referred to as **extinction** since the desired response (e.g., pleasant feelings or brand purchase) decays or dies out if learning is not repeated and reinforced. In cognitive learning, forgetting is often referred to as a **retrieval failure** since information that is available in LTM cannot be accessed, that is, retrieved from LTM into STM.

Two aspects of forgetting that are of concern to marketers are the *likelihood of forgetting* in any given situation and the *rate of forgetting*. Figure 9-7 illustrates a commonly found rate of forgetting for advertising. In this study, aided and unaided recall of four advertisements from *American Machinist* magazine was measured. As can be seen, the probability of ad recall (likelihood) dropped rapidly after five days and then stabilized (rate).

At times, marketers or regulatory groups desire to accelerate forgetting or extinction. For example, the American Cancer Society and other organizations offer programs designed to help individuals "unlearn" smoking behavior. Manufacturers want consumers to forget unfavorable publicity or outdated product images. *Corrective advertising,* a

| FIGURE 9-7 | Forgetting over Time: Magazine Advertisement |

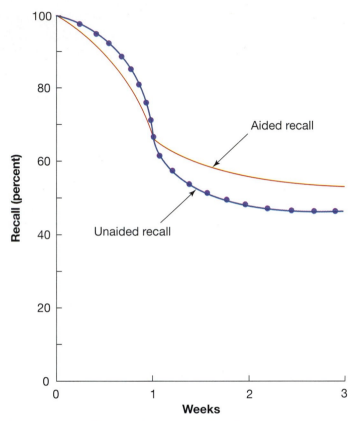

Source: LAP Report #5260.1 (New York: Weeks McGraw-Hill, undated). Reprinted with permission from McGraw-Hill Companies, Inc.

government requirement that firms remove inaccurate learning caused by past advertising, is described in Chapter 20.

Consumers forget brands, brand associations, and other information for a variety of reasons. First, learning may be weak to begin with. Second, information from competing brands and ads may cause memory interference. Third, the response environment (e.g., the retail store) may not be set up to encourage retrieval of previously learned information (e.g., from advertising). We turn to these issues next.

Strength of Learning

How can the HIV Alliance teach you to minimize your AIDS risk so that you will not forget? Or, how can Neutrogena teach you about its line of sunless tanning products so you remember key features when shopping at CVS? That is, what is required to bring about a long-lasting learned response?

One factor is strength of learning. The stronger the original learning (e.g., of nodes and links between nodes), the more likely relevant information will be retrieved when required. *Strength of learning* is enhanced by six factors: *importance, message involvement, mood, reinforcement, repetition,* and *dual coding.*

Importance   Importance refers to the value that consumers place on the information to be learned. Importance might be driven by inherent interest in the product or brand, or might be driven by the need to make a decision in the near future. The more important it is for the individual to learn a particular behavior or piece of information, the more effective and efficient he or she becomes in the learning process. This is largely due to the greater elaborative activities involved in fully processing and categorizing the material.

One emerging area of interest to marketers is how bilingual consumers process and recall second-language ads. For example, if Hispanic consumers process an ad in English will it still be as effective as when they process the same ad in Spanish? Generally speaking, processing an ad in a second language is more difficult. This tends to reduce learning and recall for ads in a consumer's second language. Does this mean that second-language ads can never be effective? The answer appears to depend on importance. When importance is high, bilingual consumers expend more processing effort to understand the second-language ad, leading to greater learning and recall.[35]

Importance is one dimension that separates high-involvement learning situations from low-involvement situations. Therefore, high-involvement learning tends to be more complete than low-involvement learning.[36] Unfortunately, marketers are most often confronted with consumers in low-involvement learning situations.

Message Involvement   When a consumer is not motivated to learn the material, processing can be increased by causing the person to become involved *with the message itself.* For example, playing an instrumental version of a popular song with lyrics related to product attributes ("Like a rock" in Chevrolet pickup ads) may cause people to "sing along," either out loud or mentally. This deepened involvement with the message, relative to merely listening to the lyrics being sung, increases the extent of processing of the message and memory of the associated features or theme.[37]

In Chapter 8 we discussed various strategies for increasing consumer attention including incongruity, rhetoric, incomplete messages, and interesting ads with plots and surprise endings.[38] These strategies also tend to enhance message involvement and thus lead to stronger learning and memory.[39]

Several issues regarding message involvement are important to consider. First, there is evidence that scent may be important to memory. One study found that positive scents present during exposure to an ad increased attention to the ad and resulted in higher brand recall. Not surprisingly, marketers are currently in the early stages of developing technologies that will allow for "scent-emitting" technologies for Internet applications and in-store kiosks![40]

A second issue is the role of suspense. Sometimes marketers wait until the very end of a message to reveal the brand name in an attempt to attract interest and attention. However, this strategy must be used with caution because waiting until the end of an ad to reveal the brand gives consumers little opportunity to integrate new information into their existing brand schemas. As a result, the associative linkages are weaker and memory is reduced. These results suggest that marketers should strongly consider mentioning the brand relatively early in any marketing message.[41]

A final issue regards message strategies that highlight a brand's personal relevance to the consumer. One such strategy is self-referencing. **Self-referencing** indicates that consumers are relating brand information to themselves. The "self" is a powerful memory schema and integrating brand information into this schema enhances learning and memory. Self-referencing can be encouraged in ads by using nostalgia appeals which encourage consumers to remember past personal experiences.[42] It can also be encouraged by using language such as "you" and "your" (second person pronoun). The CamelBak ad in

Reinforcement is anything that increases the probability that a response will be repeated in the future. It can involve a positive outcome such as providing pleasure, or the removal or avoidance of a negative outcome, such as sinus problems.

© The Procter & Gamble Company. Used by permission.

Illustration 9-1 effectively uses self-referencing. It encourages self-brand links with statements such as "allows *you* to carry more water," and "increases *your* stamina."

Mood   Get happy, learn more? Research indicates that this is indeed true. A positive mood during the presentation of information such as brand names enhances learning. A positive mood during the reception of information appears to enhance its relational elaboration—it is compared with and evaluated against more categories. This produces a more complete and stronger set of linkages among a variety of other brands and concepts, which in turn enhances retrieval (access to the information).[43]

Learning enhancement caused by a positive mood suggests the types of programs that marketers attempting to encourage consumer learning should advertise on. Likewise, it suggests that those commercials that enhance one's mood would also increase learning.[44]

Reinforcement   Anything that increases the likelihood that a given response will be repeated in the future is considered **reinforcement.** While learning frequently occurs in the absence of reinforcement, reinforcement has a significant impact on the speed at which learning occurs and the duration of its effect.

A *positive reinforcement* is a pleasant or desired consequence. A couple who likes Italian food and dining out sees an ad for a new Olive Garden restaurant in their area and decides to try it. They enjoy the food, service, and ambience. They are now more likely to select the Olive Garden next time they dine out.

A *negative reinforcement* involves the removal or the avoidance of an unpleasant consequence. In Illustration 9-5, Vicks promises to relieve sinus pain and pressure. If the ad convinces a consumer to try the sinus formula and it performs well, this consumer is likely to purchase and use it again in the future and, based on stimulus generalization, perhaps try other Vicks products as well.

Punishment is the opposite of reinforcement. It is any consequence that decreases the likelihood that a given response will be repeated in the future. If the couple who tried the Olive Garden restaurant described earlier thought that the service was bad or that the food was poorly prepared, they would be unlikely to patronize it in the future.

Obviously, it is critical for marketers to determine precisely what reinforces consumer purchases so they can design promotional messages and products that encourage initial and repeat purchases.

Repetition   Repetition enhances learning and memory by increasing the accessibility of information in memory or by strengthening the associative linkages between concepts.[45] Quite simply, the more times people are exposed to information or engage in a behavior, the more likely they are to learn and remember it. For example, ads in sports arenas have a greater effect on those who attend the games regularly than on those who attend infrequently.[46] And compared with one showing of a Miller Lite beer commercial, three showings during a championship baseball game produced two-and-one-third times the recall.[47]

The effects of repetition depend, of course, on importance and reinforcement. Less repetition of an advertising message is necessary for someone to learn the message if the subject matter is important or if there is a great deal of relevant reinforcement. Since many advertisements do not contain information of current importance to consumers or direct rewards for learning, repetition plays a critical role in the promotion process for many products.[48] As we saw earlier, classical conditioning and iconic rote learning (low-involvement learning) rely heavily on repetition.

Figure 9-8, based on a study of 16,500 respondents, shows the impact of various levels of advertising repetition over a 48-week period on brands that had either high or low levels of initial awareness. Several features stand out. First, the initial exposure has the largest impact.[49] Second, frequent repetition (once a week) outperforms limited repetition (once every other week or every four weeks). This advantage grows the longer the campaign lasts. Finally, relative gains are much greater for unknown brands.

Both the number of times a message is repeated and the timing of those repetitions affect the extent and duration of learning and memory.[50] Figure 9-9 illustrates the relationship between repetition timing and product recall for a food product. One group of homemakers, represented by the curved line in the figure, was exposed to a food product advertisement once a week for 13 consecutive weeks. For this group, product recall increased rapidly and reached its highest level during the 13th week. Forgetting occurred rapidly when advertising stopped, and recall was virtually zero by the end of the year.

A second group of homemakers was exposed to the same 13 direct-mail advertisements. However, they received one ad every four weeks. The zigzag line in the figure shows the recall pattern for this group. In this case, learning increased throughout the year, but substantial forgetting occurred between message exposures.

Given a finite budget, how should a firm allocate its advertising across a budget cycle—should it concentrate it all at once or spread it out over time? The answer depends on the task. Any time it is important to produce widespread knowledge of the product rapidly, such as during a new-product introduction, frequent (close together) repetitions should be used. This is referred to as **pulsing.** Thus, political candidates frequently hold back a significant proportion of their media budgets until shortly before the election and then use a media blitz to ensure widespread knowledge of their desirable attributes. More long-range

FIGURE 9-8   Impact of Repetition on Brand Awareness for High- and Low-Awareness Brands

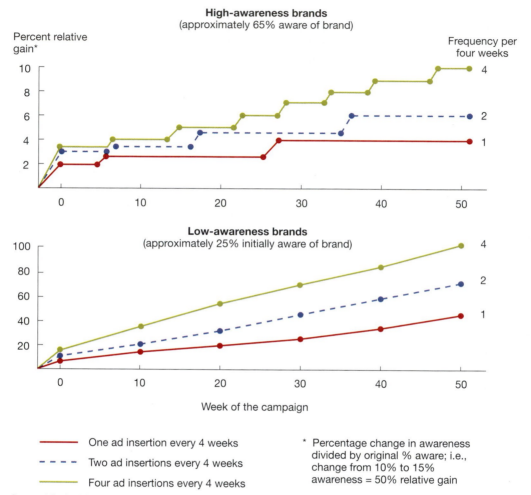

Source: *A Study of the Effectiveness of Advertising Frequency in Magazines.* © 1993 Time Inc. Reprinted by permission.

programs, such as store or brand image development, should use more widely spaced repetitions.[51]

Marketers must walk a fine line in terms of repetition. Too much repetition can cause consumers to actively shut out the message, evaluate it negatively, or disregard it, an effect called **advertising wearout.**[52] One strategy for avoiding wearout is to utilize variations on a common theme.[53] For example, ads for Target continually emphasize core brand themes and the "red dot" symbol. However, they do so in different and interesting ways including roaming animated spokes characters, a white dog with a red dot around one eye, and so on.

Dual Coding   Consumers can store (code) information in different ways. Storing the same information in different ways (dual coding) results in more internal pathways (associative links) for retrieving information. This, in turn can increase learning and memory.

One example of dual coding is when consumers learn information in two different contexts—for example, a consumer sees two ads for the same brand of dandruff shampoo,

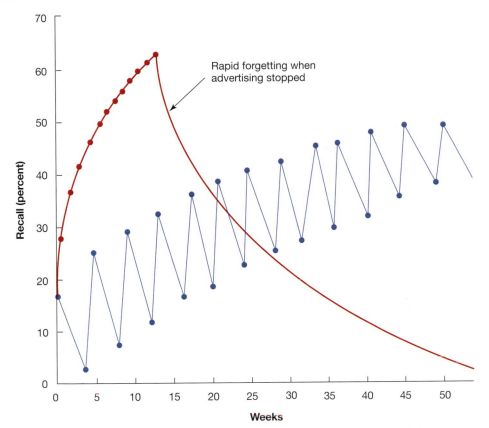

Source: Reprinted from H. J. Zielski, "The Remembering and Forgetting of Advertising," *Journal of Marketing*, January 1959, p. 240, with permission from The American Marketing Association. The actual data and a refined analysis were presented in J. L. Simon, "What Do Zielski's Data Really Show about Pulsing?" *Journal of Marketing Research*, August 1979, pp. 415–20.

one with an office theme and one with a social theme. The varied theme (context) provides multiple paths to the brand and therefore enhances consumers' ability to recall that brand name later on. Illustration 9-6 shows one theme that Clorox uses for its disinfectant products. (Illustration 3-3 in Chapter 3 shows another.) By using multiple themes for its disinfectant products, Clorox can enhance consumer memory beyond its traditional bleach products.

Another example of dual coding relates to information being stored in different memory modes, such as verbal versus visual.[54] Dual coding helps to explain why *imagery* enhances memory. High-imagery stimuli leave a dual code, because they are stored in memory on both verbal and pictorial dimensions, whereas low-imagery stimuli are only coded verbally. As a consequence, high-imagery brand names such as Camel and Mustang are substantially easier to learn and remember than low-imagery names.

Echoic memory—memory of sounds, including words—is another memory mode that appears to have characteristics distinct from visual and verbal memory.[55] This provides the opportunity for dual coding when the sound component of a message (e.g., background music) conveys similar meanings to that being conveyed by the verbal message.[56]

Learning and memory appear to be enhanced when the key ideas communicated through one mode are consistent with those communicated through other modes.[57] For

ILLUSTRATION 9-6

Using varied themes across ads can aid dual coding and enhance memory. Note the differences between this Clorox ad and that found in Illustration 3-3.

CLOROX® is a registered trademark of the CLOROX Company. Reprinted with permission. © 2005 The CLOROX Company. Reprinted with permission.

example, one study finds that having the picture (visual) and text (verbal) convey consistent ideas makes it easier for bilingual consumers to process an ad in their second language. The result is greater learning and memory of the second-language ad.[58]

Memory Interference

Sometimes consumers have difficulty retrieving a specific piece of information because other related information in memory gets in the way. This effect is referred to as **memory interference.** A common form of interference in marketing is due to competitive advertising. For example, seeing an ad for Canada Dry Ginger Ale might interfere with your memory of Mountain Dew. Competitive advertising makes it harder for consumers to recall any given advertisement and its contents. And even if they can recall the contents of a specific ad, they will often have a hard time associating that ad with a specific brand. As a consequence, competitive advertising can either reduce memory for the brand claims made in a specific advertisement or lead to brand-claim confusions across advertisements for competing brands.[59]

Competitive advertising interference increases as the number of competing ads within the same product category increases and as the similarity of these ads to each other increases. Given the high levels of advertising clutter, it should not be surprising that this is an area of concern for marketers and advertisers. The major question is *what can marketers do to decrease competitive interference?* A number of strategies exist, many of which are related to the learning and memory concepts we discussed earlier in the chapter.

Avoid Competing Advertising

One strategy is to avoid having your ad appear in the same set of ads (same pod in a TV format) as your competitors'. Some companies actually pay a premium to ensure this exclusivity. Another strategy is called *recency planning* which involves trying to plan advertising exposures so that they occur as close in time to a consumer purchase occasion as possible. The idea behind this concept is that reducing the time to purchase reduces the chances that an ad for a competing brand will be seen prior to purchase.[60]

Strengthen Initial Learning

Another strategy is to increase the strength of initial learning since stronger learning is less subject to memory interference. Evidence for the value of this strategy comes from the fact that memory interference is less pronounced in high-involvement contexts and for highly familiar brands. This is not surprising when you consider that high-involvement learning should result in stronger brand schemas and that brand schemas for familiar brands are stronger than those for unfamiliar brands.[61]

Additional evidence for the role of learning comes from advertising strategies that encourage dual coding. Specifically, brands can reduce competitive interference by showing different ad versions for the same brand (shampoo ad in office context and social context) or by varying the modality across exposures (radio ad followed by a print ad).[62]

Interestingly, while strong initial learning of a brand's key attributes can yield positive memory effects, it can also make it harder for the brand to add or change attributes. That is, the strong initial learning interferes with consumer learning and memory for new brand information.[63] This can make brand *repositioning* a challenging task. Repositioning is discussed later in the chapter.

Reduce Similarity to Competing Ads

Ads within the same product class (e.g., ads for different brands of cell phone) have been shown to increase interference, as have ads that are similar to competing ads. Similarity can be in terms of ad claims, emotional valence, and ad execution elements such as background music or pictures. Interestingly, similarity between ad execution elements can lead to memory interference even when the ads are for brands in different product categories (print ads for bleach and soda each picturing mountain scenes). Just as unique ads can break through advertising clutter to garner greater attention, unique ads are also more resistant to competitive memory interference.[64]

Provide External Retrieval Cues

Retrieval cues provide an external pathway to information that is stored in memory. The reason that brand names are so important is because they can serve as a retrieval cue. Seeing a brand name can trigger recall of brand information stored in memory, as well as retrieval of images and emotions associated with prior advertisements for the brand.

However, brand name is not always enough to trigger recall of prior advertising for the brand. For example, seeing the brand on a store shelf may not be sufficient to cue consumers' memory for prior advertising. This is of major consequence for marketers, since failure to recall prior advertising information and emotion during purchase reduces advertising effectiveness. In this case, marketers can use point-of-purchase displays or package cues that link directly back to the advertisements for that brand.[65] For example, during the "Got Milk?" campaign, in-store signage with the "Got Milk?" slogan was used to remind consumers about the TV ads which emphasized how awful it feels to run out of milk. These signs were placed in strategic locations such as the cereal and cookie aisles.

Quaker Oats applied this concept as well by placing a photo of a scene from its Life cereal commercial on the cereal box. This enhanced the ability of consumers to recall both affect and information from the commercial and was very successful.

Response Environment

Retrieval is also affected by the similarity of the retrieval (response) environment to the original learning environment and type of learning.[66] Thus, the more the retrieval situation offers cues similar to the cues present during learning, the more likely effective retrieval is to occur. One strategy is to configure the retrieval environment to resemble the original learning environment. The "Got Milk?" and Life cereal examples discussed earlier represent attempts by marketers to match the in-store retrieval environment to the learning environment by providing retrieval cues.

Another strategy is to configure the learning environment to resemble the most likely retrieval environment. Suppose a chewing gum brand knows that its retrieval environment will be in retail stores. In this case, conditioning a positive feeling to the *brand and package* by consistently pairing a visual image of the package with pleasant music would likely be most appropriate. This is because the response environment (the store shelf) visually presents consumers with brand packages. And, since learning was conditioned to a visual of the brand's package (learning environment configured to match the retrieval environment), seeing the package on the shelf will likely elicit the learned response.

BRAND IMAGE AND PRODUCT POSITIONING

Brand Image

Brand image refers to *the schematic memory of a brand.* It contains the target market's interpretation of the product's attributes, benefits, usage situations, users, and manufacturer/marketer characteristics. It is what people think of and feel when they hear or see a brand name. It is, in essence, the set of associations consumers have *learned* about the brand.[67] *Company image* and *store image* are similar except that they apply to companies and stores rather than brands.

The importance of branding and brand image can be seen in the fact that products which have traditionally been unbranded such as water, apples, and meat, are increasingly being branded. Consider the meat industry. It must deal with a number of issues, not the least of which is that many consumers see meat as difficult and time-consuming to prepare. As one industry expert said,

> A lot of consumers don't have the time and expertise to take a raw roast and cook it for six to eight hours, so what we have to do in this industry is understand that and do something about it.[68]

Tyson has responded by offering a line of fully cooked chicken, pork, and beef meals that are fast, easy, and safe to prepare. This move builds nicely on Tyson's strong reputation for quality fresh meat products and its prepackaged lunch meats. Given today's consumers' dual concerns over convenience and food safety, Tyson is well positioned with a strong and consistent image that consumers trust and can relate to (see Illustration 9-7). The ability to benefit from a brand image is called *brand equity,* which we discuss in the next section.

Courtesy Tyson Foods, Inc.

ILLUSTRATION 9-7

Brand names provide an anchor to which consumers can attach meaning. This allows marketers to invest in product improvements and communications with a reasonable possibility of benefiting from those investments.

Brand image is a major concern of both industrial and consumer good marketers. Consider the following headlines from recent marketing publications:

Volvo Plans Ad Campaign to Clarify Automaker's Image

Making Coke *Iconic* Again

P&G Bets $100 mil on Crest Brand Plan

How powerful are brand images? Think of Nike, McDonald's, Kate Spade, Hershey's, Coke, Discovery Channel, Amazon.com, and Midas. For many consumers, each of these names conjures up a rich pattern of meanings and feelings. These meanings and imagery are powerful drivers of consumer decision making which explains why strong brands also tend to be market leaders in terms of sales and profits.

Brand images can hinder as well as help products.[69] What do you think of when you hear the word *Teflon?* That will depend in part on how successful a current $40 million advertising campaign for Teflon-treated clothes is. At present, most people have a strong image of Teflon as a slick, hard, nonsticky cookware surface. Would you want your slacks to have these features? Probably not. However, you probably would like them to be stain-repellent. Thus, DuPont is spending a large sum of money to change the image of Teflon to make it compatible for use on clothing. A theme being tested for the campaign is "Cotton feels like cotton, wool feels like wool, red wine doesn't stain like red wine."

Product Positioning

Product positioning is a *decision by a marketer to try to achieve a defined brand image relative to competition within a market segment.* That is, marketers decide that they want the members of a market segment to think and feel in a certain way about a brand relative to competing brands. The term *product positioning* is most commonly applied to decisions concerning brands, but it is also used to describe the same decisions for stores, companies, and product categories.

Product positioning has a major impact on the long-term success of the brand, presuming the firm can create the desired position in the minds of consumers. A key issue in positioning relates to the need for brands to create product positions that differentiate them from competitors in ways that are meaningful to consumers.[70] A brand that fails to differentiate itself from competitors (stimulus discrimination) will generally find it difficult to generate consumer interest and sales.

Consider Saturn's positioning strategy. Saturn emphasizes value, made in America by caring workers, and dealers who care about and respect customers and who do not haggle over price. These are attributes that Saturn believes are important to its target customers. And, Saturn wants to create a differentiated position in the marketplace by being perceived as superior to its competitors on each of these attributes. Saturn will succeed to the extent that it creates the desired image in the minds of its target customers. However, as customer needs change, or as competitors improve their positions relative to Saturn, Saturn may need to consider how to change or *reposition* its brand to maintain or regain its value in the minds of customers.

An important component of brand image is the appropriate usage situations for the product or brand. Often marketers have the opportunity to influence the usage situations for which a product or brand is seen as appropriate. What do you think of when you think of cranberry sauce? Odds are that Thanksgiving and perhaps Christmas are part of your image of cranberry sauce. In fact, these are probably the only usage situations that came to mind. However, in one study, sales for cranberry sauce increased almost 150 percent over a three-month period after consumers saw advertisements promoting nontraditional uses. Thus, expanding the usage situation component of cranberry sauce's product position could dramatically increase its sales.[71]

The terms *product position* and *brand image* are often used interchangeably. In general, however, product position involves an explicit reference to a brand's image relative to another brand or the overall industry. It is characterized by statements such as "HP printers are the most reliable printers available." Brand image generally considers the firm's image without a direct comparison to a competitor. It is characterized by statements such as "HP printers are extremely reliable."

Once a marketer decides on an appropriate product position, the marketing mix is manipulated in a manner designed to achieve that position in the target market.[72] For example, Sunkist Growers offers a fruit jelly candy called Sunkist Fruit Gems which comes in various fruit flavors. It is positioned as a "healthful, natural" snack for adults and children. From a product standpoint, the candy is made from pectin (a natural ingredient from citrus peels) and contains no preservatives and less sugar than most fruit jelly candies. Thus, the product itself communicates the desired position.

However, other aspects of the marketing mix can also contribute. For example, Sunkist could distribute the candy through the produce departments of supermarkets. Notice how distribution then supports the desired product position or image. A consumer receiving a message that this is a healthful, natural product should be more receptive when the product is found near other healthful, natural products such as apples and oranges.

Marketing managers frequently fail to achieve the type of product image or position they desire because they fail to anticipate or test for consumer reactions. Toro's initial lightweight snowthrower was not successful. Why? It was named the Snowpup, and consumers interpreted this to mean that it was a toy or lacked sufficient power. Sales success came only after a more macho, power-based name was utilized—first Snowmaster and later Toro.

Perceptual Map for Automobiles **FIGURE 9-10**

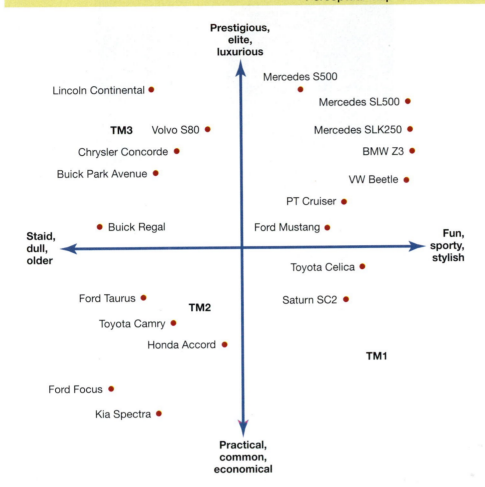

Perceptual mapping offers marketing managers a useful technique for measuring and developing a product's position. Perceptual mapping takes consumers' perceptions of how similar various brands or products are to each other and relates these perceptions to product attributes. Figure 9-10 is a perceptual map for several automobile models. This perceptual map also provides the ideal points for three market segments—TM1, TM2, and TM3. These ideal points represent the image/characteristics each segment desires in an automobile. If the models in this map were all that existed, it would indicate that TM1 consumers are not being offered the products they want. At present, they have to spend more than they want and buy a Saturn SC2 or a less sporty car than they desire such as the Honda Accord or the Kia Spectra. If this segment is large enough, one or more firms should consider developing a fun, sporty, but low-cost, economical car and target this group. If TM1 and TM2 were the only ideal points in the lower portion of the perceptual map, both the Ford Focus and the Kia Spectra would be in trouble. *Why?*

Product Repositioning

The images consumers have of brands change over time as a function of their own changing needs, as a function of changes in competitors, and as a function of changes initiated by the brand itself. For example, over the past few years, Volvo has introduced a number of

© M. Hruby.

new models targeting younger and less affluent consumers than it had in the past. As a
Volvo representative stated,

> Consumers still think of the brand primarily in terms of safety but are unclear whether the cars are
> luxury vehicles, what their average prices are, and who the brand's target is. There is less clarity
> about Volvo now than when we had one car and one wagon. We are going to explain to people
> what we are.[73]

The lack of clarity of the Volvo image may signal that it is time for new strategies to help
reposition their brand in the minds of consumers. **Product repositioning** refers to *a deliberate decision to significantly alter the way the market views a product*. This could involve
its level of performance, the feelings it evokes, the situations in which it should be used, or
even who uses it.[74]

Mug Root Beer was repositioned to be more appropriate for a younger audience (its
primary target market is 15- to 29-year-olds). To accomplish this repositioning, it was
advertised on television shows that appeal to young adults as well as on MTV. In one ad, a
young man drinks Mug while flipping the city's master light switch on and off to the beat
of a rock song. In another ad, a young man drinks Mug while talking to a prairie dog in a
pet store about freeing him from his "jail." In addition to advertising and promotion
changes, the package was redesigned to a brighter red from its original brown in order to
appeal more to this market segment (see Illustration 9-8).

Other recent repositioning efforts include,

- H&R Block is moving from being a tax preparation specialist to "the accessible
  provider of financial services to Middle America."[75]
- Infiniti is attempting to move from a diffuse luxury car image to a "new brand image
  that is about performance."[76]
- Hyundai is attempting to move from a low-price image to one that is "refined and
  elegant."[77]

Repositioning can be very difficult and costly, requiring consumers to *unlearn* old associations and replace them with new ones.[78] This can take years to accomplish. In the auto
industry, it is estimated that repositioning can take up to 10 years. According to one industry expert, "People's perceptions change very slowly."[79]

Repositioning may also require drastic action. For example, Hardee's was able to reverse plummeting sales only after completely walking away from the thin patties common in fast-food hamburgers and focusing exclusively on its now signature Thickburger made from Black Angus beef.[80] Sometimes companies will even change their brand name to allow a fresh start. For example, when Bell Atlantic and GTE Wireless merged, they changed their name to Verizon.

BRAND EQUITY AND BRAND LEVERAGE

Brand equity is *the value consumers assign to a brand above and beyond the functional characteristics of the product.*[81] For example, many people pay a significant premium for Bayer aspirin relative to store brands of aspirin although they are chemically identical.

Brand equity is nearly synonymous with the reputation of the brand. However, the term *equity* implies economic value.[82] Thus, brands with "good" reputations have the potential for high levels of brand equity, whereas unknown brands or brands with weak or negative reputations do not. The outcomes of brand equity include increased market share, decreased consumer price sensitivity, and enhanced marketing efficiency.[83]

Brand equity is based on the product position of the brand. A consumer who believes that a brand delivers superior performance, is exciting to use, and is produced by a company with appropriate social values is likely to be willing to pay a premium for the brand, to go to extra trouble to locate and buy it, to recommend it to others, to forgive a mistake or product flaw, or to otherwise engage in behaviors that benefit the firm that markets the brand. Thus, one source of economic value from a positive brand image results from consumers' behaviors toward existing items with that brand name.[84]

Another source of value for a brand image is that consumers may assume that the favorable aspects of the image associated with an existing product will apply to a new product with the same brand name. This is based on the principle of stimulus generalization described earlier in this chapter. **Brand leverage,** often termed *family branding, brand extensions,* or *umbrella branding,* refers to *marketers capitalizing on brand equity by using an existing brand name for new products.*[85] If done correctly, consumers will assign some of the characteristics of the existing brand to the new product carrying that name. Relatively recent brand extensions include Starbucks ice cream, Listerine breath strips, and Campbell's tomato juice.

However, stimulus generalization does not occur just because two products have the same brand name. There must be a connection between the products. Pace is finally leveraging its brand equity beyond salsas by extending its name into related products such as refried beans, taco sauces, and bean dip. According to Pace's brand manager,

> We feel we have the ability to expand into Mexican meals, it's just now about choosing the right products and aligning with what consumers are making.[86]

In contrast, Campbell's was not able to introduce a spaghetti sauce under the Campbell's name (it used Prego instead). Consumer research found that

> Campbell's, to consumers, says it isn't authentic Italian. Consumers figured it would be orangy and runny like our tomato soup.[87]

Successful brand leverage generally requires that the original brand have a strong positive image and that the new product fit with the original product on at least one of four dimensions:[88]

1. *Complement.* The two products are used together.
2. *Substitute.* The new product can be used instead of the original.
3. *Transfer.* Consumers see the new product as requiring the same manufacturing skills as the original.
4. *Image.* The new product shares a key image component with the original.

It is important for marketers to understand what the key "fit" criteria are for consumers. For example, one study found that consumers would prefer Fruit Loops lollipops over Fruit Loops hot cereal. Apparently the key fit criterion of concern was not the transfer of manufacturing capability, but rather the image component of taste.[89] Some brands are broad enough to be leveraged in multiple ways. For example, Porsche has a high-quality, sporty image among many consumers. It could logically extend its name to tires (complement), motorcycles (substitute), ski boats (transfer), or sunglasses (image). In fact, it has an entire line of golf accessories including a Porsche golf bag trolley with custom Porsche aluminum wheels designed to fit into the luggage compartment of its 911 Turbo and Boxster!

It is also important for marketers to understand that fit criteria may differ across consumer groups. For example, one study found that adults tend to look for deeper connections between the original product and the extension product, while children do not. So, despite the fact that crayons and guitars have virtually nothing in common, Crayola is able to successfully market both products to kids under the Crayola name![90]

Finally, it is important for marketers to realize that the more the new product category is a "stretch" for the brand, the more their advertising messages must help to explain how the products fit together. Such strategies help consumers transfer meaning from the existing brand to the new product by pointing out more subtle linkages than they might naturally think of on their own.[91] For example, Revlon tried to launch its own vitamins with the expression "Now, Revlon beauty begins from the inside-out." Notice how the slogan associates cosmetics and vitamins in terms of beauty.

Neutrogena has successfully extended its brand from a bar soap to shampoos, cleansing clothes, make-ups, and lipsticks. The extensions to shampoos and acne cleansing cloths were very consistent with the base product and image. Lipsticks are further removed, but their introduction has been successful. Illustration 9-9 shows ads for two different Neutrogena products. Notice how the tag line "Beautiful and Beneficial" for their lipstick points out key linkages between lipstick and its other products that might not have been readily apparent to some consumers.

Other examples of successful and unsuccessful brand extensions include the following:

- Gillette was unsuccessful with a facial moisturizer line under the Silkience brand name. Silkience's excellent reputation in hair care simply did not translate to face creams.
- Harley-Davidson has applied its name successfully to a wide variety of products, but its Harley-Davidson wine coolers were not successful.
- Levi Strauss failed in its attempt to market Levi's tailored suits for men.
- Country Time could not expand from lemonade to apple cider.
- LifeSavers gum did not succeed.
- Coleman successfully expanded from camping stoves and lanterns into a complete line of camping equipment.
- Oil of Olay bar soap is successful in large part due to the equity of the Oil of Olay lotion.

Brand extensions are sometimes undertaken to bolster the image of the brand rather than to capitalize on its current equity. Mercedes launched a mountain bike with its name attached mostly because mountain bikes have a hip, active image. A marketer for Mercedes says the firm wants to "appeal to a larger, wider, younger audience."[92] Similarly, Courvoisier, a

Courtesy Neutrogena.

high-end cognac brand, is extending into luxury clothing to transform itself into a "lush lifestyle brand."[93] In these cases, the new product is designed to enhance the base brand image and increase its equity.

Sometimes brand extensions are not feasible. When marketers want to target distinct market segments with a distinct image from the original brand, they generally need to create a new brand rather than extend the existing one. AT&T did this by creating the Lucky Dog Phone Co. to offer low-cost dial-around phone service to cost-focused customers. Similarly, The Gap created Old Navy to target value-oriented students and young families. Miller Brewing uses the Plank Road Brewery to market specialty beers such as Red Dog, Southpaw, and Icehouse. These new brands have images that are distinct from the original brand. Using unique brand names for this purpose avoids diluting or confusing the original brand image.

Brand extensions can also involve risks for marketers, one being that a failure of any product with a brand name can hurt all the products with the same brand name (consumers generalize both good and bad outcomes).[94] Another risk is diluting or unfavorably altering the original brand image.[95] A strong image is generally focused on a fairly narrow set of characteristics. Each additional product added to that product name alters the image somewhat. If too many or too dissimilar products are added to the brand name, the brand image may become diffuse or confused.[96] For instance, were Porsche to offer a ski boat that competed on price rather than performance, it could damage its core image, particularly among existing owners.[97] Some observers feel that Nike is in danger of such a brand dilution as it attaches its name to an ever-wider array of products.

ILLUSTRATION 9-9

Brand extensions are most likely to succeed when the new product is closer to existing products. However, the greatest rewards are sometimes associated with extensions into more distinct product categories.

SUMMARY

Consumers must learn almost everything related to being a consumer—product existence, performance, availability, values, preference, and so forth. Marketing managers, therefore, are very interested in the nature of consumer learning and memory.

Memory is the result of learning, which involves information processing. Most commonly, information goes directly into *short-term memory* for processing where two basic activities occur—maintenance rehearsal and elaborative activities. *Maintenance rehearsal* is the continual repetition of a piece of information in order to hold it in current memory. *Elaborative activities* are the use of stored experiences, values, attitudes, and feelings to interpret and evaluate information in current memory.

Long-term memory is information from previous information processing that has been stored for future use. LTM undergoes continual restructuring as new information is acquired. Information is stored in long-term memory in associative networks or schemas. Consumers often organize information in long-term memory around brands in the form of *brand schemas*. These schemas represent the brand's image in terms of key attributes, feelings, experiences, and so on.

Learning is defined as any change in the content or organization of long-term memory. Consumers learn in various ways, which can be broadly classified into high- versus low-involvement learning. *High-involvement learning* occurs when an individual is motivated to acquire the information. *Low-involvement learning* occurs when an individual is paying only limited or indirect attention to an advertisement or other message. Low-involvement learning tends to be limited due to a lack of elaborative activities.

Learning can also be classified as either conditioned or cognitive. There are two forms of conditioned learning—classical and operant. *Classical conditioning* attempts to create an association between a stimulus (e.g., brand name) and some response (e.g., behavior or feeling) and is generally low-involvement in nature. *Operant conditioning* attempts to create an association between a response (e.g., buying a brand) and some outcome (e.g., satisfaction) that serves to reinforce the response and is generally high-involvement in nature.

The *cognitive* approach to learning encompasses the mental activities of humans as they work to solve problems, cope with complex situations, or function effectively in their environment. Cognitive learning includes *iconic rote learning* (generally low involvement), *vicar-ious learning/modeling* (low or high involvement), and *analytical reasoning* (generally high involvement).

Stimulus generalization is one way of transferring learning by generalizing from one stimulus situation to other, similar ones. *Stimulus discrimination* refers to the opposite process of learning—responding differently to somewhat similar stimuli. The ability of consumers to differentiate and generalize is critical for successful brand positioning and leverage.

Once learned, information is *retrieved* from long-term memory for use in evaluations and decisions. *Retrieval failures* or *extinction* of a learned response represents a reduction in marketing effectiveness. Retrieval depends on strength of initial learning, memory interference, and the response environment. *Strength of learning* depends on six basic factors: importance, message involvement, reinforcement, mood, repetition, and dual coding. *Importance* refers to the value that the consumer places on the information to be learned—greater importance increases learning and retrieval. *Message involvement* is the degree to which the consumer is interested in the message itself—the greater the message involvement, the greater the learning and retrieval. *Reinforcement* is anything that increases the likelihood that a response will be repeated in the future—the greater the reinforcement, the greater the learning and retrieval. *Mood* is the temporary mental state or feeling of the consumer. Learning and memory appear to be greater in positive mood conditions. *Repetition* refers to the number of times that we are exposed to the information or that we engage in a behavior. Repetition increases learning and memory, but can also lead to *wearout*. *Dual coding* involves creating multiple complementary pathways to a concept in long-term memory. Dual coding increases learning and retrieval.

Memory interference occurs when consumers have difficulty retrieving a specific piece of information because other related information in memory gets in the way. A common form of memory interference is due to competitive advertising. Competitive interference increases with increased advertising clutter. But, it can be reduced by avoiding competitive clutter, strengthening learning, reducing similarity to competitor ads, and providing retrieval cues.

The *response environment* can also be critical to retrieval. Matching the response environment to the learning environment, or matching the learning environment to the response environment can enhance the ease and likelihood of retrieval.

Brand image, a market segment or individual consumer's schematic memory of a brand, is a major focus of marketing activity. *Product positioning* is a decision by a marketer to attempt to attain a defined and differentiated brand image, generally in relation to specific competitors. A brand image that matches a target market's needs and desires will be valued by that market segment. Such a brand is said to have *brand equity* because consumers respond favorably toward it in the market. In addition, these consumers may be willing to assume that other products with the same brand name will have some of the same features. Introducing new products under the same name as an existing product is referred to as *brand leverage* or *brand extension*.

KEY TERMS

Accessibility 327
Advertising wearout 342
Analogical reasoning 335
Analytical reasoning 335
Brand equity 351
Brand image 346
Brand leverage 351
Classical conditioning 331
Cognitive learning 334
Concept 325
Conditioning 330
Elaborative activities 324
Episodic memory 325
Explicit memory 328

Extinction 337
High-involvement learning 329
Iconic rote learning 334
Imagery 325
Implicit memory 328
Learning 322
Long-term memory (LTM) 323
Low-involvement learning 329
Maintenance rehearsal 323
Memory interference 344
Modeling 334
Operant conditioning 332
Perceptual mapping 349
Product positioning 347

Product repositioning 350
Pulsing 341
Punishment 341
Reinforcement 340
Retrieval failure 337
Schema 325
Script 327
Self-referencing 339
Semantic memory 325
Shaping 332
Short-term memory (STM) 323
Stimulus discrimination 336
Stimulus generalization 336
Vicarious learning 334

INTERNET EXERCISES

1. Visit one of the following Web sites. Evaluate the site in terms of its application of learning principles.
   a. www.actionvillage.com
   b. www.fogdog.com
   c. www.dior.com
   d. www.drpepper.com

2. Visit several company Web sites until you find one that you feel makes particularly effective use of one or more of the learning theories we have covered and one that makes very little use of these principles. Describe each and justify your selections.

3. Evaluate the following three Web sites in terms of their ability to create/support a good brand image and product position.
   a. www.minicooper.org
   b. www.vw.com
   c. www.bentleymotors.com

REVIEW QUESTIONS

1. What is *learning?*
2. What is *memory?*
3. Define *short-term memory* and *long-term memory*.
4. Discuss the nature of *short-term memory* in terms of its endurance and capacity.
5. What is *maintenance rehearsal?*
6. What is meant by *elaborative activities?*
7. What is meant by *imagery* in working memory?
8. What is *semantic memory?*
9. How does a *schema* differ from a *script?*
10. What is *episodic memory?*
11. Describe *low-involvement learning*. How does it differ from *high-involvement learning?*

12. What do we mean by *cognitive learning,* and how does it differ from the *conditioning theory* approach to learning?

13. Distinguish between learning via *classical conditioning* and learning that occurs via *operant conditioning.*

14. What is *iconic rote learning?* How does it differ from classical conditioning? Operant conditioning?

15. Define *modeling.*

16. What is meant by learning by *analytical reasoning?*

17. Describe *analogical reasoning.*

18. What is meant by *stimulus generalization?* When do marketers use it?

19. Define *stimulus discrimination.* Why is it important?

20. Explain *extinction* and *retrieval failure* and why marketing managers are interested in them.

21. What factors affect the *strength of learning?*

22. How does *self-referencing* relate to *strength of learning* and retrieval?

23. What is *memory interference* and what strategies can marketers use to deal with it?

24. Why is it useful to match the retrieval and learning environments?

25. What is a *brand image?* Why is it important?

26. What is *product positioning? Repositioning?*

27. What is *perceptual mapping?*

28. What is *brand equity?*

29. What does *leveraging brand equity* mean?

DISCUSSION QUESTIONS

30. How would you determine the best product position for the following?
    a. A candidate student body president at your university
    b. A breakfast cereal targeting children
    c. A nonprofit organization focused on foster care
    d. A line of power tools targeting women
    e. A brand of shampoo

31. Is low-involvement learning really widespread? Which products are most affected by low-involvement learning?

32. Almex and Company introduced a new coffee-flavored liqueur in direct competition with Hiram Walker's tremendously successful Kahlua brand. Almex named its new entry Kamora and packaged it in a bottle similar to that of Kahlua, using a pre-Columbian label design. The ad copy for Kamora reads, "If you like coffee—you'll love Kamora." Explain Almex's marketing strategy in terms of learning theory.

33. Describe the brand images the following "brands" have among students on your campus.

    a. Fraternities
    b. Your student government
    c. Jolt
    d. Hummer
    e. Navy
    f. Vegan

34. In what ways, if any, would the brand images you described in response to the previous question differ with different groups, such as (a) middle-aged professionals, (b) young blue-collar workers, (c) high school students, and (d) retired couples?

35. What role does *dual coding* play in the learning process?

36. Respond to the questions in Consumer Insight 9-1.

37. Evaluate Illustrations 9-1 through 9-5 in light of their apparent objectives and target market.

38. How would you teach teenagers an eating script that involved consistently washing one's hands first? A script for use of seat belts?

APPLICATION ACTIVITIES

39. Fulfill the requirements of Question 33 by interviewing three male and three female students.

40. Answer Question 34 based on interviews with five individuals from each group.

41. Pick a consumer convenience product, perhaps a personal care product such as suntan lotion or toothpaste, and create advertising copy stressing (a) a positive reinforcement, (b) a negative reinforcement, and (c) a punishment.

42. Find and describe three advertisements, one based on cognitive learning, another based on operant conditioning, and the third based on classical conditioning. Discuss the nature of each advertisement and how it utilizes that type of learning.

43. Find and describe three advertisements that you believe are based on low-involvement learning and three that are based on high-involvement learning. Justify your selection.

44. Select a product and develop an advertisement based on low-involvement learning and one on high-involvement learning. When should each be used (be specific)?

45. Find two advertisements for competing brands that you feel do a good job of avoiding competitive advertising interference and two that you think do not. Justify your selection.

46. Visit a grocery store and examine product packages or point-of-purchase information that could serve as retrieval cues for a brand's ongoing advertising campaign. Write a brief report of your findings and describe the nature and effectiveness of the retrieval cues utilized. Could they have been better? Explain.

47. Select a product that you feel has a good product position and one that has a weak position. Justify your selection. Describe an ad or package for each product and indicate how it affects the product's position.

48. Select a product, store, or service of relevance to students on your campus. Using a sample of students, measure its brand image. Develop a marketing strategy to improve its image.

49. Develop a campaign to reduce the risk of AIDS for students on your campus by teaching them the value of
    a. Abstinence from sex outside of marriage
    b. Safe sex

50. Find a recent brand extension that you feel will be successful and one that you feel will fail. Explain each of your choices.

REFERENCES

1. A. Klaassen, "St. Joseph," *Advertising Age,* July 9, 2001, p. 1.

2. A. A. Mitchell, "Cognitive Processes Initiated by Exposure to Advertising," in *Information Processing Research in Advertising,* ed. R. Harris (New York: Lawrence Erlbaum Associates, 1983), pp. 13–42.

3. For differing views see A. J. Malter, "An Introduction to Embodied Cognition," *Advances in Consumer Research,* vol. 23, eds. K. P. Corfman and J. G. Lynch (Provo, UT: Association for Consumer Research, 1996), pp. 272–76; and M. E. Hill, R. Radtke, and M. King, "A Transfer Appropriate Processing View of Consumer Memory," *Journal of Current Issues and Research in Advertising,* Spring 1997, pp. 1–21.

4. J. Fetto, "Call Me Vain," *American Demographics,* November 2002, p. 15.

5. See K. Mason, T. Jensen, S. Burton, and D. Roach, "The Accuracy of Brand and Attribute Judgments," *Journal of the Academy of Marketing Science,* Summer 2001, pp. 307–17; and S. Putrevu, J. Tan, and K. R. Lord, "Consumer Responses to Complex Advertisements," *Journal of Current Issues and Research in Advertising*, Spring 2004, pp. 9–24.

6. L. A. Babin and A. C. Burns, "Effects of Print Ad Pictures and Copy Containing Instructions to Imagine on Mental Imagery That Mediates Attitudes," *Journal of Advertising,* Fall 1997, pp. 33–44.

7. K. A. Braun, "Postexperience Advertising Effects on Consumer Memory," *Journal of Consumer Research,* March 1999, pp. 319–34.

8. See M. T. Pham and G. V. Johar, "Contingent Processes of Source Identification," *Journal of Consumer Research,* December 1997, pp. 249–66.

9. See E. J. Cowley, "Recovering Forgotten Information," in *Advances in Consumer Research,* vol. 21, eds. C. T. Allen and D. R. John (Provo, UT: Association for Consumer Research, 1994), pp. 58–63.

10. K. K. Desai and W. Hoyer, "Descriptive Characteristics of Memory-Based Consideration Sets," *Journal of Consumer Research,* December 2000, pp. 309–23. See also P. Nedungadi, A. Chattopadyay, and A.V. Muthukrishnan, "Category Structure, Brand Recall, and Choice," *International Journal of Research in Marketing* 18 (2001), pp. 191–202; and E. Cowley and A. A. Mitchell, "The Moderating Effect of Product Knowledge on the Learning and Organization of Product Information," *Journal of Consumer Research,* December 2003, pp. 443–54.

11. See S. E. Heckler, "The Role of Memory in Understanding and Encouraging Recycling Behavior," *Psychology & Marketing,* July 1994, pp. 375–92.

12. This discussion is based on K. B. Monroe and A. Y. Lee, "Remembering versus Knowing," *Journal of the Academy of Marketing Science,* Spring 1999, pp. 207–25. See also H. S. Krishnan and C. V. Trappey, "Nonconscious Memory Processes in Marketing," and S. J. S. Holden and M. Vanhuele, "Know the Name, Forget the Exposure," both in *Psychology & Marketing,* September 1999, pp. 451–57 and 479–96, respectively; J. W. Alba and J. W. Hutchinson, "Knowledge Calibration," *Journal of Consumer Research,* September 2000, pp. 123–48; and S. Shapiro and H. S. Krishnan, "Memory-Based Measures for Assessing Advertising Effects," *Journal of Advertising,* Fall 2001, pp. 1–13.

13. G. Venkataramani and M. T. Pham, "Relatedness, Prominence, and Constructive Sponsor Identification," *Journal of Marketing Research,* August 1999, pp. 299–312.

14. E. Cowley and M. Caldwell, "Truth, Lies, and Videotape," *Advances in Consumer Research,* vol. 28, eds. M. C. Gilly and J. Meyers-Levy (Provo, UT: Association for Consumer Research, 2001), pp. 20–25.

15. K. A. Braun, R. Ellis, and E. F. Loftus, "Make My Memory," *Psychology & Marketing,* January 2002, pp. 1–23.

16. See K. G. Grunert, "Automatic and Strategic Processes in Advertising Effects," *Journal of Marketing,* October 1996, pp. 88–101; W. E. Baker and R. J. Lutz, "An Empirical Test of an Updated Relevance–Accessibility Model of Advertising Effectiveness," *Journal of Advertising,* Spring 2000, pp. 1–13; and S. M. J. Van Osselaer and C. Janiszewski, "Two Ways of Learning Brand Associations," *Journal of Consumer Research,* September 2001, pp. 202–23.

17. S. A. Hawkins, S. J. Hoch, and J. Meyers-Levy, "Low-Involvement Learning," *Journal of Consumer Psychology* 11, no. 1 (2001), pp. 1–11.

18. See G. D. Olsen, "The Impact of Interstimulus Interval and Background Silence on Recall," and J. Sengupta, R. C. Goodstein, and D. S. Boninger, "All Cues Are Not Created Equal," both in *Journal of Consumer Research,* March 1997, pp. 295–303 and 351–61, respectively.

19. See G. Tom, "Classical Conditioning of Unattended Stimuli," *Psychology & Marketing,* January 1995, pp. 79–87; J. Kin, C. T. Allen, and F. R. Kardes, "An Investigation into the Mediational Mechanisms Underlying Attitudinal Conditioning," *Journal of Marketing Research,* August 1996, pp. 318–28; R. P. Grossman and B. D. Till, "The Persistence of Classically Conditioned Brand Attitudes," *Journal of Advertising,* Spring 1998, pp. 23–31; J. Kim, J.-S. Lim, and M. Bhargava, "The Role of Affect in Attitude Formation," *Journal of the Academy of Marketing Science,* Spring 1998, pp. 143–52; W. E. Baker, "When Can Affective Conditioning and Mere Exposure Directly Influence Brand Choice?" *Journal of Advertising,* Winter 1999, pp. 31–46; and B. D. Till and R. L. Priluck, "Stimulus Generalization in Classical Conditioning," *Psychology & Marketing,* January 2000, pp. 55–72.

20. B. D. Till and R. L. Priluck, "Conditioning of Meaning in Advertising," *Journal of Current Issues and Research in Advertising,* Fall 2001, pp. 1–8.

21. For discussions of the role of awareness in classical conditioning, see C. Janiszewski and L. Warlop, "The Influence of Classical Conditioning Procedures on Subsequent Attention to the Conditioned Brand," *Journal of Consumer Research,* September 1993, pp. 171–89; R. Priluck and B. D. Till, "The Role of Contingency Awareness, Involvement, and Need for Cognition in Attitude Formation," *Journal of the Academy of Marketing Science* 32, no. 3 (2004), pp. 329–44; and I. Kirsch, S. J. Lynn, M. Vigorito, and R. R. Miller, "The Role of Cognition in Classical and Operant Conditioning," *Journal of Clinical Psychology,* April 2004, pp. 369–92.

22. See, e.g., Kirsch, Lynn, Vigorito, and Miller, "The Role of Cognition in Classical and Operant Conditioning"; P. Reed, "Effect of Perceived Cost on Judgments Regarding the Efficacy of Investment," *Journal of Economic Psychology* 20 (1999), pp. 657–76; and W. H. Motes and A. G. Woodside, "Purchase Experiments of Extra-ordinary and Regular Influence Strategies

Using Artificial and Real Brands," *Journal of Business Research* 53 (2001), pp. 15–35.

23. B. J. Bergiel and C. Trosclair, "Instrumental Learning," *Journal of Consumer Marketing,* Fall 1985, pp. 23–28. See also W. Gaidis and J. Cross, "Behavior Modification as a Framework for Sales Promotion Management," *Journal of Consumer Marketing,* Spring 1987, pp. 65–74.

24. E. Heit, J. Briggs, and L. Bott, "Modeling the Effects of Prior Knowledge on Learning Incongruent Features of Category Members," *Journal of Experimental Psychology: Learning, Memory, and Cognition*, September 2004, pp. 1065–81.

25. See J. W. Pracejus, "Is More Always Better?" in *Advances in Consumer Research,* vol. 22, eds. F. R. Kardes and M. Sujan (Provo, UT: Association for Consumer Research, 1995), pp. 319–22; and K. P. Gwinner and J. Eaton, "Building Brand Image through Event Sponsorship," *Journal of Advertising,* Winter 1999, pp. 47–57.

26. T. P. Ballinger, M. G. Palumbo, and N. T. Wilcox, "Precautionary Saving and Social Learning across Generations," *The Economic Journal,* October 2003, pp. 920–47.

27. For a way to measure such images, see L. A. Babin and A. C. Burns, *Psychology & Marketing,* May (1998), pp. 261–78.

28. S. P. Jain and D. Maheswaran, "Motivated Reasoning," *Journal of Consumer Research,* March 2000, pp. 358–71.

29. J. Gregan-Paxton and D. R. John, "Consumer Learning by Analogy," *Journal of Consumer Research,* December 1997, pp. 266–85. See also J. Gregan-Paxton, "The Role of Abstract and Specific Knowledge in the Formation of Product Judgments," *Journal of Consumer Psychology* 11, no. 3 (2001), pp. 141–58; J. Gregan-Paxton, J. D. Hibbard, F. F. Brunel, and P. Azar, "So That's What That Is," *Psychology & Marketing,* June 2002, pp. 533–50; and J. Gregan-Paxton and P. Moreau, "How Do Consumers Transfer Existing Knowledge?" *Journal of Consumer Psychology* 13, no. 4 (2003), pp. 422–30.

30. See Till and Priluck, "Stimulus Generalization in Classical Conditioning."

31. M. Maremont, "Gillette Chief Says Cost-Cutting Plan Will Take Time," *The Wall Street Journal,* June 7, 2001, p. B2.

32. "Behind Saturn's Stumble," *Advertising Age,* January 24, 1994, p. 22.

33. "L&M Lights Up Again," *Marketing & Media Decisions,* February 1984, p. 69.

34. Ibid.

35. D. Luna and L. A. Peracchio, "Where There Is a Will . . ." *Psychology & Marketing,* July/August 2002, pp. 573–93; see also R. S. Wyer, Jr., "Language and Advertising Effectiveness," *Psychology & Marketing,* July/August 2002, pp. 693–712.

36. See R. G. M. Pieters, E. Rosbergen, and M. Hartog, "Visual Attention to Advertising," *Advances in Consumer Research,* vol. 23, eds. Corfman and Lynch, pp. 242–48; and S. M. Leong, S. H. Ang, and L. L. Tham, "Increasing Brand Name Recall in Print Advertising among Asian Consumers," *Journal of Advertising,* Summer 1996, pp. 65–81.

37. M. L. Roehm, "Instrumental vs. Vocal Versions of Popular Music in Advertising," *Journal of Advertising Research,* May 2001, pp. 49–58. See also Baker and Lutz, "An Empirical Test of an Updated Relevance–Accessibility Model."

38. L. F. Allwitt, "Effects of Interestingness on Evaluations of TV Commercials," *Journal of Current Issues and Research in Advertising,* Spring 2000, pp. 41–53; T. F. Stafford and M. R. Stafford, "The Advantages of Atypical Advertisements for Stereotyped Product Categories," *Journal of Current Issues and Research in Advertising,* Spring 2002, pp. 25–37; and T. M. Lowrey, L. J. Shrum, and T. M. Dubitsky, "The Relation between Brand-Name Linguistic Characteristics and Brand-Name Memory," *Journal of Advertising,* Fall 2003, pp. 7–17.

39. M. Wedel and R. Pieters, "Eye Fixations on Advertisements and Memory for Brands," *Marketing Science,* Fall 2000, pp. 297–312.

40. M. Morrin and S. Ratneshwar, "Does It Make Sense to Use Scents to Enhance Brand Memory?" *Journal of Marketing Research,* February 2003, pp. 10–25.

41. W. E. Baker, H. Honea, and C. A. Russell, "Do Not Wait to Reveal the Brand Name," *Journal of Advertising,* Fall 2004, pp. 77–85; see also W. E. Baker, "Does Brand Name Imprinting in Memory Increase Brand Information Retention?" *Psychology & Marketing,* December 2003, pp. 1119–35.

42. See R. E. Burnkrant and H. R. Unnava, "Effects of Self-Referencing on Persuasion," *Journal of Consumer Research,* June 1995, pp. 17–26; and P. Krishnamurthy and M. Sujan, "Retrospection versus Anticipation," *Journal of Consumer Research,* June 1999, pp. 55–69.

43. A. Y. Lee and B. Sternthal, "The Effects of Positive Mood on Memory," *Journal of Consumer Research,* September 1999, pp. 115–27; M. J. Barone, P. W. Miniard, and J. B. Romeo, "The Influence of Positive Mood on Brand Extension Evaluations," *Journal of Consumer Research,* March 2000, pp. 386–400; K. R. Lord, R. E. Burnkrant, and H. R. Unnava, "The Effects of Program-Induced Mood States on Memory for Commercial Information," *Journal of Current Issues and Research in Advertising,* Spring 2001, pp. 1–14; and S. J. Newell, K. V. Henderson, and B. T. Wu, "The Effects of Pleasure and Arousal on Recall of Advertisements during the Super Bowl," *Psychology & Marketing,* November 2001, pp. 1135–53.

44. T. Ambler and T. Burne, "The Impact of Affect on Memory of Advertising," *Journal of Advertising Research,* March 1999, pp. 25–39; and S. Youn et al., "Commercial Liking and Memory," *Journal of Advertising Research,* May 2001, pp. 7–13.

45. See P. Malaviya, J. Meyers-Levy, and B. Sternthal, "Ad Repetition in a Cluttered Environment," *Psychology & Marketing,* March 1999, pp. 99–118.

46. L. W. Turley and J. R. Shannon, "The Impact and Effectiveness of Advertisements in a Sports Arena," *Journal of Services Marketing* 14, no. 4 (2000), pp. 323–36.

47. J. O. Eastlack, Jr., "How to Get More Bang from Your Television Bucks," *Journal of Consumer Marketing,* Third Quarter 1984, pp. 25–34.

48. See Hawkins, Hoch, and Meyers-Levy, "Low-Involvement Learning."

49. See also J. P. Jones, "Single-Source Research Begins to Fulfill Its Promise," *Journal of Advertising Research,* May 1995, pp. 9–16.

50. See S. N. Singh and C. A. Cole, "The Effects of Length, Content, and Repetition on Television Commercial Effectiveness," *Journal of Marketing Research,* February 1993, pp. 91–104; C. P. Haugtveld, D. W. Schumann, W. L. Schneier, and W. L. Warren, "Advertising Repetition and Variation Strategies," *Journal of Consumer Research,* June 1994, pp. 176–89; S. N. Singh, S. Mishra, N. Bendapudi, and D. Linville, "Enhancing Memory of Television Commercials through Message Spacing," *Journal of Marketing Research,* August 1994, pp. 384–92; E. Ephron, "More Weeks, Less Weight," *Journal of Advertising Research,* May 1995, pp. 18–23; Pieters, Rosbergen, and Hartog, "Visual Attention to Advertising"; and Leong, Ang, and Tham, "Increasing Brand Name Recall."

51. For a review of spacing effects see C. Janiszewski, H. Noel, and A. G. Sawyer, "A Meta-analysis of the Spacing Effect in Verbal Learning," *Journal of Consumer Research,* June 2003, pp. 138–49.

52. See M. H. Blair and M. J. Rabuck, "Advertising Wearin and Wearout," *Journal of Advertising Research,* September 1998, pp. 7–25; D. Vakratsas and T. Ambler, "How Advertising Works," *Journal of Marketing,* January 1999, pp. 26–43; D. W. Stewart, "Advertising Wearout," *Journal of Advertising Research,* September 1999, pp. 39–42; M. C. Campbell and K. L. Keller, "Brand Familiarity and Advertising Repetition Effects," *Journal of Consumer Research,* September 2003, pp. 292–304.

53. D. Schumann, R. E. Petty, and D. S. Clemons, "Predicting the Effectiveness of Different Strategies of Advertising Variation," *Journal of Consumer Research,* September 1990, pp. 192–202.

54. W. J. Bryce and R. F. Yalch, "Hearing versus Seeing," *Journal of Current Issues and Research in Advertising,* Spring 1993, pp. 1–20; and A. C. Burns, A. Biswas, and L. A. Babin, "The Operation of Visual Imagery as a Mediator of Advertising Effects," *Journal of Advertising,* June 1993, pp. 71–85.

55. T. Clark, "Echoic Memory Explored and Applied," *Journal of Consumer Marketing,* Winter 1987, pp. 39–46. See also C. E. Young and M. Robinson, "Video Rhythms and Recall," *Journal of Advertising Research,* July 1989, pp. 22–25.

56. J. J. Kellaris, A. D. Cox, and D. Cox, "The Effect of Background Music on Ad Processing," *Journal of Marketing,* October 1993, pp. 114–25. See also M. Hahn and I. Hwang, "Effects of Tempo and Familiarity of Background Music on Message Processing in TV Advertising," *Psychology & Marketing,* December 1999, pp. 659–75.

57. K. R. Lord and S. Putrevu, "Communicating in Print," *Journal of Current Issues and Research in Advertising,* Fall 1998, pp. 1–18.

58. D. Luna and L. A. Peracchio, "Moderators of Language Effects in Advertising to Bilinguals," *Journal of Consumer Research,* September 2001, pp. 284–95.

59. See R. D. Jewell and H. R. Unnava, "When Competitive Interference Can Be Beneficial," *Journal of Consumer Research,* September 2003, pp. 283–91; and A. Kumar and S. Krishnan, "Memory Interference in Advertising," *Journal of Consumer Research,* March 2004, pp. 602–11.

60. See M. Dahlen and J. Nordfalt, "Interference Effects of a Purchase on Subsequent Advertising within the Category," *Journal of Current Issues and Research in Advertising,* Spring 2004, pp. 1–8.

61. R. J. Kent and C. T. Allen, "Competitive Interference Effects in Consumer Memory for Advertising," *Journal of Marketing,* July 1994, pp. 97–105; A. Kumar, "Interference Effects of Contextual

Cues in Advertisements on Memory for Ad Content," *Journal of Consumer Psychology* 9, no. 3 (2000), 155–66; S. Law, "Can Repeating a Brand Claim Lead to Memory Confusion?" *Journal of Marketing Research,* August 2002, pp. 366–78; and K. A. Braun-LaTour and M. S. LaTour, "Assessing the Long-Term Impact of a Consistent Advertising Campaign on Consumer Memory," *Journal of Advertising,* Summer 2004, pp. 49–61.

62. H. R. Unnava and D. Sirdeshmukh, "Reducing Competitive Ad Interference," *Journal of Marketing Research,* August 1994, pp. 403–11.

63. Jewell and Unnava, "When Competitive Interference Can Be Beneficial"; and K. L. Keller, S. E. Heckler, and M. J. Houston, "The Effects of Brand Name Suggestiveness on Advertising Recall," *Journal of Marketing,* January 1998, pp. 48–57.

64. Kumar, "Interference Effects of Contextual Cues in Advertisements on Memory for Ad Content."

65. M. C. Macklin, "The Effects of an Advertising Retrieval Cue on Young Children's Memory and Brand Evaluations," *Psychology & Marketing,* May 1994, pp. 291–311; Keller, Heckler, and Houston, "The Effects of Brand Name Suggestiveness on Advertising Recall"; and N. T. Tavassoli and Y. H. Lee, "The Differential Interaction of Auditory and Visual Advertising Elements with Chinese and English," *Journal of Marketing Research,* November 2003, pp. 468–80.

66. See J. W. Park, "Memory-Based Product Judgments," and E. J. Cowley, "Altering Retrieval Sets," both in *Advances in Consumer Research,* vol. 22, eds. Kardes and Sujan, pp. 159–64 and 323–27, respectively; and M. E. Hill and M. King, "Comparative vs. Noncomparative Advertising," *Journal of Current Issues and Research in Advertising,* Fall 2001, pp. 33–52.

67. S. M. J. Van Osselaer and J. W. Alba, "Consumer Learning and Brand Equity," *Journal of Consumer Research,* June 2000, pp. 1–16; W. R. Dillon et al., "Understanding What's in a Brand Rating," *Journal of Marketing Research,* November 2001, pp. 415–29; and K. L. Keller, "Brand Synthesis," *Journal of Consumer Research,* March 2003, pp. 595–600.

68. S. Thompson, "Meat Gets Branded," *Advertising Age,* September 24, 2001, p. 6.

69. S. M. J. Van Osselear and J. W. Alba, "Locus of Equity and Brand Extension," *Journal of Consumer Research,* March 2003, pp. 539–50.

70. For a discussion of perceived differences generated by trivial attributes, see S. M. Broniarczyk and A. D. Gershoff, "The Reciprocal Effects of Brand Equity and Trivial Attributes," *Journal of Marketing Research,* May 2003, pp. 161–75.

71. B. Wansink, "Making Old Brands New," *American Demographics,* December 1998, pp. 53–58.

72. See, e.g., C. Young, "Brain Waves, Picture Sorts®, and Branding Moments," *Journal of Advertising Research,* August 2002, pp. 42–53.

73. J. Halliday, "Volvo Plans Ad Campaign to Clarify Automaker's Image," *Advertising Age,* October 9, 2000, p. 4.

74. See V. Gerson, "Showing Customers Your Best Face," *Bank Marketing,* January 1999, pp. 26–30; and D. James, "Image Makeovers Require Gentle Touch," *Marketing News,* July 2, 2001, p. 4.

75. M. Cardona, "Block's Less Taxing Future," *Advertising Age,* January 15, 2001, p. 6.

76. J. Halliday, "New Q45 Effort," *Advertising Age,* March 2001, p. 8.

77. J. Halliday, "Hyundai and Kia Head Upscale via Different Routes," *Advertising Age,* November 1, 2004, p. 12.

78. Jewell and Unnava, "When Competitive Interference Can Be Beneficial"; and K. K. Desai and S. Ratneshwar, "Consumer Perceptions of Product Variants Positioned on Atypical Attributes," *Journal of the Academy of Marketing Science,* Winter 2003, pp. 22–35.

79. J. Halliday, "Little Else Matters," *Advertising Age,* August 16, 2004, p. 6.

80. K. Macarthur, "Hardee's," *Advertising Age*, November 1, 2004, p. S-18.

81. M. Supphellen, "Understanding Core Brand Equity," *International Journal of Marketing Research* 42, no. 3 (2000), pp. 319–38; M. M. Mackay, "Application of Brand Equity Service Measures in Service Markets," *Journal of Services Marketing* 15, no. 3 (2001), pp. 21–29; B. J. Krishnan and M. D. Hartline, "Brand Equity," *Journal of Services Marketing* 15, no. 5 (2001), pp. 328–42; M. Littman, "To Your Brand's Health," *American Demographics,* July 2001, pp. 37–39; D. A. Aaker and R. Jacobson, "The Value of Brand Attitude in High-Technology Markets," *Journal of Marketing Research,* November 2001, pp. 485–93; and S. Brown, R. V. Kozinets, and J. F. Sherry, Jr., "Teaching Old Brands New Tricks," *Journal of Marketing,* July 2003, pp. 19–33.

82. A. Chaudhuri, "How Brand Reputation Affects the Advertising-Brand Equity Link," *Journal of Advertising Research*, June 2002, pp. 33–43.

83. P. Chandon, B. Wansink, and G. Laurent, "A Benefit Congruency Framework of Sales Promotion Effectiveness," *Journal of Marketing,* October 2000, pp. 65–81.

84. M. S. Sullivan, "How Brand Names Affect the Demand of Twin Automobiles," *Journal of Marketing Research,* May 1998, pp. 154–65; T. Erdem et al., "Brand Equity, Consumer Learning, and Choice," *Marketing Letters,* August 1999, pp. 301–18; N. Dawar and M. M. Pillutla, "Impact of Product-Harm Crises on Brand Equity," *Journal of Marketing Research,* May 2000, pp. 215–26; A. O'Cass and D. Grace, "An Exploratory Perspective of Service Brand Associations," *Journal of Services Marketing* 17, no. 5 (2003), pp. 452–75; J. A. Garretson, D. Fisher, and S. Burton, "Antecedents of Private Label Attitude and National Brand Promotion Attitude," *Journal of Retailing* 78 (2002), pp. 91–99; H. Kim, W. G. Kim, and J. A. An, "The Effect of Consumer-based Brand Equity on Firms' Financial Performance," *Journal of Consumer Marketing* 20, no. 4 (2003), pp. 335–51; and M. C. Campbell and K. L. Keller, "Brand Familiarity and Advertising Repetition Effects," *Journal of Consumer Research,* September 2003, pp. 292–304.

85. See T. Erdem, "An Empirical Analysis of Umbrella Branding," *Journal of Marketing Research,* August 1998, pp. 339–51; T. Erdem and B. Sun, "An Empirical Investigation of the Spillover Effects of Advertising and Sales Promotions in Umbrella Branding," *Journal of Marketing Research,* November 2002, pp. 408–20; and J. H. Washburn, B. D. Till, and R. Priluck,

"Brand Alliance and Customer-Based Brand-Equity Effects," *Psychology & Marketing,* July 2004, pp. 487–508.

86. S. Thompson, "Campbell Extends Pace beyond Salsa," *Advertising Age,* August 30, 2004, p. 10.

87. H. Schlossberg, "Slashing through Market Clutter," *Marketing News,* March 5, 1990, p. 6.

88. V. R. Lane, "The Impact of Ad Repetition and Ad Content on Consumer Perceptions of Incongruent Extensions," *Journal of Marketing,* April 2000, pp. 80–91; K. de Ruyter and M. Wetzels, "The Role of Corporate Image and Extension Similarity in Service Brand Extensions," *Journal of Economic Psychology* 21 (2000), pp. 639–59; G. Oakenfull et al., "Measuring Brand Meaning," *Journal of Advertising Research,* September 2000, pp. 43–53; I. M. Martin and D. W. Stewart, "The Differential Impact of Goal Congruency on Attitudes, Intentions, and the Transfer of Brand Equity," and P. A. Bottomley and S. J. S. Holden, "Do We Really Know How Consumers Evaluate Brand Extensions?" both in *Journal of Marketing Research,* November 2001, pp. 471–84 and 494–500, respectively; and E. Maoz and A. M. Tybout, "The Moderating Role of Involvement and Differentiation in the Evaluation of Brand Extensions," *Journal of Consumer Psychology* 12, no. 2 (2002), pp. 119–31.

89. S. M. Broniarczyk and J. W. Alba, "The Importance of the Brand in Brand Extension," *Journal of Marketing Research,* May 1994, pp. 214–28; see also T. Meyvis and C. Janiszewski, "When Are Broader Brands Stronger Brands?" *Journal of Consumer Research,* pp. 346–57.

90. See S. Zhang and S. Sood, "'Deep' and 'Surface' Cues," *Journal of Consumer Research,* June 2002, pp. 129–41.

91. S. Bridges, K. L. Keller, and S. Sood, "Communication Strategies for Brand Extensions," *Journal of Advertising,* Winter 2000,

pp. 1–12; and R. Klink and D. C. Smith, "Threats to the External Validity of Brand Extension Research," *Journal of Marketing Research,* August 2001, pp. 326–35.

92. B. Forrest, "Two-Wheel Drives," *Men's Journal,* November 1996, p. 34.

93. V. O'Connell, "Courvoisier to Launch Clothing Line," *The Wall Street Journal,* February 13, 2004, p. B2.

94. V. Swarminathan, R. J. Fox, and S. K. Reddy, "The Impact of Brand Extension Introduction on Choice," *Journal of Marketing,* October 2001, pp. 1–15.

95. Effects can be negative or positive. See, e.g., D. R. John, B. Loken, and C. Joiner, "The Negative Impact of Extensions," *Journal of Marketing,* January 1998, pp. 19–32; Z. Gurhan-Canli and D. Maheswaran, "The Effects of Extensions on Brand Name Dilution and Enhancement," *Journal of Marketing Research,* November 1998, pp. 464–73; M. Morrin, "The Impact of Brand Extensions on Parent Brand Memory Structures and Retrieval Processes," *Journal of Marketing Research,* November 1999, pp. 517–25; C. Janiszewski and S. M. J. van Osselaer, "A Connectionist Model of Brand-Quality Associations," *Journal of Marketing Research,* August 2000, pp. 331–50; R. Ahluwalia and Z. Gurhan-Canli, "The Effects of Extensions on the Family Brand Name," *Journal of Consumer Research,* December 2000, pp. 371–81; and S. Balachander and S. Ghose, "Reciprocal Spillover Effects," *Journal of Marketing,* January 2003, pp. 4–13.

96. For exceptions, see Meyvis and Janiszewski, "When Are Broader Brands Stronger Brands?"

97. A. Kirmani, S. Sood, and S. Bridges, "The Ownership Effect in Consumer Response to Brand Line Stretches," *Journal of Marketing,* January 1999, pp. 88–101.

Courtesy Tourism New Zealand.

10

Motivation, Personality, and Emotion

■ How do people decide where to go on vacation? The answer to this question was of critical concern to New Zealand as it embarked on its first global branding initiative.[1] New Zealand, like many countries, depends on tourism as a significant source of revenue. Tourism New Zealand (TNZ) was created to investigate the tourism market and to develop New Zealand into a destination spot with a high level of emotional pull.

TNZ's first step was extensive market research, with a particular focus on the United Kingdom (U.K.). An interesting early finding was that U.K. travelers had various underlying motivations for going on vacation. Their six motivations were:

- *Energizing*—take on the world
- *Sociability*—join in/have in
- *Status*—feel superior to others
- *Connection*—getting together
- *Learning*—broaden the mind
- *Relaxation*—restore the spirit

A critical next step was to understand whether these needs and motives were different across types of traveler and travel situations. The answer was a resounding yes. Some vacationers were "Fun and Sun" types who wanted relaxation and socialization. Others were "Serious" vacationers who wanted a vacation that was prestigious, energizing, and provided opportunities for learning.

TNZ realized that they could not go after the "Fun and Sun" types. Their research clearly indicated that New Zealand was seen as potentially serious and boring due to its perceived lack of culture and night life. In addition, while warmer than the U.K., New Zealand knew that it probably couldn't compete successfully against much closer resort destinations such as Venice in terms of sun and beaches.

All of this led TNZ to the conclusion that it had to position itself to go after the more serious vacationer. Its research showed that U.K. travelers saw New Zealand as friendly, down-to-earth, unpretentious, and adventurous. In addition, New Zealand is seen as "real and authentic." As one advertising executive on the account stated,

As the world becomes increasingly "manufactured," the world's nations have become more and more homogeneous. It's become almost impossible to find meaningful differentiation. But New Zealand is different. It's an authentic country. New Zealand doesn't come prepackaged or prepared. New Zealand is for real.[2]

This insight led to a positioning strategy based on freedom and purity as expressed through the tag line "100% Pure." This tag line has a number of variations all designed to tap into emotional responses related to freedom, purity, authenticity, prestige, and adventure.

The New Zealand example illustrates that motivation, personality, and emotion are key factors in consumer decisions and marketing strategies. *Motivation* is the energizing force that activates behavior and provides purpose and direction to that behavior. It helps to answer the question of "why" consumers engage in specific behaviors. *Personality* reflects the relatively stable behavioral tendencies that individuals display across a variety of situations. It helps to answer the question of "what" behaviors consumers choose to engage in to achieve their goals. *Emotions* are strong, relatively uncontrollable feelings that affect our behavior. Emotions are triggered by a complex interplay between motives, personality, and external factors. Indeed, the three concepts are closely interrelated and are frequently difficult to separate.

THE NATURE OF MOTIVATION

Motivation is the reason for behavior. A **motive** is a construct representing an unobservable inner force that stimulates and compels a behavioral response and provides specific direction to that response. A motive is why an individual does something. The terms *need* and *motivation* are often used interchangeably. This is because when a consumer feels a gap between a desired state and his or her actual current state, a need is recognized and experienced as a drive state referred to as motivation. Needs and motives influence what consumers perceive as relevant and also influence their feelings and emotions. For example, a consumer who feels hungry is motivated to satisfy that need, will view food and ads for food as personally relevant, and will experience negative emotions prior to eating and positive emotions after eating.

As we saw in the opening vignette on New Zealand, various motivations underlie consumer behavior. There are numerous theories of motivation, and many of them offer useful insights for the marketing manager. This section describes two particularly useful approaches. The first approach, *Maslow's need hierarchy,* is a macro theory designed to account for most human behavior in general terms. The second approach, based on McGuire's work, uses a fairly detailed set of motives to account for specific aspects of consumer behavior.

Maslow's Hierarchy of Needs

Maslow's hierarchy of needs is based on four premises:[3]

1. All humans acquire a similar set of motives through genetic endowment and social interaction.

TABLE 10-1

Marketing Strategies and Maslow's Need Hierarchy

I. Physiological: Food, water, sleep, and, to an extent, sex, are physiological motives.

Products   Health foods, medicines, sports drinks, low-cholesterol foods, and exercise equipment.

Themes   BAND-AID—"Blister-proof your feet."
Quaker Oats—"Eating oatmeal is good for your heart."
NordicTrack—"Only NordicTrack gives you a total-body workout."

II. Safety: Seeking physical safety and security, stability, familiar surroundings, and so forth are manifestations of safety needs.

Products   Smoke detectors, preventive medicines, insurance, retirement investments, seat belts, burglar alarms, and sunscreen.

Themes   Sleep Safe—"We've designed a travel alarm that just might wake you in the middle of the night—because a fire is sending smoke into your room. You see, ours is a smoke alarm as well as an alarm clock."
Partnership for a Drug-Free America—"Heroin: Dying's the Easy Part."
Revo cycling glasses—"Should've worn Revo" under a picture of a wrecked bike.

III. Belongingness: Belongingness motives are reflected in a desire for love, friendship, affiliation, and group acceptance.

Products   Personal grooming, foods, entertainment, clothing, and many others.

Themes   Olive Garden Restaurants—"Italians didn't invent sharing. They just made it impossible to resist."
Tums—"You are important. You are loved. You should take your calcium."
J.C. Penney—"Wherever teens gather, you'll hear it. It's the language of terrific fit and fashion."

IV. Esteem: Desires for status, superiority, self-respect, and prestige are examples of esteem needs. These needs relate to the individual's feelings of usefulness and accomplishment.

Products   Clothing, furniture, liquors, hobbies, stores, cars, and many others.

Themes   Sheaffer—"Your hand should look as contemporary as the rest of you."
New Balance—"One more woman chasing a sunset. One more woman going a little farther. One more woman simply feeling alive. One less woman relying on someone else."
Cadillac—"Those long hours have paid off. In recognition, financial success, and in the way you reward yourself. Isn't it time you owned a Cadillac?"

V. Self-Actualization: This involves the desire for self-fulfillment, to become all that one is capable of becoming.

Products   Education, hobbies, sports, some vacations, gourmet foods, museums.

Themes   U.S. Army—"Be all you can be."
Avia—"She wasn't just training her body, she was training her mind."
Outward Bound School—"Challenges, adventure, growth."

2. Some motives are more basic or critical than others.
3. The more basic motives must be satisfied to a minimum level before other motives are activated.
4. As the basic motives become satisfied, more advanced motives come into play.

Thus, Maslow proposed a need hierarchy shared by all. Table 10-1 illustrates this hierarchy, briefly describes each level, and provides marketing examples.

Maslow's theory is a good guide to general behavior. It is not an ironclad rule, however. Numerous examples exist of individuals who sacrificed their lives for friends or ideas, or who gave up food and shelter to seek self-actualization. However, we do tend to regard such behavior as exceptional, which indicates the general validity of Maslow's overall approach.[4] It is important to remember that any given consumption behavior can satisfy more than one need. Likewise, the same consumption behavior can satisfy different needs at different times. For example, a number of motives could cause one to join the National Guard. The ad in Illustration 10-1 appeals to self-actualization.

ILLUSTRATION 10-1

Appeals to self-actualization focus on individuals challenging themselves and reaching their full potential.

Courtesy Army National Guard.

McGuire's Psychological Motives

Maslow presented a hierarchical set of five basic motives, and other researchers have proposed hundreds of additional, very specific motives. McGuire developed a classification system that organizes these various theories into 16 categories.[5] This system helps marketers isolate motives likely to be involved in various consumption situations. McGuire first divides motivation into four main categories using two criteria:

1. Is the mode of motivation cognitive or affective?
2. Is the motive focused on preservation of the status quo or on growth?

Cognitive motives focus on the person's need for being adaptively oriented toward the environment and achieving a sense of meaning. *Affective* motives deal with the need to reach satisfying feeling states and to obtain personal goals. *Preservation-oriented* motives emphasize the individual as striving to maintain equilibrium, while *growth* motives emphasize development. These four main categories are then further subdivided on the bases of source and objective of the motive:

3. Is this behavior actively initiated or in response to the environment?
4. Does this behavior help the individual achieve a new internal or a new external relationship to the environment?

The third criterion distinguishes between motives that are actively or internally aroused versus those that are a more passive response to circumstances. The final criterion is used to categorize outcomes that are internal to the individual and those focused on a relationship with the environment.

Each of McGuire's 16 motives and their implications for marketing are briefly described in the following sections.

Cognitive Preservation Motives   *Need for Consistency (active, internal)*   A basic desire is to have all facets or parts of oneself consistent with each other.[6] These facets include attitudes, behaviors, opinions, self-images, views of others, and so forth. *Cognitive dissonance* is a common motive of this type. Often making a major purchase is not consistent with the need to save money, to make other purchases, or to purchase a different brand with desirable features not in the purchased brand. This inconsistency motivates the individual to reduce it. How this is done is covered in depth in Chapter 18.

Understanding the need for consistency is also important for structuring advertising messages and developing attitude change strategies. Consumers have a need for internal consistency, so they are reluctant to accept information that disagrees with existing beliefs. Thus, marketers wishing to change attitudes must use highly credible sources or other techniques to overcome this (see Chapter 11).

Need for Attribution (active, external)   This set of motives deals with our need to determine who or what causes the things that happen to us. Do we attribute the cause of a favorable or unfavorable outcome to ourselves or to some outside force?

The fact that consumers need to attribute cause underlies an area of research known as **attribution theory.**[7] This approach to understanding the reasons consumers assign particular meanings to the behaviors of others has been used primarily for analyzing consumer reactions to promotional messages (in terms of credibility). When consumers attribute a sales motive to advice given by a salesperson or advertising message, they tend to discount the advice. In contrast, similar advice given by a friend would likely be attributed to a desire to be helpful and might therefore be accepted.

Because consumers do not passively receive messages but rather attribute sales motives and tactics to ads and the advice of sales personnel, they do not believe or they discount many sales messages.[8] Marketers use a variety of means to overcome this. One approach is to use a credible spokesperson in ads, such as in Illustration 10-2. This technique is discussed in depth in Chapter 11.

Need to Categorize (passive, internal)   People have a need to categorize and organize the vast array of information and experiences they encounter in a meaningful yet manageable way.[9] So they establish categories or mental partitions that allow them to process large quantities of information. Prices are often categorized such that different prices connote different categories of goods. Automobiles over $20,000 and automobiles under $20,000 may elicit two different meanings because of information categorized on the basis of price level. Many firms price items at $9.95, $19.95, $49.95, and so forth. One reason is to avoid being categorized in the over $10, $20, or $50 group.

Need for Objectification (passive, external)   These motives reflect needs for observable cues or symbols that enable people to infer what they feel and know. Impressions, feelings, and attitudes are subtly established by viewing one's own behavior and that of others and drawing inferences as to what one feels and thinks. In many instances, clothing plays an important role in presenting the subtle meaning of a desired image and consumer lifestyle.

Consumers generally attribute selling motives to ads and disbelieve or discount the message. One approach to gain message acceptance is to use a credible source.

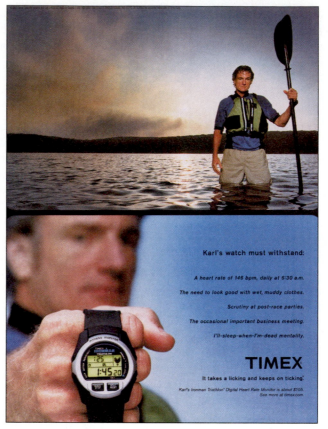

Courtesy Timex Corporation; Photo by: Platon.

This is so critical that companies such as Anheuser-Busch use clothing consulting firms to tailor clothes for executives that are consistent with the firm's desired image.

Cognitive Growth Motives   ***Need for Autonomy (active, internal)***   The need for independence and individuality is a characteristic of the American culture, as described in Chapter 2. All individuals in all cultures have this need at some level. Americans are taught that it is proper and even essential to express and fulfill this need. In contrast, in countries such as Japan, fulfillment of this need is discouraged, while fulfillment of the need for affiliation is more socially acceptable.

Owning or using products and services that are unique is one way consumers express their autonomy.[10] The increasing popularity of handmade craft goods, original art, antiques, and other unique products reflects this need. Marketers have responded to this motive by developing limited editions of products and providing wide variety and customization options. In addition, many products are advertised and positioned with independence, uniqueness, or individuality themes, as shown in Illustration 10-3.

Need for Stimulation (active, external)   People often seek variety and difference out of a need for stimulation.[11] Such variety-seeking behavior may be a prime reason for brand switching and some so-called impulse purchasing.[12] The need for stimulation is curvilinear and changes over time.[13] That is, individuals experiencing rapid change generally become satiated and desire stability, whereas individuals in stable environments become bored and desire change.

Courtesy Windsor Fashion.

Teleological Need (passive, internal)   Consumers are pattern matchers who have images of desired outcomes or end states to which they compare their current situation. Behaviors are changed and the results are monitored in terms of movement toward the desired end state. This motive propels people to prefer mass media such as movies, television programs, and books with outcomes that match their view of how the world should work (the good guys win, the hero and heroine get together, and so forth). This has obvious implications for advertising messages.

Utilitarian Need (passive, external)   These theories view the consumer as a problem solver who approaches situations as opportunities to acquire useful information or new skills. Thus, a consumer watching a situation comedy on television not only is being entertained but is learning clothing styles, etiquette, lifestyle options, and so forth. Likewise, consumers may approach ads, salespeople, and other marketing stimuli as a source of learning for future decisions as well as for the current one.

Affective Preservation Motives   ***Need for Tension Reduction (active, internal)***
People encounter situations in their daily lives that create uncomfortable levels of stress. In

Courtesy DaimlerChrysler.

order to effectively manage tension and stress, people are motivated to seek ways to reduce arousal. Recreational products and activities are often promoted in terms of tension relief. Illustration 10-4 contains a product and appeal focused on this need.

Need for Expression (active, external)   This motive deals with the need to express one's identity to others. People feel the need to let others know who and what they are by their actions, which include the purchase and use of goods. The purchase of many products such as clothing and automobiles allows consumers to express an identity to others, because these products have symbolic or expressive meanings. For example, fashion oriented watches such as Swatch satisfy much more than the functional need to tell time—they also allow consumers to express who they are.

Need for Ego Defense (passive, internal)   The need to defend one's identity or ego is another important motive. When one's identity is threatened, the person is motivated to protect his or her self-concept and utilize defensive behaviors and attitudes. Many products can provide ego defense. A consumer who feels insecure may rely on well-known brands for socially visible products to avoid any chance of making a socially incorrect purchase.

Need for Reinforcement (passive, external)   People are often motivated to act in certain ways because they were rewarded for behaving that way in similar situations in the past. This is the basis for operant learning as described in the previous chapter. Products designed to be used in public situations (clothing, furniture, and artwork) are frequently sold on the basis of the amount and type of reinforcement that will be received. Keepsake Diamonds exploits this motive with an advertisement that states, "Enter a room and you are immediately surrounded by friends sharing your excitement."

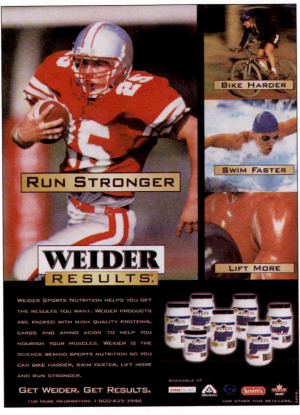

Courtesy Weider Nutrition International, Inc.

Affective Growth Motives   *Need for Assertion (active, internal)*   Many people are competitive achievers who seek success, admiration, and dominance. Important to them are power, accomplishment, and esteem. As Illustration 10-5 shows, the need for assertion underlies numerous ads.

Need for Affiliation (active, external)   Affiliation refers to the need to develop mutually helpful and satisfying relationships with others. It relates to altruism and seeking acceptance and affection in interpersonal relations. As we saw in Chapter 7, group membership is a critical part of most consumers' lives, and many consumer decisions are based on the need to maintain satisfying relationships with others. Marketers frequently use such affiliation-based themes as "Your kids will love you for it" in advertisements.[14]

Need for Identification (passive, internal)   The need for identification results in the consumer playing various roles. A person may play the role of college student, sorority member, bookstore employee, fiancée, and many others. One gains pleasure from adding new, satisfying roles and by increasing the significance of roles already adopted. Marketers encourage consumers to assume new roles (become a skateboarder) and position products as critical for certain roles ("No working mother should be without one").

Need for Modeling (passive, external)   The need for modeling reflects a tendency to base behavior on that of others. Modeling is a major means by which children learn to become consumers. The tendency to model explains some of the conformity that occurs within reference groups. Marketers utilize this motive by showing desirable types of individuals using their brands. For example, some Rolex ads devote most of their copy to a description of very successful people such as Picabo Street or Monica Kristensen. They then state that this person owns a Rolex.

MOTIVATION THEORY AND MARKETING STRATEGY

Beck's and Heineken are imported beers consumed primarily by confident, upscale, professional men. However, BBDO (a major advertising agency) found through its motivation research that Heineken consumption is driven by a desire for status, whereas Beck's is associated with a desire for individuality. Likewise, both Classico and Newman's Own spaghetti sauces are consumed by upscale, sophisticated adults. However, Classico buyers are motivated by indulgence and romance while Newman's Own buyers are showing ambition and individuality. Since the purchase of each of these brands is caused by a different motive, each requires a distinct marketing and advertising program.[15]

Consumers do not buy products; instead, they buy motive satisfaction or problem solutions. Thus, consumers do not buy perfume or cologne (or a chemical compound with certain odoriferous characteristics). Instead, they buy romance, sex appeal, sensual pleasure, sophistication, or a host of other emotional and psychological benefits. Managers must discover the motives that their products and brands can satisfy and develop marketing mixes around these motives.

An important question that often arises is "Do marketers create needs?" The answer depends in part on what is meant by the term *need*. If it is used to refer to the basic motives described in this chapter, it is clear that marketers seldom if ever *create* a need. Human genetics and experience basically determine motives. Long before marketing or advertising appeared, individuals used perfumes, clothing, and other items to gain acceptance, display status, and so forth.

However, marketers do create **demand.** Demand is *the willingness to buy a particular product or service.* It is caused by a need or motive, but it is not the motive. For example, a mouthwash ad might use a theme suggesting that without mouthwash people will not like you because you have bad breath. This message ties mouthwash to an existing need for affiliation in hopes of creating demand for the brand. Still, critics argue that unduly playing on the insecurities surrounding such needs can have negative consequences on consumer self-perceptions and behaviors. One area of profound concern is that related to body perceptions and eating disorders.

The preceding discussion makes clear the important role that motives play in consumer behavior and thus in marketing strategy. In the following sections, we examine (1) how to discover underlying purchase motives, (2) how to develop marketing strategy based on the total array of motives operating, (3) how to manage motivational conflict, and (4) the link between motivation and consumer involvement.

Discovering Purchase Motives

Suppose a marketing researcher asked a consumer why he wears Gap clothes (or owns a mountain bike, or uses cologne, or whatever). Odds are the consumer would offer several reasons, such as "They're in style," "My friends wear them," "I like the way they fit," or "They look good on me." However, there may be other reasons that the consumer is reluctant to admit or perhaps is not even aware of: "They show that I have money," "They make

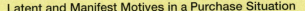

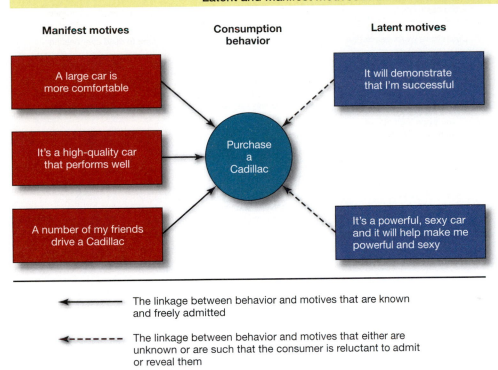

Latent and Manifest Motives in a Purchase Situation   FIGURE 10-1

Manifest motives

- A large car is more comfortable
- It's a high-quality car that performs well
- A number of my friends drive a Cadillac

Consumption behavior

Purchase a Cadillac

Latent motives

- It will demonstrate that I'm successful
- It's a powerful, sexy car and it will help make me powerful and sexy

← The linkage between behavior and motives that are known and freely admitted

←---- The linkage between behavior and motives that either are unknown or are such that the consumer is reluctant to admit or reveal them

me sexually desirable," or "They show I'm still young." All or any combination of the above motives could influence the purchase of clothes or many other items.

The first group of motives mentioned above were known to the consumer and admitted to the researcher. Motives that are known and freely admitted are called **manifest motives.** Any of the motives we have discussed can be manifest; however, motives that conform to a society's prevailing value system are more likely to be manifest than are those in conflict with such values.

The second group of motives described above either were unknown to the consumer or were such that he was reluctant to admit them. Such motives are **latent motives.** Figure 10-1 illustrates how the two types of motives might influence a purchase.

Given that a variety of manifest and latent motives may be operative in a particular purchase such as that shown in Figure 10-1, the first task of the marketing manager is to determine the combination of motives influencing the target market. Manifest motives are relatively easy to determine. Direct questions (Why did you buy a Cadillac?) will generally produce reasonably accurate assessments of manifest motives.[16]

Determining latent motives is substantially more complex. Sophisticated analytical techniques such as multidimensional scaling can sometimes provide insights into latent motives. Motivation research or **projective techniques** are designed to provide information on latent motives. Table 10-2 describes some of the more common projective techniques.

These techniques are used to enhance and enrich the insights that can be gained from more empirical sources. For example, Oreo used projective techniques in a focus group setting to gain a fuller understanding of the brand: "We had always known that Oreo evoked strong emotions but what surprised us in these focus groups was that many regarded Oreo

TABLE 10-2

Motivation Research
Techniques

I. Association Techniques	
Word association	Consumers respond to a list of words with the first word that comes to mind.
Successive word association	Consumers give the series of words that come to mind after hearing each word on the list.
Analysis and use	Responses are analyzed to see if negative associations exist. When the time to respond (response latency) is also measured, the emotionality of the word can be estimated. These techniques tap semantic memory more than motives and are used for brand name and advertising copy tests.
II. Completion Techniques	
Sentence completion	Consumers complete a sentence such as "People who buy a Cadillac _____."
Story completion	Consumers complete a partial story.
Analysis and use	Responses are analyzed to determine what themes are expressed. Content analysis—examining responses for themes and key concepts—is used.
III. Construction Techniques	
Cartoon techniques	Consumers fill in the words or thoughts of one of the characters in a cartoon drawing.
Third-person techniques	Consumers tell why "an average woman," "most doctors," or "people in general" purchase or use a certain product. Shopping lists (describe a person who would go shopping with this list) and lost wallets (describe a person with these items in his wallet) are also third-person techniques.
Picture response	Consumers tell a story about a person shown buying or using a product in a picture or line drawing.
Analysis and use	Same as for completion techniques.

as almost 'magical.' " As a result, "Unlocking the Magic of Oreo" became a campaign theme.[17]

Not only are the traditional projective techniques being used at an increasing rate, but new approaches are being developed.[18] One popular approach is **laddering,** or constructing a **means-end** or **benefit chain.**[19] A product or brand is shown to a consumer, who names all the benefits that possession or use of that product might provide. Then for each benefit mentioned, the respondent is asked to identify further benefits that the named benefit provides. This is repeated for each round of benefits until the consumer can no longer identify additional benefits.

For example, a respondent might mention "fewer colds" as a benefit of taking a daily vitamin. When asked the benefit of fewer colds, one respondent might identify "more efficient at work" and "more energy." Another might name "more skiing" and "looking better." Both use the vitamin to reduce colds but as a means to different ultimate benefits. *How should vitamin ads aimed at each of these two consumers differ?*

Marketing Strategies Based on Multiple Motives

Once a manager has isolated the combination of motives influencing the target market, the next task is to design the marketing strategy around the appropriate set of motives. This involves everything from product design to marketing communications. The nature of these decisions is most apparent in the communications area. Suppose the motives shown in Figure 10-1 are an accurate reflection of a desired target market. *What communications strategy should the manager use?*

Courtesy AstraZeneca Pharmaceuticals LP.

One consideration is the extent to which more than one motive is important. If multiple motives are important the product must provide more than one benefit and the advertising for the product must communicate these multiple benefits. A second consideration is whether the motive is manifest or latent. Communicating manifest benefits is relatively easy. For example, an advertisement for Cadillac states, "From the triple-sanded finish (once with water and twice with oil) to that superbly refined Cadillac ride, the quality comes standard on Cadillac." This is a direct appeal to a manifest motive for product quality. Direct appeals are generally effective for manifest motives, since these are motives that consumers are aware of and will discuss.

However, since latent motives often are less than completely socially desirable, indirect appeals frequently are used. The bulk of the copy of the Cadillac ad referred to above focuses on the quality of the product. However, the artwork (about 60 percent of the ad) shows the car being driven by an apparently wealthy individual in front of a luxurious club. This is a dual appeal. The direct appeal in the copy focuses on quality, while the indirect appeal in the artwork focuses on status.

While any given advertisement for a product may focus on only one or a few purchasing motives, the campaign needs to cover all the important purchase motives of the target market. In essence, the overall campaign attempts to position the product in the schematic memory of the target market in a manner that corresponds with the target market's manifest and latent motives for purchasing the product. *To what motives does the ad shown in Illustration 10-6 appeal?*

Consumers Have Fun at the Mall

Consumers can shop for utilitarian reasons related to achieving specific purchase goals. Alternatively, they can shop for hedonic reasons related to having fun. As catalogs and the Web make it easier to satisfy utilitarian motives, traditional retailers are finding that they need to examine hedonic shopping motives and related marketing strategies. A recent study uncovered six hedonic shopping motives related to McGuire's typology.[20]

- *Adventure shopping* refers to shopping for fun and adventure and relates to the need for stimulation, e.g., "I enjoy shopping. It brings me great excitement and sometimes suspense as to what I'm going to find."
- *Social shopping* refers to the enjoyment that comes from socializing and bonding while shopping and relates to the need for affiliation, e.g., "Well, I shop because it gives me a chance to spend time with my friends and family."
- *Gratification shopping* relates to shopping to reduce stress or as a self-reward and relates to the tension reduction need, e.g., "I love to go shopping. It is my biggest stress reliever."
- *Idea shopping* involves shopping to keep up with trends and fashions and relates to categorization and objectification needs, e.g., "I like new gadgets, new technology and see the new toys that are out there. It is kind of a hobby."
- *Role shopping* relates to the enjoyment that consumers feel from shopping for others and relates to the identification motivation, e.g., "I love to buy gifts for other people. It makes me feel good to buy something for someone that I know they are going to like."
- *Value shopping* involves shopping for deals and relates to assertion needs, e.g., "It's exciting, because you feel like your winning. That's like the competitive part of shopping."

Interestingly, different segments of consumers emerged depending on their level of motivation on each hedonic dimension. These segments have interesting demographic characteristics (see Chapter 4) that are important for marketers to consider. For example, there was a *minimalist* segment which is only motivated by value. This segment is comprised mostly of middle-aged males. There was also a *provider* segment motivated primarily by role and value shopping. This segment is comprised mostly of middle-aged females. There was also an *enthusiasts* segment which is motivated by all the hedonic dimensions. This segment was comprised primarily of young females.

Critical Thinking Questions

1. Can motivations vary by shopping situation (grocery versus clothes shopping)?
2. What implications do the demographic differences across shopping segments have for advertising and media selection?
3. What strategies can retailers use to target the various hedonic shopping motives?

Consumer Insight 10-1 looks at the various motives people have for shopping. Notice how some consumers have one basic motive for shopping while others have numerous motives.

Marketing Strategies Based on Motivation Conflict

With the many motives consumers have and the many situations in which these motives are activated, there are frequent conflicts between motives. The resolution of a motivational conflict often affects consumption patterns. In many instances, the marketer can analyze situations that are likely to result in a motivational conflict, provide a solution to the conflict, and attract the patronage of those consumers facing the motivational conflict. There are three types of motivational conflict of importance to marketing managers: approach–approach conflict, approach–avoidance conflict, and avoidance–avoidance conflict.

Approach–Approach Motivational Conflict   A consumer who must choose between two attractive alternatives faces **approach–approach conflict.** The more equal the attractions, the greater the conflict. A consumer who recently received a large cash gift for graduation (situational variable) might be torn between a trip to Hawaii (perhaps powered by a need for stimulation) and a new mountain bike (perhaps driven by the need for assertion). This conflict could be resolved by a timely advertisement designed to encourage one or the other action. Or a price modification, such as "buy now, pay later," could result in a resolution whereby both alternatives are selected.

Approach–Avoidance Motivational Conflict   A consumer facing a purchase choice with both positive and negative consequences confronts **approach–avoidance conflict.** A person who is concerned about gaining weight yet likes snack foods faces this type of problem. He or she may want the taste and emotional satisfaction associated with the snacks (approach) but does not want to gain weight (avoidance). The development of lower-calorie snack foods reduces this conflict and allows the weight-sensitive consumer to enjoy snacks and also control calorie intake. Similarly, many consumers want a tan but don't want to risk the skin damage and health risks associated with extended sun exposure. Neutrogena's Instant Bronze sunless tanner resolves this problem.

Avoidance–Avoidance Motivational Conflict   A choice involving only undesirable outcomes produces **avoidance–avoidance conflict.** When a consumer's old washing machine fails, this conflict may occur. The person may not want to spend money on a new washing machine, or pay to have the old one repaired, or go without one. The availability of credit is one way of reducing this motivational conflict. Advertisements emphasizing the importance of regular maintenance for cars, such as oil filter changes, also use this type of motive conflict: "Pay me now, or pay me (more) later."

Motivation and Consumer Involvement

As we have seen in previous chapters, involvement is an important determinant of how consumers process information and learn. We will also see in future chapters that involvement is an important determinant of how consumers form attitudes and make purchase decisions. **Involvement** is a motivational state caused by consumer perceptions that a product, brand, or advertisement is relevant or interesting.[21] It should not be surprising that needs play a strong role in determining what is relevant or interesting to consumers. For example, watches may be involving to consumers because they tell time (a utilitarian need), because they allow for self-expression (expressive need), or because they provide a way to fit in with a social group (affiliation need).[22] In addition, the situation itself may influence involvement. For example, some consumers may be involved with computers on an ongoing basis (enduring involvement), while others may only be involved in specific situations such as an upcoming purchase (situational involvement).

Involvement is important to marketers because it influences numerous consumer behaviors. For example, consumers who are highly involved in a specific product category such as automobiles are more likely to (1) pay attention to relevant marketing messages, (2) engage in analytical reasoning to process and learn new information, (3) seek out information from numerous sources prior to a decision, and (4) act as opinion leaders.[23]

Involvement is also important to marketers because it influences choice of marketing strategies. For example, high involvement consumers tend to be product experts and are more persuaded by ads that include detailed product information. On the other hand, low-involvement consumers lack product expertise and are more persuaded by images, emotion, and message source. As a consequence, you will often find highly informational ads for automobiles in magazines such as *Car and Driver* which are targeted at high-involvement consumers. Alternatively, image and emotional approaches are often the norm in general interest magazines where involvement is likely moderate to low.

PERSONALITY

While motivations are the energizing and directing force that makes consumer behavior purposeful and goal directed, the personality of the consumer guides and directs the behavior chosen to accomplish goals in different situations. **Personality** is *an individual's characteristic response tendencies across similar situations*. Thus, two consumers might have equal needs for tension reduction, but differ in their level of extroversion, and as a consequence, engage in very different behaviors designed to satisfy that need.

While there are many theories of personality, those found to be most useful in a marketing context are called trait theories. Trait theories examine personality as an individual difference and thus allow marketers to segment consumers as a function of their personality differences. Trait theories assume that (1) all individuals have internal characteristics or traits related to action tendencies, and (2) there are consistent and measurable differences between individuals on those characteristics. To demonstrate, imagine how you might respond if you were asked to describe the personality of a friend. You might say that one of your friends is aggressive, competitive and outgoing. What you have described are the behavioral tendencies or *traits* your friend has exhibited over time across a variety of situations. Most trait theories state that traits are inherited or formed at an early age and are relatively unchanging over the years. Differences between personality theories center on which traits or characteristics are the most important.

Multitrait Approach

Some trait research attempts to examine a consumer's entire personality profile across a set of relatively exhaustive dimensions. Specifically, *multitrait personality theory* identifies several traits that in combination capture a substantial portion of the personality of the individual. The multitrait theory used most commonly by marketers is the **Five-Factor Model.**[24] This theory identifies five basic traits that are formed by genetics and early learning. These core traits interact and manifest themselves in behaviors triggered by situations. Table 10-3 lists the five traits and some of their manifestations.

TABLE 10-3

The Five-Factor Model of Personality

Core Trait	Manifestation
Extroversion	Prefer to be in a large group rather than alone Talkative when with others Bold
Instability	Moody Temperamental Touchy
Agreeableness	Sympathetic Kind to others Polite with others
Openness to experience	Imaginative Appreciative of art Find novel solutions
Conscientiousness	Careful Precise Efficient

The Five-Factor Model has proven useful in such areas as understanding bargaining and complaining behavior[25] and compulsive shopping.[26] There is evidence that it may have validity across cultures.[27] The advantage of a multitrait approach such as this is the broad picture it allows of the determinants of behavior. For example, suppose research focused on the single dimension of extroversion and found that those who complained about a dissatisfactory purchase tended to be extroverts. *What insights does this provide for training those who deal with consumer complaints? What training insights are added if we also learn such people are conscientious?* Clearly, the more we know, the better we can satisfy these customers.

Single-Trait Approach

Single-trait theories emphasize one personality trait as being particularly relevant to understanding a particular set of behaviors. They do not suggest that other traits are nonexistent or unimportant. Rather, they study a single trait for its relevance to a set of behaviors, in our case, consumption-related behaviors. Examples of single-trait theories of relevance to marketing include those dealing with neuroticism,[28] vanity,[29] trait anxiety,[30] locus of control, sensation seeking,[31] compulsive buying,[32] materialism,[33] affect intensity,[34] and self-monitoring.[35]

Next, we examine three additional traits in more detail. We emphasize that given the strong interrelationship between motivation and personality, it is not uncommon for personality traits to evidence motivational aspects.[36] Traits labeled as "needs" often reflect these motivational bases.

Consumer Ethnocentrism   **Consumer ethnocentrism** reflects an individual difference in consumers' propensity to be biased against the purchase of foreign products.[37] Consumers low in ethnocentrism tend to be more open to other cultures, less conservative, and more open to purchasing foreign-made products. Consumers high in ethnocentrism tend to be less open to other cultures, more conservative, and more likely to reject foreign-made products in favor of domestics. As a consequence, Lexington furniture is tapping into pro-American sentiments by actively promoting the "Made in America" status of its Bob Timberlake line to retailers and consumers.[38] It is important to note, however, that consumer ethnocentrism is a global phenomenon. One study found that for Western brands trying to market in Russia, brand image mattered only for those low in ethnocentricity.[39]

Need for Cognition   *Need for cognition (NFC)* reflects an individual difference in consumers' propensity to engage in and enjoy thinking.[40] Compared to low-NFC individuals, those high in NFC engage in more effortful processing of persuasive communications, prefer verbal to visual information, and are less swayed by the opinions of others. NFC has obvious implications for marketing communications. In addition, research linking NFC to demographic characteristics such as gender (e.g., women are generally higher in NFC) helps to make this personality factor more actionable in terms of media targeting.[41]

Consumers' Need for Uniqueness   *Consumers' need for uniqueness* reflects an individual difference in consumers' propensity to pursue differentness relative to others through the acquisition, utilization, and disposition of consumer goods.[42] It affects what consumers own and value, why they own it, and how they use it. The concept fits with the increasingly common marketing practice of deliberate scarcity—producing less of an item than the predicted demand. Such a strategy helps preserve the uniqueness of the product and enhances the distinctiveness and status of those who own it.

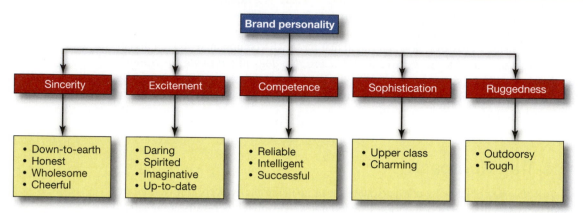

FIGURE 10-2   Dimensions of Brand Personality

Source: J. L. Aaker, "Dimensions of Brand Personality," *Journal of Marketing Research*, August 1997, p. 352. Published by the American Marketing Association; reprinted with permission.

THE USE OF PERSONALITY IN MARKETING PRACTICE

Sometimes consumers choose products that fit their personality. For example, a timid person might forgo a flashy car because "it's just not me." Other times, consumers use products to bolster an area of their personality where they feel weak. Thus, a timid person who wants to feel more assertive might drive a powerful, flashy sports car. Clearly, products and brands help consumers express their personality.

Brand image is what people think of and feel when they hear or see a brand name (Chapter 9). A particular type of image that some brands acquire is a **brand personality.** Brand personality is *a set of human characteristics that become associated with a brand.* Consumers perceive brand personalities in terms of five basic dimensions, each with several facets as shown in Figure 10-2. A scale has been developed to measure brand personality on these dimensions.[43] Modifications of this scale have been used to tap brand personality in other countries such as Russia and Chile.[44]

Marketers are paying increasing attention to brand personality given its power to influence purchases. Jaguar, Reebok, and Sprite are just a few of the many companies that are currently attempting to enhance their brand personalities to better target key customer groups. Jaguar is trying to be less "aloof," Reebok wants to be "hip and aggressive," and Sprite wants more "street cred."[45]

Researchers at Whirlpool found the following personality profiles for Whirlpool and KitchenAid appliances. Higher scores indicate the trait is more associated with the brand.[46] *What type of target market will each brand appeal to?*

Whirlpool	KitchenAid
Gentle (146)	Sophisticated (206)
Sensitive (128)	Glamorous (186)
Quiet (117)	Wealthy (180)
Good natured (114)	Elegant (178)
Sailing (125)	Theater (124)
Jazz (118)	Classical (126)

Based on their investigation, researchers at Whirlpool also drew the following conclusions about brand personality:[47]

- Consumers readily assign human characteristics to brands even if the brands are not managed or the characteristics are not wanted by the marketers.
- Brand personalities create expectations about key characteristics, performance and benefits, and related services.
- Brand personalities are often the basis for a long-term relationship with the brand.

The ability of a brand's personality to affect customer relationships is critical and we are only beginning to understand this process. One study provides early insights. Specifically, consumer relationships with "sincere" brands were found to deepen over time along the lines of a "friendship." Alternatively, consumer relationships with "exciting" brands were found to weaken over time along the lines of a "short-lived fling." This advantage for sincere brands required, however, that the brand consistently deliver high quality.[48]

Communicating Brand Personality

Marketers need to manage and communicate brand personality. As the head of Swatch Group (numerous watch brands) notes:

> My job is to sit in the bunker with a machine gun defending the distinct messages of all my brands. I am the custodian of our messages. I review every new communications campaign for every single brand.[49]

Numerous elements can be used to communicate brand personality. Three important advertising tactics include celebrity endorsers, user imagery, and executional factors.[50]

Celebrity Endorsers   Celebrity endorsers are often a useful way to personify a brand since the characteristics and meanings of the celebrity can be transferred to the brand. Examples include:[51]

- Nike and Serena Williams—edgy, individualistic brand.
- Revlon and Halle Berry—sexy, confident brand.

User Imagery   User imagery involves showing a typical user along with images of the types of activities they engage in while using the brand. User imagery helps to define who the typical user is in terms of their traits, activities, and emotions. The emotion and tone of the activities can also transfer to the brand. Examples include:[52]

- Mountain Dew—features young, active users engaged in fun and exciting activities.
- Hush Puppies—features "hip young people in a wooded setting."

Executional Factors   Executional factors go beyond the core message to include "how" it is communicated. The "tone" of the ad (serious vs. quirky), the appeal used (fear vs. humor), the logo and typeface characteristics (*scripted font* may signal sophistication), the pace of the ad, and even the media outlet chosen can all communicate a brand's personality. Examples include:[53]

- Tone—Listerine in Canada wanted a way to be both lighthearted and powerful, so they leveraged an action-hero theme from a popular movie. Listerine went from "old-fashioned and serious," to "powerful and larger than life."
- Media—Hush Puppies placed ads in fashion magazines such as *W* and *InStyle* to establish a more hip, fashionable personality.

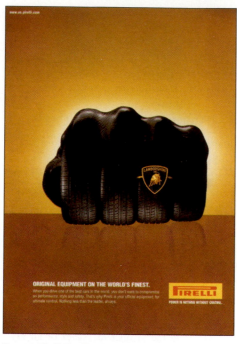

Courtesy Pirelli Tire North America.

- Pace—Molson in Canada wanted a "spirited, adventurous and slightly naughty" personality. So, they created TV ads in which "a festive Latin beat is punctuated with fast-moving, sexually charged party scenes."
- Logo—Reebok wanted to invigorate its brand toward a younger, hipper image. So, they created the new Rbk logo. According to one executive, "Creating a short code gave permission to the youth culture to look at the brand again without the old baggage."

What type of brand personality is created by the ad in Illustration 10-7? What advertising elements are being used?

EMOTION

Emotions are strong, relatively uncontrolled feelings that affect behavior.[54] Emotions are strongly linked to needs, motivation, and personality. Unmet needs create motivation which is related to the arousal component of emotion. Unmet needs generally yield negative emotions, while met needs generally yield positive emotions. As a result, products and brands that generate positive consumption emotions increase consumer satisfaction and loyalty.[55] Personality also plays a role. For example, some people are more emotional than others, a consumer trait termed *affect intensity*. Consumers higher in affect intensity experience stronger emotions and are more influenced by emotional appeals.[56]

We all experience a wide array of emotions such as anger, joy, and sadness. Think about a recent emotional experience. What characterized it? All emotional experiences tend to have several elements in common. First, emotions are often triggered by environmental events (e.g., viewing an advertisement, consuming a product that meets a need). However, they can also be initiated by internal processes such as imagery. As we have seen, advertisers frequently use imagery to evoke specific emotional responses.

Second, emotions are accompanied by *physiological changes* such as (1) eye pupil dilation, (2) increased perspiration, (3) more rapid breathing, (4) increased heart rate and blood pressure, and (5) enhanced blood sugar level. Third, emotions generally, though not necessarily, are accompanied by *cognitive thought*.[57] The types of thoughts and our ability to think rationally vary with the type and degree of emotion.[58]

A fourth characteristic is that emotions have associated *behaviors*. While the behaviors vary across individuals and within individuals across time and situations, there are unique behaviors characteristically associated with different emotions: fear triggers fleeing (avoidance) responses, anger triggers striking out (approach), grief triggers crying, and so forth.[59]

Finally, emotions involve *subjective feelings*. In fact, it is the feeling component we generally refer to when we think of emotions. Grief, joy, anger, and fear feel very different.

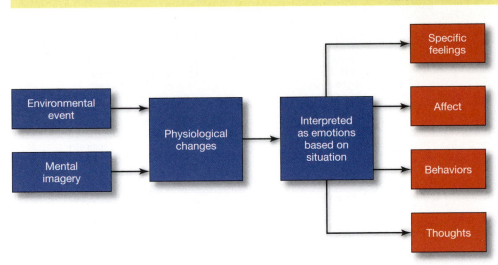

These subjectively determined feelings are the essence of emotion. These feelings have a specific component we label as the emotion, such as sad or happy. In addition, emotions carry an evaluative or a like/dislike component.

We use **emotion** to refer to the identifiable, specific feeling, and *affect* to refer to the liking/disliking aspect of the specific feeling. Emotions are generally evaluated (liked and disliked) in a consistent manner across individuals and within individuals over time, but there are cultural, individual, and situational variations.[60] For example, few of us generally want to be sad or afraid, yet we occasionally enjoy a movie or book that scares or saddens us.

Figure 10-3 reflects current thinking on the nature of emotions.

Types of Emotions

If asked, you could doubtless name numerous emotions. Thus, it is not surprising that researchers have attempted to categorize emotions into manageable clusters. Some researchers have suggested that three basic dimensions—pleasure, arousal, and dominance (PAD)—underlie all emotions. Specific emotions reflect various combinations and levels of these three dimensions. Table 10-4 lists the three primary PAD dimensions, a variety of emotions or emotional categories associated with each dimension, and indicators or items that can be used to measure each emotion.

EMOTIONS AND MARKETING STRATEGY

Although marketers have always used emotions to guide product positioning, sales presentations, and advertising on an intuitive level, the deliberate, systematic study of the relevance of emotions in marketing strategy is relatively new. For example, salespeople and other service providers frequently must deal with consumers displaying an array of emotions. Only recently have marketers developed sufficient understanding to create systematic training and marketing programs related to responding to emotional consumers.[61]

In this section, we describe strategies focused on emotion arousal and reduction as product benefits and emotion in the context of advertising.

Emotional
Dimensions,
Emotions, and
Emotional Indicators

Dimension	Emotion	Indicator/Feeling
Pleasure	Duty	Moral, virtuous, dutiful
	Faith	Reverent, worshipful, spiritual
	Pride	Proud, superior, worthy
	Affection	Loving, affectionate, friendly
	Innocence	Innocent, pure, blameless
	Gratitude	Grateful, thankful, appreciative
	Serenity	Restful, serene, comfortable, soothed
	Desire	Desirous, wishful, craving, hopeful
	Joy	Joyful, happy, delighted, pleased
	Competence	Confident, in control, competent
Arousal	Interest	Attentive, curious
	Hypoactivation	Bored, drowsy, sluggish
	Activation	Aroused, active, excited
	Surprise	Surprised, annoyed, astonished
	Déjà vu	Unimpressed, uninformed, unexcited
	Involvement	Involved, informed, enlightened, benefited
	Distraction	Distracted, preoccupied, inattentive
	Surgency	Playful, entertained, lighthearted
	Contempt	Scornful, contemptuous, disdainful
Dominance	Conflict	Tense, frustrated, conflictful
	Guilt	Guilty, remorseful, regretful
	Helplessness	Powerless, helpless, dominated
	Sadness	Sad, distressed, sorrowful, dejected
	Fear	Fearful, afraid, anxious
	Shame	Ashamed, embarrassed, humiliated
	Anger	Angry, agitated, enraged, mad
	Hyperactivation	Panicked, confused, overstimulated
	Disgust	Disgusted, revolted, annoyed, full of loathing
	Skepticism	Skeptical, suspicious, distrustful

Source: Adapted from M. B. Holbrook and R. Batra, "Assessing the Role of Emotions on Consumer Responses to Advertising," *Journal of Consumer Research,* December 1987, pp. 404–20. Copyright © 1987 by the University of the Chicago. Used by permission.

Emotion Arousal as a Product Benefit

Emotions are characterized by positive or negative evaluations. Consumers actively seek products whose primary or secondary benefit is emotion arousal.[62] Although consumers seek positive emotions the majority of the time, this is not always the case. ("The movie was so sad, I cried and cried. I loved it. You should see it.")

Many products feature emotion arousal as a primary benefit. Movies, books, and music are the most obvious examples.[63] Las Vegas, Atlantic City, and Disney World are positioned as emotion-arousing destinations, as are various types of adventure travel programs. Stores feature events and environments that arouse emotions such as excitement.[64] Recent advertisements designed to fuel consumer emotion and excitement include Bacardi rum's "Shake up your night," Pontiac G6's "Move like a shaker," and Chevrolet's "An American Revolution."

Products often arouse emotions in ways unintended by marketers. Most of us have experienced emotions such as frustration and anger as we have tried to assemble products or learn how to use new high-tech gadgets.

Emotion Reduction as a Product Benefit

As a glance at Table 10-4 indicates, many emotional states are unpleasant to most individuals most of the time. Few people like to feel sad, powerless, humiliated, or disgusted.

ILLUSTRATION 10-8

Emotional appeals can play a powerful role in developing a brand image.

Responding to this, marketers design or position many products to prevent or reduce the arousal of unpleasant emotions.

The most obvious of these products are the various over-the-counter medications designed to deal with anxiety or depression. As we saw in Consumer Insight 10-1, shopping malls, department stores, and other retail outlets are often visited to alleviate boredom or loneliness. Food and alcohol are consumed, often harmfully, to reduce stress. Flowers are heavily promoted as an antidote to sadness. Weight-loss products and other self-improvement products are frequently positioned primarily in terms of guilt-, helplessness-, shame-, or disgust-reduction benefits. Personal grooming products often emphasize anxiety reduction as a major benefit. Charities frequently stress guilt reduction or avoidance as a reason for contributing.[65]

Emotion in Advertising

Emotion arousal is often used in advertising even when emotion arousal or reduction is not a product benefit. Consider the following recent headlines:

- Under Armour taps raw emotion.
- Kleenex for Men to play on emotion in TV return.
- Emotional appeal of laundry to replace performance claims in ads.

Illustration 10-8 provides an example of the effective use of emotion to attract attention to an ad and to position a line of products. In this ad, the young girl is being introduced to her new foster mother. After a shy start, the girl tries some soup. As the girl tastes the soup she says, "My mother used to make me that soup." "So did mine," says the foster mother.

Emotional appeals can capture attention and enhance the retention of advertising messages. They can also help humanize the brand and associate feelings with it.

There's nothing more natural.

Follow the Sun.®

© 2004 Sun-Maid Growers of California.

"Why don't I tell you about my mom and then you can tell me about yours." The tag line for the campaign is "Good for the body. Good for the soul."

We are just beginning to develop a sound understanding of how emotional responses to advertising influence consumer behavior,[66] as well as what causes an ad to elicit particular emotions.[67] Therefore, the general conclusions discussed below must be regarded as tentative.[68] The effects we consider include attention, elaboration, and brand attitudes.

Emotional content in advertisements *enhances their attention, attraction, and maintenance capabilities.* Advertising messages that trigger the emotional reactions of joy, warmth, and suspense[69] are more likely to be attended to than are more neutral ads. As we saw in Chapter 8, attention is a critical early step in the perception process.

Emotions are characterized by a state of heightened physiological arousal. Individuals become more alert and active when aroused. Given this enhanced level of arousal, *emotional messages may be processed more thoroughly* than neutral messages. More effort and increased elaboration activities may occur in response to the emotional state.[70] As a consequence of this greater attention and processing, emotional ads *may be remembered better than neutral ads.*[71]

Emotional advertisements that *trigger a positively evaluated emotion will enhance liking of the ad itself.*[72] For example, warmth is a positively valued emotion that is triggered by experiencing directly or vicariously a love, family, or friendship relationship. Ads high in warmth, such as the Campbell's ad in Illustration 10-8, are liked more than neutral ads. Liking an ad has a positive impact on liking the product and purchase intentions. As you might suspect, ads that irritate or disgust consumers can create negative reactions to the advertised brand.[73]

Repeated exposure to positive-emotion-eliciting ads *may increase brand preference through classical conditioning.*[74] Repeated pairings of positive emotion (unconditioned response) with the brand name (conditioned stimulus) may result in the positive affect occurring when the brand name is presented. *Brand preference may also occur in a direct, high-involvement way.* A person having a single or few exposures to an emotional ad may simply decide they like the product. This is a much more conscious process than implied by classical conditioning. Such a process would seem likely for products involving high levels of emotional value, where ad-evoked emotion would be a relevant quality cue.

Advertising using emotional appeals is gaining popularity. For example, Zippo recently launched an emotion-based campaign for its lighters. It has eight print ads, each with a picture of an engraved lighter and a simple headline "True Love is not Disposable." A spokesperson said of the campaign, "We wanted to make a human, emotional attachment."[75] Illustration 10-9 shows how Sun-Maid is using an emotional appeal to humanize its brand and accentuate feelings of suspense and awe.

SUMMARY

Consumer motivations are energizing forces that activate behavior and provide purpose and direction to that behavior. There are numerous motivation theories. Maslow's need hierarchy states that basic motives must be minimally satisfied before more advanced motives are activated. It proposes five levels of motivation: physiological, safety, belongingness, esteem, and self-actualization.

McGuire developed a more detailed set of motives—the needs for consistency, attribution, categorization, objectification, autonomy, stimulation, desired outcomes (teleological), utility, tension reduction, expression, ego defense, reinforcement, assertion, affiliation, identification, and modeling.

Consumers are often aware of and will admit to the motives causing their behavior. These are *manifest motives*. They can be discovered by standard marketing research techniques such as direct questioning. Direct advertising appeals can be made to these motives. At other times, consumers are unable or unwilling to admit to the motives that are influencing them. These are *latent motives*. They can be determined by motivation research techniques such as word association, sentence completion, and picture response. Although direct advertising appeals can be used, indirect appeals are often necessary. Both manifest and latent motives are operative in many purchase situations.

Because of the large number of motives and the many different situations that consumers face, motivational conflict can occur. In an *approach–approach conflict,* the consumer faces a choice between two attractive alternatives. In an *approach–avoidance conflict,* the consumer faces both positive and negative consequences in the purchase of a particular product. And finally, in an *avoidance–avoidance conflict,* the consumer faces two undesirable alternatives.

Involvement is a motivational state caused by consumer perceptions that a product, brand, or advertisement is relevant or interesting. Consumer needs play a strong role in shaping involvement and marketers must adapt their strategies depending on the level (high versus low) and type (enduring versus situational) of involvement exhibited by their target audience.

The *personality* of a consumer guides and directs the behavior chosen to accomplish goals in different situations. Trait theories of personality assume that (1) all individuals have internal characteristics or traits related to action tendencies, and (2) there are consistent and measurable differences between individuals on those characteristics. Most of these theories assume that traits are formed at an early age and are relatively unchanging over the years.

Multitrait theories attempt to capture a significant portion of a consumer's total personality using a set of personality attributes. The Five-Factor Model of personality is the most widely used multitrait approach. Single-trait theories focus on one aspect of personality in an attempt to understand a limited part of consumer behavior. Various traits related specifically to consumer behavior include consumer ethnocentricity, need for cognition, and consumers' need for uniqueness.

Brands, like individuals, have personalities, and consumers tend to prefer products with brand personalities that are pleasing to them. Consumers also prefer advertising messages that portray their own or a desired personality. Brand personality can be communicated in a number of ways including celebrity endorsers, user imagery, and executional ad elements such as tone and pace.

Emotions are strong, relatively uncontrollable feelings that affect our behavior. Emotions occur when environmental events or our mental processes trigger physiological changes such as increased heart rate. These changes are interpreted as specific emotions resulting from the situation. They affect consumers' thoughts and behaviors. Marketers design and position products to both arouse and reduce emotions. Advertisements include emotion-arousing material to increase attention, degree of processing, remembering, and brand preference through classical conditioning or direct evaluation.

KEY TERMS

Approach–approach conflict 377
Approach–avoidance conflict 377
Avoidance–avoidance conflict 377
Attribution theory 367
Benefit chain 374
Brand personality 380
Consumer ethnocentrism 379
Demand 372
Emotion 383

INTERNET EXERCISES

1. Visit several company Web sites. Find and describe one that makes effective use of an appeal or theme based on the following:
   a. One of Maslow's need hierarchy levels
   b. One of McGuire's motives
   c. An emotional appeal
2. Visit several general interest or entertainment sites on the Internet that contain ads. Find and describe an ad that uses the following:
   a. One of Maslow's need hierarchy levels
   b. One of McGuire's motives
   c. An emotional appeal
3. Monitor a hobby- or product-based interest group for a week. What types of motives and emotions are involved with the activity or product? What are the marketing implications of this?
4. Search for "emotional intelligence" on Google or another search engine. What do the results of this search indicate?

DDB LIFE STYLE STUDY™ DATA ANALYSES

1. Examine the DDB data in Tables 1B through 7B. What characterizes someone who *wants to look a little different from others?* Which factors contribute most? Which of McGuire's motives does this most relate to and what are the marketing implications of your findings?
2. What characterizes someone who *views shopping as a form of entertainment* (Tables 1B through 7B)? Which factors contribute most? How do your findings relate to the information presented in Consumer Insight 10-1?
3. Some people feel (and act) more self-confident than others. Based on the DDB data (Tables 1B through 7B), what factors are most characteristic of highly confident individuals? Which of the Big Five personality dimensions does self-confidence relate most to and what are the marketing implications of your findings?

REVIEW QUESTIONS

1. What is a *motive?*
2. What is meant by a *motive hierarchy?* How does Maslow's hierarchy of needs function?
3. Describe each level of Maslow's hierarchy of needs.
4. Describe each of McGuire's motives.
5. Describe *attribution theory*.
6. What is meant by *motivational conflict,* and what relevance does it have for marketing managers?
7. What is a *manifest motive?* A *latent motive?*
8. How do you measure manifest motives? Latent motives?
9. How do you appeal to manifest motives? Latent motives?
10. Describe the following motivation research techniques:
    a. Association
    b. Completion
    c. Construction
11. What is the relationship between *involvement* and *motivation?*
12. What is *personality?*
13. What is *consumer ethnocentrism* and why is it important to global marketers?

14. How can knowledge of personality be used to develop marketing strategy?

15. What is an *emotion?*

16. What physiological changes accompany emotional arousal?

17. What factors characterize emotions?

18. How can we type or categorize emotions?

19. How do marketers use emotions in product design and positioning?

20. What is the role of emotional content in advertising?

DISCUSSION QUESTIONS

21. How could Maslow's motive hierarchy be used to develop marketing strategy for the following?
    a. UNICEF
    b. Almay skin care products
    c. Evian bottled water
    d. TGI Friday's
    e. Blackberry
    f. Crest Whitestrips

22. Which of McGuire's motives would be useful in developing a promotional campaign for the following? Why?
    a. Hyundai Sonata
    b. Precision Cuts (hair salon chain)
    c. Nokia cell phones
    d. Just for Men hair coloring
    e. Amazon.com
    f. Habitat for Humanity

23. Describe how motivational conflict might arise in purchasing, or giving to, the following:
    a. Greenpeace
    b. Hummer
    c. Target (chain store)
    d. Amp energy drink
    e. Taco Bell restaurant
    f. Home security system

24. Describe the manifest and latent motives that might arise in purchasing, shopping at, or giving to the following:
    a. Live Aid
    b. Formal shoes
    c. Bose sound system
    d. Puppy
    e. Mercedes Benz convertible
    f. iPod

25. Do marketers create needs? Do they create demand? What ethical issues are relevant?

26. Respond to the questions in Consumer-Insight 10-1.

27. How might knowledge of personality be used to develop an advertising campaign for the following?
    a. Rainforest Action Network (an environmental group)
    b. Specialized mountain bikes
    c. American Express financial services
    d. Pizza Magia
    e. J. Crew women's shoes
    f. Tiger's Milk energy bars

28. Using Table 10-3, discuss how you would use one of the core personality source traits in developing a package design for an organic, shade-grown coffee.

29. How would the media preferences of those on each end of the consumer need for uniqueness continuum differ?

30. How would the shopping behaviors of those on each end of the ethnocentrism continuum differ?

31. How would you use emotion to develop marketing strategy for each of the following?
    a. Visa card use
    b. Golf clubs
    c. Orthodontist
    d. Silk (soy milk)
    e. Honda Accord Hybrid
    f. Juno, Alaska

32. List all the emotions you can think of. Which ones are not explicitly mentioned in Table 10-4? Where would you place them in this table?

APPLICATION ACTIVITIES

33. Develop an advertisement for one of the items in Question 21 based on relevant motives from McGuire's set.

34. Repeat Question 33 using Maslow's need hierarchy.

35. Repeat Question 33 using emotions.

36. Find and copy or describe two advertisements that appeal to each level of Maslow's hierarchy. Explain why the ads appeal to the particular levels, and speculate on why the firm decided to appeal to these levels.

37. Find and copy or describe an ad that contains direct appeals to manifest motives and indirect appeals to latent motives. Explain how and why the ad is using each approach.

38. Select a product of interest and use motivation research techniques to determine the latent purchase motives for five consumers.

39. Have five students describe the personality of the following. To what extent are their descriptions similar? Why are there differences?
    a. Cancun
    b. Swatches
    c. BMW
    d. Macintosh computer
    e. Cheesecake Factory Restaurant
    f. The university bookstore

40. Find and copy an ad that you feel communicates a strong brand personality. Describe that personality in terms of the dimensions in Figure 10-2. Describe the various techniques used in the ad (e.g., celebrity endorser, user imagery, and executional factors) and how that links to the personality they are communicating.

41. Find and copy an ad with strong emotional appeals and another ad from the same product category with limited emotional appeals. Why do the companies use different appeals?
    a. Have 10 students rank or rate the ads in terms of their preferences and then explain their rankings or ratings.
    b. Have 10 different students talk about their reactions to each ad as they view it. What do you conclude?

REFERENCES

1. The opening vignette is based on N. Morgan, A. Pritchard, and R. Piggott, "New Zealand, 100% Pure," *Brand Management,* April 2002, pp. 335–54.

2. From R. Piggott, "Building a Brand for a Country," unpublished MBA dissertation, University of Hull, 2002, p. 79, as quoted in Morgan, Pritchard, and Piggott, "New Zealand, 100% Pure."

3. A. H. Maslow, *Motivation and Personality,* 2nd ed. (New York: Harper & Row, 1970).

4. See R. Yalch and F. Brunel, "Need Hierarchies in Consumer Judgments of Product Designs," *Advances in Consumer Research,* vol. 23, eds. K. P. Corfman and J. G. Lynch (Provo, UT: Association for Consumer Research, 1996), pp. 405–10.

5. W. J. McGuire, "Psychological Motives and Communication Gratification," in *The Uses of Mass Communications,* eds. J. G. Blumler and C. Katz (Newbury Park, CA: Sage, 1974), pp. 167–96; and W. J. McGuire, "Some Internal Psychological Factors Influencing Consumer Choice," *Journal of Consumer Research,* March 1976, pp. 302–19.

6. See A. G. Woodside and J.-C. Chebat, "Updating Heider's Balance Theory in Consumer Behavior," *Psychology & Marketing,* May 2001, pp. 475–95.

7. M. C. Campbell and A. Kirmani, "Consumers' Use of Persuasion Knowledge," *Journal of Consumer Research,* June 2000, pp. 69–83; and R. N. Laczniak, T. E. DeCarlo, and S. N. Ramaswami, "Consumers' Responses to Negative Word-of-Mouth Communication," *Journal of Consumer Psychology* 11, no. 31 (2001), pp. 57–73.

8. See D. M. Boush, M. Friestad, and G. M. Rose, "Adolescent Skepticism toward TV Advertising and Knowledge of Advertiser Tactics," and M. Friestad and P. Wright, "The Persuasion Knowl-edge Model," both in *Journal of Consumer Research,* June 1994, pp. 1–31 and 165–75, respectively; and M. Friestad and P. Wright, "Persuasion Knowledge," *Journal of Consumer Research,* June 1995, pp. 62–74.

9. See B. H. Schmit and S. Zhang, "Language Structure and Categorization," *Journal of Consumer Research,* September 1998, pp. 108–22; and J. A. Rosa and J. F. Porac, "Categorization Bases and Their Influence on Product Category Knowledge Structures," *Psychology & Marketing,* June 2002, pp. 503–32.

10. M. Lynn and J. Harris, "The Desire for Unique Consumer Products," *Psychology & Marketing,* September 1997, pp. 601–16.

11. R. K. Ratner, B. E. Kahn, and D. Kahneman, "Choosing Less-Preferred Experiences for the Sake of Variety," *Journal of Consumer Research,* June 1999, pp. 1–15; and R. K. Ratner and B. E. Kahn, "The Impact of Private versus Public Consumption on Variety-Seeking Behavior," *Journal of Consumer Research,* September 2002, pp. 246–57.

12. P. Leszczyc and H. Timmermans, "Store-Switching Behavior," *Marketing Letters,* no. 2 (1997), pp. 193–204; M. Trivedi, "Using Variety-Seeking-Based Segmentation to Study Promotional Response," *Journal of the Academy of Marketing Science,* Winter 1999, pp. 37–49; M. Trivedi and M. S. Morgan, "Promotional Evaluation and Response among Variety Seeking Segments," *Journal of Product and Brand Management* 12, no. 6 (2003), pp. 408–25; and J. Chen and S. Paliwoda, "The Influence of Company Name in Consumer Variety Seeking," *Brand Management,* February 2004, pp. 219–31.

13. See D. Goldman, "Pain? It's a Pleasure," *American Demographics,* January 2000, pp. 60–61; and J. J. Inman, "The Role of Sensory-Specific Satiety in Attribute-Level Variety Seeking," *Journal of Consumer Research,* June 2001, pp. 105–19.

14. See G. M. Zinkhan, J. W. Hong, and R. Lawson, "Achievement and Affiliation Motivation," *Journal of Business Research,* March 1990, pp. 135–43.

15. C. Miller, "Spaghetti Sauce Preference," *Marketing News,* August 31, 1992, p. 5.

16. For an excellent approach, see G. Berstell and D. Nitterhouse, "Looking 'Outside the Box,'" *Marketing Research,* Summer 1997, pp. 5–13.

17. C. Rubel, "Three Firms Show that Good Research Makes Good Ads," *Marketing News,* March 13, 1995, p. 18.

18. See T. Collier, "Dynamic Reenactment," *Marketing Research,* Spring 1993, pp. 35–37; G. Zaltman, "Metaphorically Speaking," *Marketing Research,* Summer 1996, pp. 13–20; and C. B. Raffel, "Vague Notions," *Marketing Research,* Summer 1996, pp. 21–23.

19. F. T. Hofstede, J.-B. E. M. Steenkamp, and M. Wedel, "International Market Segmentation Based on Consumer-Product Relations," *Journal of Marketing Research,* February 1999, pp. 1–17; C. E. Gengler, M. S. Mulvey, and J. E. Oglethorpe, "A Means-End Analysis of Mothers' Infant Feeding Choices," *Journal of Public Policy & Marketing,* Fall 1999, pp. 172–88; T. J. Reynolds and J. C. Olson, *Understanding Consumer Decision Making* (Mahwah, NJ: Lawrence Erlbaum Associates, 2001); G. S. Mort and T. Rose, "The Effect of Product Type on Value Linkages in the Means-End Chain," *Journal of Consumer Behaviour,* March 2004, pp. 221–34; and F. Huber, S. C. Beckmann, and A. Herrmann, "Means-End Analysis," *Psychology & Marketing,* September 2004, pp. 715–37.

20. This insight is based on M. J. Arnold and K. E. Reynolds, "Hedonic Shopping Motivations," *Journal of Retailing* 79 (2003), pp. 77–95; see also T. L. Childers, C. L. Carr, J. Peck, and S. Carson, "Hedonic and Utilitarian Motivations for Online Retail Shopping Behavior," *Journal of Retailing* 77 (2001), pp. 511–35.

21. See J. L. Zaichkowsky, "The Personal Involvement Inventory," *Journal of Advertising,* December 1994, pp. 59–70.

22. See P. Quester and A. L. Lim, "Product Involvement/Brand Loyalty," *Journal of Product and Brand Management* 12, no. 1 (2003), pp. 22–38.

23. See U. M. Dholakia, "A Motivational Process Model of Product Involvement and Consumer Risk Perception," *European Journal of Marketing* 35, no. 11/12 (2001), pp. 1340–60; and C.-W. Park and B.-J. Moon, "The Relationship between Product Involvement and Product Knowledge," *Psychology & Marketing,* November 2003, pp. 977–97.

24. See J. S. Wiggins, *The Five-Factor Model of Personality* (New York: Guilford Press, 1996).

25. E. G. Harris and J. C. Mowen, "The Influence of Cardinal-, Central-, and Surface-Level Personality Traits on Consumers' Bargaining and Complaint Behaviors," *Psychology & Marketing,* November 2001, pp. 1155–85.

26. J. C. Mowen and N. Spears, "Understanding Compulsive Buying among College Students," *Journal of Consumer Psychology* 8, no. 4 (1999), pp. 407–30.

27. W. Na and R. Marshall, "Validation of the 'Big Five' Personality Traits in Korea," *Journal of International Consumer Marketing* 12, no. 1 (1999), pp. 5–19.

28. See T. A. Mooradian, "Personality and Ad-Evoked Feelings," *Journal of the Academy of Marketing Science,* Spring 1996, pp. 99–109; and "I Can't Get No Satisfaction," *Psychology & Marketing,* July 1997, pp. 379–93.

29. R. G. Netemeyer, S. Burton, and D. R. Lichtenstein, "Trait Aspects of Vanity," *Journal of Consumer Research,* March 1995, pp. 612–26.

30. R. Suri and K. B. Monroe, "The Effects of Need for Cognition and Trait Anxiety on Price Acceptability," *Psychology & Marketing,* January 2001, pp. 21–42.

31. C. Boone, B. D. Brabander, and A. van Witteloostuijn, "The Impact of Personality in Five Prisoners' Dilemma Games," *Journal of Economic Psychology* 20 (1999), pp. 344–76.

32. D. J. Faber and T. C. O'Guinn, "A Clinical Screener for Compulsive Buying," *Journal of Consumer Research,* December 1992, pp. 459–69; and H. Kwak, G. M. Zinkhan, and D. E. Delorme, "Effects of Compulsive Buying Tendencies on Attitudes toward Advertising," *Journal of Current Issues and Research in Advertising,* Fall 2002, pp. 17–32.

33. See A. C. Ahuvia and N. Y. Wong, "Personality and Values Based Materialism," *Journal of Consumer Psychology* 12, no. 4 (2002), pp. 389–402.

34. M. Geuens and P. D. Pelsmacker, "Affect Intensity Revisited," *Psychology & Marketing,* May 1999, pp. 195–209; and D. J. Moore and P. M. Homer, "Dimensions of Temperament," *Journal of Consumer Psychology* 9, no. 4 (2000), pp. 231–42.

35. M. J. Dutta and B. Vanacker, "Effects of Personality on Persuasive Appeals," *Advances in Consumer Research,* vol. 27, eds. S. J. Hoch and R. J. Meyers (Provo, UT: Association for Consumer Research, 2000), pp. 119–24; and R. K. Ratner and B. E. Kahn, "The Impact of Private versus Public Consumption on Variety-Seeking Behavior," *Journal of Consumer Research,* September 2002, pp. 246–57.

36. See N. Brody and H. Ehrlichman, *Personality Psychology* (Englewood Cliffs, NJ: Prentice Hall, 1998); and A. Deponte, "Linking Motivation to Personality," *European Journal of Personality* 18 (2004), pp. 31–44.

37. See S. Sharma, T. A. Shimp, and J. Shin, "Consumer Ethnocentrism," *Journal of the Academy of Marketing Science,* Winter 1995, pp. 26–37; and G. Balabanis and A. Diamantopoulos, "Domestic Country Bias, Country-of-Origin Effects, and Consumer Ethnocentrism," *Journal of the Academy of Marketing Science,* Winter 2004, pp. 80–95.

38. J. Linville, "Lexington Touts Timberlake as "Made in America" Line," *Furniture Today,* October 13, 2003, p. 98.

39. M. Supphellen and K. Gronhaug, "Building Foreign Brand Personalities in Russia," *International Journal of Advertising* 22, no. 2 (2003), pp. 203–26.

40. C. S. Areni, M. E. Ferrell, and J. B. Wilcox, "The Persuasive Impact of Reported Group Opinions on Individuals Low vs. High in Need for Cognition," *Psychology & Marketing,* October 2000, pp. 855–75; J. Z. Sojka and J. L. Giese, "The Influence of Personality Traits on the Processing of Visual and Verbal Information," *Marketing Letters,* February 2001, pp. 91–106.

41. See, e.g., L. K. Waters and T. D. Zakrajsek, "Correlates of Need for Cognition Total and Subscale Scores," *Educational and Psychological Measurement,* Spring 1990, pp. 213–17.

42. K. T. Tian, W. O. Bearden, and G. L. Hunter, "Consumers' Need for Uniqueness," *Journal of Consumer Research,* June 2001, pp. 50–66. See also K. T. Tian and K. McKenzie, "The Long-Term Predictive Validity of the Consumers' Need for Uniqueness Scale," *Journal of Consumer Psychology* 10, no. 3 (2001), pp. 171–93.

43. J. L. Aaker, "Dimensions of Brand Personality," *Journal of Marketing Research,* August 1997, pp. 347–56; for an application to restaurants see J. A. Siguaw, A. Mattila, and J. R. Austin, "The Brand-Personality Scale," *Cornell Hotel and Restaurant Administration Quarterly,* June 1999, pp. 48–55.

44. Supphellen and Gronhaug, "Building Foreign Brand Personalities in Russia"; and J. I. Rojas-Mendez, I. Erenchun-Podlech, and E. Silva-Olave, "The Ford Brand Personality in Chile," *Corporate Reputation Review,* Fall 2004, pp. 232–51.

45. K. Greenberg, "Levinson: Jaguar Ads to Stress Quality, Youth, a Bit of Humor," *Brandweek,* April 26, 2004, p. 32; B. Russak, "Calling the Shots," *Footwear News,* October 25, 2004, p. 42; and K. MacArthur and J. Neff, "Sprite Shifts Gears in Quest for Street Cred," *Advertising Age,* January 26, 2004, p. 1.

46. B. F. Roberson, "Brand Personality and the Brand-Consumer Relationship," Whirlpool Corporation, April 5, 1994.

47. Ibid. Also see T. Triplett, "Brand Personality Must Be Managed or It Will Assume a Life of Its Own," *Marketing News,* May 9, 1994, p. 9.

48. J. Aaker, S. Fournier, and S. A. Brasel, "When Good Brands Do Bad," *Journal of Consumer Research,* June 2004, pp. 1–16.

49. W. Taylor, "Message and Muscle," *Harvard Business Review,* March 1993, p. 105.

50. For a detailed discussion see D. A. Aaker, R. Batra, and J. G. Meyers, *Advertising Management,* 4th ed. (Englewood Cliffs, NJ: Prentice Hall, 1992), ch. 8. See also, T. T. T. Wee, "Extending Human Personality to Brands," *Brand Management,* April 2004, pp. 317–30.

51. A. Nagel and M. Prior, "Revlon Gets Ready for 2005," *WWD,* August 13, 2004, p. 8; and S. Kang, "Nike, Serena Williams Partner Up," *The Wall Street Journal,* December 12, 2003, p. B2.

52. S. O'Loughlin, "Hush Puppies Steps into a New Image," *Brandweek,* June 23, 2003, p. 14.

53. Russak, "Calling the Shots"; O'Loughlin, "Hush Puppies Steps into a New Image"; "Listerine Mouthwash and PocketPaks," *Marketing Magazine,* November 18, 2002, p. C9; and M. Warren, "Molson Debuts a Saucy Brazilian," *Marketing Magazine,* March 24, 2003, p. 2.

54. For a thorough discussion, see R. P. Bagozzi, M. Gopinath, and P. U. Nyer, "The Role of Emotions in Marketing," *Journal of the Academy of Marketing Science,* Spring 1999, pp. 184–207. See also M. E. Hill et al., "The Conjoining Influences of Affect and Arousal on Attitude Formation," *Research in Consumer Behavior* 9 (2000), pp. 129–46.

55. See, e.g., D. M. Phillips and H. Baumgartner, "The Role of Consumption Emotions in the Satisfaction Response," *Journal of Consumer Psychology* 12, no. 3 (2002), pp. 243–52.

56. See, e.g., Moore and Homer, "Dimensions of Temperament."

57. See U. Nyer, "A Study of the Relationships between Cognitive Appraisals and Consumption Emotions," *Journal of the Academy of Marketing Science,* Fall 1997, pp. 296–305; and J. A. Ruth, F. F. Brunel, and C. C. Otnes, "Linking Thoughts to Feelings," *Journal of the Academy of Marketing Science,* Winter 2002, pp. 44–58.

58. See B. J. Babin, J. S. Boles, and W. R. Darden, "Salesperson Stereotypes, Consumer Emotions, and Their Impact on Information Processing," *Journal of the Academy of Marketing Science,* Spring 1995, pp. 94–105.

59. For a discussion of coping strategies, see S. Yi and H. Baumgartner, "Coping with Negative Emotions in Purchase-Related Situations," *Journal of Consumer Psychology* 14, no. 3 (2004), pp. 303–17.

60. See D. J. Moore and W. D. Harris, "Affect Intensity and the Consumer's Attitude toward High Impact Emotional Advertising Appeals," *Journal of Advertising,* Summer 1996, pp. 37–50; L. Dube and M. S. Morgan, "Trend Effects and Gender Differences in Retrospective Judgments of Consumption Emotions," *Journal of Consumer Research,* September 1996, pp. 156–62; M.-H. Huang, "Exploring a New Typology of Emotional Appeals," *Journal of Current Issues and Research in Advertising,* Fall 1997, pp. 24–37; J. L. Aaker and P. Williams, "Empathy versus Pride," *Journal of Consumer Research,* December 1998, pp. 241–61; and M. Geuens and P. D. Pelsmacker, "Affect Intensity Revisited," *Psychology & Marketing,* May 1999, pp. 195–209.

61. K. Menon and L. Dube, "Ensuring Greater Satisfaction by Engineering Salesperson Response to Customer Emotions," *Journal of Retailing* 76, no. 3 (2000), pp. 285–307; W. van Dolen et al., "Affective Consumer Responses in Service Encounters," *Journal of Economic Psychology* 22 (2001), pp. 359–76; and A. S. Mattila and C. A. Enz, "The Role of Emotions in Service Encounters," *Journal of Service Research,* May 2002, pp. 268–77.

62. See N. V. Raman, P. Chattopadhyay, and W. D. Hoyer, "Do Consumers Seek Emotional Situations?" *Advances in Consumer Research,* vol. 22, eds. F. R. Kardes and M. Sujan (Provo, UT: Association for Consumer Research, 1995), pp. 537–42; and J. A. Ruth, "Promoting a Brand's Emotion Benefits," *Journal of Consumer Psychology* 11, no. 2 (2001), pp. 99–113.

63. See K. T. Lacher and R. Mizerski, "An Exploratory Study of the Responses and Relationships Involved in the Evaluation of, and in the Intention to Purchase, New Rock Music," *Journal of Consumer Research,* September 1994, pp. 366–80.

64. See E. Sherman, A. Mathur, and R. B. Smith, "Store Environment and Consumer Purchase Behavior," *Psychology & Marketing,* July 1997, pp. 361–78.

65. B. A. Huhmann and T. P. Brotherton, "A Content Analysis of Guilt Appeals in Popular Magazine Advertisements," *Journal of Advertising,* Summer 1997, pp. 35–45.

66. M.-H. Huang, "Is Negative Affect in Advertising General or Specific?" *Psychology & Marketing,* May 1997, pp. 223–40; G. Gorn, M. T. Pham, and L. Y. Sin, "When Arousal Influences Ad Evaluation and Valence Does Not (and Vice Versa)," *Journal of Consumer Psychology* 11, no. 1 (2001), pp. 43–55; and P. Williams and J. L. Aaker, "Can Mixed Emotions Peacefully Coexist?" *Journal of Consumer Research,* March 2002, pp. 636–49.

67. H. Baumgartner, M. Sujan, and D. Padgett, "Patterns of Affective Reactions to Advertisements," *Journal of Marketing Research,*

May 1997, pp. 219–32; D. W. Miller and L. J. Marks, "The Effects of Imagery-Evoking Radio Advertising Strategies on Affective Responses," *Psychology & Marketing,* July 1997, pp. 337–60; J. D. Morris and M. A. Boone, "The Effects of Music on Emotional Response," *Advances in Consumer Research,* vol. 25, eds. J. W. Alba and J. W. Hutchinson (Provo, UT: Association for Consumer Research, 1998), pp. 518–26; and D. J. Howard and C. Gengler, "Emotional Contagion Effects on Product Attitudes," *Journal of Consumer Research,* September 2001, pp. 189–201.

68. See S. P. Brown, P. M. Homer, and J. J. Inman, "A Meta-Analysis of Relationships between Ad-Evoked Feelings and Advertising Responses," *Journal of Marketing Research,* February 1998, pp. 114–26.

69. See L. F. Alwitt, "Suspense and Advertising Responses," *Journal of Consumer Psychology* 12, no. 1 (2002), pp. 35–49.

70. H. Mano, "Affect and Persuasion," *Psychology & Marketing,* July 1997, pp. 315–35; and A. M. Isen, "An Influence of Positive Affect on Decision Making in Complex Situations," *Journal of Consumer Psychology* 11, no. 2 (2001), pp. 75–85.

71. A. Y. Lee and B. Sternthal, "The Effects of Positive Mood on Memory," *Journal of Consumer Research,* September 1999, pp. 115–27; M. J. Barone, P. W. Miniard, and J. B. Romeo, "The Influence of Positive Mood on Brand Extension Evaluations," *Journal of Consumer Research,* March 2000, pp. 386–400;

K. R. Lord, R. E. Burnkrant, and H. R. Unnava, "The Effects of Program-Induced Mood States on Memory for Commercial Information," *Journal of Current Issues and Research in Advertising,* Spring 2001, pp. 1–14; and S. J. Newell, K. V. Henderson, and B. T. Wu, "The Effects of Pleasure and Arousal on Recall of Advertisements during the Super Bowl," *Psychology & Marketing,* November 2001, pp. 1135–53.

72. See J. P. Murry, Jr., and P. A. Dacin, "Cognitive Moderators of Negative-Emotion Effects," *Journal of Consumer Research,* March 1996, pp. 439–47; and K. S. Coulter, "The Effects of Affective Responses to Media Context on Advertising Evaluations," *Journal of Advertising,* Winter 1998, pp. 41–51.

73. B. M. Fennis and A. B. Bakker, "Stay Tuned—We Will Be Right Back after These Messages," *Journal of Advertising,* Fall 2001, pp. 15–25; J. D. Morris et al., "The Power of Affect," *Journal of Advertising Research,* May/June 2002, pp. 7–17; and T. A. Shimp and E. W. Stuart, "The Role of Disgust as an Emotional Mediator of Advertising Effects," *Journal of Advertising,* Spring 2004, pp. 43–53.

74. See E. A. Groenland and J. P. L. Schoormans, "Comparing Mood-Induction and Affective Conditioning as Mechanisms Influencing Product Evaluation and Product Choice," *Psychology & Marketing,* March 1994, pp. 183–97.

75. C. Beardi, "Zippo's Eternal Flame," *Advertising Age,* August 13, 2001, p. 4.

Source: www.hsus.org/pets/pets_related_news_and_events/stamping_out_pet.overpopulation.htm/
© 2001 US Postal Service. All rights reserved.

11

Attitudes and Influencing Attitudes

■ Pet overpopulation is a major concern in the United States.[1] Each day, roughly 70,000 puppies and kittens are born. Many of these animals end up in shelters or are abandoned as strays. According to The Humane Society of the United States (HSUS), an estimated 3–4 million cats and dogs are euthanized each year. That's one animal every eight seconds. Strays live short, harsh lives riddled with disease and hunger, while also contributing to the overpopulation problem.

Organizations such as HSUS and ASPCA (The American Society for the Prevention of Cruelty to Animals) continue their crusade to convince pet owners to spay or neuter. They see spaying and neutering as a key element in reducing the number of unwanted, abandoned, and abused animals. Consider the statistics: one cat and her offspring can create 420,000 cats in seven years; one dog and her offspring can create 67,000 dogs in six years.

Based on all its potential benefits, you might think spaying and neutering would be an easy sell. You would be wrong. Efforts to convince pet owners to spay or neuter continue to come up against heavy resistance by those with strong negative attitudes toward the practice. These negative attitudes are often based on strongly held beliefs that simply have no scientific foundation.

For example, if you go to www.aspca.org you can find an informational brochure about spaying and neutering that discusses common misperceptions and tries to replace these with factual evidence, as the following excerpts demonstrate:

- *Myth:* My female cat or dog should have a litter before she is spayed.
  Fact: The sooner you spay your female, the better her health will be in the future. The longer a female goes unsprayed, the greater the likelihood of developing mammary tumors or uterine infections.
- *Myth:* Spaying or neutering will alter my pet's personality.
  Fact: Regardless of the age when spayed or neutered, your pet will remain a caring, loving,

and protective companion. Any slight changes will be positive.

- *Myth:* Companion animals will become fat and lazy if they are neutered.
  Fact: Absolutely not! Lack of exercise and overfeeding make pets fat and lazy—not neutering. Your pet will not gain weight if you provide exercise and monitor food intake.

As you can see, failure to spay or neuter does not indicate a lack of caring. On the contrary, it often appears to reflect important concerns of pet owners that are based on misperceptions. Changing these misperceptions (that is, replacing incorrect beliefs with correct beliefs) is at the heart of ongoing marketing efforts at the local, state, and federal level by organizations such as HSUS and ASPCA.

As the chapter's opening example indicates, organizations frequently attempt to alter consumer behavior by changing attitudes toward a product, service, or activity.

An **attitude** is an enduring organization of motivational, emotional, perceptual, and cognitive processes with respect to some aspect of our environment. It is a learned predisposition to respond in a consistently favorable or unfavorable manner with respect to a given object. Thus, an attitude is the way one thinks, feels, and acts toward some aspect of his or her environment such as a retail store, television program, or product.[2]

Attitudes serve four key functions for individuals:[3]

- *Knowledge function.* Some attitudes serve primarily as a means of organizing beliefs about objects or activities such as brands and shopping. These attitudes may be accurate or inaccurate with respect to objective reality, but the attitude rather than reality will often determine behaviors. For example, a consumer's attitude toward cola drinks may be "they all taste the same." This consumer would likely purchase the least expensive brand even if actual taste differences exist. Obviously, firms work hard to influence and differentiate consumers' brand attitudes.
- *Value-expressive function.* Other attitudes are formed and serve to express an individual's central values and self-concept. Thus, consumers who value nature and the environment are likely to develop attitudes about products and activities that are consistent with that value. These consumers are likely to support environmental protection initiatives, to recycle, and to purchase and use "green" products such as hybrid automobiles.
- *Utilitarian function.* This function is based on operant conditioning, as described in Chapter 9. People tend to form favorable attitudes toward objects and activities that are rewarding and negative attitudes toward those that are not. Marketers frequently promise rewards in advertising and conduct extensive product testing to be sure the products are indeed rewarding.
- *Ego-defensive function.* People form and use attitudes to defend their egos and self-images against threats and shortcomings. Products promoted as very macho may be viewed favorably by men who are insecure in their masculinity. Or individuals who feel threatened in social situations may form favorable attitudes toward stylish and popular products and brands that promise success or at least safety in such situations.

Any given attitude can perform multiple functions, although one may predominate. Marketers need to be aware of the attitude functions operating in regard to the purchase or use of their brand. Attitudes are formed as the result of all the influences we have discussed in previous chapters, and they represent an important influence on an individual's lifestyle. In this chapter, we examine attitude components, general attitude change strategies, and the effect of marketing communications on attitudes.

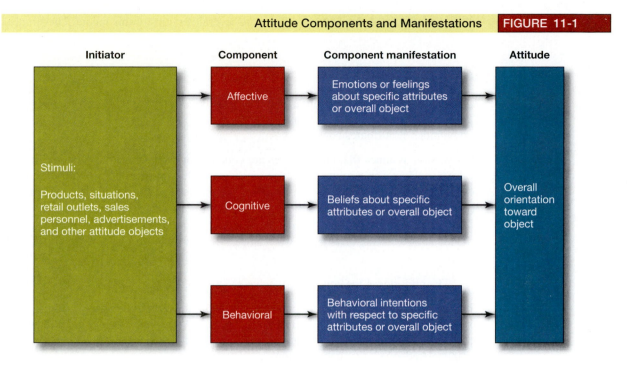

Attitude Components and Manifestations   **FIGURE 11-1**

ATTITUDE COMPONENTS

As Figure 11-1 illustrates, it is useful to consider attitudes as having three components: cognitive (beliefs), affective (feelings), and behavioral (response tendencies). Each of these attitude components is discussed in more detail below.

Cognitive Component

The **cognitive component** consists of *a consumer's beliefs about an object.* For most attitude objects, people have a number of beliefs. For example, an individual may believe that Mountain Dew

- Is popular with younger consumers
- Contains a lot of caffeine
- Is competitively priced
- Is made by a large company

The total configuration of beliefs about this brand of soda represents the cognitive component of an attitude toward Mountain Dew. Beliefs can be about the emotional benefits of owning or using a product (one can believe it would be exciting to own or drive a convertible) as well as about objective features.[4] Many beliefs about attributes are evaluative in nature; for example, high gas mileage, attractive styling, and reliable performance are generally viewed as positive beliefs. The more positive beliefs associated with a brand, the more positive each belief is, and the easier it is for the individual to recall the beliefs, the more favorable the overall cognitive component is presumed to be.[5] And because all of the components of an attitude are generally consistent, the more favorable the overall attitude is. This logic underlies what is known as the **multiattribute attitude model.**

Multiattribute Attitude Model   There are several versions of this model. The simplest is

$$A_b = \sum_{i=1}^{n} X_{ib}$$

where

A_b = Consumer's attitude toward a particular brand b
X_{ib} = Consumer's belief about brand b's performance on attribute i
n = Number of attributes considered

This version assumes that all attributes are equally important in determining our overall evaluation. However, a moment's reflection suggests that frequently a few attributes such as price, quality, or style are more important than others. Thus, it is often necessary to add an importance weight for each attribute:

$$A_b = \sum_{i=1}^{n} W_i X_{ib}$$

where

W_i = The importance the consumer attaches to attribute i

This version of the model is useful in a variety of situations. However, it assumes that more (or less) is always better. This is frequently the case. More miles to the gallon is always better than fewer miles to the gallon, all other things being equal. This version is completely adequate for such situations.

For some attributes, more (or less) is good up to a point, but then further increases (decreases) become bad. For example, adding salt to a saltless pretzel will generally improve the consumer's attitude toward the pretzel up to a point. After that point, additional amounts of salt will decrease the attitude. Thus, we need to introduce an *ideal point* into the multiattribute attitude model:

$$A_b = \sum_{i=1}^{n} W_i |I_i - X_{ib}|$$

where

I_i = Consumer's ideal level of performance on attribute i

Because multiattribute attitude models are widely used by marketing researchers and managers, we will work through an example using the weighted, ideal point model. The simpler models would work in a similar manner.

Imagine that Coca-Cola gathers data on a set of beliefs about Diet Coke from a segment of consumers (more details on measuring the various attitude components can be found in Appendix A and Appendix Table A-2). These consumers perceive Diet Coke to have the following levels of performance (the Xs) and desired performance (the Is) on four attributes:

	(1)	(2)	(3)	(4)	(5)	(6)	(7)	
Low price	___	___	_I_	_X_	___	___	___	High price
Sweet taste	___	_I_	___	___	___	_X_	___	Bitter taste
High status	___	___	_I_	___	_X_	___	___	Low status
Low calories	_IX_	___	___	___	___	___	___	High calories

This segment of consumers believes (the Xs) that Diet Coke is average priced, very bitter in taste, somewhat low in status, and extremely low in calories. Their ideal soda (the Is) would be slightly low priced, very sweet in taste, somewhat high in status, and extremely low in calories. Since these attributes are not equally important to consumers, they are assigned weights based on the relative importance a segment of consumers attaches to each.

A popular way of measuring importance weights is with a 100-point *constant-sum scale*. For example, the importance weights shown below express the relative importance of the four soft-drink attributes such that the total adds up to 100 points.

Attribute	Importance
Price	10
Taste	30
Status	20
Calories	40
	100 points

In this case, calories are considered the most important attribute, with taste slightly less important. Price is given little importance.

From this information, we can index this segment's attitude toward Diet Coke as follows:

$$A_{Diet\ Coke} = (10)(|3-4|) + (30)(|2-6|) + (20)(|3-5|) + (40)(|1-1|)$$

$$= (10)(1) + (30)(4) + (20)(2) + (40)(0)$$

$$= 170$$

This involves taking the absolute difference between the consumer's ideal soft-drink attributes and beliefs about Diet Coke's attributes and multiplying these differences by the importance attached to each attribute. In this case, the attitude index is computed as 170. Is this good or bad?

An attitude index is a relative measure, so in order to fully evaluate it, we must compare it to the segment's attitudes toward competing products or brands. However, if these consumers perceived Diet Coke to be the ideal soft drink, then all their beliefs and ideals would be equal and an attitude index of zero would be computed. Thus, the closer an attitude index calculated in this manner is to zero, the better.

We have been discussing the multiattribute view of the cognitive component as though consumers explicitly and consciously went through a series of deliberate evaluations and summed them to form an overall impression. However, this level of effort would occur only in very high-involvement purchase situations. In general, the multiattribute attitude model merely *represents* a process that is much less precise and structured than implied by the model.

Affective Component

Feelings or *emotional reactions to an object* represent the **affective component** of an attitude. A consumer who states "I like Diet Coke" or "Diet Coke is a terrible soda" is expressing the results of an emotional or affective evaluation of the product. This overall evaluation may be simply a vague, general feeling developed without cognitive information or beliefs about the product. Or it may be the result of several evaluations of the product's performance on each of several attributes. Thus, the statements "Diet Coke tastes bad" and "Diet Coke is not good for your health" imply a negative affective reaction to specific aspects of the product that, in combination with feelings about other attributes, will determine the overall reaction to the brand.

Aesthetically pleasing or interesting product designs can evoke powerful emotional responses that are such a critical aspect of the affective component of attitudes.

Courtesy Nike.

Marketers are increasingly turning their attention to the affective or "feeling" component of attitudes to provide a richer understanding of attitudes than that based solely on the cognitive or "thinking" component. As a consequence, marketers now commonly distinguish *utilitarian* or functional benefits and attitudes from *hedonic* or emotional benefits and attitudes.[6] For example, one study found that consumer acceptance of handheld Internet devices was influenced both by utilitarian benefits such as usefulness and hedonic aspects such as fun to use.[7] Another study found that in some cases hedonic aspects of giving blood such as fear and joy were stronger determinants of overall attitude toward blood donation than utilitarian beliefs.[8]

In addition, marketers are beginning to consider both form *and* function in product designs and focus considerable attention on the aesthetic aspects of design (appearance, sensory experience). The iPod and iMac are examples of products with high **aesthetic appeal** that tap consumers' affective reactions by going beyond the cognitive associations of functionality.[9] Illustration 11-1 shows an ad for a product high in aesthetic appeal.

Affective reactions to a specific product or benefit can vary by situation and individual. For example, a consumer's belief that Diet Coke has caffeine may result in positive feelings if he or she needs to stay awake to work late but negative feelings if he or she wants to get to sleep quickly. And some individuals may have positive feelings toward the belief that "Diet Coke is made by a large multinational firm," whereas others could respond negatively. Would you enjoy an experience that induced the following? "Muscles screaming. Heart pounding. Lungs feeling as if they could burst." This is the "benefit" the ad shown in

Courtesy Cycle-Ops Products.

Illustration 11-2 promises. Affective reactions to this benefit likely vary by individual and situation.

Marketers sometimes measure the affective component on verbal scales much like those used to measure the cognitive component (for more detail, see Appendix A and Appendix Table A-2). So, consumers might be asked to rate Diet Coke overall (or specific attributes such as taste) on the following dimensions by placing an *X* in the appropriate space:

	(1)	(2)	(3)	(4)	(5)	(6)	(7)	
Good	___	___	___	___	___	___	___	Bad
Like	___	___	___	___	___	___	___	Dislike
Happy	___	___	___	___	___	___	___	Sad
Pleasant	___	___	___	___	___	___	___	Unpleasant

SAM and adSAM®   However, sometimes marketers want to more directly tap feelings and emotions and bypass the cognitive processing that often goes along with verbal scales. One such measure is based on the pleasure-arousal-dominance (PAD) approach to emotions discussed in Chapter 10. This measure, termed SAM (Self-Assessment Manikin), provides visual representations of 232 "emotional adjectives" underlying PAD. SAM (and adSAM® which applies SAM specifically to ads) is a graphical character which is manipulated to visually portray emotions and more directly tap emotional responses. From a global standpoint, SAM is effective across different cultures and languages because the pictorial representations don't require translation or alteration.[10] Examples of SAM for each dimension of PAD are shown below (top panel = pleasure; middle = arousal; bottom = dominance):

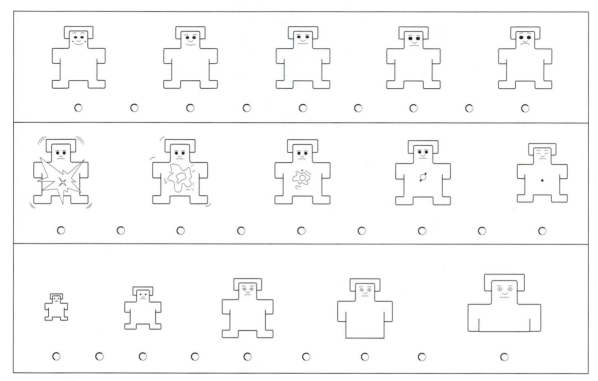

Source: adSAM®.

Behavioral Component

The **behavioral component** of an attitude is *one's tendency to respond in a certain manner toward an object or activity*. A series of decisions to purchase or not purchase Diet Coke or to recommend it or other brands to friends would reflect the behavioral component. Brand interest, as represented by tendencies to seek out the brand on store shelves or search for brand information, also reflects the behavioral component. The behavioral component provides response tendencies or behavioral intentions. *Actual behaviors reflect these intentions as they are modified by the situation in which the behavior will occur.*

Direct versus Indirect Approach   Actual behaviors and response tendencies are most often measured by fairly direct questioning (for more detail, see Appendix A and Appendix Table A-2). For example, consumers might be asked about their intentions to buy Diet Coke as follows:

How likely it is that you will buy Diet Coke the next time you purchase a soft drink (put an X in the appropriate space)?

Definitely Will	Probably Will	Might	Probably Will Not	Definitely Will Not
___	___	___	___	___

Such direct questioning may work well for most consumption, but not so well for sensitive topics like alcohol, pornography, and eating patterns where consumers may understate negative behaviors or intentions. In these cases, asking *indirect* questions such as estimating the behaviors of other people similar to themselves (neighbors, those with similar jobs, etc.) may help to reduce the bias.

Component Consistency

Figure 11-2 illustrates a critical aspect of attitudes: *All three attitude components tend to be consistent.*[11] This means that a change in one attitude component tends to produce related changes in the other components. This tendency is the basis for a substantial amount of marketing strategy.

Marketing managers are ultimately concerned with influencing behavior. But it is often difficult to influence behavior directly. Marketers generally are unable to directly cause consumers to buy, use, or recommend their products. However, consumers will often listen to sales personnel, attend to advertisements, or examine packages. Marketers can, therefore, indirectly influence behavior by providing information, music, or other stimuli that influence a belief or feeling about the product if the three components are indeed consistent with each other.

Some research has found only a limited relationship among the three components.[12] Let's examine the sources of this inconsistency by considering an example. Suppose an individual reports positive beliefs and affect toward the iPod but does not own an iPod or purchases another brand. At least seven factors may account for inconsistencies between *measures* of beliefs and feelings and *observations* of behavior.

1. *Lack of Need*—A favorable attitude requires a need or motive before it can be translated into action. Thus, the consumer may not feel a need for a portable player or might already own an acceptable, though less preferred, brand.
2. *Lack of Ability*—Translating favorable beliefs and feelings into ownership requires ability. The consumer might not have sufficient funds to purchase an iPod, thus she might purchase a less expensive brand.
3. *Failure to Consider Relative Attitudes*—In the prior example, only attitudes toward the iPod were considered. However, purchases often involve trade-offs across competing

Attitude Component Consistency   **FIGURE 11-2**

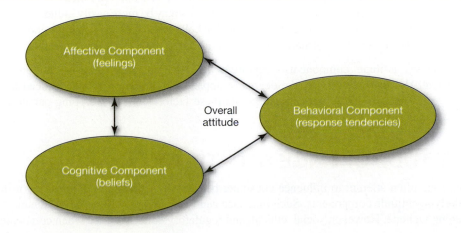

brands. Thus, a consumer may have a relatively high attitude toward iPod, but a slightly higher attitude toward a competing brand. In a choice situation, relative attitudes are a stronger predictor of behavior.

4. *Weakly Held Beliefs and Affect*—If the cognitive and affective components are weakly held, and if the consumer obtains additional information while shopping, then the initial attitudes may give way to new ones. Specifically, stronger attitudes or those attitudes held with more confidence tend to be stronger predictors of behavior.[13] Moreover, direct experience tends to yield attitudes that are more strongly and confidently held. As a consequence, companies often spend enormous amounts of money on coupons and free samples to generate direct product experience.

   In addition to direct experience, factors related to strength of learning such as importance, message involvement, reinforcement, and repetition (see Chapter 9) are also related to attitude strength since attitudes are generally learned.

5. *Failure to Consider Interpersonal Influence*—An individual's attitudes were measured above. However, many purchase decisions involve others either directly or indirectly. Thus, for example, the shopper may purchase something other than an iPod in order to better meet the needs of the entire family.

6. *Failure to Consider Situational Factors*—Brand attitudes are often measured independent of the purchase situation. However, items are purchased for, or in, specific situations. The consumer might purchase an inexpensive portable player now if she anticipates access to more sophisticated equipment in the near future.

   The **theory of reasoned action** is based in part on this concept.[14] It holds that behavioral intentions are based on a combination of the attitude toward a specific behavior, such as purchasing a brand; the social or normative beliefs about the appropriateness of the behavior; and the motivation to comply with the normative beliefs. Thus, a consumer might have a favorable attitude toward having a drink before dinner at a restaurant. However, the intention to actually order the drink will be influenced by the consumer's beliefs about the appropriateness of the action in the current situation (with friends for a fun meal, or on a job interview) and her motivation to comply with those normative beliefs.

   The role of social norms was found in a recent study of Taiwanese consumers' intentions to buy pirated DVDs. The positive influence of beliefs about cost savings was offset somewhat by the negative influence of social norms.[15]

7. *Measurement Issues*—It is difficult to measure all the relevant aspects of an attitude. Consumers may be unwilling or unable to articulate all relevant feelings and beliefs. Therefore, attitude components are sometimes more consistent than measures suggest them to be. In addition, some behavioral dimensions may be more easily influenced than others. For example, even weakly held positive beliefs about a brand may be enough to encourage additional information search but not sufficient to directly influence choice.

In summary, attitude components—cognitive, affective, and behavioral—tend to be consistent. However, as we see, the degree of apparent consistency can be reduced by a variety of factors. Marketers must incorporate these factors when developing persuasive messages and strategies.

ATTITUDE CHANGE STRATEGIES

Marketers often attempt to influence consumer behavior by changing one or more of the underlying attitude components. Such influence can be positive as we saw in the chapter's opening vignette. However, social, ethical, and regulatory concerns arise when companies

Reducing Smoking

As a result of Minnesota's settlement with the tobacco industry, the Minnesota Partnership for Action Against Tobacco (MPAAT) acquired funds to launch an antismoking campaign. It began with focus groups conducted throughout the state with both smokers and nonsmokers. In addition to other topics, the MPAAT showed participants antismoking commercials used elsewhere and asked them to rate the commercials' impact.

One finding was that just another warning about health risks would not be effective. "The overwhelming sentiment was, 'We know smoking is bad. Now we need something to move us from that understanding to action.'" As a result MPAAT decided to emphasize the devastating effects of smoking (secondhand smoke) on children and families. Many smokers still did not fully realize this, and it was felt that this knowledge would provide a fresh, strong incentive for action.

Another key finding from the focus groups was that "smokers are regular people who don't deserve to be chastised. Smoking is very tough to kick, and we didn't want to be demeaning or just tell them things they already knew." Therefore two categories of ads were created. One illustrated in hard-hitting terms the deadly impact of secondhand smoke. After this campaign ran for three months and then alternating with it, the second series of ads promoted MPAAT's 24-hour help-line. Smokers can call this line anytime for encouragement and information on quitting smoking.

A spokesperson explained the logic: "We knew we needed to be firm but also offer hope, and that's where the help-line ads came in."

The ads in both categories were brutally frank. A television commercial showed secondhand smoke becoming a ghostly hand that reaches out to choke an infant (see Illustration 11-7). A restroom poster pictured a pet bird lying dead on the floor of its cage as a result of secondhand smoke. A radio spot featured the croaky, distressed voice of a smoker who had to have her larynx and vocal cords removed because of throat cancer.

A spokesperson explained the reason for the ads' somber nature:

> We are dealing with an addiction and I think you have to be harsh about the realities of tobacco use. Quitting smoking is a task most smokers prefer to put off. MPAAT's guiding principle was to get their attention and make them see that quitting needs to happen today. You need to do that forcefully.

Critical Thinking Questions

1. What attitude component is MPAAT focusing on? What theory or assumption makes this reasonable?

2. What type of appeals is MPAAT using? Is this an appropriate use of this type of appeal?

3. How successful do you think this campaign will be? Why?

4. Does this campaign raise any ethical concerns?

---

attempt to promote potentially harmful consumption behaviors or when persuasion attempts are deemed deceptive.

Sometimes changing beliefs is enough, although sometimes it is not. For example, a challenge for antismoking campaigns is that many smokers know it's bad for their health but postpone quitting or can't quit. Thus, the belief component appears to be in place but the behavior component is not. Consumer Insight 11-1 describes how one organization is dealing with this.

Change the Cognitive Component

A common and effective approach to changing attitudes is to focus on the cognitive component.[16] As we saw in the chapter's opening example, ASPCA is working to change existing negative beliefs. The theory is that by changing these beliefs, affect and behavior will then change.

Four basic marketing strategies are used for altering the cognitive structure of a consumer's attitude.

Change Beliefs   This strategy involves shifting beliefs about the performance of the brand on one or more attributes.[17] There is some evidence that beliefs tend to be consistent with each other.[18] Thus, changing one belief about a brand may result in other beliefs changing to remain consistent with the changed belief. For example, causing consumers to believe that the Kia Sportage has a smooth ride rather than a rough ride may result in their having enhanced beliefs about its handling and safety.

Attempts to change beliefs generally involve providing facts or statements about performance. It is important to realize that some beliefs are strongly held and thus hard to change. As a consequence, marketers may have more success changing overall brand attitudes by targeting weaker brand beliefs that are more vulnerable to persuasion attempts.[19] Illustration 11-3 shows an ad for California Almonds. *What beliefs are they trying to change?*

Shift Importance   Most consumers consider some product attributes to be more important than others. Marketers often try to convince consumers that those attributes on which their brands are relatively strong are the most important. For example, General Motors uses detailed narratives of drivers in distress to emphasize the importance of instant communications and emergency assistance which their proprietary OnStar system provides.

Sometimes evaluative factors that would otherwise not be prominent to consumers can be enhanced by cues in the ad. One study created ads with references to Asian culture (e.g., picture of the Great Wall of China) to enhance "ethnic self-awareness." When ethnic self-awareness was enhanced, Asian consumers reacted more positively to ads containing an Asian spokesperson.[20]

Add Beliefs   Another approach to changing the cognitive component of an attitude is to add new beliefs to the consumer's belief structure. For example, IBM introduced a "shock absorption" feature to protect its laptops from sudden jolts, as might occur if a computer is dropped. This technological breakthrough has created a benefit that consumers will increasingly incorporate in their laptop judgments.

Change Ideal   The final strategy for changing the cognitive component is to change the perceptions of the ideal brand or situation. Thus, many conservation organizations strive to influence our beliefs about the ideal product in terms of minimal packaging, nonpolluting manufacturing, extensive use of recycled materials, and nonpolluting disposition after its useful life.

Change the Affective Component

Firms increasingly attempt to influence consumers' liking of their brands without directly influencing either beliefs or behavior. If the firm is successful, increased liking will tend to lead to increased positive beliefs,[21] which could lead to purchase behavior should a need for the product arise. Or, perhaps more common, increased liking will lead to a tendency to purchase the brand should a need arise,[22] with purchase and use leading to increased positive beliefs. Marketers use three basic approaches to directly increase affect: classical conditioning, affect toward the ad itself, and mere exposure.

Classical Conditioning   One way of directly influencing the affective component is through classical conditioning (see Chapter 9). In this approach, a stimulus the audience likes, such as music, is consistently paired with the brand name. Over time, some of the

Courtesy of the Almond Board of California.

positive affect associated with the music will transfer to the brand.[23] Other liked stimuli, such as pictures, are frequently used for this reason.

Affect toward the Ad or Web Site   As we saw in Chapter 10, liking the advertisement (attitude toward the ad, or Aad) generally increases the tendency to like the brand (attitude toward the brand, or Abr).[24] Somewhat similar results are associated with liking the Web site on which an ad appears (Aweb).[25] Using humor, celebrities, or emotional appeals

Ads can change the affective component of an attitude toward a brand without altering the belief structure if the ad itself elicits a positive response (is liked). Ads that are primarily pictorial are often used for this purpose, though the pictures themselves convey cognitive as well as emotional meanings.

Courtesy Lancaster Group; Agency: Deloge/Paris.

increases Aad and Aweb. For example, vivid Web sites with rich sensory content that appeal to multiple senses produce more positive Aweb than do less vivid sites.[26] Illustration 11-4 contains an ad that relies on positive affect.

Ads that arouse negative affect or emotions such as fear, guilt, or sorrow can also enhance attitude change. For example, an ad for a charity assisting refugees could show pictures that would elicit a variety of unpleasant emotions such as disgust or anger and still be effective.[27]

Mere Exposure   While controversial, there is evidence that affect or brand preference may also be increased by **mere exposure.**[28] That is, simply presenting a brand to an individual on a large number of occasions might make the individual's attitude toward the brand more positive. A common explanation of the mere exposure effect is that "familiarity breeds liking." Thus, the repetition of advertisements for low-involvement products may well increase liking (through enhanced familiarity) and subsequent purchase of the advertised brands without altering the initial belief structure. Mere exposure effects underlie the use of simple reminder ads as well as product placements.[29]

Classical conditioning, Aad, and mere exposure can alter affect directly and, by altering affect, alter purchase behavior without first changing beliefs. This has a number of important implications:

- Ads designed to alter affect need not contain any cognitive (factual or attribute) information.
- Classical conditioning principles should guide such campaigns.

- Aad and ad-evoked affect are critical for this type of campaign unless mere exposure is being used.
- Repetition is critical for affect-based campaigns.
- Cognitively based measures may be inappropriate to assess advertising effectiveness.

As these guidelines suggest, classical conditioning, Aad, and mere exposure tend to occur in low-involvement situations (see Chapter 9). There is at least one major exception, however. When emotions and feelings are important product performance dimensions, then such feelings and emotions are relevant to the evaluation. In these situations, Aad can readily influence Abr under high involvement. As we discussed earlier in the chapter, hedonic (versus utilitarian) products are those for which affect and emotion are relevant performance criteria. Not surprisingly, hedonic products are those for which affect, emotions, and Aad can play a role in more conscious, high-involvement settings.[30]

Change the Behavioral Component

Behavior, specifically purchase or use behavior, may precede the development of cognition and affect. Or it may occur in contrast to the cognitive and affective components. For example, a consumer may dislike the taste of diet soft drinks and believe that artificial sweeteners are unhealthy. However, rather than appear rude, the same consumer may accept a diet drink when offered one by a friend (see the earlier discussion of reasoned action, page 404). Drinking the beverage may alter her perceptions of its taste and lead to liking; this in turn may lead to increased learning, which changes the cognitive component.

Behavior can lead directly to affect, to cognitions, or to both simultaneously.[31] Consumers frequently try new brands or types of low-cost items in the absence of prior knowledge or affect. Such purchases are as much for information (Will I like this brand?) as for satisfaction of some underlying need such as hunger.

Changing behavior prior to changing affect or cognition is based primarily on operant conditioning (see Chapter 9). Thus, the key marketing task is to induce people to purchase or consume the product while ensuring that the purchase or consumption will indeed be rewarding.[32] Coupons, free samples, point-of-purchase displays, tie-in purchases, and price reductions are common techniques for inducing trial behavior. Since behavior often leads to strong positive attitudes toward the consumed brand, a sound distribution system (limited stockouts) is important to prevent current customers from trying competing brands.

INDIVIDUAL AND SITUATIONAL CHARACTERISTICS THAT INFLUENCE ATTITUDE CHANGE

Attitude change is determined by individual and situational factors as well as marketing activities.[33] Individual factors include gender, need for cognition, consumer knowledge, and ethnicity. Situational factors include program context, level of viewer distraction, and buying occasion.

Marketers continue to focus considerable attention on consumer involvement, which has both an individual (intrinsic interest) and situational (current need to make a purchase decision) component. Consumer involvement is an important motivational factor that influences elaborative processing, learning, and attitudes. The **elaboration likelihood model (ELM)** is a theory about how attitudes are formed and changed under varying conditions of involvement. Thus, the ELM integrates select individual, situational, and marketing factors to understand attitudes.[34]

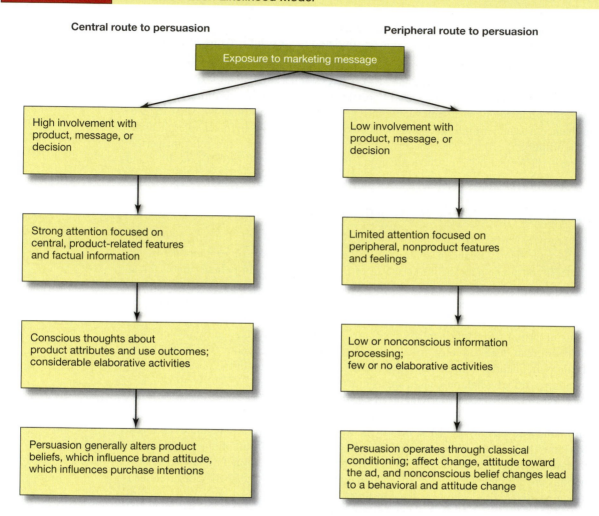

FIGURE 11-3   The Elaboration Likelihood Model

The ELM suggests that involvement is a key determinant of how information is processed and attitudes are changed. High involvement results in a *central route* to attitude change by which consumers deliberately and consciously process those message elements that they believe are relevant to a meaningful and logical evaluation of the brand (see Figure 11-3). These elements are elaborated on and combined into an overall evaluation. The multiattribute attitude model represents a high-involvement view of attitude change.

In contrast, low involvement results in a *peripheral route* to attitude change in which consumers form impressions of the brand based on exposure to readily available cues in the message regardless of their relevance to the brand or decision. Attitudes formed through the peripheral route are based on little or no elaborative processing. Classical conditioning, Aad, and mere exposure represent low-involvement views of attitude change.

The ELM suggests that vastly different communications strategies are required to communicate effectively with high- versus low-involvement consumers. In general, detailed factual information (central cues) is effective in high-involvement, central route situations. Low-involvement, peripheral route situations generally require limited information and instead rely on simple affective and cognitive cues such as pictures, music, and characteristics of people in the ad (peripheral cues). *Which persuasion route is most likely being utilized in Illustration 11-4?*

Cue Relevance and Competitive Situation

Generally speaking, compared to attitudes formed under the peripheral route, attitudes formed under the central route tend to be stronger, more resistant to counterpersuasion attempts, more accessible from memory, and more predictive of behavior.[35]

However, it is important to realize that central route processing involves extensive processing of *decision-relevant* information or cues. And, what consumers find relevant can vary by product and situation. For example, an attractive picture can be peripheral or central. In an ad for orange soda, a picture of cute puppies would be a peripheral cue (and influence attitudes under low involvement) while a picture of fresh juicy orange slices would be a central cue (and influence attitudes under high involvement).[36] Similarly, emotions likely represent a central cue for hedonic products and thus influence attitudes under high involvement.

In addition, the competitive situation can also work to enhance the role of peripheral cues even under high involvement. For example, if competing brands are comparable in terms of their product features (central cues), highly involved consumers prefer the brand with the strongest peripheral cues in its advertising.[37] The basic idea is that relative attitudes are critical in competitive settings and peripheral cues become the tie breaker between otherwise equivalent (parity) brands. As you can see, the role of peripheral cues can extend beyond low-involvement settings in certain competitive situations.

Consumer Resistance to Persuasion

Consumers are not passive to persuasion attempts. Instead, consumers are often skeptical (an individual characteristic) and resist persuasion.[38] Also, consumers frequently infer an advertiser's intent and respond in light of that presumed selling intent.[39] For example, a consumer could respond to the California Almond ad in Illustration 11-3 as follows: "Of course they're going to tell me almonds are healthy for me. They're trying to sell more almonds. I'm still not convinced." To help reduce the likelihood of such responses, the ad makes use of The American Heart Association and scientific research to bolster its health claims.

Strongly held attitudes are harder to change than weakly held attitudes. Think of something you feel strongly about—perhaps your school or your favorite sports team. What would be required to change your attitude? Clearly, it would be difficult. Consumers tend to avoid messages that are counter to their attitudes (e.g., committed smokers tend to avoid antismoking ads). And if they do encounter such messages, they tend to discount them.[40] Thus, most marketers do not try to capture sales from consumers who are committed to competing brands. Rather, they focus on those who are less committed, as these consumers are more attentive and responsive to their messages.

COMMUNICATION CHARACTERISTICS THAT INFLUENCE ATTITUDE FORMATION AND CHANGE

In this section, we describe communication techniques that can be used to form and change attitudes. Obviously, as with all aspects of consumer behavior, individual and situational characteristics interact with the communication features to determine effectiveness.

Source Characteristics

The source of a communication represents "who" delivers the message. Sources include people (famous celebrities, typical consumers), animated spokes characters (Jolly Green Giant, Mr. Peanut), and organizations (the company, a third party endorser). The source of a message is important because consumers respond differently to the same message delivered by different sources.

Source Credibility   Persuasion is easier when the target market views the message source as highly credible. **Source credibility** consists of *trustworthiness* and *expertise*. A source that has no ulterior motive to provide anything other than complete and accurate information would generally be considered trustworthy. However, product knowledge is required for a source to have expertise. Thus a friend might be trustworthy but lack expertise. Alternatively, salespeople and advertisers may have ample knowledge but be viewed with skepticism by consumers.

Individuals who are recognized experts and who have no apparent motive to mislead can be powerful sources.[41] 1-800-PetMeds® has TV advertisements in which a veterinarian discusses pain management options for your pet. Relatively unknown individuals similar to the target market can be effective spokespersons as well but for different reasons. In a **testimonial ad,** *a person, generally a typical member of the target market, recounts his or her successful use of the product, service, or idea.*[42] Similarity of the source enhances the believability and relevance of these testimonials.

Independent *third-party endorsements* by organizations such as the American Dental Association (ADA) are widely viewed as both trustworthy and expert by consumers and are actively sought by marketers. Such endorsements appear to be used by consumers as brand quality cues.[43] The remarkable success of Crest toothpaste is largely attributable to the ADA endorsement. Other examples include:

* The American Heart Association—Kellogg's Smart Start and Subway
* J. D. Power and Associates—Caldwell Banker
* Good Housekeeping Seal of Approval—Charmin Toilet Tissue

Of course, the company itself is the most obvious source of most marketing messages. This means developing a corporate reputation or image for trustworthiness can greatly enhance the impact of the firm's marketing messages.[44] Consider the following consumer quote regarding insurance companies:[45]

> I don't like insurance companies. Insurance is such a pain; it's confusing on purpose. You pay all this money in premiums, then when you have to use it, they raise your premiums like you haven't already paid for the service. So if an insurance company was trying to tell me something about AIDS or drinking and driving, I wouldn't believe one word.

Source credibility can influence persuasion in various situations. First, a credible source can enhance attitudes when consumers lack the ability or motivation to form direct judgments of the product's performance.[46] This is more of a low-involvement process. Second, a credible source can enhance message processing and acceptance. In fact, expert sources can increase attitudes in some high-involvement settings due to their perceived decision-relevance.[47]

Cultural differences can also play a role. For example, Thai consumers are more influenced by expert sources than Canadian consumers. Thai consumers are more risk averse and more likely to defer to authority, thus making them more prone to external sources of influence.[48]

La cosa más divina del universo:
mi mamá.

Ella me ayudó
a crecer
dándome
mucha leche.
La leche
contiene
9 vitaminas y
minerales
esenciales para
que
los niños
crezcan sanos,
fuertes y muy
activos.
Dale a tus hijos
tres vasos de
leche al día,
para ellos tu eres
lo más divino
del universo.

más leche, más logro.

got milk?

Courtesy National Fluid Milk Processor Promotion Board; Agency: Lowe
World Wide, Inc.

ILLUSTRATION 11-5
Ethnic celebrities are increasingly common in U.S. advertisements as a way to target specific ethnic subcultures.

One factor that can diminish the credibility of any source is if consumers believe that the firm is paying the source for his or her endorsement.[49] This is especially relevant for celebrities and athletes who are paid large sums for their endorsements.

Celebrity Sources   Celebrities are widely used in advertising. Marketers are increasingly using culturally diverse celebrities to reach an ethnically diverse U.S. population. Salma Hayek, John Leguizamo, Daisy Fuentes, Tiger Woods, Mary J. Blige, Halle Berry, Chanté Moore, and Michael Chang are just a few such celebrities with endorsement contracts with companies such as General Motors, L'Oréal, Nike, Pepsi, and MAC Viva Glam cosmetics.

A visible use of celebrity endorsers in recent years has been the mustache campaign for milk. Illustration 11-5 shows their use of Miss Universe Amelia Vega. This ad clearly targets the growing Hispanic market in the U.S. and emphasizes strong family ties (by including her mother), which resonates well with Hispanic consumers.

Celebrity sources are effective for a variety of reasons.[50]

- *Attention*—Celebrities may attract attention to the advertisement. Consumers tend to be curious about celebrities and are drawn to ads in which they appear.
- *Attitude toward the ad*—A celebrity's likeability and popularity often translate into higher Aad which can enhance brand attitudes.
- *Trustworthiness*—Despite being paid for their endorsements, celebrities often develop strong and credible public personas that consumers trust. And, this trust translates into purchases. A recent study finds that 26 percent of respondents are more likely to buy a

product endorsed by Michael Jordan, one of the most trusted celebrity athletes. This same study finds that "62 percent of consumers say endorsers' private actions are just as important as professional achievements."[51]

- *Expertise*—Some celebrities are also experts. This occurs frequently in areas such as music and sports. Companies such as Nike and Reebok build whole lines around celebrity athletes such as Lance Armstrong, Serena Williams, and Alan Iverson. Nike's partnership with Tiger Woods in golf equipment is a classic example of celebrity expertise.

- *Aspirational aspects*—Consumers may identify with or desire to emulate the celebrity. As a consequence they may imitate the behavior and style of a celebrity through purchases of similar brands and styles. For example, popular actresses often lead the way in terms of clothing and hair styles for young women.

- *Meaning transfer*—Consumers may associate known characteristics of the celebrity with attributes of the product that coincide with their own needs or desires. For example, urban youth looking for "street cred" see celebrity athletes like Alan Iverson as powerful icons. As one executive states, "He's from the streets. They admire him."[52]

As the last point suggests, effectiveness of a celebrity endorser can generally be improved by matching the image of the celebrity with the personality of the product and the actual or desired self-concept of the target market.

When the three components shown in Figure 11-4 are well matched, effective attitude formation or change can result.[53] For example, celebrity endorsements by Jimmy Connors and Joe Montana are credited with increasing Nuprin's sales almost 25 percent. Their images as maturing athletes now subject to aches and pains matched well with the target market and the product. Sometimes images don't mesh and should be avoided. For example, Burger King cancelled talks with Paris Hilton when they decided her racy image might be too extreme for their franchise.[54]

Using a celebrity as a company spokesperson creates special risks. One risk is overexposure. If a celebrity endorses many products, consumers' reactions may become less positive. Thus, marketers might consider limiting the number of products "their" celebrities endorse.[55] An additional risk is that negative behavior involving the spokesperson will affect the individual's credibility and, in turn, damage the firm's image.[56] PepsiCo has had problems with commercials featuring Madonna and Michael Jackson after these celebrities became embroiled in public controversy. Both Coca-Cola and Nike distanced themselves

FIGURE 11-4   **Matching Endorser with Product and Target Audience**

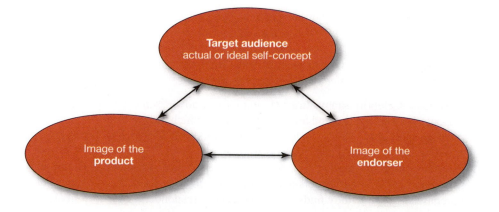

Courtesy Master Foods USA.

ILLUSTRATION 11-6

Spokescharacters are gaining popularity. They can add credibility to a message as well as attract attention. Some come to serve as a symbol of the product.

from Kobe Bryant after allegations of sexual assault. And NASCAR was quick to penalize Dale Earnhardt, Jr., for using profanity in an interview to protect its family image.

Rather than use celebrities, many firms are creating **spokescharacters.**[57] Tony the Tiger and the Green Giant are perhaps the most famous, although Geico's gecko and Aflac's duck have quickly become household names. Spokescharacters can be animated animals, people, products, or other objects. A major advantage of spokescharacters is complete image control. This eliminates many of the problems associated with real celebrities. Such characters come to symbolize the brand and give it an identity that competitors cannot easily duplicate. Illustration 11-6 shows the M&M's characters in a funny situation.

Sponsorship   **Sponsorship**, *a company providing financial support for an event* such as the Olympics or a concert, is one of the most rapidly growing marketing activities and a multibillion dollar industry.[58] Sponsorships in North America grew by 30 percent between 2000 and 2004, with most growth occurring in sports.[59] One high-profile example is Nextel's replacement of Winston as NASCAR's title sponsor.[60] The potential to generate goodwill in sports sponsorships is particularly high among rabid fans.[61] These fans may react along the lines of "Reebok supports my team, I'm going to support them."

Sponsorships often work in much the same manner as using a celebrity endorser. That is, the characteristics of the sponsored event may become associated with the sponsoring organization. Such an association is most likely and most effective when the match-up described in Figure 11-4 occurs, with the event taking the place of the endorser.[62] Thus, a financial institution sponsoring a sophisticated art show may enhance its image as being discriminating, sophisticated, elite, and serious. Or fans seeing a new, upcoming band wearing Airwalk gear may come to see Airwalk as cool and "with it."

Sponsorships can also augment the company's image as a good corporate citizen, as the following example indicates:[63]

> I think also that it [Texaco Children's Art Competition] is genuinely doing good as a result of its [sponsorship]. It is putting it [funds] into something that wouldn't be done otherwise and it is promoting and it has been promoting children's art around the country and it gets a lot of entries and all that.[64]

Reactions such as these seem likely to extend to corporate sponsorships of events tied to specific ethnic subcultures such as Native American celebrations (see Chapter 5).

In addition to enhancing attitudes, an event serves to increase awareness just like traditional advertising.[65] And, the evidence is clear that firms should promote their sponsorships through traditional media to further enhance their impact.[66]

Appeal Characteristics

As you would expect, the nature of the appeal or "how" a message is communicated affects attitude formation and change.

Fear Appeals

> The picture at the top of an ad is a snapshot of a young couple sitting together on their back deck. The headline reads: "I woke up in the hospital. Patti never woke up." The copy describes how carbon monoxide poisoning caused the tragedy. The ad, one of a series of similar ads, is for First Alert carbon monoxide detector.

Fear appeals use *the threat of negative (unpleasant) consequences if attitudes or behaviors are not altered*. Fear appeals have been studied primarily in terms of physical fear (physical harm from smoking, unsafe driving, and eating genetically modified foods), but social fears (disapproval of one's peers for incorrect clothing, bad breath, or smoking) are also used in advertising.[67]

There is some evidence that individuals avoid or distort extremely threatening messages. At the same time, fear appeals tend to be more effective as higher levels of fear are aroused. Thus, those using fear appeals want to maximize the level of fear aroused while not presenting a threat so intense as to cause the consumer to distort, reject, or avoid the message. This task is difficult because individuals respond differently to threats. Thus, the same "threatening" advertisement may arouse no fear in one individual or group and a high level of fear in another.[68]

Using a fear appeal as a way to gain attention and emphasize the dangers of secondhand smoke, the MPAAT sponsors the ad shown in Illustration 11-7 (see Consumer Insight 11-1). *Is this an effective use of a fear appeal?*

Fear appeals are frequently criticized as unethical. Frequent targets of such criticisms are fear appeals based on social anxieties about bad breath, body odor, dandruff, or soiled clothes. The thrust of these complaints is that these appeals raise anxieties unnecessarily; that is, the injury or harm that they suggest will occur is unlikely to occur or is not really harmful. Fear appeals used to produce socially desirable behaviors such as avoiding drug use or avoiding acknowledged physical risks such as carbon monoxide poisoning are subject to much less criticism.[69]

Humorous Appeals   At almost the opposite end of the spectrum from fear appeals are **humorous appeals.**[70] Ads built around humor appear to increase attention to and liking of

Courtesy Minnesota Partnership for Action Against Tobacco.

the ad, particularly for those individuals high in *need for humor*.[71] The overall effectiveness of humor is generally increased when the humor relates to the product or brand in a meaningful way and is viewed as appropriate for the product by the target audience.[72]

Illustration 11-8 shows an ad for the Citi card that makes effective use of humor. Note how the humor relates to the key benefit of fraud detection. Other humorous ads with relevance to the brand include:

- Mitsubishi's Montero Sport television commercial shows the faces of several men applying mascara, eye shadow, and lipstick as another man drives on a country road. The point is made that the drive is smooth enough to allow the makeup to be applied accurately. At the end of the commercial, the men leave the vehicle as rodeo clowns.
- The FedEx ad for its Latin America region described in the opening for Chapter 2 showed the humorous consequences (having to play a soccer match nude) of using another delivery service.

While it is generally recommended that humor be relevant, companies have been successful using humor that is only loosely tied to the product (e.g., Budweiser's lizard campaign). In these cases, humor attracts attention, and the positive emotional response may transfer to the brand via classical conditioning or Aad.[73]

Humorous ads also involve risk. What is considered funny varies across individuals, cultures, and situations.[74] Humor viewed as demeaning or insulting can cost a company image and sales. One Subway campaign had a good idea—it's OK to cheat a bit on your diet if you eat at Subway. However, this idea was lost on viewers who saw people engaging in hurtful behaviors (cutting a child's kite string) and glibly justifying it with "It's OK, I had a Subway." Subway benched this campaign. In another instance, Toyota issued a public apology to the African American community after it placed an ad in *Jet* with the headline, "Unlike your last boyfriend, it goes to work in the morning," which many viewed as insulting.

Comparative Ads   **Comparative ads** *directly compare the features or benefits of two or more brands* (see Illustration 11-9; Daewoo is the sponsor brand). Comparative ads are often more effective than noncomparative ads in generating attention, message and brand awareness, greater message processing, favorable sponsor brand attitudes, and increased purchase intentions and behaviors. However, comparative ads can also have negative consequences for the sponsor brand such as lower believability, lower attitude toward the ad and sponsor brand, and more positive attitude toward the competitor brand(s).[75] Available evidence suggests that comparative ads should follow these guidelines:[76]

ILLUSTRATION 11-8

Humor is widely used in advertising to attract attention and alter attitudes.

It didn't seem right to us, either.

With Fraud Early Warning, when we see uncharacteristic or suspicious spending, we'll alert you and stop it. It's part of Citi Identity Theft Solutions. That's using your card wisely. Call 1-888-CITICARD or visit citicards.com.

Courtesy Citi Group, Inc.

- Comparative advertising may be particularly effective for promoting new or little-known brands with strong product attributes to create its position or to upgrade their image by association. When established brands use comparative ads they may appear "defensive." This may be particularly true if comparisons are seen as overly derogatory.
- Comparative advertising is likely to be more effective if its claims are substantiated by credible sources. Also, research should be used to determine the optimal number of claims.

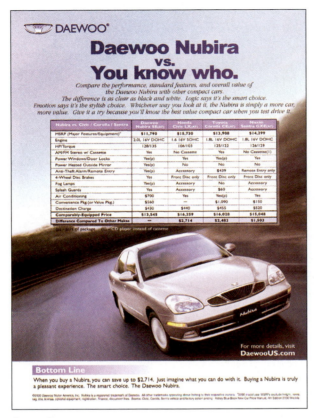

Courtesy Daewoo.

- Audience characteristics, especially brand loyalty associated with the sponsoring brand, are important. Users of the named competitor brands appear to resist comparative claims.
- Since comparative ads are more interesting than noncomparatives (and more offensive), they may be effective in stagnant categories where noncomparative ads have ceased to be effective.
- Print media appear to be better vehicles for comparative advertisements, because print lends itself to more thorough comparisons.
- Care must be used with *partially* comparative ads due to their misleading potential. A partially comparative ad contains comparative and noncomparative information and may lead consumers to believe the sponsor brand is superior on all attributes not just the compared attributes.

Emotional Appeals   Emotional or feeling ads are being used with increasing frequency. **Emotional ads** are *designed primarily to elicit a positive affective response rather than to provide information or arguments.* Emotional ads such as those that arouse feelings of warmth trigger physiological reactions (see Chapter 10). Emotional advertisements may enhance persuasion by increasing[77]

- Attention and processing of the ad and, therefore, ad recall.
- Liking of the ad.
- Product liking through classical conditioning.
- Product liking through high-involvement processes.

ILLUSTRATION 11-10

Ads such as this evoke powerful emotional responses in some individuals. These emotional responses often facilitate attitude change.

Courtesy Cease Fire, Inc.

As we discussed previously, whether emotional ads operate through classical conditioning and Aad (low involvement) or through more analytical high-involvement processes depends on the relevance of the emotion to evaluating key aspects of the product.

In addition, emotional ads appear to work better than rational or informational ads for heavy (versus light) users of a brand and more established (versus new) brands in a market. This effect may be due to the fact that heavy users and established brands already have an established knowledge base for attribute information, making emotions a more compelling differentiating feature.[78]

Illustrations 11-10 and 10-8 (see page 385) are designed to elicit emotional responses.

Value-Expressive versus Utilitarian Appeals   **Value-expressive appeals** attempt to build a personality for the product or create an image of the product user. **Utilitarian appeals** involve informing the consumer of one or more functional benefits that are important to the target market. Which is best under what conditions?

Both theory and some empirical evidence indicate that *utilitarian* appeals are most effective for functional products and *value-expressive* appeals are most effective for products designed to enhance self-image or provide other intangible benefits.[79] Thus, marketers generally should not use image (value-expressive) advertising for lawn fertilizers or factual (utilitarian) advertising for perfumes. However, many products such as automobiles, some cosmetics, and clothes serve both utilitarian and value-expressive purposes. For example,

Courtesy Toni & Guy/TIGI Linea USA, Inc.

Courtesy Merck; Agency: Prime Access, Inc.

a recent survey finds that about 40 percent of car buyers see cars as an extension of their personality, while about 60 percent see them as functional.[80] Which approach is best for these products? There is no simple answer. Some marketers opt to present both types of appeals, others focus on one or the other, and still others vary their approach across market segments. Illustration 11-11 contains an example of each approach.

Research also indicates that banner ads on Web sites should differ for the two types of products. For utilitarian products, banner ads serve primarily to transport consumers to the more detailed target ads or sites. For value-expressive products, banner ads should influence attitudes on the basis of exposure to the banner ad itself, not on clickthrough to the target ad.[81]

Message Structure Characteristics

One-Sided versus Two-Sided Messages   In advertisements and sales presentations, marketers generally present only the benefits of their product without mentioning any negative characteristics it might possess or any advantages a competitor might have. These are **one-sided messages,** since only one point of view is expressed. The idea of a **two-sided message,** presenting both good and bad points, is counterintuitive, and most marketers are reluctant to try such an approach. However, two-sided messages are generally more effective than one-sided messages in changing a strongly held attitude. One reason is because they are unexpected and increase consumer trust in the advertiser. They are particularly

ILLUSTRATION 11-11

Utilitarian appeals generally work best with functional products; value-expressive appeals work best with products designed to enhance one's image or provide other intangible benefits.

effective with highly educated consumers. One-sided messages are most effective at reinforcing existing attitudes. However, product type, situational variables, and advertisement format influence the relative effectiveness of the two approaches.[82]

Positive versus Negative Framing   **Message framing** refers to presenting one of two equivalent value outcomes either in positive or gain terms (positive framing) or in negative or loss terms (negative framing). There are various *types* of message frames and the type of frame influences whether positive or negative framing is best.[83] The simplest form appears to be **attribute framing** where only a single attribute is the focus of the frame. A classic example is describing ground beef as either 80 percent fat free (positive frame) or 20 percent fat (negative frame). In attribute framing situations, positive framing yields the most positive evaluations because it emphasizes the desirable aspects of the specific attribute.

Goal framing is where "the message stresses either the positive consequences of performing an act or the negative consequences of not performing the act."[84] The act could be purchasing a specific brand, having a yearly mammogram, and so on. In both cases the act is beneficial. However, in the positive frame, the benefits of the act are emphasized (e.g., increased chance of finding tumor) while in the negative frame, the risks of not engaging in the act are emphasized (e.g., decreased chance of finding tumor). In goal framing situations the *negative* frame is generally more effective. This is likely due to the risk-averse nature of consumers coupled with the risk-enhancing nature of the negative goal frame.

Framing effects can vary across products, consumers, and situations. Thus, decisions to use positive or negative framing should ultimately be based on research for the specific product and market.[85]

Nonverbal Components   In Chapter 9, we discussed how pictures enhance imagery and facilitate learning. Pictures, music, surrealism, and other nonverbal cues are also effective in attitude change. Emotional ads, described earlier, often rely primarily or exclusively on nonverbal content to arouse an emotional response. Nonverbal ad content can also affect cognitions about a product. For example, an ad showing a person drinking a new beverage after exercise provides information about appropriate usage situations without stating "good to use after exercise." Thus, nonverbal components can influence attitudes through affect, cognition, or both.

MARKET SEGMENTATION AND PRODUCT DEVELOPMENT STRATEGIES BASED ON ATTITUDES

Market Segmentation

Identifying market segments is a key aspect of marketing. Properly designed marketing programs should be built around the unique needs of each market segment. The importance of various attributes is one way of defining customer needs for a given product. *Segmenting consumers on the basis of their most important attribute or attributes* is called **benefit segmentation.**[86]

To define benefit segments, a marketer needs to know the importance that consumers attached to various product/service features. This allows consumers who seek the same benefits to be grouped into segments. Additional information about consumers within each segment can then be obtained to develop a more complete picture of each segment. Based on this information, separate marketing programs can be developed for each of the selected target segments.

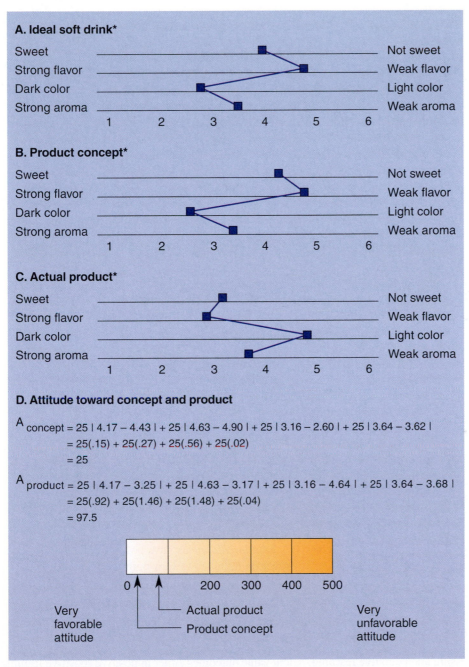

TABLE 11-1

Using the Multiattribute Attitude Model in the Product Development Process

A. Ideal soft drink*

Sweet		Not sweet
Strong flavor		Weak flavor
Dark color		Light color
Strong aroma		Weak aroma

(scale 1 2 3 4 5 6)

B. Product concept*

Sweet		Not sweet
Strong flavor		Weak flavor
Dark color		Light color
Strong aroma		Weak aroma

(scale 1 2 3 4 5 6)

C. Actual product*

Sweet		Not sweet
Strong flavor		Weak flavor
Dark color		Light color
Strong aroma		Weak aroma

(scale 1 2 3 4 5 6)

D. Attitude toward concept and product

$$A_{concept} = 25 \mid 4.17 - 4.43 \mid + 25 \mid 4.63 - 4.90 \mid + 25 \mid 3.16 - 2.60 \mid + 25 \mid 3.64 - 3.62 \mid$$
$$= 25(.15) + 25(.27) + 25(.56) + 25(.02)$$
$$= 25$$

$$A_{product} = 25 \mid 4.17 - 3.25 \mid + 25 \mid 4.63 - 3.17 \mid + 25 \mid 3.16 - 4.64 \mid + 25 \mid 3.64 - 3.68 \mid$$
$$= 25(.92) + 25(1.46) + 25(1.48) + 25(.04)$$
$$= 97.5$$

(scale: 0   200   300   400   500)

Very favorable attitude — Actual product — Product concept — Very unfavorable attitude

*Measured on a six-point semantic differential scale.

Product Development

While the importance consumers attach to key attributes provides a meaningful way to understand needs and form benefit segments, the ideal levels of performance indicate the consumers' desired level of performance in satisfying those needs. These ideal levels of performance can provide valuable guidelines in developing a new product or reformulating an existing one.

Table 11-1 describes how Coca-Cola used this approach in developing a new soft drink.[87] The first step is constructing a profile of a consumer segment's ideal level of performance on key soft drink attributes. As shown in Table 11-1, four attributes were identified for a particular type of soft drink, and ideal performance was obtained from consumer ratings.

A second step is creating a product concept that closely matches the ideal profile. The concept could be a written description, picture, or actual prototype. As section B in Table 11-1 shows, consumers evaluated the product concept developed by Coca-Cola as being fairly close to their ideal on each of the four attributes. Only color appears to be off target slightly by being a little too dark.

The next step is translating the concept into an actual product. When Coca-Cola did this and presented the product to the consumers, they did not perceive it to be similar to either the product concept or their ideal (see section C in Table 11-1). While the actual product achieved a reasonable attitude rating, the product concept scored higher (section D, Table 11-1). Thus, the product could benefit from further improvements that better align it with the ideal profile. This same basic procedure can be used to help design ads, packages, or retail outlets.

SUMMARY

Attitudes can be defined as the way people think, feel, and act toward some aspect of their environment. A result of all the factors discussed so far in the text, attitudes influence, as well as reflect, the lifestyle individuals pursue.

Attitudes have three components: cognitive, affective, and behavioral. The *cognitive component* consists of the individual's beliefs or knowledge about the object. It is generally assessed by using a version of the multiattribute attitude model. Feelings or emotional reactions to an object represent the *affective component* of the attitude and can be assessed in various ways including adSAM. The *behavioral component* reflects overt actions and statements of behavioral intentions with respect to specific attributes of the object or the overall object. In general, all three components tend to be consistent with each other.

Attitude change strategies can focus on affect, behavior, cognition, or some combination. Attempts to change affect generally rely on classical conditioning. Change strategies focusing on behavior rely more on operant conditioning. Changing cognitions usually involves information processing and cognitive learning. Whether affect and emotion influence attitudes under high involvement depends on their decision relevance.

Source credibility is composed of two dimensions: trustworthiness and expertise. Persuasion is much easier when the message source is viewed as highly credible. Celebrities are widely used as product or company spokespersons. They are most effective when their image matches the personality of the product and the actual or desired self-concept of the target market.

The appeals used to change attitudes are important and are varied. *Fear appeals* use threat of negative consequences if attitudes or behaviors are not altered. *Humorous appeals* can also be effective in influencing attitudes. However, the humorous message must remain focused on the brand or main selling point to be maximally effective.

Comparative ads produce mixed results. They are most effective for unknown brands having a strong functional advantage.

The decision to use a *value-expressive* or *utilitarian appeal* depends on whether the brand fills value-expressive or utilitarian needs. However, this is complicated when the brand fills both types of needs.

Emotional appeals have been found to have a strong effect on attitudes toward both the ad and the product.

Three aspects of the structure of the message affect its effectiveness. *Two-sided* (versus *one-sided*) *messages* can increase trust and message acceptance, but effects depend on characteristics of the individual and situation. *Message framing* effects—presenting equivalent value outcomes either in positive (positive framing) or negative (negative framing) terms—depend on type of frame. Positive *attribute framing* tends to work best whereas negative *goal framing* tends to work best. Nonverbal aspects of the ad, such as pictures, surrealism, and music, also affect attitudes.

Consumer evaluations, feelings, and beliefs about specific product features form the basis for market segmentation strategies, such as *benefit segmentation,* and for new-product development strategies.

KEY TERMS

Aesthetic appeal 400
Affective component 399
Attitude 396
Attribute framing 422
Behavioral
  component 402
Benefit segmentation 422
Cognitive component 397
Comparative ads 417

Elaboration likelihood model
  (ELM) 409
Emotional ads 419
Fear appeals 416
Goal framing 422
Humorous appeals 416
Mere exposure 408
Message framing 422
Multiattribute attitude model 397

One-sided message 421
Source credibility 412
Spokescharacters 415
Sponsorship 415
Testimonial ads 412
Theory of reasoned action 404
Two-sided message 421
Utilitarian appeals 420
Value-expressive appeals 420

INTERNET EXERCISES

1. Visit several general interest or entertainment sites on the Internet that contain ads. Find and describe an ad that attempts to change each of the following to help form or change attitudes:
   a. Affective component
   b. Cognitive component
   c. Behavioral component
2. Visit several company Web sites. Find and describe one that uses one of the following to help form or change attitudes:
   a. Credible source
   b. Celebrity source
   c. Humorous appeal

   d. Fear appeal
   e. Comparative appeal
   f. Emotional appeal
3. Visit www.adsam.com. Go to the "take a sample survey now" section, read the instructions, and take a survey which involves ratings using the adSAM approach. Evaluate adSAM compared to more cognitive approaches that utilize verbal scales.
4. Visit the American Plastics Council Web site (www.plasticsresource.com). What attitude change techniques does it use? Are they effective?

REVIEW QUESTIONS

1. What is an *attitude?*
2. What are the functions of attitudes?
3. What are the components of an attitude?
4. Are the components of an attitude consistent? What factors reduce the apparent consistency among attitude components?
5. What is the *multiattribute attitude model?*
6. What strategies can be used to change the following components of an attitude?
   a. Affective
   b. Behavioral
   c. Cognitive
7. What is meant by *mere exposure?*
8. What is the *elaboration likelihood model?*
9. Describe the *theory of reasoned action.*

10. What are the two characteristics of the source of a message that influence its ability to change attitudes? Describe each.
11. What is *source credibility?* What causes it?
12. Why are celebrity sources sometimes effective? What risks are associated with using a celebrity source?
13. Name five possible characteristics of an appeal that would influence or change attitudes. Describe each.
14. Are *fear appeals* always effective in changing attitudes? Why?
15. What characteristics should *humorous ads* have?
16. Are *emotional appeals* effective? Why?
17. Are *comparative appeals* effective? Why?

18. What is a *value-expressive appeal?* A *utilitarian appeal?* When should each be used?

19. What are the three characteristics of the message structure that influence its ability to change attitudes? Describe each.

20. What is meant by *positive message framing* and *negative message framing?* How does the effectiveness of a positive versus negative frame vary depending on whether it's a *goal frame* or *attribute frame?*

21. What are the nonverbal components of an ad? What impact do they have on attitudes?

22. When is a *two-sided message* likely to be more effective than a *one-sided message?*

23. How can attitudes guide new-product development?

24. What is a *benefit segment?*

DISCUSSION QUESTIONS

25. Which version of the multiattribute attitude model and which attributes would you use to assess student attitudes toward the following? Justify your answer.
    a. Your university
    b. BP gas station
    c. Paper grocery bags
    d. Cats as pets
    e. Jolt

26. Respond to the questions in Consumer Insight 11-1.

27. Assume you wanted to improve or create favorable attitudes among college students toward the following. Would you focus primarily on the affective, cognitive, or behavioral component? Why?
    a. ASPCA
    b. Kia automobiles
    c. Free-range chicken consumption
    d. Water skiing
    e. Not driving after drinking
    f. Using the bus for most local trips
    g. Pizza Hut
    h. Internship with local senator

28. Suppose you used the multiattribute attitude model and developed a fruit-based carbonated drink that was successful in the United States. Could you use the same model in the following countries? If not, how would it have to change?
    a. India
    b. Chile
    c. Qatar

29. Suppose you wanted to form highly negative attitudes toward smoking among college students.
    a. Which attitude component would you focus on? Why?
    b. Which message characteristic would you use? Why?
    c. What type of appeal would you use? Why?

30. What communications characteristics would you use in an attempt to improve college students' attitudes toward the following?
    a. Blackberry device
    b. BMW motorcycles
    c. Volunteering at a local shelter
    d. Vitamin supplements
    e. MADD
    f. White water rafting

31. Is it ethical to use fear appeals to increase demand for the following?
    a. Complexion medication among teenagers
    b. Tongue scrapers among adults
    c. Emergency response devices among elderly consumers
    d. Handguns for women

32. Name two appropriate and two inappropriate celebrity spokespersons for each of the products or causes in Question 30. Justify your selection.

33. What benefit segments do you think exist for attendance at the following?
    a. Live Aid concert
    b. Broadway theater presentations
    c. Major art museums
    d. X Games

APPLICATION ACTIVITIES

34. Find and copy two magazine or newspaper advertisements, one based on the affective component and the other on the cognitive component. Discuss the approach of each ad in terms of its copy and illustration and what effect it creates in terms of attitude. Also, discuss why the marketer might have taken that approach in each advertisement.

35. Repeat Activity 34 for utilitarian and value-expressive appeals.

36. Identify a television commercial that uses a humorous appeal. Then interview five individuals not enrolled in your class and measure their
    a. Awareness of this commercial
    b. Recall of the brand advertised
    c. Recall of relevant information
    d. Liking of the commercial
    e. Preference for the brand advertised

    Evaluate your results and assess the level of communication that has taken place in terms of these five consumers' exposure, attention, interpretation, and preferences for this product and commercial.

37. Describe a magazine, Internet, or television advertisement, or a package that uses the following. Evaluate the effectiveness of the ad or package.
    a. Aesthetic appeal
    b. Source credibility
    c. Celebrity source
    d. Testimonial
    e. Fear appeal
    f. Humorous appeal
    g. Emotional appeal
    h. Comparative approach
    i. Extensive nonverbal elements
    j. A two-sided appeal
    k. Positive message framing
    l. Negative message framing

38. Measure another student's ideal beliefs and belief importance for the following. Examine these ideal beliefs and importance weights and then develop a verbal description (i.e., concept) of a new brand for these items that would satisfy this student's needs. Next, measure that student's attitude toward the concept you have developed in your verbal description.
    a. Drycleaner
    b. Nice restaurant
    c. Automobile
    d. Credit card
    e. Backpack
    f. Charity

39. Use the multiattribute attitude model to assess 10 students' attitudes toward several brands in the following product categories. Measure the students' behavior with respect to these brands. Are they consistent? Explain any inconsistencies.
    a. Television news program
    b. Sports drinks
    c. Healthy dinners
    d. Formal dining
    e. Exercise
    f. Snacks

40. Develop two advertisements for the following with college students as the target. One ad should focus on the cognitive component and the other on the affective component.
    a. Listerine breath strips
    b. Hyundai SUV
    c. Sprite
    d. Reducing smoking
    e. Increasing exercise
    f. Burger King

41. Repeat Activity 40 using utilitarian and value-expressive appeals.

42. Develop a positively framed and an equivalent negatively framed message about a product attribute. Have five students react to these messages. What do you conclude?

REFERENCES

1. Discussion based on "Why Spay or Neuter?" ASPCA Brochure (2003), found at www.aspca.org; "HSUS Pet Overpopulation Estimates," HSUS Brochure (2004), found at www.hsus.org; and information from Northeast Arkansas for Animals found at www.nafacares.org.

2. See R. E. Petty, D. T. Wegener, and L. R. Fabriger, "Attitudes and Attitude Change," *Annual Review of Psychology* 48 (1997), pp. 609–38.

3. D. Katz, "The Functional Approach to the Study of Attitudes," *Public Opinion Quarterly,* Summer 1960, pp. 163–204. For discussion of a fifth function, social identity, see R. Grewal,

R. Mehta, and F. R. Kardes, "The Role of Social-Identity Function of Attitudes in Consumer Innovativeness and Opinion Leadership," *Journal of Economic Psychology* 21 (2000), pp. 233–52.

4. J. A. Ruth, "Promoting a Brand's Emotional Benefits," *Journal of Consumer Psychology* 11, no. 2 (2001), pp. 99–113.

5. See M. Wanke, G. Bohner, and A. Jurkowitsch, "There Are Many Reasons to Drive a BMW," *Journal of Consumer Research,* September 1997, pp. 170–77.

6. K. E. Voss, E. R. Spangenberg, and B. Grohmann, "Measuring the Hedonic and Utilitarian Dimensions of Consumer Attitude," *Journal of Marketing Research,* August 2003, pp. 310–20; and

T. Lageat, S. Czellar, and G. Laurent, "Engineering Hedonic Attributes to Generate Perceptions of Luxury," *Marketing Letters,* July 2003, pp. 97–109.

7. G. C. Bruner II and A. Kumar, "Explaining Consumer Acceptance of Handheld Internet Devices," *Journal of Business Research* 58 (2005), pp. 553–58.

8. C. T. Allen et al., "A Place for Emotion in Attitude Models," *Journal of Business Research* 58 (2005), pp. 494–99.

9. C. Page and P. M. Herr, "An Investigation of the Processes by Which Product Design and Brand Strength Interact to Determine Initial Affect and Quality Judgments," *Journal of Consumer Psychology* 12, no. 2 (2002), pp. 133–47.

10. J. D. Morris et al., "The Power of Affect," *Journal of Advertising Research,* May–June 2002, pp. 7–17; and J. D. Morris, "Observations: SAM," *Journal of Advertising Research,* November–December 1995, pp. 63–68.

11. For an excellent review, see P. A. Dabholkar, "Incorporating Choice into an Attitudinal Framework," *Journal of Consumer Research,* June 1994, pp. 100–18. See also Morris et al., "The Power of Affect"; and P. E. Grimm, "A_b Components' Impact on Brand Preference," *Journal of Business Research* 58 (2005), pp. 508–17.

12. R. E. Petty and J. A. Krosnick, *Attitude Strength* (Mahwah, NJ: Erlbaum, 1995); S. J. Kraus, "Attitudes and the Prediction of Behavior," *Personality and Social Psychology Bulletin* 21 (1995), pp. 58–75; R. Madrigal, "Social Identity Effects in a Belief-Attitude-Intentions Hierarchy," *Psychology & Marketing,* February 2001, pp. 145–65; and W. E. Baker, "The Diagnosticity of Advertising Generated Brand Attitudes in Brand Choice Contexts," *Journal of Consumer Psychology* 11, no. 2 (2001), pp. 129–39.

13. See, e.g., J. R. Priester et al., "The A²SC² Model," *Journal of Consumer Research,* March 2004, pp. 574–87.

14. See R. P. Bagozzi et al., "Cultural and Situational Contingencies and the Theory of Reasoned Action," *Journal of Consumer Psychology* 9, no. 2 (2000), pp. 97–106.

15. C.-C. Wang, "Factors That Influence the Piracy of DVD/VCD Motion Pictures," *Journal of American Academy of Business,* March 2005, pp. 231–37.

16. See S. A. Hawkins, S. J. Hoch, and J. Meyers-Levy, "Low-Involvement Learning," *Journal of Consumer Psychology* 11, no. 31 (2001), pp. 1–11.

17. For guidelines on structuring message arguments to enhance beliefs see C. S. Areni, "The Proposition-Probability Model of Argument Structure and Message Acceptance," *Journal of Consumer Research,* September 2002, pp. 168–87.

18. F. R. Kardes et al., "Down the Garden Path," *Journal of Consumer Psychology* 11, no. 3 (2001), pp. 159–68. See also J. Sengupta and G. V. Johar, "Effects of Inconsistent Attribute Information on the Predictive Value of Product Attitudes," *Journal of Consumer Research,* June 2002, pp. 39–56.

19. See A. Drolet and J. Aaker, "Off-Target?" *Journal of Consumer Psychology* 12, no. 1 (2002), pp. 59–68.

20. M. R. Forehand and R. Deshpande, "What We See Makes Us Who We Are," *Journal of Marketing Research,* August 2001, 336–48. See also J. K. Maher and M. Hu, "The Priming of Material Values on Consumer Information Processing of Print Advertisements," *Journal of Current Issues and Research in Advertising,* Fall 2003, pp. 21–30.

21. For a discussion of program-induced affect and extremity of beliefs, see R. Adaval, "How Good Gets Better and Bad Gets Worse," *Journal of Consumer Research,* December 2003, pp. 352–67.

22. See M. J. J. M. Candel and J. M. E. Pennings, "Attitude-Based Models for Binary Choices," *Journal of Economic Psychology* 20 (1999), pp. 547–69; and H.-P. Erb, Antoine Bioy, and D. J. Hilton, "Choice Preferences without Inferences," *Journal of Behavioral Decision Making,* July 2002, pp. 251–62.

23. See, e.g., W. E. Baker, "When Can Affective Conditioning and Mere Exposure Directly Influence Brand Choice?" *Journal of Advertising,* Winter 1999, pp. 31–46; and B. D. Till and R. L. Priluck, "Stimulus Generalization in Classical Conditioning," *Psychology & Marketing,* January 2000, pp. 55–72.

24. See, e.g., R. E. Goldsmith, B. A. Lafferty, and S. J. Newell, "The Impact of Corporate Credibility and Celebrity Credibility on Consumer Reaction to Advertisements and Brands," *Journal of Advertising,* Fall 2000, pp. 43–54; and K. S. Coulter, "An Examination of Qualitative vs. Quantitative Elaboration Likelihood Effects," *Psychology & Marketing,* January 2005, pp. 31–49.

25. J. S. Stevenson, G. C. Bruner II, and A. Kumard, "Webpage Background and Viewer Attitudes," and G. C. Bruner II and A. Kumard, "Web Commercials and Advertising Hierarchy-of-Effects," both in *Journal of Advertising Research,* January 2000, pp. 29–34 and 35–43, respectively. See also L. Dailey, "Navigational Web Atmospherics," *Journal of Business Research* 57 (2004), 795–803.

26. J. R. Coyle and E. Thorson, "The Effects of Progressive Levels of Interactivity and Vividness in Web Marketing Sites," *Journal of Advertising,* Fall 2001, pp. 65–77.

27. See M.-H. Huang, "Is Negative Affect in Advertising General or Specific?" *Psychology Marketing,* May 1997, pp. 223–40. See also P. S. Ellen and P. F. Bone, "Does It Matter if It Smells?" *Journal of Advertising,* Winter 1998, pp. 29–39.

28. A. Rindfleisch and J. J. Inman, "Explaining the Familiarity-Liking Relationship," *Marketing Letters,* no. 1 (1998), pp. 5–19; E. L. Olson and H. M. Thjomoe, "The Effects of Peripheral Exposure to Information on Brand Preference," *European Journal of Marketing* 37, no. 1/2 (2003), pp. 243–55; and G. Menon and P. Raghubir, "Ease-of-Retrieval as an Automatic Input in Judgments," *Journal of Consumer Research,* September 2003, pp. 230–43.

29. S. Auty and C. Lewis, "Exploring Children's Choice," *Psychology & Marketing,* September 2004, pp. 697–713.

30. See Ruth, "Promoting a Brand's Emotional Benefits"; R. Adaval, "Sometimes It Just Feels Right," *Journal of Consumer Research,* June 2001, pp. 1–17; M. T. Pham et al., "Affect Monitoring and the Primacy of Feelings in Judgment," *Journal of Consumer Research,* September 2001, pp. 167–88; and C. W. M. Yeung and R. S. Wyer, Jr., "Affect, Appraisal, and Consumer Judgment," *Journal of Consumer Research,* September 2004, pp. 412–24.

31. See D. S. Kempf, "Attitude Formation from Product Trial," *Psychology & Marketing,* January 1999, pp. 35–50.

32. See G. J. Gaeth et al., "Consumers' Attitude Change across Sequences of Successful and Unsuccessful Product Usage," *Marketing Letters,* no. 1 (1997), pp. 41–53; and L. A. Brannon

and T. C. Brock, "Limiting Time for Response Enhances Behavior Corresponding to the Merits of Compliance Appeals," *Journal of Consumer Psychology* 10, no. 3 (2001), pp. 135–46.

33. See, e.g., M. L. Roehm and B. Sternthal, "The Moderating Effect of Knowledge and Resources on the Persuasive Impact of Analogies," *Journal of Consumer Research,* September 2001, pp. 257–72; M. Moorman, P. C. Neijens, and E. G. Smit, "The Effects of Magazine-Induced Psychological Responses and Thematic Congruence on Memory and Attitude toward the Ad in a Real-Life Setting," *Journal of Advertising,* Winter 2002, pp. 27–40; and S. Putrevu, J. Tan, and K. R. Lord, "Consumer Responses to Complex Advertisements," *Journal of Current Issues and Research in Advertising,* Spring 2004, pp. 9–24.

34. See R. E. Petty, J. T. Cacioppo, and D. Schumann, "Central and Peripheral Routes to Advertising Effectiveness," *Journal of Consumer Research,* September 1993, pp. 135–46; F. Kokkinaki and P. Lunt, "The Effect of Advertising Message Involvement on Brand Attitude Accessibility," *Journal of Economic Psychology* 20 (1999), pp. 41–51; J. Meyers-Levy and P. Malaviya, "Consumers' Processing of Persuasive Advertisements," *Journal of Marketing* 63 (1999), pp. 45–60; and C. S. Areni, "The Effects of Structural and Grammatical Variables on Persuasion," *Psychology & Marketing,* April 2003, pp. 349–75.

35. See, e.g., Petty and Krosnick, *Attitude Strength.* For a discussion of attitude persistence under low involvement, see J. Sengupta, R. C. Goodstein, and D. S. Boninger, "All Cues Are Not Created Equal," *Journal of Consumer Research,* March 1997, pp. 351–61.

36. P. W. Miniard et al., "Picture-based Persuasion Processes and the Moderating Role of Involvement," *Journal of Consumer Research,* June 1991, pp. 92–107.

37. P. W. Miniard, D. Sirdeshmukh, and D. E. Innis, "Peripheral Persuasion and Brand Choice," *Journal of Consumer Research,* September 1992, pp. 226–39; and T. B. Heath, M. S. McCarthy, and D. L. Mothersbaugh, "Spokesperson Fame and Vividness Effects in the Context of Issue-Relevant Thinking," *Journal of Consumer Research,* March 1994, pp. 520–34; See also, B. Yoo and R. Mandhachitara, "Estimating Advertising Effects on Sales in a Competitive Setting," *Journal of Advertising Research,* September 2003, pp. 310–21; and S. S. Posavac et al., "The Brand Positivity Effect," *Journal of Consumer Research,* December 2004, pp. 643–51.

38. T. F. Mangleburg and T. Bristol, "Socialization and Adolescents' Skepticism toward Advertising," *Journal of Advertising,* Fall 1998, pp. 11–21; C. Obermiller and E. R. Spangenberg, "On the Origin and Distinctiveness of Skepticism toward Advertising," *Marketing Letters,* November 2000, pp. 311–22; and D. M. Hardesty, J. P. Carlson, and W. O. Bearden, "Brand Familiarity and Invoice Price Effects on Consumer Evaluations," *Journal of Advertising,* Summer 2002, pp. 1–15.

39. M. Friestad and P. Wright, "The Persuasion Knowledge Model," *Journal of Consumer Research,* June 1994, pp. 1–31; M. C. Campbell and A. Kirmani, "Consumers' Use of Persuasion Knowledge," *Journal of Consumer Research,* June 2000, pp. 69–83; and R. Ahluwalia and R. E. Burnkrant, "Answering Questions about Questions," *Journal of Consumer Research,* June 2004, pp. 26–42.

40. See R. Ahlusalia, "Examination of Psychological Processes Underlying Resistance to Persuasion," *Journal of Consumer Research,* September 2000, pp. 217–32; and Z. L. Tormala and R. E. Petty, "Source Credibility and Attitude Certainty," *Journal of Consumer Psychology* 14, no. 4 (2004), pp. 427–42.

41. See A. C. B. Tse, "Factors Affecting Consumer Perceptions on Product Safety," *Journal of International Consumer Marketing* 12, no. 1 (1999), pp. 39–55.

42. R. D. Reinartz, "Testimonial Ads," *Bank Marketing,* March 1996, pp. 25–30; and J. Nicholson, "Testimonial Ads Defend Client Turf," *Editor & Publisher,* October 23, 1999, p. 33.

43. D. H. Dean, "Brand Endorsement, Popularity, and Event Sponsorship as Advertising Cues Affecting Pre-Purchase Attitudes," *Journal of Advertising,* Fall 1999, pp. 1–11; and D. H. Dean and A. Biswas, "Third-Party Organization Endorsement of Products," *Journal of Advertising,* Winter 2001, pp. 41–57.

44. Goldsmith, Lafferty, and Newell, "The Impact of Corporate Credibility and Celebrity Credibility on Consumer Reaction to Advertisements and Brands"; B. A. Lafferty, R. E. Goldsmith, and S. J. Newell, "The Dual Credibility Model," *Journal of Marketing Theory and Practice,* Summer 2002, pp. 1–12; and Z. Gurhan-Canli and R. Batra, "When Corporate Image Affects Product Evaluations," *Journal of Marketing Research,* May 2004, pp. 197–205.

45. E. Haley, "Exploring the Construct of Organization as Source," *Journal of Advertising,* Summer 1996, pp. 19–35.

46. S. P. Jain and S. S. Posavac, "Prepurchase Attribute Verifiability, Source Credibility, and Persuasion," *Journal of Consumer Psychology* 11, no. 3 (2001), pp. 169–80.

47. See P. M. Homer and L. R. Kahle, "Source Expertise, Time of Source Identification, and Involvement in Persuasion," *Journal of Advertising* 19, no. 1 (1990), pp. 30–39.

48. C. Pornpitakpan and J. N. P. Francis, "The Effect of Cultural Differences, Source Expertise, and Argument Strength on Persuasion," *Journal of International Consumer Marketing* 13, no. 1 (2001), pp. 77–101.

49. D. J. Moore, J. C. Mowen, and R. Reardon, "Multiple Sources in Advertising Appeals," *Journal of the Academy of Marketing Science,* Summer 1994, pp. 234–43. See also N. Artz and A. M. Tybout, "The Moderating Impact of Quantitative Information on the Relationship between Source Credibility and Persuasion," *Marketing Letters* 10, no. 1 (1999), pp. 51–62.

50. J. Sengupta, R. C. Goodstein, and D. S. Boninger, "All Cues Are Not Created Equal"; B. Z. Erdogan, M. J. Baker, and S. Tagg, "Selecting Celebrity Endorsers," *Journal of Advertising Research,* May–June 2001, pp. 39–48; and M. R. Stafford, N. E. Spears, and C.-K. Hsu, "Celebrity Images in Magazine Advertisements," *Journal of Current Issues and Research in Advertising,* Fall 2003, pp. 13–20.

51. "Michael Jordon Trumps Tiger, Lance in Influence on Purchase Consideration," press release, Knowledge Networks, October 27, 2003 (www.knowledgenetworks.com).

52. M. Tenser, "Endorser Qualities Count More than Ever," *Advertising Age,* November 8, 2004, p. S2.

53. B. D. Till and M. Busler, "The Match-Up Hypothesis," *Journal of Advertising,* Fall 2000, pp. 1–13; Erdogan, Baker, and Tagg, "Selecting Celebrity Endorsers"; A. B. Bower and S. Landreth, "Is Beauty Best?" *Journal of Advertising,* Spring 2001, pp. 1–12; and R. Batra and P. M. Homer, "The Situational Impact of Brand

Image Beliefs," *Journal of Consumer Psychology* 14, no. 3 (2004), pp. 318–30.

54. K. Macarthur, "BK and Paris," *Advertising Age,* August 30, 2004, p. 6.

55. C. Tripp, T. D. Jensen, and L. Carlson, "The Effects of Multiple Product Endorsements by Celebrities on Consumers' Attitudes and Intentions," *Journal of Consumer Research,* March 1994, pp. 535–47; and J. R. Priester and R. E. Petty, "The Influence of Spokesperson Trustworthiness on Message Elaboration, Attitude Strength, and Advertising Effectiveness," *Journal of Consumer Psychology* 13, no. 4 (2003), pp. 408–21.

56. B. D. Till and T. A. Shimp, "Endorsers in Advertising," *Journal of Advertising,* Spring 1998, pp. 67–82; and T. A. Louie, R. L. Kulik, and R. Jacobson, "When Bad Things Happen to the Endorsers of Good Products," *Marketing Letters,* February 2001, pp. 13–23.

57. M. F. Callcott and W.-N. Lee, "Establishing the Spokes-Character in Academic Inquiry," *Advances in Consumer Research,* vol. 22, eds. F. R. Kardes and M. Sujan (Provo, UT: Association for Consumer Research, 1995), pp. 144–51; and M. F. Callcott and B. J. Phillips, "Elves Make Good Cookies," *Journal of Advertising Research,* September 1996, pp. 73–79.

58. For an excellent overview, see T. Meenaghan, "Understanding Sponsorship Effects," *Psychology & Marketing,* February 2001, pp. 95–122; see also B. Walliser, "An International Review of Sponsorship Research," *International Journal of Advertising* 22 (2003), pp. 5–40.

59. "Trade Shows Still Lag while Beverage Makers Are Top Sponsors," *Marketing News,* July 15, 2004, p. 18.

60. R. Thomaselli, "Nextel Sees Payoff as NASCAR Sponsor," *Advertising Age,* May 31, 2004, p. 3.

61. R. Madrigal, "The Influence of Social Alliances with Sports Teams on Intentions to Purchase Corporate Sponsors' Products," *Journal of Advertising,* Winter 2000, pp. 13–24.

62. S. R. McDaniel, "An Investigation of Match-Up Effects in Sport Sponsorship Advertising," *Psychology & Marketing,* March 1999, pp. 163–84; T. B. Cornwell, S. W. Pruitt, and R. V. Ness, "The Value of Winning in Motorsports," *Journal of Advertising Research,* January 2001, pp. 17–31; and N. J. Rifon et al., "Congruence Effects in Sponsorships," *Journal of Advertising,* Spring 2004, pp. 29–42.

63. B. Harvey, "Measuring the Effects of Sponsorship," *Journal of Advertising Research,* January 2001, pp. 59–65; S. Menon and B. E. Kahn, "Corporate Sponsorships of Philanthropic Activities," *Journal of Consumer Psychology* 13, no. 3 (2003), pp. 316–27. For a slightly different view, see L. R. Szykman, P. N. Bloom, and J. Blazing, "Does Corporate Sponsorship of a Socially-Oriented Message Make a Difference?" *Journal of Consumer Psychology* 14, no. 1/2 (2004), pp. 13–20.

64. T. Meenaghan, "Sponsorship and Advertising," *Psychology & Marketing,* February 2001, pp. 191–215.

65. T. Lardinoit and C. Derbaix, "Sponsorship and Recall of Sponsors," *Psychology & Marketing,* February 2001, pp. 167–90.

66. P. G. Quester and B. Thompson, "Advertising and Promotion Leverage on Arts Sponsorship Effectiveness," *Journal of Advertising Research,* January 2001, pp. 33–47; and A. M. Levin, C. Joiner, and G. Cameron, "The Impact of Sports Sponsorship on Consumers' Brand Attitudes and Recall," *Journal of Current Issues and Research in Advertising,* Fall 2001, pp. 23–31. Conflicting evidence is in T. Lardinoit and P. G. Quester. "Attitudinal Effects of Combined Sponsorship and Sponsor's Prominence on Basketball in Europe," *Journal of Advertising Research,* January 2001, pp. 48–58.

67. D. D. Schoenbachler and T. E. Whittler, "Adolescent Processing of Social and Physical Threat Communications," *Journal of Advertising,* Winter 1996, pp. 37–54; C. Pechmann et al., "What to Convey in Antismoking Advertisements for Adolescents," *Journal of Marketing,* April 2003, pp. 1–18; and M. S. LaTour and J. F. Tanner, Jr., "Randon," *Psychology & Marketing,* May 2003, 377–94.

68. P. A. Keller and L. G. Block, "Increasing the Persuasiveness of Fear Appeals," *Journal of Consumer Research,* March 1996, pp. 448–60; M. S. LaTour and H. J. Rotfeld, "There Are Threats and (Maybe) Fear-Caused Arousal," *Journal of Advertising,* Fall 1997, pp. 45–59; and M. Laroche et al., "A Cross-Cultural Study of the Persuasive Effect of Fear Appeal Messages in Cigarette Advertising," *International Journal of Advertising* 3 (2001), pp. 297–317.

69. See M. S. LaTour, R. L. Snipes, and S. J. Bliss, "Don't Be Afraid to Use Fear Appeals," *Journal of Advertising Research,* March 1996, pp. 59–66.

70. H. E. Sparks, M. G. Weinberger, and A. L. Parsons, "Assessing the Use and Impact of Humor on Advertising Effectiveness," *Journal of Advertising,* Fall 1997, pp. 17–32; T. W. Cline and J. J. Kellaris, "The Joint Impact of Humor and Argument Strength in a Print Advertising Context," *Psychology & Marketing,* January 1999, pp. 69–86; D. L. Alden, A. Mukherjee, and W. D. Hoyer, "The Effects of Incongruity, Surprise and Positive Moderators and Perceived Humor in Television Advertising," *Journal of Advertising,* Summer 2000, pp. 1–14; and K. Flaherty, M. G. Weinberger, and C. S. Gulas, "The Impact of Perceived Humor, Product Type, and Humor Style in Radio Advertising," *Journal of Current Issues and Research in Advertising,* Spring 2004, pp. 25–36.

71. T. W. Cline, M. B. Altsech, and J. J. Kellaris, "When Does Humor Enhance or Inhibit Ad Responses?" *Journal of Advertising,* Fall 2003, pp. 31–45.

72. See, e.g., H. S. Krishnan and D. Chakravarti, "A Process Analysis of the Effects of Humorous Advertising Executions on Brand Claims Memory," *Journal of Consumer Psychology* 13, no. 3 (2003), pp. 230–45.

73. H. Chung and X. Zhao, "Humour Effect on Memory and Attitude," *International Journal of Advertising* 22 (2003), pp. 117–44.

74. D. L. Fugate, J. B. Gotlieb, and D. Bolton, "Humorous Services Advertising," *Journal of Professional Services Marketing* 21, no. 1 (2000), pp. 9–22; M. F. Toncar, "The Use of Humour in Television Advertising," *International Journal of Advertising* 20 (2001), pp. 521–39; K. Macarthur, "Subway Cans Schtick to Focus on Food in Its Creative," *Advertising Age,* March 1, 2004, p. 4.

75. D. Grewal et al., "Comparative versus Noncomparative Advertising," *Journal of Marketing,* October 1998, pp. 1–15; M. E. Hill and M. King, "Comparative vs. Noncomparative Advertising," *Journal of Current Issues and Research in Advertising,*

Fall 2001, pp. 33–52; K. C. Manning et al., "Understanding the Mental Representations Created by Comparative Advertising," *Journal of Advertising,* Summer 2001, pp. 27–39; L. D. Compeau, D. Grewal, and R. Chandrashekaran, "Bits, Briefs, and Applications," *Journal of Consumer Affairs,* Winter 2002, pp. 284–94; and J. R. Priester et al., "Brand Congruity and Comparative Advertising," *Journal of Consumer Psychology* 14, no. 1/2 (2004), pp. 115–23.

76. A. Chattopadhyay, "When Does Comparative Advertising Influence Brand Attitude?" *Psychology & Marketing,* August 1998, pp. 461–75; M. J. Barone and P. W. Miniard, "How and When Factual Ad Claims Mislead Consumers," *Journal of Marketing Research,* February 1999, pp. 58–74; S. V. Auken and A. J. Adams, "Across- versus Within-Class Comparative Advertising," *Psychology & Marketing,* August 1999, pp. 429–50; A. B. Sorescu and B. D. Gelb, "Negative Comparative Advertising," *Journal of Advertising,* Winter 2000, pp. 25–40; S. P. Jain, B. Buchanan, and D. Maheswaran, "Comparative versus Noncomparative Advertising," *Journal of Consumer Psychology* 9, no. 4 (2000), pp. 201–11; A. V. Muthukrishnan, L. Warlop, and J. W. Alba, "The Piecemeal Approach to Comparative Advertising," *Marketing Letters* 12, no. 1 (2001), pp. 63–73; S. P. Jain and S. S. Posavac, "Valenced Comparisons," *Journal of Marketing Research,* February 2004, pp. 46–58; and M. J. Barone, K. M. Palan, and P. W. Miniard, "Brand Usage and Gender as Moderators of the Potential Deception Associated with Partial Comparative Advertising," *Journal of Advertising*, Spring 2004, pp. 19–28.

77. See, e.g., M. E. Hill et al., "The Conjoining Influences of Affect and Arousal on Attitude Formation," *Research in Consumer Behavior* 9 (2000), pp. 129–46; J. D. Morris et al., "The Power of Affect," *Journal of Advertising Research,* May/June 2002, pp. 7–17; M.-H. Huang, "Romantic Love and Sex," *Psychology & Marketing,* January 2004, pp. 53–73; and D. J. MacInnis and G. E. de Mello, "The Concept of Hope and Its Relevance to Product Evaluation and Choice," *Journal of Marketing,* January 2005, pp. 1–14.

78. R. K. Chandy et al., "What to Say When," *Journal of Marketing Research,* November 2001, pp. 399–414; and R. D. Jewell and H. R. Unnava, "Exploring Differences in Attitudes between Light and Heavy Brand Users," *Journal of Consumer Psychology* 14, no. 1/2 (2004), pp. 75–80.

79. J. S. Johar and M. J. Sirgy, "Value-Expressive versus Utilitarian Advertising Appeals," *Journal of Advertising,* September 1991,

pp. 23–33; S. Shavitt, "Evidence for Predicting the Effectiveness of Value-Expressive versus Utilitarian Appeals," *Journal of Advertising,* June 1992, pp. 47–51; M. E. Slama and R. B. Singley, "Self-Monitoring and Value-Expressive vs. Utilitarian Ad Effectiveness," *Journal of Current Issues and Research in Advertising,* Fall 1996, pp. 39–49; L. Dube, A. Chattopadhyay, and A. Letarte, "Should Advertising Appeals Match the Basis of Consumers' Attitudes?" *Journal of Advertising Research,* November 1996, pp. 82–89; and J.-shen Chiou, "The Effectiveness of Different Advertising Message Appeals in the Eastern Emerging Society," *International Journal of Advertising* 21 (2002), pp. 217–36.

80. D. MacDonald, "Women & Wheels," *Design Engineering,* November/December 2004, p. 24.

81. M. Dahlen and J. Bergendahl, "Informing and Transforming on the Web," *International Journal of Advertising* 20, no. 2 (2001), pp. 189–205.

82. A. E. Crowley and W. D. Hoyer, "An Integrative Framework for Understanding Two-Sided Persuasion," *Journal of Consumer Research,* March 1994, pp. 561–74; and G. Bohner et al., "When Small Means Comfortable," *Journal of Consumer Psychology* 13, no. 4 (2003), pp. 454–63.

83. I. P. Levin, S. L. Schneider, and G. J. Gaeth, "All Frames Are Not Created Equal," *Organizational Behavior and Human Decision Processes,* November 1998, pp. 149–88.

84. Ibid.

85. P. A. Keller, I. M. Lipkus, and B. K. Rimer, "Affect, Framing, and Persuasion," *Journal of Marketing Research,* February 2003, pp. 54–64; J. Meyers-Levy and D. Maheswaran, "Exploring Message Framing Outcomes When Systematic, Heuristic, or Both Types of Processing Occur," *Journal of Consumer Psychology* 14, no. 1/2 (2004), pp. 159–67; and B. Shiv, J. A. E. Britton, and J. W. Payne, "Does Elaboration Increase or Decrease the Effectiveness of Negatively versus Positively Framed Messages?" *Journal of Consumer Research,* June 2004, pp. 199–208.

86. See, e.g., J. W. Peltier and J. A. Schribrowsky, "The Use of Need-Based Segmentation for Developing Segment-Specific Direct Marketing Strategies," *Journal of Direct Marketing,* Fall 1997, pp. 53–62; and R. Ahmad, "Benefit Segmentation," *International Journal of Marketing Research* 45 (2003), pp. 373–88.

87. H. E. Bloom, "Match the Concept and the Product," *Journal of Advertising Research,* October 1977, pp. 25–27.

Chase Jarvis/Getty Images/MGH-DIL.

12

Self-Concept and Lifestyle

■ Extreme is the name of the game![1] Snowboarding, wakeboarding, artificial wall climbing, and surfing have all seen double-digit growth in recent years. This comes at a time when many traditional sports are seeing their numbers decline. Monday Night Football, a perennial favorite with top-10 prime-time ratings, has seen its audience numbers slip in recent years. Participation in team sports such as baseball, basketball, and softball have seen double-digit declines. These changes are being fueled by dramatic shifts in the interests, values, and lifestyles of the youth market.

Harvey Lauer is president of American Sports Data, Inc. (ASD), a company which examines these trends. Lauer points out that the values underlying extreme sports are very different from those of traditional team sports. While team sports key in on working together and character building, extreme sports are rooted in "fierce individualism, alienation, and defiance."

The X Games and Gravity Games are two nationally televised events for extreme sports with a growing fan base particularly among young men, a segment which marketers often find elusive and hard to reach. Extreme sports offer one way to connect, and marketers are scrambling to tap into the extreme, active, and adrenaline-pumped lifestyles that fuel this audience. Consider the following examples of marketing campaigns which blend extreme sports, culture, lifestyle, and music:

- Mountain Dew is a major sponsor of the X Games. They also have edgy ads with people engaged in extreme activities. Not surprisingly, teens increasingly see Mountain Dew as a "brand for them."
- Memorex has created action sports-theme CD-R blank media that include images of extreme sports on the discs.
- Clear Channel is partnering with NBC and Mountain Dew to create an extreme sports tour much like NASCAR's Nextel Cup Series.

- Aspen Colorado hosted the Winter X Games recently as a way to attract a younger audience and put a bit of edge into its stodgy image.
- Fender guitar sponsors athletes at the X Games. They bring a truck loaded with guitars to the event and allow athletes and fans to jam right there in the snow! According to one executive at Fender, "What these guys are doing is art with their bodies and boards. They have a real desire to pursue creative outlets beyond just riding."

According to ASD's Lauer, "These sports are an authentic slice of the wider youth culture and not just a fad." Clearly marketers should continue to look for ways to blend their brands into the lifestyles of this dynamic youth market.

In this chapter, we will discuss the meaning of lifestyle and the role it plays in developing marketing strategies. Lifestyle is, in many ways, an outward expression of one's self-concept. That is, the way an individual chooses to live, given the constraints of income and ability, is heavily influenced by that person's current and desired self-concept. Therefore, we begin the chapter with an analysis of the self-concept. We then describe lifestyles, the ways in which lifestyle is measured, and examples of how lifestyle is being used to develop marketing programs.

SELF-CONCEPT

Self-concept is defined as *the totality of the individual's thoughts and feelings having reference to himself or herself as an object.* It is an individual's perception of and feelings toward him- or herself. In other words, your self-concept is composed of the attitudes you hold toward yourself.

The self-concept can be divided into four basic parts, as shown in Table 12-1: actual versus ideal, and private versus social. The actual/ideal distinction refers to the individual's perception of *who I am now* (**actual self-concept**) and *who I would like to be* (**ideal self-concept**). The private self refers to *how I am or would like to be to myself* (**private self-concept**), and the social self is *how I am seen by others or how I would like to be seen by others* (**social self-concept**).

Interdependent/Independent Self-Concepts

The self-concept is important in all cultures. However, those aspects of the self that are most valued and most influence consumption and other behaviors vary across cultures. Researchers have found it useful to categorize self-concepts into two types—independent and interdependent, also referred to as one's separateness and connectedness.[2]

An independent construal of the self is based on the predominant Western cultural belief that individuals are inherently separate. The **independent self-concept** *emphasizes*

TABLE 12-1	Dimensions of Self-Concept	Actual Self-Concept	Ideal Self-Concept
Dimensions of a Consumer's Self-Concept	*Private self*	How I actually see myself	How I would like to see myself
	Social self	How others actually see me	How I would like others to see me

Courtesy Bonne Bell.

personal goals, characteristics, achievements, and desires. Individuals with an independent self-concept tend to be individualistic, egocentric, autonomous, self-reliant, and self-contained. They define themselves in terms of what they have done, what they have, and their personal characteristics.[3]

An interdependent construal of the self is based more on the common Asian cultural belief in the fundamental connectedness of human beings. The **interdependent self-concept** *emphasizes family, cultural, professional, and social relationships.* Individuals with an interdependent self-concept tend to be obedient, sociocentric, holistic, connected, and relation oriented. They define themselves in terms of social roles, family relationships, and commonalities with other members of their groups.

Independent and interdependent self-concepts are not discrete categories; rather, they are constructs used to describe the opposite ends of a continuum along which most cultures lie. However, as we emphasized in Chapter 2, most cultures are heterogeneous. Therefore, within a given culture, subcultures and other groups will vary on this dimension, as will individuals.[4] For example, women across cultures tend to have more of an *interdependent* self-concept than do males.[5]

Variation in the degree to which an individual or culture is characterized by an independent versus an interdependent self-concept has been found to influence message preferences, consumption of luxury goods, and the types of products preferred. For example, ads emphasizing acting alone and autonomy tend to be effective with consumers with independent self-concepts, whereas ads emphasizing group membership work better with consumers with interdependent self-concepts.[6] The ad in Illustration 12-1 should be effective with individuals whose independent self-concept is dominant.

Possessions and the Extended Self

Some products acquire substantial meaning to an individual or are used to signal particularly important aspects of that person's self to others. Belk developed a theory called the *extended self* to explain this.[7] The **extended self** consists of *the self plus possessions;* that is, people tend to define themselves in part by their possessions. Thus, some possessions are not just a manifestation of one's self-concept; they are an integral part of the person's self-identity. People are, to some extent, what they possess. If one lost key possessions, he or she would be a somewhat different individual.[8]

While these key possessions might be major items, such as one's home or automobile, they are equally likely to be smaller items with unique meanings, such as a souvenir, a photograph, a pet, or a favorite cooking pan. Such objects have meaning to the individual beyond their market value. Consider these statements from consumers who lost their possessions in natural disasters and who had ample insurance to replace them:

> Yea, we got better stuff, but it doesn't mean anything to us. It's just stuff.
>
> You can't put back or replace what you had. It was too personal—it was customized.[9]

Products become part of one's extended self for a variety of reasons. Souvenirs often become part of the extended self as representations of memories and feelings:

> You can't really tell what Paris is like . . . you know, a lot of it is just feelings; feelings you can't put into words, or [that] pictures cannot capture. . . . They [a hat and blouse] are just reminders.
>
> I had a really wonderful trip and really sort of discovered myself, you know, I learned to be independent on my own. I really didn't have the money to buy this [necklace and boomerang charm], but I decided I wanted something really permanent. . . . The boomerang is a symbol of going back there sometime.[10]

Gifts often take on important meanings as representations of relationships:

> That gift was my grandfather's ring. . . . Even now when I look at it, I think about its past with him and the journeys it took around the world in the Navy back in World War II.
>
> The key chain is special because every so often, when I think about who gave it to me, it brings back old thoughts and feelings. It is a symbol of friendship between us, and it keeps us in touch.[11]

Some products become embedded with meaning, memories, and value as they are used over time, as with an old baseball glove. At other times a single peak experience with a product such as a mountain bike can propel the product into the extended self. A **peak experience** is *an experience that surpasses the usual level of intensity, meaningfulness, and richness and produces feelings of joy and self-fulfillment.*[12] Finally, products that are acquired or used to help consumers with major life transitions (e.g., leaving home, first job, marriage) are also likely to be or become part of the extended self.[13]

Consumer Insight 12-1 describes a product that is likely to become part of one's extended self as well as one's physical self.

A scale has been developed to measure the extent to which an item has been incorporated into the extended self.[14] It is a Likert scale (see Appendix A) in which consumers

Tattoos and the Extended Self

Most products and services associated with the *extended* self are distinct from the *physical* self.[15] Until recently, exceptions to this were limited primarily to hairstyling, hair coloring, and cosmetics. One could also alter the physical self through exercise, diet, weight training, and plastic surgery. In recent years, body piercing and tattooing have become additional ways to alter both the extended self and the physical self.

For most of the past century, tattooing was not socially acceptable among most groups in the United States. The most noticeable exception was enlisted men in the Navy, and even then alcohol consumption was frequently involved in the decision to get a tattoo. This has changed sharply in recent years. Why have tattoos become socially acceptable, and what does it mean to the self-concept of those who get tattoos?

A *tattoo renaissance* began in the 1960s with the hippie movement and the evolution of skilled tattoo artists in the San Francisco area. The commercial art world and academic art historians began to pay attention to tattooing as an art form. This, in turn, attracted better tattoo artists. By the early 1990s, public figures, particularly athletes, began to wear visible tattoos, which increased their acceptability among the more venturesome members of mainstream society. And the trend continues.

Tattoos have meanings on at least three levels. First, there is the meaning associated with *having a tattoo*. While increasingly common, having a tattoo is still far from the norm. Thus, having a tattoo in and of itself makes a statement about the person. A person with a tattoo is still viewed as somewhat of a risk taker or nonconformist. Second, the *location* of the tattoo also contains meaning. The more visible the tattoo, the more rebellious or nonconforming the individual appears to be. Finally, the nature of the tattoo is a major source of meaning, both private and symbolic. Tattoos may symbolize group membership, one's interests, activities, relationships, life transitions, accomplishments, or values. Tattoos may be unique and expressive primarily of personal meanings or their meanings may be rooted in cultural practice, myths, or religion.

Critical Thinking Questions

1. How does a tattoo affect one's self-concept and become part of one's extended self?

2. Will one or more visible tattoos become the norm for younger consumers over the next 10 years?

3. How is the renaissance in tattooing similar to the revival of cigar smoking? How is it different?

express levels of agreement (from strongly agree to strongly disagree on a seven-point scale) to the following statements:

1. My _____ helps me achieve the identity I want to have.
2. My _____ helps me narrow the gap between what I am and what I try to be.
3. My _____ is central to my identity.
4. My _____ is part of who I am.
5. If my _____ is stolen from me I will feel as if my identity has been snatched from me.
6. I derive some of my identity from my _____.

Owning a product affects a person even if it does not become an important part of the person's extended self. The **mere ownership effect,** or the *endowment effect,* is *the tendency of an owner to evaluate an object more favorably than a nonowner.* This occurs almost immediately upon acquiring an object and increases with time of ownership. Thus, people tend to value an object more after acquiring it than before. People also tend to value objects they own more highly than they value similar objects owned by others.[16]

The concept of the extended self and the mere ownership effect have numerous implications for marketing strategy. One is that communications that cause potential consumers

1. Rugged	___	___	___	___	___	___	___	Delicate
2. Excitable	___	___	___	___	___	___	___	Calm
3. Uncomfortable	___	___	___	___	___	___	___	Comfortable
4. Dominating	___	___	___	___	___	___	___	Submissive
5. Thrifty	___	___	___	___	___	___	___	Indulgent
6. Pleasant	___	___	___	___	___	___	___	Unpleasant
7. Contemporary	___	___	___	___	___	___	___	Noncontemporary
8. Organized	___	___	___	___	___	___	___	Unorganized
9. Rational	___	___	___	___	___	___	___	Emotional
10. Youthful	___	___	___	___	___	___	___	Mature
11. Formal	___	___	___	___	___	___	___	Informal
12. Orthodox	___	___	___	___	___	___	___	Liberal
13. Complex	___	___	___	___	___	___	___	Simple
14. Colorless	___	___	___	___	___	___	___	Colorful
15. Modest	___	___	___	___	___	___	___	Vain

Source: N. K. Malhotra, "A Scale to Measure Self-Concepts, Person Concepts, and Product Concepts," *Journal of Marketing Research,* published by the American Marketing Association; reprinted with permission. November 1981, p. 462.

to *visualize product ownership* may result in enhanced product evaluations. Product sampling or other trial programs may have similar results.

Measuring Self-Concept

Utilizing the self-concept in marketing requires that it be measurable. The most common measurement approach is the semantic differential (see Appendix A). Malhotra has developed a set of 15 pairs of adjectives shown in Table 12-2. These have proven effective in describing the ideal, actual, and social self-concepts of individuals as well as the images of automobiles and celebrities. *Using this scale, determine your actual and desired private and social self-concepts.*

This instrument can be used to ensure a match between the self-concept (actual or ideal) of a target market, the image of a brand, and the characteristics of an advertising spokesperson. For example, in its decision to sign Serena Williams to a multi-year endorsement contract, Nike undoubtedly saw a match between the desired self-concept of young women, the desired image for Nike's women's athletic-apparel line, and the image of Serena Williams.[17]

Using Self-Concept to Position Products

People's attempts to obtain their ideal self-concept, or maintain their actual self-concept, often involve the purchase and consumption of products, services, and media.[18] This process is described in Figure 12-1. While this figure implies a rather conscious and deliberate process, many times this is not the case. For example, a person may drink diet colas because his desired self-concept includes a trim figure, but he is unlikely to think about the purchase in these terms. However, as the following statement illustrates, sometimes people do think in these terms.

And I feel if you present yourself in the right way, people will start to notice. But this leads back to image and self-worth, which can be achieved through having the right clothes and a good haircut . . . having a good portrait of yourself on the outside can eventually lead to an emotionally stable inside.[19]

The Relationship between Self-Concept and Brand Image Influence   FIGURE 12-1

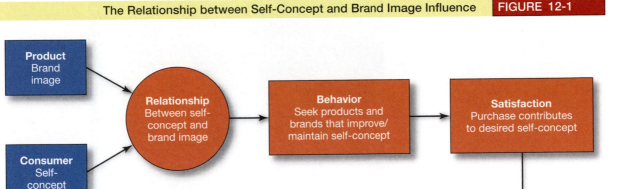

All this suggests that marketers should strive to develop product images that are consistent with the self-concepts of their target markets.[20] While everyone's self-concept is unique, there is also significant overlap across individuals and groups, which is one basis for market segmentation. For example, many consumers see themselves as environmentalists. Companies and products that create an image as being concerned about or good for the environment are likely to be supported by these consumers.

Consumers maintain and enhance their self-concepts not only by what they consume, but by what they avoid.[21] Some consumers make a point of avoiding certain product categories such as red meat or brands such as Nike as part of maintaining "who they are."

In general, consumers prefer brands that match their self-concepts. However, it is important to realize that the degree to which such "self-image congruity" influences brand preference and choice depends on a number of product, situational, and individual factors. First, self-image congruity is likely to matter more for products such as perfume where value-expressive *symbolism* is critical than for more utilitarian products such as a garage door opener. Second, self-image congruity (especially ideal social self) is likely to matter more when the situation involves *public* or *conspicuous consumption* (e.g., having a beer with friends at a bar) than when consumption is private (e.g., having a beer at home).[22] Finally, self-image congruity is likely to matter more for consumers who place heavy weight on the opinions and feelings of others (called *high self-monitors*) than for consumers who do not (called *low self-monitors*), particularly in public situations where consumption behaviors can be observed by others.[23]

Look at Illustration 12-2 and the various aspects of self-concept listed in Table 12-2. *Which aspect(s) of self-concept does this ad appeal to?*

Marketing Ethics and the Self-Concept

The self-concept has many dimensions. Marketers have been criticized for focusing too much attention on the importance of being beautiful, with *beautiful* being defined as young and slim with a fairly narrow range of facial features. Virtually all societies appear to define and desire beauty, but the intense exposure to products and advertisements focused on beauty in America today is unique. Critics argue that this concern leads individuals to develop self-concepts that are heavily dependent on their physical appearance rather than other equally or more important attributes.

Ads that position products to match the self-concept of the target market are generally successful. Such ads can appeal to the consumer's actual or ideal, private or social self.

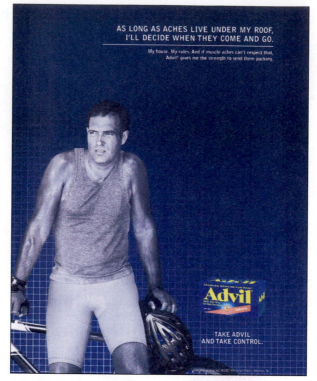

AS LONG AS ACHES LIVE UNDER MY ROOF, I'LL DECIDE WHEN THEY COME AND GO.

My house. My rules. And if muscle aches can't respect that, Advil® gives me the strength to send them packing.

Advil

TAKE ADVIL AND TAKE CONTROL.

© 2002 Wyeth Consumer Healthcare.

Consider the following statements from two young women:

I never felt that I looked right. Like I can see outfits that I'd love to wear, but I know that I could never wear them. I probably could wear them and get away with it, but I'd be so self-conscious walking around that I'd be like, "oh, my God." Like I always try to look thinner and I guess everybody does.

I am pretty content with my hair because I have good hair. I have good eyesight (laughs) so I don't have to wear glasses or anything that would make my face look different from what it is. In terms of bad points, well there is a lot. I got a lot of my father's features. I wish I had more of my mother's. My hands are pretty square. I have a kind of a big butt. Then, I don't have that great of a stomach.[24]

These young women have self-concepts that are partly negative as a result of their perceptions of their beauty relative to the standard portrayed in the media. Critics of advertising claim that most individuals, but particularly young women, acquire negative components to their self-concepts because very few can achieve the standards of beauty presented in advertising. Recent research indicates that similar negative self-evaluations occur in males as a result of idealized images of both physical attractiveness and financial success.[25]

The ethical question is complex. No one ad or company has this type of impact. It is the cumulative effect of many ads across many companies reinforced by the content of the mass media that presumably causes some to be overly focused on their physical beauty. And, as stated earlier, concern with beauty existed long before advertising.

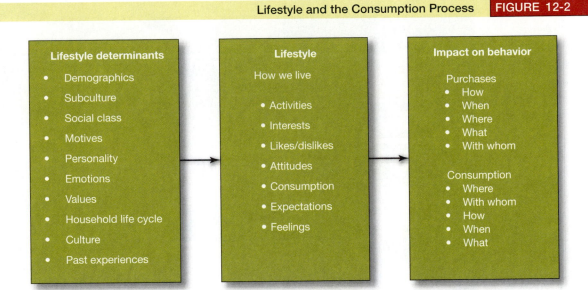

Lifestyle and the Consumption Process   FIGURE 12-2

Lifestyle determinants
- Demographics
- Subculture
- Social class
- Motives
- Personality
- Emotions
- Values
- Household life cycle
- Culture
- Past experiences

Lifestyle
How we live
- Activities
- Interests
- Likes/dislikes
- Attitudes
- Consumption
- Expectations
- Feelings

Impact on behavior
Purchases
- How
- When
- Where
- What
- With whom

Consumption
- Where
- With whom
- How
- When
- What

THE NATURE OF LIFESTYLE

As Figure 12-2 indicates, **lifestyle** is basically *how a person lives*. It is how one enacts one's self-concept, and is determined by one's past experiences, innate characteristics, and current situation. One's lifestyle influences all aspects of one's consumption behavior and is a function of inherent individual characteristics that have been shaped and formed through social interaction as the person has evolved through the life cycle.

The relationship between *lifestyle* and *self-concept* was demonstrated in a recent study comparing various lifestyle-related activities, interests, and behaviors across those with independent versus interdependent self-concepts. *Independents* were more likely to seek adventure and excitement through travel, sports, and entertainment; to be opinion leaders; and to prefer magazines over TV. *Interdependents* were more likely to engage in home and domestic-related activities and entertainment including cooking at home and from scratch. Interdependents were also more likely to engage in social activities revolving around family and the community.[26]

Individuals and households both have lifestyles. Although household lifestyles are in part determined by the individual lifestyles of the household members, the reverse is also true.

Individuals' *desired* lifestyles influence their needs and desires and thus their purchase and use behavior. Desired lifestyle determines many of a person's consumption decisions, which in turn reinforce or alter that person's lifestyle.

Marketers can use lifestyle to segment and target specific markets. As the chapter's opening vignette illustrates, companies such as Mountain Dew and Fender guitars are targeting their promotions and brands toward the lifestyles of extreme sports fans and participants. Beer brands such as Heineken and Amstel would also see this group as a highly attractive segment since they are 107 percent more likely than the average consumer to drink import beers.[27] Illustration 12-3 shows a Web site targeted at the extreme sports enthusiast.

Consumers are seldom explicitly aware of the role lifestyle plays in their purchase decisions. For example, few consumers would think, "I'll have a Starbucks coffee at a Starbucks outlet to maintain my lifestyle." However, individuals pursuing an active, social lifestyle might purchase Starbucks in part because of its convenience, its "in" status, and

This Web site targets the lifestyle of extreme sports enthusiasts.

Courtesy Concussion Magazine.

the presence of others at Starbucks outlets. Thus, lifestyle frequently provides the basic motivation and guidelines for purchases, although it generally does so in an indirect, subtle manner.

Measurement of Lifestyle

Attempts to develop quantitative measures of lifestyle were initially referred to as **psychographics.**[28] In fact, the terms *psychographics* and *lifestyle* are frequently used interchangeably. Psychographics or lifestyle studies typically include the following:

- *Attitudes*—evaluative statements about other people, places, ideas, products, and so forth.
- *Values*—widely held beliefs about what is acceptable or desirable.
- *Activities and interests*—nonoccupational behaviors to which consumers devote time and effort, such as hobbies, sports, public service, and church.
- *Demographics*—age, education, income, occupation, family structure, ethnic background, gender, and geographic location.
- *Media patterns*—the specific media the consumers utilize.
- *Usage rates*—measurements of consumption within a specified product category; often consumers are categorized as heavy, medium, light, or nonusers.

A large number of individuals, often 500 or more, provide the above information. Statistical techniques are used to place them into groups whose members have similar response patterns. Most studies use the first two or three dimensions described above to group individuals. The other dimensions are used to provide fuller descriptions of each group. Other studies include demographics as part of the grouping process.[29]

General versus Specific Lifestyle Schemes

Lifestyle measurements can be constructed with varying degrees of specificity. At one extreme, marketers can study the general lifestyle patterns of a population. These general lifestyle approaches are not specific to any one product or activity so they have broad applicability in developing marketing strategies for a wide range of products and brands. General approaches include VALS and PRIZM, which are discussed in later sections of this chapter.

At the other extreme, firms can conduct very specific lifestyle studies focused on those aspects of individual or household lifestyles most relevant to their product or service. For these studies, lifestyle measurement is product or activity specific. Specific lifestyle schemes have been used to analyze complaint behavior by elderly patients dissatisfied with their health care,[30] to understand art gallery attendance in New Zealand,[31] to determine optimal marketing strategies for tourism in Spain,[32] and to develop dining menus at U.S. college campuses.[33] Let's take an in-depth look at three specific lifestyle schemes.

Luxury Sports Cars   Porsche examined the lifestyles of its buyers. What they found surprised them a bit, because although key demographics (e.g., high education and income) were similar across their buyers, their lifestyles and motivations were quite different. The segments and their descriptions are listed below:[34]

- *Top Guns* (27 percent). Ambitious and driven, this group values power and control and expects to be noticed.
- *Elitists* (24 percent). These old-family-money "blue-bloods" don't see a car as an extension of their personality. Cars are cars no matter what the price tag.
- *Proud Patrons* (23 percent). This group purchases a car to satisfy themselves, not to impress others. A car is a reward for their hard work.
- *Bon Vivants* (17 percent). These thrill seekers and "jet-setters" see cars as enhancing their already exciting lives.
- *Fantasists* (9 percent). This group uses their car as an escape, not as a means to impress others. In fact, they feel a bit of guilt for owning a Porsche.

How would Porsche's marketing approach need to be changed across these different lifestyle segments?

Shopping   In Chapter 10 (Consumer Insight 10-1) we discussed various hedonic motives underlying consumer shopping patterns. The motives were (1) adventure (fun), (2) gratification (reward/stress reduction), (3) role (shop for others), (4) value (good deal), (5) social (bonding), and (6) idea (trends). Five shopping lifestyle segments emerged based on these motives.[35]

- *Minimalists* (12 percent). Primarily motivated by value. Least motivated by fun and adventure. Minimalists are low in appreciation of retail aesthetics (look and feel of the mall/store), low in innovativeness, and don't tend to be browsers. This group is middle-aged and 57 percent are men.
- *Gatherers* (15 percent). Primarily motivated by keeping up with trends and enjoyment of shopping for others. Least motivated by value. Gatherers are low in appreciation of retail aesthetics, low in innovativeness, but are moderate browsers. This group contains a mix of younger and older shoppers but is predominantly (70 percent) male.
- *Providers* (23 percent). Primarily motivated by enjoyment of shopping for others and value. Not motivated by fun and adventure. Providers are moderate in their appreciation of retail aesthetics, low in innovativeness, and are moderate browsers. This is the oldest group and is predominantly (83 percent) female.

- *Enthusiasts* (27 percent). Highly motivated by all hedonic aspects including fun and adventure, for which they are higher than any other group. Enthusiasts are highest in appreciation of retail aesthetics, the most innovative, and spend the most time browsing. This is the youngest group and predominantly (90 percent) female.
- *Traditionalists* (23 percent). Moderately motivated by all hedonic aspects, with gratification high on the list. Traditionalists are moderate in appreciation of retail aesthetics, highly innovative, and moderate browsers. This group contains a mix of younger and older shoppers and 58 percent are women.

Which lifestyle segment(s) do you think shop at Banana Republic? What about Target?

Technology   How technology is utilized by consumers is of critical importance to marketers. Numerous technology and Internet lifestyle profiles exist, including Pew Internet User Types, Ebates.com Dot-shoppers, and TDS Shopper Clusters: Onliners Group.[36] Forrester Research has created Technographics, a technology segmentation scheme that examines lifestyle segments across such technologies and activities as online access, PC ownership, instant messaging, and shopping online. Based on the responses of over 60,000 North American respondents, the following 10 segments emerged:[37]

- *Fast Forwards* (12 percent). Optimistic, high income, and motivated by career. Fast Forwards are time-pressed, driven, and heavy users of technology across the board. Most likely to own a PC and be online.
- *Techno-Strivers* (5 percent). Optimistic, low income, and motivated by career. Techno-Strivers are beginning to believe in the value of technology as a way to help advance their careers. More likely than average to be influenced by "what is hot." Average technology users.
- *Handshakers* (7 percent). Pessimistic, high income, and motivated by career. Handshakers are successful in their careers but have a low tolerance for technology. They are the lowest users of instant messaging and least likely to download music files. But they are still more likely than average to own a PC and be online.
- *New Age Nurturers* (8 percent). Optimistic, high income, and motivated by family. New Age Nurturers believe strongly in the value of technology for family and education. More likely than average to own a PC and be online.
- *Digital Hopefuls* (6 percent). Optimistic, low income, and motivated by family. Digital hopefuls are family-oriented technology lovers. Relatively high users of instant messaging. Perhaps due to lower income, they are less likely than average to own a PC and be online.
- *Traditionalists* (10 percent). Pessimistic, high income, and motivated by family. Traditionalists are suspicious of any technology beyond simple basics. Least likely to be influenced by "what's hot." One of the least likely groups to bank online and download music files.
- *Mouse Potatoes* (9 percent). Optimistic, high income, and motivated by entertainment. Mouse Potatoes are into interactive entertainment especially on the PC. Most likely of all groups to shop online, have a mobile phone, and bank online.
- *Gadget Grabbers* (7 percent). Optimistic, low income, and motivated by entertainment. Gadget Grabbers want affordable high-tech products. Most influenced by "what's hot," and most likely to use instant messaging and download music files. Lower income makes them slightly less likely than average to own a PC and be online.
- *Media Junkies* (6 percent). Pessimistic, high income, and motivated by entertainment. Media Junkies are especially interested in TV and such features as on-demand video.

- *Sidelined Citizens* (29 percent). Pessimistic and low income. Sidelined Citizens, by far the largest group, are frightened of technology and slow to adopt. This group is least receptive to technological innovations. Least likely to own a PC, be online, shop online, or bank online.

To which of these groups will the ad in Illustration 12-4 appeal?

While specific lifestyle studies are useful, many firms have found general lifestyle studies to be of great value also. Two popular general systems are described next.[38]

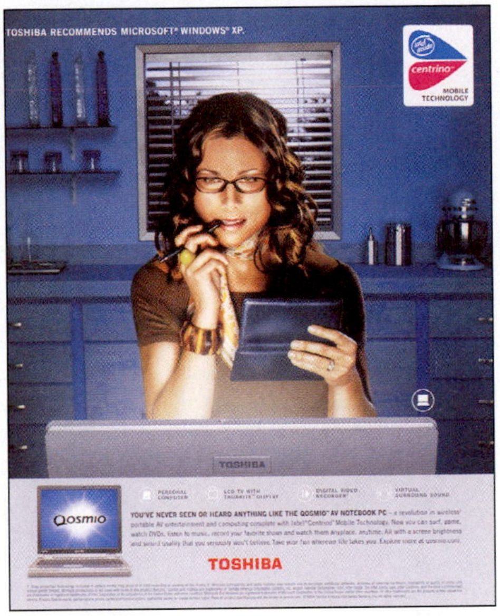

Courtesy Toshiba American Information Systems, Digital Products Divisions.

ILLUSTRATION 12-4

Forrester Research has identified 10 lifestyle segments related to technology. To which segment(s) will this ad most appeal?

THE VALS™ SYSTEM

By far the most popular application of psychographic research by marketing managers is SRI Consulting Business Intelligence's (SRIC-BI) VALS™ program. Introduced in 1978 and significantly revised in 1989, **VALS** provides a systematic classification of American adults into eight distinct consumer segments.[39]

VALS is based on enduring psychological characteristics that correlate with purchase patterns. Respondents are classified according to their *primary motivation* which serves as one of VALS's two dimensions. As we saw in Chapter 10, motives are critical determinants of behavior. Motives have strong linkages to personality and self concept. Indeed, a core premise behind VALS is that "An individual's primary motivation determines what in particular about the self or the world is the meaningful core that governs his or her activities." SRIC-BI has identified three primary motivations:

- *Ideals Motivation.* These consumers are guided in their choices by their beliefs and principles rather than by feelings or desire for social approval. They purchase functionality and reliability.
- *Achievement Motivation.* These consumers strive for a clear social position and are strongly influenced by the actions, approval, and opinions of others. They purchase status symbols.
- *Self-Expression Motivation.* These action-oriented consumers strive to express their individuality through their choices. They purchase experiences.

These three orientations determine the types of goals and behaviors that individuals will pursue. Table 12-3 provides more detailed descriptions of the goals, motivations, and behavioral tendencies of each motivational group.

The second dimension, termed *resources,* reflects the ability of individuals to pursue their dominant self-orientation. It refers to the full range of psychological, physical, demographic, and material means on which consumers can draw. Resources generally increase from adolescence through middle age and then remain relatively stable until they begin to decline with older age. Resources are an important part of VALS since they can aid or inhibit a consumer's ability to act on his or her primary motivation.

TABLE 12-3

Underlying
Differences Across
VALS™ Motivational
Types

	Primary Motivation		
	Ideals	**Achievement**	**Self-Expression**
They are	Information seeking	Goal oriented	Spontaneous
They make	Choices based on principles	Choices to enhance position	Choices to have emotional impact
They buy	Functionality and reliability	Success symbols	Experiences
They seek	Understanding	Social approval	Adventure, excitement, novelty
They pursue	Self-development	Self-improvement	Self-reliance
They resist	Impulse	Risk	Authority
They ask	What "should" I do?	What are others like me doing?	What do I feel like doing?

Source: SRI Consulting Business Intelligence, www.sric-bi.com/VALS/.

TABLE 12-4

Selected
Demographics of the
VALS™ Segments

Segment	Percent Female	Median Age	Median Income (000)
Innovators	46%	43	$104
Thinkers	49	54	76
Believers	69	50	34
Achievers	56	40	67
Strivers	41	28	22
Experiencers	42	25	47
Makers	43	45	39
Survivors	63	70	15

Source: VALS/MediaMark Research Inc. (MRI) data from *The Survey of American Consumers;* SRI Consulting Business Intelligence, www.sric-bi.com/VALS/.

TABLE 12-5   VALS Segment Selected Ownership and Activities*

	All	Innovators	Thinkers	Believers	Achievers	Strivers	Experiencers	Makers	Survivors
Own a truck	100	54	99	106	121	78	83	158	89
Drink herb tea	100	219	152	71	97	47	92	92	61
Mountain bicycle $100+	100	145	36	14	141	146	221	122	0
Attend country music performances	100	59	95	107	116	87	92	159	74

*Note: Table based on index numbers (100 = average of U.S. adult population) and provide a basis of comparison across the VALS groups and the U.S. population overall. For example, Makers are 58 percent more likely to own a truck than the average U.S. adult consumer.

Source: VALS/MediaMark Research Inc. (MRI) data from *The Survey of American Consumers;* SRI Consulting Business Intelligence, www.sric-bi.com/VALS/.

On the basis of these two concepts, SRIC-BI has identified eight general psychographic segments, as shown in Figure 12-3. Table 12-4 provides selected demographics for each segment. Table 12-5 provides information on selected product ownership and activities for each segment. Each of these segments is described briefly next.

The VALS™ Segments

Innovators   *Innovators* are successful, sophisticated, active, take-charge people with high self-esteem and abundant resources. Innovators are motivated by a blend of ideals,

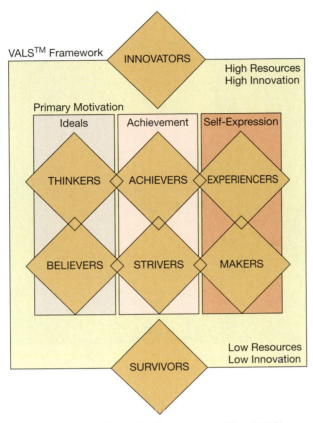

Source: SRI Consulting Business Intelligence, www.sric-bi.com/VALS/.

achievement, and self-expression. Image is important to Innovators, not as evidence of status or power but as an expression of their taste, independence, and character. Their possessions and recreation reflect a cultivated taste for the finer things in life, and they often see brands and products as extensions of their personalities.

Innovators are among the established and emerging leaders in business and government, yet they continue to grow and seek new challenges. They have a wide range of interests, are concerned with social issues, and are the most receptive to new products, ideas, and technologies. The ad in Illustration 12-5 would appeal to Innovators.

Thinkers and Believers: Ideals Motivated

Ideals-motivated consumers base their decisions on abstract idealized criteria such as quality, integrity, and tradition. They seek to behave in ways that are consistent with their views of how the world is or should be.

Thinkers are mature, satisfied, comfortable, reflective people who value order, knowledge, and responsibility. Most are well educated, and in or recently retired from professional occupations. They are well informed about world and national events and are alert to opportunities to broaden their knowledge. Content with their careers, families, and station in life, they tend to center their leisure activities on the home.

Thinkers have a moderate respect for the status quo but are open-minded about new ideas and social change. They tend to base their decisions on strongly held principles and

This ad would appeal to Innovators' desire for growth and their taste for the finer things in life.

London, tastefully delivered.

BRITISH AIRWAYS

© British Airways Plc 2005.

consequently appear calm and self-assured. Thinkers plan their purchases carefully and are particularly cautious concerning big-ticket items; they look for functionality, value, and durability in the products they buy.

Believers are conservative, conventional people with concrete beliefs based on traditional, established codes: family, church, community, and the nation. Many Believers express moral codes that are deeply rooted and literally interpreted. They follow established routines, organized in large part around their homes, families, and the social or religious organizations to which they belong. As consumers, they are conservative, predictable, and highly loyal. Believers favor American products and established brands, and are averse to change and new technology.

Achievers and Strivers: Achievement Motivated

Achievement-oriented consumers make choices to enhance their position or to facilitate their move to a more desirable group. Strivers look to others to indicate what they should be and do, whereas Achievers look to their own peer group.

Achievers are successful career- and work-oriented people who like to, and generally do, feel in control of their lives. They value consensus, predictability, and stability over risk, intimacy, and self-discovery. They are deeply committed to work and family with lives structured around family, church, and career. Achievers live conventional lives, tend to be politically conservative, and respect authority and the status quo. Image is important to them; they favor established, prestige products and services that demonstrate success to their peers. Convenience and time-saving products and services are also of interest to achievers given their hectic lifestyles.

The ad in Illustration 12-6 would appeal to Achievers.

Strivers are style conscious and trendy. They have limited education and tend to have narrow interests. Money defines success for Strivers, but they usually don't have enough of it. They favor stylish products that emulate the purchases of people with greater material wealth. Strivers have less self-confidence than Achievers. They often feel that life has given them a raw deal.

Experiencers and Makers: Self-Expression Motivated

Self-expression motivated consumers like to affect their environment in tangible ways. Makers do so by physically altering their environment at home—for example building a new patio or adding a room. Alternatively, Experiencers seek to make an impact through their dress, speech, or adventurous experiences.

Courtesy Garmin International Inc.

Experiencers are young, vital, enthusiastic, impulsive, and rebellious. They seek variety and excitement, savoring the new, the offbeat, and the risky. Still in the process of formulating life values and patterns of behavior, they quickly become enthusiastic about new possibilities but are equally quick to cool. At this stage of their lives, they are politically uncommitted, uninformed, and highly ambivalent about what they believe.

Experiencers combine an abstract disdain for conformity with an outsider's awe of others' wealth, prestige, and power. Their energy finds an outlet in exercise, sports, outdoor recreation, and social activities. Experiencers are avid consumers and spend much of their income on clothing, fast food, music, movies, and videos and technology. The ad in Illustration 12-7 would be particularly appealing to this segment.

Makers are practical people who have constructive skills and value self-sufficiency. They live within a traditional context of family, practical work, and physical recreation and have little interest in what lies outside that context. Makers express themselves and experience the world by working on it—building a house, raising children, fixing a car, or canning vegetables. Makers are politically conservative, suspicious of new ideas, respectful of government authority and organized labor, but resentful of government intrusion on individual rights. They are unimpressed by material possessions other than those with a practical or functional purpose (e.g., tools, pickup trucks, washing machines, or fishing equipment). The product shown in Illustration 12-8 would appeal to this group.

Survivors

Survivors' lives are constricted. They live simply on limited incomes but are relatively satisfied. Frequently elderly and concerned about their health, they are not active in the marketplace. Survivors show no evidence of a strong primary motivation. They buy familiar, trusted products. Their chief concerns are for security, safety and being with family. Survivors are cautious consumers who look for low prices. They represent a modest market for most products and services. As described in Chapter 4, meeting the needs of these consumers is a challenge for both marketers and public policy makers.

Courtesy Plano Molding.

GEO-LIFESTYLE ANALYSIS (PRIZM)

Claritas Inc., a leading firm in this industry, describes the logic of **geo-demographic analysis:**

> People with similar cultural backgrounds, means and perspectives naturally gravitate toward one another. They choose to live amongst their peers in neighborhoods offering affordable advantages and compatible lifestyles.
>
> Once settled in, people naturally emulate their neighbors. They adopt similar social values, tastes and expectations. They exhibit shared patterns of consumer behavior toward products, services, media and promotions.[40]

Geo-demographic analyses are based on the premise that lifestyle, and thus consumption, is largely driven by demographic factors, as described above.[41] The geographic regions analyzed can range from states and counties, to metropolitan statistical areas (urbanized areas of 50,000 people or more plus adjacent territory), to five-digit ZIP codes (1,500 to 15,000 or more households), to Census tracts (850–2,500 households), to Census blocks (8–25 households), to ZIP+4 (6–15 households), and even down to the individual household. Such data are used for target market selection, promotional emphasis, retail site selection and so forth by numerous marketers.

Claritas has taken geo-demographic analysis one step further and incorporated extensive data on product consumption and media usage patterns. They have updated their

Courtesy Central Boiler.

system based on the most recent Census data and are now able to classify down to the level of individual households. The output is a set of 66 lifestyle segments called the **PRIZM**® system (the newest version being PRIZM NE, or New Evolution). Each household in the United States can be profiled in terms of these lifestyle groups.[42]

PRIZM Social and Life Stage Groups

PRIZM organizes its 66 individual segments into broader social and lifestage groups. The broadest social groupings are based on "urbanicity." Urbanicity is determined by population density, relates to where people live and is strongly related to the lifestyles people lead. The four major social groups are:

- *Urban*—major cities with high population density.
- *Suburban*—moderately dense "suburban" areas surrounding metropolitan areas.
- *Second City*—smaller, less densely populated cities or satellites to major cities.
- *Town & Country*—low-density towns and rural communities.

The broadest life stage groups are based on age and the presence of children. As we saw in Chapter 6, these factors strongly influence consumption patterns and lifestyle. The three major life stage groups are:

- *Younger Years*—singles and couples under 45 years of age with no children.
- *Family Life*—middle aged (25–54) families with children.
- *Mature Years*—singles and couples over 45 years of age.

PRIZM gets even finer-grained detail by further dividing each social and life stage group by level of affluence, (e.g., income and wealth) since affluence is a strong demographic determinant of activities, consumption patterns and lifestyle. When possible, Claritas also merges its general PRIZM information with clients' customer databases as a way to further enhance precision.

Sample PRIZM Segments

We briefly describe eight specific segments and use them in demonstrating how PRIZM can be used in developing successful marketing strategies (for information on all 66 segments, visit www.MyBestSegments.com).

- *Young Digerati* (Urban/Younger Years—PRIZM segment 04) are young, upscale and technology savvy. They live in fashionable neighborhoods. They are highly educated professionals who are ethnically diverse including a high concentration of Asians. They live near trendy boutiques, restaurants, and bars. They shop at stores like Banana Republic, travel and scuba dive, read newspapers, and listen to online radio.
- *Blue Blood Estates* (Suburban/Family—PRIZM segment 02) are middle-aged married couples with children. They live in exclusive neighborhoods with private clubs. They are highly educated, wealthy business executives and professionals. Ethnic diversity includes a high concentration of Asians. They shop at stores like Bloomingdales. They travel extensively for business and read business magazines like *Business Week*. They also eat at fast food restaurants a lot with their kids.
- *Big Fish, Small Pond* (Town/Mature—PRIZM segment 09) are older "empty-nester" couples who are leaders in their small communities. They are affluent, typically Caucasian, college educated professionals. They shop from catalog retailers like L.L. Bean, belong to country clubs, travel, and bird watch. They are also heavy listeners of radio and read magazines like *Travel and Leisure*.
- *Pools and Patios* (Suburban/Mature—PRIZM segment 15) are evolving into older "empty-nester" couples as their children grow up and leave home. They live in older, stable neighborhoods with pools and patios in their backyards. They are college-educated, typically Caucasian, middle class managers and professionals who read the *Washington Post* and listen to classical radio. They order from QVC but will also shop Nordstrom. They travel, play the lottery, and bird watch.
- *Bohemian Mix* (Urban/Younger Years—PRIZM segment 16) are young, mobile, liberal singles. They are ethnically diverse with high concentrations of Hispanics, Asians, and African-Americans. And they are professionally diverse including students, artists and professionals with reasonably high incomes. They are early adopters who shop at stores like J. Crew, travel, play tennis and listen to online radio. They read magazines like *Maxim* and newspapers like *The New York Times*.
- *Urban Achievers* (Urban/Younger Years—PRIZM segment 31) are young singles often located in port cities. They are ethnically diverse with high concentrations of African-Americans, Asians and Hispanics as well as recent immigrants. They are college educated artists and professionals with modest incomes. They shop at stores like The Gap and eat out a lot at fast food restaurants. They go to movies, order books online, watch MTV and read magazines like *Spin* and *Vibe*.
- *Young & Rustic* (Town/Younger Years—PRIZM segment 48) are young, restless singles. They are less educated, typically Caucasian, work in low-paying blue-collar jobs, and live in tiny apartments. Despite their lower incomes, they try to live active lifestyles centered around sports, cars and dating. They eat at fast food restaurants, play

volleyball and go fishing and camping. They read magazines like S*pin, Bass Master* and *Soap Opera Weekly*.

- *Golden Ponds* (Town/Mature—PRIZM segment 55) are retired (or soon to be) singles and couples. They are less educated, work (or worked) in blue collar and farm jobs and are lower income. Many live in mobile homes or small apartments and lead sedentary lifestyles. They shop at stores like Wal-Mart, play bingo and sew. They watch a lot of daytime TV and listen to oldies radio.

Applications of PRIZM in Marketing Strategy

Marketing a Las Vegas Casino   One Las Vegas casino used PRIZM to identify its core consumers and markets and identify opportunities for future growth. They merged their own customer database with the PRIZM system in order to categorize each customer in their database into one of the 66 segments. With this data, they were able to find out which segments represented their core customers. These segments included *Young Digerati, Big Fish, Small Pond* and *Pools and Patios*. While consumers in these segments differ in various ways, they are all highly educated, affluent professionals who like to travel.

The casino also looked at which segments were least attractive for their business. These included the *Young and Rustics* and *Golden Ponds*. Given the casino's core customer, these results make sense since both of these segments are less-educated, lower-income consumers who tend to engage in sedentary activities or activities close to home.

Finally, the casino searched for attractive segments that held opportunity but were currently being underleveraged. One such segment was the *Blue Blood Estates,* which holds key similarities to the casino's core customers in terms of education, income and travel.

Having identified high-opportunity segments, the casino re-aligned and refocused its marketing efforts to specifically target those groups while also staying true to its core. By understanding their core customers, and where households that looked like their core customers existed in target markets, they were successful in attracting new and profitable customers in a cost-effective manner.

A Library Gets Hip to a Younger Crowd   Lakewood Public Library (PL) in Lakewood, Ohio, realized that a major chunk of its residents hardly ever used their library.[43] One reason for this seemed to be that the population of the city was evolving and changing in ways that Lakewood PL had not fully understood or adapted to. As Lakewood PL's manager of electronic services noted,

> Many people had a perception of Lakewood as being a city of families and senior citizens. Our experiences at the library over the past several years suggested otherwise—that it was fast becoming a city dominated by young, professional (but non-mainstream) singles.

Unfortunately, Lakewood PL didn't have a library collection that was well-suited to attract this emerging customer base. And on top of that, they didn't know enough about these consumers to make the necessary changes.

In response, Lakewood PL engaged in marketing research including PRIZM.[44] They found that two of the largest segments in Lakewood included Urban Achievers and Bohemian Mix, two young, ethnically diverse segments who were intellectually, culturally, and socially engaged. Lakewood PL felt that they could attract these consumers to their library if the content were right.

So, based on the general lifestyle and media-usage information provided by Claritas and their own expertise in library design, Lakewood PL made adjustments in content and programming to better target these groups with "a rich array of programming and diverse book and CD collections just for them." Their efforts have been quite a success, enabling Lakewood PL to draw in the younger more diverse residents now so much a part of their community.

The New Urban America: SoHo 10003   "You are where you live" (YAWYL) is a core tenant of PRIZM. And, PRIZM allows you to take a look at specific neighborhoods and get an up-close look at their distinctive composition, ethnic diversity, and lifestyle patterns. Let's take a quick tour of New York City's 10003 ZIP code, which includes or is in close proximity to chic and eclectic areas such as SoHo and the East Village and is home to the prestigious New York University. Key PRIZM segments include Bohemian Mix, Young Digerati, and Urban Achievers.

> The area indexes high as a young, tech-savvy, upwardly mobile, multicultural melting pot that most marketers of electronics, upscale clothing and imported autos often covet. Small wonder, then, that outdoor advertising here typically consists of beverage, fashion, movies and other "badge" brands looking to spark trends among nightcrawlers, show off their "coolness" factor and celebrate the diversity and independence echoing from these streets.[45]

INTERNATIONAL LIFESTYLES

The VALS and PRIZM systems presented in this chapter are oriented to the United States. In addition, VALS has systems for Japan and the United Kingdom. As we saw in Chapter 2, marketing is increasingly a global activity. If there are discernible lifestyle segments that cut across cultures, marketers can develop cross-cultural strategies around these segments. Although language and other differences would exist, individuals pursuing similar lifestyles in different cultures should be responsive to similar product features and communication themes.

Not surprisingly, a number of attempts have been made to develop such systems.[46] Large international advertising agencies and marketing research firms are leading the way. Roper Starch Worldwide, a global marketing research and consulting company, surveyed roughly 35,000 consumers across 35 countries in Asia, North and South America, and Europe.[47] Their goal was a global segmentation scheme based on core underlying values. According to one executive,

> We're looking for the bedrock values, the fundamental stable things in people's lives that determine who they are, to understand the underlying motivations that drive their attitudes as well as their behavior.[48]

Their survey uncovered six global lifestyle segments as described in Table 12-6. While these segments exist in all the countries they studied, the percentage of the population in each group varied by country. For example, Brazil had the highest proportion of Fun Seekers, a segment which Pepsi seems to be targeting in the ad shown in Illustration 12-9. Notice how the global existence of Fun Seekers allows Pepsi to have a relatively standardized approach to its advertising. Aside from language, this ad doesn't look all that different from one you might find in the United States.

Courtesy ALMAP/BBDO, São Paulo.

ILLUSTRATION 12-9

This Brazilian ad would have strong appeal to Fun Seekers.

Strivers (23 percent)—value material and professional goals and are driven by wealth, status, and power. They like computers and cell phones but have little time for media beyond newspapers. Middle aged, and skewing male, Strivers are found disproportionately (33 percent) in Asia.

Devouts (22 percent)—value duty, tradition, faith, obedience, and respect for elders. They are the least media involved and least interested in Western brands. Skewing female, Devouts are most common in developing Asia (e.g., Phillipines), Africa, and the Middle East and least common in developed Asia (e.g., Japan) and Western Europe.

Altruists (18 percent)—are interested in social issues and the welfare of society. They are well educated and older with a median age of 44. Skewing female, Altruists are most common in Latin America and Russia.

Intimates (15 percent)—value close personal relationships and family. They are heavy users of broadcast media, enjoy cooking and gardening, and are good targets for familiar consumer brands. Gender balanced, Intimates are more common in Europe and the United States (25 percent) and less common in developing Asia (7 percent).

Fun Seekers (12 percent)—value adventure, pleasure, and excitement. They are heavy users of electronic media, are fashion conscious, and like going to restaurants, bars, and clubs. Fun Seekers are the youngest, the most global in their lifestyles, roughly gender balanced, and more common in developed Asia.

Creatives (10 percent)—are interested in knowledge, education, and technology. They are the heaviest users of media, particularly books, magazines, and newspapers. They also lead the way in technology including owning a computer and surfing the net. Gender balanced, Creatives are more common in Latin America and Western Europe.

Global Lifestyle Segments, Roper Starch Worldwide.

TABLE 12-6

Global Lifestyle Segments Identified by Roper Starch Worldwide

SUMMARY

The *self-concept* is one's beliefs and feelings about one-self. There are four types of self-concept: *actual self-concept, social self-concept, private self-concept,* and *ideal self-concept.* The self-concept is important to marketers because consumers purchase and use products to express, maintain, and enhance their self-concepts.

Marketers, particularly those in international marketing, have found it useful to characterize individuals and cultures by whether they have a predominantly *independent self-concept* (the individual is the critical component) or an *interdependent self-concept* (relationships are of primary importance).

An individual's self-concept, the way one defines oneself, typically includes some of the person's possessions. The self-concept including the possessions one uses to define oneself is termed the *extended self.*

Lifestyle can be defined simply as how one lives. It is a function of one's inherent individual characteristics that have been shaped through social interaction as the person moves through his or her life cycle. It is how an individual expresses one's self-concept through actions.

Psychographics is the primary way that lifestyle is made operationally useful to marketing managers. This is a way of describing the psychological makeup or lifestyle of consumers by assessing such lifestyle dimensions as activities, interests, opinions, values, and demographics. Lifestyle measures can be macro and reflect how individuals live in general, or micro and describe their attitudes and behaviors with respect to a specific product category or activity.

The *VALS* system, developed by SRIC-BI, divides the United States into eight groups—Innovators, Thinkers, Believers, Achievers, Strivers, Experiencers, Makers, and Survivors. These groups were derived on the basis of two dimensions. The first, *primary motivation,* has three categories: *ideals* (those guided by their basic beliefs and values); *achievement* (those striving for a clear social position and influenced by others); and *self-expression* (those who seek self-expression, physical activity, variety, and excitement). The second dimension is the physical, mental, and material *resources* to pursue one's dominant motivation.

Geo-demographic analysis is based on the premise that individuals with similar lifestyles tend to live near each other. PRIZM is one system that examines demographic and consumption data down to the individual household. Based on the most recent Census data, it has developed 66 lifestyle segments organized around social groupings and life stage.

In response to the rapid expansion of international marketing, a number of attempts have been made to develop lifestyle measures applicable across cultures. Roper Starch Worldwide conducted a large multinational survey and found six global lifestyle segments based on core values.

KEY TERMS

Actual self-concept 434
Extended self 436
Geo-demographic analysis 450
Ideal self-concept 434
Independent self-concept 434

Interdependent self-concept 435
Lifestyle 441
Mere ownership effect 437
Peak experience 436
Private self-concept 434

PRIZM 451
Psychographics 442
Self-concept 434
Social self-concept 434
VALS 445

INTERNET EXERCISES

1. Visit SRIC-BI's VALS Web site (www.sric-bi.com/VALS). Complete the survey for yourself and your parents. Are you and your parents' classifications and the behaviors associated with them accurate?

2. Visit Claritas's Web site (www.claritas.com). Report on its PRIZM approach to lifestyle segmentation.

3. Visit the Lakewood Public Library Web site (www.lkwdpl.org). Has the library provided material and information on its Web site that will attract the city's Urban Achievers and Bohemian Mix segments? Explain.

DDB LIFE STYLE STUDY™ DATA ANALYSES

1. DDB measures *ideal self-concept* on various dimensions. Based on the information in Table 7A answer the following:
   a. Do any of these ideal self-concept characteristics seem to be associated with any of the *heavier user behaviors* (general, consumption, shopping)? Why do you think this is?
   b. Do any of these ideal self-concept characteristics seem to be associated with *product ownership?* Why do you think this is?
   c. Do any of these ideal self-concept characteristics seem to be associated with *television preferences?* Why do you think this is?

2. Based on the information in DDB Table 7B, identify which *ideal self-concept* characteristics are most versus least associated with the following. Explain.
   a. Enjoy shopping for items influenced by other cultures.
   b. Religion is a big part of my life.
   c. Work at trying to maintain a youthful appearance.
   d. A woman's place is in the home.
   e. I am usually among the first to try a new product.
   f. I'm an impulse buyer.
   g. In making big decisions I go with my heart rather than my head.

3. Examine the DDB data in Tables 1B through 7B. What characterizes someone who feels that (*a*) brands, (*b*) cars, or (*c*) clothing is part of his or her extended self?

REVIEW QUESTIONS

1. What is a *self-concept?* What are the four types of self-concept?
2. How do marketers use insights about the self-concept?
3. How can one measure the self-concept?
4. How does an *interdependent self-concept* differ from an *independent self-concept?*
5. What is the *extended self?*
6. What is a *peak experience?*
7. What ethical issues arise in using the self-concept in marketing?
8. What do we mean by *lifestyle?* What factors determine and influence lifestyle?

9. What is *psychographics?*
10. When is a product- or activity-specific psychographic instrument superior to a general one?
11. What are the dimensions on which VALS is based? Describe each.
12. Describe the VALS system and each segment in it.
13. What is *geo-demographic analysis?*
14. Describe the PRIZM system.
15. Describe the global lifestyle segments identified by Roper Starch Worldwide.

DISCUSSION QUESTIONS

16. Use Table 12-2 to measure your four self-concepts. To what extent are they similar? What causes the differences? To what extent do you think they influence your purchase behavior?
17. Use Table 12-2 to measure your self-concept (you choose which self-concept and justify your choice). Also measure the images of three celebrities you admire. What do you conclude?

18. Respond to the questions in Consumer Insight 12-1.
19. What possessions are part of your extended self? Why?
20. Is your self-concept predominantly independent or interdependent? Why?
21. What ethical concerns are associated with ads that portray a standardized ideal image of beauty?

22. For each of the following products, develop one ad that would appeal to a target market characterized by predominantly independent self-concepts and another ad for a target market characterized by predominantly interdependent self-concepts.
    a. Red Envelope Internet store
    b. Mini Cooper automobile
    c. Custom golf clubs
    d. Domino's pizza

23. Use the self-concept theory to develop marketing strategies for the following products:
    a. Habitat for Humanity contributions
    b. Barnesandnoble.com
    c. Army ROTC recruitment
    d. A&W root beer
    e. Swiffer WetJet
    f. Norwegian Cruiseline

24. Does VALS make sense to you? What do you like or dislike about it?

25. How would one use VALS to develop a marketing strategy?

26. Develop a marketing strategy based on VALS for
    a. J. Crew
    b. Grand Canyon Kayak vacation
    c. Sirius satellite radio
    d. Buffalo cheese
    e. Triumph motorcycles
    f. WNBA

27. Develop a marketing strategy for each of the eight VALS segments for
    a. Electric razor (for men)
    b. Vacation package
    c. DeVinci Gourmet coffee syrups
    d. HBO
    e. Facial cleansers
    f. Taco Bell

28. Does PRIZM make sense to you? What do you like or dislike about it? Is it really a measure of lifestyle?

29. How would one use PRIZM to develop a marketing strategy?

30. Develop a marketing strategy for each of the Roper Starch global lifestyle segments for the products in Question 26. What challenges do you face in trying to market these products to global market segments?

31. The following quote is from Paul Casi, president of Glenmore distilleries: "Selling cordials is a lot different from selling liquor. Cordials are like the perfume of our industry. You're really talking high fashion and you're talking generally to a different audience—I don't mean male versus female—I'm talking about lifestyle."
    a. In what ways do you think the lifestyle of cordial drinkers would differ from those who drink liquor but not cordials?
    b. How would you determine the nature of any such differences?
    c. Of what use would knowledge of such lifestyle differences be to a marketing manager introducing a new cordial?

32. How is one likely to change one's lifestyle at different stages of the household life cycle? Over one's life, is one likely to assume more than one of the VALS lifestyle profiles described?

33. To which VALS category do you belong? To which do your parents belong? Which will you belong to when you are your parents' age?

34. Based on the extreme activity lifestyles described in the chapter opening example, develop a marketing strategy for
    a. A mountain resort
    b. Wall climbing equipment
    c. In-line skates
    d. Schwinn bicycles
    e. Snowboards
    f. Video games

APPLICATION ACTIVITIES

35. Develop an instrument to measure the interdependent versus independent self-concept.

36. Use the instrument you developed in Activity 35 to measure the self-concepts of 10 male and 10 female students, all of the same nationality. What do you conclude?

37. Develop your own psychographic instrument (set of relevant questions) that measures the lifestyles of college students.

38. Using the psychographic instrument developed in Activity 37, interview 10 students (using the questionnaire instrument). On the basis of their responses, categorize them into lifestyle segments.

39. Find and copy or describe ads that would appeal to each of the eight VALS segments.

40. Find and copy or describe ads that would appeal to each of the PRIZM segments discussed in the text.

41. Repeat Activity 40 for the Roper Starch Worldwide global lifestyle segments.

42. Repeat Activity 40 for the Forrester Research Technographics segments.

REFERENCES

1. This chapter opening is based on S. Yin, "Going to Extremes," *American Demographics,* June 2001, p. 26; J. Raymond, "Going to Extremes," *American Demographics,* June 2002, pp. 28–30; "Memorex Intros CD-Rs Depicting Extreme Lifestyles," *Twice,* March 24, 2003, p. 52; W. Friedman, "NBC, Clear Channel Will Form Extreme Sports Tour," *TelevisionWeek,* November 8, 2004, p. 12; J. Blevins, "Living the X-treme Life," *Denver Post,* January 30, 2005, p. A1; and T. R. Reid, "X Games Give Aspen an Extreme Makeover," *Seattle Times,* February 1, 2005, p. A2.

2. S. Abe, R. P. Bagozzi, and P. Sadarangani, "An Investigation of Construct Validity and Generalizability of the Self-Concept," *Journal of International Consumer Marketing,* no. 3/4 (1996), pp. 97–123; and N. Y. Wong and A. C. Ahuvia, "Personal Taste and Family Face," *Psychology & Marketing,* August 1998, pp. 423–41.

3. See, e.g., E. C. Hirschman, "Men, Dogs, Guns, and Cars: The Semiotics of Rugged Individualism," *Journal of Advertising,* Spring 2003, pp. 9–22.

4. C. L. Wang and J. C. Mowen, "The Separateness-Connectedness Self-Schema," *Psychology & Marketing,* March 1997, pp. 185–207.

5. C. L. Wang et al., "Alternative Modes of Self-Construal," *Journal of Consumer Psychology* 9, no. 2 (2000), pp. 107–15.

6. See Abe, Bagozzi, and Sadarangani, "An Investigation of Construct Validity and Generalizability of the Self-Concept"; Wong and Ahuvia, "Personal Taste and Family Face"; Wang and Mowen, "The Separateness-Connectedness Self-Schema"; Wang et al., "Alternative Modes of Self-Construal"; and C. Webster and R. C. Beatty, "Nationality, Materialism, and Possession Importance," in *Advances in Consumer Research,* vol. 24, eds. M. Bruck and D. J. MacInnis (Provo, UT: Association for Consumer Research, 1997), pp. 204–10. See also, A. Reed II, "Activating the Self-Importance of Consumer Selves," *Journal of Consumer Research,* September 2004, pp. 286–95.

7. R. W. Belk, "Possessions and the Extended Self," *Journal of Consumer Research,* September 1988, pp. 139–68; and R. Belk, "Extended Self and Extending Paradigmatic Perspective," *Journal of Consumer Research,* June 1989, pp. 129–32. See also M. L. Richins, "Valuing Things" and "Special Possessions and the Expression of Material Values," both in *Journal of Consumer Research,* December 1994, pp. 504–21 and 522–31, respectively; and D. A. Laverie, R. E. Kleine III, and S. S. Kleine, "Reexamination and Extension of Kleine, Kleine, and Kernan's Social Identity Model of Mundane Consumption," *Journal of Consumer Research,* March 2002, pp. 659–69.

8. See S. S. Kleine, R. E. Kleine, III, and C. T. Allen, "How Is a Possession 'Me' or 'Not Me'?" *Journal of Consumer Research,* December 1995, pp. 327–43.

9. S. Sayre and D. Horne, "I Shop, Therefore I Am," *Advances in Consumer Research,* vol. 23, eds. K. P. Corfman and J. G. Lynch (Provo, UT: Association for Consumer Research, 1996), pp. 323–28.

10. See L. L. Love and P. S. Sheldon, "Souvenirs," *Advances in Consumer Research,* vol. 25, eds. J. W. Alba and J. W. Hutchinson (Provo, UT: Association for Consumer Research, 1998), pp. 170–74.

11. C. S. Areni, P. Kiecker, and K. M. Palan, "Is It Better to Give than to Receive?" *Psychology & Marketing,* January 1998, pp. 81–109.

12. K. J. Dodson, "Peak Experiences and Mountain Biking," *Advances in Consumer Research,* vol. 23, eds. Corfman and Lynch, pp. 317–22.

13. C. H. Noble and B. A. Walker, "Exploring the Relationships among Liminal Transitions, Symbolic Consumption, and the Extended Self," *Psychology & Marketing,* January 1997, pp. 29–47.

14. E. Sivadas and K. A. Machleit, "A Scale to Determine the Extent of Object Incorporation in the Extended Self," in *Marketing Theory and Applications,* vol. 5, eds. C. W. Park and D. C. Smith (Chicago: American Marketing Association, 1994).

15. Based on J. Watson, "Why Did You Put That There," and A. M. Velliquette, J. B. Murray, and E. H. Creyer, "The Tattoo Renaissance," both in *Advances in Consumer Research,* vol. 25, eds. Alba and Hutchinson, pp. 453–60 and 461–67, respectively; R. P. Libbon, "Why Do So Many Kids Sport Tattoos?" *American Demographics,* September 2000, p. 26; and D. Whelan, "Ink Me, Stud," *American Demographics,* December 2001, pp. 9–11.

16. S. Sen and E. J. Johnson, "Mere-Possession Effects without Possession in Consumer Choice," *Journal of Consumer Research,* June 1997, pp. 105–17; M. A. Strahilevitz and G. Loewenstein, "The Effect of Ownership History of the Valuation of Objects," *Journal of Consumer Research,* December 1998, pp. 276–89; and K. P. Nesselroade, Jr., J. K. Beggan, and S. T. Allison, "Possession Enhancement in an Interpersonal Context," *Psychology & Marketing,* January 1999, pp. 21–34.

17. S. Kang, "Nike, Serena Williams Partner Up," *The Wall Street Journal,* December 12, 2003, p. B2.

18. T. R. Graeff, "Image Congruence Effects on Product Evaluations," *Psychology & Marketing,* August 1996, pp. 481–99;

J. E. Burroughs, "Product Symbolism, Self Meaning, and Holistic Matching," *Advances in Consumer Research,* vol. 23, eds. Corfman and Lynch, pp. 463–69; R. E. Kleine and S. S. Kleine, "Consumption and Self-Schema Changes throughout the Identity Project Life Cycle," *Advances in Consumer Research,* vol. 27, eds. S. J. Hoch and R. J. Meyer (Provo, UT: Association for Consumer Research, 2000), pp. 279–85; A. Jamal and M. M. H. Goode, "Consumers and Brands," *Marketing Intelligence and Planning* 19, no. 7 (2001), pp. 482–92; A. d'Astous and M. Levesque, "A Scale for Measuring Store Personality," *Psychology & Marketing,* May 2003, pp. 455–69; and J. G. Helgeson and M. Supphellen, "A Conceptual and Measurement Comparison of Self-Congruity and Brand Personality," *International Journal of Market Research* 46, no. 2 (2004), pp. 205–33.

19. S. J. Gould, "An Interpretive Study of Purposeful, Mood Self-Regulating Consumption," *Psychology & Marketing,* July 1997, pp. 395–426.

20. See J. W. Hong and G. M. Zinkhan, "Self-Concept and Advertising Effectiveness," *Psychology & Marketing,* January 1995, pp. 53–77; A. Mehta, "Using Self-Concept to Assess Advertising Effectiveness, *Journal of Advertising Research,* January 1999, pp. 81–89; and M. J. Barone, T. A. Shimp, and D. E. Sprott, "Product Ownership as a Moderator of Self-Congruity Effects," *Marketing Letters,* February 1999, pp. 75–85.

21. E. N. Banister and M. K. Hogg, "Mapping the Negative Self," and A. M. Muniz and L. O. Hamer, "Us versus Them," both in *Advances in Consumer Research,* vol. 28, eds. M. C. Gilly and J. Meyers-Levy (Provo, UT: Association for Consumer Research, 2001), pp. 242–48 and 355–61, respectively.

22. For a broader discussion of situational factors, see T. R. Graeff, "Consumption Situations and the Effects of Brand Image on Consumers' Brand Evaluations," *Psychology & Marketing,* January 1997, pp. 49–70.

23. M. K. Hogg, A. J. Cox, and K. Keeling, "The Impact of Self-Monitoring on Image Congruence and Product/Brand Evaluation," *European Journal of Marketing* 34, no. 5/6 (2000), pp. 641–66.

24. J. Meyers-Levy and L. A. Peracchio, "Understanding the Socialized Body," *Journal of Consumer Research,* September 1995, p. 147.

25. C. S. Gulas and K. McKeage, "Extending Social Comparison," *Journal of Advertising,* Summer 2000, pp. 17–28.

26. M. J. Dutta-Bergman and W. D. Wells, "The Values and Lifestyles of Idiocentrics and Allocentrics in an Individualistic Culture," *Journal of Consumer Psychology* 12, no. 3 (2002), pp. 231–42.

27. "Sports Fans Make Surprising Choices in Beers and Wines According to Scarborough Research," Abritron Press Release (www.arbitron.com/newsroom/archive), April 24, 2002.

28. See E. H. Demby, "Psychographics Revisited," *Marketing Research,* Spring 1994, pp. 26–30.

29. See F. W. Gilbert and W. E. Warren, "Psychographic Constructs and Demographic Segments," *Psychology & Marketing,* May 1995, pp. 223–37.

30. A. L. Dolinsky et al., "The Role of Psychographic Characteristics as Determinants of Complaint Behavior by Elderly Consumers," *Journal of Hospital Marketing,* no. 2 (1998), pp. 27–51.

31. S. Todd and R. Lawson, "Lifestyle Segmentation and Museum/Gallery Visiting Behavior," *International Journal of Nonprofit and Voluntary Sector Marketing* 6, no. 3 (2001), pp. 269–77.

32. A. M. Gonzalez and L. Bello, "The Construct 'Lifestyle' in Market Segmentation," *European Journal of Marketing* 36, no. 1/2 (2002), pp. 51–85.

33. D. J. Lipke, "You Are What You Eat," *American Demographics,* October 2000, pp. 42–46.

34. Based on A. Taylor, III, "Porsche Slices Up Its Buyers," *Fortune,* January 16, 1995, p. 24.

35. Based on M. J. Arnold and K. E. Reynolds, "Hedonic Shopping Motivations," *Journal of Retailing* 79 (2003), pp. 77–95.

36. See M. J. Weiss, "Online America," *American Demographics,* March 2001, pp. 53–60.

37. Based on a Forrester Research report by J. Kolko, "Why Technographics *Still* Works," December 14, 2004. Used by permission of Forrester Research.

38. For a critical review and alternative approach, see D. B. Holt, "Poststructuralist Lifestyle Analysis," *Journal of Consumer Research,* March 1997, pp. 326–50. Alternative lifestyle systems are also described in C. Walker and E. Moses, "The Age of Self-Navigation," *American Demographics,* September 1996, pp. 36–42; and P. H. Ray, "The Emerging Culture," *American Demographics,* February 1997, pp. 29–56.

39. Based on material provided by SRI Consulting Business Intelligence.

40. *How to Use PRIZM* (Claritas Inc., 1986), p. 1.

41. See S. Mitchell, "Birds of a Feather," *American Demographics,* February 1995, pp. 40–48.

42. Based on materials provided by Claritas. Source: Claritas, Inc.

43. Based on E. St. Lifer, "Tapping into the Zen of Marketing," *Library Journal,* May 1, 2001, pp. 44–46.

44. This research was done prior to the most recent PRIZM NE system. However, the main thrust of this example is still germane.

45. B. Ebenkamp, "Urban America, Redefined," *Brandweek,* October 6, 2003, pp. 12–13.

46. For example, see M. T. Ewing, "Affluent Asia," *Journal of International Consumer Marketing* 12, no. 2 (1999), pp. 25–37.

47. This material, including information in Table 12-6, is based on S. Elliott, "Research Finds Consumers Worldwide Belong to Six Basic Groups That Cross National Lines," *The New York Times,* June 25, 1998, p. D8; and T. Miller, "Global Segments from 'Strivers' to 'Creatives,'" *Marketing News,* July 20, 1998, p. 11.

48. Elliott, "Research Finds Consumers Worldwide Belong to Six Basic Groups That Cross National Lines."

Cases

CASE 3-1   K9-Quencher Sport Drink for Dogs?

The market for pet supplies and products is large and expected to grow rapidly over the next several years. By 2007 it is expected to be a $11.1 billion market, up from $7.5 billion in 2002. Pet owners, it seems, are a very interesting and committed group of folks. Increasingly, pet owners are "humanizing" their pets, with 92 percent considering their pets to be another member of the family. According to survey results from The American Animal Hospital Association, of pet owners surveyed, 63 percent tell their pets they love them at least once a day, 59 percent celebrate their pet's birthday, and 66 percent prepare special foods for their pet!

In addition to perceptions and attitudes, there are also distinctive demographics for pet owners. Table A contains demographic data relevant to the ownership of dogs and cats and the purchase of products for them.

While brands such as Purina and Hartz are major players in the mass market for pet supplies and products, numerous smaller brands exist which fill various niches in the market. One such company is K9-Quencher, which sells flavored sports drinks for dogs through its online store and through specialty stores located around the country. K9-Quencher is a flavored powder that contains nutrients and electrolytes, much like human sports drinks. According to their Web site,

> K9-Quencher is a Sport Drink for dogs. It is a healthy, completely safe, veterinarian recommended drink. You'll find information about why you should give your dog K9-Quencher, testimonials from Veterinarians and other professionals, tips on numerous health issues related to your best friend, and links to stores that sell it. K9-Quencher is vital for many essential body functions. Just add it to the water bowl!

K9-Quencher comes in three flavors (Electryc Ice Cream, Smokin' Hot Dog, and Lickin' Chickin') and a 15-unit (1 unit per bowl of water) variety pack currently sells for $15.

Discussion Questions

1. Visit K9-Quencher's Web site (www.k9-quencher.com). What types of attitude change strategies are they utilizing? Do you think they are effective?

2. What learning approach and principles would you use to teach consumers about K9-Quenchers? Is this reflected in the company's Web site?

3. Develop a psychographic profile relating to the type of person who would be most likely to purchase K9-Quenchers. That is, generate a list of attitudes, values, activities, and interests that are specifically related to having a dog that K9-Quencher buyers would likely possess.

4. Based on the demographic data in Table A, what would be the best target(s) market for K9-Quenchers?

5. Develop an ad or marketing approach to create a positive attitude toward K9-Quenchers, focusing on the following components:
   a. Cognitive
   b. Affective
   c. Behavioral

6. Develop an ad or marketing approach to create a positive attitude toward K9-Quenchers, using the following:
   a. Humor
   b. Emotion
   c. Utilitarian appeal
   d. Value-expressive appeal
   e. Celebrity endorser
   f. Self-concept
   g. Fear

7. What sorts of products, if any, could K9-Quencher develop for cats? What type of branding strategy would you suggest if they made such a move?

Source: J. Fetto, "'Woof, Woof' Means, 'I Love You,'" *American Demographics,* February 2002, p. 11; R. Gardyn, "Animal Magnetism," *American Demographics,* May 2002, pp. 30–37; *The U.S. Market for Pet Supplies and Pet Care Products* (New York: Packaged Facts, June 2003); and information from K9-Quencher's Web site at www.k9-quencher.com, accessed August 5, 2005.

TABLE A

Demographics and
Pet Ownership

	Cat Owners	Cat Treats	Dog Owners	Dog Treats
Percent of adults	22%	10%	30%	22%
Age				
18–24 years	93	111	63	62
25–34	103	102	111	105
35–44	119	111	124	122
45–54	125	126	127	124
55–64	99	94	93	104
>64	52	57	54	59
Education				
College graduate	117	116	118	119
Some college	114	109	115	119
High school graduate	99	104	95	94
No degree	59	55	64	59
Occupation				
Professional	123	119	123	121
Managerial/administrative	123	135	121	121
Technical/clerical/sales	120	115	118	119
Precision/craft	117	105	129	128
Race/Ethnic group				
White	114	112	110	112
Black	20	26	43	36
Spanish speaking	80	75	76	79
Region				
Northeast	98	139	79	89
North Central	100	98	110	110
South	91	78	100	95
West	119	105	109	107
Household income				
<$10,000	67	75	56	63
$10,000–19,999	65	81	54	49
$20,000–29,999	87	86	76	76
$30,000–39,999	93	88	102	99
$40,000–49,999	104	85	116	111
$50,000–59,999	126	118	123	122
$60,000–74,999	121	125	133	124
$75,000+	128	129	133	142
Household structure				
Single	93	107	70	74
Married	113	107	119	118
Child <2	87	62	94	82
Child 2–5	90	64	93	73
Child 6–11	103	100	114	104
Child 12–17	128	125	134	127

Note: 100 = Average use or consumption unless a percent is indicated. Base = female homemakers.
Source: Spring 2000 Mediamark Research Inc.

CASE 3-2   Levi's Signature Stretch

Levi's sales in 1996 were $7.1 billion. In 2001, sales had declined dramatically to $4.25 billion. While the major slide appears to have halted, sales in 2003 were down again to $4.09 billion. Market share is also telling. Levi's U.S. jeans market share has dropped by a third from 18.7 percent to 12.1 percent in the past five years. Many teenagers and tweens view Levi's jeans as being for middle-aged consumers. One 19-year-old consumer said, "They're too plain. There's just not enough style to them."

TABLE A

Levi's Jean Lines

Line	Price/Range	Retail Outlets
LeviStrauss Signature		
Authentic	$20–23	Wal-Mart, Kmart, Target
Premium	$24.99	Kmart
Levi's		
Red Tab	$30–40	JC Penney, Kohls
Silver Tab	$42–51	JC Penney, Foleys
Premium	$110	Nordstrom, Urban Outfitters

How did this happen? Super success in the 1980s led to complacency and a lack of focus on evolving customer needs. Levi's created women's jeans from men's patterns, resulting in a poor fit. It treated teenage girls and women as one segment, producing jeans too tight for many moms and too high-waisted for the teens. It ignored emerging style competitors such as Calvin Klein, Old Navy, Seven, and Blue Asphalt.

Various efforts have been made by Levi's to stave off the decline and launch a comeback including new advertising and new product designs to bolster its image and relevance particularly among younger buyers. Their "Dangerously Low" campaign is one example.

Levi has also worked on distribution. For example, they tried to get into specialty chains, which are more popular with younger consumers, but met with resistance. Some chain buyers don't think the brand passes the "cool test." The VP of marketing for Wet Seal, Inc., said the chain will not carry Levi's because "it's not on the radar screen of young women now." One bright spot was their push into upscale chains such as Neiman Marcus, Saks Fifth Avenue, and Bloomingdale's. According to a buyer from Neiman Marcus, "Many customers want an all-American jean and Levi's is a name associated with that."

Currently the brightest area for Levi's is their new Signature (called LeviStrauss Signature) line, a lower-priced jean that sells through discount retailers like Kmart, Target, and ShopKo. The Signature line was introduced in 2003 and leverages the fact that 30 percent of all jeans are sold through discounter retailers. The Signature line has seen double digit growth since its introduction and now accounts for about 8 percent of Levi's sales. In what Levi's calls a "mass-tige" strategy of bringing their fashion and the unique authentic Levi's cache to more people, this latest move takes their jeans "down market." To get a sense of the possible implications of this move, consider the Levi jeans lines, price points, and retail outlets shown in Table A.

Note that all the products and product lines prominently carry the Levi's brand name. Note also that the Premium line is a relatively new part of the signature line-up currently targeting the "juniors" part of the female audience with jeans designed to have the most "fashion forward" fabrics, colors, and styles. Special embroidering details set the Premium line apart as the top end of their Signature lineup.

Critics argue that the Signature line will cannibalize sales, particularly from its Red Tab line. They also argue that going discount means an even bigger hit on their image. For example, the reaction of the Wet Seal marketing VP was "The brand's not cool when you're at Target for detergent and you see a rack of Levi's."

Levi's remains positive. As one executive noted, "People are predisposed to the brand. So, if we get the product right, they'll buy." Consider another comment by a Levi's executive when asked if the Signature line hurts their credibility in the premium market:

That's [the premium market] such a different customer. Very few brands have the elasticity that we have, but we have it, so we should use it. It is the heritage of our company. That's what makes it so strong and why people of all socio-economic levels want a pair of Levi's. We have the original patent on five-pocket jeans. The other brands are just copying us.

Discussion Questions

1. Do you think that Levi's was correct to keep the Levi Strauss name on its Signature line? Or, would they have been better off creating a completely new brand name? Present both sides of the case. Take and justify a position.

2. What do you think Levi's image is among the following? What are the marketing implications of your response?
   a. Tween girls (aged 10 to 12)
   b. Tween boys (aged 10 to 12)
   c. Teenage girls
   d. Teenage boys
   e. Women aged 21 to 35
   f. Men aged 21 to 35
   g. Women aged 36 to 55
   h. Men aged 36 to 55

3. Do you believe that the Levi's brand is as "elastic" as Levi's executives believe it is? Or, have they "overstretched" the name with the Signature line?

4. Develop the "brand schema" that you think existed for the overall Levi's brand *before* and *after* the introduction of the Signature line (i.e., an associative network map of links and nodes). What are the marketing implications of the differences?

5. Do you think there is a core image of Levi's that can survive across the wide range of prices and outlets that it operates in? What is it?

6. Should Levi's consider a special brand for the specialty chains that cater to younger, hip consumers?

7. How can Levi's use each of the following to enhance its brand image?
   a. Emotion
   b. Humor
   c. Maslow's needs
   d. McGuire's needs
   e. Brand personality
   f. Self-concept

8. How should Levi's market to teen consumers in each of the following ethnic groups?
   a. African American
   b. Arab American
   c. Asian American
   d. Asian-Indian American
   e. Native American
   f. White

Source: A. Z. Cuneo, "Ailing Levi Strauss Refits U.S. Strategy," *Advertising Age,* July 15, 2002, p. 12; L. Lee, "Why Levi's Still Looks Faded," *Business-Week,* July 22, 2002, p. 54; G. Anderson, "Target Puts Signature on Levi's Deal," *retailwire* (online), January 16, 2004; "Levi Strauss & Co. Announces Fiscal Year 2003 Financial Results" (Levi Strauss & Co., financial news release, March 1, 2004); "Levi's Dangerous Jean Therapy," *BusinessWeek,* August 8, 2005, p. 10; "Levi Strauss Seeing Green with Signature Blues," *BrandWeek,* July 25, 2005, p. 12; "Making Strides at Levi's," *BusinessWeek Online,* July 28, 2005; and information from Levi Strauss & Co.'s Web site at www.levi.com.

CASE 3-3   Marketing the California Avocado

In 1999, Integrated Marketing Works and the California Avocado Commission conducted a set of minifocus groups (five to seven participants) in an ongoing research program designed to increase their understanding of the consumption of avocados in general and California avocados in particular. This set of interviews focused on light to moderate users in geographic regions with heavy consumption (three in California and three in Colorado) and on nonusers in the light-use areas (three with nonusers and one with light/moderate users in Atlanta). All of the groups were composed of 35- to 49-year-old females who were the primary grocery shoppers for their households. On the basis of these and previous research studies, users and nonusers are described as follows.

Users derive pleasure both from the taste of avocados and from the emotional and usage situations associated with avocado consumption. The following represents the agency's view of how avocados trigger emotional or sensual responses in consumers:

Physical Avocado	Emotional
Flavor/texture	Delicious, creamy, pizzazz, special
Green	Natural, good for me, friendly
Implied occasions	Festive, feeling good, fun, up-beat, carefree, happy
Implied usage	Pizzazz, healthy, satisfying, delicious
Unique	Special, different, fun
California "aspirational"	Healthy, natural, fun, outdoors, active, feeling good

Barriers to the consumption of avocados by users are price, the fat content, and the view that they are only for special occasions.

Nonusers are actually nonretail purchasers. Many of them have had avocados in restaurants, and many are attached to the avocados. Thus, they have some of the same emotional responses to avocados as do users. They also feel the same barriers. However, in addition, they are unsure of how to purchase one (how do you select a ripe one for use today or one that will ripen for use in three or four days?) and how to peel and use them in recipes.

Until recently, California avocados have had virtually no direct competition except in the Northeast, where avocados from Mexico have been imported, and in the South where Florida avocados are available. However, with the ongoing removal of trade barriers, it is likely that competition will spread throughout the country and will involve additional countries. Therefore, the California Avocado Commission wants to develop a strong brand image and brand equity for its product. In addition, avocados compete for share of stomach with 240 other items in a typical produce department.

In light of the research and the changing competitive situation, two campaigns were prepared—one targeting light/moderate users in core market areas and one targeting nonusers in light-usage areas. A description of each campaign and wording for one of the commercials for each follow. Table A contains demographic data relevant to avocado consumption.

Core Market Campaign

Objective   Convince current users to buy California avocados more often.

Target Market   The target market is moderate to light users, women, 25 to 54, middle and upper income, families and single households. These individuals are always on the go. They are rushed in shopping and have little time for elaborate food preparation. They like the produce department and feel good about incorporating fresh and natural foods into their diets. They have rich feelings about avocados. Beyond the physical experience of eating the avocado, there is a rich experiential association that stems from usage—happy, fun festive, outdoors, natural, upbeat, satisfying, delicious, creamy, special, feeling good, carefree.

The Campaign   It will leverage attachment to the product through the physical and emotional attributes to inspire cravings for California avocados that will cause consumers to eat them more often. It will emphasize the California origin, where the best produce comes from. This will also provide an image of nat-

ural, fresh, healthy, and tasty. The unique taste will be emphasized. The tone will be evocative, natural, fun. After seeing the ad, consumers should think, "I love California avocados and I need to satisfy my cravings for them more often."

Radio Ad Copy

SOUND EFFECTS: Music under, throughout.

ANNOUNCER: In a world where love and good taste are misunderstood . . .

MAN: To hide your love is . . . not . . . good.

ANNOUNCER: In a house where love is hard to find . . .

ANNOUNCER: In a kitchen where one woman can love despite looks . . .

WOMAN: Oh avocado, dark and slightly soft when ripe. You may have bumpy skin . . . but I . . . I love you!

ANNOUNCER: In a mouth that craves great taste, there is, the Genuine California Avocado.

WOMAN: Did you ever think a burger could be like this?

MAN: (Mouth full) Hang on . . . (chewing swallows) . . . there . . . what was your question, Love?

ANNOUNCER: The Genuine California Avocado (fast, like legal disclosure). Opening in markets everywhere today. This fruit is not yet rated.

Underdeveloped Market Campaign

Objective   Convince nonpurchasers of California Avocados to buy them at retail supermarkets.

Target Market   Basically the same as for the core market. The difference is that avocados are not part of their consideration set when shopping. Since displays for avocados in these regions tend to be small, these consumers may remain unaware of them at retail. While many of them may have had and enjoyed avocados as part of a dish or salad at a restaurant, they may not be aware of its physical appearance and may not recognize it at retail.

The Campaign   It is important to differentiate the California avocado from the Florida one (there are

TABLE A

Demographics and Avocado Consumption

	Avocados	Bananas	Apples	Kiwis
Percent of adults*	15%	72%	69%	17%
Age				
18–24 years	82	86	89	115
25–34	100	95	94	92
35–44	109	100	106	111
45–54	108	105	104	117
55–64	119	104	102	98
>64	77	105	98	74
Education				
College graduate	136	106	108	130
Some college	114	101	103	115
High school graduate	72	100	97	88
No degree	88	91	92	63
Occupation				
Professional	135	109	109	150
Managerial/administrative	122	101	102	113
Technical/clerical/sales	90	99	102	96
Precision/craft	113	102	97	104
Race/Ethnic group				
White	105	104	102	101
Black	48	76	84	84
Spanish speaking	185	93	97	100
Region				
Northeast	57	99	101	96
North Central	52	106	104	111
South	79	93	93	89
West	235	105	106	111
Household income				
<$10,000	69	87	88	73
$10,000–19,999	75	91	88	71
$20,000–29,999	81	97	96	80
$30,000–39,999	101	102	101	100
$40,000–49,999	105	103	99	106
$50,000–59,999	97	102	106	113
$60,000–74,999	107	102	109	112
$75,000+	137	110	109	131
Household structure				
Single	101	86	89	96
Married	106	105	105	109
Any child in HH	102	99	103	113

Note: 100 = Average use or consumption unless a percent is indicated. Base = female homemakers.
*Purchased in the past 30 days.
Source: Spring 2000 Mediamark Research Inc.

noticeable physical differences) in order to avoid building sales for the competition. The campaign will focus on "I know I like California Avocados (guacamole) and now it's easy to enjoy them at home." Why? They aren't hard to pick, purchase, or use, and they have a taste unlike anything else. The tone will be fun, sophisticated, and natural. After seeing the ad, people should think, "I've never considered buying a California Avocado before. I know I like them and they're much easier to use than I previously thought. I should buy one next time I'm at the supermarket."

Radio Ad Copy

NARRATOR: It has come to my attention that, due to not knowing exactly what they are, some people out there are using Genuine California Avocados for things other than what they are intended. I have been instructed to tell you that

California Avocados are NOT for use as fishing line weights.

SOUND EFFECTS: Buzzer.

NARRATOR: A drain plug.

SOUND EFFECTS: Buzzer.

NARRATOR: A doggie chew-toy.

SOUND EFFECTS: Buzzer.

NARRATOR: A dish scrubber.

SOUND EFFECTS: Buzzer.

NARRATOR: A go-kart wheel.

SOUND EFFECTS: Buzzer.

NARRATOR: Or a videotape machine head-cleaner.

SOUND EFFECTS: Buzzer.

NARRATOR: California Avocados ARE intended for use in guacamole.

SOUND EFFECTS: Ding.

NARRATOR: Sliced on a sandwich.

SOUND EFFECTS: Ding.

NARRATOR: Or chopped up in salad, and other delicious uses.

SOUND EFFECTS: Ding.

NARRATOR: So whatever you do, when you see a California Avocado, think, "Man, I'm really in the mood for a Turkey Avocado Sandwich."

SOUND EFFECTS: Ding.

NARRATOR: Not, "Say, that thing is just about the same size as the hole in my heating duct?"

SOUND EFFECTS: Ding.

ANNOUNCER: This has been a word from Genuine California Avocados.

Discussion Questions

1. Evaluate these ads in terms of their ability to capture attention. How will they be interpreted?

2. How can nonusers be taught the proper way to select avocados at retail?

3. In light of increasing competition, for what product position should California Avocados strive?

4. What role does emotion play in the consumption of avocados?

5. Is there any motivational conflict in avocado consumption? If so, what should the California Avocado Commission do about it?

6. Evaluate the attitude change strategy being used.

7. Evaluate the use of humor in these ads. Propose and defend two other approaches.

8. Develop a lifestyle-based television ad to increase avocado consumption.

9. What insights, if any, are provided by the demographic data?

10. Develop a marketing campaign to increase avocado use among nonusers.

11. Visit the California Avocado Commission Web site (www.avocado.org). Evaluate its effectiveness in promoting the consumption of avocados. What behavioral principles and assumptions does it rely on?

Source: Based on materials supplied by Integrated Marketing Works. Used with permission.

CASE 3-4   Dairy Queen Sells Irradiated Burgers

Food irradiation was developed in the 1950s. It involves exposing food to ionizing energy such as gamma rays that kill all bacteria, parasites, mold, and fungus in or on agricultural products, including red meat, poultry, fresh fruits, vegetables, herbs, and spices. The U.S. Food and Drug Administration (FDA) began approving irradiation applications in 1963. By 2000, most foods could be treated with irradiation, but they had to carry a prominent "Radura" symbol (a stylized flower) along with the phrase "treated with irradiation." This scared many consumers, and few retailers carried irradiated meats.

While it sounds exotic, irradiation is similar to X-rays. As the dean of the Yale University School of Medicine and former FDA commissioner stated, "The process of irradiating food does not make food radioactive. Food that is being irradiated never comes in direct contact with radioactive material and the gamma rays or X-rays or electrons used do not have the potential to make the food radioactive."

Forbes magazine ran an article in 1999 entitled "These People Didn't Have to Die." The article described how nine adult deaths and three stillborn births were caused by tainted hot dogs sold by Sara Lee Corp. In addition to the immeasurable grief caused by the deaths, Sara Lee faced a $60 million product recall. According to the article, people have been eating irradiated fruit, vegetables, and spices for years (although other sources indicate that irradiated foods rarely appear in American supermarkets), but the pork and chicken industry still make virtually no use of it and it was not allowed on red meats until 2000. The article quotes a university scientist as saying, "It [irradiation] could have prevented this outbreak. These people didn't need to die." Although irradiation of meat products has been on the rise over the past several years in the United States, its use is still relatively low. For example, it has been estimated that less than 5 percent of the ground beef sold in the United States each year is irradiated.

Irradiation has been widely used as a food safety measure in Europe for years. Groups such as the World Health Organization and the American Medical Association endorse its use. However, it has yet to catch on in the United States. As the CEO of ConAgra stated, "ConAgra stands ready to use irradiation technology once public acceptance of irradiation becomes stronger." The primary reason that is advanced for the lack of public acceptance is a phobia about radiation and the absence of a coordinated industry effort to address this concern.

Others suggest that the public is largely indifferent but that a vocal, if small, opposition has prevented widespread acceptance. According to the *Forbes* article,

A group called Food & Water, Inc., has instilled in a fair number of consumers a visceral fear of the process, as if eating irradiated meat were the equivalent of swallowing radium capsules. Hoping to stop technology in the supermarket if they can't stop it in Washington, D.C., the irradiation opponents have run fear-mongering ad campaigns. Irradiation-bashers also say the meat should carry warning labels suggestive of what you see on hazardous materials cargo.

Despite the efforts of opponents and the lack of aggressive industry promotion, recent surveys show fairly high level of public acceptance of irradiated foods. Among the findings,

- 48 percent favor the use of irradiation to increase the safety of foods such as meat, poultry, and fish; 26 percent oppose it and 26 percent are undecided.
- Shoppers who have confidence in the safety of nationally branded products are much more favorably inclined toward irradiation than are those who doubt the safety of these brands.
- Males and frequent users of microwaves are particularly supportive of irradiation.

Another survey found that 31 percent would certainly try and 41 percent would probably try irradiated meat if it were available even if it cost more than regular meat.

One thing the food industry does agree on: Greater acceptance will require changing the name of the process from *irradiation*. As one industry spokesperson stated, "This is a word that has 'radiation' in it, and for many people, that raises [concerns]." In late 1999, at industry's urging, the FDA began consideration of changing the required use of the Radura symbol and the "treated with irradiation" label to alternatives such as "cold pasteurized" and "electronic pasteurization." In May 2002, legislation was passed and signed into law that allowed irradiated foods to be labeled as pasteurized. However, many consumers appear to find the term and concept *irradiated* much more acceptable when applied to meat than *pasteurized*. As one consumer stated, "Pasteurized steak, yuk."

Dairy Queen (DQ) did not wait for the new law to take effect. Early in 2002, it began a trial in one outlet in Minnesota which has subsequently expanded to dozens more, including a recent expansion to New Mexico. DQ ran internal tests to be certain its employees could not tell the difference between burgers made with regular meat versus irradiated meat. When they could not, the test with consumers began.

The test outlets use menu board messages, tray liners, posters, crew uniform stickers, and numerous other means to let consumers know they are being served irradiated meat and the advantages this has.

Discussion Questions

1. How will consumers respond to the irradiated meat in the Dairy Queen test?

2. What type of innovation is irradiated meat? Conduct a diffusion analysis on irradiated meat, using Table 7-3 as a guide.

3. What meaning will the new label *pasteurized* convey to the average consumer? How would you determine if this is misleading?

4. How will consumers respond to *pasteurized* steak? Is this a better term than *irradiated* steak, or *protected by irradiation?*

5. What product position should the industry try to obtain for irradiated foods?

6. How could the industry teach consumers about the benefits of irradiated foods?

7. How could the industry change the attitudes of those consumers opposed to irradiated foods?

8. How could the Food & Water, Inc., organization change the attitudes of those in favor of irradiated foods?

Source: L. Rothstein, "An Idea Whose Time Has Come—and Gone," *Bulletin of the Atomic Scientists,* July 1998, pp. 7–11; L. Freeman, " 'Irradiation' Designation May Finally Become a Sales Pitch," *Marketing News,* September 14, 1998, p. 1; M. Conlin, "These People Didn't Have to Die," *Forbes,* February 8, 1999, p. 54; A. Allen, "Ready for Irradiation," *Food Processing,* August 1999, p. 68; "Radiation Scandal," *The Ecologist,* August 1999, p. 304; "Most Await Irradiated Meat," *The Shopper Report,* April 2000, p. 1; A. J. Liddle, "DQ Field Tests Irradiated Burgers," *Nation's Restaurant News,* May 5, 2002, p. 1; *The Truth About Irradiated Meat* (Yonkers, NY: Consumer Reports, August 2003), accessed at www.consumerreports.org; and *Dairy Queen Announces Expansion of Irradiated Beef Test to New Mexico Locations* (Dairy Queen: press release, September 22, 2003).

CASE 3-5   The Psychographics of Luxury Shoppers

Marketers are always trying to fine-tune their segmentation strategies. For example, retailers may find that income is a necessary, but not sufficient, indicator of luxury spending or shopping patterns. To illustrate, Simmons Market Research recently conducted a psychographic analysis relating to luxury buying and shopping. Their analysis examined middle-class and affluent single women who were heads of their households. Their analysis also took into account demographics and life-stage factors. They identified five unique segments.

Consumer Description	Savvy Career Women	Upscale Mature Women	Educated Working Women, No Kids	Single Working Moms	Active Grandmas
Median age	41	60	33	39	61
Median income	$166,425	$69,605	$49,789	$48,916	$35,431
I am very happy with my life as it is	94	103	87	92	95
I enjoy entertaining people at home	108	112	92	98	103
It is worth paying extra for quality goods	115	127	76	75	79
Home décor is a particular interest	131	139	103	123	123
I can't resist expensive perfume/cologne	172	*	151	218	*
I like other people to think I'm rich	116	98	91	97	83
I tend to spend money without thinking	143	81	121	132	102
Most everything I wear is the highest quality	150	121	86	124	101
I spend more than I can afford for clothes	201	*	164	136	127
I plan far ahead to buy expensive items	93	95	109	100	97
Price isn't most important—what's important is getting what I want	120	108	84	101	103
Options on a car impress me	111	75	84	121	71
I prefer driving a luxury car	106	95	59	83	70
I try to keep up with changes in style/fashion	152	101	114	125	111

Note: Except for age and income (where numbers are years and dollars, respectively), 100 is national average for adults. A 94 indicates group was 6 percent less likely than average adult to agree with statement.

*Sample size too small.

Source: Reprinted with permission from the November 2002 issue of *American Demographics.* Copyright Crain Communications, Inc. 2004.

Discussion Questions

1. For which segment(s) do you feel that products are most likely to become part of the extended self? What are the marketing implications of this?

2. Which segments appear to be more motivated by functional concerns versus those motivated by the need to keep up with the latest styles and trends? What are the marketing implications of this?

3. Can you explain why Savvy Career Women place great emphasis on clothing and fashion,

while luxury automobiles really aren't that important?

4. Choose two segments which you feel would be viable but different markets for spas. Develop a marketing plan for each segment, to include core positioning statement, media venues, key product/service features, and promotional materials.

Source: See R. Gardyn, "Oh, The Good Life," *American Demographics*, November 2002, p. 33; and J. D. Zbar, "Tony Travelers Seek out Quality," *Advertising Age*, September 13, 2004, pp. 5–6.

CASE 3-6   Revlon for Men?

Males have three reasons for trying to look good (which, in American society, also implies looking young). First, one's career may be enhanced by looking good, which includes being attractive, fit appearing, and energetic (young). One businesswoman stated,

> Any guy who goes into consulting has to be attractive. It struck me one day: Every time I met a good-looking guy and asked him "So, little boy, what do you do?" he was a consultant. The ugly ones are all accountants.

A second reason for men's concern about looks is to be attractive to women. Many middle-aged men who go through divorce engage in a wide variety of "beauty" enhancement activities. Most women no longer need to rely on men for financial support, which allows them to focus more on the physical and personal characteristics of potential partners.

A final reason is a combination of ego and competitiveness. If looks matter, then competitive men will compete to look good. Knowing that one looks good or receiving compliments or "admiring glances" is also gratifying to a person's ego.

In 2003, the men's grooming market was approximately $7.7 billion, up from $3.3 billion in 1995. The market can be broken out as follows (figures below in

millions of dollars):

Fragrances	$1,935
Shaving	3,560
Deodorant	1,470
Hair care	541
Skin care	154
Bath and shower	77

Source: Based on information from *The U.S. Market for Men's Grooming Products* (New York: Packaged Facts, January 2004), pp. 51 and 62.

As you can see, the skin care market remains a relatively small part of the overall men's grooming marketing. And growth in the skin care market has been a sound but not overwhelming 7 percent a year since 1995. In the spring of 2000, men were using the following facial care products (see Table A for details):

Complexion care (all)	25.0%
Cleansers	10.5
Lotion	5.6
Cream	5.3
Scrub	3.6
Mask	2.5
Toner	2.5

Research and observation have led those in the industry to reach several conclusions. One is that men are willing to buy and experiment with all kinds and types of new fragrances and colognes, but they almost uniformly do not want anything that smells too strong or in any way draws attention to themselves. According to one expert, the challenge is

> How to entice more men to smell good, put gooey things in their hair, and oily lotions on their faces without feeling somehow unmanly?

Despite such challenges, numerous firms are entering with a variety of beauty-enhancing products that are generally positioned as skin care products. Nivea's product line and approach are described in the opening vignette for Chapter 14. There are numerous small niche marketers serving this market through online sales (use a search engine for "men's skin care products"). Some of the major participants in this emerging market are described below.

- *Clinique* promotes a three-step skin care process for men featuring Clinique Facial Soap, Clinique Scruffing Lotion (a facial cleanser), and Clinque M Lotion (a moisturizing lotion). It also offers a complete line of shaving-related products, including Cream Shave and M Shave Aloe Gel (shaving gels), Face Scrub (a facial cleaner), Post-Shave Healer, Happy for Men After Shave Balm, and Turnaround Lotion. In addition, it markets Eye Treatment Formula, Surge Extra Oil-Free Gel (a moisturizer), Non-Streak Bronzer, and deodorants.
- *Mënaji* focuses exclusively on men's cosmetic products. Its slogan is "Men don't wear makeup, they use Mënaji." Its products include the following. CAMO Concealer, in four shades, is designed to hide dark circles, age spots, and razor burn. 911 Eye Jell reduces puffiness or darkness around the eye area in about 30 minutes. Glycolic Skin Toner reduces the appearance of fine lines and wrinkles. Mënaji Mask is used once a week to thoroughly deep clean one's face. H.D.P.V. Dual Active Powder is used to eliminate oily shine without looking like pancake makeup. Mënaji Polishing Scrub is designed to be used twice a week to deep clean one's face.
- *Neutrogena Men* offers nine products for men, several of which are versions of traditional shaving products: Skin Clearing Face Bar, Skin Clearing Face Wash, Razor Defense Daily Face Scrub, Skin Clearing Shave Cream, Razor Defense Shave Gel, Skin Clearing Astringent After Shave, Skin Clearing Targeted Acne Treatment, and Razor Defense Daily Face Lotion.

Table A contains material related to the use of beauty items by men.

Discussion Questions

1. Develop a marketing strategy for Revlon to enter the men's cosmetics market with a complete product line.
2. Evaluate Clinique's men's product line and branding strategy. Suggest changes where appropriate.
3. Visit one of the Web sites listed below. Is it effective at promoting its products to men? What behavior principles and assumptions does it rely on?
   a. Clinique (www.clinique.com)
   b. Neutrogena (www.neutrogena.com)
   c. Mënaji (www.menaji.com)
   d. Gillette Complete (www.gillettecomplete.com)
4. If Revlon were to enter the men's cosmetics market, what branding strategy should it use?
5. How, if at all, could Revlon use the following as the basis for its appeal for a men's cosmetic line?
   a. Personality
   b. Emotion
   c. Self-concept
6. What motives should Clinique appeal to in promoting its men's line?
7. Persuading many men to use skin care products will require a significant attitude change. Which attitude change techniques would be most appropriate? Which would be least appropriate?
8. Design an ad for a line of men's skin care products by Revlon. Explain how it will work at each stage of the perception process.
9. What learning theories would you use to teach your target market to take proper care of their skin?
10. Which of the following would be the best target market?
    a. Demographic groups
    b. Occupational categories

TABLE A

Demographics and
Male Cosmetic Use

	Hair Coloring Products	Complexion Care Products	Cleansers	Lotion	Cream
Percent of males	9.8%	25%	10.5%	5.6%	5.3%
Age					
18–24 years	115	140	179	150	172
25–34	96	105	121	87	110
35–44	107	98	89	94	94
45–54	109	91	85	88	64
55–64	86	68	57	71	65
>64	79	95	66	120	100
Education					
College graduate	78	85	88	89	80
Some college	93	100	100	90	103
High school graduate	109	104	105	99	105
No degree	123	113	107	130	114
Occupation					
Professional	98	96	102	96	90
Managerial/administrative	76	90	94	102	105
Technical/clerical/sales	108	102	117	92	100
Precision/craft	105	98	107	93	91
Race/Ethnic group					
White	90	94	92	90	92
Black	170	140	149	160	141
Spanish speaking	108	111	114	116	149
Region					
Northeast	81	88	80	63	63
North Central	82	92	80	76	81
South	119	113	128	127	117
West	104	98	94	114	126
Household income					
<$10,000	SS	117	SS	SS	SS
$10,000–19,999	118	111	117	SS	SS
$20,000–29,999	120	115	112	131	145
$30,000–39,999	99	103	97	98	137
$40,000–49,999	128	97	100	101	106
$50,000–59,999	88	90	99	89	77
$60,000–74,999	73	95	89	71	86
$75,000+	85	91	98	89	75
Household structure					
Single	112	117	134	116	126
Married	93	95	90	94	95
Any child in HH	113	105	117	92	107

Note: 100 = Average use or consumption unless a percent is indicated.

SS = sample size too small for a reliable index.

Source: Spring 2000 Mediamark Research Inc.

  c. VALS segments
  d. PRIZM segments
11. Develop a strategy for Revlon to use to introduce a
complete line of men's cosmetics to the following
countries.
  a. Japan
  b. Germany
  c. France
  d. Mexico

12. How would you explain the differences in
usage across the demographic groups in
Table A?

Source: A. Wallenstein, "Boomers Put New Life in Hair Dye for Men," *Advertising Age,* September 1995, p. 1; A. Farnham, "You're So Vain," *Fortune,* September 9, 1996, pp. 66–82; G. Boulard, "Men's Personal Care Market," *I,* January 1999, pp. 50–54; K. Yamanouchi, "Men Wake Up to Makeup," *Hartford Courant,* May 24, 2002, p. 3; *The U.S. Market for Men's Grooming Products* (New York: Packaged Facts, January 2004).

CASE 3-7   Made in Mexico*

The passage of NAFTA greatly lowered the trade barriers among Canada, the United States, and Mexico. Many manufacturers in each country are actively evaluating opportunities to export to the other two countries, as well as facing increased competition from imports from those countries.

Productos Superior, Inc., is a leading manufacturer of appliances in Mexico. The firm is considering a major effort to market its brand in the United States. Product testing indicates that its appliances are slightly above average in terms of quality, design, and reliability compared to the brands currently sold in the United States. Productos Superior's cost structure is such that its products will cost 10 to 20 percent less than products with similar quality currently selling in the United States.

Productos Superior's management is very concerned about the image that products made in Mexico have in the United States. Because Productos Superior is virtually unknown in the United States, management is concerned that consumers will generalize any image they have of products made in Mexico onto Productos Superior's products. Although it has yet to conduct research on the image that appliances made in Mexico have in the United States, it did find a study on the general image U.S. consumers had of products made in other countries. Table A contains the results of this study, in which respondents were asked to rate "the typical product made in" on a 1 to 10 scale, with 1 being "very poor" and 10 being "excellent."

Discussion Questions

1. Should Productos Superior's management be concerned that the relatively weak image of products made in Mexico will be attached to their line of products? Why?

2. How can Productos Superior introduce its appliances and avoid consumers attaching the negative aspects of "Made in Mexico" to their brand?

3. Develop a marketing strategy, including specific ads, to introduce Productos Superior appliances into the U.S. market.

4. What product position would you try to establish for Productos Superior appliances? Why?

5. What learning approach and principles would you use to teach consumers about Productos Superior appliances?

6. How would you establish a favorable attitude for Productos Superior appliances?

7. What name and logo or tag line would you use for Productos Superior's appliance line in the United States? Why?

8. Develop an ad or marketing approach to create a positive attitude toward Productos Superior appliances, focusing on the following components:
   a. Cognitive
   b. Affective
   c. Behavioral

9. Develop an ad or marketing approach to create a positive attitude toward Productos Superior appliances, using the following:
   a. Humor
   b. Emotion
   c. Utilitarian appeal
   d. Value-expressive appeal
   e. Celebrity endorser
   f. Self-concept

10. What VALS lifestyle segment(s) would be the best target market(s) for Productos Superior appliances? Why?

Attribute	United States	Japan	Germany	Taiwan	Mexico
Quality	7.3	8.7	9.1	6.9	5.2
Style	8.2	8.5	8.7	7.1	6.7
Reliability	7.8	8.2	8.9	7.4	5.4
Price	8.3	7.9	6.2	9.1	9.0
Design	8.5	8.2	9.3	7.6	6.2
Prestige	7.4	7.3	8.2	6.9	4.3

TABLE A

U.S. Consumer Perceptions of Products Made in Other Countries

11. To what motive(s) would you appeal to induce consumers to purchase Productos Superior appliances?

12. Develop an ad for Productos Superior appliances that would attract the attention of consumers not interested in appliances. Explain how your ad will attract attention and why it will also convey the desired message or image.

*The company name and data in this case are fictitious. See B. E. Richey, P. B. Rose, and L. Dominquez, "Perceived Value of Mexican vs. U.S. Products," *Journal of Global Marketing* 13, no. 2 (1999), pp. 49–65; and G. S. Insch and J. B. McBride, "The Impact of Country-of-Origin Cues on Consumer Perceptions of Product Quality," *Journal of Business Research* 57 (2004), pp. 256–65.

CASE 3-8   Hardiplank's Pull Strategy

In 1989, James Hardie Siding Products launched a line of fiber cement home siding products. The product was guaranteed against rotting or cracking for 50 years and had a warm, textured look that vinyl siding could not match. For most of the next decade, Hardie tried the traditional "push" approach of selling the product to builders, remodelers, and home improvement centers with ads and product demonstrations.

Unfortunately, builders did not like the siding. It was heavy, was hard on saw blades, and showed any flaws in a poor frame job. In addition, there were other fiber cement sidings available so a builder or home improvement center that decided to use or carry the product would frequently buy on price.

In the late 1990s, Hardie's USA President Lewis Gries decided to build a brand image for the siding, which was named Hardiplank. The project began with a very small budget of $500,000. The head of the ad agency chosen for the project stated,

> The first step was to do some research to find out what homeowners thought about the building materials used in their homes. Our assumption was that siding was a low-interest category but that turned out to be incorrect.

The research revealed that people are very emotional about their homes. When one focuses on what building materials provide, such as safety, security, beauty, warmth, and so forth, rather than what they actually are, home buyers and remodelers care a lot. This led the team to shift from a pure push (selling to builders and retailers who would then sell to home buyers) to more of a pull strategy (selling to home buyers who would then demand the product from builders and retailers).

Advertising was shifted from homebuilding trade publications to lifestyle magazines such as *Southern Living, Sunset,* and *Coastal Living*. The ads empha-sized the emotional appeal of houses made with strong, weather-resistant materials. Trade ads were used to explain this positioning and emphasized the interest that would be generated on behalf of builders and remodelers.

Hardie's sales force also had to be trained. Historically, they had called on purchasing agents and talked price and delivery schedules. Now they needed to reach the marketing directors of major homebuilders and communicate the value this product and its emerging reputation could provide to their sales programs.

Another major effort was to put Hardiplank on model homes, in "dream homes" promoted by the lifestyle magazines, and in builder design centers.

While Hardiplank had to compete against wood siding and other fiber cement brands, vinyl was perhaps its strongest competitor. It lasted longer than wood, and builders liked it because it was easy to install. However, it did not look or feel like wood. So Hardie built displays that placed vinyl and Hardiplank side by side and encouraged consumers not only to do a visual comparison but to do a "tap test." Unlike Hardiplank, vinyl is thin and rattles when tapped. According to Louis Sawyer, CEO of Hardie's advertising agency,

> Vinyl siding met the functional requirements, but not the emotional ones. Our ads and displays spoke directly to the affluent baby boomer audience, and they appreciated the difference immediately.

Discussion Questions

1. Will Hardie's pull strategy work? Why or why not?
2. What product position is Hardie trying to establish for Hardiplank?
3. What learning approach and principle would you use to teach consumers about Hardiplank?

4. How would you develop a favorable attitude toward Hardiplank?

5. Evaluate the name Hardiplank. Suggest and justify two others.

6. Conduct a diffusion analysis from the perspective of the home buyer, and develop appropriate strategies based on this analysis.

7. Conduct a diffusion analysis from the perspective of the builder, and develop appropriate strategies based on this analysis.

8. Develop two ads to create a positive attitude toward Hardiplank, one using a cognitive approach and one using an affective approach. Which is best? Why?

9. How can Hardie use emotion in marketing Hardiplank?

Source: B. Lamons, "Another Story about an Unlikely Brand," *Marketing News,* May 27, 2002, p. 8. Lamons is president of Robert Lamons & Associates in Houston, Texas.

CASE 3-9   www.teenpregnancy.org

Pregnancy among teenagers is a major problem in the United States, much more so than in other developed nations. Despite recent declines, 34 percent of girls become pregnant before they are 20. Eighty percent of these pregnancies are unplanned, and 81 percent of the girls are unwed. About half of pregnancies end in birth, a third in abortion, and the rest in miscarriage.

The consequences of these pregnancies, particularly the unplanned out-of-wedlock ones, are severe for the mother and often the father, the child, and society.

- Teen mothers are less likely to complete high school (only one-third receive a high school diploma) and more likely to end up on welfare (nearly 80 percent of unmarried teen mothers end up on welfare).
- The children of teenage mothers have lower birth weights, are more likely to perform poorly in school, and are at greater risk of abuse and neglect.
- The sons of teen mothers are 13 percent more likely to end up in prison, and teen daughters are 22 percent more likely to become teen mothers themselves.
- It has been estimated that U.S. taxpayers spent about $40 billion to support families started by teenage mothers.

Given the high cost of teenage pregnancies, why is the rate so high in the United States? Unfortunately, there is no solid evidence to answer this question. Proposed explanations include

- Less social stigma attached to pregnancy or childbearing by unmarried teenage girls.

- Few consequences for the boys and men who father out-of-wedlock teenage pregnancies.
- The absence of clear, forceful messages from all social sectors and leaders that teenagers are too young for pregnancy and childbearing—that "parenthood is for adulthood."
- A media environment that glorifies sexuality generally, and high-risk, nonmarital sexual behavior in particular, which typically is portrayed with no serious consequences.
- Continuing arguments about whether and when sexual activity by unmarried teenagers is acceptable and about whether abstinence or contraception is the best remedy for teenage pregnancy—arguments that are often divisive and hamper the ability of communities to take action to reduce teenage pregnancy.
- Sexual abuse of young girls, which results, among other things, in an increased vulnerability to teenage pregnancy later.
- Sexual exploitation of teenage girls by men who are older, sometimes by five years or more.
- A failure of parents and communities to nurture and supervise adolescent children—to monitor and support them adequately in order to teach and enforce moral standards of behavior; to talk about and model respectful male/female relationships; and to engage them in constructive after-school activities.
- Earlier puberty combined with a later average age of marriage—a gap that has led to increasing levels of premarital intercourse and a greater number of premarital sexual partners among teenagers.
- A judgment by poor teenage girls that there is little to be gained in postponing pregnancy and parenthood.

- The failure to develop a highly accessible system of family planning services and information for teenagers or to develop contraceptive methods more suited to them.
- Insufficient information provided to children and teenagers about human sexuality, how to avoid pregnancy and sexually transmitted diseases (STDs), and related topics in reproductive health.

Several factors appear to reduce the likelihood of a teen becoming pregnant:

- The primary reason that teenage girls who have never had intercourse give for abstaining is that having sex would be against their religious or moral values. Other reasons cited include desire to avoid pregnancy, fear of contracting an STD, and not having met the appropriate partner. Three of four girls and more than half of boys report that girls who have sex do so because their boyfriends want them to.
- Teenagers who have strong emotional attachments to their parents are much less likely to become sexually active at an early age.
- Contraceptive use among sexually active teens has increased but remains inconsistent. A sexually active teen who does not use contraception has a 90 percent chance of pregnancy within one year.
- Parents rate high among many teens as trustworthy and preferred information sources on birth control. One in two teens say they trust their parents most for reliable and complete information about birth control; only 12 percent say a friend.
- Teens who have been raised by both parents (biological or adoptive) from birth have lower probabilities of having sex than teens who grew up in any other family situation. At age 16, 22 percent of girls from intact families and 44 percent of other girls have had sex at least once.
- A majority of both girls and boys who are sexually active wish they had waited. Eight in 10 girls and six in 10 boys say they wish they had waited until they were older to have sex.

In response to this issue, The National Campaign to Prevent Teen Pregnancy was founded as a nonpartisan, nonprofit organization with a primary mission to sharply reduce teen pregnancy in the United States. Its Web site www.teenpregnancy.org provides an important communication link with teens. One of the principles that guides its actions is

> The Campaign will focus on boys as well as girls, and emphasize the importance of mutual respect between the sexes; shared responsibility for children; the need for pregnancy to be undertaken with deep commitment by both partners; further, the Campaign should send a message that becoming pregnant and bringing a child into the world is an enormous responsibility, and that couples should not have a child until they are able to support, nurture, and care for that child.

The campaign has taken a multifaceted approach to achieve its goal. One component of its approach is the development of a series of public service announcements (PSAs) such as posters, magazine ads, and television commercials that are distributed widely over a long period of time.

One series of PSAs targeting teens focuses on the theme "Sex has consequences." It attempts to show teens that there is a downside to sex. Each of the six poster/magazine ads features a picture of a teen (four feature girls, two feature boys) with small text running up the left side and one large, negative term that goes horizontally across the picture of the teen (see Illustration A). Across the bottom of each is "sex has consequences / www.teenpregnancy.org." The text for each ad follows (the four ads featuring a girl are described first):

> Condoms are CHEAP. If we'd used one, I wouldn't have to tell my parents I'm pregnant.
>
> I want to be with my friends. Instead, I'm changing DIRTY diapers at home.
>
> Now that I'm home with a baby, NOBODY calls me anymore.
>
> I had sex so my boyfriend wouldn't REJECT me. Now I have a baby. And no boyfriends.
>
> My scholarship is USELESS. Now I need a job to support my baby.
>
> All it took was one PRICK to get my girlfriend pregnant. At least that's what her friends say.

Other efforts include The National Day to Prevent Teen Pregnancy, which involves having teens go online and take a quiz consisting of scenarios relating to sex, and then choose a course of action. Participation has risen dramatically from 75,000 in 2002 (first year) to 630,000 in 2005 in part due to the organization's strong community and media partnerships.

Courtesy The National Campaign to Prevent Teen Pregnancy.

Discussion Questions

1. How effective are the PSAs described above likely to be?

2. Is there any risk that these ads could make teen sex "cool" rather than dangerous?

3. Go to www.teenpregnancy.org, click on The National Day to Prevent Teen Pregnancy tab, and view the most recent version of the quiz. Look for examples of learning principles and attitude/persuasion principles that are being used within the quiz format. Evaluate their effectivness.

4. What theme or message would you use to reduce teen pregnancy? How would you convey that message?

5. Design a poster to discourage teenage girls from becoming sexually active. Justify your design in terms of the relevant concept from the text and the information in this case.

6. Design a poster to discourage teenage boys from becoming sexually active. Justify your design in terms of the relevant concept from the text and the information in this case.

7. Design a poster to encourage sexually active teenage girls to use birth control. Justify your design in terms of the relevant concept from the text and the information in this case. What is the risk that your poster will encourage nonsexually active girls to become sexually active?

8. Design a poster to encourage sexually active teenage boys to use birth control. Justify your design in terms of the relevant concept from the text and the information in this case. What is the risk that your poster will encourage nonsexually active boys to become sexually active?

9. Evaluate www.teenpregnancy.org from the perspective of a 15-year-old who is under pressure to become sexually active. Does it provide the needed information? Will it reduce the likelihood of the person becoming sexually active? Should the PSAs targeting teens list a separate site designed just for them?

10. Evaluate www.teenpregnancy.org from the perspective of a 15-year-old who is sexually active and is concerned about becoming pregnant or fathering a child. Does it provide the needed information? Will it reduce the likelihood of pregnancy? Should the PSAs targeting teens list a separate site designed just for them?

Source: Teenpregnancy.org. Used by permission of National Campaign to Prevent Teen Pregnancy.

CASE 3-10   Framing Preventive Care

Public health officials and other concerned groups have struggled for years trying to persuade women to have breast cancer examinations and men to be checked for prostate cancer. The technical ability to detect disease or disease causing conditions has exploded in recent years. There are screening tests for high cholesterol (a heart attack risk factor), high blood pressure, osteoporosis, inherited breast cancer risk, HIV, and colon cancer, among others.

The advantages of early detection are great. Some diseases may be prevented entirely by early detection of potential causes (high cholesterol). Others are treated much more effectively and efficiently if detected and treated early. Thus, early detection can save lives, suffering, and money.

Despite such advantages, the use of early detection technology remains far below an optimal level. Some of this is due to the economics of the medical system. Lower-income individuals often lack adequate health insurance and are reluctant to spend scarce financial resources on tests for problems they may not have. However, even well-insured and prosperous individuals often forgo important tests. For example, it is estimated that 20 percent of American adults have dangerously high cholesterol, and many are unaware of this fact.

Why are consumers reluctant to take steps, often quite simple and inexpensive, that could literally save their lives? Some consumers believe that they are not susceptible to a particular health problem because of their age, genetics, or general condition. Given this belief, they do not see any value in taking a test that they are sure will merely confirm what they already "know." Marketers for Lipitor, a cholesterol-lowering drug, try to counter this by showing that apparently low-risk people such as figure-skater Peggy Fleming have cholesterol levels that need treatment.

Other consumers are in the opposite camp. They are fearful that the tests might reveal a problem. Even if such a problem is correctable if caught early, it is still bad news to have any type of disease or likelihood of a disease. Further, such a diagnosis generally involves at least short-term unpleasantness—a change in diet, physical or drug treatments, and anxiety. People are ambivalent at best about seeking out potentially bad news.

In light of the above, how does a firm or a nonprofit or public agency convince consumers to use appropriate early-detection technologies?

A number of opposing advertising approaches have been suggested. Should the ad use statistics or anecdotal evidence? Should the consequences be framed in terms of losses from not being tested or gains from being tested? Examples of each of these approaches are

- *Statistical, gain:* "Many women have no family history of breast cancer and have never felt any lump in their breast. But they follow the advice of the American Cancer Society and start having annual screening mammograms when they turn fifty. Because of this, doctors are able to detect their tumors at an early, treatable stage, and they are 30 percent less likely to die of breast cancer."
- *Statistical, loss:* "Many women have no family history of breast cancer and have never felt any lump in their breast. So they don't follow the advice of the American Cancer Society to start having annual screening mammograms when they turn fifty. Because of this, doctors are not able to detect tumors at an early, treatable stage, and they are 43 percent more likely to die of breast cancer."
- *Anecdotal, gain:* "No one in Sara Johnson's family had ever gotten breast cancer, and she had never felt any lump in her breast. But she followed the advice of the American Cancer Society and started having annual screening mammograms when she turned fifty. Because of this, doctors were able to detect her breast tumor at an early, treatable stage, and now Sara can look forward to a long life, watching her grandson, Jeffrey, grow up."
- *Anecdotal, loss:* "No one in Sara Johnson's family had ever gotten breast cancer, and she had never felt any lump in her breast. So she didn't follow the advice of the American Cancer Society to start having annual screening mammograms when she turned fifty. Because of this, doctors were not able to detect her breast tumor at an early, treatable stage, and now Sara may miss out on a long life, watching her grandson, Jeffrey, grow up."

Discussion Questions

1. Which of the four ads described above will work best? What consumer behavior theory helps you come to this conclusion?

2. Evaluate the four ads in terms of their use of fear appeal. What emotional responses linked to fear do these various messages promote? What consumer

factors do you think will increase or decrease the level of fear that is experienced in response to any one of the ads (holding the ad itself constant)?

3. Create a survey to examine the effectiveness of each of the above ad formats in inducing changes in behavioral intentions (the focal behavior is your choice, and could include such things as intentions to take vitamins, engage in daily exercise, and so on). Which format works best? Why?

4. Develop a strategy to encourage people to test for a disease or health risk factor of your choice.

Source: D. Cox and A. D. Cox, "Communicating the Consequences of Early Detection," *Journal of Marketing,* July 2001, pp. 91–103; L. Sanders, "Aiming to Stay No. 1," *Advertising Age,* December 10, 2001, p. 4; and www.cdc.gov.

Consumer Decision Process

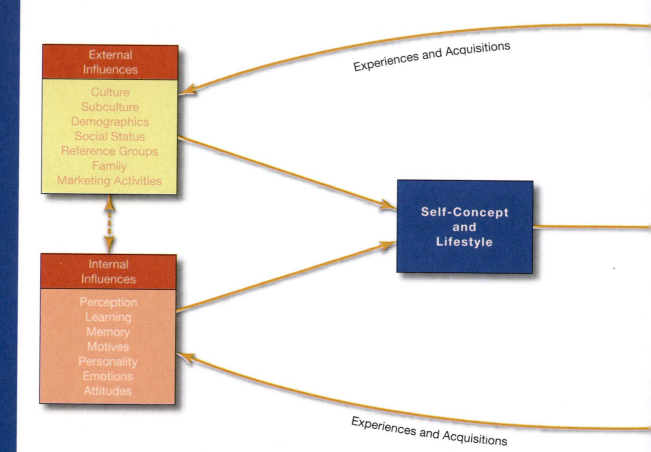

Up to now, we have focused on various sociological and psychological factors that contribute to different patterns of consumer behavior. Though these various influences play a significant role in behavior, all behavior takes place within the context of a situation. Chapter 13 provides a discussion of the impact situational variables have on consumer behavior.

Of particular importance to marketers is how situations and internal and external sources of influence affect the purchase decision process. The extended consumer decision process, shown on this page, is composed of a sequence of activities: problem recognition, information search, brand evaluation and selection, outlet choice and purchase, and postpurchase processes. However, extended decision making occurs only in those relatively rare situations when the consumer is highly involved in the purchase. Lower levels of purchase involvement produce limited or nominal decision making. Chapter 14 describes those various types of decisions and their relationship to involvement. It also analyzes the first stage of the process—problem recognition.

Information search, discussed in Chapter 15, constitutes the second stage of the consumer decision process. Chapter 16 examines the alternative evaluation and selection process. Chapter 17 deals with outlet selection and the in-store and online influences that often determine final brand choice. The final stage of the consumer decision process, presented in Chapter 18, involves behaviors after the purchase. These include postpurchase dissonance and regret, product use, satisfaction, disposition, and repurchase motivation. Both cognitive (thinking) and emotional (feeling) processes are important at each stage of the decision process.

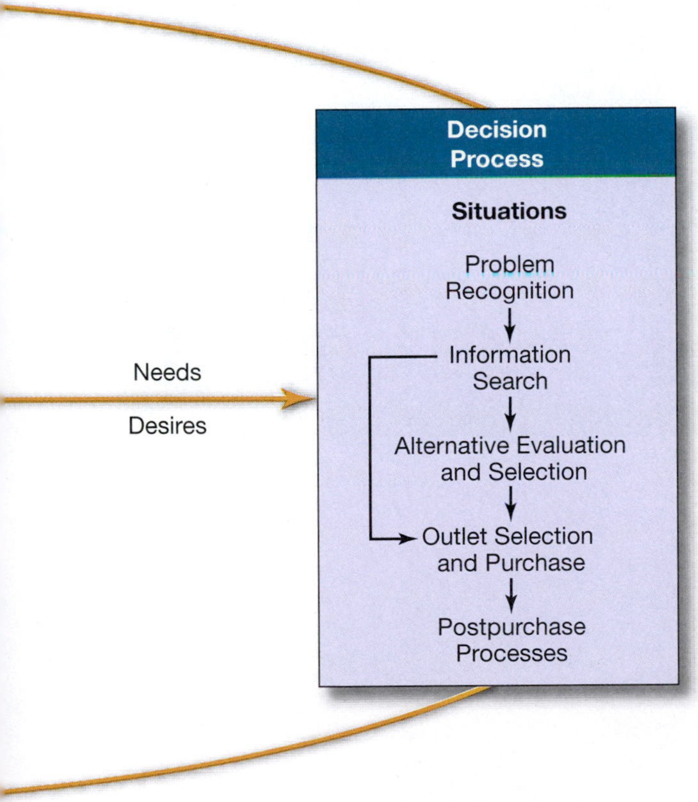

Decision Process

Situations

Problem Recognition

Needs
Desires

Information Search

Alternative Evaluation and Selection

Outlet Selection and Purchase

Postpurchase Processes

Courtesy *Fiestas The Party Magazine,* Inc.

13

Situational Influences

■ The transition from childhood to adulthood is an important life event. Different religious and ethnic subcultures have celebrations to mark the occasion.[1] For example, 13-year-old Jewish boys and girls celebrate bar mitzvahs and bat mitzvahs. Fifteen-year-old Hispanic girls celebrate quinceanera (keen-seen-yerah). These occasions are often marked with religious ceremonies and after-ceremony parties. Traditionally, these events have tended to focus on religious aspects and responsibility to family and community:

The bar mitzvah is actually an ancient solemn event marking the coming of age of a Jewish male, undertaken after study of Jewish history, traditions and Hebrew. Bat mitzvahs, for girls, are a more recent phenomenon.[2]

In Latin America, the quinceanera, a celebration dating back to the Aztecs that commemorates the spiritual and physical coming of age of a 15-year-old girl, is typically observed with a ceremony in the Catholic church and a backyard party for family members.[3]

The "after-ceremony" celebrations range from simple and inexpensive to elaborate and costly. However, the trend is definitely toward more elaborate and costly parties with modern themes, expensive catering and entertainment, and interactive activities to entertain hundreds of guests. For example:

One Jewish family hired Big Wave International to convert their synagogue into a rainforest with its own waterfall for their son's bar mitzvah.

One Hispanic family spent $30,000 to celebrate their daughter's quinceanera with "a horse-drawn, pumpkin-shaped crystal carriage with liveried servants in powdered wigs, a silver tulle gown and a gala at which 260 guests danced until dawn in the shadow of Sleeping Beauty's castle at Disneyland."[4]

Marketers are definitely tapping into this more secularized luxury trend. For example, the Hartford Civic Center and others feature events such as the "Ultimate Bar and Bat Mitzvah Showcase" where vendors can market to prospective clients. Disneyland has event planners that custom-design quinceaneras for their clients. Royal Carribbean Cruises offers quinceanera cruises for which demand has been strong. And, Mattel recently issued a limited edition Quinceanera Barbie!

The modernization and secularization have gone so far that some non-Jewish teens are having what are called faux Mitzvahs—the lavish after-party without the religious ceremony! Clearly the ongoing evolution of these ritual "coming of age" events will continue to present marketers with opportunities and challenges.

Bar and bat mitzvahs and quinceaneras are *ritual situations*. As the model we have used to organize this text indicates, the purchase decision and consumption process always occur in the context of a specific situation. Therefore, before examining the decision process, we must first develop an understanding of situations. In this chapter, we will examine the situations in which consumption occurs, the way situations influence consumption behaviors, key characteristics of situations, the nature of ritual situations, and situation-based marketing strategies.

THE NATURE OF SITUATIONAL INFLUENCE

Consumers do not respond to stimuli such as advertisements and products presented by marketers in isolation; instead, they respond to marketing influences and the situation simultaneously. To understand a consumer's behavior, we must know about the *consumer,* about the primary *stimulus* object such as a product or advertisement that the consumer is responding to, and about the *situation* in which the response is occurring.[5]

We define **situational influence** as *all those factors particular to a time and place that do not follow from a knowledge of the stable attributes of the consumer and the stimulus and that have an effect on current behavior.*[6] Thus, with one exception, the situation stands apart from the consumer and the stimulus. The exception is in the case of *temporary* (as opposed to stable) characteristics of a consumer or stimulus that are specific to the situation and sometimes even caused by it. For example, a consumer may generally be upbeat (stable trait), but just prior to viewing a firm's ad sees a disturbing news flash that puts her in a bad mood. This bad mood is a transient state (situational factor) caused by the surrounding media context in which the focal ad appears. Other such temporary conditions include illness and time pressure. Consumer involvement also includes a situation-specific component. That is, some consumers are only involved when they have to make a purchase.

A key marketing finding is that consumers often react and behave very differently depending on the situation. We discussed some of these effects in earlier chapters. For example, an ad or in-store display that might otherwise attract consumer attention may not do so in a cluttered environment (Chapter 8). Or an ad that might be persuasive in a nonpurchase situation may be much less persuasive in a purchase situation where consumers are on the market to buy (Chapter 11). The interplay between situation, marketing, and the individual is shown in Figure 13-1.

Consumer behavior occurs within four broad categories or types of situations: the communications situation, the purchase situation, the usage situation, and the disposition situation.

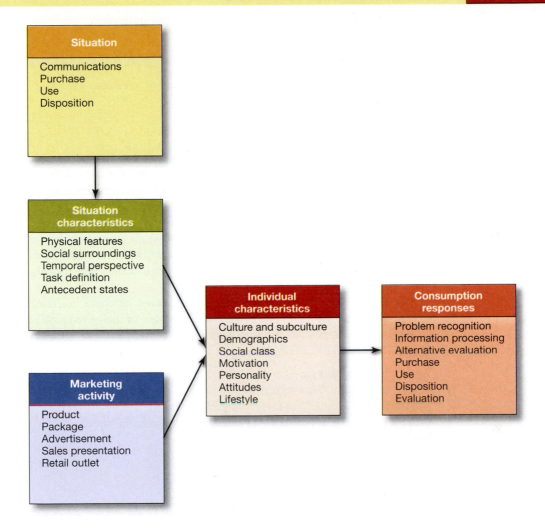

The Situation Interacts with the Marketing Activity and the Individual to Determine Behavior

FIGURE 13-1

Situation
Communications
Purchase
Use
Disposition

Situation characteristics
Physical features
Social surroundings
Temporal perspective
Task definition
Antecedent states

Marketing activity
Product
Package
Advertisement
Sales presentation
Retail outlet

Individual characteristics
Culture and subculture
Demographics
Social class
Motivation
Personality
Attitudes
Lifestyle

Consumption responses
Problem recognition
Information processing
Alternative evaluation
Purchase
Use
Disposition
Evaluation

The Communications Situation

The situation in which consumers receive information has an impact on their behavior. Whether one is alone or in a group, in a good mood or bad, in a hurry or not influences the degree to which one sees and listens to marketing communications. Is it better to advertise on a happy or sad television program? A calm or exciting program? These are some of the questions managers must answer with respect to the **communications situation.**[7] Marketers often attempt to place their ads in appropriate media contexts to enhance their effectiveness. Some even go so far as to mandate that their ads be "pulled" when programming content negative to their company or industry will appear. Recent examples include Morgan Stanley and BP. *What are the ethical implications of such policies?*[8]

A marketer is able to deliver an effective message to consumers who are interested in the product and are in a receptive communications situation. However, finding high-interest potential buyers in receptive communications situations is a difficult challenge. For example, consider the difficulty a marketer would have in communicating to you in the following communications situations:

- Your favorite team just lost the most important game of the year.
- Final exams begin tomorrow.
- Your roommates only watch comedy programs.
- You have the flu.
- You are driving home on a cold night, and your car heater doesn't work.

The Purchase Situation

The situation in which a purchase is made can influence consumer behavior. Mothers shopping with children are more apt to be influenced by the product preferences of their children than when shopping without them. A shortage of time, such as trying to make a purchase between classes, can affect the store-choice decision, the number of brands considered, and the price the shopper is willing to pay. At an even more basic level, whether or not a consumer is in a "purchase mode" influences a whole host of behaviors from advertising responses to shopping. Consider, for example, how differently you might behave at Best Buy if you were there only to browse versus being there to replace a broken DVD player.

Marketers must understand how **purchase situations** influence consumers in order to develop marketing strategies that enhance the purchase of their products. For example, how would you alter your decision to purchase a beverage in the following purchase situations?

- You are in a very bad mood.
- A good friend says "That stuff is bad for you!"
- The store you visit does not carry your favorite brand.
- There is a long line at the checkout counter as you enter the store.
- You are with someone you want to impress.

The Usage Situation

What beverage would you prefer to consume in each of the following usage situations?

- Friday afternoon after your last final exam.
- With your parents for lunch.
- After dinner on a cold, stormy evening.
- At a dinner with a friend you have not seen in several years.
- When you are feeling sad or homesick.

Marketers need to understand the **usage situations** for which their products are, or may become, appropriate. Using this knowledge, marketers can communicate how their products create consumer satisfaction in each relevant usage situation. For example, a recent study found that consuming two 1.5-cup servings of oat-based cereal a day could lower cholesterol. How could General Mills take advantage of this finding to increase sales of its oat-based cereal, Cheerios? A recent ad depicts a dad coming home late from work and having Cheerios for dinner. When asked why by his young daughter, he replies, "Because they taste just as good at night."

Research indicates that *expanded usage situation* strategies can produce major sales gains for established products.[9] For example, Kraft has attempted to expand the appropriate

ILLUSTRATION 13-1

Many products become defined for particular usage situations. Firms that are able to expand the range of usage situations deemed appropriate for their brands can capture significant sales gains.

Courtesy Coach USA, Inc.; Creative Director: Reed Krakoff;
Photographer: Steven Sebring.

usage situations for Grey Poupon mustard beyond sandwiches. In addition, Coach went away from the traditional two-occasion (everyday and dressy) approach to handbags and moved toward what they call a "usage voids" approach. Now they offer a wide range of products including weekend bags, coin purses, clutches, and wristlets in a variety of colors and fabrics (see Illustration 13-1). The goal is to get consumers more attuned to the various usage situations available in which to accessorize and then create bags to fit them.[10]

The Disposition Situation

Consumers must frequently dispose of products or product packages after or before product use. As we will examine in detail in Chapter 18, decisions made by consumers regarding the **disposition situation** can create significant social problems as well as opportunities for marketers.

Some consumers consider ease of disposition an important product attribute. These people may purchase only items that can be easily recycled. Often disposition of an existing product must occur before or simultaneously with the acquisition of the new product. For example, most consumers must remove their existing bed before using a new one. Marketers need to understand how situational influences affect disposition decisions in order to develop more effective and ethical products and marketing programs. Government and environmental organizations need the same knowledge in order to encourage socially responsible disposition decisions.

How would your disposition decision differ in these situations?

- You have finished a soft drink in a can at a mall. There is a trashcan nearby, but there is no sign of a recycling container.
- You have finished reading the newspaper after class, and you note that you are running late for a basketball game.
- You and two friends have finished soft drinks. Both your friends toss the recyclable cans into a nearby garbage container.
- A local charity will accept old refrigerators if they are delivered to the charity. Your garbage service will haul one to the dump for $15. You just bought a new refrigerator. You don't (do) know anyone with a pickup or van.

SITUATIONAL CHARACTERISTICS AND CONSUMPTION BEHAVIOR

The situations discussed above can be described on a number of dimensions which determine their influence on consumer behavior. The five key dimensions or characteristics are physical surroundings, social surroundings, temporal perspectives, task definition, and antecedent states.[11] These characteristics have been studied primarily in the United States. While the same characteristics of the situation exist across cultures, a marketer should not assume that the response to these characteristics would be the same. For example, a crowded store might cause a different emotional reaction among American consumers than among Indian consumers.[12]

Physical Surroundings

Physical surroundings include decor, sounds, aromas, lighting, weather, and configurations of merchandise or other materials surrounding the stimulus object. Physical surroundings are a widely used type of situational influence, particularly for retail applications.

The lifestyle centers we examined in Chapter 1 (Consumer Insight 1-1) show how important external factors such as the architecture, arrangement, and assortment of retailers can be in affecting consumers' shopping experiences. In addition, store interiors are often designed to create specific feelings in shoppers that can have an important cueing or reinforcing effect on purchase. All physical aspects of the store, including lighting, layout, presentation of merchandise, fixtures, floor coverings, colors, sounds, odors, and dress and behavior of sales personnel, combine to produce these feelings, which in turn influence purchase tendencies.[13] A retail clothing store specializing in extremely stylish, modern clothing would want its fixtures, furnishings, and colors to reflect an overall mood of style, flair, and newness. In addition, the store personnel should carry this theme in terms of their own appearance and apparel. Illustration 13-2 shows the interior of the Bergdorf Goodman men's store in New York City. Its target market is males with upscale incomes and taste levels. Its fixtures, design, and layout present an environment appropriate for this group. Compare this interior with that of the men's clothing section of Wal-Mart that is also shown in the illustration. It is important to note that one is not superior to the other. Each attempts to create an appropriate atmosphere for its target audience.

The sum of all the physical features of a retail environment is referred to as the **store atmosphere** or environment (see Chapter 17). A store's atmosphere influences the consumers' judgments of the quality of the store and the store's image. It also has been shown to influence shoppers' moods and their willingness to visit and linger. **Atmospherics** is *the process managers use to manipulate the physical retail environment to create specific*

Courtesy J. T. Nakaoka Associates Architects.

© Tannen Maury/The Image Works.

ILLUSTRATION 13-2

Retail store interiors should provide a physical environment consistent with the nature of the target market, the product line, and the desired image of the outlet.

Typology of Service Environments   FIGURE 13-2

Time Spent in Facility	Consumption Purpose		
	Utilitarian -- *Hedonic*		
Short [minutes]	Dry cleaner Bank	Fast food Hair salon	Facial Coffee at Starbucks
Moderate [hour(s)]	Medical appointment Legal consultation	Business dinner Exercise class	**Theater** **Sporting event**
Extended [day(s)]	Hospital Trade show	**Conference hotel** **Training center**	**Cruise** **Resort**

Note: The darker the shading, the more important the physical features of the servicescape are.

Source: Adapted from K. L. Wakefield and J. G. Blodgett, "Customer Response to Intangible and Tangible Service Factors," *Psychology & Marketing,* January 1999, p. 54. Copyright © 1999 John Wiley & Sons. Reprinted with permission of John Wiley & Sons, Inc.

mood responses in shoppers.[14] Atmospherics is also important online and is receiving increasing attention from marketers.[15]

Atmosphere is referred to as **servicescape** when describing a service business such as a hospital, bank, or restaurant.[16] Figure 13-2 classifies services according to the reason the customer is using the service and the length of time the service will be used. The consumption purpose is categorized along a continuum from strictly utilitarian, such as dry cleaning, to completely hedonic, such as a massage. The time can range from a few minutes to days or weeks. Physical characteristics and the feelings and image they create become increasingly important as hedonic motives and the time involved with the service increase. Thus, the physical characteristics of a vacation resort may be as or more important than the intangible services provided.

It is important that Figure 13-2 be interpreted correctly. It indicates that the physical environment at Starbucks is more important to the service experience than the physical features of dry cleaners are. *This does not mean that the physical aspects of dry cleaners are not important.* Indeed, an organized, professional-appearing dry cleaning establishment is likely to produce more satisfied customers than one with the opposite characteristics. What the figure does indicate is that the relative importance of tangible physical features increases as one moves to extended, hedonic consumption experiences.

Having established the importance of the physical environment, we will now examine some of its components.

Colors   As we saw in Chapter 8, certain colors and color characteristics create feelings of excitement and arousal which are related to attention. Bright colors are more arousing than dull colors. And *warm* colors such as reds and yellows are more arousing than *cool* colors such as blues and greys.[17] Which color would be best for store interiors? The answer is, it depends. For the dominant interior color, cool colors (e.g., blue) should probably be used since they increase sales and customer satisfaction.[18] However the attention-getting nature of warm colors should not be overlooked and can be used effectively as an accent color in areas where the retailer wants to attract attention and drive impulse purchases.[19] Cool colors also appear to be capable of reducing wait time perceptions by inducing feelings of relaxation.[20]

As we saw in Chapter 2, the meaning of colors varies across cultures. Therefore, this and all other aspects of the physical environment should be designed specifically for the cultures involved.

Aromas   There is increasing evidence that odors can affect consumer shopping.[21] One study found that a scented environment produced a greater intent to revisit the store, higher purchase intention for some items, and a reduced sense of time spent shopping.[22] Another study found that one aroma, but not another, increased slot machine usage in a Las Vegas casino.[23] A third study reported that a floral-scented environment increased sales of Nike shoes.[24] A fourth study found that a pleasantly scented environment enhanced brand recall and evaluations particularly for unfamiliar brands. The pleasant scent increased the time spent evaluating the brands (attention), which, in turn, increased memory.[25]

Given these results it is not surprising that a billion-dollar *environmental fragrancing* industry has developed around the use of ambient scents. However, marketers still have a lot to learn about if, when, and how scents can be used effectively in a retail environment.[26] In addition, scent preferences are highly individualized such that a pleasant scent to one individual may be repulsive to another. Moreover, some shoppers object to anything being deliberately added to the air they breathe, and others worry about allergic reactions.[27]

Music   Music influences consumers' moods, which influence a variety of consumption behaviors.[28] Is slow-tempo or fast-tempo background music better for a restaurant? Table 13-1 indicates that slow music increased gross margin for one restaurant by almost 15 percent per customer group compared with fast music. However, before concluding that all restaurants should play slow music, examine the table carefully. Slow music appears to have relaxed and slowed down the customers, resulting in more time in the restaurant and substantially more purchases from the bar. Restaurants that rely on rapid customer turnover might be better off with fast-tempo music.

TABLE 13-1

The Impact of
Background Music
on Restaurant
Patrons

Variables	Slow Music	Fast Music
Service time	29 min.	27 min.
Customer time at table	56 min.	45 min.
Customer groups leaving before seated	10.5%	12.0%
Amount of food purchased	$55.81	$55.12
Amount of bar purchases	$30.47	$21.62
Estimated gross margin	$55.82	$48.62

Source: R. E. Milliman, "The Influence of Background Music on the Behavior of Restaurant Patrons," in the *Journal of Consumer Research,* September 1986, p. 289. Copyright © 1986 by the University of Chicago. Used by permission.

Other aspects of music besides tempo are also important. For example, research suggests that matching music to the musical preferences of the target audience is critical to positive retail outcomes such as satisfaction and enjoyment, browsing time, spending, perceived service quality, and positive word of mouth. In addition, research suggests that music which creates moderate levels of arousal (versus extremely low or high) yields the most positive retail outcomes.[29]

Because of the impact that music can have on shopping behavior, firms exist to develop music programs to meet the unique needs of specific retailers. An emerging trend is having music more in the foreground so it becomes part of the shopping experience and drives store image. AEI, a major supplier of foreground music, does intense research on the demographics and psychographics of each client store's customers. The age mix, buying patterns, and traffic flows of each part of the day are analyzed. AEI characterizes their approach as:

[Creating] environments where sounds, video, lighting and architecture blend together to give a brand a voice, creating emotional attachments that encourage consumers to shop longer, increase spending and return often.[30]

Firms such as the Abercombrie & Fitch, Banana Republic, Bath & Body Works, and Eddie Bauer use companies like AEI to create appropriate and consistent shopping environments throughout their chains.

Crowding   Crowding generally produces negative outcomes for both the retail outlet and the consumer.[31] As more people enter a store or as more of the space of the store is filled with merchandise, an increasing percentage of the shoppers will experience a feeling of being crowded, confined, or claustrophobic. Most consumers find these feelings to be unpleasant and will take steps to change them. The primary means of doing so is to spend less time in the store by buying less, making faster decisions, and using less of the available information. This in turn tends to produce less satisfactory purchases, an unpleasant shopping trip, and a reduced likelihood of returning to the store.

Marketers should design their outlets in ways that will help reduce consumers' perceptions of crowding. This is difficult because retail shopping tends to occur at specific times, such as holiday weekends. Retailers must balance the expense of having a larger store than required most of the time against the cost of dissatisfied customers during key shopping periods. Using extra personnel, adding additional checkout lines, and similar measures can enhance the flow of consumers through a store during peak periods and reduce the crowding sensation.

Marketers need to be sensitive to cross-cultural differences since personal space and resulting crowding perceptions can vary from culture to culture.[32]

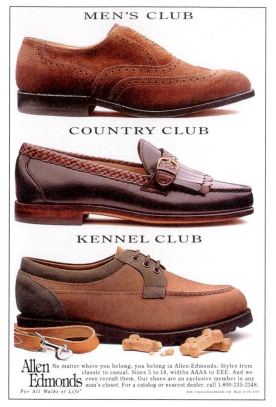

Courtesy Allen Edmonds.

Social Surroundings

Social surroundings are *the other individuals present in the particular situation*. People's actions are frequently influenced by those around them. What would you wear in each of the following situations?

- Studying alone for a final.
- Meeting at the library with a date to study for a final.
- Going to a nice restaurant with a date.
- Meeting a prospective employer for lunch.

Most people would change their apparel for at least some of these situations. Illustration 13-3 shows how Allen Edmonds designs shoes for different types of social situations.

Social influence is a significant force acting on our behavior, since individuals tend to comply with group expectations, particularly when the behavior is visible (see Chapter 7). Thus, shopping, a highly visible activity, and the use of many publicly consumed brands are subject to social influences.[33] This is particularly true of those who are highly susceptible to interpersonal influence, a stable personality trait. As just one example, a recent study finds that consumers are more likely to engage in variety seeking behavior in public (versus private) consumption situations even if it means consuming products they like less. The reason is that consumers feel that others view them more positively (more fun, interesting, exciting) if their purchases show more variety. This tendency is stronger for those more susceptible to interpersonal influence.[34]

Marketers have recently begun to examine the role of social influence on embarrassment. **Embarrassment** is a negative emotion influenced both by the product and the situation. Certain products are more embarrassing than others (condoms, hearing aids, etc.) and embarrassment is driven by the presence of others in the purchase or usage situation. Since embarrassment can deter purchases, this is an important area for marketers. One finding is that familiarity with purchasing the product reduces embarrassment, so marketers might try advertisements that show the purchase of a potentially embarrassing product in which no awkwardness or embarrassment occurs. For extremely sensitive products (e.g., adult diapers), strategies might include home delivery options with discreet labeling to completely avoid the social component.[35]

Shopping can provide a social experience outside the home for making new acquaintances, meeting existing friends, or just being near other people (Consumer Insight 10-1 discusses the social shopping motive). Some people seek status and authority in shopping since the salesperson's job is to wait on the customer. This allows these individuals a measure of respect or prestige that may otherwise be lacking in their lives. Thus, consumers, on occasion, shop *for* social situations rather than, or in addition to, products.

Frequently, marketing managers will not have any control over social characteristics of a situation. For example, when a television advertisement is sent into the home, the advertising manager cannot control whom the viewer is with at the time of reception. However, the manager can utilize the knowledge that some programs are generally viewed alone (weekday, daytime programs), some are viewed by the entire family (prime-time family comedies), and others by groups of friends (Super Bowl). The message presented can be structured to these viewing situations. Marketers can also utilize social consumption themes in their ads to enhance the likelihood that consumers will consider the social component in their decisions. For example, a recent study found that brand personality (fun and sophistication) conveyed by a celebrity endorser in an ad only enhanced purchase intentions when a social context was evoked.[36]

Temporal Perspectives

Temporal perspectives are *situational characteristics that deal with the effect of time on consumer behavior*. Time as a situational factor can manifest itself in a number of ways.[37] The amount of time available for the purchase has a substantial impact on the consumer decision process. In general, the less time there is available (i.e., increased time pressure), the shorter will be the information search, the less available information will be used, and the more suboptimal purchases will be made.[38]

Limited purchase time can also result in a smaller number of product alternatives being considered. The increased time pressure experienced by many dual-career couples and single parents tends to increase the incidence of brand loyalty, particularly for nationally branded products. The obvious implication is that these consumers feel safer with nationally branded or "known" products, particularly when they do not have the time to engage in extensive comparison shopping.

Time as a situational influence affects consumers' choice of stores and behaviors in those stores.[39] A number of retail firms have taken advantage of the temporal perspective factor. Perhaps the most successful of these is the 7-Eleven chain, which caters almost exclusively to individuals who either are in a hurry or want to make a purchase after regular shopping hours.

Internet shopping is growing rapidly in part as a result of the time pressures felt by many dual-career and single-parent households. Shopping on the Internet has two important

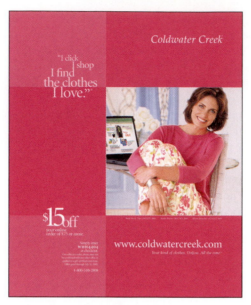

Used by permission of Coldwater Creek.

time-related dimensions. First, it has the potential to reduce the amount of time required to make a specific purchase. Second, it provides the consumer with almost total control over *when* the purchase is made (see Chapter 17). These features are among the major reasons for the rapid growth in Internet outlets and sales (see Illustration 13-4).

Task Definition

Task definition is *the reason the consumption activity is occurring.* The major task dichotomy used by marketers is between purchases for self-use versus gift giving.

Gift Giving   Consumers use different shopping strategies and purchase criteria when shopping for gifts versus shopping for the same item for self-use.[40] Consumers give gifts for many reasons. Social expectations and ritualized consumption situations such as birthdays often require gift giving independent of the giver's actual desires.[41] Gifts are also given to elicit return favors in the form of either gifts or actions. And, of course, gifts are given as an expression of love and caring.[42]

The type of gift given and desired varies by occasion and gender.[43] One study found that wedding gifts tend to be *utilitarian* while birthday gifts tend to be *fun.* Thus, both the general task definition (gift giving) and the specific task definition (gift-giving occasion) influence purchase behavior, as does the relationship between the giver and the recipient.

Gift giving produces anxieties on the part of both givers and receivers.[44] Gifts communicate symbolic meaning on several levels. The gift item itself generally has a known, or knowable, price that can be interpreted as a measure of the esteem the giver has for the receiver. The image and functionality of the gift implies the giver's impression of the image and personality of the receiver. It also reflects on the image and thoughtfulness of the giver.

The nature of a gift can signify the type of relationship the giver has or desires with the receiver.[45] A gift of stationery implies a very different desired relationship between two individuals than does a gift of cologne. Consider the following:

> The biggest moment of revelation, the moment I knew he was "serious" about me, was when he showed up with a gift for my daughter. Other men had shown the typical false affection for her in order to get on my good side, but he was only civil and polite to her, never gushy. One day, however, he showed up with a very nice skateboard for my daughter. . . . The gift marked a turning point in our relationship. I think for him it marked the time that he decided it would be OK to get serious about a woman with a child.[46]

As the example above indicates, the act of giving/receiving a gift can alter the relationship between the giver and receiver. In addition, items received as gifts often take on meaning associated with the relationship or the giver. For example a gift may be cherished and protected because it symbolizes an important friendship.[47]

Of course, gift giving is culture specific (see Chapter 2).[48] For example, in characterizing gift giving in Korea (collectivist) compared to the United States (individualistic), one expert summarized:

> Koreans reported more gift giving occasions, a wider exchange network, more frequent giving of practical gift items, especially cash gifts, strong face-saving and group conformity motivations, more social pressure to reciprocate, higher gift budget, and frequent workplace giving.[49]

Antecedent States

Features of the individual person that are not lasting characteristics, such as momentary moods or conditions, are called **antecedent states.** For example, most people experience states of depression or excitement from time to time that are not normally part of their individual makeup.

Moods   **Moods** are *transient feeling states that are generally not tied to a specific event or object.*[50] They tend to be less intense than emotions and may operate without the individual's awareness. Although moods may affect all aspects of a person's behavior, they generally do not completely interrupt ongoing behavior as an emotion might. Individuals use such terms as *happy, cheerful, peaceful, sad, blue,* and *depressed* to describe their moods.

Moods both affect and are affected by the consumption process.[51] Moods influence decision processes, the purchase and consumption of various products, and perceptions of service.[52] Positive moods appear to be associated with increased browsing and impulse purchasing. Negative moods also increase impulse and compulsive purchasing in some consumers. One explanation is that some shopping behaviors play both a mood maintenance (positive moods) and mood enhancement (negative moods) role.[53]

Mood can also play an important role in the communications situation. Such effects are often called *program context effects* and relate to the nature of the programming surrounding the focal ad (see Chapter 8). The television, radio, and magazine content viewed just prior to the focal ad can influence consumers' moods and arousal levels, which, in turn, influence their information-processing activities.[54] A basic finding is that ad and brand attitudes are often influenced in a mood-congruent manner. Thus, a TV show that puts a consumer in a positive mood (elicits positive affective reactions) should improve ad and brand attitudes compared to one that puts the consumer in a negative mood. However, in cases where so-called negative programming is also liked by the viewer (a sad movie that a viewer loves), then program liking can still provide a positive boost in ad and brand attitudes.[55] Given such complexities, marketers must pretest their ads in contexts as close to their expected programming environment as possible.

Consumers actively manage their mood states (see Illustration 13-5).[56] That is, consumers often seek situations, activities, or objects that will alleviate negative moods or enhance positive ones. Products and services are one means consumers use to manage their mood states. Thus, a person feeling bored, sad, or down might view a situation comedy on television, go to a cheerful movie, visit a fun store, eat at an upbeat restaurant, or purchase a new compact disc, shirt, or other fun product.[57] Consumers may engage in such mood-regulating behavior both at a nonconscious level and also at a deliberate, conscious level:

> [T]here are certain products that I purchase specifically to make me feel better. For instance, occasionally, I enjoy smoking a cigar. Certainly the cigar serves no other purpose than to make me feel good.
>
> While other cosmetics, perfumes and nice clothes can make me feel good, they seldom have the same power to transform my temperament like a manicure and pedicure can.[58]

© 2005 Jelly Belly Candy Company. ® Registered trademark of Jelly Belly Candy. Used with permission from Jelly Belly Candy Company.

Marketers attempt to influence moods and to time marketing activities with positive mood-inducing events.[59] Many companies prefer to advertise during light television programs because viewers tend to be in a good mood while watching these shows. Restaurants, bars, shopping malls, and many other retail outlets are designed to induce positive moods in patrons. As discussed earlier, music is often played for this reason. Finally, marketers can position their products and services in terms of mood enhancement.

Momentary Conditions   Whereas moods reflect states of mind, *momentary conditions reflect temporary states of being* such as being tired, being ill, having extra money, being broke, and so forth. However, for conditions, as for moods, to fit under the definition of antecedent states, they must be momentary and not constantly with the individual. Hence, an individual who is short of cash only momentarily will act differently from someone who is always short of cash.[60]

As with moods, individuals attempt to manage their momentary conditions, often through the purchase or consumption of products and services. For example, individuals feeling tired or sleepy during the day may drink a cup of coffee or a soft drink or eat a candy bar. Massages are consumed to relieve sore muscles. A variety of medications are sold to relieve physical discomfort associated with overexertion, colds, allergies, and so forth. Pawnshops provide cash for individuals temporarily needing funds, as do banks and other financial institutions. Thus, a great deal of marketing activity is directed toward momentary conditions. Illustration 13-6 is an ad for a product designed to relieve a momentary condition.

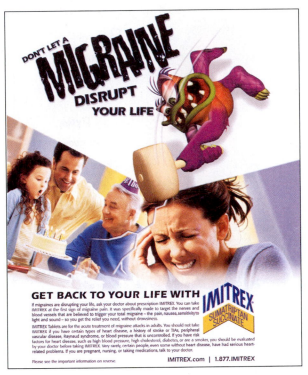

Copyright GlaxoSmithKline. Used with permission.

RITUAL SITUATIONS

Rituals are receiving increasing attention by marketing scholars and practitioners. A **ritual situation** can be described as a socially defined occasion that triggers a set of interrelated behaviors that occur in a structured format and that have symbolic meaning.[61] Ritual situations can range from completely private to completely public. A completely private ritual situation would be an individual's decision to drink a private toast or say a private prayer on the anniversary of an event with special meaning to the individual. A couple that celebrates their first date by returning to the same restaurant every year is involved in a more public ritual. Weddings tend to be even more public. Finally, national and global holidays present very public ritual situations.

Ritual situations are of major importance to marketers because they often involve prescribed consumption behaviors. Every major American holiday (ritual situation) has consumption rituals associated with it. For example, more than 60 percent of the toy industry's sales occur at Christmas.

While there is significant variation across individuals and households, there is enough shared behavior that marketers can develop products and promotions around the common ritual situations that arise each year. For example, candy marketers produce and promote a wide array of candies for Valentine's Day and Halloween. Illustration 13-7 shows how an Internet firm is capitalizing on the consumption rituals associated with high school proms.

Marketers also attempt to change or create consumption patterns associated with ritual situations.[62] Mother's Day is a $10 billion occasion in which card giving is largely a ritual behavior created by marketers.[63] Halloween cards are now being promoted as part of the Halloween ritual.[64] And as we saw in the chapter's opening example, many firms seek to make their products and services part of the consumption pattern associated with

Ritual situations generally have consumption patterns associated with them. This Internet firm makes a wide selection of prom dresses available to girls no matter where they live.

Courtesy BestPromDresses.com; Art Direction: Merrill Singer Design.

"coming of age." The same is true for most other rites of passage in America such as graduation.

Ritual situations can also result in injurious consumption. Binge or excessive drinking is a serious health and social problem on many college campuses. Recent research suggests that this can be understood as a ritual behavior (see Consumer Insight 13-1). When approached from this perspective, more effective strategies for minimizing such behaviors may result.

SITUATIONAL INFLUENCES AND MARKETING STRATEGY

In the previous sections, we described a variety of marketing strategies based on situational influences. Here we will focus more specifically on the process by which such strategies can be developed.

It is important to note that individuals do not encounter situations randomly. Instead, most people "create" many of the situations they face. Thus, individuals who choose to engage in physically demanding sports such as jogging, tennis, or racquetball are indirectly choosing to expose themselves to the situation of "being tired" or "being thirsty." This allows marketers to develop products, advertising, and segmentation strategies based on the situations that individuals selecting various lifestyles are likely to encounter.

After identifying the different situations that might involve the consumption of a product, marketers must determine which products or brands are most likely to be purchased or consumed across those situations. One method of approaching this is to jointly scale situations and products. An example is shown in Figure 13-3. Here, *use situations* that ranged from "private consumption at home" to "consumption away from home where there is a concern for other people's reaction to you" were scaled in terms of their similarity and relationship to products appropriate for that situation.

Binge drinking has been described as one of the most significant health and social issues on college campuses.[65] It is associated with deaths due to alcohol poisoning and traffic accidents, unplanned and unsafe sex, physical and sexual assaults, crime, nontraffic accidents, interpersonal problems, cognitive impairment, and poor academic performance. Despite widespread publicity about its dangers and efforts by university officials to curb it, binge drinking continues to be a problem. One explanation for its persistence is that it has become an important ritual of college life on many campuses.

The social occasions that trigger binge drinking can range from private ones, such as birthdays, to shared ones, such as sports events on campus, traditional "drinking nights," and bar specials.

> We have our routine. We go to one bar because they have a special. When that's ended, we go next door to a dance place because ladies get in free until 12. We stay until 11:30 and we go next door and get in free there.

> If it is a day game like at 1:00 P.M., we usually start drinking around 11:00 A.M. and just drink throughout the game. . . . If it was a 7:00 P.M. game, it [drinking] would start around 4:00 P.M.

Binge drinking also has a set of interrelated behaviors that participants follow, with variations across groups and campuses. As can be seen, some of these behaviors place the participants at serious risk.

> I and the other girls don't eat much on the day we go drinking because if you have a full stomach, you

really can't get drunk. If we're going drinking at night, we eat lunch around noon and won't eat for the rest of the day.

People tend to go where they know their friends are going versus places where they don't know anyone. It is very much a pattern.

Sometimes we do put ourselves into risky situations as far as driving under the influence. But, when the situation arises, how else are we going to get home?

As with all ritual behaviors, binge drinking has meaning and rewards for its participants.

> It was fun feeling drunk . . . laughing, have fun and being in a social situation where a lot of people are the same way. Everyone decided to collectively go there for that reason and have a good time.

> You don't want the guys to go "Oh, she's not the type of person that likes to have fun." The guys we hang around with think it is cool to have a couple of beers.

> The joke is that once you turn 21, it's not exciting anymore. The thrill of getting through that door and trying to get served is gone because you are legal.

Critical Thinking Questions

1. Do you agree that binge drinking by college students is a form of ritual behavior?

2. Utilizing the idea that binge drinking among college students is a ritual behavior, develop a commercial to minimize this type of behavior.

For use situation I, "to clean my mouth upon rising in the morning," toothpaste and mouthwash are viewed as most appropriate (see Figure 13-3). However, use situation II, "before an important business meeting late in the afternoon," involves both consumption away from home and a concern for the response from others. As a result, mint-flavored gums or candies are preferred. *Where do you think a product like Listerine Breath Strips would be located on this map?*

Determining how products are *currently used* across situations can help the marketer develop appropriate advertising and positioning strategies. In our example, Wrigley's might advertise its Spearmint Gum as having breath-freshening capabilities that make it appropriate for use in social situations away from home. Or a marketer may try to change

FIGURE 13-3   Use Situations and Product Positioning

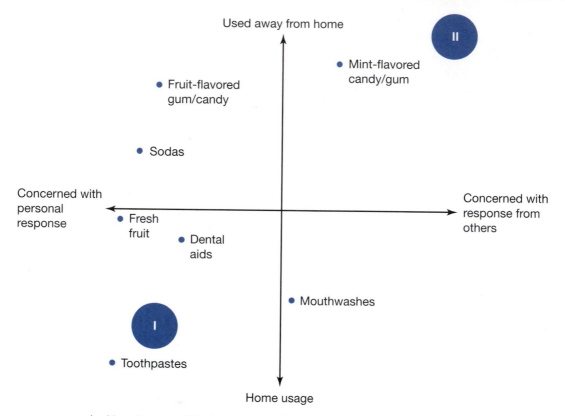

I = Use situation: "To clean my mouth upon rising in the morning."
II = Use situation: "Before an important business meeting late in the afternoon."

the situations for which a product is used. In Figure 13-3, mouthwash is not seen as appropriate for consumption away from home. What if a version of Scope was developed that one swallowed after use? Could it successfully be promoted for use away from home? Would it be able to compete against breath strips? Illustration 13-8 shows one of a series of ads designed to convince consumers that French wine is appropriate for casual social situations, not just very special celebrations (the primary current use situation).

Another approach for developing situation-based marketing strategies is to follow these five steps:[66]

1. Use observational studies, focus group discussions, depth interviews, and secondary data to discover the various usage situations that influence the consumption of the product.
2. Survey a larger sample of consumers to better understand and quantify how the product is used and the benefits sought in the usage situation by the market segment.
3. Construct a person–situation segmentation matrix. The rows are the major usage situations and the columns are groups of users with unique needs or desires. Each cell contains the key benefits sought. (Table 13-2 illustrates such a matrix for suntan lotion.) Then:
4. Evaluate each cell in terms of potential (sales volume, price level, cost to serve, competitor strength, and so forth).
5. Develop and implement a marketing strategy for those cells that offer sufficient profit potential given your capabilities.

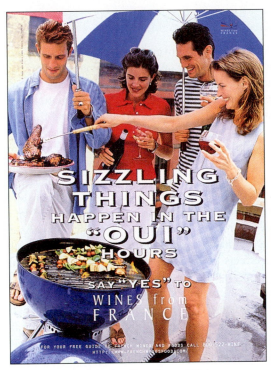

Courtesy Food and Wines from France/Sopexa U.S.A.

Suntan Lotion Use Situation	Potential Users of Suntan Lotion				
	Young Children	Teenagers	Adult Women	Adult Men	General Situation Benefits
Beach/boat activities	Prevent sunburn/skin damage	Prevent sunburn while tanning	Prevent sunburn/skin change/dry skin	Prevent sunburn	Container floats
Home/pools sunbathing	Prevent sunburn/skin damage	Tanning without sunburn	Tanning without skin damage or dry skin	Tanning without sunburn/skin damage	Lotion won't stain clothes or furniture
Tanning booth		Tanning	Tanning with moisturizer	Tanning	Designed for sunlamps
Snow skiing		Prevent sunburn	Prevent sunburn/ skin damage/ dry skin	Prevent sunburn	Antifreeze formula
Person benefits	Protection	Tanning	Protection and tanning with soft skin	Protection and tanning	

Source: Adapted from P. Dickson, "Person–Situation: Segmentation's Missing Link," *Journal of Marketing*, Fall 1982, pp. 56–64. Published by the American Marketing Association. Reprinted with permission.

SUMMARY

Marketing managers should view the consumer and the marketing activities designed to affect and influence that consumer in light of the situations that the consumer faces. A *consumer situation* is a set of factors outside of and removed from stable characteristics of the individual consumer and focal stimulus. Four categories of situations are communications, purchase, usage, and disposition situations.

Situations have been classified into a scheme of five objectively measured variables. *Physical surroundings* include geographical and institutional location, decor, sound, aromas, lighting, weather, and displays of merchandise or other material surrounding the product. Retailers are particularly concerned with the effects of physical surroundings. The sum of all the physical features of a retail environment is referred to as the *store atmosphere* or environment. *Atmospherics* is the process managers use to manipulate the physical retail environment to create specific mood responses in shoppers. Atmosphere is referred to as *servicescape* when describing a service business such as a hospital, bank, or restaurant.

Social surroundings deal with other persons present who could have an impact on the individual consumer's behavior. The characteristics of the other persons present, their roles, and their interpersonal interactions are potentially important social situational influences.

Temporal perspectives relate to the effect of time on consumer behavior, such as effects of time of day, time since last purchase, time since or until meals or payday, and time constraints imposed by commitments.

Convenience stores have evolved and been successful by taking advantage of the temporal perspective factor.

Task definition reflects the purpose or reason for engaging in the consumption behavior. The task may reflect different buyer and user roles anticipated by the individual. For example, a person shopping for dishes to be given as a wedding present is in a different situation from a person buying dishes for personal use.

Antecedent states are features of the individual person that are not lasting or relatively enduring characteristics. *Moods* are temporary states of depression or high excitement, and so on, which all people experience. *Momentary conditions* are such things as being tired, ill, having a great deal of money (or none at all), and so forth.

A *ritual situation* can be described as a set of interrelated behaviors that occur in a structured format, that have symbolic meaning, and that occur in response to socially defined occasions. Ritual situations can range from completely private to completely public. They are of major importance to marketers because they often involve prescribed consumption behaviors.

Situational influences may have direct influences, but they also interact with product and individual characteristics to influence behavior. In some cases, the situation will have no influence whatsoever, because the individual's characteristics or choices are so intense that they override everything else. But the situation is always potentially important and therefore of concern to marketing managers.

KEY TERMS

Antecedent states 495
Atmospherics 488
Communications situation 485
Disposition situation 487
Embarrassment 493
Moods 495

Physical surroundings 488
Purchase situation 486
Ritual situation 497
Servicescape 489
Situational influence 484
Social surroundings 492

Store atmosphere 488
Task definition 494
Temporal perspectives 493
Usage situation 486

INTERNET EXERCISES

1. Visit several online malls. How would you characterize this shopping situation relative to shopping at an actual mall?

2. What type of online environment does Amazon.com have?

3. Prepare a report listing and describing several useful sites for gathering current information about ritual situations such as marriages, high school graduation, Thanksgiving, or proms.

4. Evaluate WeddingWindow.com.

REVIEW QUESTIONS

1. What is meant by the term *situation?* Why is it important for a marketing manager to understand situational influences on purchasing behavior?

2. What are *physical surroundings* (as a situational variable)? Give an example of how they can influence the consumption process.

3. How does crowding affect shopping behavior?

4. What is *store atmosphere?*

5. What is *atmospherics?*

6. What is a *servicescape?*

7. What are *social surroundings* (as a situational variable)? Give an example of how they can influence the consumption process.

8. What is *temporal perspective* (as a situational variable)? Give an example of how it can influence the consumption process.

9. What is *task definition* (as a situational variable)? Give an example of how it can influence the consumption process.

10. Why do people give gifts?

11. How might the receipt of a gift affect the relationship between the giver and the receiver?

12. What are *antecedent conditions* (as a situational variable)? Give an example of how they can influence the consumption process.

13. What is a *mood?* How does it differ from an *emotion?* How do moods influence consumption behavior?

14. How do people manage their moods?

15. How do moods differ from *momentary conditions?*

16. What is meant by the statement, "Situational variables may interact with product or personal characteristics"?

17. Are individuals randomly exposed to situational influences? Why or why not?

18. What are *ritual situations?* Why are they important?

19. Describe a process for developing a situation-based marketing strategy.

DISCUSSION QUESTIONS

20. Discuss the potential importance of each type of situational influence in developing a marketing strategy to promote the purchase of (gifts to/shopping at):
    a. Audubon Society
    b. Applebee's
    c. Wakeboard
    d. Coca-Cola Zero
    e. Health insurance
    f. Old Navy

21. What product categories seem most susceptible to situational influences? Why?

22. Flowers are appropriate gifts for women for many situations but seem to be appropriate for men only when they are ill. Why is this so? How might 1-800-FLOWERS change this?

23. How could the store atmosphere at the following be improved?
    a. The main library on campus
    b. The bank lobby near campus
    c. A Mexican restaurant near campus
    d. A convenience store near campus
    e. The student advising office

24. Speculate on what a matrix like the one shown in Table 13-2 would look like for the following:
    a. Lemonade
    b. Eyewear
    c. Ice cream
    d. Shoes
    e. Bicycles
    f. Coffee

25. Does Table 13-1 have implications for outlets other than restaurants? If yes, which ones and why?

26. Do your shopping behavior and purchase criteria differ between purchases made for yourself and purchases made as gifts? How?

27. Describe a situation in which a mood (good or bad) caused you to make an unusual purchase.

28. Describe a relatively private ritual that you or someone you know has. What, if any, consumption pattern is associated with it?

29. Describe the consumption rituals your family has associated with the following ritual situations:
    a. Family birthdays
    b. Summer vacations
    c. Winter holiday
    d. Halloween
    e. Mother's Day
    f. Father's Day
    g. New Year's Eve

30. Respond to the questions in Consumer Insight 13-1.

APPLICATION ACTIVITIES

31. Interview five people who have recently purchased the following. Determine the role, if any, played by situational factors.
    a. A book
    b. Jewelry
    c. Luxury automobile
    d. A fast-food restaurant meal
    e. A cup of coffee
    f. Life insurance

32. Interview a salesperson for the following. Determine the role, if any, this individual feels situational variables play in his or her sales.
    a. Renter's insurance
    b. BMX bikes
    c. Fine chocolates
    d. Flowers

33. Conduct a study using a small (five or so) sample of your friends in which you attempt to isolate the situational factors that influence the type, brand, or amount of the following purchased or used.
    a. Health club
    b. Briefcase
    c. Movie attendance
    d. Volunteer work
    e. TV dinners
    f. Audio books

34. Create a list of 10 to 20 use situations relevant to campus area restaurants. Then interview 10 students and have them indicate which of these situations they have encountered, and ask them to rank order these situations in terms of how likely they are to occur. Discuss how a restaurant could use this information in trying to appeal to the student market.

35. Visit three stores selling the same product line. Describe how the atmosphere differs across the stores. Why do you think these differences exist?

36. Visit three local coffee shops. Describe how the servicescapes differ across the shops. Why do you think these differences exist?

37. What kind of online atmosphere does each of the following have? How would you improve it?
    a. HyundaiUSA.com
    b. Harley-Davidson.com
    c. Phatfarmstore.com
    d. Charities.org
    e. Cabelas.com
    f. Mountaindew.com

38. Copy or describe an advertisement that is clearly based on a situational appeal. Indicate
    a. Which situational variable is involved
    b. Why the company would use this variable
    c. Your evaluation of the effectiveness of this approach

39. Create a graduation gift, anniversary gift, and self-use ad for the following. Explain the differences across the ads:
    a. Savings bond
    b. Gourmet coffee maker
    c. Magazine subscription
    d. Set of dishes
    e. Blender
    f. Watch

40. Interview five students and determine instances where their mood affected their purchases. What do you conclude?

41. Interview five students and determine the consumption rituals they have with respect to the following. What do you conclude?
    a. New Year's Day
    b. Spring break
    c. Memorial Day
    d. Valentine's Day
    e. Mother's Day
    f. Father's Day

REFERENCES

1. This vignette is based on E. Bernstein, "You Don't Have to Be Jewish to Want a Bar Mitzvah," *The Wall Street Journal,* January 14, 2004, p. A1; T. Weiss, "Event Companies Cater Rising Demand for Elaborate Bar, Bat Mitzvahs," *Knight Ridder Tribune Business News,* March 10, 2004, p. 1; A. Chozick, "Fairy-Tale Fifteenths," *The Wall Street Journal,* October 15, 2004, p. B1; and D. M. Alba, "New Mexico Hispanics Emphasize 'Quinceanera' Celebrations," *Knight Ridder Tribune Business News,* February 7, 2005, p. 1.

2. Bernstein, "You Don't Have to Be Jewish to Want a Bar Mitzvah."

3. Chozick, "Fairy-Tale Fifteenths."

4. Ibid.

5. See K. S. Lim and M. A. Razzaque, "Brand Loyalty and Situational Effects," *Journal of International Consumer Marketing,* no. 4 (1997), pp. 95–115.

6. R. W. Belk, "Situational Variables and Consumer Behavior," *Journal of Consumer Research,* December 1975, p. 158.

7. See K. R. France and C. W. Park, "The Impact of Program Affective Valence and Level of Cognitive Appraisal on Advertising Processing and Effectiveness," *Journal of Current Issues and Research in Advertising,* Fall 1997, pp. 1–21; A. B. Aylesworth and S. B. MacKenzie, "Context Is Key," *Journal of Advertising,* Summer 1998, pp. 17–31; K. R. Lord, R. E. Burnkrant, and H. R. Unnava, "The Effects of Program-Induced Mood States on Memory for Commercial Information," *Journal of Current Issues and Research in Advertising,* Spring 2001, pp. 1–14; S. Shapiro, D. J. MacInnis, and C. Whan Park, "Understanding Program-Induced Mood Effects," *Journal of Advertising,* Winter 2002, pp. 15–26; P. De Pelsmacker, M. Geuens, and P. Anckaert, "Media Context and Advertising Effectiveness," *Journal of Advertising,* Summer 2002, pp. 49–61; and S. Jun et al., "The Influence of Editorial Context on Consumer Response to Advertisements in a Specialty Magazine," *Journal of Current Issues and Research in Advertising,* Fall 2003, pp. 1–11.

8. L. Sanders and J. Halliday, "BP Institutes 'Ad-Pull' Policy for Print Publications," *AdAge.com,* May 24, 2005.

9. B. Wansink, "Making Old Brands New," *American Demographics,* December 1997, pp. 53–58.

10. E. Byron, "Case by Case," *The Wall Street Journal,* November 17, 2004, p. A1.

11. Ibid.; and I. Sinha, "A Conceptual Model of Situation Type on Consumer Choice Behavior and Consideration Sets," in *Advances in Consumer Research,* vol. 21, eds. C. T. Allen and D. R. John (Provo, UT: Association for Consumer Research, 1994), pp. 477–82.

12. See J. A. F. Nicholls et al., "Situational Influences on Shoppers," *Journal of International Consumer Marketing* 9, no. 2 (1996), pp. 21–39; and J. A. F. Nicholls, T. Li, and S. Roslow, "Oceans Apart," *Journal of International Consumer Marketing* 12, no. 1 (1999), pp. 57–72.

13. See E. Sherman, A. Mathur, and R. B. Smith, "Store Environment and Consumer Purchase Behavior," *Psychology & Marketing,* July 1997, pp. 361–78; and J. Baker et al., "The Influence of Multiple Design Cues on Perceived Merchandise Value and Patronage Intentions," *Journal of Marketing,* April 2002, pp. 120–41.

14. For an extensive review see L. W. Turley and R. E. Milliman, "Atmospheric Effects on Shopping Behavior," *Journal of Business Research* 49 (2000), pp. 193–211. See also, A. d'Astous, "Irritating Aspects of the Shopping Environment," and A. Sharma and T. F. Stafford, "The Effect of Retail Atmospherics on Customers' Perceptions of Salespeople and Customer Persuasion," both in *Journal of Business Research* 49 (2000), pp. 149–156 and 183–191, respectively.

15. P. Sautter, M. R. Hyman, and V. Lukosius, "E-Tail Atmospherics," *Journal of Electronic Commerce Research* 5, no. 1 (2004), pp. 14–24.

16. M. J. Bitner, "Servicescapes," *Journal of Marketing,* April 1992, pp. 57–71. See also, K. L. Wakefield and J. G. Blodgett, "The Effect of the Servicescape on Customers' Behavioral Intentions in Leisure Service Settings," *Journal of Services Marketing* 6 (1996), pp. 45–61; and K. D. Hoffman, S. W. Kelley, and B. C. Chung, "A CIT Investigation of Servicescape Failures and Associated Recovery Strategies," *Journal of Services Marketing* 17, no. 4/5 (2003), pp. 322–40.

17. G. J. Gorn, A. Chattopadhyay, T. Yi, and D. W. Dahl, "Effects of Color as an Executional Cue in Advertising," *Management Science,* October 1997, pp. 1387–99.

18. See J. A. Bellizzi and R. E. Hite, "Environmental Color, Consumer Feelings, and Purchase Likelihood," *Psychology & Marketing,* September 1992, pp. 347–63.

19. B. E. Kahn and L. McAlister, *Grocery Revolution* (Reading, MA: Addison-Wesley, 1997).

20. G. J. Gorn, A. Chattopadhyay, J. Sengupta, and S. Tripathi, "Waiting for the Web," *Journal of Marketing Research,* May 2004, pp. 215–25.

21. D. J. Mitchell, B. E. Kahn, and S. C. Knasko, "There's Something in the Air," *Journal of Consumer Research,* September 1995, pp. 229–38.

22. E. R. Spangenberg, A. E. Crowley, and P. W. Henderson, "Improving the Store Environment," *Journal of Marketing,* April 1996, pp. 67–80.

23. A. R. Hirsch, "Effects of Ambient Odors on Slot-Machine Usage in a Las Vegas Casino," *Psychology & Marketing,* October 1995, pp. 585–94.

24. M. Wilkie, "Scent of a Market," *American Demographics,* August 1995, pp. 40–49.

25. M. Morrin and S. Ratneshwar, "The Impact of Ambient Scent on Evaluation, Attention, and Memory for Familiar and Unfamiliar Brands," *Journal of Business Research* 49 (2000), pp. 157–65.

26. P. F. Bone and P. S. Ellen, "Scents in the Marketplace," *Journal of Retailing* 75, no. 2 (1999), pp. 243–62.

27. P. Sloan, "Smelling Trouble," *Advertising Age,* September 11, 1995, p. 1.

28. See S. Oakes, "The Influence of the Musicscape within Service Environments," *Journal of Services Marketing* 4, no. 7 (2000), pp. 539–56.

29. J. D. Herrington and L. M. Capella, "Effect of Music in Service Environments," *Journal of Services Marketing* 10, no. 2 (1996), pp. 26–41; M. K. Hui, L. Dube, and J.-C. Chebat, "The Impact of Music on Consumers' Reactions to Waiting for Services," *Journal of Retailing,* Spring 1997, pp. 87–104; J. C. Sweeney and F. Wyber, "The Role of Cognitions and Emotions in the Music-Approach-Avoidance Behavior Relationship," *Journal of Services Marketing* 16, no. 1 (2002), pp. 51–69; and C. Caldwell and S. A. Hibbert, "The Influence of Music Tempo and Musical Preference on Restaurant Patrons' Behavior," *Psychology & Marketing,* November 2002, pp. 895–917.

30. B. Zimmers, "Business Deals Put AEI Music CEO in Good Mood," *Puget Sound Business Journal,* June 23, 2000, p. 44; see also C. A. Olson, "Shopping to the Music Made Easy," *Billboard,* July 31, 1999, pp. 73–74.

31. See K. A. Machleit, S. A. Eroglu, and S. P. Mantel, "Perceived Retail Crowding and Shopping Satisfaction," *Journal of Consumer Psychology* 9, no. 1 (2000), pp. 29–42.

32. For general servicescape differences see B. D. Keillor, G. T. M. Hult, and D. Kandemir, "A Study of the Service Encounter in Eight Countries," *Journal of International Marketing* 12, no. 1 (2004), pp. 2–35.

33. See B. Dubois and G. Laurent, "The Functions of Luxury," *Advances in Consumer Research,* vol. 23, eds. K. P. Corfman and J. G. Lynch (Provo, UT: Association for Consumer Research, 1996), pp. 470–77; Y. Zhang and B. Gelb, "Matching Advertising Appeals to Culture," *Journal of Advertising,* Fall 1996, pp. 29–46; and T. R. Graeth, "Consumption Situations and the Effects of Brand Image on Consumers' Brand Evaluations," *Psychology & Marketing,* January 1997, pp. 49–70.

34. R. K. Ratner and B. E. Kahn, "The Impact of Private versus Public Consumption on Variety-Seeking Behavior," *Journal of Consumer Research,* September 2002, pp. 246–57.

35. See, e.g., D. W. Dahl, R. V. Manchanda, and J. J. Argo, "Embarrassment in Consumer Purchase," *Journal of Consumer Research,* December 2001, pp. 473–81.

36. R. Batra and P. M. Homer, "The Situational Impact of Brand Image Beliefs," *Journal of Consumer Psychology* 14, no. 3 (2004), pp. 318–30.

37. See B. L. Gross, "Consumer Response to Time Pressure," *Advances in Consumer Research,* vol. 21, eds. Allen and John, pp. 120–24; L. A. Brannon and T. C. Brock, "Limiting Time for Responding Enhances Behavior Corresponding to the Merits of Compliance Appeals," *Journal of Consumer Psychology* 10, no. 3 (2001), pp. 135–46; and R. Suri and K. B. Monroe, "The Effects of Time Constraints on Consumers' Judgments of Prices and Products," *Journal of Consumer Research,* June 2003, pp. 92–104.

38. S. M. Nowlis, "The Effect of Time Pressure on the Choice of Brands That Differ in Quality, Price, and Product Features," *Marketing Letters,* October 1995, pp. 287–96; R. Dhar and S. M. Nowlis, "The Effect of Time Pressure on Consumer Choice Deferral," *Journal of Consumer Research,* March 1999, pp. 369–84; and R. Pieters and L. Warlop, "Visual Attention during Brand Choice," *International Journal of Research in Marketing,* February 1999, pp. 1–16.

39. P. Van Kenhove, K. De Wulf, and W. Van Waterschoot, "The Impact of Task Definition on Store-Attribute Saliences and Store Choice," *Journal of Retailing* 75, no. 1 (1999), pp. 125–37; P. Van Kenhove and K. De Wulf, "Income and Time Pressure," *International Review of Retail, Distribution and Consumer Research,* April 2000, pp. 149–66.

40. See B. H. Schmitt and C. J. Shultz II, "Situational Effects on Brand Preferences for Image Products," *Psychology & Marketing,* August 1995, pp. 433–46.

41. T. M. Lowrey, C. C. Otnes, and J. A. Ruth, "Social Influences on Dyadic Giving over Time," *Journal of Consumer Research,* March 2004, pp. 547–58.

42. For a review and framework, see D. Larsen and J. J. Watson, "A Guide Map to the Terrain of Gift Value," *Psychology & Marketing,* August 2001, pp. 889–906; see also G. Saad and T. Gill, "An Evolutionary Psychology Perspective on Gift Giving among Young Adults," *Psychology & Marketing,* September 2003, pp. 765–84.

43. M. A. McGrath, "Gender Differences in Gift Exchanges," *Psychology & Marketing,* August 1995, pp. 371–93; K. M. Palan, C. S. Areni, and P. Kiecker, "Gender Role Incongruency and Memorable Gift Exchange Experiences," and J. F. Durgee and T. Sego, "Gift-Giving as a Metaphor for Understanding New Products That Delight," both in *Advances in Consumer Research,* vol. 28, eds. M. C. Gilly and J. Meyers-Levy (Provo, UT: Association for Consumer Research, 2001), pp. 51–57 and 64–69, respectively; and Saad and Gill, "An Evolutionary Psychology Perspective on Gift Giving among Young Adults."

44. D. B. Wooten, "Qualitative Steps toward an Expanded Model of Anxiety in Gift-Giving," *Journal of Consumer Research,* June 2000, pp. 84–95.

45. See, e.g., J. A. Ruth, C. C. Otnes, and F. F. Brunel, "Gift Receipt and the Reformulation of Interpersonal Relationships," *Journal of Consumer Research,* March 1999, pp. 385–402.

46. R. W. Belk and G. S. Coon, "Gift Giving as Agapic Love," *Journal of Consumer Research,* December 1993, pp. 404–5.

47. C. S. Areni, P. Kiecker, and K. M. Palan, "Is It Better to Give than to Receive?" *Psychology & Marketing,* January 1998, pp. 81–109.

48. A. Joy, "Gift Giving in Hong Kong and the Continuum of Social Ties," *Journal of Consumer Research,* September 2001, pp. 239–55; and S. L. Lotz, S. Shim, and K. C. Gehrt, "A Study of Japanese Consumers' Cognitive Hierarchies in Formal and Informal Gift-Giving Situations," *Psychology & Marketing,* January 2003, pp. 59–85.

49. S.-Y. Park, "A Comparison of Korean and American Gift-Giving Behaviors," *Psychology & Marketing,* September 1998, pp. 577–93.

50. See R. P. Bagozzi, M. Gopinath, and P. U. Nyer, "The Role of Emotion in Marketing," *Journal of the Academy of Marketing Science,* Spring 1999, pp. 184–206; and H. T. Luomala and M. Laaksonen, "Contributions from Mood Research," *Psychology & Marketing,* March 2000, pp. 195–233.

51. M. B. Holbrook and M. P. Gardner, "Illustrating a Dynamic Model of the Mood-Updating Process in Consumer Behavior," *Psychology & Marketing,* March 2000, pp. 165–94.

52. See, e.g., J.-C. Chebat et al., "Impact of Waiting Attribution and Consumer's Mood on Perceived Quality," *Journal of Business Research,* November 1995, pp. 191–96; J. P. Forgas and J. Ciarrochi,

"On Being Happy and Possessive," *Psychology & Marketing,* March 2001, pp. 239–60; and R. Adaval, "Sometimes It Just Feels Right," *Journal of Consumer Research,* June 2001, pp. 1–17.

53. D. W. Rook and M. P. Gardner, "In the Mood," *Research in Consumer Behavior* 6 (1993), pp. 1–28; W. R. Swinyard, "The Effects of Mood, Involvement, and Quality of Store Experience on Shopping Intentions," *Journal of Consumer Research,* September 1993, pp. 271–80; and R. J. Faber and G. A. Christenson, "In the Mood to Buy," *Psychology & Marketing,* December 1996, pp. 803–19.

54. See endnote 7.

55. See, e.g., K. S. Coulter, "The Effects of Affective Responses to Media Context on Advertising Evaluations," *Journal of Advertising,* Winter 1998, pp. 41–51.

56. H. T. Luomala and M. Laaksonen, "A Qualitative Exploration of Mood-Regulatory Self-Gift Behaviors," *Journal of Economic Psychology* 20 (1999), pp. 147–82.

57. H. Mano, "The Influence of Pre-Existing Negative Affect on Store Purchase Intentions," *Journal of Retailing* 75, no. 2 (1999), pp. 149–73.

58. S. J. Gould, "An Interpretive Study of Purposeful, Mood Self-Regulating Consumption," *Psychology & Marketing,* July 1997, pp. 395–426.

59. See M. G. Meloy, "Mood-Driven Distortion of Product Information," *Journal of Consumer Research,* December 2000, pp. 345–58.

60. See P. A. Walsh and S. Spiggle, "Consumer Spending Patterns," in *Advances in Consumer Research,* vol. 21, eds. Allen and John, pp. 35–40; and N. Karlsson, T. Garling, and M. Selart, "Explanations of Prior Income Changes on Buying Decisions," *Journal of Economic Psychology* 20 (1999), pp. 449–63.

61. See B. Gainer, "Ritual and Relationships," *Journal of Business Research,* March 1995, pp. 253–60.

62. See C. C. Otnes and L. M. Scott, "Something Old, Something New," *Journal of Advertising,* Spring 1996, pp. 33–50.

63. "$10 Billion for Mom," *CNNmoney* (online), April 21, 2004.

64. A. Z. Cuneo, "Using Halloween to Scare Up Sales," *Advertising Age,* October 8, 2001, p. 4.

65. D. Treise, J. M. Wolburg, and C. C. Otnes, "Understanding the 'Social Gifts' of Drinking Rituals," *Journal of Advertising,* Summer 1999, pp. 17–30.

66. For a similar approach see R. Brodie, "Segmentation and Market Structure When Both Consumer and Situational Characteristics Are Explanatory," *Psychology & Marketing,* September 1992, pp. 395–408.

© M. Hruby.

14

Consumer Decision Process and Problem Recognition

■ In 2001, Beiersdorf, marketers of the Nivea brand, introduced its Nivea for Men line in the United States.[1] Nivea for Men has been very popular in Europe for the past 10 years. However, according to the director of marketing for Beiersdorf Inc. USA,

American men are the most powerful men in the world in finance and the Internet. However, in terms of styling, they lag 15–20 years behind their European counterparts.

Nivea for Men currently consists of numerous products within a four-step facial care system:

Step One: Cleanse Face   Wash your face twice a day with Double Action Face Wash. Soap free, it clears away everyday dirt and excess oils without drying out your skin.

Wash your face three or four times a week with Exfoliating Face Scrub. It deeply cleanses and purifies to help clear away dry, rough skin, built-up dirt and helps prevent clogged pores.

Step Two: Shave   Use Mild Shaving Gel every time you shave. It gives you an extra thick lather for a closer, smoother shave. Enriched with unique moisturizers, it improves the condition of your skin while shaving and helps to protect against razor burn and skin dryness.

For sensitive skin use Sensitive Shaving Gel. Enriched with soothing Aloe and moisturizing agents, it protects your skin while shaving. Unscented and free of dyes, it minimizes the risk of irritation.

Step Three: Apply After Shave   Use After Shave Balm every time you shave to help calm the irritations that are caused by shaving. It soothes and moisturizes the skin after shaving, and noticeably improves the condition of your skin.

For sensitive skin use Sensitive After Shave Balm. This light, unscented, easily absorbed balm moisturizes the skin without burning it.

Step Four: Moisturize   Use Moisturizing Lotion every day to provide valuable moisture to the skin. It leaves skin smooth and protected.

Currently, 98 percent of American men wash their faces with bar soap despite the fact that many have dry skin, which soap can exacerbate. Beiersdorf is betting millions that they can change that pattern.

The time is right—American men are ready. Because of tough competition in the workplace, the changing dynamics between men and women, and the increased societal value placed upon youth, American men of all ages are now realizing that looking good can give them a significant advantage, both in professional and personal areas.

Problem recognition is the first stage of the consumer decision process. For Nivea for Men to succeed in America, Beiersdorf must cause significant numbers of American men to recognize a problem with their current methods of facial care. If Beiersdorf can trigger problem recognition, consumers may then proceed to evaluate, purchase, and use their product line.

This chapter examines the nature of the consumer decision process and analyzes the first step in that process—problem recognition. Within problem recognition, we focus on (1) the process of problem recognition, (2) the uncontrollable determinants of problem recognition, and (3) marketing strategies based on the problem recognition process.

TYPES OF CONSUMER DECISIONS

The term *consumer decision* produces an image of an individual carefully evaluating the attributes of a set of products, brands, or services and rationally selecting the one that solves a clearly recognized need for the least cost. It has a rational, functional connotation. Consumers do make many decisions in this manner; however, many other decisions involve little conscious effort. Further, many consumer decisions focus not on brand attributes but rather on the feelings or emotions associated with acquiring or using the brand or with the situation in which the product is purchased or used. Thus, a brand may be selected not because of an attribute (price, style, functional characteristics) but because "it makes me feel good" or "my friends will like it."[2]

Although purchases and related consumption behavior driven by emotional or situational needs have characteristics distinct from the traditional attribute-based model, the decision process model provides useful insights into all types of consumer purchases. As we describe the process of consumer decision making in this and the next four chapters, we will indicate how it helps us understand emotion-, situation-, and attribute-based decisions.

Consumer decisions are frequently the result of a single problem, for example, running low on gasoline. At other times, they result from the convergence of several problems, such as an aging automobile and a growing feeling of inadequacy or low self-esteem. Furthermore, once the decision process begins, it may evolve and become more complex with multiple goals. A consumer noticing a simple need for gas may want to minimize the price paid, avoid one or more brands because of their environmental record, and decide to find a station with food service attached. This consumer may wind up choosing between a station with a lower price and its own food service, or another station with a higher price but with a preferred food outlet such as Taco Bell attached, or perhaps spending the extra time to buy gas at one and food at the other.[3]

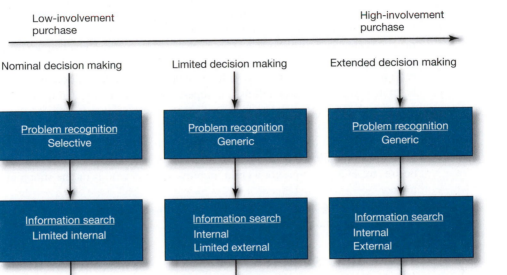

Low-involvement purchase → High-involvement purchase

Nominal decision making	Limited decision making	Extended decision making
Problem recognition Selective	**Problem recognition** Generic	**Problem recognition** Generic
Information search Limited internal	**Information search** Internal Limited external	**Information search** Internal External
	Alternative evaluation Few attributes Simple decision rules Few alternatives	**Alternative evaluation** Many attributes Complex decision rules Many alternatives
Purchase	Purchase	Purchase
Postpurchase No dissonance Very limited evaluation	**Postpurchase** No dissonance Limited evaluation	**Postpurchase** Dissonance Complex evaluation

As Figure 14-1 indicates, there are various types of consumer decision processes.[4] As the consumer moves from a very low level of involvement *with the purchase* to a high level of involvement, decision making becomes increasingly complex. While purchase involvement is a continuum, it is useful to consider nominal, limited, and extended decision making as general descriptions of the types of processes that occur along various points on the continuum. Keep in mind that the types of decision processes are not distinct but rather blend into each other.

Before describing each type of decision process, the concept of purchase involvement must be clarified. We define **purchase involvement** as *the level of concern for, or interest in, the purchase process triggered by the need to consider a particular purchase.* Thus, purchase involvement is a *temporary state* of an individual or household. It is influenced by the interaction of individual, product, and situational characteristics.

Note that purchase involvement is *not* the same as **product involvement** or enduring involvement. A consumer may be very involved with a brand (Starbucks or Saturn) or a product category (coffee or cars) and yet have a very low level of involvement with a particular purchase of that product because of brand loyalty, time pressures, or other reasons. For example, think of your favorite brand of soft drink or other beverage. You may be quite loyal to that brand, think it is superior to other brands, and have strong, favorable feelings about it. However, when you want a soft drink, you probably just buy your preferred brand without much thought.

Or a consumer may have a rather low level of involvement with a product (school supplies or automobile tires) but have a high level of purchase involvement because he or she desires to set an example for a child, impress a friend who is on the shopping trip, or save money.

The following sections provide a brief description of how the purchasing process changes as purchase involvement increases.

Nominal Decision Making

Nominal decision making, sometimes referred to as *habitual decision making,* in effect *involves no decision per se.* As Figure 14-1 indicates, a problem is recognized, internal search (long-term memory) provides a single preferred solution (brand), that brand is purchased, and an evaluation occurs only if the brand fails to perform as expected. Nominal decisions occur when there is very low involvement with the purchase.

A completely nominal decision does not even include consideration of the "do not purchase" alternative. For example, you might notice that you are nearly out of Aim toothpaste and resolve to purchase some the next time you are at the store. You don't even consider not replacing the toothpaste or purchasing another brand. At the store, you scan the shelf for Aim and pick it up without considering alternative brands, its price, or other potentially relevant factors.

Nominal decisions can be broken into two distinct categories: brand loyal decisions and repeat purchase decisions. These two categories are described briefly below and examined in detail in Chapter 18.

Brand Loyal Purchases
At one time, you may have been highly involved in selecting a brand of toothpaste and, in response, used an extensive decision-making process. Having selected Aim as a result of this process, you may now purchase it without further consideration, even though using the best available toothpaste is still important to you. Thus, you are committed to Aim because you believe it best meets your overall needs and you have formed an emotional attachment to it (you like it). You are brand loyal. It will be very difficult for a competitor to gain your patronage.

In this example, you have a fairly high degree of product involvement but a low degree of purchase involvement because of your brand loyalty. Should you encounter a challenge to the superiority of Aim, perhaps through a news article, you would most likely engage in a high-involvement decision process before changing brands.

Repeat Purchases
In contrast, you may believe that all ketchup is about the same and you may not attach much importance to the product category or purchase. Having tried Del Monte and found it satisfactory, you now purchase it whenever you need ketchup. Thus, you are a repeat purchaser of Del Monte ketchup, but you are not committed to it.

Should you encounter a challenge to the wisdom of buying Del Monte the next time you need ketchup, perhaps because of a point-of-sale price discount, you would probably engage in only a limited decision process before deciding on which brand to purchase.

Limited Decision Making

Limited decision making involves internal and limited external search, few alternatives, simple decision rules on a few attributes, and little postpurchase evaluation. It covers the middle ground between nominal decision making and extended decision making. In its simplest form (lowest level of purchase involvement), limited decision making is similar to nominal decision making. For example, while in a store you may notice a point-of-purchase display for Jell-O and pick up two boxes without seeking information beyond your memory that "Jell-O tastes good," or "Gee, I haven't had Jell-O in a long time." In addition, you may have considered no other alternative except possibly a very limited examination of a "do not buy" option. Or you may have a decision rule that you buy the cheapest brand of instant coffee available. When you run low on coffee (problem recognition), you simply examine coffee prices the next time you are in the store and select the cheapest brand.

Limited decision making also occurs in response to some emotional or situational needs. For example, you may decide to purchase a new brand or product because you are bored with the current, otherwise satisfactory, brand. This decision might involve evaluating only the newness or novelty of the available alternatives.[5] Or you might evaluate a purchase in terms of the actual or anticipated behavior of others. For example, you might order or refrain from ordering wine with a meal depending on the observed or expected orders of your dinner companions.

In general, limited decision making involves recognizing a problem for which there are several possible solutions. There is internal and a limited amount of external search. A few alternatives are evaluated on a few dimensions using simple selection rules. The purchase and use of the product are given very little evaluation afterward, unless there is a service problem or product failure.

Extended Decision Making

As Figure 14-1 indicates, **extended decision making** involves an extensive internal and external information search followed by a complex evaluation of multiple alternatives and significant postpurchase evaluation. It is the response to a high level of purchase involvement. After the purchase, doubt about its correctness is likely and a thorough evaluation of the purchase takes place. Relatively few consumer decisions reach this level of complexity. However, products such as homes, personal computers, and complex recreational items such as backpacks and stereo systems are frequently purchased via extended decision making.

Even decisions that are heavily emotional may involve substantial cognitive efforts. For example, a consumer may agonize over a decision to take a ski trip or visit parents even though the needs being met and the criteria being evaluated are largely emotions or feelings rather than attributes per se, and are therefore typically fewer in number with less external information available.

As Figure 14-1 illustrates, problem recognition is the first stage of the decision process. We will describe this stage and discuss the marketing applications associated with it in the balance of this chapter. We devote the next four chapters to the remaining four stages of the consumer decision process and discuss the relevant marketing applications in those chapters.

Our discussion of the decision process is based primarily on studies conducted in America. Although the evidence is limited, it appears that consumers in other cultures use similar processes.[6]

THE PROCESS OF PROBLEM RECOGNITION

A day rarely passes in which a person does not face multiple problems that are resolved by consuming products and services. Routine problems of depletion, such as the need to get gasoline as the gauge approaches empty or the need to replace a frequently used food item, are readily recognized, defined, and resolved. The unexpected breakdown of a major appliance such as a refrigerator creates an unplanned problem that is also easily recognized but is often more difficult to resolve. Recognition of other problems, such as the need for a camera phone or a GPS system in the car, may take longer, as they may be subtle and evolve slowly over time.

Feelings, such as boredom, anxiety, or the "blues," may arise quickly or slowly over time. Such feelings are often recognized as problems subject to solution by purchasing behavior (I'm sad, I think I'll go shopping/to a movie/to a restaurant). At other times, such feelings may trigger consumption behaviors without deliberate decision making. A person feeling restless may eat snack food without really thinking about it. In this case, the problem remains unrecognized (at the conscious level) and the solutions tried are often inappropriate (eating may not reduce restlessness).

Marketers develop products to help consumers solve problems. They also attempt to help consumers recognize problems, sometimes well in advance of their occurrence (see Illustration 14-1).

The Nature of Problem Recognition

Problem recognition is the first stage in the consumer decision process. **Problem recognition** is the result of a discrepancy between a desired state and an actual state that is sufficient to arouse and activate the decision process.[7] An **actual state** is the way an individual perceives his or her feelings and situation to be at the present time. A **desired state** is the way an individual *wants* to feel or be at the present time. For example, you probably don't want to be bored on Friday night. If you find yourself alone and becoming bored, you would treat this as a problem because your actual state (being bored) and your desired state (being pleasantly occupied) are different. You could then choose to consume a television program, rent a video, call a friend, go out, or take a wide array of other actions.

The kind of action taken by consumers in response to a recognized problem relates directly to the problem's importance to the consumer, the situation, and the dissatisfaction or inconvenience created by the problem.

Without recognition of a problem, there is no need for a decision. This condition is shown in Figure 14-2, when there is no discrepancy between the consumer's desired state (what the consumer would like) and the actual state (what the consumer perceives as already existing). Thus, if Friday night arrives and you find yourself engrossed in a novel, your desire to be pleasantly occupied (desired state) and your condition of enjoying a novel would be consistent, and you would have no reason to search for other activities.

On the other hand, when there is a discrepancy between a consumer desire and the perceived actual state, recognition of a problem occurs. Figure 14-2 indicates that any

© Veterinary Pet Insurance Company.

time the desired state is perceived as being greater than or less than the actual state, a problem exists. For example, being pleasantly occupied (desired state) would generally exceed being bored (actual state) and result in problem recognition. However, if your roommate suddenly showed up with a rowdy party, you might find yourself with more stimulation (actual state) than the medium level you actually desire. This too would result in problem recognition.

In Figure 14-2, consumer desires are shown to be the result of the desired lifestyle of the consumer (as described in Chapter 12) and the current situation (time pressures, physical surroundings, and so forth, as described in Chapter 13). Thus, a consumer whose self-concept and desired lifestyle focus on outdoor activities will desire frequent participation in such activities. A current situation of new snow in the mountains or warm weather at the beach would tend to increase that person's desire to be engaged in outdoor sports.

Perceptions of the actual state are also determined by a consumer's lifestyle and current situation. Consumers' lifestyles are a major determinant of their actual state because that is how they choose to live given the constraints imposed by their resources. Thus, a consumer who has chosen to raise a family, have significant material possessions, and pursue a demanding career is likely to have little free time for outdoor activities (actual state). The current situation—a day off work, a big project due, or a sick child—also has a major impact on how consumers perceive the actual situation.

It is important to note that it is the consumer's *perception* of the actual state that drives problem recognition, not some objective reality. Consumers who smoke cigars may

FIGURE 14-2   The Process of Problem Recognition

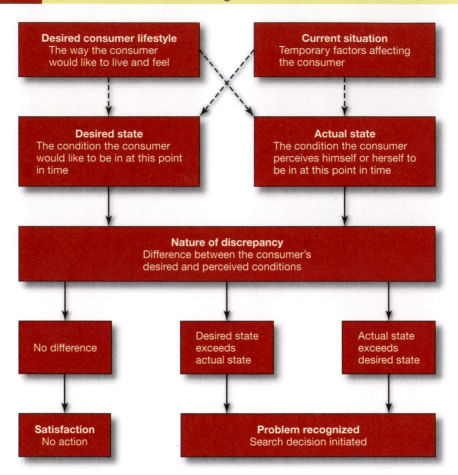

believe that this activity is not harming their health because they do not inhale. These consumers do not recognize a problem with this behavior despite the reality that it is harmful.

The Desire to Resolve Recognized Problems   The level of one's desire to resolve a particular problem depends on two factors: (1) *the magnitude of the discrepancy between the desired and actual states,* and (2) *the relative importance of the problem.* An individual could desire to have a car that averages at least 25 miles per gallon while still meeting certain size and power desires. If his or her current car obtains an average of 22 miles per gallon, a discrepancy exists, but it may not be large enough to motivate the consumer to proceed to the next step in the decision process.

On the other hand, a large discrepancy may exist and the consumer may not proceed to information search because the *relative importance* of the problem is small. A consumer may desire a new Volkswagen and own a 15-year-old Toyota. The discrepancy is large. However, the relative importance of this particular discrepancy may be small compared to other consumption problems such as those related to housing, utilities, and food. Relative importance is a critical concept because all consumers have budget constraints, time constraints, or both. Only the relatively more important problems are likely to be solved. In general, importance is determined by how critical the problem is to the maintenance of the consumer's desired lifestyle.

Types of Consumer Problems

Consumer problems may be either active or inactive. An **active problem** is *one the consumer is aware of or will become aware of in the normal course of events*. An **inactive problem** is *one of which the consumer is not aware*. (This concept is very similar to the concept of felt need discussed in the "Diffusion of Innovations" section of Chapter 7.) The following example should clarify the distinction between active and inactive problems.

Timberlane Lumber Co. acquired a source of supply of Honduran pitch pine. This natural product lights at the touch of a match even when damp and burns for 15 to 20 minutes. It will not flare up and is therefore relatively safe. It can be procured in sticks 15 to 18 inches long and 1 inch in diameter. These sticks can be used to ignite fireplace fires, or they can be shredded and used to ignite charcoal grills.

Prior to marketing the product, Timberlane commissioned a marketing study to estimate demand and guide in developing marketing strategy. Two large samples of potential consumers were interviewed. The first sample was asked how they lit their fireplace fires and what problems they had with this procedure. Almost all of the respondents used newspaper, kindling, or both, and very few experienced any problems. The new product was then described, and the respondents were asked to express the likelihood that they would purchase such a product. Only a small percentage expressed any interest. However, a sample of consumers that were paid to use the new product for several weeks felt it was a substantial improvement over existing methods and expressed a strong desire to continue using the product. Thus, the problem was there (because the new product was strongly preferred over the old by those who tried it), but most consumers were not aware of it. This is an *inactive problem*. Before the product can be successfully sold, the firm must activate problem recognition.

In contrast, a substantial percentage of those interviewed about lighting charcoal fires expressed a strong concern about the safety of liquid charcoal lighter. These individuals expressed great interest in purchasing a safer product. This is an *active problem*. Timberlane need not worry about problem recognition in this case. Instead, it can concentrate on illustrating how its product solves the problem that the consumers already know exists.

As this example indicates, active and inactive problems require different marketing strategies. Active problems require the marketer only to convince consumers that its brand is the superior solution. Consumers are already aware of the problem. In contrast, inactive problems require the marketer to convince consumers that they *have* the problem *and* that the marketer's brand is a superior solution to the problem. This is a much more difficult task.

Illustration 14-2 shows two ads, one of which is designed to activate a problem that is inactive for many pet owners. Note that an important component of the ad is to alert pet owners that the appearance of their young dog may not reveal an unhealthy level of body fat. Thus, it attempts to cause a change in their perception of the actual state and trigger the recognition of an inactive problem. In contrast, the Abreva ad assumes that these consumers are aware of the problem. It focuses on its unique ability to solve the problem.

Courtesy Nestle Purina Pet Care.

Abreva® is a trademark of the GlaxoSmithKline Group of Companies.

UNCONTROLLABLE DETERMINANTS OF PROBLEM RECOGNITION

A discrepancy between what is desired by a consumer and what the consumer has is the necessary condition for problem recognition. A discrepancy can be the result of a variety of factors that influence consumer desires, perceptions of the existing state, or both. These factors are often beyond the direct influence of the marketing manager, such as a change in family composition. Figure 14-3 summarizes the major nonmarketing factors that influence problem recognition. The marketing factors influencing problem recognition are discussed in the next section of this chapter.

Most of the nonmarketing factors that affect problem recognition are fairly obvious and logical. Most were described in some detail in prior chapters. For example, as we discussed in Chapter 2, a person's culture affects almost all aspects of his or her desired state. Thus, the desire to be recognized as an independent, unique person with distinctive behaviors and possessions differs sharply between American and Japanese consumers because of cultural influences.

Previous decisions and individual development were not discussed in earlier chapters. A previous decision to buy a bike or skis could lead to a current desire to have a car rack to carry them. A decision to become a home owner may trigger desires for numerous home and garden items. Past decisions may also deplete purchasing power with the result that fewer problems are recognized or are assigned sufficient importance to trigger action.[8] Consumer Insight 14-1 examines the role that prior consumption plays in driving consumers to seek variety in their future purchases.

You probably have a favorite breakfast cereal. However, do you switch around to other brands, flavors, or varieties from time to time because you get bored or are curious about other alternatives? If the answer is yes you are engaging in variety-seeking.[9] Variety-seeking is a challenge because it means that consumers switch brands for reasons beyond a company's control.

However, there is hope. Research shows that consumers are more likely to become bored (satiated) on sensory attributes such as taste more than on non-sensory attributes such as brand name. Basically this means that consumers don't switch because they are bored with the brand but because they are bored with a specific attribute of the brand such as its taste. This effect is called *sensory-specific satiety* and it is a major driver of consumer variety-seeking in foods such as tortilla chips, cake mixes, and cereal bars.

The good news for brand managers is that offering variety on key sensory attributes can increase loyalty to the brand even if consumers engage in variety-seeking. This is because consumers can switch among the various options *within* the brand (e.g., from Kellogg's Froot Loops to Kellogg's Frosted Flakes) and the brand still gets the sale.

Critical Thinking Questions

1. What effect do you think variety-seeking has had on the proliferation of food products in the supermarket?

2. What other products have sensory attributes other than taste that might be prone to satiation effects?

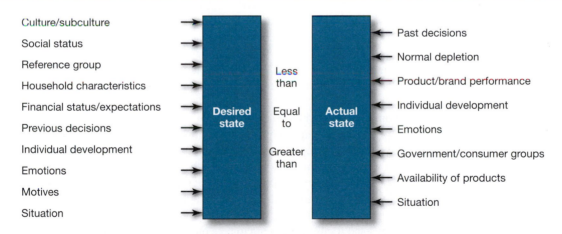

Nonmarketing Factors Affecting Problem Recognition   **FIGURE 14-3**

Individual development causes many changes in the desired state. As people age, their needs and desires evolve noticeably. An ad for Scotch appearing in men's magazines recognizes this—its headline, "When you were young, you didn't like girls either," appears over a picture of an attractive woman and a bottle of Scotch. As individuals gain skills, their desires related to those skills change. Beginning skiers, musicians, and gardeners typically desire products and capabilities that will no longer be appropriate as their skills increase.

Government agencies and various consumer groups actively attempt to trigger problem recognition, often in relation to the consumption of various products. Warning labels on alcohol and cigarettes are just two examples of these types of efforts. Illustration 14-3 is an ad used by the American Cancer Society to increase problem recognition related to the dangers of smoking.

Government agencies and nonprofit groups often attempt to generate problem recognition in consumers. This is often done in an attempt to change behaviors that are harmful to the individual or society.

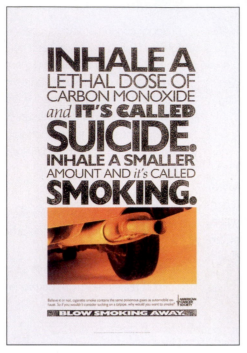

Courtesy The American Cancer Society.

MARKETING STRATEGY AND PROBLEM RECOGNITION

Marketing managers have four concerns related to problem recognition. First, they need to know the problems consumers are facing. Second, they must know how to develop the marketing mix to solve consumer problems. Third, managers occasionally want to cause consumers to recognize problems. Finally, there are times when they desire to suppress problem recognition among consumers. The remainder of this chapter discusses these issues.

Discovering Consumer Problems

A wide variety of approaches are used to determine the problems consumers face. The most common approach undoubtedly is *intuition;* that is, a manager can analyze a given product category and logically determine where improvements could be made. Thus, soundless vacuum cleaners or lawnmowers are logical solutions to potential consumer problems. The difficulty with this approach is that the problem identified may actually be of low importance to most consumers. Therefore, several research techniques are also employed.

A common research technique is the *survey,* which asks relatively large numbers of individuals about the problems they are facing. This was the technique used by Timberlane, as described earlier. A second common technique is *focus groups*. Focus groups are composed of 8 to 12 similar individuals—such as male college students, lawyers, or teenage girls—brought together to discuss a particular topic. A moderator is present to keep the discussion moving and focused on the topic, but otherwise the sessions are free flowing (see Appendix A for more details).

Both surveys and focus groups tend to take one of three approaches to problem identification: *activity analysis, product analysis,* or *problem analysis*. A fourth approach, *human factors research,* does not rely on surveys or focus groups. *Emotion research,* a fifth effort, attempts to discover the role emotions play in problem recognition.

Activity Analysis   Activity analysis focuses on a particular activity such as preparing dinner, maintaining the lawn, or swimming. The survey or focus group attempts to determine what problems consumers encounter during the performance of the activity. For example, Johnson Wax had a national panel of women report on how they cared for their hair and the problems they encountered. Their responses revealed a perceived problem with oiliness that existing brands could not resolve. As a result, Johnson Wax developed Agree Shampoo and Agree Crème Rinse, both of which were successful. More recently, shampoos have been developed specifically for the hair-related problems associated with swimming in chlorinated pools.

Product Analysis   Product analysis is similar to activity analysis but examines the purchase or use of a particular product or brand. Thus, consumers may be asked about problems associated with using their mountain bikes or laptop computers. Curlee Clothing used focus groups to analyze the purchase and use of men's clothing. The results indicated a high level of insecurity in purchasing men's clothing. This insecurity was combined with a distrust of both the motivations and competence of retail sales personnel. As a result, Curlee initiated a major effort to train retail sales personnel through specially prepared films and training sessions.

Problem Analysis   Problem analysis takes the opposite approach from the previous techniques. It starts with a problem and asks respondents to indicate which activities, products, or brands are associated with (or perhaps could eliminate) those problems. For example, a study dealing with packaging problems could include questions such as,

_____ packages are hard to open.

Packages of _____ are hard to reseal.

_____ doesn't pour well.

Packages of _____ don't fit on the shelf.

Packages of _____ waste too many resources.

A recent survey examined a pervasive problem in America—namely, getting and staying organized. The study found that 89 percent of adults feel that they could use help organizing some aspect of their lives. In addition, 54 percent say they have or would purchase products or hire a service to get organized.[10] Marketers are responding with TV shows like "Mission: Organization" and stores like Organized Living devoted solely to home-organization solutions. There is even a blog devoted to the topic (http://organized-living.com/tipblog.htm)!

Human Factors Research   Human factors research attempts to determine human capabilities in areas such as vision, strength, response time, flexibility, and fatigue and the effect on these capabilities of lighting, temperature, and sound. Many methods can be employed in human factors research. However, observational techniques such as slow-motion and time-lapse photography, video recording, and event recorders are particularly useful.

This type of research can sometimes identify functional problems that consumers are unaware of. For example, it can be used in the design of such products as vacuum cleaners, lawnmowers, kitchen utensils, and computers to minimize user fatigue. The growth in carpal tunnel syndrome (injury resulting from repeating the same movements such as inputting data into a computer over time) has resulted in substantial interest in this area.

Emotion Research   Marketers are increasingly conducting research on the role of emotions in problem recognition and resolution. Common approaches are focus group research and personal interviews that examine the emotions associated with certain problems. Surveys can also be used (see Table 10-4 for specific measures). For example, researchers are beginning to examine how consumers cope with the negative emotions associated with product or service failures. Findings suggest that certain emotions (e.g., anger) are associated with certain coping strategies (e.g., confrontation). This type of research is critical to marketers in helping them to anticipate consumer reactions to problems and train their customer service personnel to respond appropriately.[11] For subtle or sensitive problems and emotions, projective techniques (see Table 10-2) may be necessary.[12]

Courtesy McNeil Nutritionals LLC.

Responding to Consumer Problems

Once a consumer problem is identified, the manager may structure the marketing mix to solve the problem. This can involve developing a new product or altering an existing one, modifying channels of distribution, changing pricing policy, or revising advertising strategy. For example, in Illustration 14-4 the product is being positioned as a unique solution to a problem.

As you approach graduation, you will be presented with opportunities to purchase insurance, acquire credit cards, and solve other problems associated with the onset of financial independence and a major change in lifestyle. These opportunities reflect various firms' knowledge that many individuals in your situation face problems that their products will help solve.

Weekend and night store hours and, in part, the rapid growth of Internet stores are a response of retailers to the consumer problem of limited weekday shopping opportunities. Solving this problem has become particularly important to families with both spouses employed.

The examples described above represent only a small sample of the ways in which marketers react to consumer problem recognition. Each firm must be aware of the consumer problems it can solve, which consumers have these problems, and the situations in which the problems arise.

Helping Consumers Recognize Problems

There are occasions when the manager will want to cause problem recognition rather than react to it. In the earlier example, Timberlane faced having to activate problem recognition in order to sell its product as a fireplace starter. Toy marketers are attempting to reduce their dependence on the Christmas season by activating problem recognition at other times of the year. For example, Fisher-Price has had "rainy day" and "sunny day" promotions in the spring and summer months. Illustrations 14-1 and 14-2, presented earlier, show attempts to activate problem recognition.

Generic versus Selective Problem Recognition   Two basic approaches to causing problem recognition are *generic problem recognition* and *selective problem recognition*. These are analogous to the economic concepts of generic and selective demand.

Generic problem recognition involves a *discrepancy that a variety of brands within a product category can reduce*. Generally, a firm will attempt to influence generic problem recognition when the problem is latent or of low importance and one of the following conditions exists:

- It is early in the product life cycle.
- The firm has a high percentage of the market.
- External search after problem recognition is apt to be limited.
- It is an industrywide cooperative effort.

Courtesy National Fluid Milk Processor Promotion Board; Agency: Lowe Worldwide, Inc.

ILLUSTRATION 14-5

This ad will generate problem recognition that any brand of milk could resolve. This is known as generic problem recognition.

Telephone sales programs often attempt to arouse problem recognition, in part because the salesperson can then limit external search to one brand. Advertising for food-related cooperatives such as milk, beef, and pork frequently focuses on generic problem recognition. Illustration 14-5 is an example of one of the most notable ongoing campaigns of this type. Note that the copy attempts to make individuals aware of the need for calcium that milk provides but does not promote any particular brand of milk.

Firms with large market shares in a product category often focus on generic problem recognition because any sales increase will probably come to their brands. However, a smaller firm that generates generic problem recognition for its product category may be generating more sales for its competitors than for itself. But even firms with large market share can lose share if generic problem recognition campaigns are not done carefully. In the early 1990s, Borden increased marketing efforts for its popular Creamette pasta brand substantially and promoted recipes using pasta. Its sales increased only 1.6 percent, compared with the industry's growth of 5.5 percent.[13] Its efforts apparently helped the sales of its competitors more than its own sales.

Selective problem recognition involves *a discrepancy that only one brand can solve.* The ad shown in Illustration 14-6 is focused on creating selective problem recognition. Firms attempt to cause selective problem recognition to gain or maintain market share, whereas increasing generic problem recognition generally results in an expansion of the total market.

Approaches to Activating Problem Recognition   How can a firm influence problem recognition? Recall that problem recognition is a function of the (1) *importance* and

This ad will generate problem recognition that is best solved by one brand. This is known as selective problem recognition.

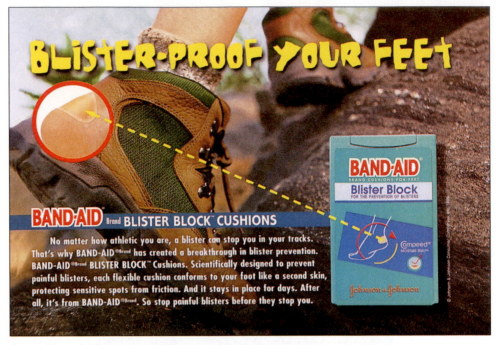

Courtesy Johnson & Johnson.

This ad attempts to influence the desired state by showing how white and bright teeth can be.

© The Procter & Gamble Company. Used by permission.

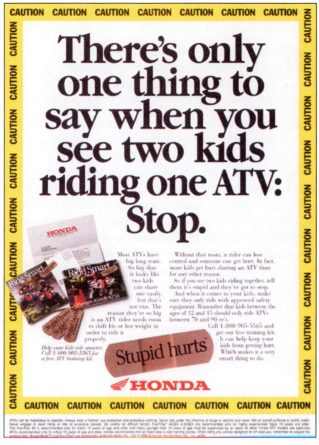

Courtesy American Honda Company.

ILLUSTRATION 14-8

Many adults may not be aware that two kids riding on one ATV is unsafe. This ad triggers problem recognition by altering perceptions of the safety of the existing state.

(2) *magnitude* of a discrepancy between the desired state and an existing state. Thus, a firm can attempt to influence the size of the discrepancy by altering the desired state or perceptions of the existing state. Or the firm can attempt to influence perceptions of the importance of an existing discrepancy.

Many marketing efforts attempt to *influence the desired state;* that is, marketers often advertise the benefits their products will provide, hoping that these benefits will become desired by consumers. The ad in Illustration 14-7 attempts to influence the desired state by showing how white and bright teeth can be.

It is also possible to *influence perceptions of the existing state* through advertisements. Many personal care and social products take this approach. "Even your best friend won't tell you . . ." or "Kim is a great worker but this coffee . . ." are examples of messages designed to generate concern about an existing state. The desired state is assumed to be fresh breath and good coffee. These messages are designed to cause individuals to question if their existing state coincides with this desired state.

The Honda ad in Illustration 14-8 attempts to make parents and other adults aware that the common practice (actual state) of two children riding one ATV is not as safe as it may appear, thus triggering problem recognition that it is hoped will result in parents' restricting such behaviors.

Critics frequently question the ethics of activating problem recognition. This is particularly true for problems related to status or social acceptance. This debate is generally discussed in terms of marketers "creating needs," which we discussed in Chapter 10.

The Timing of Problem Recognition   Consumers often recognize problems at times when purchasing a solution is difficult or impossible, as the following examples demonstrate:

- We decide we need snow chains when caught in a blizzard.
- We become aware of a need for insurance *after* an accident.
- We desire a flower bed full of tulips in the spring but forgot to plant bulbs in the fall.
- We want cold medicine when we are sick but don't feel like driving to the store.

In some instances, marketers attempt to help consumers solve such problems after they arise. For example, some pharmacies will make home deliveries. However, the more common strategy is to trigger problem recognition in advance of the actual problem (see Illustration 14-1). That is, it is often to the consumer's and marketer's advantage for the consumer to recognize and solve potential problems *before* they become actual problems.

Some companies, particularly insurance companies, attempt to initiate problem recognition through mass media advertising; others rely more on point-of-purchase displays and other in-store influences (see Chapter 17). Retailers, as well as manufacturers, are involved in this activity. For example, prior to snow season, the following sign was placed on a large rack of snow shovels in the main aisle of a large hardware store:

> REMEMBER LAST WINTER
> WHEN YOU *NEEDED*
> A SNOW SHOVEL?
> THIS YEAR
> BE PREPARED!

Suppressing Problem Recognition

As we have seen, competition, consumer organizations, and governmental agencies occasionally introduce information in the marketplace that triggers problem recognition that particular marketers would prefer to avoid. The American tobacco industry has made strenuous attempts to minimize consumer recognition of the health problems associated with cigarette smoking. For example, a Newport cigarette advertisement showed a happy, laughing couple under the headline, "Alive with pleasure." This could easily be interpreted as an attempt to minimize any problem recognition caused by the mandatory warning at the bottom of the advertisement: "Warning: The Surgeon General has determined that cigarette smoking is dangerous to your health."

Obviously marketers do not want their current customers to recognize problems with their brands. Effective quality control and distribution (limited out-of-stock situations) are important in this effort. Packages and package inserts that assure the consumer of the wisdom of their purchase are also common.

SUMMARY

Consumer decision making becomes more extensive and complex as *purchase involvement* increases. The lowest level of purchase involvement is represented by *nominal decisions:* a problem is recognized, long-term memory provides a single preferred brand, that brand is purchased, and only limited postpurchase evaluation occurs. As one moves from *limited decision making* toward *extended decision making,* information search increases, alternative evaluation becomes more extensive and complex, and postpurchase evaluation becomes more thorough.

Problem recognition involves the existence of a discrepancy between the consumer's desired state (what the consumer would like) and the actual state (what the consumer perceives as already existing). Both the desired state and the actual state are influenced by the consumer's lifestyle and current situation. If the discrepancy between these two states is sufficiently large and important, the consumer will begin to search for a solution to the problem.

A number of factors beyond the control of the marketing manager can affect problem recognition. The desired state is commonly influenced by (1) culture/subculture, (2) social status, (3) reference groups, (4) household characteristics, (5) financial status/expectations, (6) previous decisions, (7) individual development, (8) motives, (9) emotions, and (10) the current situation. The actual state is influenced by (1) past decisions, (2) normal depletion, (3) product/brand performance, (4) individual development, (5) emotions, (6) government/consumer groups, (7) availability of products, and the (8) current situation.

Before marketing managers can respond to problem recognition generated by outside factors, they must be able to *identify* consumer problems. Surveys and focus groups using *activity, product,* or *problem analysis* are commonly used. *Human factors research* approaches the same task from an observational perspective. *Emotion research* focuses on the role of emotions in problem recognition and resolution.

Once managers are aware of problem recognition patterns among their target market, they can react by designing the marketing mix to solve the recognized problem. This may involve product development or repositioning, a change in store hours, a different price, or a host of other marketing strategies.

Marketing managers often want to influence problem recognition rather than react to it. They may desire to generate *generic problem recognition,* a discrepancy that a variety of brands within a product category can reduce, or to induce *selective problem recognition,* a discrepancy that only one brand in the product category can solve.

Attempts to *activate problem recognition* generally do so by focusing on the desired state. However, attempts to make consumers aware of negative aspects of the existing state are also common. In addition, marketers attempt to influence the timing of problem recognition by making consumers aware of potential problems before they arise.

Finally, managers may attempt to minimize or suppress problem recognition by current users of their brands.

KEY TERMS

Active problem   517
Actual state   514
Desired state   514
Extended decision making   513

Generic problem recognition   522
Inactive problem   517
Limited decision making   513
Nominal decision making   512

Problem recognition   514
Product involvement   512
Purchase involvement   511
Selective problem recognition   523

INTERNET EXERCISES

1. Visit several general interest or entertainment Web sites that contain ads. Find and describe an ad that attempts to trigger problem recognition. How does it do this?

2. Visit several company Web sites. Find and describe one that attempts to trigger problem recognition. How does it do this?

3. Monitor several chat sites or interest groups for a week. Prepare a report on how a marketer could learn about the consumption problems of consumers by doing this.

REVIEW QUESTIONS

1. What is meant by *purchase involvement?* How does it differ from product involvement?

2. How does consumer decision making change as purchase involvement increases?

3. What is the role of *emotion* in the consumer decision process?

4. How do *nominal, limited,* and *extended decision making* differ? How do the two types of nominal decision making differ?

5. What is *problem recognition?*

6. What influences the motivation to resolve a recognized problem?

7. What is the difference between an *active* and an *inactive problem?* Why is this distinction important?

8. How does lifestyle relate to problem recognition?

9. What are the main uncontrollable factors that influence the *desired* state?

10. What are the main uncontrollable factors that influence the *existing* state?

11. How can you measure problem recognition?

12. In what ways can marketers react to problem recognition? Give several examples.

13. How does *generic problem recognition* differ from *selective problem recognition?* Under what conditions would a firm attempt to influence generic problem recognition? Why?

14. How can a firm cause problem recognition? Give examples.

15. How can a firm suppress problem recognition?

DISCUSSION QUESTIONS

16. What products do you think *generally* are associated with nominal, limited, and extended decision making? Under what conditions, if any, would these products be associated with a different form of decision making?

17. What products do you think *generally* are purchased or used for emotional reasons? How would the decision process differ for an emotion-driven purchase compared to a more functional purchase?

18. What products do you think *generally* are associated with brand loyal decision making and which with repeat purchase decision making? Justify your response.

19. Describe a purchase you made using nominal decision making, one using limited decision making, and one using extended decision making. What caused you to use each type of decision process?

20. Describe two recent purchases you have made. What uncontrollable factors, if any, triggered problem recognition? Did they affect the desired state, the actual state, or both?

21. How would you measure consumer problems among the following?
    a. College students
    b. Children aged 2 to 4
    c. Internet shoppers
    d. New residents in a town
    e. Vegans
    f. Newly married couples

22. How would you determine the existence of consumer problems of relevance to a marketer of the following?
    a. Women's spa
    b. Internet retail outlets
    c. Online health food store
    d. Public library
    e. Alaskan fishing lodge
    f. Mountain bikes

23. Discuss the types of products that resolve specific problems that occur for most consumers at different stages of their household life cycle.

24. How would you activate problem recognition among college students for the following?
    a. United Way blood drive
    b. Student recreation center
    c. A vegan diet
    d. Rooms To Go
    e. Using a designated driver if drinking
    f. Laundry service

25. How would you influence the time of problem recognition for the following?
    a. Fire alarm battery replacement
    b. Gift basket
    c. Car tune-up
    d. Air conditioner filters
    e. Health insurance
    f. Vitamins

26. Respond to the questions in Consumer Insight 14-1.

APPLICATION ACTIVITIES

27. Interview five students and identify three consumer problems they have recognized recently. For each problem, determine
    a. The relative importance of the problem.
    b. How the problem occurred.
    c. What caused the problem (i.e., change in desired or actual states).
    d. What action they have taken.

e. What action is planned to resolve each problem.

28. Find and describe an advertisement that is attempting to activate problem recognition. Analyze the advertisement in terms of the type of problem and the action the ad is suggesting. Also, discuss any changes you would recommend to improve the effectiveness of the ad in terms of activating problem recognition.

29. Interview three students and identify recent instances when they engaged in nominal, limited, and extended decision making (a total of nine decisions). What specific factors appear to be associated with each type of decision?

30. Interview three students and identify five products that each buys using a nominal decision process. Identify those that are based on brand loyalty and those that are merely repeat purchases. What characteristics, if any, distinguish the brand loyal products from the repeat products?

31. Find and describe an advertisement or point-of-purchase display that attempts to influence the timing of problem recognition. Evaluate its likely effectiveness.

32. Using two consumers from a relevant market segment, conduct an activity analysis for an activity that interests you. Prepare a report on the marketing opportunities suggested by your analysis.

33. Using two consumers from a relevant market segment, conduct a product analysis for a product that interests you. Prepare a report on the marketing opportunities suggested by your analysis.

34. Conduct a problem analysis, using a sample of five college freshmen. Prepare a report on the marketing opportunities suggested by your analysis.

35. Interview five smokers and ascertain what problems they see associated with smoking.

36. Interview someone from the local office of the American Cancer Society concerning their attempts to generate problem recognition among smokers.

REFERENCES

1. Based on V. MacDonald, "Nivea for Men Debuts in U.S.," *Happi-Household & Personal Products Industry,* April 2001, p. 50; and "A More Sophisticated Male Shopper Emerges," *MMR,* May 13, 2002, p. 34.

2. See B. Shiv and J. Huber, "The Impact of Anticipating Satisfaction on Consumer Choice," *Journal of Consumer Research,* September 2000, pp. 202–16; and M. T. Pham et al., "Affect Monitoring and the Primacy of Feelings in Judgment," *Journal of Consumer Research,* September 2001, pp. 167–88.

3. See J. R. Bettman, M. F. Luce, and J. W. Payne, "Constructive Consumer Choice," *Journal of Consumer Research,* December 1998, pp. 187–217.

4. For more complex but valuable approaches, see Bettman, Luce, and Payne, "Constructive Consumer Choice"; and R. Lawson, "Consumer Decision Making within a Goal-Driven Framework," *Psychology & Marketing,* August 1997, pp. 427–49.

5. M. Trivedi, F. M. Bass, and R. C. Rao, "A Model of Stochastic Variety-Seeking," *Marketing Science,* Summer 1994, pp. 274–97; S. Menon and B. E. Kahn, "The Impact of Context on Variety Seeking in Product Choice," *Journal of Consumer Research,* December 1995, pp. 285–95; and R. K. Ratner, B. E. Kahn, and D. Kahneman, "Choosing Less-Preferred Experiences for the Sake of Variety," *Journal of Consumer Research,* June 1999, pp. 1–15.

6. See W. J. McDonald, "Developing International Direct Marketing Strategies with a Consumer Decision-Making Content Analysis," *Journal of Direct Marketing,* Autumn 1994, pp. 18–27; and W. J. McDonald, "American versus Japanese Consumer Decision Making," *Journal of International Consumer Marketing* 7, no. 3 (1995), pp. 81–93.

7. See C. J. Hill, "The Nature of Problem Recognition and Search in the Extended Health Care Decision," *Journal of Services Marketing* 15, no. 6 (2001), pp. 454–79.

8. D. Soman, "Effects of Payment Mechanism on Spending Behavior," *Journal of Consumer Research,* March 2001, pp. 460–74.

9. This insight is based on H. C. M. Van Trijp, W. D. Hoyer, and J. J. Inman, "Why Switch? Product Category-Level Explanations for True Variety-Seeking Behavior," *Journal of Marketing Research,* August 1996, pp. 281–92; and J. J. Inman, "The Role of Sensory-Specific Satiety in Attribute-Level Variety Seeking," *Journal of Consumer Research,* June 2001, pp. 105–20.

10. J. Fetto, "Get It Together," *American Demographics,* April 2003, pp. 10–11.

11. S. Yi and H. Baumgartner, "Coping with Negative Emotions in Purchase-Related Situations," *Journal of Consumer Psychology* 14, no. 3 (2004), pp. 303–17.

12. See, e.g., G. Zaltman, "Metaphorically Speaking," *Marketing Research,* Summer 1996, pp. 13–20; and C. B. Raffel, "Vague Notions," *Marketing Research,* Summer 1996, pp. 21–23.

13. E. Lesly, "Why Things Are So Sour at Borden," *BusinessWeek,* November 22, 1993, p. 84.

Courtesy Nike, Inc.

15

Information Search

The ability of consumers to search for information has increased radically since the advent of the Internet. The Internet allows easy access to manufacturers' Web sites, to other consumers, and to third parties such as consumer groups and government agencies. It also greatly expands the ability of marketers to provide information to consumers. Marketers can provide information to consumers who are directly seeking information about the firm's products, typically through the company's or brand's home page or Web site. Marketers can also provide consumers information that they are not explicitly seeking by placing ads in other sites on the Web.

Internet strategies continue to evolve. However, most companies go well beyond simply providing company and product information in an electronic format. Consider the following:[1]

- Nike's Web site has various pages relating to its shoe and apparel lines. However, they go well beyond a simple place to find out information about shoes. For example, runners can create their own online training log, learn about upcoming events, learn about runner communities, download running-related Nike wallpaper, and become a member and receive access to members-only services and the NikeRunning.com Newsletter.

- Kodak's site has various sections which provide product information to both amateur consumers and professional users. For cinematographers (and aspiring film students), Kodak offers film-comparison software, interviews with cinematographers, and information about their student film program. For their consumer market, they offer Kodak EasyShare Gallery, where digital pictures can be stored, printed, and shared online for free. For NASCAR fans, they also post ongoing information about team Kodak Racing.

- Kraft Foods' site provides quick and easy help with food planning and preparation. It has a searchable recipe box, delivers recipes by e-mail for those who sign up, and has a recipe connection center where members can post their favorite recipes for others to use. They have their *food and family* online magazine and a section with tips on healthy living. With increased broadband use, Kraft has also created a video-based "Cooking School" where consumers can watch video clips on how to prepare specific dishes.

Note that each of these Web sites provides basic product information similar to that which a consumer could get from a brochure or catalog. However, each site goes much further than this. They provide application and usage suggestions often personalized for each consumer. They add value for the consumer both in terms of providing easily accessible product information and by adding other information, activities, and applications of relevance to the consumer. These firms want consumers to use their sites not only when explicitly seeking product specific information but on a regular basis for a variety of purposes. This is one way a firm can build a relationship with the consumer.

Consumers continually recognize problems and opportunities, so internal and external searches for information to solve these problems are ongoing processes. Searching for information is not free. Information search involves mental as well as physical activities that consumers must perform. It takes time, energy, and money and can often require giving up more desirable activities.

The benefits of information search, however, often outweigh the costs of search. For example, a search may produce a lower price, a preferred style of merchandise, a higher-quality product, or greater confidence in the choice. In addition, the physical and mental processes involved in information search are, on occasion, rewarding in themselves.

Finally, marketers must keep in mind that consumers acquire a substantial amount of relevant information without deliberate search—through low-involvement learning (see Chapter 9).

THE NATURE OF INFORMATION SEARCH

Suppose your television quit working, or you noticed that you were low on gas, or you felt particularly restless, or you decided you needed a bicycle. What would you do in response to each of these recognized problems? The odds are you would first remember how you usually solve this type of problem. This might produce a satisfactory solution (I'd better stop at the next BP station and fill up), which you would proceed to implement. Or you might decide that you needed to get additional information (I'll check the Yellow Pages to see who repairs my brand of television).

Once a problem is recognized, relevant information from long-term memory is used to determine if a satisfactory solution is known, what the characteristics of potential solutions are, what are appropriate ways to compare solutions, and so forth. This is **internal search.** If a resolution is not reached through internal search, then the search process is focused on external information relevant to solving the problem. This is **external search,** which can involve independent sources, personal sources, marketer-based information, and product experience. We discuss these sources in more detail later in the chapter. It is important to note that even in extended decision making with extensive external search, the initial internal search generally produces a set of guides or decision constraints that limit and guide external search. Such constraints might be a price range, a set of manufacturers, "must have" performance criteria, and so forth.[2]

Many problems are resolved by the consumer using only previously stored information. If, in response to a problem, a consumer recalls a single, satisfactory solution (brand or store), no further information search or evaluation may occur. The consumer purchases the recalled brand and *nominal decision making* has occurred. For example, a consumer who catches a cold may recall that Dristan nasal spray provided relief in the past. He or she then purchases Dristan at the nearest store without further information search or evaluation.

Likewise, a consumer might notice a new product in a store because of the attention-attracting power of a point-of-purchase display. He or she reads about the attributes of the product and recalls an unresolved problem that these attributes would resolve. The purchase is made without seeking additional information. This represents *limited decision making,* involving mainly internal information.

Had the consumer in the preceding example gone on and looked for other brands that would perform the same task or looked at another store for a lower price, we would have had an example of limited decision making using both internal and external information. As we move into *extended decision making,* the relative importance of external information search tends to increase.[3]

Deliberate external search also occurs in the absence of problem recognition. **Ongoing search** is done both *to acquire information for possible later use and because the process itself is pleasurable.* For example, individuals highly involved with an activity, such as tennis are apt to seek information about tennis-related products on an ongoing basis without a recognized problem with their existing tennis equipment (recall that enduring involvement is characteristic of opinion leaders). This search could involve offline and online activities such as reading ads in tennis magazines, visiting tennis equipment shops, participating in tennis-related blogs, and so on. These activities would provide the individual both pleasure and information for future use.

TYPES OF INFORMATION SOUGHT

A consumer decision requires information on the following:[4]

1. The appropriate evaluative criteria for the solution of a problem.
2. The existence of various alternative solutions.
3. The performance level or characteristic of each alternative solution on each evaluative criterion.

Information search, then, seeks each of these three types of information, as shown in Figure 15-1.

Evaluative Criteria

Suppose you are provided with money to purchase a notebook computer, perhaps as a graduation present. Assuming you have not been in the market for a computer recently, your first thought would probably be, "What features do I want in a computer?" You would then engage in internal search to determine the features or characteristics required to meet your

FIGURE 15-1   Information Search in Consumer Decisions

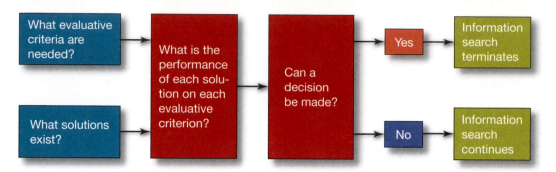

needs. These desired characteristics are your *evaluative criteria.* If you have had limited experience with computers, you might also engage in external search to learn which characteristics a good computer should have. You could check with friends, read reviews in *PC Magazine,* talk with sales personnel, visit computer Web sites, post questions on an online discussion board, or personally inspect several computers.

Thus, one potential objective of both internal and external search is *the determination of appropriate evaluative criteria.* Government agencies and consumer organizations want consumers to use sound evaluative criteria such as the nutrition content of foods. Marketers want consumers to use evaluative criteria that match their brand's strengths. Thus, both marketers and government agencies provide information designed to influence the evaluative criteria used by consumers. The ad in Illustration 15-1 encourages consumers to use five primary evaluative criteria when choosing a portable computer. Implied in the ad is that using too many evaluative criteria produces unneeded capabilities and an unnecessarily high price.

A detailed discussion of evaluative criteria appears in Chapter 16.

Appropriate Alternatives

After, and while, searching for appropriate evaluative criteria, you would probably seek *appropriate alternatives*—in this case brands or, possibly, stores. Again, you would start with an internal search. You might say to yourself, "IBM, Compaq, Toshiba, Apple, NEC, Sony, Fujitsu, and HP all make notebook computers. After my brother's experience, I'd never buy Fujitsu. I've heard good things about IBM, Apple, and Compaq. I think I'll check them out." The eight brands you thought of as potential solutions are known as the **awareness set.** The awareness set is composed of three subcategories of considerable importance to marketers. The three brands that you have decided to investigate are known as the **evoked set,** or the **consideration set.**[5] An evoked set is *those brands or products one will evaluate for the solution of a particular consumer problem.* It is important to note that the evoked set or consideration set will vary depending on the usage situation. For example, a person might choose from among cereal (perhaps several brands), a bagel, an Egg McMuffin, or just a cup of coffee for a weekday breakfast option but might consider eggs, waffles, or leftover pizza for a weekend breakfast.[6] Note that while evoked sets are frequently composed of brands from a single product category (brands of cereals or computers), this need not be the case.[7] For example, one landscaping company found that

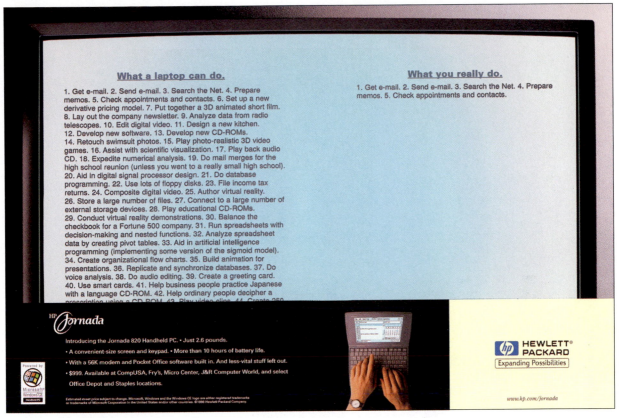

Courtesy Hewlett-Packard Company.

consumers often view landscaping as a "home improvement decision." As a consequence, their landscaping services often compete with other home improvement products such as interior decorating instead of, or in addition to, other landscaping services.

If you do not have an evoked set for notebook computers, or lack confidence that your evoked set is adequate, you will probably engage in external search to learn about additional alternatives. You may also learn about additional acceptable brands such as Acer and Sharp as an incidental aspect of moving through the decision process. Thus, an important outcome of information search is the development of a *complete* evoked set.

Whenever you are satisfied with your evoked set, your information search will focus on the performance of the brands in your evoked set on the evaluative criteria. Thus, the evoked set is of particular importance in structuring subsequent information search and purchase.

The brand you found completely unworthy of further consideration is a member of what is called the **inept set.** Brands in the inept set are *actively disliked or avoided by the consumer.* Positive information about these brands is not likely to be processed even if it is readily available.

In our example, Sony, Toshiba, NEC, and HP were brands of which you were aware but were basically indifferent toward. They compose what is known as an **inert set.** Consumers will generally accept favorable information about brands in the inert set, although they do not seek out such information. Brands in this set are generally acceptable when

ILLUSTRATION 15-1

Consumers often search for information on the appropriate evaluative criteria to use. This ad seeks to influence the criteria used as well as position HP on those criteria.

preferred brands are not available. Thus, the eight brands in the initial awareness set can be subdivided as follows:

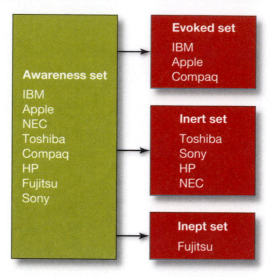

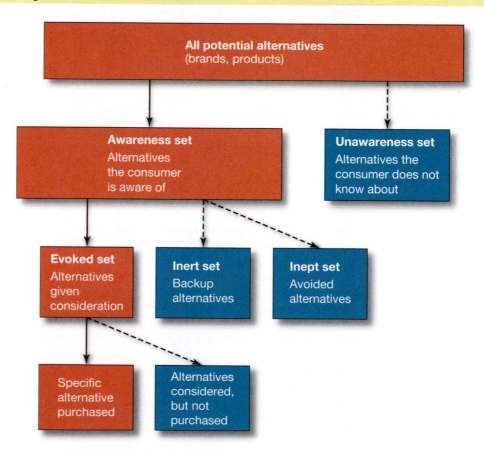

FIGURE 15-2   Categories of Decision Alternatives

Awareness and Evoked Sets for Various Products   FIGURE 15-3

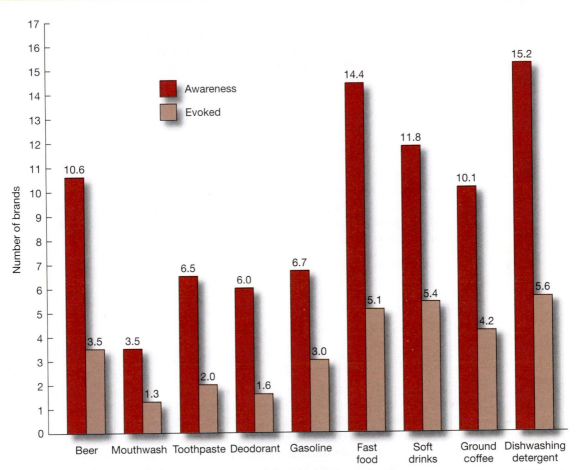

Source: J. Roberts, "A Grounded Model of Consideration Set Size and Composition," in *Advances in Consumer Research,* vol. 26, ed. T. K. Skrull (Provo, UT: Association for Consumer Research, 1989), p. 750.

Figure 15-2 illustrates the general relationships among these classes of alternatives. Figure 15-3 illustrates the results of several studies comparing the size of the awareness and evoked sets for a variety of products. Notice that in all cases, the evoked set is substantially smaller than the awareness set. Because the evoked set generally is the one from which consumers make final evaluations and decisions, *marketing strategy that focuses only on creating awareness may be inadequate.* Thus, marketers must strive to have consumers recall their brand in response to a recognized problem *and* consider the brand a worthy potential solution.

A similar process operates with respect to retail outlet selection.[8]

Alternative Characteristics

To choose among the brands in the evoked set, the consumer compares them on the relevant evaluative criteria. This process requires the consumer *to gather information about each brand on each pertinent evaluative criterion.* In our example of a computer purchase, you might collect information on the price, memory, processor, weight, screen clarity, and software package for each brand you are considering.

In summary, consumers engage in internal and external search for (1) appropriate evaluative criteria, (2) the existence of potential solutions, and (3) the characteristics of potential solutions. However, extensive search generally occurs for only a few consumption decisions. Nominal and limited decisions that involve little or no active external search are the rule. In addition, consumers acquire substantial information without deliberate search through low-involvement learning. Finally, while our discussion has focused on searching for functional information, emotions and feelings are important in many purchases.

SOURCES OF INFORMATION

Refer again to our notebook computer example. We suggested that you might recall what you know about computers, check with friends and an online discussion board, consult *Consumer Reports* and read reviews in *PC Magazine,* talk with sales personnel, or personally inspect several computers to collect relevant information. These represent the five primary sources of information available to consumers:

- *Memory* of past searches, personal experiences, and low-involvement learning.
- *Personal sources,* such as friends, family, and others.
- *Independent sources,* such as magazines, consumer groups, and government agencies.
- *Marketing sources,* such as sales personnel, Web sites, and advertising.
- *Experiential sources,* such as inspection or product trial.[9]

It is important to note that each of these sources has an online and offline component. That is, memory could be from prior information search offline or on the Internet; offline personal sources correspond to online chatrooms, blogs, and user groups; independent sources such as *Consumer Reports* magazine correspond to online independent sources and portals; offline marketing sources such as TV advertising and brochures correspond to online banner ads and corporate Web sites.[10] And given the importance of product experiences in the attitude formation and purchase process, marketers are increasingly looking for ways to allow consumers to at least simulate an experience with their products via the Internet.[11] These sources are shown in Figure 15-4. Consumers decide how many and which sources of information to use at both the macro (personal sources) and micro (specific individuals) levels. Thus, a purchase decision requires a subset of decisions concerning information seeking.[12]

Internal information is the primary source used by most consumers most of the time (nominal and limited decision making). However, note that information in long-term memory was *initially* obtained from external sources. Thus, a consumer may resolve a consumption problem using only or mainly stored information. At some point, however, the individual acquired that information from an external source, such as direct product experience, friends, or low-involvement learning.

Marketing-originated messages are only one of five potential information sources, and they are frequently reported to be of limited *direct* value in consumer decisions.[13] However, marketing activities influence all five sources. Thus, the characteristics of the product, the distribution of the product, and the promotional messages about the product provide the underlying or basic information available in the market. An independent source such as *Consumer Reports* bases its evaluation on the functional characteristics of the product. Personal sources such as friends also must base their information on experience with the product or its promotion, or on other sources that have had contact with the product or its promotion.

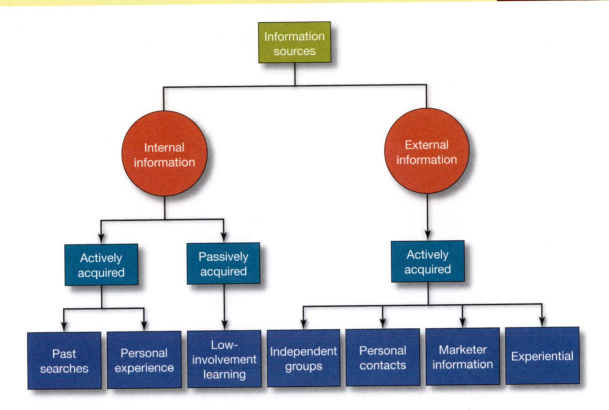

A substantial amount of marketing activity is designed to influence the information that consumers will receive from nonmarketing sources. For example, when Johnson & Johnson introduced a new-formula baby bath,

> Product information, demonstrations, monographs, journal ads, and direct-mail programs were targeted at pediatricians and nurses to capitalize on health care professionals' direct contact with new mothers. Print ads and coupons appeared in baby care publications, and a film exploring the parent–infant bonding process was distributed to teaching centers, hospitals, and medical schools.

In addition, although consumers may not use (or believe they use) advertising or other marketer-provided data as immediate input into many purchase decisions, there is no doubt that continual exposure to advertising frequently influences the perceived need for the product, the composition of the awareness and evoked sets, the evaluative criteria used, and beliefs about the performance levels of each brand.[14] As a consequence, the long-term influence of advertising and other marketer-provided information on consumer decision making and sales can be substantial.

Information Search on the Internet

The Internet gives consumers unprecedented access to information. One study estimates global Internet usage at 1.35 billion people by 2007, which is more than a 100 percent increase in just five years! This same study forecasts that there will be 247 million Internet users in North America by 2007, compared with 265.5 million in Western Europe,

562.8 million in Asia Pacific, and 100.9 million in Central/South America.[15] While the United States had the highest number of Internet users in 2004 (185.6 million), China (99.8 million)[16] will likely surpass the United States in a few years. The Asia Pacific region already overshadows all other regions of the world. And their growth rate in terms of Internet usage remains well above that of North America. *What are the marketing implications of such global trends for American businesses?*

Just as there are global differences, Figure 15-5 shows that the Internet is not used equally by all segments of the adult U.S. population.[17] It is important to keep several points in mind while examining this figure. First, the differences shown in this figure have been rapidly decreasing and are expected to continue to do so, with growth in lower-use segments often outpacing that found in higher-use segments.[18] Second, the estimate for Hispanics is specifically for English-speaking Hispanics. Research examining overall Hispanic usage generally finds lower use due to language barriers.[19] Third, as the baby boomers age, the large usage gap between those 65 and over and the rest of the population should decline sharply as these older consumers take their online skills into their latter years.[20] Finally, children and teenagers are also an important online market segment. One study from 2003 shows that children as young as three years old are using the Internet and that Internet usage increases steadily from children to tweens to teens.[21]

The following list represents the top 10 activities of adult Internet users (number represents percent who have ever engaged in the activity):[22]

E-mail	91%
Use search engine to find information	***84***
Search for a map or driving directions	84
Do an Internet search to answer a specific question	80
Research a product/service before buying it	***78***
Check the weather	78
Look for information on a hobby or interest	77
Get travel information	73
Get news	72
Buy a product	***67***

© Pew Internet and American Life Project.

This information shows just how important the Internet is in the search and decision process. Indeed, research suggests that the Internet is a preferred source of product-related information among Internet users.[23] Consider the following:[24]

- *Online information is expected:* A Pew survey finds that 79 percent of Internet users *expect* to find information about a product or brand of interest to them on a company's Web site.

- *Online information boosts offline sales:* A Pew survey finds that 47 percent of Internet users are more likely to purchase a company's product offline if its Web site provides product-related information.

- *Online sources are viewed as valuable:* A DoubleClick study finds that corporate Web sites outstrip traditional TV and print advertising as an information source in 6 out of 10 product/service categories. A study of automobile buyers finds that 58 percent rate an Internet source (versus an offline source) as the most valuable.

- *Online sources reduce salespersons role:* A DoubleClick study finds that 51 percent of Internet users across 11 product/service categories required considerably less assistance from a salesperson on their current purchase compared to their last. Two studies of automobile buyers found similar results.

Demographics of U.S. Adult Internet Users   FIGURE 15-5

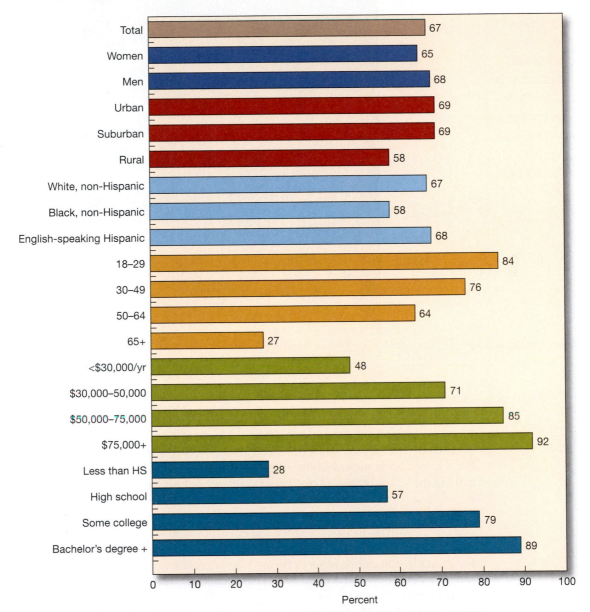

Source: "Demographics of Adult Internet Users," © Pew Internet & American Life Project, Washington D.C. May 18, 2005.

Obviously, traditional media can be effective at guiding consumers' information search activities to company Web sites as shown in Illustration 15-2.

Search engines such as Google, Yahoo, and MSN are an important search tool for consumers. A recent DoubleClick study examined search engine use in a 12-week period preceding an online purchase. Four product categories and 7 to 8 retailers within each of these categories were tracked using their panel of 1.5 million U.S. Internet users. They found that 50 percent of online purchases were preceded by information search using a search engine. Perhaps more interesting was the nature of search, where search terms were

Courtesy Expedia, Inc.

categorized as *brand only* (retailer's brand), *generic* (general product-related terms), and *brand-item* (brand plus generic). As shown in Figure 15-6, most of the search leading up to the purchase was generic—that is, general product-related terms that did not include any of the retailers being tracked in the study. As you might expect, generic search dominated early in the search process (3 to 12 weeks out), while branded search dominated just prior to purchase.[25] *What strategic implications do these results hold for online marketers?*

As we have seen, the Internet influences consumer information search. Obvious advantages of the Internet include the speed and efficiency with which vast amounts of information can be obtained. The result can be a more efficient search process and better decisions. For example, automobile buyers who used the Internet were able to make decisions faster and get a better buy—on average by $741.[26] Economic considerations appear to be a major motivator of online searching.[27]

Despite these and other benefits, one of the challenges facing consumers is sifting through the mountains of available information on the Internet. Thus, *information overload* (see Chapter 8) can be a major factor on the Internet. General search engines are useful. However, more specialized services and tools continue to evolve to more specifically aid consumers in their search and decision making.[28] For example, there are numerous shopping services on the Internet that can search out the lowest prices for specific items, search out online retailers of specific merchandise, suggest specific brands based on your prior purchases or prespecified criteria, and so on (see Illustration 15-3). These services use **bots,** which are software "robots" that do the shopping/searching for users, and are therefore often referred to as *shopping bots.* Examples include bizrate.com, mysimon.com, and excite.com.

The Nature of Search Using Online Search Engines   FIGURE 15-6

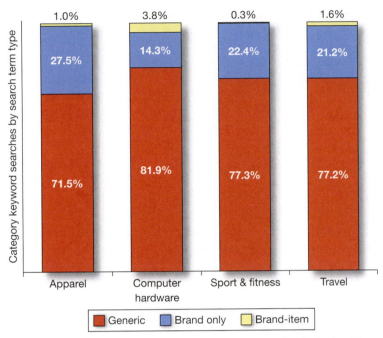

Source: "The Nature of Search Using Online Search Engines," *Search Before the Purchase* (New York: DoubleClick), February 2005, p. 2. Copyright: DoubleClick, Inc., 2005.

Courtesy mysimon.com.

ILLUSTRATION 15-3

Online shopping services are increasingly popular as a way for consumers to deal with the enormous amount of information on the Internet.

Some shopping bots offer relatively simple services such as price comparisons, sorting options by price, and so on. Other sites are more sophisticated. For example, Active Buyers Guide combines user input and proprietary software (Adaptive Recommendation Technology) to mimic the trade-offs that consumers make in the buying process so they can rank order the options. Thus, not only does Active Buyers Guide help consumers form their evoked set, it also provides them with guidance about how to choose from among the brands in that set (more on choice in Chapter 16). Amazon.com is an example of a site that combines online shopping with a relatively sophisticated bot that can make recommendations to you while you shop based on your prior purchases.[29]

In addition to marketer-based information, the Internet contains personal sources of information in bulletin boards and chat rooms as well as in the brand review features associated with some shopping services.[30] One study finds that consumers are increasingly using online WOM (word-of-mouth) as an information source prior to automobile purchases.[31] WOM and personal sources are highly influential due to consumer trust in these sources (Chapter 7).

Marketing Strategy and Information Search on the Internet   The online environment is continually evolving. For example, early on, the online consumer population was relatively homogeneous and characterized as younger, white, educated, and male. As the online population increasingly mirrors the general population, segmentation and target marketing are becoming increasingly critical to online success. Consider the following:

> Where higher education marketing is different is the complexity of the audiences. A college . . . in particular has to please—if you are talking about the institutional Web site—alumni, donors, current students, prospective students, parents (and) the media. It's daunting sometimes.

Furman University decided that its general Web site was inadequate for admissions. So, they created a separate Web site to target high school students interested in their institution. The site is designed to specifically target this tech-savvy group with virtual tours, message boards, and online student journals (with no editing by administration!).[32]

Obviously, universities are not the only ones who must deal with diverse consumer needs and characteristics. For example, consumers of various ethnicities in the U.S. often prefer and primarily use ethnic (versus mainstream) Web sites.[33] Global marketers must adapt as well. A recent study finds that Japanese Web sites use less individualistic approaches than do U.S. Web sites.[34]

More specifically, with respect to the Internet's role in information search and decision making, marketers have at least three major strategic issues to deal with:

1. How can they drive their information to consumers?
2. How can they drive consumers to their information?
3. How (if at all) can online selling be utilized or integrated with existing channels?

The first two issues are addressed in this section. The third will be covered in Chapter 17.

The first issue—*driving a firm's information to consumers*—is important since consumers are not always actively searching. One way is through Web advertising, including *banner ads*. Internet advertising spending is growing at around 25 percent per year and is projected to be $13.1 billion in 2007. This represents a marked increase from 2002 ($5.7 billion) but still is a relatively small proportion of total advertising expenditures in the United States (around $250 billion).[35] Broadband is changing the nature of online advertising, allowing for more use of streaming media. For example, in response to data showing that half of all new car buyers visit the Web prior to visiting a dealer, Honda placed its national TV ads for the Odyssey minivan on at least 14 Web sites. Viewers could click off the video or view it and ask for additional information. This goes beyond the traditional banner ad approach, and yet both drive the brand and information to the consumer.[36]

E-mail is also an important tool for pushing information to consumers. A study by DoubleClick shows that many consumers see e-mail as a replacement for direct mail. However, spam (unsolicited e-mails) continues to be a major concern and irritant. *Permission-based e-mail* (PBE) in which the consumer "opts in" to receive e-mail appears to be something consumers are highly receptive to. Even with PBE, marketers need to be careful—too many e-mails that lack relevance may still be viewed as spam![37]

The second issue—*driving consumers to a firm's information*—is a daunting and important task given the explosion in the amount and sources of information on the Web. Companies have Web sites to which they want consumers to go and return frequently.[38] Various strategies are possible. As we saw in Illustration 15-2, offline media are one avenue for calling attention to a Web site.

Banner ads are another way to drive traffic to Web sites. While clickthrough rates (percentage who click through to the corporate Web site) are generally low, marketers are looking beyond immediate clickthrough to measures that include brand awareness, brand attitudes, and purchase intentions. The idea is that boosting awareness and attitudes will drive *long-term* Web site visits and purchases. Behavioral targeting appears to improve banner performance across various outcomes including clickthrough rates.[39] **Behavioral targeting** *involves tracking consumer click patterns on a Web site and using that information to decide on banner ad placement.* For example, Snapple wanted to market its Snapple-a-Day product to health-conscious women. Snapple set its target as women who had visited iVillage's diet and fitness area three times in the prior 45 days. For those visitors, Snapple then delivered banner ads wherever they happened to be on the iVillage site. Behavioral targeting produced much better results for Snapple than standard Web-placement models because the ad and product were highly relevant to the targeted customer.[40]

As we saw earlier, online consumers are heavy users of search engines. Since search results are ordered and consumers often don't *drill down* beyond the first page of listings, keyword selection and other techniques relating to search engine optimization are critical for the firm in terms of getting their Web site the highest priority listing for the most appropriate search terms. **Search engine optimization** (SEO) *involves techniques designed to ensure that a company's Web pages "are accessible to search engines and focused in ways that help improve the chances they will be found."*[41] Programs such as Google's Adword program, in which companies pay for "sponsored" listings for specific search terms, are also available. The DoubleClick search-engine results suggest that consumers often begin their searches with general product-related terms. Therefore, finding and optimizing around the most likely generic search terms used by consumers would be a recommended strategy for getting the brand in front of the consumer during the decision process and increasing the odds that the consumer will visit the Web site as a consequence.

Web site design is also critical. While we will discuss this issue more in Chapter 17, it is clear that driving *ongoing and repeat* traffic to a Web site requires such factors as relevant and frequently updated content. That is, firms must provide consumers with ongoing incentives to return to their Web sites. Techniques can include product-related news features, user-related discussion forums, updates on new products and features, and so on. In fact, many Web sites now offer consumers the option to receive regular e-mail updates which can trigger site visits.[42]

AMOUNT OF EXTERNAL INFORMATION SEARCH

Marketing managers are particularly interested in external information search, as this provides them with direct access to the consumer. How much external information search do consumers actually undertake? Most purchases are a result of nominal or limited decision making and therefore involve limited external search immediately prior to purchase. This is particularly true for relatively low-priced convenience goods such as soft drinks, canned foods, and detergents. Therefore, the discussion in this section focuses on major purchases such as appliances, professional services, and automobiles. Intuitively, we would expect substantial amounts of direct external search prior to such purchases.

Various measures of external information search have been used: (1) number of stores visited, (2) number of alternatives considered, (3) number of personal sources used, and (4) overall or combination measures. Each of these measures of search effort assesses a different aspect of behavior, yet each measure supports one observation: *external information search is skewed toward limited search, with the greatest proportion of consumers performing little external search immediately prior to purchase.* For example, surveys of *shopping behavior* have shown a significant percentage of all durable purchases are made after the consumer has visited only one store.[43] The *number of alternatives* considered also shows a limited amount of prepurchase search. Although the number of alternative brands or models considered tends to increase as the price of the product increases, for some product categories, such as watches, almost half of the purchasers considered only one brand *and* one model. Another study found that 27 percent of the purchasers of major appliances considered only one brand.[44] And while Internet use increased automobile search, those who used the Internet still examined only three models.[45]

Eight separate studies spanning almost 50 years, two product categories, four services, and two countries show remarkable consistency in terms of the total external information search undertaken. Consumers can be classified in terms of their total external information search as (1) nonsearchers—little or no search, (2) limited information searchers—low to moderate search, and (3) extended information searchers—high search.[46]

Country/Product/Year	Nonsearchers	Limited Searchers	Extended Searchers
America/appliances/1955	65%	25%	10%
America/appliances/1972	49	38	13
America/appliances/1974	65	27	08
Australia/automobiles/1981	24	58	18
America/appliances/1989	24	45	11
America/professional services/1989	55	38	07
Australia/professional services/1995	53	35	12
America/automobiles/2003	20	40	20

As this information suggests, most consumers engage in minimal external information search immediately prior to the purchase of consumer durables and important professional services. The level of search for less important items is even lower. However, limited information search does not necessarily mean that the consumer is not following a sound purchasing strategy. Nor does it mean that substantial amounts of internal information are not being used.

COSTS VERSUS BENEFITS OF EXTERNAL SEARCH

Why do buyers often engage in so little external search immediately prior to the purchase even for important durable goods and services? Part of the answer lies in the differences between the buyers' perceptions of the benefits and costs of search associated with a particular purchase situation.[47] The benefits of external information search can be tangible, such as a lower price, a preferred style, or a higher-quality product. Or the benefits can be intangible—reduced risk, greater confidence in the purchase, or the search itself can even provide enjoyment.[48] Perceptions of these benefits are likely to vary with the consumer's experience in the market, his or her media habits, and the extent to which the consumer interacts with others or belongs to different reference groups. Therefore, one reason for limited external search in many cases is that consumers do not perceive significant benefits resulting from such an effort.

Furthermore, acquisition of external information is not free, and consumers may engage in limited search because the costs of search exceed the perceived benefits. The costs of search can be both monetary and nonmonetary. Monetary costs include the cost of transportation, parking, lost wages, charges for child care, and so forth. Nonmonetary costs of search are less obvious but may have an even greater impact than monetary costs. Almost every external search effort involves time and physical and psychological effort. Frustration and conflict between the search task and other more desirable activities, as well as fatigue, may shorten or otherwise alter the search effort. The Internet clearly has the potential to greatly lower search costs. When it does, it has been shown to increase search and result in better consumer decisions and a more enjoyable shopping experience.[49]

In this section, we examine four basic types of factors that influence the expected benefits and perceived costs of search: *market characteristics, product characteristics, consumer characteristics,* and *situation characteristics.*[50] These four factors and their components are shown in Table 15-1.

Market Characteristics

Market characteristics include the number of alternatives, price range, store distribution, and information availability. It is important to keep in mind that it is the consumer's perception of, or beliefs about, the market characteristics that influence shopping behavior, *not* the actual characteristics.[51] While beliefs and reality are usually related, often they are not identical.

Obviously, the greater the *number of alternatives* (products, stores, brands) available to resolve a particular problem, the more external search there is likely to be. At the extreme, there is no need to search for information in the face of a complete monopoly such as utilities or driver's licenses.

However, if too many models and brands are available, information overload may cause consumers to shop less. In particular, a wide range of models or brands may make the search process virtually impossible if the models vary across stores. That is, if one store has two brands with five models each and a second store has the same two brands but with five different models each, the consumer must compare 20 distinct brands/models. In response, many consumers will limit their shopping to a single retail outlet. This leads some marketers to develop a large number of models so that key accounts can have exclusive models and avoid direct price competition with other retailers on those exact models.[52]

TABLE 15-1		
Factors Affecting External Search Immediately Prior to Purchase	**Influencing Factor**	**Increasing the Influencing Factor Causes External Search To:**

Influencing Factor	Increasing the Influencing Factor Causes External Search To:
I. Market Characteristics	
A. Number of alternatives	Increase
B. Price range	Increase
C. Store concentration	Increase
D. Information availability	Increase
1. Advertising	
2. Point-of-purchase	
3. Web sites	
4. Sales personnel	
5. Packaging	
6. Experienced consumers	
7. Independent sources	
II. Product Characteristics	
A. Price	Increase
B. Differentiation	Increase
C. Positive products	Increase
III. Consumer Characteristics	
A. Learning and experience	Decrease
B. Shopping orientation	Mixed
C. Social status	Increase
D. Age and household life cycle	Mixed
E. Product involvement	Mixed
F. Perceived risk	Increase
IV. Situation Characteristics	
A. Time availability	Increase
B. Purchase for self	Decrease
C. Pleasant surroundings	Increase
D. Social surroundings	Mixed
E. Physical/mental energy	Increase

The *perceived range of prices* among equivalent brands in a product class is a major factor in stimulating external search. For example, shopping 36 retail stores in Tucson for five popular branded toys produced a total low cost of $51.27 and a total high cost of $105.95. Clearly, efficient shopping for these products in this market would provide a significant financial gain. Pricing strategies such as price matching can affect consumer price perceptions. A recent study suggests that consumers interpret such policies as signaling lower prices which, under high search costs, yields less search.[53]

It appears that the percentage savings available from shopping may be as important as the dollar amount. Consumers who perceive the chance to save $50 when purchasing a $200 item may be motivated to engage in search but not if the same savings were available for a $5,000 item.[54]

Store distribution—the number, location, and distances between retail stores in the market—affects the number of store visits a consumer will make before purchase. Because store visits take time, energy, and in many cases money, a close proximity of stores will often increase this aspect of external search.[55]

In general, *information availability,* including format, is directly related to information use.[56] However, too much information can cause information overload and the use of less information. In addition, readily available information tends to produce learning over time, which may reduce the need for additional external information immediately prior to a purchase.[57] *Advertising, point-of-purchase displays, Web sites, sales personnel, packages, other consumers,* and *independent sources* such as *Consumer Reports* are major sources of consumer information.

Product Characteristics

Product *differentiation*—feature and quality variation across brands—is associated with increased external search.

In addition, consumers appear to enjoy shopping for *positive products*—those whose acquisition results in positive reinforcement. Thus, shopping for flowers and plants, dress clothing, sports equipment, and cameras is viewed as a positive experience by most consumers. In contrast, shopping for *negative products*—those whose primary benefit is negative reinforcement (removal of an unpleasant condition)—is viewed as less pleasant. Shopping for groceries, extermination services, and auto repairs is not enjoyed by most individuals. Other things being equal, consumers are more likely to engage in external search for positive products.[58]

Consumer Characteristics

A variety of consumer characteristics affect perceptions of expected benefits, search costs, and the need to carry out a particular level of external information search.[59] As described earlier, the first step a consumer normally takes in response to a problem or opportunity is a search of memory for an appropriate solution. If the consumer finds a solution that he or she is confident is satisfactory, external search is unlikely. Thus, confidence in one's knowledge of existing solutions is an important determinant of search. However, as Consumer Insight 15-1 illustrates, consumers often do not know what they think they know!

A satisfying *experience* with a particular brand is a positively reinforcing process. It increases the probability of a repeat purchase of that brand and decreases the likelihood of external search. As a result, external search is generally greater for consumers who have limited purchase experience with brands in a particular product category.[60]

However, there is evidence that at least some familiarity with a product class is necessary for external search to occur. For example, external search prior to purchasing a new automobile is high for consumers who have a high level of *general knowledge about cars* and low for those who have a substantial level of knowledge about existing brands.[61] Thus, consumers facing a completely unfamiliar product category may feel threatened by the amount of new information or may simply lack sufficient knowledge to conduct an external search.

External search tends to increase with various measures of *social status* (education, occupation, and income), though middle-income individuals search more than those at higher or lower levels. *Age* of the shopper is inversely related to information search. External search appears to decrease as the age of the shopper increases. This may be explained in part by increased learning and product familiarity gained with age. New households and individuals moving into new stages of the *household life cycle* have a greater need for external information than established households.

Consumers tend to form general approaches or patterns of external search. These general approaches are termed *shopping orientations*.[62] While individuals will exhibit substantial variation from the general pattern across situations and product categories, many do take a stable shopping approach to most products across a wide range of situations. Other individuals engage in extensive ongoing information search because they are market mavens, as described in Chapter 7.

Consumers who are *highly involved with a product category* generally seek information relevant to the product category on an ongoing basis.[63] This ongoing search and the knowledge base it produces may reduce their need for external search immediately before a purchase. However, this may vary with the nature of their involvement with the product

Do You Know What You Think You Know?

A recent study concluded that "consumers are overconfident—they think they know more than they actually do."[64] Consumers who are motivated to purchase the lowest-priced groceries available and who "know" that store A has the lowest prices are likely to shop at store A. If, instead, store B is equally accessible and has the same items at a lower price, both the consumers and the more efficient store suffer from this lack of accurate knowledge.

Two aspects of consumer knowledge are important. One is the knowledge, memory, or belief itself and its correspondence to objective reality (accuracy). The other is the consumer's confidence that his or her belief is accurate. The more confident an individual is in his or her belief, the more likely he or she is to act accordingly without seeking additional information. Unfortunately, research reveals that the correspondence (calibration) between confidence and accuracy is sometimes quite low.

There are a variety of types of knowledge where a low level of calibration frequently occurs to the detriment of consumers and firms. Some of these include

Memory of facts—"Saturn scores highest of all small cars on most customer satisfaction ratings." Consumers tend to be more confident in this type of knowledge than accuracy levels justify.

Memory of events—"John had to have his Saturn repaired three times the first year he owned it." Again, individuals tend to be more confident in their memories than is justified.

Belief polarization—"I like the looks of the new Saturn. The new Saturn handles well." Research shows that consumers who form a preference for a brand on one dimension tend to form positive, sometimes inaccurate, beliefs about other attributes.

Belief validity—"The Saturn costs more than the Kia so it is a higher quality car." Both general (higher price equals higher quality) and specific beliefs (Volvo is the safest car in a crash) are often unexamined for accuracy when consumers make decisions.

Personal forecasts—"I can afford a new Saturn because I'll earn a bonus next year." Research indicates that consumers are often very confident in overly optimistic assessments of the occurrence of desirable personal events.

A large variety of complex factors account for the low levels of calibration that frequently occur between the accuracy of one's knowledge and one's confidence in that knowledge. For example, memory is often not just inaccurate but distorted. People tend to remember things in a manner consistent with a prior judgment; that is, they make a decision, then "remember" facts or events in a manner consistent with the decision. Or as individuals become predisposed toward a choice, they remember mainly those aspects of the past that are consistent with the predisposition.

Critical Thinking Questions

1. What, if any, implications does the above have for our educational system?

2. What are the primary marketing implications of the above?

category. One study found that wine enthusiasts who desired variety engaged in significantly more external search than those who were less interested in variety.[65]

Perceived Risk The **perceived risk** associated with unsatisfactory product performance, either instrumental or symbolic, increases information search prior to purchase.[66] Higher perceived risk is associated with increased search and greater reliance on personal sources of information and personal experiences.

Perceived risk is a function of the individual, the product, and the situation. It varies from one consumer to another and for the same consumer from one product to another and from one situation to another. For example, the purchase of a bottle of wine may not involve much perceived risk when buying for one's own consumption. However, the choice of wine may involve considerable perceived risk when buying wine for a dinner party for one's boss. Likewise, it might be perceived as risky if the individual has little knowledge and is buying an expensive bottle for personal consumption.

While perceived risk varies across consumers and situations, some products and services are generally seen as riskier than others (see Table 17-2).[67] Likewise, perceived risk is high for products whose failure to perform as expected would result in a high

- *Social cost* (e.g., a new suit that is not appreciated by one's peers).
- *Financial cost* (e.g., an expensive vacation during which it rained all the time).
- *Time cost* (e.g., an automobile repair that required the car to be taken to the garage, left, and then picked up later).
- *Effort cost* (e.g., a computer that is loaded with important software before the hard drive crashes).
- *Physical cost* (e.g., a new medicine produces a harmful side effect).

Situation Characteristics

As indicated in Chapter 13, situational variables can have a major impact on search behavior. For example, recall that one of the primary reactions of consumers to crowded store conditions is to minimize external information search. *Temporal perspective* is probably the most important situational variable with respect to search behavior. As the time available to solve a particular consumer problem decreases, so does the amount of external information search.[68]

Gift-giving situations (*task definition*) tend to increase perceived risk, which, as we have seen, increases external search. Likewise, multiple-item purchase tasks such as buying a bike and a bike rack or several items for a meal produce increased levels of information search.[69] Shoppers with limited physical or emotional energy (*antecedent state*) will search for less information than others. Pleasant *physical surroundings* increase the tendency to search for information, at least *within* that outlet. *Social surroundings* can increase or decrease search, depending on the nature of the social setting (see Chapter 13 for a more complete discussion of these issues).

MARKETING STRATEGIES BASED ON INFORMATION SEARCH PATTERNS

Sound marketing strategies take into account the nature of information search engaged in by the target market prior to purchase. Two dimensions of search are particularly appropriate: the type of decision influences the level of search, and the nature of the evoked set influences the direction of the search. Table 15-2 illustrates a strategy matrix based on these two dimensions. This matrix suggests the six marketing strategies discussed in the

Position	Target Market Decision-Making Pattern		
	Nominal Decision Making (no search)	Limited Decision Making (limited search)	Extended Decision Making (extensive search)
Brand in evoked set	Maintenance strategy	Capture strategy	Preference strategy
Brand not in evoked set	Disrupt strategy	Intercept strategy	Acceptance strategy

TABLE 15-2

Marketing Strategies Based on Information Search Patterns

TM® 3 Musketeers is a registered trademark of Mars, Incorporated and its affiliates. They are used with permission. Mars, Incorporated is not associated with McGraw-Hill Companies or Michael J. Hruby & Associates. Advertisement printed with permission of Mars, Incorporated. © Mars, Inc., 2002.

ILLUSTRATION 15-4

Firms with a significant group of loyal or repeat purchasers must continually improve their products and communicate their advantages to their consumers.

following sections. As you will see, while there is considerable overlap between the strategies, each has a unique thrust.

Maintenance Strategy

If the brand is purchased habitually by the target market, the marketer's strategy is to maintain that behavior. This requires consistent attention to product quality, distribution (avoiding out-of-stock situations), and a reinforcement advertising strategy. In addition, the marketer must defend against the disruptive tactics of competitors. Thus, it needs to maintain product development and improvements and to counter short-term competitive strategies such as coupons, point-of-purchase displays, or rebates.

Morton salt and Del Monte canned vegetables have large repeat purchaser segments that they have successfully maintained. Budweiser, Marlboro, and Crest have large brand-loyal purchaser segments. They have successfully defended their market positions against assaults by major competitors in recent years. In contrast, Liggett & Myers lost 80 percent of its market share when it failed to engage in maintenance advertising.[70] Quality control problems caused Schlitz to lose substantial market share.

Illustration 15-4 shows part of Masterfoods USA's maintenance strategy for its 3 Musketeers® candy bar against the challenge of multiple competitors. Note that the ad stresses the improvements that Masterfoods USA has made in the candy.

Courtesy White Wave.

Disrupt Strategy

If the brand is not part of the evoked set and the target market engages in nominal decision making, the marketer's first task is to *disrupt* the existing decision pattern. This is a difficult task since the consumer does not seek external information or even consider alternative brands before a purchase. Low-involvement learning over time could generate a positive product position for our brand, but this alone would be unlikely to shift behavior.

In the long run, a major product improvement accompanied by attention-attracting advertising could shift the target market into a more extensive form of decision making. In the short run, attention-attracting advertising aimed specifically at breaking habitual decision making can be successful. Free samples, coupons, rebates, and tie-in sales are common approaches to disrupting nominal decision making. Likewise, striking package designs and point-of-purchase displays may disrupt a habitual purchase sequence.[71] Comparative advertising is also often used for this purpose.

Illustration 15-5 is an example of a disrupt strategy. Silk has found that once consumers try its various soymilk products, many prefer them. However, most consumers drink either cow's milk or no milk at all. Therefore, Silk has tried a number of ways to disrupt these behaviors and induce trial. In this attention-attracting ad, Silk uses humor and a direct challenge.

Capture Strategy

Limited decision making generally involves a few brands that are evaluated on only a few criteria such as price or availability. Much of the information search occurs at the point-of-purchase or in readily available media prior to purchase. If the brand is one given this type of consideration by the target market, the marketer's objective is to capture as large a share of their purchases as practical.

Because these consumers engage in limited search, the marketer needs to know where they search and what information they are looking for. In general, the marketer will want to supply information, often on price and availability, in their Web site, in local media through cooperative advertising, and at the point-of-purchase through displays and adequate shelf space. The marketer will also be concerned with maintaining consistent product quality and adequate distribution.

Intercept Strategy

If the target market engages in limited decision making and the brand is not part of their evoked set, the objective will be to intercept the consumer during the search for information on the brands in the evoked set or during general search for related information. Again, the emphasis will be on local media with cooperative advertising and at the point-of-purchase with displays, shelf space, package design, and so forth. Coupons can also be effective. The marketer will have to place considerable emphasis on attracting the consumers' attention as they will not be seeking information on the brand. The behavioral targeting strategy used by Snapple on iVillage's Web site is a great example of an online intercept strategy. As one ad executive stated:

> The big trick with this product was changing [the audience's perception] of Snapple-a-Day from an on-the-go, quirky product to something that has real health benefits for women and that has to be more of a planned purchase.[72]

The promotion shown in Illustration 15-6 would be effective as part of a capture or intercept strategy.

In addition to the strategies mentioned above, low-involvement learning, product improvements, and free samples can be used to move the brand into the target market's evoked set.

Preference Strategy

Extended decision making with the brand in the evoked set requires a preference strategy. Because extended decision making generally involves several brands, many attributes, and a number of information sources, a simple capture strategy may not be adequate. Instead, the marketer needs to structure an information campaign that will result in the brand being preferred by members of the target market.

The first step is a strong position on those attributes important to the target market.[73] This is discussed in considerable detail in Chapter 16. Next, information must be provided in all the appropriate sources. This may require extensive advertising to groups that do not purchase the item but recommend it to others (e.g., druggists for over-the-counter drugs, veterinarians and county agents for agricultural products). Independent groups should be encouraged to test the brand, and sales personnel should be provided detailed information on the brand's attributes. In addition, it may be wise to provide the sales personnel with extra motivation (e.g., extra commissions paid by the manufacturer) to recommend the

Courtesy Pizza Hut, Inc.

product. Point-of-purchase displays and pamphlets should also be available. A well-designed Web site is essential.

The OnStar ad shown in Illustration 15-7 (actually one page of a multi-page ad) is part of an effective preference strategy. It assumes an involved search, provides detailed information relative to multiple product attributes, and offers a Web site where consumers can find out even more.

Acceptance Strategy

Acceptance strategy is similar to preference strategy. However, it is complicated by the fact that the target market is not seeking information about the brand. Therefore, in addition to the activities involved in the preference strategy described above, the marketer must attract the consumers' attention or otherwise motivate them to learn about the brand. Consider the following quote by Lee Iacocca while he was head of Chrysler:

> Our biggest long-term job is to get people in [the showroom] to see how great these cars are—to get some traffic—and let them compare, so we're going head to head on price and value.[74]

Because of this situation, Chrysler implemented an acceptance strategy. In addition to product improvements and heavy advertising, Chrysler literally paid consumers to seek information about their cars! They did this by offering cash to individuals who would test drive a Chrysler product prior to purchasing a new car.

Long-term advertising designed to enhance low-involvement learning is another useful technique for gaining acceptance. Extensive advertising with strong emphasis on attracting

This ad assumes an extended search process. It provides substantial data on numerous product features.

© 2005 General Motors Archive.

attention can also be effective. The primary objective of these two approaches is not to sell the brand; rather, they seek to move the brand into the evoked set. Then, when a purchase situation arises, the consumer will seek additional information on this brand.

Finally, the Internet can play an important role in an acceptance strategy. As the search-engine results of DoubleClick indicate, keyword searches prior to a purchase tend to be generic. This opens up important opportunities for companies which are not in the evoked set to engage in search engine optimization strategies (including paying for specific keywords) to give their brand exposure to the consumer during the decision process—hopefully to the point of moving the brand into consumers' evoked sets. Obviously, a well-designed Web site is a critical part of this strategy.

SUMMARY

Following problem recognition, consumers may engage in extensive internal and external search, limited internal and external search, or only internal search. Information may be sought on (1) the appropriate *evaluative criteria* for the solution of the problem, (2) the existence of various *alternative solutions,* and (3) the *performance* of each alternative solution on each evaluative criterion.

Most consumers, when faced with a problem, can recall a limited number of brands that they feel are proba-

bly acceptable solutions. These acceptable brands, the *evoked set* (also known as the consideration set), are the initial ones that the consumer seeks additional information on during the remaining internal and external search process. Therefore, marketers are very concerned that their brands fall within the evoked set of most members of their target market.

Consumer internal information (information stored in memory) may have been actively acquired in previous searches and personal experiences or it may have been passively acquired through low-involvement learning. In addition to their own *memory,* consumers can seek information from four major types of external sources: (1) *personal sources,* such as friends and family; (2) *independent sources,* such as consumer groups, paid professionals, and government agencies; (3) *marketing sources,* such as sales personnel and advertising; and (4) *experiential sources,* such as direct product inspection or trial.

The Internet is commonly used as a source of information. While the Internet can decrease the costs of information search and lead to enhanced decisions, it can also lead to information overload. Online services that utilize *shopping bots* are increasingly popular with consumers as a means of establishing their consideration sets and for aiding in the decision itself. Marketing segmentation and targeted approaches are increasingly common as online users become more diverse. Marketers must be concerned with both driving their information to consumers and driving consumers to their information. Traditional offline media, Web advertising, search engine optimization, and behavioral targeting can help to accomplish these goals.

Explicit external information search *after* problem recognition is limited. This emphasizes the need to communicate effectively with consumers prior to problem recognition. Characteristics of the market, the product, the consumer, and the situation interact to influence the level of search.

It is often suggested that consumers generally should engage in relatively extensive external search prior to purchasing an item. However, this view ignores the fact that information search is not free. It takes time, energy, money, and can often require giving up more desirable activities. Therefore, consumers should engage in external search only to the extent that the expected benefits such as a lower price or a more satisfactory purchase outweigh the expected costs.

Sound marketing strategy takes into account the nature of information search engaged in by the target market. The level of search and the brand's position in or out of the evoked set are two key dimensions. Based on these two dimensions, six potential information strategies are suggested: (1) *maintenance,* (2) *disrupt,* (3) *capture,* (4) *intercept,* (5) *preference,* and (6) *acceptance.*

KEY TERMS

Awareness set 534
Behavioral targeting 545
Bots 542
Consideration set 534

Evoked set 534
External search 532
Inept set 535
Inert set 535

Internal search 532
Ongoing search 533
Perceived risk 550
Search engine optimization 545

INTERNET EXERCISES

1. The demographic composition of Internet users in the United States is changing over time as are the activities that users engage in. Go to the Pew Internet and American Life Project Web site (www.pewinternet.org). Go to the section on trends and report on how demographics and activities have changed from those reported in the text (generally from 2004/5).

2. The Conference Board (www.conference-board.org) gives periodic updates on what it calls the Consumer Internet Barometer. Report on the various dimensions they track and the major issues and perceptions of online users.

3. Go to www.searchenginewatch.com under their *search engine submission tips* section. Examine the various resources in this section including strategies for search engine optimization (SEO). Prepare a brief report on the various techniques involved in SEO.

4. Find and describe a magazine ad that is particularly effective at causing readers to consult a Web site. Why is it effective?

5. Visit a firm's Web site in one of the product categories listed below. Report on the strategies this firm uses (if any) to generate repeat traffic. Which strategies are most effective?

a. Automobiles
b. Cosmetics
c. Notebook computers
d. Food products company
e. Health care organization
f. Charities focused on poverty relief

6. Use an Internet shopping service such as mysimon.com to determine the "best buy" for a product that interests you. Evaluate this process. How could it be improved? If you were actually going to make the purchase, would you buy this one or would you purchase elsewhere? Why?

7. Visit Amazon.com, epionions.com, or a similar site. Examine the product reviews provided by other customers. How useful do you think these are? What could make them more useful?

8. Click on two banner ads for similar products. Describe where you encountered the banner ads and evaluate each banner ad and the target site. Do you feel like behavioral targeting was being used? Explain.

DDB LIFE STYLE STUDY™ DATA ANALYSES

1. Using the DDB data (Tables 1B through 7B) describe the major determinants of the following search-related behaviors and beliefs. What are the marketing implications?
   a. Consult consumer reports before making major purchases
   b. Information in advertising helps me make better decisions
   c. The Internet is the best place to get information about products and services

2. Some consumers feel more *technology savvy* than others. Examine the DDB data in Tables 1B through 7B to determine what characterizes one who is likely to feel tech savvy.

3. Using Table 3B, specifically examine the relationship between consumer perceptions of being tech savvy and the three search-related variables in Question 1. What are the relationships and implications?

REVIEW QUESTIONS

1. When does *information search* occur? What is the difference between internal and external information search?

2. What kind of information is sought in an external search for information?

3. What are *evaluative criteria* and how do they relate to information search?

4. How does a consumer's *awareness set* influence information search?

5. What roles do the *evoked set, inert set,* and *inept set* play in a consumer's information search?

6. What are the primary sources of information available to consumers?

7. What is the *Internet?*

8. What is *behavioral targeting?*

9. What is *search engine optimization?*

10. How do *nonsearchers, limited information searchers,* and *extended information searchers* differ in their search for information?

11. What factors might influence the search effort of consumers who are essentially one-stop shoppers? How do these factors differ in terms of how they influence limited information searchers and extended information searchers?

12. What factors have to be considered in the total cost of the information search? How might these factors be different for different consumers?

13. Explain how different *market characteristics* affect information search.

14. How do different *consumer characteristics* influence a consumer's information search effort?

15. How do *product characteristics* influence a consumer's information search effort?

16. How do *situational characteristics* influence a consumer's information search effort?

17. Describe the information search characteristics that should lead to each of the following strategies:
    a. Maintenance
    b. Disrupt

    c. Capture
    d. Intercept
    e. Preference
    f. Acceptance

18. Describe each of the strategies listed in Question 17.

DISCUSSION QUESTIONS

19. Pick a product/brand that you believe would require each strategy in Table 15-2 (six products in total). Justify your selection. Develop a specific marketing strategy for each (six strategies in total).

20. Of the products shown in Figure 15-3, which product class is most likely to exhibit the most brand switching? Explain your answer in terms of the information provided in Figure 15-3.

21. Use the Active Buyers Guide Web site to help you choose a brand of digital camera. Do you feel like the rankings it provided reflect your underlying preferences and attribute trade-offs? Do you see any potential problems related to consumers using shopping bots to aid in making their decisions? Explain.

22. Have you used an Internet shopping service such as mysimon.com? If so, what is your evaluation of it? If no, why not?

23. What information sources do you think students on your campus use when acquiring the items listed below? Consider the various sources listed in Figure 15-4 in developing your answer. Do you think there will be individual differences? Why?
    a. Movies
    b. Restaurants
    c. Apartment
    d. Dorm furnishings
    e. Fitness equipment
    f. A charity contribution
    g. Dress clothes
    h. Father's Day gifts

24. What factors contribute to the size of the awareness set, evoked set, inert set, and inept set?

25. Discuss factors that may contribute to external information search and factors that act to reduce external search for information before purchase or adoption of the following:
    a. Car repairs
    b. A pet
    c. Exercise club
    d. Formal wear
    e. Vegetarianism
    f. Counseling services

26. Is it ever in the best interest of a marketer to encourage potential customers to carry out an extended prepurchase search? Why or why not?

27. What implications for marketing strategy does Figure 15-2 suggest?

28. What implications for online marketing strategy does Figure 15-6 suggest?

29. What role, if any, should the government play in ensuring that consumers have easy access to relevant product information? How should it accomplish this?

30. Respond to the questions in Consumer Insight 15-1.

31. Describe a recent purchase in which you engaged in extensive search and one in which you did little prepurchase search. What factors caused the difference?

32. What is your awareness set, evoked set, inert set, and inept set for the following? In what ways, if any, do you think your sets will differ from the average member of your class? Why?
    a. MP3 players
    b. Energy bars
    c. Sports drinks
    d. Jewelry stores
    e. Book stores
    f. Internet shopping services
    g. Restaurants

APPLICATION ACTIVITIES

33. Develop an appropriate questionnaire and complete Question 23 using information from five students not in your class. Prepare a report discussing the marketing implications of your findings.

34. For the same products listed in Question 32, ask five students to list all the brands they are aware of in each product category. Then have them indicate which ones they might buy (evoked set), which ones they are indifferent toward (inert set), and which brands they strongly dislike and would not purchase (inept set). What are the marketing implications of your results?

35. Develop a short questionnaire designed to measure the information search consumers engage in prior to purchasing an expensive recreational or entertainment item or service. Your questionnaire should include measures of types of information

sought, as well as sources that provide this information. Also include measures of the relevant consumer characteristics that might influence information search, as well as some measure of past experience with the products. Then interview two recent purchasers of each product, using the questionnaire you have developed. Analyze each consumer's response and classify each consumer in terms of information search. What are the marketing implications of your results?

36. For each strategy in Table 15-2, find one brand that appears to be following that strategy. Describe in detail how it is implementing the strategy.

37. Develop a questionnaire to determine which products college students view as positive and which they view as negative. Measure the shopping effort associated with each type. Explain your overall results and any individual differences you find.

REFERENCES

1. Based on information found on the various corporate Web sites.

2. G. Punji and R. Brookes, "Decision Constraints and Consideration-Set Formation in Consumer Durables," *Psychology & Marketing,* August 2001, pp. 843–63.

3. An outstanding discussion of the trade-off consumers make between memory-based decisions (internal search) and external search is in J. R. Bettman, M. F. Luce, and J. W. Payne, "Constructive Consumer Choice Processes," *Journal of Consumer Research,* December 1998, pp. 187–217.

4. For a more comprehensive view, see R. Lawson, "Consumer Decision Making within a Goal-Driven Framework," *Psychology & Marketing,* August 1997, pp. 427–49.

5. S. Shapiro, D. J. MacInnis, and S. E. Heckler, "The Effects of Incidental Ad Exposure on the Formation of Consideration Sets," *Journal of Consumer Research,* June 1997, pp. 94–104; S. S. Posavac, D. M. Sanbonmatsu, and E. A. Ho, "The Effects of the Selective Consideration of Alternatives on Consumer Choice and Attitude-Decision Consistency," *Journal of Consumer Psychology* 12, no. 3 (2002), pp. 203–13; F. R. Kardes et al., "Consideration Set Overvaluation," *Journal of Consumer Psychology* 12, no. 4 (2002), pp. 353–61; and T. Erdem and J. Swait, "Brand Credibility, Brand Consideration, and Choice," *Journal of Consumer Research,* June 2004, pp. 191–98.

6. P. Aurier, S. Jean, and J. L. Zaichkowsky, "Consideration Set Size and Familiarity with Usage Context," *Advances in Consumer Research,* vol. 27, eds. S. J. Hoch and R. J. Meyer (Provo, UT: Association for Consumer Research, 2000), pp. 307–13; and K. K. Desai and W. D. Hoyer, "Descriptive Characteristics of Memory-Based Consideration Sets," *Journal of Consumer Research,* December 2000, pp. 309–23.

7. E. M. Felcher, P. Malaviya, and A. L. McGill, "The Role of Taxonomic and Goal-Derived Product Categorization in, within, and across Category Judgments," *Psychology & Marketing,* August 2001, pp. 865–87.

8. R. R. Brand and J. J. Cronin, "Consumer-Specific Determinants of the Size of Retail Choice Sets," *Journal of Services Marketing* 11, no. 1 (1997), pp. 19–38.

9. See S. C. Mooy and H. S. J. Robben, "How Consumers Learn from and about Products," *Advances in Consumer Research,* vol. 25, eds. J. W. Alba and J. W. Hutchinson (Provo, UT: Association for Consumer Research, 1998), pp. 318–23.

10. L. R. Klein and G. T. Ford, "Consumer Search for Information in the Digital Age," *Journal of Interactive Marketing,* Summer 2003, pp. 29–49; and B. T. Ratchford, M.-Soo Lee, and D. Talukdar, "The Impact of the Internet on Information Search for Automobiles," *Journal of Marketing Research,* May 2003, pp. 193–209.

11. H. Li, T. Daugherty, and F. Biocca, "The Role of Virtual Experience in Consumer Learning," *Journal of Consumer Psychology* 13, no. 4 (2003), pp. 395–407; A. E. Schlosser, "Experience Products in the Virtual World," *Journal of Consumer Research,* September 2003, pp. 184–98; and D. A. Griffith and Q. Chen, "The Influence of Virtual Direct Experience (VDE) on On-line Ad Message Effectiveness," *Journal of Advertising,* Spring 2004, pp. 55–68.

12. C. B. Jarvis, "An Exploratory Investigation of Consumers' Evaluations of External Information Sources in Prepurchase Search," *Advances in Consumer Research,* vol. 25, eds. Alba and Hutchinson, pp. 446–51; and M. Laroche, C. Kim, and T. Matsui, "Which Decision Heuristics Are Used in Consideration Set

Formation?" *Journal of Consumer Marketing* 20, no. 3 (2003), pp. 192–209.

13. For a review and conflicting evidence, see A. A. Wright and J. G. Lynch, Jr., "Communications Effects of Advertising versus Direct Experience When Both Search and Experience Attributes Are Present," *Journal of Consumer Research,* March 1995, pp. 108–18.

14. See C. F. Mela, S. Gupta, and D. R. Lehmann, "The Long-Term Impact of Promotion and Advertising on Consumer Brand Choice," *Journal Marketing Research,* May 1997, pp. 248–61; and M. J. Sirgy et al., "Does Television Viewership Play a Role in the Perception of Quality of Life," *Journal of Advertising,* Spring 1998, pp. 125–42.

15. "International Wired and Wireless Activity Forges Ahead in the Global Arena," *Marketing News,* July 15, 2004, p. 16.

16. *Worldwide Internet Users Will Top 1 Billion in 2005* (Arlington Heights, IL: Computer Industry Almanac, Inc., press release, September 3, 2004).

17. *Demographics of Internet Users* (Washington, DC: Pew Internet & American Life Project, May 18, 2005), available online at www.pewinternet.org.

18. See, e.g., *Internet Becomes More Mainstream* (New York: Mediamark Research Inc., press release, July 16, 2002).

19. *A Nation Online* (Washington, DC: U.S. Department of Commerce, September 2004).

20. *Older Americans and the Internet* (Washington, DC: Pew Internet & American Life Project, March 25, 2004).

21. *A Nation Online.*

22. *Internet Activities* (Washington, DC: Pew Internet & American Life Project, May 18, 2005).

23. S. Hays, "Has Online Advertising Finally Grown Up?" *Advertising Age,* April 1, 2002, p. C1.

24. *Counting on the Internet* (Washington, DC: Pew Internet & American Life Project, December 29, 2002); Klein and Ford, "Consumer Search for Information in the Digital Age,"; Ratchford, Lee, and Talukdar, "The Impact of the Internet on Information Search for Automobiles,"; and *DoubleClick's Touchpoints II* (New York: DoubleClick research report, March 2004).

25. *Search Before the Purchase* (New York: DoubleClick research report, February 2005).

26. Ratchford, Lee, and Talukdar, "The Impact of the Internet on Information Search for Automobiles."

27. J. L. Joines, C. W. Scherer, and D. A. Scheufele, "Exploring Motivations for Consumer Web Use and their Implications for E-commerce," *Journal of Consumer Marketing* 20, no. 2 (2003), pp. 90–108.

28. L. Gentry and Roger Calantone, "A Comparison of Three Models to Explain Shop-Bot Use on the Web," *Psychology & Marketing,* November 2002, pp. 945–56.

29. For detailed discussion and possible consequences, see A. Ansari, S. Essegaier, and R. Kohli, "Internet Recommendation Systems," *Journal of Marketing Research,* August 2000, pp. 363–75; D. Lacobucci, P. Arabie, and A. Bodapati, "Recommendation Agents on the Internet," *Journal of Interactive Marketing,* Summer 2000, pp. 2–11; G. Haubl and K. B. Murray, "Preference Construction and Persisitence in Digital Market-

places," *Journal of Consumer Psychology* 13, no. 1/2 (2003), pp. 75–91; K. Diehl, L. J. Kornish, and J. G. Lynch, Jr., "Smart Agents," *Journal of Consumer Research,* June 2003, pp. 56–71; and V. Swaminathan, "The Impact of Recommendation Agents on Consumer Evaluation and Choice," *Journal of Consumer Psychology* 13, no. 1/2 (2003), pp. 93–101.

30. B. Bickart and R. M. Schindler, "Internet Forums as Influential Sources of Consumer Information," *Journal of Interactive Marketing,* Summer 2001, pp. 31–40; and P. Chatterjee, "Online Reviews," *Advances in Consumer Research,* vol. 28, eds. M. C. Gilly and J. Meyers-Levy (Provo, UT: Association for Consumer Research, 2001), pp. 129–33.

31. Klein and Ford, "Consumer Search for Information in the Digital Age."

32. A. Parmar, "Student e-union," *Marketing News,* April 1, 2004, pp. 14–15.

33. "Ethnic Groups Online," *eMarketer,* June 20, 2005.

34. N. Singh and H. Matsuo, "Measuring Cultural Adaptation on the Web," in *Advances in Consumer Research,* vol. 30, eds. P. A. Keller and D. W. Rook (Provo, UT: Association for Consumer Research, 2003), pp. 271–72.

35. "Internet," *Marketing News,* July 15, 2004, p. 15.

36. J. Halliday, "Half Hit Web Before Showrooms," *Advertising Age,* October 4, 2004, p. 76.

37. E-mail material based on *DoubleClick's 2004 Consumer E-mail Study* (New York: DoubleClick, October 2004).

38. J. S. Ilfeld and R. S. Winer, "Generating Web Traffic," *Journal of Advertising Research,* October 2002, pp. 49–61.

39. W. Dou, R. Linn, and S. Yang, "How Smart are 'Smart Banners'?" *Journal of Advertising Research* 41, no. 4 (2001), pp. 31–43.

40. K. Oser, "Snapple Effort Finds Women as They Browse," *Advertising Age,* May 3, 2004, p. 22.

41. D. Sullivan, "Intro to Search Engine Optimization," *SearchEngineWatch.com,* October 14, 2002.

42. See, e.g., T. P. Novak, D. L. Hoffman, and Y.-F. Yung, "Measuring the Customer Experience in Online Environments," *Marketing Science,* Winter 2000, pp. 22–42; and J. R. Coyle and E. Thorson, "The Effects of Progressive Levels of Interactivity and Vividness in Web Marketing Sites," *Journal of Advertising,* Fall 2001, pp. 65–77.

43. R. A. Westbrook and C. Farnell, "Patterns of Information Source Usage among Durable Goods Buyers," *Journal of Marketing Research,* August 1979, pp. 303–12; and J. E. Urbany, P. R. Dickson, and W. L. Wilkie, "Buyer Uncertainty and Information Search," *Journal of Consumer Research,* September 1989, pp. 208–15.

44. Urbany, Dickson, and Wilkie, "Buyer Uncertainty and Information Search"; and *Warranties Rule Consumer Follow-Up* (Washington DC: Federal Trade Commission, 1984), p. 26.

45. Ratchford, Lee, and Talukdar, "The Impact of the Internet on Information Search for Automobiles."

46. G. Katona and E. Mueller, "A Study of Purchase Decisions," in *Consumer Behavior: The Dynamics of Consumer Reaction,* ed. L. Clark (New York University Press, 1955), pp. 30–87; J. Newman and R. Staelin, "Prepurchase Information Seeking for

New Cars and Major Household Appliances," *Journal of Marketing Research,* August 1972, pp. 249–57; J. Claxton, J. Fry, and B. Portis, "A Taxonomy of Prepurchase Information Gathering Patterns," *Journal of Consumer Research,* December 1974, pp. 35–42; G. C. Kiel and R. A. Layton, "Dimensions of Consumer Information Seeking Behavior," *Journal of Marketing Research,* May 1981, pp. 233–39; J. B. Freiden and R. E. Goldsmith, "Prepurchase Information-Seeking for Professional Services," *Journal of Services Marketing,* Winter 1989, pp. 45–55; Urbany, Dickson, and Wilkie, "Buyer Uncertainty and Information Search"; G. N. Souter and M. M. McNeil, *Journal of Professional Services Marketing* 11, no. 2 (1995), pp. 45–60; and Klein and Ford, "Consumer Search for Information in the Digital Age."

47. For more elaborate models, see S. Moorthy, B. T. Ratchford, and D. Talukdar, "Consumer Information Search Revisited," *Journal of Consumer Research,* March 1997, pp. 263–77; and S. Putrevu and B. T. Ratchford, "A Model of Search Behavior with an Application to Grocery Shopping," *Journal of Retailing,* no. 4 (1997), pp. 463–86.

48. See W. K. Darley, "The Relationship of Antecedents of Search and Self-Esteem to Adolescent Search Effort," *Psychology & Marketing,* August 1999, pp. 409–27.

49. J. G. Lynch, Jr., and D. Ariely, "Wine Online," *Marketing Science,* Winter 2000, pp. 83–103; D. Ariely, "Controlling the Information Flow," *Journal of Consumer Research,* September 2000, pp. 233–48; and Ratchford, Lee, and Talukdar, "The Impact of the Internet on Information Search for Automobiles."

50. For a similar model of online search, see S. Kulviwat, C. Guo, and N. Engchanil, "Determinants of Online Search," *Internet Research* 14, no. 3 (2004), pp. 245–53.

51. D. R. Lichtenstein, N. M. Ridgway, and R. G. Netemeyer, "Price Perceptions and Consumer Shopping Behavior," *Journal of Marketing Research,* May 1993, pp. 234–45.

52. M. N. Bergen, S. Dutta, and S. M. Shugan, "Branded Variants," *Journal of Marketing Research,* February 1996, pp. 9–19.

53. J. Srivastava and N. Lurie, "A Consumer Perspective on Price-Matching Refund Policies," *Journal of Consumer Research,* September 2001, pp. 296–307.

54. D. Grewal and H. Marmorstein, "Market Price Variation, Perceived Price Variation, and Consumers' Price Search Decisions for Durable Goods," *Journal of Consumer Research,* December 1994, pp. 453–60.

55. See B. G. C. Dellaert, "Investigating Consumers' Tendency to Combine Multiple Shopping Purposes and Destinations," *Journal Marketing Research,* May 1998, pp. 177–89.

56. See C. Moorman, "Market-Level Effects of Information," *Journal Marketing Research,* February 1998, pp. 82–98; and A. D. Miyazaki, D. E. Sprott, and K. C. Manning, "Unit Prices on Retail Shelf Labels," *Journal of Retailing* 76, no. 1 (2000), pp. 93–112.

57. See C. M. Fisher and C. J. Anderson, "The Relationship between Consumer Attitudes and Frequency of Advertising in Newspapers for Hospitals," *Journal of Hospital Marketing* 7, no. 2 (1993), pp. 139–56.

58. S. Widrick and E. Fram, "Identifying Negative Products," *Journal of Consumer Marketing,* no. 2 (1983), pp. 59–66.

59. See D. D'Rozario and S. P. Douglas, "Effect of Assimilation on Prepurchase Information-Search Tendencies," *Journal of Consumer Psychology* 8, no. 2 (1999), pp. 187–209; and C. Merrill, "Where the Cars Are Caliente," *American Demographics,* January 2000, pp. 56–59.

60. C. M. Heilman, D. Bowman, and G. P. Wright, "The Evolution of Brand Preferences and Choice Behaviors of Consumers New to a Market," *Journal of Marketing Research,* May 2000, pp. 139–55. See also, D. Mazursky, "The Effects of Invalidating Information on Consumers' Subsequent Search Patterns," *Journal of Economic Psychology,* April 1998, pp. 261–77.

61. See G. E. Smith, M. P. Venkatraman, and R. R. Dholakia, "Diagnosing the Search Cost Effort," *Journal of Economic Psychology* 20 (1999), pp. 285–314; and B. T. Ratchford, "The Economics of Consumer Knowledge," *Journal of Consumer Research,* March 2001, pp. 397–411. See also, J. A. Barrick and B. C. Spilker, "The Relations between Knowledge, Search Strategy, and Performance in Unaided and Aided Information Search," *Organizational Behavior and Human Decision Processes* 90 (2003), pp. 1–18.

62. See J. R. Lumpkin; "Shopping Orientation Segmentation of the Elderly Consumer," *Journal of the Academy of Marketing Science,* Spring 1985, pp. 271–89; T. Williams, M. Slama, and J. Rogers, "Behavioral Characteristics of the Recreational Shopper," *Journal of Academy of Marketing Science,* Summer 1985, pp. 307–16; J. R. Lumpkin, J. M. Hawes, and W. R. Darden, "Shopping Patterns of the Rural Consumer," *Journal of Business Research,* February 1986, pp. 63–81; and W. W. Moe, "Buying, Searching, or Browsing," *Journal of Consumer Psychology* 13, no. 1/2 (2003), pp. 29–39.

63. See U. M. Dholakia, "Involvement-Response Models of Joint Effects," *Advances in Consumer Research,* vol. 25, eds. Alba and Hutchinson, pp. 499–506.

64. This insight is based on J. W. Alba and J. W. Hutchinson, "Knowledge Calibration," *Journal of Consumer Research,* September 2000, pp. 123–49.

65. T. H. Dodd, B. E. Pinkleton, and A. W. Gustafson, *Psychology & Marketing,* May 1996, pp. 291–304. See also J. R. McColl-Kennedy and R. E. Fetter, Jr., "An Empirical Examination of the Involvement to External Search Relationship," *Journal of Services Marketing* 15, no. 2 (2001), pp. 82–98.

66. G. R. Dowling and R. Staelin, "A Model of Perceived Risk and Intended Risk-Handling Activity," *Journal of Consumer Research,* June 1994, pp. 119–34. See also J. B. Smith and J. M. Bristor, "Uncertainty Orientation," *Psychology & Marketing,* November 1994, pp. 587–607.

67. A. Chaudhuri, "Product Class Effects on Perceived Risk," *International Journal of Research in Marketing,* May 1998, pp. 157–68; and K. Mitra, M. C. Reiss, and L. M. Capella, "An Examination of Perceived Risk, Informational Search, and Behavioral Intentions," *Journal of Services Marketing* 13, no. 3 (1999), pp. 208–28.

68. See, e.g., M. W. H. Weenig and M. Maarleveld, "The Impact of Time Constraint on Information Search Strategies in Complex Choice Tasks," *Journal of Economic Psychology* 23 (2002), pp. 689–702. For an exception, see C. J. Hill, "The Nature of Problem Recognition and Search in the Extended Health Care

Decision," *Journal of Services Marketing* 15, no. 6 (2001), pp. 454–79.

69. A. G. Abdul-Muhmin, "Contingent Decision Behavior," *Journal of Consumer Psychology* 8, no. 1 (1999), pp. 91–111.

70. "L&M Lights Up Again," *Marketing and Media Decisions,* February 1984, p. 69.

71. L. L. Garber, "The Package Appearance in Choice," in *Advances in Consumer Research,* vol. 22, eds. F. R. Kardes and M. Sujan (Provo, UT: Association for Consumer Research, 1995), pp. 653–60.

72. Oser, "Snapple Effort Finds Women as They Browse."

73. See, e.g., Erdem and Swait, "Brand Credibility, Brand Consideration, and Choice."

74. R. Gray, "Chrysler Hinges Price on Popularity," *Advertising Age,* October 5, 1981, p. 7.

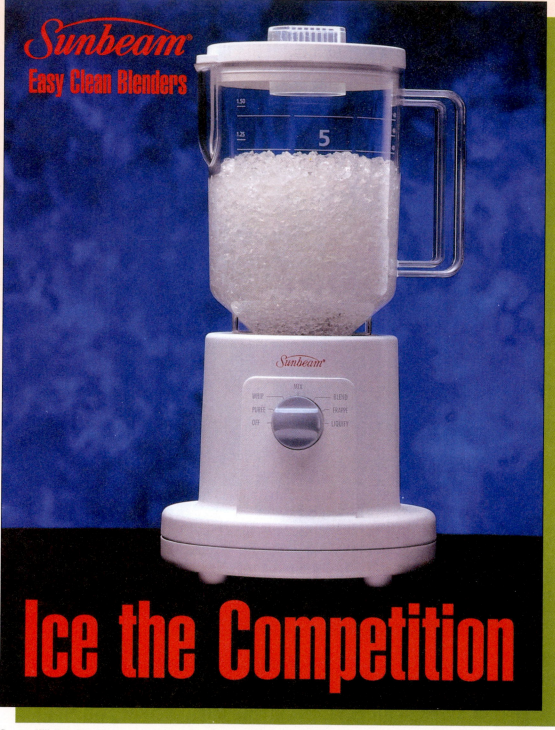

564

Courtesy Hill, Knowlton, Sancor.

16

Alternative Evaluation and Selection

■ Sunbeam Appliance Company successfully redesigned its many lines of small kitchen appliances. The redesign of its food processor line illustrates the four-stage process used:

1. A *consumer usage and attitude survey* was used to determine how and for what purpose products in the product category are used, frequency of use, brand ownership, brand awareness, and attitudes toward the product.

2. A *consumer attribute and benefit survey* was used to provide importance ratings of product attributes and benefits desired from the product category, along with perceptions of the degree to which each brand provides the various attributes and benefits.

3. A *conjoint analysis study* (a technique described in this chapter) was used to provide data on the structure of consumers' preferences for product features and their willingness to trade one feature for more of another feature. Conjoint analysis provides the relative

importance *each* consumer attaches to various levels of each potential product feature. This allows individuals with similar preference structures to be grouped into market segments.

4. *Product line sales and market share simulations* were used to determine the best set of food processors to bring to the market. Based on the preference structures and sizes of the market segments discovered in step 3 and the perceived characteristics of competing brands, the market share of various Sunbeam product sets was estimated using computer simulations.

The above process involved interviewing hundreds of product category users. Twelve different product attributes were tested and four distinct market segments were uncovered. The existing product line was replaced with four new models (down from six) targeted at three of the four segments. The results were increased market share, reduced costs, and increased profitability.[1]

| FIGURE 16-1 | Alternative Evaluation and Selection Process |

The opening example describes Sunbeam's successful analysis of consumers' desired product benefits (evaluative criteria) and the manner in which they choose between products with differing combinations of benefits. The process by which consumers evaluate and choose among alternatives is illustrated in Figure 16-1.

We will organize our discussion around four basic areas. First, we will provide an overview of the processes consumers use to select among alternatives. Then, the nature and characteristics of evaluative criteria (the benefits the product should provide) will be described. After examining evaluative criteria, we will focus on the ability of consumers to judge the performance of products on the evaluative criteria. Finally, we will examine the decision rules that consumers use in selecting one alternative from those considered.

It is important to remember that many purchases involve little or no evaluation of alternatives. Nominal decisions do not require the evaluation of any alternatives. The last purchase is repeated without considering other information. Limited decisions may involve comparing a few brands (small evoked set) on one or two dimensions (I'll buy Heinz or Del Monte ketchup, depending on which is cheaper at Safeway).

HOW CONSUMERS MAKE CHOICES

Any attempt to describe a complex, nonlinear process such as consumer choice necessarily simplifies it and removes much of its richness. Thus, our discussion will make consumer choice seem more logical, structured, rational, and deliberate than it often is. Fortunately, we have all made numerous consumer choices and we know that they are frequently circular, emotional, incomplete, and based on expediency rather than optimality. We also know that the situation plays an important role in the processes we use to make consumer choices. For example, when we are tired or hurried, we are very likely to use different choice processes than we would if we had more energy or time.

A substantial amount of research and marketing strategy has assumed a rational consumer decision maker with well-defined, stable preferences. The consumer is also assumed to have sufficient skills to calculate which option will maximize his or her value, and will choose on this basis. This approach is referred to as *rational choice theory*. The task in rational choice theory is to *identify* or discover the one optimal choice for the decision confronting the decision maker. The decision maker simply collects information on the levels of the attributes of the alternatives, applies preexisting values to those levels, applies the appropriate choice rule, and the superior option is revealed.

Consumer choice goals are usually described in terms such as "getting the least expensive calculator with the functions I need" or "selecting a dress that makes me feel great." These are the specific purchase goals or outcomes the consumer wants to obtain. A **metagoal** refers to *the general nature of the outcome being sought*.[2] The purchase goals just described are examples of a metagoal of *maximizing the accuracy of the decision*. This is the only goal assumed in many studies of consumer decision making. However, other metagoals exist.

Consumers often seek to *minimize the cognitive effort required for the decision*. This is often the goal in nominal and limited decision making. However, it can also play an important role in extended decision making as well. Consumers seeking to minimize effort tend to use simple choice rules, consider fewer alternatives, place more importance on the dominant attribute, and evaluate fewer attributes of each alternative.[3] Consumers may also delay or avoid the decision.[4]

Choices that involve conflicts between valued goals such as an attractive, low-effort lawn versus the use of pesticides and herbicides can generate significant negative emotions.[5] Thus, another consumer metagoal is to *minimize the experience of negative emotion while making the decision*. One strategy consumers use for this purpose is to avoid or delay the decision and stay with the status quo.

A fourth metagoal is to *maximize the ease with which a decision can be justified*. Consumers are social beings and often feel compelled to justify a decision to others or to themselves.[6] This is particularly true for luxury items and items that are different or more extravagant than those used by one's reference groups. Anticipating the need for such justifications can affect how a consumer makes the initial decision.

These metagoals are not mutually exclusive.[7] In fact, many decisions are characterized by multiple goals with differing levels of importance. Further, the relative importance of the goals may change as the consumer moves through the decision process. For example, a consumer deciding to purchase a lawnmower may begin with maximizing the accuracy of the decision as the primary goal. However, as the consumer learns of the vast number of brands, models, and features, minimizing effort may become increasingly important. As the consumer learns of incompatible features (the model that pollutes the least costs the most and does not perform as well), minimizing negative emotion may become more salient.

Critical Thinking Questions

1. Do you agree with the four metagoals described above? What others do you think are common?

2. What are the marketing implications of each of the metagoals described above (assume all four are widely used by consumers)?

In reality, all consumers have **bounded rationality**—*a limited capacity for processing information*. Moreover, consumers often have goals that are different from, or in addition to, selecting the optimal alternative (see Consumer Insight 16-1). Further, recent research indicates that preferences are not stable. That is, if an individual is comparing brands A and B, he or she might prefer brand A. However, if brand C is added to the evoked set, the consumer's preference might shift to brand B.[8] Therefore, for many decisions consumers do not engage in a strictly rational choice; instead, they construct a decision process that is appropriate for the situation at hand.

In addition, many consumer decisions do not involve the comparison of brands on their features at all. Instead, they are based on emotional responses to the brand or overall impressions of the brand. In this section, we will examine three types of consumer choice processes: affective choice, attitude-based choice, and attribute-based choice. Keep in mind that these are not mutually exclusive and combinations may be used in a single decision.

Affective Choice

Consider a consumer buying an alarm clock. She inspects several models, noticing many differences among them. Some models have a snooze-alarm feature, some don't. Some have a battery backup, others don't. The models also vary on wake-to-music or -to-alarm feature, top-mounted versus side controls, push-button versus rotary or sliding switches, lighted alarm-set indicator, automatic FM frequency control, the type of finish, and the price. She reviews her relative preference for these diverse features and chooses the model that gives her the best combination of the desired features.

Now consider her buying a dress for an upcoming big social event. Scanning a rack full of dresses in a store, she pulls out a few that seemed nice. One of them particularly caught her eye: she tries it on, and thinks she looks great in it. She tries another one which she thought made her look too conservative. A third one made her look too sexy. Somehow, the first one looked so right for her: a few more minutes of contemplation about what a great impression she would make donning that dress in the party, and she has made up her mind about that dress.[9]

The purchase of the alarm clock is an example of an attribute-based choice, discussed in the following section. It is based on a conscious evaluation of the various features of the clocks considered. The purchase of the dress is primarily an **affective choice.** Affective choices tend to be more holistic in nature. The brand is not decomposed into distinct components, each of which is evaluated separately from the whole. The evaluation of such products is generally focused on the way they will make the user feel as they are used. The evaluation itself is often based exclusively or primarily on the immediate emotional response to the product or service:

I'm getting married, and we were looking for a place to have the wedding and we had been to about five or six places . . . this (place) was not quite right . . . and this other place was not quite right . . . but then we went to a place called The Highlander in Glens Falls. I went in the lobby and I knew immediately that this was right. It was immaculately clean, the floor was not just marble but inlaid different types of patterns on the floor . . . its restaurant, the doors were lead and glass and you just knew that this was right. . . . You go in there and sure enough they had a wedding coordinator.[10]

Decisions based on affect use the "How do I feel about it" heuristic or decision rule.[11] Consumers imagine or picture using the product or service and evaluate the feeling that this use will produce.[12] For example, a consumer choosing between a weekend at a bed-and-breakfast on a beach and a weekend in a nice hotel in a city might imagine each episode to see how he or she feels. The decision would then be made largely or completely on these expected feelings.

Affective choice is most likely when the underlying motive is consummatory rather than instrumental. **Consummatory motives** *underlie behaviors that are intrinsically rewarding to the individual involved.* **Instrumental motives** *activate behaviors designed to achieve a second goal.* For example, one person might read a best-seller for the pleasure of reading the book (consummatory motive), whereas another might read the same book to be able to appear "with it" to his or her friends (instrumental motive).[13] Illustration 16-1 shows ads appealing to each of these motives.

Marketers continue to learn more about affect-based decisions.[14] It is clear that such decisions require different strategies than the more cognitive decisions generally considered in marketing. For those decisions that are likely to be affective in nature (largely triggered by consummatory motives), marketers should design products and services that will provide the appropriate emotional responses.[15] They also should help consumers

Courtesy Häagen-Dazs.

Courtesy FreshLook Cosmetic Contact Lenses.

visualize how they will feel during and after the consumption experience.[16] This is particularly important for new brands or products and services. Consumers who have experience with a product or brand have a basis for imagining the affective response it will produce. Those who do not may incorrectly predict the feelings the experience will produce. For example, individuals imagining a whitewater rafting trip may conclude that it would produce feelings of terror rather than exhilaration. Illustration 16-2 shows an ad that helps consumers envision the positive experiences and accompanying feelings they would have if they owned a Toyota Solara.

Attribute-Based versus Attitude-Based Choice Processes

Consider the following two processes a consumer might use to purchase a digital camera:

Process 1: After consulting the Internet to determine what features she is most interested in, the consumer then goes to her local electronics store and compares the various brands on the features most important to her—namely, camera size, zoom, automatic features, and storage size. She mentally ranks each model on these attributes and her general impression of each model's quality. On the basis of these evaluations, she chooses the Olympus SportZoom.

ILLUSTRATION 16-1

The Häagen-Dazs ad appeals to the consummatory motive associated with the pleasure of consuming the product. The FreshLook ad appeals to an instrumental motive by positioning the contact lenses as a means to the end of being attractive.

This ad encourages an affect-based choice by encouraging consumers to imagine the pleasure they will derive from owning the product.

Courtesy Saatchi & Saatchi/Los Angeles.

Process 2: The consumer remembers that her friend's Olympus SportZoom worked well and looked "good"; her parents had a Kodak Easyshare that also worked well but was rather large and bulky; and her old Fujifilm FinePix had not performed as well as she had expected. At her local electronics store she sees that the Olympus and Kodak models are about the same price and decides to buy the Olympus SportZoom.

The first example above is attribute-based choice. **Attribute-based choice** *requires the knowledge of specific attributes at the time the choice is made, and it involves attribute-by-attribute comparisons across brands.* The second example above is attitude-based choice. **Attitude-based choice** *involves the use of general attitudes, summary impressions, intuitions, or heuristics; no attribute-by-attribute comparisons are made at the time of choice.*[17] There can also be combinations of these forms. A common combination would be for an evoked set (also known as a consideration set) to be formed using attitude-based processing, with the final choice being made on the basis of a brand-by-brand comparison.

Attribute-based choices require the comparison of each specific attribute across all the brands considered. This is a much more effortful and time-consuming process than the global comparisons made when attitude-based choice is involved. It also tends to produce a more nearly optimal decision.

Motivation, information availability, and situational factors interact to determine which choice process will be used. As one would suspect, the greater the motivation to make an optimal decision, the more likely an attribute-based choice will be made. In general, the importance of making an optimal decision increases with the value of the item being considered and consequences of a nonoptimal decision. Thus, attribute-based processing is more likely for a laptop computer or an athletic shoe for a marathoner than it is for an inexpensive calculator or an athletic shoe to wear around campus.

Courtesy Visa USA.

Courtesy ASICS Tiger, Inc.

The easier it is to access complete attribute-by-brand information, the more likely attribute-based processing will be used. This can be used by marketers of brands that have important attribute-based advantages but that lack strong reputations or images in the target market. The approach would be to provide attribute-based comparisons in an easy-to-process format such as a brand-by-attribute matrix. Such a matrix could be presented in ads, on packages, in point-of-purchase displays, in brochures, or on the brand's Web site. A firm using such a strategy should use an appropriate comparison format and structure the information so that its brand will be the focal point of comparison.[18] This could be done by listing it first, perhaps in bold or colored type.

A variety of situations influence which choice approach is most likely. As we saw in Chapter 13, task definition influences the importance assigned to purchases, with gift purchases often being assigned more importance than similar purchases for oneself. Thus, gift purchases would be more likely to produce attribute-based decision processes. Time pressure is a major determinant of choice process used, with increasing time pressures producing more use of attitude-based decisions.

It is important to note that many decisions, even for important products, appear to be attitude-based. Recall from the previous chapter that most individuals collect very little product information from external sources immediately before a purchase. They are most likely making attitude-based decisions.

The ads in Illustration 16-3 illustrate the differences between attribute-based and attitude-based choice strategies. The Visa ad focuses on features and emphasizes its

ILLUSTRATION 16-3

The Visa ad encourages attribute-based choice with primacy given to its enhanced purchasing power, upgraded services, and rewards. Ads that assume or encourage attitude-based choice, such as the ASICS ad, focus on brand, overall performance, and image rather than specific product features.

Tamron USA, Inc. 2002.

enhanced purchasing power, upgraded services, and rewards. In contrast, the ASICS ad focuses on the brand and an overall impression of the product and its users.

Marketers for most products and services, even expensive, important ones, have a dual task. They must provide information and experiences that produce a strong attitude-based position (for those consumers making an attitude-based choice) *and* they must provide performance levels and supporting information that will result in preference among those consumers making attribute-based choices.

EVALUATIVE CRITERIA

As the prior discussion described, consumers often make decisions based on affect or on overall attitude toward the brand or to minimize effort or negative emotion. Many of these types of decisions involve very little consideration of specific product features. However, most decisions involve an evaluation of the likely performance of the product or service on one or more dimensions. **Evaluative criteria** are *the various dimensions, features, or benefits a consumer looks for in response to a specific problem.* Before purchasing a computer, you might be concerned with cost, speed, memory, operating system, display, and warranty. These would be your evaluative criteria. Someone else could approach the same purchase with an entirely different set of evaluative criteria.

Nature of Evaluative Criteria

Evaluative criteria are typically product features or attributes associated with either benefits desired by customers or the costs they must incur. Thus, many consumers who want to

Reprinted by permission of the Andrew Jergen Company.

Courtesy Beiersdorf, Inc.

avoid cavities use toothpaste that contains fluoride. For these consumers, fluoride is an evaluative criterion associated with the benefit cavity prevention. In this case, the evaluative criterion and the desired benefit are not identical, and fluoride is important as a feature only to the extent that it helps prevent cavities. In such cases, marketers should emphasize the benefit the feature will provide the consumer, not just the feature itself. The ad in Illustration 16-4 focuses on the ability of the Tamron zoom lens to capture memories, not on its technical specifications.

In other situations, the product feature and the benefit or cost are the same. For example, price is often an evaluative criterion that is identical to one aspect of cost (although it can also be a quality signal as discussed in Chapter 8).

As we saw earlier, products and services purchased primarily for emotional reasons may involve anticipating the effect of purchase or use on feelings rather than on analysis of product attributes per se. Likewise, a product purchased for use in a social situation often involves anticipation of the reaction of others to the product instead of an analysis of its attributes. In these cases, the anticipated feelings or reactions would be the evaluative criteria.

Evaluative criteria can differ in type, number, and importance. The *type of evaluative criteria* a consumer uses in a decision varies from *tangible* cost and performance features to *intangible* factors such as style, taste, prestige, feelings generated, and brand image.[19]

Illustration 16-5 shows how two similar products stress very different types of evaluative criteria. The Jergens ad stresses tangible attributes and technical performance. The Nivea ad focuses on intangible attributes and feelings.

Evaluative criteria may exist in terms of extremes (lower price or more miles per gallon is better), limits (it must not cost more than $100; it must get more than 25 miles per gallon), or ranges (any price between $85 and $99 is acceptable).[20] For new product categories, consumers must often determine which levels of a various criteria are desirable. For example, a consumer who buys a barbecue grill for the first time and has very limited experience with such grills may have to determine if he prefers gas to charcoal, domed or traditional shape, appropriate size, and so forth. After purchase and use, these preference levels are likely to become more firmly established and stable.[21]

For fairly simple products such as toothpaste, soap, or facial tissue, consumers use relatively few evaluative criteria. On the other hand, the purchase of an automobile, stereo system, or house may involve numerous criteria. Characteristics of the individual (such as product familiarity and age) and characteristics of the purchase situation (such as time pressure) also influence the number of evaluative criteria considered.[22] For example, recent research shows that time pressure reduces the amount of ingredient information that consumers examine in making choices about packaged goods.[23]

The *importance* that consumers assign to each evaluative criterion is of great interest to marketers. Three consumers could use the same six evaluative criteria shown in the following table when considering a notebook computer. However, if the importance rank they assigned each criterion varied as shown, they would likely purchase different brands.

Criterion	Importance Rank for		
	Consumer A	Consumer B	Consumer C
Price	1	6	3
Processor	5	1	4
Display quality	3	3	1
Memory	6	2	5
Weight	4	4	2
After-sale support	2	5	6

Consumer A is concerned primarily with cost and support services. Consumer B wants computing speed and power. Consumer C is concerned primarily with ease of use. If each of these three consumers represented a larger group of consumers, we would have three distinct market segments based on the importance assigned the same criteria.

Evaluative criteria, and the importance that individuals assign them, influence not only the brands selected but if and when a problem will be recognized. For example, consumers who attach more importance to automobile styling and product image relative to comfort and cost buy new cars more frequently than do those with the opposite importance rankings.[24]

Marketers must understand the criteria consumers use to evaluate their brands for two reasons. First, as we saw in the opening example, understanding these criteria is essential for developing or communicating appropriate brand features to the target market. In addition, marketers frequently want to influence the evaluative criteria used by consumers.[25]

Measurement of Evaluative Criteria

Before a marketing manager or a public policy decision maker can develop a sound strategy to affect consumer decisions, he or she must determine

- Which evaluative criteria are used by the consumer.
- How the consumer perceives the various alternatives on each criterion.
- The relative importance of each criterion.

Consumers sometimes will not or cannot verbalize their evaluative criteria for a product. Therefore, it is often difficult to determine which criteria they are using in a particular brand-choice decision, particularly if emotions or feelings are involved. This is even more of a problem when trying to determine the relative importance they attach to each evaluative criterion.

Determination of Which Evaluative Criteria Are Used

To determine which criteria are used by consumers in a specific product decision, the marketing researcher can utilize either direct or indirect methods of measurement. *Direct* methods include asking consumers what criteria they use in a particular purchase or, in a focus group setting, noting what consumers say about products and their attributes. Of course, direct measurement techniques assume that consumers can and will provide data on the desired attributes.

In the research that led to the development of Sunbeam's new food processor line, consumers readily described their desired product features and benefits. However, direct questioning is not always as successful. For example, Hanes Corporation suffered substantial losses ($30 million) on its L'erin cosmetics line when, *in response to consumer interviews,* it positioned it as a functional rather than a romantic or emotional product. Eventually, the brand was successfully repositioned as glamorous and exotic, although consumers did not *express* these as desired attributes.[26]

Indirect measurement techniques differ from direct in that they assume consumers will not or cannot state their evaluative criteria. Hence, frequent use is made of indirect methods such as **projective techniques** (see Table 10-2), which allow the respondent to indicate the criteria someone else might use. The "someone else" will likely be a projection of the respondent, of course—thus, the marketer can indirectly determine the evaluative criteria that would be used.

Perceptual mapping is another useful indirect technique for determining evaluative criteria. First, consumers judge the similarity of alternative brands. This generally involves the consumer looking at possible pairs of brands and indicating which pair is most similar, which is second most similar, and so forth until all pairs are ranked. These similarity judgments are processed via a computer to derive a perceptual map of the brands. No evaluative criteria are specified by the consumer. The consumer simply ranks the similarity between all pairs of alternatives, and a perceptual configuration is derived in which the consumer's still unnamed evaluative criteria are the dimensions of the configuration.

For example, consider the perceptual map of beers shown in Figure 16-2. This configuration was derived from a consumer's evaluation of the relative similarity of these brands of beer. The horizontal axis is characterized by physical characteristics such as taste, calories, and fullness. The vertical axis is characterized by price, quality, and status. Naming each axis, and thus each evaluative criterion, is done using judgment. This procedure allows marketers to understand consumers' perceptions and the evaluative criteria they use to differentiate brands.

There may be attributes that consumers consider important but that they do not use in choosing among brands.[27] Such attributes will generally not be discovered in the techniques we have described. This situation would occur when consumers consider all brands either to be equivalent on the attribute or to be above their desired level. Thus, a consumer might consider all brands of bottled water to be safe to drink (not contaminated). Therefore, they do not use this as a criterion when comparing brands.

Determination of Consumers' Judgments of Brand Performance on Specific Evaluative Criteria

A variety of methods are available for measuring consumers' judgments of brand performance on specific attributes. These include *rank ordering scales, semantic differential scales,* and *Likert scales* (see Appendix A and Appendix Table A-2). The semantic differential scale is probably the most widely used technique.

| FIGURE 16-2 | Perceptual Mapping of Beer Brand Perceptions |

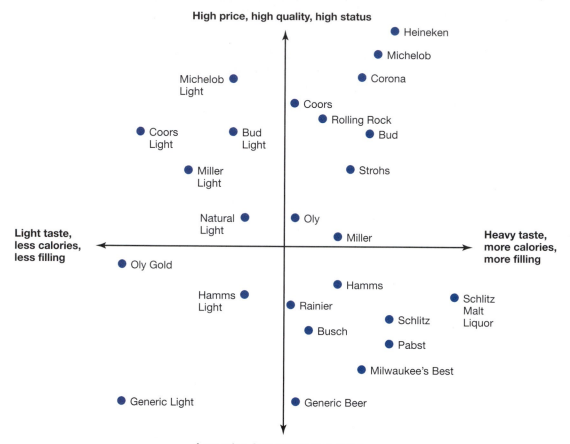

None of these techniques are very effective at measuring emotional responses to products or brands. Projective techniques can provide some insights. SAM, the graphical approach designed to more directly tap into the Pleasure-Arousal-Dominance dimensions of emotions (see Chapter 11), is also a useful option.

Determination of the Relative Importance of Evaluative Criteria   The importance assigned to evaluative criteria can be measured either by direct or by indirect methods. No matter which technique is used, the usage situation should be specified as attribute importance varies with the situation. The *constant sum scale* is the most common method of direct measurement (see Chapter 11, page 399).

The most popular indirect measurement approach is **conjoint analysis.** In conjoint analysis, the consumer is presented with a set of products or product descriptions in which the evaluative criteria vary. For example, the consumer may be presented with the description of 24 different notebook computers that vary on four criteria. Two might be

Pentium M 2.0 GHz	Pentium M 1.6 GHz
Wireless enabled (yes)	Wireless enabled (no)
5.1 pounds	3.5 pounds
$2,000	$1,500

The consumer ranks all 24 such descriptions in terms of his or her preference for those combinations of features. Using these preference ranks, sophisticated computer programs derive the relative importance consumers assign to each level of each attribute tested (see Appendix A and Appendix Figure A-1 for details).

Conjoint analysis was used in the Sunbeam example that opened this chapter. Sunbeam tested 12 different attributes, such as price, motor power, number of blades, bowl shape, and so forth. As stated earlier, four segments emerged *based on the relative importance of these attributes*. In order of importance, the key attributes for two segments were

Cheap/Large Segment	**Multispeed/Multiuse Segment**
$49.99 price	$99.99 price
4-quart bowl	2-quart bowl
Two speeds	Seven speeds
Seven blades	Functions as blender and mixer
Heavy-duty motor	Cylindrical bowl
Cylindrical bowl	Pouring spout

INDIVIDUAL JUDGMENT AND EVALUATIVE CRITERIA

If you were buying a notebook computer, you would probably make direct comparisons across brands on features such as price, weight, and display clarity. These comparative judgments may not be completely accurate. For example, the display that is the easiest to read in a five-minute trial may not be the easiest to read over a two-hour work session. For other attributes, such as quality, you might not be able to make direct comparisons. Instead, you might rely on brand name or price to indicate quality. In addition, consumer perceptions of the importance of product features are influenced by various external factors. The accuracy of direct judgments, the use of one attribute to indicate performance on another (surrogate indicator), and variations in attribute importance are critical issues for marketers.

Accuracy of Individual Judgments

The average consumer is not adequately trained to judge the performance of competing brands on complex evaluative criteria such as quality or durability. For more straightforward criteria, however, most consumers can and do make such judgments. Prices generally can be judged and compared directly. However, even this can be complex. Is a six-pack of 12-ounce cans of Coca-Cola selling for $2.49 a better buy than two liters priced at 99 cents each? Consumer groups have pushed for unit pricing (pricing by common measurements such as cost per ounce) to make such comparisons simpler. The federal truth-in-lending law was passed to facilitate direct price comparisons among alternative lenders.

The ability of an individual to distinguish between similar stimuli is called **sensory discrimination** (see Chapter 8). This could involve such variables as the sound of stereo systems, the taste of food products, or the clarity of display screens. The minimum amount that one brand can differ from another with the difference still being noticed is referred to as the *just noticeable difference (j.n.d.)*. As we saw in Chapter 8, this ability is not well developed in most consumers. In general, research indicates that *individuals typically do not notice relatively small differences between brands or changes in brand attributes*. In addition, the complexity of many products and services as well as the fact that some aspects of

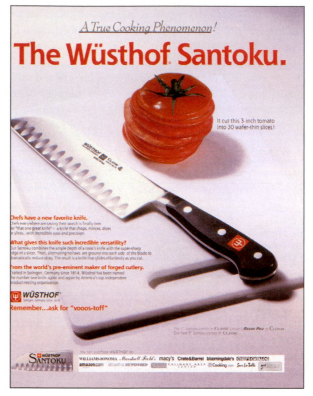

Courtesy Wüsthof-Trident of America, Inc.

performance can be judged only after extensive use makes accurate brand comparisons difficult.[28]

The inability of consumers to accurately evaluate many products can result in inappropriate purchases (buying a lower-quality product at a higher price than necessary).[29] This is a major concern of regulatory agencies and consumer groups as well as for marketers of high-value brands.

Use of Surrogate Indicators

Consumers frequently use an observable attribute of a product to indicate the performance of the product on a less observable attribute.[30] For example, a consumer might infer that since a product has a relatively high price it must also be high quality. *An attribute used to stand for or indicate another attribute* is known as a **surrogate indicator.** As discussed in Chapter 8, consumers often use such factors as price, advertising intensity, warranties, brand, and country of origin as surrogate indicators of quality—what we termed quality signals. Illustration 16-6 shows how Wüsthof takes advantage of Germany's reputation for engineering and manufacturing excellence.

In general, surrogate indicators operate more strongly when consumers lack the expertise to make informed judgments on their own, when consumer motivation or interest in the decision is low, and when other quality-related information is lacking. Unfortunately, the relationship between surrogate indicators and functional measures of quality is often modest at best.[31] Obviously, when consumers rely on surrogates that have little relationship to actual quality, they are likely to make suboptimal decisions.

Surrogate indicators are based on consumers' beliefs that two features such as price level and quality level generally go together. Consumers also form beliefs that certain variables do not go together—such as *lightweight* and *strong; rich taste* and *low calories;* and *high fiber* and *high protein.*[32] Marketers attempting to promote the presence of two or more variables that many consumers believe to be mutually exclusive have a high risk of failure unless very convincing messages are used. Thus, it is important for marketers to fully understand consumers' beliefs about the feasible relationships of attributes related to their products.

The Relative Importance and Influence of Evaluative Criteria

The importance of evaluative criteria varies among individuals and also within the same individual over time. That is, while consumers often have a general sense of how important various criteria are, this can be influenced by a number of factors. These include:

- *Usage situation*—The situation in which a product or service is used (Chapter 13) can have important influences on the criteria used to make a choice. For example, speed of service and convenient location may be very important in selecting a restaurant over a lunch break but relatively unimportant when selecting a restaurant for a special occasion.[33]
- *Competitive context*—Generally speaking, the lower the variance across competing brands on a given evaluative criteria, the less influence it is likely to have in the decision process.[34] For example, you might think that the weight of a notebook computer is important. However, if all the brands you are considering weigh between 3.5 and 5 pounds, this attribute may suddenly become less of a factor in your decision.

    When one evaluative criterion becomes less important, others generally become more important. We saw this in Chapter 11, where *decision irrelevant* advertising cues (peripheral cues) such as endorser fame became more important determinants of brand choice when competing brands were comparable in terms of important product features (central cues) such as price and quality.[35]
- *Advertising effects*—Advertising can affect the importance of evaluative criteria in a number of ways. For example, an ad that increases attention and elaborative processing of an attribute can increase its perceived importance and/or influence in the decision.[36] As we saw in Chapters 8 and 9, contrast, prominence, and imagery are just a few of the tactics that can be used to enhance attention and elaboration.

    A recent study suggests the power of imagery. Specifically, when consumers were encouraged to elaborate on prior usage experiences for a given product, attributes strongly related to the quality of the usage experience became much more important. As a consequence, they chose brands that were stronger on use-related attributes (e.g., suction power for a vacuum cleaner) over brands that were stronger on transaction-related attributes such as price.[37]

Evaluative Criteria, Individual Judgments, and Marketing Strategy

Obviously, marketers must understand the evaluative criteria consumers use relative to their products and develop products that excel on these features. All aspects of the marketing communications mix must then communicate this excellence.

Marketers must also recognize and react to the ability of individuals to judge evaluative criteria, as well as to their tendency to use surrogate indicators. For example, most new consumer products are initially tested against competitors in **blind tests.** A blind test is one in which *the consumer is not aware of the product's brand name.* Such tests enable the marketer to evaluate the functional characteristics of the product and to determine if an advantage over a particular competitor has been obtained without the contaminating, or halo, effects of the brand name or the firm's reputation. *Can you see any drawbacks to only using blind tests in evaluating the market potential of products?*

Marketers also make direct use of surrogate indicators. Andecker is advertised as "the most expensive taste in beer." This is an obvious attempt to utilize the price–quality relationship that many consumers believe exists for beer. On occasion, prices are raised to increase sales because of the presumed price–quality relationship. For example, a new mustard packaged in a crockery jar did not achieve significant sales priced at 49 cents, but it did at $1.[38]

Marketers frequently use brand names as an indicator of quality. Elmer's glue emphasized the well-established reputation of its brand in promoting a new super glue (ads for Elmer's Wonder Bond said "Stick with a name you can trust"). Firms with a limited reputation can sometimes form *brand alliances* with a reputable firm and gain from the quality associated with the known brand. Thus, a new brand of ice cream that used a branded ingredient such as M&Ms would gain from M&Ms quality image.[39] Country-of-origin themes such as "Made in America," "Italian Styling," or "German Engineering" are also common.

Marketers must also understand the various factors that can influence consumer perceptions of the importance of evaluative criteria. Understanding that attributes may be important but wield relatively little influence on consumer decisions due to similarity across competitors is a critical insight. It speaks to the need for marketing managers to examine critical points of differentiation on which the brand can be positioned. Advertising themes that emphasize specific usage occasions for which the brand is particularly appropriate can be effective, as can strategies such as imagery that draw consumer attention to an attribute on which the firm's brand is particularly strong.

DECISION RULES FOR ATTRIBUTE-BASED CHOICES

As we describe some of the choice rules consumers use to select among alternatives, remember that these rules are representations of imprecise and often nonconscious or low-effort mental processes. The following example is a good representation of a consumer using a complex choice rule (compensatory with one attribute weighted heavily):

> I really liked the Ford [minivan] a lot, but it had the back tailgate that lifted up instead of the doors that opened. I suspect that if that had been available we might have gone with the Ford instead because it was real close between the Ford and the GM. The lift gate in the back was the main difference, and we went with the General Motors because we liked the doors opening the way they did. I loved the way the Ford was designed on the inside. I loved the way it drove. I loved the way it felt and everything, but you are there manipulating all these kids and groceries and things and you have got to lift this thing, and it was very awkward. It was hard to lift, and if you are holding something you have got to steer all the kids back, or whack them in the head. So that was a big thing. You know it was a lot cheaper than the GM. It was between $1,000 and $2,000 less than General Motors, and because money was a factor, we did go ahead and actually at one point talk money with a [Ford] dealer. But we couldn't get the price difference down to where I was willing to deal with that tailgate is what it comes down to.[40]

Despite the fact that the choice rules we describe are not precise representations of consumer decisions, they do enhance our understanding of how consumers make decisions and provide guidance for marketing strategy.

TABLE 16-1

Performance Levels
on the Evaluative
Criteria for Six
Notebook
Computers

Evaluative Criteria	Consumer Perceptions*					
	WinBook	HP	Compaq	Dell	IBM	Toshiba
Price	5	3	3	4	2	1
Weight	3	4	5	4	3	4
Processor	5	5	5	2	5	5
Battery life	1	3	1	3	1	5
After-sale support	3	3	4	3	5	3
Display quality	3	3	3	5	3	3

*1 = Very poor; 5 = Very good.

Suppose you have six notebook computers in your evoked set and that you have assessed them on six evaluative criteria: price, weight, processor, battery life, after-sale support, and display quality. Further, suppose that each brand excels on one attribute but falls short on one or more of the remaining attributes, as shown in Table 16-1.

Which brand would you select? The answer would depend on the decision rule you utilize. Consumers commonly use five decision rules: conjunctive, disjunctive, elimination-by-aspects, lexicographic, and compensatory. More than one rule may be used in any given decision. The most common instance of this is using a relatively simple rule to reduce the number of alternatives considered and then to apply a more complex rule to choose among the remaining options.[41] An example would be eliminating from consideration all those apartments that are too far from campus or that rent for more than $700 per month (conjunctive decision rule). The choice from among the remaining apartments might involve carefully trading off among features such as convenience of location, price, presence of a pool, size of rooms, and so forth (compensatory rule).

The first four rules we will describe are *noncompensatory* rules. This means that a high level of one attribute cannot offset a low level of another. In the apartment example, the consumer would not consider an apartment that was right next to campus if it cost more than $700 per month. An excellent location could not compensate for an inappropriate price. In contrast, the last rule we will describe is a *compensatory* rule in which consumers average across attribute levels. This allows a high level of one value to offset a low value of another.

Finally, note that the conjunctive and disjunctive decision rules may produce a set of acceptable alternatives, whereas the remaining rules generally produce a single "best" alternative.

Conjunctive Decision Rule

The **conjunctive decision rule** establishes minimum required performance standards for each evaluative criterion and selects the first or all brands that meet or exceed these minimum standards. Thus, in making the decision on the computer, you would say, "I'll consider all (or I'll buy the first) brands that are acceptable on the attributes I think are important." For example, assume that the following represent your minimum standards:

Price	3
Weight	4
Processor	3
Battery life	1
After-sale support	2
Display quality	3

This ad assures consumers that the Talkabout has every feature they might need. This is consistent with consumers using a conjunctive decision rule.

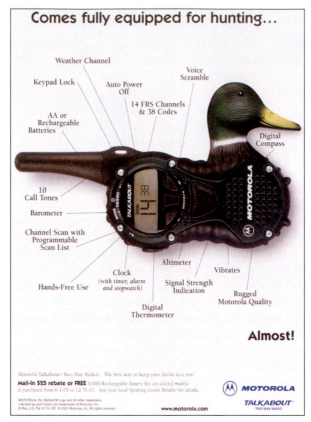

Courtesy Motorola, Inc. Consumer Products.

Any brand of computer falling below any of these minimum standards (cutoff points) would be eliminated from further consideration. Referring to Table 16-1, we can see that four computers are eliminated—IBM, WinBook, Dell, and Toshiba. These are the computers that failed to meet all the minimum standards. Under these circumstances, the two remaining brands may be equally satisfying. Or you might use another decision rule to select a single brand from these two alternatives.

Because individuals have limited ability to process information, the conjunctive rule is frequently used to reduce the size of the information processing task to some manageable level. This is often done in the purchase of such products as homes, computers, and bicycles; in the rental of apartments; or in the selection of vacation options. A conjunctive rule is used to eliminate alternatives that are out of a consumer's price range, are outside the location preferred, or do not offer other desired features. After eliminating those alternatives not providing these features, the consumer may use another decision rule to make a brand choice among those remaining alternatives that satisfy these minimum standards.

The conjunctive decision rule is commonly used in many low-involvement purchases as well. In such a purchase, the consumer generally evaluates a set of brands one at a time and selects the first brand that meets all the minimum requirements.

If the conjunctive decision rule is used by a target market, it is critical to meet or surpass the consumers' minimum requirement on each criterion. For low-involvement purchases, consumers often purchase the first brand that does so. For such products, extensive distribution and dominant shelf space are important. It is also necessary to understand how consumers "break ties" if the first satisfactory option is not chosen. The ad in Illustration 16-7 assures consumers that the Motorola Talkabout has every feature they might need.

Disjunctive Decision Rule

The **disjunctive decision rule** *establishes a minimum level of performance for each important attribute* (often a fairly high level). All brands that meet or exceed the performance level for *any* key attribute are considered acceptable. Using this rule, you would say, "I'll consider all (or buy the first) brands that perform really well on any attribute I consider to be important." Assume that you are using a disjunctive decision rule and the attribute cutoff points shown below:

Price	5
Weight	5
Processor	Not critical
Battery life	Not critical
After-sale support	Not critical
Display quality	5

You would find WinBook (price), Compaq (weight), and Dell (display quality) to warrant further consideration (see Table 16-1). As with the conjunctive decision rule, you might purchase the first brand you find acceptable, use another decision rule to choose among the three, or add additional criteria to your list.

When the disjunctive decision rule is used by a target market, it is critical to meet or surpass the consumers' requirements on at least one of the key criteria. This should be emphasized in advertising messages and on the product package. Because consumers often purchase the first brand that meets or exceeds one of the requirements, extensive distribution and dominant shelf space are important. Again, it is also necessary to understand how consumers break ties if the first satisfactory option is not chosen. Illustration 16-8 stresses one important attribute of the Eureka Mountain Pass tent—speed of setting up.

Elimination-by-Aspects Decision Rule

The **elimination-by-aspects decision rule** requires the consumer to rank the evaluative criteria in terms of their importance and to establish a cutoff point for each criterion. All brands are first considered on the most important criterion. Those that do not meet or exceed the cutoff point are dropped from consideration. If more than one brand remains in the set after this first elimination phase, the process is repeated on those brands for the second most important criterion. This continues until only one brand remains. Thus, the consumer's logic is, "I want to buy the brand that has a high level of an important attribute that other brands do not have."

Consider the rank order and cutoff points shown below. What would you choose using the elimination-by-aspects rule?

	Rank	Cutoff Point
Price	1	3
Weight	2	4
Display quality	3	4
Processor	4	3
After-sale support	5	3
Battery life	6	3

Printed with permission of the Eureka!® Tent Brand, Johnson Outdoors, Inc.

Price would eliminate IBM and Toshiba (see Table 16-1). Of those remaining, Compaq, HP, and Dell meet or exceed the weight hurdle (WinBook is eliminated). Notice that Toshiba also meets the minimum weight requirement but would not be considered because it had been eliminated in the initial consideration of price. Only Dell meets or exceeds the third requirement, display quality.

Using the elimination-by-aspects rule, you end up with a choice that has all the desired features of all the other alternatives, plus one more.

For a target market using the elimination-by-aspects rule, it is critical to meet or surpass the consumers' requirements on one more (in order) of the criteria used than the competition. This competitive superiority should be emphasized in advertising messages and on the product package. Firms can also attempt to alter the relative importance that consumers assign to the evaluative criteria. The ad in Illustration 16-9 is consistent with this rule. It indicates that Lynx Black Cat Irons match competitors on some features (oversized club head) and also have desirable features other competitors do not have (Elastomer cartridge).

Lexicographic Decision Rule

The **lexicographic decision rule** *requires the consumer to rank the criteria in order of importance.* The consumer then selects the brand that performs *best* on the most important attribute. If two or more brands tie on this attribute, they are evaluated on the second most important attribute. This continues through the attributes until one brand outperforms the

Courtesy Golfsmith International, Inc., 2005.

others. The consumer's thinking is something like this: "I want to get the brand that does best on the attribute of most importance to me. If there is a tie, I'll break it by choosing the one that does best on my second most important criterion."

The lexicographic decision rule is similar to the elimination-by-aspects rule. The difference is that the lexicographic rule seeks maximum performance at each stage, whereas the elimination-by-aspects seeks satisfactory performance at each stage. Thus, using the lexicographic rule and the data from the elimination-by-aspects example above would result in the selection of WinBook, because it has the best performance on the most important attribute. Had WinBook been rated a 4 on price, it would be tied with Dell. Then, Dell would be chosen based on its superior weight rating.

When this rule is being used by a target market, the firm should try to be superior to the competition on *the* key attribute. This competitive superiority should be emphasized in advertising. It is essential that the product at least equal the performance of all other competitors on the most important criterion. Outstanding performance on lesser criteria will not matter if a competitor is superior on the most important attribute. If a competitive advantage is not possible on the most important feature, attention should be shifted to the second most important (assuming equal performance on the most important one). If it is not possible to meet or beat the competition on the key attribute, the firm must attempt to make another attribute more important.

The ad shown in Illustration 16-10 emphasizes that Orbitz has more low fares than any other travel site. This ad would be particularly effective for consumers who use a lexicographic rule and consider low fares as the most important attribute.

ILLUSTRATION 16-10

Consumers using a lexicographic decision rule select the brand or service that performs best on their most important attribute.

Courtesy Orbitz.

Compensatory Decision Rule

The four previous rules are *noncompensatory* decision rules, because very good performance on one evaluative criterion cannot compensate for poor performance on another evaluative criterion. On occasion, consumers may wish to average out some very good features with some less attractive features of a product in determining overall brand preference. Consider the following example:

> PepsiCo's Frito-Lay will introduce a new single-serve canister line called Go Snacks this January backed by $60 million in marketing in hopes that consumers' desire for convenience outweighs their concern for price.[42]

The new snacks are in a single-serving size container with resealable cup lids designed to fit easily into car beverage-holders as well as backpacks and lunch boxes. However, it is priced at $1.29 per serving, which is more than many large bags of chips cost. Frito-Lay knows that price is important to customers but believes that the added convenience of the new packaging will more than offset the higher price. That is, it assumes its target market will use a compensatory decision rule for this product.

The **compensatory decision rule** states that *the brand that rates highest on the sum of the consumer's judgments of the relevant evaluative criteria will be chosen.* This can be illustrated as

$$R_b = \sum_{i=1}^{n} W_i B_{ib}$$

where

R_b = Overall rating of brand b
W_i = Importance or weight attached to evaluative criterion i
B_{ib} = Evaluation of brand b on evaluative criterion i
n = Number of evaluative criteria considered relevant

This is the same as the multiattribute attitude model described in Chapter 11. If you used the relative importance scores shown below, which brand would you choose using the compensatory rule?

	Importance Score
Price	30
Weight	25
Processor	10
Battery life	05
After-sale support	10
Display quality	20
Total	100

Using this rule, Dell has the highest preference (see Table 16-1). The calculations for Dell are as follows:

$$\begin{aligned} R_{\text{Dell}} &= 30(4) + 25(4) + 10(2) + 5(3) + 10(3) + 20(5) \\ &= 120 + 100 + 20 + 15 + 30 + 100 \\ &= 385 \end{aligned}$$

Products and services targeting consumers likely to use a compensatory rule can offset low performance on some features with relatively high performance on others. However, it is important to have a performance level at or near the competition on the more important features because they receive more weight in the decision than do other attributes. Recall the description of the minivan purchase from the beginning of this section. This customer preferred most of the features of the Ford but bought the GM because Ford was very weak on one key attribute. However, the consumer did express a willingness to change the decision had the price differential been greater. Thus, for compensatory decisions, the total mix of the relevant attributes must be considered to be superior to those of the competition.

Summary of Decision Rules

As shown below, each decision rule yields a somewhat different choice. Therefore, marketers must understand which decision rules are being used by target consumers in order to position a product within this decision framework.

Decision Rule	Brand Choice
Conjunctive	HP, Compaq
Disjunctive	Dell, Compaq, WinBook
Elimination-by-aspects	Dell
Lexicographic	WinBook
Compensatory	Dell

Research clearly indicates that people do use these decision rules.[43] Low-involvement purchases generally involve relatively simple decision rules (conjunctive, disjunctive, elimination-by-aspects, or lexicographic), because consumers will attempt to minimize the mental cost of such decisions.[44] High-involvement decisions and purchases involving considerable perceived risk tend to increase evaluation efforts and often may involve not only more complex rules (compensatory) but stages of decision making, with different attributes being evaluated using different rules at each stage.[45] Of course, individual, product, and situational characteristics also influence the type of decision rule used.[46]

A marketing manager must first determine which rule or combination of rules the target consumers will most likely use in a particular purchase situation, then develop the appropriate marketing strategy.

SUMMARY

During and after the time that consumers gather information about various alternative solutions to a recognized problem, they evaluate the alternatives and select the course of action that seems most likely to solve the problem. Consumer choices are sometimes based on extremely simple decision rules such as "buy the cheapest brand available." At other times, they are extremely complex, involving multiple stages and processes.

There are a number of ways consumers make choices. *Affective choice* is most likely when the underlying motive is consummatory rather than instrumental. *Consummatory motives* underlie behaviors that are intrinsically rewarding to the individual involved. *Instrumental motives* activate behaviors designed to achieve a secondary goal.

Affective choice tends to be holistic in nature. The brand is not decomposed into distinct components, each of which is evaluated separately from the whole. The evaluation of such products is generally focused on the way they will make the user *feel* as they are used. Decisions based on affect are said to use the "How do I feel about it" heuristic or decision rule. Consumers imagine or picture using the product or service and evaluate the feeling that this use will produce.

Attribute-based choice requires the knowledge of the specific attributes of the alternatives at the time the choice is made, and it involves attribute-by-attribute comparisons across brands. *Attitude-based choice* involves the use of general attitudes, summary impressions, intuitions, or heuristics; no attribute-by-attribute comparisons are made at the time of choice. There can also be combinations of these forms. A common combination would be for the evoked or consideration set to be formed using attitude-based processing, with the final choice being made on the basis of a brand-by-brand comparison on the price attribute.

Rational choice theory assumes a rational decision maker with well-defined preferences that do not depend on how the options are presented. Each option or alternative in a choice set is assumed to have a value to the consumer that depends only on the characteristics of that option. The consumer is also assumed to have sufficient skill to calculate which option will maximize his or her value and will choose on this basis.

Although useful, rational choice theory is incomplete. An emerging view is that many choices are constructed by the consumer as the decision is made. All consumers have *bounded rationality*—a limited capacity for processing information. In addition, consumers often have goals that are different from, or in addition to, selecting the optimal alternative. A *metagoal* refers to the general nature of the outcome being sought in a decision. Four metagoals characterize many consumer choices—maximizing the accuracy of the decision, minimizing the cognitive effort required for the decision, minimizing the experience of negative emotion while making the decision, and maximizing the ease with which a decision can be justified. These goals may shift in importance as the consumer moves through the decision process.

Evaluative criteria are the various features or benefits a consumer looks for in response to a specific problem. They are the performance levels or characteristics consumers use to compare different brands in light of their particular consumption problem. The number, type, and importance of evaluative criteria used differ from consumer to consumer and across product categories. And, the importance of various evaluative criteria can be influenced by usage situation, competitive context, and advertising.

The measurement of (1) which evaluative criteria are used by the consumer, (2) how the consumer perceives the various alternatives on each criterion, and (3) the relative importance of each criterion is a critical first step in utilizing evaluative criteria to develop marketing strategy. The measurement task is not easy; however, a number of techniques ranging from direct questioning to projective techniques and multidimensional scaling are available.

Evaluative criteria such as price, size, and color can be judged easily and accurately by consumers. Other criteria, such as quality, durability, and health benefits, are much more difficult to judge. In such cases, consumers often use price, brand name, or some other variable as a *surrogate indicator* of quality.

When consumers judge alternative brands on several evaluative criteria, they must have some method to select one brand from the various choices. Decision rules serve this function. A decision rule specifies how a consumer compares two or more brands. Five commonly used decision rules are *disjunctive, conjunctive, lexicographic, elimination-by-aspects,* and *compensatory.* The decision rules work best with functional products and cognitive decisions. Marketing managers must be aware of the decision rule(s) used by the target market, because different decision rules require different marketing strategies.

KEY TERMS

Affective choice 568
Attitude-based choice 570
Attribute-based choice 570
Blind tests 579
Bounded rationality 567
Compensatory decision rule 587
Conjoint analysis 576

Conjunctive decision rule 581
Consummatory motives 568
Disjunctive decision rule 583
Elimination-by-aspects decision rule 583
Evaluative criteria 572
Instrumental motives 568

Lexicographic decision rule 584
Metagoal 567
Perceptual mapping 575
Projective techniques 575
Sensory discrimination 577
Surrogate indicator 578

INTERNET EXERCISES

1. Monitor several chat sites or interest groups for a week. Prepare a report on how a marketer could learn about the following used by consumers by doing this.
   a. Evaluative criteria
   b. Decision rules

2. Use Dell's "Notebook Advisor" feature to select a notebook computer (hint: go to www.dell.com, select "small business," then click on "notebook," then select notebook advisor). What decision rule or combination of rules does this decision aid reflect? What type of consumer

would be most likely to utilize this advisor function?

3. Visit ski-europe.com. Use their "SkiMatcher Resort Finder" feature to select a vacation destination for you or your family. On what decision rule does this feature appear to be based?

4. Visit three Web sites for brands in the same product category. Using the brand information provided and the manner in which it is provided, determine what decision rule each brand appears to assume its market uses. If there are differences, how would you explain them?

DDB LIFE STYLE STUDY™ DATA ANALYSES

1. Based on the DDB Tables 1B through 7B, what characterizes an individual who would say, "In making big decisions, I go with my heart rather than my head"? How does this relate to affective decision making? What are the marketing implications of this?

REVIEW QUESTIONS

1. What is *rational choice* theory?

2. What is meant by *bounded rationality?*

3. What is a *metagoal?*

4. What are four common metagoals for consumer decisions?

5. What is *affective choice* and when is it most likely to occur?

6. What is the difference between *consummatory motives* and *instrumental motives?*

7. How does *attribute-based choice* differ from *attitude-based choice?* When is each most likely?

8. What are *evaluative criteria* and on what characteristics can they vary?

9. How can you determine which evaluative criteria consumers use?

10. What methods are available for measuring consumers' judgments of brand performance on specific attributes?

11. How can the importance assigned to evaluative criteria be assessed?

12. What is *sensory discrimination,* and what role does it play in the evaluation of products? What is meant by a *just noticeable difference?*

13. What are *surrogate indicators?* How are they used in the consumer evaluation process?

14. What factors influence the *importance* of evaluative criteria?

15. What is the *conjunctive decision rule?*

16. What is the *disjunctive decision rule?*

17. What is the *elimination-by-aspects decision rule?*

18. What is the *lexicographic decision rule?*

19. What is the *compensatory decision rule?*

20. How can knowledge of consumers' evaluative criteria and criteria importance be used in developing marketing strategy?

21. How can knowledge of the decision rules consumers might use in a certain purchase assist a firm in developing marketing strategy?

DISCUSSION QUESTIONS

22. Respond to the questions in Consumer Insight 16-1.

23. Would you use an attribute-based or an attitude-based decision approach to purchasing (or renting or giving to) the following? Which, if any, situational factors would change your approach?

   a. A present for your romantic partner

   b. A movie

   c. A motorcycle

d. A cat
e. A personal trainer
f. Athletic shoes
g. A new shampoo
h. A spring break cruise
i. A camera phone
j. Habitat for Humanity

24. Repeat Question 23, but speculate on how your instructor would answer. In what ways might his or her answer differ from yours? Why?

25. For which, if any, of the options in Question 23 would you make an affective decision? What role would situational factors play?

30. Identify five products for which surrogate indicators may be used as evaluative criteria in a brand choice decision. Why are the indictors used, and how might a firm enhance their use (i.e., strengthen their importance)?

31. The table below represents a particular consumer's evaluative criteria, criteria importance, acceptable level of performance, and judgments of performance with respect to several brands of mopeds. Discuss the brand choice this consumer would make when using the lexicographic, compensatory, and conjunctive decision rules.

Evaluative Criteria	Criteria Importance	Minimum Acceptable Performance	Alternative Brands					
			Motron	Vespa	Cimatti	Garelli	Puch	Motobecane
Price	30	4	2	4	2	4	2	4
Horsepower	15	3	4	2	5	5	4	5
Weight	5	2	3	3	3	3	3	3
Gas economy	35	3	4	4	3	2	4	5
Color selection	10	3	4	4	3	2	5	2
Frame	5	2	4	2	3	3	3	3

Note: 1 = Very poor; 2 = Poor; 3 = Fair; 4 = Good; and 5 = Very good.

26. What metagoals might you have, and what would be their relative importance to you, in purchasing (or renting or giving to) the options in Questions 23?

27. List the evaluative criteria and the importance of each that you would use in purchasing (or renting or giving to) the options in Question 23. Would situational factors change the criteria? The importance weights? Why?

28. Repeat Question 27, but speculate on how your instructor would answer. In what ways might his or her answer differ from yours? Why?

29. Describe a purchase decision for which you used affective choice, one for which you used attitude-based choice, and one for which you used attribute-based choice. Why did the type of decision process you used vary?

32. Describe the decision rule(s) you used or would use in buying, renting, or giving to the options listed for Question 23. Would you use different rules in different situations? Which ones? Why? Would any of these involve an affective choice?

33. Describe your last two major and your last two minor purchases. What role did emotions or feelings play? How did they differ? What evaluative criteria and decision rules did you use for each? Why?

34. Discuss surrogate indicators that could be used to evaluate the perceived quality of the products or activities listed in Question 23.

APPLICATION ACTIVITIES

35. Interview five students about a recent purchase decision. What metagoals characterize these different decisions? Do your results support Consumer Insight 16-1? How would you explain any differences?

36. Conduct an extensive interview with two students who recently made a major purchase. Have them describe the process they went through. Report your results. If each represented a market segment, what are the strategy implications?

37. Develop a list of evaluative criteria that students might use in evaluating alternative apartments they might rent. After listing these criteria, go to the local newspaper or student newspaper, select several apartments, and list them in a table similar to the one in Question 31. Then have five other students evaluate this information and have each indicate the apartment they would rent if given only those alternatives. Next, ask them to express the importance they attach to each evaluative criterion, using a 100-point constant sum scale. Finally, provide them with a series of statements that describe different decision rules and ask them to indicate the one that best describes the way they made their choice. Calculate the choice they should have made given their importance ratings and stated decision rules. Have them explain any inconsistent choices. Report your results.

38. Develop a short questionnaire to elicit the evaluative criteria consumers might use in selecting the following. Also, have each respondent indicate the relative importance he or she attaches to each of the evaluative criteria. Then, working with several other students, combine your information and develop a segmentation strategy based on consumer evaluative criteria and criteria importance. Finally, develop an advertisement for each market segment to indicate that their needs would be served by your brand.
    a. Cologne/perfume
    b. Running shoes
    c. Movie
    d. Nice restaurant
    e. Credit card
    f. Charity
    g. Home theatre system
    h. Health club

39. Set up a taste-test experiment to determine if volunteer taste testers can perceive a just noticeable difference between three different brands of the following. To set up the experiment, store each test brand in a separate but identical container and label the containers L, M, and N. Provide volunteer taste testers with an adequate opportunity to evaluate each brand before asking them to state their identification of the actual brands represented as L, M, and N. Evaluate the results and discuss the marketing implications of these results.
    a. Colas
    b. Diet colas
    c. Lemon-lime drinks
    d. Carbonated waters
    e. Chips
    f. Orange juices

40. For a product considered high in social status, develop a questionnaire that measures the evaluative criteria of that product, using both a *direct* and an *indirect* method of measurement. Compare the results and discuss their similarities and differences and which evaluative criteria are most likely to be utilized in brand choice.

41. Find and copy or describe an ad that uses a surrogate indicator. Is it effective? Why? Why do you think the firm uses this approach?

42. Find and copy or describe an ad that attempts to change the importance consumers assign to product class evaluative criteria. Is it effective? Why? Why do you think the firm uses this approach?

43. Find and copy or describe two ads that are based on affective choice. Why do you think the firm uses this approach? Are the ads effective? Why?

44. Interview a salesperson for one of the following products. Ascertain the evaluative criteria, importance weights, decision rules, and surrogate indicators that he or she believes consumers use when purchasing this product. What marketing implications are suggested if their beliefs are accurate for large segments?
    a. Luxury cars
    b. Kitchen furniture
    c. Air purification system
    d. Cosmetics
    e. Ski clothes
    f. Fine art

REFERENCES

1. A. L. Page and H. F. Rosenbaum, "Redesigning Product Lines with Conjoint Analysis," *Journal of Product Innovation Management,* no. 4 (1987), pp. 120–37.

2. J. R. Bettman, M. F. Luce, and J. W. Payne, "Constructive Consumer Choice Processes," *Journal of Consumer Research,* December 1998, pp. 187–217.

3. See C. A. Mandrik, "Consumer Heuristics," *Advances in Consumer Research,* vol. 23, eds. K. P. Corfman and J. G. Lynch (Provo, UT: Association for Consumer Research, 1996), pp. 301–7; and J. Swait and W. Adamowicz, "The Influence of Task Complexity on Consumer Choice," *Journal of Consumer Research,* June 2001, pp. 135–48.

4. See R. Dhar and S. M. Nowlis, "The Effects of Time Pressure on Consumer Choice Deferral," *Journal of Consumer Research,* March 1999, pp. 369–84.

5. See E. C. Garbarino and J. A. Edell, "Cognitive Effort, Affect, and Choice," *Journal of Consumer Research,* September 1997, pp. 147–58; M. F. Luce, "Choosing to Avoid," *Journal of Consumer Research,* March 1998, pp. 409–33; M. F. Luce, J. W. Payne, and J. R. Bettman, "Emotional Trade-Off Difficulty and Choice," *Journal of Marketing Research,* May 1999, pp. 143–59; and A. Drolet and M. F. Luce, "The Rationalizing Effects of Cognitive Load on Emotion-Based Trade-off Avoidance," *Journal of Consumer Research,* June 2004, pp. 63–77.

6. See C. L. Brown and G. S. Carpenter, "Why Is the Trivial Important?" *Journal of Consumer Research,* March 2000, pp. 372–85; and J. J. Inman and M. Zeelenberg, "Regret in Repeat Purchase versus Switching Decisions," *Journal of Consumer Research,* June 2002, pp. 116–28.

7. In addition, there are other goals and goal frameworks. For a recent discussion of one such example, namely, the self-regulatory goals of promotion versus prevention, see A. Chernev, "Goal-Attribute Compatibility in Consumer Choice," *Journal of Consumer Psychology* 14, no. 1/2 (2004), pp. 141–50.

8. J. R. Doyle et al., "The Robustness of the Asymmetrically Dominated Effect," *Psychology & Marketing,* May 1999, pp. 225–43; M. Bhargava, J. Kim, and R. K. Srivastava, "Explaining Context Effects on Choice Using a Model of Comparative Judgment," *Journal of Consumer Psychology* 9, no. 3 (2000), pp. 167–77; and R. Dhar, S. M. Nowlis, and S. J. Sherman, "Trying Hard or Hardly Trying," *Journal of Consumer Psychology* 9, no. 4 (2000), pp. 189–200. See also A. Drolet, "Inherent Rule Variability in Consumer Choice," *Journal of Consumer Research,* December 2002, pp. 293–305.

9. B. Mittal, "A Study of the Concept of Affective Choice Mode for Consumer Decisions," in *Advances in Consumer Research,* vol. 21, eds. C. T. Allen and D. R. John (Provo, UT: Association for Consumer Research, 1994), p. 256.

10. J. F. Durgee and G. C. O'Connor, "Why Some Products 'Just Feel Right,'" in *Advances in Consumer Research,* vol. 22, eds. F. R. Kardes and M. Sujan (Provo, UT: Association for Consumer Research, 1995), p. 652.

11. See M. T. Pham et al., "Affect Monitoring and the Primacy of Feelings in Judgment," *Journal of Consumer Research,* September 2001, pp. 167–87.

12. M. T. Pham, "Representativeness, Relevance, and the Use of Feelings in Decision Making," *Journal of Consumer Research,* September 1998, pp. 144–59.

13. See also R. Dhar and K. Wertenbroch, "Consumer Choice between Hedonic and Utilitarian Goods," *Journal of Marketing Research,* February 2000, pp. 60–71.

14. See B. Shiv and A. Fedorikhin, "Heart and Mind in Conflict," *Journal of Consumer Research,* December 1999, pp. 278–91.

15. J. A. Ruth, "Promoting a Brand's Emotional Benefits," *Journal of Consumer Psychology* 11, no. 2 (2001), pp. 99–113; and J. C. Sweeney and G. N. Soutar, "Consumer Perceived Value," *Journal of Retailing* 77 (2001), pp. 203–20.

16. See P. Krishnamurthy and M. Sujan, "Retrospection versus Anticipation," *Journal of Consumer Research,* June 1999, pp. 55–69. See also B. Shiv and J. Huber, "The Impact of Anticipating Satisfaction on Consumer Choice," *Journal of Consumer Research,* September 2000, pp. 202–16; and C. P. S. Fong and R. S. Wyer Jr., "Cultural, Social, and Emotional Determinants of Decisions under Uncertainty," *Organizational Behavior and Human Decision Processes* 90 (2003), pp. 304–22.

17. This section is based on S. P. Mantell and F. R. Kardes, "The Role of Direction of Comparison, Attribute-Based Processing, and Attitude-Based Processing in Consumer Preference," *Journal of Consumer Research,* March 1999, pp. 335–52. For a discussion of the specific role of advertising based attitudes, see W. E. Baker, "The Diagnosticity of Advertising Generated Brand Attitudes in Brand Choice Contexts," *Journal of Consumer Psychology* 11, no. 2 (2001), pp. 129–39.

18. See R. Dhar, S. M. Nowlis, and S. J. Sherman, "Comparison Effects on Preference Construction," *Journal of Consumer Research,* December 1999, pp. 293–306.

19. P. H. Bloch, "Seeking the Ideal Form," *Journal of Marketing,* July 1995, pp. 16–29; and Dhar and Wertenbroch, "Consumer Choice between Hedonic and Utilitarian Goods." See also, D. Horsky, P. Nelson, and S. S. Posavac, "Stating Preference for the Ethereal but Choosing the Concrete," *Journal of Consumer Psychology* 14, no. 1/2 (2004), pp. 132–40.

20. G. Kalyanaram and J. D. C. Little, "An Empirical Analysis of Latitude of Price Acceptance in Consumer Package Goods," *Journal of Consumer Research,* December 1994, pp. 408–18.

21. See S. Hoeffler and D. Ariely, "Constructing Stable Preferences," *Journal of Consumer Psychology* 8, no. 2 (1999), pp. 113–39; and A. V. Muthukrishnan and F. R. Kardes, "Persistent Preferences for Product Attributes," *Journal of Consumer Research,* June 2001, pp. 89–102.

22. D. J. Mitchell, B. E. Kahn, and S. C. Knasko, "There's Something in the Air," *Journal of Consumer Research,* September 1995, pp. 229–38; D. R. Lichtenstein, R. G. Netemeyer, and S. Burton, "Assessing the Domain Specificity of Deal Proneness,"

Journal of Consumer Research, December 1995, pp. 314–26; D. R. Lichtenstein, S. Burton, and R. G. Netemeyer, "An Examination of Deal Proneness across Sales Promotion Types," *Journal of Retailing,* no. 2 (1997), pp. 283–97; and V. Ramaswamy and S. S. Srinivasan, "Coupon Characteristics and Redemption Intentions," *Psychology & Marketing,* January 1998, pp. 50–80.

23. R. Pieters and L. Warlop, "Visual Attention during Brand Choice," *International Journal of Research in Marketing* 16 (1999), pp. 1–16.

24. B. L. Bagus, "The Consumer Durable Replacement Buyer," *Journal of Marketing,* January 1991, pp. 42–51.

25. A. Kirmani and P. Wright, "Procedural Learning, Consumer Decision Making, and Marketing Choice," *Marketing Letters* 4, no. 1 (1993), pp. 39–48; G. S. Carpenter, R. Glazer, and K. Nakamoto, "Meaningful Brands from Meaningless Differentiation," *Journal of Marketing Research,* August 1994, pp. 339–50; and S. M. Broniarczyk and A. D. Gershoff, "Meaningless Differentiation Revisited," *Advances in Consumer Research,* vol. 24, eds. M. Bruck and D. J. MacInnis (Provo, UT: Association for Consumer Research, 1997), pp. 223–28.

26. B. Abrams, "Hanes Finds L'eggs Methods Don't Work with Cosmetics," *The Wall Street Journal,* February 3, 1983, p. 33.

27. See R. Dhar and S. J. Sherman, "The Effect of Common and Unique Features in Consumer Choice," *Journal of Consumer Research,* December 1996, pp. 193–203; and A. Chernev, "The Effect of Common Features on Brand Choice," *Journal of Consumer Research,* March 1997, pp. 304–11.

28. See S. H. Ang, G. J. Gorn, and C. B. Weinberg, "The Evaluation of Time-Dependent Attributes," *Psychology & Marketing,* January 1996, pp. 19–35.

29. P. M. Parker, "Sweet Lemons," *Journal of Marketing Research,* August 1995, pp. 291–307; S. Shapiro and M. T. Spence, "Factors Affecting Encoding, Retrieval, and Alignment of Sensory Attributes in a Memory-Based Brand Choice Task," *Journal of Consumer Research,* March 2002, pp. 603–17; and B.-K. Lee and W.-N. Lee, "The Effect of Information Overload on Consumer Choice Quality in an On-Line Environment," *Psychology & Marketing,* March 2004, pp. 159–83.

30. See A. Kirmani and A. R. Rao, "No Pain, No Gain," *Journal of Marketing,* April 2000, pp. 66–79.

31. See, e.g., V. P. Norris, "The Economic Effects of Advertising," *Current Issues and Research in Advertising,* 1984, pp. 39–134; S. Burton and D. R. Lichtenstein, "Assessing the Relationship between Perceived and Objective Price-Quality," in *Advances in Consumer Research,* vol. 27, eds. M. E. Goldberg, G. Gorn, and R. W. Pollay (Provo, UT: Association for Consumer Research, 1990), pp. 715–22; and D. J. Faulds, O. Grunewald, and D. Johnson, "A Cross-National Investigation of the Relationship between the Price and Quality of Consumer Products," *Journal of Global Marketing* 8, no. 1 (1994), pp. 7–25.

32. K. M. Elliott and D. W. Roach, "Are Consumers Evaluating Your Products the Way You Think and Hope They Are?" *Journal of Consumer Marketing,* Spring 1991, pp. 5–14; and J. Baumgartner, "On the Utility of Consumers' Theories in Judgments of

Covariation," *Journal of Consumer Research,* March 1995, pp. 634–43.

33. See S. Ratneshwar et al., "Benefit Salience and Consumers' Selective Attention to Product Features," *International Journal of Research in Marketing* 14 (1997), pp. 245–59; R. Dhar and I. Simonson, "Making Complementary Choices in Consumption Episodes," *Journal of Marketing Research,* February 1999, pp. 29–44; and J. K. H. Lee and J. H. Steckel, "Consumer Strategies for Purchasing Assortments within a Single Product Class," *Journal of Retailing* 75, no. 3 (1999), pp. 387–403.

34. See, e.g., P. W. J. Verlegh, H. N. J. Schifferstein, and D. R. Wittink, "Range and Number-of-Levels Effects in Derived and Stated Measures of Attribute Importance," *Marketing Letters* 13, no. 1 (2002), pp. 41–52.

35. See, e.g., T. B. Heath, M. S. McCarthy, and D. L. Mothersbaugh, "Spokesperson Fame and Vividness Effects in the Context of Issue-Relevant Thinking," *Journal of Consumer Research,* March 1994, pp. 520–34.

36. M. P. Gardner, "Advertising Effects on Attributes Recalled and Criteria Used for Brand Evaluations," *Journal of Consumer Research,* December 1983, pp. 310–18; S. B. MacKenzie, "The Role of Attention in Mediating the Effect of Advertising on Attribute Importance," *Journal of Consumer Research,* September 1986, pp. 174–95; and G. D. Olsen, "Creating the Contrast," *Journal of Advertising,* Winter 1995, pp. 29–44.

37. C. Huffman, "Elaboration on Experience," *Psychology & Marketing,* August 1997, pp. 451–74.

38. K. B. Monroe, *Pricing* (New York: McGraw-Hill, 1979), p. 38.

39. A. R. Rao, L. Qu, and R. W. Ruekert, "Signaling Unobservable Product Quality through a Brand Ally," *Journal of Marketing Research,* May 1999, pp. 258–68; and C. Janiszewski and S. M. J. van Osselaer, "A Connectionist Model of Brand-Quality Associations," *Journal of Marketing Research,* August 2000, pp. 331–50.

40. C. J. Thompson, "Interpreting Consumers," *Journal Marketing Research,* November 1997, p. 443. Published by the American Marketing Association; reprinted with permission.

41. See G. Haubl and V. Trifts, "Consumer Decision Making in Online Shopping Environments," *Marketing Science,* Winter 2000, pp. 2–21.

42. S. Thompson, "Snacks to Go," *Advertising Age,* October 1, 2001, p. 4.

43. M. L. Ursic and J. G. Helgeson, "The Impact of Choice and Task Complexity on Consumer Decision Making," *Journal of Business Research,* August 1990, pp. 69–86; P. L. A. Dabholkar, "Incorporating Choice into an Attitudinal Framework," *Journal of Consumer Research,* June 1994, pp. 100–18; and T. Elrod, R. D. Johnson, and J. White, "A New Integrated Model of Noncompensatory and Compensatory Decision Strategies," *Organizational Behavior and Human Decision Processes* 95 (2004), pp. 1–19.

44. See E. Coupey, "Restructuring," *Journal of Consumer Research,* June 1994, pp. 83–99.

45. See D. L. Alden, D. M. Stayman, and W. D. Hoyer, "Evaluation Strategies of American and Thai Consumers," *Psychology & Marketing,* March 1994, pp. 145–61; and J. E. Russo and F. Lecleric, "An Eye-Fixation Analysis of Choice Processes for Consumer Nondurables," *Journal of Consumer Research,* September 1994, pp. 274–90.

46. See J. G. Helgeson and M. L. Ursic, "Information Load, Cost/Benefit Assessment and Decision Strategy Variability," *Journal of the Academy of Marketing Science,* Winter 1993, pp. 13–20; W. J. McDonald, "The Roles of Demographics, Purchase Histories, and Shopper Decision-Making Styles in Predicting Consumer Catalog Loyalty," *Journal of Direct Marketing,* Summer 1993, pp. 55–65; M. S. Yadav, "How Buyers Evaluate Product Bundles," *Journal of Consumer Research,* September 1994, pp. 342–53; A. V. Muthukrishnan, "Decision Ambiguity and Incumbent Brand Advantage," *Journal of Consumer Research,* June 1995, pp. 98–109; and D. E. Hansen and J. G. Helgeson, "Consumer Response to Decision Conflict from Negatively Correlated Attributes," *Journal of Consumer Psychology* 10, no. 3 (2001), pp. 150–69.

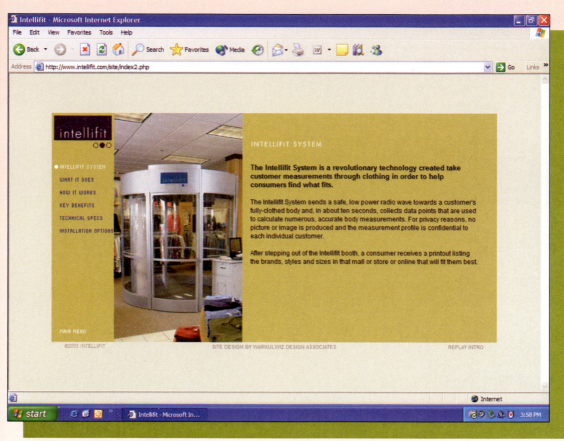

Courtesy Intellifit Corporation.

17

Outlet Selection and Purchase

◼ Technology continues to transform the way consumers shop and make purchases. Internet shopping is one of the more obvious examples. But there are numerous other ways in which retailers are using technology to enhance the in-store experience, influence consumer choices, and ease the purchase process. Consider the following:

- Consumers, manufacturers, and retailers continue to be frustrated with the sizing system used in apparel. Consumers end up having to try on numerous brands and items to find what fits. There is also the issue of returns when items don't fit as intended. To combat this problem, Intellifit has developed a product called the Size-atron. It is a full-body scanner that collects full body measurements in 10 seconds. It then prints out a confidential ticket indicating which brands and sizes will fit the best and which retailers have them. They are also using the aggregated anonymous data to help retailers and manufacturers match their approach to sizing to "create and stock clothes that fit real people." Clients include David's Bridal, Dockers, and Federated Department Stores.[1]

- IBM has developed the Shopping Buddy, a computerized touchscreen PC that can be attached to shopping carts. Stop & Shop is trying out this new technology in a number of its stores. The Shopping Buddy makes for a better in-store experience by allowing customers to do such things as order deli items remotely so they don't have to wait in line, scan and bag their items as they go to speed checkout, and browse recipes as they shop. While grocery retailing tends to be a highly competitive price-driven industry, technologies such as the Shopping Buddy are a reaction to research indicating that customers would pay more for groceries if the shopping experience were more positive.[2]

- Ever forget to take your wallet/purse to the store and you only find out when you are ready to check out? Retailers are addressing this issue with fingerprint technology. For example, Piggly Wiggly is testing a "Pay By Touch" system in which consumers register their fingerprint and then pay by having their finger scanned at checkout—no need for cash or credit card! As with all forms of identity, fingerprint technology will have to overcome consumer concerns regarding privacy issues.[3]

Technology will continue to transform retailing as marketers work to increase the shopping experience and attract customers to their retail outlets. *What's next on the retail horizon?*

Selecting a retail outlet involves the same process as selecting a brand, as described in the previous chapters.[4] That is, the consumer recognizes a problem that requires an outlet to be selected, engages in internal and possibly external search, evaluates the relevant alternatives, and applies a decision rule to make a selection. We are not going to repeat our discussion of these steps. Instead we will describe the evaluative criteria that consumers frequently use in choosing retail outlets, consumer characteristics that influence the criteria used, and in-store/online characteristics that affect the amounts and brands purchased.

OUTLET CHOICE VERSUS PRODUCT CHOICE

Outlet selection is obviously important to managers of retail firms such as Amazon.com, Sears, and L. L. Bean. However, it is equally important to consumer goods marketers. There are three basic sequences a consumer can follow when making a purchase decision: (1) brand (or item) first, outlet second; (2) outlet first, brand second; or (3) brand and outlet simultaneously.

Our model and discussion in the previous two chapters suggest that brands are selected first and outlets second. This situation may arise frequently. For example, a consumer considering buying a notebook computer may first select a brand and then purchase it from the outlet with the lowest price (or easiest access, best image, service, or other relevant attributes). However stores rather than brands can form the evoked set.[5] In our computer example, the consumer might be familiar with one store—Campus Computers—and decide to visit that store and select a computer from the brands available there. A third strategy is to compare the brands in one's evoked set at the stores in the evoked set. The decision would involve a simultaneous evaluation of both store and product attributes. Thus, a consumer might choose between a second preferred computer at a store with friendly personnel and excellent service facilities versus a favorite computer at an impersonal outlet with no service facilities.

The appropriate marketing strategies for both retailers and manufacturers differ depending on the decision sequence generally used by the target market. How would a manufacturer's strategy differ depending on whether the brand or store was selected first? A brand-first decision sequence would suggest strategies such as brand image and feature advertising, brand availability advertising (e.g., manufacturer ad introduces the brand and indicates "available now at . . . "), and possibly a limited distribution strategy. An outlet-first choice would tend to produce a focus on point-of-purchase materials, distribution through key outlets, and programs to encourage good shelf space and support from store personnel. Table 17-1 highlights additional strategic implications.

TABLE 17-1

Marketing Strategy
Based on the
Consumer Decision
Sequence

Decision Sequence	Level in the Channel	
	Retailer	Manufacturer
(1) *Outlet First, Brand Second*	Retailer image advertising Margin management on shelf space, displays Location analysis Appropriate pricing	Distribution in key outlets Point-of-purchase, shelf space, and position Programs to strengthen existing outlets
(2) *Brand First, Outlet Second*	Many brands and/or key brands Co-op ads featuring brands Price special on brands Retailer-sponsored search-engine links	More exclusive distribution Brand availability advertising Brand image management
(3) *Simultaneous*	Margin training for sales personnel Multiple brands/key brands High-service or low-price structure	Programs targeted at retail sales personnel Distribution in key outlets Co-op advertising

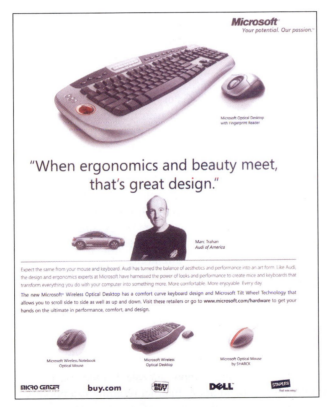

Courtesy Microsoft Corporation.

ILLUSTRATION 17-1

Marketers often use
advertising to create
brand demand and
to direct consumers
to appropriate
outlets.

Manufacturers often provide advertising dollars to retailers in exchange for featuring their products in the retailers' ads. At other times, the manufacturer lists one or more retailers as a source for its products. This both creates product demand and directs consumers to the appropriate retail outlet (see Illustration 17-1). Retailers often share in the cost of such ads. In other cases, firms use retailers' names in the ads as an inducement for the retailer to carry or display the brand.

THE RETAIL SCENE

We use *retail outlet* to refer to any source of products or services for consumers. In earlier editions of this text, we used the term *store*. However, increasingly consumers see or hear descriptions of products in catalogs, direct-mail pieces, or various print media; on television or radio; or on the Internet; they then acquire the products through mail, telephone, or computer orders. Generally referred to as **in-home shopping,** these sources represent a small but rapidly growing percentage of total retail sales. Consider this view of the future of retailing:

> You're watching "Seinfeld" on TV, and you like the jacket he's wearing. You click on it with your remote control. The show pauses and a Windows-style dropdown menu appears at the top of the screen, asking if you want to buy it. You click "yes." The next menu offers you a choice of colors; you click on black. Another menu lists your credit cards asking which one you'll use for this purchase. Click on MasterCard or whatever. Which address should the jacket go to, your office or your home or your cabin? Click on one address and you're done—the menus disappear and "Seinfeld" picks up where it left off.
>
> Just as you'll already have taught the computer about your credit cards and addresses, you will have had your body measured by a 3-D version of supermarket scanners, so the system will know your exact size. And it will send the data electronically to a factory, where robots will custom tailor the jacket to your measurements. An overnight courier service will deliver it to your door the next morning.[6]

Far-fetched? The quote is from Bill Gates, founder of Microsoft! While "Seinfeld" is now seen only in reruns and we are not yet near this level of sophistication in retailing, parts of the scenario are possible. As we saw in the chapter opener, consumers can have their bodies scanned and get recommendations about brands, sizes, and retail outlets. A consumer can also have a "mass-produced" bicycle designed for his or her body size and produced in an automated factory in a matter of days. So while Gates's vision may still be a bit futuristic, at least some aspects of it have already begun to emerge. Clearly, retailing is one of the most exciting areas of business in most developed economies.

We describe Internet (online) retailing and store (bricks and mortar) retailing in the next sections. We focus on Internet retailing because of its increasing prominence and rapid growth. However, other forms of nonstore retailing (e.g., catalogs, telemarketing, direct mail, television, and so forth) continue to be important and, in some cases, are being integrated with the Internet to produce powerful *multi-channel* approaches. These multi-channel approaches are also discussed.

Internet Retailing

In Chapter 15 we saw the increasingly important role that the Internet plays as an information source prior to purchase. In addition, Internet retailing is a booming and increasingly competitive business, as shown below in the estimates by eMarketer.[7]

	2003	2008
U.S. consumers 14 and older who are online (millions)	142	161
U.S. consumers 14 and older who have bought online (millions)	83	111
Average annual U.S. online expenditures	$675	$1,248
Total U.S. retail expenditures online (billions)	$94	$232

Forrester Research categorized products and services into three groups based on their purchase characteristics relative to Internet shopping:

- *Replenishment goods:* moderate cost, high-frequency purchases. Items that are relatively expensive and easy to ship will be most successful. Examples include health care items such as vitamins, beauty aids, and gourmet foods.
- *Researched items:* high-information, big-ticket planned purchases. Internet sales will be led by items with low style content and those for which "touch" is not important. Examples are leisure travel, computer hardware, and consumer electronics.
- *Convenience items:* low-risk discretionary items. Internet sales will be most successful for those where huge selection and deep discounts are important and easy shipping is available. Examples are books, CDs, flowers, and event tickets.[8]

As Figure 17-1 indicates, there is substantial growth across all categories. One of the more interesting categories is apparel, where lack of touch can be a major barrier for nonstore retailers. Apparel is one of the largest sales categories on the Internet and one of the fastest growing. Part of the reason for this is the rapid growth in Internet shopping by women, traditionally heavy purchasers of clothing from catalogs. As recent research suggests, this experience and comfort with other forms of in-home retailing appears to be transferring to the online context.[9] The growth of apparel also suggests that online marketers are increasingly finding ways to deal with the "touch" issue. For example, zoom features which allow for better viewing of items are now used by most online retailers.[10] In addition, across product categories including apparel, consumers are utilizing multiple channels in combination to satisfy their shopping needs. These various shopping channels often have complementary benefits that, when combined, can maximize a consumer's experience. For example, consumers may browse a catalog or retail store and then buy online.

Internet sales are growing rapidly and are expected to represent 12 percent of total retail sales by 2010.[11] These numbers likely underrepresent the role of the Internet since they do not include offline sales that are influenced by online marketing efforts. The penetration of Internet sales (as a percent of all sales in a category) is increasing and is substantial for categories such as computer hard/software (48 percent), tickets (28 percent), travel (26 percent), and books (20 percent).[12]

Consumers shop online for reasons similar to those for shopping from catalogs:[13]

Reason	Online Shopping	Catalog Shopping
Convenience	67%	62%
Price was right	41	40
Unique merchandise	33	40
Past experience with company	28	39
Wanted product delivered	16	31
No time to go to store	13	17
Recommendation from a friend	7	7
Impulse	4	5

Catalog Age. Reprinted with the permission of Primedia Business Magazines & Media Inc. Copyright 2001. All rights reserved.

Until recently, many industry experts predicted the demise of catalogs. However, catalogs and the Internet appear to work in a complementary fashion. For example, a recent study finds that when consumers received a physical catalog it nearly doubled their chances of buying at the retailer's Web site and increased their spending by 16 percent.[14]

| FIGURE 17-1 | Online Sales by Categories (in $ Billions) |

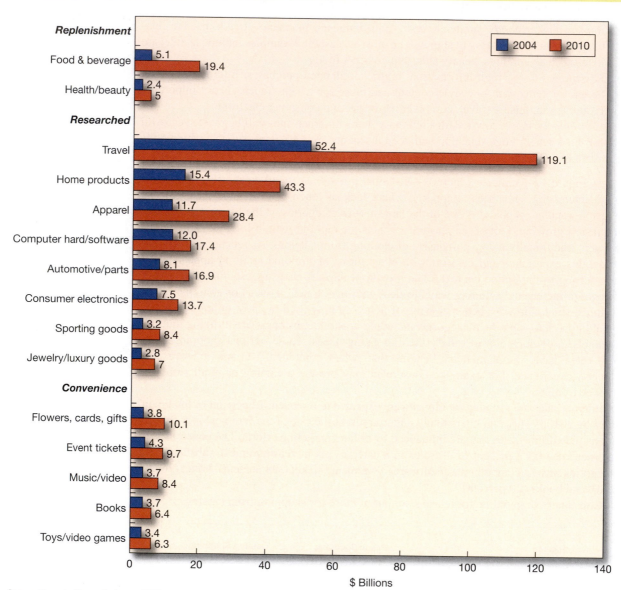

Source: Forrester Research, August 2004.

Barriers to Internet Shopping   For some products, people, and situations, the Internet offers a better combination of selection, convenience, price, and other attributes than do catalogs, traditional stores, or other outlets. However, for most purchases, most consumers still prefer and utilize traditional retail outlets. Many barriers still exist to online purchasing, not the least of which is the lack of Internet access. However, many who are online still have never made a purchase. A Forrester Research study found the following reasons among those who are online who have never made a purchase online.[15] Research suggests similar reasons for Asian consumers as well.[16]

Reason	Percent
Credit card security concerns	62%
Lack of "touch"	55
Want to research online and buy offline	24
Delivery costs too high	22
Heard about bad online buying experiences of others	21

Concerns over credit card provision online are just one aspect of more general online privacy concerns. **Online privacy concerns** *relate to consumer fears regarding how personal information about them that is gathered online might be used.* Online privacy concerns include targeting children, being inundated with marketing messages, and identity theft.[17] While privacy concerns exist for many other purchase environments such as catalog purchases and "club card" purchases at traditional stores,[18] they appear to be multiplied when the information is provided over the Internet. Online privacy concerns represent a major challenge to Internet commerce with one estimate putting lost sales at $24.5 billion in 2006.[19]

Enhancing consumer control is one approach to the issue. For example, firms can take an "opt in" approach where the consumer chooses how the firm can use any information provided.[20] Research suggests that many consumers are quite willing to provide substantial personal data online if they are assured that its use will be limited to prespecified purposes and that they will receive some benefit from providing it.[21] Unfortunately, this can remove many of the benefits of the Internet for both consumers and companies:

> On the one hand, consumers want companies to read their minds and give them what they want. On the other hand, that means companies have to collect information, data mine, and create profiles, which makes consumers feel like they're being tracked and exploited.[22]

As a consequence, companies must move beyond control to build and sustain highly trusted online images and relationships.[23] This involves such factors as having adequate privacy policies in place, utilizing security verification systems such as VeriSign, and handling consumer information responsibly. Such images are built over time as consumers gain greater experience and confidence with online purchasing and with specific online retailers. Just as brand name can be a surrogate quality indicator (Chapter 16), so too can it be a surrogate for information safety and security online.

The lack of touch or ability to physically handle, test, or try products prior to purchase is the second largest concern and affects product categories such as apparel and home decorating where it can be difficult to simulate experience attributes (e.g., fit for apparel, color and texture for home decorating).[24] Internet marketers are becoming much more sophisticated in terms of creating *virtual product experiences* using such techniques as 3D simulations and rich media, made practical by the increased penetration of broadband. For example, MVM (My Virtual Model) is available on various online apparel sites (see Illustration 17-2). MVM allows customers to create virtual models by entering their body dimensions and then "try on" the retailer's clothes to see how they "fit."[25]

Characteristics of Online Shoppers   Obviously, online shoppers must first be Internet users. As we saw in Chapter 15, Internet users tend to have higher income and education levels than the general population although these differences are diminishing. Currently, online shoppers tend to be younger and more affluent than the average Internet user. In addition, while men and women are roughly equally split in terms of Internet use,

ILLUSTRATION 17-2

MVM helps to mitigate barriers to Internet shopping for clothes. MVM has more than 9.4 million registered users, 8 million garment try-ons per month, and 200,000 new registered users each month.

Courtesy My Virtual Model, Inc.

women are emerging as the stronger Internet buyers.[26] As we noted above, this has important implications for many categories in which women are the primary purchasers or where they have strong purchase influence.

Interestingly, research is now going beyond demographics to better understand online shopping in terms of such factors as online experience and attitudes and behaviors regarding the Internet and online shopping. For example, one study shows that those who purchase online tend to have more experience in the online environment and thus build up the necessary knowledge, skills, and confidence. The effect is dramatic—those who have been online 10 or more years were found to spend roughly 75 percent more than those who have been online two years or less.[27]

Another study identified eight online shopper segments based on a holiday purchase occasion.[28] These segments and recommended marketing strategies for each are as follows:

- *Shopping Lovers* (11 percent of online households [HHs], 24 percent of online spending) enjoy buying online and do so frequently. They are competent computer users and will likely continue their shopping habits. They also spread the word to others about joys of online shopping whenever they have the opportunity. They represent an ideal target for retailers.
- *Adventurous Explorers* (9 percent of online HHs, 30 percent of online spending) are a small segment that presents a large opportunity. They require little special attention by Internet vendors because they believe online shopping is fun. They are likely the opinion leaders for all things online. Retailers should nurture and cultivate them to be online community builders and shopping advocates.
- *Suspicious Learners* (10 percent of online HHs, 15 percent of online spending) constitute another small segment with growth potential. Their reluctance to purchase online more often hinges on their lack of computer training, but they are open to new ways of

doing things. In contrast to more fearful segments, they don't have a problem giving a computer their credit card number. Further guidance and training would help coax them into online buying.

- *Business Users* (13 percent of online HHs, 19 percent of online spending) are among the most computer literate. They use the Internet primarily for business purposes. They take a serious interest in what it can do for their professional life. They don't view online shopping as novel and aren't usually champions of the practice.

- *Fearful Browsers* (11 percent of online HHs, 5 percent of online spending) are on the cusp of buying online. They are capable Internet and computer users, spending a good deal of time "window shopping." They could become a significant buying group if their fears about credit card security, shipping charges, and buying products sight unseen were overcome.

- *Shopping Avoiders* (16 percent of online HHs, 3 percent of online spending) have an appealing income level, but their values make them a poor target for online retailers. They don't like to wait for products to be shipped to them, and they like seeing merchandise in person before buying. They have online shopping issues that retailers will not easily be able to overcome.

- *Technology Muddlers* (20 percent of online HHs, 3 percent of online spending) face large computer literacy hurdles. They spend less time than any other segment online and show little excitement about increasing their online comfort level. They are not an attractive market for online retailers.

- *Fun Seekers* (12 percent of online HHs, 2 percent of online spending) are the least wealthy and least educated market segment. They see entertainment value in the Internet, but buying things online frightens them. Although security and privacy issues might be overcome, the spending power of the segment suggests that only a marginal long-term payback would be possible.

A recent study of Asian consumers yielded a similar set of segments, with online buyers tending to have more positive attitudes about, and experience with, online shopping and purchasing than traditional in-store buyers.[29]

Store-Based Retailing

The vast majority of retail sales take place in physical stores, and this will remain true for the foreseeable future. However traditional store-based retailing is certainly vulnerable in ways that play into the hands of in-home retailers. Consider the results of a Roper survey asking consumers why they don't like shopping in stores:[30]

Reason	Percent
Salespeople are poorly informed	74%
Waiting in long lines	73
Hard time finding things	64
Parking and traffic	64
Dealing with crowds	58
Hard to get someone to wait on you	54
The time it takes to shop	38
Don't like shopping	34

Source: From Roper Reports Telephone Survey, August 2003.

Obviously, for many people in-store shopping is perceived as neither fun nor an efficient use of time. However, retailers are fighting back with an explosion of store-based retailing

Courtesy Mall of America.

activities and technologies to improve the shopping experience.[31] Lifestyle centers are emerging to generate excitement and adapt to the changing shopping habits of consumers as we saw in Consumer Insight 1-1. Brand stores are emerging as major sales volume outlets as well as promotional devices for brands such as Levi's, Nike, Reebok, and OshKosh B'Gosh. The Sharper Image and similar outlets function as adult toy stores where one can play with the latest fun items for adults.

Other approaches are being tried including kiosks, mini-stores, and stores within stores. Sunglass Hut operates small kiosks in malls, airports, and other high-traffic areas. Giant superstores such as Staples, Home Depot, Costco, and Blockbuster are opening mini-stores in small towns, tiny shopping centers, and downtown areas.[32] And fast-food restaurants operate stores inside other outlets such as Wal-Mart, Home Depot, and gas stations.

Traditional department stores are fighting back by creating "destination areas" within their stores that enhance their overall image and drive ongoing store traffic. For example, Parisians (part of the Saks Department Store Group) has a day spa and nail salon. They have also developed Club Libby Lu for girls where they can have birthday parties, get makeovers with friends, and so on. Club Libby Lu pushes the excitement and social aspects of shopping and terms its customers VIPs—Very Important Princesses!

Courtesy Eastern Mountain Sports.

Target has "reinvented the whole discount store concept." It has "been able to carve out the ultimate retail positioning with both a perception of having the highest-quality products and, at the same time, a perception of being a low-price leader." It is predicted that soon Target will be the second-largest retailer in the United States (Wal-Mart is the largest).[33]

Malls are becoming giant entertainment centers. For example, the Mall of America near Minneapolis is built around an amusement park. It also has a miniature golf course, 9 nightclubs, 45 restaurants, a 14-screen movie complex, and a wedding chapel (see Illustration 17-3).[34] Retailing is clearly an exciting, competitive area. Those retailers who best understand their consumers will be the ones to prosper in the future.

The Internet as Part of a Multi-Channel Strategy

There is a tendency to think of Internet retailers as distinct from store-based retailers and other forms of in-home shopping such as catalogs. However, *pure play* Internet retailers such as eBay, Amazon.com, and Priceline are only part of the picture. Most large store-based retailers and catalog firms also have Internet sales sites. In fact, such multi-channel retail strategies are increasingly essential.[35] Thus, firms such as Eddie Bauer and The Gap actively market through physical retail stores, catalogs, and the Internet. In fact, over 70 percent of the top 100 online retailers in the United States are multi-channel retailers.[36]

A multi-channel approach can take many forms and can be successful for a number of reasons. For example, regional in-store retailers such as Eastern Mountain Sports can use the Internet to instantly become national and international in scope (see Illustration 17-4). On the flip side, the Internet allows traditional retailers such as JCPenney and Saks Fifth Avenue to reach smaller communities where they could not otherwise operate economically.

| FIGURE 17-2 | Multi-Channel Shoppers Often Browse in One Channel and Purchase in Another |

The arrow start point indicates where consumer browse occurs; the arrow end point indicates where the consumer buy occurs. For example, 19 percent browsed/searched in the catalog and then purchased the product at the retail store.

Source: DoubleClick, Inc., Multi-Channel Shopping Study (New York, NY: 2004). Copyright: DoubleClick, Inc., 2005.

Another option is the use of Internet shopping kiosks in traditional outlets. These kiosks allow consumers to purchase items not carried at that store or that are out of stock. In addition, consumers can use this service to purchase items for delivery to their homes or to be delivered as gifts. As a consequence, these kiosks represent a complementary rather than competing channel.

The increased use of a multi-channel approach relates to shifts in consumer shopping patterns.[37] Specifically, consumers are increasingly likely to be **multi-channel shoppers**—that is consumers who browse and/or purchase in more than one channel. Research by DoubleClick suggests the following:

- Multi-channel shoppers spend more than single-channel shoppers, with triple-channel shoppers (Internet, catalog, and retail store) spending the most.
- Multi-channel shoppers often browse/search in one channel and use that information to make a purchase in another channel. For example, a consumer might research jewelry at JCPenney's Web site but make the purchase at a JCPenney store.

Figure 17-2 shows the *channel-switching* behavior engaged in by multi-channel shoppers who browsed in one channel but purchased in another. Consistent with Chapter 15, many consumers browse/research online but then purchase offline in retail stores. However, the overall message here is that consumers are utilizing multiple channels in *complementary* ways since no retailing format is optimal on all dimensions. Thus, the Internet can be used to overcome a lack of informed salespeople or the inconvenience of researching products in-store, while in-store can provide "touch" and immediacy of purchasing.[38] Figure 17-2 also emphasizes the ongoing importance of catalogs as drivers of both online and retail store purchases.

ATTRIBUTES AFFECTING RETAIL OUTLET SELECTION

The selection of a specific retail outlet involves a comparison of the alternative outlets on the consumer's evaluative criteria. This section considers a number of evaluative criteria commonly used by consumers to select retail outlets. While much of the research on outlet selection relates to choosing among retail stores (e.g., JCPenney versus Sears), when applicable we also draw linkages to choosing among online retailers (e.g., Buybooks.com versus Amazon.com) based on emerging evidence.

Outlet Image

A given consumer's or target market's perception of all the attributes associated with a retail outlet is generally referred to as the **store image.** This is the same as the concept of *brand image* discussed in Chapter 9. One study found the following nine dimensions and 23 components of these nine dimensions of store image.[39] Notice that the store atmosphere component is primarily affective or feeling in nature.

<table>
<tr><th colspan="2">Store Image</th></tr>
<tr><th>Dimension</th><th>Components</th></tr>
<tr><td>Merchandise</td><td>Quality, selection, style, and price</td></tr>
<tr><td>Service</td><td>Layaway plan, sales personnel, easy return, credit, and delivery</td></tr>
<tr><td>Clientele</td><td>Customers</td></tr>
<tr><td>Physical facilities</td><td>Cleanliness, store layout, shopping ease, and attractiveness</td></tr>
<tr><td>Convenience</td><td>Location and parking</td></tr>
<tr><td>Promotion</td><td>Advertising</td></tr>
<tr><td>Store atmosphere</td><td>Congeniality, fun, excitement, comfort</td></tr>
<tr><td>Institutional</td><td>Store reputation</td></tr>
<tr><td>Posttransaction</td><td>Satisfaction</td></tr>
</table>

Source: J. D. Lindquist, "Meaning of Image," *Journal of Retailing,* Winter 1974, pp. 29–38.

This study focused on stores; the components and probably the dimensions will require adjusting for use with other types of retail outlets. For example, a recent study of *online retailer image* found the following seven dimensions and related components which influenced online outlet selection.[40] *Which dimensions and components of store image translate the most to an online context and which the least?*

<table>
<tr><th colspan="2">Online Retailer Image</th></tr>
<tr><th>Dimension</th><th>Components</th></tr>
<tr><td>Usefulness</td><td>Good product offers and information, value, aligned with interests</td></tr>
<tr><td>Enjoyment</td><td>Fun, attractive, pleasant to browse</td></tr>
<tr><td>Ease of use</td><td>Easy to use and navigate, flexible site</td></tr>
<tr><td>Trustworthiness</td><td>Reputation, information safety and security</td></tr>
<tr><td>Style</td><td>Helpful, friendly, knowledgeable, calm</td></tr>
<tr><td>Familiarity</td><td>Advertising online and offline, general familiarity</td></tr>
<tr><td>Settlement</td><td>Fast and flexible delivery and transactions</td></tr>
</table>

Source: Reprinted from H. van der Heijden and T. Verhage, "Online Store Image," *Information and Management,* 41, 2004, pp. 609–617.

As these studies suggest, overall retailer image (both Internet and store-based) relates to both functional and affective dimensions. The importance of the affective component cannot be underestimated. A study that focused on the affective component of store image or personality found the following differences across stores (the higher the number, the more the component fits the outlet):[41]

Store	Affective Component			
	Pleasant	Unpleasant	Active	Sleepy
Penney's	18.5	12.8	13.7	14.3
Kmart	15.2	12.6	14.8	12.9
Macy's	25.2	7.2	19.0	6.7
Sharper Image	23.5	7.8	22.4	6.9
Victoria's Secret	25.5	9.5	16.0	12.7

Source: Reprinted from W.R. Darden and B.J. Badin, "Exploring the Concept of Affective Quality," *Journal of Business Research*, February 1994, p. 106.

Notice that JCPenney and Kmart are about as strong on the unpleasant component as on the pleasant component, and they are viewed as being neither active nor sleepy. This suggests that shopping motives will have to come from price, selection, or other functional features. In contrast, Macy's is a pleasant, active place to shop. Consumers will shop at stores such as Macy's because they are pleasant and active rather than, or in addition to, their functional characteristics. Victoria's Secret and The Sharper Image are both pleasant places to shop, but the former is a less active experience than the latter. *What do these affective results suggest for JCPenney's marketing strategy?*

Marketers make extensive use of image data in formulating retail strategies.[42] First, marketers control many of the elements that determine an outlet's image. Second, differing groups of consumers desire different things from various types of retail outlets. Thus, a focused, managed image that matches the target market's desires is essential for most retailers.

Target has been able to develop an image as a source of high-quality, stylish products for relatively low prices. One of the ways it does this is by developing and promoting its own exclusive, stylish merchandise (see Illustration 17-5).

Other outlets concentrate on one or more attributes that are important to a segment of consumers or that are important to most consumers in certain situations. For example, online superstores such as Amazon.com and Buy.com focus heavily on breadth of merchandise and price. Alternatively, stores like 7-Eleven focus almost exclusively on convenience (easy access, extended hours, and quick service) for consumers in those situations where convenience is the key attribute.

Retailer Brands

Closely related to store image are **store brands.** At the extreme, the store or outlet is the brand. The Gap, Victoria's Secret, and Body Shop International are examples. All the items carried in the store are the store's own brand. Traditionally, retailers carried only manufacturers' brands, and only a few, such as Sears and Wards, developed their own house or store brands. In the 1970s, many stores began to develop store brands as low-price alternatives to national brands, and many continue with this approach.[43]

Increasingly, however, retailers such as Wal-Mart and Target are developing and promoting high-quality brands with either the store's name or an independent name. Such brands not only provide attractive margins for these outlets; if they are developed appropriately, they also become an important attribute of the outlet. That is, they are another

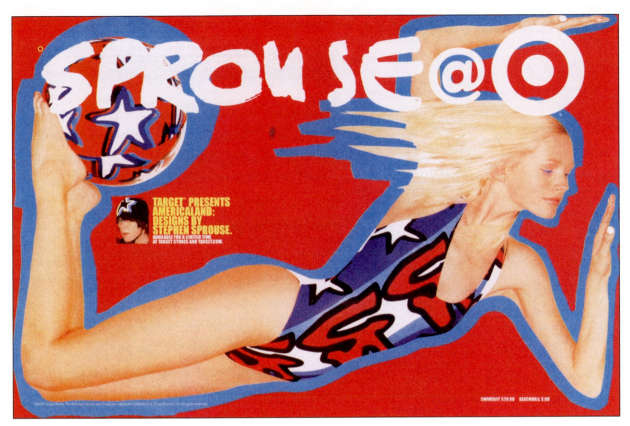

Courtesy Target Corporations.

reason for the consumer to shop that store.[44] And importantly, no other outlet can carry this brand. The key to success of store brands seems clear—high quality at a reasonable price. The traditional pattern of providing reasonable quality at a low price is no longer necessarily optimal.[45] In fact, emphasizing quality over price may be particularly beneficial if the brand carries the store's name or will become associated with the store.

Retail Advertising

Retailers use advertising to communicate their attributes, particularly sale prices, to consumers. It is clear that price advertising can attract people to stores. Revealing results were obtained in a major study involving newspaper ads in seven cities for a range of product categories (motor oil, sheets, digital watches, pants, suits, coffee makers, dresses, and mattresses). The impact of the retail advertisements varied widely by product category. For example, 88 percent of those who came to the store in response to the advertisement for motor oil purchased the advertised item, compared with only 16 percent of those responding to the dress ad. Approximately 50 percent of the shoppers overall purchased the advertised item that attracted them to the store.

As Figure 17-3 illustrates, purchases of the advertised item understate the total impact of the ad. *Sales of additional items to customers who came to purchase an advertised item* are referred to as **spillover sales.** Spillover sales in this study equaled sales of the advertised items; that is, for every $1 spent on the sale item by people who came to the store in response to the advertising, another $1 was spent on some other item(s) in the store.[46]

ILLUSTRATION 17-5

This stylish swimsuit was designed by artist Stephen Sprouse. It was available for a limited time at Target stores and Target.com for $29.99.

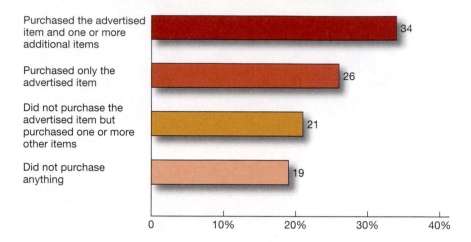

FIGURE 17-3   **Expenditures of Individuals Drawn to a Store by an Advertised Item**

Another study produced the results shown below:[47]

	Reason for Visiting Store	
Action	**Purchase Promoted Item**	**Other Reason**
Dollars spent on promoted items	$11.30	$3.27
Dollars spent on regular items	18.48	21.90
Total	29.78	25.17
Store profit	5.64	5.77

Retailers evaluating the benefits of price or other promotions must consider the impact on overall store sales and profits, not just those of the advertised item. And while a large percentage of retail advertising stresses price, particularly sales price, studies continue to show that price is frequently not the prime reason consumers select a retail outlet.[48] Thus, many retailers could benefit by emphasizing service, selection, or the affective benefits of their outlets. Affective benefits may be particularly effective for hedonic rather than utilitarian products.[49]

Online retailers advertise in mass media both to attract consumers to their sites and to build an image. Price and value are clearly important attributes for online shoppers,[50] and many sites promote this feature. In addition, recent research suggests that customization of online promotions such as e-mail to better match the characteristics and needs of target customers can dramatically increase online store traffic.[51]

Price Advertising Decisions   Retailers face three decisions when they consider using price advertising:

1. How large a price discount should be used?
2. Should comparison or reference prices be used?
3. What verbal statements should accompany the price information?

Consumers tend to assume that any advertised price represents a price reduction or sale price. Showing a comparison price increases the perceived savings significantly. However, the strength of the perception varies with the manner in which the comparison or reference price is presented. A **reference price** is *a price with which other prices are compared.* In the claim, "Regularly $9.95, now only $6.95," $9.95 is the reference price. An **external reference price** is *a price presented by a marketer for the consumer to use to compare with the current price.* An **internal reference price** is *a price or price range[52] that a consumer retrieves from memory to compare with a price in the market.*[53]

Although there are situational influences and individual differences,[54] most consumers understand external reference prices and are influenced by them but do not completely believe them.[55] The reason for the lack of belief is the practice of some retailers of using inflated reference prices. These inflated prices could be "suggested list prices" in markets where virtually all sales are at a lower level. Or they may reflect prices that the store set for the merchandise originally that were too high and produced few sales. The price reduction being shown then merely corrects an earlier pricing error but does not provide meaningful benefit to the consumer. Since price and sale advertising have a strong impact on consumer purchases, the FTC and many states have special guidelines and regulations controlling their use.[56]

The best approach for retailers seems to be to present the sale price and (1) the dollar amount saved if it is large, (2) the percentage saved when it is large, and (3) both if both are large. Thus, $10 savings on a $200 item should show the dollar savings but not the percentage savings. A $10 saving on a $20 item could emphasize both the dollar and the percentage savings. A $1 saving on a $3 item should focus on the percentage savings.[57] The regular price could be shown in any of these conditions.[58] The regular price (the price on which the savings are calculated) should be the price at which the store normally sells a reasonable volume of the brand being discounted.

Such words or phrases as "now only," "compare at," or "special" appear to enhance the perceived value of a sale. However, this varies by situation, initial price level and discount size, consumer group, and retail outlet.[59] Is "50 percent off" or "buy one, get one free" likely to be perceived as a better value? It depends in large part on the nature of the item being promoted. For stock-up items such as detergent, they are viewed as equivalent. However, for perishable items such as bread, the "50 percent off" is seen as a better value.[60]

Retailers need to use caution in how they use price advertising. Such advertising signals not only the price of the advertised items but also the price level of the store.[61] And because price level, quality, service, and other important attributes are often linked in the consumer's mind, inappropriate price advertising can have a negative effect on the store's image.[62]

The ad in Illustration 17-6 places primary emphasis on the dollar savings but also shows the reference price and the sale price. Since the dollar savings are relatively large, the research we have reviewed suggests that this is a sound strategy.

Outlet Location and Size

Location plays an important role in consumer store choice. If all other things are approximately equal, the consumer generally will select the closest store.[63] Likewise, the size of an outlet is an important factor. Unless the customer is particularly interested in fast service or convenience, he or she would tend to prefer larger outlets over smaller outlets, all other things being equal.[64] Interestingly, some of the major online players are "superstores" such as Amazon.com. Thus, retailer size appears to play a role online as well.

The **retail attraction model,** also called the **retail gravitation model,** is used to calculate the level of store attraction based on store size and distance from the consumer. In the retail gravitation model, store size is measured in square footage and assumed to be a measure of breadth of merchandise. The distance or travel time to a store is assumed to be a measure of the effort, both physical and psychological, to reach a given retail area.

Courtesy The Sharper Image.

The effect of distance or travel time varies by product.[65] For a convenience item or minor shopping good, distance is important, since shoppers are unwilling to travel very far for such items. However, major high-involvement purchases such as automobiles or specialty items such as wedding dresses generate greater willingness to travel.

Willingness to travel also varies with the size of the shopping list for that trip.[66] Thus, a consumer who would not be willing to travel very far to purchase three or four convenience items may willingly go much farther if 20 or 30 such items are to be purchased on the same trip.

Consumers often combine shopping trips and purposes.[67] Thus, a consumer may visit a health club, have lunch with a friend, pick up the laundry, shop for food for the next few days, and pick up a prescription on one trip. Thus, retail patronage is in part a function of an outlet's location in relation to other outlets and consumers' travel patterns. Combining outlets or adding departments in response to such shopping patterns can produce value for customers and increased revenue for the firm.[68] For example, supermarkets such as Safeway and Albertson's have added pharmacies to their outlets.

CONSUMER CHARACTERISTICS AND OUTLET CHOICE

The preceding discussion by and large has focused on store attributes independently of the specific characteristics of the consumers in the target market. However, different consumers have vastly differing desires and reasons for shopping. This section of the chapter examines two consumer characteristics that are particularly relevant to store choice: perceived risk and shopper orientation.

Perceived Risk

The purchase of products involves the risk that they may not perform as expected. As described in Chapter 15, such a failure may result in a high

- *Social cost* (e.g., a hairstyle that is not appreciated by one's peers).
- *Financial cost* (e.g., an expensive pair of shoes that become too uncomfortable to wear).
- *Time cost* (e.g., a television repair that requires the set to be taken to the shop, left, and then picked up later).
- *Effort cost* (e.g., a computer disk that is loaded with several hours of work before it fails).
- *Physical cost* (e.g., a new medicine that produces a harmful side effect).

TABLE 17-2

The Economic and
Social Risk of Various
Types of Products

| Social Risk | Economic Risk | |
	Low	High
Low	Wine (personal use)	Personal computer
	Socks	Auto repairs
	Kitchen supplies	Clothes washer
	Pens/pencils	Insurance
	Gasoline	Doctor/lawyer
High	Fashion accessories	Business suits
	Hairstyles	Living room furniture
	Gifts (inexpensive)	Automobile
	Wine (entertaining)	Snowboard
	Deodorant	Ski suit

The first of these is generally termed *social risk;* the next three are often considered to be *economic risk.* Product categories vary in the level and type of risk generally associated with them.[69] Table 17-2 shows that socks and gasoline are low in economic and social risk, while hairstyles and small gifts are low in economic risk but high in social risk. Other products, such as personal computers and auto repairs, are low in social risk but high in economic risk. Finally, automobiles and living room furniture are high in both economic and social risk.[70] Table 17-2 also indicates the role of the situation in perceived risk. Wine is shown as low in both social and economic risk when used for personal consumption but high in social risk when served while entertaining.

The perception of these risks differs among consumers, depending in part on their past experiences and lifestyles. For this reason, **perceived risk** is considered a consumer characteristic as well as a product characteristic.[71] For example, while many individuals would feel no social risk associated with the brand of car owned, others would.

Like product categories, retail outlets are perceived as having varying degrees of risk. Traditional outlets are perceived as low in risk, whereas more innovative outlets such as online are viewed as higher risk.[72]

The above findings lead to a number of insights into retailing strategy,[73] including the following:

- Nontraditional outlets need to minimize the perceived risk of shopping particularly if they sell items with either high economic or social risk. Lands' End attempts to reduce perceived risk by emphasizing toll-free ordering, 24-hour toll-free customer service telephones with trained assistants, and a 100 percent satisfaction guarantee. Word of mouth from satisfied customers reinforces these advertised policies.
- Nontraditional outlets need brand-name merchandise in those product categories with high perceived risk. Most Internet retailers feature such items.
- Traditional outlets and Web sites of well-known retailers have a major advantage with high-perceived-risk product lines. These lines should generally be their primary strategy focus. Low-risk items can be used to round out the overall assortment.
- Economic risks can be reduced through warranties, reasonable return policies, security verification systems, and so forth. As we've seen, such factors are critical to online shopping where financial security concerns are high. Social risk is harder to reduce. A skilled sales force, known brands, and satisfaction guarantees can help reduce this type of risk.

Illustration 17-7 shows how L.L. Bean reduces perceived risk by guaranteeing complete satisfaction no matter how long you own their clothing.

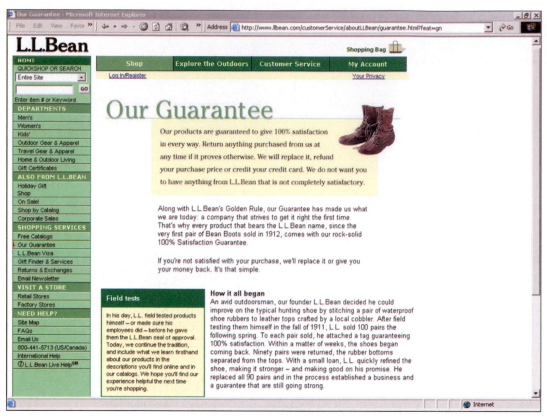

Courtesy L.L. Bean, Inc.

Shopping Orientation

Individuals go shopping for more complex reasons than simply acquiring a product or set of products. Diversion from routine activities, exercise, sensory stimulation, social interactions, learning about new trends, and even acquiring interpersonal power ("bossing" clerks) are nonpurchase reasons for shopping.[74] Of course, the relative importance of these motives varies both across individuals and within individuals over time as the situation changes.[75] See again Illustration 17-3, which shows how malls can provide an inviting environment for activities in addition to shopping.

   A shopping style that puts particular emphasis on certain activities or shopping motivations is called a **shopping orientation.** Shopping orientations are closely related to general lifestyle and are subject to similar influences. A recent study used projective techniques to ascertain the ways college students approach shopping.[76] It had consumers "Think about an animal that best describes you as a shopper . . . [and] explain what it is about your behavior that makes this animal an appropriate metaphor." This projective approach uncovered six shopping orientations:

1. *Chameleons* indicated that their shopping styles are situation-specific or constantly changing. Their shopping approach is based on product type, shopping impetus, and purchase task.
2. *Collectors/Gatherers* are characterized by their propensity to stockpile items and to purchase large quantities to either save money or alleviate the need for shopping. They attempt to get the best price and take advantage of retailer guarantees.

3. *Foragers* are particular and are motivated to purchase only the desired items. They are willing to search extensively and have little store loyalty. They like to shop alone.

4. *Hibernants* are indifferent toward shopping. Their shopping patterns are opportunistic rather than need driven and they will often postpone even required purchases.

5. *Predators* are purposive and speed oriented in their shopping. They plan before shopping and like to shop alone. They don't enjoy shopping and tend to shop outlets where they are assured of getting the items they need quickly.

6. *Scavengers* enjoy shopping both to make purchases and as an activity. They like to go to sales and consider shopping to be entertainment. They make numerous unplanned purchases.

The opportunities for developing segment-specific marketing strategies are clearly evident.[77] For example, Predators might respond to home delivery. Scavengers would respond well to entertainment-focused malls and outlets. However, as a single store attempts to target more of the segments, the risk of failure with all groups increases, as many of their desires are, if not mutually exclusive, difficult to meet within the same outlet. *Which of these groups would shop at Wal-Mart? Banana Republic? Sears? Which are the best targets for Internet outlets?*

IN-STORE AND ONLINE INFLUENCES ON BRAND CHOICES

It is not uncommon to enter a retail outlet with the intention of purchasing a particular brand but to leave with a different brand or additional items. Influences operating within the retail outlet induce additional information processing and subsequently affect the final purchase decision. This portion of the chapter examines six variables that singularly and in combination influence brand decisions inside a retail outlet: *point-of-purchase materials, price reductions, outlet atmosphere, stockout situations, Web site design,* and *sales personnel.* Our focus is specifically on factors within *physical stores* or *online retailer Web sites* that influence purchase behavior. We begin by examining the extent and nature of unplanned purchases.

The Nature of Unplanned Purchases

The fact that consumers often purchase brands different from or in addition to those planned has led to an interest in unplanned purchases. **Unplanned purchases** are defined as *purchases made in a retail outlet that are different from those the consumer planned to make prior to entering that retail outlet.* While the term *unplanned purchase* implies a lack of rationality or alternative evaluation, this is not necessarily true. For example, the decision to purchase Del Monte rather than Green Giant peas because Del Monte is on sale is certainly not illogical.

Viewing most in-store and online purchase decisions as the result of additional information processing within the retail outlet leads to more useful marketing strategies than does viewing such purchases as random or illogical.[78] This approach allows the marketer to utilize knowledge of the target market, its motives, and the perception process to increase sales of specific items. The Point-of-Purchase Advertising International (POPAI) uses the following definitions regarding in-store purchases:

- *Specifically planned.* A specific brand or item decided on before visiting the store and purchased as planned.

| FIGURE 17-4 | Supermarket Decisions: Two-Thirds Are Made In-Store |

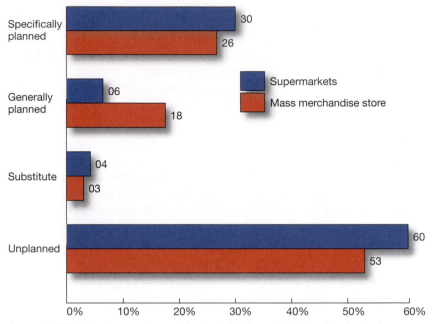

Source: *The 1995 POPAI Consumer Buying Habits Study* (Washington, DC, Point-of-Purchase Institute, www.popai.com, 1995 ©), p. 18.

- *Generally planned.* A prestore decision to purchase a product category such as vegetables but not the specific item.
- *Substitute.* A change from a specifically or generally planned item to a functional substitute.
- *Unplanned.* An item bought that the shopper did not have in mind on entering the store.
- *In-store decisions.* The sum of generally planned, substitute, and unplanned purchases.

Unplanned purchases as defined above can be further subdivided into two categories—reminder purchases and impulse purchases. A *reminder purchase* would occur when a consumer notices Band-Aids in a store and remembers that she is almost out at home.[79] An **impulse purchase** would occur when a consumer sees a candy bar in the store and purchases it with little or no deliberation as the result of a sudden, powerful urge to have it.[80]

Figure 17-4 and Table 17-3 illustrate the extent of purchasing (in the United States and Canada) that is not specifically planned. It reveals that consumers make most item or brand decisions *after* entering the store. Interestingly, high levels of in-store decision making have also been found in the U.K. (76 percent), France (76 percent), Belgium (69 percent), Holland (80 percent), Australia (70 percent), and Brazil (88 percent).[81] *Can you explain differences in terms of cultural values?*

As a consequence, marketers not only must strive to position their brand in the target market's evoked set but also must attempt to influence the in-store and online decisions of their potential consumers. Retailers not only must attract consumers to their outlets but should structure the purchasing environment in a manner that provides maximum encouragement for unplanned purchases, particularly of high-margin items.[82] The appropriate way to do this would depend on the type of unplanned purchase associated with the product category.

TABLE 17-3

In-Store Purchase
Behavior

Product	Specifically Planned	Generally Planned	+	Substituted	+	Unplanned	=	In-Store Decisions
Total study average*	30%	61%		4%		60%		70%
Hair care*	23	4		5		68		77
Magazines/newspapers*	11	3		1		84		89
Oral hygiene products*	30	5		5		61		71
Automotive oil*	21	—		—		79		79
Tobacco products*	32	6		—		61		68
Coffee*	42	5		6		47		58
First-aid products*	7	10		—		83		93
Cereal*	33	9		6		52		67
Soft drinks*	40	3		5		51		60
Mixers	23	6		4		68		77
Fresh fruits, vegetables*	67	7		1		25		33
Cold remedies†	28	35		19		18		72
Toothpaste/toothbrushes†	38	31		16		15		62
Antacids/laxatives†	39	37		12		12		61
Facial cosmetics†	40	34		11		15		60

Sources: *1995 POPAI Consumer Buying Habits Study* (Englewood, NJ: Point-of-Purchase Advertising Institute, 1995); †*1992 POPAI/Horner Canadian Drug Store Study* (Englewood, NJ: Point-of-Purchase Advertising Institute, 1992).

The Sales Impact of Shelf-Based Point-of-Purchase Materials   **FIGURE 17-5**

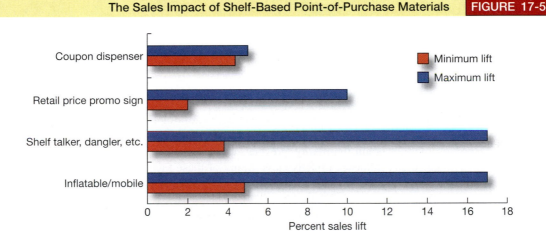

Source: *2001 POPAI P-O-P Measures UP: Learnings from the Supermarket Class of Trade Study* (Washington, DC, Point-of-Purchase Advertising International, www.Popai.com).

We now turn our attention to some of the strategies that manufacturers and retailers can use to influence in-store and online decisions.

Point-of-Purchase Materials

Point-of-purchase (P-O-P) materials are common in the retailing of many products, and the impact these materials have on brand sales can be substantial. Recent research by POPAI examined the sales increase or "lift" generated by the addition of various types of P-O-P materials in supermarkets.[83] They examined both store-shelf and product-display materials. Shelf-based materials are placed in the main shelf for the product category and include price signage, coupon dispensers, shelf talkers, and dangling signage. Product display materials are those included with product displays located at end of aisle (end caps), on the store floor, etc. Figure 17-5 provides a visual representation of the lift provided by four different shelf-based P-O-P materials.

Point-of-purchase
displays are effec-
tive across cultures.

Courtesy Federation of Swiss Milk Producers.

Courtesy Matsushita Electric Works, Ltd.

This figure demonstrates that the effectiveness of P-O-P materials can vary substantially. Effectiveness can also vary across brands and products. Factors such as frequency of promotion, brand familiarity, prevalence of certain types of P-O-P, and extent of P-O-P change can influence effectiveness. Many of these factors relate to the ability to capture consumer attention (Chapter 8). Consider the following comment from a POPAI report:

> When consumers visit the main shelf and the same types of P-O-P advertisements are presented from week to week and brand-to-brand, they appear to be less receptive to the message.[84]

Thus, the relative prevalence of price promotion signs and coupon dispensers may help to explain why they provide less lift than do other approaches. Despite variability across type, category, and brand, P-O-P materials are an important and increasingly measurable in-store influence.[85] Illustration 17-8 shows two successful point-of-purchase displays from different cultures.

Price Reductions and Promotional Deals

Price reductions and promotional deals (coupons, multiple-item discounts, and gifts) are generally accompanied by the use of some point-of-purchase materials. Therefore, the relative impact of each is sometimes not clear.[86] Nonetheless, there is ample evidence that in-store price reductions affect decision making and choice.[87] The general pattern, observed in the United States, the United Kingdom, Japan, and Germany, is a sharp increase in sales when the price is first reduced, followed by a return to near-normal sales over time or after the price reduction ends.[88]

Why Do So Many Retail Prices End in 99?

Retail prices typically end just below a round number (a number ending in one or more zeros), such as $24.95 rather than $25.00 or $2.49 rather than $2.50.[89] Having the last two digits (the rightmost digits) be 99 is particularly popular for lower-priced goods, with 95 being more common for higher-priced items. Why? Even numbers are probably easier to remember and compare, and adding the cost of several items together is certainly simpler with round numbers.

Two theoretical explanations have been advanced, and both have received support in empirical studies. Both are probably valid but for different consumers or situations. The first and most supported explanation is the "left-to-right" theory. Multidigit numbers are processed left-to-right. As we saw in Chapters 9, 15, and 16, consumers frequently seek to minimize or at least reduce their information processing efforts. Therefore, they may ignore or pay little attention to the rightmost digits in a price. The number of digits receiving limited attention depends on the total number present.

Thus, a price of $.99 may be interpreted as $.90, but one of $119.99 may be viewed as $110. To the extent that such a mechanism operates, marketers using 99 or 95 rightmost digits are receiving the highest possible price relative to the price consumers will perceive.

Another explanation is the sale-association theory. While many prices end in 99 normally, it is even more common for reduced-price items. Therefore, consumers may associate (low-involvement learning) a 99 ending price as a sale or bargain price.

Critical Thinking Questions

1. Is it ethical for retailers to set prices with 99 as rightmost digits knowing that consumers will interpret the price to be lower than it is?

2. Why don't consumers simply round up to the next larger number? Wouldn't it be easier to think of $9.99 as $10.00 rather than as $9.90 or even $9.00?

Sales increases in response to price reductions come from four sources:[90]

1. Current brand users may buy ahead of their anticipated needs (stockpiling). Stockpiling often leads to increased consumption of the brand, since it is readily available.
2. Users of competing brands may switch to the reduced price brand. These new brand buyers may or may not become repeat buyers of the brand.
3. Nonproduct category buyers may buy the brand because it is now a superior value to the substitute product or to "doing without."
4. Consumers who do not normally shop at the store may come to the store to buy the brand.

High-quality brands tend to benefit more than brands from lower quality tiers when prices are reduced, and they suffer less when prices are raised.[91]

As discussed earlier under price advertising, consumers judge store quality and image in part on the basis of the number and nature of reduced price items in the store.[92] Therefore, retailers need to carefully consider their sale price policies in light of both the sales of the discounted items and the impact these discounts will have on the store image. In addition, shoppers who purchase a large number of items at one time prefer stores with "everyday low prices"—all items in the store have relatively low prices but few are reduced beyond that level ("on sale")—to stores with somewhat higher standard prices but many sale items.[93] Is a shirt from an Internet retailer priced at $24.95 plus $5.00 shipping and handling a better or worse deal than the same shirt priced at $29.95 with shipping and handling free? Consumers tend to perceive the former to be a better deal than the latter. Research has shown that *partitioned prices* (the first scenario above) produced greater demand and a lower recalled total cost than the combined price (the second scenario).[94]

Consumer Insight 17-1 explores an additional retailing pricing phenomenon, the tendency to end prices in 99.

Retail Web site designs should create an appropriate atmosphere or feelings as well as provide content and functionality.

Courtesy RedEnvelope, Inc.

Outlet Atmosphere

Store atmosphere is influenced by such attributes as lighting, layout, presentation of merchandise, fixtures, floor coverings, colors, sounds, odors, and the dress and behavior of sales and service personnel (see Chapter 13).

Atmosphere is referred to as **servicescape** when describing a service business such as a hospital, bank, or restaurant.[95] **Atmospherics** is the process managers use to manipulate the physical retail or service environment to create specific mood responses in shoppers. Internet retailers also have *online atmospheres* that are determined by graphics, colors, layout, content, entertainment features, interactivity, tone, and so forth.[96] *What type of atmosphere is portrayed in the Red Envelope site as shown in Illustration 17-9?*

A store's atmosphere affects the shopper's mood/emotions and willingness to visit and linger. It also influences the consumer's judgments of the quality of the store and the store's image.[97] Similarly, recent research shows that online atmospherics influence shopping behavior. For example, one study found that designing a Web site to elicit affective responses such as pleasure and arousal leads to increased willingness to browse.[98] Another study found that when a Web site offers restricted navigation, negative emotions (due to consumers' felt loss of control) occur which lead to Web site avoidance.[99] Perhaps more important, positive mood/emotion induced while in the store or Web site increases satisfaction with the store or Web site, which can produce repeat visits and store loyalty.[100]

A major component of store atmosphere is the *number, characteristics, and behavior of other customers*.[101] Crowding must be considered since it can generate negative emotions and reduce browsing. And training staff how to appropriately deal with unruly customers is critical since the behaviors of other customers can influence the overall atmosphere.[102]

Music can have a major impact on the store environment (see Chapter 13). It can influence the time spent in the store or restaurant, the mood of the consumer, and the overall impression of the outlet.[103] However, it is important to match the music to the target audience. As shown below, baby boomers responded positively to classic rock music in a supermarket setting, but older adults did not:[104]

	Baby Boomers			Older Adults		
	Classic Rock	**Big Band**	**Top 40**	**Classic Rock**	**Big Band**	**Top 40**
Items purchased	31	11	15	4	12	14
Dollars spent	34	21	21	16	17	24
Shopping minutes	27	16	29	21	30	28

Marketers are also beginning to investigate the impact of *odors* on shopping behaviors (see Chapter 13).[105] Early studies suggest that odors can have a positive effect on the shopping experience, particularly if they are consistent with other aspects of the atmosphere such as the music being played.[106] However, like music, odor preference varies across customers, so caution must be used to ensure that the aroma is not offensive to target customers.[107]

Figure 17-6 illustrates the way store atmosphere influences shopper behavior. Several things in this figure are noteworthy. First, the physical environment interacts with individual characteristics. Thus, an atmosphere that would produce a favorable response in teenagers might produce a negative response in older shoppers. Second, store atmosphere influences sales personnel and customers, whose interactions then influence each other. Finally, while this model focuses on store-based retailing, emerging research will continue to advance our understanding of online atmospherics.

Stockouts

Stockouts, *the store being temporarily out of a particular brand,* obviously affect a consumer's purchase decision. The customer then must decide whether to buy the same brand but at another store, switch brands, delay the purchase and buy the desired brand later at the same store, or forgo the purchase altogether. In addition, the consumer's verbal behaviors and attitudes may change. Table 17-4 summarizes the impacts that a stockout situation may have.

TABLE 17-4

Impact of a Stockout Situation

I. Purchase Behavior
  A. Purchase a substitute size, brand or product at the original store. The substitute brand/product may or may not replace the regular brand in future purchases.
  B. Delay the purchase until the brand is available at the original store.
  C. Forgo the purchase entirely.
  D. Purchase the desired brand at a second store. All of the items initially desired may be purchased at the second store or only the stockout items. The second store may or may not replace the original store on future shopping trips.

II. Verbal Behavior
  A. The consumer may make negative comments to peers about the original store.
  B. The consumer may make positive comments to peers about the substitute store.
  C. The consumer may make positive comments to peers about the substitute brand/product.

III. Attitude Shifts
  A. The consumer may develop a less favorable attitude toward the original store.
  B. The consumer may develop a more favorable attitude toward the substitute store.
  C. The consumer may develop a more favorable attitude toward the substitute brand/product.

FIGURE 17-6   Store Atmosphere and Shopper Behavior

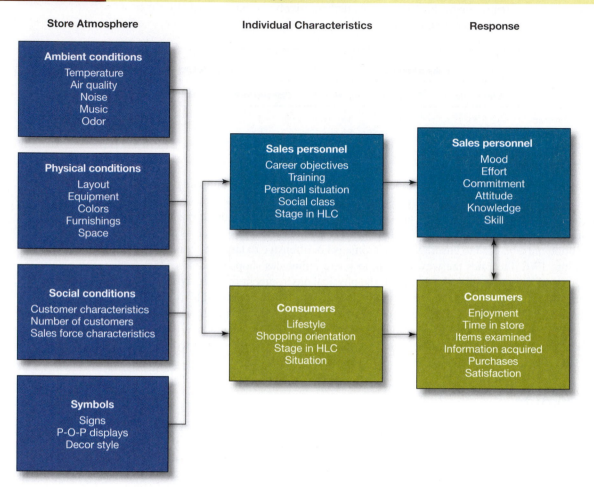

Source: Adapted from M. J. Bitner, "Servicescapes," *Journal of Marketing,* April 1, 1992, pp. 57–71. Published by the American Marketing Association; reprinted with permission.

Three types of perceived costs affect the likely response of a consumer to a stockout.[108] *Substitution costs* refer to the reduction in satisfaction the consumer believes a replacement size, brand, or product will provide. This is a function of the consumer's commitment or loyalty to the preferred brand and the perceived similarity of potential substitutes.[109] *Transaction costs* refer to the mental, physical, time, and financial costs of purchasing a substitute product or brand. *Opportunity costs* are the reduction in satisfaction associated with forgoing or reducing consumption of the product. How these costs will be perceived and thus which of the outcomes, or combinations of outcomes, in Table 17-4 will occur depends on the particular consumer, product, and situation.

Web Site Functioning and Requirements

Recent research suggests that only 5 percent of those who visit an online outlet make a purchase.[110] One reason for this is that consumers often research online then buy in traditional stores. However, losses also occur during the online shopping process, when consumers who planned to make a purchase do not. One study finds that 57 percent of consumers abandon their online shopping carts without making a purchase, with the overall result being that for every $1 spent online, roughly $4 is left in abandoned shopping carts.[111] Various Web site factors can hamper online purchasing including security issues, return policies, and desired items being out of stock.[112] DoubleClick found the following reasons for shopping cart abandonment:[113]

Additional charges (e.g., shipping) too high	84%
Buying process (complicated, confusing, technical difficulties)	44
Changed mind	32
Desired item not available	24
Inaccurate initial product description	5

Copyright: DoubleClick, Inc., 2005.

Clearly, there are many areas in which the design and functioning of retail Web sites can be improved. Obviously, managing shipping charges is important and companies are responding. Amazon offers Amazon.com *Prime,* a member-based program where consumers pay a fixed annual fee for free second-day shipping and reduced-rate overnight. Complexity of the online buying process is also a problem. As a consequence online retailers such as T.J. Maxx are adopting simplified shopping-cart technology that streamlines the online checkout process.[114] Security is an ongoing concern. Various Web site strategies are possible as we discussed earlier. In addition, credit card companies are getting into the game with *single-use numbers*. Consumers who were offered and adopted this controlled payment option increased their online purchases between 50 and 200 percent.[115]

Sales Personnel

For most low-involvement purchases in the United States, self-service is predominant. As purchase involvement increases, the likelihood of interaction with a salesperson also increases. Thus, most studies of effectiveness in sales interactions have focused on high-involvement purchases such as insurance, automobiles, or industrial products. There is no simple explanation for effective sales interactions. Instead, the effectiveness of sales efforts is influenced by the interactions of

* The salesperson's knowledge, skill, and authority.
* The nature of the customer's buying task.
* The customer–salesperson relationship.

Thus, specific research is required for each target market and product category to determine the optimal personnel selling strategy.

Consider the following shopping experience:

> I also had lousy service in the store. The sales guy seemed to be trying to sell me the cheaper shoe to get me out the door. . . . The thing that irritated me was that I thought I was a fairly knowledgeable shopper and I thought that they should understand some of these things. . . . They weren't very knowledgeable. . . . I got the impression they didn't like their jobs.[116]

Is this consumer likely to return to this outlet? Will he recommend it to his friends? It is clear that knowledgeable, helpful salespeople enhance the shopping experience, while those who are not have the opposite effect.

In the online context, marketers are testing so-called "pop-up" sales clerks that interact with customers as they shop on their Web site. HP uses a pop-up chat box that will connect the customer with a live customer service representative if he or she wishes. This is new territory and marketers would be wise to proceed with caution given the potential annoyance factor.[117]

PURCHASE

Once the consumer has selected the brand and retail outlet, he or she must complete the transaction. This involves what is normally called *purchasing* or *renting* the product. In traditional retail environments, this was straightforward and did not generally stop or delay purchases, with the possible exception of major and more complex purchases such as a home or car. However, as we saw earlier, many consumers starting to make an online purchase quit without making one for a variety of reasons. Increasing the percentage of potential purchasers who actually purchase is a major challenge for most online retailers.

Credit plays a major role in consumer purchases, and fingerprint technology is being tested as we saw earlier. And, research indicates that the ability to pay by credit card rather than cash substantially increases consumers' willingness to pay and the amount they purchase.[118] Thus, it may be to the retailer's advantage to encourage credit card use even though it must pay a percentage of these sales to the credit card companies.

Businesses need to simplify the actual purchase as much as possible. This involves strategies as simple as managing the time spent in line at the checkout register to more complex operations such as computerized credit checks to minimize credit authorization time. Many businesses appear to overlook the fact that the actual purchase act is generally the last contact the consumer will have with the store on that trip. Although first impressions are important, so are final ones. Store personnel need to be not only efficient at this activity but also helpful and personable. And online retailers need to minimize the complexity, hassle, and stress involved.

SUMMARY

Consumers generally must select outlets as well as products. There are three general ways these decisions can be made: (1) *simultaneously;* (2) *item first, outlet second;* or (3) *outlet first, item second.* Both the manufacturer and the retailer must be aware of the decision sequence used by their target market, as it will have a major impact on their marketing strategy.

Internet retailing and other forms of in-home retailing including catalogs are increasingly important retail outlets. While store-based retailing continues to dominate in terms of overall sales, consumers increasingly use in-home options such as the Internet and catalogs in combination with retail stores in what is known as *multi-channel shopping.* Retailers often operate in vari-

ous formats (catalog, retail store, and Internet) to leverage the benefits that consumers derive from each.

The decision process used by consumers to select a retail outlet is the same as the process described for selecting a brand. The only difference is in the nature of the evaluative criteria used. Retail outlet *image* is an important evaluative criterion. Store-based image and online retailer image are both important, although the dimensions consumers use to judge them vary. *Store brands* can both capitalize on a store's image and enhance, or detract from, it. *Outlet location and size* are important with closer and larger outlets generally being preferred over more distant and smaller ones. Consumer characteristics such as *perceived risk* and *shopping orientation* are also important determinants of outlet choice.

While in a retail outlet, consumers often purchase a brand or product that differs from their plans before entering. Such purchases are referred to as *unplanned purchases*. Most of these decisions are the result of additional information processing induced by in-store or online stimuli. However, some are impulse purchases made with little or no deliberation in response to a sud-den, powerful urge to buy or consume the product. Such variables as *point-of-purchase displays, price reductions, outlet atmosphere, Web site design, sales personnel,* and brand or product *stockouts* can have a major impact on sales patterns.

Once the outlet and brand have been selected, the consumer must acquire the rights to the item. This often involves credit, but fingerprint approaches are also being tested.

KEY TERMS

Atmospherics 622
External reference price 613
Impulse purchase 618
In-home shopping 600
Internal reference price 613
Multi-channel shopper 608
Online privacy concerns 603

Perceived risk 615
Reference price 613
Retail attraction (gravitation) model 613
Servicescape 622
Shopping orientation 616
Spillover sales 611

Stockouts 623
Store atmosphere 622
Store brands 610
Store image 609
Unplanned purchases 617

INTERNET EXERCISES

1. Visit three Internet retail outlets and evaluate them on the dimensions of Internet retailer image discussed in the text. Are there other dimensions or components you might add? Explain.

2. Visit two Internet retailers for the same product category. Evaluate the outlet atmosphere of each. What, if anything, in the atmosphere provides the following?
   a. Encouragement for impulse purchases
   b. Nonpurchase reasons for visiting

   c. Risk reduction
   d. Service
   e. Fun

3. Visit two online retailers and select an item of interest. Go through the checkout process up to the last step (don't buy it unless you want it!). What aspects of the process at each store might cause a user to stop before completing the purchase?

DDB LIFE STYLE STUDY™ DATA ANALYSES

1. Based on the DDB Tables 1B through 7B, what most characterizes those who feel *making purchases over the Internet with a credit card is too risky?* What are the online marketing implications?

2. Using the DDB Tables 1B through 7B, describe the characteristics of those who have purchased event (concert/play/sports) tickets online. What is the role of the *tech savvy* trait in terms of this behavior?

3. What most characterizes someone who frequently uses mail order catalogs to make purchases (DDB Tables 1A through 7A)? Does there seem to be any relationship between characteristics of Internet buyers (Question 2) and catalog buyers? Explain.

4. What are the characteristics of heavy *store brand* buyers (Tables 1A through 7A)? What are the retail implications?

REVIEW QUESTIONS

1. The consumer faces the problems of both what to buy and where to buy it. How do these two types of decisions differ?

2. How does the sequence in which the brand/outlet decision is made affect the brand strategy? The retailer strategy?

3. How is the retail environment changing?

4. Describe Internet retailing.

5. What is *multi-channel shopping* and what implications does it hold for retailer strategy?

6. What is meant by *online privacy concern?* Why is it a particularly important issue for online shoppers?

7. Describe the eight segments of online shoppers.

8. What is a *store image,* and what are its dimensions and components?

9. Describe *Internet retailer image* and compare/contrast it with *store image.*

10. What is a *store brand?* How do retailers use store brands?

11. What key decisions do retailers make with respect to retail price advertising?

12. What is meant by the term *spillover sales?* Why is it important?

13. How does the size of and distance to a retail outlet affect store selection and purchase behavior?

14. How is store choice affected by the *perceived risk* of a purchase?

15. What is meant by *social risk?* How does it differ from *economic risk?*

16. What is a *shopping orientation?*

17. Describe six motivation-based shopping orientations of college students.

18. What is meant by an *in-store purchase decision?* Why is it important?

19. What is meant by an *impulse purchase?* Why is it important?

20. Once in a particular retail outlet, what in-store and/or online characteristics can influence brand and product choice? Give an example of each.

21. Describe the impact of point-of-purchase displays on retail sales.

22. Describe the impact of price reductions and deals on retail sales.

23. What is meant by *store atmosphere? Online atmosphere?* How do they affect consumer behavior?

24. What is a *servicescape?*

25. Why do consumers planning to make a purchase at an online outlet often fail to do so?

26. What are frequent problems consumers encounter while shopping online?

27. What can happen in response to a *stockout?*

DISCUSSION QUESTIONS

28. Name two product categories for which the brand is generally selected first and the outlet second, two for which the reverse is true, and two for which these decisions are generally made simultaneously. Justify your selections. How should marketing strategy differ across these products?

29. Does the image of a retail outlet affect the image of the brands it carries? Do the brands carried affect the image of the retail outlet?

30. What challenges face multi-channel retailers in managing their image across channel?

31. Respond to the questions in Consumer Insight 17-1.

32. How are social and economic risks associated with the following products likely to affect the outlet choice behavior of consumers? How would the perception of these risks differ by consumer? Situation?
    a. Nice sweaters
    b. Athletic shoes (for running)
    c. Wine (as a gift)
    d. Hairdresser
    e. Mountain bike
    f. Mouthwash
    g. DVD player
    h. Movie for a date

33. Describe an appropriate strategy for an online store such as Target for each of the motivation-based shopping orientations described in the text (pages 616–617).

34. Describe an appropriate strategy for an online store such as J. Crew for each of the eight online shopper types described in the text (pages 604–605).

35. The motivation-based shopping orientations described in the text were developed using a small sample of students. Do you think these are accurate descriptions of the shopping orientations of students on your campus? How should they be modified?

36. How should retailer strategies to encourage unplanned purchases differ depending on the type of unplanned purchase generally associated with the product category?

37. What in-store characteristics could traditional retailers use to enhance the probability of purchase among individuals who visit a store? Describe each factor in terms of how it should be used, and describe its intended effect on the consumer for the following products:
    a. Cologne
    b. Ice cream
    c. Coffee after a meal
    d. Flowers from a supermarket
    e. Herbal supplements
    f. Motor oil

38. What site characteristics could online retailers use to enhance the probability of purchase among individuals who visit their sites? Describe each factor in terms of how it should be used, and describe its intended effect on the consumer for the following products:
    a. Dorm furniture from Target.com
    b. Electronics from Amazon.com
    c. Laptop from HP.com
    d. Backpack from REI.com
    e. Apparel from JCPenney.com
    f. Cosmetics from Macys.com
    g. Tools from Sears.com

39. What type of store atmosphere is most appropriate for each of the following retailer types? Why?
    a. Bookstore serving college students
    b. Cosmetic section of Sears
    c. Auto dealership service department
    d. Consumer electronics
    e. Mercedes automobiles
    f. Inexpensive furniture
    g. Thai food restaurant

40. Repeat Question 39 (except for c and g) for online retailers.

41. How would you respond to a stockout of your preferred brand of the following? What factors other than product category would influence your response?
    a. Suntan lotion
    b. Cereal
    c. Deodorant
    d. Dress shirt/blouse
    e. Perfume/aftershave lotion
    f. Soft drink

APPLICATION ACTIVITIES

42. Describe the current state of Internet retailing.

43. Pick a residential area in your town and develop a gravitational model for (a) nearby supermarkets or (b) shopping malls. Conduct telephone surveys to test the accuracy of your model.

44. Develop a questionnaire to measure the image of the following. Have 10 other students complete these questionnaires. Discuss the marketing implications of your results.
    a. Target
    b. Amazon.com
    c. Papa Johns
    d. Local coffee shop
    e. eBay
    f. Wal-Mart
    g. Banana Republic

45. Have 10 students on your campus describe their shopping orientations in terms of animals as discussed in the section of the text on motivation-based shopping orientations. Combine your descriptions with those of two other students. Do any patterns emerge? Do they match those described in the text? How would you explain the differences?

46. For several of the products listed in Table 17-3, interview several students not enrolled in your class and ask them to classify their last purchase as specially planned, generally planned, substitute, or unplanned. Then combine your results with those of your classmates to obtain an estimate of student behavior. Compare student behavior with the behavior shown in Table 17-3 and discuss any similarities or differences.

47. Arrange with a local retailer (convenience store, drugstore, or whatever) to temporarily install a point-of-purchase display. Then set up a procedure to unobtrusively observe the frequency of evaluation and selection of the brand before and while the display is up. Describe your findings.

48. Visit two retail stores selling the same type of merchandise and prepare a report on their use of P-O-P materials. Explain any differences.

49. Interview the manager of a drug, department, or grocery store on their views of P-O-P materials and price advertising.

50. Develop an appropriate questionnaire and construct a new version of Table 17-2, using products relevant to college students. What are the marketing implications of this table?

51. Determine, through interviews, the general shopping orientations of students on your campus. What are the marketing implications of your findings?

52. Interview 10 students on your campus and determine their attitudes toward and use of the Internet and online shopping. Place each into one of the eight online shopper segments described in the text. Do they fit into these segments? Combine your results with those of four other students. What do you conclude?

REFERENCES

1. S. Schubert, "The Size-atron," *Business 2.0,* June 2005, p. 2c; and information from the Intellifit's Web site.

2. P. Bhatnagar, "Supermarkets Strike Back," *CNNMoney* (online), May 2, 2005.

3. W. M. Bulkeley, "Cash, Credit–or Prints?" *The Wall Street Journal,* October 11, 2004, pp. B1 and B4.

4. See, e.g., M. Laaksonen, "Retail Patronage Dynamics," *Journal of Business Research,* September 1993, pp. 3–174.

5. R. R. Brand and J. J. Cronin, "Consumer-Specific Determinants of the Size of Retail Choice Sets," *Journal of Services Marketing,* no. 1 (1997), pp. 19–38.

6. S. Sherman, "Will the Information Superhighway Be the Death of Retailing," *Fortune,* April 18, 1994, p. 17.

7. *E-Commerce in the U.S.* (New York: eMarketer, Research Report, May 2005).

8. J. L. McQuivey et al., "On-Line Retail Strategies," *The Forrester Report,* November 1998, p. 5. See also, A. Bhatnagar, S. Misra, and H. R. Rao, "On Risk, Convenience, and Internet Shopping Behavior," *Communications of the Association for Computing Machinery* 43 (2000), pp. 98–105.

9. E. Yoh et al. "Consumer Adoption of the Internet," *Psychology & Marketing,* December 2003, pp. 1095–1118.

10. *Forrester Research Projects U.S. eCommerce to Hit Nearly $230 Billion in 2008* (Cambridge, MA: Forrester Research, Inc., press release, August 5, 2003).

11. *Forrester Research Projects U.S. Online Retail Sales to Top $300 Billion by 2010* (Cambridge, MA: Forrester Research, Inc., press release, August 23, 2004).

12. *Online Retail Sales, Profitability Continue Climb, According to Shop.org/Forrester Research* (Washington, DC: Shop.org, press release, May 24, 2005).

13. S. Chiger, "Consumer Shopping Survey: Part III," *Catalog Age,* November 1, 2001, pp. 1–4. See also, P. Miller, "Live from NEMOA," *Multichannel Merchant* (online), March 27, 2003.

14. "USPS Study Shows Mailed Catalogs Boost Online Spending," *directmag.com,* September 28, 2004.

15. *Why Some Consumers Don't Buy Online* (Cambridge, MA: Forrester Research, Inc., research report, 2005).

16. See, e.g., A. K. Kau, Y. E. Tang, and S. Ghose, "Typology of Online Shoppers," *Journal of Consumer Marketing* 20, no. 2 (2003), pp. 139–56.

17. P. Paul, "Mixed Signals," *American Demographics,* July 2001, pp. 45–49.

18. See S. Sayre and D. Horne, "Trading Secrets for Savings," *Advances in Consumer Research,* vol. 27, eds. S. J. Hoch and R. J. Meyer (Provo, UT: Association for Consumer Research, 2000), pp. 151–55; and J. E. Phelps, G. D'Souza, and G. J. Nowak, "Antecedents and Consequences of Consumer Privacy Concerns," *Journal of Interactive Marketing,* Autumn 2001, pp. 2–17.

19. Jupiter Media Metrix, Inc., June 2002.

20. For a description of the FTC's approach in this area and its fit with consumer concerns, see K. B. Sheehan and M. G. Hoy, "Dimensions of Privacy Concern among Online Consumers," *Journal of Public Policy & Marketing,* Spring 2000, pp. 62–73. See also J. Phelps, G. Nowak, and E. Ferrell, "Privacy Concerns and Consumer Willingness to Provide Personal Information," *Journal of Public Policy & Marketing,* Spring 2000, pp. 27–41; and K. B. Sheehan and T. W. Gleason, "Online Privacy," *Journal of Current Issues and Research in Advertising,* Spring 2001, pp. 31–41.

21. See R. Gardyn, "Swap Meet," *American Demographics,* July 2001, pp. 51–55.

22. Paul, "Mixed Signals."

23. See, e.g., A. D. Miyazaki and A. Fernandez, "Consumer Perceptions of Privacy and Security Risks for Online Shopping," *Journal of Consumer Affairs* 35, no. 1 (2001), pp. 27–44; E. B. Andrade, V. Kaltcheva, and B. Weitz, "Self-Disclosure on the Web," *Advances in Consumer Research,* vol. 29, eds S. M. Broniarczyk and K. Nakamoto (Provo, UT: Association for Consumer Research, 2002), pp. 350–53; A. D. Miyazaki and S. Krishnamurthy, "Internet Seals of Approval," *Journal of Consumer Affairs* 36, no. 1 (2002), pp. 28–49; G. R. Milne and M. J. Culnan, "Strategies for Reducing Online Privacy Risks," *Journal of Interactive Marketing,* Summer 2004, pp. 15–29; and T. B. White, "Consumer Disclosure and Disclosure Avoidance," *Journal of Consumer Psychology* 14, no. 1/2 (2004), pp. 41–51.

24. See, e.g., K.-Pin Chiang and R. R. Dholakia, "Factors Driving Consumer Intention to Shop Online," *Journal of Consumer Psychology* 13, no. 1/2 (2003), pp. 177–83.

25. L. R. Klein, "Creating Virtual Product Experiences," *Journal of Interactive Marketing,* Winter 2003, pp. 41–55; and J. Nantel, "My Virtual Model," *Journal of Interactive Marketing*, Summer 2004, pp. 73–86.

26. *Online Retail Sales, Profitability Continue Climb, According to Shop.org/Forrester Research.*

27. S. M. Kerner, "More Broadband Usage Means More Online Spending," *clickz.com,* October 8, 2004.

28. Adapted from W. R. Swinyard and S. M. Smith, "Why People (Don't) Shop Online," *Psychology & Marketing,* July 2003, pp. 567–97. For an alternative typology, see A. J. Rohm and V. Swaminathan, "A Typology of Online Shoppers Based on Shopping Motivations," *Journal of Business Research* 57 (2004), pp. 748–57.

29. Kau, Tang, and Ghose, "Typology of Online Shoppers."

30. From Roper Reports Telephone Survey, August 2003.

31. See A. Z. Cuneo, "What's in Store?" *Advertising Age,* February 25, 2002, p. 1; and R. V. Kozinets et al., "Themed Flagship Brand Stores in the New Millennium," *Journal of Retailing* 78 (2002), pp. 17–29.

32. S. A. Forest, "Look Who's Thinking Small," *BusinessWeek,* May 17, 1999, pp. 67–70.

33. A. Z. Cuneo, "On Target," *Advertising Age,* December 11, 2000, p. 1.

34. K. Labich, "What It Will Take to Keep People Hanging Out at the Mall," *Fortune,* May 1995, pp. 102–6.

35. R. Gulati and J. Garino, "Getting the Right Mix of Bricks & Clicks," *Harvard Business Review,* May 2000, pp. 107–14.

36. M. Brohan, "The Top 400 Guide," *InternetRetailer.com,* June 2005.

37. The remainder of this section based on *Multi-Channel Shopping Study* (New York: DoubleClick, Research Report, January 2004).

38. See also, K. C. Gehrt and R.-N. Yan, "Situational, Consumer, and Retailer Factors Affecting Internet, Catalog, and Store Shopping," *International Journal of Retail and Distribution Management* 32, no. 1 (2004), pp. 5–18.

39. J. D. Lindquist, "Meaning of Image," *Journal of Retailing,* Winter 1974, pp. 29–38; see also M. R. Zimmer and L. L. Golden, "Impressions of Retail Stores," *Journal of Retailing,* Fall 1988, pp. 265–93.

40. H. van der Heijden and T. Verhagen, "Online Store Image," *Information and Management* 41 (2004), 609–17. See also, J. R. Coyle and E. Thorson, "The Effects of Progressive Levels of Interactivity and Vividness in Web Marketing Sites," *Journal of Advertising,* Fall 2001, pp. 65–77; C. Page and E. Lepkowska-White, "Web Equity," *Journal of Consumer Marketing* 19, no. 3 (2002), pp. 231–48; E. J. Johnson, S. Bellman, and G. L. Lohse, "Cognitive Lock-In and the Power Law of Practice," *Journal of Marketing,* April 2003, pp. 62–75; and P. Katerattanakul and K. Siau, "Creating a Virtual Store Image," *Communications in ACM,* December 2003, pp. 226–32.

41. W. R. Darden and B. J. Badin, "Exploring the Concept of Affective Quality," *Journal of Business Research,* February 1994, p. 106.

42. See N. Sirohi, E. W. McLaughlin, and D. R. Witink, "A Model of Consumer Perceptions and Store Loyalty Intentions for a Supermarket Retailer," *Journal of Retailing,* no. 2 (1998), pp. 223–45.

43. See S. Burton, D. R. Lichtenstein, R. G. Netemeyer, and J. A. Garretson, "A Scale for Measuring Attitude toward Private

Label Products," *Journal of the Academy of Marketing Science,* Fall 1998, pp. 293–306.

44. See M. Corstjens and R. Lal, "Building Store Loyalty through Store Brands," *Journal of Marketing Research,* August 2000, pp. 281–91.

45. P. S. Richardson, A. K. Jain, and A. Dick, "Household Store Brand Proneness," *Journal of Retailing,* no. 2 (1996), pp. 159–85. For a conflicting view, see K. L. Ailawadi, S. A. Neslin, and K. Gegdenk, "Pursuing the Value-Conscious Consumer," *Journal of Marketing,* January 2001, pp. 71–89.

46. *The Double Dividend* (New York: Newspaper Advertising Bureau Inc., February 1977).

47. F. J. Mulhern and D. T. Padgett, "The Relationship between Retail Price Promotions and Regular Price Purchases," *Journal of Marketing,* October 1995, pp. 83–90. For similar results, see S. Burton, D. R. Lichtenstein, and R. G. Netemeyer, "Exposure to Sales Flyers and Increased Purchases in Retail Supermarkets," *Journal of Advertising Research,* September 1999, pp. 7–14.

48. See, e.g., V. Severin, J. J. Louviere, and A. Finn, "The Stability of Retail Shopping Choices over Time and across Countries," *Journal of Retailing* 77 (2001), pp. 185–202.

49. See, e.g., P. Chandon, B. Wansink, and G. Laurent, "A Benefit Congruency Framework of Sales Promotion Effectiveness," *Journal of Marketing,* October 2000, pp. 65–81.

50. See, e.g., van der Heijden and Verhagen, "Online Store Image."

51. A. Ansari and C. F. Mela, "E-Customization," *Journal of Marketing Research,* May 2003, pp. 131–45.

52. See C. Janiszewski and D. R. Lichtenstein, "A Range Theory of Price Perception," *Journal of Consumer Research,* March 1999, pp. 353–68.

53. See R. A. Briesch, L. Krishnamurthi, and T. Mazumdar, "A Comparative Analysis of Reference Price Models," *Journal of Consumer Research,* September 1997, pp. 202–14; R. W. Niedrich, S. Sharma, and D. H. Wedell, "Reference Price and Price Perceptions," *Journal of Consumer Research,* December 2001, pp. 339–54; and P. K. Kopalle, and J. Lindsey-Mullikin, "The Impact of External Reference Price on Consumer Price Expectations," *Journal of Retailing* 79 (2003), pp. 225–36. For a different approach, see K. B. Monroe and A. Y. Lee, "Remembering versus Knowing," *Journal of the Academy of Marketing Science,* Spring 1999, pp. 207–25.

54. See V. Kumar, K. Karande, and W. J. Reinartz, "The Impact of Internal and External Reference Prices on Brand Choice," *Journal of Retailing,* no. 3 (1998), pp. 401–26.

55. T. A. Suter and S. Burton, "Reliability and Consumer Perceptions of Implausible Reference Prices in Retail Prices," *Psychology & Marketing,* January 1996, pp. 37–54; M. S. Yadav and K. Seiders, "Is the Price Right?" *Journal of Retailing,* no. 3 (1998), pp. 311–29; and L. D. Compeau and D. Grewal, "Comparative Price Advertising," *Journal of Public Policy & Marketing,* Fall 1998, pp. 257–73. See also, M. J. Barone, K. C. Manning, and P. W. Miniard, "Consumer Response to Retailers' Use of Partially Comparative Pricing," *Journal of Marketing,* July 2004, pp. 37–47.

56. See A. Biswas et al., "Consumer Evaluation of Reference Price Advertisements," *Journal of Public Policy & Marketing,* Spring 1999, pp. 52–65.

57. T. B. Heath, S. Chatterjee, and K. R. France, "Mental Accounting and Changes in Price," *Journal of Consumer Research,* June 1995, pp. 90–97.

58. See S.-F. S. Chen, K. B. Monroe, and Y.-C. Lou, "The Effects of Framing Price Promotion Messages on Consumers' Perceptions and Purchase Intentions," *Journal of Retailing,* no. 3 (1998), pp. 353–72; and M. R. Stafford and T. F. Stafford, "The Effectiveness of Tensile Pricing Tactics in the Advertising of Services," *Journal of Advertising,* Summer 2000, pp. 45–60.

59. See A. Biswas and S. Burton, "Consumer Perceptions of Tensile Price Claims in Advertisements," *Journal of the Academy of Marketing Science,* Summer 1993, pp. 217–30; K. N. Rajendran and G.-J. Tellis, "Contextual and Temporal Components of Reference Price," *Journal of Marketing,* January 1994, pp. 22–39; and D. Grewal, H. Marmorstein, and A. Sharma, "Communicating Price Information through Semantic Cues," *Journal of Consumer Research,* September 1996, pp. 148–55.

60. I. Sinha and M. F. Smith, "Consumers' Perceptions of Promotional Framing of Price," *Psychology & Marketing,* March 2000, pp. 257–75.

61. See D. Simester, "Signaling Price Image Using Advertised Prices," *Marketing Science* 14, no. 2 (1995), pp. 166–88; and J. Srivastave and N. Lurie, "A Consumer Perspective on Price-Matching Refund Policies," *Journal of Consumer Research,* September 2001, pp. 296–307.

62. G. S. Bobinski, Jr., D. Cox, and A. Cox, "Retail 'Sale' Advertising, Perceived Retailer Credibility, and Price Rationale," *Journal of Retailing,* no. 3 (1996), pp. 291–306.

63. See, e.g., Severin, Louviere, and Finn, "The Stability of Retail Shopping Choices over Time and across Countries."

64. See I. Simonson, "The Effect of Product Assortment on Buyer Preferences," and R. E. Stassen, J. D. Mittelstaedt, and R. A. Mittelstaedt, "Assortment Overlap," both in *Journal of Retailing* 75, no. 3 (1999), pp. 347–70 and 371–86, respectively.

65. C. S. Craig, A. Ghosh, and S. McLafferty, "Models of the Retail Location Process: A Review," *Journal of Retailing,* Spring 1984, pp. 5–33.

66. See D. R. Bell, T.-H. Ho, and C. S. Tang, "Determining Where to Shop," *Journal Marketing Research,* August 1998, pp. 352–69.

67. See B. G. C. Dellaert et al., "Investigating Consumers' Tendency to Combine Multiple Shopping Purposes and Destinations," *Journal Marketing Research,* May 1998, pp. 177–88.

68. See P. R. Messinger and C. Narasimhan, "A Model of Retail Formats Based on Consumers' Economizing on Shopping Time," *Marketing Science,* no. 1 (1997), pp. 1–23.

69. A. Chaudhuri, "Product Class Effects on Perceived Risk," *International Journal of Research in Marketing,* May 1998, pp. 157–68; and R. Batra and I. Sinha, "Consumer-Level Factors Moderating the Success of Private Label Brands," *Journal of Retailing* 76, no. 2 (2000), pp. 175–91.

70. Based on V. Prasad, "Socioeconomic Product Risk and Patronage Preferences of Retail Shoppers," *Journal of Marketing,* July 1975, p. 44.

71. G. R. Dowling and R. Staelin, "A Model of Perceived Risk and Intended Risk-Handling Activity," *Journal of Consumer Research,* June 1994, pp. 119–34; L. W. Turley and R. P. LeBlanc,

"An Exploratory Investigation of Consumer Decision Making in the Service Sector," *Journal of Services Marketing* 7, no. 4 (1993), pp. 11–18; and J. B. Smith and J. M. Bristor, "Uncertainty Orientation," *Psychology & Marketing,* November 1994, pp. 587–607.

72. Settle, Alreck, and McCorkle, "Consumer Perceptions of Mail/Phone Order Shopping Media"; C. R. Jasper and S. J. Ouellette, "Consumers' Perception of Risk and the Purchase of Apparel from Catalogs," *Journal of Direct Marketing,* Spring 1994, pp. 23–36; and D. Biswas and A. Biswas, "The Diagnostic Role of Signals in the Context of Perceived Risks in Online Shopping," *Journal of Interactive Marketing,* Summer 2004, pp. 30–45.

73. See also J. C. Sweeney, G. N. Soutar, and L. W. Johnson, "The Role of Perceived Risk in the Quality-Value Relationship," *Journal of Retailing* 75, no. 1 (1999), pp. 75–105.

74. See K. L. Wakefield and J. Baker, "Excitement at the Mall," *Journal of Retailing* 74, no. 4 (1998), pp. 515–39; H. McDonald, P. Darbyshire, and C. Jevons, "Shop Often, Buy Little," *Journal of Global Marketing* 13, no. 4 (2000), pp. 53–71; J. A. F. Nicholls et al., "Inter-American Perspectives from Mall Shoppers," *Journal of Global Marketing* 15, no. 1 (2001), pp. 87–103; B. Jin and J.-O. Kim, "Discount Store Retailing in Korea," *Journal of Global Marketing* 15, no. 2 (2001), pp. 81–107; and J. L. Joines, C. W. Scherer, and D. A. Scheufele, "Exploring Motivations for Consumer Web Use and Their Implications for E-commerce," *Journal of Consumer Marketing* 20, no. 2 (2003), pp. 90–108.

75. See M. A. Eastlick and R. A. Feinberg, "Gender Differences in Mail-Catalog Patronage Motives," *Journal of Direct Marketing,* Spring 1994, pp. 37–44; "The Call of the Mall," *EDK Forecast,* October 1994, pp. 1–3; "Black, Hip, and Primed to Shop," *American Demographics,* September 1996, pp. 52–58; and J. A. F. Nicholls et al., "The Seven Year Itch?" *Journal of Consumer Marketing* 19, no. 2 (2002), pp. 149–65.

76. D. N. Hassay and M. C. Smith, "Fauna, Foraging and Shopping Motives," *Advances in Consumer Research,* vol. 23, eds. K. P. Corfman and J. G. Lynch (Provo, UT: Association for Consumer Research, 1996), pp. 510–15. Reprinted with permission of the Association for Consumer Research.

77. See N. Paden and R. Stell, "Using Consumer Shopping Orientations to Improve Retail Web Site Design," *Journal of Professional Services Marketing* 20, no. 2 (2000), pp. 73–85; and K. E. Reynolds and S. E. Beatty, "A Relationship Customer Typology," *Journal of Retailing* 75, no. 4 (1999), pp. 509–23.

78. See J. E. Russo and F. Lecleric, "An Eye Fixation Analysis of Choice Processes for Consumer Nondurables," *Journal of Consumer Research,* September 1994, pp. 274–90.

79. See L. G. Block and V. G. Morwitz, "Shopping Lists as an External Memory Aid for Grocery Shopping," *Journal of Consumer Psychology* 8, no. 4 (1999), pp. 343–75.

80. See D. W. Rook and R. J. Fisher, "Normative Influences on Impulsive Buying Behaviors," *Journal of Consumer Research,* December 1995, pp. 305–13; R. Puri, "Measuring and Modifying Consumer Impulsive Buying Behavior," *Journal of Consumer Psychology* 5, no. 2 (1996), pp. 87–113; U. M. Dholakia, "Temptation and Resistance," *Psychology & Marketing,*

November 2000, pp. 955–82; and R. F. Baumeister, "Yielding to Temptation," *Journal of Consumer Research,* March 2002, pp. 670–76.

81. R. Liljenwall, "Global Trends in Point-of-Purchase Advertising," in *The Power of Point-of-Purchase Advertising,* ed. R. Liljenwall (Washington, DC: Point-of-Purchase Advertising International, 2004), p. 191.

82. See S. E. Beatty and M. E. Ferrell, "Impulse Buying," *Journal of Retailing,* no. 2 (1998), pp. 169–91; and M. Koufaris, "Applying the Technology Acceptance Model and Flow Theory to Online Consumer Behavior," *Information Systems Research,* June 2002, pp. 205–23.

83. *P-O-P Measures Up* (Washington, DC: Point-of-Purchase Advertising Institute, 2001).

84. Ibid.

85. See *POPAI/Horner Drug Store Study* (Englewood, NJ: Point-of-Purchase Advertising Institute, 1992); A. J. Greco and L. E. Swayne, "Sales Response of Elderly Consumers to P-O-P Advertising," *Journal of Advertising Research,* September 1992, pp. 43–53; *POPAI/Kmart/Procter & Gamble Study of P-O-P Effectiveness* (Englewood, NJ: Point-of-Purchase Advertising Institute, 1993); *P-O-P Measures Up*; and T. Lee, "Experts Say Point-of-Purchase Advertising Can Influence Shoppers' Choices," *Knight Ridder Tribune Business News,* January 19, 2002. For an exception, see C. S. Areni, D. F. Duhan, and P. Kiekeer, "Point-of-Purchase Displays, Product Organization, and Brand Purchase Likelihoods," *Journal of the Academy of Marketing Science,* Fall 1999, pp. 428–41.

86. See E. T. Anderson and D. I. Simester, "The Role of Sale Signs," *Marketing Science,* no. 2 (1998), pp. 139–55.

87. See, e.g., G. A. Taylor, "Coupon Response in Services," *Journal of Retailing* 77 (2001), pp. 139–51; C. M. Heilman, K. Nakamoto, and A. G. Rao, "Pleasant Surprises," *Journal of Marketing Research,* May 2002, pp. 242–52; and D. M. Hardesty and W. O. Bearden, "Consumer Evaluations of Different Promotion Types and Price Presentations," *Journal of Retailing* 79 (2003), pp. 17–25.

88. A. S. C. Ehrenberg, K. Hammond, and G. J. Goodhardt, "The After-Effects of Price-Related Consumer Promotions," *Journal of Advertising Research,* July 1994, pp. 11–21; and P. Papatla and L. Krishnamurthi, "*Journal of Marketing Research,* February 1996, pp. 20–36.

89. Based on R. M. Schindler and T. M. Kibarian, "Increased Consumer Sales Response through Use of 99-Ending Prices," *Journal of Retailing,* no. 2 (1996), pp. 187–99; M. Stiving and R. S. Winer, "An Empirical Analysis of Price Endings with Scanner Data," *Journal of Consumer Research,* June 1997, pp. 57–67; R. M. Schindler and P. N. Kiby, "Patterns of Rightmost Digits Used in Advertised Prices," September 1997, pp. 192–201; and R. M. Schindler, "Relative Price Level of 99-Ending Prices," *Marketing Letters,* August 2001, pp. 239–47.

90. See C. F. Mela, K. Jedidi, and D. Bowman, "The Long-Term Impact of Promotions on Consumer Stockpiling Behavior," *Journal of Marketing Research,* May 1998, pp. 250–62; and J. E. Urbany, P. R. Dickson, and A. G. Sawyer, "Insights into Cross- and Within-Store Price Search," *Journal of Retailing* 76, no. 2 (2000), pp. 243–58.

91. K. Sivakumar and S. P. Raj, "Quality Tier Competition," *Journal of Marketing,* July 1997, pp. 71–84; and S. M. Nowlis and I. Simonson, "Sales Promotions and the Choice Context as Competing Influences on Consumer Decision Making," *Journal of Consumer Psychology* 9, no. 1 (2000), pp. 1–16.

92. D. Grewal, R. Krishnan, J. Baker, and N. Borin, "The Effect of Store Name, Brand Name, and Price Discounts on Consumers' Evaluations and Purchase Intentions," *Journal of Retailing,* no. 3 (1998), pp. 331–52.

93. D. R. Bell and J. M. Lattin, "Shopping Behavior and Consumer Preference for Store Price Format," *Marketing Science,* no. 1 (1998), pp. 66–88. See also R. Lal and R. Rao, "Supermarket Competition," *Marketing Science,* no. 1 (1997), pp. 60–80.

94. V. G. Morwitz, E. A. Greenleaf, and E. J. Johnson, "Divide and Prosper," *Journal of Consumer Research,* November 1998, pp. 453–63.

95. K. L. Wakefield and J. G. Blodgett, "The Effect of the Servicescape on Customers' Behavioral Intentions in Leisure Service Settings," *Journal of Services Marketing,* no. 6 (1996), pp. 45–61; and K. L. Wakefield and J. G. Blodgett, "Customer Response to Intangible and Tangible Service Factors," *Psychology & Marketing,* January 1999, pp. 51–68; and B. D. Keillor, G. T. M. Hult, and D. Kandemir, "A Study of the Service Encounter in Eight Countries," *Journal of International Marketing* 12, no. 1 (2004), pp. 9–35.

96. See C. Mathwick, N. Malhotra, and E. Rigdon, "Experiential Value," *Journal of Retailing* 77 (2001), pp. 39–56; P. D. Lynch, R. J. Kent, and S. S. Srinivasan, "The Global Internet Shopper," *Journal of Advertising Research,* May 2001, pp. 15–23; T. P. Novak, D. L. Hoffman, and A. Duhachek, "The Influence of Goal-Directed and Experiential Activities on Online Flow Experiences," *Journal of Consumer Psychology* 13, no. 1/2 (2003), pp. 3–16; and A. P. Vrechopoulos et al., "Virtual Store Layout," *Journal of Retailing* 80, no. 1 (2004), pp. 13–22.

97. E. Sherman, A. Mathur, and R. B. Smith, "Store Environment and Consumer Purchase Behavior," *Psychology & Marketing,* July 1997, pp. 361–78; and J. Baker et al., "The Influence of Multiple Store Environment Cues on Perceived Merchandise Value and Patronage Intentions," *Journal of Marketing,* April 2002, pp. 120–41.

98. S. A. Eroglu, K. A. Machleit, and L. M. Davis, "Emprical Testing of a Model of Online Store Atmospherics and Shopper Responses," *Psychology & Marketing,* February 2003, pp. 139–50. See also, S. Menon and B. Kahn, "Cross-Category Effects of Induced Arousal and Pleasure on the Internet Shopping Experience," *Journal of Retailing* 78 (2002), pp. 31–40.

99. L. Dailey, "Navigational Web Atmospherics," *Journal of Business Research* 57 (2004), pp. 795–803.

100. B. Babin and W. R. Darden, "Good and Bad Shopping Vibes," *Journal of Business Research,* March 1996, pp. 210–60; K. Chang, "The Impact of Perceived Physical Environments on Customers' Satisfaction and Return Intentions," *Journal of Professional Services Marketing* 21, no. 2 (2000), pp. 75–85; D. Grewal et al., "The Effects of Wait Expectations and Store Atmosphere Evaluations on Patronage Intentions in Service-Intensive Retail Stores," *Journal of Retailing* 79 (2003), pp. 259–68; Menon and Kahn, "Cross-Category Effects of In-

duced Arousal and Pleasure on the Internet Shopping Experience"; and Eroglu, Machleit, and Davis, "Empirical Testing of a Model of Online Store Atmospherics and Shopper Responses."

101. See K. A. Machleit, S. A. Eroglu, and S. P. Mantel, "Perceived Retail Crowding and Shopping Satisfaction," *Journal of Consumer Psychology* 9, no. 1 (2000), pp. 29–42; and K. Harris and S. Baron, "Consumer-to-Consumer Conversations in Service Settings," *Journal of Service Research,* February 2004, pp. 287–303.

102. S. J. Grove and R. P. Fisk, "The Impact of Other Customers on Service Experiences," *Journal of Retailing,* no. 1 (1997), pp. 63–85.

103. See, e.g., S. Oakes, "The Influence of Musicscape within Service Environments," *Journal of Services Marketing* 4, no. 7 (2000), pp. 539–56; J. C. Sweeney and F. Wyber, "The Role of Cognitions and Emotions in the Music-Approach-Avoidance Behavior Relationship," *Journal of Services Marketing* 16, no. 1 (2002), pp. 51–69; and C. Caldwell and S. A. Hibbert, "The Influence of Music Tempo and Musical Preference on Restaurant Patrons' Behavior," *Psychology & Marketing,* November 2002, pp. 895–917.

104. C. S. Gulas and C. D. Schewe, "Atmospheric Segmentation," in *Enhancing Knowledge Development in Marketing,* eds. R. Achrol and A. Mitchell (Chicago: American Marketing Association, 1994), pp. 325–30. Similar results are in J. D. Herrington and L. M. Capella, "Effects of Music in Service Environments," *Journal of Services Marketing,* no. 2 (1996), pp. 26–41.

105. D. J. Mitchell, B. E. Kahn, and S. C. Knasko, "There's Something in the Air," *Journal of Consumer Research,* September 1995, pp. 229–38; A. R. Hirsch, "Effects of Ambient Odors on Slot-Machine Usage in a Las Vegas Casino," *Psychology & Marketing,* October 1995, pp. 585–94; M. Wilkie, "Scent of a Market," *American Demographics,* August 1995, pp. 40–49; P. Sloan, "Smelling Trouble," *Advertising Age,* September 11, 1995, p. 1; E. R. Spangenberg, A. E. Crowley, and P. W. Henderson, "Improving the Store Environment," *Journal of Marketing,* April 1996, pp. 67–80; and P. F. Bone and P. S. Ellen, "Scents in the Marketplace," *Journal of Retailing* 75, no. 2 (1999), pp. 243–62.

106. A. S. Mattila and J. Wirtz, "Congruency of Scent and Music as a Driver of In-Store Evaluations and Behavior," *Journal of Retailing* 77, no. 2 (2001), pp. 273–89.

107. See A. M. Fiore, X. Yah, and E. Yoh, "Effects of Product Display and Environmental Fragrancing on Approach Responses and Pleasurable Experiences," *Psychology & Marketing,* January 2000, pp. 27–54.

108. K. Campo, E. Gijsbrechts, and P. Nisol, "Towards Understanding Consumer Response to Stock-Outs," *Journal of Retailing* 76, no. 2 (2000), pp. 219–42.

109. G. J. Fitzsimons, "Consumer Response to Stockouts," *Journal of Consumer Research,* September 2000, pp. 249–67.

110. *E-Commerce Site Trend Report* (New York: DoubleClick, Research Report, November 2004).

111. Ibid.

112. S. L. Wood, "Remote Purchase Environments," *Journal of Marketing Research,* May 2001, pp. 157–69; information

reported by Pacific Online, Inc., www.pon.net/service/ecommerce/etailors, July 30, 2002; J. Goldeen, "Consumers More Likely to Stay Loyal to Stores with Easy Return Policy," *Knight Ridder Tribune Business News,* December 25, 2003, p. 1; and V. Vara, "Tabs on Tech," *The Wall Street Journal Online,* November 8, 2004.

113. *Holiday Multi-Channel Retail Study* (New York: DoubleClick, Research Presentation, July 15, 2005).

114. M. Prince, "Online Retailers Turn to New Shopping Carts Drive Sales," *The Wall Street Journal Online,* November 10, 2004.

115. "Single-use Numbers Increase Confidence, Boost Online Spending, Study Says," *InternetRetailer.com,* February 3, 2005.

116. B. B. Stern, G. J. Thompson, and E. J. Arnould, "Narrative Analysis of a Marketing Relationship," *Psychology & Marketing,* no. 3 (1998), pp. 195–214.

117. M. Higgins, "Pop-Up Sales Clerks," *The Wall Street Journal,* April 15, 2004, pp. D1, D2.

118. D. Prelec and D. Simester, "Always Leave Home without It," *Marketing Letters*, February 2001, pp. 5–12; and D. Soman, "Effects of Payment Mechanism on Spending Behavior," *Journal of Consumer Research,* March 2001, pp. 460–74.

© NFL.com

18

Postpurchase Processes, Customer Satisfaction, and Customer Commitment

■ Many firms now send consumers e-mail newsletters on a regular basis. The purpose of these letters is less to generate immediate sales than it is to build a relationship with customers. For example, Procter & Gamble sponsors a Web site called HomeMadeSimple.com that sends subscribers a monthly e-mail newsletter designed to help consumers achieve "easy living." According to a P&G spokesperson, "The ultimate goal is to build strong relationships with our customers."

The NFL has launched a similar program to supplement its Web site. It hopes to build a more personal relationship with its fans through a weekly e-mail newsletter. The newsletters provide a preview of the team's next game, information on trades, cuts, injuries, and so forth. There are also links to various NFL and team sites.

According to the NFL, "the e-mail newsletters are the most direct, most customized and the most critical to fan development." The NFL.com newsletter is customized by team and then further tailored to match the individual fan's specific interests.

The newsletter is not interactive: "We haven't gone to the full community model where fans can interact through message boards. But we are able to communicate with them by watching what they are interested in. We know what pieces of the newsletter they're clicking on. It allows us to better tailor the merchandising to the individual fan." Subscribers are informed when they register that they will be monitored to allow for customized information. They are invited to visit and update their profiles.[1]

FIGURE 18-1   **Postpurchase Consumer Behavior**

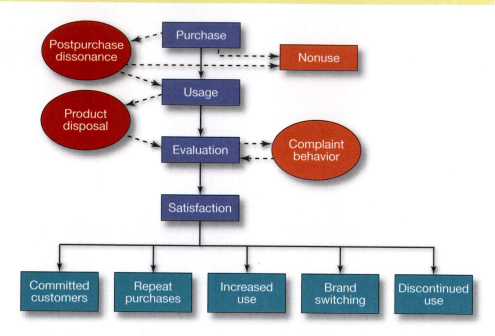

Customer relationship programs are common in American firms. The objective of such programs is to increase the satisfaction, commitment, and retention of key customers. In this chapter, we will examine the postpurchase processes that produce customer satisfaction and commitment and the marketing strategies these processes suggest.

Figure 18-1 illustrates the relationships among the postpurchase processes. As the figure indicates, some purchases are followed by a phenomenon called *postpurchase dissonance*. This occurs when a consumer doubts the wisdom of a purchase he or she has made. Other purchases are followed by nonuse. The consumer keeps or returns the product without using it. Most purchases are followed by product use, even if postpurchase dissonance is present. Product use often requires the disposition of the product package or the product itself. During and after use, the purchase process and the product are evaluated by the consumer. Unsatisfactory evaluations may produce complaints by those consumers. Appropriate responses by the firm may reverse the initial dissatisfaction among those who complained. The result of all these processes is a final level of satisfaction, which in turn can result in a loyal, committed customer, one who is willing to repurchase, or a customer who switches brands or discontinues using the product category.

POSTPURCHASE DISSONANCE

I still like it [a dining room set] a whole lot better than what we used to have. But I think if we had taken longer we would have gotten more precisely what we wanted. I mean we got a great deal. You couldn't get that for that price, so I am happy with the money part of it, but some days I wish we had spent more and gotten something a bit different.[2]

This is a common consumer reaction after making a difficult, relatively permanent decision. Doubt or anxiety of this type is referred to as **postpurchase dissonance.**[3] Figure 18-1 indicates that some, but not all, consumer purchase decisions are followed by postpurchase dissonance. The probability of a consumer experiencing postpurchase dissonance, as well as the magnitude of such dissonance, is a function of

- *The degree of commitment or irrevocability of the decision.* The easier it is to alter the decision, the less likely the consumer is to experience dissonance.
- *The importance of the decision to the consumer.* The more important the decision, the more likely dissonance will result.
- *The difficulty of choosing among the alternatives.* The more difficult it is to select from among the alternatives, the more likely the experience and magnitude of dissonance. Decision difficulty is a function of the number of alternatives considered, the number of relevant attributes associated with each alternative, and the extent to which each alternative offers attributes not available with the other alternatives.
- *The individual's tendency to experience anxiety.* Some individuals have a higher tendency to experience anxiety than do others. The higher the tendency to experience anxiety, the more likely the individual will experience postpurchase dissonance.

Dissonance occurs because making a relatively permanent commitment to a chosen alternative requires one to give up the attractive features of the unchosen alternatives. This is inconsistent with the desire for those features. Thus, nominal and most limited decision making will not produce postpurchase dissonance, because these decisions do not consider attractive features in an unchosen brand that do not also exist in the chosen brand. For example, a consumer who has an evoked set of three brands of detergent could consider them to be equivalent on all relevant attributes except price and, therefore, always purchases the least expensive brand. Such a purchase would not produce postpurchase dissonance.

Because most high-involvement purchase decisions involve one or more of the factors that lead to postpurchase dissonance, these decisions often are accompanied by dissonance. And since dissonance is unpleasant, consumers generally attempt to avoid or reduce it.

Decisions that involve giving up some or all of a desirable feature to obtain a slightly more desirable feature often generate negative emotions while the decision is being made. These negative emotions may be sufficient to cause the consumer to avoid or delay the decision (I'll just keep this car a while longer).[4] This suggests that firms marketing products such as automobiles, vacation homes, expensive vacation packages, and similar products train their salespeople to help minimize these negative emotions. Advertising that emphasizes the fun and positive emotions of the decision outcome and incentive programs that encourage consumers to continue with the purchase process could also be effective.

Consumers may also use decision rules designed to minimize the experience of postpurchase doubt. Such a rule or tactic would focus on minimizing the regret or doubt that a decision might produce rather than maximizing the value or benefits of the decisions.[5] The following choice exemplifies this rule:

> And I think that fear was one reason that we bought the General Motors van because we were afraid that if we bought the Ford . . . Well, there is a feeling that if something is too much less, then you start asking yourself why is it that much less. . . . We had read how Ford uses more automatization in their manufacturing and we knew that it cost them less to make a car than GM. So we knew that there was a real reason for why theirs is so much cheaper, but you keep asking yourself, "Am I going to kick myself for this? Am I going to wish that I spent more and gotten the other one?"[6]

After the purchase is made, the consumer may utilize one or more of the following approaches to reduce dissonance:

- Increase the desirability of the brand purchased.
- Decrease the desirability of rejected alternatives.

Advertisements for high-involvement purchase items can serve to confirm the wisdom of a purchase as well as influence new purchasers.

© 2002 BMW of North America, LLC. Used with permission. The BMW name and logo are registered trademarks.

- Decrease the importance of the purchase decision.
- Reverse the purchase decision (return the product before use).

Although postpurchase dissonance may be reduced by internal reevaluations, searching for additional external information that serves to confirm the wisdom of a particular choice is also a common strategy. Naturally, information that supports the consumer's choice acts to bolster confidence in the correctness of the purchase decision.

The consumer's search for, or heightened receptiveness to, information *after* the purchase greatly enhances the role that advertising and follow-up sales efforts can have. To build customer confidence in choosing their brand, many marketers of consumer durables such as major appliances and automobiles send recent purchasers direct-mail materials designed in large part to confirm the wisdom of the purchase. Local retailers can place follow-up calls to make sure the customer is not experiencing any problems with the car or appliance and to reduce any dissonance. Obviously e-mail is an option as well. For example, Johnston & Murphy (high-end footwear and accessories) sends follow-up e-mails thanking customers for their recent purchase, pointing them to their Web site, and soliciting feedback. Such communications can go a long way in reducing dissonance and increasing satisfaction.

Many advertisements help recent purchasers confirm the wisdom of their purchase as well as attract new purchasers. Imagine a consumer who just purchased a BMW 5 Series after a lengthy and difficult decision process involving it and several other options. At this point he or she would be very receptive to positive information about the 5 Series and likely to read the ad shown in Illustration 18-1.

A concept very similar to postpurchase dissonance is **consumption guilt.** Consumption guilt occurs when *negative emotions or guilt feelings are aroused by the use of a product or a service.* A person driving a large car may experience some negative feelings due to concern over resource utilization and pollution. The example below illustrates consumption guilt quite clearly:

> I have to count calories much more than I did before. I still buy a sundae once in a while but the joy of eating ice cream will probably forever be connected with guilt over eating something so unhealthy. When I think about it, I realize that most products make me feel good and bad at the same time.[7]

Marketers of products whose target markets might experience consumption guilt need to focus on validating the consumption of the product. They need to find ways to give the consumer permission or a rationale for indulging in that consumption act.[8]

As Consumer Insight 18-1 indicates, consumers also engage in "what if" thinking after and sometimes before purchases.

What If?

Counterfactual thinking refers to imagining the outcome if a different decision had been made in the past.[9] These thoughts are generally in the form of a conditional proposition such as "If I had a convertible instead of this sedan, I would be a lot happier now." Typically the antecedent (*if*) refers to an action or decision by an individual. The consequence (*then*) generally describes a state of being in evaluative terms (*happy*). Counterfactual thinking can be negative (I'd be better off had I made a different choice) or positive (I'd be worse off had I made a different choice). Such thoughts are different from cognitive dissonance in that the antecedent—a convertible in this case—might not have been considered at the time of the original decision.

Prefactual thinking is the same as counterfactual except it occurs before a decision is made. A common form of such thinking is "If I buy this notebook computer today and it goes on sale somewhere else next week, I'll really regret it." Research shows that this particular type of purchase barrier can be removed by price guarantees. These guarantees not only reduce the negative effect such thinking produces but tend to increase long-term satisfaction even if they were not exercised.

Marketers often encourage counterfactual and prefactual thinking. State lotteries are one industry that frequently uses ads that directly encourage people to imagine what they would do with the money had they won (counterfactual) or if they win (prefactual) the lottery. Likewise, resorts and cruise lines encourage prefactual thinking about the pleasures of using their services. Firms seek to reassure purchasers of major items that they did indeed make an optimal decision, which decreases negative counterfactual thinking.

Critical Thinking Questions

1. What ethical issues, if any, are there with state lotteries encouraging counterfactual and prefactual thinking about winning the lottery?

2. Why is counterfactual thinking so common among consumers (it is common)?

PRODUCT USE AND NONUSE

Product Use

Most consumer purchases involve nominal or limited decision making and therefore arouse little or no postpurchase dissonance. Instead, the purchaser or some other member of the household uses the product without first worrying about the wisdom of the purchase. And as Figure 18-1 shows, even when postpurchase dissonance occurs, it is still generally followed by product use.

Marketers need to understand how consumers use their products for a variety of reasons. Understanding both the functional and symbolic ways in which a product is used can lead to more effective product designs. For example, Nike uses observation of basketball players at inner-city courts to gain insights into desired functional and style features. One insight gained through these observations is that the process of putting on and tying/buckling basketball shoes before a match is full of meaning and symbolism. In many ways, it is the equivalent of a knight putting on armor before a jousting match or combat. Nike has used this insight in several aspects of its shoe designs.

Use innovativeness refers to *a consumer using a product in a new way.*[10] Marketers who discover new uses for their products can greatly expand sales. Two products famous for this are Arm & Hammer's baking soda and WD-40. Arm & Hammer discovered that consumers were using its baking soda for a variety of noncooking uses such as deodorizing refrigerators. It now advertises such uses. WD-40, a lubricant, is renowned for the wide array of applications that consumers suggest for it, including as an additive to fish bait and for removing gum from a carpet.

Many firms attempt to obtain relevant information on product usage via surveys using standard questionnaires. Such surveys can lead to new-product development, indicate new uses or markets for existing products, or indicate appropriate communications themes. For example, *what marketing strategies are suggested by the following uses of a microwave oven?*[11]

Use	Times Per Month
Reheat food	11.4
Cook food	2.6
Cook frozen food (TV dinner)	2.3
Boil water (for coffee)	2.1
Defrost food	1.6

Surveys can provide useful information, but observation, depth interviews, and case studies often produce deeper insights:

- During the summer, several Chicago organizations offer "architectural boat cruises" on the Chicago River. They compete on the architectural credentials of their guides, the sites shown, and the boats used. One company did a standard survey and virtually all the respondents checked "interest in architecture" as a "very important" or "extremely important" reason for taking the cruise. However, depth research with 50 passengers showed that architecture was a relatively minor reason for their being there. Most of the Chicago residents were there as a means to entertain out-of-town guests on a nice day. This finding resulted in very different positioning and advertising themes for the sponsoring firm.
- A few years back, a number of upscale frozen gourmet dinner entrées were introduced with great expectations—which none achieved. Researchers observed the frozen food cases that still sold the product and found that, while most consumers ignored it, a few bought substantial quantities. Interviews with these consumers revealed that they were not using them for home meals but rather were preparing them in the office microwave for lunch. They stated that good restaurants were too slow, inconvenient, and expensive for lunch and fast-food places lacked quality and nutrition. This led to opportunities to reposition a line for office-based lunch consumption.[12]

Marketers can frequently take advantage of the fact that the use of one product may require or suggest the use of other products (see Illustration 18-2). Consider the following product sets: houseplants and fertilizer, bikes and helmets, cameras and carrying cases, sport coats and ties, and dresses and shoes. In each case, the use of the first product is made easier, more enjoyable, or safer by the use of the related product. Retailers can promote such items jointly, display them together, or train their sales personnel to make relevant complementary sales.

Stringent product liability laws and aggressive civil suits also are forcing marketing managers to examine how consumers use their products. These laws have made firms responsible for harm caused by products *not only when the product is used as specified by the manufacturer but in any reasonably foreseeable use of the product*. Thus, the manufacturer must design products with both the primary purpose *and* other potential uses in mind. This requires substantial research into how consumers actually use products.

When marketers discover confusion about the proper way to use a product, it is often to their advantage to teach consumers how to use it and engage in marketing communications that increase the chances of proper use. After all, how many consumers blame themselves when a product failure occurs due to their own failure to follow usage instructions?[13] At other times, a firm can gain a competitive advantage by redesigning the product so that it is easier to use properly.

Product Nonuse

As Figure 18-1 indicates, not all purchases are followed by product use. **Product nonuse** occurs when a consumer actively acquires a product that is not used or used only sparingly relative to its potential use.[14]

For many products and most services, the decisions to purchase and to consume are made simultaneously. A person who orders a meal in a restaurant is also deciding to eat the meal at that time. However, a decision to purchase food at a supermarket requires a second decision to prepare and consume the food. The second decision occurs at a different point in time and in a different environment from the first. Thus, nonuse can occur because the situation or the purchaser changes between the purchase and the potential usage occasion. For example, a point-of-purchase display featuring a new food item shown as part of an appealing entrée might cause a consumer to imagine an appropriate usage situation and to purchase the product. However, without the stimulus of the display, the consumer may not remember the intended use or may just never get around to it. Nonuse situations such as the following are common:[15]

Courtesy Unione Industriali Pastai Italiani.

ILLUSTRATION 18-2

Marketers can leverage the fact that certain products are used together by developing product mixes consisting of complementary products.

> Wok—"I wanted to try and cook stirfry, but I didn't take time out to use it."
>
> Skirt—"My ingenious idea was that I'd lose a few pounds and fit into the size 4 rather than gain a few and fit into the size 6. Obviously, I never lost the weight, so the skirt was snug."
>
> Gym membership—"Couldn't get in the groove to lift."

In such cases, the consumer has wasted money and the marketer is unlikely to get repeat sales or positive referrals. Many such purchases are difficult for the marketer to correct after the purchase. In other cases, consumers would have used the product if reminded or motivated at the proper time. In the last example above, good records would indicate that this member was not using the gym. A personal letter, e-mail, or telephone invitation to come in might be enough to get this person started.

Campbell Soup Company has conducted research that shows that most homes have several cans of Campbell's soup on hand. Therefore, a major goal of its ads is to encourage people to consume soup at the next appropriate meal through such tactics as radio commercials aired prior to mealtime. Since consumers have the product available, the task is not to encourage purchase but to motivate near-term consumption.

The ad in Illustration 18-3 would serve to encourage both the purchase of Campbell's soup and the near-term consumption of soup already on hand.

The division between the initial purchase decision and the decision to consume is particularly strong with catalog and online purchases. In effect, two decisions are involved

ILLUSTRATION 18-3

Advertisements can encourage purchases, consumption of previously purchased items, or both.

Courtesy Campbell Soup Company.

in these purchases—the initial decision to order the product, and a second decision to keep or return the item when it is received. Not only is it likely that several days will have passed between the two decisions, but substantially different information is available at the "keep or return" decision point. In particular, consumers can physically touch, try on, or otherwise experience the item.

Obviously, online and catalog retailers want to maximize the percentage of items kept rather than returned. Intuitively, one might think that a strict return policy would accomplish this. However, such a policy might also reduce the number of initial orders. In fact, a liberal return policy appears to maximize initial orders and may also minimize returns. Such a policy reduces perceived risk and signals higher quality (surrogate indicator), which increases initial orders. Consumers also tend to perceive items ordered under liberal return policies as having higher quality after receiving them, which reduces returns.[16]

DISPOSITION

Disposition of the product or the product's container may occur before, during, or after product use. Or for products that are completely consumed, such as an ice cream cone, no disposition may be involved.

The United States produces several hundred million tons of household and commercial refuse a year, more than 1,500 pounds per person, not including industrial waste.[17] Many landfills are rapidly being filled. Collection and dumping costs for most urban and suburban areas continue to climb. Environmental concerns involving dioxins, lead, and mercury are growing. Clearly, disposition is a major concern for marketers.

Millions of pounds of product packages are disposed of every day. These containers are thrown away as garbage or litter, used in some capacity by the consumer, or recycled. Creating packages that utilize a minimal amount of resources is important for economic reasons as well as being a matter of social responsibility. Many firms are responding to this issue, as the examples below illustrate:

- Rubbermaid repositioned its trash barrel line to a recycling container line. The new line has four models designed to store newspapers, cans, bottles, and yard waste.
- Procter & Gamble uses recycled paper in 80 percent of its product packaging and is packaging liquid Spic and Span, Tide, Cheer, and Downy in containers made from recycled packages.

For many product categories, a physical product continues to exist even though it may no longer meet a consumer's needs. A product may no longer function physically (instrumental function) in a manner desired by a consumer. Or it may no longer provide the symbolic meaning desired by the consumer. An automobile that no longer runs is an example of instrumental function, while one that runs but is out of style is an example of symbolic function. In either case, once a replacement purchase is made, or even before the purchase, a disposition decision must be made.

Exploding demand and short product life-spans for high-tech gadgets such as cell phones, personal computers, and various other personal electronics devices is creating growing concerns over **e-waste.** Both instrumental and symbolic considerations can drive e-waste. The Environmental Protection Agency (EPA) estimates that "63 million personal computers became obsolete in 2003, potentially creating four billion pounds of e-waste."[18] Consumer and corporate solutions are necessary and evolving. For example:

- eBay has created a PC recycling program called "Rethink" which attempts to coordinate efforts across companies and the U.S. EPA, as well as increase awareness about disposal options. These include trade-ins, selling on eBay, charity donations, and so on. Their Web site http://rethink.ebay.com/ is a major source of information and a major thrust of their initiative.[19]
- Companies such as HP, Office Depot, and PrintPal are engaged in ongoing efforts related to print cartridges. For example, HP provides a self-addressed, postage paid, envelope in which you can return used ink cartridges to their recycling center. Office Depot offers discounts on new cartridges to those who bring in their used cartridges. And PrintPal offers a filler kit which allows consumers to reuse their cartridges.

Figure 18-2 illustrates the various alternatives for disposing of a product or package. Unfortunately, while "throw it away" is only one of many disposition alternatives, it is by far the most widely used by consumers. Environmental groups work hard to change these behaviors, as do some firms (see Illustration 18-4). Other firms, however, continue to use unnecessary or hard to recycle packaging and product components. Some of these same firms also spend millions of dollars campaigning against stricter laws on recycling and product/package disposition.

Product Disposition and Marketing Strategy

Why should a marketing manager be concerned about the disposition of a used product? Perhaps the best reason is the cumulative effect that these decisions have on the quality of the environment and the lives of current and future generations. However, there are also short-term economic reasons for concern. Disposition decisions affect the purchase

FIGURE 18-2   **Disposition Alternatives**

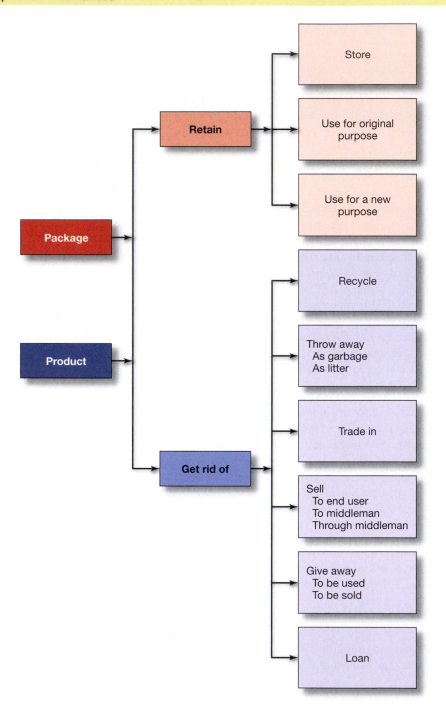

decisions of both the individual making the disposition and other individuals in the market for that product category.

There are five major ways in which disposition decisions can affect a firm's marketing strategy. First, for most durable goods consumers are reluctant to purchase a new item until they have "gotten their money's worth" from the old one. These consumers mentally

© 2002 Rechargeable Battery Recycling Corporation.

depreciate the value of a durable item over time. If the item is not fully mentally depreciated, they are reluctant to write it off by disposing of it to acquire a new one. Allowing old items to be traded in is one way to overcome this reluctance.[20]

Second, disposition sometimes must occur before acquisition of a replacement because of space or financial limitations. For example, because of a lack of storage space, a family living in an apartment may find it necessary to dispose of an existing bedroom set before acquiring a new one. Or someone may need to sell his current bicycle to raise supplemental funds to pay for a new bicycle. Thus, it is to the manufacturer's and retailer's advantage to assist the consumer in the disposition process.

Third, frequent decisions by consumers to sell, trade, or give away used products may result in a large used-product market that can reduce the market for new products. A **consumer-to-consumer sale** occurs when *one consumer sells a product directly to another with or without the assistance of a commercial intermediary.* Garage sales, swap meets, flea markets, classified ads, and postings on electronic bulletin boards are growing rapidly. And companies such as eBay and Yahoo! Auctions are flourishing due to consumer demand to buy and sell used items.

In addition to consumer-to-consumer sales, consumers may give or sell their used items to resellers. Thrift stores, featuring used clothing, appliances, and furniture, run by both commercial and nonprofit groups, are an important part of the economy.

A fourth reason for concern with product disposition is that the United States is not completely a throwaway society. Many Americans continue to be very concerned with waste and how their purchase decisions affect waste.[21] Such individuals might be willing to purchase, for example, a new vacuum cleaner if they were confident that the old one would be rebuilt and resold. However, they might be reluctant to throw their old vacuums away or to go to the effort of reselling the machines themselves. Thus, manufacturers and retailers could take steps to ensure that products are reused.

The fifth reason is that environmentally sound disposition decisions benefit society as a whole and thus the firms that are part of that society. Firms' owners and employees live and work in the same society and environment as many of their consumers. Their environment and lives are affected by the disposition decisions of consumers. Therefore, it is in their best interest to develop products, packages, and programs that encourage proper disposition decisions.

PURCHASE EVALUATION AND CUSTOMER SATISFACTION

As we saw in Figure 18-1, a consumer's evaluation of a purchase can be influenced by the purchase process itself, postpurchase dissonance, product use, and product/package disposition. Further, the outlet or the product or both may be involved in the evaluation. Consumers may evaluate each aspect of the purchase, ranging from information availability to price to retail service to product performance. In addition, satisfaction with one component, such as the product itself, may be influenced by the level of satisfaction with other components, such as the salesperson.[22] For many products, this is a dynamic process, with the factors that drive satisfaction evolving over time.[23] However, keep in mind that nominal decisions and many limited decisions are actively evaluated only if some factor, such as an obvious product malfunction, directs attention to the purchase.[24]

The Evaluation Process

A particular alternative such as a product, brand, or retail outlet is selected because it is thought to be a better overall choice than other alternatives considered in the purchase process. Whether that particular item is selected because of its presumed superior functional performance or because of some other reason, such as a generalized liking of the item or outlet, the consumer has a level of expected performance for it. The expected level of performance can range from quite low (this brand or outlet isn't very good, but it's the only one available and I'm in a hurry) to quite high.[25] As you might suspect, expectations and perceived performance are not independent. Up to a point, consumers tend to perceive performance to be in line with their expectations.[26]

While and after using the product, service, or outlet, the consumer will perceive some level of performance. This perceived performance level could be noticeably above the expected level, noticeably below the expected level, or at the expected level. As Table 18-1 indicates, satisfaction with the purchase is primarily a function of the initial performance expectations and perceived performance relative to those expectations.[27]

Table 18-1 shows that an outlet or brand whose performance confirms a low-performance expectation generally will result in neither satisfaction nor dissatisfaction but rather with what can be termed *nonsatisfaction*. That is, the consumer is not likely to feel disappointment or engage in complaint behavior. However, this purchase will not reduce the likelihood that the consumer will search for a better alternative the next time the problem arises.

A brand whose perceived performance falls below expectations generally produces dissatisfaction. If the discrepancy between performance and expectation is sufficiently large, or if initial expectations were low, the consumer may restart the entire decision process. Most likely, he or she will place an item performing below expectations in the

TABLE 18-1

Expectations,
Performance, and
Satisfaction

Perceived Performance Relative to Expectation	Expectation Level	
	Below Minimum Desired Performance	**Above Minimum Desired Performance**
Better	Satisfaction*	Satisfaction/Commitment
Same	Nonsatisfaction	Satisfaction
Worse	Dissatisfaction	Dissatisfaction

*Assuming the perceived performance surpasses the minimum desired level.

inept set (see Chapter 15) and no longer consider it. In addition, the consumer may complain or initiate negative word-of-mouth communications.

When perceptions of product performance match expectations that are at or above the minimum desired performance level, satisfaction generally results. Likewise, performance above the minimum desired level that exceeds a lower expectation tends to produce satisfaction. Satisfaction reduces the level of decision making the next time the problem is recognized; that is, a satisfactory purchase is rewarding and encourages one to repeat the same behavior in the future (nominal decision making). Satisfied customers are also likely to engage in positive word-of-mouth communications about the brand.

Product performance that exceeds expected performance will generally result in satisfaction and sometimes in commitment. Commitment, discussed in depth in the next section, means that the consumer is enthusiastic about a particular brand and is somewhat immune to actions by competitors.

Table 18-1 focuses on only the chosen alternative. However, the evaluation of the chosen alternative is somewhat dependent on the quality of the set of alternatives from which it was selected. A clearly superior choice may be held to lower standards than one that was nearly equal to one or more unchosen alternatives.[28] Other situational factors such as mood also affect how individuals evaluate products and services,[29] as do individual characteristics[30] and the general shopping environment.[31]

The need to develop realistic consumer expectations poses a difficult problem for the marketing manager. For a brand or outlet to be selected, the consumer must view it as superior on the relevant combination of attributes. Therefore, the marketing manager naturally wants to emphasize its positive aspects. If such an emphasis creates expectations in the consumer that the item cannot fulfill, a negative evaluation may occur. Negative evaluations can produce brand switching, unfavorable word-of-mouth communications, and complaint behavior. Thus, the marketing manager must balance enthusiasm for the product with a realistic view of the product's attributes.

Determinants of Satisfaction and Dissatisfaction   Because performance expectations and actual performance are major factors in the evaluation process, we need to understand the dimensions of product and service performance. A major study of the reasons customers switch service providers found competitor actions to be a relatively minor cause. Most customers did not switch from a satisfactory provider to a better provider. Instead, they switched because of perceived problems with their current service provider. The nature of these problems and the percentage listing each as a reason they changed providers follow (the percentages sum to more than 100 because many customers listed several reasons that caused them to switch):[32]

- *Core service failure* (44 percent)—mistakes (booking an aisle rather than the requested window seat), billing errors, and service catastrophes that harm the customer (the dry cleaners ruined my wedding dress).

- *Service encounter failures* (34 percent)—service employees were uncaring, impolite, unresponsive, or unknowledgeable.
- *Pricing* (30 percent)—high prices, price increases, unfair pricing practices, and deceptive pricing.
- *Inconvenience* (21 percent)—inconvenient location, hours of operation, waiting time for service or appointments.
- *Responses to service failures* (17 percent)—reluctant responses, failure to respond, and negative responses (it's your fault).
- *Attraction by competitors* (10 percent)—more personable, more reliable, higher quality, and better value.
- *Ethical problems* (7 percent)—dishonest behavior, intimidating behavior, unsafe or unhealthy practices, or conflicts of interest.
- *Involuntary switching* (6 percent)—service provider or customer moves, or a third-party payer such as an insurance company requires a change.

Other studies have found that waiting time has a major impact on evaluations of service. Consumers have particularly negative reactions to delays over which they believe the service provider has control and during which they have little to occupy their time.[33] *What are the marketing strategy implications of these results?*

Other research has found that negative performance on a feature such as waiting time or ease of use has a stronger effect on satisfaction than does positive performance on that same feature.[34] This suggests that both products and services focus on meeting expectations across all relevant features before maximizing performance on a few.

Not surprisingly, the nature and extent of personal contact with customers in service encounters are of critical importance in determining customer satisfaction. Although extended, personalized customer contact is expensive, it is very effective at increasing satisfaction and repeat purchase intentions.[35] However, increasingly services are delivered by self-service technologies such as ATMs and online stores. A recent study found the following dissatisfaction-causing incidents:[36]

Incident Type	Example
Technology failure	The ATM broke down. Kept my card. I had to have the card reissued.
Service design flaw	I did not realize that some ATM machines limit how much you can get out. The machine did not tell me I went over my limit for the day. It just spit my card back out so I kept trying . . .
Process failure	After a month passed from placing my original order, I e-mailed the customer service center at Disney with my order confirmation number. They had lost my order.
Technology design flaw	I was trying to order books from a book club online. The system was confusing, and I ordered two copies of the same title without knowing it.
Customer failure	I was attempting to get money from an ATM and couldn't remember my number. I was leaving for Japan in an hour and it took my card.

Many firms now guarantee their services. These guarantees can range from inclusive and general—"Satisfaction guaranteed"—to specific in terms of coverage and pay out—"Delivery in 30 minutes or it's free." Such service guarantees can increase expected performance levels and patronage—but can also increase costs.[37]

For many products, there are two dimensions to performance: instrumental, and expressive or symbolic. **Instrumental performance** relates *to the physical functioning of the product.* **Symbolic performance** relates to *aesthetic or image-enhancement performance.*

For example, the durability of a sport coat is an aspect of instrumental performance, whereas styling represents symbolic performance. Complete satisfaction requires adequate performance on both dimensions. However, for at least some product categories such as clothing "Dissatisfaction is caused by a failure of instrumental performance, while complete satisfaction also requires the symbolic functions to perform at or above the expected levels."[38]

In addition to symbolic and instrumental performance, products also provide affective performance. **Affective performance** is *the emotional response that owning or using the product or outlet provides.*[39] It may arise from the instrumental or symbolic performance or from the product itself; for example, a suit that produces admiring glances or compliments may produce a positive affective response. Or the affective performance may be the primary product benefit, such as for an emotional movie or novel.

We are just beginning to understand the factors that lead to satisfaction with online retailers. One study found that convenience, site design, and financial security are the dominant factors. These are illustrated by the following statements from focus groups:[40]

> It is easy to browse for books online. There is only a select group of authors that I read and I want to read everything they write. . . . I can give them the name of the author and a list will pop up (convenience, satisfaction).
>
> It seems to take forever to navigate down far enough into the site to find what I'm looking for. And frankly, I've gotten really tired of the advertising (site design, dissatisfaction).
>
> I don't like giving my credit card to someone online. They keep it on file. I don't like the thought of someone having my card number on file (financial security, dissatisfaction).

Another study found that Web site design (including adequate product information and selection), reliability of order fulfillment, privacy and financial security, and customer service can play a role. In addition, some factors were more important for some consumers than others. For example, privacy/security was more important for frequent buyers and customer service was more important for buyers than browsers.[41] Finally, while these studies examined U.S. online shopping, a study of German consumers finds similar drivers of satisfaction with online retailers.[42]

DISSATISFACTION RESPONSES

Figure 18-3 illustrates the major options available to a dissatisfied consumer.[43] The first decision is whether or not to take any external action. By taking no action, the consumer decides to live with the unsatisfactory situation. This decision is a function of the importance of the purchase to the consumer, the ease of taking action,[44] the consumer's existing level of overall satisfaction with the brand or outlet,[45] and the characteristics of the consumer involved.[46] It is important to note that even when no external action is taken, the consumer is likely to have a less favorable attitude toward the store or brand.

Consumers who take action in response to dissatisfaction generally pursue one or more of five alternatives. As Figure 18-3 indicates, the most favorable of these alternatives from a company's standpoint is for consumers to complain to them. This at least gives the company a chance to resolve the problem. Many times, however, consumers do not complain to the company, but instead take actions such as switching brands, engaging in negative word-of-mouth (WOM), and so on.

Consumers are satisfied with the vast majority of their purchases. Still, because of the large number of purchases they make each year, most individuals experience dissatisfaction with some of their purchases. For example, one study asked 540 consumers if they

FIGURE 18-3   **Dissatisfaction Responses**

could recall a case in which one or more of the grocery products they normally purchase were defective. They recalled 1,307 separate unsatisfactory purchases.

These purchases produced the following actions (the study did not measure negative word-of-mouth actions such as warning friends):

- 25 percent of these unsatisfactory purchases resulted in brand switching.
- 19 percent caused the shopper to stop buying the products.
- 13 percent led to an in-store inspection of future purchases.
- 3 percent produced complaints to the manufacturer.
- 5 percent produced complaints to the retailer.
- 35 percent resulted in the item being returned.

In a similar study of durable goods, 54 percent of the dissatisfied customers said they would not purchase the brand again (brand switching), and 45 percent warned their friends (negative WOM) about the product.[47]

As we discussed in Chapter 7, WOM is a critical factor in consumer behavior. Consumers trust WOM more than many other sources and, therefore, tend to rely on it heavily when making decisions. Unfortunately for companies, when it comes to WOM, there appears to be an asymmetry—that is, dissatisfaction yields more WOM than does satisfaction. One estimate puts the ratio at 2 to 1, with consumers telling twice as many people about a negative product or service experience than a positive one.[48]

One of the reasons for the asymmetry in WOM is the motivational force behind the emotions surrounding dissatisfaction, which can range from disappointment to frustration to rage. The results clearly point to the fact that the stronger the negative emotion, the more consumers are motivated to hurt the company in some way. That is, rather than trying to explain their problem to the company in hopes of fixing the situation, angry customers want to "get even." Learning how to avoid situations which would provoke such negative emotions is critical as is training of customer-service employees to identify and deal with these strong emotions when they occur.[49]

Obviously, marketers should strive to minimize dissatisfaction *and* to effectively resolve dissatisfaction when it occurs. However, marketers also need to strive to maximize the chances that consumers will complain to their firm rather than engage in negative WOM and brand switching. We discuss these issues next.

Marketing Strategy and Dissatisfied Consumers

I feel mad. I put it in my Christmas letter to 62 people across the country. I mean, I told everybody don't buy one of these things because the transmission is bad.[50]

The above example is a marketer's nightmare. And the ease of communicating by e-mail and on Web sites/blogs makes such scenarios even more frightening:

I'm the founder of this Web site and like everyone else, I got scammed by First USA. Of course, at the time I thought it was just me. After battling First USA and getting nowhere, I decided to throw up a quick Web page. I was surprised when I got bombarded with e-mails from people saying the same thing happened to them. Since then, this site has grown tremendously.[51]

Firms need to satisfy consumer expectations by (1) creating reasonable expectations through promotional efforts and (2) maintaining consistent quality so the reasonable expectations are fulfilled. Since dissatisfied consumers tend to engage in negative WOM and since WOM is such a powerful decision influence, one dissatisfied consumer can cause a ripple or multiplier effect in terms of discouraging future sales. Movies are a great example of how powerful negative *buzz* about a new movie can quickly kill its box office take even in the face of strong promotional support from the studio.

When a consumer is dissatisfied, the most favorable consequence is for the person to communicate this dissatisfaction to the firm but to no one else. This alerts the firm to problems, enables it to make amends where necessary, and minimizes negative word-of-mouth communications. Many firms have discovered that customers whose complaints are resolved to their satisfaction are sometimes even more satisfied than are those who did not experience a problem in the first place.[52] This appears to be more likely when the problem is minor or moderate rather than severe,[53] and when problems are isolated rather than ongoing.[54]

Unfortunately, many individuals do not communicate their dissatisfaction to the firm involved. Some people find it difficult to complain due to a lack of resources (e.g., income and education), while others have personality traits (e.g., introversion) that make the complaint process emotionally painful.[55] Consider the following:

I find it hard to say anything when I'm unhappy [with a purchase]. It takes talking to myself all the way to the store. I say, "how do I say that?" I practice it. If I can get my husband to do it, I will. I'm very uncomfortable, even afterwards. I don't want people to think that I'm such a crab or not be liked or not think, "That's not such a nice lady."[56]

As we saw in Chapter 2, cultural factors also play a role. However, demographics, personality, and culture do not completely explain consumers' generally negative attitude toward complaining. Companies often make it difficult to complain or are unresponsive to complaints. As a consequence, consumers "learn" that complaining to the company is not worth the effort. Thus, it is critical that companies not only create processes and an atmosphere that encourages consumers to direct their complaints to them, but also train and empower their employees to respond to and resolve consumer problems in a timely and effective manner.[57]

Toll free call centers and hotlines are one approach used by many companies. These can be effective in handling complaints and also an opportunity to learn how to improve. Procter & Gamble provides the following examples of benefits received from its hot line:

- Duncan Hines brownie mix: "We learned that people in high-altitude areas need special instructions for baking, and these soon were added to the packages. We also found that one of the recipes on a box label was confusing, so we changed it."
- Toothpaste: "We spotted a pattern of people complaining that they couldn't get the last bit of toothpaste out of the tube without it breaking, so the tubes were strengthened."
- P&G also receives calls with positive testimonials. These are forwarded to the appropriate advertising agency, where they are analyzed for insights into why people like the product. Several P&G campaigns have been based on these unsolicited consumer comments.[58]

Obviously consumers increasingly expect to be able to express complaints via e-mail. Initial research shows firms that receive and respond quickly to such complaints can greatly increase customer satisfaction.[59]

Although hot lines and other procedures increase the ease with which consumers can express a complaint, they are not sufficient. Most consumers who complain want a tangible result. Further, the results desired vary by customer type and the nature of the problem, requiring customized response capabilities.[60] Failure to deal effectively with this expectation can produce increased dissatisfaction. Therefore, firms need to resolve the cause of consumer complaints, not just give the consumers the opportunity to complain.[61]

In fact, for many firms, retaining customers by encouraging and responding effectively to complaints is more economical than attracting new customers through advertising or other promotional activities. It has been estimated that it costs only one-fifth as much to retain an old customer as to obtain a new one.[62] Training *front-line employees* who deal directly with customers to use appropriate communication styles and empowering them to resolve problems as they arise is one way firms can increase customer satisfaction and retention.[63]

Unfortunately, many corporations are not organized to effectively resolve and learn from consumer complaints. This area represents a major opportunity for many businesses.[64] Consider the following:[65]

> When Sprint's new CEO Gary Forsee joined the company last March, he wanted to know why hundreds of millions of dollars were being spent on bringing in new wireless customers, while existing unsatisfied customers went out the back door. Mr. Forsee, a 30-year veteran of telephone companies including AT&T and BellSouth, wanted Sprint to put customer service in its place, right next to customer acquisition. So, Sprint changed—a lot.
>
> In fact, Sprint business units were completely reorganized around a new focus: the customer experience. No longer are customers acquired and then "thrown over the wall" to customer service. Marketing, customer service and sales are no longer three different silos, but reside in a combined unit working together.

Sprint's companywide approach has already yielded dividends, with customer turnover down since the reorganization. Travelocity is another example of a company that is aligning its processes to proactively deal with customer issues and the customer experience in an online context (Illustration 18-5).

ILLUSTRATION 18-5

Travelocity is aligning its internal processes toward proactively responding to consumer issues and needs.

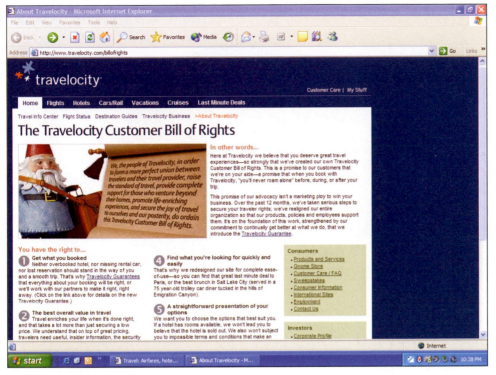

Courtesy Click Here/Online Media.

CUSTOMER SATISFACTION, REPEAT PURCHASES, AND CUSTOMER COMMITMENT

Pizza Hut's customer satisfaction department conducts an aggressive customer satisfaction campaign at all of its company-owned outlets. A key part of the campaign is a major, ongoing survey of several thousand customers per week.

A percentage of all customers who have pizza delivered or who take it out are telephoned within 24 hours. The interview is limited to four minutes. A system is in place to ensure that at least 60 days elapse before a customer is interviewed again. In addition, one out of every 20 to 30 dine-in customers is given a coupon at the bottom of their receipt and a toll-free number to call to participate in a six-minute interview. Two-thirds of those who respond to this offer do so within 24 hours, so the dining experience is still fresh in their memory.

Half of the store manager's quarterly bonus is linked to the survey results. Thus, it serves as a motivational and control device for the managers. In addition, it identifies problems quickly and allows managers to solve them before the image of the outlet or of Pizza Hut is harmed.

The surveys have identified systemwide problems as well as issues at individual stores. When Pizza Hut launched its Stuffed Crust Pizza, initial sales were strong, but repeat sales did not materialize. The surveys revealed the nature of the problems associated with the new product and enabled the firm to take corrective action. It also provided insights that Pizza Hut can use in future new-product introductions.[66]

Pizza Hut is typical of the many American firms that have responded to increased competition by focusing their efforts on producing satisfied customers rather than on

Creating Committed Customers Is Increasingly the Focus of Marketing Strategy

producing short-term sales. However, given increasingly sophisticated and value-conscious consumers and multiple brands that perform at satisfactory levels, producing satisfied customers is necessary but not sufficient for many marketers. Instead, the objective is to produce committed or brand-loyal customers.

Figure 18-4 illustrates the composition of the buyers of a particular brand at any point in time. Of the total buyers, some percentage will be satisfied with the purchase. As we have seen, marketers are spending considerable effort to make this percentage as high as possible. The reason is that, while many satisfied customers will switch brands,[67] satisfied customers are much more likely to become or remain repeat purchasers than are dissatisfied customers.[68] **Repeat purchasers** continue to buy the same brand though they do not have an emotional attachment to it.

As we saw earlier, some dissatisfied customers may also become or remain repeat purchasers. These individuals perceive the **switching costs**—*the costs of finding, evaluating, and adopting another solution*—to be too high.[69] However, they may engage in negative word-of-mouth and are vulnerable to competitors' actions.

Repeat purchasers are desirable, but *mere* repeat purchasers are vulnerable to competitor actions. That is, they are buying the brand out of habit or because it is readily available where they shop, or because it has the lowest price, or for similar superficial reasons. These customers have no commitment to the brand. They are not brand loyal. **Brand loyalty** is defined as

a biased (i.e., nonrandom) behavioral response (i.e., purchase/recommend) expressed over time by a decision-making unit with respect to one or more alternative brands out of a set of such brands that is a function of psychological (decision-making, evaluative) processes.[70]

Service and store loyalty are generally defined in the same or a similar manner.[71] Thus, a consumer loyal to a brand (store or service), or a **committed customer,** has an emotional attachment to the brand or firm. The customer likes the brand in a manner somewhat similar to friendship. Consumers use expressions such as "I trust this brand," "I like this outlet," and "I believe in this firm" to describe their commitment:

> I tried it myself one time and eventually adopted a taste for it. Now I drink it all the time. I have it every morning after I come in from my run. I drink it after I clean the house. I always have a glass of it in my hand. That's me. I am very loyal to Gatorade. I would say that I am very loyal to that. I know they have other brands of that now, I see coupons all the time, but I have never even picked up a bottle of them. Never even tried them. Because I like Gatorade a lot. I really do.[72]

Brand loyalty can arise through identification, where a consumer believes the brand reflects and reinforces some aspect of his or her self-concept. This type of commitment is most common for symbolic products such as beer and automobiles. It is also likely in service situations that involve extended interpersonal encounters.[73] Research in services has also found that loyalty can arise from *consumer comfort*. Consumer comfort is "a psychological state wherein a customer's anxiety concerning a service has been eased, and he or she enjoys peace of mind and is calm and worry free concerning service encounters with [a specific] provider."[74] Service employees likely play a strong role in developing comfort given the high-contact nature of many services. Brand loyalty may also arise through performance so far above expected that it delights the customer.[75] Such superior performance can be related to the product, the firm itself, or, as mentioned earlier, the manner in which the firm responds to a complaint or a customer problem.

Given the above, it is obvious that it is more difficult to develop brand-loyal consumers for some product categories than for others. Indeed, for low-involvement product categories with few opportunities for truly distinct performance or customer service, most firms should focus on creating satisfied repeat purchasers rather than loyal or committed customers.[76]

Committed customers are unlikely to consider additional information when making a purchase. They are also resistant to competitors' marketing efforts—for example, coupons. Even when loyal customers do buy a different brand to take advantage of a promotional deal, they generally return to their original brand for their next purchase.[77] Committed customers are more receptive to line extensions and other new products offered by the same firm. They are also more likely to forgive an occasional product or service failure.[78]

Finally, committed customers are likely to be a source of positive word-of-mouth communications. This is extremely valuable to a firm. Positive word-of-mouth communications from a committed customer increase the probability both of the recipient becoming a customer and of the recipient sharing the positive comments with a third person[79]—"I haven't eaten at Aron's yet, but Kim raves about the food and service."

It is for these reasons that many marketers have attempted to create committed customers as well as satisfied customers. Committed customers are much more profitable to the firm than mere repeat purchasers, who in turn are more profitable than occasional buyers.[80]

Repeat Purchasers, Committed Customers, and Profits

Churn is a term used to refer to *turnover in a firm's customer base*. If a firm has a base of 100 customers and 20 leave each year and 20 new ones become customers, it has a churn rate of 20 percent. Reducing churn is a major objective of many firms today. Why? It typically costs more to obtain a new customer than to retain an existing one, and new customers generally are not as profitable as longer-term customers. Consider the profits generated by one credit card firm's customers over time:[81]

Year	Profits
Acquisition cost	($51)
Year 1	$30
Year 2	$42
Year 3	$44
Year 4	$49
Year 5	$55

Acquisition costs include such expenses as advertising, establishing the account, mailing the card, and so forth. First-year profits are low because many new customers are acquired as a result of a promotional deal of some type. In addition, their initial usage rate tends to be low and they don't use all the features. This is a common pattern for both consumer and industrial products. Auto service profits per customer increased from $25 the first year to $88 in the fifth year, and an industrial laundry found they went from $144 to $258.

Figure 18-5 shows the sources of the growth of profit per customer over time. *Price premium* refers to the fact that repeat and particularly committed customers tend to buy the brand consistently rather than waiting for a sale or continually negotiating price. *Referrals* refers to profits generated by new customers acquired as a result of recommendations from

---

FIGURE 18-5   **Sources of Increased Customer Profitability over Time**

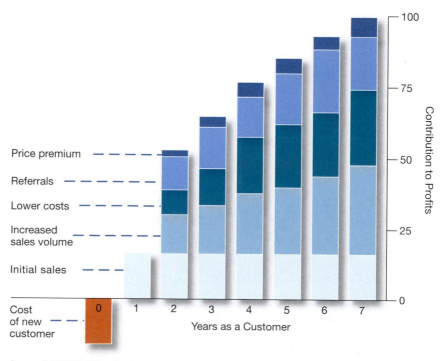

Source: © 1999 TIME Inc. Reprinted by permission.

existing customers. *Lower costs* occur because both the firm and the customer learn how to interact more efficiently over time. Finally, customers tend to use a wider array of a firm's products and services over time.[82]

Although committed customers are most valuable to a firm, reducing churn can have a major impact on profit even if the retained customers are primarily repeat purchasers. Reducing the number of customers who leave a firm in a year increases the average life of the firm's customer base.[83] As we saw earlier, the longer a customer is with a firm, the more profits the firm derives from that customer. Thus, a stable customer base tends to be highly profitable per customer. Reducing the number of customers who leave various types of firms each year by 5 percent has been found to increase the average profits per customer as follows:[84]

Firm Type	Percent Increase in Average Profits per Customer
Auto service	30%
Branch banks	85
Credit card	75
Credit insurance	25
Insurance brokerage	50
Industrial laundry	45

The motivation for marketers to retain customers is obvious. Phil Bressler, the co-owner of five Domino's Pizza outlets in Maryland, found that a regular customer was worth more than $5,000 over the 10-year life of the franchise agreement. He makes sure that every employee in every store is constantly aware of that number. Poor service or a bad attitude may cost the outlet several thousands of dollars, not just the $10 or $15 that might be lost on the single transaction![85]

However, as Consumer Insight 18-2 indicates, retaining some customers is more profitable than retaining others.

Repeat Purchasers, Committed Customers, and Marketing Strategy

An important step in developing a marketing strategy for a particular segment is to specify the objectives being pursued. Several distinct possibilities exist:

1. Attract new users to the product category.
2. Capture competitors' current customers.
3. Encourage current customers to use more.
4. Encourage current customers to become repeat purchasers.
5. Encourage current customers to become committed customers.

Each of the objectives listed above will require different strategies and marketing mixes. The first two objectives require the marketer to convince potential customers that the marketer's brand will provide superior value to not using the product or to using another brand. Advertisements promising superior benefits, coupons, free trials, and similar strategies are common approaches. While some firms are content to consider the sale the last step, smart firms now realize the critical importance of retaining customers after the initial sale. This is true even for infrequently purchased items—rather than repeat sales, the marketer wants positive, or at least neutral, word-of-mouth communications.

Consumer Insight   18-2

Not All Customers are Created Equal

Sophisticated data systems allow many firms to closely monitor the profitability as well as preferences of individual customers.[86] For example, every one of Continental Airlines' gate, reservation, and service agents can instantly access the history and economic value of every customer. This information includes very personal data such as past disagreements with gate agents. As a company vice president said, "We even know if they put their eyeshades on and go to sleep."

As you would expect, there are wide variations in profitability across customers. For example, at a typical commercial bank, the top 20 percent of customers generate six times more revenue than they cost. In contrast, the bottom 20 percent generate three to four times more costs than they do revenue.

In many industries, firms now utilize this individual profitability information to segment customers into service levels. Highly profitable customers receive excellent service, whereas those who generate low or negative profits receive little or no service.

At one electric utility, the top 350 business clients are served by six customer service representatives. The next 700 are served by six more, and the remaining 30,000 are served by two. The 300,000 residential customers must deal with an automated 800 number.

Centura Banks of Raleigh, N.C., rates its 2 million customers on a profitability scale from one to five. "Ones" get substantial personal attention; "fives" do not.

First Union codes its credit card customers with colors that appear when their accounts appear on a service rep's screen. Green (profitable) customers are granted waivers and otherwise given white-glove treatment. Red (unprofitable) customers have no bargaining power. Yellow (marginal profit) customers are given a moderate level of accommodation.

Critical Thinking Questions

1. What ethical issues, if any, do you see from collecting and using individual data this way?

2. What risks, if any, do you see from this approach to providing service?

The last three objectives listed earlier focus on marketing to the firm's current customers. All require customer satisfaction as a necessary precondition. As Figure 18-6 indicates, this requires that the firm deliver the value expected by the customer. Techniques for creating satisfied customers were described earlier. Marketing efforts focused on a firm's current customers are generally termed *relationship marketing*.

FIGURE 18-6	Customer Satisfaction Outcomes

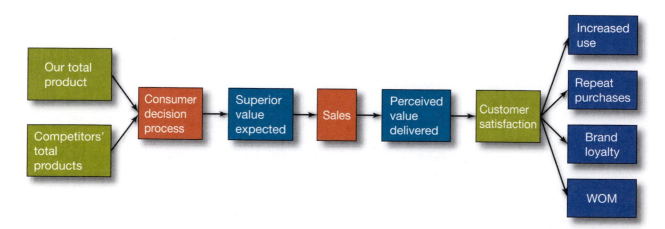

Relationship Marketing   *An attempt to develop an ongoing, expanding exchange relationship with a firm's customers* is called **relationship marketing.**[87] In many ways, it seeks to mimic the relationships that existed between neighborhood stores and their customers many years ago. In these relationships, the store owner knew the customers not only as customers but also as friends and neighbors. The owner could anticipate their needs and provide help and advice when needed. Relationship marketing attempts to accomplish the same results, but because of the large scale of most operations, the firm must use databases, customized mass communications, and advanced employee training and motivation.[88]

Consider the following example:

Lees Supermarkets, a family-owned and -operated company, started a Shoppers Club that records the purchases of members. Frequent or heavy shoppers are offered special incentives and deals. These offers can be customized on the basis of past purchasing patterns. In addition, last Thanksgiving, 600 regular, high-volume members were rewarded with free turkeys. Such an unexpected reward can produce delight and loyalty among key customers.[89]

Relationship marketing has five key elements:[90]

1. Developing a core service or product around which to build a customer relationship.
2. Customizing the relationship to the individual customer.
3. Augmenting the core service or product with extra benefits.
4. Pricing in a manner to encourage loyalty.
5. Marketing to employees so that they will perform well for customers.

This list of elements makes it clear that relationship marketing is centered on understanding consumer needs at the individual consumer level.[91]

A substantial amount of effort is currently being focused on **customer loyalty programs.** However, many of these programs are designed to generate repeat purchases rather than committed customers.[92] In addition to frequent-flier programs offered by most major airlines, programs designed to generate repeat purchases include the following:

- Marriott has Marriott Rewards. Members earn points for staying at Marriott hotels and are classified into Silver, Gold, or Platinum, based on number of stays per year. This classification system and their large customer database helps Marriott customize its amenities and promotions based on each customer's individual profile.
- Sports franchises use card-based reward programs where members earn points for attending events and can redeem these points for team memorabilia, food, and drinks. Teams can also use the member data to create personalized communications and offerings, including season-ticket packages to their most attractive members.[93]

Although programs such as those described above are often effective at generating repeat purchases, they do not necessarily create committed customers.[94] Committed customers have a reasonably strong emotional attachment to the product or firm. Generating committed customers requires that the firm consistently meet or exceed customer expectations. Further, customers must believe that the firm is treating them fairly and is, to some extent at least, concerned about their well-being. Thus, *generating committed customers requires a customer-focused attitude in the firm.* It also requires that this attitude be translated into actions that meet customers' needs.[95]

Air France attempts to create committed customers through the services it provides its passengers and an extensive frequent-flier program that gives increasing rewards the more one flies (see Illustration 18-6). It even provides a specialized program for petroleum industry professionals to better serve their specific needs.

ILLUSTRATION 18-6

Successful customer loyalty programs are based on understanding the needs of key customers and providing benefits of value to them.

Courtesy AirFrance Airlines.

Research is beginning to investigate online loyalty. While differences in type of site and purpose of visit (buying versus browsing) are likely to exist, evidence supports Figure 18-6 in suggesting that perceived value and satisfaction are important determinants of online loyalty just as they are for products, services, and traditional retail outlets.[96] In addition, research has identified factors unique to online settings that drive e-loyalty. For example, one study finds security/privacy to be critical.[97] Other research identifies customization/personalization, interactivity, convenience, and online community as factors that drive *e-loyalty,* WOM, and willingness to pay.[98] Interestingly, the importance of these factors seems to depend on the amount of Internet experience. For example, personalization is more important for those with greater online experience while community is more important for those with less online experience.[99]

SUMMARY

Following some purchases, consumers experience doubts or anxiety about the wisdom of the purchase. This is known as *postpurchase dissonance.* It is most likely to occur (1) among individuals with a tendency to experience anxiety, (2) after an irrevocable purchase, (3) when the purchase was important to the consumer, and (4) when it involved a difficult choice between two or more alternatives.

Whether or not the consumer experiences dissonance, most purchases are followed by product use. This use may be by the purchaser or by some other member of the purchasing unit. Monitoring product usage can indicate new uses for existing products,

needed product modifications, appropriate advertising themes, and opportunities for new products. Product liability laws have made it increasingly important for marketing managers to be aware of all potential uses of their products.

Product nonuse is also a concern. Both marketers and consumers suffer when consumers buy products that they do not use or use less than they intended. Thus, marketers frequently attempt to influence the decision to use the product as well as the decision to purchase the product.

Disposition of the product or its package may occur before, during, or after product use. Understanding disposition behavior is important to marketing managers because of the ecological concerns of many consumers, the costs and scarcity of raw materials, and the activities of federal and state legislatures and regulatory agencies. *E-waste* is an emerging area of concern related to disposition.

Postpurchase dissonance, product usage, and disposition are potential influences on the purchase evaluation process. Consumers develop certain expectations about the ability of the product to fulfill instrumental and symbolic needs. To the extent that the product meets these needs, satisfaction is likely to result. When expectations are not met, dissatisfaction is the likely result.

Taking no action; switching brands, products, or stores; and engaging in negative WOM (e.g., warning friends) are all common reactions to a negative purchase evaluation. A marketing manager generally should encourage dissatisfied consumers to complain directly to the firm and to no one else. Unfortunately, only a fairly small, unique set of consumers tends to complain. Developing strategies and processes that minimize the costs and hassles of complaining are critical in encouraging dissatisfied consumers to complain to the firm.

After the evaluation process and, where applicable, the complaint process, consumers have some degree of repurchase motivation. There may be a strong motive to avoid the brand, a willingness to repurchase it some of the time, a willingness to repurchase it all of the time, or some level of brand loyalty or customer commitment, which is a willingness to repurchase coupled with a psychological commitment to the brand. As online retailing continues to grow, marketers are examining ways in which e-satisfaction and e-loyalty can be bolstered.

Marketing strategy does not always have the creation of brand loyalty as its objective. Rather, the manager must examine the makeup of the brand's current and potential consumers and select the specific objectives most likely to maximize the overall organizational goals.

Relationship marketing attempts to develop an ongoing, expanding exchange relationship with a firm's customers. It is used to increase brand usage, repeat sales, or customer commitment.

KEY TERMS

Affective performance 651
Brand loyalty 656
Churn 657
Committed customer 656
Consumer-to-consumer sales 647
Consumption guilt 640

Customer loyalty programs 661
E-waste 645
Instrumental performance 650
Postpurchase dissonance 638
Product nonuse 643
Relationship marketing 661

Repeat purchasers 656
Switching costs 656
Symbolic performance 650
Use innovativeness 641

INTERNET EXERCISES

1. Monitor several product- or activity-related chat sites or interest groups for a week. Prepare a report on how a marketer could learn about the following by doing this.
   a. Customer satisfaction levels and customer commitment
   b. Product use
   c. Customer evaluation processes

2. Join Active.com. Evaluate its weekly e-mail newsletter.

3. Find a company site that helps the company in terms of relationship marketing. Describe and evaluate this effort.

4. Find an independent complaint Web site (go to Yahoo and search for "complaints about _____") for the following firms. What insights does it provide? How should the targeted company respond?
   a. Wal-Mart
   b. Disney
   c. Saturn

5. How should marketers use airlinequality.com/main/forum.htm.

6. Find a product, company, or brand site that helps the consumer use a product properly or effectively. Describe and evaluate this effort.

DDB LIFE STYLE STUDY™ DATA ANALYSES

1. What characterizes individuals who feel they have acquired too much debt (DDB Tables 1B through 7B)? What are the marketing implications of this? What are the regulatory implications of this?

2. Using DDB Tables 1B through 7B, what characterizes people who become committed enough to favorite brands to resist other brands when they are on sale? What are the marketing implications of this?

REVIEW QUESTIONS

1. What are the major postpurchase processes engaged in by consumers?

2. How does the type of decision process affect the postpurchase processes?

3. What is *postpurchase dissonance?* What characteristics of a purchase situation are likely to contribute to postpurchase dissonance?

4. What actions do consumers take to avoid postpurchase dissonance before the purchase?

5. In what ways can a consumer reduce postpurchase dissonance?

6. What is *consumption guilt?*

7. What is *counterfactual thinking?*

8. What is *prefactual thinking?*

9. What is *use innovativeness?*

10. What is meant by *product nonuse,* and why is it a concern of marketers?

11. What is meant by the disposition of products and product packaging, and why does it interest governmental regulatory agencies and marketers?

12. What is *e-waste* and why is it a growing concern?

13. What factors influence consumer satisfaction? In what way do they influence consumer satisfaction?

14. What is the difference between *instrumental* and *symbolic performance,* and how does each contribute to consumer satisfaction?

15. What is *affective performance?*

16. What courses of action can a consumer take in response to dissatisfaction? Which are used most often?

17. What determines satisfaction for online retailers?

18. What would marketers like consumers to do when dissatisfied? How can marketers encourage this?

19. What is *churn?* How does it affect profits?

20. What are the sources of increased profits from longer-term customers?

21. What is the relationship between *customer satisfaction, repeat purchases,* and *committed customers?*

22. What is the difference between *repeat purchasers* and *committed customers?*

23. What are *switching costs?*

24. Why are marketers interested in having committed customers?

25. What are five objectives that a marketing strategy for a particular segment might have? How will marketing strategies differ across the five objectives that a firm might have for a particular segment?

26. What is *relationship marketing?* What strategies are involved?

27. What are *loyalty programs?* What do most of them actually do?

28. What factors influence e-loyalty?

DISCUSSION QUESTIONS

29. How should retailers deal with consumers immediately after purchase to reduce postpurchase dissonance? What specific action would you recommend, and what effect would you intend it to have on the recent purchaser of (gift of) the following?
   a. PBS donation
   b. Airline vacation package

    c. Dance lessons

    d. New car

    e. Microwave oven

    f. Tropical fish

30. What type of database should your university maintain on its students? In general, what ethical concerns surround the use of such databases by institutions and companies?

31. How should manufacturers deal with consumers immediately after purchase to reduce postpurchase dissonance? What specific action would you recommend, and what effect would you intend it to have on the recent purchaser of the following?

    a. Laptop computer

    b. Expensive watch

    c. Cell phone

    d. Corrective eye surgery

32. Respond to the questions in Consumer Insight 18-1.

33. Discuss how you could determine how consumers actually use the following. How could this information be used to develop marketing strategy?

    a. Blender

    b. Telephone message machine

    c. Online banking services

    d. Movies on demand

    e. Hair color

    f. Hotel reward points

34. How would you go about measuring consumer satisfaction among purchasers of the following? What questions would you ask, what additional information would you collect, and why? How could this information be used for evaluating and planning marketing programs?

    a. Cell phone service

    b. Spiegel.com

    c. Car insurance

    d. Six Flags theme parks

    e. Upscale furniture

    f. Customized computers

35. What level of product dissatisfaction should a marketer be content with in attempting to serve a particular target market? What characteristics contribute to dissatisfaction, regardless of the marketer's efforts?

36. Describe the last time you were dissatisfied with a purchase. What action did you take? Why?

37. Are you a *mere* repeat purchaser of any brand, service, or outlet? Why are you not a committed customer? What, if anything, would make you a committed customer?

38. Respond to the questions in Consumer Insight 18-2.

39. How could an automobile dealership use the service segmentation strategy described in Consumer Insight 18-2?

40. Are you a committed customer to any brand, service, or outlet? Why?

41. Design a customer loyalty program for the following.

    a. Dry cleaning service

    b. Grocery store chain

    c. Cosmetics line

    d. Catering service

APPLICATION ACTIVITIES

42. Develop a brief questionnaire to determine product nonuse among college students and the reasons for it. With four other classmates, interview 50 students. What do you conclude?

43. Develop a questionnaire designed to measure consumer satisfaction of a clothing purchase of $50 or more. Include in your questionnaire items that measure the product's instrumental, symbolic, and affective dimensions of performance, as well as what the consumer wanted on these dimensions. Then, interview several consumers to obtain information on actual performance, expected performance, and satisfaction. Using this information, determine if consumers received what they expected (i.e., evaluation of performance) and relate any difference to consumer expressions of satisfaction. What are the marketing implications of your results?

44. Develop a survey to measure student dissatisfaction with service purchases. For purchases they were dissatisfied with, determine what action they took to resolve this dissatisfaction and what the end result of their efforts was. What are the marketing implications of your findings?

45. Develop a questionnaire to measure repeat purchase behavior and brand loyalty. Measure the repeat purchase behavior and brand loyalty of 10 students with respect to the following. Determine why the brand loyal students are brand loyal.
    a. Batteries
    b. Spaghetti sauce
    c. Coffee
    d. Light bulbs
    e. Clothing stores
    f. Online stores

46. With the cooperation of a durables retailer, assist the retailer in sending a postpurchase letter of thanks to every other customer immediately after purchase. Then, approximately two weeks after purchase, contact the same customers (both those who received the letter and those who did not) and measure their purchase satisfaction. Evaluate the results.

47. Interview a grocery store manager, a department store manager, and a restaurant manager. Determine the types of products their customers are most likely to complain about and the nature of those complaints.

48. Measure 10 students' disposition behaviors with respect to the following. Determine why they use the alternatives they do.
    a. Car battery
    b. Cell phones
    c. Mattress
    d. Televisions
    e. Plastic items

49. Interview 20 students to determine which, if any, customer loyalty programs they belong to, what they like and dislike about them, and the impact they have on their attitudes and behaviors. What opportunities do your results suggest?

REFERENCES

1. E. O. Lawler, "Fine Line between Added Value, Spam," *Advertising Age,* October 29, 2001, p. 54.

2. G. J. Thompson, "Interpreting Consumers," *Journal of Marketing Research,* November 1997, p. 444. Published by the American Marketing Association; reprinted with permission.

3. See J. C. Sweeney, D. Hausknecht, and G. N. Soutar, "Cognitive Dissonance after Purchase," *Psychology & Marketing,* May 2000, pp. 369–85.

4. M. F. Luce, "Choosing to Avoid," *Journal of Consumer Research,* March 1998, pp. 409–33.

5. See M. Tsiros and V. Mittal, "Regret," *Journal of Consumer Research,* March 2000, pp. 401–17; J. J. Hetts et al., "The Influence of Anticipated Counterfactual Regret on Behavior," *Psychology & Marketing,* April 2000, pp. 345–68; and A. D. J. Cooke, T. Meyvis, and A. Schwartz, "Avoiding Future Regret in Purchase-Timing Decisions," *Journal of Consumer Research,* March 2001, pp. 447–59.

6. See Thompson, "Interpreting Consumers." See endnote 2.

7. S. J. Gould, "An Interpretative Study of Purposeful, Mood Self-Regulating Consumption," *Psychology & Marketing,* July 1997, pp. 395–426.

8. See, e.g., R. Kivetz and I. Simonson, "Self-Control for the Righteous," *Journal of Consumer Research,* September 2002, pp. 199–217.

9. Based on N. J. Roese, "Counterfactual Thinking and Marketing," A. R. McConnel et al., "What If I Find It Cheaper Someplace Else?" and J. Landman and R. Petty, "It Could Have Been You," all in *Psychology & Marketing,* April 2000, pp. 277–80, 281–98, and 299–321, respectively. See also, S. B. Walchli and J. Landman, "Effects of Counterfactual Thought on Postpurchase Consumer Affect," *Psychology & Marketing,* January 2003, pp. 23–46.

10. See S. Ram and H.-S. Jung, "Innovativeness in Product Usage," and N. M. Ridgway and L. L. Price, "Exploration in Product Usage," both in *Psychology & Marketing,* January 1994, pp. 57–69 and 70–84, respectively; and K. Park and C. L. Dyer, "Consumer Use Innovative Behavior," in *Advances in Consumer Research,* vol. 22, eds. F. R. Kardes and M. Sujan (Provo, UT: Association for Consumer Research, 1995), pp. 566–72.

11. S. Ram and H. J. Jung, "The Conceptualization and Measurement of Product Usage," *Journal of the Academy of Marketing Science,* Winter 1990, pp. 67–76.

12. G. Berstell and D. Nitterhouse, "Looking 'Outside the Box,'" *Marketing Research,* Summer 1997, pp. 5–11. See also K. Parker, "How Do You Like Your Beef?" *American Demographics,* January 2000, pp. 35–37.

13. V. A. Taylor and A. B. Bower, "Improving Product Instruction Compliance," *Psychology & Marketing,* March 2004, pp. 229–45; and D. Bowman, C. M. Heilman, and P. B. Seetharaman, "Determinants of Product-Use Compliance Behavior," *Journal of Marketing Research,* August 2004, pp. 324–38.

14. A. B. Bower and D. E. Sprott, "The Case of the Dusty Stair-Climber," in *Advances in Consumer Research,* vol. 22, eds. Kardes and Sujan, pp. 582–87. See also B. Wansink and R. Deshpande, *Marketing Letters* 5, no. 1 (1994), pp. 91–100.

15. Bower and Sprott, "The Case of the Dusty Stair-Climber," p. 585.

16. S. L. Wood, *Journal of Marketing Research,* May 2001, pp. 157–69.

17. For detailed statistics visit the U.S. Environmental Protection Agency Web site at www.epa.org.

18. F. Abrams, "Electronic Waste Recycling Gathers Steam in the United States," www.circuitree.com, July 2005.

19. "eBay Launches PC Recycling and Reuse Initiative," *TWICE,* February 7, 2005, p. 22.

20. E. M. Okada, "Trade-ins, Mental Accounting, and Product Replacement Decisions," *Journal of Consumer Research,* March 2001, pp. 433–66.

21. A. Biswas, "The Recycling Cycle," *Journal of Public Policy & Marketing,* Spring 2000, pp. 93–105.

22. See B. G. Goff, J. S. Boles, D. N. Bellenger, and C. Stojack, "The Influence of Salesperson Selling Behaviors on Customer Satisfaction with Products," *Journal of Retailing,* no. 2 (1997), pp. 171–83.

23. V. Mittal, P. Kumar, and M. Tsiros, "Attribute-Level Performance, Satisfaction, and Behavioral Intentions over Time," *Journal of Marketing,* April 1999, pp. 88–101; and R. J. Slotegraff and J. J. Inman, "Longitudinal Shifts in the Drivers of Satisfaction with Product Quality," *Journal of Marketing Research,* August 2004, pp. 269–80.

24. See, e.g., A. S. Mattila, "The Impact of Cognitive Inertia on Postconsumption Evaluation Processes," *Journal of the Academy of Marketing Science* 31, no. 3 (2003), pp. 287–99.

25. See, e.g., K. E. Clow, D. L. Kurtz, J. Ozment, and B. S. Ong, "The Antecedents of Consumer Expectations of Services," *Journal of Services Marketing,* no. 4 (1997), pp. 230–48.

26. See J. Ozment and E. A. Morash, "The Augmented Service Offering for Perceived and Actual Service Quality," *Journal of the Academy of Marketing Science,* Fall 1994, pp. 352–63; and G. B. Voss, A. Parasuraman, and D. Grewal, "The Roles of Price, Performance, and Expectations in Determining Satisfaction in Service Exchanges," *Journal of Marketing,* October 1998, pp. 48–61.

27. For discussions of both conceptual and measurement issues, see K. Gupta and D. Stewart, "Customer Satisfaction and Customer Behavior," *Marketing Letters,* no. 3 (1996), pp. 249–63; P. J. Danaher, "Using Conjoint Analysis to Determine the Relative Importance of Service Attributes," *Journal of Retailing,* no. 2 (1997), pp. 235–60; R. N. Bolton and K. N. Lemon, "A Dynamic Model of Customers' Usage of Services," *Journal of Marketing Research,* May 1999, pp. 171–86; C. P. Bebko, "Service Intangibility and Its Impact on Customer Expectations," *Journal of Services Marketing* 14, no. 1 (2000), pp. 9–26; B. Bickart and N. Schwartz, "Service Experiences and Satisfaction Judgments," *Journal of Consumer Psychology* 11, no. 1 (2001), pp. 29–41; D. M. Szymanski and D. H. Henard, "Customer Satisfaction," *Journal of the Academy of Marketing Science,* Winter 2001, pp. 16–35; J. C. Sweeney and G. N. Soutar, "Consumer Perceived Value," *Journal of Retailing* 77 (2001), pp. 203–20; P. K. Kopalle and D. R. Lehmann, "Strategic Management of Expectations," *Journal of Marketing Research,* August 2001, pp. 386–94; J. Wirtz and A. Mattila, "Exploring the Role of Alternative Perceived Performance Measures and Needs-Congruency in the Customer Satisfaction Process," *Journal of Consumer Psychology* 11, no. 3 (2001), pp. 181–92; and E. Garbarino and M. S. Johnson, "Effects of Consumer Goals on Attribute Weighting, Overall Satisfaction, and Product Usage," *Psychology & Marketing,* September 2001, pp. 929–49. A different view is S. Fournier and D. G. Mick, "Rediscovering Satisfaction," *Journal of Marketing,* October 1999, pp. 5–23.

28. See C. Droge, D. Halstead, and R. D. Mackoy, "The Role of Competitive Alternatives in the Postchoice Satisfaction Formation Process," *Journal of the Academy of Marketing Science,* Winter 1997, pp. 18–30.

29. A. Mattila, "An Examination of Consumers' Use of Heuristic Cues in Making Satisfaction Judgments," *Psychology & Marketing,* August 1998, pp. 477–500.

30. See, e.g., T. A. Mooradian and J. M. Oliver, "I Can't Get No Satisfaction," *Psychology & Marketing,* July 1997, pp. 379–92; and R. A. Preng and T. J. Page, Jr., "The Impact of Confidence in Expectations on Consumer Satisfaction," *Psychology & Marketing,* November 2001, pp. 1187–1204.

31. M. Griffin, B. J. Babin, and D. Modianos, "Shopping Values of Russian Consumers," *Journal of Retailing* 76, no. 31 (2000), pp. 33–52.

32. S. M. Keaveney, "Customer Switching Behavior in Service Industries," *Journal of Marketing,* April 1995, pp. 71–82. See also D. Grace and A. O'Cass, "Attributions of Service Switching," *Journal of Services Marketing* 14, no. 4 (2001), pp. 300–21; and V. Mittal, J. M. Katrichis, and P. Kumar, "Attribute Performance and Customer Satisfaction over Time," *Journal of Services Marketing* 15, no. 5 (2001), pp. 343–56.

33. See, e.g., S. Taylor, "The Effects of Filled Waiting Time and Service Provider Control over the Delay on Evaluations of Service," *Journal of the Academy of Marketing Science,* Winter 1995, pp. 38–48; and M. K. Hui, M. V. Thakor, and R. Gill, "The Effect of Delay Type and Service Stage on Consumers' Reactions to Waiting," *Journal of Consumer Research,* March 1998, pp. 469–79.

34. V. Mittal, W. T. Ross, Jr., and P. M. Baldsare, "The Asymmetric Impact of Negative and Positive Attribute-Level Performance on Overall Satisfaction and Repurchase Levels," *Journal of Marketing,* January 1998, pp. 33–47. See also G. J. Gaeth et al., "Consumers' Attitude Change across Sequences of Successful and Unsuccessful Product Usage," *Marketing Letters,* no. 1 (1997), pp. 41–53.

35. See B. Mittal and W. M. Lassar, "The Role of Personalization in Service Encounters," *Journal of Retailing,* no. 1 (1996), pp. 95–109; R. A. Spreng and R. D. Mackoy, "An Empirical Examination of a Model of Perceived Service Quality and Satisfaction," *Journal of Retailing,* no. 2 (1996), pp. 210–14; N. Sirohi, E. W. McClaughlin, and D. R. Wittink, "A Model of Consumer Perceptions and Store Loyalty Intentions for a Supermarket Retailer," *Journal of Retailing,* no. 2 (1998), pp. 223–45; and W. O. Bearden, M. K. Malhotra, and K. H. Uscategui, "Customer Contact and the Evaluation of Service Experiences," *Psychology & Marketing,* December 1998, pp. 793–809.

36. M. L. Meuter et al., "Self-Service Technologies," *Journal of Marketing,* July 2000, pp. 50–64. See also M. J. Bitner and M. L. Meuter, "Technology Infusion in Service Encounters," and A. Parasuraman and D. Grewal, "The Impact of Technology on the Quality-Value-Loyalty Chain," both in *Journal of the Academy of Marketing Science,* Winter 2000, pp. 138–49 and 168–74, respectively.

37. See G. H. G. McDougall, T. Levesque, and P. VanderPlaat, "Designing the Service Guarantee," *Journal of Services Marketing,* no. 4 (1998), pp. 278–93; and A. M. Ostrom and D. Iacobucci, "The Effect of Guarantees on Consumers' Evaluation of Services," *Journal of Services Marketing,* no. 5 (1998), pp. 362–78.

38. I. E. Swan and L. J. Combs, "Product Performance and Consumer Satisfaction: A New Concept," *Journal of Marketing,* April 1976, pp. 25–33.

39. See H. Mano and R. L. Oliver, "Assessing the Dimensionality and Structure of the Consumption Experience," *Journal of Consumer Research,* December 1993, pp. 451–66; and L. W. Turley and D. L. Bolton, "Measuring the Affective Evaluations of Retail Service Environments," *Journal of Professional Services Marketing* 19, no. 1 (1999), pp. 31–44. See also, S. M. Nowlis, N. Mandel, and D. B. McCabe, "The Effect of a Delay between Choice and Consumption on Consumption Enjoyment," *Journal of Consumer Research,* December 2004, pp. 502–10.

40. D. M. Szymanski and R. T. Hise, "e-Satisfaction," *Journal of Retailing* 76, no. 3 (2000), pp. 309–22. See also Q. Chen and W. D. Wells, ".Com Satisfaction and .Com Dissatisfaction," *Advances in Consumer Research,* vol. 28, eds. M. C. Gilly and J. Meyers-Levy (Provo, UT: Association for Consumer Research, 2001), pp. 34–39.

41. M. Wolfinbarger and M. C. Gilly, "eTailQ," *Journal of Retailing* 79 (2003), pp. 183–98.

42. H. Evanschitzky et al., "E-satisfaction," *Journal of Retailing* 80 (2004), pp. 239–47.

43. See., e.g., J. Singh, "A Typology of Consumer Dissatisfaction Response Styles," *Journal of Retailing,* Spring 1990, pp. 57–97; J. Singh, "Voice, Exit, and Negative Word-of-Mouth Behaviors," *Journal of the Academy of Marketing Science,* Winter 1990, pp. 1–15; K. Gronhaug and O. Kvitastein, "Purchases and Complaints," *Psychology & Marketing,* Spring 1991, pp. 21–35; and S. W. Kelley and M. A. Davis, "Antecedents to Customer Expectations for Service Recovery," *Journal of the Academy of Marketing Science,* Winter 1994, pp. 52–61.

44. M. A. Jones, D. L. Mothersbaugh, and S. E. Beatty, "Switching Barriers and Repurchase Intentions in Services," *Journal of Retailing* 76, no. 2 (2000), pp. 259–74; J. Lee, J. Lee, and L. Feick, "The Impact of Switching Costs on the Customer Satisfaction-Loyalty Link," *Journal of Services Marketing* 15, no. 1 (2001), pp. 35–48; and I. Roos, B. Edvardsson, and A. Gustafsson, "Customer Switching Patterns in Competitive and Noncompetitive Service Industries," *Journal of Service Research,* February 2004, pp. 256–71.

45. M. A. Jones and J. Suh, "Transaction-Specific Satisfaction and Overall Satisfaction," *Journal of Services Marketing* 14, no. 2 (2000), pp. 147–59.

46. See, e.g., K. P. N. Morel, T. B. C. Poiesz, and H. A. M. Wilkie, "Motivation, Capacity and Opportunity to Complain," in *Advances in Consumer Research,* vol. 24, eds. M. Bruck and D. J. MacInnis (Provo, UT: Association for Consumer Research, 1997), pp. 464–69.

47. See also S. P. Brown and R. F. Beltramini, "Consumer Complaining and Word-of-Mouth Activities," in *Advances in Consumer Research,* vol. 16, ed. T. K. Srull (Provo, UT: Association for Consumer Research, 1989), pp. 9–11; and J. E. Swan and R. L. Oliver, "Postpurchase Communications by Consumers," *Journal of Retailing,* Winter 1989, pp. 516–33.

48. J. Goodman and S. Newman, "Understanding Customer Behavior and Complaints," *Quality Progress,* January 2003, pp. 51–55. For additional research and statistics, visit www.tarp.com.

49. See, e.g., A. K. Smith and R. N. Bolton, "The Effect of Consumers' Emotional Responses to Service Failures on Their Recovery Effort Evaluations and Satisfaction Judgments," *Journal of the Academy of Marketing Science,* Winter 2002, pp. 5–23; N. N. Bechwati and M. Morrin, "Outraged Consumers," *Journal of Consumer Psychology* 13, no. 4 (2003), pp. 440–53; and R. Bougie, R. Pieters, and M. Zeelenberg, "Angry Customers Don't Come Back, They Get Back," *Journal of the Academy of Marketing Science,* Fall 2003, pp. 377–93.

50. Thompson, "Interpreting Consumers."

51. L. J. Harrison-Walker, "E-Complaining," *Journal of Services Marketing* 15, no. 5 (2001), pp. 397–412.

52. See R. A. Spreng, G. D. Harrell, and R. D. Mackoy, "Service Recovery," *Journal of Services Marketing* 9, no. 1 (1995), pp. 15–23; and L. Dube and M. F. Maute, "Defensive Strategies for Managing Satisfaction and Loyalty in the Service Industry," *Psychology & Marketing,* December 1998, pp. 775–91. For an alternative view see T. W. Andreassen, "From Disgust to Delight," *Journal of Service Research,* August 2001, pp. 39–49.

53. S. Weun, S. E. Beatty, and M. A. Jones, "The Impact of Service Failure Severity on Service Recovery Evaluations and Post-Recovery Relationships," *Journal of Services Marketing* 18, no. 2 (2004), pp. 133–46.

54. J. G. Maxham II and R. G. Netemeyer, "A Longitudinal Study of Complaining Customers' Evaluations of Multiple Service Failures and Recovery Efforts," *Journal of Marketing,* October 2002, pp. 57–71.

55. A literature review and model is in N. Stephens and K. P. Gwinner, "Why Don't Some People Complain?" *Journal of the Academy of Marketing Science,* Summer 1998, pp. 172–89. See also A. L. Dolinsky et al., "The Role of Psychographic Characteristics as Determinants of Complaint Behavior," *Journal of Hospital Marketing,* no. 2 (1998), pp. 27–51; and E. G. Harris and J. C. Mowen, "The Influence of Cardinal-, Central-, and Surface-Level Personality Traits on Consumers' Bargaining and Complaining Behavior," *Psychology & Marketing,* November 2001, pp. 1115–85.

56. Ibid.

57. See, e.g., C. Kim et al., "The Effect of Attitude and Perception on Consumer Complaint Intentions," *Journal of Consumer Marketing* 20, no. 4 (2003), pp. 352–71.

58. J. A. Prestbo, "At Procter & Gamble, Success Is Largely Due to Heeding Consumer," *The Wall Street Journal,* April 29, 1980, p. 23.

59. J. Strauss and D. J. Hill, "Consumer Complaints by E-Mail," *Journal of Interactive Marketing,* Winter 2001, pp. 63–73. See also, A. S. Mattila and J. Wirtz, "Consumer Complaining to Firms," *Journal of Services Marketing* 18, no. 2 (2004), pp. 147–55.

60. See A. K. Smith, R. N. Bolton, and J. Wagner, "A Model of Customer Satisfaction with Service Encounters Involving Failure and Recovery," *Journal of Marketing Research,* August 1999, pp. 356–72; A. Palmer, R. Beggs, and C. KeownMcMullan, "Equity and Repurchase Intention Following Service Failure," *Journal of Services Marketing* 14, no. 6 (2000), pp. 513–28;

A. S. Mattila, "The Effectiveness of Service Recovery in a Multi-Industry Setting," *Journal of Services Marketing* 15, no. 7 (2001), pp. 583–96; J. G. Maxham III and R. G. Netemeyer, "Modeling Customer Perceptions of Complaint Handling over Time," *Journal of Retailing* 78 (2002), pp. 239–52; M. Davidow, "Organizational Responses to Customer Complaints," *Journal of Service Research,* February 2003, pp. 225–50; and C. Homburg and A. Furst, "How Organizational Complaint Handling Drives Customer Loyalty," *Journal of Marketing,* July 2005, pp. 95–114.

61. See C. Goodwin and I. Ross, "Consumer Evaluations of Response to Complaints," *Journal of Consumer Marketing,* Spring 1990, pp. 39–47; and J. G. Blodgett, D. J. Hill, and S. S. Tax, "The Effects of Distributive, Procedural, and Interactional Justice on Postcomplaint Behavior," *Journal of Retailing,* no. 2 (1997), pp. 185–210.

62. P. Sellers, "What Customers Really Want," *Fortune,* June 4, 1990, pp. 58–62.

63. B. A. Sparks, G. L. Bradley, and V. J. Callan, "The Impact of Staff Empowerment and Communication Style on Customer Evaluations," *Psychology & Marketing,* August 1997, pp. 475–93.

64. See F. F. Reichheld, "Learning from Customer Defections," *Harvard Business Review,* March 1996, pp. 56–69. See also H. Estelami, "The Profit Impact of Consumer Complaint Solicitation across Market Conditions," *Journal of Professional Services Marketing* 20, no. 1 (1999), pp. 165–95; and N. A. Morgan, E. W. Anderson, and V. Mittal, "Understanding Firms' Customer Satisfaction Information Usage," *Journal of Marketing,* July 2005, pp. 131–51.

65. B. S. Bulik, "Brands Spotlight Customer Experience," *Advertising Age,* April 19, 2004, pp. 1 and 14.

66. C. Rubel, "Pizza Hut Explores Customer Satisfaction," *Marketing News,* March 25, 1996, p. 15. Published by the American Marketing Association; reprinted with permission.

67. T. O. Jones and W. E. Sasser, Jr., "Why Satisfied Customers Defect," *Harvard Business Review,* November 1995, pp. 88–95; P. P. Leszczyc and H. J. P. Timmermans, "Store-Switching Behavior," *Marketing Letters,* no. 2 (1997), pp. 193–204; B. Mittal and W. M. Lassar, "Why Do Customer Switch?" *Journal of Services Marketing,* no. 3 (1998), pp. 177–94; and C. Homburg and A. Giering, "Personal Characteristics as Moderators of the Relationship between Customer Satisfaction and Loyalty," *Psychology & Marketing,* January 2001, pp. 43–66.

68. See V. Mittal and W. Kamakura, "Satisfaction, Repurchase Intent, and Repurchase Behavior," *Journal of Marketing Research,* February 2001, pp. 131–42.

69. For a discussion of switching costs and repurchase intentions, see Jones, Mothersbaugh, and Beatty, "Switching Barriers and Repurchase Intentions in Services"; P. G. Patterson and T. Smith, "A Cross-Cultural Study of Switching Barriers and Propensity to Stay with Service Providers," *Journal of Retailing* 79 (2003), pp. 107–20; and T. A. Burnham, J. K. Frels, and V. Mahajan, "Consumer Switching Costs," *Journal of the Academy of Marketing Science,* Spring 2003, pp. 109–126.

70. J. Jacoby and D. B. Kyner, "Brand Loyalty versus Repeat Purchasing Behavior," *Journal of Marketing Research,* February 1973, pp. 1–9. See also S. Rundle-Thiele and M. M. Mackay, "Assessing the Performance of Brand Loyalty Measures," *Journal of Services Marketing* 15, no. 7 (2001), pp. 529–46; A. Chaudhuri and M. B. Holbrook, "The Chain of Effects from Brand Trust and Brand Affect to Brand Performance," *Journal of Marketing,* April 2001, pp. 81–93; C. F. Curasi and K. N. Kennedy, "From Prisoners to Apostles," *Journal of Services Marketing* 16, no. 4 (2002), pp. 322–41; and V. Liljander and I. Roos, "Customer-Relationship Levels," *Journal of Services Marketing* 16, no. 7 (2002), pp. 593–614.

71. See, e.g., R. G. Javalgi and C. R. Moberg, "Service Loyalty," *Journal of Services Marketing,* no. 3 (1997), pp. 165–79.

72. S. Fournier, "Consumers and Their Brands," *Journal of Consumer Research,* March 1998, p. 355.

73. See E. Garbarino and M. S. Johnson, "The Different Roles of Satisfaction, Trust, and Commitment in Customer Relationships," *Journal of Marketing,* April 1999, pp. 70–87; J. Singh and D. Sirdeshmukh, "Agency and Trust Mechanisms in Consumer Satisfaction and Loyalty Judgments," *Journal of the Academy of Marketing Science,* Winter 2000, pp. 150–67; D. Sirdeshmukh, J. Singh, and B. Sabol, "Consumer Trust, Value, and Loyalty in Relational Exchanges," *Journal of Marketing,* January 2002, pp. 15–37; and C. B. Battacharya and S. Sen, "Consumer-Company Identification," *Journal of Marketing,* April 2003, pp. 76–88.

74. D. F. Spake et al., "Consumer Comfort in Service Relationships," *Journal of Service Research,* May 2003, pp. 316–32.

75. R. L. Olvier, R. T. Rust, and S. Varki, "Customer Delight," *Journal of Retailing,* no. 3 (1997), pp. 311–36; and R. T. Rust and R. L. Oliver, "Should We Delight the Customer?" *Journal of the Academy of Marketing Science,* Winter 2000, pp. 86–94.

76. R. L. Oliver, "Whence Consumer Loyalty," *Journal of Marketing,* Special Issue 1999, pp. 33–44.

77. See J. Deighton, C. M. Henderson, and S. A. Neslin, "The Effects of Advertising on Brand Switching and Repeat Purchasing," *Journal of Marketing Research,* February 1994, pp. 28–43.

78. See D. Bejou and A. Palmer, "Service Failure and Loyalty," *Journal of Services Marketing,* no. 1 (1998), pp. 7–22; and R. L. Hess Jr., S. Ganesan, and N. M. Klein, "Service Failure and Recovery," *Journal of the Academy of Marketing Science,* Spring 2003, pp. 127–45.

79. M. Johnson, G. M. Zinkham, and G. S. Ayala, "The Impact of Outcome, Competency, and Affect on Service Referral," *Journal of Services Marketing,* no. 5 (1998), pp. 397–415.

80. E. W. Anderson, C. Fornell, R. T. Rust, "Customer Satisfaction, Productivity, and Profitability," *Marketing Science,* no. 2 (1997), pp. 129–45.

81. F. F. Reichheld and W. E. Sasser, Jr., "Zero Defections," *Harvard Business Review,* September 1990, pp. 105–11; and R. Jacob, "Why Some Customers Are More Equal than Others," *Fortune,* September 19, 1994, pp. 215–24. See also V. A. Zeithaml, "Service Quailty, Profitablity, and the Economic Worth of Customers," *Journal of the Academy of Marketing Science,* Winter 2000, pp. 67–85.

82. For additional research examining these various outcomes, see T. Hennig-Thurau, K. P. Gwinner, and D. D. Gremler, "Understanding Relationship Marketing Outcomes," *Journal of Service Research,* February 2002, pp. 230–47; P. C. Verhoef, P. H. Franses, and J. C. Hoekstra, "The Effect of Relational Constructs on Customer Referrals and Number of Services Purchased From

a Multiservice Provider," *Journal of the Academy of Marketing Science* 30, no. 3 (2002), pp. 202–16; H. S. Bansal, P. G. Irving, and S. F. Taylor, "A Three-Component Model of Customer Commitment to Service Providers," *Journal of the Academy of Marketing Science* 32, no. 3 (2004), pp. 234–50; and C. Homburg, N. Koschate, and W. D. Hoyer, "Do Satisfied Customers Really Pay More?" *Journal of Marketing,* April 2005, pp. 84–96.

83. See S. Li, "Survival Analysis," *Marketing Research,* Fall 1995, pp. 17–23.

84. Reichheld and Sasser, "Zero Defections," p. 110.

85. See also S. Lingle, "How Much Is a Customer Worth?" *Bank Marketing,* August 1995, pp. 13–16.

86. Based on D. Brady, "Why Service Sucks," *BusinessWeek,* October 23, 2000, pp. 118–28. See also J. Ganesh, M. J. Arnold, and K. E. Reynolds, "Understanding the Customer Base of Service Providers," *Journal of Marketing,* July 2000, pp. 65–87.

87. See G. S. Day, "Managing Market Relationships," *Journal of the Academy of Marketing Science,* Winter 2000, pp. 24–30.

88. See the special issue on relationship marketing, *Journal of the Academy of Marketing Science,* Fall 1995; and G. E. Gengler and P. P. Leszczyc, "Using Customer Satisfaction Research for Relationship Marketing," *Journal of Direct Marketing,* Winter 1997, pp. 23–29.

89. L. Freeman, "Marketing the Market," *Marketing News,* March 2, 1998, p. 1. Other examples are in G. B. Voss and Z. G. Voss, "Implementing a Relationship Marketing Program," *Journal of Services Marketing,* no. 11 (1997), pp. 278–98; B. G. Yovovich, "Scanners Reshape the Grocery Business," *Marketing News,* February 16, 1998, p. 1; and G. Brewer, "The Customer Stops Here," *Sales & Marketing Management,* March 1998, pp. 31–36.

90. L. L. Berry, "Relationship Marketing of Services," *Journal of the Academy of Marketing Science,* Fall 1995, pp. 236–45.

91. See N. Bendapudi and L. L. Berry, "Customers' Motivations for Maintaining Relationships with Service Providers," *Journal of Retailing,* no. 1 (1997), pp. 15–37.

92. See G. Levin, "Marketers Flock to Loyalty Offers," *Advertising Age,* May 24, 1993, p. 13; C. Miller, "Rewards for the Best Customers," *Marketing News,* July 5, 1993, p. 1; J. Fulkerson, "It's in the Cards," *American Demographics,* July 1996, pp. 38–43; and J. Passingham, "Grocery Retailing and the Loyalty Card," *Journal of the Market Research Society,* January 1998, pp. 55–63.

93. J. Raymond, "Home Field Advantage," *American Demographics,* April 2001, pp. 34–36.

94. See L. O'Brien and C. Jones, "Do Rewards Really Create Loyalty?" *Harvard Business Review,* May 1995, pp. 75–82; R. N. Bolton, P. K. Kannan, and M. D. Bramlett, "Implications of Loyalty Programs Membership and Service Experiences for Customer Retention and Value," *Journal of the Academy of Marketing Science,* Winter 2000, pp. 95–108; and A. W. Magi, "Share of Wallet in Retailing," *Journal of Retailing* 79 (2003), pp. 97–106.

95. See F. Rice, "The New Rules of Superlative Services," and P. Sellers "Keeping the Buyers," both in *Fortune,* Autumn–Winter 1993, pp. 50–53 and 56–58, respectively; and G. A. Conrad, G. Brown, and H. A. Harmon, "Customer Satisfaction and Corporate Culture," *Psychology & Marketing,* October 1997, pp. 663–74.

96. J. Holland and S. M. Baker, "Customer Participation in Creating Site Brand Loyalty," *Journal of Interactive Marketing,* Autumn 2001, pp. 34–45; R. E. Anderson and S. S. Srinivasan, "E-Satisfaction and E-Loyalty," *Psychology & Marketing,* February 2003, pp. 123–38; L. C. Harris and M. M. H. Goode, "The Four Levels of Loyalty and the Pivotal Role of Trust," *Journal of Retailing* 80 (2004), pp. 139–58.

97. J. Gummerus et al., "Customer Loyalty to Content-based Web Sites," *Journal of Services Marketing* 18, no. 3 (2004), pp. 175–86.

98. S. S. Srinivasan, R. Anderson, and K. Ponnavolu, "Customer Loyalty in E-commerce," *Journal of Retailing* 78 (2002), pp. 41–50.

99. H. Thorbjornsen et al., "Building Brand Relationships Online," *Journal of Interactive Marketing,* Summer 2002, pp. 17–34.

Cases

CASE 4-1   Adidas Goes High Tech

Adidas is trying to alter the very nature of the athletic footwear market. After three years of product development, they have created the Adidas 1, a $250 running shoe that uses a computer sensor in the heel of the shoe to adjust the amount of cushion in real time 1,000 times per second. Adidas executives are ecstatic:

> Adidas executives believe the shoe could be their iPod, a technology so ready for prime-time that it can be adapted to the company's basketball and soccer shoes and eventually enter the profitable league of "gotta-have" sneakers among urban youth. Says a hopeful Erich Stamminger, CEO of Adidas North America: "This is the biggest thing to hit this industry in decades."

Early signs are positive, including an endorsement by *Runner's World*'s Warren Greene. However, there are concerns including price, which is more than 50 percent higher than the most expensive sneaker currently on the market. In addition, the technology adds weight to the shoe which can be a big deal to serious runners.

Number 3 Adidas (in the United States) is counting on this technology to give them an edge over their closest rivals, Nike (number 1) and Reebok (number 2), who are also developing sensor technology of their own.

Discussion Questions

1. What type of innovation is the Adidas 1?
2. How might Adidas encourage problem recognition among potential users?
3. Do you think price will be used as a quality surrogate among the innovators who will be the first to buy the Adidas 1? Explain.
4. Are the innovators who first buy Adidas 1 likely to use a compensatory or noncompensatory decision rule? Explain.
5. Describe how you think Adidas should plan for the diffusion of its sensor technology (not just the Adidas 1 shoe). Think in terms of what types of consumers the market will/should consist of in terms of users (e.g., professional vs. amateur, sport, type of shoe, etc.) at each of the following stages:
   a. Innovator market
   b. Early adopter market
   c. Majority (mass) market
6. Based on your response to Question 5, what types of decision making (affective, attitude-based, attribute-based) should Adidas attempt to encourage for each of the identified markets? Explain.
7. Develop an advertisement for each of the markets identified in Question 5. Identify such factors as core positioning, theme, copy points, visuals, and so on.
8. Develop a retail strategy for Adidas (type and number of outlets) as its technology moves from the innovator, to early adopter, and finally to the mass market.
9. How might Adidas capitalize on reference group influence, WOM, and buzz to influence the diffusion process for its new technology? Outline a strategy for creating a cascading influence from innovators, to early adopters, to the mass market.

Source: "The Machine of a New Sole," *BusinessWeek*, March 14, 2005, p. 99.

CASE 4-2   Supermarket Shopping in Europe

The Point-of-Purchase Advertising Institute (POPAI) conducted a major study of supermarket shopping in four European countries. Almost 3,000 consumers age 16 or older were interviewed while shopping at a major supermarket. Respondents were first screened to ascertain that they were on a "major shopping trip" before the interview. Part of the results are shown in Table A.

TABLE A		UK	Holland	Belgium	France
Age					
55 and over (%)		32%	32%	15%	22%
35–54 (%)		49	48	50	43
Under 35 (%)		20	20	34	35
Female (%)		84	87	83	77
Shop alone (%)		57	79	65	62
How often do you use this store?					
Some of the time (%)		18	32	47	27
Most of the time (%)		32	52	32	24
All of the time (%)		50	16	21	49
Average time on a major trip (minutes)		48	23	38	53
Number of items bought on major trip		30	15	14	26
Number of major trips per week		1.1	1.2	1.1	1.0
Total number of grocery trips per week		2.1	3.4	3.4	3.7
Use a written shopping list (%)		61	70	74	76
Store is over 5 km from home (%)		32	9	24	46
Amount spent ($)		74	36	52	86
Shopping patterns					
Visited aisles where intended purchases were (%)		29	45	51	45
Visited most aisles (%)		35	28	34	38
Visited all aisles (%)		36	27	15	17
In-store decision making					
Specifically planned (%)		25	20	31	24
Generally planned (%)		8	24	9	12
Substitute (%)		4	4	4	6
Unplanned (%)		64	53	56	58

Cross-Country Variations in Major Shopping Trips to Supermarkets

Source: "Cross-Country Variations in Major Shopping Trips to Supermarkets," *The 1997/98 POPAI Europe Consumer Buying Habits Study* (Paris, France: POPAI Europe, 1998).

Discussion Questions

1. What are the most significant shopping differences across these four countries?

2. What causes the most significant shopping differences across these four countries?

3. What are the strategy implications of the most significant shopping differences across these four countries for an EU-wide supermarket chain?

4. What, if any, are the strategy implications of the most significant shopping differences across these four countries for a manufacturer of products sold in supermarkets throughout the EU?

CASE 4-3   A Shifting Retail Scene—Can Blockbuster Survive?

There's no question about it—consumers prefer to watch movies at home. A recent survey finds that 73 percent prefer watching a movie at home to going to the theater. You might think that's good news for Blockbuster. Think again. While Blockbuster is still the dominant player in the movie rental business, they have been slow to recognize or adapt to competitive threats. These include:

- *Consumer purchases of new DVDs.* Consumers appear to want to own movies, and studios now offer relatively low-priced movies through discounters like Wal-Mart. While Blockbuster now buys used DVDs from consumers and resells them at a considerable markup, they admit that they can't match the low new-DVD prices offered by the discount chains.

- *Online rentals.* Netflix, while still a relatively small player in the overall market, offers fixed-rate prices for prespecified numbers of movies which are ordered online and delivered direct to consumers' homes (usually a business day once the order is shipped). Consumers keep the movies as long as they like and get replacements when they return the old movies. Blockbuster has basically matched this program with its own version. One challenge is that it requires consumers to plan ahead rather than spontaneously stopping by the rental store on the spur of the moment. Changing this behavior could be easier said than done.

- Video-on-demand (VOD) offered by cable companies. While still relatively new, this service could revolutionize the industry *and* make obsolete all existing models including online models like Netflix. VOD offers the convenience of in-home ordering, instant delivery, and automatic billing. Assuming studios back the system and rental options remain current and broad, this could spell the end for Blockbuster as we know it.

As one analyst notes,

> Blockbuster's problems are not just a tale of a business struggling with technological obsolescence, but a compelling illustration of how more general changes in consumer behavior can affect a business.

Blockbuster has taken steps as we've seen. First, they eliminated the late charge (sort of), but it cost them $50 million in advertising and $250 million in revenues. In addition, since consumers who don't return the movie in the designated time are billed for the cost of the movie minus rental fees on the assumption they have decided to purchase it, lawsuits surrounding the misleading nature of the "no late fee" claim have surfaced. Other steps have included matching the Netflix online model with one of their own. Perhaps the brightest spot for Blockbuster is video games, which account for 20 percent of their business.

Discussion Questions

1. Detail the various options available for movie rentals. List what you feel are the most important evaluative criteria on which to judge these options. Do the evaluative criteria depend on consumer characteristics?

2. What are some of the "must have" attributes and features for online and VOD to spread to the mass market?

3. What marketing strategies can be developed to "teach" consumers to plan ahead for their entertainment needs?

4. Are there any benefits to the "brick and mortar" stores operated by Blockbuster that exist or could be developed that would be unique from VOD and get consumers into Blockbuster stores?

5. How might Blockbuster leverage its current strength in video games to make it a stronger part of its business model?

6. What, if any, switching barriers exist in a consumer's decision to switch from the traditional in-store Blockbuster model to other options like online and VOD? Are these barriers higher for some consumers than others?

7. Create an advertising campaign for Blockbuster to *increase* consumers' sense of regret or so-called "buyers' remorse" at having purchased a DVD (or many DVDs) they probably won't watch again and paid substantially more than the rental fee. Consider such appeals as:
   a. Emotional appeal
   b. Testimonials
   c. Utilitarian appeal

Source: "Poll: Most Prefer to Watch Movies at Home," *CNN.com,* accessed June 17, 2005; and D. McGinn, "Rewinding a Video Giant," *Newsweek,* June 27, 2005, pp. E9–E14.

CASE 4-4   Is Sears on Target?

As a 1992 story on Sears in *Advertising Age* explained,

> The task facing Sears is very, very difficult. Sears has to set completely new strategies that are responsive to the new realities. For one thing, it has to make its stores attractive. Consumers have a myriad of retailing choices, and they are also conservative and frugal. Retailers first must make them want to spend and second induce them to spend at their store. Sears is not good at that; it doesn't stand out, and *it doesn't stand for anything* [italics added]. Do you know any woman who wants a Sears' cocktail dress? Its hard goods get in the way of its soft goods and vice versa.

Sears decided to tackle this challenge head-on. It closed 113 outdated stores, replaced its phone book–thick, all-inclusive catalog with 23 specialty catalogs; started carrying popular brands; accepted credit cards other than its own; moved its clothing lines to more fashionable items; and started a $4 billion renovation project for its remaining stores.

In 1993, it launched its "Softer Side of Sears" campaign to draw middle-income women shoppers to Sears' soft goods and fashion items. The campaign cleverly juxtaposed things such as hammers, batteries, and tires versus items such as satiny robes, stylish black dresses, and sexy shoes. The idea was to get women between the ages of 25 and 54 into the stores, a group that controls at least 70 percent of all dollars spent at Sears. In one ad a woman said, "I came in for a DieHard—and I left with something drop dead," showing a model in a sexy black dress. Sears' advertising agency was able to tweak the idea to cover dozens of categories. Eventually, it evolved the tag line into "Come See the Many Sides of Sears."

One reason for the strategy was research revealing that while women were the primary purchasers of Sears' major hard goods, Kenmore appliances, and Craftsman tools, they went elsewhere for fashion and personal items. Sears had few major brands of apparel to offer, and its store brands were not widely popular.

Sears' chairman Arthur Martinez described the goal of the campaign as follows:

> We've listened carefully to the women who shop at Sears for their families and homes and we know that they want affordable, fashionable apparel for themselves. We want the campaign to disarm the skeptics and pleasantly surprise our customers and feature the kind of merchandise that's on our sales floor right now.

Initial results were encouraging. Sales and profit increases were above the industry average for the next three years. Revenue per square foot of selling space increased from $289 at year-end 1992 to $353 at the end of 1995. However, by late 1999, Sears was announcing depressed earnings, a managerial shake-up, a 1,400 employee layoff at its headquarters, and a new marketing campaign.

A new campaign was developed to be more value focused, with the theme "The Good Life at a Great Price. Guaranteed. Sears." Mark A. Cohen, Sears' executive vice president of marketing, said,

> Whether we like it or not, we're in a price game war, a value shootout with all our competition. With the "softer side" campaign, the customer feedback has been "We love the commercials, imagery and models, but we don't find those goods at Sears."

The campaign tops off a series of changes initiated by the retailer, including offering trendier brand-name clothing, reaching out to younger consumers with concert tours and teenage advisory panels, remodeling its stores, and selling merchandise on the Internet.

Cohen said the campaign, which continues to target women, is intended to emphasize Sears' entire product line, positioning the chain as a one-stop-shopping destination for so-called lifestyle brands and products. These include Lands' End which it acquired in June of 2002 and Covington apparel. Other highlights include Craftsman Kids and even DeWalt boots!

The Future?

Some experts say the rescue of the company from the brink of bankruptcy in 1992 only delayed the inevitable. Middle-priced stores such as Sears, JCPenney, and the late Montgomery Ward are being squeezed from both ends, by higher-priced competitors such as Macy's and Bloomingdale's and discount and specialty shops such as Wal-Mart, Target, and Abercrombie & Fitch. This is referred to as the *hourglass phenomenon,* and Sears appears to be in the middle where few customers are.

Sears will continue to face strong competition for its clothing and soft goods from powerful retailers such as Target and JCPenney, which is focusing exclusively in this area. Its hard goods positioning will continue to place it in direct competition with Lowe's and Home Depot.

"There's much more competition, and Sears, at its core, still has a cost structure that is quite a bit higher than their competition," one Chicago analyst said. "What happened was that companies like Wal-Mart came along. They were able to build a different model and grew up with a better cost structure from the get-go." The merger with Kmart in 2005 may help to improve both retailers' cost structures if economies of scale can be realized. This may be difficult, however, since both will continue to operate under their own nameplates.

Table A provides demographic data on shoppers at different outlets.

Discussion Questions

1. What is Sears' store image and position? What should it be?
2. Evaluate the new positioning strategy compared to the old.
3. To what extent does the Lands' End acquisition help Sears' image? Do you feel that it will help to draw consumers into their stores? Does your answer depend on the nature of the customer? Explain.
4. What criteria do the groups listed below use to select an outlet to purchase (*i*) dress clothes, (*ii*) casual clothes, (*iii*) power tools, and (*iv*) appliances?
   a. Teenagers
   b. Retired men

TABLE A

Demographics and
Retail Shopping

	Sears	JCPenney	Target	Gap
Percent adults using	25%	33%	34%	13%
Gender				
Male	103	86	90	86
Female	98	113	109	113
Age				
18–24	70	84	103	154
25–34	87	88	110	139
35–44	106	104	117	121
45–54	111	113	105	101
55–64	116	109	89	38
>64	108	102	64	24
Education				
College graduate	105	105	123	159
Some college	105	107	110	115
High school graduate	104	101	90	77
No degree	79	81	73	46
Occupation				
Professional	104	111	128	161
Managerial/administrative	100	110	128	155
Technical/clerical/sales	103	107	113	133
Precision/craft	107	79	96	84
Race/Ethnic Group				
White	102	100	102	99
Black	88	105	77	89
Spanish speaking	91	89	116	115
Region				
Northeast	117	92	38	138
North Central	107	116	135	99
South	90	93	83	81
West	94	102	146	97
Household Income				
<$10,000	57	70	58	61
$10,000–19,999	76	81	63	50
$20,000–29,999	93	99	82	59
$30,000–39,999	105	104	95	74
$40,000–49,999	111	104	108	91
$50,000–59,999	112	107	106	92
$60,000–74,999	115	115	121	124
$75,000+	109	105	127	167
Household Structure				
Single	76	85	99	131
Married	112	108	107	101

Note: 100 = Average use or consumption unless a percent is indicated. Base = All adults.
Source: Spring 2000 Mediamark Research, Inc.

    c. Middle-aged professional men
    d. Young professional women
    e. Older working-class women

5. How should Sears determine the type of atmospherics it should have?

6. How would you encourage consumers who come to Sears for hard goods to purchase clothing items?

7. Develop a marketing strategy for Sears targeting the following groups.
    a. Hispanics

    b. African Americans
    c. Teenagers
    d. Middle-class women 25 to 50
    e. Middle-class men over 50

Source: S. Hume, "Sears' Next Struggle," *Advertising Age,* October 5, 1992, p. 4; "Sears Trades Its 'Softer Side' for Fresher Image," *Los Angeles Times,* August 18, 1999, p. C5; J. Mann, "Sears Unable to Deliver on Ad Campaign's Promises," *Kansas City Star,* August 24, 1999; B. Garfield, "Sears Abandons Softer Side," *Advertising Age,* August 27, 2001; D. Eboghdady, "2 Chains Take Different Paths," *Register Guard,* April 24, 2002, p. 10D; and *Kmart and Sears Complete Merger to Form Sears Holdings Corporation* (Sears press release, March 24, 2005).

CASE 4-5   Vespa Boutiques

Vespa was a popular motor scooter in the United States until it withdrew from the market as a result of its inability to meet federal emission standards. In 2000 it returned. Its introduction included sponsoring the New York Marathon with new Vespas leading the race and the winners receiving a new 2001 Vespa. The Vespa ads appearing during the marathon showed a small red dot on a white screen. The dot moves closer, weaving to the tune "Flight of the Bumblebee." Soon it becomes clear that the dot is a Vespa. The tagline is "Vespa is back."

The opening of the first retail outlet for Vespa was celebrated a few weeks later at Paramount Studio's original *Roman Holiday* set with a fund raiser for Audrey Hepburn's children's charity. Ms. Hepburn helped make Vespas famous when she zipped around Rome on one in the popular movie *Roman Holiday*.

After the introductory period, Vespa launched a new tagline—"Vespa, the fun and only"—around a series of black-and-white pictures of twentyish models posing on the scooters. The ads ran in upscale magazines in cities where Vespa dealers were located or planned. In addition, teams of 12 models visited cafés and colleges in many of these cities. Their mission was described as "looking cool, sipping coffee, and tacitly pitching the Vespa."

In 2002, both Vespa and local dealer groups began to use sexy, hip advertising with the tagline "Life is better with Vespa." A 30-second spot by the company is

> Set in a backyard on a summer afternoon; a young man appears to heap praise on a woman reading in a nearby lawn chair. "You take me places I've never been before," he says in an Italian accent as he praises "her" curves and sleek figure. "Your petite but powerful body will purr with excitement when we are together." When he continues with "I must mount you now," the camera pans out to reveal a new Vespa, which he climbs aboard.

Vespa of Greater New York launched ads that showcase words ending in "issimo," such as "vroomisimo," and "sexissimo," and feature "barely clothed women sprawled over and around Vespas." In the San Francisco area, three billboards were developed that featured a woman's hands, arms, or legs grasping a male driver. A spokesman states, "Vespa is a passion brand that has been discovered by style leaders. Vespa is the sexiest way to get from A to B, and its Italian heritage allows us to own that."

In 2005, Vespa launched yet another advertising campaign entitled "Make Your Reality a Dream." The company awarded this campaign to KraftWorks because of "their unique approach that coupled the stylish Vespa heritage with the modernity of urban life. KraftWorks understands the romance that surrounds Vespa, as well as the obsession it engenders in its owners."

While Vespa's general marketing and advertising strategy is certainly unique for a motor scooter, its distribution strategy is even more so. Vespa is distributed through a limited but growing number of Vespa boutiques. These outlets will sell only Vespas, Vespa merchandise, and espresso and pastries. Vespa merchandise will include product accessories, helmets, and such items as Vespa brand watches. The Vespa Web site describes the boutiques as follows:

> Since 1946, Vespa has been synonymous with entertainment, pleasure, freedom; feelings directly influencing the design of the new Vespa boutiques—unique retail environments created to showcase all the products which comprise the Vespa Lifestyle.

One expert on brand development has expressed surprise that Vespa, a utilitarian product in Europe, is positioning itself as a luxury brand in the United States: "To me, why would you want one? For prestige? Nah. It's the ultimate run-around machine."

Discussion Questions

1. What brand image is Vespa creating?
2. What outlet image is Vespa creating?
3. Are the outlet and brand images consistent?
4. If Vespa were to reposition as a utilitarian, fun, "run-around machine," how would the ads change?
5. If Vespa were to reposition as a utilitarian, fun, "run-around machine," would the existing distribution system be appropriate? How should it change?
6. What are the pros and cons of Vespa distributing through a mass merchant such as Sears or through multibrand retailers?
7. Evaluate Vespa's Web site (www.vespausa.com).
8. Describe the decision process a typical consumer would use with respect to this product. What are the marketing implications of this?
9. Should management attempt to trigger problem recognition for the Vespa? Why? If they decided to, how should they do it?

10. What information sources is a consumer likely to use regarding the purchase of a Vespa?

11. What decision rule(s) is a consumer likely to use in the purchase of a Vespa?

12. Is the purchase of a Vespa likely to be a family purchase decision? If so, what roles will each family member play?

13. What will determine customer satisfaction and commitment to Vespa?

14. How would you define the target market for Vespas?

Source: J. Halliday, "Scooters and Pastry," *Advertising Age,* November 6, 2000, p. 4; K. Greenberg, "Reintroduced Vespa Takes a New Turn," *Brandweek,* May 28, 2001, p. 1; S. J. Heim, "Vespa's Sex Appeal Promoted in KBP Ads," *Adweek Western Edition,* April 22, 2002, p. 2; M. Anderson, "Vespa Gets Sexy in New Dealer Ads," *Adweek Eastern Edition,* May 13, 2002, p. 1; K. Roundtree, "Viewpoint Studios Intros Racy TV Work for Vespa," *Adweek New England Edition,* July 2002, p. 1; and "Make Your Reality a Dream," *internetAutoGuide.com,* Featured News Article, August 3, 2005.

CASE 4-6   Hyundai's Turnaround

In 1998, Hyundai was at a crossroads in the U.S. market. After a decade of dwindling sales and nagging quality concerns, they needed to do something to turn their brand around. And they took some bold moves. Among them:

• A 10-year, 100,000 mile warranty
• Quality improvements
• Product line and pricing reconfiguration
• "Buy-in" from their dealers, a critical customer link

The changes were dramatic and so were the results. Sales jumped from a low of 90,200 vehicles in 1998 to 400,200 in 2003! And in 2004, Hyundai tied with Honda for second place in the J.D. Power Initial Quality Survey, and only one point behind the leader Toyota.

Obviously Hyundai has come a long way. However, they realize there are still obstacles to overcome. Consider a story related by Chris Perry, Hyundai Motor America's National Advertising Manager:

> During a product clinic, where we introduce one of our new models, we asked people to tell us what they thought of Hyundai. A woman in the focus group said, "Wow, I just love that vehicle, but I've worked too hard to drive a Hyundai."

Perry goes on to state:

> Now, this [the focus group statement] happened a couple of years ago, and perceptions of Hyundai have improved quite a bit since then. But we still think of that comment to remind ourselves that we have a long way to go, in spite of our sales success. In fact, research from NOP World Automotive shows that a large percentage of new vehicle intenders who are aware of Hyundai say that they would not consider purchasing the brand. A lot of this lingering reluctance has to do with product cycles. Most experts say that in our industry it takes one to two product cycles for perceptions to catch up to reality.

Indeed, it appears that Hyundai continues to have mixed brand associations that may help to explain the "I've worked too hard to drive a Hyundai" statement. On the plus side—great warranty, good value, affordable, independent minded, and a perception that Hyundai is probably better than its reputation. On the minus side—unfamiliar, cheap, low quality, economy car, and boring. And despite its quality improvements, Hyundai's Korean heritage may still be a problem area. A recent *American Demographics* study found that U.S. consumers "of all ages, incomes and education levels gave Korea the lowest marks for car quality."

In taking its next steps, Hyundai has worked with NOP to conduct a segmentation analysis. One intriguing finding is that within their critical target markets consumers "strive for an authentic lifestyle."

Obviously, Hyundai is on the right track. Where they go in the future remains to be seen.

Discussion Questions

1. What role do you feel Hyundai's 10-year, 100,000 mile warranty played in its turnaround? Can you relate this to postpurchase dissonance? Would this warranty be as important an evaluative criterion today as it was 10 years ago? Explain.

2. How much influence do you think Hyundai's value-pricing strategy plays in consumers' ongoing mixed perceptions about Hyundai's quality?

3. Based on Hyundai's efforts thus far, have they been taking more of a utilitarian approach or a value-expressive approach in their overall strategy and marketing efforts?

4. Assume that Hyundai successfully upgrades its quality image among all U.S. consumers so that they are universally recognized for high quality. Will this result in greater sales and loyalty? Are there other factors driving consumer decisions and satisfaction that

Hyundai could focus on *beyond* quality that could drive even greater sales increases?

5. To which VALS segment(s) does the woman belong who indicated "I've worked too hard to drive a Hyundai?" If Hyundai sticks with its current positioning efforts, do you think this person will ever change her mind?

6. Research indicates that "authenticity" is critical to Hyundai's target consumers. To what VALS segments do you think these consumers belong?

7. Based on your answers to Questions 5 and 6, which VALS segment(s) would you strive to target. Justify your selection. Develop an advertising campaign for one of these chosen segments to include core positioning statement, theme, copy points, and visuals. Justify your ad in terms of the characteristics of your selected target segment.

Source: D. Kiley, "Hyundai Improves Dramatically in Quality Survey," *USA Today* (online), April 28, 2004; B. Johnson, "American Consumers Largely Ignore 'Made in USA' Pitch," *AdAge.com*, June 6, 2005; and C. Perry, "Driving Your Brand Forward . . . by Narrowing Your Focus," *NOP World Perspectives* (online), Spring 2005.

CASE 4-7   Muddy Boots Mercantile

It has often been assumed that the Internet would eventually make catalogs obsolete. Catalog marketers, the logic went, would migrate to an online setting and then shut down their catalog operations. However, this doesn't appear to be happening. As we saw in Chapter 17, catalogs can spur online buying and Internet sites can spur catalog buying. As a consequence of the complementarities currently existing between catalog and Internet channels, catalog marketers who have migrated online also maintain their catalog businesses. Lillian Vernon, Fingerhut, and Spiegel are examples of this model, which take advantage of the multi-channel shopping behaviors that have emerged in the consumer market.

Another model is emerging and flies in the face of what used to be considered conventional wisdom in the e-commerce era. That model is one of using an Internet Web site to *launch* into catalogs. A recent example is Muddy Boots Mercantile.

Muddy Boots Mercantile (www.muddybootsmercantile.com) is a new online retail business created in 2003 to serve the needs of gardeners. While there are many other sources of garden-related merchandise (traditional retail, catalogs and online), the creators of Muddy Boots identified the growth of e-commerce and the growth of gardening as a lifestyle passion as an opportunity to secure a percentage of the category.

A 2003 study by the National Gardening Association helped them determine that the most desirable target market for their garden-related products would be "an upscale, well-educated female audience between the ages of 35 and 55." With a tagline of "Beautiful and Useful Garden Goods," their merchandising goal was to have products that were both functional and aesthetically pleasing to appeal to their upscale gardener target audience.

Muddy Boots considered the "reverse" migration from online to catalog from the very start. Their logic centered on the following information: catalog marketers generally find that "cold call" sending of their catalogs results in response rates around 1 percent, while sending their catalogs to customers who have purchased from them before boosts that rate to around 6 percent. This finding is not new by any means. Marketers have long known that past behavior is a strong predictor of future behavior. So, Muddy Boots planned to work this to their advantage by building up a database of customers from their online business and then using that information to launch into catalogs.

Muddy Boots launched its first printed catalog in 2004 and consumers can make purchases in a number of ways including online and mail/fax.

Discussion Questions

1. Visit Muddy Boots Mercantile Web site (www.muddybootsmercantile.com). Evaluate their site with respect to:
   a. Appropriateness for their target audience
   b. The image it projects and its match with their goal to combine aesthetics with function
   c. Online retailer image
   d. Its privacy policy
   e. Ease of online purchasing
   f. Ease of information search

2. Evaluate the Muddy Boots Web site and evaluate it with respect to various aspects that have been found to relate to *e-loyalty*.
   a. Personalization
   b. Interactivity

c. Convenience
d. Online community

3. Based on your answers to Questions 1 and 2, suggest changes/modifications that you would make to the Muddy Boots Web site.

4. From the consumer standpoint, what complementary strengths do catalogs and Web sites leverage that makes them jointly useful as shopping tools?

Source: D. L. Duffy, "Using Online Retailing as a Springboard for Catalog Marketing," *Journal of Consumer Marketing* 21, no. 3 (2004), pp. 221–25; and www.muddybootsmercantile.com.

CASE 4-8   Increasing Egg Consumption

In 1945, per capita egg consumption was 402. By 1997, that figure had dropped to 236. Consumption rebounded somewhat to an estimated 254 in 1999, but has remained relatively flat ever since, with 2003 consumption at 259. The sharp decline in per capita egg consumption has a number of causes. General changes in lifestyles and eating patterns have favored the use of cereals and other prepared foods over eggs. The massive advertising of cereal companies has caused consumers to shift their breakfast preferences away from eggs (the leading cereal brand often has an ad budget five times larger than the budget of the American Egg Board).

While the two factors described above hampered egg sales, the 1960s association of high cholesterol levels with heart disease had a devastating impact. Many mass media reports from 1960s through the 1990s emphasized the importance of cholesterol reduction as a means of reducing heart disease. Eggs have perhaps the highest concentration of cholesterol of any food product. The early reports recommended sharply reducing dietary cholesterol (cholesterol that one eats such as that found in eggs). This caused many consumers to recognize a problem with their current eating patterns (particularly egg consumption) and to seek and consume alternatives.

As research continued, it became increasingly clear that dietary cholesterol was not nearly the culprit it was initially thought to be. Instead, cholesterol produced by one's own body is the major problem. The consumption of fats, particularly saturated fats, tends to increase cholesterol, particularly the most harmful type, in many people. However, eggs and other cholesterol-containing foods continued to be shunned by consumers.

Starting in 1996, several fairly widely reported studies have shown that moderate amounts of dietary cholesterol (egg) consumption do not pose a risk of increased body cholesterol for most consumers. However, even these studies have produced only a modest resurgence in egg consumption—per capita consumption of shell eggs has increased less than an egg a month since 1996.

The American Egg Board (AEB)

The AEB is the industry association that promotes eggs. To provide information about consumers' attitudes and knowledge about eggs and to assess the effectiveness of its "I Love Eggs" campaign (its previous marketing effort), the AEB completed a three-part consumer research study in early 1998. More than one-third of consumers reported feeling better about eggs than they did just two years earlier, and most consumers in 1998 admit that they are no longer as concerned about consuming cholesterol as they were before.

Research also showed that convenience is still a major problem for eggs, particularly on weekdays when the time spent at breakfast is growing shorter. In addition, many consumers are not aware of the nutritional positives that eggs have to offer, particularly the quality of protein in an egg. Surprisingly, AEB research showed that another barrier to increased egg consumption is that consumers don't even think of eggs at breakfast.

In 1998, the AEB spent $20 million promoting eggs, with $11 million devoted to advertising. This was a sharp increase from prior years and was associated with a new theme: "If It Ain't Eggs, It Ain't Breakfast." The president of the AEB stated, "When consumers think about breakfast, we want them to think about eggs." The campaign tried to reach consumers when they were thinking about breakfast by sponsoring NBC's "Today Show" concert series.

Launched in the spring of 1998, the new campaign shifted the American Egg Board's focus from combating negative publicity about eggs and cholesterol to celebrating the nutritional positives of eggs and protein. The ads stated that one large egg a day makes good nutritional sense as part of a balanced diet. The ads continued to use the "Incredible egg" and the "I love eggs" slogans.

The 1998 AEB Annual Report describes the campaign as follows:

The "If It Ain't Eggs" campaign grew out of the idea that although a cold bowl of cereal or a bagel on the run might be fast, and they might fill you up, they just aren't breakfast. The television and radio campaign uses music to remind people about their favorite family meal in a fun, folksy way. It is a shift from changing attitudes about cholesterol to changing behavior and encouraging consumers to eat eggs more often.

The television commercial features three generations coming together to prepare a family breakfast with eggs as the centerpiece. It includes mouthwatering footage of a variety of egg dishes in order to "trigger the crave" for eggs. As permission to eat the eggs they love, the spot includes a protein message to educate consumers about the nutritional benefits of eggs.

The overall campaign goal to "Capture the Weekend Breakfast" remained intact. More breakfasts continue to be eaten on weekends, and most weekend breakfasts still don't include eggs. Thus, weekend breakfast remains AEB's greatest opportunity to increase consumption. Television and radio advertising was emphasized during three-day holiday weekends throughout the year to encourage consumers to include eggs in the additional breakfast occasion.

In addition to advertising, the AEB engages in consumer education and generates significant publicity. It describes some of its educational activities as follows:

For hard-to-reach young parents and their children, a new booklet, *We Are Eggstra Special,* was developed and distributed to over 163,000 chain and individually owned day care centers, Head Start facilities, and elementary schools with prekindergarten and kindergarten classes as well as to early childhood education district supervisors.

The booklet features hands-on activities for children not yet old enough to read—elementary math measurements, simple science and art projects, songs, poems, raps, and other language arts activities and, of course, cooking—all within a multicultural theme. Included in the mailing was a reproducible letter to parents announcing the program and providing both nutrition and food safety tips. With the completion of the preschool program, AEB has now provided accurate, up-to-date information to teachers at all levels of childhood education.

Seven years after its original release, *The Incredible Journey from Hen to Home* was given a facelift and an update. With jazzed-up colors and a new pocket folder, the material for fourth- through sixth-grade use was particularly revised in the areas of nutrition and food safety to include the Food Guide Pyramid and Fight BAC! campaign.

More than 104,000 copies of the new *Journey* kit edition were sent to schools nationwide at the end of the year.

Following up on the previously released kit for active older adult programs, three new issues of a coordinating *Rediscover Eggs!* newsletter were sent to 4,000 retirement living communities, neighborhood senior centers, and nutrition sites. Each issue—bearing the seal of the American Academy of Family Physicians Foundation for credibility—contained articles on nutrition and food safety, recipes, egg craft instructions, and answers to common questions.

A video was produced to coordinate with *The Incredible Classroom Eggsperience* middle/high school print kit produced last year. The film was mailed to 25,000 family and consumer science department heads, media specialists, and classroom educators.

The AEB attempts to influence opinion leaders in a variety of ways including a recipe contest conducted among members of the International Association of Culinary Professionals (IACP) in conjunction with their Kids in the Kitchen Network section. In terms of general publicity, the AEB focused on generating widespread attention for a study published in the *Journal of the American College of Nutrition,* which showed that even people with moderately high cholesterol can eat two eggs a day. A multidimensional publicity campaign resulted in positive news stories in leading national magazines such as *Good Housekeeping* and *First for Women;* a syndicated story by the Gannett News Service reaching more than 500 newspapers across the country; and feature television segments on "Dr. Dean," a syndicated health program, and FOX's "Good Day New York."

As of 2005, AEB is even online with its Incredible Edible Egg Web site. It continues to use the "Incredible Egg" theme song and their Web site (www.aeb.org) includes egg recipes, information about nutrition, and a "Kids and Family" section designed to be both fun and educational.

Table A provides demographic data relevant to egg consumption.

Discussion Questions

1. Consumers appear to have recognized a problem with egg consumption. Why is it so difficult to get them to "unrecognize" this problem?

2. Why don't consumers eat more eggs?

3. According to the research, eggs are not in the evoked set for breakfast for many consumers. What can the AEB do to change this?

	Heavy User**	Light User***	Egg Substitute****
Percent of respondents	34%	28%	12%
Age			
18–24	83	135	78
25–34	101	95	82
35–44	120	89	84
45–54	106	89	81
55–64	99	94	142
>64	78	118	141
Education			
College graduate	82	114	102
Some college	101	97	80
High school graduate	105	93	96
No degree	110	101	137
Occupation			
Professional	85	106	102
Managerial/Administrative	85	114	83
Technical/Clerical/Sales	98	98	76
Precision/Craft	99	98	121
Race/Ethnic Group			
White	101	100	96
Black	92	104	126
Spanish speaking	120	91	110
Region			
Northeast	92	109	116
North central	97	106	88
South	107	92	104
West	99	98	91
Household Income			
<$10,000	90	131	135
$10,000–19,999	95	107	107
$20,000–29,999	106	96	92
$30,000–39,999	99	96	88
$40,000–49,999	109	86	95
$50,000–59,999	117	89	92
$60,000–74,999	110	88	78
$75,000+	89	103	108
Household Structure			
Single	76	125	87
Married	114	84	99
Child <2	114	88	87
Child 2–5	122	77	78
Child 6–11	130	70	79
Child 12–17	131	70	94

TABLE A

Demographics and
Egg Consumption*

*100 = Average use or consumption unless a percent is indicated. Base = Female homemakers.

**More than two dozen in last 30 days.

***Less than two dozen in last 30 days.

****Any in last 30 days.

Source: Spring 2000 Mediamark Research, Inc.

4. What decision process do consumers use to decide what to have for breakfast during the week? During the weekend?

5. What evaluative criteria do consumers use in selecting a food for breakfast? Do these change from weekdays to weekends?

6. What insights do the demographic data offer the AEB?

7. How can the AEB use situations to increase egg consumption?

8. Evaluate the AEB's Web site (www.aeb.org).

Sources: J. Pollack, "Egg Board Budgets $11 Mil," *Advertising Age,* May 25, 1998, p. 10; J. Neff, "The Great Egg Breakthrough," *Food Processing,* January 1998, p. 25; American Egg Board Web site (www.aeb.org); and A. M. Miraglio, "The Return of the Egg," *Food Product Design* (online), April 2005.

Organizations as Consumers

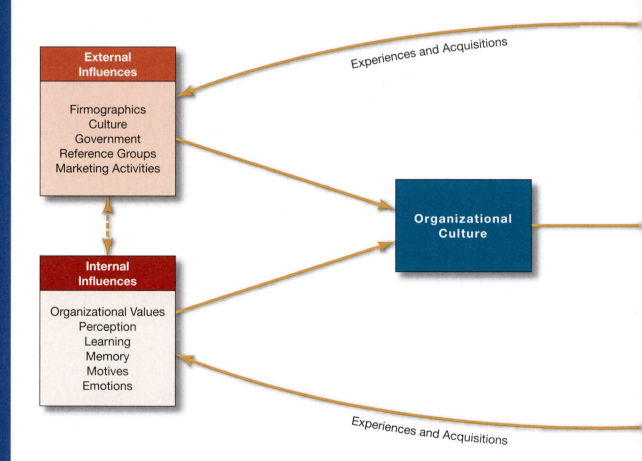

External Influences

Firmographics
Culture
Government
Reference Groups
Marketing Activities

Internal Influences

Organizational Values
Perception
Learning
Memory
Motives
Emotions

Organizational Culture

Experiences and Acquisitions

Experiences and Acquisitions

The stereotype of organizational buying behavior is one of a cold, efficient, economically rational process. Computers rather than humans could easily, and perhaps preferably, fulfill this function. In reality, nothing could be further from the truth. In fact, organizational consumer behavior is as human as individual and household consumer behavior.

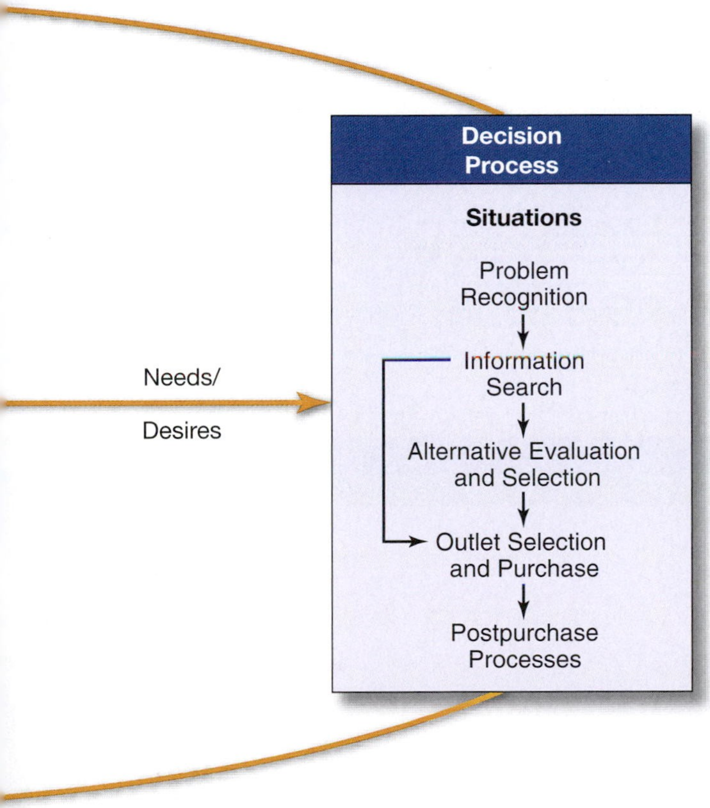

Organizations pay price premiums for well-known brands and for prestige brands. They avoid risk and fail to properly evaluate products and brands both before and after purchase. Individual members of organizations use the purchasing and consumption process as a political arena and attempt to increase their personal, departmental, or functional power through purchasing. Marketing communications are perceived and misperceived by organization members. Likewise, organizations learn correct and incorrect information about the world in which they operate.

Organizational purchase decisions take place in situations with varying degrees of time pressure, importance, and newness. They typically involve more people and criteria than do individual or household decisions. Thus, the study of organizational buying behavior is a rich and fun-filled activity.

On this and the facing page is a version of our model of consumer behavior modified for organizational buying. Chapter 19 explains these modifications.

Needs/
Desires

Decision Process

Situations

Problem Recognition

↓

Information Search

↓

Alternative Evaluation and Selection

↓

Outlet Selection and Purchase

↓

Postpurchase Processes

683

Courtesy New Pig Corporation.

19

Organizational Buyer Behavior

■ It may sound funny to say it this way, but businesses are customers too! They have needs and wants, are influenced by internal factors like values, and by external factors like reference groups. Relationships matter, as do efforts to build and foster brand image. Understanding what drives businesses, and the people who run them, is critical to marketing success. Consider the following:

Segmentation—While small and moderate-sized businesses often get lost in the shuffle, marketers increasingly realize that this segment has a lot of potential. However, tapping this potential requires adapting to the unique needs and wants of this customer base. For example, in the North American IT industry, slightly more than half of all spending comes from companies with less than 1,000 employees. IBM is aggressively courting these customers with a program called IBM Express which offers flexible and reasonably priced products and services tailored to this market.[1]

Technology—Technology helps businesses in many ways. An interesting twist is in the area of online business networking (think Friendster for business), particularly for salespeople. Consider the following:

Most business networking sites work in similar ways. You can create a profile with your name, title, and other basic information, then have the option of uploading your personal address book and inviting colleagues to join the network. After you sign up you can search the database by job title, geographic location, company name, and more. If the site indicates you know someone who knows a person at a company you want to pursue, you can request an introduction. If that person agrees to be an intermediary, you exchange information with his contact, and go from there.[2]

Sites such as LinkedIn, Ryze, and Spoke offer online networking services and results are encouraging. However, having a strong set of intermediaries is critical and the less direct a linkage you have to the person you want to contact, the lower the chances of success.

Branding—Think brands don't matter in the world of organizational buying? Don't tell that to New Pig Corporation. New Pig makes products such as absorbent socks (pigs) for soaking up oil spills on factory floors. New Pig has built a strong brand reputation not only by providing innovative products, delivering on its quality and service promises, but also with unique marketing efforts built around its name. For example, they have giveaways such as pig hats, "Oink" T-shirts, piggy banks, and so on. This all might sound a bit over the edge. However, New Pig's loyal customers seem to love it and have, themselves, become apostles for the brand. One customer went so far as wearing her pig hat to get married—now that's devotion![3]

Purchase decisions by businesses are often described as "rational" or "economic." However, as the chapter opener suggests, various factors beyond functional utility influence organizational decisions. This is not so surprising when you consider that businesses and other organizations are made up of individuals, and that these individuals, not "the organization," make the purchase decisions.

Understanding organizational purchasing requires many of the same concepts used to understand individual consumer or household needs (see Illustration 19-1). Although larger and often more complex than individual consumers and households, organizations too develop preferences, memories, and behaviors through perceptions, information processing, and experience. Likewise, organizations develop cultures that create relatively stable patterns of behaviors over time and across situations.

Like households, organizations make different types of buying decisions. In some instances, these buying decisions are routine replacement decisions for a frequently purchased commodity product or service such as paper or pens. At the other end of the continuum, organizations face new, complex purchase decisions that require careful problem definition, extensive information search, a long and often technical evaluation process, perhaps a negotiated purchase, and a long period of use and postpurchase evaluation.

Because there are many similarities between analyzing consumer behavior and analyzing organizational buyer behavior, our basic conceptual model of buyer behavior still holds. However, organizations are not just a collection of individuals. Organizations do develop unique rules and cultures that influence the behavior of their members. Thus, it is important that we understand the unique characteristics of organizations that relate to their purchasing behavior.

Figure 19-1 shows our basic model of buyer behavior modified to be applicable to an organizational buying context. We will begin our discussion by examining the organization decision process. Then we will examine the internal and external factors that determine organizational culture, the organizational equivalent of household lifestyle.

ORGANIZATIONAL PURCHASE PROCESS

Organizational buying decisions are often compared to family purchases. While useful, there are important distinctions. Organizations generally have relatively objective and clearly articulated criteria, such as profit maximization, that guide purchases. Families lack such explicit, overarching goals.

Courtesy Tekelec.

Most organizational purchases are made by individuals unknown to other organizational members and most purchases have little effect on most other members of the organization. On the other hand, many family purchases are inherently emotional and strongly affect the relationships between the family members.[4] For example, the decision to buy a child a requested toy or new school clothes is more than an acquisition; it is a symbol of love and commitment to the child. Such processes are not likely to operate with such intensity for most organizational buying decisions, although emotions certainly can play a role.

Finally, businesses often engage in reciprocal purchases (they buy from their customers when possible), form strategic alliances with their suppliers, and are proactive in helping suppliers develop products that meet their unique needs. These are not common options for households. Thus, while organizational decision making has some things in common with family decision making, it is not the same.

Decision-Making Unit

Decision-making units (DMUs) are the individuals (representing functional areas and management) within an organization who participate in making a given purchase decision. These often function as **buying centers** when they consist of individuals from various areas of the firm, such as accounting, engineering, manufacturing, and marketing, who meet specifically to make a purchase decision. They are often relatively permanent for recurring decisions and ad hoc for nonroutine ones. Large, highly structured organizations ordinarily involve more individuals in a purchase decision than do smaller, less formal organizations. Important decisions are likely to involve individuals from a wider variety of functional areas and organizational levels than are less important purchase decisions.

FIGURE 19-1   **Overall Model of Organizational Buyer Behavior**

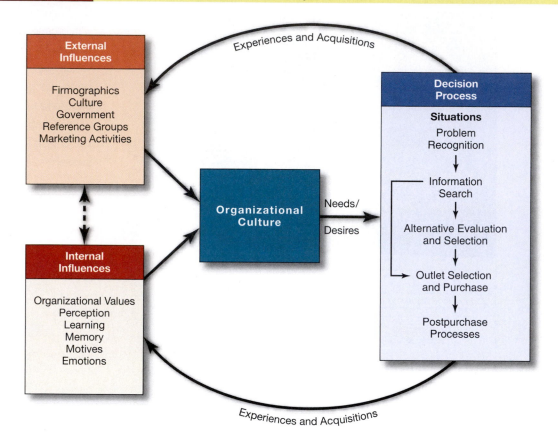

The following describes a Hewlett-Packard salesperson's view of the DMU and the buying process for very expensive imaging systems for large hospitals:

> Selling in the hospital market is a two-stage process and the buying cycle ranges from 3 to 12 months. In the first stage, I deal with medical professionals. They are most concerned with image quality, product reliability, and service. I must establish relationships and awareness of our products' functionality and reliability with a number of people, and the product demonstration is critical.
>
> The second stage is negotiations with administrators, who are more driven by price and cost issues. But much depends on the hospital's situation. For example, if a hospital is renowned for cancer treatment, they want the best available systems in that area and are more price sensitive with other equipment.[5]

In Table 19-1, we see that buyers in retail and wholesale firms assign different priorities to the performance of suppliers than do the operations people in those same firms. Organizations marketing to these firms must meet the needs of each group and communicate that to each group. Note that focusing only on the buyers, a common strategy, is not likely to be successful.

How the final purchase decision is made is in part determined by individual power, expertise, the degree of influence each functional area possesses in this type of decision, how the organization resolves group decision conflicts, and the nature of the decision.[6]

TABLE 19-1

Service Attribute
Importance for Retail
and Wholesale
Buyers and
Operations Personnel

Attribute*	Buyer Rating	Operations Rating
Ease of placing orders	**4.01**	3.71
Line-item availability	**4.55**	4.31
Packages clearly identified	4.46	**4.82**
Meets appointments	4.46	**4.73**
Delivers when requested	**4.87**	4.70
Delivered sorted and segregated	4.36	**4.75**
Palletizing/unitizing capability	3.72	**4.37**
Master carton packaging quality	3.81	**4.48**
Shelf unit packaging quality	3.97	**4.29**
Complete/accurate documentation	4.54	**4.81**
Well-documented deal/style codes	4.36	**4.60**
Length of order cycle	**4.14**	3.61
Consistency of order cycle	**4.38**	3.88

*Measured on a 1 to 5 scale with 5 being very important and 1 being not at all important. All are significantly different at the .05 level.

Source: Adapted from M. B. Cooper, C. Droge, and P. J. Daugherty, "How Buyers and Operations Personnel Evaluate Service," *Industrial Marketing Management*, no. 20 (1991), p. 83, with permission from Elsevier.

Members of the decision-making unit play various roles, such as information gatherer, key influencer, decision maker, purchaser, or user. A plant manager could play all five roles, while corporate engineers may simply be sources of information.

Decision-making units are likely to vary over the product life cycle (new products versus older ones). Consider the changes in the decision-making unit that took place in the purchase of microprocessors by an original equipment manufacturer over the stages of the microprocessor's product life cycle. Early stages in the life of the new microprocessor presented a difficult, important decision that required a large DMU. As the product grew in its utilization, a simpler decision evolved, as did a change in the structure of the DMU. Finally, as the microprocessor moved into a mature stage, it became a routine low-priority decision involving primarily the purchasing function. These changes are illustrated below:

Stage of Product Life Cycle	Size of DMU	Key Functions Influencing the Purchase Decision
Introduction	Large	Engineering and R&D
Growth	Medium	Production and top management
Maturity	Small	Purchasing

Purchase Situation

The buying process is influenced by the importance of the purchase and the complexity and difficulty of the choice. Simple, low-risk, routine decisions are generally made by an individual or even an automated process without extensive effort. At the other extreme are decisions that are complex and have major organizational implications. A continuum of purchase situations lies between these two extremes. A useful categorization of organizational purchase situations is provided in Table 19-2 and described in the following paragraphs.[7]

Note that this is similar to the purchase involvement construct discussed in Chapter 14. For consumers, we divided the purchase involvement continuum into three categories—nominal,

Organizational
Purchase Situations
and Buying
Responses

	Straight Rebuy	Modified Rebuy	New Task
Situational characteristics			
Purchase importance	Low	Moderate	High
Choice complexity	Low	Moderate	High
Purchasing characteristics			
Size of DMU	Very small	Medium	Large, evolving
Level of DMU	Low	Mid-level	Top of organization
Time to decision	very brief	Moderate	Long
Information search	None/very limited	Moderate	Extensive
Analysis techniques	None/price comparisons	Several	Extensive, complex
Strategic focus	None	Limited	Dominates

limited, and extended. These correspond closely to the straight rebuy, modified rebuy, and new task purchase situations shown in Table 19-2.

Straight Rebuy   This situation occurs when the purchase is of minor importance and is not complex. This is generally the case when reordering basic supplies and component parts. In such cases, the reordering process may be completely automated or done routinely by clerical personnel. Such purchases are often handled under a contract that is reviewed and perhaps rebid periodically. Price or reliability tend to be the dominant evaluative criteria. No consideration is given to strategic issues.

Modified Rebuy   This strategy is used when the purchase is moderately important to the firm or the choice is more complex. This typically involves a product or service that the organization is accustomed to purchasing but the product or the firm's needs have changed. Or, because the product is important to the firm (it is simple but the firm uses a lot of it or it is an important component of the firm's output), the firm may periodically reevaluate brands or suppliers. The DMU is likely to include several representatives, including some midlevel managers. More information is gathered and more evaluative criteria are analyzed. Strategic issues also begin to play a role.

New Task   This approach tends to occur when the buying decision is very important and the choice is quite complex. This would involve decisions on such things as an initial sales automation system or a new advertising agency. The buying organization will typically have had little experience with the decision and perhaps with the product or service. The DMU is likely to be large and evolve over time. Top management will be involved in the decision, and strategic issues will be of prime importance. The time involved is frequently quite long; for example, from problem recognition to implementation of a sales automation system typically takes 21 to 30 months.

Clearly, the marketing strategy and tactics for one particular type of purchase situation would be inappropriate for others. Thus, marketers must understand the purchase task confronting their organizational consumers and develop appropriate marketing strategies.

Steps in the Organizational Decision Process

Because organizational decisions typically involve more individuals in more complex decision tasks than do individual or household decisions, marketing efforts to affect this process are much more complex.[8] Shown in Table 19-3 are stages in the decision process and sources of influence at each stage in a large insurance company's decision to add microcomputers to its office management function. Altogether there were 12 separate sources of influence, each with different levels of influence and affecting different stages of the purchase decision process.

TABLE 19-3

Decision Process in
Purchasing
Microcomputers for a
Large Insurance
Company

Stages of the Purchase Decision Process	Key Influences within Decision-Making Unit	Influences Outside the Decision-Making Unit
Problem recognition	Office manager Sales manager	Field sales agents Administrative clerks Accounting manager Microcomputer sales representative
Information search	Data processing manager Office manager Purchasing manager	Operations personnel Microcomputer sales representative Other corporate users Office systems consultant
Alternative evaluation	General management Data processing manager Office manager Sales manager Purchasing manager	Office systems consultant Microcomputer sales representative
Purchase decision	General management Office manager Purchasing manager	
Product usage	Office manager Sales manager	Field sales agents Administrative clerks Accounting personnel Microcomputer sales representative
Evaluation	Office manager Sales manager General management	Field sales agents Administrative clerks Accounting personnel

To have a chance to win this large contract, a selling firm must provide relevant information to each source of influence. This is not a simple task, given that each source of influence has different motives and different criteria for evaluating alternative products, as well as different media habits.

Problem Recognition   In Table 19-3, the sales manager and office manager played the key role in recognizing the need to add microcomputers to their organization. In this instance, a continuing problem between field sales agents and internal administrative clerks led the office manager and sales manager to recognize the problem. Aiding their recognition of the problem were accounting personnel and microcomputer sales representatives who called on the office manager. The combination of these sources of influence eventually led to an increased level of importance and the subsequent stage of information search.

Table 19-4 shows that in high-tech markets, the head of a department is most likely to recognize a problem or need to purchase. Perhaps more important is that purchasing managers are not a source of problem recognition. This points out the danger of salespeople calling on purchasing agents only. As shown in Table 19-4, problem recognition and determining specifications often occur without much involvement of purchasing personnel.

Information Search   Information search can be both formal and informal.[9] Site visits to evaluate a potential vendor, laboratory tests of a new product or prototype, and investigation of possible product specifications are part of formal information search. Informal information search can occur during discussions with sales representatives, while attending trade shows, or when reading industry-specific journals. Industrial buyers search for information both to help make the best decision and to support their actions and recommendations within the organization.[10]

For complex technology products, organizational buyers often hire consultants both to provide information and to help evaluate alternatives. Consider the role played by

TABLE 19-4

Group Involvement in
the Decision Process
in High-Tech
Organizations

Stages of Decision Process	Percent Involved in Each Stage of Decision Process					
	Board of Directors	Top Management	Head of Department	Lab Technician or Operator	Purchasing Manager or Buyer	Finance Manager Accountant
Recognizing the need to purchase	7%	26%	70%	30%	0%	3%
Determining product specifications	0	33	74	33	3	0
Deciding which suppliers to consider	3	33	56	14	19	0
Obtaining quotations and proposals	0	26	52	19	14	3
Evaluating quotations and proposals	7	63	63	3	11	7
Final product or supplier selection	21	48	48	7	11	0

Source: Reprinted from R. Abratt, "Industrial Buying in Hi-Tech Markets," *Industrial Marketing Management* 15 (1986), p. 295. Copyright 1986; reprinted with permission from Elsevier Science.

consultants in the purchase of sales automation systems:

> The second step in the buying cycle was to evaluate the potential to automate existing processes. . . . Customers were usually not equipped to do this in-house. It was common for SA consultants to help them. Their deep understanding of the industry, and their skills and experience, made them the best option for this step.
>
> In the third step, the customer decided how the different functions to be automated were related, and determined how data was to be collected, stored, and analyzed. This again was usually done by SA consultants with the support of the customer's information systems department.
>
> The customer decided the type of SA software and hardware to be purchased. . . . Here again, the customer relied heavily on the consultant.[11]

Increasingly, organizational buyers are searching for product and price information on the Internet. Kyocera offers an online tool that businesses can use to determine ownership costs and savings (see Illustration 19-2; note that the ad, as shown here, is not full size).

Evaluation and Selection   The evaluation of possible vendors and selection of a given vendor often follow a **two-stage decision process.**[12] The first stage is making the buyer's approved vendor list. A conjunctive decision process is very common. In this manner, the organization can screen out potential vendors that do not meet all its minimum criteria. In a government missile purchase, 41 potential manufacturers of a given missile electronics system were first identified. After site visits to inspect manufacturing capability and resources, the organization pared this list of 41 down to 11 that met the government's minimum criteria.

A second stage of organizational decision making could involve other decision rules, such as disjunctive, lexicographic, compensatory, or elimination-by-aspects. For the government purchase discussed above, a lexicographic decision process was next used, with the most important criterion being price. Using this decision rule, the organization selected two vendors.

The process of evaluation and selection is further complicated by the fact that different members of the decision-making unit have differing evaluative criteria.[13] Recall the difference in criteria for imaging systems between hospital administrators and medical

Courtesy Kyocera Mita America, Inc.

professionals described earlier. Table 19-5 shows that purchasing, management, engineering, and operations use differing sets of performance criteria. For example, purchasing is more concerned with pricing policies, terms and conditions, and order status; engineers are more concerned with product knowledge, product operations, and applications knowledge. A salesperson calling on these accounts would need to understand and respond to the unique as well as the shared criteria of these purchase influencers.

It is generally assumed that business purchases are strictly economic, with the goal of maximizing the profits of the purchasing organization.[14] However, power, prestige, security, and similar noneconomic criteria also play important roles in business purchase decisions.[15] Research finds that there are organizations that buy "green," similar to the "green consumers" described in Chapter 3. These organizations have policies or individual champions for socially responsible buying behavior by the organization.[16] Firms wishing to do business with these organizations must meet their requirements for products produced in an environmentally sound manner. The ad in Illustration 19-3 would appeal to these firms.

Brand image and equity also play a role in the evaluation process for organizations. Obviously, brand can be a surrogate indicator of quality (see Chapter 16). And research suggests that while brand may not always be the most important consideration, it can result in organizational buyers paying a price premium.[17]

TABLE 19-5

Evaluative Criteria
and Organizational
Role

Evaluative Criteria Used in Purchase Decision	Functional Role in Organization			
	Purchasing	Management	Engineering	Operations
Vendor offers broad line	X	X		
Many product options available	X	X		
Ease of maintenance of equipment			X	X
Competence of service technicians		X	X	X
Overall quality of service		X	X	
Product warranty	X	X	X	X
Delivery (lead time)				X
Time needed to install equipment	X			X
Construction costs	X		X	X
Vendor has the lowest price	X	X	X	
Financial stability of vendor	X		X	X
Vendor willing to negotiate price	X			
Vendor reputation for quality	X	X	X	
Salesperson competence		X	X	X
Compatibility with equipment	X	X		
Available computer interface	X			

Source: Adapted from D. H. McQuiston and R. G. Walters, "The Evaluative Criteria of Industrial Buyers: Implications for Sales Training," *The Journal of Business and Industrial Marketing,* Summer–Fall 1989, p. 74.

ILLUSTRATION 19-3

Firms make decisions for more than economic reasons.

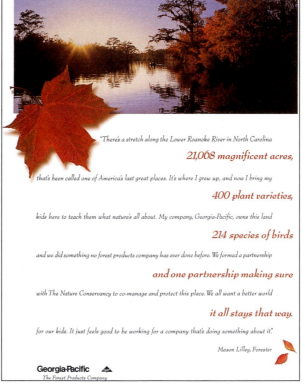

Courtesy Georgia Pacific.

Purchase and Decision Implementation   Once the decision to buy from a particular organization has been made, the method of purchase must be determined. From the seller's point of view, this means how and when they will get paid. In many purchases, payment is not made until delivery. Others involve progress payments. For a firm working on the construction of a building or highway or developing a new military aircraft that will take several years, payment timing is critical.

On an international basis, purchase implementation and method of payment are even more critical. Some countries prohibit the removal of capital from their country without an offsetting purchase. This led Caterpillar Tractor Company to sell earthmoving equipment in South America in exchange for raw materials, such as copper, which it could sell or use in its manufacturing operations.

Terms and conditions—payments, warranties, delivery dates, and so forth—are both complex and critical in business-to-business markets. One U.S. manufacturer of steam turbines lost a large order to a foreign manufacturer because its warranty was written too much to the advantage of the seller.

Firms marketing to organizations increasingly use the Internet to sell their products directly to customers or through online wholesalers (see Illustration 19-4).[18] They also use it to generate leads for telephone or direct sales calls and to solicit orders either on the Internet or via an 800 number.

Usage and Postpurchase Evaluation   After-purchase evaluations of products are typically more formal for organizational purchases than are household evaluations of purchases. In mining applications, for example, a product's life is broken down into different components such that total life-cycle cost can be assessed. Many mines will operate different brands of equipment side by side to determine the life-cycle costs of each before repurchasing one in larger quantities.

A major component of postpurchase evaluation is the service the seller provides during and after the sale.[19] Table 19-6 indicates the importance that one group of customers and managers assigned to different aspects of after-sales service. Notice that the managers did not have a very good understanding of what was important to their customers. Clearly, this firm needs a better understanding of its customers' needs.

Similar to households, dissatisfied organizational buyers may switch suppliers or engage in negative word-of-mouth communications.[20] Firms marketing to organizations pursue strategies similar to those followed by consumer marketers in dealing with dissatisfied customers. They seek to minimize dissatisfaction and to encourage those who become dissatisfied to complain to them and to no one else.[21]

Otis Elevator uses customer problems and a sophisticated database not only to increase customer satisfaction but to improve the design and functioning of its elevators:

> Otis Elevator's centralized service center, OtisLine, handles 1.2 million calls a year. Half are for unscheduled repairs. When answering such a call, the service rep punches in a code that identifies the customer's building. Immediately, a record of the equipment and its repair history appears. A series of canned questions elicits the essential new information. Within minutes, a radio message dispatches the appropriate Otis technician to the building.
>
> This fast, efficient postproblem service is only a minor part of the picture. The technician completes a report on the problem and the needed repairs. A full-time 20-member engineering team reviews each case and has the computer scan for similar cases. The results may involve a design change in an elevator model or a change in the recommended maintenance schedule.[22]

The Internet is a major source of supply for many organizational buyers.

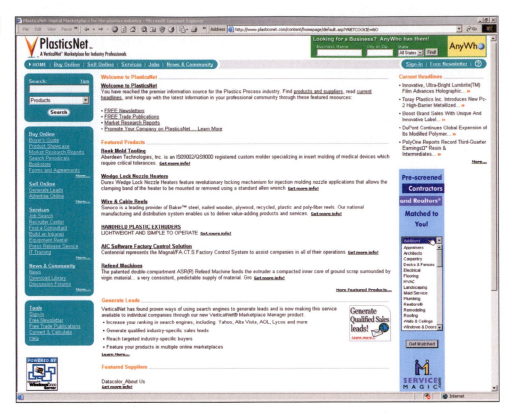

TABLE 19-6

Customer and Management Perceptions of the Importance of After-Sale Services

After-Sales Service Item	Importance of Service Item			Ratings of Service		
	Customers	Managers	Gap	Customers	Managers	Gap
Attitude and behavior of technician	11.5	8.4	3.1	7.04	7.56	−0.52
Availability of technical service staff	16.1	12.9	3.2	7.64	8.12	−0.48
Repair time when service needed	15.4	17.4	−2.0	6.36	7.71	−1.35
Dispatch of breakdown call	15.5	9.8	5.7	6.92	7.57	−0.65
Availability of spare parts during call	10.0	10.1	−0.1	7.16	7.49	−0.33
Service contract options	5.2	6.8	−1.6	6.88	7.48	−0.60
Price–performance ratio for services rendered	8.1	14.5	−6.4	6.12	7.30	−1.18
Response time when service needed	18.2	20.1	−1.9	5.92	7.09	−1.17

Source: Reprinted from H. Kasper and J. Lemmink. "After-Sales Service Quality: Views between Industrial Customers and Service Managers," *Industrial Marketing Management* 18 (1989), p. 203, with permission from Elsevier.

Relationship marketing is at least as important in industrial marketing as it is in consumer marketing.[23] The basic idea at the organizational level is for the seller to work closely with the buyer over time with the objective of enhancing the buyer's profits or operations while also making a profit. Consumer Insight 19-1 describes a successful example of organizational relationship marketing.

Organizational Relationship Marketing

W.W. Grainger distributes maintenance, repair, and operating (MRO) supplies to organizational buyers. To enhance its services to its customers, it formed Grainger Consulting Services (GCS), which helps customers understand and minimize the total cost of MRO supplies management.

Pharma Labs (a disguised name) is a pharmaceuticals manufacturer. GCS worked with Pharma on a fee basis to analyze its MRO supplies cost. It applied its models and research methods to four primary areas: processes (from how the need for items is identified to payment of invoices), products (product price, usage factors, brand standardization and application), inventory (on-hand value and carrying costs), and suppliers (performance, consolidation, and value-adding services provided).

Among other outcomes of the study, GCS recommended that Pharma consolidate its MRO supplies purchases. Pharma agreed and initiated a national account agreement with Grainger. Grainger placed a representative on site with Pharma to manage the purchase and inventory processes. This freed a Pharma maintenance technician who had been purchasing MRO supplies full-time to return to more value-adding activities in his department.

After six months, the various actions taken by Pharma based on the GCS report produced $387,000 in cost savings. Grainger's sales to Pharma increased from $50,000 to $350,000 per year! Thus, both companies benefited from their relationship.

Critical Thinking Questions

1. Is this truly relationship marketing? Why or why not?

2. What opportunities does Grainger's approach suggest for other types of firms marketing to organizations? To households?

Source: J. C. Anderson and J. A. Narus, "Business Marketing," *Harvard Business Review*, November 1998, pp. 53–65.

The Internet's Role in the Organizational Decision Process

Just as the Internet has become a major force in consumer decisions, so too is it an important tool in organizations. In fact, business-to-business (B-to-B) e-commerce in the United States is projected at anywhere from $1 trillion to over $3 trillion![24] As we have seen, the Internet can play a variety of roles in the decision process from lead generation, to information provision, to efficient and automated order fulfillment.[25] Yankelovich and Harris Interactive surveyed purchasers and purchase influencers within organizations about the Internet's role relative to other sources for "providing information," and "influencing/supporting decisions." The percentages are those who said a source was either somewhat or extremely valuable:[26]

	Information	Decision
B-to-B magazines	56%	51%
B-to-B trade shows	51	49
Salespeople	48	47
B-to-B Web sites	47	44
Professional organizations	44	40
Online database services	34	29
Newspapers	34	23
General business press	17	11
Television business networks	15	11

Business-to-Business Media Study Final Report (October 14, 2001), p. 14. © American Business Media

As this information shows, the Internet rivals salespeople, trade shows, and trade magazines as a source of information and influence. In terms of Web site design, recent research suggests that site organization (easy to navigate), customization, privacy/security, information value, and personalization are important drivers of B-to-B Web site effectiveness.[27] These characteristics are similar to those found to be important in business-to-consumer (B-to-C) contexts (see Chapter 17).

Having examined organizational purchasing behavior in some detail, let us now apply the balance of our revised model to further our understanding of organizations as consumers.

ORGANIZATIONAL CULTURE

At the hub of our consumer model of buyer behavior is self-concept and lifestyle. Organizations also have a type of self-concept in the beliefs and attitudes the organization members have about the organization and how it operates. Likewise, organizations have a type of lifestyle in that they have distinct ways of operating. We characterize these two aspects of an organization as its **organizational culture** (see Figure 19-1). Organizational culture is much like lifestyle in that organizations vary dramatically in how they make decisions and how they approach problems involving risk, innovation, and change.[28] The term **corporate culture** is often used to refer to the organizational culture of a business firm.

Organizational culture reflects and shapes organizational needs and desires, which in turn influence how organizations make decisions. For example, the Environmental Protection Agency, the Red Cross, and IBM are three large organizations. Each has a different organizational culture that influences how it gathers information, processes information, and makes decisions.

EXTERNAL FACTORS INFLUENCING ORGANIZATIONAL CULTURE

Firmographics

We discussed earlier the important role of consumer demographics in understanding consumer behavior. Firmographics are equally important. **Firmographics** involve both *organization characteristics*—for example, size, activities, objectives, location, and industry category—*and characteristics of the composition of the organization*—for example, gender, age, education, and income distribution of employees.

Size   Large organizations are more likely to have a variety of specialists who attend to purchasing, finance, marketing, and general management; in smaller organizations, one or two individuals may have these same responsibilities. Larger organizations are generally more complex because more individuals participate in managing the organization's operations. That there are often multiple individuals involved in the purchase decision in a large organization means advertising and sales force efforts must be targeted at various functions in the firm. Each message might need to emphasize issues of concern only to that function. The same purchase decision in a smaller firm might involve only the owner or manager. Different media would be required to reach this person, and one message would need to address all the key purchase issues.

Activities and Objectives   The activities and objectives of organizations influence their style and behavior. For example, the Navy, in procuring an avionics system for a new fighter plane, operates differently than Boeing does in purchasing a similar system for a commercial aircraft. The Navy is a government organization carrying out a public objective, whereas Boeing seeks a commercial objective at a profit.

TABLE 19-7

Organizational
Activities Based on
Organizational
Objective and Nature
of Activity

General Organizational Objective	Nature of Organizational Activity		
	Routine	Complex	Technical
Commercial	Office management	Human resource management	New-product development
Governmental	Highway maintenance	Tax collection	Space exploration
Nonprofit	Fund raising	Increase number of national parks	Organ donor program
Cooperative	Compile industry statistics	Establish industry standards	Applied research

Table 19-7 is a matrix that provides examples of the interface between broad organizational objectives and activities. Organizational objectives can be categorized as commercial, governmental, nonprofit, and cooperative. The general nature of organizational activity is described as routine, complex, or technical. For example, a government organization purchasing highway maintenance services would operate differently from a government organization procuring missiles. Likewise, a cooperative wholesale organization set up as a buying cooperative for several retailers would have a different organizational culture from a cooperative research institute set up by firms in the semiconductor industry. And a nonprofit organization involved in organ donations is likely to differ from one organized to gather industry statistics.

Commercial firms can be usefully divided into public firms (stock is widely traded) and private firms (one or a few individuals own a controlling share of the firm). In public firms, management is generally expected to operate the firm in a manner that will maximize the economic gains of the shareholders. These organizations face consistent pressures to make economically sound, if not optimal, decisions.

However, about half of all business purchases involve privately held firms whose CEO is often the controlling shareholder. In this situation, the firm can and frequently does pursue objectives other than profit maximization. One study found that the following motives drive the management of such firms:[29]

- Building a place for the entire family to work and be involved.
- Having complete, autocratic control over an environment.
- Build a lasting "empire."
- Becoming wealthy.
- Doing what the family expects.
- Avoiding corporations or working for others.
- Obtaining status.
- Improving the world or the environment.

Segmenting these firms according to the motives of the owners is a useful approach for developing sales messages. For example, Micron Electronics targeted the owners and managers of smaller, entrepreneurial firms. Its ads positioned it as understanding and caring about the needs and concerns of these individuals more than the larger firms do. One ad stated, "They wouldn't give you the time of day. They said you weren't a player. . . . They're holding on line three." Sun Trust is also clearly targeting this group with an ad designed to appeal to concerns regarding long-term wealth management (Illustration 19-5).

Location   As we saw in Chapter 5, there are a number of regional subcultures in the United States. These subcultures influence organizational cultures as well as individual

Courtesy SunTrust Banks, Inc.

lifestyles. For example, firms on the West Coast tend to be more informal in their operations than those on the East Coast. Dress is more casual, relationships are less formalized, and business is on more of a personal level in the West than elsewhere in the country. The Midwest and South also have unique business styles. Marketing communications and sales force training need to reflect these differences.

Location-based differences are magnified when doing business in foreign cultures. Firms that open branches outside their home countries frequently experience some difficulties managing the workforce and operating within the local community. Selling to organizations outside a firm's home culture poses as many challenges as selling to households in that culture (see Chapter 2). For example,

> To get a bank in China's Sichuan province last year to buy more than 100 ATMs, Diebold had to offer the bank 23 units for free. Diebold's distributor was coerced into buying a floor in a building the bank had invested in. And the distributor, as well as Thorpe McConville, Diebold's general manager and CEO, and Kevin Wu, a deputy GM, needed to get approval from 10 people in a variety of the bank's departments. "You've always got to meet with 8 to 12 people, all of whom have a different agenda," Wu says. "And you've got to be prepared for political chaos."
>
> The sales cycle took six months. McConville paid four visits to Sichuan, each time taking the prospects out for lunch, dinner, or karaoke.[30]

Industry Category   Two firms can be similar in terms of size (large), location (Illinois), activity (manufacturing), objective (profit), and ownership (public), and still have sharply differing cultures due in part to being in differing industries. If one of the two firms described above manufactured heavy equipment and the other computers, we would expect differing cultures to exist.

Organization Composition   Organization cultures influence the behaviors and values of those who work in the organizations. However, the types of individuals who work in the organization also heavily influence organization cultures. An organization composed primarily of young, highly educated, technically oriented people (say, a software engineering firm) will have a different culture from an organization composed primarily of older, highly educated, nontechnical individuals (say, an insurance firm). While the culture of most organizations is influenced more by the characteristics of the founder and top managers, the overall composition of the organizational membership is also important.[31]

Macrosegmentation   Organizations with distinguishing firmographics can be grouped into market segments through a process called **macrosegmentation.** These segments, based on differences in needs due to firmographics, are called *macrosegments.*[32] Micron Electronics' decision to focus on smaller firms, described earlier, is an example. First Chicago, one of America's largest banks, stated,

> We've tried too long to be everything to everyone. We're in the process of rolling out a strategy in all our branches where we segment customers and tailor our marketing campaigns to those segments.

Two of the macrosegments the bank is targeting are midsized and small businesses. Each segment will have a marketing team that focuses on that segment.[33]

Culture/Government

Variations in values and behaviors across cultures affect organizations as well as individuals.[34] For example, in most American firms shareholder or owner wealth is a dominant decision criterion. Corporate downsizing has resulted in hundreds of thousands of workers and managers losing their jobs in order to enhance profitability. These actions have been acceptable in American society. Similar corporate behavior would not be accepted in much of Europe or Japan. In these societies, worker welfare is often on a par with or above concern about corporate profit. Plant closure laws, layoff regulations, and worker benefits tend to be much higher than in America.

In America, Japan, and most of Europe, bribery and similar approaches for making sales are not acceptable, and these governments enforce a wide array of laws prohibiting such behaviors. In America, both the legal and social constraints against bribery are strong enough to make corporate gift giving from a supplier to a buyer difficult or impossible.[35] In other parts of the world, "bribes" are an expected part of many business transactions. This poses a difficult ethical dilemma for firms doing business in these regions. Ignoring any legal constraints imposed by the American government, *should an American firm provide an expensive "gift" to the purchasing agent in a foreign country where it is common knowledge that such gifts are essential to do business with the country's firms?*

In many parts of the world, businesses and governments are partners or at least work closely together. In the United States, an arm's-length or even adversarial relationship is more common. One example of this is Microsoft's ongoing battle with the U.S. government. *How do you think this might influence Microsoft's culture over time?*

Reference Groups

Reference groups influence organizational behavior and purchasing decisions. Perhaps the most powerful type of reference group in industrial markets is that of lead users. **Lead users** are *innovative organizations that derive a great deal of their success from leading*

FIGURE 19-2   **Combining Lead User and Infrastructure Reference Groups**

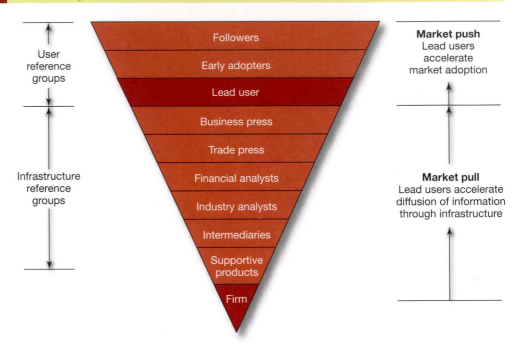

Source: Roger Best and Reinhard Angellhard, "Strategies for Leveraging a Technology Advantage," *Handbook of Business Strategy,* 1988.

change. As a result, their adoption of a new product, service, technology, or manufacturing process is watched and often emulated by the majority.[36] This statement from a Hewlett-Packard salesperson illustrates their role:

> Another aspect of hospital buying behavior is the role of key accounts. A pyramid of influence operates in this market, with smaller and medium-sized hospitals often relying on larger research and teaching hospitals for technology cues. Therefore, maintaining a strong position in influential hospitals is critical.[37]

Other reference groups such as trade associations, financial analysts, and dealer organizations also influence an organization's decision to buy or not buy a given product, or to buy or not buy from a given supplier. **Reference group infrastructure** refers to *the flow of purchase influence within an industry.* As an example, the success of a new technology product depends on how the firm influences the reference groups located along the continuum separating it from its market. The more the firm gains positive endorsement or use throughout this infrastructure, the greater its chances of customers treating it as a preferred source of supply.

If we combine the concept of lead users with reference group infrastructure, as shown in Figure 19-2, we have a more comprehensive picture of organizational reference group systems. Because the lead users play such a critical role, their adoption of a product, technology, or vendor can influence the overall infrastructure in two powerful ways. First, a lead-user decision to adopt a given supplier's innovative product adds credibility to the product and supplier. This in turn has a strong positive impact on the infrastructure that stands between the firm and its remaining target customers. Second, a lead-user decision to purchase will have a direct impact on firms inclined to follow market trends.

The strategy implication of this is clear. Marketers of new industrial products, particularly technology products, should focus initial efforts on securing sales to visible lead users.

INTERNAL FACTORS INFLUENCING ORGANIZATIONAL CULTURE

Organizational Values

IBM and Apple Computer both manufacture and market computers. However, each organization has a distinct organizational culture. IBM is corporate, formal, and takes itself seriously. Apple is less formal, creative, and promotes a more open organizational culture. Marketing managers must understand these differences in order to best serve the respective organizational needs.

As you examine the eight common business values shown below, think of how IBM might differ from Apple, Macy's from Target, Amazon.com from Buy.com, or FedEx from the U.S. Postal Service. Each is a large organization, but each has a unique set of values that underlies its organizational culture. To the degree that organizations differ on these values, a firm marketing to them will have to adapt its marketing approach.

1. Risk taking is admired and rewarded.
2. Competition is more important than cooperation.
3. Hard work comes first, leisure second.
4. Individual efforts take precedence over collective efforts.
5. Any problem can be solved.
6. Active decision making is essential.
7. Change is positive and is actively sought.
8. Performance is more important than rank or status.

The values as stated above are representative of an innovative organization that seeks change, views problems as opportunities, and rewards individual efforts.[38] It is hard to imagine the U.S. Postal Service or many other bureaucratic organizations encouraging such values. On the other hand, these values underlie many high-technology startup organizations.

The ad in Illustration 19-6 would appeal to organizations and individuals with an orientation toward efficiency and active problem solving.

Perception

To process information, a firm must go through the same sequential stages of exposure, attention, and interpretation as consumers. Of course, given the more complex nature of organizations, the processes involved are also more complex.[39] A business customer develops certain images of seller organizations from their products, people, and organizational activities. Like people, organizations have memories and base their decisions on images or memories they have developed. Once an image is formed by an organization, it is very difficult to change. Therefore, it is important for an organization to develop a sound communications strategy to build and reinforce a desired image or brand position.[40]

Illustration 19-7 shows an ad from 3M's 1, 2, 3M campaign, which was very successful. The challenge was to unify 3M's 60,000 products and provide the organization with a meaningful image. It was important to show that not only are 3M products exciting

Ads should appeal to the values of the organizations they are targeting. This ad will appeal to businesses and individuals that value efficiency and active problem solving.

Courtesy Business Objects Americas, Inc.

Well-done industrial advertising campaigns will often work across cultures to enhance the image of the firm.

Courtesy 3M.

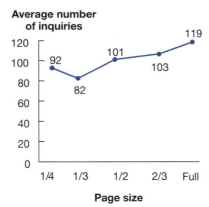

Impact of Ad Size on Inquiries   FIGURE 19-3

Source: *CARR Report No. 250.1,* CARR-Cahners
Advertising Research Report, September 2, 2005.
Used by permission.

technologically but they are useful and make a difference in peoples' lives. The campaign was highly successful in the United States, France, Latin America, and Australia. Research showed that perception of 3M as an innovative company with innovative products went from 10 to 51 percent, overall favorable impression of 3M increased from 65 to 85 percent, and the likelihood of recommending 3M and its products moved from 71 to 91 percent.[41]

Ad size and repetition have a positive effect on awareness and action. One major study found a 20 percent gain in awareness when two or more ads are placed in the same issue of a specialized business magazine compared with only one.[42] The size of the advertisement also affects action in the form of inquiries generated by the advertisement. A study of 500,000 inquiries to ads run in *Plastic World, Electronics Design News,* and *Design News* found that full-page ads were much more effective at generating inquiries than smaller ads (see Figure 19-3).

The potential power of industrial advertising can be seen in its impact on sales of an industrial safety product. Sales in the first year of the ad campaign increased almost fourfold, with advertising in one trade publication using an eight-page advertising schedule: six black-and-white ads and two color ads. When three color spreads were added to the schedule, sales continued to climb. When ad frequency was again increased, this time to six black-and-white single-page ads and 11 color spreads, product sales rose to 6.7 times pre-campaign sales.[43]

While advertising plays an important role in communicating to organizations, direct sales calls are the most important element of the communications mix in most industrial markets. This is the case despite the high cost of such calls:[44]

Industry	Average Cost per Sales Call
Manufacturing	$159
Service	106
Retail	99
Wholesale distribution	81
All companies	113

One reason for the significant role of salespeople is that businesses are not just economic entities. Business buyers prefer to do business with firms they know, like, and trust. Those relationships are most often formed between members of the firms involved, with sales personnel being the most common representative of the selling organization. As one successful salesperson stated,

> You have to have a great product but you also have to make the customer like you as a salesperson.[45]

Learning

Like individuals, organizations learn through their experiences and perceptions.[46] Positive experiences with vendors are rewarding and tend to be repeated. Purchasing processes and procedures that prove effective tend to be institutionalized in rules and policies. Likewise, negative experiences with vendors produce learning and avoidance behavior, and purchasing procedures that don't work are generally discarded. Developing the capacity to learn efficiently is increasingly a key to organizational success.[47]

Motives and Emotions

Organizational decisions tend to be less emotional than many consumer purchase decisions. However, because humans with psychological needs and emotions influence these decisions, this aspect of marketing to an organizational customer cannot be overlooked or underestimated.

Quite often there is considerable personal or career risk in organizational purchase decisions. The risk of making a bad purchase decision can elicit feelings of self-doubt or psychological discomfort. These are personal emotions that will influence purchase decisions. FedEx appeals to risk avoidance with ads that ask, in essence,

> How do you explain to your boss that the important papers didn't arrive but you saved the company $5 by using a less expensive overnight mail service?

SUMMARY

Like households, organizations make many buying decisions. In some instances, these buying decisions are routine replacement decisions; at other times, they involve new, complex purchase decisions. Three purchase situations are common to organizational buying: *straight rebuy, modified rebuy,* and *new task.* Each of these purchase situations will elicit different organizational behaviors.

The organizational decision process involves problem recognition, information search, evaluation and selection, purchase implementation, and postpurchase evaluation. As with household decisions, the Internet is an important element across various phases of the organizational decision process, including the information search and decision phases. A conjunctive process is typical in establishing an evoked set, and other decision rules are used for selecting a specific vendor. While functional attributes such as price and quality certainly play a critical role, brand image can also be important,

in some cases even increasing the prices that organizational buyers are willing to pay.

Purchase implementation is more complex and the terms and conditions more important than in household decisions. How payment is made is of major importance. Finally, use and postpurchase evaluation are often quite formal. Many organizations will conduct detailed in-use tests to determine the life-cycle costs of competing products or spend considerable time evaluating a new product before placing large orders. Satisfaction depends on a variety of criteria and on the opinions of many different people. To achieve customer satisfaction, each of these individuals has to be satisfied with the criteria important to him or her.

Organizations have a style or manner of operating that we characterize as organizational culture. *Firmographics* (organization characteristics such as size, activities, objectives, location, and industry category, and characteristics of the composition of the organization such as the gender, age, education, and income distribution of employees) have a major influence on organizational culture. The process of grouping buyer organizations into market segments on the basis of similar firmographics is called *macrosegmentation*.

Reference groups play a key role in business-to-business markets. *Reference group infrastructures* exist in most organizational markets. These reference groups often include third-party suppliers, distributors, industry experts, trade publications, financial analysts, and key customers. *Lead users* have been shown to be a key reference group that influences both the reference group infrastructure and other potential users.

Other external influences on organizational culture include the local culture in which the organization oper-

ates and the type of government it confronts. Internal factors affecting organizational culture include organizational values, perception, learning, memory, motives, and emotions.

Organizations hold values that influence the organization's style. Individuals in the organization also hold these values in varying degrees. Organizations also develop images, have motives, and learn. Seller organizations can affect how they are perceived through a variety of communication alternatives. Print advertising, direct mail, sales calls, and the Internet are common. Whereas organizations have rational motives, their decisions are influenced and made by people with emotions. A seller organization has to understand and satisfy both to be successful.

KEY TERMS

Buying center 687
Corporate culture 698
Decision-making units
   (DMUs) 687

Firmographics 698
Lead users 701
Macrosegmentation 701
Organizational culture 698

Reference group infrastructure 702
Terms and conditions 695
Two-stage decision process 692

INTERNET EXERCISES

1. Evaluate the Otis Elevator Web site (www.otis.com).

2. Visit Sun Microsystem's Web site (www.sun.com). How does their site leverage the power of reference groups in an organizational setting?

3. Evaluate *Advertising Age*'s Web site (www.adage.com).

4. Pick an industrial market and compare the Web sites of three firms. Which is best? Why?

REVIEW QUESTIONS

1. How can an organization have a culture? What factors contribute to different organizational cultures?

2. How would different organizational activities and objectives affect organizational culture?

3. What are *organizational values?* How do they differ from personal values?

4. What are *firmographics* and how do they influence organizational culture?

5. Define *macrosegmentation* and describe the variables used to create a macrosegmentation of an organizational market.

6. What types of reference groups exist in organizational markets?

7. What are *lead users* and how do they influence word-of-mouth communication and the sales of a new product?

8. What is a *decision-making unit?* How does it vary by purchase situation?

9. How can a seller organization influence perceptions of a buyer organization?
10. What are *organizational motives?*
11. What is a *two-stage decision process?*
12. Why is purchase implementation a critical part of the organizational decision process?
13. What are the three purchase situations commonly encountered by organizations? How do organizations typically respond to each situation?
14. In what ways does the Internet play a role in the organizational decision process?

DISCUSSION QUESTIONS

15. Describe three organizations with distinctly different organizational cultures. Explain why they have different organizational cultures and the factors that have helped shape the style of each.
16. Respond to the questions in Consumer Insight 19-1.
17. Describe how IBM might vary in its organizational culture from the following. Justify your response.
    a. Dell Computer
    b. Compaq
    c. Apple
18. Discuss how the following pairs differ from each other in terms of organizational activities and objectives. Discuss how these differences influence organizational cultures.
    a. Wal-Mart, Target
    b. DHL, the US Post Office
    c. Buy.com, Banana Republic
    d. Mercedes Benz, Kraft Foods
19. What role does brand/brand image play in the organizational decision process?
20. Discuss how Compaq might use a macrosegmentation strategy to sell computers to businesses.
21. Discuss how a small biotechnology firm could influence the reference group infrastructure and the lead users to accelerate adoption of its products in the market.
22. "Industrial purchases, unlike consumer purchases, do not have an emotional component." Comment.
23. For each of the three purchase situations described in the chapter (Table 19-2), describe a typical purchase for the following:
    a. McDonald's
    b. A local radio station
    c. Starbucks
    d. Your university
    e. Rite Aid drugstores

APPLICATION ACTIVITIES

24. Interview an appropriate person at a large and at a small organization and ask each to identify purchase situations that could be described as straight rebuy, modified rebuy, and new task. For each organization and purchase situation, determine the following:
    a. Size and functional representation of the decision-making unit
    b. The number of choice criteria considered
    c. Length of the decision process
    d. Number of vendors or suppliers considered
25. Review two issues of a magazine targeting organization buyers or purchase influencers. What percent of the ads contain emotional or other noneconomic appeals?
26. Interview a representative from a commercial, governmental, and nonprofit organization. For each, determine its firmographics, activities, and objectives. Then relate these differences to differences in the organizational cultures of the organizations.
27. Interview a person responsible for purchasing for a business or government agency. Have that person describe and evaluate any attempts at relationship marketing by its suppliers. What do you conclude?
28. For a given organization, identify its reference groups. Create a hierarchical diagram, as shown in Figure 19-2, and discuss how this organization could influence groups that would in turn create

favorable communication concerning this organization.

29. Interview a manager at a business or government agency who has recently been involved in an important purchase decision (e.g., a capital equipment acquisition). Have them describe the key influences at each phase of the decision process as shown in Table 19-3. Discuss how this information might be used in developing a marketing strategy for this industry.

REFERENCES

1. J. Gilbert, "Small but Mighty," *Sales & Marketing Management,* January 2004, pp. 30–35.

2. D. Tynan, "Tech Advantage," *Sales & Marketing Management,* April 2004, pp. 46–51.

3. B. Lamons, "Even Small Companies Can Build Big Brands," *Marketing News,* October 27, 2003, pp. 7–8.

4. See J. Park, P. Tansuhaj, and E. R. Spangenberg, "An Emotion-Based Perspective of Family Purchase Decisions," *Advances in Consumer Research,* vol. 22, eds. F. R. Kardes and M. Sujan (Provo, UT: Association for Consumer Research, 1995), pp. 723–28.

5. F. V. Cespedes, "Hewlett-Packard Imaging Systems Division," Harvard Business School case 9-593-080, September 6, 1994, p. 4.

6. R. Ventakesh, A. K. Kohli, and G. Zaltman, "Influence Strategies in Buying Centers," *Journal of Marketing,* October 1995, pp. 71–82; and M. A. Farrell and B. Schroder, "Influence Strategies in Organizational Buying Decisions," *Industrial Marketing Management* 25 (1996), pp. 393–403.

7. See W. J. Johnson and J. E. Lewin, "Organizational Buying Behavior," *Journal of Business Research,* January 1996, pp. 1–15; and E. J. Wilson, R. C. McMurrian, and A. G. Woodside, "How Buyers Frame Problems," *Psychology & Marketing,* June 2001, pp. 617–55.

8. S. J. Puri and C. M. Sashi, "Anatomy of a Complex Computer Purchase," *Industrial Marketing Management,* January 1994, pp. 17–27; and E. Day and J. C. Barksdale, Jr., "Organizational Purchasing of Professional Services," *Journal of Business and Industrial Marketing* 9, no. 3 (1994), pp. 44–51.

9. See A. M. Weiss and J. B. Heide, "The Nature of Organizational Search in High-Technology Markets," *Journal of Marketing Research,* May 1993, pp. 220–33.

10. P. M. Doney and G. M. Armstrong, "Effects of Accountability on Symbolic Information Search and Information Analysis by Organizational Buyers," *Journal of the Academy of Marketing Science,* Winter 1996, pp. 57–65.

11. D. Narayandas, "SalesSoft, Inc.," Harvard Business School case 9-596-112, March 24, 1998.

12. J. B. Heide and W. M. Weiss, "Vendor Consideration and Switching Behavior for Buyers in High-Technology Markets," *Journal of Marketing,* July 1995, pp. 30–43.

13. J. E. Stoddard and E. F. Fern, "Buying Group Choice," *Psychology & Marketing,* January 2002, pp. 59–90.

14. See K. N. Thompson, B. J. Coe, and J. R. Lewis, "Gauging the Value of Suppliers' Products," *Journal of Business and Industrial Marketing* 9, no. 2 (1994), pp. 29–40.

15. See, e.g., A. Kumar and D. B. Grisaffe, "Effects of Extrinsic Attributes on Perceived Quality, Customer Value, and Behavioral Intentions in B2B Settings," *Journal of Business-to-Business Marketing* 11, no. 4 (2004), pp. 43–63.

16. M. E. Drumwright, "Socially Responsible Organizational Buying," *Journal of Marketing,* July 1994, pp. 1–19. See also, D. Pujari, K. Peattie, and G. Wright, "Organizational Antecedents of Environmental Responsiveness in Industrial New Product Development," *Industrial Marketing Management* 33 (2004), pp. 381–91.

17. M. Bendixen et al., "Brand Equity in the Business-to-Business Market," *Industrial Marketing Management* 33 (2004), pp. 371–80. See also, P. Michell, J. King, and J. Reast, "Brand Values Related to Industrial Products," *Industrial Marketing Management* 30 (2001), pp. 415–25.

18. See, e.g., G. S. Lynn et al., "Factors Impacting the Adoption and Effectiveness of the World Wide Web in Marketing," *Industrial Marketing Management* 31 (2002), pp. 35–49; and H. Min and W. P. Galle, "E-Purchasing," *Industrial Marketing Management* 32 (2003), pp. 227–33.

19. K. Smith, "Service Aspects of Industrial Products," *Industrial Marketing Management* 27 (1998), pp. 83–93.

20. S. Y. Lam et al., "Customer Value, Satisfaction, Loyalty, and Switching Costs," *Journal of the Academy of Marketing Science* 32, no. 3 (2004), pp. 293–311.

21. S. W. Hansen, J. E. Swan, and T. L. Powers, "Encouraging 'Friendly' Complaint Behavior in Industrial Markets," *Industrial Marketing Management* 25 (1996), pp. 271–81.

22. J. W. Verity, "The Gold Mine of Data in Customer Service," *BusinessWeek,* March 21, 1994, p. 113.

23. See, e.g., A. Walter et al., "Functions of Industrial Supplier Relationships and their Impact on Relationship Quality," *Industrial Marketing Management* 32 (2003), pp. 159–69; J. N. Sheth and R. H. Shah, "Till Death Do Us Part . . . But Not Always," *Industrial Marketing Management* 32 (2003), pp. 627–31; and T. L. Keiningham, T. Perkins-Munn, and H. Evans, "The Impact of Customer Satisfaction on Share-of-Wallet in a Business-to-Business Environment," *Journal of Service Research*, August 2003, pp. 37–50.

24. "Regional B-to-B E-Commerce Projections," *Marketing News,* July 7, 2003, p. 20; and "U.S. B-to-B E-Commerce," *Marketing News,* July 15, 2004, p. 17.

25. H. H. Bauer, M. Grether, and M. Leach, "Building Customer Relations over the Internet," *Industrial Marketing Management* 31 (2002), pp. 155–63; J. B. MacDonald and K. Smith, "The Effects of Technology-Mediated Communication on Industrial Buyer

Behavior," *Industrial Marketing Management* 33 (2004), pp. 107–16; G. Easton and L. Araujo, "Evaluating the Impact of B2B E-commerce," *Industrial Marketing Management* 32 (2003), pp. 431–39; and L. M. Hunter et al., "A Classification of Business-to-Business Buying Decisions," *Industrial Marketing Management* 33 (2004), pp. 145–54.

26. *Business-to-Business Media Study Final Report*, prepared by Yankelovich Partners and Harris Interactive (Rochester, NY: Harris Interactive, October 4, 2001), p. 14.

27. G. Chakraborty, V. Lala, and D. Warren, "What Do Customers Consider Important in B2B Web sites?" *Journal of Advertising Research,* March 2003, pp. 50–61.

28. See S. Kitchell, "Corporate Culture, Environmental Adaptation, and Innovation Adoption," *Journal of the Academy of Marketing Science,* Summer 1995, pp. 195–205; and P. Berthon, L. F. Pitt, and M. T. Ewing, "Corollaries of the Collective," *Journal of the Academy of Marketing Science,* Spring 2001, pp. 135–50.

29. K. M. File and R. A. Prince, "A Psychographic Segmentation of Industrial Family Businesses," *Industrial Marketing Management,* May 1996, pp. 223–34.

30. G. Brewer, "An American in Shanghai," *Sales & Marketing Management,* November 1997, p. 42. See also N. D. Albers-Miller and B. Gelb, "Business Advertising Appeals as a Mirror of Cultural Dimensions," *Journal of Advertising,* Winter 1996, pp. 57–70.

31. See J. E. Stoddard and E. F. Fern, "Risk-Taking Propensity in Supplier Choice," *Psychology & Marketing,* October 1999, pp. 563–82.

32. See R. L. Griffith and L. G. Pol, "Segmenting Industrial Markets," *Industrial Marketing Management,* January 1994, pp. 39–46.

33. G. Brewer, "Selling an Intangible," *Sales & Marketing Management,* January 1998, pp. 52–58. See also S. P. Kalafatis and V. Cheston, "Normative Models and Practical Applications of Segmentation in Business Markets," *Industrial Marketing Management* 26 (1997), pp. 519–30.

34. See, e.g., C. Nakata and K. Sivakumar, "Instituting the Marketing Concept in a Multinational Setting," *Journal of the Academy of Marketing Science* 29, no. 3 (2001), pp. 255–75.

35. See F. Gibb, "To Give or Not to Give," *Sales & Marketing Management,* September 1994, pp. 136–39.

36. A. N. Link and J. Neufeld, "Innovation vs. Imitation: Investigating Alternative R&D Strategies," *Applied Economics,* no. 18 (1986), pp. 1359–63.

37. Cespedes, "Hewlett-Packard Imaging Systems Division."

38. For a discussion of innovativeness, see G. T. M. Hult, R. F. Hurley, and G. A. Knight, "Innovativeness," *Industrial Marketing Management* 33 (2004), pp. 429–38.

39. D. I. Gilliland and W. J. Johnston, "Toward a Model of Business-to-Business Marketing Communications Effects," *Industrial Marketing Management* 26 (1997), pp. 15–29.

40. See S. M. Mudambi, P. Doyle, and V. Wong, "An Exploration of Branding in Industrial Markets," *Industrial Marketing Management* 26 (1997), pp. 433–46; J. Lapierre, "The Role of Corporate Image in the Evaluation of Business-to-Business Professional Services," *Journal of Professional Services Marketing,* no. 1 (1998), pp. 21–41; and D. H. McQuiston, "Successful Branding of a Commodity Product," *Industrial Marketing Management* 33 (2004), pp. 345–54.

41. L. Hochwald, "It's the Sizzle That Sells," *Sales & Marketing Management,* April 1997, p. 51.

42. *CARR Report No. 120.3* (Boston: Cahners Publishing Co., undated).

43. "Study: Increase Business Ads to Increase Sales," *Marketing News,* March 14, 1988, p. 13.

44. M. Marchetti, "Hey Buddy, Can You Spare $113.25?" *Sales & Marketing Management,* August 1997, pp. 69–77.

45. G. Conlon, "A Day in the Life of Sales," *Sales & Marketing Management,* September 1997, pp. 42–63.

46. See J. M. Sinkula, "Market Information Processing and Organizational Learning," *Journal of Marketing,* January 1994, pp. 35–45; G. T. M. Hult and E. L. Nichols, Jr., "The Organizational Buyer Behavior Learning Organization," *Industrial Marketing Management,* May 1996, pp. 197–207; and S. J. Bell, G. J. Whitwell, and B. A. Lukas, "Schools of Thought in Organizational Learning," *Journal of the Academy of Marketing Science,* Winter 2002, pp. 70–86.

47. D. A. Garvin, "Building a Learning Organization," *Harvard Business Review,* July 1993, pp. 78–91; S. F. Slater and J. C. Narver, "Market Orientation and the Learning Organization," *Journal of Marketing,* July 1995, pp. 63–74; and G. T. M. Hult, "Cultural Competitiveness in Global Sourcing," *Industrial Marketing Management* 31 (2002), pp. 25–34.

Cases

CASE 5-1 RAEX LASER Steel

The global steel market is plagued with overcapacity and slow growth. Annual growth between 1980 and 2003 has been less than 1 percent. This has created fierce competition and a perception among industrial buyers that steel is a commodity. The result has been that in many cases the deciding factor in a purchase decision is price with resulting downward pressure on profitability.

One strategy that some steel manufacturers have used is to cut operating costs in order to help protect profit margins. Another strategy that some manufacturers have been attempting is a product differentiation approach accompanied by a strong brand name around which to build a distinctive image. But is branding useful in an industrial (B-to-B) context? The answer appears to be yes:

> [I]ndustrial firms hold very positive views about the benefits of brand names and feel that branding is valuable to marketing success and is a major corporate asset. In addition, industrial firms perceive a number of competitive differential benefits in the use of manufacturer brands, with quality, reliability, and performance rated as primary factors.

Clearly industrial marketers see value in branding. However, do industrial buyers? The answer here depends on the extent to which the brand (*a*) creates benefits of value to buyers and (*b*) consistently delivers these core benefits. When these two factors are present, brand name becomes the symbol of these benefits and core values and provides for differentiation in the marketplace. In addition, consistent delivery over time results in increased trust, stronger relationships, and enhanced loyalty.

Rautaruukki Ojy (RO) is a steel manufacturer in Finland. It has a strong reputation in Europe but is relatively small. Rather than go the cost-cutting route, it decided to take the differentiation route. Its opportunity came when laser cutting technology became available. After hearing initial grumbling about steel quality problems associated with laser cutting, RO conducted intensive research to understand the nature of the problem/opportunity.

RO found that laser cutting involves preprogrammed computer settings. These settings involve considerable setup time, so users want to be able to save the cutting specs for reuse later on. However, this requires very high consistency in terms of the chemical composition and quality of the steel both within a batch of steel and across batches. The nature of the industry was also one where companies outsourced their laser cutting needs to specialty "job shops." Order quantity from these job shops was highly variable and not predictable. Given the technical nature of laser cutting, an educated customer service department was also critical.

As a result of this research, RO created RAEX LASER brand steel. The value components included:

- Consistent quality steel within and across batches to meet laser cutting specifications.
- Flexibility in order size acceptance through its distributors. The supply chain for RO is one of manufacturer (RO) to distributors, to end users (job shops who do laser cutting). Since the job shops had highly variable order size needs and they were unpredictable, RO had to provide flexibility in order size fulfillment. In managing supply, RO also created a cooperative atmosphere among their distributors whereby they would share inventories if needed in order to keep the supply chain running. Educational seminars and an annual retreat are part of this process.
- Customer service. Since education was critical, RO engaged in extensive training of its internal customer service personnel to provide them with the tools to deliver the highest customer service possible.

The results have been very positive. Sales have been on the increase since the introduction of the RAEX LASER brand and its value components. Customer loyalty has increased and buyers are now willing to pay a *price premium* to get RAEX LASER steel and all that goes with it. And their efforts even caught the attention of the largest laser cutter manufacturer, which now recommends RAEX to new buyers of its machines!

Discussion Questions

1. Create a diagram linking the value drivers for RAEX LASER steel to buyer satisfaction, trust, relationship quality, and loyalty. Explain how RAEX branding was much more than a promotion-driven process.

2. Should promotion and advertising come first or last in the brand building process? Does this depend on whether the promotion is targeted at the "external consumer" (in this case the job shops) or the "internal consumers" (in this case customer service employees)? Explain.

3. Discuss the importance of "internal marketing efforts" discussed in Question 2 to the success of RAEX's branding strategy.

4. Are buyers of RAEX LASER just "paying more for the name" or is it due to the economic benefits associated with the name? What, if any, economic benefits accrue to buyers of RAEX LASER steel?

5. Does the fact that job shops use brand name in their decision process mean that they are irrational decision makers?

6. Describe the various ways in which reference groups and word-of-mouth might operate in this setting.

7. Could RO use the RAEX name to expand beyond laser applications? Which of its value propositions do you think would transfer successfully?

Source: D. H. McQuiston, "Successful Branding of a Commodity Product," *Industrial Marketing Management* 33 (2004), pp. 345–54; and www.ruukki.com.

CASE 5-2 Mack Trucks' Integrated Communications Campaign

For 90 years Mack Trucks dominated the construction and refuse segments of the Class 8 (large) truck market. In fact, the expression "Built like a Mack truck" came to stand for solid, rugged construction. Unfortunately, 70 percent of the demand for large trucks is in the highway or over-the-road hauling segment, and this is also the segment with the highest growth rate.

Until the late 1980s, Mack did not compete effectively in the over-the-road segments. In 1990, Mack was purchased by the French automaker Renault. A plan to become a major competitor in the critical highway market segment was developed and implemented. The first stage involved the development and launch of two new over-the-road truck lines. According to Brian Taylor, Mack's vice president of marketing,

> We developed a product line that had good ergonomics. It was roomy and it had a smooth ride, but we faced a challenge with communicating those changes to our customers.

To meet this challenge, the firm initiated a series of research studies with the goal of developing an integrated communications campaign.

Research Studies

Four basic sources of information were used to guide the development of the integrated campaign.

1. Perceptual maps were derived that identified how Mack trucks were perceived relative to competing brands. The maps revealed that they were viewed as durable but not very comfortable.

2. Focus group sessions and one-on-one interviews with current and prospective Mack customers isolated additional driver and operator needs and concerns. This research helped identify the criteria the trucks would need to meet to be in the buyer's consideration set.

3. Industry trade publications frequently conduct surveys of fleet operators, truck owners, and truck drivers. These surveys cover a wide range of issues, including desired truck features and shortcomings. These surveys were obtained and analyzed.

4. News clippings and other sources of data describing quality or service problems Mack had experienced in the past were also studied.

These studies indicated that Mack faced a significant communications challenge. According to Taylor, "'Built like a Mack truck' served us well in our core business, but it did not have a good connotation in the over-the-road segment. And that was a perception we had to change." A consultant on the project stated the challenge this way: "We had to create a campaign—an impression—in which customers would be willing to suspend their disbelief that Mack was more than they knew."

Objectives

Three primary objectives were developed for the campaign:

1. Change the perception of Mack trucks from "rugged, tough, and uncomfortable to drive," to "the most comfortable and driveable over-the-road trucks."
2. Change the perception of Mack engines from "heavy, expensive, and low tech," to "ideal for over-the-road applications, very economical and reliable."
3. Increase the number of over-the-road fleet buyers who have Mack in their consideration sets.

Accomplishing these objectives would require a change in Mack's current positioning from

Mack is a great old brand. But they can't compete for my business because they don't have a package that meets my needs.

to

Mack's turning things around. The CH model with the E7 engine is the right combination for my fleet. Plus, these guys really want my business.

This leads to the following positioning statement:

The new Mack is the proud result of combining Mack tradition and unequaled driveability.

The Communications Strategy

The communications strategy integrated advertising, sales promotion, direct marketing, and public relations. For the advertising campaign, Mack's traditional bulldog was made hip in six new print ads with racing stripes, sunglasses, a champagne glass, or other symbols of change and uniqueness. The ads were colorful with limited text. Each focused on one key attribute such as fuel economy. The tagline for the campaign was "Drive one and you'll know."

The sales promotion program consisted of the "Bulldog National Test Drive Tour." This tour allowed truckers to test drive a new Mack truck at truck stops and trade shows throughout the country.

The direct marketing program included an 800 number in all print advertising that readers could use to get information about the nearest dealer, the test drive promotion, or to request specific model information. The "Fleet Focus" part of the campaign mailed materials to nearly 1,200 non-Mack fleet customers urging them to consider Mack in their next purchase and providing material to support that recommendation. Dealers were provided qualified lead cards generated from the 800 number, the test drives, and the direct-mail program.

Throughout the campaign, numerous news releases and articles were provided to trade publications. There was also an eight-city media tour in which Mack discussed its commitment to the public and the over-the-road segment. Mack redesigned the quarterly, 24-page *Bulldog* magazine to reflect the firm's customer service orientation.

Discussion Questions

1. Predict the likely success of this program. Explain. What, if anything, would you change?
2. Is a "hip" bulldog an appropriate symbol for a serious industrial product like a truck?
3. Why are Mack and its agencies so concerned with customer perception when its products are so good?
4. What criteria do you think fleet buyers have for including a brand in their consideration set? How do you think they choose from among the brands in the consideration set?
5. Why did the "built like a Mack truck" theme not work for the over-the-road segment?
6. How would you alter the campaign for use in these countries?
    a. Japan
    b. Germany
    c. China
    d. Brazil

Source: Reprinted with permission from the September 18, 1995, issue of *Advertising Age.* Copyright Crain Communications, Inc. 1995.

Consumer Behavior and Marketing Regulation

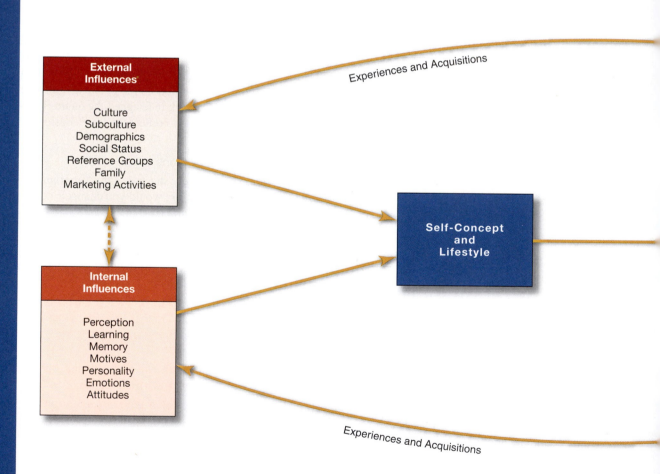

External Influences

Culture
Subculture
Demographics
Social Status
Reference Groups
Family
Marketing Activities

Internal Influences

Perception
Learning
Memory
Motives
Personality
Emotions
Attitudes

Self-Concept and Lifestyle

Experiences and Acquisitions

Experiences and Acquisitions

Throughout the text, we have emphasized that knowledge of consumer behavior is as important to those who would regulate consumer behavior as it is to those who engage in marketing activities. Government officials, consumer advocates, and citizens all need to understand consumer behavior to develop, enact, and enforce appropriate rules and regulations for marketing activities. Consumers in particular need to understand their own behaviors and how their purchase and consumption behaviors help determine the type of marketplace and society we have.

In this section, we will analyze the role of consumer behavior principles in regulating marketing practices.

We will pay particular attention to the regulation of marketing activities focused on children. We also discuss regulations covering advertising, product, and pricing practices aimed at adults.

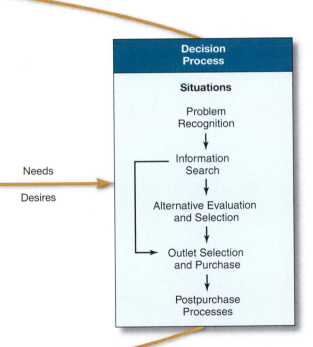

Needs

Desires

Marketing Regulation and Consumer Behavior

A battle is raging over childhood obesity.[1] On the one hand consumer groups, lawyers, and policy makers often claim that food marketing and advertising are major contributing factors. For example, both the American Psychological Association (APA) and the Kaiser Family Foundation recently issued reports that summarize the findings of numerous studies relating to media, food consumption, and obesity among children. Among the conclusions:

- Over the decades that childhood obesity has increased, so too has the amount of advertising to children. They both cite one source suggesting that children are exposed to 40,000 ads per year, up from 20,000 in the 1970s.
- Much of the advertising to children is food related and often in categories historically known for high sugar and/or fat content including candy, cereal, and fast food.
- Food advertising appears to be capable of influencing the food consumption choices of children in terms of both brands and food categories.

On the other hand food marketers and their proponents often argue that a strong, solid link between food advertising and obesity has not been established and further suggest that inactivity and parents are to blame.

The debate has gotten so intense that Senate hearings have been conducted. In addition, the Federal Trade Commission (FTC) and Health and Human Services (HHS) recently brought together industry, media, medical, and government representatives for a two-day workshop on marketing, self-regulation, and childhood obesity. In her opening remarks, Deborah Majoras, chairman of the FTC, was quick to point out the complex and multifaceted nature of the problem:[2]

There are many alleged "suspects": developers for the suburban sprawl that puts us in our cars, not on our feet; schools for cutting physical education programs and meeting budget shortfalls through vending machine sales; video and computer games for competing with more physical play time; parents for overindulging their children and failing to set a good example and buy healthy foods; restaurants for increasing portion sizes; and the food industry for an abundance of good-tasting, convenient, affordable, calorie-laden foods, which are marketed in ways that directly appeal to children.

Majoras also made it clear, however, that the food industry must be accountable and play a positive proactive role:[3]

[F]rom the FTC's perspective, based on years of experience with advertising, a government ban on children's food advertising is neither wise nor viable. It would be, however, equally unwise for industry to maintain the status quo. Not only is downplaying the concerns of consumers bad business, but if industry fails to demonstrate good faith commitment to this issue and to take positive steps, others may step in and act in its stead.

To their credit, those in the food, advertising, and entertainment industries have taken steps in the right direction. Some examples include:

- Kraft has created healthier offerings and is eliminating or limiting some forms of advertising in programming targeted at children of certain ages.
- McDonald's offers healthy options in its Happy Meals.
- Nickelodeon and Warner Brothers are licensing their characters for healthier products such as fruits and vegetables.

Many, even those in the industry, admit that these efforts are just a start. In addition, critics contend that money not spent in one area (e.g., traditional TV ads) is often shifted to other areas (Web sites) that are increasingly effective in targeting children.

As the opening example indicates, marketing practices are sometimes controversial. Marketing is a highly visible, important activity. It affects the lives of individuals, the success of nonprofit groups, and the profits of businesses. As indicated throughout the text, there are many issues where the appropriate ethical action for marketers is not clear-cut. As a marketing manager, you will face many such situations in your career. However, society has declared that some marketing actions are clearly inappropriate. It has done so by enacting laws and regulations that prohibit or require specific marketing actions. In this chapter, we examine the regulation of marketing practices. Regulating marketing activities requires the same level of understanding of consumer behavior as does managing marketing programs. Our consideration of the regulation of marketing practices will separate regulations designed to protect children from those designed to protect adults.

REGULATION AND MARKETING TO CHILDREN

The regulation of marketing activities aimed at children focuses primarily on product safety, advertising and promotions, and privacy protection. Product safety issues focus on appropriate product design and materials. We will concentrate on privacy protection and advertising and other promotional activities[4] targeting children as consumers. The regulation of these activities rests heavily on theories of children's consumer behavior, particularly their information-processing skills.

There are a variety of state, federal, and voluntary guidelines and rules governing marketing to children. Despite these rules, many feel that some marketers continue to take advantage of children and that the overall marketing system, particularly advertising, is socializing children to value things (products) rather than intangibles such as relationships and integrity.

One basis for the concern over marketing to children is based on *Piaget's stages of cognitive development* (Chapter 6), which indicate that children lack the ability to fully process and understand information, including marketing messages, until around 12 years of age.[5] This and related theories are the basis for most regulation of advertising aimed at children and, according to critics, for some marketing programs that deliberately exploit children.

Concerns about the Ability of Children to Comprehend Commercial Messages

The American advertising industry's primary self-regulatory body, the National Advertising Division of the Council of Better Business Bureaus, maintains a special unit to review advertising aimed at children—the **Children's Advertising Review Unit (CARU).** Two of the seven principles that underlie CARU's guidelines for advertising directed to children relate to their ability to comprehend commercial messages:[6]

1. Advertisers should always take into account the level of knowledge, sophistication, and maturity of the audience to which their message is primarily directed. Younger children have a limited capacity for evaluating the credibility of information they receive. They also may lack the ability to understand the nature of the personal information they disclose on the Internet. Advertisers, therefore, have a special responsibility to protect children from their own susceptibilities.

2. Realizing that children are imaginative and that make-believe play constitutes an important part of the growing-up process, advertisers should exercise care not to exploit unfairly the imaginative quality of children. Unreasonable expectations of product quality or performance should not be stimulated either directly or indirectly by advertising.

Some of the specific guidelines relating to information processing that guide CARU's policing of children's advertising are shown in Table 20-1.

CARU and others are interested in the impact that the *content* of children's advertising has, as well as the ability of children to process advertising messages. However, our current

TABLE 20-1

Information Processing–Related Guidelines of CARU

1. Care should be taken not to exploit a child's imagination. Fantasy, including animation, is appropriate for younger as well as older children. However, it should not create unattainable performance expectations nor exploit the younger child's difficulty in distinguishing between the real and the fanciful.
2. The performance and use of a product should be demonstrated in a way that can be duplicated by the child for whom the product is intended.
3. All price representations should be clearly and concisely set forth. Price minimizations such as "only" or "just" should not be used.
4. Program personalities, live or animated, should not be used to sell products, premiums, or services in or adjacent to programs primarily directed to children in which the same personality or character appears.
5. Children have difficulty distinguishing product from premium. If product advertising contains a premium message, care should be taken that the child's attention is focused primarily on the product. The premium message should be clearly secondary.

Source: *Self-Regulatory Guidelines for Children's Advertising* (Council of Better Business Bureaus, Inc., Children's Advertising Review Unit, 2003).

focus is limited to children's abilities to *comprehend* advertising messages. There are two main components to this concern: (1) Do children understand the selling intent of commercials? and (2) Can children understand specific aspects of commercials, such as comparisons?

Do Children Understand the Selling Intent of Commercials?

Research suggests that younger children have at least some difficulty understanding the selling intent of commercials.[7] Currently, the advertising industry strives to separate children's commercials from the programs by prohibiting overlapping characters and by using *separators* such as "We will return after these messages."

This problem is growing in intensity, as children's products are often the "stars" of animated children's films and television programs. Increasingly, product lines and television programs (and movies) are being designed jointly with the primary objective being sales of the toy line. Parents have expressed concerns ranging from the effects that toy-based programming has on their children's behaviors and emotional development to the fear that such programming may replace other more creative and child-oriented programs.[8]

This concern has led to a variety of proposals to restrict or eliminate such programs. These proposals have produced an ongoing debate about who controls the television set. One argument is that it is the parent's responsibility to monitor and regulate their children's viewing behaviors. If a sufficient number of parents find such programs inappropriate and refuse to let their children watch them, advertisers will quit sponsoring them and they will no longer be available. Another argument is that today's time-pressured parents do not have time to screen all the shows their children watch. Furthermore, tremendous peer pressure can develop for children to watch a particular show or own the products associated with it. Denying a child the right to watch such a show then causes arguments and resentments. Therefore, society should set appropriate standards within which broadcasters should operate. *Which, if either, of these views matches your own?*

Can Children Understand the Words and Phrases in Commercials?

The second aspect of comprehension involves specific words or types of commercials that children might misunderstand. For example, research indicates that disclaimers such as "Part of a nutritious breakfast," "Each sold separately," and "Batteries not included," are ineffective with preschool children.[9] Not only do young children have a difficult time understanding these phrases, but an analysis of Saturday morning advertising aimed at children revealed that most such disclaimers are presented in a manner that does not meet the Federal Trade Commission's "Clear and Conspicuous" requirements for such disclaimers.[10]

For example, one toy ad contained this disclaimer: "TV Teddy comes with one tape. Other tapes sold separately." However, it appeared near the bottom of the screen in lettering that measured only 3.5 percent of the screen height against a multicolor background. It was not repeated by an announcer and appeared for less than three seconds. A child would have to read at 200 words per minute to read the message! Unfortunately, this treatment of the disclaimer is more the rule than the exception.

CARU has special rules for comparison advertising and prohibits price minimizations such as "only" and "just." It also suggests specific phrasing for certain situations, such as "your mom or dad must say it's OK before you call" rather than "ask your parents' permission." Recent cases involving CARU and the information-processing skills of children include the following:

• Trendmasters' Rumble Robots advertising depicted the highest level of performance of the robot, which requires the purchase of upgrades, rather than the performance of the one available in the standard package. It changed this commercial at CARU's request.[11]

- Nabisco, Inc., agreed to change its advertising for KoolStuf Oreo Toaster Pastries after CARU brought a consumer complaint to its attention. The commercial showed Oreo cookies going into a toaster and popping up as KoolStuf toaster pastries. A four-year-old saw the commercial and tried to do the same thing by putting Oreos into a toaster. When they melted, he tried to remove them with a pair of metal tongs before being stopped by his mother.[12]
- Rose Art Industries agreed to alter its packaging after CARU concluded that the size of the product relative to the size of the child shown in the package picture could lead a child to believe the Super Lite toy is larger than it is.[13]

The Federal Trade Commission (FTC) applied sanctions to Lewis Galoob Toys and its ad agency. The ads cited showed a doll dancing and a toy airplane flying, both of which require human assistance. The ads also failed to disclose that assembly was required for certain toy sets. Finally, the firm failed to "clearly and conspicuously" disclose that two toys shown together had to be purchased separately. An FTC spokesperson noted that the ads never appeared on network stations and speculated that the networks' internal review processes for children's ads would have precluded their being shown.[14]

Concerns about the Effects of the Content of Commercial Messages on Children

Even if children accurately comprehend television ads, there are concerns about the effects the content of these messages has on children. These concerns stem in part from the substantial amount of time American children spend viewing television. The large amount of time children devote to watching television, including commercials, gives rise to two major areas of concern:

- The impact of commercial messages on children's values.
- The impact of commercial messages on children's health and safety.

Five of the seven basic principles that underline CARU's guidelines for advertising directed at children focus on these concerns (the other two are concerned with children's information-processing capabilities). They are:[15]

1. Recognizing that advertising may play an important role in educating the child, advertisers should communicate information in a truthful and accurate manner and in language understandable to young children with full recognition that the child may learn practices from advertising which can affect his or her health and well-being.
2. Advertisers are urged to capitalize on the potential of advertising to influence behavior by developing advertising that, wherever possible, addresses itself to positive and beneficial social behavior, such as friendship, kindness, honesty, justice, generosity and respect for others.
3. Care should be taken to incorporate minority and other groups in advertisements in order to present positive and pro-social roles and role models wherever possible. Social stereotyping and appeals to prejudice should be avoided.
4. Although many influences affect a child's personal and social development, it remains the prime responsibility of the parents to provide guidance for children. Advertisers should contribute to this parent–child relationship in a constructive manner.
5. Products and content which are inappropriate for children should not be advertised or promoted directly to children.

Several of the specific guidelines derived from these principles are provided in Table 20-2.

TABLE 20-2

Examples of Specific
Guidelines of the
Children's Advertising
Review Unit

1. Representation of food products should be made so as to encourage sound use of the product with a view toward healthy development of the child and development of good nutritional practices. Advertisements representing mealtime should clearly and adequately depict the role of the product within the framework of a balanced diet. Snack foods should be clearly represented as such, and not as substitutes for meals.
2. Children should not be urged to ask parents or others to buy products. Advertisements should not suggest that a parent or adult who purchases a product or service for a child is better, more intelligent, or more generous than one who does not. Advertising directed toward children should not create a sense of urgency or exclusivity, for example, by using words like "now" and "only."
3. Benefits attributed to the product or service should be inherent in its use. Advertisements should not convey the impression that possession of a product will result in more acceptance of a child by his or her peers. Conversely, it should not be implied that lack of a product will cause a child to be less accepted by his or her peers. Advertisements should not imply that purchase and use of a product will confer upon the user the prestige, skills, or other special qualities of characters appearing in advertising.
4. Advertisements should not portray adults or children in unsafe situations, or in acts harmful to themselves or others. For example, when athletic activities (such as bicycle riding or skateboarding) are shown, proper precautions and safety equipment should be depicted.

Source: *Self-Regulatory Guidelines for Children's Advertising* (Council of Better Business Bureaus, Inc., Children's Advertising Review Unit, 2003).

Health and Safety CARU challenged a television commercial for 4Wheelers by Skechers, which ran during traditional children's viewing time. The ad featured teens skating and performing a stunt without the use of any safety gear such as helmets or pads. According to CARU, this violates the fourth guideline in Table 20-2. Skechers appealed the ruling, stating that there are no children shown in the commercial; protective gear while skating or rollerblading is not required by law; it warns purchasers to "always" wear protective gear in the safety pamphlet that comes with the product; and the skates are not being portrayed in an athletic or sporting manner.[16] *What do you think? Was CARU correct or was Skechers?*

In many instances, children and teenagers are exposed to advertising directed at adults. For example, research indicates that tobacco ads routinely reach a high percentage of 12- to 17-year-olds when placed in popular consumer magazines (many doubt that this is unintended).[17]

Even ads clearly not targeting children can have potentially harmful consequences:

> A television commercial for Calgonite automatic dishwasher detergent showed a woman inside an automatic dishwasher. The commercial was withdrawn voluntarily after CARU received a complaint that a three-year-old child had climbed into a dishwasher shortly after viewing the commercial.[18]

The problem caused by the Calgonite commercial illustrates the difficulty marketers face. This commercial was not aimed at children nor shown during a children's program. The fact that children watch prime-time television extensively places an additional responsibility on marketers.[19]

Ensuring that advertisements portray only safe uses of products is sometimes difficult, but it is not a controversial area. Advertising of health-related products, particularly snack foods and cereals, is much more controversial. The bulk of the controversy focuses on the heavy advertising emphasis placed on sugared and high-fat products. Advertising sugared products such as presweetened breakfast cereals does increase their consumption. However, this same advertising may also increase the consumption of related products, such as milk. What is not known, and probably cannot be determined, are the eating patterns that would exist in the absence of such advertising. That is, if children did not know about cereals such as Cap'n Crunch, would they eat a more nutritious breakfast, a less nutritious breakfast, or perhaps no breakfast at all?

Recently, children were attracted to nutellausa.com through a sweepstakes featuring Nutella's celebrity endorser, Kobe Bryant, that appeared in *Sports Illustrated for Kids,* as well as its Web site, sikids.com. This caused the following problem:

> On the site, the firm made several claims comparing the dietary benefits of its product, Nutella, a hazelnut spread, with those of peanut butter. The Web site had been promoting the fact that, compared to leading peanut butter, Nutella has 37 percent less fat and 87 percent less sodium. However, the site omitted a comparison of a key nutritional concern for children—sugar content. Nutella has a sugar content of 21 grams in one serving as opposed to 2 grams or 3 grams in a serving of peanut butter. CARU's position was that, taking into consideration government guidelines and medical community recommendations on sugar consumption, children could get the wrong impression about the overall dietary benefits of Nutella as opposed to peanut butter. The firm altered the claims.[20]

Unfortunately, some marketers have not been very responsible in this area as discussed in the opening example regarding childhood obesity and the role of food marketing and advertising (see also Case 2-9). It should be noted that some successful marketers of products consumed by children, such as Coca-Cola and PepsiCo, do not advertise on children's shows.[21]

Values   Advertising is frequently criticized as fostering overly materialistic, self-focused, and short-term values in children:

> We cannot afford to raise a generation of children that measures its own value by the insignia on their clothes—not by the compassion in their hearts or the knowledge in their minds.[22]

One reason is the magnitude of advertising focused on kids. One estimate is that marketers spend $15 billion per year advertising to children.[23] In addition, estimates of the number of TV ads that children are exposed to ranges from 18,000 to 40,000 per year.[24] Obviously, these numbers are conservative in terms of total ad exposure since they exclude other popular media such as the Internet. Many are concerned that this consistent pressure to buy and own things is producing negative values in children.

Numerous cosmetics companies are now targeting children as young as 8 with products and advertising. Most position the products in terms of fun rather than sensuality. For example, Disney's products are packaged in boxes with pictures of Tinkerbell, Winnie the Pooh, and similar characters.[25] According to an industry expert, girls 8 to 12 are now wearing platform heels and "low-rise jeans, tight miniskirts and midriff-baring T-shirts."[26]

There is also an increase in concern about looking thin and eating disorders in children as young as 6.[27] Many find this apparent shortening of childhood and the related body image problems inappropriate. They assign a large part of the blame to the marketing of products such as cosmetics and personalities such as Britney Spears.

Summary of Advertising and Children   Available evidence suggests that the vast majority of ads meet CARU guidelines.[28] CARU reviews thousands of ads every year and has over a 95 percent success rate in resolving issues related to children's advertising.[29] However, given the enormous amount of time children spend with all forms of media, most will see many ads that are in violation of these guidelines. In addition, these guidelines do not address such issues as advertising high-fat foods. Nor do they, nor could they, oppose generating desires for products that many families cannot afford. Nonetheless, CARU has greatly enhanced the level of responsibility in advertising aimed at children. Many consumer advocates would like it to expand the areas it covers and increase the stringency of its rules.

Controversial Marketing Activities Aimed at Children

There are a number of marketing activities targeted at children in addition to television advertising that are controversial and for which various regulatory proposals are being considered. For example, violent entertainment products (movies, videos, and music) labeled for those 17 and older were, until recently, routinely marketed to kids. Highly publicized acts of violence by teenagers produced threats of regulation and improved self-regulation by the industries.[30] However, it remains a problem.

Another area of ongoing concern is kids' clubs which typically provide membership certificates, a magazine or Web site, the chance to win prizes, and discounts or coupons for products offered by the sponsor. Kids' clubs vary widely in what they offer the members and how ethically they are run. A major concern is that these clubs disguise commercial messages—for example when ad messages come disguised as "advice from your club."[31]

Three additional issues are described in this section.

Mobile Marketing and Children   Sometimes referred to as the "Third Screen," cell phones are an increasingly integral part of our lives. And marketers see younger children as the next big growth market. Consider the following:

> Appealing to kids is rich terrain for wireless companies, which have already locked up nearly 70 percent of the U.S. population through service contracts. In the past year, the industry's biggest growth has come from 14- to 24-year-olds buying from specialized brands like Virgin Mobile or Boost Mobile LLC. Now, 55 percent of teens have wireless phones, so companies see green in the even younger market, where 25 percent of kids 12 and under own phones, according to the Yankee Group.[32]

Various types of promotional efforts are being used including:[33]

- *Ringtones*—Customized ringtones are quite the craze. Movies have gotten into the mix in a big way and allow downloads of ringtones such as Samantha's "nose wiggle" ring tone for the movie *Bewitched*. An example targeting an even younger audience is the Pokemon ringtone.
- *Mobile games*—General mobile games are a major market. Increasingly, mobile games are being customized to a brand or event. *Batman Begins* was promoted with a mobile game custom designed around the movie. In the U.K., Dennis the Menace mobile games will be distributed which feature characters from the comic strip.
- *Text-in contests*—Text message codes are being used by numerous companies for contests and other promotions. Text in a specific code provided in an ad or on the package and you can enter to win various prizes. Recent examples include Starburst and Nesquick.

The ability for marketers to infiltrate yet another media domain with promotions and materials that are seen as further blurring the line between advertising and entertainment has many parents and consumer advocate groups worried. When Disney recently announced that it would, in a partnership with Sprint, offer cellular phone service targeted specifically at children in the 8- to 12-year range, concerns grew even stronger. Consider an excerpt from a letter to Congress by Commercial Alert, a nonprofit consumer advocate group:

> If Disney Corporation and the others just wanted to give children a way to contact parents in emergencies, that would be one thing. The telecommunications companies—to parents at least—are playing up this angle. Telecommunications lobbyists in Washington will harp on it as well.

But despite the industry's rhetoric, Disney and the telecommunications companies really want to use children as conduits to their parents' wallets. And marketers want another way to bypass parents and speak directly to the nation's children.

Advertising Age reported on July 11th that many corporations, including McDonald's, Coca-Cola, and Timex, are moving "from small [mobile phone advertising] tests to all-out campaign[s]." Children already are bombarded with too much advertising. They don't need more advertising through their mobile phones, whether it is telemarketing, text message marketing, adver-games, or any other type of commercial messages.[34]

Obviously, the battle lines are being drawn. *Which side of this debate do you come down on more—that of the marketers or the consumer advocates? Does your answer depend on the age of the children and the nature of the tactics utilized?*

Commercialization of Schools

There has been ongoing concern and controversy around the commercialization of elementary and high schools. Schools are often motivated by money as budgets continue to be tight. The issue of commercialization covers a broad sphere of activities. Consumers Union has the following classification system:[35]

- *In-school ads*—Ads in such places as school buses, scoreboards, bulletin boards, as well as coupons and free samples. For example, Word of Mouse provides free mousepads to schools ranging from grade schools to colleges. Each colorful pad contains four age-appropriate ads for Web sites. Other aspects might include schools selling naming rights to companies and distributing ads in student newspapers. For example, advertisers can now get national runs in high-school newspapers through Campus Media Group.

  Kraft recently announced that it would stop school advertising aimed at younger children. However, Krispy Kreme has come under fire for offering free donuts to children who get "A"s on their report cards.

- *Ads in classroom*—Ads in classroom magazines and television programs. This also includes ads in magazines distributed in school libraries. Channel One has created substantial controversy in this area. It provides 12 minutes of news to participating schools, but contains two minutes of commercials. Research indicates that the commercials impact students.[36]

  Recently, *Time* and *Newsweek* were applauded for agreeing to remove tobacco ads from school library editions of *Time, Sports Illustrated,* and *Newsweek.*

- *Corporate-sponsored educational materials and programs*—Also called sponsored educational materials or SEMs. SEMs are teaching materials provided by corporations, usually for free. They come in various forms including posters, activity sheets, and multimedia teaching aids.

  While many criteria can be used to evaluate these materials, one of the main criteria is the level of commercialism. Highly commercialized SEMs that are thinly veiled ads with little educational value draw the most scrutiny. However, there are trade-offs in that compliance with a completely noncommercial standard would greatly reduce the motivation of firms to provide valuable (sometimes) material to the schools.[37]

- *Corporate-sponsored contests and incentive programs*—When companies gain access through various contests and incentives including prizes such as travel, free pizza, and so on.

Another area of great concern includes direct sales, usually by food products companies. Carbonated beverages are increasingly under pressure as a result of health concerns related to obesity and juvenile diabetes. As a result, Coca-Cola recently announced its own guidelines in selling to "K through 12" schools which its bottlers have agreed to adhere to.

These include not selling carbonated beverages during the school day at elementary schools (its other products such as sports drinks and water can be sold) and not selling carbonated beverages in cafeterias in middle and high schools (still offered through vending machines). Pepsi already had similar guidelines in place.[38]

Internet Marketing and Children   Children are major users of the Internet. Not surprisingly, marketers use the Internet to communicate with kids. Two major concerns have emerged: invading children's privacy and exploitation of children through manipulative sales techniques. We will consider the online privacy issue in the next section.

Concern regarding manipulative Internet practices often revolves around the creation of sites that blur the line between entertainment and advertising. This goes back to concerns touched on earlier in terms of difficulties that children have in discerning selling intent and their ability to distinguish commercial from noncommercial content. An emerging concern is "adver-games." These customized games which are placed on a company's Web site prominently feature or integrate the company's brands and products as part of the game itself. Consider the following excerpt:

> Kraft's Nabiscoworld.com features adver-games for at least 17 brands, plus classic games such as chess, mah-jongg and backgammon. Some games integrate brands into the play. In Ritz Bits Sumo Wrestling, for example, players control either the Creamy Marshmallow or the Chocolatey Fudge cracker in a belly-smacking showdown, which results in the "S'more"-flavored cracker.[39]

An early set of guidelines set forth by The Center for Media Education (CME) recommends the following principles for development of online commercial services:[40]

1. Personal information should not be collected from children, nor should personal profiles of children be sold to third parties.
2. Advertising and promotions targeted at children should be clearly labeled and separated from content.
3. Children's content areas should not be directly linked to advertising sites.
4. There should be no direct interaction between children and product spokespersons.
5. There should be no online microtargeting of children (commercial or promotions developed for individual children), and no direct-response marketing.

Two examples of companies putting Principle 2 to work are Kraft and Burger King. Kraft has an "Ad Break" icon that is an explicit indication that the material is a commercial message designed to sell them something. Burger King Kids section has various notices where they indicate "Hey Kids! This is Advertising!" *What effect, if any, do you think such notifications have on the effectiveness of this online advertising to children? Should so-called adver-games be subject to such notification?*

Children's Online Privacy Issues

Online privacy relates to the collection and use of information from Web sites. Collecting information from children is a sensitive issue, as well it should be, given all we know about their information processing deficits relative to adults. An example of an online children's privacy issue involved the KidsCom communications playground (targeting kids 4 to 8), which required children to provide their name, age, sex, and e-mail address in order to enter the site. It also requested their favorite TV show, music groups, and the name of the child who referred them to KidsCom. Once in the playground, they could earn "KidsCash," which could be redeemed for prizes by supplying additional personal information. KidsCom has since been modified (see their privacy statement at www.kidscom.com).

TABLE 20-3

Key Provisions of
COPPA

The act requires that commercial Web sites that collect personal information from children under 13 obtain prior parental consent before they collect that information. The act only applies to Web sites, or portions thereof, directed to children or to Web sites that knowingly collect personal information from children under 13. The act does not apply to nonprofits.

Notice: Parents have the right to be notified about data collection and use practices. The parent must be informed about what information will be collected, how it will be used, and to whom and in what form the information will be disclosed to others. The notice must be prominently displayed and unavoidable.

Prior Parental Consent: With certain exceptions, information cannot be collected from children, used or disclosed unless the Web site operator has obtained verifiable parental consent through "reasonable effort."

Prevention of Further Use: Parents have the right to prevent further use of already collected personal identifying information and to prevent future collection of information from the child.

Collection of Personal Information Must Be Limited: The collection of personal identifying information for a child's participation in a game, prize, offer, or other activity on the Web site must be limited to what is reasonably necessary for the activity.

Access to Information: Parents of children under 13 have the right to access and review a description of the specific types of personal identifying information collected from the child and Web site operators must provide reasonable means to the parent to obtain the information itself that has been collected from the child.

Concern over the invasion of children's privacy prompted Congress to pass the **Children's Online Privacy Protection Act (COPPA)** in October 1998. It authorizes the FTC to develop specific rules to implement the provisions of the act as described in Table 20-3.

Rules based on these guidelines became effective in April 2000. A survey of children-oriented Web sites a year later reached the following conclusions:

1. Children's commercial Web sites have modified their data collection practices and limited the amount of data being collected.
2. More children's commercial Web sites that collect personally identifiable data are posting privacy policy notices informing parents of what they are collecting and how it will be used.
3. A few sites have developed creative solutions to adapt to COPPA and still allow children to have an interactive experience without revealing identifying information such as their e-mail address.
4. A majority of sites do not have a "clear and prominent" link to privacy policies.
5. Children's sites that have a link for feedback, such as e-mail, often overlook this as a data collection point.
6. A majority of sites did not obtain prior parental consent or provide parental notice as required by COPPA.
7. In attempting to restrict children under 13 from entering personal identifying information, some sites use methods that could encourage age falsification.[41]

Clearly COPPA had a positive impact in its first year. CARU adopted similar but more detailed rules. Privacy issues now dominate CARU cases:

- The language "tipped off" children that they must be over 13 to use the interactive services offered on the site by stating: "U.S. law prohibits Alta Vista from registering anyone under the age of 13 without parental permission. Please verify your age below." It then asked prospective registrants if they were "less than 13 years old" or "13 or older." Those who registered could access all areas of the site, some of which were clearly inappropriate for children.[42]

Education is an important aspect of the FTC's fight against online privacy invasion among children.

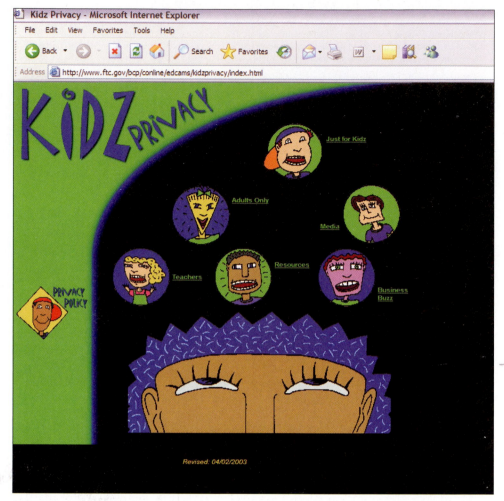

© 2005 Federal Trade Commission.

- Pinkspage, the fan site for the artist Pink, did not contain a privacy statement. In addition, CARU was concerned that a visitor of any age could submit personal identifying information such as an e-mail or street address at the "Fan Club" registration.[43]
- Scan-command.com features online games designed to be played by children ages 8 and up. It recently agreed to cease collecting parents' offline contact information from children under 13 without prior parental consent. It also agreed to obtain parental consent before allowing children to sign up as a "scan-command.com agent," which, among other things, enables them to participate in a message board.[44]

The importance of consumer education also plays a prominent role in the FTC's approach. This can be seen in the fact that it has created a privacy Web site designed to educate kids and parents about online privacy issues (see Illustration 20-1).

REGULATION AND MARKETING TO ADULTS

Regulation of marketing activities aimed at adults focuses on marketing communications, product features, and pricing practices. There is increasing demand for regulation to protect the privacy of adults, particularly on the Internet. Consider the following:

> American Express announced plans to sell extensive information on its cardholders to merchants. These data would be combined with data on 175 million Americans compiled by Knowledge-Base. KnowledgeBase has information on age, marital status, family composition, household ownership, and so forth. By combining this demographic data with American Express purchase records, American Express plans to develop mailing lists of customers most likely to buy certain products. It will sell these lists to other firms. Cardholders can keep their names off the list by calling or writing American Express but the company has no plans to explicitly inform its customers of this use of their purchase records.

Many consumers find this use of information about their purchase histories and personal characteristics to be intrusive. Many magazines sell their subscription lists to various firms who use the information for direct marketing campaigns. Some charities sell or otherwise make available their donor lists. While the dissemination of credit card, subscription, and donation data is a concern, most attention is currently focused on the privacy of data collected on the Internet.[45]

One of the reasons the concern about Internet privacy is so strong is that data are often collected without the consumer explicitly providing it. A person visiting a Web site can have that fact recorded (his or her IP address at a minimum) as well as what parts of the site are visited, what information is requested, what links are accessed, and so forth without consent or even knowledge. Other information may be collected in a more direct manner. Information from various sites and sources can be pooled to develop individual profiles. Consumer Insight 20-1 provides the FTC's evolving and ongoing approach to regulating Internet privacy practices.

The Better Business Bureau has a Code of Online Business Practices that is "designed to guide ethical business-to-consumer conduct in electronic commerce." It provides three broad requirements, each with substantial details and examples, with respect to information practices:

- Post and adhere to a privacy policy that is open, transparent, and meets generally accepted fair information principles.
- Provide adequate security for the type of information collected, maintained, or transferred to third parties.
- Respect customers' preferences regarding unsolicited e-mail.

Marketing Communications

There are three major concerns focused on the information that marketers provide to consumers, generally in the form of advertisements—the accuracy of the information provided, the adequacy of the information provided, and the cumulative impact of marketing information on society's values. We will briefly look at advertising's impact on society's values before focusing on the accuracy and adequacy of consumer information.

Advertising and Values   We discussed the impact of advertising on values in the previous section on advertising to children. The concern is the same for advertising directed at adults—the long-term effect of a constant flow of messages emphasizing materialistic or narcissistic values may be negative for both individuals and society. For example, an ad for Musk by Alyssa Ashley appeared in a magazine read by teenage females. It consisted of a picture of a teenage girl on the back of a motorcycle driven by a scruffy looking man with long hair, a beard, and a tattoo. The girl's dress is pulled up to the top of her thigh. The only other content was a picture of the product package and the headline—"Sometimes even

Online Privacy and the Federal Trade Commission

In May 2000, the Federal Trade Commission issued its third report on online privacy issues to Congress.[46] This report concluded that self-regulation was not providing adequate privacy regulation and recommended national legislation. It recommended that consumer-oriented commercial Web sites that collect personal identifying information from or about consumers comply with four standards.

1. *Notice*—Web sites would be required to provide consumers clear and conspicuous notice of their information practices, including what information they collect, how they collect it (e.g., directly or through nonobvious means such as cookies), how they use it, how they provide *choice, access*, and *security* to consumers, whether they disclose the information collected to other entities, and whether other entities are collecting information through the site.

2. *Choice*—Web sites would be required to offer consumers choices as to how their personal identifying information is used beyond the use for which the information was provided (e.g., to consummate a transaction). Such choice would encompass both internal secondary uses (such as marketing back to consumers) and external secondary uses (such as disclosing data to other entities).

3. *Access*—Web sites would be required to offer consumers reasonable access to the information a Web site has collected about them, including a reasonable opportunity to review information and to correct inaccuracies or delete information.

4. *Security*—Web sites would be required to take reasonable steps to protect the security of the information they collect from consumers.

However, in 2001 the new chairman of the FTC concluded that "it is too soon to conclude that we can fashion workable legislation." At the same time, he did conclude that privacy protection in general and online privacy protection in particular are important issues. He indicated that the FTC was going to increase the resources it devotes to privacy protection by 50 percent.

While legislative initiatives (e.g., OPPA which was designed to incorporate the four key features above) continue to be debated, the FTC's position as of 2005 described on their Web site is:

> A key part of the Commission's privacy program is making sure companies keep the promises they make to consumers about privacy and, in particular, the precautions they take to secure consumers' personal information. To respond to consumers' concerns about privacy, many Web sites post privacy policies that describe how consumers' personal information is collected, used, shared, and secured. Indeed, almost all the top 100 commercial sites now post privacy policies. Using its authority under Section 5 of the FTC Act, which prohibits unfair or deceptive practices, the Commission has brought a number of cases to enforce the promises in privacy statements, including promises about the security of consumers' personal information. The Commission has also used its unfairness authority to challenge information practices that cause substantial consumer injury.[47]

Thus, in dealing with online privacy, the FTC operates within already established legislative guidelines.

Critical Thinking Questions

1. Should there be national legislation such as that proposed above? Why or why not?

2. In the absence of legislation, how should a firm collect and use data from those who visit its Web site?

---

good girls want to be bad." Many would argue that this ad promotes inappropriate values and behaviors.

Most ads for women's cosmetics and clothing emphasize beauty or sex appeal as major benefits. Each individual ad is probably harmless. However, critics charge that when people see such themes repeated thousands of times for hundreds of products, they learn to consider a person's looks to be more important than other attributes.[48] This can lead to injurious consumption patterns such as excessive tanning or inappropriate dieting despite knowledge of the associated health hazard.[49] These harmful effects may be most severe

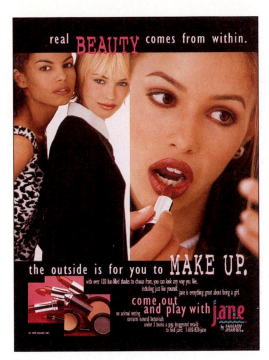

ILLUSTRATION 20-2

This ad has been praised for its positive portrayal of young women.

in younger women.[50] Further, those who cannot afford such products or who are not "good-looking" suffer. Others argue that individuals have been concerned with their looks and possessions in virtually all cultures and times. They argue that advertising does not cause a society's values; it merely reflects them.

Portrayals of beauty and casual attitudes toward sex are not the only ways advertisements are argued to influence values. The portrayal of women in the mass media in general and in advertising in particular often has been limited to stereotypical roles or as decoration.[51] This in turn can influence the concepts girls develop of themselves and their role choices. Of course, many firms now portray females in a more positive, realistic fashion. The ad for Jane, shown in Illustration 20-2, emphasizes positive values while still promoting a beauty enhancement product. A Nike campaign generated a positive response from many women as well as advertising critics. A television ad in the campaign combined quick camera takes and slow-motion shots of teenage girls on a playground, with images of girls playing on swing sets and monkey bars. The sound portion is a variety of girls' voices describing the long-term benefits of female participation in sports:

> I will like myself more; I will have more self-confidence if you let me play sports. If you let me play, I will be 60 percent less likely to get breast cancer. I will suffer less depression if you let me play sports.
>
> I will be more likely to leave a man who beats me. If you let me play, I will be less likely to get pregnant before I want to; I will learn what it means to be strong.[52]

The manner in which ethnic groups, the elderly, and other social groups are portrayed in ads and the mass media can affect the way members of these groups view themselves as well as the way others see them.[53] Marketers need to ensure that their ads reflect the diversity of the American society in a manner that is realistic and positive for all the many groups involved. These portrayals should involve both the content of the ads and the shows sponsored by the ads.[54] For example, the relative absence of Hispanic roles and actors on network television has been an ongoing concern among Hispanics, although evidence suggests that this is changing.[55]

Consumer Information Accuracy

The salesperson tells you, "My brand is the best there is." Does he or she need scientific proof to make such a statement? At what point does permissible puffery become misleading and illegal? Does it vary by the situation? The consumer group involved?[56]

An ad shows a pair of attractive female legs. The headline reads, "Her legs are insured for $1,000,000. Her policy came with one minor stipulation. Schick Silk Effects." Schick Silk Effects is a women's razor. How do you interpret this ad? Many would assume that the insurance company insisted on her using only this brand as a condition of the policy. This suggests that the insurance company considers this razor to be very good at protecting women's legs while they shave. However, in exceedingly fine print at the very bottom of the ad is this disclaimer: "Policy condition included by insurer at the request of Warner-Lambert Co." Warner-Lambert is the firm that markets Silk Effects. In other words, the firm that owns the razor had the requirement that this razor be used placed in the insurance policy. This leads to a very different interpretation of the ad. *Should this ad be illegal? Is it unethical?*

Research shows that the more baking soda toothpaste contains, the more effective it is in cleaning away plaque and deep stains. How much baking soda should a brand of toothpaste contain before it can be called "baking soda" toothpaste? There is no rule. Arm & Hammer's contains 65 percent baking soda, but Crest Baking Soda Toothpaste has only 20 percent.[57] *Should there be rules for names such as this or is the required listing of the contents enough?*

Illustration 20-3 shows several major national brands and several competing brands with similar packages. *Are consumers misled by such packages? Or are these legitimate attempts to position competing products as being similar to the brand leaders?*[58]

Because of such problems, various businesses, consumer groups, and regulatory agencies are deeply concerned with the interpretation of marketing messages. However, determining the exact meaning of a marketing message is not a simple process. The National Advertising Division (NAD) of the Council of Better Business Bureaus recently asked Bayer to alter an *accurate* commercial for Aleve. The commercial accurately stated that Aleve provided longer-lasting relief with a smaller dosage than Tylenol ("Just 2 Aleve can stop the pain all day, it would take 8 Tylenol to do that"). The concern was that this would unintentionally convey a message of superior efficacy (it would stop more pain than Tylenol).[59]

Table 20-4 illustrates some of the areas where controversy over the interpretation of various marketing messages has existed.

TABLE 20-4

Regulation and the Interpretation of Marketing Messages

- Gillette was forced to relabel 6.5 million M3 Power razor packages when a court ruled that the claim "gentle micropulses stimulate hair up and away from skin" was literally false. The court indicated that "The use of the term 'up and away' in conjunction with the term 'stimulates' is literally false as it connotes an angle change."[60]
- The 4th U.S. Circuit Court of Appeals ruled that meat from a turkey thigh can be called a "turkey ham" even if it contains no pork. A lower court had reached the opposite conclusion. The ruling appeared to rely heavily on a technical definition of the term *ham*.
- Maximum Strength Anacin's claim that it is "the maximum strength allowed" was ruled illegal because it "implies that an appropriate authority has authorized the sale of products like Maximum Strength Anacin." No such authorization exists.
- Keebler Company's claim of "Baked not fried" for Wheatables and Munch'ems snack crackers was challenged before the NAD. While the crackers are baked, they are sprayed with vegetable oil after baking and have a fat content similar to fried products.
- Under the Federal Trademark Dilution Act (FTDA), Hasbro was able to stop the use of the Internet name candyland.com for a sexually explicit Web site because the site would injure the value of its registered trademark Candy Land (a line of children's games). Courts have generally held that only the owners of registered trademarks can use them as Web site addresses.

ILLUSTRATION 20-3

Is imitation the sincerest form of flattery or a source of consumer confusion?

© Paul F. Kilmer.

Obtaining accurate assignments of meaning is made even more difficult by the variation in information-processing skills and motivations among different population groups.[61] For example, this warning was ruled inadequate in a product liability case involving a worker who was injured while inflating a truck tire:

Always inflate tire in safety cage or use a portable lock ring guard. Use a clip-on type air chuck with remote valve so that operator can stand clear during tire inflation.

The court held that (1) "there is a duty to warn *foreseeable* users of all hidden dangers" and (2) "in view of the unskilled or semiskilled nature of the work and the existence of many in the workforce who do not read English, warnings *in the form of symbols* might have been appropriate since the employee's ability to take care of himself was limited."[62]

Thus, marketers must often go to considerable lengths to provide messages that the relevant audience will interpret correctly.

Fortunately, marketers are developing considerable knowledge on how to effectively present difficult messages about such issues as product risks, nutrition, and affirmative disclosures (see Chapter 8). In addition, consumer research is being used by both marketers and the courts to determine if an ad is misleading.[63]

Regulating the explicit verbal content of ads is difficult. Regulating the more subtle meanings implied by the visual content of ads is much more difficult.[64] For example, some are critical of beer advertisements that portray active young adults in groups having fun and consuming beer. These critics contend that the visual message of these ads is that alcohol consumption is the appropriate way for young adults to be popular and have fun.

Both government and business self-regulatory groups have begun regulating visual communications.

- The FTC challenged ads for Beck's beer that featured young adults drinking on a sailing ship. It charged that the ads promoted unsafe marine conduct.
- The NAD required Balance Bar to drop all claims referring to clinical studies and *visuals of physicians* in its advertising after ruling that its formula was not proved to be "clinically effective for the general population."

Corrective advertising is advertising run by a firm to cause consumers to unlearn inaccurate information they acquired as a result of the firm's earlier advertising. Three examples of corrective advertising messages follow:

- "Do you recall some of our past messages saying that Domino sugar gives you strength, energy, and stamina? Actually, Domino is not a special or unique source of strength, energy, and stamina. No sugar is, because what you need is a balanced diet and plenty of rest and exercise."
- "If you've wondered what some of our earlier advertising meant when we said Ocean Spray cranberry juice cocktail has more food energy than orange juice or tomato juice, let us make it clear: we didn't mean vitamins and minerals. Food energy means calories. Nothing more.

  "Food energy is important at breakfast since many of us may not get enough calories, or food energy, to get off to a good start. Ocean Spray cranberry juice cocktail helps because it contains more food energy than most other breakfast drinks.

  "And Ocean Spray cranberry juice cocktail gives you and your family vitamin C plus a great wake-up taste. It's . . . the other breakfast drink."
- Sugar Information, Inc.: "Do you recall the messages we brought you in the past about sugar? How something with sugar in it before meals could help you curb your appetite? We hope you didn't get the idea that our little diet tip was any magic formula for losing weight. Because there are no tricks or shortcuts; the whole diet subject is very complicated. Research hasn't established that consuming sugar before meals will contribute to weight reduction or even keep you from gaining weight."

Although the effectiveness of corrective advertising has been debated, the FTC considers it a useful tool in protecting the public. Likewise, firms injured by the false claims of competitors often request it as a remedy (Power Bar requested the FTC to require Balance Bar to run corrective ads concerning the clinical claims described earlier). Indeed, the threat of lawsuits by competitors can serve as a strong deterrent of comparative advertising. For example, Procter & Gamble is revisiting its aggressive advertising strategy across its various brands in light of all the substantial litigation it has created (e.g., lawsuits by Playtex, J&J-Merck, Kimberly-Clark, and Georgia Pacific).[65]

With regard to corrective advertising, a court ruling has challenged the conditions under which the FTC can require it. Significantly, the challenge centers on how strongly the false impression must be learned before corrective advertising is necessary to erase it.[66]

Adequacy of Consumer Information   It is important that consumers have not only accurate information but adequate information as well. To ensure information adequacy, a number of laws have been passed, such as the federal truth-in-lending legislation.

Nutritional labeling has been required for years and was significantly revised in 1990. Research findings on the impact of such labels are mixed, but the labels do provide valuable information to many consumers. A consistent stream of consumer behavior research since these rules were enacted has uncovered a number of potential improvements in the manner in which the information should be presented. Unfortunately, as with many such

Courtesy Integrated Solutions, LLC.

ILLUSTRATION 20-4

The new trans fat rule will require packaging adaptations by companies and will serve as a way for certain brands to differentiate themselves from the competition on an attribute of importance to consumers.

programs, those who are relatively disadvantaged in terms of education and income are least able to use this type of information.[67]

A new FDA labeling rule deals with trans fats. While the Nutritional Labeling and Education Act (NLEA) of 1990 led to the nutrition fact box on food packaging which includes a line for total fat, the new rule which companies must comply with by January 1, 2006, will require a new line for trans fats as well. The logic behind this change, which will have costs to companies in terms of research into trans fat content and label redesign, includes:

> The latest health threat is so-called trans fats, which are hydrogenated oils used to make margarine, deep fried foods, cookies, cakes and crackers. They give foods the texture consumers expect, and help foods stay fresh longer than alternative ingredients. Trans fats have an effect similar to saturated fats in the body and raise the level of LDL (bad) cholesterol, but they also lower HDL (good) cholesterol levels. Because of this, the U.S. Food and Drug Administration . . . issued a ruling requiring food manufacturers to modify their package labels to reflect the *total amount* of trans fats used in their products.[68]

Obviously, this ruling will provide opportunities for some food marketers and challenges for others. Given consumer health concerns, marketers of products such as Weetabix (Illustration 20-4) can use trans fats as a point of differentiation not just in the nutrition facts box but also in more prominent locations like the box front.

Marketers, consumer groups, and public officials would like consumers to have all the information they need to make sound choices. One approach is to provide all potentially relevant information. This approach is frequently recommended by regulatory agencies and is required for some product categories such as drugs.

Problems with this approach can arise, however. The assumption behind the full-disclosure approach is that each consumer will utilize those specific information items required for the particular decision. Unfortunately, consumers frequently do not react in this manner. This is true particularly for low-involvement purchases, but can also be true of higher-involvement purchases as well. Instead, consumers may experience *information overload* (see Chapter 8) and ignore all or most of the available data. For example,

A federal act required banks belonging to the Federal Reserve to explain to their customers the detailed protections built into money transfer systems available in electronic banking. Thus, Northwestern National Bank of Minneapolis was forced to create and mail a pamphlet explaining Amended Regulation E to its 120,000 customers. At a cost of $69,000 the bank created and mailed the 4,500-word pamphlet.

In 100 of the pamphlets, the bank placed a special paragraph that offered the reader $10 just for finding that paragraph. The pamphlets were mailed in May and June. As of August, not one person had claimed the money![69]

An example in the drug category is that a relatively simple, one-page advertisement for Flonase nasal spray required the second full page of small type shown in Illustration 20-5 telling of dosage, precautions, and warnings in order to comply with federal full-disclosure regulations. Examine Illustration 20-5 carefully. Would you read this ad? Many marketers claim that such ads add to the costs of advertising and therefore reduce the available consumer information without an offset in consumer benefit.[70] Many consumer advocates agree that the current approach is not meeting the needs of consumers.

A new issue confronting marketers and regulators is disclosure in Internet advertising. Disclosure involves providing relevant qualifiers to advertising claims such as "limited to stock on hand," or "available at participating outlets only." The FTC requires disclosures to be "clear and conspicuous" and this standard has been translated into clear guidelines for print, television, and radio ads. What constitutes "clear and conspicuous" on the Internet? Is it a banner? A pop-up? Does it need a frame around it? This is yet another area where knowledge of consumer information processing and consumer research can help produce effective regulatory guidelines.

Product Issues

Consumer groups have two major concerns with products—*Are they safe?* and *Are they environmentally sound?* A variety of federal and state agencies are involved in ensuring that products are safe to use. The most important are the Food and Drug Administration and the Consumer Product Safety Commission. Product safety is generally not a controversial issue. However, it is impossible to remove all risk from products.

Should tricycles be banned? Accidents involving tricycles are a major cause of injury to young children. Manufacturers, consumer groups, and individuals differ on where the line should be drawn and who should draw it. Some feel that tricycles should indeed be banned. Others feel that parents should decide if their children should ride tricycles. However, both would agree that information on both the risks of tricycle riding and ways of reducing the

ILLUSTRATION 20-5

Do consumers benefit from this level of required information, or does information overload set in?

FLONASE® **BRIEF SUMMARY**
(fluticasone propionate)
Nasal Spray, 0.05% w/w

SHAKE GENTLY BEFORE USE.

For Intranasal Use Only.

The following is a brief summary only; see full prescribing information for complete product information.

CONTRAINDICATIONS: FLONASE Nasal Spray is contraindicated in patients with a hypersensitivity to any of its ingredients.

WARNINGS: The replacement of a systemic glucocorticoid with a topical glucocorticoid can be accompanied by signs of adrenal insufficiency, and in addition some patients may experience symptoms of withdrawal, e.g., joint and/or muscular pain, lassitude, and depression. Patients previously treated for prolonged periods with systemic glucocorticoids and transferred to topical glucocorticoids should be carefully monitored for acute adrenal insufficiency in response to stress. In those patients who have asthma or other clinical conditions requiring long-term systemic glucocorticoid treatment, too rapid a decrease in systemic glucocorticoids may cause a severe exacerbation of their symptoms.

The use of FLONASE Nasal Spray with alternate-day systemic prednisone could increase the likelihood of hypothalamic-pituitary-adrenal (HPA) suppression compared with a therapeutic dose of either one alone. Therefore, FLONASE Nasal Spray should be used with caution in patients already receiving alternate-day prednisone treatment for any disease. In addition, the concomitant use of FLONASE Nasal Spray with other inhaled glucocorticoids could increase the risk of signs or symptoms of hypercorticism and/or suppression of the HPA axis.

Patients who are on immunosuppressant drugs are more susceptible to infections than healthy individuals. Chickenpox and measles, for example, can have a more serious or even fatal course in patients on immunosuppressant doses of corticosteroids. In such patients who have not had these diseases, particular care should be taken to avoid exposure. How the dose, route, and duration of corticosteroid administration affects the risk of developing a disseminated infection is not known. The contribution of the underlying disease and/or prior corticosteroid treatment to the risk is also not known. If exposed to chickenpox, prophylaxis with varicella zoster immune globulin (VZIG) may be indicated. If exposed to measles, prophylaxis with pooled intramuscular immunoglobulin (IG) may be indicated. (See the respective package inserts for complete VZIG and IG prescribing information.) If chickenpox develops, treatment with antiviral agents may be considered.

PRECAUTIONS:
General: Rarely, immediate hypersensitivity reactions or contact dermatitis may occur after the intranasal administration of fluticasone propionate. Rare instances of wheezing, nasal septum perforation, cataracts, glaucoma, and increased intraocular pressure have been reported following the intranasal application of glucocorticoids.

Use of excessive doses of glucocorticoids may lead to signs or symptoms of hypercorticism, suppression of HPA function, and/or suppression of growth in children or teenagers. Knemometry studies in asthmatic children on orally inhaled glucocorticoids showed inhibitory effects on short-term growth rate. The relationship between short-term changes in lower leg growth and long-term effects on growth is unclear at this time. Physicians should closely follow the growth of adolescents taking glucocorticoids, by any route, and weigh the benefits of glucocorticoid therapy against the possibility of growth suppression if an adolescent's growth appears slowed.

Although systemic effects have been minimal with recommended doses of FLONASE Nasal Spray, potential risk increases with larger doses. Therefore, larger than recommended doses of FLONASE Nasal Spray should be avoided.

When used at larger doses, systemic glucocorticoid effects such as hypercorticism and adrenal suppression may appear. If such changes occur, the dosage of FLONASE Nasal Spray should be discontinued slowly consistent with accepted procedures for discontinuing oral glucocorticoid therapy.

In clinical studies with fluticasone propionate administered intranasally, the development of localized infections of the nose and pharynx with *Candida albicans* has occurred only rarely. When such an infection develops, it may require treatment with appropriate local therapy and discontinuation of treatment with FLONASE Nasal Spray. Patients using FLONASE Nasal Spray over several months or longer should be examined periodically for evidence of *Candida* infection or other signs of adverse effects on the nasal mucosa.

FLONASE Nasal Spray should be used with caution, if at all, in patients with active or quiescent tuberculous infections; untreated fungal, bacterial, or systemic viral infections; or ocular herpes simplex.

Because of the inhibitory effect of glucocorticoids on wound healing, patients who have experienced recent nasal septal ulcers, nasal surgery, or nasal trauma should not use a nasal glucocorticoid until healing has occurred.

Information for Patients: Patients being treated with FLONASE Nasal Spray should receive the following information and instructions. This information is intended to aid them in the safe and effective use of this medication. It is not a disclosure of all possible adverse or intended effects.

Patients should be warned to avoid exposure to chickenpox or measles and, if exposed, to consult their physician without delay.

Patients should use FLONASE Nasal Spray at regular intervals as directed since its effectiveness depends on its regular use. A decrease in nasal symptoms may occur as soon as 12 hours after starting therapy with FLONASE Nasal Spray. Results in several clinical trials indicate statistically significant improvement within the first day or two of treatment; however, the full benefit of FLONASE Nasal Spray may not be achieved until treatment has been administered for several days. The patient should not increase the prescribed dosage but should contact the physician if symptoms do not improve or if the condition worsens. For the proper use of the nasal spray and to attain maximum improvement, the patient should read and follow carefully the patient's instructions accompanying the product.

Carcinogenesis, Mutagenesis, Impairment of Fertility: Fluticasone propionate demonstrated no tumorigenic potential in studies of oral doses up to 1.0 mg/kg (3 mg/m² as calculated on a surface area basis) for 78 weeks in the mouse or inhalation of up to 57 mcg/kg (336 mcg/m²) for 104 weeks in the rat.

Fluticasone propionate did not induce gene mutation in prokaryotic or eukaryotic cells in vitro. No significant clastogenic effect was seen in cultured human peripheral lymphocytes in vitro or in the mouse micronucleus test when administered at high doses by the oral or subcutaneous routes. Furthermore, the compound did not delay erythroblast division in bone marrow.

FLONASE® (fluticasone propionate) Nasal Spray, 0.05%

No evidence of impairment of fertility was observed in reproductive studies conducted in rats dosed subcutaneously with doses up to 50 mcg/kg (295 mcg/m²) in males and females. However, prostate weight was significantly reduced in rats.

Pregnancy: Teratogenic Effects: Pregnancy Category C: Subcutaneous studies in the mouse and rat at 45 and 100 mcg/kg, respectively (135 and 590 mcg/m², respectively, as calculated on a surface area basis), revealed fetal toxicity characteristic of potent glucocorticoid compounds, including embryonic growth retardation, omphalocele, cleft palate, and retarded cranial ossification.

In the rabbit, fetal weight reduction and cleft palate were observed following subcutaneous doses of 4 mcg/kg (48 mcg/m²).

However, following oral administration of up to 300 mcg/kg (3.6 mg/m²) of fluticasone propionate to the rabbit, there were no maternal effects nor increased incidence of external, visceral, or skeletal fetal defects. No fluticasone propionate was detected in the plasma in this study, consistent with the established low bioavailability following oral administration (see CLINICAL PHARMACOLOGY section of full prescribing information).

Less than 0.008% of the dose crosses the placenta following oral administration to rats (100 mcg/kg, 590 mcg/m²) or rabbits (300 mcg/kg, 3.6 mg/m²).

There are no adequate and well-controlled studies in pregnant women. Fluticasone propionate should be used during pregnancy only if the potential benefit justifies the potential risk to the fetus. Experience with oral glucocorticoids since their introduction in pharmacologic, as opposed to physiologic, doses suggests that rodents are more prone to teratogenic effects from glucocorticoids than humans. In addition, because there is a natural increase in glucocorticoid production during pregnancy, most women will require a lower exogenous glucocorticoid dose and many will not need glucocorticoid treatment during pregnancy.

Nursing Mothers: It is not known whether fluticasone propionate is excreted in human breast milk. Subcutaneous administration of tritiated drug to lactating rats (10 mcg/kg, 59 mcg/m²) resulted in measurable radioactivity in both plasma and milk. Because other glucocorticoids are excreted in human milk, caution should be exercised when FLONASE Nasal Spray is administered to a nursing woman.

Pediatric Use: The safety and effectiveness of FLONASE Nasal Spray in children below 12 years of age have not been established. Oral glucocorticoids have been shown to cause growth suppression in children and teenagers with extended use. If a child or teenager on any glucocorticoid appears to have growth suppression, the possibility that they are particularly sensitive to this effect of glucocorticoids should be considered (see PRECAUTIONS).

Geriatric Use: A limited number of patients above 60 years of age (n=132) have been treated with FLONASE Nasal Spray in US and non-US clinical trials. While the number of patients is too small to permit separate analysis of efficacy and safety, the adverse reactions reported in this population were similar to those reported by younger patients.

ADVERSE REACTIONS: In controlled US studies, 2,427 patients received treatment with intranasal fluticasone propionate. In general, adverse reactions in clinical studies have been primarily associated with irritation of the nasal mucous membranes, and the adverse reactions were reported with approximately the same frequency by patients treated with the vehicle itself. The complaints did not usually interfere with treatment. Less than 2% of patients in clinical trials discontinued because of adverse events; this rate was similar for vehicle and active comparators.

Systemic glucocorticoid side effects were not reported during controlled clinical studies up to 6 months' duration with FLONASE Nasal Spray. If recommended doses are exceeded, however, or if individuals are particularly sensitive or if in conjunction with systemically administered glucocorticoids, symptoms of hypercorticism, e.g., Cushing's syndrome, could occur.

The following incidence of common adverse reactions is based upon seven controlled clinical trials in which 536 patients (57 girls and 108 boys aged 4 to 11 years, 137 female and 234 male adolescents and adults) were treated with FLONASE Nasal Spray 200 mcg once daily over 2 to 4 weeks and two controlled clinical trials in which 246 patients (119 female and 127 male adolescents and adults) were treated with FLONASE Nasal Spray 200 mcg once daily over 6 months.

Incidence Greater than 1% (Causal Relationship Possible):
Respiratory: Epistaxis, nasal burning (incidence 3% to 6%); blood in nasal mucus, pharyngitis, nasal irritation (incidence 1% to 3%).
Neurological: Headache (incidence 1% to 3%).

Incidence Less than 1% (Causal Relationship Possible): ***Respiratory:*** Sneezing, runny nose, nasal dryness, sinusitis, nasal congestion, bronchitis, nasal ulcer, nasal septum excoriation.
Neurological: Dizziness.
Special Senses: Eye disorder, unpleasant taste.
Digestive: Nausea and vomiting, xerostomia.
Skin and Appendages: Urticaria.

Postmarketing Experience: In addition to the events from clinical trials, the following have been reported during postmarketing experience.

Hypersensitivity reactions, including angioedema, skin rash, edema of the face and tongue, pruritus, urticaria, bronchospasm, wheezing, dyspnea, and anaphylaxis/anaphylactoid reactions, which in rare instances were severe.

Alteration or loss of sense of taste and/or smell and, rarely, nasal septal perforation.

OVERDOSAGE: There are no data available on the effects of acute or chronic overdosage with FLONASE Nasal Spray. Intranasal administration of 2 mg (10 times the recommended dose) of fluticasone propionate twice daily for 7 days to healthy human volunteers was well tolerated. Single oral doses up to 16 mg have been studied in human volunteers with no acute toxic effects reported. Repeat oral doses up to 80 mg daily for 10 days in volunteers and repeat oral doses up to 10 mg daily for 14 days in patients were well tolerated. Adverse reactions were of mild or moderate severity, and incidences were similar in active and placebo treatment groups. Acute overdosage with this dosage form is unlikely since one bottle of FLONASE Nasal Spray contains approximately 8 mg of fluticasone propionate. Chronic overdosage may result in signs/symptoms of hypercorticism (see PRECAUTIONS).

GlaxoWellcome

Glaxo Wellcome Inc. October 1996
Research Triangle Park, NC 27709 RL-367
Made in England GLA-01-038M

©1997 Glaxo Wellcome Inc. All rights reserved.
Printed in USA. FLN511R0 July 1997

Courtesy Glaxo-Wellcome, Inc.

risk should be made available to purchasers, though there is disagreement on who should make the information available and how it should be made available. Of course, tricycles represent only one of many products subject to such a debate.

We examined consumers' desires for environmentally sound products in some detail in Chapter 3. As indicated there, many consumers want products whose production, use, and disposition produce minimal environmental harm. Many marketers are striving to produce such products. Nonetheless, consumer groups continue to push for more stringent regulation in this area.

Potentially injurious products such as guns, tobacco products, and alcoholic beverages are subject to a wide variety of regulations at the federal, state, and even city level. So-called safer cigarettes such as R. J. Reynolds' Eclipse brand with its claim "may present less risk of cancer" are drawing significant attention.[71]

Pricing Issues

Consumer groups want prices that are fair (generally defined as competitively determined) and accurately stated (contain no hidden charges). The FTC is the primary federal agency involved in regulating pricing activities.

Perhaps the most controversial pricing area today is the use of reference prices. An **external reference price** is *a price provided by the manufacturer or retailer in addition to the actual current price of the product.* Such terms as "compare at $X," "usually $X," "suggested retail price $Y—our price only $X" are common ways of presenting reference prices (see Chapter 17, page 613). The concern arises when the reference price is one at which no or few sales actually occur. Most states and the federal government have regulations concerning the use of reference prices, but they are difficult to enforce. Given the history of abuse of reference prices, it is not surprising that many consumers are skeptical of them.

SUMMARY

Marketing to children is a major concern to regulators and consumer groups. A major reason for this concern is evidence based on Piaget's theory of cognitive development that children are not able to fully comprehend commercial messages. This has led to rules issued by both the Federal Trade Commission and the Children's Advertising Review Unit (CARU) of the National Advertising Division of the Council of Better Business Bureaus. These rules focus mainly on being sure that commercials are clearly separated from the program content and that the words and pictures in the commercials do not mislead children having limited cognitive skills.

In addition to concerns about children's comprehension of advertisements, there is concern about the effect of the content of commercials on children. The extensive advertising of high-fat and high-sugar products raises a concern about its effect on the health of children. Since children watch a substantial amount of prime-time television, there is also a danger that ads aimed at adults will inspire children to take inappropriate actions. In addition, there is concern that the enormous amount of advertising that children view will lead to values that are overly materialistic.

There are a number of marketing activities aimed at children other than television advertising that cause concerns. Marketing to children through mobile devices is an emerging concern. Corporate programs that place strong sales messages in "educational" materials supplied to schools have also come under attack. Children's advocates are now particularly concerned about marketing to children on the Internet. The federal government has passed legislation to protect children's online privacy (Children's Online Privacy Protection Act). CARU also has guidelines on this topic.

Regulators and business alike are also concerned that adults receive accurate and adequate information about products. The cumulative impact of numerous ads focusing on narcissistic values and product ownership on society's values is a controversial issue.

The regulators and responsible marketers want consumers to have sufficient, adequate information to make sound purchase decisions. Attempts to regulate the amount of information provided sometimes overlook information overload and are not effective.

The focus of consumer concern and regulation of products is twofold: Are they safe? and Are they environmentally sound?

Concern with pricing is that prices be fair and accurately presented in a manner that allows comparison across brands.

KEY TERMS

Children's Advertising Review
    Unit (CARU) 719

Children's Online Privacy
    Protection Act (COPPA) 727

Corrective advertising 734
External reference price 738

INTERNET EXERCISES

1. Visit the Federal Trade Commission Web site (www.ftc.gov). Describe the issues and concerns the FTC is concerned with in terms of consumer protection and marketing.

2. Visit the CARU Web site (www.caru.org). Examine the past six months' news releases. Place each case in a category (such as privacy protection). What do you conclude?

3. Visit the TrustE Web site (www.truste.org). Evaluate its approach to privacy. Will such a seal increase consumer confidence in a site? Justify your response.

4. Visit one of the sites listed below. Evaluate the effectiveness of the site in terms of marketing to children and the degree to which it meets the requirements of COPPA (Table 20-3).

   a. www.nick.com
   b. www.barbie.com
   c. www.nabiscoworld.com
   d. www.kelloggsfunktown.com/funktown/index2.htm.

5. Visit three companies' Web sites. Evaluate their privacy statements and policy.

6. Visit the Better Business Bureau Web site (www.bbb.org). Describe the issues the BBB is concerned with in terms of consumer protection and marketing to adults.

7. Visit an adult-oriented site such as Mike's Hard Lemonade (www.mikeshardlemonade.com). How hard would it be for a 10-year-old to access inappropriate content on this site?

DDB LIFE STYLE STUDY™ DATA ANALYSES

1. Based on DDB Tables 1B through 7B, what characterizes individuals who feel *TV commercials place too much emphasis on sex?* What are the marketing and regulatory implications of this?

2. Using the DDB Tables (1B through 7B), determine what characterizes people who *avoid buying products advertised on shows with sex or violence.* What are the marketing and regulatory implications of this?

3. What characterizes individuals who feel that *advertising directed at children should be taken off TV* (DDB Tables 1B through 7B)? What are the marketing and regulatory implications of this?

4. Based on DDB Tables 1B through 7B, what characterizes those who feel that *there is not enough ethnic diversity in commercials today?* What are the marketing and regulatory implications of this?

REVIEW QUESTIONS

1. What are the major concerns in marketing to children?

2. What are the two main issues concerning children's ability to comprehend advertising messages?

3. What is *CARU?* What does it do? What are some of its rules?

4. What are the major concerns about the *content* of commercial messages targeting children?

5. What are the issues concerning the impact of advertising on children's health and safety?

6. What are the issues concerning the impact of advertising on children's values?

7. What are the concerns associated with mobile marketing to children?

8. What is meant by "commercialization of schools"? What are the various areas in which

commercialization can occur and what are the major concerns?

9. Why are consumer advocates worried about marketing to kids on the Internet?

10. Describe the key provisions of *COPPA*.

11. How effective was COPPA in its first year?

12. What are the major concerns with marketing communications targeting adults?

13. What are the issues concerning the impact of advertising on adults' *values?*

14. What are the concerns with *consumer information accuracy?*

15. What are the concerns with *consumer information adequacy?*

16. What is *information overload?*

17. What is *corrective advertising?*

18. What are the major regulatory issues with respect to products?

19. What are the major regulatory issues with respect to prices?

20. What is *unit pricing?*

21. What is a *reference price?* What is the concern with reference prices?

DISCUSSION QUESTIONS

22. A television advertisement for General Mills' Total cereal made the following claim: "It would take 16 ounces of the leading natural cereal to equal the vitamins in 1 ounce of fortified Total." The Center for Science in the Public Interest filed a petition against General Mills claiming that the advertisement is deceptive. It was the center's position that the claim overstated Total's nutritional benefits because the cereal is not 16 times higher in other factors important to nutrition.
   a. Is the claim misleading? Justify your answer.
   b. How should the FTC proceed in cases such as this?
   c. What are the implications of cases such as this for marketing management?

23. Turkey ham looks like ham and tastes like ham but it contains no pork; it is all turkey. A nationwide survey of consumers showed that most believed the meat product contained both turkey and ham. The USDA approved this label based on a dictionary definition for the term *ham:* the thigh cut of meat from the hind leg of any animal. Discuss how consumers processed information concerning this product and used this information in purchasing this product. (One court ruled the label to be misleading but was overruled by a higher court.)
   a. Is the label misleading?
   b. How should the FTC proceed in such cases?

24. How much and what type of (if any) advertising should be allowed on television programs aimed at children of the following ages?
   a. Under 6
   b. 6 to 9
   c. 10 to 12

25. Should there be special rules governing the advertising of food and snack products to children?

26. Does advertising influence children's values? What can the FTC or CARU do to ensure that positive values are promoted? Be precise in your responses.

27. What rules, if any, should govern mobile marketing to children?

28. What rules, if any, should govern marketing to kids on the Internet?

29. What rules, if any, should govern advertising and promotional messages presented in the classroom?

30. Does advertising influence or reflect a society's values?

31. Do you agree that beer advertisements portraying groups of active young adults having fun while consuming beer teach people that the way to be popular and have fun is to consume alcohol?

32. Respond to the questions in Consumer Insight 20-1.

33. Do you think corrective advertising works? Evaluate the three corrective messages described in the text on page 734.

34. "Since riding tricycles is a major cause of accidental injury to young children, the product should be banned." State and defend your position on this issue (the first part of the statement is true).

35. To what extent, if at all, do you use nutrition labels to guide your purchases? Why?

36. Do you believe reference prices generally reflect prices at which substantial amounts of the product are normally sold? Does this vary by store, season, or other circumstances?

APPLICATION ACTIVITIES

37. Watch two hours of Saturday morning children's programming on a commercial channel (not public broadcasting). Note how many commercials are run. What products are involved? What are the major themes? Would hundreds of hours of viewing these commercials over the course of several years have any impact on children's values or behaviors?

38. With parental consent, interview a child 2 to 4 years of age, one between 5 and 7, and one between 8 and 10. Determine their understanding of the selling intent and techniques of television commercials.

39. Interview two grade school teachers and get their responses to material provided by corporations and their level of educational versus commercial content.

40. Repeat Question 37 for prime-time television and adults.

41. Find and copy or describe an ad that you feel is misleading. Explain why.

42. Visit a large supermarket. Identify the best and worst breakfast cereal focused on children considering both cost and nutrition. What do you conclude?

REFERENCES

1. Based on B. Young, "Does Food Advertising Influence Children's Food Choices?" *International Journal of Advertising* 22 (2003), pp. 441–59; *The Role of Media in Childhood Obesity* (Washington, DC: Kaiser Family Foundation, Research Report, February 2004); D. Kunkel et al., *Report of the APA Task Force on Advertising to Children* (Washington, DC: American Psychological Association, February 20, 2004); M. M. Cardona, "Marketers Bite Back as Fat Fight Flares Up," *Advertising Age,* March 1, 2004, pp. 3 and 35; J. Pereira, "Coming Up Next . . ." *The Wall Street Journal,* March 15, 2004, pp. B1 and B3; D. J. Wood, "Anti-ad Crusaders Miss Point," *Advertising Age,* April 12, 2004, p. 30; J. Pereira, "Junk-Food Games," *The Wall Street Journal,* May 3, 2004, pp. B1 and B4; S. Vranica, "Kraft Limits on Kids' Ads May Cheese Off Rivals," *The Wall Street Journal Online,* January 13, 2005, p. B3; I. Teinowitz, "Politicians Feast on Food Fight," *Advertising Age,* March 14, 2005, pp. 1 and 37; R. Berman, "Sloth, Not Ads, Is Responsible for Fat Kids," *Advertising Age,* April 18, 2005, p. 30; I. Teinowitz, "Marketer Obesity Efforts Get Low Consumer Marks," *AdAge.com,* June 7, 2005; I. Teinowitz, "Food Industry Braces for Two-Day FTC Hearing," *AdAge.com,* July 13, 2005; and D. Majoras, *FTC/HHS Marketing, Self-Regulation, and Childhood Obesity Workshop* (Washington, DC: Federal Trade Commission, Opening Remarks, July 15, 2005), at http://www.ftc.gov/speeches/majoras.

2. Majoras, *FTC/HHS Marketing, Self-Regulation, and Childhood Obesity Workshop.*

3. Ibid.

4. For an overview of this area, see S. Bandyopadhyay, G. Kindra, and L. Sharp, "Is Television Advertising Good for Children?" *International Journal of Advertising* 20, no. 1 (2001), pp. 89–116.

5. See D. R. John, "Consumer Socialization of Children," *Journal of Consumer Research,* December 1999, pp. 183–209.

6. *Self-Regulatory Guidelines for Children's Advertising* (Council of Better Business Bureaus, Inc. Children's Advertising Review Unit, 2003).

7. See M. C. Martin, "Children's Understanding of the Intent of Advertising," *Journal of Public Policy & Marketing,* Fall 1997, pp. 205–16.

8. L. Carlson, R. N. Laczniak, and D. D. Muehling, "Understanding Parental Concern about Toy-Based Programming," *Journal of Current Issues and Research in Advertising,* Fall 1994, pp. 59–72.

9. M. A. Stutts and G. G. Hunnicutt, "Can Young Children Understand Disclaimers?" *Journal of Advertising,* no. 1 (1987), pp. 41–46.

10. R. H. Kolbe and D. D. Muehling, "An Investigation of the Fine Print in Children's Television Advertising," *Journal of Current Issues and Research in Advertising,* Fall 1995, pp. 77–95; and D. D. Muehling and R. H. Kolbe, "A Comparison of Children's and Prime-Time Fine-Print Advertising Disclosure Practices," *Journal of Advertising,* Fall 1998, pp. 37–47.

11. "Trendmasters Addresses CARU Concerns," CARU, Council of Better Business Bureaus, October 3, 2001.

12. "Nabisco Puts Safety First in TV Ads," CARU, Council of Better Business Bureaus, October 4, 2000.

13. "Rose Art Industries, Inc., and Hasbro Participate in CARU Self-Regulatory Forum," CARU, Council of Better Business Bureaus, February 22, 2000.

14. S. W. Colford, "FTC Hits Galoob, Agency for Ads," *Advertising Age,* December 10, 1990, p. 62.

15. *Self-Regulatory Guidelines for Children's Advertising.*

16. "Skechers USA, Inc. Appeals CARU Decision," CARU, Council of Better Business Bureaus, April 10, 2002.

17. See J. B. Cohen, "Playing to Win," D. M. Krugman and K. W. King, "Teenage Exposure to Cigarette Advertising in Popular Consumer Magazines," and K. J. Kelly et al., "The Use of Human Models and Cartoon Characters in Magazine Advertisements for Cigarettes, Beer, and Nonalcoholic Beverages," all in *Journal of Public Policy & Marketing,* Fall 2000, pp. 155–67, 183–88, and 189–200, respectively.

18. "B-M Drops Spots after Query by NAD," *Advertising Age,* April 20, 1981, p. 10.

19. See C. Preston, "The Unintended Effects of Advertising upon Children," *International Journal of Advertising* 18, no. 3 (1999), pp. 363–76.

20. "Ferrero U.S.A. Cooperates with CARU on Comparative Claims," CARU, Council of Better Business Bureaus, December 20, 2001.

21. Cardona, "Marketers Bite Back as Fat Fight Flares Up."

22. H. Clinton, "FTC Action," *Advertising Age,* October 9, 2000, p. 58. For an opposing view, see R. Bergler, "The Effects of Commercial Advertising on Children," *International Journal of Advertising* 18, no. 4 (1999), pp. 411–25.

23. "Advertising Strategies to Target Kids Raise Questions," *10News.com,* July 11, 2005.

24. See, e.g., *The Role of Media in Childhood Obesity* (Washington, DC: Kaiser Family Foundation); and P. M. Ippolito, *TV Advertising to Children 1977 v. 2004* (Washington, DC: Bureau of Economics, FTC, Research Presentation, July 14, 2005).

25. M. M. Cardona, "Young Girls Targeted by Makeup Companies," *Advertising Age,* November 27, 2000, p. 15.

26. M. Scott, "Girls Clamoring for Grown-Up Shoe Styles," *Marketing News,* November 19, 2001, p. 25.

27. M. Irvine, "More Young Children Fret over Body Image," *Eugene Register Guard,* July 23, 2001, p. 1.

28. S. W. Colford, "Top Kid TV Offender: Premiums," *Advertising Age,* April 29, 1991, p. 52.

29. *Guidance for Food Advertising Self-Regulation* (New York: National Advertising Review Council, White Paper, May 28, 2004).

30. See K. Anders, "Marketing and Policy Considerations for Violent Video Games," *Journal of Public Policy & Marketing,* Fall 1999, pp. 270–73; I. Teinowitz, "FTC Report Refuels Debate on Violent Entertainment," *Advertising Age,* April 30, 2001, p. 4; I. Teinowitz, "Violence Revisited," *Advertising Age,* December 3, 2001, p. 3; and I. Teinowitz, "Entertainment Gets a Pass," *Advertising Age,* December 10, 2001, p. 16.

31. See *Selling America's Kids* (Yonkers, NY: Consumers Union Educational Services, 1990), p. 15.

32. Y. Noguchi, "Connecting with Kids, Wirelessly," *Washington Post,* July 7, 2005, p. A1.

33. See "Blue Sphere Games Announces Licence Agreement with DC Thomson," *phonegamereview.com,* May, 25, 2005; A. Z. Cuneo, "Marketers Get Serious about the 'Third Screen,'" *Advertising Age,* July 11, 2005, p. 6; and "Please Hold," *Dallas Morning News,* July 14, 2005.

34. *Children's Advocates Ask Congress to Investigate Marketing of Mobile Phones to Kids* (Portland, OR: Commercial Alert, press release, www.commercialalert.org, July 26, 2005).

35. Classification scheme and descriptions come from *Captive Kids* (Yonkers, NY: Consumers Union, 1995 Research Report, copyright 1998). Various examples, unless otherwise listed, from Teinowitz, "Marketer Obesity Efforts Get Low Consumer Marks"; M. M. Cardona, "High School Papers Group to Take Ads," *Advertising Age,* March 29, 2004, p. 13; "NAAG Bans Tobacco Ads in Library Magazines," *Promo Magazine* (online), June 21, 2005; and *Krispy Kreme in Florida Schools* (Portland, OR: Commercial Alert, press release, www.commercialalert.org, August 30, 2004).

36. See J. E. Brand and B. S. Greenberg, "Commercials in the Classroom," *Journal of Advertising Research,* January 1994, pp. 18–27.

37. See S. Thompson, "Pepsi Hits High Note with Students," *Advertising Age,* October 9, 2000, p. 30; and S. Jarvis, "Lesson Plans," *Marketing News,* June 18, 2001, p. 1.

38. C. Terhune, "Coke's Guidelines for Soft Drinks in Schools Faces Some Criticism," *The Wall Street Journal,* November 17, 2003, p. A6.

39. Pereira, "Junk-Food Games," p. B1.

40. K. Montgomery and S. Pasnik, *Web of Deception* (Washington, DC: Center for Media Education, 1996).

41. *Children's Online Privacy Protection Act—The First Year* (Washington, DC: Center for Media Education, April 2001), p. 4.

42. "Alta Vista Makes Changes," CARU, Council of Better Business Bureaus, February 14, 2001.

43. "CARU Refers Fansite of Singer Pink to Federal Trade Commission," CARU, Council of Better Business Bureaus, April 10, 2002.

44. "Scan-Command.Com Works with CARU," CARU, Council of Better Business Bureaus, April 17, 2002.

45. See K. B. Sheehan and M. G. Hoy, "Flaming, Complaining, and Abstaining," *Journal of Advertising,* Fall 1999, pp. 37–51; K. B. Sheehan, "An Investigation of Gender Differences in On-Line Privacy Concerns," *Journal of Interactive Marketing,* Autumn 1999, pp. 24–38; and E. M. Caudill and P. E. Murphy, "Consumer Online Privacy," J. Phelps, G. Nowak, and E. Ferrell, "Privacy Concerns and Consumer Willingness to Provide Personal Information," and K. B. Sheehan and M. G. Hoy, "Dimensions of Privacy Concern among Online Consumers," all in *Journal of Public Policy & Marketing,* Spring 2000, pp. 7–19, 27–41, and 62–73, respectively. See also K. B. Sheehan and T. W. Gleason, "Online Privacy," *Journal of Current Issues and Research in Advertising,* Spring 2001, pp. 31–41; P. Paul, "Mixed Signals," and R. Gardyn, "Swap Meet," both in *American Demographics,* July 2001, pp. 47 and 51–55, respectively; and J. E. Phelps, G. D'Souza, and G. J. Nowak, "Antecedents and Consequences of Consumer Privacy Concerns," *Journal of Interactive Marketing,* Autumn 2001, pp. 2–17.

46. Based on R. Pitofsky, "Privacy Online," testimony before the U.S. Senate, May 25, 2000; and T. J. Muris, "Protecting Consumers' Privacy: 2002 and Beyond," speech at the Privacy 2001 Conference, both available at www.ftc.gov.

47. Taken from the FTC Web site at www.ftc.gov/privacy/privacyinitiatives/promises.html, accessed July 31, 2005.

48. See B. G. Englis, M. R. Solomon, and R. D. Ashmore, "Beauty *before* the Eyes of Beholders," *Journal of Advertising,* June 1994, pp. 49–64; C. R. Wiles, J. A. Wiles, and A. Tjernlund, "The Ideology of Advertising," *Journal of Advertising Research,* May, 1996, pp. 57–66; M. C. Martin and J. W. Gentry, "Stuck in the Model Trap," *Journal of Advertising,* Summer 1997, pp. 19–33; M. K. Hogg, M. Bruce, and K. Hough, "Female Images in Advertising," *International Journal of Advertising* 18, no. 4 (1999), pp. 445–73; and T. Reichert, "The Prevalence of Sexual Imagery in Ads Targeted to Young Adults," *Journal of Consumer Affairs,* Winter 2003, pp. 403–12.

49. S. Burton, R. G. Netemeyer, and D. R. Lichtenstein, "Gender Differences for Appearance-Related Attitudes and Behaviors," *Journal of Public Policy & Marketing,* Fall 1994, pp. 60–75.

50. R. Gustafson, M. Popovich, and S. Thompson, "Subtle Ad Images Threaten Girls More," *Marketing News,* June 4, 2001, p. 12.

51. For research in these areas, see R. W. Pollay and S. Lysonski, "In the Eye of the Beholder," *Journal of International Consumer Marketing* 6, no. 2 (1993), pp. 25–43; D. Walsh, "Safe Sex in Advertising," *American Demographics,* April 1994, pp. 24–30; and R. H. Kolbe and D. Muehling, "Gender Roles and Children's Television Advertising," *Journal of Current Issues and Research in Advertising,* Spring 1995, pp. 49–64.

52. C. Rubel, "Marketers Giving Better Treatment to Females," *Marketing News,* April 22, 1996, p. 10.

53. See L. Langmeyer, "Advertising Images of Mature Adults," *Journal of Current Issues and Research in Advertising,* Fall 1993, pp. 81–91; C. R. Taylor and J. Y. Lee, "Not in *Vogue*," *Journal of Public Policy & Marketing,* Fall 1994, pp. 239–45; T. H. Stevenson and P. E. McIntyre, "A Comparison of the Portrayal and Frequency of Hispanics and Whites in English Language Television Advertising," and M. T. Elliott, "Differences in the Portrayal of Blacks," both in *Journal of Current Issues and Research in Advertising,* Spring 1995, pp. 65–86; J. M. Bristor, R. G. Lee, and M. R. Hunt, "Race and Ideology," *Journal of Public Policy & Marketing,* Spring 1995, pp. 48–59; E. J. Wilson and A. Biswas, "The Use of Black Models in Specialty Catalogs," *Journal of Direct Marketing,* Autumn 1995, pp. 47–56; and K. Karande and A. Grbavac, "Acculturation and the Use of Asian Models in Print Advertisements," *Enhancing Knowledge Development in Marketing* (Chicago: American Marketing Association, 1996), pp. 347–52.

54. See L. J. Shrum, "Television and Persuasion," *Psychology & Marketing,* March 1999, pp. 119–40.

55. See, e.g., *Fall Colors* (Oakland, CA: Children Now, 2003–04).

56. See A. Simonson and M. B. Holbrook, "Permissible Puffery versus Actionable Warranty in Advertising and Salestalk," *Journal of Public Policy & Marketing,* Fall 1993, pp. 216–33.

57. J. Pollack, "Arm & Hammer Brand Fights Toothpaste Rivals," *Advertising Age,* July 27, 1998, p. 2.

58. See J.-N. Kapferer, "Brand Confusion," *Psychology & Marketing,* September 1995, pp. 551–68; and D. J. Howard, R. A. Kerin, and C. Gengler, "The Effects of Brand Name Similarity on Brand Source Confusion," *Journal of Public Policy & Marketing,* Fall 2000, pp. 250–64.

59. "Bayer & McNeil Participate in NAD Self-Regulatory Process," CARU, Council of Better Business Bureaus, July 8, 2002.

60. Gillette example from J. Neff, "Court Rules against Gillette Razor Package Claim," *AdAge.com,* June 23, 2005.

61. C. A. Cole and G. J. Gaeth, "Cognitive and Age-Related Differences in the Ability to Use Nutritional Information in a Complex Environment," *Journal of Marketing Research,* May 1990, pp. 175–84; and W. Mueller, "Who Reads the Label?" *American Demographics,* January 1991, pp. 36–40.

62. B. Reid, "Adequacy of Symbolic Warnings," *Marketing News,* October 25, 1985, p. 3.

63. M. L. Retsky, "Survey Research Is Useful in False Advertising Cases," *Marketing News,* April 27, 1998, p. 8; M. L. Retsky, "Misleading Ads Could Be as Litigious as Outright Lies," *Marketing News,* August 3, 1998, p. 5; and I. L. Preston, "Dilution and Negation of Consumer Information by Antifactual Content," *Journal of Consumer Affairs,* Summer 2003, pp. 1–21.

64. See G. V. Johar, "Consumer Involvement and Deception from Implied Advertising Campaigns," *Journal of Marketing Research,* August 1995, pp. 267–79.

65. S. Ellison and B. Steinberg, "P&G Is Settling Disputes on Ads as Suits Pile Up," *The Wall Street Journal,* November 26, 2003, pp. B1 and B3.

66. I. Teinowitz, "FTC Faces Test of Ad Power," *Advertising Age,* March 30, 1998, p. 26.

67. See, e.g., A. Mitra et al., "Can the Educationally Disadvantaged Interpret the FDA-Mandated Nutrition Facts Panel?" *Journal of Public Policy & Marketing,* Spring 1999, pp. 106–17; J. A. Garretson and S. Burton, "Effects of Nutrition Facts Panel Values, Nutrition Claims, and Health Claims," *Journal of Public Policy & Marketing,* Fall 2000, pp. 213–27; G. Baltas, "The Effects of Nutrition Information on Consumer Choice," *Journal of Advertising Research,* March 2001, pp. 57–63; and S. K. Balasubramanian and C. Cole, "Consumers' Search and Use of Nutrition Information," *Journal of Marketing,* July 2002, pp. 112–27.

68. D. L. Vence, "The Lowdown on Trans Fats," *Marketing News,* March 15, 2004, pp. 13–14.

69. "$10 Sure Thing," *Time,* August 4, 1980, p. 51. See also M. A. Eastlick, R. Feinberg, and C. Trappey, "Information Overload in Mail Catalog Shopping," *Journal of Direct Marketing,* Autumn 1993, pp. 14–19. For a different explanation, see Y. Ganzach and P. Ben-Or, "Information Overload, Decreasing Marginal Responsiveness, and the Estimation of Nonmonotonic Relationships in Direct Marketing," *Journal of Direct Marketing,* Spring 1996, pp. 7–12.

70. See M. Wilkie, "Rx Marketers 'Test' FDA Guides on Print DTC Ads," *Advertising Age,* April 6, 1998, p. 18.

71. V. O'Connell, "As 'Safer Smokes' Multiply, States Probe Marketing Claims," *The Wall Street Journal,* May 18, 2004, pp. B1 and B10.

Cases

CASE 6-1   Children's Online Privacy Protection

Table A provides a grid which can be used to evaluate how well various Web sites targeted toward children under 13 years of age adhere to the components of COPPA (Children's Online Privacy Protection Act). Each row represents one of the key provisions of COPPA (for more detail on each provision, see Table 20-3, pg. 727). Each column represents a different company Web site.

Each company Web site can be rated in terms of its adherence to each COPPA provision on the following scale: 1 = very poor; 2 = poor; 3 = adequate; 4 = good; 5 = very good. Alternatively, a check-box procedure might be used in which a checkmark is placed in each cell where the provision is met.

Discussion Questions

1. Visit at least three Web sites designed to appeal to children under 13 (e.g., Nick.com, Disney.com and so on) and complete the COPPA Evaluation Grid.
2. Prepare a report including the COPPA Evaluation Grid and discuss how well these companies appear to be adhering to the COPPA provisions. Are there areas in which you see room for improvement? Explain.
3. Do you feel COPPA is adequate? Detail any areas where COPPA could be strengthened in order to better protect children's online privacy.
4. CARU (Children's Advertising Review Unit) has its own self-regulatory program which is an FTC-approved Safe Harbor. Participants (companies) who adhere to CARU's Guidelines are deemed in compliance with COPPA. Visit CARU's Online Privacy Program area at www.caru.org/program/index.asp and address the following:
   a. In what ways do CARU's guidelines (under CARU's compliance checklist tab) help companies to interpret the broad mandates of COPPA?
   b. Do CARU's guidelines help you make finer-grade assessments of the companies you evaluated in Questions 1 and 2 above? Do your assessments remain the same or do they change? Explain.
   c. Describe and evaluate any tools provided by CARU to help companies evaluate their Web sites with respect to children's online privacy.

TABLE A

COPPA Evaluation Grid

COPPA Provision	Company A	Company B	Company C
Notice			
Prior Parental Consent			
Prevention of Further Use			
Limited Collection of Personal Information			
Access to Information			

CASE 6-2   Safer Cigarettes?

In November 2001, Brown & Williamson Tobacco placed Advance cigarettes into Indianapolis stores for a sales test. Ads supporting the brand feature part of a man's or woman's face focusing on one clear eye. The headline is "New ADVANCE . . . A step in the right direction." The tagline is "All of the taste . . . Less of the toxins." The text credits the toxin reduction to a "revolutionary new filter design," and a "patented new method for growing tobacco." The text again states "Less toxins and great taste." In addition to the required Surgeon General's warning, the ads contain a boxed statement: "There is no such thing as a safe cigarette, nor is there enough medical information to know if Advance with less toxins will lower health risks." This statement is also on the back of the package.

There are four views of the likely impact of this product and its message. Brown & Williamson obviously feels it meets a market need. It uses the "less toxins" claim because

> It seems to be the clearest and most impactful statement we could make of the facts that are behind Advance and the product itself. We did not want to get into polysyllabic chemical names.

One analyst feels that the tagline will backfire and remind smokers of the harmful effects of smoking:

> People are aware of the fact that when they purchase cigarettes, there are significant adverse health consequences, but it doesn't seem to be a winning proposition to remind them every time.

Mathew Myers, president of the Campaign for Tobacco-Free Kids, feels it is unethical and misleading:

> It's always a good thing to remove a known carcinogen from cigarettes, but it is irresponsible to make statements in marketing that will lead consumers to believe that the product is safer. And that's exactly what happens when a manufacturer touts a product as having fewer toxins, no matter how many disclaimers they put on it.

A final view is expressed by an analyst who sees very little demand for a safer or less toxic cigarette:

> Cigarette smokers are risk-takers. If they're truly concerned about health, they quit.

Discussion Questions

1. Which of the four positions described above is (are) most likely accurate? Why?
2. Why would consumers believe that Advance is safer, if not a safe, cigarette despite the disclaimer?
3. What are the ethical issues Brown & Williamson should have considered before launching this product?
4. What regulations, if any, should be applied to promoting toxin reduction in cigarettes?
5. Less educated individuals are much more likely to smoke and smoke heavily (if 100 equals an average rate of heavy smoking within a group, college graduates score 48, those who attended college are 86, those with high school degrees are 120, and those who did not graduate from high school are 151). Does this fact impose additional ethical or regulatory requirements concerning how Brown & Williamson communicates about Advance?

Source: C. B. DiPasquale, "B&W Smoke Boasts Fewer Toxins," *Advertising Age,* November 5, 2001, p. 3; "Blowing Smoke," *Advertising Age,* November 12, 2001, p. 26; B. Garfield, "Softly Lit or Blunt, 'Less Toxic' Cigarette Ads Hint at Health," *Advertising Age,* November 12, 2001; and C. B. DiPasquale, "B&W Leads Lower-Toxin Pitch," *Advertising Age,* June 24, 2002, p. S22.

Appendix A
Consumer Research Methods

In this appendix, we want to provide you with some general guidelines for conducting research on consumer behavior. While these guidelines will help you get started, a good marketing research text is indispensable if you need to conduct a consumer research project or evaluate a consumer research proposal.

SECONDARY DATA

Secondary data is basically existing information or data. Any research project should begin with a thorough search for existing information relevant to the project at hand. Internal data such as past studies, sales reports, and accounting records should be consulted. External data, including reports, magazines, government organizations, trade associations, marketing research firms, advertising agencies, academic journals, trade journals, and books, should be thoroughly researched.

Computer searches are fast, economical means of conducting such searches. University and large public libraries, as well as companies, often subscribe to various databases that can be invaluable sources of information, reports, and data. These include, but are not limited to, (*a*) ABI Inform—electronic access to trade and academic publications, (*b*) MarketResearch.com—an online source of detailed industry reports, (*c*) Simmons Market Research Bureau data, (*d*) Mediamark data, and (*e*) Standard Rate and Data (SRDS). Publicly available demographic information can be found at the U.S. Census (www.census.gov). And a great source for global information is *The World Fact Book* (www.cia.gov/cia/publications/factbook/).

PRIMARY DATA COLLECTION: ISSUES AND METHODS

If the specific information required is not available from secondary sources, we must gather primary data. Primary data is information or data that we collect for the first time in order to answer a specific research question. Thus, we might use the U.S. Census data to better understand the demographics driving gardening (secondary data), but conduct a survey (primary data) to collect information regarding the specific brand name we will use for our new garden tool.

Sampling

Collecting primary data generally involves talking to or observing consumers. However, it could involve asking knowledgeable others, such as sales personnel, about the consumers. In either case, time and cost constraints generally preclude us from contacting every single potential consumer. Therefore, most consumer research projects require a sample—a deliberately selected portion of the larger group. This requires a number of critical decisions, as described below. Mistakes made at this point are difficult to correct later in the study. The key decisions are briefly described below.

Define the Population   The first step is to define the consumers in which we are interested. Do we want to talk to current brand users, current product-category users, or potential product-category users? Do we want to talk with the purchasers, the users, or everyone involved in the purchase process? The population as we define it must reflect the behavior on which our marketing decision will be based.

Specify the Sampling Frame   A sampling frame is a list or grouping of individuals or households that reflects the population of interest. A phone book and shoppers at a given shopping mall can each serve as a sampling frame. Perfect sampling frames contain every member of the population one time. Phone books do not have households with unlisted numbers; many people do not visit shopping malls, while others visit them frequently. This is an area in which we generally must do the best we can without expecting a perfect frame. However, we must be very alert for biases that may be introduced by imperfections in our sampling frame.

Select a Sampling Method   The major decision at this point is between a random (probability) sample and a nonrandom sample. Nonrandom samples, particularly judgment samples, can provide good results. A judgment sample involves the deliberate selection of knowledgeable consumers or individuals. For example, a firm might decide to interview the social activity officers of fraternities and sororities to estimate campus attitudes toward a carbonated wine drink aimed at the campus market. Such a sample might provide useful insights. However, it might also be biased, since such individuals are likely to have a higher level of income and be more socially active than the average student.

The most common nonrandom sample, the convenience sample, involves selecting sample members in the manner most convenient for the researcher. It is subject to many types of bias and should generally be avoided.

Random or probability samples allow some form of a random process to select members from a sample frame. It may be every third person who passes a point-of-purchase display, house addresses selected by using a table of random numbers, or telephone numbers generated randomly by a computer. If random procedures are used, we can calculate the likelihood that our sample is not representative within specified limits.

Determine Sample Size   Finally, we must determine how large a sample to talk to. If we are using random sampling, there are formulas that can help us make this decision. In general, the more diverse our population is and the more certain we want to be that we have the correct answer, the more people we will need to interview.

DATA COLLECTION METHODS

Depth Interviews

Depth interviews can involve one respondent and one interviewer, or they may involve a small group (8 to 15 respondents) and an interviewer. The latter are called **focus group interviews,** and the former are termed **individual depth interviews** or one-on-ones. Groups of four or five are often referred to as minigroup interviews. Depth interviews in general are commonly referred to as qualitative research. Individual depth interviews involve a one-to-one relationship between the interviewer and the respondent. The interviewer does not have a specific set of prespecified questions that must be asked according to the order imposed by a questionnaire. Instead, there is freedom to create questions, to probe those responses that appear relevant, and generally to try to develop the best set of data in any way practical. However, the interviewer must follow one rule: He or she must not consciously try to affect the content of the answers given by the respondent. The respondent must feel free to reply to the various questions, probes, and other, more subtle ways of encouraging responses in the manner deemed most appropriate.

Individual depth interviews are appropriate in six situations:

1. Detailed probing of an individual's behavior, attitudes, or needs is required.
2. The subject matter under discussion is likely to be of a highly confidential nature (e.g., personal investments).
3. The subject matter is of an emotionally charged or embarrassing nature.
4. Certain strong, socially acceptable norms exist (e.g., child care) and the need to conform in a group discussion may influence responses.
5. A highly detailed (step-by-step) understanding of complicated behavior or decision-making patterns (e.g., planning the family holiday) is required.
6. The interviews are with professional people or with people on the subject of their jobs (e.g., finance directors).

Focus group interviews can be applied to (1) basic need studies for product ideas creation, (2) new-product ideas or concept exploration, (3) product-positioning studies, (4) advertising and communications research, (5) background studies on consumers' frames of reference, (6) establishment of consumer vocabulary as a preliminary step in questionnaire development, and (7) determination of attitudes and behaviors.

The standard focus group interview involves 8 to 12 individuals. Normally, the group is designed to reflect the characteristics of a particular market segment. The respondents are selected according to the relevant sampling plan and meet at a central location that generally has facilities for taping or filming the interviews. The discussion itself is led by a moderator. The competent moderator attempts to develop three clear stages in the one- to three-hour interview: (1) establish rapport with the group, structure the rules of group interaction, and set objectives; (2) attempt to provoke intense discussion in the relevant areas; and (3) attempt to summarize the group's responses to determine the extent of agreement. In general, either the moderator or a second person prepares a summary of each session after analyzing the session's transcript.

Observation

Observation can be used when (1) the behaviors of interest are public; (2) they are repetitive, frequent, or predictable; and (3) they cover a relatively brief time span. An observational study requires five decisions:

1. *Natural versus contrived situation.* Do we wait for a behavior to occur in its natural environment, or do we create an artificial situation in which it will occur?
2. *Open versus disguised observation.* To what extent are the consumers aware that we are observing their behavior?
3. *Structured versus unstructured observation.* Will we limit our observations to predetermined behaviors, or will we note whatever occurs?
4. *Direct or indirect observations.* Will we observe the behaviors themselves or merely the outcomes of the behaviors?
5. *Human or mechanical observations.* Will the observations be made mechanically or by people?

Physiological Measures

Physiological measures are direct observations of physical responses to a stimulus such as an advertisement. These responses may be controllable, such as eye movements, or uncontrollable, such as the galvanic skin response. Eye-tracking cameras allow researchers to determine how long a consumer looks at each element in a stimulus, such as a point-of-purchase display, ad, or package, and the sequence in which they are examined. Galvanic skin response can be measured (via a lie detector) to detect the intensity of emotional responses to ads or packages.

Projective Techniques

Projective techniques are designed to measure feelings, attitudes, and motivations that consumers are unable or unwilling to reveal otherwise. They are based on the theory that the description of vague objects requires interpretation, and this interpretation can be based only on the individual's own attitudes, values, and motives.

Table 10-2 provides descriptions and examples of the more common projective techniques.

Surveys

Surveys are systematic ways of gathering information from a large number of people. They generally involve the use of a structured or semi-structured questionnaire. Surveys can be administered by mail, telephone, in person, or online. Personal interviews generally take place in shopping malls and are referred to as mall intercept interviews.

Each approach has advantages and disadvantages.

- **Personal interviews** allow the use of complex questionnaires, product demonstrations, and the collection of large amounts of data. They can be completed in a relatively short period of time. However, they are very expensive and are subject to interviewer bias.
- **Telephone surveys** can be completed rapidly, provide good sample control (who answers the questions), and are relatively inexpensive. Substantial amounts of data can be collected, but it must be relatively simple. Interviewer bias is possible.
- **Mail surveys** take the longest to complete and must generally be rather short. They can be used to collect modestly complex data, and they are very economical. Interviewer bias is not a problem.
- **Online surveys** are increasingly popular since they are highly cost effective (respondents enter the data), fast, and easy to conduct. A major concern with online survey research historically has been the demographic skew or bias due to income, education, ethnic, and gender gaps. As the online population continues to become more representative of the general population, such concerns will be reduced.

A major concern in survey research is nonresponse bias. In most surveys, fewer than 50 percent of those selected to participate in the study actually do participate. In telephone and personal interviews, many people are not at home or refuse to cooperate. In mail surveys, many people refuse or forget to respond.

We can increase the response rate by callbacks in telephone and home personal surveys. The callbacks should be made at different times and on different days. Monetary inducements (enclosing $1) increase the response rate to mail surveys, as do prenotification (a card saying that a questionnaire is coming) and reminder postcards.

If less than a 100 percent response rate is obtained, we must be concerned that those who did not respond differ from those who did. A variety of techniques are available to help us estimate the likelihood and nature of nonresponse error.

Experimentation

Experimentation involves changing one or more variables (product features, package color, advertising theme) and observing the effect the change has on another variable (consumer attitude, repeat purchase behavior, learning). The variable(s) that is changed is called an *independent variable*. The "change" is called a "manipulation," which simply means that we are systematically varying a factor at different levels. For example, if we presented different groups of consumers with a product priced at $1.00, $1.50, and $2.00, then we would have manipulated price at three levels.

The variable(s) that may be affected by the manipulation(s) is called a *dependent variable*. The objective in experimental design is to structure the situation so that any change in the dependent variable is very likely to have been caused by a change in the independent variable. The way this is done is through high levels of "control," which generally means that we manipulate variables of interest and hold all other factors constant. Thus, we could present three different product concepts that differed only in terms of price. Everything else, including design, package color, and so on, would be held constant (or remain the same) across the different price levels. The logic is that since only the manipulated variable changed, we have high confidence that it was the reason (cause) for any observed changes in the dependent variable.

There are numerous experimental designs depending on the number and level of independent variables the researcher wishes to investigate. There are different kinds of experiments that reflect the level of control that we can achieve. In a laboratory experiment, we carefully control for all outside influences and can conclude with confidence that our independent variables *caused* the changes in our dependent variable(s). Lab experiments thus yield high levels of *internal validity*.

In a field experiment, we conduct our study in the most relevant environment possible. This generally means giving up the pristine control of a lab setting. However, the reason for doing so is to see how consumers actually react in "real world" settings. Field experiments are important because they help to establish *external validity*—which is the extent to which our results are likely to hold true in real world settings. This can mean that unusual outside influences may distort our results (that is, reduce internal validity). However, careful planning can often avoid these unusual influences.

Conjoint Analysis: Examining Attribute Importance Using Experimentation Conjoint analysis is an application of experimentation. In conjoint analysis, the consumer is presented with a set of products or product descriptions in which the potential evaluative criteria vary (are manipulated). For example, consider a notebook manufacturer who is interested in the importance of four different attributes: Processor (2 levels: Pentium M 1.6 Ghz versus Pentium M 2.0 Ghz), Wireless enabled (2 levels: yes versus no), weight (2 levels: 3.5 lbs. versus 5.1 lbs.), and price (3 levels: $1,000, $1,500, and $2,000). This would result in 24 different notebook computer configurations ($2 \times 2 \times 2 \times 3 = 24$) that vary on four criteria. Two might be

Pentium M 2.0 GHz	Pentium M 1.6 GHz
Wireless enabled (yes)	Wireless enabled (yes)
5.1 pounds	3.5 pounds
$1,500	$2,000

The consumer ranks all 24 such descriptions in terms of his or her preference for those combinations of features. Based on these preference ranks, sophisticated computer

Using Conjoint Analysis to Determine the Importance of Evaluative Criteria for a Notebook Computer

Design features

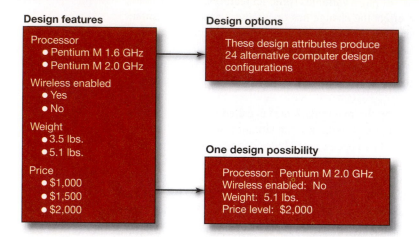

Processor
• Pentium M 1.6 GHz
• Pentium M 2.0 GHz

Wireless enabled
• Yes
• No

Weight
• 3.5 lbs.
• 5.1 lbs.

Price
• $1,000
• $1,500
• $2,000

Design options

These design attributes produce 24 alternative computer design configurations

One design possibility

Processor: Pentium M 2.0 GHz
Wireless enabled: No
Weight: 5.1 lbs.
Price level: $2,000

Consumer preferences

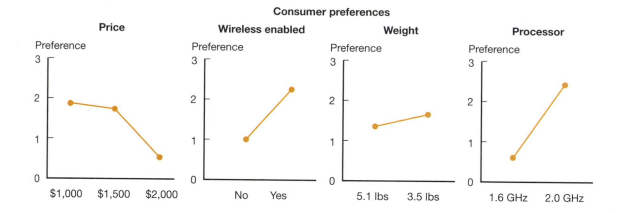

Price — Preference vs. $1,000 / $1,500 / $2,000

Wireless enabled — Preference vs. No / Yes

Weight — Preference vs. 5.1 lbs / 3.5 lbs

Processor — Preference vs. 1.6 GHz / 2.0 GHz

Relative importance

Evaluative criteria	Importance
Processor	45%
Weight	5
Wireless enabled	25
Price	25

■ Processor is the most important feature in this example, and Pentium M 2.0 GHz is the preferred option.

■ While price and wireless enabled are also important, price becomes important only between $1,500 and $2,000.

programs derive the relative importance consumers assign to each level of each attribute tested.

For example, in Figure A-1, imagine a consumer was asked to rank in terms of overall preference 24 different computer designs featuring different levels of four key evaluative criteria. The preferences were then analyzed in light of the variations in the attributes. The

1. *Preliminary decisions*
   Exactly what information is required?
   Exactly who are the target respondents?
   What method of communication will be used to reach these respondents?
2. *Decisions about question content*
   Is this question really needed?
   Is this question sufficient to generate the needed information?
   Can the respondent answer the question correctly?
   Will the respondent answer the question correctly?
   Are there any external events that might bias the response to the question?
3. *Decisions about the response format*
   Can this question best be asked as an open-ended, multiple-choice, or dichotomous question?
4. *Decisions concerning question phrasing*
   Do the words used have but one meaning to all the respondents?
   Are any of the words or phrases loaded or leading in any way?
   Are there any implied alternatives in the question?
   Are there any unstated assumptions related to the question?
   Will the respondents approach the question from the frame of reference desired by the researcher?
5. *Decisions concerning the question sequence*
   Are the questions organized in a logical manner that avoids introducing errors?
6. *Decisions on the layout of the questionnaire*
   Is the questionnaire designed in a manner to avoid confusion and minimize recording errors?
7. *Pretest and revise*
   Has the final questionnaire been subjected to a thorough pretest, using respondents similar to those who will be included in the final survey?

result is a preference curve for each evaluative criterion that reflects the importance of that attribute. Based on Figure A-1, processor is a particularly important evaluative criterion for this consumer while weight (at least in the range examined) is of almost no importance.

Conjoint analysis is limited to the attributes listed by the researcher. Thus, a conjoint analysis of soft-drink attributes would not indicate anything about calorie content unless the researcher listed it as a feature. The Sunbeam study (opening example in Chapter 16) did not test such attributes as brand name, color, weight, or safety features. If an important attribute is omitted, incorrect market share predictions are likely to result. In addition, conjoint analysis is not well suited for measuring the importance of emotional or feeling-based product choices. For example, what types of attributes would you use to perform a conjoint analysis of perfumes?

Questionnaire Design

All surveys and many experiments use questionnaires as data collection devices. A questionnaire is simply a formalized set of questions for eliciting information. It can measure (1) behavior—past, present, or intended; (2) demographic characteristics—age, gender, income, education, occupation; (3) level of knowledge; and (4) attitudes and opinions. The process of questionnaire design is outlined in Table A-1.

Attitude Scales

Attitudes are frequently measured on specialized scales as detailed below. The instructions indicate that the consumer is to mark the blank that best indicates how accurately one or the other term describes or fits the attitude object.

Various types of attitude scales exist. These include the following:

Noncomparative Rating Scale   Noncomparative rating scales require the consumer to evaluate an object or an attribute of the object without directly comparing it to another object. An example would be *"How do you like the taste of Diet Pepsi?"*

Like it very much	Like it	Dislike it	Strongly dislike it
_____	_____	_____	_____

Comparative Rating Scale   Comparative rating scales provide a direct comparison point (a named competitor, "your favorite brand," "the ideal brand"). An example would be *"How do you like the taste of Tom's of Maine compared to Ultra Bright?"*

Like it much more	Like it more	Like it about the same	Like it less	Like it much less
_____	_____	_____	_____	_____

Semantic Differential Scale   The semantic differential scale requires the consumer to rate an item on a number of scales bounded at each end by one of two bipolar adjectives. For example: *"Rate the Honda Accord on the following attributes."*

Fast _____ _____ _____ _____ _____ _____ _____ Slow

Fancy _____ _____ _____ _____ _____ _____ _____ Plain

The end positions indicate "extremely," the next pair in from the ends indicate "very," the middlemost pair indicate "somewhat," and the middle position indicates "neither/nor."

Likert Scale   Likert scales ask consumers to indicate a degree of agreement or disagreement with each of a series of statements related to the attitude object, such as the following:

1. *Macy's is one of the most attractive stores in town.*

Strongly agree	Agree	Neither agree nor disagree	Disagree	Strongly disagree
_____	_____	_____	_____	_____

2. *The service at Macy's is not satisfactory.*

Strongly agree	Agree	Neither agree nor disagree	Disagree	Strongly disagree
_____	_____	_____	_____	_____

To analyze responses each response category is assigned a numerical value. For example, in the Likert scales above we could assign values such as 1 (Strongly agree) through 5 (Strongly disagree). Or a $+2$ through -2 system could be used with zero representing the neutral point (neither agree nor disagree).

Measuring the Three Attitude Components

As we discussed in Chapter 11, attitude can be broken into its cognitive, affective, and behavioral components. Table A-2 provides a detailed set of items for each attitude component.

Cognitive Component (Measuring Beliefs about Specific Attributes Using the Semantic Differential Scale)

Diet Coke

Strong taste	____	____	____	____	____	____	____	Mild taste
Low priced	____	____	____	____	____	____	____	High priced
Caffeine free	____	____	____	____	____	____	____	High in caffeine
Distinctive in taste	____	____	____	____	____	____	____	Similar in taste to most

Affective Component (Measuring Feelings about Specific Attributes or the Overall Brand Using Likert Scales)

	Strongly Agree	Agree	Neither Agree nor Disagree	Disagree	Strongly Disagree
I like the taste of Diet Coke.	____	____	____	____	____
Diet Coke is overpriced.	____	____	____	____	____
Caffeine is bad for your health.	____	____	____	____	____
I like Diet Coke.	____	____	____	____	____

Behavioral Component (Measuring Actions or Intended Actions)

The last soft drink I consumed was a ____.
I usually drink ____ soft drinks.
What is the likelihood you will buy Diet Coke
   the next time you purchase a soft drink?

    ____ Definitely will buy
    ____ Probably will buy
    ____ Might buy
    ____ Probably will not buy
    ____ Definitely will not buy

EVALUATING ADVERTISING EFFECTS

A successful advertisement, or any other marketing message, must accomplish four tasks:

1. *Exposure*. It must physically reach the consumer.
2. *Attention*. The consumer must attend to it.
3. *Interpretation*. It must be properly interpreted.
4. *Memory*. It must be stored in memory in a manner that will allow retrieval under the proper circumstances.

Advertising evaluation covers all of these tasks. However, most of the effort is focused on attention and, to a lesser extent, memory.

Measures of Exposure

Exposure to print media is most frequently measured in terms of circulation. Data on circulation are provided by a variety of commercial firms. However, frequently these data are not broken down in a manner consistent with the firm's target market. Thus, a firm may be targeting the lower-middle social class, but circulation data may be broken down by income rather than social class.

Diary reports, in which respondents record their daily listening patterns, and telephone interviews are the two methods used to measure radio listening. Television viewing is measured primarily by **people meters** (mechanical observation), which are electronic devices that automatically determine if a television is turned on and, if so, to which channel. They allow each household member to log on when viewing by punching an identifying button. The demographics of each potential viewer are stored in the central computer so viewer profiles can be developed.

Web sites can automatically record (mechanical observation) the number of total and unique (from distinct computers) visits per time period. Banner ads and the sites on which they appear are often evaluated on the *clickthrough rate*—the percentage of site visitors or total number of people who click on the banner ad.

Measures of Attention

The attention-attracting powers of commercials, packages, and Web sites can be partially measured in a direct manner using **eye tracking** (mechanical observation) or eye fixations. While a consumer looks at images of print ads, billboards, store shelves, packages, or Web sites, a camera underneath the screen sends an invisible beam of light off the consumer's pupil. The camera indicates exactly what the consumer is attending to. This technology allows marketers to determine (1) what parts of the message were attended to, (2) what sequence was used in viewing the message, and (3) how much time was spent on each part.

Indirect measures of attention, which also tap at least some aspects of memory, include theater tests, day-after recall, recognition tests, and Starch scores. *Theater tests* involve showing commercials along with television programs in a theater. Viewers complete questionnaires designed to measure which commercials, and what aspects of those commercials, attracted their attention. **Day-after recall (DAR)** is the most popular method of measuring the attention-getting power of television commercials. Individuals are interviewed the day after a commercial is aired on a program they watched. Recall of the commercial and recall of specific aspects of the commercial (assessed through questionnaires) are interpreted as a reflection of the amount of attention.

DAR measures of television commercials have been criticized as favoring rational, factual, hard-sell ads and high-involvement products while discriminating against feeling, emotional, soft-sell ads. However, for many product/target market combinations, the latter approach may be superior. In response, substantial work has been done to develop recognition measures for television commercials. In **recognition tests,** the commercial of interest, or key parts of it, along with other commercials are shown to target-market members. Recognition of the commercial, or key parts of it, is the measure.

Starch scores are the most popular technique for evaluating the attention-attracting power of print ads. The respondents are shown advertisements from magazine issues they have recently read. For each advertisement, they indicate which parts (headlines, illustrations, copy blocks) they recall reading. Three main scores are computed:

1. *Noted*. The percentage of people who recall seeing the ad in that issue.
2. *Seen-associated*. The percentage of those who recall reading a part of the ad that clearly identifies the brand or advertiser.
3. *Read most*. The percentage of those who recall reading 50 percent or more of the copy.

Starch scores allow an indirect measure of attention to the overall ad and to key components of the ad.

Measures of Interpretation

Marketers investigating *interpretation* can use any number of the research methods we've discussed including focus groups, surveys, and projective techniques. A critical task for marketers is to move beyond cognitive interpretation and tap emotions and feelings as well. Techniques such as the adSAM discussed in Chapter 11 can be quite useful in this regard.

Appendix B
Consumer Behavior Audit*

In this appendix, we provide a list of key questions to guide you in developing marketing strategy from a consumer behavior perspective. This audit is no more than a checklist to minimize the chance of overlooking a critical behavioral dimension. It does not guarantee a successful strategy. However, thorough and insightful answers to these questions should greatly enhance the likelihood of a successful marketing program.

Our audit is organized around the key decisions that marketing managers must make. The first key decision is the selection of the target market(s) to be served. This is followed by the determination of a viable product position for each target market. Finally, the marketing mix elements—product, place, price, and promotion—must be structured in a manner consistent with the desired product position. This process is illustrated in Figure B-1.

MARKET SEGMENTATION

Market segmentation is the process of dividing all possible users of a product into groups that have similar needs the products might satisfy. Market segmentation should be done prior to the final development of a new product. In addition, a complete market segmentation analysis should be performed periodically for existing products. The reason for continuing segmentation analyses is the dynamic nature of consumer needs.

A. External influences
   1. Are there cultures or subcultures whose value system is particularly consistent (or inconsistent) with the consumption of our product?
   2. Is our product appropriate for male or female consumption? Will ongoing gender-role changes affect who consumes our product or how it is consumed?
   3. Do ethnic, social, regional, or religious subcultures have different consumption patterns relevant to our product?
   4. Do various demographic or social-strata groups (age, gender, urban/suburban/rural, occupation, income, education) differ in their consumption of our product?
   5. Is our product particularly appropriate for consumers with relatively high (or low) incomes compared to others in their occupational group (ROCI)?
   6. Can our product be particularly appropriate for specific roles, such as students or professional women?
   7. Would it be useful to focus on specific adopter categories?
   8. Do groups in different stages of the household life cycle have different consumption patterns for our product? Who in the household is involved in the purchase process?
B. Internal influences
   1. Can our product satisfy different needs or motives in different people? What needs are involved? What characterizes individuals with differing motives?

*Revised by Richard Pomazal of Wheeling College.

| FIGURE B-1 | Consumer Influences Drive Marketing Decisions |

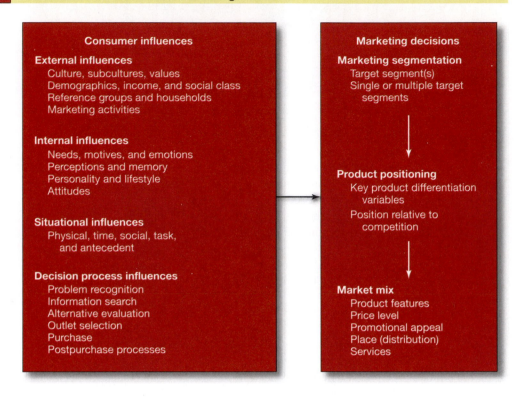

<table>
<tr><td>

Consumer influences

External influences
  Culture, subcultures, values
  Demographics, income, and social class
  Reference groups and households
  Marketing activities

Internal influences
  Needs, motives, and emotions
  Perceptions and memory
  Personality and lifestyle
  Attitudes

Situational influences
  Physical, time, social, task,
    and antecedent

Decision process influences
  Problem recognition
  Information search
  Alternative evaluation
  Outlet selection
  Purchase
  Postpurchase processes

</td><td>

Marketing decisions

Marketing segmentation
  Target segment(s)
  Single or multiple target
    segments

Product positioning
  Key product differentiation
    variables
  Position relative to
    competition

Market mix
  Product features
  Price level
  Promotional appeal
  Place (distribution)
  Services

</td></tr>
</table>

2. Is our product uniquely suited for particular personality types? Self-concepts?
3. What emotions, if any, are affected by the purchase and/or consumption of this product?
4. Is our product appropriate for one or more distinct lifestyles?
5. Do different groups have different attitudes about an ideal version of our product?

C. Situational influences
   1. Can our product be appropriate for specific types of situations instead of (or in addition to) specific types of people?

D. Decision process influences
   1. Do different individuals use different evaluative criteria in selecting the product?
   2. Do potential customers differ in their loyalty to existing products/brands?

PRODUCT POSITION

A product position is the way the consumer thinks of a given product/brand relative to competing products/brands. A manager must determine what a desirable product position would be for each market segment of interest. This determination is generally based on the answers to the same questions used to segment a market, with the addition of the consumer's perceptions of competing products/brands. Of course, the capabilities and motivations of existing and potential competitors must also be considered.

A. Internal influences
    1. What is the general semantic memory structure for this product category in each market segment?
    2. What is the ideal version of this product in each market segment for the situations the firm wants to serve?
B. Decision process influences
    1. Which evaluative criteria are used in the purchase decision? Which decision rules and importance weights are used?

PRICING

The manager must set a pricing policy that is consistent with the desired product position. Price must be broadly conceived as everything a consumer must surrender to obtain a product. This includes time and psychological costs as well as monetary costs.

A. External influences
    1. Does the segment hold any values relating to any aspect of pricing, such as the use of credit or conspicuous consumption?
    2. Does the segment have sufficient income, after covering living expenses, to afford the product?
    3. Is it necessary to lower price to obtain a sufficient relative advantage to ensure diffusion? Will temporary price reductions induce product trial?
    4. Who in the household evaluates the price of the product?
B. Internal influences
    1. Will price be perceived as an indicator of status?
    2. Is economy in purchasing this type of product relevant to the lifestyle(s) of the segment?
    3. Is price an important aspect of the segment's attitude toward the brands in the product category?
    4. What is the segment's perception of a fair or reasonable price for this product?
C. Situational influences
    1. Does the role of price vary with the type of situation?
D. Decision process factors
    1. Can a low price be used to trigger problem recognition?
    2. Is price an important evaluative criterion? What decision rule is applied to the evaluative criteria used? Is price likely to serve as a surrogate indicator of quality?
    3. Are consumers likely to respond to in-store price reductions?

DISTRIBUTION STRATEGY

The manager must develop a distribution strategy that is consistent with the selected product position. This involves the selection of outlets if the item is a physical product, or the location of the outlets if the product is a service.

A. External influences
    1. What values do the segments have that relate to distribution?
    2. Do the male and female members of the segments have differing requirements of the distribution system? Do working couples, single individuals, or single parents within the segment have unique needs relating to product distribution?

3. Can the distribution system capitalize on reference groups by serving as a means for individuals with common interests to get together?

4. Is the product complex such that a high-service channel is required to ensure its diffusion?

B. Internal influences

1. Will the selected outlets be perceived in a manner that enhances the desired product position?

2. What type of distribution system is consistent with the lifestyle(s) of each segment?

3. What attitudes does each segment hold with respect to the various distribution alternatives?

C. Situational influences

1. Do the desired features of the distribution system vary with the situation?

D. Decision process factors

1. What outlets are in the segment's evoked set? Will consumers in this segment seek information in this type of outlet?

2. Which evaluative criteria does this segment use to evaluate outlets? Which decision rule?

3. Is the outlet selected before, after, or simultaneously with the product/brand? To what extent are product decisions made in the retail outlet?

PROMOTION STRATEGY

The manager must develop a promotion strategy, including advertising, nonfunctional package design features, publicity, promotions, and sales force activities that are consistent with the product position.

A. External factors

1. What values does the segment hold that can be used in our communications? Which should be avoided?

2. How can we communicate to our chosen segments in a manner consistent with the emerging gender-role perceptions of each segment?

3. What is the nonverbal communication system of each segment?

4. How, if at all, can we use reference groups in our advertisements?

5. Can our advertisements help make the product part of one or more role-related product clusters?

6. Can we reach and influence opinion leaders?

7. If our product is an innovation, are there diffusion inhibitors that can be overcome by promotion?

8. Who in the household should receive what types of information concerning our product?

B. Internal factors

1. Have we structured our promotional campaign such that each segment will be exposed to it, attend to it, and interpret it in the manner we desire?

2. Have we made use of the appropriate learning principles so that our meaning will be remembered?

3. Do our messages relate to the purchase motives held by the segment? Do they help reduce motivational conflict if necessary?

4. Are we considering the emotional implications of the ad and/or the use of our product?

5. Is the lifestyle portrayed in our advertisements consistent with the desired lifestyle of the selected segments?
6. If we need to change attitudes via our promotion mix, have we selected and properly used the most appropriate attitude-change techniques?

C. Situational influences
1. Does our campaign illustrate the full range of appropriate usage situations for the product?

D. Decision process influences
1. Will problem recognition occur naturally, or must it be activated by advertising? Should generic or selective problem recognition be generated?
2. Will the segment seek out or attend to information on the product prior to problem recognition, or must we reach them when they are not seeking our information? Can we use low-involvement learning processes effectively? What information sources are used?
3. After problem recognition, will the segment seek out information on the product/brand, or will we need to intervene in the purchase decision process? If they do seek information, what sources do they use?
4. What types of information are used to make a decision?
5. How much and what types of information are acquired at the point of purchase?
6. Is postpurchase dissonance likely? Can we reduce it through our promotional campaign?
7. Have we given sufficient information to ensure proper product use?
8. Are the expectations generated by our promotional campaign consistent with the product's performance?
9. Are our messages designed to encourage repeat purchases, brand loyal purchases, or neither?

PRODUCT

The marketing manager must be certain that the physical product, service, or idea has the characteristics required to achieve the desired product position in each market segment.

A. External influences
1. Is the product designed appropriately for all members of the segment under consideration, including males, females, and various age groups?
2. If the product is an innovation, does it have the required relative advantage and lack of complexity to diffuse rapidly?
3. Is the product designed to meet the varying needs of different household members?

B. Internal influences
1. Will the product be perceived in a manner consistent with the desired image?
2. Will the product satisfy the key purchase motives of the segment?
3. Is the product consistent with the segment's attitude toward an ideal product?

C. Situational influences
1. Is the product appropriate for the various potential usage situations?

D. Decision process influences
1. Does the product/brand perform better than the alternatives on the key set of evaluative criteria used by this segment?

2. Will the product perform effectively in the foreseeable uses to which this segment may subject it?
3. Will the product perform as well or better than expected by this segment?

CUSTOMER SATISFACTION AND COMMITMENT

Marketers must produce satisfied customers to be successful in the long run. It is often to a firm's advantage to go beyond satisfaction and create committed or loyal customers.

1. What factors lead to satisfaction with our product?
2. What factors could cause customer commitment to our brand or firm?

NAME INDEX

CASE INDEX

SUBJECT INDEX